Dianne Kirtley

W9-BZP-930

THE QUILL READER

JOCELYN SILER

University of Montana

KATE GADBOW

University of Montana

MARK MEDVETZ

University of Montana

HARCOURT COLLEGE PUBLISHERS

Fort Worth   Philadelphia   San Diego   New York   Orlando   Austin   San Antonio
Toronto   Montreal   London   Sydney   Tokyo

PUBLISHER	Earl McPeek
ACQUISITIONS EDITOR	Julie McBurney
MARKET STRATEGIST	John Myers
DEVELOPMENTAL EDITOR	Camille Adkins
PROJECT EDITOR	G. Parrish Glover
ART DIRECTOR	Sue Hart
PRODUCTION MANAGER	Cindy Young

ISBN: 0-15-507945-X
Library of Congress Catalog Card Number: 99-067032

Copyright © 2000 by Harcourt, Inc.

All rights reserved. No part of this publication may be reproduced or transmitted in any form or by any means, electronic or mechanical, including photocopy, recording, or any information storage and retrieval system, without permission in writing from the publisher.

Requests for permission to make copies of any part of the work should be mailed to: Permissions Department, Harcourt, Inc., 6277 Sea Harbor Drive, Orlando, FL 32887-6777.

Copyrights and Acknowledgments appear on pages 879–886, which constitutes a continuation of the copyright page.

Address for Domestic Orders
Harcourt College Publishers, 6277 Sea Harbor Drive, Orlando, FL 32887-6777
800-782-4479

Address for International Orders
International Customer Service
Harcourt, Inc., 6277 Sea Harbor Drive, Orlando, FL 32887-6777
407-345-3800
(fax) 407-345-4060
(e-mail) hbintl@harcourtbrace.com

Address for Editorial Correspondence
Harcourt College Publishers, 301 Commerce Street, Suite 3700,
Fort Worth, TX 76102

Web Site Address
http://www.harcourtcollege.com

Harcourt College Publishers will provide complimentary supplements or supplement packages to those adopters qualified under our adoption policy. Please contact your sales representative to learn how you qualify. If as an adopter or potential user you receive supplements you do not need, please return them to your sales representative or send them to: Attn: Returns Department, Troy Warehouse, 465 South Lincoln Drive, Troy, MO 63379.

Printed in the United States of America

9 0 1 2 3 4 5 6 7 8 039 9 8 7 6 5 4 3 2 1

Harcourt College Publishers

We designed every aspect of the Quill Reader, from its organization and reading and writing chapters to its selections, to encourage students to become active members of the reading community. From our first early discussions about the book, we envisioned it as an invitation and introduction to the life-changing process of interactive, critical reading.

Therefore, in order to lead students from personal concerns toward larger cultural and philosophical ones, we have organized the thematic sections in the book to progress from early chapters on the individual and the individual's place in society through middle chapters centering on cultural and historic matters to the final chapters focusing on art and on philosophy and religion.

In addition, rather than include closed, text-specific discussion questions or assignments at the ends of chapters, we have designed open, conceptual assignments that are integrated throughout the first two introductory chapters. Chapter One, Strategies for Critical Reading, and Chapter Two, Responding by Writing, connect the reading and writing processes and introduce students to general principles that can be applied to the reading of all texts. Rather than lead students toward a particular "correct" judgment of a text's meaning, the critical reading strategies in Chapter One invite students to read interactively by making evidence-supported cases for their judgments of meaning; any judgment that can be supported with evidence from the text is considered a credible judgment.

Furthermore, so as not to influence students' readings of selections nor to limit what they might learn about the writers whose work appears here, we have introduced each selection with only the date and place of original publication. In place of the standard biographical notes about writers and summaries of selections that tend to shut down independent inquiry and group discussion, in Chapter One we have included assignments that direct students to research authors and to discuss the results of their research with classmates. Our own experience with author-search assignments has shown us that they enhance the reading process in a number of significant ways. In the process of researching, students learn how to be more active and interactive readers; the biographical and critical information students encounter helps flesh out writers into three dimensional people whose ideas are discussed and challenged by other writers and thinkers. In addition, reading biographical and critical information about a particular writer often leads students to read other texts written by that writer.

Finally, and most importantly, we have brought together what we believe to be the finest and most diverse selection of readings ever assembled in a college text. The texts included here are diverse in a number of ways: they are contemporary and ancient, brief as well as long, written by students as well as professionals; and they represent a variety of genres. Internet "zines" are included along with classic essays; student selections include prose poems as well as academic research papers. In the chapter on philosophy and religion, alongside selections by Sartre and Plato, we have included an excerpt from Neil Gaiman's comic-book novel *Death—The Time of Your Life.* In addition, we are particularly proud that many of the readings here are anthologized for the first time.

Choosing the reading selections (reading and rereading them) has been the most exciting part of this project. Although many of the selections included here were favorites suggested by one or another of us, many were altogether new reading experiences. We invite you to follow us as readers, and we wish you good reading—and great thinking.

We are grateful to the following reviewers for their advice on the drafting and revision of the book: Deborah Barberousse, Montgomery Community College; Dan Butcher, Southeastern Louisiana University; Scott Douglass, Chattanooga State Technical Community College; Paul Heilker, Vriginia Tech; Michael Léger, University of Texas at Arlington; and Judy Pearce, Montgomery College. Also we thank the following employees of Harcourt College Publishers for their guidance and support: Julie McBurney, Acquisitions Editor; Camille Adkins; Senior Developmental Editor; Parrish Glover, Project Editor; Sue Hart, Art Director; and Cindy Young, Production Manager.

JOCELYN SILER
KATE GADBOW
MARK MEDVETZ

BRIEF CONTENTS

soon to become

College Publishers

A Harcourt Higher Learning Company

Soon you will find Harcourt Brace's distinguished innovation, leadership, and support under a different name . . . a new brand that continues our unsurpassed quality, service, and commitment to education.

We are combining the strengths of our college imprints into one worldwide brand: Harcourt Our mission is to make learning accessible to anyone, anywhere, anytime—reinforcing our commitment to lifelong learning.

We'll soon be Harcourt College Publishers. Ask for us by name.

**One Company
"Where Learning
Comes to Life."**

CONTENTS

   To write one's life is to live it twice, and the second living is both spiritual and
   historical.

CHAPTER 9

NATURE AND THE ENVIRONMENT   563

STRATEGIES FOR CRITICAL READING

Jean-Honoré Fragonard, A Young Girl Reading, oil on canvas, 32×25½″.

The painting of the young girl reading might lead you to conclude that reading is a passive activity. Looking at the young girl with the book in her hand, it's easy to imagine a silence broken only by the occasional sound of a page being turned. The truth is, however, reading is anything but passive. Reading involves so many mental processes that our brains are more active when we are reading than when we are engaged in any other endeavor. When we read, we interact with the text: We predict what will happen next; we recall things that details in the text have triggered in our memories; we feel emotions; and we make judgments about what we think the text means. Furthermore, no two people read the same text in exactly the same way. When we read, we bring our personal, social, and educational histories to the reading, and those histories influence the meaning we take from the texts we encounter.

Although all reading is interactive, the most effective reading is also actively **critical**. The ability to be a critical reader is essential—not only for success in college and your chosen career, but also for your development as a thinker and a human being. Critical reading is the interactive process of understanding and learning from and responding to written texts. When you read critically, you actively converse with the texts you encounter; you listen to and learn from what other people have written, and then you decide for yourself what *you* think. Reading texts critically gives you not only the opportunity to share in other people's perspectives and ideas, but also the knowledge to thoughtfully agree or disagree with other people's points of view. In addition, careful critical reading can help you unlock texts that at first seem beyond your understanding.

Although you won't have time to incorporate **discussion** into all your college reading assignments, it's important to keep in mind that reading, like writing, is enhanced by collaboration. More often than not, we extend and clarify our knowledge by interacting with others. That's why it's a good idea to think of your classmates and instructors as collaborative partners. Discuss your reading with them, and listen carefully to their responses. Use them as resources to test and expand your ideas.

Writing is an even more crucial part of the reading process. Initially, you write **informally**—on your own or in collaboration with others—to explore the meaning of a text and to begin to frame responses to it; later, you may write to communicate your conclusions to other people by constructing a formal responsive paper. Several of the steps of the critical reading process outlined below entail **writing** because understanding a difficult text involves making your conversation with it permanent on a written page. Only when that conversation is recorded in writing can you revisit it and refine your responses.

THE CRITICAL READING PROCESS

Preread
Read Holistically
Analyze the Speaker
Determine the Message
Determine the Audience
Determine the Purpose
Write in Response

PREREAD

Active prereading provides you with a preliminary context by providing clues about the subject and the author's attitudes toward that subject. It also focuses your reading and helps you decode complicated texts more efficiently. You may wish to employ all of the following prereading strategies or only some of them, depending on the complexity of the text you're reading.

RESEARCH THE AUTHOR.   Using the resources in your college library (and/or using the Internet) to do an author search can provide you with information about the writer's background and values. One of the most useful databases for author information is LION (Literature on Line). In addition to giving you access to author Web pages, LION can lead you to biographical information, reviews, criticism, interviews, and full text essays, poems, plays, and fiction.

RESEARCH THE PLACE AND DATE OF PUBLICATION.   The place of first publication can give you clues about the text's probable audience and that audience's values. The date of publication will enable you to put the text into a historical context.

DEFINE THE GENRE.   Is the text fiction (novel, short story)? Is it nonfiction (essay, textbook chapter, scientific or news report)?

DEFINE THE SCOPE.   Is the text complete, or is it an excerpt from a chapter or a section of a longer work?

UNLOCK THE TEXT.   **Read the first three paragraphs** slowly, focusing on those things you know and understand. When you get to the end of the third paragraph, stop reading and take stock; **summarize** what you think has gone on in the text up to that point. What do you know about the subject of the text so far? If you're confused, go back and focus on the sentences you don't understand. **Reread** them, searching for meaning. Then

predict what direction you think the text will take next. As you continue to read, compare your predictions with what unfolds on the page. After each of the remaining paragraphs, pause again to summarize, reread if necessary, and predict.

ACTIVITY 1.1 Choose one of the selections from this book and preread it according to the above directions.

READ HOLISTICALLY

In the holistic reading stage, you read the text straight through and begin to actively converse with it.

ANNOTATE. At this stage of the critical reading process, you will want to have a pen and a highlighting marker on hand to **annotate** the text. Mark passages that confuse or compel you, that you agree or disagree with strongly, or that express major ideas. Record your questions and responses in the margins.

RESEARCH UNKNOWNS. The purpose of active critical reading is to discern, as closely as you can, the meaning of a text. Therefore, it's crucial to **research** unfamiliar words or references in the text. Use the research resources in your school's library.

ACTIVITY 1.2 Annotate and research the unknowns of one of the selections in this book.

KEEP A READING JOURNAL. Expand on your annotations by exploring one or more of them in a reading journal. Consider your attitudes toward the subject of the selection, and your agreements and disagreements with the author. How are your attitudes different from those of the author? In what ways are they similar? What experiences in your personal, cultural, and educational histories may have influenced your responses to the text?

ACTIVITY 1.3 Following the directions for annotating and journaling, write a reading journal entry for one of the selections in this book.

ANALYZE THE SPEAKER

Behind every piece of writing is a writer, a unique human being who uses written language to express a point of view on a subject. However, a writer has many more facets than can be revealed in one particular text. A given text will reveal only one limited, carefully constructed part, and that part is called **the speaker.** A good way to begin getting at the meaning of a text is to learn whatever **facts** you can about the speaker and his or her **emotional** and **rational responses.** Analyzing the speaker in this way will help you focus on the language and developmental material that reveal the writer's judgments about the subject.

FACTS.   List, and support with evidence from the text, as many **facts** as you can about the speaker. For example, can you determine the speaker's gender, profession, age, and era? Keep in mind that facts are indisputable.

EMOTIONS.   Where in the text does the speaker reveal or describe his or her emotional responses? Does the speaker also describe the emotions of another person? Identify any emotions that the speaker describes.

ATTITUDES.   Unlike emotional responses, a speaker's **attitudes** are thoughtful conclusions or **evidence-supported judgments** that the speaker has drawn about the subjects being written about. Although an emotional response can, after some thought, lead to an attitude, an attitude is an intellectual rather than an emotional response. Identify text passages in which the speaker expresses particular **conclusions** he or she has drawn about the subjects of his or her writing. In addition, identify the **evidence** the speaker uses to support each conclusion.

| ACTIVITY 1.4 | Either on you own or in collaboration with one or more classmates, analyze the speaker in one of the selections in this book. Follow the suggestions listed above.

| ACTIVITY 1.5 | In the form of a reading journal entry, explore the results of Activity 1.4. What traits of the speaker did your analysis reveal?

DETERMINE THE MESSAGE

The **message** of a particular text is the speaker's **main idea** or **thesis.** Usually, a focused judgment or a **claim** about the subject is supported throughout the text by judgments and evidence that specifically relate to it. For example, suppose a persuasive essay about capital punishment has as its message: "Capital punishment is wrong because it is dehumanizing." The essay should then contain evidence-supported judgments about why and how capital punishment is dehumanizing. Notice that the message is a focused **claim** ("Capital punishment is wrong *because* it is dehumanizing"), rather than a general statement ("Capital punishment is wrong").

Writers want their audiences to agree with the messages of the texts they construct, and to be moved to further thought or action. The message of a text is usually stated in one or two sentences. If the message isn't openly stated, it should be revealed in the sum total of the speaker's "attitudes."

| ACTIVITY 1.6 |
Either on your own or in collaboration with one or more classmates, follow the suggestions above and determine the message of one of the selections in this book.

DETERMINE THE AUDIENCE

Most pieces of writing are directed at a specific and discernible audience. Determining who that audience is can help you understand the text and the writer's purpose in writing it. Considerations of audience directly affect the language and developmental material a writer chooses to include in a text. For example, a writer who intended to reach a highly educated audience would make different choices in language and developmental material than if he or she wanted to reach an audience of young children. The age, gender, and values, and the educational and socioeconomic levels of an audience all affect the choices a writer makes as he or she constructs a text. Studying the language and developmental material in a text, and making judgments about their meaning and complexity, should lead you to a detailed determination of audience.

| ACTIVITY 1.7 |
Either on your own or in collaboration with one or more classmates, follow the suggestions above to determine the audience for one of the selections in this book.

DETERMINE THE PURPOSE

Purpose is always intimately connected to audience. The writer's **specific purpose** is the **change** he or she desires in the **audience's knowledge or its way of thinking or acting.** Purpose is not as specific as message; a writer may send many different messages through the medium of many different texts, and each one may be intended to accomplish the same purpose.

| ACTIVITY 1.8 |
Either on your own or in collaboration with one or more classmates, follow the suggestions above to determine the purpose of one of the selections in this book.

WRITE IN RESPONSE

As I said earlier, writing is a crucial part of the critical reading process. If you have engaged in any of the writing activities presented in this chapter so far, you have already begun to formulate written responses to your reading. To take your responses to a higher level, construct a formal paper by engaging in one of the activities included below.

ACTIVITY 1.9 Choose one of the emotional responses you identified in Activity 1.3. Then, focus on a time in your own life when you experienced a similar response. Then describe, in writing, the remembered situation and your response to it.

ACTIVITY 1.10 Choose an "attitude" (a conclusive judgment) you identified in Activity 1.3 that you agree with and one you disagree with. Then, in the form of two written responses, explain why you agree and why you disagree. Use evidence from your own experience to support your explanation.

ACTIVITY 1.11 After you have engaged in Activity 1.6 (to determine the message of a text), write a response statement in which you explain your agreements or disagreements with the text's message. Use your own knowledge and experience as supportive evidence for your position.

RESPONDING
BY WRITING

As suggested earlier, writing is an integral part of the critical reading process. Writing **informally** in a **reading journal** allows you to search for meaning in texts. Your journal becomes a permanent record of your interactive conversations with the texts you read, and it gives you a place to hold on to ideas and explore them more fully. In addition, writing **formally** for an **external audience** about the texts you encounter helps you expand your conversations with those texts and allows you to communicate your critical responses to other people.

Whether you write formally or informally, understanding the **writing process** and using it consciously will help you become a better writer. The writing process has five basic steps:

1. Prewriting
2. Drafting
3. Revising
4. Editing
5. Proofreading

PREWRITING

Prewriting is the exploratory step of the writing process. When you prewrite in response to a written text, you put critical pressure on the ideas expressed in the text and on your own responses to them. You test and evaluate the conclusions and evidence in the text by comparing them with your own experience; however, you test and evaluate your own judgments about the subject as well. Entries in a reading journal can often be the starting place for formal papers.

The basic goal of prewriting is to generate enough material so that you have a firm place to begin drafting. In addition to being the stage of the writing process where you generate and evaluate your ideas about the subject of writing, prewriting is also where you **analyze the writing situation** and **decide on a working message** for the text you're constructing.

STRATEGIES FOR GENERATING IDEAS

If you have trouble getting started prewriting about a text, the following strategies are particularly useful for prewriting in response to readings.

FREEWRITING.   To freewrite, **just write nonstop** about a subject until you've generated as much language as possible. Don't take your pen off the page (or your fingers off the keyboard). If necessary, repeat the last word that pops into your head until a new one comes along. Don't think too deeply; just keep focusing on the subject, and let the language take you where it will.

LOOPING. Looping is **enhanced freewriting.** After you have freely explored your subject for ten or fifteen minutes, go back and underline the most meaningful thing that you have written down. Using it as a focus, freewrite again. Keep repeating the process until you find a focus for your writing.

DOUBLE-ENTRY NOTES. Some writers begin with double-entry notes. Draw a line down the center of a blank sheet of paper. On the left side, free-associate **(brainstorm)** and write down as many words related to the subject as you can, until you've exhausted the possibilities. Then, on the right side, **comment on each word.** In your comments, go into more detail. Supply examples and evidence, but also record your reflections and conclusive judgments about the specifics that you have listed on the left side of the page.

ANALYZING THE WRITING SITUATION

Every writing assignment that you're given is actually a **writing situation** that has its own unique system of choices and constraints. A writing situation is defined by the **writer** who's writing, the **audience** to whom the piece of writing is addressed, the **subject** that's being written about, and the **purpose** that the writer is trying to accomplish. As part of prewriting, it's important to analyze the elements of the particular writing situation at hand. Those elements will have a major impact on the choices you make as you write.

SUBJECT. The **subject** you're writing about—the text you're responding to—determines the choices you make as you write. For example, if you're assigned to write a paper responding to one of the readings in this book, it would be important for you to focus on that reading and not stray off into a discussion about a different subject that has no relevance.

WRITER. What you write is ultimately created by you, the **writer,** an individual human being with unique personal and educational histories. Given the same writing assignment, no two people would produce exactly the same text.

AUDIENCE. Just as the person you are influences what you choose to put down on the page, the **audience** to whom you're writing also influences your choices. For example, no matter what your age, a letter to your mother describing your weekend activities will be very different from a letter to your best friend describing the same weekend.

PURPOSE. What you write will also be affected by the **purpose** you have for writing. Your purpose in any writing situation is the specific **change** in knowledge, thought, or action that you desire from your audience. Sometimes, your general purpose for writing will be **writer-based.** Journals and class notes are examples of writer-based writing. If your purpose is writer-based, you'll write to change your knowledge or your way of thinking or acting, and no external audience will be in the writing equation. You might write in a journal to **learn** and **understand** by exploring what you think. And as you learn and understand, you might **express** your ideas and feelings about the subject of your writing. At other times, or at the same time, you might write to **remember.** The process of writing will help you to fix facts or concepts—or your own emotional responses—in your memory. You might also write to **observe** sensory experiences; writing down what you receive through your senses will help you understand your sensory experiences more clearly.

Often, however, you will be writing primarily to **change** an audience other than yourself. Then, your general purpose for writing might be to **inform** your audience or to **explain** concepts. You might write to **persuade** others to accept a particular point of view or take some course of action. At other times, your purpose will be to **explore** ideas with your audience by sharing your reflections and posing questions. In addition, or in combination with other general purposes, you might write to **entertain** your audience by engaging their wit and imagination.

DECIDING ON A WORKING MESSAGE

The **message** of the text you create is simply that text's **main idea** or **thesis.** In most college writing, the message is a focused judgment or **claim** about the subject that is then supported throughout the text by judgments and evidence that specifically relate to it. As a writer, your aim is to get the audience to agree with the message of your text and then be moved to further thought or action about the subject of writing. Usually, you state the message in your text in one or two sentences. Less frequently, you might decide, for one reason or another, not to openly state the message; in those instances, the message would be implied by the sum total of the material included in the text.

Whether you state the message openly or not, you should have at least a tentative idea of your message before you begin drafting.

DRAFTING

Drafting is the stage of the writing process where you begin to bring your responses together into a formed paper. Drafting gives you the opportunity to expand on old ideas and formulate new ones. Read and reread your draft as you write, and look for new ways of viewing the text you're responding to. As you draft, revise your writing and thinking by cutting, adding, and rearranging material, and by rewording.

The more choices you have made up to this point, the easier drafting will be. Your draft should flow right out of your prewriting. As you draft, keep in mind your audience, your purpose, and your message.

AUDIENCE.   Imagine yourself in conversation with your audience as you write. What do they know or need to know? What are their possible points of view on the text you are responding to?

PURPOSE.   How do you want to change your audience? Will what is emerging on your page or computer screen get the change you want?

MESSAGE.   As you draft, keep your working message foremost (write it across the top of your draft, or tape a written copy of it to the top of your computer screen) and test it frequently against what you put down on the page.

During the drafting step, new responses to the text will come to you, and vague responses will coalesce into solid conclusions. Test your working message and your new discoveries against each other. Go back and fill in details, or, if you have established some momentum, leave yourself notes in your emerging text.

As you write, you may come to resting places (perhaps you have finished relating an anecdote that illustrates your responsive position, or maybe you have drawn a significant conclusion). If you get stuck at one of these places, go back to the beginning of your draft and read aloud what you have gotten down so far. Reading can help you to find your next direction.

If you find the draft dying on you, analyze why. Go back through the process. Check your message. If it still seems workable, you may need to spend more time exploring your responses to the text. A rereading of it or a conversation with a member of the class or with the instructor might help. Perhaps you need to think more deeply about the subject. Solitary time with a notebook and pen might be the answer.

REVISING

If possible, **workshop** your response in a collaborative group. The draft you bring to your collaborative partners should be your best effort—a finished piece of writing, not a "rough draft." Think of your workshop partners as your first line of defense against a judgmental audience that is waiting at the end of the writing process.

If possible, put your draft aside for a day or two before you begin rewriting, but continue thinking critically about both the text and your response to it. Getting a little distance on your writing while continuing your encounter with the subject can help you to see holes in your response that need to be plugged.

If, as you rewrite, you find you have questions about how well parts of your text are working, write down your concerns in the form of brief notes, and take, both your notes and your written response I to a trusted classmate or your instructor. Presenting a collaborative partner with specific questions can make rewriting more active and interactive.

EDITING

Polish your text as you write the final draft. Focus on paragraphs, transitions, and any habitual problems with spelling, punctuation, and sentence structure.

PROOFREADING

If possible, put your response away for at least a couple of hours before you proofread. Proofread for small careless errors by reading your text aloud, preferably to another person.

WRITING ACTIVITIES

ACTIVITY 2.1 After critically reading one of the selections in this book, write an essay in which you explain your agreement or disagreement with that text's message. Use your own experience and knowledge as supportive evidence for your position.

ACTIVITY 2.2 Choose an emotional response described in one of the selections in this book. Then write an essay in which you describe a time in your own life when you had a similar response.

ACTIVITY 2.3 After critically reading a selection from this book, choose, from the selection, one conclusive judgment you agree with and one judgment you disagree with. Then write one essay explaining your agreement and another explaining your disagreement.

| **ACTIVITY 2.4** | Consider your preconceived judgments about the subject of one of the selections in this book. |

Then write an essay in which you explore how your social and educational histories might have influenced you to draw the conclusions you did.

| **ACTIVITY 2.5** | If reading a selection from this book has changed your perspective on a subject, write an |

essay in which you describe the change and explain why you think it took place.

| **ACTIVITY 2.6** | Rewrite any of the papers you wrote in response to an activity listed above, but add re- |

search to the writing process.

GROWING UP

MEMORY AND IMAGINATION

■

Patricia Hampl

This piece was originally published in The Dolphin Reader *in 1985.*

When I was seven, my father, who played the violin on Sundays with a nicely tortured flair which we considered artistic, led me by the hand down a long, unlit corridor in St. Luke's School basement, a sort of tunnel that ended in a room full of pianos. There many little girls and a single sad boy were playing truly tortured scales and arpeggios in a mash of troubled sound. My father gave me over to Sister Olive Marie, who did look remarkably like an olive.

Her oily face gleamed as if it had just been rolled out of a can and laid on the white plate of her broad, spotless wimple. She was a small, plump woman; her body and the small window of her face seemed to interpret the entire alphabet of olive: her face was a sallow green olive placed upon the jumbo ripe olive of her black habit. I trusted her instantly and smiled, glad to have my hand placed in the hand of a woman who made sense, who provided the satisfaction of being what she was: an Olive who looked like an Olive.

My father left me to discover the piano with Sister Olive Marie so that one day I would join him in mutually tortured piano-violin duets for the edification of my mother and brother who sat at the table meditatively spooning in the last of their pineapple sherbet until their part was called for: they put down their spoons and clapped while we bowed, while the sweet ice in their bowls melted, while the music melted, and we all melted a little into each other for a moment.

But first Sister Olive must do her work. I was shown middle C, which Sister seemed to think terribly important. I stared at middle C and then glanced away for a second. When my eye returned, middle C was gone, its slim finger lost in the complicated grasp of the keyboard. Sister Olive struck it again, finding it with laughable ease. She emphasized the importance of middle C, its central position, a sort of North Star of sound. I remember thinking, "Middle C is the belly button of the piano," an insight whose originality and accuracy stunned me with pride. For the first time in my life I was astonished by metaphor. I hesitated to tell the kindly Olive for some reason; apparently I understood a true metaphor is a risky business, revealing of the self. In fact, I have never, until this moment of writing it down, told my first metaphor to anyone.

Sunlight flooded the room; the pianos, all black, gleamed. Sister Olive, dressed in the colors of the keyboard, gleamed; middle C shimmered with meaning and I resolved never—never—to forget its location: it was the center of the world.

Then Sister Olive, who had had to show me middle C twice but who seemed to have drawn no bad conclusions about me anyway, got up and went to the windows on the opposite wall. She pulled the shades down, one after the other. The sun was too bright, she said. She sneezed as she stood at the windows with the sun shedding its glare over her. She sneezed and sneezed, crazy little convulsive sneezes, one after another, as helpless as if she had the hiccups.

"The sun makes me sneeze," she said when the fit was over and she was back at the piano. This was odd, too odd to grasp in the mind. I associated sneezing with colds, and colds with rain, fog, snow, and bad weather. The sun, however, had caused Sister Olive to sneeze in this wild way, Sister Olive who gleamed benignly and who was so certain of the location of the center of the world. The universe wobbled a bit and became unreliable. Things were not, after all, necessarily what they seemed. Appearance deceived: here was the sun acting totally out of character, hurling this woman into sneezes, a woman so mild that she was named, so it seemed, for a bland object on a relish tray.

I was given a red book, the first Thompson book, and told to play the first piece over and over at one of the black pianos where the other children were crashing away. This, I was told, was called practicing. It sounded alluringly adult, practicing. The piece itself consisted mainly of middle C, and I excelled, thrilled by my savvy at being able to locate that central note amidst the cunning camouflage of all the other white keys before me. Thrilled too by the shiny red book that gleamed, as the pianos did, as Sister Olive did, as my eager eyes probably did. I sat at the formidable machine of the piano and got to know middle C intimately, preparing to be as tortured as I could manage one day soon with my father's violin at my side.

But at the moment Mary Katherine Reilly was at my side, playing something at least two or three lessons more sophisticated than my piece. I believe she even struck a chord. I glanced at her from the peasantry of single notes, shy, ready to pay homage. She turned toward me, stopped playing, and sized me up.

Sized me up and found a person ready to be dominated. Without introduction she said, "My grandfather invented the collapsible opera hat."

I nodded, I acquiesced, I was hers. With that little stroke it was decided between us—that she should be the leader, and I the side-kick. My job was admiration. Even when she added, "But he didn't make a penny from it. He didn't have a patent"—even then, I knew and she knew that this was not an admission of powerlessness, but the easy candor of a master, of one who can afford a weakness or two.

With the clairvoyance of all fated relationships based on dominance and submission, it was decided in advance: that when the time came for us to play duets, I should always play second piano, that I should spend my allowance to buy her the Twinkies she craved but was not allowed to have, that finally, I should let her copy from my test paper, and when confronted by our teacher, confess with convincing hysteria that it was I, I who had cheated, who had reached above myself to steal what clearly belonged to the rightful heir of the inventor of the collapsible opera hat. . . .

There must be a reason I remember that little story about my first piano lesson. In fact, it isn't a story, just a moment, the beginning of what could perhaps become a story. For the memoirist, more than for the fiction writer, the story seems already *there*, already accomplished and fully achieved in history ("in reality," as we naively say). For the memoirist, the writing of the story is a matter of transcription.

That, anyway, is the myth. But no memoirist writes for long without experiencing an unsettling disbelief about the reliability of memory, a hunch that memory is not, after a, *just* memory. I don't know why I remembered this fragment about my first piano lesson. I don't, for instance, have a single recollection of my first arithmetic lesson, the first time I studied Latin, the first time my grandmother tried to teach me to knit. Yet these things occurred too, and must have their stories.

It is the piano lesson that has trudged forward, clearing the haze of forgetfulness, showing itself bright with detail more than thirty years after the event. I did not choose to remember the piano lesson. It was simply there, like a book that has always been on the shelf, whether I ever read it or not, the binding and title showing as I skim across the contents of my life. On the day I wrote this fragment I happened to take that memory, not some other, from the shelf and paged through it. I found more detail, more event, perhaps a little more entertainment than I had expected, but the memory itself was there from the start. Waiting for me.

Or was it? When I reread what I had written just after I finished it, I realized that I had told a number of lies. I *think* it was my father who took me the first time for my piano lesson—but maybe he only took me to meet my teacher and there was no actual lesson that day. And did I even know then that he played the violin—didn't he take up his violin again much later, as a result of my piano playing, and not the reverse? And is it even remotely accurate to describe as "tortured" the musicianship of a man who began every day by belting out "Oh What a Beautiful Morning" as he shaved?

More: Sister Olive Marie did sneeze in the sun, but was her name Olive? As for her skin tone—I would have sworn it was olive-like; I would have been willing to spend the better part of an afternoon trying to write the exact description of imported Italian or Greek olive her face suggested: I wanted to get it right. But now, were I to write that passage over, it is her intense black eyebrows I would see, for suddenly they seem the central fact of that face, some indicative mark of her serious and patient nature. But the truth is, I don't remember the woman at all. She's a sneeze in the sun and a finger touching middle C. That, at least, is steady and clear.

Worse: I didn't have the Thompson book as my piano text. I'm sure of that because I remember envying children who did have this wonderful book with its pictures of children and animals printed on the pages of music.

As for Mary Katherine Reilly. She didn't even go to grade school with me (and her name isn't Mary Katherine Reilly—but I made that change on purpose). I met her in Girl Scouts and only went to school with her later, in high school. Our relationship was not really one of leader and follower; I played first piano most of the time in duets. She certainly never copied anything from a test paper of mine: she was a better student, and cheating just wasn't a possibility with her. Though her grandfather (or someone in her family) did invent the collapsible opera hat and I remember that she was proud of that fact, she didn't tell me this news as a deft move in a childish power play.

So, what was I doing in this brief memoir? Is it simply an example of the curious relation a fiction writer has to the material of her own life? Maybe. That may have some value in itself. But to tell the truth (if anyone still believes me capable of telling the truth), I wasn't writing fiction. I was writing memoir—or was trying to. My desire was to be accurate. I wished to embody the myth of memoir: to write as an act of dutiful transcription.

Yet clearly the work of writing narrative caused me to do something very different from transcription. I am forced to admit that memoir is not a matter of transcription, that memory itself is not a warehouse of finished stories, not a static gallery of framed pictures. I must admit that I invented. But why?

Two whys: why did I invent, and then, if a memoirist must inevitably invent rather than transcribe, why do I—why should anybody—write memoir at all?

I must respond to these impertinent questions because they, like the bumper sticker I saw the other day commanding all who read it to QUESTION AUTHORITY, challenge my authority as a memoirist and as a witness.

It still comes as a shock to realize that I don't write about what I know: I write in order to find out what I know. Is it possible to convey to a reader the enormous degree of blankness, confusion, hunch, and uncertainty lurking in the act of writing? When I am the reader, not the writer, I too fall into the lovely illusion that the words before me (in a story by Mavis Gallant, an essay by Carol Bly, a memoir by M. F. K. Fisher), which *read* so inevitably, must also have been *written* exactly as they appear, rhythm and cadence, language and syntax, the powerful waves of the sentences laying themselves on the smooth beach of the page one after another faultlessly.

But here I sit before a yellow legal pad, and the long page of the preceding two paragraphs is a jumble of crossed-out lines, false starts, confused order. A mess. The mess of my mind trying to find out what it wants to say. This is a writer's frantic, grabby mind, not the poised mind of a reader ready to be edified or entertained.

I sometimes think of the reader as a cat, endlessly fastidious, capable, by turns, of mordant indifference and riveted attention, luxurious, recumbent, and ever poised. Whereas the writer is absolutely a dog, panting and moping, too eager for an affectionate scratch behind the ears, lunging frantically after any old stick thrown in the distance.

The blankness of a new page never fails to intrigue and terrify me. Sometimes, in fact, I think my habit of writing on long yellow sheets comes from an atavistic fear of the writer's stereotypic "blank white page." At least when I begin writing, my page isn't utterly blank; at least it has a wash of color on it, even if the absence of words must finally be faced on a yellow sheet as truly as on a blank white one. Well, we all have our ways of whistling in the dark.

If I approach writing from memory with the assumption that I know what I wish to say, I assume that intentionality is running the show. Things are not that simple. Or perhaps writing is even more profoundly simple, more telegraphic and immediate in its choices than the grating wheels and chugging engine of logic and rational intention. The heart, the guardian of intuition with its secret, often fearful intentions, is the boss. Its commands are what a writer obeys—often without knowing it. Or, I do.

That's why I'm a strong adherent of the first draft. And why it's worth pausing for a moment to consider what first draft really is. By my lights, the piano lesson memoir is a first draft. That doesn't mean it exists here exactly as I first wrote it. I like to think I've cleaned it up from the first time I put it down on paper. I've cut some adjectives here, toned down the hyperbole there, smoothed a transition, cut a repetition—that sort of housekeeperly tidying-up. But the piece remains a first draft because I haven't yet gotten to know it, haven't given it a chance to tell me anything. For me, writing a first draft is a little like meeting someone for the first time. I come away with a wary acquaintanceship, but the real friendship (if any) and genuine intimacy—that's all down the road. Intimacy with a piece of writing, as with a person, comes from paying attention to the revelations it is capable of giving, not by imposing my own preconceived notions, no matter how well-intentioned they might be.

I try to let pretty much anything happen in a first draft. A careful first draft is a failed first draft. That may be why there are so many inaccuracies in the piano lesson memoir: I didn't censor, I didn't judge. I kept moving. But I would not publish this piece as a memoir on its own in its present state. It isn't the "lies" in the piece that give me pause, though a reader has a right to expect a memoir to be as accurate as the writer's memory can make it. No, it isn't the lies themselves that makes the piano lesson memoir a first draft and therefore "unpublishable."

The real trouble: the piece hasn't yet found its subject; it isn't yet about what it wants to be about. Note: what *it* wants, not what I want. The difference has to do with the relation a memoirist—any writer, in fact—has to unconscious or half-known intentions and impulses in composition.

Now that I have the fragment down on paper, I can read this little piece as a mystery which drops clues to the riddle of my feelings, like a culprit who wishes to be apprehended. My narrative self (the culprit who has invented) wishes to be discovered by my reflective self, the self who wants to understand and make sense of a half-remembered story about a nun sneezing in the sun. . . .

We only store in memory images of value. The value may be lost over the passage of time (I was baffled about why I remembered that sneezing nun, for example), but that's the implacable judgment of feeling: *this*, we say somewhere deep within us, is something I'm hanging on to. And of course, often we cleave to things because they possess heavy negative charges. Pain likes to be vivid.

Over time, the value (the feeling) and the stored memory (the image) may become estranged. Memoir seeks a permanent home for feeling and image, a habitation where they can live together in harmony. Naturally, I've had a lot of experiences since I packed away that one from the basement of St. Luke's School; that piano lesson has been effaced by waves of feeling for other moments and episodes. I persist in believing the event has value—after all, I remember it—but in writing the memoir I did not simply relive the experience. Rather, I explored the mysterious relationship between all the images I could round up and the even more impacted feelings that caused me to store the images safely away in memory. Stalking the relationship, seeking the congruence between stored image and hidden emotion—that's the real job of memoir.

By writing about the first piano lesson, I've come to know things I could not know otherwise. But I only know these things as a result of reading this first draft. While I was writing, I was following the images, letting the details fill the room of the page and use the furniture as they wished. I was their dutiful servant—or thought I was. In fact, I was the faithful retainer of my hidden feelings which were giving the commands.

I really did feel, for instance, that Mary Katherine Reilly was far superior to me. She was smarter, funnier, more wonderful in every way— that's how I saw it. Our friendship (or she herself) did not require that I become her vassal, yet perhaps in my heart that was something I wanted; I wanted a way to express my feeling of admiration. I suppose I waited until this memoir to begin to find the way.

Just as, in the memoir, I finally possess that red Thompson book with the barking dogs and bleating lambs and winsome children. I couldn't (and still can't) remember what my own music book was, so I grabbed the name and image of the one book I could remember. It was only in reviewing the piece after writing it that I saw my inaccuracy. In pondering this "lie," I came to see what I was up to: I was getting what I wanted. At last.

The truth of many circumstances and episodes in the past emerges for the memoirist through details (the red music book, the fascination with a nun's name and gleaming face), but these details are not merely information, not flat facts. Such details are not allowed to lounge. They must work. Their work is the creation of symbol. But it's more accurate to call it *recognition* of symbol. For meaning is not "attached" to the detail by the memoirist; meaning is revealed. That's why a first draft is important. Just as the first meeting (good or bad) with someone who later becomes the beloved is important and is often reviewed for signals, meanings, omens and indications.

Now I can look at that music book and see it not only as "a detail," but for what it is, how it *acts*. See it as the small red door leading straight into the dark room of my childhood longing and disappointment. That red book *becomes* the palpable evidence of that longing. In other words, it becomes symbol. There is no symbol, no life-of-the-spirit in the general of the abstract. Yet a writer wishes—indeed all of us wish—to speak about profound matters that are, like it or not, general and abstract. We wish to talk to each other about life and death, about love, despair, loss, and innocence. We sense that in order to live together we must learn to speak of peace, of history, of meaning and values. Those are a few.

We seek a means of exchange, a language which will renew these ancient concerns and make them wholly and pulsingly ours. Instinctively, we go to our store of private images and associations for our authority to speak of these weighty issues. We find, in our details and broken and obscured images, the language of symbol. Here memory impulsively reaches out its arms and embraces imagination. That is the resort to invention. It isn't a lie, but an act of necessity, as the innate urge to locate personal truth always is.

All right. Invention is inevitable. But why write memoir? Why not call it fiction and be done with all the hashing about, wondering where memory stops and imagination begins? And if memoir seeks to talk about "the big issues," about history and peace, death and love—why not leave these reflections to those with expert and scholarly knowledge? Why let the common or garden variety memoirist into the club? I'm thinking again of that bumper sticker: why Question Authority?

My answer, of course, is a memoirist's answer. Memoir must be written because each of us must have a created version of the past. Created: that is, real, tangible, made of the stuff of a life lived in place and in history. And the down side of any created thing as well; we must live with a version that attaches us to our limitations, to the inevitable subjectivity of our points of view. We must acquiesce to our experience and our gift to transform experience into meaning and value. You tell me your story, I'll tell you my story.

If we refuse to do the work of creating this personal version of the past, someone else will do it for us. That is a scary political fact. "The struggle of man against power," a character in Milan Kundera's novel *The Book of Laughter and Forgetting* says, "is the struggle of memory against forgetting." He refers to willful political forgetting, the habit of nations and those in power (Question Authority!) to deny the truth of memory in order to disarm moral and ethical power. It's an efficient way of control-ling masses of people. It doesn't even require much bloodshed, as long as people are entirely willing to give over their personal memories. Whole histories can be rewritten. As Czeslaw Milosz said in his 1980 Nobel Prize lecture, the number of books published that seek to deny the existence of the Nazi death camps now exceeds one hundred.

What is remembered is what *becomes* reality. If we "forget" Auschwitz, if we "forget" My Lai, what then do we remember? And what is the pur-pose of our remembering? If we think of memory naively, as a simple story, logged like a documentary in the archive of the mind, we miss its beauty but also its function. The beauty of memory rests in its talent for rendering detail, for paying homage to the senses, its capacity to love the particles of life, the richness and idiosyncrasy of our existence. The func-tion of memory, on the other hand, is intensely personal and surprisingly political.

Our capacity to move forward as developing beings rests on a healthy relation with the past. Psychotherapy, that widespread method of mental health, relies heavily on memory and on the ability to retrieve and organ-ize images and events from the personal past. We carry our wounds and perhaps even worse, our capacity to wound, forward with us. If we learn not only to tell our stories but to listen to what our stories tell us—to write the first draft and then return for the second draft—we are doing the work of memoir.

Memoir is the intersection of narration and reflection, of story-telling and essay-writing. It can present its story *and* reflect and consider the meaning of the story. It is a peculiarly open form, inviting broken and in-complete images, half-recollected fragments, all the mass (and mess) of detail. It offers to shape this confusion—and in shaping, of course it nec-essarily creates a work of art, not a legal document. But then, even legal documents are only valiant attempts to consign the truth, the whole truth, and nothing but the truth to paper. Even they remain versions.

Locating touchstones—the red music book, the olive Olive, my father's violin playing—is deeply satisfying. Who knows why? Perhaps we all sense that we can't grasp the whole truth and nothing but the truth of our experience. Just can't be done. What can be achieved, however, is a ver-sion of its swirling, changing wholeness. A memoirist must acquiesce to selectivity, like any artist. The version we dare to write is the only truth, the only relationship we can have with the past. Refuse to write your life and you have no life. At least, that is the stern view of the memoirist.

Personal history, logged in memory, is a sort of slide projector flashing images on the wall of the mind. And there's precious little order to the slides in the rotating carousel. Beyond that confusion, who knows who is running the projector? A memoirist steps into this darkened room of flashing, unorganized images and stands blinking for a while. Maybe for a long while. But eventually, as with any attempt to tell a story, it is nec-essary to put something first, then something else. And so on, to the end.

That's a first draft. Not necessarily the truth, not even *a* truth sometimes, but the first attempt to create a shape.

The first thing I usually notice at this stage of composition is the appalling inaccuracy of the piece. Witness my first piano lesson draft. Invention is screamingly evident in what I intended to be transcription. But here's the further truth: I feel no shame. In fact, it's only now that my interest in the piece truly quickens. For I can see what isn't there, what is shyly hugging the walls, hoping not to be seen. I see the filmy shape of the next draft. I see a more acute version of the episode or—this is more likely—an entirely new piece rising from the ashes of the first attempt.

The next draft of the piece would have to be a true re-vision, a new seeing of the materials of the first draft. Nothing merely cosmetic will do—no rough buffing up the opening sentence, no glossy adjective to lift a sagging line, nothing to attempt covering a patch of gray writing. None of that. I can't say for sure, but my hunch is the revision would lead me to more writing about my father (why was I so impressed by that ancestral inventor of the collapsible opera hat? Did I feel I had nothing as remarkable in my own background? Did this make me feel inadequate?). I begin to think perhaps Sister Olive is less central to this business than she is in this draft. She is meant to be a moment, not a character.

And so I might proceed, if I were to undertake a new draft of the memoir. I begin to feel a relationship developing between a former self and me.

And, even more compelling, a relationship between an old world and me. Some people think of autobiographical writing as the precious occupation of a particularly self-absorbed person. Maybe, but I don't buy that. True memoir is written in an attempt to find not only a self but a world.

The self-absorption that seems to be the impetus and embarrassment of autobiography turns into (or perhaps always was) a hunger for the world. Actually, it begins as hunger for *a* world, one gone or lost, effaced by time or a more sudden brutality. But in the act of remembering, the personal environment expands, resonates beyond itself, beyond its "subject," into the endless and tragic recollection that is history.

We look at old family photographs in which we stand next to black, boxy Fords and are wearing period costumes, and we do not gaze fascinated because there we are young again, or there we are standing, as we never will again in life, next to our mother. We stare and drift because there we are . . . historical. It is the dress, the black car that dazzle us now and draw us beyond our mother's bright arms which once caught us. We reach into the attractive impersonality of something more significant than ourselves. We write memoir, in other words. We accept the humble position of writing a version rather than "the whole truth."

I suppose I write memoir because of the radiance of the past—it draws me back and back to it. Not that the past is beautiful. In our commercial memoir, in history, the death camps *are* back there. In intimate life too, the record is usually pretty mixed. "I could tell you stories . . ." people say and drift off, meaning terrible things have happened to them.

But the past is radiant. It has the light of lived life. A memoirist wishes to touch it. No one owns the past, though typically the first act of new political regimes, whether of the left or the right, is to attempt to re-write history, to grab the past and make it over so the end comes out right. So their power looks inevitable.

No one owns the past, but it is a grave error (another age would have said a grave sin) not to inhabit memory. Sometimes I think it is all we really have. But that may be a trifle melodramatic. At any rate, memory possesses authority for the fearful self in a world where it is necessary to have authority in order to Question Authority.

There may be no more pressing intellectual need in our culture than for people to become sophisticated about the function of memory. The political implications of the loss of memory are obvious. The authority of memory is a personal confirmation of selfhood. To write one's life is to live it twice, and the second living is both spiritual and historical, for a memoir reaches deep within the personality as it seeks its narrative form and also grasps the life-of-the-times as no political treatise can.

Our most ancient metaphor says life is a journey. Memoir is travel writing, then, notes taken along the way, telling how things looked and what thoughts occurred. But I cannot think of the memoirist as a tourist. This is the traveller who goes on foot, living the journey, taking on mountains, enduring deserts, marveling at the lush green places. Moving through it all faithfully, not so much a survivor with a harrowing title to tell as a pilgrim, seeking, wondering.

LONGING AND BLISS

Megan McNamer

This essay first appeared in the March 6, 1995, Sports Illustrated.

It had to do, in part, with the seasons and the weather. The game peaked at a time of year that was between times, that otherwise felt depressing, with only an occasional tremulous flutter. Valentine's Day, followed by Ash Wednesday. Walking down an alley you would see a sugar-candy heart melting in the slush. The inscription: SUM DISH. This meshes in my memory with all those winters—raw and ugly, sloppy if the wind was a chinook. Life had a dull kind of chaos to it. But inside those gymnasiums it was clean and warm and still. It was whatever I wanted it to be. And that's why I grew up loving basketball.

It all began in grade school with the St. Margaret's Huskies ("Hard to beat, hard to beat"). This was in Cut Bank, Mont., up on the Hi-Line, a series of wind-stripped little towns linked by the railroad tracks and the long ribbon of U.S. Highway 2. At St. Margaret's we were two grades to a room, with no gym of our own and no association with the Public-ers (a word we considered interchangeable with Publicans, Christ's adversaries), so all our games were away. We played kids from tiny Heart Butte or from Star School, the Catholic-run boarding school near Browning on the Blackfeet Reservation. I remember wood-burning stoves just beyond the baskets. They burned any player who reached for an errant shot. I remember another court with only one basket, so the game had to be improvised accordingly. Basketball had limits, barriers. But it seemed full of consequence.

I, of course, was sidelined. It was the '60s in rural Montana, and I was a girl. By junior high school I acknowledged my position as spectator. But that didn't diminish my interest in the game. If anything it started to take on more weight. I switched my focus from the surroundings to the players.

I watched a Blackfeet player, Jim Kennedy, launch a midcourt shot that left his long fingers milliseconds before the final blast of the buzzer. The ball arced for a silent eternity, then swished back to earth amid a human roar. It sounded as though Lindbergh had landed in Paris. The Cut Bank High School Wolves lost a preliminary game in the State B Tournament to the Browning High School Indians by one pivotal point. My best friend Julie and I cried.

I watched Don Wetzel from Cut Bank—also a Blackfeet, compact and quick—steal the ball at the final moment and dunk it in a victory over the Shelby Coyotes, causing my best friend Shelly and me to cry.

I watched a Conrad Cowboy named Dick Harte make another of those long shots, changing fate in the nick of time. And I knew that the KSEN radio announcer was at that very moment screaming, "Heartbreaker by Harte!" as always, his words bouncing off the stars and down into Canada.

I watched those players for clues to myself. I was concerned with chance, a sudden upset, a ball flirting with the rim. But I was also concerned with certainty. I desired the players, and I desired a certain way to be. Long-limbed and loose. Sweating victory. In this respect, there was something both satisfying and heartrending about basketball. It was charged with against-odds possibility.

We would saddle up with chains and set out—the mother of my best friend Robyn driving—for 80 miles through snow flurries, ignoring the winter-storm warnings, skirting the eventual ROAD CLOSED sign. Homing in on Havre, the B squad game on the radio as our signal, we would have the car heater going full blast, making our wet-nyloned feet stink.

Once there, it was time to head for the bathroom and prepare. Put on our best blouses. Stuff our bras with Kleenex. Take out the curlers and spray the spit curls. Tease and comb our hair into smooth helmets. Erase our faces and apply a ghostly mask of white lipstick and black mascara.

The A squad game would begin, the important game. There were boundaries, rules, it would go on only so long. And while it lasted, the clock ticking away, I could forget the long drive, the rocky night, wind, Lent, death. My own gawky self. I existed within the game, which had an almost organic pattern, a coherence all its own.

From the starting lineup to the end of the bench, the players were extraordinary. In their shiny uniforms (usually something and gold) they were stars, all of them, even Tom, my winter-prom date, who was just getting his growth. When emerging from the mysterious locker room, he had a momentary glow.

This phenomenon wasn't new. Buzz—a guy my father's age, a growly, barrel-shaped, sleepy St. Bernard of a man, now a chef modestly successful restaurateur surrounded by a hazy halo of cigarette smoke—was in his youth a Hi-Line high school basketball star. He was lean, of course, and flashing. The town fathers, as he tells it, would stop him on the street and give him money. Not to play harder, not to rig the game. Just for being, on Saturday night, Buzz.

My dad was a basketball star for Shelby, as were his brothers. He and my uncle Bob had tight curls that popped back into place after each flurry of play. They would have traded any amount of time on the bench for the pleasure of flipping their hair out of their eyes just once, one smooth swoosh. I guess they sensed something we all knew intuitively: Basketball was only partly about baskets, balls and the various tactics for getting balls into baskets. It was mostly about bodies.

Poor exposed elbows, winter-pale legs, soft, first-growth hair matted with sweat. Those high school bodies were sort of pitiful. But they were in motion. They kaleidoscoped right past the cheerleaders, who had a physical presence I always found discouragingly at rest.

Cheerleaders in the 1960s wore dress shields. They kept their faces flat. They shouted *V!-I!-C!-T!-O!-R!-Y!*, but their performance didn't seem goal-oriented. They repeated the same motions no matter what was happening on the floor. There was no sense of evolution in their actions.

For a while I wanted to be a cheerleader myself. I wanted the social endorsement that went with being a cheerleader; I wanted the attention. I wanted *something*, and this was what was given me to want. But, for all that, I really didn't want to stand positioned on the center line, traveling neither to the left nor to the right.

Being a cheerleader seemed so static: Be cute and things will come to you. This might sound similar to being Buzz on a Saturday night, but there was a difference. It had to do with desire. Bodies, at their best, are always wanting—in both senses of the word. Those high school basketball players had zits and skinny legs, but they were trained to summon passion. And they were rewarded with a kind of redemption. They were gracelessness turned to grace.

I eventually played in the pep band, a negligible role in the overall mix. Everyone liked hearing our songs. Distorted and stumbling, they nevertheless added jazz to the main event. But we might as well have been a human jukebox or itinerant musicians from the street, the way fans averted their eyes. We weren't in motion, we weren't quite still. We were just something odd in our stiff, hot uniforms with their high-water pants. At tournaments, in the crush of the crowd, pep bands from various towns were positioned here and there in a cordoned-off gulag. Deep within our boardlike band suits, we perspired. But we enjoyed a bit of importance then. We were court eunuchs at the royal palace.

As a member of the band, the closest I ever came to insinuating my body into the orchestrated whole that is basketball was when I performed my solo cymbal crash during *The Star-Spangled Banner*. I would take one step onto the floor and clear a little room. "And the rockets' red glare. . . . " *Crash!* It occurred to me that I could tamper with the scheme of an evening by being innovative at this point—by executing a modest pratfall or by substituting a triangle's tiny *ping* for the big metallic crash.

But I didn't.

I believed in the drama of basketball; I didn't want to break the spell. And my band position—betwixt and between—was not so bad. It afforded a good vantage point and excellent camouflage. I could become nearly invisible, making it easier for me to dream. And I could really see the players.

Later I had a similar experience while in a community production of *Jesus Christ, Superstar.* There was a rabble-sized cast, dramatic music, an emotional text. I was leper and had to spend most of my time underneath the stage. I would peep through a little gauze-covered porthole (the stage was built on risers), waiting for my cue. Then I would writhe out at various intervals, along with other strategically placed lepers, to clutch at the Savior's robes.

While I was waiting, I would watch the sandaled feet of the Apostles. Because there were so many bodies, with so much happening on the stage, each second of the show was carefully blocked. The Apostles' every move was scripted and meant to be executed just so. The actors, I'm sure, were thinking mainly about their arm gestures (supplicating) and their facial expressions (agonized), just as I did for those few moments when I twisted into view. But from my porthole I was looking at the Apostles' feet, which were right at the level of my eyes. And I was fascinated with what a good job the feet were doing. They moved so confidently, always doing the right thing to contribute to the overall moment. I suppose that if I had seen the whole supplicating, agonized effect from somewhere in row M, I might have thought, Well, this is, after all, community theater. But at foot level I was in Nazareth.

The basketball players of my memory also followed a script with a limited number of positions and modes of execution. Still, their bodies moved spontaneously, intuitively. Maybe that was why they seemed so full of promise to those of us who couldn't play.

Of course the players yearned to indulge in grand gestures—the hair toss, the full-body prostration, the moment of prayer at the free throw line—and sometimes they did. But like actors or dancers caught up in a performance, they didn't know, or didn't appear to know, what their feet were doing. And so it seemed as if they were involved in the truest dance of all.

"The more constraints one imposes, the more one frees one's self of the chains that shackle the spirit."

Stravinsky wrote that in *The Poetics of Music*. "In art," he continued, "as in everything else, one can build only upon a resisting foundation."

By focusing on feet, as gender-equal as any body part can be, I injected myself into the art of basketball. And then the players, with their peculiar constrained grace, affected me. They were, I think now, like male divas of the Chinese opera, women in brackets—beating wings within a tightly defined space. I watched the game, and I was in it; the real actors were me and not-me. We were agents in a combustive play. It was about all of unknown life. For the length of a game, we were an ignited dream.

In my flat band suit I could picture myself any way I wanted. I imagined that I would eventually emerge into the world looking something like them, those leaping players, instead of taking any other form—the domesticated cheerleaders, for example—that I could see.

After high school I stopped watching basketball. I left Cut Bank and considered my departure to be the true beginning of life. All those games had been mere rehearsal. It was time to take the floor.

And then last winter I went to a game, my first in more than 20 years. My six-year-old son, Patrick, and I perched up among the rafters of Dahlberg Arena at the University of Montana in Missoula. I went under the guise of a good mother; Patrick, I said, should get a glimpse of the world of organized sports. He obligingly sat beside me, content with his plastic pom-pom and tiny megaphone—free, for being cute.

Neither of us quite knew what we would see.

There it was, the gleaming yellow-gold of the gym floor, a warm, squeaky contrast to midwinter muck. And there it was, I felt it, that familiar, light-headed sensation of being inside a large windless space. There was the band, duly in its place, having just finished *Satisfaction*. (Our warm-up song was always *Taste of Honey*.)

And there were the cheerleaders: Janes of a regimental jungle, each with one sturdy shoulder bared. Some were being flung about by strong and happy boys in sweaters. Some intoned a dispassionate chant before a *very* large crowd—8,000 or so, certainly as many as had ever watched Cut Bank play Shelby.

And there *they* were. The satin-shorted idols of my youth, wheeling stars in this cozy universe, apostles of grace, dancers at the altar, saints on a saffron stage. . . . There they were. Working up the same celestial sweat.

Women.

Every one of them.

As I entered the real world to begin my true life, other women, younger women—girls from the Hi-Line—started playing basketball for real.

It began, the thump-and-rush rhythm of the game. I watched April Sather from Havre move methodically down the court, fluttering the fingers of her left hand in a semimenacing signal. I watched Malia Kipp, a Blackfeet player from Browning, assume a stance that was both polite and wary, her legs pivoting in perfect synchrony with the game. I looked at the program. The players on the UM team were all from Montana, mostly small towns. Jodi Hinrichs, from Fairfield, hung her head at the free throw line as if in deep repentance, then slipped the ball soundlessly through the net.

I was moved. I was jealous and joyful. I was filled with longing and with bliss.

I saw the players as high school boys, Wolves, Coyotes. They were Buzz, skinny again, Uncle Bob, his hair straight. They were Blackfeet warriors on horses. Lindbergh landing in Paris again and again. They were stars of the Chinese opera, released. They were loose-limbed and glowing. They were slender men in masquerade, and they were women unmasked. They were me. They were me and not-me.

GUN CRAZY

Dorothy Allison

This is a chapter from Allison's 1994 book Skin: Talking About Sex, Class, and Literature.

When we were little, my sister and I would ride with the cousins in the back of my uncle Bo's pickup truck when he drove us up into the foothills where we could picnic and the men could go shooting. I remember standing up behind the cab, watching the tree branches filter the bright Carolina sunshine, letting the wind push my hair behind me, and then wrestling with my cousin, Butch, until my aunt yelled at us to stop.

"Ya'll are gonna fall out," she was always screaming, but we never did. Every stop sign we passed was pocked with bullet holes.

"Fast flying bees," Uncle Jack told us with a perfectly serious expression.

"Hornets with lead in their tails," Bo laughed.

My mama's youngest brother, Bo, kept his guns, an ought-seven rifle and a lovingly restored old Parker shotgun, wrapped in a worn green army blanket. A fold of the blanket was loosely stitched down a third of its length to make a cloth bag, the only sewing Bo ever did in his life. He kept his cleaning kit—a little bag of patches and a plastic bottle of gun oil—in the blanket pouch with the guns. Some evenings he would spread the blanket out in front of the couch and sit there happily cleaning his guns slowly and thoroughly. All the while he would sip cold beer and talk about what a fine time a man could have with his weapons out in the great outdoors. "You got to sit still, perfectly still," he'd say, nod, and sip again, then dab a little more gun oil on the patch he was running through the rifle barrel.

"Oh, you're good at that," someone would always joke.

"The man an't never shot an animal once in his life," Bo's wife, Nessa, told us. "Shot lots of bottles, whiskey bottles, beer bottles, coke-cola bottles. The man's one of the great all-time bottle destroyers."

I grinned. Stop signs and bottles, paper targets and wooden fences. My uncles loved to shoot, it was true, but the only deer they ever brought home was one found drowned in a creek and another that Uncle Jack hit head-on one night when he was driving his Pontiac convertible with the busted headlights.

"Let me help you," I begged my uncle Bo one night when he had pulled out his blanket kit and started the ritual of cleaning his gun. I was eleven, shy but fearless. Bo just looked at me over the angle of the cigarette jutting out of the corner of his mouth. He shook his head.

"I'd be careful," I blurted.

"Nessa, you hear this child?" Bo yelled in the direction of the kitchen and then turned back to me. "An't no such thing as careful where girls and guns are concerned." He took the cigarette out of his mouth and gave me another of those cool, distant looks. "You an't got no business thinking about guns."

"But I want to learn to shoot."

He laughed a deep throaty laugh, coughed a little, then laughed again. "Girls don't shoot," he told me with a smile. "You can do lots of things, girl, but not shooting. That just an't gonna happen."

I glared at him and said, "I bet Uncle Jack will teach me. He knows how careful I can be."

Bo shook his head and tucked the cigarette back in the corner of his mouth. "It an't about careful, it's about you're a girl. You can whine and wiggle all you wont. An't nobody in this family gonna teach you to shoot." His face was stern, his smile completely gone. "That just an't gonna happen."

When I was in high school my best girlfriend was Anne, whose mama worked in the records division at the local children's hospital. One Sunday Anne invited me to go over to the woods out behind the mental hospital, to a hollow there where we could do some plinking.

"Plinking?"

"You know, plinking. Shooting bottles and cans." She pushed her hair back off her face and smiled at me. "If there's any water we'll fill the bottles up and watch it shoot up when the glass breaks. That's my favorite thing."

"You got a gun?" My mouth was hanging open.

"Sure. Mama gave me a rifle for my birthday. Didn't I tell you?"

"I don't think so." I looked away, so she wouldn't see how envious I felt. Her mama had given her a gun for her sixteenth birthday! I had always thought Anne's mama was something special, but that idea was simply amazing.

Anne's mama refused to cook, smoked Marlboros continuously, left the room any time any of her three children mentioned their dead father, and drank cocktails every evening while leaning back in her Lazy-Boy lounge chair and wearing dark eyeshades. "Don't talk to me," she'd hiss between yellow stained teeth. "I got crazy people and drunken orderlies talking at me all day long. I come home, I want some peace and quiet."

"My mama thinks a woman should be able to take care of herself," Anne told me.

"Right," I agreed. "She's right." Inside, I was seething with envy and excitement. Outside, I kept my face smooth and noncommittal. I wanted to shoot, wanted to shoot a shotgun like all my uncles, pepper stop signs and scare dogs. But I'd settle for a rifle, the kind of rifle a woman like Anne's mama would give her sixteen-year-old daughter.

That Sunday I watched closely as Anne slid a bullet into the chamber of her rifle and sighted down the gully to the paper target we had set up thirty feet away. Anne looked like Jane Fonda in *Cat Ballou* after she lost her temper—fierce, blonde, and competent. I swallowed convulsively and wiped sweaty palms on my jeans. I would have given both my big toes to have been able to stand like that, legs apart, feet planted, arms up, and the big rifle perfectly steady as the center circle target was fissured with little bullet holes.

Anne was myopic, skinny, completely obsessed with T. E. Lawrence, and neurotically self-conscious with boys, but holding that rifle tight to her shoulder and peppering the target, she looked different—older and far more interesting. She looked sexy, or maybe the gun looked sexy, I wasn't sure. But I wanted that look. Not Anne, but the power. I wanted to hold a rifle steady, the stock butting my shoulder tightly while I hit the target dead center. My mouth went dry. Anne showed me how to aim the gun a little lower than the center of the target.

"It shoots a little high," she said. "You got to be careful not to let it jump up when it fires." She stood behind me and steadied the gun in my hands. I put the little notch at the peak of the barrel just under the target, tightened my muscles, and pulled the trigger. The rifle still jerked up a little, but a small hole appeared at the outer edge of the second ring of the target.

"Goddamn!" Anne crowed. "You got it, girl." I let the barrel of the rifle drop down, the metal of the trigger guard smooth and warm under my hand.

You got to hold still, I thought. Perfectly still. I sighted along the barrel again, shifting the target notch to the right of the jars Anne had set up earlier. I concentrated, focused, felt my arm become rigid, stern and strong. I pulled back on the trigger slowly, squeezing steadily, the way in the movies they always said it was supposed to be done. The bottle exploded, water shooting out in a wide fine spray.

"Goddamn!" Anne shouted again. I looked over at her. Her glasses had slipped down on her nose and her hair had fallen forward over one eye. Sun shone on her sweaty nose and the polished whites of her teeth. She was staring at me like I had stared at her earlier, her whole face open with pride and delight.

LIVING IN TONGUES

Luc Sante

This essay first appeared in The New York Times Magazine *in 1997.*

The first thing you have to understand about my childhood is that it mostly took place in another language. I was raised speaking French, and did not begin learning English until I was nearly seven years old. Even after that, French continued to be the language I spoke at home with my parents. (I still speak only French with them to this day.) This fact inevitably affects my recall and evocation of my childhood, since I am writing and primarily thinking in English. There are states of mind, even people and events, that seem inaccessible in English, since they are defined by the character of the language through which I perceived them. My second language has turned out to be my principal tool, my means for making a living, and it lies close to the core of my self-definition. My first language, however, is coiled underneath, governing a more primal realm.

French is a pipeline to my infant self, to its unguarded emotions and even to its preserved sensory impressions. I can, for example, use language as a measure of pain. If I stub my toe, I may profanely exclaim, in English, "Jesus!" But in agony, such as when I am passing a kidney stone, I become uncharacteristically reverent, which is only possible for me in French. *"Petit Jésus!"* I will cry, in the tones of nursery religion. When I babble in the delirium of fever or talk aloud in my sleep, I have been told by others, I do so in French. But French is also capable of summoning up a world of lost pleasures. The same idea, expressed in different languages, can have vastly different psychological meanings. If, for example, someone says in English, "Let's go visit Mr. and Mrs. X," the concept is neutral, my reaction determined by what I think of Mr. and Mrs. X. On the other hand, if the suggestion is broached in French, *"Allons dire bonjour,"* the phrasing affects me more powerfully than the specifics. *"Dire bonjour"* calls up a train of associations: for some reason, I see my great-uncle Jules Stelmes, dead at least thirty years, with his fedora and his enormous white mustache and his soft dark eyes. I smell coffee and the raisin bread called *cramique,* hear the muffled bong of a parlor clock and the repetitive commonplaces of chitchat in the drawling accent of the Ardennes, people rolling their r's and leaning hard on their initial *h*'s. I feel a rush-caned chair under me, see white curtains and starched tablecloths, can almost tap my feet on the cold ceramic tiles, perhaps the trompe-l'oeil pattern that covered the entire floor surface of my great-uncle Albert Remacle's farmhouse in Viville. I am sated, sleepy, bored out of my mind.

A large number of French words and turns of phrase come similarly equipped with dense associative catalogues, which may contain a ghostly impression of the first time I understood their use in speech. On the other hand, nearly all English words and phrases have a definite point of origin, which I can usually recall despite the overlaying patina acquired through years of use. Take that word "patina," for example. I don't remember how old I was when I first encountered it, but I know that I immediately linked it to the French *patiner,* meaning "to skate," so that its use calls up an image of a crosshatched pond surface.

Other English words have even more specific histories. There is "coffee," which I spotted on a can of Chock Full o' Nuts in our kitchen in Westfield, New Jersey, in 1960, when I was six. I learned to spell it right away because I was impressed by its insistent doubling of *f*'s and *e*'s. The creative spellings reveled in by commerce in the early 1960s tended to be unhelpful. I didn't know what to make of "kleen" or "Sta-Prest," and it took me some time to appreciate the penguin's invitation on the glass door of the pharmacy: "Come in, it's KOOL inside." Then there was the local dry-cleaning establishment whose signs promised "one-hour Martinizing." I struggled for years to try and plumb that one, coming up with increasingly baroque scenarios.

■ ■ ■

When I started first grade, my first year of American schooling—I had begun school in Belgium at three and a half, in a pre-kindergarten program that taught basic reading, writing, and arithmetic—I knew various words in English, but not how to construct a sentence. My first day remains vivid in its discomfort: I didn't know how to ask to go to the toilet. In addition, my mother had dressed me in a yellow pullover over a white shirt-collar dickey. It was a warm day, and the nun in charge suggested I take off my sweater. Since I didn't understand, she came over and yanked it off me, revealing my sleeveless undershirt.

As the weeks and months went on, I gradually learned how to speak and comprehend the new language, but between home and school, and school and home, I would pass through a sort of fugue state lasting an hour or two during which I could not use either language. For a while, my mother tackled this problem by tutoring me in French grammar and vocabulary as soon as I got home. It never crossed my parents' minds that we should begin employing English as the household tongue. For one thing, my parents' command of it was then rudimentary—I was rapidly outpacing them—and for another, they were never certain that our American sojourn was to be permanent. We were economic refugees, to use the current expression, victims of the collapse of the centuries-old textile industry centered in my native city of Verviers, but my parents' loyalty to their own country was unquestioned.

For several years our family kept up a sort of double role. We were immigrants whose income bobbed just above the poverty line, thanks to my father's capacity for working swing shifts and double shifts in factories (and thanks to the existence of factory jobs); but we were also tourists. As soon as we could afford a used car we began methodically visiting every state park, historical site, and roadside attraction within a reasonable radius, taking hundreds of snapshots—some to send to my grandparents, but many more that were intended for our delectation later on, when we were safely back in Belgium, recalling our fascinating hiatus in the land of large claims and vast distances. This was not to be, owing to family deaths and diverse obligations and uneasily shifting finances, but my parents kept up their faith in an eventual return, and a concomitant relative detachment from the American way of life.

Our household was a European outpost. My parents made earnest attempts to replicate Belgian food, a pursuit that involved long car trips to the then rural middle of Staten Island to purchase leeks from Italian farmers, and expeditions to German butcher shops in Union and Irvington, New Jersey, to find a version of *sirop*—a dense concentrate of pears and apples that is the color and texture of heavy-gauge motor oil and is spread on bread—and various unsatisfactory substitutions. Neither cottage cheese nor ricotta could really pass for the farmer cheese called *makée* (*sirop* and *makée* together make *caca de poule*), but we had little choice in the matter, just as club soda had to stand in for *eau gazeuse,* since we lived in suburbs far from the seltzer belt, and parsley could only ever be a distant cousin to chervil. Desires for gooseberries and red currants, for familiar varieties of apricots and strawberries and potatoes and lettuce, for "real" bread and "real" cheese and "real" beer, simply had to be suppressed.

It wasn't easy constructing a version of Belgium in an apartment in a wooden house, with wood floors and Salvation Army furniture and sash windows and no cellar—not that the situation didn't present certain advantages, such as central heating, hot running water, and numerous appliances, none of which my parents could afford in Belgium, where we had actually been more prosperous. "Belgium" became a mental construct, its principal constituent material being language. We spoke French, thought in French, prayed in French, dreamed in French. Relatives kept us supplied with a steady stream of books and periodicals, my father with his Marabout paperbacks, my mother with the magazine *Femme d'Aujourd'hui* (Woman of Today), and me with history books for kids and comic magazines, in particular *Spirou*, which I received every week. Comics occupy a place in Belgian popular culture roughly comparable to that held in America by rock-and-roll, and like every other Belgian child, I first aspired to become a cartoonist. The comics I produced were always in French and clearly set in Belgium. (I couldn't abide American superhero adventures, although I did love *Mad* and the Sunday funnies, which were more commensurate with a Belgian turn of mind.) Somehow, though, I decided I wanted to become a writer when I was ten, and having made that decision never thought of writing in any language but English. Even so, I continued to conduct my internal monologues in French until late adolescence. For me the French language long corresponded to the soul, while English was the world.

My parents learned the language of their adopted country not without some difficulty. My father could draw on what remained of his high school English, complete with pronunciation rules that wavered between Rhenish German and the BBC, but otherwise my parents had arrived equipped only with the 1945 edition of a conversation manual entitled *L'Anglais sans peine* (English Without Toil). This volume, published by the Assimil firm of Paris and Brussels, is sufficiently embedded in Francophone consciousness that you can still raise a snicker by quoting its opening phrase, "My tailor is rich." (English speakers, of course, will have no idea what you are talking about.) The book could not have been much help, especially since its vocabulary and references were attuned not to 1960s America but to Britain in the 1930s: "The Smiths had wired ahead the time of their arrival, and were expected for lunch at Fairview." This was also true of their other textbook, a reader called *Short Narratives* published in Ghent: "The proprietor of an eating-house ordered some bills to be printed for his window, with the words, 'Try our mutton pies!'" There were also some evening classes at the YMCA in Summit, New Jersey, where we eventually settled, but I don't recall their lasting very long.

My parents' circle of acquaintances was almost entirely Belgian. My father had grown up in a tenement apartment in Verviers downstairs from the Dosquet family, whose children became his closest friends. The second daughter, Lucy, married an American GI after the war and they went to live in his native northern New Jersey. In 1953, her younger brother, Léopold (known as Pol), who was the same age as my father, followed suit with his wife, Jeanne. They were enthusiastic about the States and wrote rapturous letters. In 1957, when the prospects of my father's employer, an iron foundry that manufactured wool-carding machinery, were beginning to look grim, Jeanne Dosquet returned on a visit, and we all spent a week at the seaside resort of De Panne, at a socialist hostelry called the Hôtel Germinal, where plans were made for our own emigration.

After our arrival, we briefly shared an apartment with the Dosquets, a tight and uncomfortable situation. They introduced my parents to such Belgians as they had met by chance, in particular the three Van Hemmelrijk sisters and their mother, bourgeois French-speaking Antwerpers who had somehow ended up in America in straitened circumstances. There were others, too: a couple from Dolhain, near Verviers, who worked as caretakers of an estate in Tuxedo Park, New York, and another French-speaking Fleming, whom I only ever knew as Marie-Louise *"du facteur,"* because she had once been married to a mailman. She contributed another item to my burgeoning English vocabulary. One evening, while we were all watching television, Cesar Romero appeared on the screen: "Such a handsome man!" Marie-Louise exclaimed in English. To this day, any appearance of the word "handsome" calls up, in my mind's eye, the faint but unmistakable impression of Cesar Romero.

Even non-Belgian acquaintances tended to be foreigners whose grasp of the local tongue was as limited as ours. In Summit, our downstairs neighbors for a while were Hungarians named Szivros, who had fled their country after the doomed Budapest uprising Of 1956. Since we did not yet own a television, Mrs. Szivros would stand at the foot of the stairs of an evening and call up, "Missis, missis! *Million Dollar Movie!*" Given the landscape, then, it is not surprising that my parents were somewhat at sea, knocked about among languages.

Sometimes, especially under pressure, my parents would reach for one tongue or the other and find themselves instead speaking Walloon, the native patois of southern Belgium. Walloon, now moribund, is usually identified as a dialect of French, whereas it is actually as old as the patois of Île-de-France, which became the official language—the eleventh edition of the *Encyclopedia Britannica* in fact describes it as the northernmost Romance language. Like English, Walloon incorporates a substantial body of words that derives from Old Low German, so that it could, if unconsciously, seem like the middle ground between English and French. An often-told story in my family related how Lucy Dosquet, when her GI suitor arrived looking like a slob, angrily ordered him in Walloon, *"Louke-tu el mireu!"* He understood perfectly, and studied his reflection.

■ ■ ■

Walloon was the household tongue of all the relatives of my grandparents' generation. Their parents in turn might have spoken nothing else; that no one bothered to establish rules for the writing of Walloon until the very beginning of this century, just in time for its decline in currency, partly accounts for the fact that nearly everyone in the family tree before my grandparents' time was illiterate. Walloon enjoyed a brief literary flowering that started in the 1890s but was largely killed off by World War I. My paternal grandfather acted in the Walloon theater in Verviers during its heyday, and my father followed in his footsteps after World War II, but by then it had largely become an exercise in nostalgia. Today, only old people still speak Walloon, and poor ones at that, since its use is considered rude by merchants, businessmen, and the middle class in general, and young people simply don't care. Young Walloons nowadays have been formed by television, movies, and pop music, much of it emanating from France, and they have seemingly acquired the Parisian accent *en bloc.*

I was raised in a Belgian bubble, though, which means, among other things, that my speech is marked by the old Verviers Walloon accent, which causes observant Belgians some confusion. They can't reconcile that accent with the American flavor that has inevitably crept in, nor with my age and apparent class status. My French speech is also peppered with archaisms; I find myself unconsciously saying, for example, *"auto"* instead of *"voiture"* to mean "car," or *"illustré"* instead of *"revue"* to mean "magazine," expressions redolent of the thirties and forties, if not earlier.

The sound of Walloon, on those rare occasions when I hear it, affects me emotionally with even more force than French does. Hearing, as I did a few months ago, an old man simply greeting his friend by saying, *"Bôd-jou, Djôsef,"* can move me nearly to tears. But, of course, I hear much more than just "Hiya, Joe"—I hear a ghostly echo of my maternal grandfather greeting his older brother, Joseph Nandrin, for one thing, and I also hear the table talk of countless generations of workers and farmers and their wives, not that I particularly wish to subscribe to notions of collective ethnic memory. Walloon is a good-humored, long-suffering language of the poor, naturally epigrammatic, ideal for both choleric fervor and calm reflection, wry and often psychologically acute—reminiscent in some ways of Scottish and in some ways of Yiddish. Walloon is often my language of choice when, for instance, I am sizing up people at a party, but I have no one to speak it with at home. (My wife hails from Akron, Ohio.) I sometimes boast that, among the seven million people in New York City, I am the only Walloon speaker, which may or may not be true.

My three languages revolve around and inform one another. I live in an English-speaking world, of course, and for months on end I may speak nothing else. I do talk with my parents once a week by phone, but over the years we have developed a family dialect that is so motley it amounts to a Creole. I cannot snap back and forth between languages with ease, but need to be surrounded by French for several days before I can properly recover its rhythm, and so recover my idiomatic vocabulary—a way of thinking rather than just a set of words—and not merely translate English idioms. This means that I am never completely present at any given moment, since different aspects of my self are contained in different rooms of language, and a complicated apparatus of air locks prevents the doors from being flung open all at once. Still, there are subterranean correspondences between the linguistic domains that keep them from stagnating. The classical order of French, the Latin-Germanic dialectic of English, and the onomatopoeic-peasant lucidity of Walloon work on one another critically, help enhance precision, and reduce cant.

I like to think that this system helps fortify me in areas beyond the merely linguistic. I am not rootless but multiply rooted. This makes it impossible for me to fence off a plot of the world and decide that everyone dwelling outside those boundaries is "other." I am grateful to the accidents of my displaced upbringing, which taught me several kinds of irony. Ethnically, I am about as homogeneous as it is possible to be: aside from one great-grandmother who came from Luxembourg, my gene pool derives entirely from an area smaller than the five boroughs of New York City. I was born in the same town as every one of my Sante forebears at least as far back as the mid-sixteenth century, which is as far back as the records go. Having been transplanted from my native soil, though, and having had to construct an identity in response to a double set of demands, one from my background and one from my environment, I have become permanently "other." The choice I am faced with is simple: either I am at home everywhere or I am nowhere at all; either I realize my ties to human beings of every race and nationality or I will die, asphyxiated by the vacuum. Mere tolerance is idle and useless—if I can't recognize myself in others, no matter how remote in origin or behavior they might appear, I might as well declare war upon myself.

BREAKING CLEAN

Judy Blunt

This piece was originally published in Northern Lights *in 1991.*

I rarely go back to the ranch where I was born or to the neighboring land where I bore the fourth generation of a cattle dynasty. My people live where hardpan and sagebrush flats give way to the Missouri River Breaks, a country so harsh and wild and distant that it must grow its own replacements, as it grows its own food, or it will die. Hereford cattle grow slick and mean foraging along the cutbanks for greasewood shoots and buffalo grass. A two-hour trip over gumbo roads will take you to the lone main street of the nearest small town.

"Get tough," my father snapped in irritation as I dragged my feet at the edge of a two-acre potato field. He gave me a gunnysack and started me down the rows pulling the tough fanweed that towered over the potato plants. I was learning then the necessary lessons of weeds and seeds and blisters. My favorite story as a child was of how I fainted in the garden when I was eight. My mother had to pry my fingers from around the handle of the hoe, she said, and she also said I was stupid not to wear a hat in the sun. But she was proud. My granddad hooted with glee when he heard about it.

"She's a hell of a little worker," he said, shaking his head. I was a hell of a little worker from that day forward, and I learned to wear a hat.

I am sometimes amazed at my own children, their incredulous outrage if they are required to do the dishes twice in one week, their tender self-absorption with minor bumps and bruises. As a mom I've had to teach myself to croon over thorn scratches, admire bloody baby teeth, and sponge the dirt from scraped shins. But in my mind, my mother's voice and that of her mother still compete for expression. "Oh for Christ's sake, you aren't hurt!" they're saying, and for a moment I struggle. For a moment I want to tell this new generation about my little brother calmly spitting out a palm full of tooth chips and wading back in to grab the biggest calf in the branding pen. I want to tell them how tough I was, falling asleep at the table with hands too sore to hold a fork, or about their grandmother, who cut off three fingers on the blades of a sickle mower and finished the field before she came in to get help. For a moment I'm terrified I'll slip and tell them to get tough.

Like my parents and grandparents, I was born and trained to live there. I could rope and ride and jockey a John Deere swather as well as my brothers, but being female, I also learned to bake bread and can vegetables and reserve my opinion when the men were talking. When a bachelor neighbor twice my age began courting me when I was sixteen, my parents were proud and hopeful. He and his father ran a good, tight spread with over a thousand head of cattle. They held a thirty-thousand-acre lease. They drove new Chevy pickups.

After supper one spring evening, my mother and I stood in the kitchen. She held her back stiff as her hands shot like pistons into the mound of bread dough on the counter. I stood tough beside her. On the porch, Jack had presented my father with a bottle of whiskey and was asking Dad's permission to marry me. I wanted her to grab my cold hand and tell me how to run. I wanted her to smooth the crumpled letter from the garbage can and read the praise of my high school principal. I wanted her to tell me what I could be.

She rounded the bread neatly and efficiently and began smoothing lard over the top, intent on her fingers as they tidied the loaves.

"He's a good man," she said finally.

In the seventh grade this year, my daughter has caught up with the culture shock and completed her transition from horse to bicycle, from boot-cut Levi's to acid-washed jeans. She delights me with her discoveries. Knowing little of slumber parties, roller skates, or packs of giggling girls, sometimes I'm more her peer than her parent. She writes, too; long, sentimental stories about lost puppies that find homes and loving two-parent families with adventurous daughters. Her characters are usually right back where they started, rescued and happy by the end of the story. She watches television now.

"Do you hate Daddy?" she asked once, from the depths of a divorced child's sadness.

"Your daddy," I replied, "is a good man."

In the manner of good ranchmen, my father and Jack squatted on their haunches on the porch facing each other. The whiskey bottle rested on the floor between them. Jack's good white shirt was buttoned painfully around his neck. Dad had pushed his Stetson back, and a white band of skin glowed above his dark face, smooth and strangely delicate. When I moved to the doorway, their conversation was shifting from weather and cattle to marriage. As Dad tilted back heavily on one heel to drink from the neck of the bottle, Jack looked down and began to plot our life with one finger in the dust on the floor.

"I been meaning to stop by . . . ," Jack said to the toe of his boot. He looked up to catch Dad's eye. Dad nodded and looked away.

"You figured a spot yet?" He spoke deliberately, weighing each word. Like all the big ranches out there, Jack's place had been pieced together from old homesteads and small farms turned back to grass.

"Morgan place has good buildings," Jack replied, holding Dad's gaze for a moment. He shifted the bottle to his lips and passed it back to Dad.

"Fair grass on the north end, but the meadows need work," Dad challenged. Jack shifted slightly to the left, glancing to the west through the screen door. The setting sun was balanced on the blue tips of the pines in the distance. He worked at the stiffness of his collar, leaving gray smudges of dust along his throat. Settling back, he spoke with a touch of defiance.

"If a person worked it right . . ." Then his eyes found his boots again. He held his head rigid, waiting.

Dad smoothed one hand along his jaw as if in deep thought, and the two men squatted silently for several minutes. Then Dad drew a long breath and blew it out.

"Old Morgan used to get three cuttings on a rain year," he said at last. Jack's head rose, and he met my father's steady look.

"A person could make a go of it," he said, and Dad nodded slightly. I moved against the doorjamb. It was darker now, and the light from the kitchen threw my shadow across to the floorboards between them. My silhouette was long and thin, barely touching their boots on either side.

"A person could make a go of it," Jack repeated softly. Dad's shoulders lifted slightly and dropped in mock defeat. He placed a hand on each knee and pushed himself up, Jack rising beside him and they shook hands, grinning. Twisting suddenly, Dad reached down and grabbed the whiskey. He held it high in a toast, then leaned forward and tapped Jack's chest with the neck of the bottle.

"And you, you cocky son of a bitch! Don't you try planting anything too early, understand?" They were still laughing when they entered the kitchen.

I talk to my father twice a year now, on Christmas and Father's Day. We talk about the yearling weights and the rain, or the lack of rain. My parents lost a daughter when I moved away, but they will have Jack forever. He is closer to them in spirit than I am in blood, and shares their bewilderment and anger at my rejection of their life. As the ultimate betrayal, I have taken Jack's sons, interrupting the perfect rites of passage. The move was hardest on the boys, for here they are only boys. At the ranch they were men in training, and they mourn this loss of prestige.

"I used to drive tractor for my dad," my eldest son relates to his friends now, and they scoff. "You're only eleven years old," they laugh and he's frustrated to bitter tears. He will go back, that one. He will have to. But he will return an outsider, and his father knows this. The first son of the clan to cross the county line and survive will find it easier to leave a second time if he has to. If he spends his life there, he will still have memories of symphonies and tennis shoes and basketball. If he marries and has children, he will raise them knowing that, at least technically, boys can cry.

I stuck with the bargain sealed on my parents' porch for over twelve years, although my faith in martyrdom as a way of life dwindled. I collected children and stress-related disorders the way some of the women collected dress patterns and ceramic owls. It was hard to shine when all the good things had already been done. Dorothy crocheted tissue covers and made lampshades from Styrofoam egg cartons. Pearle looped thick, horrible rugs from rags and denim scraps. Helen gardened a half acre of land and raised two hundred turkeys in her spare time. And everyone attended the monthly meetings of the Near and Far Club to answer roll call with her favorite new recipe.

These were the successful ranchwomen who moved from barn to kitchen to field with patient, tireless steps. I kept up with the cycles of crops and seasons and moons, and I did it all well. I excelled. But I couldn't sleep. I quit eating. It wasn't enough.

I saved for three years and bought my typewriter from the Sears, Roebuck catalog. I typed the first line while the cardboard carton lay around it in pieces. I wrote in a cold sweat on long strips of freezer paper that emerged from the keys thick and rich with ink. At first I only wrote at night when the children and Jack slept, emptying myself onto the paper until I could lie down. Then I began writing during the day, when the men were working in the fields. The children ran brown and wild and happy. The garden gave birth and died with rotting produce fat under its vines. The community buzzed. Dorothy offered to teach me how to crochet.

One day Jack's father, furious because lunch for the hay crew was late, took my warm, green typewriter to the shop and killed it with a sledgehammer.

A prescribed distance of beige plush separated us. On a TV monitor nearby, zigzag lines distorted our images. Jack's face looked lean and hard. My face showed fear and exhaustion. The years were all there in black and white. Mike, our marriage counselor, stood behind the video camera adjusting the sound level. We were learning to communicate, Jack and I. We each held a sweaty slip of paper with a list of priority topics we had prepared for this day. Our job was to discuss them on camera. Next week we would watch our debate and learn what areas needed improvement. We talked by turns, neither allowed to interrupt the other, for three minutes on each topic.

Jack was indignant, bewildered by my topics. I, on the other hand, could have written his list myself. Somewhere in a dusty file drawer is a film of an emaciated, haggard woman hesitantly describing her needs and dreams to a tight-jawed man who twists his knuckles and shakes his head because he wants to interrupt her, and he can't. His expression shows that he doesn't know this woman; she's something he never bargained for. When it's over, they are both shaking and glad to get away.

"Jack," Mike once asked, "how often do you tell your wife you love her?"

"Oh, I've told her that before," he replied cautiously. I cut into the conversation from my corner of the ring.

"You only told me you love me once, and that was the day we were married." I said.

"Well." Jack said, injured and defensive. "I never took it back, did I?"

The break, when it came, was so swift and clean that I sometimes dream I went walking in the coulee behind the ranch house and emerged on the far side of the mountains. It's different here—not easier, but different. And it's enough.

SHAME
—■—
Dick Gregory

"Shame" is from Gregory's 1964 book Nigger: An Autobiography.

I never learned hate at home, or shame. I had to go to school for that. I was about seven years old when I got my first big lesson. I was in love with a little girl named Helene Tucker, a light-complected little girl with pigtails and nice manners. She was always clean and she was smart in school. I think I went to school then mostly to look at her. I brushed my hair and even got me a little old handkerchief. It was a lady's handkerchief, but I didn't want Helene to see me wipe my nose on my hand. The pipes were frozen again, there was no water in the house, but I washed my socks and shirt every night. I'd get a pot, and go over to Mister Ben's grocery store, and stick my pot down into his soda machine. Scoop out some chopped ice. By evening the ice melted to water for washing. I got sick a lot that winter because the fire would go out at night before the clothes were dry. In the morning I'd put them on, wet or dry, because they were the only clothes I had.

Everybody's got a Helene Tucker, a symbol of everything you want. I loved her for her goodness, her cleanness, her popularity. She'd walk down my street and my brothers and sisters would yell, "Here comes Helene," and I'd rub my tennis sneakers on the back of my pants and wish my hair wasn't so nappy and the white folks' shirt fit me better. I'd run out on the street. If I knew my place and didn't come too close, she'd wink at me and say hello. That was a good feeling. Sometimes I'd follow her all the way home, and shovel the snow off her walk and try to make friends with her Momma and her aunts. I'd drop money on her stoop late at night on my way back from shining shoes in the taverns. And she had a Daddy, and he had a good job. He was a paper hanger.

I guess I would have gotten over Helene by summertime, but something happened in that classroom that made her face hang in front of me for the next twenty-two years. When I played the drums in high school it was for Helene and when I broke track records in college it was for Helene and when I started standing behind microphones and heard applause I wished Helene could hear it too. It wasn't until I was twenty-nine years old and married and making money that I finally got her out of my system. Helene was sitting in that classroom when I learned to be ashamed of myself.

It was on a Thursday. I was sitting in the back of the room, in a seat with a chalk circle drawn around it. The idiot's seat, the troublemaker's seat.

The teacher thought I was stupid. Couldn't spell, couldn't read, couldn't do arithmetic. Just stupid. Teachers were never interested in finding out that you couldn't concentrate because you were so hungry, because you hadn't had any breakfast. All you could think about was noontime, would it ever come? Maybe you could sneak into the cloakroom and steal a bite of some kid's lunch out of a coat pocket. A bite of something. Paste. You can't really make a meal of paste, or put it on bread for a sandwich, but sometimes I'd scoop a few spoonfuls out of the big paste jar in the back of the room. Pregnant people get strange tastes. I was pregnant with poverty. Pregnant with dirt and pregnant with smells that made people turn away, pregnant with cold and pregnant with shoes that were never bought for me, pregnant with five other people in my bed and no Daddy in the next room, and pregnant with hunger. Paste doesn't taste too bad when you're hungry.

The teacher thought I was a troublemaker. All she saw from the front of the room was a little black boy who squirmed in his idiot's seat and made noises and poked the kids around him. I guess she couldn't see a kid who made noises because he wanted someone to know he was there.

It was on a Thursday, the day before the Negro payday. The eagle always flew on Friday. The teacher was asking each student how much his father would give to the Community Chest. On Friday night, each kid would get the money from his father, and on Monday he would bring it to the school. I decided I was going to buy a Daddy then. I had money in my pocket from shining shoes and selling papers, and whatever Helene Tucker pledged for her Daddy I was going to top it. And I'd hand the money right in. I wasn't going to wait to Monday to buy me a Daddy.

I was shaking, scared to death. The teacher opened her book and started calling out names alphabetically.

"Helene Tucker?"

"My Daddy said he'd give two dollars and fifty cents."

"That's very nice, Helene. Very, very nice indeed."

That made me feel pretty good. It wouldn't take too much to top that. I had almost three dollars in dimes and quarters in my pocket. I stuck my hand in my pocket and held onto the money, waiting for her to call my name. But the teacher closed her book after she called everybody else in the class.

I stood and raised my hand.

"What is it now?"

"You forgot me."

She turned toward the blackboard. "I don't have time to be playing with you, Richard."

"My Daddy said he'd . . ."

"Sit down, Richard, you're disturbing the class."

"My Daddy said he'd give . . . fifteen dollars."

She turned around and looked mad. "We are collecting this money for you and your kind, Richard Gregory. If your Daddy can give fifteen dollars you have no business being on relief."

"I got it right now, I got it right now, my Daddy gave it to me to turn in today, my Daddy said . . ."

"And furthermore," she said, looking right at me, her nostrils getting big and her lips getting thin and her eyes opening wide. "We know you don't have a Daddy."

Helene Tucker turned around, her eyes full of tears. She felt sorry for me. Then I couldn't see her too well because I was crying, too.

"Sit down, Richard."

And I always thought the teacher kind of liked me. She always picked me to wash the blackboard on Friday, after school. That was a big thrill, it made me feel important. If I didn't wash it, come Monday the school might not function right.

"Where are you going, Richard?"

I walked out of school that day, and for a long time I didn't go back very often. There was shame there.

Now there was shame everywhere. It seemed like the whole world had been inside that classroom, everyone had heard what the teacher had said, everyone had turned around and felt sorry for me. There was shame in going to the Worthy Boys Annual Christmas Dinner for you and your kind, because everyone knew what a worthy boy was. Why couldn't they just call it the Boys Annual Dinner, why'd they have to give it a name? There was shame in wearing the brown and orange and white plaid mackinaw the welfare gave to 3,000 boys. Why'd it have to be the same for everybody so when you walked down the street the people could see you were on relief? It was a nice warm mackinaw and it had a hood, and my Momma beat me and called me a little rat when she found out I stuffed it in the bottom of a pail full of garbage way over on Cottage Street. There was shame in running over to Mister Ben's at the end of the day and asking for his rotten peaches, there was shame in asking Mrs. Simmons for a spoonful of sugar, there was shame in running out to meet the relief truck. I hated that truck, full of food for you and your kind. I ran into the house and hid when it came. And then I started to sneak through alleys, to take the long way home so the people going into White's Eat Shop wouldn't see me. Yeah, the whole world heard the teacher that day, we all know you don't have a Daddy.

It lasted for a while, this kind of numbness. I spent a lot of time feeling sorry for myself. And then one day I met this wino in a restaurant. I'd been out hustling all day, shining shoes, selling newspapers, and I had googobs of money in my pocket. Bought me a bowl of chili for fifteen cents, and a cheeseburger for fifteen cents, and a Pepsi for five cents, and a piece of chocolate cake for ten cents. That was a good meal. I was eating when this old wino came in. I love winos because they never hurt anyone but themselves.

The old wino sat down at the counter and ordered twenty-six cents worth of food. He ate it like he really enjoyed it. When the owner, Mister Williams, asked him to pay the check, the old wino didn't lie or go through his pocket like he suddenly found a hole.

He just said: "Don't have no money."

The owner yelled: "Why in hell you come in here and eat my food if you don't have no money? That food cost me money."

Mister Williams jumped over the counter and knocked the wino off his stool and beat him over the head with a pop bottle. Then he stepped back and watched the wino bleed. Then he kicked him. And he kicked him again.

I looked at the wino with blood all over his face and I went over. "Leave him alone, Mister Williams. I'll pay the twenty-six cents."

The wino got up, slowly, pulling himself up to the stool, then up to the counter, holding on for a minute until his legs stopped shaking so bad. He looked at me with pure hate. "Keep your twenty-six cents. You don't have to pay, not now. I just finished paying for it."

He started to walk out, and as he passed me, he reached down and touched my shoulder. "Thanks, sonny, but it's too late now. Why didn't you pay before?"

I was pretty sick about that. I waited too long to help another man.

THE GANGSTER WE ARE ALL LOOKING FOR

Lê Thi Diem Thúy

This essay was published in The Massachusetts Review *in 1997.*

Vietnam is a black-and-white photograph of my grandparents sitting in bamboo chairs in their front courtyard. They are sitting tall and proud, surrounded by chickens and roosters. Their feet are separated from the dirt by thin sandals. My grandfather's broad forehead is shining. So too are my grandmother's famed sad eyes. The animals are obliviously pecking at the ground. This looks like a wedding portrait, though it is actually a photograph my grandparents had taken late in life, for their children, especially for my mother. When I think of this portrait of my grandparents in the last years of their life, I always envision a beginning. To what or where, I don't know, but always a beginning.

When my mother, a Catholic schoolgirl from the South, decided to marry my father, a Buddhist gangster from the North, her parents disowned her. This is in the photograph, though it is not visible to the eye. If it were, it would be a deep impression across the soft dirt of my grandparents' courtyard. Her father chased her out of the house, beating her with the same broom she had used every day of her life, from the time she could stand up and sweep to the morning of the very day she was chased away.

The year my mother met my father, there were several young men work-ing at her house, running errands for her father, pickling vegetables with her mother. It was understood by everyone that these men were courting my mother. My mother claims she had no such understanding.

She treated these men as brothers, sometimes as uncles even, later ex-claiming in self-defense, "I didn't even know about love then."

Ma says love came to her in a dark movie theater. She doesn't remember what movie it was or why she'd gone to see it, only that she'd gone alone and found herself sitting beside him. In the dark, she couldn't make out his face but noticed he was handsome. She wondered if he knew she was watching him out of the corner of her eye. Watching him without embar-rassment or shame. Watching him with a strange curiosity, a feeling that made her want to trace and retrace his silhouette with her fingertips until she'd memorized every feature and could call his face to her in any dark place she passed through. Later, in the shadow of the beached fishing boats on the blackest nights of the year, she would call him to mind, his face a warm companion for her body on the edge of the sea.

In the early days of my parents' courtship, my mother told stories. She confessed elaborate dreams about the end of war: foods she'd eat (a ban-quet table, mangoes piled high to the ceiling); songs she'd make up and sing, clapping her hands over her head and throwing her hair like a horse's mane; dances she'd do, hopping from one foot to the other. Unlike the responsible favorite daughter or sister she was to her family, with my father, in the forest, my mother became reckless, drunk on her youth and the possibility of love. Ignoring the chores to be done at home, she rolled her pants up to her knees, stuck her bare feet in puddles, and learned to smoke a cigarette.

She tied a vermilion ribbon in her hair. She became moody. She did her chores as though they were favors to her family, forgetting that she ate the same rice and was dependent on the same supply of food. It seemed to her the face that stared back at her from deep inside the family well was the face of a woman she had never seen before. At night she lay in bed and thought of his hands, the way his thumb flicked down on the lighter and brought fire to her cigarette. She began to wonder what the forests were like before the trees were dying. She remembered her father had once de-scribed to her the smiling broadness of leaves, jungles thick in the tangle of rich soil.

One evening, she followed my father in circles through the forest, sup-posedly in search of the clearing that would take them to his aunt's house. They wandered aimlessly into darkness, never finding the clearing or the aunt she knew he never had.

"You're not from here," she said.

"I know."

"So tell me, what's your aunt's name?"

"Xuan."

"Spring?"

"Yes."

She laughed. I can't be here, she thought.

"My father will be looking for me—"

"I'll walk you home. It's not too late."

In the dark, she could feel his hand extending toward her, filling the space between them. They had not touched once the entire evening and now he stood offering his hand to her. She stared at him for a long time. There was a small scar on his chin, curved like her fingernail. It was too dark to see this. She realized she had memorized his face.

My first memory of my father's face is framed by the coiling barbed wire of a prison camp in South Vietnam. My mother's voice crosses through the wire. She is whispering his name and, in this utterance, caressing him. Over and over she calls him to her: "Anh Minh, Anh Minh." His name becomes a tree she presses her body against. The act of calling blows around them like a warm breeze, and when she utters her own name, it is the second half of a verse that began with his. She drops her name like a pebble is dropped into a well. She wants to be engulfed by him. "Anh Minh, em My. Anh Minh. Em, em My."

She is crossing through barbed wire the way some people step through open windows. She arrives warm, the slightest film of sweat on her bare arms. She says, "It's me, it's me." Shy and formal and breathless, my parents are always meeting for the first time. Savoring the sound of a name, marveling at the bone structure.

I trail behind them, the tip of their dragon's tail. I am suspended like a silk banner from the body of a kite. They flick me here and there. I twist and turn in the air, connected to them by this fabric that worms spin.

For a handful of pebbles and my father's sharp profile my mother left home and never returned. Imagine a handful of pebbles. The casual way he tossed them at her as she was walking home from school with her girlfriends. He did this because he liked her and wanted to let her know. Boys are dumb that way, my mother told me. A handful of pebbles, to be thrown in anger, in desperation, in joy. My father threw them in love. Ma says they touched her like warm kisses, these pebbles he had been holding in the sun. Warm kisses on the curve of her back, sliding down the crook of her arm, grazing her ankles and landing around her feet in the hot sand.

What my father told her could have been a story. There was no one in the South to confirm the details of his life. He said he came from a semi-aristocratic Northern family. Unlacing his boot, he pulled out his foot and told her to pay close attention to how his second toe was significantly longer than his other toes. "A sure sign of aristocracy," he claimed. His nose was high, he said, because his mother was French, one of the many mistresses his father kept. He found this out when he was sixteen. That year, he ran away from home and came south.

"There are thieves, gamblers, drunks I've met who remind me of people in my family. It's the way they're dreamers. My family's a garden full of dreamers lying on their backs, staring at the sky, drunk and choking on their dreaming." He said this while leaning against a tree, his arms folded across his bare chest, his eyes staring at the ground, his shoulders golden.

She asked her mother, "What does it mean if your second toe is longer than your other toes?"

"It means . . . your mother will die before your father," her mother said.

"I heard somewhere it's a sign of aristocracy."

"Huh! What do we know about aristocracy?"

My father's toes fascinated my mother. When she looked at his bare feet she saw ten fishing boats, two groups of five. Within each group, the second boat ventured ahead, leading the others. She would climb a tree, stand gripping the branch with her own toes, and stare down at his. She directed him to stand in the mud. There, she imagined what she saw to be ten small boats surrounded by black water, a fleet of junks journeying in the dark.

She would lean back and enjoy this vision, never explaining to him what it was she saw. She left him to wonder about her senses as he stood, cigarette in hand, staring at her trembling ankles, not moving until she told him to.

I was born in the alley behind my grandparents' house. At three in the morning my mother dragged herself out of the bed in the small house she and my father lived in after they married.

He was in prison, so, alone, she began to walk. She cut a crooked line on the beach. Moving in jerky steps, like a ball tossed on the waves, she seemed to be thrown along without direction. She walked to the schoolhouse, sat on the sand, and leaned against the first step. She felt grains of sand pressing against her back. Each grain was a minute pinprick that became increasingly painful to her. She felt as though her back would break out in a wash of blood. She thought, I am going to bleed to death. We are going to die.

In front of the schoolhouse lay a long metal tube. No one knew where it came from. It seemed always to have been there. Children hid in it, crawled through it, spoke to one another at either end of it, marched across it, sat on it, and confided secrets beside it. There had been so little to play with at the school recesses. This long metal tube became everything. A tarp was suspended over it, to shield it from the sun. The tube looked like a blackened log that sat in a room without walls. When the children sat in a line on the tube, their heads bobbing this way and that in conversation, it seemed they were sitting under a canopied raft.

The night I was born, my mother looked at this tube and imagined it to be the badly burnt arm of a dying giant whose body was buried in the sand. She could not decide if he had been buried in the sand and was trying to get out or if he had tried to bury himself in the sand but was unable to pull his arm under in time. In time for what? She had heard a story about a girl in a neighboring town who was killed during a napalm bombing. The bombing happened on an especially hot night when this girl had walked to the beach to cool her feet in the water, They found her floating on the sea. The phosphorus from the napalm made her body glow like a lantern. In her mind, my mother built a canopy for this girl. She started to cry, thinking of the buried giant, the floating girl, these bodies stopped in midstep, on their way somewhere.

She began to walk toward the tube. She had a sudden urge to be inside it. The world felt dangerous to her and she was alone. At the mouth of the tube she bent down; her belly blocked the opening. She tried the other side, the other mouth. Again her belly stopped her. "But I remember," she muttered out loud, "as a girl I sometimes slept in here." This was what she wanted now, to sleep inside the tube.

"Tall noses come from somewhere—"
   "Not from here."
   "Not tall noses."

Eyes insinuate, moving from her nose to mine then back again. Mouths suck air in, form it into the darkest shade of contempt, then spit it at her feet as she walks by. I am riding on her hip. I am the new branch that makes the tree bend, but she walks with her head held high. She knows where she pulled me from. No blue eye.

Ma says war is a bird with a broken wing flying over the countryside, trailing blood and burying crops in sorrow. If something grows in spite of this, it is both a curse and a miracle. When I was born, she cried when I cried, knowing I had breathed war in and she could never shake it out of me. Ma says war makes it dangerous to breathe, though she knows you die if you don't. She says she could have thrown me against the wall, breaking me until I coughed up this war which is killing us all. She could have stomped on it in the dark and danced on it like a madwoman dancing on gravestones. She could have ground it down to powder and spit on it, but didn't I know? War has no beginning and no end. It crosses oceans like a splintered boat filled with people singing a sad song.

Every morning Ahn wakes up in the house next to mine, a yellow duplex she and I call a townhouse because we found out from a real estate ad that a townhouse is a house that has an upstairs and a downstairs. My father calls Ahn the "chicken-egg girl." Each morning Ahn's mother loads a small pushcart with stacks of eggs and Ahn walks all over Linda Vista selling eggs. Her back yard is full of chickens and roosters. Sometimes you can see a rooster fly up and balance itself on the back gate, and it will crow and crow, off and on, all day long until dark comes.

We live in the country of California, the province of San Diego, the village of Linda Vista. We live in old Navy Housing, bungalows that were built in the 1940s and '50s. Since the 1980s these bungalows have housed Vietnamese, Cambodian, and Laotian refugees from the Vietnam War. When we moved in, we had to sign a form promising not to push fish bones down the garbage disposal.

We live in a yellow row house on Westinghouse Street. Our house is one story, made of wood and plaster. We are connected to six two-story houses and another one-story house at the other end. Across from our row of houses, separated by a field of brown dirt, sits another row of yellow houses, same as ours and facing us like a sad twin. Linda Vista is full of houses like ours, painted in peeling shades of olive green, baby blue, and sunbaked yellow.

There's new Navy Housing on Linda Vista Road, the long street that takes you out of here. We see the people there watering their lawns, the children riding pink tricycles up and down the cul-de-sacs. We see them in Victory Supermarket, buying groceries with cash. In Kelley Park they have picnics and shoot each other with water guns. At school their kids are Most Popular, Most Beautiful, Most Likely to Succeed. Though there are more Vietnamese, Cambodian, and Laotian kids at the school, we are not Most of anything in the yearbook. They call us Yang because one year a bunch of Laotian kids with the last name Yang came to our school. The Navy Housing kids started calling all the refugee kids Yang.

Yang. Yang. Yang.

Ma says living next to Ahn's family reminds her of Vietnam because the blue tarp suspended above Ahn's back yard is the bright blue of the South China Sea. Ma says isn't it funny how sky and sea follow you from place to place as if they too were traveling and not just the boat that travels across or between them. Ma says even Ahn reminds her of Vietnam, the way she sets out for market each morning.

Ba becomes a gardener. Overnight. He buys a truck full of equipment and a box of business cards from Uncle Twelve, who is moving to Texas to become a fisherman. The business cards read "Tom's Professional Gardening Service" and have a small, green embossed picture of a man pushing a lawn mower. The man's back is to the viewer, so no one who doesn't already know can tell it's not Ba. He says I can be his secretary because I speak the best English. If you call us on the business phone, you will hear me say: "Hello, you have reached Tom's Professional Gardening Service. We are not here right now, but if you leave us a message, we will get back to you as soon as possible. Thank you."

It is hot and dusty where we live. Some people think it's dirty, but they don't know much about us. They haven't seen our gardens full of lemongrass, mint, cilantro, and basil. They've only seen the pigeons pecking at day-old rice and the skinny cats and dogs sitting in the skinny shade of skinny trees as they drive by. Have they seen the berries we pick which turn our lips and fingertips red? How about the small staircase Ba built from our bedroom window to the back yard so I would have a short cut to the clothesline? How about the Great Wall of China which snakes like a river from the top of the steep Crandall Street hill to the slightly curving bottom? Who has seen this?

It was so different at the Green Apartment. We had to close the gate behind us every time we came in. It clanged heavily, and I imagined a host of eyes, upstairs and downstairs, staring at me from behind slightly parted curtains. There were four palm trees planted at the four far corners of the courtyard and a central staircase that was narrow at the top and fanned out at the bottom. The steps were covered in fake grass, like the set of an old Hollywood movie, the kind that stars an aging beauty who wakes up to find something is terribly wrong.

We moved out of the Green Apartment after we turned on the TV one night and heard that our manager and his brother had hacked a woman to pieces and dumped her body into the Pacific Ocean in ten-gallon garbage bags that washed onto the shore. Ma said she didn't want to live in a place haunted by a murdered lady. So we moved to Linda Vista, where she said there were a lot of Vietnamese people like us, people whose only sin was a little bit of gambling and sucking on fish bones and laughing hard and arguing loudly.

Ma shaved all her hair off in Linda Vista because she got mad at Ba for gambling her money away and getting drunk every week watching *Monday Night Football*. Ba gave her a blue baseball cap to wear until her hair grew back, and she wore it backward, like a real bad-ass.
 After that, some people in Linda Vista said that Ma was crazy and Ba was crazy for staying with her. But what do some people know?

When the photograph came, Ma and Ba got into a fight. Ba threw the fish tank out the front door and Ma broke all the dishes. They said they never should've been together.
 Ma's sister had sent her the photograph from Vietnam. It came in a stiff envelope. There was nothing inside but the photograph, as if anything

more would be pointless. Ma started to cry. "Child," she sobbed, over and over again. She wasn't talking about me. She was talking about herself.

Ba said, "Don't cry. Your parents have forgiven you."

Ma kept crying anyway and told him not to touch her with his gangster hands. Ba clenched his hands into tight fists and punched the walls.

"What hands?! What hands?!" he yelled. "Let me see the gangster! Let me see his hands!" I see his hands punch hands punch hands punch blood.

Ma is in the kitchen. She has torn the screen off the window. She is punctuating the pavement with dishes, plates, cups, rice bowls. She sends them out like birds gliding through the sky with nowhere in particular to go. Until they crash. Then she exhales "Huh!" in satisfaction.

I am in the hallway gulping air. I breathe in the breaking and the bleeding. When Ba plunges his hands into the fish tank, I detect the subtle tint of blood in water. When he throws the fish tank out the front door, yelling, "Let me see the gangster!" I am drinking up spilled water and swallowing whole the beautiful colored tropical fish before they hit the ground, caking themselves in brown dirt until just the whites of their eyes remain, blinking at the sun.

All the hands are in my throat, cutting themselves on broken dishes, and the fish swim in circles; they can't see for all the blood.

Ba jumps in his truck and drives away.

When I grow up I am going to be the gangster we are all looking for.

The neighborhood kids are standing outside our house, staring in through the windows and the open door. Even Ahn, our chicken-egg seller. I'm sure their gossiping mothers sent them to spy on us. I run out front and dance like a crazy lady, dance like a fish, wiggle my head and throw my body so everything eyes nose tongue comes undone. At first they laugh but then they stop, not knowing what to think. Then I stop and stare each one of them down.

"What're you looking at?" I ask.

"Lookin' at you," one boy says, half giggling.

"Well," I say, with my hand on my hip and my head cocked to one side, "I'm looking at you too," and I give him my evil one-eye look, focusing all my energy into one eye. I stare at him hard like my eye is a bullet and he can be dead.

I turn my back on them and walk into the house.

I find Ma sitting in the windowsill. The curve of her back is inside the bedroom while the rest of her body is outside, on the first step Ba built going from the bedroom to the garden. Without turning to look at me, she says, "Let me lift you into the attic."

"Why?"

"We have to move your grandparents in."

I don't really know what she is talking about, but I say O.K. anyway.

We have never needed the attic for anything. In fact, we have never gone up there. When we moved my grandparents in, Ma simply lifted me up and I pushed the attic door open with one hand, while with the other I slipped in the stiff envelope containing the photograph of my grandparents. I pushed it the length of my arm and down to my fingertips. I pushed it so far it was beyond reach, but Ma said it was enough, they had come to live with us, and sometimes you don't need to see or touch people to know they're there.

Ba came home drunk that night and asked to borrow my blanket. I heard him climbing the tree in the back yard. It took him a long time. He kept missing the wooden blocks that run up and down the tree like a ladder. Ba put them in when he built the steps going from the bedroom window into the garden. If you stand on the very top block, your whole body is hidden by tree branches. Ba put those blocks in for me, so I could win at hide-and-go-seek.

When Ba finally made it onto the roof, he lay down over my room and I could hear him rolling across my ceiling. Rolling and crying. I was scared he would roll off the edge and kill himself, so I went to wake Ma.

She was already awake. She said it would be a good thing if he rolled off. But later I heard someone climb the tree, and all night two bodies rolled across my ceiling. Slowly and firmly they pressed against my sleep, the Catholic schoolgirl and the Buddhist gangster, two dogs chasing each other's tails. They have been running like this for so long, they have become one dog one tail.

Without any hair and looking like a man, my mother is still my mother, though sometimes I can't see her even when I look and look and look so long all the colors of the world begin to swim and bob around me. Her hands always bring me up, her big peasant hands with the flat, wide nails, wide like her nose and just as expressive. I will know her by her hands and her walk which is at once slow and urgent, the walk of a woman going to the market with her goods securely bound to her side. Even walking empty-handed, my mother suggests invisible bundles whose contents no one but she can unravel. And if I never see her again, I will know my mother by the smell of sea salt and the prints of my own bare feet crossing sand, running to and away from, to and away from, family.

When the eviction notice came, we didn't believe it so we threw it away. It said we had a month to get out. The houses on our block had a new owner who wanted to tear everything down and build better housing for the community. It said we were priority tenants for the new complex, but we couldn't afford to pay the new rent so it didn't matter. The notice also said that if we didn't get out in time, all our possessions would be confiscated in accordance with some section of a law book or manual we were supposed to have known about but had never seen. We couldn't believe the eviction notice so we threw it away.

The fence is tall, silver, and see-through. Chainlink, it rattles when you shake it and wobbles when you lean against it. It circles the block like a bad dream. It is not funny like a line of laundry whose flying shirts and empty pants suggest human birds and vanishing acts. This fence presses sharply against your brain. We three stand still as posts. Looking at it, then at each other—this side and that—out of the corners of our eyes. What are we thinking?

At night we come back with three uncles. Ba cuts a hole in the fence and we step through. Quiet, we break into our own house through the back window. Quiet, we steal back everything that is ours. We fill ten-gallon garbage bags with clothes, pots and pans, flip-flops, the porcelain figure of Mary, and our wooden Buddha. In the arc of four flashlights we find our favorite hairbrushes behind bedposts. When we are done, we are clambering and breathless. We can hear police cars coming to get us, though it's quiet.

We tumble out the window like people tumbling across continents. We are time traveling, weighed down by heavy furniture and bags of precious junk. We find ourselves leaning against Ba's yellow truck. Ma calls his name, her voice reaching like a hand feeling for a tree trunk in darkness.

In the car, Ma starts to cry. "What about the sea?" she asks. "What about the garden?" Ba says we can come back in the morning and dig up the stalks of lemongrass and fold the sea into a blue square. Ma is sobbing. She is beating the dashboard with her fists. "I want to know," she says, "I want to know, I want to know . . . who is doing this to us?" Hiccupping, she says, "I want to know why, why there's always a fence. Why there's always someone on the outside wanting someone . . . something on the inside and between them . . . this . . . sharp fence. Why are we always leaving like this?"

Everyone is quiet when Ma screams.

"Take me back!" she says. "I can't go with you. I've forgotten my mother and father. I can't believe . . . Anh Minh, we've left them to die. Take me back."

Ma wants Ba to stop the car, but Ba doesn't know why. The three uncles, sitting in a line in the back of the truck, think Ma is crazy. They yell in through the window, "My, are you going to walk back to Vietnam?"

"Yeah, are you going to walk home to your parents' house?"

In the silence another laughs.

Ba puts his foot on the gas pedal. Our car jerks forward, then plunges down the Crandall Street hill. Ma says, "I need air, water . . ." I roll the window down. She puts her head in her hands. She keeps crying, "Child." Outside, I see the Great Wall of China. In the glare of the streetlamps, it is just a long strip of cardboard.

In the morning, the world is flat. Westinghouse Street is lying down like a jagged brushstroke of sunburnt yellow. There is a big sign inside the fence that reads

COMING SOON:
CONDOMINIUMS   TOWNHOUSES   FAMILY HOMES

Beside these words is a watercolor drawing of a large, pink complex.

We stand on the edge of the chainlink fence, sniffing the air for the scent of lemongrass, scanning this flat world for our blue sea. A wrecking ball dances madly through our house. Everything has burst wide open and sunk down low. Then I hear her calling them. She is whispering, "Ma/Ba, Ma/Ba." The whole world is two butterfly wings rubbing against my ear.

Listen . . . they are sitting in the attic, sitting like royalty. Shining in the dark, buried by a wrecking ball. Paper fragments floating across the surface of the sea.

Not a trace of blood anywhere except here, in my throat, where I am telling you all this.

IN THE KITCHEN

Henry Louis Gates Jr.

This essay is from Gates' book Colored People, *published in 1994.*

We always had a gas stove in the kitchen, though electric cooking became fashionable in Piedmont, like using Crest toothpaste rather than Colgate, or watching Huntley and Brinkley rather than Walter Cronkite. But for us it was gas, Colgate, and good ole Walter Cronkite, come what may. We used gas partly out of loyalty to Big Mom, Mama's mama, because she was mostly blind and still loved to cook, and she could feel her way better with gas than with electric.

But the most important thing about our gas-equipped kitchen was that Mama used to do hair there. She had a "hot comb"—a fine-tooth iron instrument with a long wooden handle—and a pair of iron curlers that opened and closed like scissors: Mama would put them into the gas fire until they glowed. You could smell those prongs heating up.

I liked what that smell meant for the shape of my day. There was an intimate warmth in the women's tones as they talked with my mama while she did their hair. I knew what the women had been through to get their hair ready to be "done," because I would watch Mama do it herself. How that scorched kink could be transformed though grease and fire into a magnificent head of wavy hair was a miracle to me. Still is.

Mama would wash her hair over the sink, a towel wrapped round her shoulders, wearing just her half-slip and her white bra. (We had no shower until we moved down Rat Tail Road into Doc Wolverton's house, in 1954.) After she had dried it, she would grease her scalp thoroughly

with blue Bergamot hair grease, which came in a short, fat jar with a picture of a beautiful colored lady on it. It's important to grease your scalp
real good, my mama would explain, to keep from burning yourself.

Of course, her hair would return to its natural kink almost as soon
as the hot water and shampoo hit it. To me, it was another miracle how
hair so "straight" would so quickly become kinky again once it even approached some water.

My mama had only a "few" clients whose heads she "did"—and did, I
think, because she enjoyed it, rather than for the few dollars it brought in.
They would sit on one of our red plastic kitchen chairs, the kind with the
shiny metal legs, and brace themselves for the process. Mama would
stroke that red-hot iron, which by this time had been in the gas fire for a
half hour or more, slowly but firmly through their hair, from scalp to
strand's end. It made a scorching, crinkly sound, the hot iron did, as it
burned its way though the damp kink, leaving in its wake the straightest
of hair strands, each of them standing up long and tall but drooping at the
end, like the top of a heavy willow tree. Slowly, steadily, with deftness and
grace, Mama's hands would transform a round mound of Odetta kink into
a darkened swamp of everglades. The Bergamot made the hair shiny; the
hear of the hot iron gave it a brownish-red cast. Once all the hair was as
straight as God allows kink to get, Mama would take the well-heated curling iron and twirl the straightened strands into more or less loosely
wrapped curls. She claimed that she owed her strength and skill as a hair-
dresser to her wrists, and her little finger would poke out the way it did
when she sipped tea. Mama was a southpaw, who wrote upside down and
backwards to produce the cleanest, roundest letters you've ever seen.

The "kitchen" she would all but remove from sight with a pair of
shears bought for this purpose. Now, the *kitchen* was the room in which
we were sitting, the room where Mama did hair and washed clothes, and
where each of us bathed in a galvanized tub. But the word has another
meaning, and the "kitchen" I'm speaking of now is the very kinky bit of
hair at the back of the head, where our neck meets the shirt collar. If there
ever was one part of our African past that resisted assimilation, it was the
kitchen. No matter how hot the iron, no matter how powerful the chemical, no matter how stringent the mashed-potatoes-and-lye formula of a
man's "process," neither God nor woman nor Sammy Davis, Jr., could
straighten the kitchen. The kitchen was permanent, irredeemable, invin-
cible kink. Unassimilably African. No matter what you did, no matter
how hard you tried, nothing could dekink a person's kitchen. So you
trimmed it off as best you could.

When hair had begun to "turn," as they'd say, or return to its natural
kinky glory, it was the kitchen that turned first. When the kitchen started
creeping up the back of the neck, it was time to get your hair done again.
The kitchen around the back, and nappy edges at the temples.

Sometimes, after dark, Mr. Charlie Carroll would come to have his hair
done. Mr. Charlie Carroll was very light-complected and had a ruddy

nose, the kind of nose that made me think of Edmund Gwenn playing Kris Kringle in *Miracle on 34th Street.* At the beginning, they did it after Rocky and I had gone to sleep. It was only later that we found out he had come to our house so Mama could iron his hair—not with a comb and curling iron but with our very own Proctor-Silex steam iron. For some reason, Mr. Charlie would conceal his Frederick Douglass mane under a big white Stetson hat, which I never saw him take off. Except when he came to our house, late at night, to have his hair pressed.

(Later, Daddy would tell us about Mr. Charlie's most prized piece of knowledge, which the man would confide only after his hair had been pressed, as a token of intimacy. "Not many people know this," he'd say in a tone of circumspection, "but George Washington was Abraham Lincoln's daddy." Nodding solemnly, he'd add the clincher: "A white man told me." Though he was in dead earnest, this became a humorous refrain around the house—"a white man told me"—used to punctuate especially preposterous assertions.)

My mother furtively examined my daughters' kitchens whenever we went home for a visit in the early eighties. It became a game between us. I had told her not to do it, because I didn't like the politics it suggested of "good" and "bad" hair. "Good" hair was straight. "Bad" hair was kinky. Even in the late sixties, at the height of Black Power, most people could not bring themselves to say "bad" for "good" and "good" for "bad." They still said that hair like white hair was "good," even if they encapsulated it in a disclaimer like "what we used to call 'good.'"

Maggie would be seated in her high chair, throwing food this way and that, and Mama would be cooing about how cute it all was, remembering how I used to do the same thing, and wondering whether Maggie's flinging her food with her left hand meant that she was going to be a southpaw too. When my daughter was just about covered with Franco-American SpaghettiOs, Mama would seize the opportunity and wipe her clean, dipping her head, tilted to one side, down under the back of Maggie's neck. Sometimes, if she could get away with it, she'd even rub a curl between her fingers, just to make sure that her bifocals had not deceived her. Then she'd sigh with satisfaction and relief, thankful that her prayers had been answered. No kink . . . yet. "Mama!" I'd shout, pretending to be angry. (Every once in a while, if no one was looking, I'd peek too.)

I say "yet" because most black babies are born with soft, silken hair. Then, sooner or later, it begins to "turn," as inevitably as do the seasons or the leaves turn on a tree. And if it's meant to turn, it *turns,* no matter how hard you try to stop it. People once thought baby oil would stop it. They were wrong.

Everybody I knew as a child wanted to have good hair. You could be as ugly as homemade sin dipped in misery and still be thought attractive if you had good hair. Jesus Moss was what the girls at Camp Lee, Virginia, had called Daddy's hair during World War II. I know he played that thick head of hair for all it was worth, too. Still would, if he could.

My own hair was "not a bad grade," as barbers would tell me when they cut my head for the first time. It's like a doctor reporting the overall results of the first full physical that he had given you. "You're in good shape" or "Blood pressure's kind of high; better cut down on salt."

I spent much of my childhood and adolescence messing with my hair. I definitely wanted straight hair. Like Pop's.

When I was about three, I tried to stick a wad of Bazooka bubble gum to that straight hair of his. I suppose what fixed that memory for me is the spanking I got for doing so: he turned me upside down, holding me by the feet, the better to paddle my behind. Little *nigger*, he shouted, walloping away. I started to laugh about it two days later, when my behind stopped hurting.

When black people say "straight," of course, they don't usually mean "straight" literally, like, say, the hair of Peggy Lipton (the white girl on *The Mod Squad*) or Mary of Peter, Paul and Mary fame; black people call that "stringy" hair. No, "straight" just means not kinky, no matter what contours the curl might take. Because Daddy had straight hair, I would have done *anything* to have straight hair—and I used to try everything to make it straight, short of getting a process, which only riffraff were dumb enough to do.

Of the wide variety of techniques and methods I came to master in the great and challenging follicle prestidigitation, almost all had two things in common: a heavy, oil-based grease and evenly applied pressure. It's no accident that many of the biggest black companies in the fifties and six-ties made hair products. Indeed, we do have a vast array of hair grease. And I have tried it all, in search of that certain silky touch, one that leaves neither the hand nor the pillow sullied by grease.

I always wondered what Frederick Douglass put on *his* hair, or Phillis Wheatley. Or why Wheatley has that rag on her head in the little engrav-ing in the frontispiece of her book. One thing is for sure: you can bet that when Wheatley went to England to see the Countess of Huntington, she did not stop by the Queen's Coiffeur on the way. So many black people still get their hair straightened that it's a wonder we don't have a national holiday for Madame C. J. Walker, who invented the process for straighten-ing kinky hair, rather than for Dr. King. Jheri-curled or "relaxed"—it's still fried hair.

I used all the greases, from sea-blue Bergamot, to creamy vanilla Duke (in its orange-and-white jar), to the godfather of grease, the formi-dable Murray's. Now, Murray's was some *serious* grease. Whereas Berg-amot was like oily Jell-O and Duke was viscous and sickly sweet, Murray's was light brown and *hard*. Hard as lard and twice as greasy, Daddy used to say whenever the subject of Murray's came up. Murray's came in an orange can with a screw-on top. It was so hard that some people would put a match to the can, just to soften it and make it more manageable. In the late sixties, when Afros came into style, I'd use

Afro-Sheen. From Murray's to Duke to Afro-Sheen: that was my progression in black consciousness.

We started putting hot towels or washrags over our greased-down Murray's-coated heads, in order to melt the wax into the scalp and follicles. Unfortunately, the wax had a curious habit of running down your neck, ears, and forehead. Not to mention your pillowcase.

Another problem was that if you put two palmfuls of Murray's on your head, your hair turned white. Duke did the same thing. It was a challenge: if you got rid of the white stuff, you had a magnificent head of wavy hair. Murray's turned kink into waves. Lots of waves. Frozen waves. A hurricane couldn't have blown those waves around.

That was the beauty of it. Murray's was so hard that it froze your hair into the wavy style you brushed it into. It looked really good if you wore a part. A lot of guys had parts *cut* into their hair by a barber, with clippers or a straight-edge razor. Especially if you had kinky hair—in which case you'd generally wear a short razor cut, or what we called a Quo Vadis.

Being obsessed with our hair, we tried to be as innovative as possible. Everyone knew about using a stocking cap, because your father or your uncle or the older guys wore them whenever something really big was about to happen, secular or sacred, a funeral or a dance, a wedding or a trip in which you confronted official white people, or when you were trying to look really sharp. When it was time to be clean, you wore a stocking cap. If the event was really a big one, you made a new cap for the occasion.

A stocking cap was made by asking your mother for one of her hose, cutting it with a pair of scissors about six inches or so from the open end, where the elastic goes to the top of the thigh. Then you'd knot the cut end, and behold—a conical-shaped hat or cap, with an elastic band that you pulled down low on your forehead and down around your neck in the back. A good stocking cap, to work well, had to fit tight and snug, like a press. And it had to fit that tightly because it *was* a press: it pressed your hair with the force of the hose's elastic. If you greased your hair down real good and left the stocking cap on long enough—*voilà:* you got a head of pressed-against-the-scalp waves. If you used Murray's, and if you wore a stocking cap to sleep, you got a *whole lot* of waves. (You also got a ring around your forehead when you woke up, but eventually that disappeared.)

And then you could enjoy your concrete 'do. Swore we were bad, too, with all that grease and those flat heads. My brother and I would brush it out a bit in the morning so it would look—ahem—"natural."

Grown men still wear stocking caps, especially older men, who generally keep their caps in their top drawer, along with their cuff links and their see-through silk socks, their Maverick tie, their silk handkerchief, and whatever else they prize most.

A Murrayed-down stocking cap was the respectable version of the process, which, by contrast, was most definitely not a cool thing to have, at least if you weren't an entertainer by trade.

Zeke and Keith and Poochie and a few other stars of the basketball team all used to get a process once or twice a year. It was expensive, and to get one you had to go to Pittsburgh or D.C. or Uniontown, someplace where there were enough colored people to support a business. They'd disappear, then reappear a day or two later, strutting like peacocks, their hair burned slightly red from the chemical lye base. They'd also wear "rags" or cloths or handkerchiefs around it when they slept or played basketball. Do-rags, they were called. But the result was *straight* hair with a hint of wave. No curl. Do-it-yourselfers took their chances at home with a concoction of mashed potatoes and lye.

The most famous process, outside of what Malcolm X describes in his *Autobiography* and maybe that of Sammy Davis, Jr., was Nat King Cole's. Nat King Cole had patent-leather hair.

"That man's got the finest process money can buy." That's what Daddy said the night Cole's TV show aired on NBC, November 5, 1956. I remember the date because everyone came to our house to watch it and to celebrate one of Daddy's buddies' birthdays. Yeah, Uncle Joe chimed in, they can do shit to his hair that the average Negro can't even *think* about—secret shit.

Nat King Cole was *clean*. I've had an ongoing argument with a Nigerian friend about Nat King Cole for twenty years now. Not whether or not he could sing; any fool knows that he could sing. But whether or not he was a handerkerchief-head for wearing that patent-leather process.

Sammy Davis's process I detested. It didn't look good on him. Worse still, he liked to have a fried strand dangling down the middle of his forehead, shaking it out from the crown when he sang. But Nat King Cole's hair was a thing unto itself, a beautifully sculpted work of art that he and he alone should have had the right to wear.

The only difference between a process and a stocking cap, really, was taste; yet Nat King Cole—unlike, say, Michael Jackson—looked *good* in his process. His head looked like Rudolph Valentino's in the twenties, and some say it was Valentino that the process imitated. But Nat King Cole wore a process because it suited his face, his demeanor, his name, his style. He was as clean as he wanted to be.

I had forgotten all about Nat King Cole and that patent-leather look until the day in 1971 when I was sitting in an Arab restaurant on the island of Zanzibar, surrounded by men in fezzes and white caftans, trying to learn how to eat curried goat and rice with the fingers of my right hand, feeling two million miles from home, when all of a sudden the old transistor radio sitting on top of a china cupboard stopped blaring out its Swahili music to play "Fly Me to the Moon" by Nat King Cole. The restaurant's din was not affected at all, not even by half a decibel. But in my mind's eye, I saw it: the King's sleek black magnificent tiara. I managed, barely, to blink back the tears.

A CLACK OF TINY SPARKS:
REMEMBRANCES OF A GAY BOYHOOD

Bernard Cooper

Harper's Magazine *first printed this essay in January of 1991.*

Theresa Sanchez sat behind me in ninth-grade algebra. When Mr. Hubbley faced the blackboard, I'd turn around to see what she was reading; each week a new book was wedged inside her copy of *Today's Equations*. The deception worked; from Mr. Hubbley's point of view, Theresa was engrossed in the value of X, but I knew otherwise. One week she perused *The Wisdom of the Orient,* and I could tell from Theresa's contemplative expression that the book contained exotic thoughts, guidelines handed down from high. Another week it was a paperback novel whose title, *Let Me Live My Life,* appeared in bold print atop every page, and whose cover, a gauzy photograph of a woman biting a strand of pearls, head thrown back in an attitude of ecstasy, confirmed my suspicion that Theresa Sanchez was mature beyond her years. She was the tallest girl in school. Her bouffant hairdo, streaked with blond, was higher than the flaccid bouffants of other girls. Her smooth skin, plucked eyebrows, and painted fingernails suggested hours of pampering, a worldly and sensual vanity that placed her within the domain of adults. Smiling dimly, steeped in daydreams, Theresa moved through the crowded halls with a languid, self-satisfied indifference to those around her. "You are merely children," her posture seemed to say. "I can't be bothered." The week Theresa hid *101 Ways to Cook Hamburger* behind her algebra book, I could stand it no longer and, after the bell rang, ventured a question.

"Because I'm having a dinner party," said Theresa. "Just a couple of intimate friends."

No fourteen-year-old I knew had ever given a dinner party, let alone used the word "intimate" in conversation. "Don't you have a mother?" I asked.

Theresa sighed a weary sigh, suffered my strange inquiry. "Don't be so naive," she said. "Everyone has a mother." She waved her hand to indicate the brick school buildings outside the window. "A higher education should have taught you that." Theresa draped an angora sweater over her shoulders, scooped her books from the graffiti-covered desk, and just as she was about to walk away, she turned and asked me, "Are you a fag?"

There wasn't the slightest hint of rancor or condescension in her voice. The tone was direct, casual. Still I was stunned, giving a sidelong glance to make sure no one had heard. "No," I said. Blurted really, with too much defensiveness, too much transparent fear in my response. Octaves lower than usual, I tried a "Why?"

Theresa shrugged. "Oh, I don't know. I have lots of friends who are fags. You remind me of them." Seeing me bristle, Theresa added, "It was just a guess." I watched her erect, angora back as she sauntered out the classroom door.

She had made an incisive and timely guess. Only days before, I'd invited Grady Rogers to my house after school to go swimming. The instant Grady shot from the pool, shaking water from his orange hair, freckled shoulders shining, my attraction to members of my own sex became a matter I could no longer suppress or rationalize. Sturdy and boisterous and gap-toothed, Grady was an inveterate backslapper, a formidable arm wrestler, a wizard at basketball. Grady was a boy at home in his body.

My body was a marvel I hadn't gotten used to; my arms and legs would sometimes act of their own accord, knocking over a glass at dinner or flinching at an oncoming pitch. I was never singled out as a sissy, but I could have been just as easily as Bobby Keagan, a gentle, intelligent, and introverted boy reviled by my classmates. And although I had always been aware of a tacit rapport with Bobby, a suspicion that I might find with him a rich friendship, I stayed away. Instead, I emulated Grady in the belief that being seen with him, being like him, would somehow vanquish my self-doubt, would make me normal by association.

Apart from his athletic prowess, Grady had been gifted with all the trappings of what I imagined to be a charmed life: a fastidious, aproned mother who radiated calm, maternal concern; a ruddy, stoic father with a knack for home repairs. Even the Rogerses' small suburban house in Hollywood, with its spindly Colonial furniture and chintz curtains, was a testament to normalcy.

Grady and his family bore little resemblance to my clan of Eastern European Jews, a dark and vociferous people who ate with abandon—matzo and halvah and gefilte fish; foods the goyim couldn't pronounce—who cajoled one another during endless games of canasta, making the simplest remark about the weather into a lengthy philosophical discourse on the sun and the seasons and the passage of time. My mother was a chain-smoker, a dervish in a frowsy housedress. She showed her love in the most peculiar and obsessive ways, like spending hours extracting every seed from a watermelon before she served it in perfectly bite-sized, geometric pieces. Preoccupied and perpetually frantic, my mother succumbed to bouts of absentmindedness so profound she'd forget what she was saying midsentence, smile and blush and walk away. A divorce attorney, my father wore roomy, iridescent suits, and the intricacies, the deceits inherent in his profession, had the effect of making him forever tense and vigilant. He was "all wound up," as my mother put it. But when he relaxed, his laughter was explosive, his disposition prankish: "Walk this way," a waitress would say, leading us to our table, and my father would mimic the way she walked, arms akimbo, hips liquid, while my mother and I were wracked with laughter. Buoyant or brooding, my parents' moods were unpredictable, and in a household fraught with extravagant emotion it was odd and awful to keep my longing secret.

One day I made the mistake of asking my mother what a "fag" was. I knew exactly what Theresa had meant but hoped against hope it was not what I thought; maybe "fag" was some French word, a harmless term like "naive." My mother turned from the stove, flew at me, and grabbed me by the shoulders. "Did someone call you that?" she cried.

"Not me," I said. "Bobby Keagan."

"Oh," she said, loosening her grip. She was visibly relieved. And didn't answer. The answer was unthinkable.

For weeks after, I shook with the reverberations from that afternoon in the kitchen with my mother, pained by the memory of her shocked expression and, most of all, her silence. My longing was wrong in the eyes of my mother, whose hazel eyes were the eyes of the world, and if that longing continued unchecked, the unwieldy shape of my fate would be cast, and I'd be subjected to a lifetime of scorn.

During the remainder of the semester, I became the scientist of my own desire, plotting ways to change my yearning for boys into a yearning for girls. I had enough evidence to believe that any habit, regardless of how compulsive, how deeply ingrained, could be broken once and for all: The plastic cigarette my mother purchased at the Thrifty pharmacy—one end was red to approximate an ember, the other ran like a filtered tip— was designed to wean her from the real thing. To change a behavior required self-analysis, cold resolve, and the substitution of one thing for another: plastic, say, for tobacco. Could I also find a substitute for Grady? What I needed to do, I figured, was kiss a girl and learn to like it.

This conclusion was affirmed one Sunday morning when my father, seeing me wrinkle my nose at the pink slabs of lox he layered on a bagel, tried to convince me of its salty appeal. "You should try some," he said. "You don't know what you're missing."

"It's loaded with protein," added my mother, slapping a platter of sliced onions onto the dinette table. She hovered above us, cinching her housedress, eyes wet from onion fumes, the mock cigarette dangling from her lips.

My father sat there chomping with gusto, emitting a couple of hearty grunts to dramatize his satisfaction. And still I was not convinced. After a loud and labored swallow, he told me I may not be fond of lox today, but sooner or later I'd learn to like it. One's tastes, he assured me, are destined to change.

"Live," shouted my mother over the rumble of the Mixmaster. "Expand your horizons. Try new things." And the room grew fragrant with the batter of a spice cake.

The opportunity to put their advice into practice, and try out my plan to adapt to girls, came the following week when Debbie Coburn, a member of

Mr. Hubbley's algebra class, invited me to a party. She cornered me in the hall, furtive as a spy, telling me her parents would be gone for the evening and slipping into my palm a wrinkled sheet of notebook paper. On it were her address and telephone number, the lavender ink in a tidy cursive. "Wear cologne," she advised, wary eyes darting back and forth. "It's a make-out party. Anything can happen."

The Santa Ana wind blew relentlessly the night of Debbie's party, careening down the slopes of the Hollywood hills, shaking the road signs and stoplights in its path. As I walked down Beachwood Avenue, trees thrashed, surrendered their leaves, and carob pods bombarded the pavement. The sky was a deep but luminous blue, the air hot, abrasive, electric. I had to squint in order to check the number of the Coburns' apartment, a three-story building with glitter embedded in its stucco walls. Above the honeycombed balconies was a sign that read BEACHWOOD TERRACE in lavender script resembling Debbie's.

From down the hall, I could hear the plaintive strains of Little Anthony's "I Think I'm Going Out of My Head." Debbie answered the door bedecked in an Empire dress, the bodice blue and orange polka dots, the rest a sheath of black and white stripes. "Op art," proclaimed Debbie. She turned in a circle, then proudly announced that she'd rolled her hair in orange juice cans. She patted the huge unmoving curls and dragged me inside. Reflections from the swimming pool in the courtyard, its surface ruffled by wind, shuddered over the ceiling and walls. A dozen of my classmates were seated on the sofa or huddled together in corners, their whispers full of excited imminence, their bodies barely discernible in the dim light. Drapes flanking the sliding glass doors bowed out with every gust of wind, and it seemed that the room might lurch from its foundations and sail with its cargo of silhouettes into the hot October night.

Grady was the last to arrive. He tossed a six-pack of beer into Debbie's arms, barreled toward me, and slapped my back. His hair was slicked back with Vitalis, lacquered furrows left by the comb. The wind hadn't shifted a single hair. "Ya ready?" he asked, flashing the gap between his front teeth and leering into the darkened room. "You bet," I lied.

Once the beers had been passed around, Debbie provoked everyone's attention by flicking on the overhead light. "Okay," she called. "Find a partner." This was the blunt command of a hostess determined to have her guests aroused in an orderly fashion. Everyone blinked, shuffled about, and grabbed a member of the opposite sex. Sheila Garabedian landed beside me—entirely at random, though I wanted to believe she was driven by passion—her timid smile giving way to plain fear as the light went out. Nothing for a moment but the heave of the wind and the distant banter of dogs. I caught a whiff of Sheila's perfume, tangy and sweet as Hawaiian Punch. I probed her face with my own, grazing the small scallop of an ear, a velvety temple, and though Sheila's trembling made me want to stop, I persisted with my mission until I found her lips, tightly sealed as a private letter. I held my mouth over hers and gathered her shoulders closer, resigned to the possibility that, no matter how long we stood there, Sheila would be too scared to kiss me back. Still, she exhaled through her nose, and I listened to the squeak of every breath as though it were a sigh of inordinate pleasure. Diving within myself, I monitored my heartbeat and respiration, trying to will stimulation into being, and all the while an image intruded, an image of Grady erupting from our pool, rivulets of water sliding down his chest. "Change," shouted Debbie, switching on the light. Sheila thanked me, pulled away, and continued her routine of gracious terror with every boy throughout the evening. It didn't matter whom I held—Margaret Sims, Betty Vernon, Elizabeth Lee—my experiment was a failure; I continued to picture Grady's wet chest, and Debbie would bellow "change" with such fervor, it could have been my own voice, my own incessant reprimand.

Our hostess commandeered the light switch for nearly half an hour. Whenever the light came on, I watched Grady pivot his head toward the newest prospect, his eyebrows arched in expectation, his neck blooming with hickeys, his hair, at last, in disarray. All that shuffling across the carpet charged everyone's arms and lips with static, and eventually, between low moans and soft osculations, I could hear the clack of tiny sparks and see them flare here and there in the dark like meager, short-lived stars.

I saw Theresa, sultry and aloof as ever, read three more books—*North American Reptiles, Bonjour Tristesse,* and *MGM: A Pictorial History*—before she vanished early in December. Rumors of her fate abounded. Debbie Coburn swore that Theresa had been "knocked up" by an older man, a traffic cop, she thought, or a grocer. Nearly quivering with relish, Debbie told me and Grady about the home for unwed mothers in the San Fernando Valley, a compound teeming with pregnant girls who had nothing to do but touch their stomachs and contemplate their mistake. Even Bobby Keagan, who took Theresa's place behind me in algebra, had a theory regarding her disappearance colored by his own wish for escape; he imagined that Theresa, disillusioned with society, booked passage to a tropical island, there to live out the rest of her days without restrictions or ridicule. "No wonder she flunked out of school," I overheard Mr. Hubbley tell a fellow teacher one afternoon. "Her head was always in a book."

Along with Theresa went my secret, or at least the dread that she might divulge it, and I felt, for a while, exempt from suspicion. I was, however, to run across Theresa one last time. It happened during a period of torrential rain that, according to reports on the six o'clock news, washed houses from the hillsides and flooded the downtown streets. The halls of Joseph Le Conte Junior High were festooned with Christmas decorations: crepe-paper garlands, wreaths studded with plastic berries, and one requisite Star of David twirling above the attendance desk. In Arts and Crafts, our teacher, Gerald (he was the only teacher who allowed us— *required* us—to call him by his first name), handed out blocks of balsa wood and instructed us to carve them into bugs. We would paint eyes and antennae with tempera and hang them on a Christmas tree he'd made the previous night. "Voilà," he crooned, unveiling his creation from a burlap sack. Before us sat a tortured scrub, a wardrobe-worth of wire hangers that were bent like branches and soldered together. Gerald credited his inspiration to a Charles Addams cartoon he's seen in which Morticia, grimly preparing for the holidays, hangs vampire bats on a withered pine. "All that red and green," said Gerald. "So predictable. So *boring*."

As I chiseled a beetle and listened to rain pummel the earth, Gerald handed me an envelope and asked me to take it to Mr. Kendrick, the drama teacher. I would have thought nothing of his request if I hadn't seen Theresa on my way down the hall. She was cleaning out her locker, blithely dropping the sum of its contents—pens and textbooks and mimeographs—into a trash can. "Have a nice life," she sang as I passed. I mustered the courage to ask her what had happened. We stood alone in the silent hall, the reflections of wreaths and garlands submerged in brown linoleum.

"I transferred to another school. They don't have grades or bells, and you get to study whatever you want." Theresa was quick to sense my incredulity. "Honest," she said. "The school is progressive." She gazed into a glass cabinet that held the trophies of track meets and intramural spelling bees. "God," she sighed, "this place is so . . . barbaric." I was still trying to decide whether or not to believe her story when she asked me where I was headed. "Dear," she said, her exclamation pooling in the silence, "that's no ordinary note, if you catch my drift." The envelope was blank and white; I looked up at Theresa, baffled. "Don't be so naive," she muttered, tossing an empty bottle of nail polish into the trash can. It struck bottom with a resolute thud. "Well," she said, closing her locker and breathing deeply, "bon voyage." Theresa swept through the double doors and in seconds her figure was obscured by rain.

As I walked toward Mr. Kendrick's room, I could feel Theresa's insinuation burrow in. I stood for a moment and watched Mr. Kendrick through the pane in the door. He paced intently in front of the class, handsome in his shirt and tie, reading from a thick book. Chalked on the blackboard behind him was THE ODYSSEY BY HOMER. I have no recollection of how Mr. Kendrick reacted to the note, whether he accepted it with pleasure or embarrassment, slipped it into his desk drawer or the pocket of his shirt. I have scavenged that day in retrospect, trying to see Mr. Kendrick's expression, wondering if he acknowledged me in any way as his liaison. All I recall is the sight of his mime through a pane of glass, a lone man mouthing an epic, his gestures ardent in empty air.

Had I delivered a declaration of love? I was haunted by the need to know. In fantasy, a kettle shot steam, the glue released its grip, and I read the letter with impunity. But how would such a letter begin? Did the common endearments apply? This was a message between two men, a message for which I had no precedent, and when I tried to envision the contents, apart from a hasty, impassioned scrawl, my imagination faltered.

Once or twice I witnessed Gerald and Mr. Kendrick walk together into the faculty lounge or say hello at the water fountain, but there was nothing especially clandestine or flirtatious in their manner. Besides, no matter how acute my scrutiny, I wasn't sure, short of a kiss, exactly what to look for—what semaphore of gesture, what encoded word. I suspected there were signs, covert signs that would give them away, just as I'd unwittingly given myself away to Theresa.

In the school library, a *Webster's* unabridged dictionary lay on a wooden podium, and I padded toward it with apprehension; along with clues to the bond between my teachers, I risked discovering information that might incriminate me as well. I had decided to consult the dictionary during lunch period, when most of the students would be on the playground. I clutched my notebook, moving in such a way as to appear both studious and nonchalant, actually believing that, unless I took precautions, someone would see me and guess what I was up to. The closer I came to the podium, the more obvious, I thought, was my endeavor; I felt like the model of The Visible Man in our science class, my heart's undulations, my overwrought nerves legible through transparent skin. A couple of kids riffled through the card catalogue. The librarian, a skinny woman whose perpetual whisper and rubber-soled shoes caused her to drift through the room like a phantom, didn't seem to register my presence. Though I'd looked up dozens of words before, the pages felt strange beneath my fingers. *Homer* was the first word I saw. *Hominid. Homogenize.* I feigned interest and skirted other words before I found the word I was after. Under the heading HO•MO•SEX•U•AL was the terse definition: *adj. Pertaining to, characteristic of, or exhibiting homosexuality.—n. A homosexual person.* I read the definition again and again, hoping the words would yield more than they could. I shut the dictionary, swallowed hard, and, none the wiser, hurried away.

As for Gerald and Mr. Kendrick, I never discovered evidence to prove or dispute Theresa's claim. By the following summer, however, I had overheard from my peers a confounding amount about homosexuals: They wore green on Thursday, couldn't whistle, hypnotized boys with a piercing glance. To this lore, Grady added a surefire test to ferret them out.

"A test?" I said.

"You ask a guy to look at his fingernails, and if he looks at them like this"—Grady closed his fingers into a fist and examined his nails with manly detachment—"then he's okay. But if he does this"—he held out his hands at arm's length, splayed his fingers, and coyly cocked his head— "you'd better watch out." Once he'd completed his demonstration, Grady peeled off his shirt and plunged into our pool. I dove in after. It was early June, the sky immense, glassy, placid. My father was cooking spareribs on the barbecue, an artist with a basting brush. His apron bore the caricature of a frazzled French chef. Mother curled on a chaise lounge, plumes of smoke wafting from her nostrils. In a stupor of contentment she took another drag, closed her eyes, and arched her face toward the sun.

Grady dog-paddled through the deep end, spouting a fountain of chlo-rinated water. Despite shame and confusion, my longing for him hadn't diminished; it continued to thrive without air and light, like a luminous fish in the dregs of the sea. In the name of play, I swam up behind him, encircled his shoulders, astonished by his taut flesh. The two of us flailed, pretended to drown. Beneath the heavy press of water, Grady's orange hair wavered, a flame that couldn't be doused.

I've lived with a man for seven years. Some nights, when I'm half-asleep and the room is suffused with blue light, I reach out to touch the expanse of his back, and it seems as if my fingers sink into his skin, and I feel the pleasure a diver feels the instant he enters a body of water.

I have few regrets. But one is that I hadn't said to Theresa, "Of course I'm a fag." Maybe I'd have met her friends. Or become friends with her. Imagine the meals we might have concocted: hamburger Stroganoff, Swedish meatballs in a sweet translucent sauce, steaming slabs of Salis-bury steak.

ASIANS

—■—

Richard Rodriguez

"Asians" is Chapter 8 of Rodriguez's 1992 book Days of Obligation: An Argument with My Mexican Father.

For the child of immigrant parents the knowledge comes like a slap: America exists.

America exists everywhere in the city—on billboards; frankly in the smell of burgers and French fries. America exists in the slouch of the crowd, the pacing of traffic lights, the assertions of neon, the cry of free-dom overriding the nineteenth-century melodic line.

Grasp the implications of American democracy in a handshake or in a stranger's Jeffersonian "hi." America is irresistible. Nothing to do with choosing.

Our parents came to America for the choices America offers. What the child of immigrant parents knows is that here is inevitability.

A Chinese boy says his high-school teacher is always after him to stand up, speak up, look up. Yeah, but then his father puts him down at home: "Since when have you started looking your father in the eye?"

I'd like you to meet Jimmy Lamm. Mr. Lamm was an architect in Saigon. Now he is a cabbie in San Francisco. Stalled in traffic in San Fran-cisco, Jimmy tells me about the refugee camp in Guam where, for nearly two years, he and his family were quartered before their flight to Amer-ica. A teenager surfs by on a skateboard, his hair cresting in purple spikes like an iron crown, his freedom as apparent, as deplorable, as Huck Finn's.

Damn kid. Honk. Honk.

The damn kid howls with pleasure. Flips us the bird.

Do you worry that your children will end up with purple hair?

Silence.

Then Jimmy says his children have too much respect for the struggle he and his wife endured. His children would never betray him so.

On the floor of Jimmy Lamm's apartment, next to the television, is a bowl of fruit and a burning wand of joss.

He means: his children would never *choose* to betray him.

Immigrant parents re-create a homeland in the parlor, tacking up post-cards or calendars of some impossible blue—lake or sea or sky.

The child of immigrant parents is supposed to perch on a hyphen, taking only the dose of America he needs to advance in America.

At the family picnic, the child wanders away from the spiced food and faceless stories to watch some boys playing baseball in the distance.

■ ■ ■

My Mexican father still regards America with skepticism from the high window of his morning paper. "Too much freedom," he says. Though he has spent most of his life in this country, my father yet doubts such a place as the United States of America exists. He cannot discern boundaries. How else to describe a country?

My father admires a flower bed on a busy pedestrian street in Zurich—he holds up the *National Geographic* to show me. "You couldn't have that in America," my father says.

When I was twelve years old, my father said he wished his children had Chinese friends—so polite, so serious are Chinese children in my father's estimation. The Spanish word he used was *formal.*

I didn't have any Chinese friends. My father did. Seventh and J Street was my father's Orient. My father made false teeth for several Chinese dentists downtown. When a Chinese family tried to move in a few blocks away from our house, I heard a friend's father boast that the neighbors had banded together to "keep out the Japs."

Many years pass.

In college, I was reading *The Merchant of Venice*—Shylock urging his daughter to avoid the temptation of the frivolous Christians on the lido. Come away from the window, Shylock commands. I heard my father's voice:

Hear you me, Jessica.
Lock up my doors, and when you hear the drum
And the vile squealing of the wry-necked fife,
Clamber not you up to the casements then,
Nor thrust your head into the public street
To gaze on Christian fools with varnished faces,
But stop my house's ears, I mean my casements.
Let not the sound of shallow foppery enter
My sober house.

■ ■ ■

I interview the mother on Evergreen Street for the *Los Angeles Times*. The mother says they came from Mexico ten years ago, and—look—already they have this nice house. Each year the kitchen takes on a new appliance.

Outside the door is Los Angeles; in the distance, the perpetual orbit of traffic. Here old women walk slowly under paper parasols, past the Vietnam vet who pushes his tinkling ice-cream cart past little green lawns, little green lawns, little green lawns. (Here teenagers have black scorpions tattooed into their biceps.)

Children here are fed and grow tall. They love Christmas. They laugh at cartoons. They go off to school with children from Vietnam, from Burbank, from Hong Kong. They get into fights. They come home and they say dirty words. Aw, Ma, they say. Gimme a break, they say.

The mother says she does not want American children. It is the thing about Los Angeles she fears, the season of adolescence, of Huck Finn and Daisy Miller.

Foolish mother. She should have thought of that before she came. She will live to see that America takes its meaning from adolescence. She will have American children.

■   ■   ■

The best metaphor of America remains the dreadful metaphor—the Melting Pot. Fall into the Melting Pot, ease into the Melting Pot, or jump into the Melting Pot—it makes no difference—you will find yourself a stranger to your parents, a stranger to your own memory of yourself.

A Chinese girl walks to the front of the classroom, unfolds several ruled pages, and begins to read her essay to a trio of judges (I am one of her judges).

The voice of the essay is the voice of an immigrant. Stammer and elision approximate naïveté (the judges squirm in their chairs). The narrator remembers her night-long journey to the United States aboard a Pan Am jet. The moon. Stars. Then a memory within a memory: in the darkened cabin of the Plane, sitting next to her sleeping father, the little girl remembers bright China.

Many years pass.

The narrator's voice hardens into an American voice; her diction takes on rock and chrome. There is an ashtray on the table. The narrator is sitting at a sidewalk café in San Francisco. She is sixteen years old. She is with friends. The narrator notices a Chinese girl passing on the sidewalk. The narrator remembers bright China. The passing girl's face turns toward hers. The narrator recognizes herself in the passing girl—herself less assimilated. Their connective glance lasts only seconds. The narrator is embarrassed by her double—she remembers the cabin of the plane, her sleeping father, the moon, stars. The stranger disappears.

End of essay.

The room is silent as the Chinese student raises her eyes from the text.

One judge breaks the silence. Do you think your story is a sad story?

No, she replies. It is a true story.

What is the difference?

(Slowly, then.)

When you hear a sad story you cry, she says. When you hear a true story you cry even more.

■ ■ ■

The U.S. Army took your darling boy, didn't they? With all his allergies and his moles and his favorite flavors. And when they gave him back, the crystals of his eyes had cracked. You weren't sure if this was the right baby. The only other institution as unsentimental and as subversive of American individuality has been the classroom.

In the nineteenth century, even as the American city was building, Samuel Clemens romanced the nation with a celebration of the wildness of the American river, the eternal rejection of school and shoes. But in the red brick cities, and on streets without trees, the river became an idea, a learned idea, a shared idea, a civilizing idea, taking all to itself. Women, usually women, stood in front of rooms crowded with the children of immigrants, teaching those children a common language. For language is not just another classroom skill, as today's bilingualists would have it. Language is *the* lesson of grammar school. And from the schoolmarm's achievement came the possibility of a shared history and a shared future. To my mind, this achievement of the nineteenth-century classroom was an honorable one, comparable to the opening of the plains, the building of bridges. Grammar-school teachers forged a nation.

A century later, my own teachers encouraged me to read *Huckleberry Finn*. I tried several times. My attempts were frustrated by the dialect voices. (*You don't know about me without you have read . . .*) There was, too, a confidence in Huck I shied away from and didn't like and wouldn't trust. The confidence was America.

Eventually, but this was many years after, I was able to read in Huck's dilemma—how he chafed so in autumn—a version of my own fear of the classroom: Huck as the archetypal bilingual child. And, later still, I discerned in Huck a version of the life of our nation.

This nation was formed from a fear of the crowd. Those early Puritans trusted only the solitary life. Puritans advised fences. Build a fence around all you hold dear and respect other fences. Protestantism taught Americans to believe that America does not exist—not as a culture, not as shared experience, not as a communal reality. Because of Protestantism, the American *ideology* of individualism is always at war with the experience of our lives, our *culture.* As long as we reject the notion of culture, we are able to invent the future.

Lacking any plural sense of ourselves, how shall we describe Americanization, except as loss? The son of Italian immigrant parents is no longer Italian. America is the country where one stops being Italian or Chinese or German.

And yet notice the testimony of thousands of bellhops in thousands of hotel lobbies around the world: Americans exist. There is a recognizable type—the accent, of course; the insecure tip; the ready smile; the impatience; the confidence of an atomic bomb informing every gesture.

When far from home, Americans easily recognize one another in a crowd. It is only when we return home, when we live and work next to one another, that Americans choose to believe anew in the fact of our separateness.

Americans have resorted to the idea of a shared culture only at times of international competition; at times of economic depression; during war; during periods of immigration. Nineteenth-century nativists feared Catholics and Jews would undermine the Protestant idea of America. As the nineteenth-century American city crowded with ragpickers, and crucifix-kissers, and garlic-eaters, yes, and as metaphors of wildness attached to the American city, nativists consoled themselves with a cropped version of America—the small white town, the general store, the Elks Hall, the Congregational church.

To this day, political journalists repair to the "heartland" to test the rhetoric of Washington or New York against true America.

But it was the antisociability of American Protestantism which paradoxically allowed for an immigrant nation. Lacking a communal sense, how could Americans resist the coming of strangers? America became a multiracial, multireligious society precisely because a small band of Puritans did not want the world.

The American city became the fame of America worldwide.

In time, the American city became the boast of America. In time, Americans would admit their country's meaning resided in the city. America represented freedom—the freedom to leave Europe behind, the freedom to re-create one's life, the freedom to re-create the world. In time, Americans came to recognize themselves in the immigrant—suitcase in hand, foreign-speaking, bewildered by the city. The figure of the immigrant became, like the American cowboy, a figure of loneliness, and we trusted that figure as descriptive of Protestant American experience. We are a nation of immigrants, we were able to say.

Now "Hispanics and Asians" have replaced "Catholics and Jews" in the imaginations of nativists. The nativist fear is that non-European immigrants will undo the European idea of America (forgetting that America was formed against the idea of Europe).

We are a nation of immigrants—most of us say it easily now. And we are working on a new cliché to accommodate new immigrants: the best thing about immigrants, the best that they bring to America, we say, is their "diversity." We mean they are not us—the Protestant creed.

■ ■ ■

In the late nineteenth century, when much of San Francisco was sand dunes, city fathers thought to plant a large park running out to the edge of the sea. Prescient city fathers. San Francisco would become crowded. Someday there would be the need for a park at the edge of the sea.

Having reached the end of the continent, Americans contemplated finitude. The Pacific Coast was ominous to the California imagination. The Pacific Coast was an Asian horizon. The end of us was the beginning of them. Old duffers warned, "Someday there will be sampans in the harbor."

With one breath people today speak of Hispanics and Asians—the new Americans. Between the two, Asians are the more admired—the model minority—more protestant than Protestants; so hardworking, self-driven; so bright. But the Asian remains more unsettling to American complacence, because the Asian is culturally more foreign.

Hispanics may be reluctant or pushy or light or dark, but Hispanics are recognizably European. They speak a European tongue. They worship or reject a European God. The shape of the meat they eat is identifiable. But the Asian?

Asians rounded the world for me. I was a Mexican teenager in America who had become an Irish Catholic. When I was growing up in the 1960s, I heard Americans describing their nation as simply bipartate: black and white. When black and white America argued, I felt I was overhearing some family quarrel that didn't include me. Korean and Chinese and Japanese faces in Sacramento rescued me from the simplicities of black and white America.

I was in high school when my uncle from India died, my Uncle Raj, the dentist. After Raj died, we went to a succession of Chinese dentists, the first Asian names I connected with recognizable faces; the first Asian hands.

In the 1960s, whole blocks of downtown Sacramento were to be demolished for a redevelopment. The *Sacramento Bee* reported several Chinese businessmen had declared their intention to build a ten-story office building downtown with a pagoda roof. About that same time, there was another article in the *Bee*. Mexican entrepreneurs would turn Sixth and K into a Mexican block with cobblestones, restaurants, colonial façades. My father was skeptical concerning the Mexican enterprise. "Guess which one will never get built?" my father intoned from the lamplight, snapping the spine of his newspaper.

Dr. Chiang, one of our family dentists, had gone to the University of the Pacific. He encouraged the same school for me. Our entire conversational motif, repeated at every visit, was college—his path and my plans.

Then there was Dr. Wang.

Not Dr. Wang! My sister refused. Dr. Wang didn't bother with Novocaine. Dr. Wang's office was a dark and shabby place.

My father said we owed it to Dr. Wang to be his patients. Dr. Wang referred business to my father.

Dr. Wang joked about my long nose. "Just like your father." And again: "Just like your father," as he pulled my nose up to open my mouth. Then China entered my mouth in a blast of garlic, a whorl of pain.

The Chinese businessmen built a ten-story office building downtown with a pagoda roof. Just as my father predicted they would.

■ ■ ■

Americans must resist the coming of fall, the starched shirt, the inimical expectation of the schoolmarm, because Americans want to remain individual. The classroom will teach us a language in common. The classroom will teach a history that implicates us with others. The classroom will tell us that we belong to a culture.

American educators, insofar as they are Americans, share with their students a certain ambivalence, even a resistance, to the public lessons of school. Witness the influence of progressivism on American education, a pedagogy that describes the primary purpose of education as fostering independence of thought, creativity, originality— notions that separate one student from another.

The hardest lesson for me, as for Huck Finn, as for the Chinese kid in the fifth paragraph of this chapter, was the lesson of public identity. What I needed from the classroom was a public life. The earliest necessity for any student is not individuality but something closer to the reverse. With Huck, I needed to learn the names of British kings and dissident Protestants, because they were the beginning of us. I read the writings of eighteenth-century white men who powdered their wigs and kept slaves, because these were the men who shaped the country that shaped my life.

Today Huck Finn would emerge as the simple winner in the contest of public education. Today Huck's schoolmarm would be cried down by her students as a tyrannical supremacist.

American educators have lost the confidence of their public institution. The failure represents, in part, an advance for America: the advance of the postwar black civil-rights movement. As America became radically integrated, Americans were less inclined to claim a common identity. It was easier to speak of an American "we" when everyone in the classroom was the same color. And then, as America became integrated, the black civil-rights movement encouraged a romantic secession from the idea of America—Americans competed with one another to claim victimization for themselves, some fence for themselves as minorities.

A second factor undermining the classroom's traditional function has been the large, non-European immigration of the last two decades. It was one thing to imagine a common culture when most immigrants came from Europe. A grammar-school teacher in California may now have students from fifty-four language groups in her class, as does one grammar-school teacher I know. How shall she teach such an assembly anything singular?

Or the college professor who lectures on Shakespeare. Most of his students are Asian. He was grading papers on *The Merchant of Venice* last term when he suddenly realized most of his Asian students had no idea what it meant that Shylock was a Jew.

Teachers and educational bureaucrats bleat in chorus: we are a nation of immigrants. The best that immigrants bring to America is diversity. American education should respect diversity, celebrate diversity. Thus the dilemma of our national diversity becomes (with a little choke on logic) the solution to itself. But diversity is a liquid noun. Diversity admits everything, stands for nothing.

There are influential educators today, and I have met them, who believe the purpose of American education is to instill in children a pride in their ancestral pasts. Such a curtailing of education seems to me condescending; seems to me the worst sort of missionary spirit. Did anyone attempt to protect the white middle-class student of yore from the ironies of history? Thomas Jefferson—that great democrat—was also a slaveowner. Need we protect black students from complexity? Thomas Jefferson, that slaveowner, was also a democrat. American history has become a pageant of exemplary slaves and black educators. Gay studies, women's studies, ethnic studies—the new curriculum ensures that education will be flattering. But I submit that America is not a tale for sentimentalists.

If I am a newcomer to your country, why teach me about my ancestors? I need to know about seventeenth-century Puritans in order to make sense of the rebellion I notice everywhere in the American city. Teach me about mad British kings so I will understand the American penchant for iconoclasm. Then teach me about cowboys and Indians; I should know that tragedies created the country that will create me.

Once you toss out Benjamin Franklin and Andrew Jackson, you toss out Navajos. You toss out immigrant women who worked the sweatshops of the Lower East Side. Once you toss out Thomas Jefferson, you toss out black history.

A high-school principal tells me there are few black students in his school, but—oh my!—in the last decade his school has changed its color, changed its accent; changed memory. Instead of Black History Week, his school now observes "Newcomers' Week." But does not everyone in America have a stake in black history? To be an American is to belong to black history.

To argue for a common culture is not to propose an exclusionary culture or a static culture. The classroom is always adding to the common text, because America is a dynamic society. Susan B. Anthony, Martin Luther King, Jr., are inducted into the textbook much as they are canonized by the U.S. Postal Service, not as figures of diversity, but as persons who implicate our entire society.

Sherlock Holmes?

I know a lot of teachers. Yet another teacher faces an eighth-grade class of Filipino immigrants. Boy-oh-boy, she would sure like to watch me try to teach her eighth-grade Filipino students to read Conan Doyle.

For example, she says: Meerschaum—a kind of pipe. Well, a pipe—you know, you smoke? Pen knife. Bell pull. Harley Street. Hobnail boots. Dressing gown. Fez. Cockney. Turkish delight. Pall Mall. Wales . . . Well, they know what whales are, she says mordantly. It's too hard. It's too hard for Conan Doyle, that's for damn sure.

But for Shakespeare?

A high-school counselor tells me her school will soon be without a football team. Too few whites and blacks are enrolled; Hispanic and Asian kids would rather play soccer. As I listen to her, a thought occurs to me: she hates football. She looks for the demise of football. Perhaps what she wants most from Hispanic and Asian children is the same reassurance earlier generations of Americans sought from European immigrants, the reassurance—the hope—that an immigrant can undo America, can untie the cultural knot.

Now the American university is dismantling the American canon in my name. In the name of my father, in the name of Chinese grocers and fry cooks and dentists, the American university disregards the Judeo-Christian foundation of the American narrative. The white university never asked my father whether or not his son should read Milton, of course. Hispanics and Asians have become the convenient national excuse for the accomplishment of what America has always wanted done—the severing of memory, the dismantlement of national culture. The end of history.

Americans are lonely now. Hispanics and Asians represent to us the alternatives of communal cultures at a time when Americans are demoralized. Americans are no longer sure that economic invincibility derives from individualism. Look at Japan! Americans learn chopsticks. Americans lustily devour what they say they fear to become. Sushi will make us lean, corporate warriors. Mexican Combination Plate #3, smothered in mestizo gravy, will bum a hole through our hearts.

No belief is more cherished by Americans, no belief is more typical of America, than the belief that one can choose to be free of American culture. One can pick and choose. Learn Spanish. Study Buddhism. . . . My Mexican father was never so American as when he wished his children might cultivate Chinese friends.

■ ■ ■

Many years pass.

Eventually I made my way through *Huckleberry Finn.* I was, by that time, a graduate student of English, able to trail Huck and Jim through thickets of American diction and into a clearing. Sitting in a university library, I saw, once more, the American river.

There is a discernible culture, a river, a thread, connecting Thomas Jefferson to Lucille Ball to Malcolm X to Sitting Bull. The panhandler at one corner is related to the pamphleteer at the next, who is related to the bank executive who is related to the Punk wearing a FUCK U T-shirt. The immigrant child sees this at once. But then he is encouraged to forget the vision.

When I was a boy who spoke Spanish, I saw America whole. I realized that there was a culture here because I lived apart from it. I didn't like America. Then I entered the culture. I entered the culture as you did, by going to school. I became Americanized. I ended up believing in choices as much as any of you do.

What my best teachers realized was their obligation to pass on to their students a culture in which the schoolmarm is portrayed as a minor villain.

■ ■ ■

When I taught Freshman English at Berkeley, I took the "F" bus from San Francisco. This was about the time when American educators were proclaiming Asians to be "whiz kids" and Asian academic triumphs fed the feature pages of American newspapers. There were lots of Asians on the "F" bus.

One day, sitting next to a Chinese student on the bus, I watched him study. The way he worried over the text was troubling to me. He knew something about the hardness of life, the seriousness of youth, that America had never taught me. I turned away; I looked out the bus window; I got off the bus at my usual stop. But consider the two of us on the "F" bus headed for Berkeley: the Chinese student poring over his text against some terrible test. Me sitting next to him, my briefcase full of English novels; lucky me. The Asian and the Hispanic. We represented, so many Americans then imagined, some new force in America, a revolutionary change, an undoing of the European line. But it was not so.

Immigrant parents send their children to school (simply, they think) to acquire the skills to "survive" in America. But the child returns home as America. Foolish immigrant parents.

By eight o'clock that morning—the morning of the bus ride— I stood, as usual, in a classroom in Wheeler Hall, lecturing on tragedy and comedy. Asian kids at the back of the room studied biochemistry, as usual, behind propped-up Shakespeares. I said nothing, made no attempt to recall them. At the end of the hour, I announced to the class that, henceforward, class participation would be a consideration in grading. Asian eyes peered over the blue rims of their Oxford Shakespeares.

Three Asian students came to my office that afternoon. They were polite. They had come to ask about the final exam—what did they need to know?

They took notes. Then one student (I would have said the most Americanized of the three) spoke up: "We think, Mr. Rodriguez, that you are prejudiced against Asian students. Because we do not speak up in class."

I made a face. Nonsense, I blustered. Freshman English is a course concerned with language. Is it so unreasonable that I should expect students to speak up in class? One Asian student is the best student in class . . . and so forth.

I don't remember how our meeting concluded. I recall my deliberation when I gave those three grades. And I think now the students were just. I did have a bias, an inevitable American bias, that favored the talkative student. Like most other American teachers, I equated intelligence with liveliness or defiance.

Another Asian student, a woman, an ethnic Chinese student from Vietnam or Cambodia, ended up with an F in one of my classes. It wasn't that she had no American voice, or even that she didn't know what to make of Thoreau. She had missed too many classes. She didn't even show up for the Final.

On a foggy morning during winter break, this woman came to my office with her father to remonstrate.

I was too embarrassed to look at her. I spoke to her father. She sat by the door.

I explained the five essay assignments. I showed him my grade book, the blank spaces next to her name. The father and I both paused a long time over my evidence. I suggested the university's remedial writing course. . . . *Really, you know, her counselor should never have . . .*

In the middle of my apology, he stood up; he turned and walked to where his daughter sat. I could see only his back as he hovered over her. I heard the slap. He moved away.

And then I saw her. She was not crying. She was looking down at her hands composed neatly on her lap.

Jessica!

LAKOTA WOMAN

Mary Crow Dog

This piece is an excerpt from the book Lakota Woman *by Mary Crow Dog with Richard Erdoes, published in 1990.*

It is not the big, dramatic things so much that get us down, but just being Indian, trying to hang on to our way of life, language, and values while being surrounded by an alien, more powerful culture. It is being an iyeska, a half-blood, being looked down upon by whites and full-bloods alike. It is being a backwoods girl living in a city, having to rip off stores in order to survive. Most of all it is being a woman. Among Plains tribes, some men think that all a woman is good for is to crawl into the sack with them and mind the children. It compensates for what white society has done to them. They were famous warriors and hunters once, but the buffalo is gone and there is not much rep in putting a can of spam or an occasional rabbit on the table.

As for being warriors, the only way some men can count coup nowadays is knocking out another skin's teeth during a barroom fight. In the old days a man made a name for himself by being generous and wise, but now he has nothing to be generous with, no jobs, no money; and as far as our traditional wisdom is concerned, our men are being told by the white missionaries, teachers, and employers that it is merely savage superstition they should get rid of if they want to make it in this world. Men are forced to live away from their children, so that the family can get ADC—Aid to Dependent Children. So some warriors come home drunk and beat up their old ladies in order to work off their frustration. I know where they are coming from. I feel sorry for them, but I feel even sorrier for their women.

To start from the beginning, I am a Sioux from the Rosebud Reservation in South Dakota. I belong to the "Burned Thigh," the Brule Tribe, the Sicangu in our language. Long ago, so the legend goes, a small band of Sioux was surrounded by enemies who set fire to their tipis and the grass around them. They fought their way out of the trap but got their legs burned and in this way acquired their name. The Brules are part of the Seven Sacred Campfires, the seven tribes of the Western Sioux known collectively as Lakota. The Eastern Sioux are called Dakota. The difference between them is their language. It is the same except that where we Lakota pronounce an *L,* the Dakota pronounce a *D.* They cannot pronounce an *L* at all. In our tribe we have this joke: "What is a flat tire in Dakota?" Answer: "A b*d*owout."

The Brule, like all Sioux, were a horse people, fierce riders and raiders, great warriors. Between 1870 and 1880 all Sioux were driven into reservations, fenced in and forced to give up everything that had given meaning to their life—their horses, their hunting, their arms, everything. But under the long snows of despair the little spark of our ancient beliefs and pride kept glowing, just barely sometimes, waiting for a warm wind to blow that spark into a flame again.

My family was settled on the reservation in a small place called He-Dog, after a famous chief. There are still some He-Dogs living. One, an old lady I knew, lived to be over a hundred years old. Nobody knew when she had been born. She herself had no idea, except that when she came into the world there was no census yet, and Indians had not yet been given Christian first names. Her name was just He-Dog, nothing else. She always told me, "You should have seen me eighty years ago when I was pretty." I have never forgotten her face—nothing but deep cracks and gullies, but beautiful in its own way. At any rate very impressive.

On the Indian side my family was related to the Brave Birds and Fool Bulls. Old Grandpa Fool Bull was the last man to make flutes and play them, the old-style flutes in the shape of a bird's head which had the elk power, the power to lure a young girl into a man's blanket. Fool Bull lived a whole long century, dying in 1976, whittling his flutes almost until his last day He took me to my first peyote meeting while I was still a kid.

He still remembered the first Wounded Knee, the massacre. He was a young boy at that time, traveling with his father, a well-known medicine man. They had gone to a place near Wounded Knee to take part in a Ghost Dance. They had on their painted ghost shirts which were supposed to make them bulletproof. When they got near Pine Ridge they were stopped by white soldiers, some of them from the Seventh Cavalry, George Custer's old regiment, who were hoping to kill themselves some Indians. The Fool Bull band had to give up their few old muzzle-loaders, bows, arrows, and even knives. They had to put up their tipis in a tight circle, all bunched up, with the wagons on the outside and the soldiers surrounding their camp, watching them closely. It was cold, so cold that the trees were crackling with a loud noise as the frost was splitting their trunks. The people made a fire the following morning to warm themselves and make some coffee and then they noticed a sound beyond the crackling of the trees: rifle fire, salvos making a noise like the ripping apart of a giant blanket; the boom of cannon and the rattling of quick-firing Hotchkiss guns. Fool Bull remembered the grown-ups bursting into tears, the women keening: "They are killing our people, they are butchering them!" It was only two miles or so from where Grandfather Fool Bull stood that almost three hundred Sioux men, women, and children were slaughtered. Later grandpa saw the bodies of the slain, all frozen in ghostly attitudes, thrown into a ditch like dogs. And he saw a tiny baby sucking at his dead mother's breast.

I wish I could tell about the big deeds of some ancestors of mine who fought at the Little Big Horn, or the Rosebud, counting coup during the Grattan or Fetterman battle, but little is known of my family's history before 1880. I hope some of my great-grandfathers counted coup on Custer's men, I like to imagine it, but I just do not know. Our Rosebud people did not play a big part in the battles against generals Crook or Custer. This was due to the policy of Spotted Tail, the all-powerful chief at the time. Spotted Tail had earned his eagle feathers as a warrior, but had been taken East as a prisoner and put in jail. Coming back years later, he said that he had seen the cities of the whites and that a single one of them contained more people than could be found in all the Plains tribes together, and that every one of the wasičuns' factories could turn out more rifles and bullets in one day than were owned by all the Indians in the country. It was useless, he said, to try to resist the wasičuns. During the critical year of 1876 he had his Indian police keep most of the young men on the reservation, preventing them from joining Sitting Bull, Gall, and Crazy Horse. Some of the young bucks, a few Brave Birds among them, managed to sneak out trying to get to Montana, but nothing much is known. After having been forced into reservations, it was not thought wise to recall such things. It might mean no rations, or worse. For the same reason many in my family turned Christian, letting themselves be "whitemanized." It took many years to reverse this process.

My sister Barbara, who is four years older than me, says she remembers the day when I was born. It was late at night and raining hard amid thunder and lightning. We had no electricity then, just the old-style kerosene lamps with the big reflectors. No bathroom, no tap water, no car. Only a few white teachers had cars. There was one phone in He-Dog, at the trading post. This was not so very long ago, come to think of it. Like most Sioux at that time my mother was supposed to give birth at home, I think, but something went wrong, I was pointing the wrong way, feet first or stuck sideways. My mother was in great pain, laboring for hours, until finally somebody ran to the trading post and called the ambulance. They took her—us—to Rosebud, but the hospital there was not yet equipped to handle a complicated birth, I don't think they had surgery then, so they had to drive mother all the way to Pine Ridge, some ninety miles distant, because there the tribal hospital was bigger. So it happened that I was born among Crazy Horse's people. After my sister Sandra was born the doctors there performed a hysterectomy on my mother, in fact sterilizing her without her permission, which was common at the time, and up to just a few years ago, so that it is hardly worth mentioning. In the opinion of some people, the fewer Indians there are, the better. As Colonel Chivington said to his soldiers: "Kill 'em all, big and small, nits make lice!"

I don't know whether I am a louse under the white man's skin. I hope I am. At any rate I survived the long hours of my mother's labor, the stormy drive to Pine Ridge, and the neglect of the doctors. I am an iyeska, a breed, that's what the white kids used to call me. When I grew bigger they stopped calling me that, because it would get them a bloody nose. I am a small woman, not much over five feet tall, but I can hold my own in a fight, and in a free-for-all with honkies I can become rather ornery and do real damage. I have white blood in me. Often I have wished to be able to purge it out of me. As a young girl I used to look at myself in the mirror, trying to find a clue as to who and what I was. My face is very Indian, and so are my eyes and my hair, but my skin is very light. Always I waited for the summer, for the prairie sun, the Badlands sun, to tan me and make me into a real skin.

The Crow Dogs, the members of my husband's family, have no such problems of identity. They don't need the sun to tan them, they are full-bloods—the Sioux of the Sioux. Some Crow Dog men have faces which make the portrait on the buffalo Indian nickel look like a washed-out white man. They have no shortage of legends. Every Crow Dog seems to be a legend in himself, including the women. They became outcasts in their stronghold at Grass Mountain rather than being whitemanized. They could not be tamed, made to wear a necktie or go to a Christian church. All during the long years when practicing Indian beliefs was forbidden and could be punished with jail, they went right on having their ceremonies, their sweat baths and sacred dances. Whenever a Crow Dog got together with some relatives, such as those equally untamed, unregenerated Iron Shells, Good Lances, Two Strikes, Picket Pins, or Hollow Horn Bears, then you could hear the sound of the can gleska, the drum, telling all the world that a Sioux ceremony was in the making. It took courage and suffering to keep the flame alive, the little spark under the snow.

The first Crow Dog was a well-known chief. On his shield was the design of two circles and two arrowheads for wounds received in battle— two white man's bullets and two Pawnee arrow points. When this first Crow Dog was lying wounded in the snow, a coyote came to warm him and a crow flew ahead of him to show him the way home. His name should be Crow Coyote, but the white interpreter misunderstood it and so they became Crow Dogs. This Crow Dog of old became famous for killing a rival chief, the result of a feud over tribal politics, then driving voluntarily over a hundred miles to get himself hanged at Deadwood, his wife sitting beside him in his buggy; famous also for finding on his arrival that the Supreme Court had ordered him to be freed because the federal government had no jurisdiction over Indian reservations and also because it was no crime for one Indian to kill another. Later, Crow Dog became a leader of the Ghost Dancers, holding out for months in the frozen caves and ravines of the Badlands. So, if my own family lacks history, that of my husband more than makes up for it.

Our land itself is a legend, especially the area around Grass Mountain where I am living now. The fight for our land is at the core of our existence, as it has been for the last two hundred years. Once the land is gone, then we are gone too. The Sioux used to keep winter counts, picture writings on buffalo skin, which told our people's story from year to year. Well, the whole country is one vast winter count. You can't walk a mile without coming to some family's sacred vision hill, to an ancient Sun Dance circle, an old battleground, a place where something worth remembering happened. Mostly a death, a proud death or a drunken death. We are a great people for dying. "It's a good day to die!" that's our old battle cry. But the land with its tar paper shacks and outdoor privies, not one of them straight, but all leaning this way or that way, is also a land to live on, a land for good times and telling jokes and talking of great deeds done in the past. But you can't live forever off the deeds of Sitting Bull or Crazy Horse. You can't wear their eagle feathers, freeload off their legends. You have to make your own legends now. It isn't easy.

THE BOY

Marie Howe

This poem is from Howe's 1998 book What the Living Do.

My older brother is walking down the sidewalk into the suburban
    summer night:
white T-shirt, blue jeans—to the field at the end of the street.

Hangers Hideout the boys called it, an undeveloped plot, a pit
    overgrown
with weeds, some old furniture thrown down there,

and some metal hangers clinking in the trees like wind chimes.
He's running away from home because our father wants to cut his hair.

And in two more days our father will convince me to go to him—you know
where he is—and talk to him: No reprisals. He promised. A small parade
   of kids

in feet pajamas will accompany me, their voices like the first peepers
   in spring.
And my brother will walk ahead of us home, and my father

will shave his head bald, and my brother will not speak to anyone the next
month, not a word, not *pass the milk,* nothing.

What happened in our house taught my brothers how to leave, how to walk
down a sidewalk without looking back.

I was the girl. What happened taught me to follow him, whoever he was,
calling and calling his name.

DOG HEAVEN

Stephanie Vaughn

This short story appeared in The New Yorker *and is collected in Vaughn's 1990 book*
Sweet Talk.

E very so often that dead dog dreams me up again.
   It's twenty-five years later. I'm walking along 42nd Street in Manhattan, the sounds of the city crashing beside me—horns, gearshifts, insults—sombody's chewing gum holding my foot to the pavement, when
that dog wakes from his long sleep and imagines me.

   I'm sweet again. I'm sweet-breathed and flat-limbed. Our family is stationed at Fort Niagara, and the dog swims his red heavy fur into the black
Niagara River. Across the street from the officers' quarters, down the
steep shady bank, the river, even this far downstream, has been clocked at
nine miles per hour. The dog swims after the stick I have thrown.

   "Are you crazy?" my grandmother says, even though she is not fond of
dog hair in the house, the way it sneaks into the refrigerator every time
you open the door. "There's a current out there! It'll take that dog all the
way to Toronto."

   "The dog knows where the backwater ends and the current begins," I
say, because it is true. He comes down to the river all the time with my
father, my brother MacArthur, or me. You never have to yell the dog away
from the place where the river water moves like a whip.

   Sparky Smith and I had a game we played called knockout. It involved
a certain way of breathing and standing up fast that caused the blood to

leave the brain as if a plug had been jerked from the skull. You came to again just as soon as you were on the ground, the blood sloshing back, but it always seemed as if you had left the planet, had a vacation on Mars, and maybe stopped back at Fort Niagara half a lifetime later.

There weren't many kids my age on the post, because it was a small command. Most of its real work went on at the missile batteries flung like shale along the American-Canadian border. Sparky Smith and I hadn't been at Lewiston-Porter Central School long enough to get to know many people, so we entertained ourselves by meeting in a hollow of trees and shrubs at the far edge of the parade ground and telling each other seventh-grade sex jokes that usually had to do with keyholes and door-knobs, hot dogs and hotdog buns, nuns, priests, preachers, schoolteachers, and people in blindfolds.

When we ran out of sex jokes, we went to knockout and took turns catching each other as we fell like a cut tree toward the ground. Whenever I knocked out, I came to on the grass with the dog barking, yelping, crouching, crying for help, "Wake up! Wake up!" he seemed to say. "Do you know your name? Do you know your name? My name is Duke! My name is Duke!" I'd wake to the sky with the urgent call of the dog in the air, and I'd think, Well, here I am, back in my life again.

Sparky Smith and I spent our school time smiling too much and running for office. We wore mittens instead of gloves, because everyone else did. We made our mothers buy us ugly knit caps with balls on top—caps that in our previous schools would have identified us as weird but were part of the winter uniform in upstate New York. We wobbled onto the ice of the post rink, practicing in secret, banged our knees, scraped the palms of our hands, so that we would be invited to skating parties by civilian children.

"You skate?" With each other we practiced the cool look.

"Oh, yeah. I mean, like I do it some—I'm not a racer or anything."

Every morning we boarded the Army-green bus—the slime-green, dead-swamp-algae-green bus—and rode it to the post gate, past the concrete island where the MPs stood in their bulletproof booth. Across from the gate, we got off at a street corner and waited with the other Army kids, the junior-high and high-school kids, for the real bus, the yellow one with the civilian kids on it. Just as we began to board, the civilian kids—there, were only six of them but eighteen of us—would begin to sing the Artillery song with obscene variations one of them had invented. Instead of "Over hill, over dale," they sang things like "Over boob, over tit." For a few weeks, we sat in silence watching the heavy oak trees of the town give way to apple orchards and potato farms, and we pretended not to hear. Then one day Sparky Smith began to sing the real Artillery song, the booming song with caissons rolling along in it, and we all joined in and took over the bus with our voices.

When we ran out of verses, one of the civilian kids, a football player in high school, yelled, "Sparky is a *dog's* name. Here Sparky, Sparky,

Sparky." Sparky rose from his seat with a wounded look, then dropped to the aisle on his hands and knees and bit the football player in the calf. We all laughed, even the football player, and Sparky returned to his seat.

"That guy's just lucky I didn't pee on his leg," Sparky said.

Somehow Sparky got himself elected homeroom president and me homeroom vice president in January. He liked to say, "In actual percentages—I mean in actual per capita terms—we are doing much better than the civilian kids." He kept track of how many athletes we had, how many band members, who among the older girls might become a cheerleader. Listening to him even then, I couldn't figure out how he got anyone to vote for us. When he was campaigning, he sounded dull and serious, and anyway he had a large head and looked funny in a knit cap. He put up a homemade sign in the lunchroom, went from table to table to find students from 7-B to shake hands with, and said to me repeatedly, as I walked along a step behind and nodded, "Just don't tell them that you're leaving in March. Under no circumstances let them know that you will not be able to finish out your term."

In January, therefore, I was elected homeroom vice president by people I still didn't know (nobody in 7-B rode our bus—that gave us an edge), and in March my family moved to Fort Sill, in Oklahoma. I surrendered my vice presidency to a civilian girl, and that was the end for all time of my career in public office.

Two days before we left Fort Niagara, we took the dog, Duke, to Charlie Battery, fourteen miles from the post, and left him with the mess sergeant. We were leaving him for only six weeks, until we could settle in Oklahoma and send for him. He had stayed at Charlie Battery before, when we visited our relatives in Ohio at Christmastime. He knew there were big meaty bones at Charlie Battery, and scraps of chicken, steak, turkey, slices of cheese, special big-dog bowls of ice cream. The mess at Charlie Battery was Dog Heaven, so he gave us a soft, forgiving look as we walked with him from the car to the back of the mess hall.

My mother said, as she always did at times like that, "I wish he knew more English." My father gave him a fierce manly scratch behind the ear. My brother and I scraped along behind with our pinched faces.

"Don't you worry," the sergeant said. "He'll be fine here. We like this dog, and he likes us. He'll run that fence perimeter all day long. He'll be his own early-warning defense system. Then we'll give this dog everything he ever dreamed of eating." The sergeant looked quickly at my father to see if the lighthearted reference to the defense system had been all right. My father was in command of the missile batteries. In my father's presence, no one spoke lightly of the defense of the United States of America—of the missiles that would rise from the earth like a wind and knock out (knock out!) the Soviet planes flying over the North Pole with their nuclear bombs. But Duke was my father's dog, too, and I think that my father had the same wish we all had—to tell him that we were going to send for him, this was just going to be a wonderful dog vacation.

"Sergeant Mozley has the best mess within five hundred miles," my father said to me and MacArthur.

We looked around. We had been there for Thanksgiving dinner when the grass was still green. Now, in late winter, it was a dreary place, a collection of rain-streaked metal buildings, standing near huge dark mounds of earth. In summer, the mounds looked something like the large grassy mounds in southern Ohio, the famous Indian mounds, softly rounded and benignly mysterious. In March, they were black with old snow. Inside the mounds were the Nike missiles, I supposed, although I didn't know for sure where the missiles were. Perhaps they were hidden in the depressions behind the mounds.

Once during "Fact Monday" in Homeroom 7-B, our teacher, Miss Bintz, had given a lecture on nuclear weapons. First she put a slide on the wall depicting an atom and its spinning electrons.

"Do you know what this is?" she said, and everyone in the room said, "An atom," in one voice, as if we were reciting a poem. We liked "Fact Monday" sessions because we didn't have to do any work for them. We sat happily in the dim light of her slides through lectures called "Nine Chapters in the Life of a Cheese" ("First the milk is warmed, then it is soured with rennet"), "The Morning Star of English Poetry" ("As springtime suggests the beginning of new life, so Chaucer stands at the beginning of English poetry"), and "Who's Who Among the Butterflies" ("The monarch—*Danaus plexipus*—is king"). Sparky liked to say that Miss Bintz was trying to make us into third-graders again, but I liked Miss Bintz. She had high cheekbones and a passionate voice. She believed, like the adults in my family, that a fact was something solid and useful, like a penknife you could put in your pocket in case of emergency.

That day's lecture was "What Happens to the Atom When It Is Smashed." Miss Bintz put on the wall a black-and-white slide of four women who had been horribly disfigured by the atomic blast at Hiroshima. The room was half darkened for the slide show. When she surprised us with the four faces of the women, you could feel the darkness grow, the silence in the bellies of the students.

"And do you know what this is?" Miss Bintz said. No one spoke. What answer could she have wanted from us, anyway? She clicked the slide machine through ten more pictures—close-ups of blistered hands, scarred heads, flattened buildings, burned trees, maimed and naked children staggering toward the camera as if the camera were food, a house, a mother, a father, a friendly dog.

"Do you know what this is?" Miss Bintz said again. Our desks were arranged around the edge of the room, creating an arena in the center. Miss Bintz entered that space and began to move along the front of our desks, looking to see who would answer her incomprehensible question.

"Do you know?" She stopped in front of my desk.

"No," I said.

"Do you know?" She stopped next at Sparky's desk.

Sparky looked down and finally said, "It's something horrible."

"That's right," she said. "It's something very horrible. This is the effect of an atom smashing. This is the effect of nuclear power." She turned to gesture at the slide, but she had stepped in front of the projector, and the smear of children's faces fell across her back. "Now let's think about how nuclear power got from the laboratory to the scientists to the people of Japan." She had begun to pace again. "Let's think about where all this devastation and wreckage actually comes from. You tell me," she said to a large crouching boy named Donald Anderson. He was hunched over his desk, and his arms lay before him like tree limbs.

"I don't know," Donald Anderson said.

"Of course you do," Miss Bintz said. "Where did all of this come from?"

None of us had realized yet that Miss Bintz's message was political. I looked beyond Donald Anderson at the drawn window shades. Behind them were plate-glass windows, a view of stiff red-oak leaves, the smell of wood smoke in the air. Across the road from the school was an orchard, beyond that a pasture, another orchard, and then the town of Lewiston, standing on the Niagara River seven miles upstream from the long row of red-brick Colonial houses that were the officers' quarters at Fort Niagara. Duke was down the river, probably sniffing at the reedy edge, his head lifting when ducks flew low over the water. Once the dog had come back to our house with a live fish in his mouth, a carp. Nobody ever believed that story except those of us who saw it: me, my mother and father and brother, my grandmother.

Miss Bintz had clicked to a picture of a mushroom cloud and was now saying, "And where did the bomb come from?" We were all tired of "Fact Monday" by then. Miss Bintz walked back to where Sparky and I were sitting. "You military children," she said. "You know where the bomb comes from. Why don't you tell us?" she said to me.

Maybe because I was tired, or bored, or frightened—I don't know—I said to Miss Bintz, looking her in the eye, "The bomb comes from the mother bomb."

Everyone laughed. We laughed because we needed to laugh, and because Miss Bintz had all the answers and all the questions and she was pointing them at us like guns.

"Stand up," she said. She made me enter the arena in front of the desks, and then she clicked the machine back to the picture of the Japanese women. "Look at this picture and make a joke," she said. What came next was the lecture she had been aiming for all along. The bomb came from the United States of America. We in the United States were worried about whether another country might use the bomb, but in the whole history of the human species only one country had ever used the worst weapon ever invented. On she went, bombs and airplanes and bomb tests, and then she got to the missiles. They were right here, she said, not more than ten miles away. Didn't we all know that? "You know that, don't you?" she said to me. If the missiles weren't hidden among our orchards, the planes from the Soviet Union would not have any reason to drop bombs on top of Lewiston-Porter Central School.

I had stopped listening by then and realized that the pencil I still held in my hand was drumming a song against my thigh. Over hill, over dale. I looked back at the wall again, where the mushroom cloud had reappeared, and my own silhouette stood wildly in the middle of it. I looked at Sparky and dropped the pencil on the floor, stooped down to get it, looked at Sparky once more, stood up, and knocked out.

Later, people told me that I didn't fall like lumber, I fell like something soft collapsing, a fan folding in on itself, a balloon rumpling to the floor. Sparky saw what I was up to and tried to get out from behind his desk to catch me, but it was Miss Bintz I fell against, and she went down, too. When I woke up, the lights were on, the mushroom cloud was a pale ghost against the wall, voices in the room sounded like insect wings, and I was back in my life again.

"I'm so sorry," Miss Bintz said. "I didn't know you were an epileptic."

At Charlie Battery, it was drizzling as my parents stood and talked with the sergeant, rain running in dark tiny ravines along the slopes of the mounds.

MacArthur and I had M&Ms in our pockets, which we were allowed to give to the dog for his farewell. When we extended our hands, though, the dog lowered himself to the gravel and looked up at us from under his tender red eyebrows. He seemed to say that if he took the candy he knew we would go, but if he didn't perhaps we would stay here at the missile battery and eat scraps with him.

We rode back to the post in silence, through gray apple orchards, through small upstate towns, the fog rising out of the rain like a wish. MacArthur and I sat against opposite doors in the back seat, thinking of the loneliness of the dog.

We entered the kitchen, where my grandmother had already begun to clean the refrigerator. She looked at us, at our grim children's faces—the dog had been sent away a day earlier than was really necessary—and she said, "Well, God knows you can't clean the dog hair out of the house with the dog still in it."

Whenever I think of an Army post, I think of a place the weather cannot touch for long. The precise rectangles of the parade grounds, the precisely pruned trees and shrubs, the living quarters, the administration buildings, the PX and commissary, the nondenominational church, the teen club, snack bar, the movie house, the skeet-and-trap field, the swimming pools, the runway, warehouses, the officers' club, the NCO club. Men marching, women marching, saluting, standing at attention, at ease. The bugle will trumpet reveille, mess call, assembly, retreat, taps through a hurricane, a tornado, flood, blizzard. Whenever I think of the clean squared look of a military post, I think that if one were blown down today in a fierce wind, it would be standing again tomorrow in time for reveille.

The night before our last full day at Fort Niagara, an arctic wind slipped across the lake and froze the rain where it fell, on streets, trees, power lines, rooftops. We awoke to a fabulation of ice, the sun shining like a weapon, light rocketing off every surface except the surfaces of the Army's clean streets and walks.

MacArthur and I stood on the dry, scraped walk in front of our house and watched a jeep pass by on the way to the gate. On the post, everything was operational, but in the civilian world beyond the gate power lines were down, hanging like daggers in the sun, roads were glazed with ice, cars were in ditches, highways were impassable. No yellow school buses were going to be on the roads that morning.

"This means we miss our very last day in school," MacArthur said. "No goodbyes for us."

We looked up at the high, bare branches of the hard maples, where drops of ice glimmered.

"I just want to shake your hand and say so long," Sparky said. He had come out of his house to stand with us. "I guess you know this means you'll miss the surprise party."

"There was going to be a party?" I said.

"Just cupcakes," Sparky said. "I sure wish you could stay the school year and keep your office."

"Oh, who cares!" I said, suddenly irritated with Sparky, although he was my best friend. "Jesus," I said, sounding to myself like an adult—like Miss Bintz maybe, when she was off duty. "Jesus," I said again. "What kind of office is home-goddamn-room vice president in a crummy country school?"

MacArthur said to Sparky, "What kind of cupcakes were they having?"

I looked down at MacArthur and said, "Do you know how totally ridiculous you look in that knit cap? I can't wait until we get out of this place."

"Excuse me," MacArthur said. "Excuse me for wearing the hat you gave me for my birthday."

It was then that the dog came back. We heard him calling out before we saw him, his huge woof-woof. "My name is Duke! My name is Duke! I'm your dog! I'm your dog!" Then we saw him streaking through the trees, through the park space of oaks and maples between our house and the post gate. Later the MPs would say that he stopped and wagged his tail at them before he passed through the gate, as if he understood that he should be stopping to show his ID card. He ran to us, bounding across the crusted, glass-slick snow—ran into the history of our family, all the stories we would tell about him after he was dead. Years and years later, whenever we came back together at the family dinner table, we would start the dog stories. He was the dog who caught the live fish with his mouth, the one who stole a pound of butter off the commissary loading dock and brought it to us in his soft bird dog's mouth without a tooth mark on the package. He was the dog who broke out of Charlie Battery the morning of an ice storm, traveled fourteen miles across the needled grasses and frozen pastures, through the prickly frozen mud of orchards, across backyard fences in small towns, and found the lost family.

The day was good again. When we looked back at the ice we saw a fairyland. The red-brick houses looked like ice castles. The ice-coated trees, with their million dreams of fight, seemed to cast a spell over us.

"This is for you," Sparky said, and handed me a gold-foiled box. Inside were chocolate candies and a note that said, "I have enjoyed knowing you this year. I hope you have a good life." Then it said, "P.S. Remember this name. Someday I'm probably going to be famous."

"Famous as what?" MacArthur said.

"I haven't decided yet," Sparky said.

We had a party. We sat on the front steps of our quarters, Sparky, MacArthur, the dog, and I, and we ate all the chocolates at 8 o'clock in the morning. We sat shoulder to shoulder, the four of us, and looked across the street through the trees at the river, and we talked about what we might be doing a year from then. Finally, we finished the chocolates and stopped talking and allowed the brilliant light of that morning to enter us.

Miss Bintz is the one who sent me the news about Sparky four months later. BOY DROWNS IN SWIFT CURRENT. In the newspaper story, Sparky takes the bus to Niagara Falls with two friends from Lewiston-Porter. It's a searing July day, 100 degrees in the city, so the boys climb down the gorge into the river and swim in a place where it's illegal to swim, 2 miles downstream from the Falls. The boys Sparky is tagging along with— they're both student-council members as well as football players, just the kind of boys Sparky himself wants to be—have sneaked down to this swimming place many times: a cove in the bank of the river, where the water is still and glassy on a hot July day, not like the water raging in the middle of the river. But the current is a wild invisible thing, unreliable, whipping out with a looping arm to pull you in. "He was only three feet in front of me," one of the boys said. "He took one more stroke and then he was gone."

We were living in civilian housing not far from the post. When we had the windows open, we could hear the bugle calls and the sound of the cannon firing retreat at sunset. A month after I got the newspaper clipping about Sparky, the dog died. He was killed, along with every other dog on our block, when a stranger drove down our street one evening and threw poisoned hamburger into our front yards.

All that week I had trouble getting to sleep at night. One night I was still awake when the recorded bugle sounded taps, the sound drifting across the Army fences and into our bedrooms. Day is done, gone the sun. It was the sound of my childhood in sleep. The bugler played it beautifully, mournfully, holding fast to the long, high notes. That night I listened to the cadence of it, to the yearning of it. I thought of the dog again, only this time I suddenly saw him rising like a missile into the air, the red glory of his fur flying, his nose pointed heavenward. I remembered the dog leaping high, prancing on his hind legs the day he came back from Charlie Battery, the dog rocking back and forth, from front legs to hind legs, dancing, sliding across the ice of the post rink later that day, as Sparky, MacArthur, and I played crack-the-whip, holding tight to each other, our skates careening and singing. "You're AWOL! You're AWOL!" we cried at the dog. "No school!" the dog barked back. "No school!" We skated across the darkening ice into the sunset, skated faster and faster, until we seemed to rise together into the cold, bright air. It was a good day, it was a good day, it was a good day.

TRAIN

Joy Williams

This short story is from Williams's collection Taking Care, *first published in 1972.*

Inside, the Auto-Train was violet. Both little girls were pleased because it was their favorite color. Violet was practically the only thing they agreed on. Danica Anderson and Jane Muirhead were both ten years old. They had traveled from Maine to Washington, D.C., by car with Jane's parents and were now on the train with Jane's parents and 109 other people and 42 automobiles on the way to Florida where they lived. It was September. Danica had been with Jane since June. Danica's mother was getting married again and she had needed the summer months to settle down and have everything nice for Dan when she saw her in September. In August, her mother had written Dan and asked what she could do to make things nice for Dan when she got back. Dan replied that she would like a good wall-hung pencil sharpener and satin sheets. She would like cowboy bread for supper. Dan supposed that she would get none of these things. Her mother hadn't even asked her what cowboy bread was.

The girls explored the entire train, north to south. They saw everyone but the engineer. Then they sat down in their violet seats. Jane made faces at a cute little toddler holding a cloth rabbit until he started to cry. Dan took out her writing materials and began writing to Jim Anderson. She was writing him a postcard.

"Jim," she wrote, "I miss you and I will see you any minute. When I see you we will go swimming right away."

"That is real messy writing," Jane said. "It's all scrunched together. If you were writing to anyone other than a dog, they wouldn't be able to read it at all."

Dan printed her name on the bottom of the card and embellished it all with X's and O's.

"Your writing to Jim Anderson is dumb in about twelve different ways. He's a *golden retriever,* for Godssakes."

Dan looked at her friend mildly. She was used to Jane yelling at her and expressing disgust and impatience. Jane had once lived in Manhattan. She had developed certain attitudes. Jane was a treasure from the city of New York currently on loan to the state of Florida where her father, for the last two years, had been engaged in running down a perfectly good investment in a marina and dinner theater. Jane liked to wear scarves tied around her head. She claimed to enjoy grapes and brown sugar and sour cream for dessert more than ice cream and cookies. She liked artichokes. She *adored* artichokes. She *adored* the part in the New York City Ballet's *Nutcracker Suite* where the Dew Drops and the candied Petals of Roses dance to the "Waltz of the Flowers." Jane had seen the *Nutcracker* four *times,* for Godssakes.

Dan and Jane and Jane's mother and father had all lived with Jane's grandmother in her big house in Maine all summer. The girls hadn't seen that much of the Muirheads. The Muirheads were always "cruising." They were always "gunk-holing," as they called it. Whatever that was, Jane said, for Godssakes. Jane's grandmother had a house on the ocean and knew how to make pizza and candy and sail a canoe. She called pizza 'za. She sang hymns in the shower. She sewed sequins on their jeans and made them say grace before dinner. After they said grace, Jane's grandmother would ask forgiveness for things done and left undone. She would, upon request, lie down and chat with them at night before they went to sleep. Jane was crazy about her grandmother and was quite a nice person in her presence. One night, at the end of summer, Jane had had a dream in which men dressed in black suits and white bathing caps had broken into her grandmother's house and taken all her possessions and put them in the road. In Jane's dream, rain fell on all her grandmother's things. Jane woke up weeping. Dan had wept too. Jane and Dan were friends.

The train had not yet left the station even though it was two hours past the posted departure time. An announcement had just been made that said that a two-hour delay was built into the train's schedule.

"They make up the time at night," Jane said. She plucked the postcard from Dan's hand. "This is a good one," she said. "I think you're sending it to Jim Anderson just so you can save it yourself." She read aloud, "This is a photograph of the Phantom Dream Car crashing through a wall of burning television sets before a cheering crowd at the Cow Palace in San Francisco."

At the beginning of the summer, Dan's mother had given her one hundred dollars, four packages of new underwear and three dozen stamped postcards. Most of the cards were plain but there were a few with odd pictures on them. Dan's mother wanted to hear from her twice weekly throughout the summer. She had married a man named Jake, who was a carpenter. Jake had already built Dan three bookcases. This seemed to be the extent of what he knew how to do for Dan.

"I only have three left now," Dan said, "but when I get home, I'm going to start my own collection."

"I've been through that phase," Jane said. "It's just a phase. I don't think you're much of a correspondent. You wrote, 'I got sunburn, Love, Dan'. . . 'I bought a green Frisbee. Love, Dan'. . . 'Mrs. Muirhead has swimmer's ear. Love, Dan'. . . 'Mr. Muirhead went water-skiing and cracked his rib. Love, Dan'. . . When you write to people you should have something to say."

Dan didn't reply. She had been Jane's companion for a long time, and was wearying of what Jane's mother called her "effervescence."

Jane slapped Dan on the back and hollered, "Danica Anderson, for Godssakes! What is a clod like yourself doing on this fabulous journey!"

Together, the girls made their way to the Starlight Lounge in Car 7 where Mr. and Mrs. Muirhead told them they would be enjoying cocktails. They hesitated in the car where the train's magician was with his audience, watching him while he did the magic silks trick, the cut and restored handkerchief trick, the enchanted salt shaker trick, and the dissolving quarter trick. The audience, primarily retirees, screamed with pleasure.

"I don't mind the tricks," Jane whispered to Dan, "but the junk that gets said drives me crazy."

The magician was a young man with a long spotted face. He did a lot of card forcing. Again and again, he called the card that people chose from a shuffled deck. Each time that the magician was successful, the audience participant yelled and smiled and in general acted thrilled. Jane and Dan passed on through.

"You don't really choose," Jane said. "He just makes you think you choose. He does it all with his pinky." She pushed Dan forward into the Starlight Lounge where Mrs. Muirhead was on a banquette staring out the window at a shed and an unkempt bush which was sliding slowly past. She was drinking a martini. Mr. Muirhead was several tables away talking to a young man wearing jeans and a yellow jacket. Jane did not sit down. "Mummy," she said, "can I have your olive?"

"Of course not," Mrs. Muirhead said, "it's soaked in gin."

Jane, Dan in tow, went to her father's table. "Daddy," Jane demanded, "why aren't you sitting with Mummy? Are you and Mummy having a fight?"

Dan was astonished at this question. Mr. and Mrs. Muirhead fought continuously and as bitterly as vipers. Their arguments were baroque, stately, and although frequently extraordinary, never enlightening. At breakfast, they would be quarreling over an incident at a cocktail party the night before or a dumb remark made fifteen years ago. At dinner, they would be howling over the fate, which they called by many names, which had given them one another. Forgiveness, charity and cooperation were qualities unknown to them. They were opponents *pur sang*. Dan was sure that one morning, Jane would be called from her classroom and told as gently as possible by Mr. Mooney, the school principal, that her parents had splattered one another's brains all over the lanai.

Mr. Muirhead looked at the children sorrowfully and touched Jane's check.

"I am not sitting with your mother because I am sitting with this young man here. We are having a fascinating conversation."

"Why are you always talking to young men?" Jane asked.

"Jane, honey," Mr. Muirhead said, "I will answer that." He took a swallow of his drink and sighed. He leaned forward and said earnestly, "I talk to so many young men because your mother won't let me talk to young women." He remained hunched over, patting Jane's cheek for a moment, and then leaned back.

The young man extracted a cigarette from his jacket and hesitated. Mr. Muirhead gave him a book of matches. "He does automobile illustrations," Mr. Muirhead said.

The young man nodded. "Belly bands. Pearls and flakes. Flames. All custom work."

Mr. Muirhead smiled. He seemed happier now. Mr. Muirhead loved conversations. He loved "to bring people out." Dan supposed that Jane had picked up this pleasant trait from her father and distorted it in some perversely personal way.

"I bet you have a Trans Am yourself," Jane said.

"You are so-o-o right," the young man said. "It's ice-blue. You like ice-blue? Maybe you're too young." He extended his hand showing a large gaudy stone in a setting that seemed to be gold. "Same color as this ring," he said.

Dan nodded. She could still be impressed by adults. Their mysterious, unreliable images still had the power to attract and confound her, but Jane was clearly not interested in the young man. She demanded much of life. She had very high standards when she wanted to. Mr. Muirhead ordered the girls ginger ales and the young man and himself another round of drinks. Sometimes the train, in the mysterious way of trains, would stop, or even reverse, and they would pass unfamiliar scenes once more. The same green pasture filled with slanty light, the same row of clapboard houses, each with the shades of their windows drawn against the heat, the same boats on their trailers, waiting on dry land. The moon was rising beneath a spectacular lightning and thunder storm. People around them were commenting on it. Close to the train, a sheen of dark birds flew low across a dirt road.

"Birds are only flying reptiles, I'm sure you're all aware," Jane said suddenly.

"Oh my God, what a horrible thought!" Mr. Muirhead said. His face had become a little slack and his hair had become somewhat disarranged.

"It's true, it's true," Jane sang. "Sad but true."

"You mean like lizards and snakes?" the young man asked. He snorted and shook his head.

"*Glorified* reptiles certainly," Mr. Muirhead said, recovering a bit of his sense of time and place.

Dan suddenly felt lonely. It was not homesickness, although she would have given anything at that moment to be poking around in her little aluminum boat with Jim Anderson. She wouldn't even be living any longer in the place she thought of as "home." The town was the same but the place was different. The house where she had been a little tiny baby and had lived her whole life belonged to someone else now. Over the summer, her mother and Jake had bought another house which Jake was going to fix up.

"Reptiles have scales," the young man said, "or else they are long and slimy."

Dan felt like bawling. She could feel the back of her eyes swelling up like cupcakes. She was surrounded by strangers saying crazy things, and had been for quite some while. Even her own mother said crazy things in a reasonable way that made Dan know she was a stranger too. Dan's mother told Dan everything. Her mother told her she wouldn't have to worry about having brothers or sisters. Her mother discussed the particular nature of the problem with her. Half the things Dan's mother told her, Dan didn't want to know. There would be no brothers and sisters. There would be Dan and her mother and Jake, sitting around the house together, caring deeply for one another, sharing a nice life together, not making any mistakes.

Dan excused herself and started toward the lavatory on the level below. Mrs. Muirhead called to her as she approached and handed her a folded piece of paper. "Would you be kind enough to give this to Mr. Muirhead?" she asked. Dan gave Mr. Muirhead the note and went down to the lavatory. She sat on the little toilet as the train rocked along and cried.

After a while, she heard Jane's voice saying, "I hear you in here, Danica Anderson. What's the matter with you?"

Dan didn't say anything.

"I know it's you," Jane said. "I can see your stupid shoes and your stupid socks."

Dan blew her nose, pushed the button on the toilet and said, "What did the note say?"

"I don't know," Jane said. "Daddy ate it."

"He ate it!" Dan exclaimed. She opened the door of the stall and went to the sink. She washed her hands and splashed her face with water. She giggled. "He really ate it?"

"Everybody is looped in that Starlight Lounge," Jane said. Jane patted her hair with a hairbrush. Jane's hair was full of tangles and she never brushed hard enough to get them out. She looked at Dan by looking in the mirror. "Why were you crying?"

"I was thinking about your grandma," Dan said. "She said that one year she left the Christmas tree up until Easter."

"Why were you thinking about my grandma!" Jane yelled.

"I was thinking about her singing," Dan said, startled. "I like her singing."

In her head, Dan could hear Jane's grandmother singing about Death's dark waters and sinking souls, about Mercy Seats and the Great Physician. She could hear the voice rising and falling through the thin walls of the Maine house, borne past the dark screens and into the night.

"I don't want you thinking about my grandma," Jane said, pinching Dan's arm.

Dan tried not to think of Jane's grandma. Once, she had seen her fall coming out of the water. The beach was stony. The stones were round and smooth and slippery. Jane's grandmother had skinned her arm and bloodied her lip.

The girls went into the corridor and saw Mrs. Muirhead standing there. Mrs. Muirhead was deeply tanned. She had put her hair up in a twist and a wad of cotton was noticeable in her left ear. The three of them stood together, bouncing and nudging against one another with the motion of the train.

"My ear is killing me," Mrs. Muirhead said. "I think there's something they're not telling me. It crackles and snaps in there. It's like a bird breaking seeds in there." She touched the bone between cheekbone and ear. "I think the doctor I was seeing should lose his license. He was handsome and competent, certainly, but on my last visit, he was vacuuming my ear and his secretary came in to ask him a question and she put her hand on his neck. She stroked his neck, his secretary! While I was sitting there having my ear vacuumed!" Mrs. Muirhead's cheeks were flushed.

The three of them gazed out the window. The train must have been clipping along, but things outside, although gone in an instant, seemed to be moving slowly. Beneath a street light, a man was kicking his pickup truck.

"I dislike trains," Mrs. Muirhead said. "I find them depressing."

"It's the oxygen deprivation," Jane said, "coming from having to share the air with all these people."

"You're such a snob, dear," Mrs. Muirhead sighed.

"We're going to supper now," Jane said.

"Supper," Mrs. Muirhead said. "Ugh."

The children left her looking out the window, a disconsolate, pretty woman wearing a green dress with a line of frogs dancing around it.

The dining car was almost full. The windows reflected the eaters. The countryside was dim and the train pushed through it.

Jane steered them to a table where a man and woman silently labored over their meal.

"My name is Crystal," Jane offered, "and this is my twin sister, Clara."

"Clara!" Dan exclaimed. Jane was always inventing drab names for her.

"We were triplets," Jane went on, "but the other died at birth. Cord got all twisted around his neck or something."

The woman looked at Jane and smiled.

"What is your line of work?" Jane persisted brightly.

There was silence. The woman kept smiling, then the man said, "I don't do anything, I don't have to do anything. I was injured in Vietnam and they brought me to the base hospital and worked on reviving me for forty-five minutes. Then they gave up. They thought I was dead. Four hours later, I woke up in the mortuary. The Army gives me a good pension." He pushed his chair away from the table and left.

Dan looked after him, astonished, a cold roll raised halfway to her mouth. "Was your husband really dead for all that while?" she asked.

"My husband, ha!" the woman said. "I'd never laid eyes on that man before the 6:30 seating."

"I bet you're a professional woman who doesn't believe in men," Jane said slyly.

"Crystal, how did you guess! It's true, men are a collective hallucination of women. It's like when a group of crackpots get together on a hilltop and see flying saucers." The woman picked at her chicken.

Jane looked surprised, then said, "My father went to a costume party once wrapped from head to foot in aluminum foil."

"A casserole," the woman offered.

"No! A spaceman, an alien astronaut!"

Dan giggled, remembering when Mr. Muirhead had done that. She felt that Jane had met her match with this woman.

"What do you do!" Jane fairly screamed. "You won't tell us!"

"I do drugs," the woman said. The girls shrank back. "Ha," the woman said. "Actually, I test drugs for pharmaceutical companies. And I do research for a perfume manufacturer. I am involved in the search for human pheromones."

Jane looked levelly at the woman.

"I know you don't know what a pheromone is, Crystal. To put it grossly, a pheromone is a smell that a person has that can make another person do or feel a certain thing. It's an irresistible signal."

Dan thought of mangrove roots and orange groves. Of the smell of gas when the pilot light blew out on Jane's grandmother's stove. She liked the smell of the Atlantic Ocean when it dried upon your skin and the smell of Jim Anderson's fur when he had been rained upon. There were smells that could make you follow them, certainly.

Jane stared at the woman, tipping forward slightly in her seat.

"Relax, will you, Crystal, you're just a child. You don't even *have* a smell yet," the woman said. "I test all sorts of things. Sometimes I'm part of a control group and sometimes I'm not. You never know. If you're part of the control group, you're just given a placebo. A placebo, Crystal, is something that is nothing, but you don't know it's nothing. You think you're getting something that will change you or make you feel better or healthier or more attractive or something, but you're not really."

"I know what a placebo is," Jane muttered.

"Well that's terrific, Crystal, you're a prodigy." The woman removed a book from her handbag and began to read it. The book had a denim jacket on it which concealed its title.

"Ha!" Jane said, rising quickly and attempting to knock over a glass of water. "My name's not Crystal!"

Dan grabbed the glass before it fell and hurried after her. They returned to the Starlight Lounge. Mr. Muirhead was sitting with another young man. This young man had a blond beard and a studious manner.

"Oh, this is a wonderful trip!" Mr. Muirhead said exuberantly. "The wonderful people you meet on a trip like this! This is the most fascinating young man. He's a writer. Been everywhere. He's putting together a book on cemeteries of the world. Isn't that some subject? I told him anytime he's in our town, stop by our restaurant, be my guest for some stone crab claws."

"Hello," the young man said to the girls.

"We were speaking of Père-Lachaise, the legendary Parisian cemetery," Mr. Muirhead said. "So wistful. So grand and romantic. Your mother and I visited it, Jane, when we were in Paris. We strolled through it on a clear crisp autumn day. The desires of the human heart have no boundaries, girls. The mess of secrets in the human heart are without number. Witnessing Père-Lachaise was a very moving experience. As we strolled, your mother was screaming at me, Jane. Do you know why, honey-bunch? She was screaming at me because back in New York, I had garaged the car at the place on East 84th Street. Your mother said that the people in the place on East 84th Street never turned the ignition all the way off to the left and were always running down the battery. She said that there wasn't a soul in all of New York City who didn't know that the people running the garage on East 84th Street were idiots who were always ruining batteries. Before Père-Lachaise, girls, this young man and I were discussing the Panteón, just outside of Guanajuato in Mexico. It so happens that I am also familiar with the Panteón. Your mother wanted some tiles for the foyer so we went to Mexico. You stayed with Mrs. Murphy, Jane. Remember? It was Mrs. Murphy who taught you how to make egg salad. In any case, the Panteón is a walled cemetery, not unlike the Campo Santo in Genoa, Italy, but the reason everybody goes there is to see the mummies. Something about the exceptionally dry air in the mountains has preserved the bodies and there's a little museum of mummies. It's grotesque of course, and it certainly gave me pause. I mean it's one thing to think we will all gather together in a paradise of fadeless splendor like your grandma thinks, lamby-lettuce, and it's another thing to think as the Buddhists do that latent possibilities withdraw into the heart at death, but do not perish, thereby allowing the being to be reborn, and it's one more thing, even, to believe like a Goddamn scientist in one of the essential laws of physics which states that no energy is ever lost. It's one thing to think any of those things, girls, but it's quite another to be standing in that little museum looking at those miserable mummies. The horror and indignation were in their faces still. I almost cried aloud, so vivid was my sense of the fleetingness of this life. We made our way into the fresh air of the courtyard and I bought a package of cigarettes at a little stand which sold postcards and films and such. I reached into my pocket for my lighter and it appeared that my lighter was not there. It seemed that I had lost my lighter. The lighter was a very good one that your mother had bought me the Christmas before, Jane, and your mother started screaming at me. There was a very gentle, warm rain falling, and there were bougainvillea petals on the walks. Your mother grasped my arm and reminded me that the lighter had been a gift from her. Your mother reminded me of the blazer she had bought for me. I spilled buttered popcorn on it at the movies and you can still see the spot. She reminded me of the hammock she bought for my fortieth birthday, which I allowed to rot in the rain. She recalled the shoulder bag she bought me, which I detested, it's true. It was somehow left out in the yard and I mangled it with the lawn-mower. Descending the cobbled hill into Guanajuato, your mother recalled every one of her gifts to me, offerings both monetary and of the heart. She pointed out how I had mishandled and betrayed every one."

No one said anything. "Then," Mr. Muirhead continued, "there was the Modena Cemetery in Italy."

"That hasn't been completed yet," the young man said hurriedly. "It's a visionary design by the architect Aldo Rossi. In our conversation, I was just trying to describe the project to you."

"You can be assured," Mr. Muirhead said, "that when the project is finished and I take my little family on a vacation to Italy, as we walk, together and afraid, strolling through the hapless landscape of the Modena Cemetery, Jane's mother will be screaming at me."

"Well, I must be going," the young man said. He got up.

"So long," Mr. Muirhead said.

"Were they really selling postcards of the mummies in that place?" Dan asked.

"Yes, they were, sweetie-pie," Mr. Muirhead said. "In this world there is a postcard of everything. That's the kind of world this is."

The crowd was getting boisterous in the Starlight Lounge. Mrs. Muirhead made her way down the aisle toward them and with a deep sigh, sat beside her husband. Mr. Muirhead gesticulated and formed words silently with his lips as though he was talking to the girls.

"What?" Mrs. Muirhead said.

"I was just telling the girls some of the differences between men and women. Men are more adventurous and aggressive with greater spatial and mechanical abilities. Women are more consistent, nurturant and aesthetic. Men can see better than women, but women have better hearing," Mr. Muirhead said.

"Very funny," Mrs. Muirhead said.

The girls retired from the melancholy regard Mr. and Mrs. Muirhead had fixed upon one another, and wandered through the cars of the train, occasionally returning to their seats to fuss in the cluttered nests they had created there. Around midnight, they decided to revisit the game car where earlier, people had been playing backgammon, Diplomacy, anagrams, crazy eights and Clue. They were still at it, variously throwing down queens of diamonds, moving troops through Asia Minor and accusing Colonel Mustard of doing it in the conservatory with a wrench. Whenever there was a lull in the playing, they talked about the accident.

"What accident?" Jane demanded.

"Train hit a Buick," a man said. "Middle of the night." The man had big ears and a tattoo on his forearm.

"There aren't any good new games," a woman complained. "Haven't been for years and years."

"Did you fall asleep?" Jane said accusingly to Dan.

"When could that have happened?" Dan said.

"We didn't see it," Jane said, disgusted.

"Two teenagers escaped without a scratch," the man said. "Lived to laugh about it. They are young and silly but it's no joke to the engineer. The engineer has a lot of paperwork to do after he hits something. The engineer will be filling out forms for a week." The man's tattoo said MOM and DAD.

"Rats," Jane said.

The children returned to the darkened dining room where *Superman* was being shown on a small television set. Jane instantly fell asleep. Dan watched Superman spin the earth backward so he could prevent Lois Lane from being smothered in a rock slide. The train shot past a group of old lighted buildings. SEWER KING, a sign said. When the movie ended, Jane woke up.

"When we lived in New York," she said muzzily, "I was sitting in the kitchen one afternoon doing my homework and this girl came in and sat down at the table. Did I ever tell you this? It was the middle of the winter and it was snowing. This person just came in with the snow on her coat and sat right down at the table."

"Who was she?" Dan asked.

"It was me, but I was old. I mean I was about thirty years old or something."

"It was a dream," Dan said.

"It was the middle of the afternoon, I tell you! I was doing my homework. She said, 'You've never lifted a finger to help me.' Then she asked me for a glass with some ice in it."

After a moment, Dan said, "It was probably the cleaning lady."

"Cleaning lady! Cleaning lady for Godssakes, what do you know about cleaning ladies!"

Dan felt her hair bristle as though someone were running a comb through it back to front, and realized she was mad, madder than she'd been all summer, for all summer she'd only felt humiliated when Jane was nasty to her.

"Listen up," Dan said, "don't talk to me like that anymore."

"Like what," Jane said cooly.

Dan stood up and walked away, leaving Jane sitting there, not realizing what had happened to her. Jane was saying, "The thing I don't understand is how she ever got into that apartment. My father had about a dozen locks on the door."

Dan sat in her seat in the quiet, dark coach and looked out at the dark night. She tried to recollect how it seemed dawn happened. Things just sort of rose out, she guessed she knew. There was nothing you could do about it. She thought of Jane's dream in which the men in white bathing caps were pushing all her grandma's things out of the house and into the street. The inside became empty and the outside became full. Dan was beginning to feel sorry for herself. She was alone, with no friends and no parents, sitting on a train between one place and another, scaring herself with someone else's dream in the middle of the night. She got up and walked through the rocking cars to the Starlight Lounge for a glass of water. After 4 A.M. it was no longer referred to as the Starlight Lounge. They stopped serving drinks and turned off the electric stars. It became just another place to sit. Mr. Muirhead was sitting there, alone. He must have been on excellent terms with the stewards because he was drinking a Bloody Mary.

"Hi, Dan!" he said.

Dan sat opposite him. After a moment she said, "I had a very nice summer. Thank you for inviting me."

"Well, I hope you enjoyed your summer, sweetie," Mr. Muirhead said.

"Do you think Jane and I will be friends forever?" Dan asked.

Mr. Muirhead looked surprised. "Definitely not. Jane will not have friends. Jane will have husbands, enemies, and lawyers." He cracked ice noisily with his white teeth. "I'm glad you enjoyed your summer, Dan, and I hope you're enjoying your childhood. When you grow up, a shadow falls. Everything's sunny and then this big goddamn *wing* or something passes overhead."

"Oh," Dan said.

"Well, I've only heard that's the case actually," Mr. Muirhead said. "Do you know what I want to be when I grow up?" He waited for her to smile. "When I grow up I want to become an Indian so I can use my Indian name."

"What is your Indian name?" Dan asked, smiling.

"My Indian name is 'He Rides a Slow Enduring Heavy Horse.'"

"That's a nice one," Dan said.

"It is, isn't it?" Mr. Muirhead said, gnawing ice.

Outside, the sky was lightening. Daylight was just beginning to flourish on the city of Jacksonville. It fell without prejudice on the slaughterhouses, Dairy Queens and courthouses, on the car lots, sabal palms and a billboard advertisement for pies.

The train went slowly around a long curve, and looking backward, past Mr. Muirhead, Dan could see the entire length of it moving ahead. The bubble-topped cars were dark and sinister in the first flat and hopeful light of the morning.

Dan took the three postcards she had left out of her bookbag and looked at them. One showed Thomas Edison beneath a banyan tree. One showed a little tar-paper shack out in the middle of the desert in New Mexico where men were supposed to have invented the atomic bomb. One was a "quicky" card showing a porpoise balancing a grapefruit on the top of his head.

"Oh, I remember those," Mr. Muirhead said, picking up the "quicky" card. "You just check off what you want." He read aloud, *"How are you? I am fine ( ) lonesome ( ) happy ( ) sad ( ) broke ( ) flying high ( )."* Mr. Muirhead chuckled. He read, *"I have been good ( ) no good ( ). I saw The Gulf of Mexico ( ) The Atlantic Ocean ( ) The Orange Groves ( ) Interesting Attractions ( ) You in My Dreams ( )."*

"I like this one," Mr. Muirhead said, chuckling.

"You can have it," Dan said. "I'd like you to have it."

"You're a nice little girl," Mr. Muirhead said. He looked at his glass and then out the window. "What do you think was on that note Mrs. Muirhead had you give me?" he asked. "Do you think there's something I've missed?"

On Your Feet . . . On Your Heart

Stacy Alexander

Stacy Alexander is a twenty-five-year-old college
freshman with two children and a graphic artist
husband. A few months ago, she was juggling
motherhood with a job as a certified nurse's
assistant at an Alzheimer's care facility. These
days, Stacy is astonished by how much fun being a
university student is.

As I ponder the countless ways in which I could
compare my childhood view of the world to my present
view, the recurring image in my mind's eye is my
daughter, Madison. I think about walking into her
preschool classroom to pick her up after I've finished
"grown-up school." Small children, ages three to five,
are scattered around the busy room, all engaged in
various activities, ranging from finger-painting to
playing dress-up. I spot Madison at the birdseed table,
diligently sifting through the large tub full of birdseed
with a plastic rake, searching for hidden treasures.
Maddie glances up and notices me. Her tiny, elfin face
immediately lights up. She drops the rake and a handful
of birdseed on the floor and dashes toward me. I then
experience what I like to think of as a deep, sort of
psychic maternal moment. I look at my daughter and I see
myself as a little girl and I remember looking very much
like her and being four and feeling that complete and
unconditional adoration for my mother. Sometimes, looking
into Madison's face can be an experience similar to
peering into an age-altering mirror.

How easy life was when I simply had to emit some sort
of high-pitched wail and an adult would appear to cure
whatever was currently ailing me. If I was sick, my only
obligation was to cry and perhaps vomit. Between my mother
and my father, I received a sufficient amount of sympathy,
coddling, and chewable Tylenol. That was a time when
adults always seemed to be in control of things. My dad
was a superhero because he could juggle and do one-handed

push-ups. My mother always knew just what to do if I was hurt or sick and she always brought a surprise home when she went to the store.

I suppose that my being "the mom" and creating the magic of Santa and The Easter Bunny and bringing surprises back from the store makes me a grown-up. Thus, I now know that my naïve childhood assessment of adults being all-knowing and always having their shit together, so to speak, was merely an illusion. Nonetheless, I do enjoy allowing my children to continue believing that I'm perfect while they're still young and gullible.

Still, I occasionally feel sadness somewhere inside, knowing that my current rank as goddess, in Madison's and my son Justin's minds, will inevitably dissipate with time. I don't recall exactly when in my childhood that it happened, but some sort of social metamorphosis occurred within me. My opinion of my parents, and most adults in general, changed. They were demoted, in my mind, from being my all-knowing heroes to annoying sources of embarrassment and an occasional lecture, though they really didn't seem to know much.

There were many times when I would walk several paces behind my mom or dad at the mall so as not to be inadvertently seen with them by a classmate. I remember being extremely pissed off at my dad once because he had the audacity to stop at K-mart while driving me and my best friend home from school. Was he so clueless that he didn't realize the social faux pas it was, in the fifth grade, to let my friends see that my dad shopped at Kmart? His blatant disregard for my feelings was not only annoying and rude, but also embarrassing, as most everything seemed to be then.

It seems that there may be no way to avoid that period during childhood when your parents stop being your source of happiness and, instead, become an obstacle between you and fun. Sometimes I visualize Madison, in the all-too-near future, looking at me as if she can't fathom that a person as stupid as I am exists. She'll respond to my questions or advice by rolling her eyes or giving me a look that says, "Why are you talking to me?" I imagine her desperately begging me to stop bragging about all of the bargains I scored at Target or The Goodwill!

I am reminded of something that an elderly woman with Alzheimer's disease once said to me that surprised me with its truthfulness. She said, "When your children are young, they step on your feet, and when they are older, they step on your heart." For today, I will enjoy being adored in the unique and special way that young children adore their mothers, as I did mine. In the future, when my presence embarrasses my children or they no longer choose to share the details of their lives with me, I will try to remember to take comfort in the knowledge that I will eventually get them back. Never again will they see me the way that they do now, as the center of their tiny world, the solver of virtually all problems. But they *will* respect and like me again. They will come to realize that I am only human and they will forgive my mistakes. They will see that I really did know what I was talking about for all of those years.

4

IMAGES OF SELF

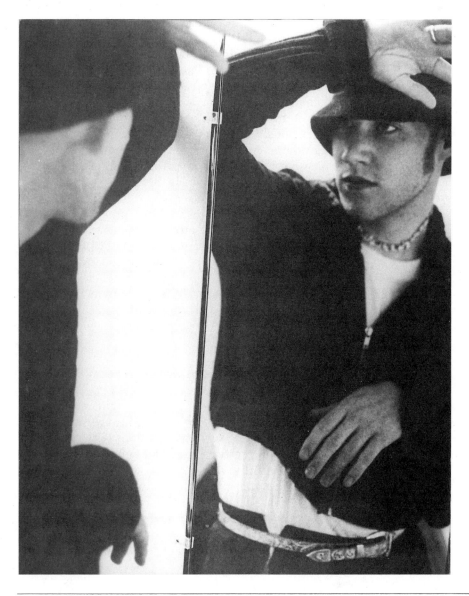

ON SELF-RESPECT

■

Joan Didion

This essay appeared in Didion's book Slouching Toward Bethlehem, *first published in 1961.*

Once, in a dry season, I wrote in large letters across two pages of a notebook that innocence ends when one is stripped of the delusion that one likes oneself. Although now, some years later, I marvel that a mind on the outs with itself should have nonetheless made painstaking record of its every tremor, I recall with embarrassing clarity the flavor of those particular ashes. It was a matter of misplaced self-respect.

I had not been elected to Phi Beta Kappa. This failure could scarcely have been more predictable or less ambiguous (I simply did not have the grades), but I was unnerved by it; I had somehow thought myself a kind of academic Raskolnikov, curiously exempt from the cause-effect relationships which hampered others. Although even the humorless nineteen-year-old that I was must have recognized that the situation lacked real tragic stature, the day that I did not make Phi Beta Kappa nonetheless marked the end of something, and innocence may well be the word for it. I lost the conviction that lights would always turn green for me, the pleasant certainty that those rather passive virtues which had won me approval as a child automatically guaranteed me not only Phi Beta Kappa keys but happiness, honor, and the love of a good man; lost a certain touching faith in the totem power of good manners, clean hair, and proven competence on the Stanford-Binet scale. To such doubtful amulets had my self-respect been pinned, and I faced myself that day with the nonplused apprehension of someone who has come across a vampire and has no crucifix at hand.

Although to be driven back upon oneself is an uneasy affair at best, rather like trying to cross a border with borrowed credentials, it seems to me now the one condition necessary to the beginnings of real self-respect. Most of our platitudes notwithstanding, self-deception remains the most difficult deception. The tricks that work on others count for nothing in that very well-lit back alley where one keeps assignations with oneself: no winning smiles will do here, no prettily drawn lists of good intentions. One shuffles flashily but in vain through one's marked cards—the kindness done for the wrong reason, the apparent triumph which involved no real effort, the seemingly heroic act into which one had been shamed. The dismal fact is that self-respect has nothing to do with the approval of others—who are, after all, deceived easily enough; has nothing to do with reputation, which, as Rhett Butler told Scarlett O'Hara, is something people with courage can do without.

To do without self-respect, on the other hand, is to be an unwilling audience of one to an interminable documentary that details one's failings, both real and imagined, with fresh footage spliced in for every screening. *There's the glass you broke in anger, there's the hurt on X's face; watch now, this next scene, the night Y came back from Houston, see how you muff this one.* To live without self-respect is to lie awake some night, beyond the reach of warm milk, phenobarbital, and the sleeping hand on the coverlet, counting up the sins of commission and omission, the trusts betrayed, the promises subtly broken, the gifts irrevocably wasted through sloth or cowardice or carelessness. However long we postpone it, we eventually lie down alone in that notoriously uncomfortable bed, the one we make ourselves. Whether or not we sleep in it depends, of course, on whether or not we respect ourselves.

To protest that some fairly improbable people, some people who *could not possibly respect themselves,* seem to sleep easily enough is to miss the point entirely, as surely as those people miss it who think that self-respect has necessarily to do with not having safety pins in one's underwear. There is a common superstition that "self-respect" is a kind of charm against snakes, something that keeps those who have it locked in some unblighted Eden, out of strange beds, ambivalent conversations, and trouble in general. It does not at all. It has nothing to do with the face of things, but concerns instead a separate peace, a private reconciliation. Although the careless, suicidal Julian English in *Appointment in Samarra* and the careless, incurably dishonest Jordan Baker in *The Great Gatsby* seem equally improbable candidates for self-respect, Jordan Baker had it, Julian English did not. With that genius for accommodation more often seen in women than in men, Jordan took her own measure, made her own peace, avoided threats to that peace: "I hate careless people," she told Nick Carraway. "It takes two to make an accident."

Like Jordan Baker, people with self-respect have the courage of their mistakes. They know the price of things. If they choose to commit adultery, they do not then go running, in an excess of bad conscience, to receive absolution from the wronged parties; nor do they complain unduly of the unfairness, the undeserved embarrassment, of being named corespondent. In brief, people with self-respect exhibit a certain toughness, a kind of moral nerve; they display what was once called *character,* a quality which, although approved in the abstract, sometimes loses ground to other, more instantly negotiable virtues. The measure of its slipping prestige is that one tends to think of it only in connection with homely children and United States senators who have been defeated, preferably in the primary, for reelection. Nonetheless, character—the willingness to accept responsibility for one's own life—is the source from which self-respect springs.

Self-respect is something that our grandparents, whether or not they had it, knew all about. They had instilled in them, young, a certain discipline, the sense that one lives by doing things one does not particu-larly want to do, by putting fears and doubts to one side, by weighing im-mediate comforts against the ability of larger, even intangible, comforts. It seemed to the nineteenth century admirable, but not remarkable, that Chinese Gordon put on a clean white suit and held Khartoum against the Mahdi; it did not seem unjust that the way to free land in California involved death and difficulty and dirt. In a diary kept during the winter of 1846, an emigrating twelve-year-old named Narcissa Cornwall noted coolly: "Father was busy reading and did not notice that the house was being filled with strange Indians until Mother spoke about it." Even lack-ing any clue as to what Mother said, one can scarcely fail to be impressed by the entire incident: the father reading, the Indians filing in, the mother choosing the words that would not alarm, the child duly recording the event and noting further that those particular Indians were not, "fortu-nately for us," hostile. Indians were simply part of the *donnée.*

In one guise or another, Indians always are. Again, it is a question of recognizing that anything worth having has its price. People who respect themselves are willing to accept the risk that the Indians will be hostile, that the venture will go bankrupt, that the liaison may not turn out to be one in which *every day is a holiday because you're married to me.* They are willing to invest something of themselves; they may not play at all, but when they do play, they know the odds.

That kind of self-respect is a discipline, a habit of mind that can never be faked but can be developed, trained, coaxed forth. It was once sug-gested to me that, as an antidote to crying, I put my head in a paper bag. As it happens, there is a sound physiological reason, something to do with oxygen, for doing exactly that, but the psychological effect alone is incalculable: it is difficult in the extreme to continue fancying oneself Cathy in *Wuthering Heights* with one's head in a Food Fair bag. There is a similar case for all the small disciplines, unimportant in themselves; imagine maintaining any kind of swoon, commiserative or carnal, in a cold shower.

But those small disciplines are available only insofar as they represent larger ones. To say that Waterloo was won on the playing fields of Eton is not to say that Napoleon might have been saved by a crash program in cricket; to give formal dinners in the rain forest would be pointless did not the candlelight flickering on the liana call forth deeper, stronger dis-ciplines, values instilled long before. It is a kind of ritual, helping us to remember who and what we are. In order to remember it, one must have known it.

To have that sense of one's intrinsic worth which constitutes self-respect is potentially to have everything: the ability to discriminate, to love and to remain indifferent. To lack it is to be locked within oneself, paradoxically incapable of either love or indifference. If we do not respect ourselves, we are on the one hand forced to despise those who have so few resources as to consort with us, so little perception as to remain blind to our fatal weaknesses. On the other, we are peculiarly in thrall to everyone we see, curiously determined to live out—since our self-image is untenable—their false notions of us. We flatter ourselves by thinking this compulsion to please others an attractive trait: a gist for imaginative empathy, evidence of our willingness to give. Of *course* I will play Francesca to your Paolo, Helen Keller to anyone's Annie Sullivan: no expectation is too misplaced, no role too ludicrous. At the mercy of those we cannot but hold in contempt, we play roles doomed to failure before they are begun, each defeat generating fresh despair at the urgency of divining and meeting the next demand made upon us.

It is the phenomenon sometimes called "alienation from self." In its advanced stages, we no longer answer the telephone, because someone might want something; that we could say *no* without drowning in self-reproach is an idea alien to this game. Every encounter demands too much, tears the nerves, drains the will, and the specter of something as small as an unanswered letter arouses such disproportionate guilt that answering it becomes out of the question. To assign unanswered letters their proper weight, to free us from the expectations of others, to give us back to ourselves—there lies the great, the singular power of self-respect. Without it, one eventually discovers the final turn of the screw: one runs away to find oneself, and finds no one at home.

BORGES AND MYSELF

—◾—

Jorge Luis Borges

This piece, translated from Spanish by Norman Thomas di Giovanni, appeared in Borges's 1968 book The Aleph and Other Stories 1933–1969.

I t's to the other man, to Borges, that things happen. I walk along the streets of Buenos Aires, stopping now and then—perhaps out of habit—to look at the arch of all old entranceway or a grillwork gate; of Borges I get news through the mail and glimpse his name among a committee of professors or in a dictionary of biography. I have a taste for hourglasses, maps, eighteenth-century typography, the roots of words, the smell of coffee, and Stevenson's prose; the other man shares these likes, but in a showy way that turns them into stagy mannerisms. It would be an exaggeration to say that we are on bad terms; I live, I let myself live, so that Borges can weave his tales and poems, and those tales and poems are my justification. It is not hard for me to admit that he has managed to write a few worthwhile pages, but these pages cannot save me, perhaps because what is good no longer belongs to anyone—not even the other man—but rather to speech or tradition. In any case, I am fated to become lost once and for all, and only some moment of myself will survive in the other man. Little by little, I have been surrendering every-thing to him, even though I have evidence of his stubborn habit of falsifi-cation and exaggerating. Spinoza held that all things try to keep on being themselves; a stone wants to be a stone and the tiger, a tiger. I shall re-main in Borges, not in myself (if it is so that I am someone), but I recog-nize myself less in his books than in those of others or than in the laborious tuning of it guitar. Years ago, I tried ridding myself of him and I went from myths of the outlying slums of the city to games with time and infinity, but those games are now part of Borges and I will have to turn to other things. And so, my life is a running away, and I lose every-thing and everything is left to oblivion or to the other man.

Which of us is writing this page I don't know.

BEING A MAN
—■—

Paul Theroux

This essay appears in Theroux's 1985 book Sunrise with Seamonsters.

There is a pathetic sentence in the chapter "Fetishism" in Dr. Nor-man Cameron's book *Personality Development and Psychopathology.* It goes, "Fetishists are nearly always men; and their commonest fetish is a woman's shoe." I cannot read that sentence without thinking that it is just one more awful thing about being a man—and perhaps it is an important thing to know about us.

I have always disliked being a man. The whole idea of manhood in America is pitiful, in my opinion. This version of masculinity is a little like having to wear an ill-fitting coat for one's entire life (by contrast, I imagine femininity to be an oppressive sense of nakedness). Even the ex-pression "Be a man!" strikes me as insulting and abusive. It means: Be stupid, be unfeeling, obedient, soldierly and stop thinking. Man means "manly"—how can one think about men without considering the terrible ambition of manliness? And yet it is part of every man's life. It is a hideous and crippling lie; it not only insists on difference and connives at superiority, it is also by its very nature destructive—emotionally damag-ing and socially harmful.

The youth who is subverted, as most are, into believing in the mascu-line ideal is effectively separated from women and he spends the rest of his life finding women a riddle and a nuisance. Of course, there is a female version of this male affliction. It begins with mothers encourag-ing little girls to say (to other adults) "Do you like my new dress?" In a sense, little girls are traditionally urged to please adults with a kind of coquettishness, while boys are enjoined to behave like monkeys toward each other. The nine-year-old coquette proceeds to become womanish in a subtle power game in which she learns to be sexually indispensable, socially decorative and always alert to a man's sense of inadequacy.

Femininity—being lady-like—implies needing a man as witness and seducer; but masculinity celebrates the exclusive company of men. That is why it is so grotesque; and that is also why there is no manliness without inadequacy—because it denies men the natural friendship of women.

It is very hard to imagine any concept of manliness that does not belittle women, and it begins very early. At an age when I wanted to meet girls—let's say the treacherous years of thirteen to sixteen—I was told to take up a sport, get more fresh air, join the Boy Scouts, and I was urged not to read so much. It was the 1950s and if you asked too many questions about sex you were sent to camp—boy's camp, of course: the nightmare. Nothing is more unnatural or prison-like than a boy's camp, but if it were not for them we would have no Elks' Lodges, no pool rooms, no boxing matches, no Marines.

And perhaps no sports as we know them. Everyone is aware of how few in number are the athletes who behave like gentlemen. Just as high school basketball teaches you how to be a poor loser, the manly attitude toward sports seems to be little more than a recipe for creating bad marriages, social misfits, moral degenerates, sadists, latent rapists and just plain louts. I regard high school sports as a drug far worse than marijuana, and it is the reason that the average tennis champion, say, is a pathetic oaf.

Any objective study would find the quest for manliness essentially right-wing, puritanical, cowardly, neurotic and fueled largely by a fear of women. It is also certainly philistine. There is no book-hater like a Little League coach. But indeed all the creative arts are obnoxious to the manly ideal, because at their best the arts are pursued by uncompetitive and essentially solitary people. It makes it very hard for a creative youngster, for any boy who expresses the desire to be alone seems to be saying that there is something wrong with him.

It ought to be clear by now that I have something of an objection to the way we turn boys into men. It does not surprise me that when the President of the United States has his customary weekend off he dresses like a cowboy—it is both a measure of his insecurity and his willingness to please. In many ways, American culture does little more for a man than prepare him for modeling clothes in the L.L. Bean catalog. I take this as a personal insult because for many years I found it impossible to admit to myself that I wanted to be a writer. It was my guilty secret, because being a writer was incompatible with being a man.

There are people who might deny this, but that is because the American writer, typically, has been so at pains to prove his manliness that we have come to see literariness and manliness as mingled qualities. But first there was a fear that writing was not a manly profession—indeed, not a profession at all. (The paradox in American letters is that it has always been easier for a woman to write and for a man to be published.) Growing up, I had thought of sports as wasteful and humiliating, and the idea of manliness was a bore. My wanting to become a writer was not a flight from that oppressive role-playing, but I quickly saw that it was at odds with it. Everything in stereotyped manliness goes against the life of the mind. The Hemingway personality is too tedious to go into here, and in any case his exertions are well known, but certainly it was not until this aberrant behavior was examined by feminists in the 1960s that any male writer dared question the pugnacity in Hemingway's fiction. All the bullfighting and arm wrestling and elephant shooting diminished Hemingway as a writer, but it is consistent with a prevailing attitude in American writing: one cannot be a male writer without first proving that one is a man.

It is normal in America for a man to be dismissive or even somewhat apologetic about being a writer. Various factors make it easier. There is a heartiness about journalism that makes it acceptable—journalism is the manliest form of American writing and, therefore, the profession the most independent-minded women seek (yes, it is an illusion, but that is my point). Fiction-writing is equated with a kind of dispirited failure and is only manly when it produces wealth—money is masculinity. So is drinking. Being a drunkard is another assertion, if misplaced, of manliness. The American male writer is traditionally proud of his heavy drinking. But we are also a very literal-minded people. A man proves his manhood in America in old-fashioned ways. He kills lions, like Hemingway; or he hunts ducks, like Nathanael West; or he makes pronouncements like, "A man should carry enough knife to defend himself with," as James Jones once said to a *Life* interviewer. Or he says he can drink you under the table. But even tiny drunken William Faulkner loved to mount a horse and go fox hunting, and Jack Kerouac roistered up and down Manhattan in a lumberjack shirt (and spent every night of *The Subterraneans* with his mother in Queens). And we are familiar with the lengths to which Norman Mailer is prepared, in his endearing way, to prove that he is just as much a monster as the next man.

When the novelist John Irving was revealed as a wrestler, people took him to be a very serious writer; and even a bubble reputation like Eric *(Love Story)* Segal's was enhanced by the news that he ran the marathon in a respectable time. How surprised we would be if Joyce Carol Oates were revealed as a sumo wrestler or Joan Didion active in pumping iron. "Lives in New York City with her three children" is the typical woman writer's biographical note, for just as the male writer must prove he has achieved a sort of muscular manhood, the woman writer—or rather her publicists—must prove her motherhood.

There would be no point in saying any of this if it were not generally accepted that to be a man is somehow—even now in feminist-influenced America—a privilege. It is on the contrary an unmerciful and punishing burden. Being a man is bad enough; being manly is appalling (in this sense, women's lib has done much more for men than for women). It is the sinister silliness of men's fashions, and a clubby attitude in the arts. It is the subversion of good students. It is the so-called Dress Code of the Ritz-Carlton Hotel in Boston, and it is the institutionalized cheating in college sports. It is the most primitive insecurity.

And this is also why men often object to feminism but are afraid to explain why: of course women have a justified grievance, but most men believe—and with reason—that their lives are just as bad.

JUST WALK ON BY: A BLACK MAN PONDERS HIS POWER TO ALTER PUBLIC SPACE

Brent Staples

This essay first appeared in Ms. *magazine in 1986.*

My first victim was a woman—white, well dressed, probably in her early twenties. I came upon her late one evening on a deserted street in Hyde Park, a relatively affluent neighborhood in an otherwise mean, impoverished section of Chicago. As I swung onto the avenue behind her, there seemed to be a discreet, uninflammatory distance between us. Not so. She cast back a worried glance. To her, the youngish black man—a broad six feet two inches with a beard and billowing hair, both hands shoved into the pockets of a bulky military jacket—seemed menacingly close. After a few more quick glimpses, she picked up her pace and was soon running in earnest. Within seconds she disappeared into a cross street.

That was more than a decade ago. I was twenty-two years old, a graduate student newly arrived at the University of Chicago. It was in the echo of that terrified woman's footfalls that I first began to know the unwieldy inheritance I'd come into—the ability to alter public space in ugly ways. It was clear that she thought herself the quarry of a mugger, a rapist, or worse. Suffering a bout of insomnia, however, I was stalking sleep, not defenseless wayfarers. As a softy who is scarcely able to take a knife to a raw chicken—let alone hold it to a person's throat—I was surprised, embarrassed, and dismayed all at once. Her flight made me feel like an accomplice in tyranny. It also made it clear that I was indistinguishable from the muggers who occasionally seeped into the area from the surrounding ghetto. That first encounter, and those that followed, signified that a vast, unnerving gulf lay between nighttime pedestrians—particularly women—and me. And I soon gathered that being perceived as dangerous is a hazard in itself. I only needed to turn a corner into a dicey situation, or crowd some frightened, armed person in a foyer somewhere, or make an errant move after being pulled over by a policeman. Where fear and weapons meet—and they often do in urban America—there is always the possibility of death.

In that first year, my first away from my hometown, I was to become thoroughly familiar with the language of fear. At dark, shadowy intersections in Chicago, I could cross in front of a car stopped at a traffic light and elicit the *thunk, thunk, thunk, thunk* of the driver—black, white, male, or female—hammering down the door locks. On less traveled streets after dark, I grew accustomed to but never comfortable with people who crossed to the other side of the street rather than pass me. Then there 122 were the standard unpleasantries with police, doormen, bouncers, cabdrivers, and others whose business is to screen out troublesome individuals *before* there is any nastiness.

I moved to New York nearly two years ago and I have remained an avid night walker. In central Manhattan, the near-constant crowd cover minimizes tense one-on-one street encounters. Elsewhere—visiting friends in SoHo, where sidewalks are narrow and tightly spaced buildings shut out the sky—things can get very taut indeed.

Black men have a firm place in New York mugging literature. Norman Podhoretz in his famed (or infamous) 1963 essay, "My Negro Problem—And Ours," recalls growing up in terror of black males; they "were tougher than we were, more ruthless," he writes—and as an adult on the Upper West Side of Manhattan, he continues, he cannot constrain his nervousness when he meets black men on certain streets. Similarly, a decade later, the essayist and novelist Edward Hoagland extols a New York where once "Negro bitterness bore down mainly on other Negroes." Where some see mere panhandlers, Hoagland sees "a mugger who is clearly screwing up his nerve to do more than just *ask* for money." But Hoagland has "the New Yorker's quick-hunch posture for broken-field maneuvering," and the bad guy swerves away.

I often witness that "hunch posture," from women after dark on the warrenlike streets of Brooklyn where I live. They seem to set their faces on neutral and, with their purse straps strung across their chests bandolier style, they forge ahead as though bracing themselves against being tackled. I understand, of course, that the danger they perceive is not a hallucination. Women are particularly vulnerable to street violence, and young black males are drastically overrepresented among the perpetrators of that violence. Yet these truths are no solace against the kind of alienation that comes of being ever the suspect, against being set apart, a fearsome entity with whom pedestrians avoid making eye contact.

It is not altogether clear to me how I reached the ripe old age of twenty-two without being conscious of the lethality nighttime pedestrians attributed to me. Perhaps it was because in Chester, Pennsylvania, the small, angry industrial town where I came of age in the 1960s, I was scarcely noticeable against a backdrop of gang warfare, street knifings, and murders. I grew up one of the good boys, had perhaps a half-dozen fistfights. In retrospect, my shyness of combat has clear sources.

Many things go into the making of a young thug. One of those things is the consummation of the male romance with the power to intimidate. An infant discovers that random flailings send the baby bottle flying out of the crib and crashing to the floor. Delighted, the joyful babe repeats those motions again and again, seeking to duplicate the feat. Just so, I recall the points at which some of my boyhood friends were finally seduced by the perception of themselves as tough guys. When a mark cowered and surrendered his money without resistance, myth and reality merged—and paid off. It is, after all, only manly to embrace the power to frighten and intimidate. We, as men, are not supposed to give an inch of our lane on the highway; we are to seize the fighter's edge in work and in play and even in love, we are to be valiant in the face of hostile forces.

Unfortunately, poor and powerless young men seem to take all this nonsense literally. As a boy, I saw countless tough guys locked away; I have since buried several, too. They were babies, really—a teenage cousin, a brother of twenty-two, a childhood friend in his midtwenties— all gone down in episodes of bravado played out in the streets. I came to doubt the virtues of intimidation early on. I chose, perhaps even unconsciously, to remain a shadow—timid, but a survivor.

The fearsomeness mistakenly attributed to me in public places often has a perilous flavor. The most frightening of these confusions occurred in the late 1970s and early 1980s when I worked as a journalist in Chicago. One day, rushing into the office of a magazine I was writing for with a deadline story in hand, I was mistaken for a burglar. The office manager called security and, with an ad hoc posse, pursued me through the labyrinthine halls, nearly to my editor's door. I had no way of proving who I was. I could only move briskly toward the company of someone who knew me.

Another time I was on assignment for a local paper and killing time before an interview. I entered a jewelry store on the city's affluent Near North Side. The proprietor excused herself and returned with an enormous red Doberman pinscher straining at the end of a leash. She stood, the dog extended toward me, silent to my questions, her eyes bulging nearly out of her head. I took a cursory look around, nodded, and bade her good night. Relatively speaking, however, I never fared as badly as another black male journalist. He went to nearby Waukegan, Illinois, a couple of summers ago to work on a story about a murderer who was born there. Mistaking the reporter for the killer, police hauled him from his car at gunpoint and but for his press credentials would probably have tried to book him. Such episodes are not uncommon. Black men trade tales like this all the time.

In "My Negro Problem—And Ours," Podhoretz writes that the hatred he feels for blacks makes itself known to him through a variety of avenues—one being his discomfort with that "special brand of paranoid touchiness" to which he says blacks are prone. No doubt he is speaking here of black men. In time, I learned to smother the rage I felt at so often being taken for a criminal. Not to do so would surely have led to madness—via that special "paranoid touchiness" that so annoyed Pod-horetz at the time he wrote the essay.

I began to take precautions to make myself less threatening. I move about with care, particularly late in the evening. I give a wide berth to nervous people on subway platforms during the wee hours, particularly when I have exchanged business clothes for jeans. If I happen to be enter-ing a building behind some people who appear skittish, I may walk by, let-ting them clear the lobby before I return, so as not to seem to be following them. I have been calm and extremely congenial on those rare occasions when I've been pulled over by the police.

And on late-evening constitutionals along streets less traveled by, I employ what has proved to be an excellent tension-reducing measure: I whistle melodies from Beethoven and Vivaldi and the more popular classical composers. Even steely New Yorkers hunching toward night-time destinations seem to relax, and occasionally they even join in the tune. Virtually everybody seems to sense that a mugger wouldn't be warbling bright, sunny selections from Vivaldi's *Four Seasons*. It is my equivalent of the cowbell that hikers wear when they know they are in bear country.

SPLIT AT THE ROOT: AN ESSAY
ON JEWISH IDENTITY

■

Adrienne Rich

This piece is an abridged form of an essay that appeared in Rich's 1986 book Blood, Bread, and Poetry: Selected Prose 1979–1985.

For about fifteen minutes I have been sitting chin in hand in front of the typewriter, staring out at the snow. Trying to be honest with my-self, trying to figure out why writing this seems to be so dangerous an act, filled with fear and shame, and why it seems so necessary. It comes to me that in order to write this I have to be willing to do two things: I have to claim my father, for I have my Jewishness from him and not from my gentile mother, and I have to break his silence, his taboos; in order to claim him I have in a sense to expose him.

And there is, of course, the third thing: I have to face the sources and the flickering presence of my own ambivalence as a Jew; the daily, mun-dane anti-Semitisms of my entire life.

These are stories I have never tried to tell before. Why now? Why, I asked myself sometime last year, does this question of Jewish identity float so impalpably, so ungraspably around me, a cloud I can't quite see the outlines of, which feels to me to be without definition?

And yet I've been on the track of this longer than I think.

In a long poem written in 1960, when I was thirty-one years old, I described myself as "Split at the root, neither Gentile nor Jew, / Yankee nor Rebel." I was still trying to have it both ways: to be neither/nor, trying to live (with my Jewish husband and three children more Jewish in ancestry than I) in the predominantly gentile Yankee academic world of Cambridge, Massachusetts.

But this begins, for me, in Baltimore, where I was born in my father's workplace, a hospital in the black ghetto, whose lobby contained an immense white marble statue of Christ.

My father was then a young teacher and researcher in the department of pathology at the Johns Hopkins Medical School, one of the very few Jews to attend or teach at that institution. He was from Birmingham, Alabama; his father, Samuel, was Ashkenazic, an immigrant from Austria-Hungary and his mother, Hattie Rice, a Sephardic Jew from Vicksburg, Mississippi. My grandfather had had a shoe store in Birmingham, which did well enough to allow him to retire comfortably and to leave my grandmother income on his death. The only souvenirs of my grandfather, Samuel Rich, were his ivory flute, which lay on our living-room mantel and was not to be played with; his thin gold pocket watch, which my father wore; and his Hebrew prayer book, which I discovered among my father's books in the course of reading my way through his library. In this prayer book there was a newspaper clipping about my grandparents' wedding, which took place in a synagogue.

My father, Arnold, was sent in adolescence to a military school in the North Carolina mountains, a place for training white southern Christian gentlemen. I suspect that there were few, if any, other Jewish boys at Colonel Bingham's, or at "Mr. Jefferson's university" in Charlottesville, where he studied as an undergraduate. With whatever conscious forethought, Samuel and Hattie sent their son into the dominant southern WASP culture to become an "exception," to enter the professional class. Never, in describing these experiences, did he speak of having suffered— from loneliness, cultural alienation, or outsiderhood. Never did I hear him use the word *anti-Semitism*.

It was only in college, when I read a poem by Karl Shapiro beginning "To hate the Negro and avoid the Jew / is the curriculum," that it flashed on me that there was an untold side to my father's story of his student years. He looked recognizably Jewish, was short and slender in build with dark wiry hair and deep-set eyes, high forehead, and curved nose.

My mother is a gentile. In Jewish law I cannot count myself a Jew. If it is true chat "we think back through our mothers if we are women" (Virginia Woolf)—and I myself have affirmed this—then even according to lesbian theory, I cannot (or need not?) count myself a Jew.

The white southern Protestant woman, the gentile, has always been there for me to peel back into. That's a whole piece of history in itself, for my gentile grandmother and my mother were also frustrated artists and intellectuals, a lost writer and a lost composer between them. Readers and annotators of books, note takers, my mother a good pianist still, in her eighties. But there was also the obsession with ancestry, with "background," the southern talk of family, not as people you would necessarily know and depend on, but as heritage, the guarantee of "good breeding." There was the inveterate romantic heterosexual fantasy, the mother telling the daughter how to attract men (my mother often used the word "fascinate"); the assumption that relations between the sexes could only be romantic, that it was in the woman's interest to cultivate "mystery," conceal her actual feelings. Survival tactics of a kind, I think today, knowing what I know about the white woman's sexual role in the southern racist scenario. Heterosexuality as protection, but also drawing white women deeper into collusion with white men.

It would be easy to push away and deny the gentile in me—that white southern woman, that social christian. At different times in my life I have wanted to push away one or the other burden of inheritance, to say merely *I am a woman; I am a lesbian*. If I call myself a Jewish lesbian, do I thereby try to shed some of my southern gentile white woman's culpability? If I call myself only through my mother, is it because I pass more easily through a world where being a lesbian often seems like outsiderhood enough?

According to Nazi logic, my two Jewish grandparents would have made me a *Mischling, first-degree*—nonexempt from the Final Solution.

The social world in which I grew up was christian virtually without needing to say so—christian imagery, music, language, symbols, assumptions everywhere. It was also a genteel, white, middle-class world in which "common" was a term of deep opprobrium. "Common" white people might speak of "niggers"; *we* were taught never to use that word—*we* said "Negroes" (even as we accepted segregation, the eating taboo, the assumption that black people were simply of a separate species). Our language was more polite, distinguishing us from the "rednecks" or the lynch-mob mentality. But so charged with negative meaning was even the word "Negro" that as children we were taught never to use it in front of black people. We were taught that any mention of skin color in the presence of colored people was treacherous, forbidden ground. In a parallel way, the word *Jew* was not used by polite gentiles. I sometimes heard my best friend's father, a Presbyterian minister, allude to "the Hebrew people" or "people of the Jewish faith." The world of acceptable folk was white, gentile (christian, really), and had "ideals" (which colored people, white "common" people, were not supposed to have). "Ideals" and "manners" included not hurting someone's feelings by calling her or him a Negro or a Jew—naming the hated identity. This is the mental framework of the 1930s and 1940s in which I was raised.

(Writing this, I feel dimly like the betrayer: of my father, who did not speak the word; of my mother, who must have trained me in the messages; of my caste and class; of my whiteness itself.)

Two memories: I am in a play reading at school of *The Merchant of Venice.* Whatever Jewish law says, I am quite sure I was *seen* as Jewish (with a re-assuringly gentile mother) in that double vision that bigotry allows. I am the only Jewish girl in the class, and I am playing Portia. As always, I read my part aloud for my father the night before, and he tells me to convey, with my voice, more scorn and contempt with the word *Jew:* "Therefore, Jew. . ." I have to say the word out, and say it loudly. I was encouraged to pretend to be a non-Jewish child acting a non-Jewish character who has to speak the word *Jew* emphatically. Such a child would not have had trouble with the part. But *I* must have had trouble with the part, if only because the word itself was really taboo. I can see that there was a kind of terrible, bitter bravado about my father's way of handling this. And who would not dissociate from Shylock in order to identify with Portia? As a Jewish child who was also a female, I loved Portia—and, like every other Shake-spearean heroine, she proved a treacherous role model.

A year or so later I am in another play, *The School for Scandal*, in which a notorious spendthrift is described as having "many excellent friends . . . among the Jews." In neither case was anything explained, either to me or to the class at large, about this scorn for Jews and the disgust surrounding Jews and money. Money, when Jews wanted it, had it, or lent it to others, seemed to take on a peculiar nastiness; Jews and money had some peculiar and unspeakable relation.

At the same school—in which we had Episcopalian hymns and prayers, and read aloud through the Bible morning after morning—I gained the impression that Jews were in the Bible and mentioned in English litera-ture, that they had been persecuted centuries ago by the wicked Inquisi-tion, but that they seemed not to exist in everyday life. These were the 1940s, and we were told a great deal about the Battle of Britain, the noble French Resistance fighters, the brave, starving Dutch—but I did not learn of the resistance of the Warsaw ghetto until I left home.

I was sent to the Episcopal church, baptized and confirmed, and at-tended it for about five years, though without belief. That religion seemed to have little to do with belief or commitment; it was liturgy that mattered, not spiritual passion. Neither of my parents ever entered that church, and my father would not enter *any* church for any reason—wedding or funeral. Nor did I enter a synagogue until I left Baltimore. When I came home from church, for a while, my father insisted on reading aloud to me from Thomas Paine's *The Age of Reason*—a diatribe against institutional religion. Thus, he explained, I would have a balanced view of these things, a choice. He—they—did not give me the choice to be a Jew. My mother explained to me when I was filling out forms for college that if any question was asked about "religion," I should put down "Episcopalian" rather than "none"—to seem to have no religion, she implied, dangerous.

But it was white social christianity, rather than any particular christian sect, that the world was founded on. The very word *Christian* was used as a synonym for virtuous, just, peace-loving, generous, etc., etc. The norm was christian: "Religion: none" was indeed not acceptable. Anti-Semitism was so intrinsic as not to have a name. I don't recall exactly being taught that the Jews killed Jesus—"Christ killer" seems too strong a term for the bland Episcopal vocabulary—but certainly we got the impression that the Jews had been caught out in a terrible mistake, failing to recognize the true Messiah, and were thereby less advanced in moral and spiritual sensibility. The Jews had actually allowed *money-lenders in the Temple* (again, the unexplained obsession with Jews and money). They were of the past, archaic, primitive, as older (and darker) cultures are supposed to be primitive; christianity was lightness, fairness, peace on earth, and combined the feminine appeal of "The meek shall inherit the earth" with the masculine stride of "Onward, Christian Soldiers."

Sometime in 1946, while still in high school, I read in the newspaper that a theater in Baltimore was showing films of the Allied liberation of the Nazi concentration camps. Alone, I went downtown after school one afternoon and watched the stark, blurry, but unmistakable newsreels. When I try to go back and touch the pulse of that girl of sixteen, growing up in many ways so precocious and so ignorant, I am overwhelmed by a memory of despair, a sense of inevitability more enveloping than any I had ever known. Anne Frank's diary and many other personal narratives of the Holocaust were still unknown or unwritten. But it came to me that every one of those piles of corpses, mountains of shoes and clothing had contained, simply, individuals, who had believed, as I now believed of myself, that they were intended to live out a life of some kind of meaning, that the world possessed some kind of sense and order; yet *this* had happened to them. And I, who believed my life was intended to be so interesting and meaningful, was connected to those dead by something—not just mortality but a taboo name, a hated identity. Or was I—did I really have to be? Writing this now, I feel belated rage that I was so impoverished by the family and social worlds I lived in, that I had to try to figure out by myself what this did indeed mean for me. That I had never been taught about resistance, only about passing. That I had no language for anti-Semitism itself.

When I went home and told my parents where I had been, they were not pleased. I felt accused of being morbidly curious, not healthy, sniffing around death for the thrill of it. And since, at sixteen, I was often not sure of the sources of my feelings or of my motives for doing what I did, I probably accused myself as well. One thing was clear: There was nobody in my world with whom I could discuss those films. Probably at the same time, I was reading accounts of the camps in magazines and newspapers; what I remember were the films and having questions that I could not even phrase, such as *Are those men and women "them" or "us"?*

To be able to ask even the child's astonished question *Why do they hate us so?* means knowing how to say "we." The guilt of not knowing, the guilt of perhaps having betrayed my parents or even those victims, those survivors, through mere curiosity—these also froze in me for years the impulse to find out more about the Holocaust.

1947: I left Baltimore to go to college in Cambridge, Massachusetts, left (I thought) the backward, enervating South for the intellectual, vital North. New England also had for me some vibration of higher moral rectitude, of moral passion even, with its seventeenth-century Puritan self-scrutiny, its nineteenth-century literary "flowering," its abolitionist righteousness, Colonel Shaw and his black Civil War regiment depicted in granite on Boston Common. At the same time, I found myself, at Radcliffe, among Jewish women. I used to sit for hours over coffee with what I thought of as the "real" Jewish students, who told me about middle-class Jewish culture in America. I described my background—for the first time to strangers—and they took me on, some with amusement at my illiteracy, some arguing that I could never marry into a strict Jewish family, some convinced I didn't "look Jewish," others that I did. I learned the names of holidays and foods, which surnames are Jewish and which are "changed names"; about girls who had had their noses "fixed," their hair straightened. For these young Jewish women, students in the late 1940s, it was acceptable, perhaps even necessary, to strive to look as gentile as possible; but they stuck proudly to being Jewish, expected to marry a Jew, have children, keep the holidays, carry on the culture.

I felt I was testing a forbidden current, that there was danger in these revelations. I bought a reproduction of a Chagall portrait of a rabbi in striped prayer shawl and hung it on the wall of my room. I was admittedly young and trying to educate myself, but I was also doing something that *is* dangerous: I was flirting with identity.

One day that year I was in a small shop where I had bought a dress with a too-long skirt. The shop employed a seamstress who did alterations, and she came in to pin up the skirt on me. I am sure that she was a recent immigrant, a survivor. I remember a short, dark woman wearing heavy glasses, with an accent so foreign I could not understand her words. Something about her presence was very powerful and disturbing to me. After marking and pinning up the skirt, she sat back on her knees, looked up at me, and asked in a hurried whisper: "You Jewish?" Eighteen years of training in assimilation sprang into the reflex by which I shook my head, rejecting her, and muttered, "No."

What was I actually saying "no" to? She was poor, older, struggling with a foreign tongue, anxious; she had escaped the death that had been intended for her, but I had no imagination of her possible courage and foresight, her resistance—I did not see in her a heroine who had perhaps saved many lives, including her own. I saw the frightened immigrant, the seamstress hemming the skirts of college girls, the wandering Jew. But I was an American college girl having her skirt hemmed. And I was frightened myself, I think, because she had recognized me ("It takes one to know one," my friend Edie at Radcliffe had said) even if I refused to recognize myself or her, even if her recognition was sharpened by loneliness or the need to feel safe with me.

But why should she have felt safe with me? I myself was living with a false sense of safety.

There are betrayals in my life that I have known at the very moment were betrayals: this was one of them. There are other betrayals committed so repeatedly, so mundanely, that they leave no memory trace behind, only a growing residue of misery, of dull, accreted self-hatred. Often these take the form not of words but of silence. Silence before the joke at which everyone is laughing: the anti-woman joke, the racist joke, the anti-Semitic joke. Silence and then amnesia. Blocking it out when the oppressor's language starts coming from the lips of one we admire, whose courage and eloquence have touched us: *She didn't really mean that; he didn't really say that.* But the accretions build up out of sight, like scale inside a kettle.

1948: I come home from my freshman year at college, flaming with new insights, new information. I am the daughter who has gone out into the world, to the pinnacle of intellectual prestige, Harvard, fulfilling my father's hopes for me, but also exposed to dangerous influences. I have already been reproved for attending a rally for Henry Wallace and the Progressive party. I challenge my father: "Why haven't you told me that I am Jewish? Why do you never talk about being a Jew?" He answers measuredly, "You know that I have never denied that I am a Jew. But it's not important to me. I am a scientist, a deist. I have no use for organized religion. I choose to live in a world of many kinds of people. There are Jews I admire and others whom I despise. I am a person, not simply a Jew." The words are as I remember them, not perhaps exactly as spoken. But that was the message. And it contained enough truth—as all denial drugs itself on partial truth—so that it remained for the time being unanswerable, leaving me high and dry, split at the root, gasping for clarity, for air.

At that time Arnold Rich was living in suspension, waiting to be appointed to the professorship of pathology at Johns Hopkins. The appointment was delayed for years, no Jew ever having held a professional chair in that medical school. And he wanted it badly. It must have been a very bitter time for him, since he had believed so greatly in the redeeming power of excellence, of being the most brilliant, inspired man for the job. With enough excellence, you could presumably make it stop mattering that you were Jewish; you could become the *only* Jew in the gentile world, a Jew so "civilized," so far from "common," so attractively combining southern gentility with European cultural values that no one would ever

confuse you with the raw, "pushy" Jews of New York, the "loud, hysterical" refugees from eastern Europe, the "overdressed" Jews of the urban
South.

We—my sister, mother, and I—were constantly urged to speak quietly
in public, to dress without ostentation, to repress all vividness or spontaneity, to assimilate with a world which might see us as too flamboyant.
I suppose that my mother, pure gentile though she was, could be seen as
acting "common" or "Jewish" if she laughed too loudly or spoke aggres-
sively. My father's mother, who lived with us half the year, was a model of
circumspect behavior, dressed in dark blue or lavender, retiring in company, ladylike to an extreme, wearing no jewelry except a good gold chain,
a narrow brooch, or a string of pearls. A few times, within the family, I
saw her anger flare, felt the passion she was repressing. But when Arnold
took us out to a restaurant or on a trip, the Rich women were always
tuned down to some WASP level my father believed, surely, would protect
us all—maybe also make us unrecognizable to the "real Jews" who
wanted to seize us, drag us back to the *shtetl*, the ghetto, in its many
manifestations.

For, yes, that *was* a message—that some Jews would be after you, once
they "knew," to rejoin them, to re-enter a world that was messy, noisy,
unpredictable, maybe poor—"even though," as my mother once wrote
me, criticizing my largely Jewish choice of friends in college, "some of
them will be the most brilliant, fascinating people you'll ever meet." I
wonder if that isn't one message of assimilation—of America—that the
unlucky or the unachieving want to pull you backward, that to identify
with them is to court downward mobility, lose the precious chance of
passing, of token existence. There was always within this sense of Jewish
identity a strong class discrimination. Jews might be "fascinating" as
individuals but came with huge unruly families who "poured chicken
soup over everyone's head" (in the phrase of a white southern male
poet). Anti-Semitism could thus be justified by the bad behavior of certain Jews; and if you did not effectively deny family and community,
there would always be a remote cousin claiming kinship with you who
was the "wrong kind" of Jew.

*I have always believed his attitude toward other Jews depended on who they
were. . . . It was my impression that Jews of this background looked down on
Eastern European Jews, including Polish Jews and Russian Jews, who generally
were not as well educated.* This from a letter written to me recently by a gentile who had worked in my father's department, whom I had asked about
anti-Semitism there and in particular regarding my father. This inform-
ant also wrote me that it was hard to perceive anti-Semitism in Baltimore
because the racism made so much more intense an impression: *I would almost have to think that blacks went to a different heaven than the whites, because
the bodies were kept in a separate morgue, and some white persons did not even
want blood transfusions from black donors.* My father's mind was predictably
racist and misogynist; yet as a medical student he noted in his journal

that southern male chivalry stopped at the point of any white man in a streetcar giving his seat to an old, weary black woman standing in the aisle. Was this a Jewish insight—an outsider's insight, even though the outsider was striving to be on the inside?

Because what isn't named is often more permeating than what is, I believe that my father's Jewishness profoundly shaped my own identity and our family existence. They were shaped both by external anti-Semitism and my father's self-hatred, and by his Jewish pride. What Arnold did, I think, was call his Jewish pride something else: achievement, aspiration, genius, idealism. Whatever was unacceptable got left back under the rubric of Jewishness or the "wrong kind" of Jews—uneducated, aggressive, loud. The message I got was that we were really superior: Nobody else's father had collected so many books, had traveled so far, knew so many languages. Baltimore was a musical city, but for the most part, in the families of my school friends, culture was for women. My father was an amateur musician, read poetry, adored encyclopedic knowledge. He prowled and pounced over my school papers, insisting I use "grown-up" sources; he criticized my poems for faulty technique and gave me books on rhyme and meter and form. His investment in my intellect and talent was egotistical, tyrannical, opinionated, and terribly wearing. He taught me, nevertheless, to believe in hard work, to mistrust easy inspiration, to write and rewrite; to feel that I *was* a person of the book, even though a woman; to take ideas seriously. He made me feel, at a very young age, the power of language and that I could share it.

The Riches were proud, but we also had to be very careful. Our behavior had to be more impeccable than other people's. Strangers were not to be trusted, nor even friends; family issues must never go beyond the family; the world was full of potential slanderers, betrayers, *people who could not understand.* Even within the family, I realize that I never in my whole life knew what my father was really feeling. Yet he spoke—monologued—with driving intensity. You could grow up in such a house mesmerized by the local electricity, the crucial meanings assumed by the merest things. This used to seem to me a sign that we were all living on some high emotional plane. It was a difficult force field for a favored daughter to disengage from.

Easy to call that intensity Jewish; and I have no doubt that passion is one of the qualities required for survival over generations of persecution. But what happens when passion is rent from its original base, when the white gentile world is softly saying "Be more like us and you can be almost one of us"? What happens when survival seems to mean closing off one emotional artery after another? His forebears in Europe had been forbidden to travel or expelled from one country after another, had special taxes levied on them if they left the city walls, had been forced to wear special clothes and badges, restricted to the poorest neighborhoods. He had wanted to be a "free spirit," to travel widely, among "all kinds of people." Yet in his prime of life he lived in an increasingly withdrawn world, in his house up on a hill in a neighborhood where Jews were not supposed to be able to buy property, depending almost exclusively on interactions with his wife and daughters to provide emotional connectedness. In his home, he created a private defense system so elaborate that even as he was dying, my mother felt unable to talk freely with his colleagues or others who might have helped her. Of course, she acquiesced in this.

The loneliness of the "only," the token, often doesn't feel like loneliness but like a kind of dead echo chamber. Certain things that ought to don't resonate. Somewhere Beverly Smith writes of women of color "inspiring the behavior" in each other. When there's nobody to "inspire the behavior," act out of the culture, there is an atrophy, a dwindling, which is partly invisible.

Sometimes I feel I have seen too long from too many disconnected angles: white. Jewish, anti-Semite, racist, anti-racist, once-married, lesbian, middle-class, feminist, exmatriate southerner, *split at the root*—that I will never bring them whole. I would have liked, in this essay, to bring together the meanings of anti-Semitism and racism as I have experienced them and as I believe they intersect in the world beyond my life. But I'm not able to do this yet. I feel the tension as I think, make notes: *If you really look at the one reality, the other will waver and disperse.* Trying in one week to read Angela Davis and Lucy Davidowicz, trying to hold throughout to a feminist, a lesbian, perspective—what does this mean? Nothing has trained me for this. And sometimes I feel inadequate to make any statement as a Jew; I feel the history of denial within me like an injury, a scar. For assimilation has affected *my* perceptions; those early lapses in meaning, those blanks, are with me still. My ignorance can be dangerous to me and to others.

Yet we can't wait for the undamaged to make our connections for us; we can't wait it to speak until we are perfectly clear and righteous. There is no purity and, in our lifetimes, no end to this process.

This essay, then, has no conclusions: It is another beginning for me. Not just a way of saying, in 1982 Right Wing America, I, *too, will wear the yellow star.* It's a moving into accountability, enlarging the range of accountability. I know that in the rest of my life, the next half century or so, every aspect of my identity will have to be engaged. The middle-class white girl taught to trade obedience for privilege. The Jewish lesbian raised to be a heterosexual gentile. The woman who first heard oppression named and analyzed in the black Civil Rights struggle. The woman with three sons, the feminist who hates male violence. The woman limping with a cane, the woman who has stopped bleeding are also accountable. The poet who knows that beautiful language can lie, that the oppressor's language sometimes sounds beautiful. The woman trying, as part of her resistance, to clean up her act.

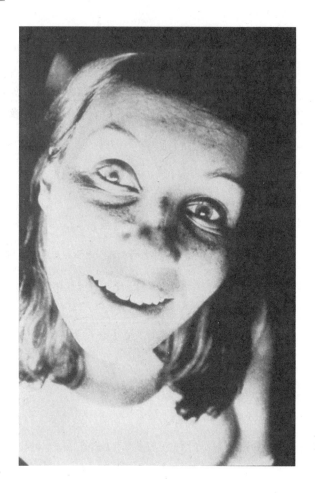

HUNGER

———■———

Maggie Helwig

This piece was originally published in TIME *in 1989.*

onsider that it is now normal for North American women to have eating disorders. Consider that anorexia—deliberate starvation—and bulimia—self-induced vomiting—and obsessive patterns for weight-controlling exercise are now the ordinary thing for young women, and are spreading at a frightening rate to older women, to men, to ethnic groups and social classes that were once "immune." Consider that some surveys suggest that 80 per cent of the women on an average university campus have borderline-to-severe eating disorders; that it is almost impossible to get treatment unless the problem is life-threatening; that, in fact, if it is not life-threatening it is not considered a problem at all. I once sat in a seminar on nutritional aspects of anorexia, and ended up listening to people tell me how to keep my weight down. All this is happening in one of the richest countries in the world, a society devoted to consumption. Amazing as it may seem, we have normalized anorexia and bulimia, even turned them into an industry.

We've also trivialized them: made them into nothing more than an exaggerated conformity with basically acceptable standards of behavior. Everyone wants to be thin and pretty, after all. Some people take it a little too far; you have to get them back on the right track, but it's all a question of knowing just how far is proper.

The consumer society has gone so far we can even buy into hunger.

But that is not what it's about. You do not stuff yourself with food and force yourself to vomit just because of fashion magazines. You do not reduce yourself to the condition of a skeleton in order to be attractive. This is not just a problem of proportion. This is the nightmare of consumerism acted out in women's bodies.

This is what we are saying as we starve: it is not all right. It is not all right. It is not all right.

There've always been strange or disordered patterns of eating, associated mainly with religious extremism or psychological problems (which some, not myself, would say were the same thing). But the complex of ideas, fears, angers and actions that make up contemporary anorexia and bulimia seems to be of fairly recent origin. Anorexia did not exist as a recognized pattern until the 1960s, and bulimia not until later than that—and at first they were deeply shocking. The idea that privileged young women (the first group to be affected) were voluntarily starving themselves, sometimes to death, or regularly sticking their fingers down their throats to make themselves throw up, shook the culture badly. It was a fad, in a sense, the illness of the month, but it was also a scandal, and a source of something like horror.

Before this, though, before anorexia had a widely recognized name, one of the first women to succumb to it had made her own scandalous stand, and left a body of writing that still has a lot to say about the real meaning of voluntary hunger.

Simone Weil was a brilliant, disturbed, wildly wrong-headed and astonishingly perceptive young French woman who died from the complications of self-starvation in America during World War II, at the age of 34. She never, of course, wrote directly about her refusal to eat—typically for any anorexic, she insisted she ate perfectly adequate amounts. But throughout her philosophical and theological writing (almost all of it fragments and essays collected after her death), she examines and uses the symbolism of hunger, eating and food.

Food occupied, in fact, a rather important and valued position in her philosophy—she once referred to food as "the irrefutable proof of the reality of the universe," and at another time said that the foods served at Easter and Christmas, the turkey and *marron glacés,* were "the true meaning of the feast"; although she could also take the more conventional puritan position that desire for food is a "base motive." She spoke often of eating God (acceptable enough in a Christian context) and of being eaten by God (considerably less so). The great tragedy of our lives, she said, is that we cannot really eat God; and also "it may be that vice, depravity and crime are almost always . . . attempts to eat beauty."

But it is her use of the symbolism of hunger that explains her death. "We have to go down into ourselves to the abode of the desire which is not imaginary. Hunger: we imagine kinds of food, but the hunger itself is real: we have to fasten onto the hunger."

Hunger, then, was a search for reality, for the irreducible need that lies beyond all imaginary satisfactions. Weil was deeply perturbed by the "materialism" of her culture; though she probably could not have begun to imagine the number of imaginary and illusory "satisfactions" now available. Simply, she wanted truth. She wanted to reduce herself to the point where she would *know* what needs, and what foods, were real and true.

Similarly, though deeply drawn to the Catholic faith, she refused to be baptized and to take Communion (to, in fact, eat God). "I cannot help wondering whether in these days when so large a proportion of humanity is sunk in materialism, God does not want there to be some men and women who have given themselves to him and to Christ and who yet remain outside the Church." For the sake of honesty, of truth, she maintained her hunger.

Weil, a mystic and a political activist simultaneously until the end of her short life—she was one of the first French intellectuals to join the Communist party and one of the first to leave, fought in the Spanish civil war and worked in auto factories—could not bear to have life be less than a total spiritual and political statement. And her statement of protest, of dissatisfaction, her statement of hunger, finally destroyed her.

The term anorexia nervosa was coined in the 19th century, but it was not until sometime in the 1960s that significant—and constantly increasing—numbers of well-off young women began dying of starvation, and not until the early 1970s that it became public knowledge.

It is the nature of our times that the explanations proffered were psychological and individualistic; yet, even so, it was understood as being, on some level, an act of protest. And of course symbolically, it could hardly be other—it was, simply, a hunger strike. The most common interpretation, at that point, was that it was a sort of adolescent rebellion against parental control, an attempt, particularly, to escape from an overcontrolling mother. It was a fairly acceptable paradigm for the period, although many mothers were justifiably disturbed; sometimes deeply and unnecessarily hurt. The theory still has some currency, and is not entirely devoid of truth.

But can it be an accident that this happened almost precisely to coincide with the growth of the consumer society, a world based on a level of material consumption that, by the end of the 1960s, had become very nearly uncontrollable? Or with the strange, underground guilt that has made "conspicuous consumption" a matter of consuming vast amounts and *hiding it,* of million-dollar minimalism? With the development of what is possibly the most emotionally depleted society in history, where the only "satisfactions" seem to be the imaginary ones, the material buy-offs?

To be skeletally, horribly thin makes one strong statement. It says, I am hungry. What I have been given is not sufficient, not real, not true, not acceptable. I am starving. To reject food, whether by refusing it or by vomiting it back, says simply, I will not consume. I will not participate. This is not real.

Hunger is the central nightmare image of our society. Of all the icons of horror the last few generations have offered us, we have chosen, above all, pictures of hunger—the emaciated prisoners of Auschwitz and Belsen, Ethiopian children with bloated bellies and stick-figure limbs. We carry in our heads these nightmares of the extreme edge of hunger.

And while we may not admit to guilt about our level of consumption in general, we admit freely to guilt about eating, easily equate food with "sin." We cannot accept hunger of our own, cannot afford to consider it.

It is, traditionally, women who carry our nightmares. It was women who became possessed by the Devil, women who suffered form "hysterical disorders," women who, in all popular culture, are the targets of the "monster." One of the roles women are cast in is that of those who act out the subconscious fears of their society. And it is women above all, in this time, who carry our hunger.

It is the starving women who embody the extremity of hunger that terrifies and fascinates us, and who insist that they are not hungry. It is the women sticking their fingers down their throats who act out the equation of food and sin, who deny hunger and yet embody endless, unfulfilled appetite. It is these women who live through every implication of our consumption and our hunger, our guilt and ambiguity and our awful need for something real to fill us.

We have too much; and it is poison.

■　■　■

As eating disorders became increasingly widespread, they also became increasingly trivialized, incorporated into a framework already "understood" all too well. Feminist writers had, early on, noted that anorexia had to be linked with the increasingly thinness of models and other glamor icons, as part of a larger cultural trend. This is true enough as a starting point, for the symbolic struggle being waged in women's bodies happens on many levels, and is not limited to pathology cases. Unfortunately, this single starting point was seized on by "women's magazines" and popularizing accounts in general. Anorexia was now understandable, almost safe really, it was just fashion gone out of control. Why, these women were *accepting* the culture, they just needed a sense of proportion. What a relief.

Now it could be condoned. Now it could, in fact, become the basis for an industry; could be incorporated neatly into consumer society. According to Jane Fonda the solution to bulimia is to remain equally unhealthily thin by buying the 20-minute workout and becoming an obsessive fitness follower (at least for those who can afford it). The diet clinic industry, the Nutrisystem package, the aerobics boom. An advertising industry that plays equally off desire and guilt, for they now reinforce each other. Thousands upon thousands of starving, tormented women, not "sick" enough to be taken seriously, not really troubled at all.

One does not reduce oneself to the condition of a skeleton in order to be fashionable. One does not binge and vomit daily as an acceptable means of weight control. One does not even approach or imagine or dream of these things if one is not in some sort of trouble. If it were as simple as fashion, surely we would not be so ashamed to speak of these things, we would not feel that either way, whether we eat or do not eat, we are doing something wrong.

I was anorexic for eight years. I nearly died. It was certainly no help to me to be told I was taking fashion too far—I knew perfectly well that had nothing to do with it. It did not help much to be told I was trying to escape from my mother, since I lived away from home and was in only occasional contact with my family; it did not help much to be approached on an individualistic, psychological level. In fact, the first person I was able to go to for help was a charismatic Catholic, who at least understood that I was speaking in symbols of spiritual hunger.

I knew that I had something to say, that things were not all right, that I had to make that concretely, physically obvious. I did not hate or look down on my body—I spoke through it and with it.

Women are taught to take guilt, concern, problems, onto themselves personally; and especially onto their bodies. But we are trying to talk about something that is only partly personal. Until we find new ways of saying it and find the courage to talk to the world about the world, we will speak destruction to ourselves. We must come to know what we are saying—and say it.

RING LEADER

Natalie Kusz

Allure *magazine first published this essay in 1997.*

I was thirty years old when I had my right nostril pierced, and back-home friends fell speechless at the news, lapsing into long telephone pauses of the sort that June Cleaver would employ if the Beave had ever called to report, "Mom, I'm married. His name's Eddie." Not that I resemble a Cleaver or have friends who wear pearls in the shower, but people who have known me the longest would say that for me to *draw* attention to my body rather than to work all out to *repel* it is at least as out of character as the Beave's abrupt urge for his-and-his golf ensembles. A nose ring, they might tell you, would be my last choice for a fashion accessory, way down on the list with a sag-enhancing specialty bra or a sign on my butt reading "Wide Load."

The fact is, I grew up ugly—no, worse than that, I grew up *unusual*—that unforgivable sin among youth. We lived in Alaska, where, despite what you might have heard about the Rugged Individualist, teenagers still adhere to the universal rules of conformity: if Popular Patty wears contact lenses, then you will by gum get contacts too, or else pocket those glasses and pray you can distinguish the girls' bathroom door from the boys'. The bad news was that I had only one eye, having lost the other in a dog attack at age seven: so although contacts, at half the two-eyed price, were easy to talk my parents into, I was still left with an eye patch and many facial scars, signs as gaudy as neon, telling everyone, "Here is a girl who is Not Like You." And Not Like Them, remember, was equivalent to Not from This Dimension, only half (maybe one third) as interesting.

The rest of my anatomy did nothing to help matters. I come from a long line of famine-surviving ancestors—on my father's side, Polish and Russian, on my mother's, everything from Irish to French Canadian—and thus I have an excellent, thrifty, Ebenezer Scrooge of a metabolism. I can ingest but a single calorie, and before quitting time at the Scrooge office, my system will have spent that calorie to replace an old blood cell, to secrete a vital hormone, to send a few chemicals around the old nervous system, and still have enough left over to deposit ten fat cells in my inner thigh—a nifty little investment for the future, in case the Irish potato famine ever recurs. These metabolic wonders are delightful if you are planning a move to central Africa, but for an American kid wiggling to Jane Fonda as if her life depended on it (which, in high school, it did), the luckiest people on earth seemed to be anorexics, those wispy and hollow-cheeked beings whose primary part in the locker room drama was to stand at the mirror and announce, "My God, I disgust myself, I am *so fat*." While the other girls recited their lines ("No, Samantha, don't talk like that, you're beautiful, you really *are!*"), I tried to pull on a gym shirt without removing any other shirt first, writhing inside the cloth like a cat trapped among the bedsheets.

Thus, if you add the oversized body to the disfigured face, and add again my family's low income and my secondhand wardrobe, you have a formula for pure, excruciating teenage angst. Hiding from public scrutiny became for me, as for many people like me, a way of life. I developed a bouncy sense of humor, the kind that makes people say, "That Natalie, she is always so *up*," and keeps them from probing for deep emotion. After teaching myself to sew, I made myself cheap versions of those Popular Patty clothes or at least the items (*never* halter tops, although this was the seventies) that a large girl could wear with any aplomb. And above all, I studied the other kids, their physical posture, their music, their methods of blow-dryer artistry, hoping one day to emerge from my body, invisible. I suppose I came as close to invisibility as my appearance would allow, for if you look at the yearbook photos from that time, you will find on my face the same "too cool to say 'cheese'" expression as on Popular Patty's eleven-man entourage.

But at age thirty, I found myself living in the (to me) incomprehensible politeness of America's Midwest, teaching at a small private college that I found suffocating, and anticipating the arrival of that all-affirming desire of college professors everywhere, that professional certification indicating you are now "one of the family": academic tenure. A first-time visitor to any college campus can easily differentiate between tenured and nontenured faculty by keeping in mind a learning institution's two main expectations: (1) that a young professor will spend her first several years on the job proving herself indispensable (sucking up), working to advance the interests of the college (sucking up), and making a name for herself in her field of study (sucking up); and (2) that a senior, tenured professor, having achieved indispensability, institutional usefulness, and fame will thereafter lend her widely recognized name to the school's public relations office, which will use that name to attract prospective new students and faculty, who will in turn be encouraged to call on senior professors for the purpose of asking deep, scholarly questions (sucking up). Thus, a visitor touring any random campus can quickly distinguish tenured faculty persons from nontenured ones simply by noting the habitual shape and amount of chapping of their lips.

I anticipated a future of senior-faculty meetings with academia's own version of Popular Patty—not a nubile, cheerleading fashion plate, but a somber and scholarly denture wearer who, under the legal terms of tenure, cannot be fired except for the most grievous unprofessional behavior, such as igniting plastique under the dean's new Lexus. When that official notice landed in my In box, my sucking-up days would be over. I would have arrived. I would be family.

I couldn't bear it. In addition to the fact that I possessed all my own teeth, I was unsuited to Become As One with the other tenured beings because I was by nature boisterous, a collector of Elvis memorabilia, and given to not washing my car—in short, I was and always would be from Alaska.

Even in my leisure hours, my roots made my life of that period disorienting. Having moved to the immaculate Midwest from the far-from-immaculate wilderness, I found myself incapable of understanding, say, the nature of cul-de-sacs, those little circles of pristine homes where all the children were named Chris, and where all the parents got to vote on whether the Johnsons (they were all Johnsons) could paint their house beige. I would go to potluck suppers where the dishes were foreign to me, and twelve people at my table would take a bite, savor it with closed eyes, and say, "Ah, Tater Tot casserole. Now *that* takes me back." It got to the point where I felt defensive all the time, professing my out-of-townness whenever I was mistaken for a local, someone who understood the conversational subtexts and genteel body language of a Minnesotan. Moreover, I could never be sure what I myself said to these people with my subtextual language or my body. For all I knew, my posture during one of those impossible kaffeeklatsches proclaimed to everyone, "I am about to steal the silverware," or "I subscribe to the beliefs of Reverend Sun Myung Moon."

I grew depressed. Before long, I was feeling nostalgic for Alaskan eccentricities I had avoided even when I had lived there—unshaven legs and armpits, for example, and automobiles held together entirely by duct tape. I began decorating my office with absurd and nonprofessional items: velvet paintings, Mr. Potato Head, and a growing collection of snow globes from each of the fifty states. Students took to coming by to play with Legos, or to blow bubbles from those little circular wands, and a wish started to grow in my brain, a yearning for some way to transport the paraphernalia around with me, to carry it along as an indication that I was truly unconventional at heart.

So the week that I received tenure, when they could no longer fire me and when a sore nose would not get bumped during the course of any future sucking-up maneuver, I entered a little shop in the black-leather part of town and emerged within minutes with my right nostril duly pierced. The gesture was, for me, a celebration, a visible statement that said, "Assume nothing. I might be a punk from Hennepin Avenue, or a belly dancer with brass knuckles in my purse." Polite as was the society of that region, my colleagues never referred to my nose, but I could see them looking and wondering a bit, which was exactly the thing I had wanted—a lingering question in the minds of the natives, the possibility of forces they had never fathomed.

After this, my comfort level changed some, and almost entirely for the better. I had warned my father, who lived with me those years, that I was thinking of piercing my nose. When I arrived home that day and the hole was through the side instead of the center—he had expected, I found out, a Maori-style bone beneath the nostrils—he looked at me, his color improved, and he asked if I wanted chicken for dinner. So that was all fine. At school, students got over their initial shock relatively quickly, having already seen the trailer-park ambience of my office, and they became less apt to question my judgment on their papers; I could hear them thinking. She looks like she must understand *something* about where I'm coming from. And my daughter—this is the best part of all—declared I was the hippest parent she knew, and decided it was O.K. to introduce me to her junior high friends; even Cool Chris—the Midwestern variety of Popular Patty—couldn't boast a body-pierced mom.

I have since moved away from Minnesota, and old friends (those of the aforementioned June Cleaver–type stunned silence) have begun to ask if I have decided to stop wearing a nose stud now that my initial reason for acquiring it has passed. And here, to me, is the interesting part: the answer, categorically, is no. Nonconformity, or something like it, may have been the initial reason behind shooting a new hole through my proboscis, but a whole set of side effects, a broad and unexpected brand of liberation, has provided me a reason for keeping it. Because the one-eyed fat girl who couldn't wear Popular Patty's clothes, much less aspire to steal her boyfriends, who was long accustomed to the grocery-store stares of adults and small children ("Mommy, what happened to that fat lady's face?"), who had learned over the years to hide whenever possible, slathering her facial scars with cover stick, is now—am I dreaming?—in charge. I have now, after all, deliberately chosen a "facial flaw," a remarkable aspect of appearance. Somehow now, the glances of strangers seem less invasive, nothing to incite me to nunhood; a long look is just that—a look—and what of it? I've invited it, I've made room for it, it is no longer inflicted upon me against my will.

NAVIGATING THE DARK WORLD

Stephen Kuusisto

This excerpt from Kuusisto's forthcoming book Navigating the Dark World *appeared in the August 1996* Harper's Magazine.

In a photo I can't find anymore, a dozen blind men sit at a table in a coffee warehouse. It's 1885, the "Gilded Age," and there's something grand about American progress, a palpable thing transmitted by telephone and electric light. Sunlight from the windows pierces the room, catching the blind men at their table. They look as if they might be sitting in Barnum's center ring: a novelty, twelve blind men drinking coffee. It's an oddity of proportion: the benighted in a vast industrial room, their faces lit by towering sunbeams, each one unaware of the camera's invasion. They're shown in varying aspects of consideration, with head tilted up or down or slightly to the side, as if a confidence were about to be shared with the empty air. Their faces have that particular blankness that comes from introversion, a childish submission to a mood.

A caption says that these are "blind coffee tasters." The photo tells us that there's something of the "savant" about them; they've sharpened their intuitions, they wear the contemplative mask of people who know something. But it's more than that: it's a dreamy appearance, a far-off look, the "hypnogogic state" between waking and sleep that fascinated Edgar Allan Poe. Even in this temple of American progress, the faces of the blind excite superstition.

■ ■ ■

In a taxi riding down Broadway, I hear the driver mumbling and I lean forward to catch his words. He's talking to me—do I mind if he asks me a question? He has noticed my white cane. He wants to know if I can see anything. His tone is a somber whisper: he's talking like a man who will soon make a confession. I wonder if he wants to know if I can count money. I tell him I can see a little bit. By his accent I guess he's from the Caribbean. Haiti?

First he tells me how his aunt lost her sight. He snips his fingers—that's how fast it was. Does she have friends, people to help her? How are her spirits? These are my questions. He doesn't care about these issues. It turns out that we're talking about more than his aunt. We're navigating the realm of sudden blindness, the land of dark spells and sad fortunes, the world of voodoo.

Now the driver tells me about his aunt: "A beautiful girl, nice hair, nice teeth, very fine! Let me tell you, she was a beauty. But she goes with the voodoo man, even though the voodoo man has a wife, she goes with him. She cooks for him and looks after him. Everyone tells her not to have anything to do with this man, but she don't listen. One day, when the voodoo man's wife is gone, she goes to his house and tells him that she's going to clean up. She opens the door to the voodoo man's closet. She could feel a wind blow right through her head, and then she was blind!"

He puts special emphasis on the word "blind." I look at the high-speed stained glass of my own myopic Manhattan as the cab now races down Fifth Avenue. I ask the driver if his aunt has people to look after her. "No," he says. "No one will go near her—she has the voodoo now."

When we get to my street, the driver is disappointed to discover that I can count my money by myself.

■ ■ ■

Legally blind, I know the eternal Freudian slip of misread signs and advertisements, the whirlwind of colors and halos, a road of mental escapades. It's a fun-house world of things appearing and disappearing, waves crowding on a beach, ferns swaying behind a thin curtain.

A friend calls me to say she'll meet me in half an hour. She drives a red Chrysler. I walk down to the street and approach the car. I reach for the door on the passenger's side and give it a tug, but it's locked. I rap on the window, but my friend doesn't seem to hear. I rap again, tug on the door, rap and tug. Then I walk around to her side of the car. When I lean down to the window, I see at last the face of a genuinely terrified Chinese woman. I motion to her to roll down her window. She won't. I try to explain my mistake in sign language—pointing to my eyes, telling her loudly that I've mistaken her car for that of a friend. I begin backing away from her into the street like an ungainly kid on roller skates.

■ ■ ■

It's the word "blind" I've been running from. I began with my mother's fear that, as a category, blindness meant a reduced life for her child. To her credit, she strove to give me an ordinary boyhood, one with bicycles and motorboats. I learned to pilot a boat without seeing where I was going. I navigated by an odd series of convulsive impressions and memories. Sometimes an adult would say, "Can you see that breakwater over there? Aim to the left of it." But I could barely see what they were talking about. I just aimed the boat and hit the throttle.

■ ■ ■

Today I ran six miles and collided with a pair of shopping carts in the tricky shade of several trees. I ran from sunlight into dark. A big crash of cymbals. Rimsky-Korsakov. I nearly gelded myself.

■ ■ ■

My mother told the school officials that she wouldn't send me to the Perkins School for the Blind. She would enroll me in public school. Sitting at the front of the class, I would hunch over a special desk with a top that raised like an architect's table so that my books might be closer to my eyes.

My days at school taught me to wish for perfect eyes, to walk as though I could really see, to emerge regularly from my narrowed province and ride a bicycle as if, eyes closed and moving fast, I might be impervious to disgrace.

One day, a boy I thought to be a friend stole my glasses in the middle of a lunch-hour recess. To this day, I can picture my panicked self, the boy clutching my glasses at a safe distance and watching me drift about. Blinded instantly and put on display, I was a sea lion, measureless and unwieldy. More than thirty years have passed, but I'm still horrified by how it felt to belong so thoroughly to other people, to be, in effect, their possession.

■ ■ ■

The whims of architects have enormous power over my experience of vision: a postmodern shopping mall with its cantilevered floors and mirrored walls—all lit by indirect lighting and high-intensity bulbs—can reduce my momentum. The darkness of restaurants and bars quickens and tightens my chest. I edge along the bar, without poise, feeling sudden reverberations of alarm. In a room designed for urbane and sexy people, I feel that boyhood panic, but conjure a different image—myself as an old man holding objects close to his face.

■ ■ ■

In the great Prado museum in Madrid, I find that I cannot see the famous paintings of Velázquez and Goya because they are hanging behind ropes that prohibit the insane from drawing too near. So I see oceans of mud in vast, gilded frames instead of the ceremonial world of the court or the sprawl of lusty peasants.

I walk through the immense museum looking for shafts of sunlight and watching the swirling dust motes. The light in the Prado is alternately prismatic and dark as a jail. I stand in the sunbeams under the oval skylights and watch the world break up into rainbows. Then I turn a corner into a great, vaulted darkness of nonbeing where an important painting hangs behind a veil, black as an abandoned lighthouse.

■ ■ ■

Last night I heard a woman on the radio talking about her experiences with menopause—she'd had to put her head in the freezer, she felt her body betraying her, etc. It was the unfairness of it: her body was doing this to her too soon; she was old already, in her early forties. "Me too," I said to the radio. "Me too!" I'm already a very old man.

WHITE MEN CAN'T DRUM
—————————■—————————
Sherman Alexie

The New York Times Magazine *first published this essay in 1992.*

L ast year on the local television news, I watched a short feature on a meeting of the Confused White Men chapter in Spokane, Washington. They were all wearing war bonnets and beating drums, more or less. A few of the drums looked as if they might have come from Kmart, and one or two men just beat their chests.

"It's not just the drum," said the leader of the group. "It's the idea of a drum."

I was amazed at the lack of rhythm and laughed, even though I knew I supported a stereotype. But it's true: White men can't drum. They fail to understand that a drum is more than a heartbeat. Sometimes it is the sound of thunder, and many times it just means some Indians want to dance.

As a Native American, I find it ironic that even the most ordinary moments of our lives take on ceremonial importance when adopted by the men's movement. Since Native American men have become role models for the men's movement, I find it vital to explain more fully some of our traditions to avoid any further misinterpretation by white men.

Peyote is not just an excuse to get high.

A Vision Quest cannot be completed in a convention room rented for that purpose.

Native Americans can be lousy fathers and sons, too.

A warrior does not necessarily have to scream to release the animal that is supposed to reside inside every man. A warrior does not necessarily have an animal inside him at all. If there happens to be an animal, it can be a parakeet or a mouse just as easily as it can be a bear or a wolf.

When a white man adopts an animal, he often chooses the largest animal possible. Whether this is because of possible phallic connotations or a kind of spiritual steroid abuse is debatable. I imagine a friend of mine, John, who is white, telling me that his spirit animal is the Tyrannosaurus rex. "But John," I would reply gently, "those things are all dead."

As a "successful" Native American writer, I have been asked to lecture at various men's gatherings. The pay would have been good—just a little more reparation I figured—but I turned down the offers because I couldn't have kept a straight face. The various topics I have been asked to address include "Native Spirituality and Animal Sexuality," "Finding the Inner Child," and "Finding the Lost Father." I figure the next step would be a meeting on "Finding the Inner Hunter When Shopping at the Local Supermarket."

Much of the men's movement focuses on finding things that are lost. I fail to understand how Native American traditions can help in that search, especially considering how much we have lost ourselves. The average life expectancy of a Native American male is about 50 years—middle age for a white man—and that highlights one of the most disturbing aspects of the entire men's movement. It blindly pursues Native solutions to European problems but completely neglects to provide European solutions to Native problems. Despite the fact that the drum still holds spiritual significance, there is not one Indian man alive who has figured our how to cook or eat a drum.

As Adrian C. Louis, the Paiute poet, writes, "We all have to go back with pain in our fat hearts to the place we grew up to grow out of." In their efforts to find their inner child, lost father, or car keys, white males need to go way back. In fact, they need to travel back to the moment when Christopher Columbus landed in America, fell to his knees on the sand and said, "But my mother never loved me."

That is where the real discovery begins.

Still, I have to love the idea of so many white men searching for answers from the same Native traditions that were considered heathen and savage for so long. Perhaps they are popular among white men precisely because they are heathen and savage. After all, these are the same men who look as if they mean to kill each other over Little League baseball games.

I imagine the possibilities for some good Indian humor and sadness mixed all together.

I imagine that Lester FallsApart, a full-blood Spokane, made a small fortune when he gathered glass fragments from shattered reservation car-wreck windshields and sold them to the new-age store as healing crystals.

I imagine that six white men traveled to a powwow and proceeded to set up shop and drum for the Indian dancers, who were stunned and surprised by how much those white men sounded like clumsy opera singers.

I imagine that white men turn to an old Indian man for answers. I imagine Dustin Hoffman. I imagine Kevin Costner. I imagine Daniel Day Lewis. I imagine Robert Bly.

Oh, these men who do all of the acting and none of the reacting.

My friend John and I were sitting in the sweatlodge. No. We were actually sitting in the sauna of the Y.M.C.A. when he turned to me. "Sherman," he said, "considering the chemicals, the stuff we eat, the stuff that hangs in the air, I think the sweatlodge has come to be a purifying ceremony, you know? White men need that, to use an Indian thing to get rid of all the pollution in our bodies. Sort of a spiritual enema."

"That's a lot of bull," I replied savagely.

"What do you mean?"

"I mean that the sweatlodge is a church, not a free clinic."

The men's movement seems designed to appropriate and mutate so many aspects of Native traditions. I worry about the possibilities: men's movement chain stores specializing in portable sweatlodges; the "Indians 'R' Us" commodification of ritual and artifact; white men who continue to show up at powwows in full regalia and dance.

Don't get me wrong. Everyone at a powwow can dance. They all get their chance. Indians have round dances, corn dances, owl dances, intertribal dances, interracial dances, female dances, and yes, even male dances. We all have our places within those dances.

I mean, honestly, no one wants to waltz to a jitterbug song, right?

Perhaps these white men should learn to dance within their own circle before they so rudely jump into other circles. Perhaps white men need to learn more about patience before they can learn what it means to be a man, Indian or otherwise.

Believe me, Arthur Murray was not a Native American.

Last week my friend John called me up on the telephone. Late at night. "Sherman," he said, "I'm afraid. I don't know what it means to be a man. Tell me your secrets. Tell me how to be a warrior."

"Well, John," I said, "a warrior did much more than fight, you know? Warriors fed their families and washed the dishes. Warriors went on Vision Quests and listened to their wives when they went on Vision Quests, too. Warriors picked up their dirty clothes and tried not to watch football games all weekend."

"Really?"

"Really," I said. "Now go back to sleep."

I hung up the phone and turned on the television because I knew it would be a long time before sleep came back to me. I flipped through channels rapidly. There was "F Troop" on one channel, "Dances With Wolves" on another, and they were selling authentic New Mexico Indian jewelry on the shopping channel.

What does it mean to be a man? What does it mean to be Indian? What does it mean to be an Indian man? I press the mute button on the remote control so that everyone can hear the answer.

FROM RACHEL AND HER CHILDREN
————————————■————————————

Jonathan Kozol

This piece is an excerpt from Kozol's 1991 book Rachel and Her Children: Homeless Families in America.

T he first thing that has to be said about the homelessness problem," writes Thomas J. Main in the *New York Times,* "is that solving it is going to take time. There are no quick fixes. . . ." The author criticizes those who wish "to improve allegedly 'damaging' conditions" in the shelters. His concern is less with the conditions in the shelters than with those who live there. "Homeless families," he writes, "seem to have greater behavioral and psychological problems than similar non-homeless families." He speculates that "such families" are "less able to adapt" to a tight housing market than the rest of us.

This is correct. Families whose welfare rental limit is $270 in New York City do not adapt well to a market where the lowest tents begin around $400. Heads of families not on welfare, earning minimum wages of $560, don't adapt successfully to rentals that consume three quarters of their income.

"Can anything be done?" The writer answers that we need more research: "Such work could do for the study of homelessness what the development of the poverty line did for the study of poverty; it does not solve the problem but it imposes a sorely needed discipline . . . on the discussion."

What does it do for someone with no home?

We may wonder if the author would propose such patience if he were, just once, in Holly's situation. We know, of course, that he would not be patient in that case; he would act with the dispatch of any frightened parent. But the distance he has already created by his clinical finality makes it impossible for him to see himself in Holly's situation. This is one reason why I think we ought to view the use of psychiatric labels, especially by those who aren't physicians, with considerable caution. It can too easily create a distance that does more than to alleviate our fears; it may at length permit us to be rather cruel and, even worse, a little smug and comfortable in our detachment.

Labeling a homeless woman as defective ("less able to adapt," to use his words) also leads us to avoid some of the documented causes of her suffering.

"A Cold-Blooded Assault on Poor People." This headline in the *Washington Post* precedes an article by William Raspberry. "Programs for low-income Americans," he writes, represent "just over a tenth of the federal budget," but are "ticketed" for one third of the 1987 Regan budget cuts. "Are appropriations for low-income housing so excessively generous," he asks, "that it makes sense to cut them by a third?" Do indigent people waste so many of our dollars on "imagined illness," he asks, "that a $20 billion cut in Medicaid over the next five years" is justified? "Do housing repair grants, rural housing programs, emergency food assistance, legal services and the Work Incentive Program" represent such foolishly misguided policies that "they should be terminated altogether, as the president proposes?"

The essay by Mr. Main speaks of the "behavioral and psychological problems" of the homeless. What of the behavioral peculiarities of those who place a child in a "pigpen" a few minutes from the White House? What of the behavior of a president who tells us that there is no hunger in the land, while children die of diarrhea caused by malnutrition, or because their mothers were malnourished—both the consequence, at least in part, of policies he has advanced?

"A continuously rising level of child abuse and homelessness," writes New York City Council President Andrew Stein, "is not a force of nature. . . ." This is a point he is compelled to make because we tend so easily to speak of homelessness as an unauthored act: something sad, perhaps the fault of those who have no homes, more likely that of chance. Homelessness "happens," like a flood or fire or a devastating storm—what legal documents, insurance forms, might call "an act of God." But homelessness is not an act of God. It is an act of man. It is done by people like ourselves. It is done to people such as Benjamin.

Phrases such as "no quick fix" do more than to dilute a sense of urgency; they also console us with the incorrect impression that we are, no matter with what hesitation, moving in the right direction. All available statistics make it clear that this is not the case.

"Federal housing assistance programs have been cut a full 64 percent since 1980," according to Manhattan Borough President David Dinkins in a study released in March of 1987, "from $32 billion to $9 billion in the current fiscal year."

In 1996, the Department of Housing and Urban Development subsidized construction of only 25,000 housing units nationwide. When Gerald Ford was president, 200,000 units were constructed. Under President Carter, 300,000 units were constructed.

"For each dollar authorized for national defense in 1980, nineteen cents were authorized for subsidized housing programs," according to another recent study. In 1984, only *three* cents were authorized for housing for each military dollar. This is neither a "quick fix" nor a "slow fix." It is an aggressive fix against the life and health of undefended children.

Mr. Stein poses a challenging scenario. "Imagine the mayor of New York calling an urgent news conference," he writes, "to announce that the crisis of the city's poor children had reached such proportions that he was mobilizing the city's talents for a massive rescue effort. . . ." Some such drastic action, he asserts, is warranted "because our city is threatened by the spreading blight of a poverty even crueler in some ways than that of the Great Depression half a century ago."

We hear this voice of urgency too rarely. Instead, we are told that all these children we have seen—those who cannot concentrate in school because they are too hungry and must rest their heads against their desks to stifle stomach pains, those who sleep in "pigpens," those who travel sixty miles twice a day to glean some bit of education from a school at which they will arrive too late for breakfast and may find themselves denied a lunch because of presidential cuts—must wait a little while and be patient and accept the fact that there is "no quick fix" for those who are too young to vote and whose defeated parents have no lobbyists in Washington or City Hall.

There is a degree of cruelty at stake when those who aren't in pain assume the privilege to counsel moderation in addressing the despair of those who are, or when those who have resources to assuage such pain urge us to be patient in denial of such blessings to the poor. It is still more cruel when those who make such judgments are, as they are bound to be, articulate adults and those who are denied are very frail and very small and very young.

No quick fix, the essayist decrees, for Laura's children. No quick fix for Raisin or for Doby or for Angelina. There is no quick fix for those we do not see as having human claims upon us. We move fast for those we love, more patiently for those we neither love nor know nor feel that we could ever be. This is the great danger in the clinical detachment that allows us to assign the destitute their labels.

The debate persists as to how many homeless people are the former patients of large mental hospitals, deinstitutionalized in the 1970s. Many homeless *individuals* may have been residents of such institutions. In cities like New York, however, where nearly half the homeless people are small children, with an average age of six, such suppositions obviously make little sense. Six-year-olds were not deinstitutionalized before their birth. Their parents, with an average age of twenty-seven, are not likely to have been the residents of mental hospitals when they were still teenagers. But there is a reason for the repetition of such arguments in face of countervailing facts. In a sense, when we refer to "institutions"—those from which we think some of the homeless come, those to which we think they ought to be consigned—we are creating a new institution of our own: the abstract institution of an airtight capsule ("underclass," "behavioral problem," "nonadaptive" or "psychotic") that will not allow their lives to touch our own. Few decent people or responsible physicians wish to do this; but the risk is there. The homeless are a nightmare. Holly's story is a nightmare. It is natural to fear and try to banish nightmares. It is not natural to try to banish human beings.

The distancing we have observed receives its most extreme expression in the use of language such as "undeserving." This is, in some sense, the ultimate act of disaffiliation and the most decisive means of placing all these families and their children in a category where they can't intrude upon our dreams.

A classic nineteenth-century distinction draws the line between two categories of the poor: those who are "fit" to survive, and those who aren't. Of the latter, Herbert Spencer wrote: "The whole effort of nature is to get rich of such, to clear the world of them and make room for better." Few people would use such words today; but several prominent authors do accept the basic notion of a line between two categories of the indigent: those who merit something in the way of mercy or forgiveness, those who don't. If such a distinction may be made at all without some injury to our humanity, we need at least to ask if those who fall into the former category (the "deserving") have deserved—and, if so, how they have deserved—precisely the abysmal treatment they receive.

Holly and Benjamin presumably are two of the deserving. Annie Harrington and Gwen and Mr. Allesandro and their children may also be regarded as deserving. If they are, I should think that they deserve a little better than they get. It is true that they receive "a free lunch," holidays and weekends not included. They also get "a free ride" if they can survive for thirty months within the Martinique Hotel in order to be eligible to use a public van to search the city for apartments. This much is permitted the deserving. What, then, of the ones who are the less deserving? The deserving group receives so little that it isn't easy to imagine what remains to be denied. Life itself, perhaps, may be denied. That would then become the final penalty for failure.

Even if some of us feel comfortable with such extreme distinctions and are not embarrassed to wield quite so sharp a blade, will we not feel hesitant to let that blade fall also on the child of the adult who has been found lacking? For an answer to this question, we may listen to the words of a conservative author named Charles Murray. "The notion," he writes, is to reduce the reproduction of poor children by intensifying the unpleasantness of circumstances that precede their birth, rendering "unwed parenthood," in Murray's words, "contemptible." But how does one apply this stigma to the parent without savaging the child too? Undesirable existence is the child of contemptible conception One word of contagion necessarily entails the next. The social worker does not enter into dialogue with Benjamin, but with his mother. If the mother is contaminated in his eyes, the child's likelihood of finding a benign reception in the world is undermined as well.

KEEPING CLOSE TO HOME: CLASS AND EDUCATION

—————————•—————————

bell hooks

This essay is an excerpt from hooks's 1989 book Talking Back: Thinking Feminist, Thinking Black.

We are both awake in the almost dark of 5 A.M. Everyone else is sound asleep. Mama asks the usual questions. Telling me to look around, make sure I have everything, scolding me because I am uncertain about the actual time the bus arrives. By 5:30 we are waiting outside the closed station. Alone together, we have a chance to really talk. Mama begins.

Angry with her children, especially the ones who whisper behind her back, she says bitterly, "Your childhood could not have been that bad. You were fed and clothed. You did not have to do without—that's more than a lot of folks have and I just can't stand the way y'all go on." The hurt in her voice saddens me. I have always wanted to protect mama from hurt, to ease her burdens. Now I am part of what troubles. Confronting me, she says accusingly, "It's not just the other children. You talk too much about the past. You don't just listen." And I do talk. Worse, I write about it.

Mama has always come to each of her children seeking different responses. With me she expresses the disappointment, hurt, and anger of betrayal: anger that her children are so critical, that we can't even have the sense to like the presents she sends. She says, "From now on there will be no presents. I'll just stick some money in a little envelope the way the rest of you do. Nobody wants criticism. Everybody can criticize me but I am supposed to say nothing." When I try to talk, my voice sounds like a twelve year old. When I try to talk, she speaks louder, interrupting me, even though she has said repeatedly, "Explain it to me, this talk about the past." I struggle to return to my thirty-five year old self so that she will know by the sound of my voice that we are two women talking together. It is only when I state firmly in my very adult voice, "Mama, you are not listening," that she becomes quiet. She waits. Now that I have her attention, I fear that my explanations will be lame, inadequate. "Mama," I begin, "people usually go to therapy because they feel hurt inside, because they have pain that will not stop, like a wound that continually breaks open, that does not heal. And often these hurts, that pain has to do with things that have happened in the past, sometimes in childhood, often in childhood, or things that we believe happened." She wants to know, "What hurts, what hurts are you talking about?" "Mom, I can't answer that. I can't speak for all of us, the hurts are different for everybody. But the point is you try to make the hurt better, to heal it, by understanding how it came to be. And I know you feel mad when we say something happened or hurt that you don't remember being that way, but the past isn't like that, we don't have the same memory of it. We remember things differently. You know that. And sometimes folk feel hurt about stuff and you just don't know or didn't realize it, and they need to talk about it. Surely you understand the need to talk about it."

Our conversation is interrupted by the sight of my uncle walking across the park toward us. We stop to watch him. He is on his way to work dressed in a familiar blue suit. They look alike, these two who rarely discuss the past. This interruption makes me think about life in a small town. You always see someone you know. Interruptions, intrusions are part of daily life. Privacy is difficult to maintain. We leave our private space in the car to greet him. After the hug and kiss he has given me every year since I was born, they talk about the day's funerals. In the distance the bus approaches. He walks away knowing that they will see each other later. Just before I board the bus I turn staring into my mother's face. I am momentarily back in time, seeing myself eighteen years ago, at this same bus stop, staring into my mother's face, continually turning back, waving farewell as I returned to college—that experience which first took me away from our town, from family. Departing was as painful then as it is now. Each movement away makes return harder. Each separation intensifies distance, both physical and emotional.

To a southern black girl from a working-class background who had never been on a city bus, who had never stepped on an escalator, who had never travelled by plane, leaving the comfortable confines of a small town Kentucky life to attend Stanford University was not just frightening; it was utterly painful. My parents had not been delighted that I had been accepted and adamantly opposed my going so far from home. At the time, I did not see their opposition as an expression of their fear that they would lose me forever. Like many working-class folks, they feared what college education might do to their children's minds even as they unenthusiastically acknowledged its importance. They did not understand why I could not attend a college nearby, an all-black college. To them, any college would do. I would graduate, become a school teacher, make a decent living and a good marriage. And even though they reluctantly and skeptically supported my educational endeavors, they also subjected them to constant harsh and bitter critique. It is difficult for me to talk about my parents and their impact on me because they have always felt wary, ambivalent, mistrusting of my intellectual aspirations even as they have been caring and supportive. I want to speak about these contradictions because sorting through them, seeking resolution and reconciliation has been important to me both as it affects my development as a writer, my effort to be fully self-realized, and my longing to remain close to the family and community that provided the groundwork for much of my thinking, writing, and being.

Studying at Stanford, I began to think seriously about class differences. To be materially underprivileged at a university where most folks (with the exception of workers) are materially privileged provokes such thought. Class differences were boundaries no one wanted to face or talk about. It was easier to downplay them, to act as though we were all from privileged backgrounds, to work around them, to confront them privately in the solitude of one's room, or to pretend that just being chosen to study at such an institution meant that those of us who did not come from privilege were already in transition toward privilege. To not long for such transition marked one as rebellious, as unlikely to succeed. It was a kind of treason not to believe that it was better to be identified with the world of material privilege than with the world of the working class, the poor. No wonder our working-class parents from poor backgrounds feared our entry into such a world, intuiting perhaps that we might learn to be ashamed of where we had come from, that we might never return home, or come back only to lord it over them.

Though I hung with students who were supposedly radical and chic, we did not discuss class. I talked to no one about the sources of my shame, how it hurt me to witness the contempt shown the brown-skinned Filipina maids who cleaned our rooms, or later my concern about the $100 a month I paid for a room off-campus which was more than half of what my parents paid for rent. I talked to no one about my efforts to save money, to send a little something home. Yet these class realities separated me from fellow students. We were moving in different directions. I did not intend to forget my class background or alter my class allegiance. And even though I received an education designed to provide me with a bourgeois sensibility, passive acquiescence was not my only option. I knew that I could resist. I could rebel. I could shape the direction and focus of the various forms of knowledge available to me. Even though I sometimes envied and longed for greater material advantages (particularly at vacation times when I would be one of few if any students remaining in the dormitory because there was no money for travel), I did not share the sensibility and values of my peers. That was important—class was not just about money; it was about values which showed and determined behavior. While I often needed more money, I never needed a new set of beliefs and values. For example, I was profoundly shocked and disturbed when peers would talk about their parents without respect, or would even say that they hated their parents. This was especially troubling to me when it seemed that these parents were caring and concerned. It was often explained to me that such hatred was "healthy and normal." To my white, middle-class California roommate, I explained the way we were taught to value our parents and their care, to understand that they were obligated to give us care. She would always shake her head, laughing all the while, and say, "Missy, you will learn that it's different here, that we think differently." She was right. Soon, I lived alone, like the one Mormon student who kept to himself as he made a concentrated effort to remain true to his religious beliefs and values. Later in graduate school I found that classmates believed "lower class" people had no beliefs and values. I was silent in such discussions, disgusted by their ignorance.

Carol Stack's anthropological study, *All Our Kin,* was one of the first books I read which confirmed my experiential understanding that within black culture (especially among the working class and poor, particularly in southern states), a value system emerged that was counter-hegemonic, that challenged notions of individualism and private property so important to the maintenance of white-supremacist, capitalist patriarchy. Black folk created in marginal spaces a world of community and collectivity where resources were shared. In the preface to *Feminist Theory: from margin to center,* I talked about how the point of difference, this marginality, can be the space for the formation of an oppositional world view. That world view must be articulated, named if it is to provide a sustained blueprint for change. Unfortunately, there has existed no consistent framework for such naming. Consequently both the experience of this difference and documentation of it (when it occurs) gradually loses presence and meaning.

Much of what Stack documented about the "culture of poverty," for example, would not describe interactions among most black poor today irrespective of geographical setting. Since the black people she described did not acknowledge (if they recognized it in theoretical terms) the oppositional value of their world view, apparently seeing it more as a survival strategy determined less by conscious efforts to oppose oppressive race and class biases than by circumstance, they did not attempt to establish a framework to transmit their beliefs and values from generation to generation. When circumstances changed, values altered. Efforts to assimilate the values and beliefs of privileged white people, presented through media like television, undermine and destroy potential structures of opposition.

Increasingly, young black people are encouraged by the dominant culture (and by those black people who internalize the values of this hegemony) to believe that assimilation is the only possible way to survive, to succeed. Without the framework of an organized civil rights or black resistance struggle, individual and collective efforts at black liberation that focus on the primacy of self-definition and self-determination often go unrecognized. It is crucial that those among us who resist and rebel, who survive and succeed, speak openly and honestly about our lives and the nature of our personal struggles, the means by which we resolve and reconcile contradictions. This is no easy task. Within the educational institutions where we learn to develop and strengthen our writing and analytical skills, we also learn to think, write, and talk in a manner that shifts attention away from personal experience. Yet if we are to reach our people and all people, if we are to remain connected (especially those of us whose familial backgrounds are poor and working-class), we must understand that the telling of one's personal story provides a meaningful example, a way for folks to identify and connect.

Combining personal with critical analysis and theoretical perspectives can engage listeners who might otherwise feel estranged, alienated. To speak simply with language that is accessible to as many folks as possible is also important. Speaking about one's personal experience or speaking with simple language is often considered by academics and/or intellectuals (irrespective of their political inclinations) to be a sign of intellectual weakness or even anti-intellectualism. Lately, when I speak, I do not stand in place—reading my paper, making little or no eye contact with audiences—but instead make eye contact, talk extemporaneously, digress, and address the audience directly. I have been told that people assume I am not prepared, that I am anti-intellectual, unprofessional (a concept that has everything to do with class as it determines actions and behavior), or that I am reinforcing the stereotype of black as non-theoretical and gutsy.

Such criticism was raised recently by fellow feminist scholars after a talk I gave at Northwestern University at a conference on "Gender, Culture, Politics" to an audience that was mainly students and academics. I deliberately chose to speak in a very basic way, thinking especially about the few community folks who had come to hear me. Weeks later, KumKum Sangari, a fellow participant who shared with me what was said when I was no longer present, and I engaged in quite rigorous critical dialogue about the way my presentation had been perceived primarily by privileged white female academics. She was concerned that I not mask my knowledge of theory, that I not appear anti-intellectual. Her critique compelled me to articulate concerns that I am often silent about with colleagues. I spoke about class allegiance and revolutionary commitments, explaining that it was disturbing to me that intellectual radicals who speak about transforming society, ending the domination of race, sex, class, cannot break with behavior patterns that reinforce and perpetuate domination, or continue to use as their sole reference point how we might be or are perceived by those who dominate, whether or not we gain their acceptance and approval.

This is a primary contradiction which raises the issue of whether or not the academic setting is a place where one can be truly radical or subversive. Concurrently, the use of a language and style of presentation that alienates most folks who are not also academically trained reinforces the notion that the academic world is separate from real life, that everyday world where we constantly adjust our language and behavior to meet diverse needs. The academic setting is separate only when we work to make it so. It is a false dichotomy which suggests that academics and/or intellectuals can only speak to one another, that we cannot hope to speak with the masses. What is true is that we make choices, that we choose our audiences, that we choose voices to hear and voices to silence. If I do not speak in a language that can be understood, then there is little chance for dialogue. This issue of language and behavior is a central contradiction all radical intellectuals, particularly those who are members of oppressed groups, must continually confront and work to resolve. One of the clear and present dangers that exists when we move outside our class of origin, our collective ethnic experience, and enter hierarchical institutions which daily reinforce domination by race, sex, and class, is that we gradually assume a mindset similar to those who dominate and oppress, that we lose critical consciousness because it is not reinforced or affirmed by the environment. We must be ever vigilant. It is important that we know who we are speaking to, who we most want to hear us, who we most long to move, motivate, and touch with our words.

When I first came to New Haven to teach at Yale, I was truly surprised by the marked class divisions between black folks—students and professors—who identify with Yale and those black folks who work at Yale or in surrounding communities. Style of dress and self-presentation are most often the central markers of one's position. I soon learned that the black folks who spoke on the street were likely to be part of the black community and those who carefully shifted their glance were likely to be associated with Yale. Walking with a black female colleague one day, I spoke to practically every black person in sight (a gesture which reflects my upbringing), an action which disturbed my companion. Since I addressed black folk who were clearly not associated with Yale, she wanted to know whether or not I knew them. That was funny to me. "Of course not," I answered. Yet when I thought about it seriously, I realized that in a deep way, I knew them for they, and not my companion or most of my colleagues at Yale, resemble my family. Later that year, in a black women's support group I started for undergraduates, students from poor backgrounds spoke about the shame they sometimes feel when faced with the reality of their connection to working-class and poor black people. One student confessed that her father is a street person, addicted to drugs, someone who begs from passersby. She, like other Yale students, turns away from street people often, sometimes showing anger or contempt; she hasn't wanted anyone to know that she was related to this kind of person. She struggles with this, wanting to find a way to acknowledge and affirm this reality, to claim this connection. The group asked me and one another what we [should] do to remain connected, to honor the bonds we have with working-class and poor people even as our class experience alters.

Maintaining connections with family and community across class boundaries demands more than just summary recall of where one's roots are, where one comes from. It requires knowing, naming, and being ever-mindful of those aspects of one's past that have enabled and do enable one's self-development in the present, that sustain and support, that enrich. One must also honestly confront barriers that do exist, aspects of that past that do diminish. My parents' ambivalence about my love for reading led to intense conflict. They (especially my mother) would work to ensure that I had access to books, but would threaten to burn the books or throw them away if I did not conform to other expectations. Or they would insist that reading too much would drive me insane. Their ambivalence nurtured in me a like uncertainty about the value and significance of intellectual endeavor which took years for me to unlearn. While this aspect of our class reality was one that wounded and diminished, their vigilant insistence that being smart did not make me a "better" or "superior" person (which often got on my nerves because I think I wanted to have that sense that it did indeed set me apart, make me better) made a profound impression. From them I learned to value and respect various skills and talents folk might have, not just to value people who read books and talk about ideas. They and my grandparents might say about somebody, "Now he don't read nor write a lick, but he can tell a story," or as my grandmother would say, "call out the hell in words."

Empty romanticization of poor or working-class backgrounds undermines the possibility of true connection. Such connection is based on understanding difference in experience and perspective and working to mediate and negotiate these terrains. Language is a crucial issue for folk whose movement outside the boundaries of poor and working-class backgrounds changes the nature and direction of their speech. Coming to Stanford with my own version of a Kentucky accent, which I think of always as a strong sound quite different from Tennessee or Georgia speech, I learned to speak differently while maintaining the speech of my region, the sound of my family and community. This was of course much easier to keep up when I returned home to stay often. In recent years, I have endeavored to use various speaking styles in the classroom as a teacher and find it disconcerts those who feel that the use of a particular patois excludes them as listeners, even if there is translation into the usual, acceptable mode of speech. Learning to listen to different voices, hearing different speech challenges the notion that we must all assimilate—share a single, similar talk—in educational institutions. Language reflects the culture from which we emerge. To deny ourselves daily use of speech patterns that are common and familiar, that embody the unique and distinctive aspect of our self is one of the ways we become estranged and alienated from our past. It is important for us to have as many languages on hand as we can know or learn. It is important for those of us who are black, who speak in particular patois as well as standard English, to express ourselves in both ways.

Often I tell students from poor and working-class backgrounds that if you believe what you have learned and are learning in schools and universities separates you from your past, this is precisely what will happen. It is important to stand firm in the conviction that nothing can truly separate us from our pasts when we nurture and cherish that connection. An important strategy for maintaining contact is ongoing acknowledgment of the primacy of one's past, of one's background, affirming the reality that such bonds are not severed automatically solely because one enters a new environment or moves toward a different class experience.

Again, I do not wish to romanticize this effort, to dismiss the reality of conflict and contradiction. During my time at Stanford, I did go through a period of more than a year when I did not return home. That period was one where I felt that it was simply too difficult to mesh my profoundly disparate realities. Critical reflection about the choice I was making, particularly about why I felt a choice had to be made, pulled me through this difficult time. Luckily I recognized that the insistence on choosing between the world of family and community and the new world of privileged white people and privileged ways of knowing was imposed upon me by the outside. It is as though a mythical contract had been signed somewhere which demanded of us black folks that once we entered these spheres we would immediately give up all vestiges of our underprivileged past. It was my responsibility to formulate a way of being that would allow me to participate fully in my new environment while integrating and maintaining aspects of the old.

One of the most tragic manifestations of the pressure black people feel to assimilate is expressed in the internalization of racist perspectives. I was shocked and saddened when I first heard black professors at Stanford downgrade and express contempt for black students, expecting us to do poorly, refusing to establish nurturing bonds. At every university I have attended as a student or worked at as a teacher, I have heard similar attitudes expressed with little or no understanding of factors that might prevent brilliant black students from performing to their full capability. Within universities, there are few educational and social spaces where students who wish to affirm positive ties to ethnicity—to blackness, to working-class backgrounds—can receive affirmation and support. Ideologically, the message is clear—assimilation is the way to gain acceptance and approval from those in power.

Many white people enthusiastically supported Richard Rodriguez's vehement contention in his autobiography, *Hunger of Memory*, that attempts to maintain ties with his Chicano background impeded his progress, that he had to sever ties with community and kin to succeed at Stanford and in the larger world, that family language, in his case Spanish, had to be made secondary or discarded. If the terms of success as defined by the standards of ruling groups within white-supremacist, capitalist patriarchy are the only standards that exist, then assimilation is indeed necessary. But they are not. Even in the face of powerful structures of domination, it remains possible for each of us, especially those of us who are members of oppressed and/or exploited groups as well as those radical visionaries who may have race, class, and sex privilege, to define and determine alternative standards, to decide on the nature and extent of compromise. Standards by which one's success is measured, whether student or professor, are quite different from those of us who wish to resist reinforcing the domination of race, sex, and class, who work to maintain and strengthen our ties with the oppressed, with those who lack material privilege, with our families who are poor and working-class.

When I wrote my first book, *Ain't I a Woman: black women and feminism*, the issue of class and its relationship to who one's reading audience might be came up for me around my decision not to use footnotes, for which I have been sharply criticized. I told people that my concern was that footnotes set class boundaries for readers, determining who a book is for. I was shocked that many academic folks scoffed at this idea. I shared that I went into working-class black communities as well as talked with family and friends to survey whether or not they ever read books with footnotes and found that they did not. A few did not know what they were, but most folks saw them as indicating that a book was for college-educated people. These responses influenced my decision. When some of my more radical, college-educated friends freaked out about the absence of footnotes, I seriously questioned how we could ever imagine revolutionary transformation of society if such a small shift in direction could be viewed as threatening. Of course, many folks warned that the absence of footnotes would make the work less credible in academic circles. This information also highlighted the way in which class informs our choices. Certainly I did feel that choosing to use simple language, absence of footnotes, etc. would mean I was jeopardizing the possibility of being taken seriously in academic circles but then this was a political matter and a political decision. It utterly delights me that this has proven not to be the case and that the book is read by many academics as well as by people who are not college-educated.

Always our first response when we are motivated to conform or compromise within structures that reinforce domination must be to engage in critical reflection. Only by challenging ourselves to push against oppressive boundaries do we make the radical alternative possible, expanding the realm and scope of critical inquiry. Unless we share radical strategies, ways of rethinking and revisioning with students, with kin and community, with a larger audience, we risk perpetuating the stereotype that we succeed because we are the exception, different from the rest of our people. Since I left home and entered college, I am often asked, usually by white people, if my sisters and brothers are also high achievers. At the root of this question is the longing for reinforcement of the belief in "the exception" which enables race, sex, and class biases to remain intact. I am careful to separate what it means to be exceptional from a notion of "the exception."

Frequently I hear smart black folks, from poor and working-class backgrounds, stressing their frustration that at times family and community do not recognize that they are exceptional. Absence of positive affirmation clearly diminishes the longing to excel in academic endeavors. Yet it is important to distinguish between the absence of basic positive affirmation and the longing for continued reinforcement that we are special. Usually liberal white folks will willingly offer continual reinforcement of us as exceptions—as special. This can be both patronizing and very seductive. Since we often work in situations where we are isolated from other black folks, we can easily begin to feel that encouragement from white people is the primary or only source of support and recognition. Given the internalization of racism, it is easy to view this support as more validating and legitimizing than similar support from black people. Still, nothing takes the place of being valued and appreciated by one's own, by one's family and community. We share a mutual and reciprocal responsibility for affirming one another's successes. Sometimes we have to talk to our folks about the fact that we need their ongoing support and affirmation, that it is unique and special to us. In some cases we may never receive desired recognition and acknowledgment of specific achievements from kin. Rather than seeing this as a basis for estrangement, for severing connection, it is useful to explore other sources of nourishment and support.

I do not know that my mother's mother ever acknowledged my college education except to ask me once, "How can you live so far away from your people?" Yet she gave me sources of affirmation and nourishment, sharing the legacy of her quilt-making, of family history, of her incredible way with words. Recently, when our father retired after more than thirty years of work as a janitor, I wanted to pay tribute to this experience, to identify links between his work and my own as writer and teacher. Reflecting on our family past, I recalled ways he had been an impressive example of diligence and hard work, approaching tasks with a seriousness of concentration I work to mirror and develop, with a discipline I struggle to maintain. Sharing these thoughts with him keeps us connected, nurtures our respect for each other, maintaining a space, however large or small, where we can talk.

Open, honest communication is the most important way we maintain relationships with kin and community as our class experience and backgrounds change. It is as vital as the sharing of resources. Often financial assistance is given in circumstances where there is no meaningful contact. However helpful, this can also be an expression of estrangement and alienation. Communication between black folks from various experiences of material privilege was much easier when we were all in segregated communities sharing common experiences in relation to social institutions. Without this grounding, we must work to maintain ties, connection. We must assume greater responsibility for making and maintaining contact, connections that can shape our intellectual visions and inform our radical commitments.

The most powerful resource any of us can have as we study and teach in university settings is full understanding and appreciation of the richness, beauty, and primacy of our familial and community backgrounds. Maintaining awareness of class differences, nurturing ties with the poor and working-class people who are our most intimate kin, our comrades in struggle, transforms and enriches our intellectual experience. Education as the practice of freedom becomes not a force which fragments or separates, but one that brings us closer, expanding our definitions of home and community.

SPIKES AND SLOW WAVES

Caroline Patterson

The literary journal Epoch *first published this essay in 1995.*

I sat at the kitchen table, eating a muffin, surrounded by my five best friends. It was the morning after a slumber party and I had had three hours of sleep, but bursts of energy seemed to collect and explode inside me.

Last night in a dark bedroom we talked about what we hoped for and what we dreamed about; this morning, in a bright kitchen, we were trying to get one another to confess our crushes. My friends turned to me. I smiled and drew a finger across my lips. "C'mon," Sarah said, her eyes glittering. "You can tell *us*."

I looked at them and began to talk. Sentences flew out of my mouth, distant as if they belonged to someone else, but as soon as I said them, I realized they were thoughts I had had for a long, long time. I felt clear, all-powerful, like I could hear and understand everything almost before it was said. Warmth flooded my hands and legs in an all-encompassing, almost sexual breath, my skin felt tight, and a balloon of happiness floated up from my heart to clog my throat.

Then it burst and I travelled to the other side, to the hollow sadness that permeated so many of my days, but this time the sadness seemed to shrink the room. I listened to one conversation, then another, but the sentences scooted out before I could fasten my mind on them, like small animals scattering before a giant's footstep. "Alone. Like. Want." The words rose up from the table, disconnected and senseless. My friends' faces looked round and sweaty. Glitter sparkled at the edge of my vision, but when I turned to it, it disappeared.

The things I saw—the copper pots over the stove, Paula coming across the kitchen with a basket of muffins, the field of snow where a lone horse stood, his back to the wind—separated into a series of stills that flipped from one to the other, like an old motion picture. Sound hummed and swelled. Something crawled up my neck and into my brain. The right side of my face went numb. The images dissolved, and I saw nothing but a scattering of salt across the table, the swirled grain of the wood.

I told myself I needed good, fresh air. I drew a breath. The world vanished.

"You fainted," my mother said, smoothing back the hair from my forehead as I lay on the couch. I wondered how she got here and why everyone stood whispering over me. My arms and legs were limp, like someone had wrung the starch from them. My stomach clenched. I turned away, vomited.

"I'm sorry," I said to the faces. Tears twisted up inside me, and I swallowed them back.

"It's okay," someone said. "We're your friends."

I was too tired to figure out who said this. Too tired to care. I pulled the blanket up over me. My mother gathered my things, and helped me stand. As we walked across the white carpet, someone patted my back. "Take it easy," someone else said, her voice quiet as if she were speaking to a child. My legs wobbled at the door, then we squeezed through the frame, and walked slowly to the car.

"I fainted," I told everyone at school the next week. With the world once more beneath my feet, I relished the drama. I had always loved books about sickly girls and miraculous recoveries and I craved the sympathy elicited by broken bones and rheumatic fever. Once, when my best friends were angry with me, I jumped again and again from the playhouse roof, trying to break a bone, but I couldn't make myself fall on my arm. I loved the idea that I was delicate, for I had always recovered from measles and strep throats with an infuriating swiftness. I was always healthy, durable, round-faced me.

"You turned blue and your arms and legs thrashed around," my friend Sally told me later. She fixed her frank, blue eyes on me. "You can't tell me," she cocked an arm on her hip, "that that was a faint."

Sally was right. What I have is epilepsy, what ancients called the "sacred illness," a condition brought on by an excessive electrical discharge in the brain. It is a condition I share with Napoleon, Van Gogh, Dostoyevsky, and 2.5 million other Americans. Some have petit mal seizures—conditions where they hear voices, songs, see colors, detect strong scents or simply wring their hands; some have tics or are paralyzed by a inexplicable feeling of terror or "daymares," as a friend of mine called them.

I have grand mal seizures or, in the neurologist's lingo, generalized tonic-clonic seizures. I lose consciousness, fall out of the world and begin to convulse. In the Vogul tribe of Siberia, I would have been a shaman. In the Andaman Islands, I would have been a magician. In Salem, Massachusetts, they would have drowned me as a witch. In eighteenth-century Europe, I would have been locked up in an insane asylum or in my family's house as the daughter who had "spells," "fits," or "falling sickness." In late 1970s America, I was an object of curiosity and I loved it.

That spring of 1973, I didn't know what I had. I was tested for diabetes, low blood sugar, epilepsy, and meningitis. I drank thick sugary drinks, gave vials of blood, watched as pink and green curlers were glued to my head or huge needles were inserted into my spine and I endured the resulting pimples, sore arms, sticky hair and blinding headaches with a cheerful stoicism. As doctors, nurses, and technicians pondered my charts and poked and prodded me, I imagined myself a dimestore heroine struck down by illness, ripe for miraculous recovery. I was to the white-jackets what I was to myself: a giant, unsolvable mystery.

The tests confirmed this: the initial results were negative. Doctors shook their heads, checked their charts, suggested more tests.

During this time, I had another seizure in an English class. I was shaky and afraid to meet my classmates' faces the next day, but as soon as my friends rushed up to me, breathless, saying, "How are you?" "What happened?" a curious pride swelled up inside me, and bore me up through the rest of the day.

Six months later at Mayo Clinic, I was put through more tests—head X-rays, a CAT scan, and another more elaborate EEG, where, wired like the bride of Frankenstein, I watched the small arm of the EEG waver and dance across graph paper, charting the lift and fall of my brain waves. I counted, tapped my feet, drew breath after breath, and passed out. As a nurse wheeled me out of the office, I spied my electro-encephalogram on the technician's desk. There above the black spikes and slow waves, the classic brain wave pattern of the epileptic, was my name: Caroline Patterson. And below it, stamped in bright red ink, was the word: "ABNORMAL."

"You can do most things," the doctor told me as my parents and I sat in his glaring white office. "But you might want to tell the people around you—your teachers, your friends, your coaches—about your condition. It's up to you."

"My theory, doctor," my father said, "is that people are just basically curious." As he crossed his legs, his pants rode up to expose the flesh-colored plastic of his wooden leg. "That's what I've found with my cancer. I just *tell* people about it. And you know what? If you tell them, then they haven't got anything over you."

"That's true," the doctor said, and turned to me. "You can ski, play sports, run, hike, even drive."

"Of course she can," my mother said, her voice clipped and resolute. She was anxious for this to be over. She didn't believe in succumbing to illness. It was something to be fought with vigor and tight-lipped determination. It was something to be conquered. "She's just fine. She's just like anybody else."

"But you do need to take special caution," the doctor said, looking over his glasses at me. "Don't, for example, swim alone."

Just tell them. Be honest. You're just like anybody else. I followed my parent's advice for the next ten years. I studied, partied, skied, drove, gave recitals—and had the fits of depression and odd, bursting joys of any young woman. I told people about my epilepsy, I did not try to hide it, and the effects were surprising, even heartbreaking. Once, upon mentioning it, the daughter of a casual acquaintance caught my arm as I walked out of the room. "I have epilepsy, too," she whispered, her eyes dark. Then she told me that when she was diagnosed, her mother had sat on one side of the hospital room crying uncontrollably, while her father stood in the door saying, "Well it's obvious what side of the family this comes from."

My life was fairly ordinary, except that at any moment I could suddenly fall out from the real world, my hum-drum existence skewed, and I would be transported from one moment to the next. One minute I'd be at school or in a restaurant; the next I'd wake up as my mother, doctor, or ambulance driver touched my arm. "You're all right," they'd say. "Rest. Everything's okay now."

Younger children rode roller coasters or the Zipper, teenagers drove fast, drank hard or took hallucinogens to release them, for a moment, from the tedious process of growing up. To release them from laws of gravity or perception and carry them into a dimension where the air was alive with color and movement. I had seizures. What we had in common was the seductive release into what our blood told us we wanted—spine-tingling speed and the exhilaration of approaching, then becoming out of control.

This is not to say that seizures were fun. The limpness, the exhaustion, the vomiting, and the "feeling of terrible guilt" Dostoyevsky describes, of having failed some invisible test of normalcy, were not fun at all. But, over and over again, my epilepsy and I played a game of cat-and-mouse. Somedays I'd get no sleep, drink too much, and I'd be fine. I'd win. Other days, the epilepsy pounced.

I believed that the world would take care of me, and more often than not, it did. After a Washington D.C. visit, I tore across Union Station, my pack thumping my back, bolting past grim-faced commuters, porters, and beggars holding out their rattling cups. As I approached my train, the doors closed, wheels churned, and in the corner of my eyes, the air sparkled.

I woke in the emergency room of the George Washington Hospital. A doctor stood over me. "You had a seizure," he said. "Shit," I said and sat up. "Where's my stuff?" He laughed. "You need to rest." He put his hand on my shoulder. "I suspect that's advice you don't take too often." I lay back on the bed and smiled at his tanned face and his beautiful white teeth. For a minute, I wanted to marry him. "Your pack's at the station. Just take it slow," he said and shut the door.

When I got back to the station, I slowly made my way to the porter's desk. "You're the one had the fits," the old porter said. "Now, we got your pack, don't worry yourself one bit." His voice was deep and kind and it unhinged me. "Thank you. This was nice of you," I said, my throat tight as I reached for my backpack. He insisted on carrying it for me. I was too exhausted to refuse. As we made our way to the platform, he walked alongside me. "Now don't you worry, little lady," he said. "You'll make that train. Don't you hurry one little bit."

One night I was driving north from Boston, and at the New Hampshire border, I stopped at a state information center to use the restroom. As I headed outside, along the wall-sized photographs of covered bridges and flaming forests, the greying, bulb-nosed attendant looked up at me and said, "Do you believe in God?" I shrugged and said, "Yes, I guess so." A few hours before a young woman told him she did not believe there was a God. He was sincerely distressed about this. "How could she not believe in God?" he kept asking me as I edged toward the door. "What would she have left?" As I put my hand on the door handle, he asked my name. When I told him, he said, "Well I'll say a prayer for you, Caroline."

Three days later, police lights swirled across my windshield, and from far away I could hear the squawk of a radio, a knock at my window. "You all right?" the officer said, leaning close enough to smell my breath as snow blew into the car. "You have a fit or something?" "I'm fine," I said, trying to inject some life in my voice. "I must have hit black ice." The words felt thick and clotted my tongue. I didn't want to tell him I'd had a seizure because I'd lose my insurance. "You're damn lucky you hit that snowbank," the policeman said as he wrote out his citation. "Otherwise you'd be dead."

I crept home along the interstate's slow lane, shaken and terrified, protected by a stranger's prayers.

In the fall of 1978, I was in an auto mechanics class at the Alaska Skills Center in Seward, learning how to change tires, fix starter motors, and adjust the balance on carburetors. Three months earlier, I had graduated from Amherst College in American Studies. That fall I sat in a white-walled classroom, the air sharp with the smells of grease and metal and cigarette smoke surrounded by nine men, all of us in blue coveralls.

As we waited for class to begin, the men joked back and forth. "Hey Nelson," someone shouted. "Gonna watch a movie?" "Fuck you," Nelson shouted back. The instructor came in, wiping his greasy hands on a towel. He was in blue coveralls too, but his name, "Ken" was stitched on his breast pocket. "All right, you guys," he said, and walked over to the projector. "Shut your traps. It's time you learned something."

The film began to roll. We watched men fall from buildings, reel back from electric shocks. A man ran his hand through a saw, and blood gushed from the deep wound. Another man groaned and held his left leg. Below his hand, a bone, white and naked, jutted out from the bloody skin. "These are victims of industrial accidents," said the crewcut narrator as he looked squarely at us. "And *you've* got to be prepared to deal with them." As we watched in stony silence, the narrator told us how to make tourniquets and splint broken bones in a voice as calm as if he were giving us the weather.

Then a woman dressed in a white hospital gown looked out at the camera with dark, lifeless eyes. A black headpiece was fitted over her head. "This was part of a scientific experiment," the narrator cooed, "so that we may learn more about that widely misunderstood condition called epilepsy." As the electric shock coursed through her body, she stiffened, her eyes rolled back, she choked and gargled. Her limbs jerked and twitched. As she writhed, her hands shook in front of her.

This was repeated again and again with one sad-eyed patient after another. As we watched their heads loll back and their limbs quiver, some guys in the classroom started to titter. Someone shouted, "Looks like Nelson after a few sixpacks!" "Fuck you," Nelson said. My hands began to shake. As the announcer droned on about sticking rulers in the patient's mouths, and holding their limbs down to keep them from thrashing, I got up and half-ran for the door. I made it out of the room and into the shop, where surrounded by half-built starter motors and disassembled tires, I began to cry.

I was not upset by the laughter of my classmates. In many ways, the film was so cruel, I too felt a hysterical need to laugh. What upset me, more than anything, was the realization that in those moments when my world went blank, this was happening to me. I wasn't just absent from the world for a while: I was jerking, twitching, peeing my pants, and biting my tongue. I had known this before in an abstract way, but until this moment, it had never been real. I had never really believed I existed in those times that for me were blank. Because they didn't exist for me, I believed they didn't exist for anyone. Suddenly, a seizure was not a moment of simple transport. It was a moment of where—in front of classmates, strangers and lovers—consciousness, self-consciousness and control were gone—and there was nothing I could do about it.

My face flamed.

I continued to behave as if my condition were something to constantly test and triumph over, but by the spring of 1982, I was losing. I was living in Boston, working at a publishing house, and I was having seizures once a month. Previously, I had one or two seizures a year—now I was regularly falling down stairs, hitting my head on furniture, driving off the road.

My HMO doctor routinely scolded me for driving and not getting enough sleep, then increased my dosages of dilantin and phenobarbital. I took handfuls of pills. I could drink coffee until I went to bed, sleep as soon as my head hit the pillow, and I had to set three alarms to wake me in the morning. At work, my boss would give me some instructions, and by the time I walked down the hall, I couldn't remember what she'd said.

It never occurred to me to tell her what was happening because my body and my mind had always seemed completely separate to me. And inside the prison of your flesh, you do not realize you have changed. What is normal is always relative and over time I had begun to accept this groggy, slow, forgetful self. Then, at my semi-annual review, my boss told me my job was on the line.

The doctor, meanwhile, had thrown up her hands. "I don't know what's wrong," she told me, exasperated, when a blood test confirmed that my medication levels were still low. "You're on more medication than any patient I have!"

It was as if the world had abandoned me. I was in danger of losing a job I loved, and I was blacking out once a month with no end in sight. I no longer lived near family who would take care of me and set me back on my feet. I was on my own, but I hardly had the energy to take care of myself. Each day was a struggle to swim to the surface of my life through the mud of my consciousness. My energy, my body, my mind were no longer allies, no longer something I could count on. I was sluggish, dopey, spacey, alien. I was losing hold.

Through a friend, I got the name of one of the best neurologists in Boston. He confirmed my experience: yes, I was having problems. Yes, the drugs reduced my intellect and memory by as much as thirty percent. After that first visit, I cried the Red Line home from relief: I wasn't losing my mind. From gratitude: there was hope. There were other medications, such as a drug called Tegretol that did a better job controlling seizures, and didn't have the mind-blurring effects of dilantin and phenobarbital. From pride: I had taken my problems in hand and solved them.

I used to shape that experience into a success story: I had prevailed over bad doctors and medicine to regain my clarity, my control. I had triumphed over my epilepsy. But one of the most difficult things about a lifelong condition is that success is, more often than not, temporary. "It is in sickness that we are compelled to recognize that we do not live alone," Marcel Proust writes, "but are chained to a being from a different realm, from who we are worlds apart, who has no knowledge of us and by whom it is impossible to make ourselves understood: our body."

Six years later, I was sitting at a desk in a pastel-colored office of a regional magazine. The room was thick with abundant, spiky plants. Plate glass windows looked out on a green expanse of lawn the employees called the putting green. There were volleyball courts, and flower-decked courtyards for the employees' coffee breaks. It was the land of the pleasant.

A long stream of visitors on one of the twice-daily tours filed through the office, gazing at the writers and their blinking computer screens. The hostess stopped and gestured in our direction. "This, folks, is the Travel Department," she said. "Now isn't that a job we'd all want? Travel for money?"

I was in front of my computer, working on a story, as the room began to buckle and roll, grow dark around the edges, and a flash of electricity seemed to jolt my brain. Not now, I prayed, please not now. Some ancient self seemed to take over, and I told myself, "Look out the window, you'll be okay. Get one deep breath of fresh air. Prop your head in your left hand, you'll make it." I gripped the edge of the desk, avoiding the sea of faces smiling down at me, and made a deal with myself: "Make it till noon, you're home free."

The "lightening storms" as I called them had returned. Once again, in this game of touch tag, I was losing. In Boston, I had made a deal: If I take care of my body, then I can trust the world again. It seemed to work. Now my body had betrayed me.

The visitors moved down the aisle toward Art.

For the first time, I didn't tell anyone at work that I had seizures. For the first time, I felt ashamed at the possibility that gnawed the edges of every day. I was new at the magazine and I wanted to fit in: I wanted to look and act like everyone else and instead I felt like a freak.

I was thirty-three, long past the age where a love of drama made up for the embarrassment of seizures. Now there was a real price to maintaining control. Seizures could cost me independence and respect; they could cost me my dignity. Seizures were no longer something to be challenged. They were something to be feared.

After several months, I walked into my boss's office and shut the door. I wanted to be casual, no-nonsense. "It's no big deal," I said as I told him, but even my face seemed to disobey me. A sudden rush of emotion jerked and twitched my mouth. He was very understanding. I apologized over and over. "I guess you think you hired a whole person," I said as he touched my arm. "Instead you got damaged goods."

As a travel writer, I had to regularly venture into the world. Each time I did, it was with a mixture of trepidation and constant watchfulness: what was the twinge? That blip at the edge of my vision? Was I shaking from too much coffee or was it the beginning—? At the thought, fear bloomed in my stomach, and as strangers talked to me about their toy museums or logging festivals or luxury bed and breakfasts, I ached to be somewhere safe. In my apartment listening to my husband padding about, in my bed with its comforting jumble of covers. Instead of a reckless, thrilling place of adventure, the world had become strange, hostile, terrifying. A craving for safety seized up my life, but my body was always threatening anarchy.

That same year, 1989, I got a letter from the Department of Motor Vehicles saying that my driver's license was "suspended indefinitely," and it was as if my passport to adulthood had been cancelled. My husband, Fred, started driving me to the grocery store. I took buses and subways to scout stories. When I travelled out of town, I asked the people I interviewed for rides because I could not rent a car. Why? they'd ask. Medical problems, I'd say, and I'd see them brace themselves and look closer into my face. I felt as if I had to constantly tell the world: I am helpless. I am no longer a resident in the country of the normal.

I kept close track of concerts or museum exhibits in San Francisco, yet the logistics of getting there seemed overwhelming. Instead, I spent weekends lying on my bed, chastising myself for my cowardliness. Where was the person who hopped freights at twenty? Who hitchhiked across country for Thanksgiving? Who was this woman who was now afraid to walk out of her apartment?

At that time, I developed an odd, unconscious habit. At the end of an interview or a doctor's appointment, I'd unzip my purse, take out my keys, and begin to rub them as I talked. The act was not practical—there was no car outside waiting for me. Instead, it was as if the keys were a talisman—and the weight, the cold metal, and the dull jingle made me whole. Gave me power. Made me, once again, part of the world.

At five P.M. on October 17, 1989, I was in my shrink's office. As I started to talk, there was a jolt. The room began to rock. We got up and walked to the doorway. In the hallway, dozens of people I had never seen before— shrinks and patients—stood white-faced, their hands dangling. The floor rippled. Joists creaked and groaned. And as the trees outside dipped and swayed and a Bay Bridge overpass sixty miles north of us collapsed on a man named "Buck," the first thing I thought was now everyone will know what a seizure is like.

A year later, I had a full-blown, grand mal seizure at work. When Fred arrived, studio lights and cameras were pushed to the side in the photography studio and the air was thick with the squeals and squawks of radios. In the center of the room, nine paramedics stood in a circle, and beneath them, I lay on the stretcher—my face tinged blue and my skirt stained with urine.

Later, Fred told me that when he came, one of the paramedics was bent over me, barking, "What is your name? Do you know where you are?"

"She's out of it," he told her. "She's just had a seizure and she can't answer you."

The woman ignored him. "What is your name?" she said, louder.

"Look, she's unconscious. She's always like this," Fred said. "She just needs to sleep."

"We don't know that. She might have a concussion. Besides, Jack," she said, glaring at him, "I'm the paramedic. Who are you?"

"I'm her husband," he said. "I'm the one who's always there. She needs rest, not to go to the hospital and rack up some big ambulance bill just so they can give her medicine and let her sleep. I can do that at home. Just let me take her home."

"Once she's on the stretcher," the woman said. "She's ours."

Who did I belong to? The paramedic? My husband? This was one of the most important questions I had to face, one of the most insidious struggles I had to fight: the fight to take charge of my own condition.

Soon after I met my husband, we were up at a cabin in Montana. We were newly in love, and it was summertime, warm, and a full moon shimmered across the lake. I walked down for a swim. I took off my clothes, and dove into the water.

Fred was at the cabin window, watching me. He knew, of course, about my epilepsy—I had a seizure one of the first nights I slept with him. He told me that as he watched my windmilling arms, white disappearing into the black water, he thought to himself, if she had one now, I would never find her. He wondered if he should go get me. He thought of my parents, how they shook their heads at my seizures, not from a lack of concern, but a belief that this was a fate they were resigned to.

As he walked down the path to the lake, I shouted, "Come out. The water's warm. It feels wonderful."

"I'll watch," he said, realizing these chances I took were a necessary part of me, a part of my spirit, and as he stood on the dock and listened to the steady lap of my strokes, his voice trailed in echo, "Watch."

After we were married, things changed. He could see the connection between my late nights, my drinking and my seizures. Look, he said, you cannot do this to yourself. You're not like everyone else.

The idea infuriated me.

One night, a friend and I sat talking at the kitchen table. At two, Fred came out, his hair rumpled, and said, "Look, you've got to go to bed. You work at 8:00 in the morning, and you've got to sleep." Then he stalked back into the bedroom.

"I'm so sorry," my friend said, gathering her things. "Do you think he's mad?"

"Only at me," I said. I waved my hand, forced a laugh. "Just ignore him. He'll get over it." But I was stiff-lipped with anger and embarrassment and the need to put the best face on it.

When she was gone, I went back to the bedroom. "Don't *ever* do that to me," I said.

"Don't your friends realize that you've got to take care of yourself?" he said. "That you need sleep or you drop?"

"That's my business," I said.

"It's *not* just your business," he said. "Who do you think picks you up?"

"I take care of myself."

"But you don't," he said.

Everything he said was true—I needed to be more vigilant about my medicine, I needed to get more rest and slow down or I wound up tighter and tighter until I spun out of control. I had to change this, but I didn't. Instead, transferring some age-old rebellion from my parents to my husband, I fought him instead.

But I was right too. When you have a lifelong condition like epilepsy, people want to take care of you. When you abdicate responsibility for yourself, others try to take it for you. It is an impulse of kindness. Of concern. And it is deadly, for it deprives you of your own experience. It deprives you of the necessary fall that precedes the climb to responsibility.

This changed between us that terrible winter in Palo Alto because I was scared. I was always at the mercy of the unpredictable beast—I could not conquer it once and have done with it. The scaffolding of belief and denial that had always supported me fell away, and I became terrified of the world. It was the first time I felt to my bones how truly fragile I was. Like Adam, when God called to him after he had eaten the forbidden apple, "I was afraid, because I was naked."

There are voices, terrors that belong to that realm of the dimmed consciousness, to the place where the brain is firing in loud pops and bursts and the world shrinks away from the echoey swamp of a mind reeling from a power outage. There are also moments of sheer joy, odd, reeling moments when the very particles in the air rush at me, and I seem to be looking into the other side of the world. Even the terror is a gift for, like a dragon at the mouth of a cave, it warns me where I cannot go.

I was with a friend in a dark, Bavarian-style restaurant. The waiter came up. "I've got your food here," he said in a steady, quiet voice, and as he set down my plate, I stiffened. The room dimmed and receded. "What's wrong?" my friend said. "You look like you've seen a ghost."

I could make nothing of it. Don't be silly, I told myself. Nothing's wrong. I calmed down and dug into my hot roast beef. Walking back to work, it came to me. The man's quiet voice sounded like an EMT who, several weeks before, had sat by my guernsey, quietly talking, as the ambulance whined and careened down Storrow Drive. It was not a memory I owned until that minute, until the man's sonorous voice tripped it. And it did not travel alone, but rushed back filled with the emotions of other moments—that terror of lost time, that terror of waking up as a white-jacketed stranger bent over me and said, over the crackling radio, "How are we feeling?"

There is the deep, warm voice of another man, saying, "I want to help you." I was in a job interview when I had one of three conscious seizures I have had in my life. As I perched on the edge my of my chair, dressed in my wool suit and nylons, words thickened in my mouth. I shook. My arms and legs began to jerk. I leaned against the desk, as wave after wave seized me, desperately wanting not to fall and expose my underwear. The man was a difficult, feckless boss, but I'll never forget how kind his voice was at that moment. "If you could only speak," he pleaded. "If you could only tell me how to help you."

The rapidly accelerating, speedy moments that a seizure is coming on are moments of wild joy, of communion. The neurologists call them auras, and some people experience certain smells or colors. Dostoyevsky said he felt "entirely in harmony with myself and the whole world, and this feeling is so strong and so delightful that for a few seconds of such bliss one would gladly give up ten years of one's life."

I was driving home from visiting friends, ignited by our conversation. As I drove, the bumpy, maple-lined street cast before me endless, exciting possibilities—stories, essays, books; travels on the trans-Siberian Express, bike trips across Spain. This was the slowly unfolding path of my life, lined with friends, lovers, writing. I could do anything. My heart soared. As the moonlight flooded the bald face of Mount Jumbo, I felt the warm breath of God.

Oliver Sacks describes epilepsy as a "simultaneous gift and affliction." In Palo Alto, I received several gifts: a good doctor and a way out of the lightning storms that plagued me. But most of all, I received the gift of submission.

Chekhov describes writing as a "long patience" and I would use the same description for illness. As exhilaration turned to dread, novelty to a feared reality, I learned I didn't have ultimate control over this quirky misfiring of the brain. I believed this disease was mine. I learned I was not, finally, like everyone else and it was time to accept that.

My long rebellion finally gave way. I began to submit to epilepsy's de-mands—but slowly, unwillingly. I am a stubborn patient. I stopped strug-gling through long, queasy mornings at work and went home, where I lay in bed and worried about work. I adopted the practicality that dealing with an illness demands, and stopped acting as if getting enough sleep and putting medicine in little boxes marked with days of the week were an admission of failure, a capitulation to a safe, dull life. I became reck-less in more important ways—I began to write fiction.

I attended a few sessions of an Epilepsy Support group. I sat at the table with an old man who worked in a pie factory, a teenager who'd just wrecked his parent's car, and a young, frightened-looking woman who never spoke. I kept thinking, "I'm not like these people. Look at them. Their lives are a mess." But as we began to talk about insurance, doctors, the outrageous cost of medication (epilepsy is the most expensive neuro-logical disorder there is), I took off my coat. I went back the next week, then I stopped: I was still not driving and it was difficult to organize a ride. But more than anything, I did not want to be completely defined by my illness.

I still don't. But I don't try to beat the oddsmaker anymore. The days, when I feel the flash and spark of an overactive brain or dark gnaws the edge of my vision, I have learned to respect the signs. My victories are no longer conquests; they are concessions. "It's all right," I say to myself as I turn around and walk home. "You're safe." I tell myself as I take off my clothes, turn back the covers on the bed, and lie down. "You're all right. Take it easy. Rest."

IN THE CANON, FOR ALL THE WRONG REASONS

Amy Tan

This piece, published in Harper's *Magazine, is an excerpt from the essay "Required Reading and Other Dangerous Subjects," first published in the literary journal* The Threepenny Review.

Several years ago I learned that I had passed a new literary milestone. I had made it to the Halls of Education under the rubric of "Multicultural Literature," also known in many schools as "Required Reading."

Thanks to this development, I now meet students who proudly tell me they're doing their essays, term papers, or master's theses on me. By that they mean that they are analyzing not just my books but me—my grade-school achievements, youthful indiscretions, marital status, as well as the movies I watched as a child, the slings and arrows I suffered as a minority, and so forth—all of which, with the hindsight of classroom literary investigation, prove to contain many Chinese omens that made it inevitable that I would become a writer.

Once I read a master's thesis on feminist writings, which included examples from *The Joy Luck Club*. The student noted that I had often used the number four, something on the order of thirty-two or thirty-six times—in any case, a number divisible by four. She pointed out that there were four mothers, four daughters, four sections of the book, four stories per section. Furthermore, there were four sides to a mah jong table, four directions of the wind, four players. More important, she postulated, my use of the number four was a symbol for the four stages of psychological development, which corresponded in uncanny ways to the four stages of some type of Buddhist philosophy I had never heard of before. The student recalled that the story contained a character called Fourth Wife, symbolizing death, and a four-year-old girl with a feisty spirit, symbolizing regeneration.

In short, her literary sleuthing went on to reveal a mystical and rather Byzantine puzzle, which, once explained, proved to be completely brilliant and precisely logical. She wrote me a letter and asked if her analysis had been correct. How I longed to say "absolutely."

The truth is, if there are symbols in my work they exist largely by accident or through someone else's interpretive design. If I wrote of "an orange moon rising on a dark night," I would more likely ask myself later if the image was a cliché, not whether it was a symbol for the feminine force rising in anger, as one master's thesis postulated. To plant symbols like that, you need a plan, good organizational skills, and a prescient understanding of the story you are about to write. Sadly, I lack those traits.

All this is by way of saying that I don't claim my use of the number four to be a brilliant symbolic device. In fact, now that it's been pointed out to me in rather astonishing ways, I consider my overuse of the number to be a flaw.

Reviewers and students have enlightened me about not only how I write but why I write. Apparently, I am driven to capture the immigrant experience, to demystify Chinese culture, to point out the differences between Chinese and American culture, even to pave the way for other Asian American writers.

If only I were that noble. Contrary to what is assumed by some students, reporters, and community organizations wishing to bestow honors on me, I am not an expert on China, Chinese culture, mah jong, the psychology of mothers and daughters, generation gaps, immigration, illegal aliens, assimilation, acculturation, racial tension, Tiananmen Square, the Most Favored Nation trade agreements, human rights, Pacific Rim economics, the purported one million missing baby girls of China, the future of Hong Kong after 1997, or, I am sorry to say, Chinese cooking. Certainly I have personal opinions on many of these topics, but by no means do my sentiments and my world of make-believe make me an expert.

So I am alarmed when reviewers and educators assume that my very personal, specific, and fictional stories are meant to be representative down to the nth detail not just of Chinese Americans but, sometimes, of all Asian culture. Is Jane Smiley's *A Thousand Acres* supposed to be taken as representative of all of American culture? If so, in what ways? Are all American fathers tyrannical? Do all American sisters betray one another? Are all American conscientious objectors flaky in love relationships?

Over the years my editor has received hundreds of permissions requests from publishers of college textbooks and multicultural anthologies, all of them wishing to reprint my work for "educational purposes." One publisher wanted to include an excerpt from *The Joy Luck Club*, a scene in which a Chinese woman invites her non-Chinese boyfriend to her parents' house for dinner. The boyfriend brings a bottle of wine as a gift and commits a number of social gaffes at the dinner table. Students were supposed to read this excerpt, then answer the following question: "If you are invited to a Chinese family's house for dinner, should you bring a bottle of wine?"

In many respects, I am proud to be on the reading lists for courses such as Ethnic Studies, Asian American Studies, Asian American Literature, Asian American History, Women's Literature, Feminist Studies, Feminist Writers of Color, and so forth. What writer wouldn't want her work to be read? I also take a certain perverse glee in imagining countless students, sleepless at three in the morning, trying to read *The Joy Luck Club* for the next day's midterm. Yet I'm also not altogether comfortable about my book's status as required reading.

Let me relate a conversation I had with a professor at a school in southern California. He told me he uses my books in his literature class but he makes it a point to lambast those passages that depict China as backward or unattractive. He objects to any descriptions that have to do with spitting, filth, poverty, or superstitions. I asked him if China in the 1930s and 1940s was free of these elements. He said, No, such descriptions are true; but he still believes it is "the obligation of the writer of ethnic literature to create positive, progressive images."

I secretly shuddered and thought, Oh well, that's southern California for you. But then, a short time later, I met a student from UC Berkeley, a school that I myself attended. The student was standing in line at a book signing. When his turn came, he swaggered up to me, then took two steps back and said in a loud voice, "Don't you think you have a responsibility to write about Chinese men as positive role models?"

In the past, I've tried to ignore the potshots. A *Washington Post* reporter once asked me what I thought of another Asian American writer calling me something on the order of "a running dog whore sucking on the tit of the imperialist white pigs."

"Well," I said, "you can't please everyone, can you?" I pointed out that readers are free to interpret a book as they please, and that they are free to appreciate or not appreciate the result. Besides, reacting to your critics makes a writer look defensive, petulant, and like an all-around bad sport.

But lately I've started thinking it's wrong to take such a laissez-faire attitude. Lately I've come to think that I must say something, not so much to defend myself and my work but to express my hopes for American literature, for what it has the potential to become in the twenty-first century—that is, a truly American literature, democratic in the way it includes many colorful voices.

Until recently, I didn't think it was important for writers to express their private intentions in order for their work to be appreciated; I believed that any analysis of my intentions belonged behind the closed doors of literature classes. But I've come to realize that the study of literature does have its effect on how books are being read, and thus on what might be read, published, and written in the future. For that reason, I do believe writers today must talk about their intentions—if for no other reason than to serve as an antidote to what others say our intentions should be.

For the record, I don't write to dig a hole and fill it with symbols. I don't write stories as ethnic themes. I don't write to represent life in general. And I certainly don't write because I have answers. If I knew everything there is to know about mothers and daughters, Chinese and Americans, I wouldn't have any stories left to imagine. If I had to write about only positive role models, I wouldn't have enough imagination left to finish the first story. If I knew what to do about immigration, I would be a sociologist or a politician and not a long-winded storyteller.

So why do I write?

Because my childhood disturbed me, pained me, made me ask foolish questions. And the questions still echo. Why does my mother always talk about killing herself? Why did my father and brother have to die? If I die, can I be reborn into a happy family? Those early obsessions led to a belief that writing could be my salvation, providing me with the sort of freedom and danger, satisfaction and discomfort, truth and contradiction I can't find in anything else in life.

I write to discover the past for myself. I don't write to change the future for others. And if others are moved by my work—if they love their mothers more, scold their daughters less, or divorce their husbands who were not positive role models—I'm often surprised, usually grateful to hear from kind readers. But I don't take either credit or blame for changing their lives for better or for worse.

Writing, for me, is an act of faith, a hope that I will discover what I mean by "truth." I also think of reading as an act of faith, a hope that I will discover something remarkable about ordinary life, about myself. And if the writer and the reader discover the same thing, if they have that connection, the act of faith has resulted in an act of magic. To me, that's the mystery and the wonder of both life and fiction—the connection between two individuals who discover in the end that they are more the same than they are different.

And if that doesn't happen, it's nobody's fault. There are still plenty of other books on the shelf. Choose what you like.

SILENT DANCING

Judith Ortiz Cofer

This piece is an excerpt from Cofer's 1990 memoir Silent Dancing: A Partial Remembrance of a Puerto Rican Childhood.

We have a home movie of this party. Several times my mother and I have watched it together, and I have asked questions about the silent revelers coming in and out of focus. It is grainy and of short duration, but it's a great visual aid to my memory of life at that time. And it is in color—the only complete scene in color I can recall from those years.

We lived in Puerto Rico until my brother was born in 1954. Soon after, because of economic pressures on our growing family, my father joined the United States Navy. He was assigned to duty on a ship in Brooklyn Yard—a place of cement and steel that was to be his home base in the States until his retirement more than twenty years later. He left the Island first, alone, going to New York City and tracking down his uncle who lived with his family across the Hudson River in Paterson, New Jersey. There my father found a tiny apartment in a huge tenement that had once housed Jewish families but was just being taken over and transformed by Puerto Ricans, overflowing from New York City. In 1955 he sent for us. My mother was only twenty years old, I was not quite three, and my brother was a toddler when we arrived at El Building, as the place had been christened by its newest residents.

My memories of life in Paterson during those first few years are all in shades of gray. Maybe I was too young to absorb vivid colors and details, or to discriminate between the slate blue of the winter sky and the darker hues of the snow-bearing clouds, but that single color washes over the whole period. The building we lived in was gray, as were the streets, filled with slush the first few months of my life there. The coat my father had bought for me was similar in color and too big; it sat heavily on my thin frame.

I do remember the way the heater pipes banged and rattled, startling all of us out of sleep until we got so used to the sound that we automatically shut it out or raised our voices above the racket. The hiss from the valve punctuated my sleep (which has always been fitful) like a nonhuman presence in the room—a dragon sleeping at the entrance of my childhood. But the pipes were also a connection to all the other lives being lived around us. Having come from a house designed for a single family back in Puerto Rico—my mother's extended-family home—it was curious to know that strangers lived under our floor and above our heads, and that the heater pipe went through everyone's apartment. (My first spanking in Paterson came as a result of playing tunes on the pipes in my room to see if there would be an answer.) My mother was as new to this concept of beehive life as I was, but she had been given strict orders by my father to keep the doors locked, the noise down, ourselves to ourselves.

It seems that Father had learned some painful lessons about prejudice while searching for an apartment in Paterson. Not until years later did I hear how much resistance he had encountered with landlords who were panicking at the influx of Latinos into a neighborhood that had been Jewish for a couple of generations. It made no difference that it was the American phenomenon of ethnic turnover which was changing the urban core of Paterson, and that the human flood could not be held back with an accusing finger.

"You Cuban?" one man had asked my father, pointing at his name tag on the navy uniform—even though my father had the fair skin and light brown hair of his northern Spanish background, and the name Ortiz is as common in Puerto Rico as Johnson is in the United States.

"No," my father had answered, looking past the finger into his adversary's angry eyes. "I'm Puerto Rican."

"Same shit." And the door closed.

My father could have passed as European, but we couldn't. My brother and I both have our mother's black hair and olive skin, and so we lived in

El Building and visited our great-uncle and his fair children on the next block. It was their private joke that they were the German branch of the family. Not many years later that area too would be mainly Puerto Rican. It was as if the heart of the city map were being gradually colored brown—*café con leche* brown. Our color.

The movie opens with a sweep of the living room. It is "typical" immigrant Puerto Rican decor for the time: the sofa and chairs are square and hard-looking, upholstered in bright colors (blue and yellow in this instance) and covered with the transparent plastic that furniture salesmen then were so adept at convincing women to buy. The linoleum on the floor is light blue; where it had been subjected to spike heels, as it was in most places, there were dime-size indentations all over it that cannot be seen in this movie. The room is full of people dressed up: dark suits for the men, red dresses for the women. When I have asked my mother why most of the women are in red that night, she has shrugged and said, "I don't re-member. Just a coincidence." She doesn't have my obsession for assigning sym-bolism to everything.

The three women in red sitting on the couch are my mother, my eighteen-year-old cousin, and her brother's girlfriend. The novia *is just up from the Island, which is apparent in her body language. She sits up formally, her dress pulled over her knees. She is a pretty girl, but her posture makes her look insecure, lost in her full-skirted dress, which she has carefully tucked around her to make room for my gorgeous cousin, her future sister-in-law. My cousin has grown up in Paterson and is in her last year of high school. She doesn't have a trace of what Puerto Ricans call* la mancha *(literally, the stain: the mark of the new immi-grant—something about the posture, the voice, or the humble demeanor that makes it obvious to everyone the person has just arrived on the mainland). My cousin is wearing a tight, sequined, cocktail dress. Her brown hair has been light-ened with peroxide around the bands, and she is holding a cigarette expertly be-tween her fingers, bringing it up to her mouth in a sensuous arc of her arm as she talks animatedly. My mother, who has come up to sit between the two women, both only a few years younger than herself, is somewhere between the poles they represent in our culture.*

It became my father's obsession to get out of the barrio, and thus we were never permitted to form bonds with the place or with the people who lived there. Yet El Building was a comfort to my mother, who never got over yearning for *la isla*. She felt surrounded by her language: the walls were thin, and voices speaking and arguing in Spanish could be heard all day. *Salsas* blasted out of radios, turned on early in the morning and left on for company. Women seemed to cook rice and beans perpetually—the strong aroma of boiling red kidney beans permeated the hallways.

Though Father preferred that we do our grocery shopping at the su-permarket when he came home on weekend leaves, my mother insisted that she could cook only with products whose labels she could read. Consequently, during the week I accompanied her and my little brother to La Bodega—a hole-in-the-wall grocery store across the street from El Building. There we squeezed down three narrow aisles jammed with various products. Goya and Libby's—those were the trademarks that were trusted by her *mamá,* so my mother bought many cans of Goya beans, soups, and condiments, as well as little cans of Libby's fruit juices for us. And she also bought Colgate toothpaste and Palmolive soap. (The finale *e* is pronounced in both these products in Spanish, so for many years I believed that they were manufactured on the Island. I remember my surprise at first hearing a commercial on television in which "Colgate" rhymed with "ate.") We always lingered at La Bodega, for it was there that Mother breathed best, taking in the familiar aromas of the foods she knew from Mamá's kitchen. It was also there that she got to speak to the other women of El Building without violating outright Father's dictates against fraternizing with our neighbors.

Yet Father did his best to make our "assimilation" painless. I can still see him carrying a real Christmas tree up several flights of stairs to our apartment, leaving a trail of aromatic pine. He carried it formally, as if it were a flag in a parade. We were the only ones in El Building that I knew of who got presents on both Christmas and *día de Reyes,* the day when the Three Kings brought gifts to Christ and to Hispanic children.

Our supreme luxury in El Building was having our own television set. It must have been a result of Father's guilt feelings over the isolation he had imposed on us, but we were among the first in the barrio to have one. My brother quickly became an avid watcher of Captain Kangaroo and Jungle Jim, while I loved all the series showing families. By the time I started first grade, I could have drawn a map of Middle America as exemplified by the lives of characters in *Father Knows Best, The Donna Reed Show, Leave It to Beaver, My Three Sons,* and (my favorite) *Bachelor Father,* where John Forsythe treated his adopted teenage daughter like a princess because he was rich and had a Chinese houseboy to do everything for him. In truth, compared to our neighbors in El Building, *we* were rich. My father's navy check provided us with financial security and a standard of living that the factory workers envied. The only thing his money could not buy us was a place to live away from the barrio—his greatest wish, Mother's greatest fear.

In the home movie the men are shown next, sitting around a card table set up in one corner of the living room, playing dominoes. The clack of the ivory pieces was a familiar sound. I heard it in many houses on the Island and in many apartments in Paterson. In Leave It to Beaver, *the Cleavers played bridge in every other episode; in my childhood, the men started every social occasion with a hotly debated round of dominoes. The women would sit around and watch, but they never participated in the games.*

Here and there you can see a small child. Children were always brought to parties and, whenever they got sleepy, were put to bed in the host's bedroom. Babysitting was a concept unrecognized by the Puerto Rican women I knew: a responsible mother did not leave her children with any stranger. And in a culture where children are not considered intrusive, there was no need to leave the children at home. We went where our mother went.

Of my preschool years I have only impressions: the sharp bite of the wind in December as we walked with our parents toward the brightly lit stores downtown; how I felt like a stuffed doll in my heavy coat, boots, and mittens; how good it was to walk into the five-and-dime and sit at the counter drinking hot chocolate. On Saturdays our whole family would walk downtown to shop at the big department stores on Broadway. Mother bought all our clothes at Penney's and Sears, and she liked to buy her dresses at the women's specialty shops like Lerner's and Diana's. At some point we'd go into Woolworth's and sit at the soda fountain to eat.

We never ran into other Latinos at these stores or when eating out, and it became clear to me only years later that the women from El Building shopped mainly in other places—stores owned by other Puerto Ricans or by Jewish merchants who had philosophically accepted our presence in the city and decided to make us their good customers, if not real neighbors and friends. These establishments were located not downtown but in the blocks around our street, and they were referred to generically as La Tienda, El Bazar, La Bodega, La Botánica. Everyone knew what was meant. These were the stores where your face did not turn a clerk to stone, where your money was as green as anyone else's.

One New Year's Eve we were dressed up like child models in the Sears catalogue: my brother in a miniature man's suit and bow tie, and I in black patent-leather shoes and a frilly dress with several layers of crinoline underneath. My mother wore a bright red dress that night, I remember, and spike heels; her long black hair hung to her waist. Father, who usually wore his navy uniform during his short visits home, had put on a dark civilian suit for the occasion: we had been invited to his uncle's house for a big celebration. Everyone was excited because my mother's brother Hernan—a bachelor who could indulge himself with luxuries— had bought a home movie camera, which he would be trying out that night.

Even the home movie cannot fill in the sensory details such a gathering left imprinted in a child's brain. The thick sweetness of women's perfumes mixing with the ever-present smells of food cooking in the kitchen: meat and plantain *pasteles,* as well as the ubiquitous rice dish made special with pigeon peas—*gandules*—and seasoned with precious *sofrito* sent up from the Island by somebody's mother or smuggled in by a recent traveler. *Sofrito* was one of the items that women hoarded, since it was hardly ever in stock at La Bodega. It was the flavor of Puerto Rico.

The men drank Palo Viejo rum, and some of the younger ones got weepy. The first time I saw a grown man cry was at a New Year's Eve party: he had been reminded of his mother by the smells in the kitchen.

But what I remember most were the boiled *pasteles*, plantain or yucca rectangles stuffed with corned beef or other meats, olives, and many other savory ingredients, all wrapped in banana leaves. Everybody had to fish one out with a fork. There was always a "trick" *pastel*—one without stuffing—and whoever got that one was the "New Year's Fool."

There was also the music. Long-playing albums were treated like precious china in these homes. Mexican recordings were popular, but the songs that brought tears to my mother's eyes were sung by the melancholy Daniel Santos, whose life as a drug addict was the stuff of legend. Felipe Rodríguez was a particular favorite of couples, since he sang about faithless women and brokenhearted men. There is a snatch of one lyric that has stuck in my mind like a needle on a worn groove: *De piedra ha de ser mi cama, de piedra la cabezera . . . la mujer que a mi me quiera . . . ha de quererme de veras. Ay, Ay, Ay, corazón, porque no amas . . .* I must have heard it a thousand times since the idea of a bed made of stone, and its connection to love, first troubled me with its disturbing images.

The five-minute home movie ends with people dancing in a circle—the creative filmmaker must have set it up, so that all of them could file past him. It is both comical and sad to watch silent dancing. Since there is no justification for the absurd movements that music provides for some of us, people appear frantic, their faces embarrassingly intense. It's as if you were watching sex. Yet for years, I've had dreams in the form of this home movie. In a recurring scene, familiar faces push themselves forward into my mind's eye, plastering their features into distorted close-ups. And I'm asking them: "Who is *she?* Who is the old woman I don't recognize? Is she an aunt? Somebody's wife? Tell me who she is."

"See the beauty mark on her cheek a big as a hill on the lunar landscape of her face—well, that runs in the family. The women on your father's side of the family wrinkle early; it's the price they pay for that fair skin. The young girl with the green stain on her wedding dress is *la novia*—just up from the Island. See, she lowers her eyes when she approaches the camera, as she's supposed to. Decent girls never look at you directly in the face. *Humilde,* humble, a girl should express humility in all her actions. She will make a good wife for your cousin. He should consider himself lucky to have met her only weeks after she arrived here. If he marries her quickly, she will make him a good Puerto Rican-style wife; but if he waits too long, she will be corrupted by the city, just like your cousin there."

"She means me. I do what I want. This is not some primitive island I live on. Do they expect me to wear black mantilla on my head and go to mass every day? Not me. I'm an American woman, and I will do as I please. I can type faster than anyone in my senior class at Central high, and I'm going to be a secretary to a lawyer when I graduate. I can pass for an American girl anywhere—I've tried it. At least for Italian, anyway—I never speak Spanish in public. I hate these parties, but I wanted the dress. I look better than any of these *humildes* here. *My* life is going to be different. I have an American boyfriend. He is older and has a car. My parents don't know it, but I sneak out of the house late at night sometimes to be with him. If I marry him, even my name will be American. I hate rice and beans—that's what makes these women fat."

"Your *prima* is pregnant by that man she's been sneaking around with. Would I lie to you? I'm your *tiá política,* your great-uncle's common-law wife—the one he abandoned on the Island to go marry your cousin's mother. *I* was not invited to this party, of course, but I came anyway. I came to tell you that story about your cousin that you've always wanted to hear. Do you remember the comment your mother made to a neighbor that has always haunted you? The only thing you heard was your cousin's name, and then you saw your mother pick up your doll from the couch and say: 'It was as big as this doll when they flushed it down the toilet.' This image has bothered you for years, hasn't it? You had nightmares about babies being flushed down the toilet, and you wondered why anyone would do such a horrible thing. You didn't dare ask your mother about it. She would only tell you that you had not heard her right, and yell at you for listening to adult conversations. But later, when you were old enough to know about abortions, you suspected.

"I am here to tell you that you were right. Your cousin was growing an *americanito* in her belly when this movie was made. Soon after, she put something long and pointy into her pretty self, thinking maybe she could get rid of the problem before breakfast and still make it to her first class at the high school. Well, *niña,* her screams could be heard downtown. Your aunt, her *mamá,* who had been a midwife on the Island, managed to pull the little thing out. Yes, they probably flushed it down the toilet. What else could they do with it—give it a Christian burial in a little white casket with blue bows and ribbons? Nobody wanted that baby—least of all the father, a teacher at her school with a house in West Paterson that he was filling with real children, and a wife who was a natural blonde.

"Girl, the scandal sent your uncle back to the bottle. And guess where your cousin ended up? Irony of ironies. She was sent to a village in Puerto Rico to live with a relative on her mother's side: a place so far away from civilization that you have to ride a mule to reach it. A real change in scenery. She found a man there—women like that cannot live without male company—but believe me, the men in Puerto Rico know how to put a saddle on a woman like her. *La gringa,* they call her. Ha, ha, ha. *La gringa* is what she always wanted to be . . ."

The old woman's mouth becomes a cavernous black hole I fall into. And as I fall, I can feel the reverberations of her laughter. I hear the echoes of her last mocking words: *la gringa, la gringa!* And the conga line keeps moving silently past me. There is no music in my dream for the dancers.

When Odysseus visits Hades to see the spirit of his mother, he makes an offering of sacrificial blood, but since all the souls crave an audience with the living, he has to listen to many of them before he can ask questions. I, too, have to hear the dead and the forgotten speak in my dream. Those who are still part of my life remain silent, going around and around in their dance. The others keep pressing their faces forward to say things about the past.

My father's uncle is last in line. He is dying of alcoholism, shrunken and shriveled like a monkey, his face a mass of wrinkles and broken arteries. As he comes closer I realize that in his features I can see my whole family. If you were to stretch that rubbery flesh, you could find my father's face, and deep within *that* face—my own. I don't want to look into those eyes ringed in purple. In a few years he will retreat into silence, and take a long, long time to die. *Move back, Tío,* I tell him. *I don't want to hear what you have to say. Give the dancers room to move. Soon it will be midnight. Who is the New Year's Fool this time?*

THEME FOR ENGLISH B
—■—

Langston Hughes

This poem is from The Collected Poems of Langston Hughes, *first published in 1926.*

The instructor said,

> Go home and write
> a page tonight.
> And let that page come out of you—
> Then, it will be true.

I wonder if it's that simple?

I am twenty-two, colored, born in Winston-Salem.
I went to school there, then Durham, then here
to this college on the hill above Harlem.
I am the only colored student in my class.
The steps from the hill lead down to Harlem,
through a park, then I cross St. Nicholas,
Eighth Avenue, Seventh, and I come to the Y,
the Harlem Branch Y, where I take the elevator
up to my room, sit down, and write this page:

It's not easy to know what is true for you or me
at twenty-two, my age. But I guess I'm what

I feel and see and hear. Harlem, I hear you:
hear you, hear me—we two—you, me talk on this page.
(I hear New York, too.) Me—who?

Well, I like to eat, sleep, drink, and be in love.
I like to work, read, learn, and understand life.
I like a pipe for a Christmas present,
or records—Bessie, bop, or Bach.

I guess being colored doesn't make me not like
the same things other folks like who are other races.
So will my page be colored that I write?
Being me, it will not be white.
But it will be
a part of you, instructor.
You are white—
yet a part of me, as I am a part of you.
That's American.

Sometimes perhaps you don't want to be a part of me.
Nor do I often want to be a part of you.
But we are, that's true!
As I learn from you,
I guess you learn from me—
although you're older—and white—
and somewhat more free.

This is my page for English B.

THE THINGS THEY CARRIED

Tim O'Brien

This short story is from O'Brien's 1990 story collection The Things They Carried.

First Lieutenant Jimmy Cross carried letters from a girl named Martha, a junior at Mount Sebastian College in New Jersey. They were not love letters, but Lieutenant Cross was hoping, so he kept them folded in plastic at the bottom of his rucksack. In the late afternoon, after a day's march, he would dig his foxhole, wash his hands under a canteen, unwrap the letters, hold them with the tips of his fingers, and spend the last hour of light pretending. He would imagine romantic camping trips into the White Mountains in New Hampshire. He would sometimes taste the envelope flaps, knowing her tongue had been there. More than anything, he wanted Martha to love him as he loved her, but the letters were mostly chatty, elusive on the matter of love. She was a virgin, he was almost sure. She was an English major at Mount Sebastian, and she wrote beautifully about her professors and roommates and midterm exams, about her respect for Chaucer and her great affection for Virginia Woolf. She often quoted lines of poetry; she never mentioned the war, except to say, Jimmy, take care of yourself. The letters weighed 10 ounces. They were signed Love, Martha, but Lieutenant Cross understood that Love was only a way of signing and did not mean what he sometimes pretended it meant. At dusk, he would carefully return the letters to his rucksack. Slowly, a bit distracted, he would get up and move among his men, checking the perimeter, then at full dark he would return to his hole and watch the night and wonder if Martha was a virgin.

The things they carried were largely determined by necessity. Among the necessities or near-necessities were P-38 can openers, pocket knives, heat tabs, wristwatches, dog tags, mosquito repellent, chewing gum, candy, cigarettes, salt tablets, packets of Kool-Aid, lighters, matches, sewing kits, Military Payment Certificates, C rations, and two or three canteens of water. Together, these items weighed between 15 and 20 pounds, depending upon a man's habits or rate of metabolism. Henry Dobbins, who was a big man, carried extra rations; he was especially fond of canned peaches in heavy syrup over pound cake. Dave Jensen, who practiced field hygiene, carried a toothbrush, dental floss, and several hotel-sized bars of soap he'd stolen on R&R in Sydney, Australia. Ted Lavender, who was scared, carried tranquilizers until he was shot in the head outside the village of Than Khe in mid-April. By necessity, and because it was SOP, they all carried steel helmets that weighed 5 pounds including the liner and camouflage cover. They carried the standard fatigue jackets and trousers. Very few carried underwear. On their feet they carried jungle boots—2.1 pounds—and Dave Jensen carried three pairs of socks and a can of Dr. Scholl's foot powder as a precaution against trench foot. Until he was shot, Ted Lavender carried 6 or 7 ounces of premium dope, which for him was a necessity. Mitchell Sanders, the RTO, carried condoms. Norman Bowker carried a diary. Rat Kiley carried comic books. Kiowa, a devout Baptist, carried an illustrated New Testament that had been presented to him by his father, who taught Sunday school in Oklahoma City, Oklahoma. As a hedge against bad times, however, Kiowa also carried his grandmother's distrust of the white man, his grandfather's old hunting hatchet. Necessity dictated. Because the land was mined and booby-trapped, it was SOP for each man to carry a steel-centered, nylon-covered flak jacket, which weighed 6.7 pounds, but which on hot days seemed much heavier. Because you could die so quickly, each man carried at least one large compress bandage, usually in the helmet band for easy access. Because the nights were cold, and because the monsoons were wet, each carried a green plastic poncho that could be used as a raincoat or ground-sheet or makeshift tent. With its quilted liner, the poncho weighed almost 2 pounds, but it was worth every ounce. In April, for instance, when Ted Lavender was shot, they used his poncho to wrap him up, then to carry him across the paddy, then to lift him into the chopper that took him away.

They were called legs or grunts.

To carry something was to hump it, as when Lieutenant Jimmy Cross humped his love for Martha up the hills and through the swamps. In its intransitive form, to hump meant to walk, or to march, but it implied burdens far beyond the intransitive.

Almost everyone humped photographs, In his wallet, Lieutenant Cross carried two photographs of Martha. The first was a Kodacolor snapshot signed Love, though he knew better. She stood against a brick wall. Her eyes were gray and neutral, her lips slightly open as she stared straight-on at the camera. At night, sometimes, Lieutenant Cross wondered who had taken the picture, because he knew she had boyfriends, because he loved her so much, and because he could see the shadow of the picture-taker spreading out against the brick wall. The second photograph had been clipped from the 1968 Mount Sebastian yearbook. It was an action shot—women's volleyball—and Martha was bent horizontal to the floor, reaching, the palms of her hands in sharp focus, the tongue taut, the expression frank and competitive. There was no visible sweat. She wore white gym shorts. Her legs, he thought, were almost certainly the legs of a virgin, dry and without hair, the left knee cocked and carrying her entire weight, which was just over 100 pounds. Lieutenant Cross remembered touching that left knee. A dark theater, he remembered, and the movie was *Bonnie and Clyde,* and Martha wore a tweed skirt, and during the final scene, when he touched her knee, she turned and looked at him in a sad, sober way that made him pull his hand back, but he would always remember the feel of the tweed skirt and the knee beneath it and the sound of the gunfire that killed Bonnie and Clyde, how embarrassing it was, how slow and oppressive. He remembered kissing her goodnight at the dorm door. Right then, he thought, he should've done something brave. He should've carried her up the stairs to her room and tied her to the bed and touched that left knee all night long. He should've risked it. Whenever he looked at the photographs, he thought of new things he should've done.

What they carried was partly a function of rank, partly of field specialty.

As a first lieutenant and platoon leader, Jimmy Cross carried a compass, maps, code books, binoculars, and a .45-caliber pistol that weighed 2.9 pounds fully loaded. He carried a strobe light and the responsibility for the lives of his men.

As an RTO, Mitchell Sanders carried the PRC-25 radio, a killer, 26 pounds with its battery.

As a medic, Rat Kiley carried a canvas satchel filled with morphine and plasma and malaria tablets and surgical tape and comic books and all the things a medic must carry, including M&Ms for especially bad wounds, for a total weight of nearly 20 pounds.

As a big man, therefore a machine gunner, Henry Dobbins carried the M-60, which weighed 23 pounds unloaded, but which was almost always loaded. In addition, Dobbins carried between 10 and 15 pounds of ammunition draped in belts across his chest and shoulders.

As PFCs or Spec 4s, most of them were common grunts and carried the standard M-16 gas-operated assault rifle. The weapon weighed 7.5 pounds unloaded, 8.2 pounds with its full twenty-round magazine. Depending on numerous factors, such as topography and psychology, the riflemen carried anywhere from twelve to twenty magazines, usually in cloth bandoliers, adding on another 8.4 pounds at minimum, 14 pounds at maximum. When it was available, they also carried M-16 maintenance gear—rods and steel brushes and swabs and tubes of LSA oil—all of which weighed about a pound. Among the grunts, some carried the M-79 grenade launcher, 5.9 pounds unloaded, a reasonably light weapon except for the ammunition, which was heavy. A single round weighed 10 ounces. The typical load was twenty-five rounds. But Ted Lavender, who was scared, carried thirty-four rounds when he was shot and killed outside Than Khe, and he went down under an exceptional burden, more than 20 pounds of ammunition, plus the flak jacket and helmet and rations and water and toilet paper and tranquilizers and all the rest, plus the unweighed fear. He was dead weight. There was no twitching or flopping. Kiowa, who saw it happen, said it was like watching a rock fall, or a big sandbag or something—just boom, then down—not like the movies where the dead guy rolls around and does fancy spins and goes ass over teakettle—not like that, Kiowa said, the poor bastard just flat-fuck fell. Boom. Down. Nothing else. It was a bright morning in mid-April. Lieutenant Cross felt the pain. He blamed himself. They stripped off Lavender's canteens and ammo, all the heavy things, and Rat Kiley said the obvious, the guy's dead, and Mitchell Sanders used his radio to report one US KIA and to request a chopper. Then they wrapped Lavender in his poncho. They carried him out to a dry paddy, established security, and sat smoking the dead man's dope until the chopper came. Lieutenant Cross kept to himself. He pictured Martha's smooth young face, thinking he loved her more than anything, more than his men, and now Ted Lavender was dead because he loved her so much and could not stop thinking about her. When the dustoff arrived, they carried Lavender aboard. Afterward they burned Than Khe. They marched until dusk, then dug their holes, and that night Kiowa kept explaining how you had to be there, how fast it was, how the poor guy just dropped like so much concrete. Boom-down, he said. Like cement.

In addition to the three standard weapons—the M-60, M-16, and M-79—they carried whatever presented itself, or whatever seemed appropriate as a means of killing or staying alive. They carried catch-as-catch-can. At various times, in various situations, they carried M-14s and CAR-15s and Swedish Ks and grease guns and captured AK-47s and Chi-Coms and RPGs and Simonov carbines and black market Uzis and .38 caliber Smith & Wesson handguns and 66 mm LAWs and shotguns and silencers and blackjacks and bayonets and C-4 plastic explosives. Lee Strunk carried a slingshot; a weapon of last resort, he called it. Mitchell Sanders carried brass knuckles. Kiowa carried his grandfather's feathered hatchet. Every third or fourth man carried a Claymore antipersonnel mine—3.5 pounds with its firing device. They all carried fragmentation grenades—14 ounces each. They all carried at least one M-18 colored smoke grenade—24 ounces. Some carried CS or tear gas grenades. Some carried white phosphorus grenades. They carried all they could bear, and then some, including a silent awe for the terrible power of the things they carried.

In the first week of April, before Lavender died, Lieutenant Jimmy Cross received a good-luck charm from Martha. It was a simple pebble, an ounce at most. Smooth to the touch, it was a milky white color with flecks of orange and violet, oval shaped, like a miniature egg. In the accompanying letter, Martha wrote that she had found the pebble on the Jersey shoreline, precisely where the land touched water at high tide, where things came together but also separated. It was this separate-but-together quality, she wrote, that had inspired her to pick up the pebble and to carry it in her breast pocket for several days, where it seemed weightless, and then to send it through the mail, by air, as a token of her truest feelings for him. Lieutenant Cross found this romantic. But he wondered what her truest feelings were, exactly, and what she meant by separate-but-together. He wondered how the tides and waves had come into play on that afternoon along the Jersey shoreline when Martha saw the pebble and bent down to rescue it from geology. He imagined bare feet. Martha was a poet, with the poet's sensibilities, and her feet would be brown and bare, the toenails unpainted, the eyes chilly and somber like the ocean in March, and though it was painful, he wondered who had been with her that afternoon. He imagined a pair of shadows moving along the strip of sand where things came together but also separated. It was phantom jealousy, he knew, but he couldn't help himself. He loved her so much. On the march, through the hot days of early April, he carried the pebble in his mouth, turning it with his tongue, tasting sea salt and moisture. His mind wandered. He had difficulty keeping his attention on the war. On occasion he would yell at his men to spread out the column, to keep their eyes open, but then he would slip away into daydreams, just pretending, walking barefoot along the Jersey shore, with Martha, carrying nothing. He would feel himself rising. Sun and waves and gentle winds, all love and lightness.

What they carried varied by mission.

When a mission took them to the mountains, they carried mosquito netting, machetes, canvas tarps, and extra bug juice.

If a mission seemed especially hazardous, or if it involved a place they knew to be bad, they carried everything they could. In certain heavily mined AOs, where the land was dense with Toe Poppers and Bouncing Betties, they took turns humping a 28-pound mine detector. With its headphones and big sensing plate, the equipment was a stress on the lower back and shoulders, awkward to handle, often useless because of the shrapnel in the earth, but they carried it anyway, partly for safety, partly for the illusion of safety.

On ambush, or other night missions, they carried peculiar little odds and ends. Kiowa always took along his New Testament and a pair of moccasins for silence. Dave Jensen carried night-sight vitamins high in carotene. Lee Strunk carried his slingshot; ammo, he claimed, would never be a problem. Rat Kiley carried brandy and M&Ms candy. Until he was shot, Ted Lavender carried the starlight scope, which weighed 6.3 pounds with its aluminum carrying case. Henry Dobbins carried his girl-friend's pantyhose wrapped around his neck as a comforter. They all carried ghosts. When dark came, they would move out single file across the meadows and paddies to their ambush coordinates, where they would quietly set up the Claymores and lie down and spend the night waiting.

Other missions were more complicated and required special equipment. In mid-April, it was their mission to search out and destroy the elaborate tunnel complexes in the Than Khe area south of Chu Lai. To blow the tunnels, they carried 1-pound blocks of pentrite high explosives, four blocks to a man, 68 pounds in all. They carried wiring, detonators, and battery-powered clackers. Dave Jensen carried earplugs. Most often, before blowing the tunnels, they were ordered by higher command to search them, which was considered bad news, but by and large they just shrugged and carried out orders. Because he was a big man, Henry Dobbins was excused from tunnel duty. The others would draw numbers. Before Lavender died there were seventeen men in the platoon, and whoever drew the number 17 would strip off his gear and crawl in headfirst with a flashlight and Lieutenant Cross's .45-caliber pistol. The rest of them would fan out as security. They would sit down or kneel, not facing the hole, listening to the ground beneath them, imagining cobwebs and ghosts, whatever was down there—the tunnel walls squeezing in—how the flashlight seemed impossibly heavy in the hand and how it was tunnel vision in the very strictest sense, compression in all ways, even time, and how you had to wiggle in—ass and elbows—a swallowed-up feeling—and how you found yourself worrying about odd things: Will your flashlight go dead? Do rats carry rabies? If you screamed, how far would the sound carry? Would your buddies hear it? Would they have the courage to drag you out? In some respects, though not many, the waiting was worse than the tunnel itself. Imagination was a killer.

On April 16, when Lee Strunk drew the number 17, he laughed and muttered something and went down quickly. The morning was hot and very still. Not good, Kiowa said. He looked at the tunnel opening, then out across a dry paddy toward the village of Than Khe. Nothing moved. No clouds or birds or people. As they waited, the men smoked and drank Kool-Aid, not talking much, feeling sympathy for Lee Strunk but also feeling the luck of the draw. You win some, you lose some, said Mitchell Sanders, and sometimes you settle for a rain check. It was a tired line and no one laughed.

Henry Dobbins ate a tropical chocolate bar. Ted Lavender popped a tranquilizer and went off to pee.

After five minutes, Lieutenant Jimmy Cross moved to the tunnel, leaned down, and examined the darkness. Trouble, he thought—a cave-in maybe. And then suddenly, without willing it, he was thinking about Martha. The stresses and fractures, the quick collapse, the two of them buried alive under all that weight. Dense, crushing love. Kneeling, watching the hole, he tried to concentrate on Lee Strunk and the war, all the dangers, but his love was too much for him, he felt paralyzed, he wanted to sleep inside her lungs and breathe her blood and be smothered. He wanted her to be a virgin and not a virgin, all at once. He wanted to know her. Intimate secrets: Why poetry? Why so sad? Why that grayness in her eyes? Why so alone? Not lonely, just alone—riding her bike across campus or sitting off by herself in the cafeteria—even dancing, she danced alone—and it was the aloneness that filled him with love. He remembered telling her that one evening. How she nodded and looked away. And how, later, when he kissed her, she received the kiss without returning it, her eyes wide open, not afraid, not a virgin's eyes, just flat and uninvolved.

Lieutenant Cross gazed at the tunnel. But he was not there. He was buried with Martha under the white sand at the Jersey shore. They were pressed together, and the pebble in his mouth was her tongue. He was smiling. Vaguely, he was aware of how quiet the day was, the sullen paddies, yet be could not bring himself to worry about matters of security. He was beyond that. He was just a kid at war, in love. He was twenty-four years old. He couldn't help it.

A few moments later Lee Strunk crawled out of the tunnel. He came up grinning, filthy but alive. Lieutenant Cross nodded. and closed his eyes while the others clapped Strunk on the back and made jokes about rising from the dead.

Worms, Rat Kiley said. Right out of the grave. Fuckin' zombie.

The men laughed. They all felt great relief.

Spook city, said Mitchell Sanders.

Lee Strunk made a funny ghost sound, a kind of moaning, yet very happy, and right then, when Strunk made that high happy, moaning sound, when he went *Ahooooo,* right then Ted Lavender was shot in the head on his way back from peeing. He lay with his mouth open. The teeth were broken. There was a swollen black bruise under his left eye. The cheekbone was gone. Oh shit, Rat Kiley said, the guy's dead. The guy's dead, he kept saying, which seemed profound—the guy's dead. I mean really.

The things they carried were determined to some extent by superstition. Lieutenant Cross carried his good-luck pebble. Dave Jensen carried a rabbit's foot. Norman Bowker, otherwise a very gentle person, carried a thumb that had been presented to him as a gift by Mitchell Sanders. The thumb was dark brown, rubbery to the touch, and weighed, 4 ounces at most. It had been cut from a VC corpse, a boy of fifteen or sixteen. They'd found him at the bottom of an irrigation ditch, badly burned, flies in his mouth and eyes. The boy wore black shorts and sandals. At the time of his death he had been carrying a pouch of rice, a rifle, and three magazines of ammunition.

You want my opinion, Mitchell Sanders said, there's a definite moral here.

He put his hand on the dead boy's wrist. He was quiet for a time, as if counting a pulse, then he patted the stomach, almost affectionately, and used Kiowa's hunting hatchet to remove the thumb.

Henry Dobbins asked what the moral was.

Moral?

You know. *Moral.*

Sanders wrapped the thumb in toilet paper and handed it across to Norman Bowker. There was no blood. Smiling, he kicked the boy's head, watched the flies scatter, and said, It's like with that old TV show—*Paladin.* Have gun, will travel.

Henry Dobbins thought about it.

Yeah, well, he finally said. I don't see no moral.

There it *is,* man.

Fuck off.

They carried USO stationery and pencils and pens. They carried Sterno, safety pins, trip flares, signal flares, spools of wire, razor blades, chewing tobacco, liberated joss sticks and statuettes of the smiling Buddha, candles, grease pencils, *The Stars and Stripes,* fingernail clippers, Psy Ops leaflets, bush hats, bolos, and much more. Twice a week, when the resupply choppers came in, they carried hot chow in green mermite cans and large canvas bags filled with iced beer and soda pop. They carried plastic water containers, each with a 2-gallon capacity. Mitchell Sanders carried a set of starched tiger fatigues for special occasions. Henry Dobbins carried Black Flag insecticide. Dave Jensen carried empty sandbags that could be filled at night for added protection. Lee Strunk carried tanning lotion. Some things they carried in common. Taking turns, they carried the big PRC-77 scrambler radio, which weighed 30 pounds with its battery. They shared the weight of memory. They took up what others could no longer bear. Often, they carried each other, the wounded or weak. They carried infections. They carried chess sets, basketballs, Vietnamese-English dictionaries, insignia of rank, Bronze Stars and Purple Hearts, plastic cards imprinted with the Code of Conduct. They carried diseases, among them malaria and dysentery. They carried lice and ringworm and leeches and paddy algae and various rots and molds. They carried the land itself—Vietnam, the place, the soil—a powdery orange-red dust that covered their boots and fatigues and faces. They carried the sky. The whole atmosphere, they carried it, the humidity, the monsoons, the stink of fungus and decay, all of it, they carried gravity. They moved like mules. By daylight they took sniper fire, at night they were mortared, but it was not battle, it was just the endless march, village to village, without purpose, nothing won or lost. They marched for the sake of the march. They plodded along slowly, dumbly, leaning forward against the heat, unthinking, all blood and bone, simple grunts, soldiering with their legs, toiling up the hills and down into the paddies and across the rivers and up again and down, just humping, one step and then the next and then another, but no volition, no will, because it was automatic, it was anatomy, and the war was entirely a matter of posture and carriage, the hump was everything, a kind of inertia, a kind of emptiness, a dullness of desire and intellect and conscience and hope and human sensibility. Their principles were in their feet. Their calculations were biological. They had no sense of strategy or mission. They searched the villages without knowing what to look for, not caring, kicking over jars of rice, frisking children and old men, blowing tunnels, sometimes setting fires and sometimes not, then forming up and moving on to the next village, then other villages, where it would always be the same. They carried their own lives. The pressures were enormous. In the heat of early afternoon, they would remove their helmets and flak jackets, walking bare, which was dangerous but which helped ease the strain. They would often discard things along the route of march. Purely for comfort, they would throw away rations, blow their Claymores and grenades, no matter, because by nightfall the resupply choppers would arrive with more of the same, then a day or two later still more, fresh watermelons and crates of ammunition and sunglasses and woolen sweaters—the resources were stunning—sparklers for the Fourth of July, colored eggs for Easter—it was the great American war chest—the fruits of science, the smokestacks, the canneries, the arsenals at Hartford, the Minnesota forests, the machine shops, the vast fields of corn and wheat—they carried like freight trains; they carried it on their backs and shoulders—and for all the ambiguities of Vietnam, all the mysteries and unknowns, there was at least the single abiding certainty that they would never be at a loss for things to carry.

After the chopper took Lavender away, Lieutenant Jimmy Cross led his men into the village of Than Khe. They burned everything. They shot chickens and dogs, they trashed the village well, they called in artillery and watched the wreckage, then they marched for several hours through the hot afternoon, and then at dusk, while Kiowa explained how Lavender died, Lieutenant Cross found himself trembling.

He tried not to cry. With his entrenching tool, which weighed 5 pounds, he began digging a hole in the earth.

He felt shame. He hated himself. He had loved Martha more than his men, and as a consequence Lavender was now dead, and this was something he would have to carry like a stone in his stomach for the rest of the war.

All he could do was dig. He used his entrenching tool like an ax, slashing, feeling both love and hate, and then later, when it was full dark, he sat at the bottom of his foxhole and wept. It went on for a long while. In part, he was grieving for Ted Lavender, but mostly it was for Martha, and for himself, because she belonged to another world, which was not quite real, and because she was a junior at Mount Sebastian College in New Jersey, a poet and a virgin and uninvolved, and because he realized she did not love him and never would.

Like cement, Kiowa whispered in the dark. I swear to God—boom, down. Not a word.

I've heard this, said Norman Bowker.

A pisser, you know? Still zipping himself up. Zapped while zipping.

All right, fine. That's enough.

Yeah, but you had to see it, the guy just—

I *heard*, man. Cement. So why not shut the fuck *up?*

Kiowa shook his head sadly and glanced over at the hole where Lieutenant Jimmy Cross sat watching the night. The air was thick and wet. A warm dense fog had settled over the paddies and there was the stillness that precedes rain.

After a time Kiowa sighed.

One thing for sure, he said. The lieutenant's in some deep hurt. I mean that crying jag—the way he was carrying on—it wasn't fake or anything, it was real heavy-duty hurt. The man cares.

Sure, Norman Bowker said.

Say what you want, the man does care.

We all got problems.

Not Lavender. No, I guess not, Bowker said. Do me a favor, though.

Shut up?

That's a smart Indian. Shut up.

Shrugging, Kiowa pulled off his boots. He wanted to say more, just to lighten up his sleep, but instead he opened his New Testament and arranged it beneath his head as a pillow. The fog made things seem hollow and unattached. He tried not to think about Ted Lavender, but then he was thinking how fast it was, no drama, down and dead, and how it was hard to feel anything except surprise. It seemed unchristian. He wished he could find some great sadness, or even anger, but the emotion wasn't there and he couldn't make it happen. Mostly he felt pleased to be alive. He liked the smell of the New Testament under his cheek, the leather and ink and paper and glue, whatever the chemicals were. He liked hearing the sounds of night. Even his fatigue, it felt fine, the stiff muscles and the prickly awareness of his own body, a floating feeling. He enjoyed not being dead. Lying there, Kiowa admired Lieutenant Jimmy Cross's capacity for grief. He wanted to share the man's pain, he wanted to care as Jimmy Cross cared. And yet when he closed his eyes, all he could think was Boom-down, and all he could feel was the pleasure of having his boots off and the fog curling in around him and the damp soil and the Bible smells and the plush comfort of night.

After a moment Norman Bowker sat up in the dark.

What the hell, he said. You want to talk, *talk*. Tell it to me.

Forget it.

No, man, go on. One thing I hate, it's a silent Indian.

For the most part they carried themselves with poise, a kind of dignity. Now and then, however, there were times of panic, when they squealed or wanted to squeal but couldn't, when they twitched and made moaning sounds and covered their heads and said Dear Jesus and flopped around on the earth and fired their weapons blindly and cringed and sobbed and begged for the noise to stop and went wild and made stupid promises to themselves and to God and to their mothers and fathers, hoping not to die. In different ways, it happened to all of them. Afterward, when the firing ended, they would blink and peek up. They would touch their bodies, feeling shame, then quickly hiding it. They would force themselves to stand. As if in slow motion, frame by frame, the world would take on the old logic—absolute silence, then the wind, then sunlight, then voices. It was the burden of being alive. Awkwardly, the men would reassemble themselves, first in private, then in groups, becoming soldiers again. They would repair the leaks in their eyes. They would check for casualties, call in dustoffs, light cigarettes, try to smile, clear their throats and spit and begin cleaning their weapons. After a time someone would shake his head and say, No lie, I almost shit my pants, and someone else would laugh, which meant it was bad, yes, but the guy had obviously not shit his pants, it wasn't that bad, and in any case nobody would ever do such a thing and then go ahead and talk about it. They would squint into the dense, oppressive sunlight. For a few moments, perhaps, they would fall silent, lighting a joint and tracking its passage from man to man, inhaling, holding in the humiliation. Scary stuff, one of them might say. But then someone else would grin or flick his eyebrows and say, Roger-dodger, almost cut me a new asshole, *almost.*

There were numerous such poses. Some carried themselves with a sort of wistful resignation, others with pride or stiff soldierly discipline or good humor or macho zeal. They were afraid of dying but they were even more afraid to show it.

They found jokes to tell.

They used a hard vocabulary to contain the terrible softness. *Greased* they'd say. *Offed, lit up, zapped while zipping.* It wasn't cruelty, just stage presence. They were actors. When someone died, it wasn't quite dying, because in a curious way it seemed scripted, and because they had their lines mostly memorized, irony mixed with tragedy, and because they called it by other names, as if to encyst and destroy the reality of death itself. They kicked corpses. They cut off thumbs. They talked grunt lingo. They told stories about Ted Lavender's supply of tranquilizers, how the poor guy didn't feel a thing, how incredibly tranquil he was.

There's a moral here, said Mitchell Sanders.

They were waiting for Lavender's chopper, smoking the dead man's dope. The moral's pretty obvious, Sanders said, and winked. Stay away from drugs. No joke, they'll ruin your day every time.

Cute, said Henry Dobbins.

Mind blower, get it? Talk about wiggy. Nothing left, just blood and brains.

They made themselves laugh.

There it is, they'd say. Over and over—there it is, my friend, there it is—as if the repetition itself were an act of poise, a balance between crazy and almost crazy, knowing without going, there it is, which meant be cool, let it ride, because Oh yeah, man, you can't change what can't be changed, there it is, there it absolutely and positively and fucking well *is.*

They were tough.

They carried all the emotional baggage of men who might die. Grief, terror, love, longing—these were intangibles, but the intangibles had their own mass and specific gravity, they had tangible weight. They carried shameful memories. They carried the common secret of cowardice barely restrained, the instinct to run or freeze or hide, and in many respects this was the heaviest burden of all, for it could never be put down, it required perfect balance and perfect posture. They carried their reputations. They carried the soldier's greatest fear, which was the fear of blushing. Men killed, and died, because they were embarrassed not to. It was what had brought them to the war in the first place, nothing positive, no dreams of glory or honor, just to avoid the blush of dishonor. They died so as not to die of embarrassment. They crawled into tunnels and walked point and advanced under fire. Each morning, despite the unknowns, they made their legs move. They endured. They kept humping. They did not submit to the obvious alternative, which was simply to close the eyes and fall. So easy, really. Go limp and rumble to the ground and let the muscles unwind and not speak and not budge until your buddies picked you up and lifted you into the chopper that would roar and dip its nose and carry you off to the world. A mere matter of falling, yet no one ever fell. It was not courage, exactly; the object was not valor. Rather, they were too frightened to be cowards.

By and large they carried these things inside, maintaining the masks of composure. They sneered at sick call. They spoke bitterly about guys who had found release by shooting off their own toes or fingers. Pussies, they'd say. Candy-asses. It was fierce, mocking talk, with only a trace of envy or awe, but even so the image played itself out behind their eyes.

They imagined the muzzle against flesh. So easy: squeeze the trigger and blow away a toe. They imagined it. They imagined the quick, sweet pain, then the evacuation to Japan, then a hospital with warm beds and cute geisha nurses.

And they dreamed of freedom birds.

At night, on guard, staring into the dark, they were carried away by jumbo jets. They felt the rush of takeoff. *Gone!* they yelled. And then velocity—wings and engines—a smiling stewardess—but it was more than a plane, it was a real bird, a big sleek silver bird with feathers and talons and high screeching. They were flying. The weights fell off; there was nothing to bear. They laughed and held on tight, feeling the cold slap of wind and altitude, soaring, thinking *It's over, I'm gone!*—they were naked, they were light and free—it was all lightness, bright and fast and buoyant, light as light, a helium buzz in the brain, a giddy bubbling in the lungs as they were taken up over the clouds and the war, beyond duty, beyond gravity and mortification and global entanglements—*Sin loi!* they yelled. *I'm sorry, mother-fuckers, but I'm out of it, I'm goofed, I'm on a space cruise, I'm gone!*—and it was a restful, unencumbered sensation just riding the light waves, sailing that big silver freedom bird over the mountains and oceans, over America, over the farms and great sleeping cities and cemeteries and highways and the golden arches of McDonald's, it was flight, a kind of fleeing, a kind of falling, failing higher and higher, spinning off the edge of the earth and beyond the sun and through the vast, silent vacuum where there were no burdens and where everything weighed exactly nothing—*Gone!* they screamed, *I'm sorry but I'm gone!*—and so at night, not quite dreaming, they gave themselves over to lightness, they were carried, they were purely borne.

On the morning after Ted Lavender died, First Lieutenant Jimmy Cross crouched at the bottom of his foxhole and burned Martha's letters. Then he burned the two photographs. There was a steady rain falling, which made it difficult, but he used heat tabs and Sterno to build a small fire, screening it with his body, holding the photographs over the tight blue flame with the tips of his fingers.

He realized it was only a gesture. Stupid, he thought. Sentimental, too, but mostly just stupid.

Lavender was dead. You couldn't burn the blame.

Besides, the letters were in his head. And even now, without photographs, Lieutenant Cross could see Martha playing volleyball in her white gym shorts and yellow T-shirt. He could see her moving in the rain.

When the fire died out, Lieutenant Cross pulled his poncho over his shoulders and ate breakfast from a can.

There was no great mystery, he decided.

In those burned letters Martha had never mentioned the war, except to say, Jimmy, take care of yourself. She wasn't involved. She signed the letters Love, but it wasn't love, and all the fine lines and technicalities did not matter. Virginity was no longer an issue. He hated her. Yes, he did. He hated her. Love, too, but it was a hard, hating kind of love.

The morning came up wet and blurry. Everything seemed part of everything else, the fog and Martha and the deepening rain.

He was a soldier, after all.

Half smiling, Lieutenant Jimmy Cross took out his maps. He shook his head hard, as if to clear it, then bent forward and began planning the day's march. In ten minutes, or maybe twenty, he would rouse the men and they would pack up and head west, where the maps showed the country to be green and inviting. They would do what they had always done.

The rain might add some weight, but otherwise it would be one more day layered upon all the other days.

He was realistic about it. There was that new hardness in his stomach. He loved her but he hated her.

No more fantasies, he told himself.

Henceforth, when he thought about Martha, it would be only to think that she belonged elsewhere. He would shut down the daydreams. This was not Mount Sebastian, it was another world, where there were no pretty poems or midterm exams, a place where men died because of carelessness and gross stupidity. Kiowa was right. Boom-down, and you were dead, never partly dead.

Briefly, in the rain, Lieutenant Cross saw Martha's gray eyes gazing back at him.

He understood.

It was very sad, he thought. The things men carried inside. The things men did or felt they had to do.

He almost nodded at her, but didn't.

Instead he went back to his maps. He was now determined to perform his duties firmly and without negligence. It wouldn't help Lavender, he knew that, but from this point on he would comport himself as an officer. He would dispose of his good-luck pebble. Swallow it, maybe, or use Lee Strunk's slingshot, or just drop it along the trail. On the march he would impose strict field discipline. He would be careful to send out flank security, to prevent straggling or bunching up, to keep his troops moving at the proper pace and at the proper interval. He would insist on clean weapons. He would confiscate the remainder of Lavender's dope. Later in the day, perhaps, he would call the men together and speak to them plainly. He would accept the blame for what had happened to Ted Lavender. He would be a man about it. He would look them in the eyes, keeping his chin level, and he would issue the new SOPs in a calm impersonal tone of voice, a lieutenant's voice, leaving no room for argument or discussion. Commencing immediately, he'd tell them, they would no longer abandon equipment along the route of march. They would police up their acts. They would get their shit together, and keep it together, and maintain it neatly and in good working order.

He would not tolerate laxity. He would show strength, distancing himself.

Among the men there would be grumbling, of course, and maybe worse, because their days would seem longer and their loads heavier, but Lieutenant Jimmy Cross reminded himself that his obligation was not to be loved but to lead. He would dispense with love; it was not now a factor. And if anyone quarreled or complained, he would simply tighten his lips and arrange his shoulders in the correct command posture. He might give a curt little nod. Or he might not. He might just shrug and say, Carry on, then they would saddle up and form into a column and move out toward the villages west of Than Khe.

All the Difference

Isaac Grenfell
Isaac Grenfell is a college sophomore and
convenience store clerk.

Manhood isn't simply something one finds, like change
in a couch or car keys. It is something that must be
handed down from older men to those young enough to be
impressed by it yet old enough to grasp it. Manhood, I've
noticed, is pretty rare among males my age. Many think it
is something to be found in the bottom of a liquor bottle
or in the crotch of a teenage girl. But the quest for
manhood is futile unless that quest is focused inwardly.
That was a lesson I happened to learn before I made any
potentially harmful major decisions in my life.

Interestingly enough, my father was not the source of
this lesson. Rather, it came from the father of my
brother-in-law. In all of my life, Bruce is one of the
most peculiar characters that I have ever met. In
appearance, he is like a cross between Alfred Hitchcock
and Pablo Neruda. In ideology, he is like a combination
of Timothy Leary and Alexander Solzhenitsen. He has a
pretentious third-generation English drawl, a prominent
nose and an equally prominent belly, and an ever-present
corn cob pipe in which he always has a bowl of pot. As a
younger man, he taught art (drawing, specifically), but
now is retired, always bouncing from one mental home to
another.

It so happened that he was to spend the summer of
three years ago mining for precious gems in central
Montana. Seeking an escape from the dull drag of a
typical summer, I volunteered to join him.

He picked me up in a beaten-up old Volvo. I packed
lightly, bringing only a tent and a week's worth of
clothes, which I could easily parlay into two. All of our
baggage was crammed into the back seat, as the trunk was
filled entirely with digging equipment and Gatorade.
After loading my stuff into the car, we promptly headed
for York, a tiny hamlet near Helena.

On the drive to York, Bruce and I spoke of a wide range of subjects, from the state of U.S. prisons to French law and its influence on American bureaucracy (Montana's State Government has a Department of Cattle). All the while, he was puffing away at his pipe (nobody suspected that some old man puffing away at a corn cob pipe would be smoking pot). Intermittently, he would offer the pipe to me as if it were some sort of peace pipe. Each time, though, I would decline, pretending to have some sort of moral objection (as if a 15-year-old would have any deep moral insight into anything).

I lived in a mind filled with public school dogma which taught me that up was up, down was down, and never the twain shall meet. Bruce lived in a world of psychedelic experience, of fighting to get innocent people out of prison, of rejection of the arrogant attitudes which permeate every institution in our society. Until that point, any learning experience I had had consisted of obediently nodding and accepting any truth put before me. I thought that I was fairly intelligent, as I had experienced unlimited praise for my intellectual prowess, which in reality was nothing more than regurgitating anything put before me. So, when Bruce told me bluntly over a cheeseburger dinner, "You're not a very bright kid," I was speechless. I mean, what's the comeback for that, "Oh yes I am!?" I sat there and looked over at a sign hanging above the grill that read, "Jack-In-The-Box: We cook the shit out of our burgers!" Upon reading that, I thought, maybe this guy is right. Maybe I just fit nicely into the system.

Everyone should try working in a gravel pit in July in front of the Sun God. It's fun. I understood quickly why he filled the trunk with Gatorade. I used about half of it during the first day. Shoveling, hauling, sifting, shoveling, hauling, sifting . . . the act of working in the heat, the smell of sweat and melting vinyl, hardened my soul and my work ethic very quickly. The first day I was there, I kept thinking, "Why am I doing this? I'm stuck in this hell-pit for a week and a half!" But once the digging was over for the day, I understood. We sifted through the sorted gravel, inch by inch, pebble by

pebble, for our objective—sapphires! While they are
monetarily pretty worthless, they make nice gifts, and
they are my birthstone. It's odd that nature could craft
something as rare and as beautiful as the purple-blue
luminescent stone among those piles and piles of
knapweek-covered gravel. It's as if, in searching for
those sapphires among the dust and worthless rocks, I was
also searching for something inside of my soul, something
I could put in a box and say, "There, that's what I'm
here for!" I know where to dig now, I just need to hit
the mother lode.

5

WORK

Linton Park, *Flax Scutching Bee*, 1885, bed ticking, 31½×50½".

"AN AMBASSADOR OF WASHINGTON DC"
OR THE BEST WORST JOB I EVER HAD

■

Al Hoff

Al Hoff wrote the following selection for the second issue of the zine McJob.

Good morning—I'll be your tour guide at Arlington Cemetery today. I'd like
to remind you to keep your hands and head inside the bus at all times. Our
first scheduled stop will be the Kennedy Gravesite. . . .

Yeah, that's me—I was the tour guide, the spiel-giver, the question-
answerer on those goofy zoo-buses that make loops around the historical
sites in Washington DC and Arlington Cemetery. Hey, it wasn't just a $4
an hour miserable dead-end job—we were instructed to view ourselves as
"ambassadors of Washington DC," that one treasured memory of the visit
to the Nation's Capital that customers would take home.

It was one of the suckiest jobs I've held but in some ways, I have to love
it. No other bad job provided me with such an unlimited supply of anec-
dotes and even after all these years I bet I'm one of less than 500 people in
the U.S.A. who can recite off exactly how high the Washington Monument
is—five hundred and fifty-five feet, five and one-eighth inches, but sinking slowly.

THE JOB

I answered the ad in the newspaper for tour guides, passed the "good
personality" interview (evidently, the scraggly double-processed peroxide hair I had at the time was not a negative factor!) and was signed
up for 2 weeks of training—training wage $3.25. Training consisted of
driving around and around the route while the suggested spiel was
given over and over again. At the completion of training, you took a
written test and did a real-life spiel on the bus. You had earned your
name tag.

There were two routes—a 45 to 60 minute loop within Arlington
Cemetery and the complete Mall and Capitol Hill tour (1–2 hours). What
sucked? Well, first and foremost, any job where you deal with the public
sucks. The public is rude, sloppy, smelly, noisy, forever eating and drinking and astonishingly ignorant. I don't expect people to know who donated the Whistler paintings to the Smithsonian, but asking who *lives* in
the Washington Monument? Which building *the President* lives in? And
no! every tree in bloom is NOT a cherry blossom tree! People exhibited
some of the worst behavior at Arlington Cemetery. Even though, I'd spell
out clearly that Arlington was still a functioning cemetery and not an
amusement park, they'd still hang out of the bus window videotaping
some poor bastard's funeral.

Other miseries of the job included DC weather (cold in the winter, rainy in the spring [people wouldn't get off the bus] and indescribably hot and humid in the summer), getting stuck in traffic (not just that you'd have to keep up some patter, but there was no seat for the tour giver—you sat on this hot lump of metal that was the engine. When stopped, there was no ventilation and you just sat sucking up engine fumes.)—and the hours. Be there at 7:30 A.M. Leave at 8:00 P.M. It's a weekend or holiday? Well, those are our busiest days! Everybody work! I took the triple hit of Spring Break, Easter and Cherry Blossom Festival working 27 straight days—spewing out the same facts hour after hour after hour.

EMPLOYEES

There were bus drivers and tour spielers. The bus drivers were mostly DC firemen or DC Metrobus drivers who were making some spare cash. They also had some sort of union and got fairly good money to essentially drive in a circle in areas where other vehicles were prohibited. The tour-spielers fell into three groups: (1) high school graduates looking for any job (2) oddballs who truly loved the tour business and were on their 9th fun-filled year and (3) assorted losers. The assorted losers category included me, the grandson of a 40's movie star, a girl so dyslexic she could barely function and a man who claimed to have been a friend of Elvis Presley's in Memphis. (When I challenged this, he brought in snapshots of himself and Elvis, proving *me* wrong. When he wasn't passing out candy, he also shilled for Jesus.)

BOSSMAN

There was no true "boss"—just a rotating set of "supervisors" who got to carry walkie-talkies. Their job was simply assigning you to a bus and discussions were generally limited to "Hoff! Arlington! Bus 21!" I was well-liked amongst the supervisors because I showed up regularly and on time and did whatever they said to do. (While I was there, one tour spieler just walked off the bus *in mid-tour*, never to return.)

THE UNIFORM

This was provided, it was bad and no substitutions allowed. A blue polyester flared skirt, two poly-cotton shirts (one to wear, one to launder—the endless handwash cycle) and a blue windbreaker with the company logo on it. That'll keep you toasty in the winter! The summer season saw the introduction of a polo shirt with the logo. It was excruciatingly embarrassing to have to travel home on the subway in these clothes and I lived in fear of people asking me questions.

JOB ENVIRONMENT

If you weren't on a bus spieling, you were to remain "on call" in one of the two trailers provided for the drivers and tour givers—one was behind some construction at Arlington, the other behind the snack bar at the Lincoln Memorial. They were tiny single room trailers, with a soda machine, candy machine and small fridge. No bathroom. Some chairs. On an average day you could spend half your time in the trailer. We were prohibited from sitting outside in the sun and fresh air—in case we picked our noses or something and belied our "ambassador" status.

There wasn't anything to do but sit with the other losers, smoke and eat candy bars. Remember, for every hour you sat around bored shitless you were making another $4 (before taxes). The trailer was a Title VII nightmare. We sat around in the one small room and mostly the guys talked—whether white or black girls gave better head, what was wrong with fags or how hard someone had partied the night before. Firemen would provide totally disgusting tales of horrors they'd seen on the job. Some of the workers were unhappy listening to all this—but there was nowhere to go.

PERKS

Without question the biggest perk was something that almost no one cared about—and that was information. You learned more than you ever wanted to about Washington DC, the museums, the monuments, the marble used, the name of the architect, the year he died and where *he* was buried, the name of the first ship sunk in World War I and what distinguished it from the ships that came after it, the names of all the Challenger astronauts as well as every flowering plant or tree, and where every port-a-potty was. (The downside of this is that for YEARS after I had this job, not one friend, or friend of a friend, or anybody else's family came to town without me being enlisted to "give the tour.")

With your uniform on, in your off-hours, you were free to take the bus tour as many times as you wished (seating permitted, of course). At the end of the day, this might mean a free ride to a subway stop on the route, but you still had to listen to someone else's spiel. This was encouraged, you might learn something. It was strongly recommended in our spare time (!) we ride around on the buses when the Tour Fanatics were giving the spiel. Arrrgghhh.

STEALING POTENTIAL

Zero, unless you counted acquiring arcane knowledge for free. The final pay checks were withheld until you returned the hideous uniform and the nametag. I kept my nametag as a memento and got my last paycheck by writing an angry but intelligently worded letter to Payroll demanding it. Sometimes, the bus drivers would beat up the candy machine and distribute the free chips and gum. Big whoop.

DON'T TELL A SOUL

Our status as "ambassadors" was strictly governed and this included much editorial control over what we could and could not say on the tour. Frankly, this restriction fascinated me and I often tried to work around it. It was to be a neutral tour—anything that smacked of partisan politics, scandal or unpleasantness was forbidden. You were not to use the term "soldier" (that might offend former Navy personnel)—the term "serviceman" was preferred. It was the "Korean Conflict" and the "Vietnam Conflict" (technically, undeclared wars). (I held my tongue when people asked directions to the "*Vietnamese* Memorial," as tempting a lead-in as that was!) The Civil War was only to be spoken of in the most general terms and we were to take care to present the Confederate side in favorable terms as well—DC is below the Mason-Dixon line where this is still a sensitive issue.

My favorite restriction was that you were never ever ever to use the term "coming up on your right/left" (as in "coming up on your left will be the Lincoln Memorial") in Arlington Cemetery. It was feared that some tourist might think that something, or more horrifying, *someone* was coming up from the earthen graves! "Coming up on your right, the Father of the Nuclear Navy, Admiral Rickover—now a crazed, flesh-eating ZOMBIE!!!"

Well, I'm all for the First Amendment, but even more so, I'm for interesting tours and it used to frustrate me greatly that I couldn't point out interesting and scandalous things—that's where Congressman Mills got caught skinny-dipping with the stripper, that's Oliver North's office (it was during the Iran-Contra mess), that's the Howard Johnson where the Watergate break-in and bugging was run from, and that the "eternal" flame at JFK's gravesite goes out sometimes in the rain.

THE END

It's funny but I have no memory of quitting, though I most certainly did. By all means, visit the nation's capital—but don't call me! Ride the bus like everybody else. Make the tour interesting by asking lots of awkward questions, and please, keep your hands and head inside the bus at all times.

WORK

—■—

Bertrand Russell

The following selection is from Russell's 1930 book The Conquest of Happiness.

 hether work should be placed among the causes of happiness or among the causes of unhappiness may perhaps be regarded as a

doubtful question. There is certainly much work which is exceedingly irksome, and an excess of work is always very painful. I think, however, that, provided work is not excessive in amount, even the dullest work is to most people less painful than idleness. There are in work all grades, from mere relief of tedium up to the profoundest delights, according to the nature of the work and the abilities of the worker. Most of the work that most people have to do is not in itself interesting, but even such work has certain great advantages. To begin with, it fills a good many hours of the day without the need of deciding what one shall do. Most people, when they are left free to fill their own time according to their own choice, are at a loss to think of anything sufficiently pleasant to be worth doing. And whatever they decide on, they are troubled by the feeling that something else would have been pleasanter. To be able to fill leisure intelligently is the last product of civilization, and at present very few people have reached this level. Moreover the exercise of choice is in itself tiresome. Except to people with unusual initiative it is positively agreeable to be told what to do at each hour of the day, provided the orders are not too unpleasant. Most of the idle rich suffer unspeakable boredom as the price of their freedom from drudgery. At times, they may find relief by hunting big game in Africa, or by flying round the world, but the number of such sensations is limited, especially after youth is past. Accordingly the more intelligent rich men work nearly as hard as if they were poor, while rich women for the most part keep themselves busy with innumerable trifles of whose earth-shaking performance they are firmly persuaded.

Work therefore is desirable, first and foremost, as a preventive of boredom, for the boredom that a man feels when he is doing necessary though uninteresting work is as nothing in comparison with the boredom that he feels when he has nothing to do with his days. With this advantage of work another is associated, namely that it makes holidays much more delicious when they come. Provided a man does not have to work so hard as to impair his vigor, he is likely to find far more zest in his free time than an idle man could possibly find.

The second advantage of most paid work and of some unpaid work is that it gives chances of success and opportunities for ambition. In most work success is measured by income, and while our capitalistic society continues, this is inevitable. It is only where the best work is concerned that this measure ceases to be the natural one to apply. The desire that men feel to increase their income is quite as much a desire for success as for the extra comforts that a higher income can procure. However dull work may be, it becomes bearable if it is a means of building up a reputation, whether in the world at large or only in one's own circle. Continuity of purpose is one of the most essential ingredients of happiness in the long run, and for most men this comes chiefly through their work. In this respect those women whose lives are occupied with housework are much less fortunate than men, or than women who work outside the home. The domesticated wife does not receive wages, has no means of bettering herself, is taken for granted by her husband (who sees practically nothing of what she does), and is valued by him not for her housework but for quite other qualities. Of course this does not apply to those women who are sufficiently well-to-do to make beautiful houses and beautiful gardens and become the envy of their neighbors; but such women are comparatively few, and for the great majority housework cannot bring as much satisfaction as work of other kinds brings to men and to professional women.

The satisfaction of killing time and of affording some outlet, however modest, for ambition, belongs to most work, and is sufficient to make even a man whose work is dull happier on the average than a man who has no work at all. But when work is interesting, it is capable of giving satisfaction of a far higher order than mere relief from tedium. The kinds of work in which there is some interest may be arranged in a hierarchy. I shall begin with those which are only mildly interesting and end with those that are worthy to absorb the whole energies of a great man.

Two chief elements make work interesting; first, the exercise of skill, and second, construction.

Every man who has acquired some unusual skill enjoys exercising it until it has become a matter of course, or until he can no longer improve himself. This motive to activity begins in early childhood: a boy who can stand on his head becomes reluctant to stand on his feet. A great deal of work gives the same pleasure that is to be derived from games of skill. The work of a lawyer or a politician must contain in a more delectable form a great deal of the same pleasure that is to be derived from playing bridge. Here of course there is not only the exercise of skill but the outwitting of a skilled opponent. Even where this competitive element is absent, however, the performance of difficult feats is agreeable. A man who can do stunts in an aeroplane finds the pleasure so great that for the sake of it he is willing to risk his life. I imagine that an able surgeon, in spite of the painful circumstances in which his work is done, derives satisfaction from the exquisite precision of his operations. The same kind of pleasure, though in a less intense form, is to be derived from a great deal of work of a humbler kind. All skilled work can be pleasurable, provided the skill required is either variable or capable of indefinite improvement. If these conditions are absent, it will cease to be interesting when a man has acquired his maximum skill. A man who runs three-mile races will cease to find pleasure in this occupation when he passes the age at which he can beat his own previous record. Fortunately there is a very considerable amount of work in which new circumstances call for new skill and a man can go on improving, at any rate until he has reached middle age. In some kinds of skilled work, such as politics, for example, it seems that men are at their best between sixty and seventy, the reason being that in such occupations a wide experience of other men is essential. For this reason successful politicians are apt to be happier at the age of seventy than any other men of equal age. Their only competitors in this respect are the men who are the heads of big businesses.

There is, however, another element possessed by the best work, which is even more important as a source of happiness than is the exercise of skill. This is the element of constructiveness. In some work, though by no means in most, something is built up which remains as a monument when the work is completed. We may distinguish construction from destruction by the following criterion. In construction the initial state of affairs is comparatively haphazard, while the final state of affairs embodies a purpose: in destruction the reverse is the case; the initial state of affairs embodies a purpose, while the final state of affairs is haphazard, that is to say, all that is intended by the destroyer is to produce a state of affairs which does not embody a certain purpose. This criterion applies in the most literal and obvious case, namely the construction and destruction of buildings. In constructing a building a previously made plan is carried out, whereas in destroying it no one decides exactly how the materials are to lie when the demolition is complete. Destruction is of course necessary very often as a preliminary to subsequent construction; in that case it is part of a whole which is constructive. But not infrequently a man will engage in activities of which the purpose is destructive without regard to any construction that may come after. Frequently he will conceal this from himself by the belief that he is only sweeping away in order to build afresh, but it is generally possible to unmask this pretense, when it is a pretense, by asking him what the subsequent construction is to be. On this subject it will be found that he will speak vaguely and without enthusiasm, whereas on the preliminary destruction he has spoken precisely and with zest. This applies to not a few revolutionaries and militarists and other apostles of violence. They are actuated, usually without their own knowledge, by hatred: the destruction of what they hate is their real purpose, and they are comparatively indifferent to the question what is to come after it. Now I cannot deny that in the work of destruction as in the work of construction there may be joy. It is a fiercer joy, perhaps at moments more intense, but it is less profoundly satisfying, since the result is one in which little satisfaction is to be found. You kill your enemy, and when he is dead your occupation is gone, and the satisfaction that you derive from victory quickly fades. The work of construction, on the other hand, when completed is delightful to contemplate, and moreover is never so fully completed that there is nothing further to do about it. The most satisfactory purposes are those that lead on indefinitely from one success to another without ever coming to a dead end; and in this respect it will be found that construction is a greater source of happiness than destruction. Perhaps it would be more correct to say that those who find satisfaction in construction find in it greater satisfaction than the lovers of destruction can find in destruction, for if once you have become filled with hate you will not easily derive from construction the pleasure which another man would derive from it.

At the same time few things are so likely to cure the habit of hatred as the opportunity to do constructive work of an important kind.

The satisfaction to be derived from success in a great constructive enterprise is one of the most massive that life has to offer, although unfortunately in its highest forms it is open only to men of exceptional ability. Nothing can rob a man of the happiness of successful achievement in an important piece of work, unless it be the proof that after all his work was bad. There are many forms of such satisfaction. The man who by a scheme of irrigation has caused the wilderness to blossom like the rose enjoys it in one of its most tangible forms. The creation of an organization may be a work of supreme importance. So is the work of those few statesmen who have devoted their lives to producing order out of chaos, of whom Lenin is the supreme type in our day. The most obvious examples are artists and men of science. Shakespeare says of his verse: "So long as men can breathe, or eyes can see, so long lives this." And it cannot be doubted that the thought consoled him for misfortune. In his sonnets he maintains that the thought of his friend reconciled him to life, but I cannot help suspecting that the sonnets he wrote to his friend were even more effective for this purpose than the friend himself. Great artists and great men of science do work which is in itself delightful; while they are doing it, it secures them the respect of those whose respect is worth having, which gives them the most fundamental kind of power, namely power over men's thoughts and feelings. They have also the most solid reasons for thinking well of themselves. This combination of fortunate circumstances ought, one would think, to be enough to make any man happy. Nevertheless it is not so. Michael Angelo, for example, was a profoundly unhappy man, and maintained (not, I am sure, with truth) that he would not have troubled to produce works of art if he had not had to pay the debts of his impecunious relations. The power to produce great art is very often, though by no means always, associated with a temperamental unhappiness, so great that but for the joy which the artist derives from his work, he would be driven to suicide. We cannot, therefore, maintain that even the greatest work must make a man happy; we can only maintain that it must make him less unhappy. Men of science, however, are far less often temperamentally unhappy than artists are, and in the main the men who do great work in science are happy men, whose happiness is derived primarily from their work.

One of the causes of unhappiness among intellectuals in the present day is that so many of them, especially those whose skill is literary, find no opportunity for the independent exercise of their talents, but have to hire themselves out to rich corporations directed by Philistines, who insist upon their producing what they themselves regard as pernicious nonsense. If you were to inquire among journalists in either England or America whether they believed in the policy of the newspaper for which they worked, you would find, I believe, that only a small minority do so; the rest, for the sake of a livelihood, prostitute their skill to purposes which they believe to be harmful. Such work cannot bring any real satisfaction, and in the course of reconciling himself to the doing of it, a man has to make himself so cynical that he can no longer derive whole-hearted satisfaction from anything whatever. I cannot condemn men who undertake work of this sort, since starvation is too serious an alternative, but I think that where it is possible to do work that is satisfactory to a man's constructive impulses without entirely starving, he will be well advised from the point of view of his own happiness if he chooses it in preference to work much more highly paid but not seeming to him worth doing on its own account. Without self-respect genuine happiness is scarcely possible. And the man who is ashamed of his work can hardly achieve self-respect.

The satisfaction of constructive work, though it may, as things are, be the privilege of a minority, can nevertheless be the privilege of a quite large minority. Any man who is his own master in his work can feel it; so can any man whose work appears to him useful and requires considerable skill. The production of satisfactory children is a difficult constructive work capable of affording profound satisfaction. Any woman who has achieved this can feel that as a result of her labor the world contains something of value which it would not otherwise contain.

Human beings differ profoundly in regard to the tendency to regard their lives as a whole. To some men it is natural to do so, and essential to happiness to be able to do so with some satisfaction. To others life is a series of detached incidents without directed movement and without unity. I think the former sort are more likely to achieve happiness than the latter, since they will gradually build up those circumstances from which they can derive contentment and self-respect, whereas the others will be blown about by the winds of circumstances now this way, now that, without ever arriving at any haven. The habit of viewing life as a whole is an essential part both of wisdom and of true morality, and is one of the things which ought to be encouraged in education. Consistent purpose is not enough to make life happy, but it is an almost indispensable condition of a happy life. And consistent purpose embodies itself mainly in work.

SHOESHINING

Malcolm X

This selection is excerpted from The Autobiography of Malcolm X, *which was published in 1964.*

When I got home, Ella said there had been a telephone call from somebody named Shorty. He had left a message that over at the Roseland State Ballroom, the shoeshine boy was quitting that night, and Shorty had told him to hold the job for me.

"Malcolm, you haven't had any experience shining shoes," Ella said. Her expression and tone of voice told me she wasn't happy about my taking that job. I didn't particularly care, because I was already speech-less thinking about being somewhere close to the greatest bands in the world. I didn't even wait to eat any dinner.

The ballroom was all lighted when I got there. A man at the front door was letting in members of Benny Goodman's band. I told him I wanted to see the shoeshine boy, Freddie.

"You're going to be the new one?" he asked. I said I thought I was, and he laughed, "Well, maybe you'll hit the numbers and get a Cadillac, too." He told me that I'd find Freddie upstairs in the men's room on the second floor.

But downstairs before I went up, I stepped over and snatched a glimpse inside the ballroom. I just couldn't believe the size of that waxed floor! At the far end, under the soft, rose-colored lights, was the bandstand with the Benny Goodman musicians moving around, laughing and talking, arranging their horns and stands.

A wiry, brown-skinned, conked fellow upstairs in the men's room greeted me. "You Shorty's homeboy?" I said I was, and he said he was Freddie. "Good old boy," he said. "He called me, he just heard I hit the big number, and he figured right I'd be quitting." I told Freddie what the man at the front door had said about a Cadillac. He laughed and said, "Burns them white cats up when you get yourself something. Yeah, I told them I was going to get me one—just to bug them."

Freddie then said for me to pay close attention, that he was going to be busy and for me to watch but not get in the way, and he'd try to get me ready to take over at the next dance, a couple of nights later.

As Freddie busied himself setting up the shoeshine stand, he told me, "Get here early . . . your shoeshine rags and brushes by this footstand . . . your polish bottles, paste wax, suede brushes over here . . . everything in place, you get rushed, you never need to waste motion . . ."

While you shined shoes, I learned, you also kept watch on customers inside, leaving the urinals. You darted over and offered a small white hand towel. "A lot of cats who ain't planning to wash their hands, some-times you can run up with a towel and shame them. Your towels are really your best hustle in here. Cost you a penny apiece to launder—you always get at least a nickel tip."

The shoeshine customers, and any from the inside rest room who took a towel, you whiskbroomed a couple of licks. "A nickel or a dime tip, just give 'em that," Freddie said. "But for two bits, Uncle Tom a little—white cats especially like that. I've had them to come back two, three times a dance."

From down below, the sound of the music had begun floating up. I guess I stood transfixed. "You never seen a big dance?" asked Freddie. "Run on awhile, and watch."

There were a few couples already dancing under the rose-covered lights. But even more exciting to me was the crowd thronging in. The most glamorous-looking white women I'd ever seen—young ones, old ones, white cats buying tickets at the window, sticking big wads of green bills back into their pockets, checking the women's coats, and taking their arms and squiring them inside.

Freddie had some early customers when I got back upstairs. Between the shoeshine stand and thrusting towels to me just as they approached the wash basin, Freddie seemed to be doing four things at once. "Here, you can take over the whiskbroom," he said, "just two or three licks—but let 'em feel it."

When things slowed a little, he said, "You ain't seen nothing tonight. You wait until you see a spooks' dance! Man, our own people carry *on!*" Whenever he had a moment, he kept schooling me. "Shoelaces, this drawer here. You just starting out, I'm going to make these to you as a present. Buy them for a nickel a pair, tell cats they need laces if they do, and charge two bits."

Every Benny Goodman record I'd ever heard in my life, it seemed, was filtering faintly into where we were. During another customer lull, Freddie let me slip back outside again to listen. Peggy Lee was at the mike singing. Beautiful! She had just joined the band and she was from North Dakota and had been singing with a group in Chicago when Mrs. Benny Goodman discovered her, we had heard some customers say. She finished the song and the crowd burst into applause. She was a big hit.

"It knocked me out, too, when I first broke in here," Freddie said, grinning, when I went back in there. "But, look, you ever shined any shoes?" He laughed when I said I hadn't, excepting my own. "Well, let's get to work. I never had neither." Freddie got on the stand and went to work on his own shoes. Brush, liquid polish, brush, paste wax, shine rag, lacquer sole dressing . . . step by step, Freddie showed me what to do.

"But you got to get a whole lot faster. You can't waste time!" Freddie showed me how fast on my own shoes. Then, because business was tapering off, he had time to give me a demonstration of how to make the shine rag pop like a firecracker. "Dig the action?" he asked. He did it in slow motion. I got down and tried it on his shoes. I had the principle of it. "Just got to do it faster," Freddie said. "It's a jive noise, that's all. Cats tip better, they figure you're knocking yourself out!"

WORKERS
■

Studs Terkel

"Workers" is excerpted from Terkel's 1974 book Working.

I. TERRY MASON, AIRLINE STEWARDESS

She has been an airline stewardess for six years. She is twenty-six-years old, recently married. "The majority of airline stewardesses are from small towns. I myself am from Nebraska. It's supposed to be one of the nicest professions for a woman—if she can't be a model or in the movies. All the great benefits: flying around the world, meeting all those people. It is a nice status symbol.

"I have five older sisters and they were all married before they were twenty. The minute they got out of high school, they would end up getting married. That was the thing everybody did, was get married. When I told my parents I was going to the airlines, they got excited. They were so happy that one of the girls could go out and see the world and spend some time being single. I didn't get married until I was almost twenty-five. My mother especially thought it would be great that I could have the ambition, the nerve to go to the big city on my own and try to accomplish being a stewardess."

When people ask you what you're doing and you say stewardess, you're really proud, you think it's great. It's like a stepping stone. The first two months I started flying I had already been to London, Paris, and Rome. And me from Broken Bow, Nebraska. But after you start working, it's not as glamorous as you thought it was going to be.

They like girls that have a nice personality and that are pleasant to look at. If a woman has a problem with blemishes, they take her off. Until the appearance counselor thinks she's ready to go back on. One day this girl showed up, she had a very slight black eye. They took her off. Little things like that.

We had to go to stew school for five weeks. We'd go through a whole week of makeup and poise. I didn't like this. They make you feel like you've never been out in public. They showed you how to smoke a cigarette, when to smoke a cigarette, how to look at a man's eyes. Our teacher, she had this idea we had to be sexy. One day in class she was showing us how to accept a light for a cigarette from a man and never blow it out. When he lights it, just look in his eyes. It was really funny, all the girls laughed.

It's never proper for a woman to light her own cigarette. You hold it up and of course you're out with a guy who knows the right way to light the cigarette. You look into their eyes as they're lighting your cigarette and you're cupping his hand, but holding it just very light, so that he can feel your touch and your warmth. (Laughs.) You do not blow the match out. It used to be really great for a woman to blow the match out when she looked in his eyes, but she said now the man blows the match out.

The idea is not to be too obvious about it. They don't want you to look too forward. That's the whole thing, being a lady but still giving out that womanly appeal, like the body movement and the lips and the eyes. The guy's supposed to look in your eyes. You could be a real mean woman. You're a lady and doing all these evil things with your eyes.

She did try to promote people smoking. She said smoking can be part of your conversation. If you don't know what to say, you can always pull out a cigarette. She says it makes you more comfortable. I started smoking when I was on the airlines.

Our airline picks the girl-next-door type. At one time they wouldn't let us wear false eyelashes and false fingernails. Now it's required that you wear false eyelashes, and if you do not have the right length nails, you wear false nails. Everything is supposed to be becoming to the passenger.

That's the whole thing: meeting all these great men that either have great business backgrounds or are good looking or different. You do meet a lot of movie stars and a lot of political people, but you don't get to really visit with them that much. You never really get to go out with these men. Stewardesses are impressed only by name people. But a normal millionaire that you don't know you're not impressed about. The only thing that really thrills a stewardess is a passenger like Kennedy or movie stars or somebody political. Celebrities.

I think our average age is twenty-six. But our supervisors tell us what kind of makeup to wear, what kind of lipstick to wear, if our hair is not the right style for us, if we're not smiling enough. They even tell us how to act when you're on a pass. Like last night I met my husband. I was in plain clothes. I wanted to kiss him. But I'm not supposed to kiss anybody at the terminal. You're not supposed to walk off with a passenger, hand in hand. After you get out of the terminal, that's all yours.

The majority of passengers do make passes. The ones that do make passes are married and are business people. When I tell them I'm married, they say, "I'm married and you're married and you're away from home and so am I and nobody's gonna find out." The majority of those who make passes at you, you wouldn't accept a date if they were friends of yours at home.

After I was a stewardess for a year, and I was single, I came down to the near North Side of Chicago, which is the swinging place for singles. Stewardess, that was a dirty name. In a big city, it's an easy woman. I didn't like this at all. All these books—*Coffee, Tea and Me.*

I lived in an apartment complex where the majority there were stewardesses. The other women were secretaries and teachers. They would go to our parties and they would end up being among the worst. They never had stories about these secretaries and nurses, but they sure had good ones about stewardesses.

I meet a lot of other wives or single women. The first minute they start talking to me, they're really cold. They think the majority of stewardesses are snobs or they may be jealous. These women think we have a great time, that we are playgirls, that we have the advantage to go out with every type of man we want. So when they first meet us, they really turn off on us.

When you first start flying, the majority of girls do live in apartment complexes by the airport. The men they meet are airport employees: ramp rats, cleaning airplanes and things like that, mechanics, and young pilots, not married, ones just coming in fresh.

After a year we get tired of that, so we move into the city to get involved with men that are usually young executives, like at Xerox or something. Young businessmen in the early thirties and late twenties, they really think stewardesses are the gals to go out with if they want to get so far. They wear their hats and their suits and in the winter their black gloves. The women are getting older, they're getting twenty-four, twenty-five. They get involved with bartenders too. Stewardesses and bartenders are a pair. (Laughs.)

One time I went down into the area of swinging bars with two other girls. We just didn't want anybody to know that we were stewardesses, so we had this story made up that we were going to a women's college in Colorado. That went over. We had people that were talking to us, being nice to us, being polite. Down there, they wouldn't even be polite. They'd buy you drinks but then they'd steal your stool if you got up to go to the restroom. But when they knew you weren't stewardesses, just young ladies that were going to a women's college, they were really nice to us.

They say you can spot a stewardess by the way she wears her makeup. At that time we all had short hair and everybody had it cut in stew school exactly alike. If there's two blondes they have their hair cut very short, wearing the same shade of makeup, and they get into uniform, people say, "Oh, you look like sisters." Wonder why? (Laughs.)

The majority of us were against it because they wouldn't let you say how *you'd* like your hair cut, they wouldn't let you have your own personality, *your* makeup, *your* clothes. They'd tell you what length skirts to wear. At one time they told us we couldn't wear anything one inch above the knees. And no pants at that time. It's different now.

Wigs used to be forbidden. Now it's the style. Now it's permissible for nice women to wear wigs, eyelashes, and false fingernails. Before it was the harder looking women that wore them. Women showing up in pants, it wasn't ladylike. Hot pants are in now. Most airlines change styles every year.

She describes stewardess schools in the past as being like college dorms: it was forbidden to go out during the week; signing in and out on Friday and Saturday nights. "They've cut down stewardess school quite a bit. Cut down on how-to-serve meal classes and paperwork. A lot of girls get on aircraft these days and don't know where a magazine is, where the tray tables are for passengers. . . . Every day we used to have an examination. If you missed over two questions, that was a failure. They'd ask us ten questions. If you failed two tests out of the whole five weeks, you would have to leave. Now they don't have any exams at all. Usually we get a raise every year. We haven't been getting that lately."

We have long duty hours. We can be on duty for thirteen hours. But we're not supposed to fly over eight hours. This is in a twenty-four-hour period. During the eight hours, you could be flying from Chicago to Flint, to Moline, short runs. You stop twenty minutes. So you get to New York finally, after five stops, let's say. You have an hour on your own. But you have to be on the plane thirty minutes before departure time. How many restaurants can serve you food in thirty minutes? So you've gone thirteen hours, off and on duty, having half-hours and no time to eat. This is the normal thing. If we have only thirty minutes and we don't have time to eat, it's our hard luck.

Pilots have the same thing too. They end up grabbing a sandwich and eating in the cockpit. When I first started flying we were not supposed to eat at all on the aircraft, even though there was an extra meal left over. Now we can eat in the buffet. We have to stand there with all those dirty dishes and eat our meals—if there's one left over. We cannot eat in the public eye. We cannot bring it out if there's an extra seat. You can smoke in the cockpit, in the restrooms, but not in the public's eye.

"We have a union. It's a division of the pilot's union. It helps us out on duty time and working privileges. It makes sure that if we're in Cleveland and stuck because of weather and thirteen hours have gone by, we can go to bed. Before we had a union the stew office would call and say, 'You're working another seven.' I worked one time thirty-six hours straight."

The other day I had fifty-five minutes to serve 101 coach passengers, a cocktail and full-meal service. You do it fast and terrible. You're very rude. You don't mean to be rude, you just don't have time to answer questions. You smile and you just ignore it. You get three drink orders in a hurry. There's been many times when you miss the glass, pouring, and you pour it in the man's lap. You just don't say I'm sorry. You give him a cloth and you keep going. That's the bad part of the job.

Sometimes I get tired of working first class. These people think they're great, paying for more, and want more. Also I get tired of coach passengers asking for something that he thinks he's a first-class passenger. We get this attitude of difference from our airlines. They're just dividing the class of people. If we're on a first-class pass, the women are to wear a dress or a nice pants suit that has a matching jacket, and the men are to dress with suit jacket and tie and white shirt. And yet so many types of first-class passengers: some have grubby clothes, jeans and moccasins and everything. They can afford to dress the way they feel. . . .

If I want to fly first class, I pay the five dollars difference. I like the idea of getting free drinks, free champagne, free wine. In a coach, you don't. A coach passenger might say, "Could I have a pillow?" So you give him a pillow. Then he'll say, "Could you bring me a glass of water?" A step behind him there's the water fountain. In first class, if the guy says, "I want a glass of water," even if the water fountain is right by his arm, you'd bring it for him. We give him all this extra because he's first class. Which isn't fair. . . .

When you're in a coach, you feel like there's just heads and heads and heads of people. That's all you can see. In first class, being less people, you're more relaxed, you have more time. When you get on a 727, we have one coatroom. Our airline tells us you hang up first class coats only. When a coach passenger says, "Could you hang up my coat?" most of the time I'll hang it up. Why should I hang up first class and not coach?

One girl is for first class only and there's two girls for coach. The senior girl will be first class. That first-class girl gets used to working first class. If she happens to walk through the coach, if someone asks her for something, she'll make the other girls do it. The first stew always stays at the door and welcomes everybody aboard and says good-by to everybody when they leave. That's why a lot of girls don't like to be first class.

There's an old story on the airline. The stewardess asks if he'd like something to drink, him and his wife. He says, "I'd like a martini." The stewardess asks the wife, "Would you like a drink?" She doesn't say anything, and the husband says, "I'm sorry, she's not used to talking to the help." (Laughs.) When I started flying, that was the first story I heard.

I've never had the nerve to speak up to anybody that's pinched me or said something dirty. Because I've always been afraid of these onion letters. These are bad letters. If you get a certain amount of bad letters, you're fired. When you get a bad letter you have to go in and talk to the supervisor. Other girls now, there are many of 'em that are coming around and telling them what they feel. The passenger reacts: She's telling me off! He doesn't believe it. Sometimes the passenger needs it.

One guy got his steak and he said, "This is too medium, I want mine rarer." The girl said, "I'm sorry, I don't cook the food, it's precooked." He picked up the meal and threw it on the floor. She says, "If you don't pick the meal up right now, I'll make sure the crew members come back here and make you pick it up." (With awe) She's talking right back at him and loud, right in front of everybody. He really didn't think she would yell at him. Man, he picked up the meal. . . . The younger girls don't take that guff any more, like we used to. When the passenger is giving you a bad time, you talk back to him.

It's always: the passenger is right. When a passenger says something mean, we're supposed to smile and say, "I understand." We're supposed to *really* smile because stewardesses' supervisors have been getting reports that the girls have been back-talking passengers. Even when they pinch us or say dirty things, we're supposed to smile at them. That's one thing they taught us at stew school. Like he's rubbing your body somewhere, you're supposed to just put his hand down and not say anything and smile at him. That's the main thing, smile.

When I first went to class, they told me I had a crooked smile. She showed me how to smile. She said, "Kinda press a little smile on"—which I did. "Oh, that's great," she said, "that's a *good* smile." But I couldn't do it. I didn't feel like I was doing it on my own. Even if we're sad, we're supposed to have a smile on our face.

I came in after a flight one day, my grandfather had died. Usually they call you up or meet you at the flight and say, "We have some bad news for you." I pick up this piece of paper in my mailbox and it says, "Mother called in. Your grandfather died today." It was written like, say, two cups of sugar. Was I mad! They wouldn't give me time off for the funeral. You can only have time off for your parents or somebody you have lived with. I have never lived with my grandparents. I went anyway.

A lot of our girls are teachers, nurses, everything. They do this part-time, 'cause you have enough time off for another kind of job. I personally work for conventions. I work electronic and auto shows. Companies hire me to stay in their booth and talk about products. I have this speech to tell. At others, all I do is pass out matches or candy. Nowadays every booth has a young girl in it.

People just love to drink on airplanes. They feel adventurous. So you're serving drinks and meals and there's very few times that you can sit down. If she does sit down, she's forgotten how to sit down and talk to passengers. I used to play bridge with passengers. But that doesn't happen any more. We're not supposed to be sitting down, or have a magazine or read a newspaper. If it's a flight from Boston to Los Angeles, you're supposed to have a half an hour talking to passengers. But the only time we can sit down is when we go to the cockpit. You're not supposed to spend any more than five minutes up there for a cigarette.

We could be sitting down on our jump seat and if you had a supervisor on board, she would write you up—for not mixing with the crowd. We're supposed to be told when she walks on board. Many times you don't know. They do have personnel that ride the flights that don't give their names—checking, and they don't tell you about it. Sometimes a girl gets caught smoking in the cabin. Say it's a long flight, maybe a night flight. You're playing cards with a passenger and you say, "Would it bother you if I smoke?" And he says no. She would write you up and get you fired for smoking in the airplane.

They have a limit on how far you can mix. They want you to be sociable, but if he offers you a cigarette, not to take it. When you're outside, they encourage you to take cigarettes.

You give your time to everybody, you share it, not too much with one passenger. Everybody else may be snoring away and there's three guys, maybe military, and they're awake 'cause they're going home and excited. So you're playing cards with 'em. If you have a supervisor on, that would be a no-no. They call a lot of things no-no's.

They call us professional people but they talk to us as very young, childishly. They check us all the time on appearance. They check our weight every month. Even though you've been flying twenty years, they check you and say that's a no-no. If you're not spreading yourself around passengers enough, that's a no-no. Not hanging up first-class passenger's coats, that's a no-no, even though there's no room in the coatroom. You're supposed to somehow make room. If you're a pound over, they can take you off flight until you get under.

Accidents? I've never yet been so scared that I didn't want to get in the airplane. But there've been times at take offs, there's been something funny. Here I am thinking, What if I die today? I've got too much to do. I can't die today. I use it as a joke.

I've had emergencies where I've had to evacuate the aircraft. I was coming back from Las Vegas and being a lively stewardess I stayed up all night, gambled. We had a load full of passengers. The captain tells me we're going to have an emergency landing in Chicago because we lost a pin out of the nose gear. When we land, the nose gear is gonna collapse. He wants me to prepare the whole cabin for the landing, but not for two more hours. And not to tell the other stewardesses, because they were new girls and would get all excited. So I had to keep this in me for two more hours, wondering, Am I gonna die today? And this is Easter Sunday. And I was serving the passengers drinks and food and this guy got mad at me because his omelet was too cold. And I was gonna say, "You just wait, buddy, you're not gonna worry about that omelet." But I was nice about it, because I didn't want to have trouble with a passenger, especially when I have to prepare him for an emergency.

I told the passengers over the intercom: "The captain says it's just a precaution, there's nothing to worry about." I'm just gonna explain how to get out of the airplane fast, how to be in a braced position. They can't wear glasses or high heels, purses, things out of aisles, under the seats. And make sure everybody's pretty quiet. We had a blind woman on with a dog. We had to get people to help her off and all this stuff.

They were fantastic. Nobody screamed, cried, or hollered. When we got on the ground, everything was fine. The captain landed perfect. But there was a little jolt, and the passengers started screaming and hollering: They held it all back and all of a sudden we got on the ground, blah.

I was great. (Laughs.) That's what was funny. I thought, I have a husband now. I don't know how he would take it, my dying on an airplane. so I thought, I can't die. When I got on the intercom, I was so calm. Also we're supposed to keep a smile on our face. Even during an emergency, you're supposed to walk through the cabin and make everybody feel comfortable with a smile. When you're on the jump seat everybody's looking at you. You're supposed to sit there, holding your ankles, in a position to get out of that airplane fast with a big fat smile on your face.

Doctors tell stewardesses two bad things about them. They're gonna get wrinkles all over their face because they smile with their mouth and their eyes. And also with the pressurization on the airplane, we're not supposed to get up while we're climbing because it causes varicose veins in our legs. So they say being a stewardess ruins your looks.

A lot of stewardesses wanted to be models. The Tanya girl used to be a stewardess on our airline. A stewardess is what they could get and a model is what they couldn't get. They weren't the type of person, they weren't that beautiful, they weren't that thin. So their second choice would be stewardess.

What did you want to be? I wanted to get out of Broken Bow, Nebraska. (Laughs.)

POSTSCRIPT "Everytime I go home, they all meet me at the airplane. Not one of my sisters has been on an airplane. All their children think that Terry is just fantastic, because their mom and dad—my sisters and their husbands—feel so stupid. 'Look at us. I wish I could have done that.' I know they feel bad, that they never had the chance. But they're happy I can come home and tell them about things. I send them things from Europe. They get to tell all their friends that their sister's a stewardess. They get real excited about that. The first thing they come out and say, 'One of my sisters is a stewardess.'

"My father got a promotion with his company and they wrote in their business news that he had a family of seven, six girls and a boy, and one girl is a stewardess in Chicago. And went on to say what I did, and didn't say a word about anything else."

II. ROBERTA VICTOR, HOOKER

She had been a prostitute, starting at the age of fifteen. During the first five or six years, she worked as a high-priced call girl in Manhattan. Later she was a streetwalker. . . .

You never used your own name in hustling. . . . I used a different name practically every week. If you got busted, it was more difficult for them to find out who you really were. The role one plays when hustling had nothing to do with who you are. It's only fitting and proper you take another name.

There were certain names that were in great demand. Every second hustler had the name Kim or Tracy or Stacy and a couple others that were in vogue. These were all young women from seventeen to twenty-five, and we picked these very non-ethnic-oriented WASP names, rich names.

A hustler is any woman in American society. I was the kind of hustler who received money for favors granted rather than the type of hustler who signs a lifetime contract for her trick. Or the kind of hustler who carefully reads women's magazines and learns what it is proper to give for each date, depending on how much money her date or trick spends on her.

The favors I granted were not always sexual. When I was a call girl, men were not paying for sex. They were paying for something else. They were either paying to act out a fantasy or they were paying for companionship or they were paying to be seen with a well-dressed young woman. Or they were paying for somebody to listen to them. They were paying for a *lot* of things. Some men were paying for sex that *they* felt was deviant. They were paying so that nobody would accuse them of being perverted or dirty or nasty. A large proportion of these guys asked things that were not at all deviant. Many of them wanted oral sex. They felt they couldn't ask their wives or girl friends because they'd be repulsed. Many of them wanted somebody to talk dirty to them. Every good call girl in New York used to share her book and we all knew the same tricks.

We know a guy who used to lie in a coffin in the middle of his bedroom and he would see the girl only once. He got his kicks when the door would be open, the lights would be out, and there would be candles in the living room, and all you could see was his coffin on wheels. As you walked into the living room, he'd suddenly sit up. Of course, you screamed. He got his kicks when you screamed. Or the guy who set a table like the Last Supper and sat in a robe and sandals and wanted you to play Mary Magdalene. (Laughs.)

I was about fifteen, going on sixteen. I was sitting in a coffee shop in the Village, and a friend of mine came by. She said: "I've got a cab waiting. Hurry up. You can make fifty dollars in twenty minutes." Looking back, I wonder why I was so willing to run out of the coffee shop, get in a cab, and turn a trick. It wasn't traumatic because my training had been in how to be a hustler anyway.

I learned it from the society around me, just as a woman. We're taught how to hustle, how to attract, hold a man, and give sexual favors in return. The language that you hear all the time, "Don't sell yourself cheap." "Hold out for the highest bidder." "Is it proper to kiss a man good night on the first date?" The implication is it may not be proper on the first date, but if he takes you out to dinner on the second date, it's proper. If he brings you a bottle of perfume on the third date, you should let him touch you above the waist. And go on from here. It's a market place transaction.

Somehow I managed to absorb that when I was quite young. So it wasn't even a moment of truth when this woman came into the coffee shop and said; "Come on." I was back in twenty-five minutes and I felt no guilt.

She was a virgin until she was fourteen. A jazz musician, with whom she had fallen in love, avoided her. "So I went out to have sex with somebody to present him with an accomplished fact. I found it nonpleasurable. I did a lot of sleeping around before I ever took money."

A precocious child, she was already attending a high school of demanding academic standards. "I was very lonely. I didn't experience myself as being attractive. I had always felt I was too big, too fat, too awkward, didn't look like a Pepsi-Cola ad, was not anywhere near the American Dream. Guys were mostly scared of me. I was athletic, I was bright, and I didn't know how to keep my mouth shut. I didn't know how to play the games right.

"I understood very clearly they were not attracted to me for what I was, but as a sexual object. I was attractive. The year before I started hustling there were a lot of guys that wanted to go to bed with me. They didn't want to get involved emotionally, but they did want to ball. For a while I was willing to accept that. It was feeling intimacy, feeling close, feeling warm.

"The time spent in bed wasn't unpleasant. It just wasn't terribly pleasant. It was a way of feeling somebody cared about me, at least for a moment. And it mattered that I was there, that I was important. I discovered that in bed it was possible. It was one skill that I had and I was proud of my reputation as an amateur.

"I viewed all girls as being threats. That's what we were all taught. You can't be friends with another woman, she might take your man. If you tell her anything about how you really feel, she'll use it against you. You smile at other girls and you spend time with them when there's nothing better to do, but you'd leave any girl sitting anywhere if you had an opportunity to go somewhere with a man. Because the most important thing in life is the way men feel about you."

How could you forget your first trick? (Laughs.) We took a cab to midtown Manhattan, we went to a penthouse. The guy up there was quite well known. What he really wanted to do was watch two women make love, and then he wanted to have sex with me. It was barely sex. He was almost finished by the time we started. He barely touched me and we were finished.

Of course, we faked it, the woman and me. The ethic was: You don't participate in a sexual act with another woman if a trick is watching. You always fake it. You're putting something over on him and he's paying for something he didn't really get. That's the only way you can keep any sense of self-respect.

The call girl ethic is very strong. You were the lowest of the low if you allowed yourself to feel anything with a trick. The bed puts you on their level. The way you maintain your integrity is by acting all the way through. It's not too far removed from what most American women do— which is to put on a big smile and act.

It was a tremendous kick. Here I was doing absolutely nothing, *feeling* nothing, and in twenty minutes I was going to walk out with fifty dollars in my pocket. That just made me feel absolutely marvelous. I came downtown. I can't believe this! I'm not changed, I'm the same as I was twenty minutes ago, except that now I have fifty dollars in my pocket. It really was tremendous status. How many people could make fifty dollars for twenty minutes' work? Folks work for eighty dollars take-home pay. I worked twenty minutes for fifty dollars clear, no taxes, nothing! I was still in school, I was smoking grass, I was shooting heroin, I wasn't hooked yet, and I had money. It was terrific.

After that, I made it my business to let my friend know that I was available for more of these situations. (Laughs.) She had good connections. Very shortly I linked up with a couple of others who had a good call book.

Books of phone numbers are passed around from call girl to call girl. They're numbers of folks who are quite respectable and with whom there is little risk. They're not liable to pull a knife on you, they're not going to cheat you out of money. Businessmen and society figures. There's three or four groups. The wealthy executive, who makes periodic trips into the city and is known to several girls. There's the social figure, whose name appears quite regularly in the society pages and who's a regular once-a-week John. Or there's the quiet, independently wealthy type. Nobody knows how they got their money. I know one of them made his money off munitions in World War II. Then there's the entertainer. There's another crowd that runs around the night spots, the 21 Club. . . .

These were the people whose names you saw in the paper almost every day. But I knew what they were really like. Any John who was obnoxious or aggressive was just crossed out of your book. You passed the word around that this person was not somebody other people should call.

We used to share numbers—standard procedure. The book I had I got from a guy who got it from a very good call girl. We kept a copy of that book in a safe deposit box. The standard procedure was that somebody new gave half of what they got the first time for each number. You'd tell them: "Call so-and-so, that's a fifty-dollar trick." They would give you twenty-five dollars. Then the number was theirs. My first book, I paid half of each trick to the person who gave it to me. After that, it was my book.

The book had the name and phone number coded, the price, what the person wants, and the contact name. For four years I didn't turn a trick for less than fifty dollars. They were all fifty to one hundred dollars and up for twenty minutes, an hour. The understanding is: it doesn't get conducted as a business transaction. The myth is that it's a social occasion.

You're expected to be well dressed, well made up, appear glad to see the man. I would get a book from somebody and I would call and say, "I'm a friend of so-and-so's, and she thought it would be nice if we got together." The next move was his. Invariably he'd say, "Why don't we do that? Tonight or tomorrow night. Why don't you come over for a drink?" I would get very carefully dressed and made up. . . .

There's a given way of dressing in that league—that's to dress well but not ostentatiously. You have to pass doormen, cabdrivers. You have to look as if you belong in those buildings on Park Avenue or Central Park West. You're expected not to look cheap, not to look hard. Youth is the premium. I was quite young, but I looked older, so I had to work very hard at looking my age. Most men want girls who are eighteen. They really want girls who are younger, but they're afraid of trouble.

Preparations are very elaborate. It has to do with beauty parlors and shopping for clothes and taking long baths and spending money on preserving the kind of front that gives you a respectable address and telephone and being seen at the right clubs and drinking at the right bars. And being able to read the newspapers faithfully, so that not only can you talk about current events, you can talk about the society columns as well.

It's a social ritual. Being able to talk about what is happening and learn from this great master, and be properly respectful and know the names that he mentions. They always drop names of their friends, their contacts, and their clients. You should recognize these. Playing a role. . . .

At the beginning I was very excited. But in order to continue I had to turn myself off. I had to disassociate who I was from what I was doing.

It's a process of numbing yourself. I couldn't associate with people who were not in the life—either the drug life or the hustling life. I found I couldn't turn myself back on when I finished working. When I turned myself off, I was numb—emotionally, sexually numb.

At first I felt like I was putting one over on all the other poor slobs that would go to work at eight-thirty in the morning and come home at five. I was coming home at four in the morning and I could sleep all day. I really thought a lot of people would change places with me because of the romantic image: being able to spend two hours out, riding cabs, and coming home with a hundred dollars. I could spend my mornings doing my nails, going to the beauty parlor, taking long baths, going shopping. . . .

It was usually two tricks a night. That was easily a hundred, a hundred and a quarter. I always had money in my pocket. I didn't know what the inside of a subway smelled like. Nobody traveled any other way except by cab. I ate in all the best restaurants and I drank in all the best clubs. A lot of people wanted you to go out to dinner with them. All you had to do was be an ornament.

Almost all the call girls I knew were involved in drugs. The fast life, the night hours. At after-hours clubs, if you're not a big drinker, you usually find somebody who has cocaine, 'cause that's the big drug in those places. You wake up at noon, there's not very much to do till nine or ten that night. Everybody else is at work, so you shoot heroin. After a while the work became a means of supplying drugs, rather than drugs being something we took when we were bored.

The work becomes boring because you're not part of the life. You're the part that's always hidden. The doormen smirk when you come in, 'cause they know what's going on. The cabdriver, when you give him a certain address—he knows exactly where you're going when you're riding up Park Avenue at ten o'clock at night, for Christ sake. You leave there and go back to what? Really, to what? To an emptiness. You've got all this money in your pocket and nobody you care about.

When I was a call girl I looked down on streetwalkers. I couldn't understand why anybody would put themselves in that position. It seemed to me to be hard work and very dangerous. What I was doing was basically riskless. You never had to worry about disease. These were folks who you know took care of themselves and saw the doctor regularly. Their apartments were always immaculate and the liquor was always good. They were always polite. You didn't have to ask them for money first. It was always implicit: when you were ready to leave, there would be an envelope under the lamp or there'd be something in your pocketbook. It never had to be discussed.

I had to work an awful lot harder for the same money when I was a streetwalker. I remember having knives pulled on me, broken bottles held over my head, being raped, having my money stolen back from me, having to jump out of a second-story window, having a gun pointed at me.

As a call girl, I had lunch at the same places society women had lunch. There was no way of telling me apart from anybody else in the upper tax bracket. I made my own hours, no more than three or so hours of work an evening. I didn't have to accept calls. All I had to do was play a role.

As a streetwalker, I didn't have to act. I let myself show the contempt I felt for the tricks. They weren't paying enough to make it worth performing for them. As a call girl, I pretended I enjoyed it sexually. You have to act as if you had an orgasm. As a streetwalker, I didn't. I used to lie there with my hands behind my head and do mathematics equations in my head or memorize the keyboard typewriter.

It was strictly a transaction. No conversation, no acting, no myth around it, no romanticism. It was purely a business transaction. You always asked for your money in front. If you could get away without undressing totally, you did that.

It's not too different than the distinction between an executive secretary and somebody in the typing pool. As an executive secretary you really identify with your boss. When you're part of the typing pool, you're a body, you're hired labor, a set of hands on the typewriter. You have nothing to do with whoever is passing the work down to you. You do it as quickly as you can.

What led you to the streets?

My drug habit. It got a lot larger. I started looking bad. All my money was going for drugs. I didn't have any money to spend on keeping myself up and going to beauty parlors and having a decent address and telephone.

If you can't keep yourself up, you can't call on your old tricks. You drop out of circulation. As a call girl, you have to maintain a whole image. The trick wants to know he can call you at a certain number and you have to have a stable address. You must look presentable, not like death on a soda cracker.

I looked terrible. When I hit the streets, I tried to stick to at least twenty dollars and folks would laugh. I needed a hundred dollars a night to maintain a drug habit and keep a room somewhere. It meant turning seven or eight tricks a night. I was out on the street from nine o'clock at night till four in the morning. I was taking subways and eating in hamburger stands.

For the first time I ran the risk of being busted. I was never arrested as a call girl. Every once in a while a cop would get hold of somebody's book. They would call one of the girls and say, "I'm a friend of so-and-so's." They would try to trap them. I never took calls from people I didn't know. But on the streets, how do you know who you're gonna pick up?

As a call girl, some of my tricks were upper echelon cops, not patrolmen. Priests, financiers, garment industry folks, bigtimers. On the street, they ranged from *junior* executive types, blue-collar workers, upwardly striving postal workers, college kids, suburban white collars who were in the city for the big night, restaurant workers. . . .

You walk a certain area, usually five or six blocks. It has a couple of restaurants, a couple of bars. There's the step in-between: hanging out in a given bar, where people come to you. I did that briefly.

You'd walk very slowly, you'd stop and look in the window. Somebody would come up to you. There was a ritual here too. The law says in order to arrest a woman for prostitution, she has to mention money and she has to tell you what she'll do for the money. We would keep within the letter of the law, even though the cops never did.

Somebody would come up and say, "It's a nice night, isn't it?" "Yes." They'd say, "Are you busy?" I'd say, "Not particularly." "Would you like to come with me and have a drink?" You start walking and they say, "I have fifteen dollars or twelve dollars and I'm very lonely." Something to preserve the myth. Then they want you to spell out exactly what you're willing to do for the money.

I never approached anybody on the street. That was the ultimate risk. Even if he weren't a cop, he could be some kind of supersquare, who would call a cop. I was trapped by cops several times.

The first one didn't even trap me as a trick. It was three in the morning. I was in Chinatown. I ran into a trick I knew. We made contact in a restaurant. He went home and I followed him a few minutes later. I knew the address. I remember passing a banana truck. It didn't dawn on me that it was strange for somebody to be selling bananas at three in the morning. I spent about twenty minutes with my friend. He paid me. I put the money in my shoe. I opened the door and got thrown back against the wall. The banana salesman was a vice squad cop. He'd stood on the garbage can to peer in the window. I got three years for that one.

I was under age. I was four months short of twenty-one. They sent me to what was then called Girls' Term Court. They wouldn't allow me a lawyer because I wasn't an adult, so it wasn't really a criminal charge. The judge said I was rehabilitable. Instead of giving me thirty days, he gave me three years in the reformatory. It was very friendly of him. I was out on parole a couple of times before I'd get caught and sent back.

I once really got trapped. It was about midnight and a guy came down the street. He said he was a postal worker who just got off the shift. He told me how much money he had and what he wanted. I took him to my room. The cop isn't supposed to undress. If you can describe the color of his shorts, it's an invalid arrest. Not only did he show me the color of his shorts, he went to bed with me. Then he pulled a badge and a gun and busted me.

He lied to me. He told me he was a narc and didn't want to bust me for hustling. If I would tell him who was dealing in the neighborhood, he'd cut me loose. I lied to him, but he won. He got me to walk out of the building past all my friends and when we got to the car, he threw me in. (Laughs.) It was great fun. I did time for that—close to four years.

What's the status of the streetwalker in prison?

It's fine. Everybody there has been hustling. It's status in reverse. Anybody who comes in saying things like they could never hustle is looked down on as being somewhat crazy.

She speaks of a profound love she had for a woman who she's met in prison; of her nursing her lover after the woman had become blind.

"I was out of the country for a couple of years. I worked a house in Mexico. It had heavy velour curtains—a Mexican version of a French whorehouse. There was a reception area, where the men would come and we'd parade in front of them.

"The Mexicans wanted American girls. The Americans wanted Mexican girls. So I didn't get any American tricks. I had to give a certain amount to the house for each trick I turned and anything I negotiated over that amount was mine. It was far less than anything I had taken in the States.

"I was in great demand even though I wasn't a blonde. A girl-friend of mine worked there two nights. She was Norwegian and very blonde. Every trick who came in wanted her. Her head couldn't handle it all. She quit after two nights. So I was the only American.

"That was really hard work. The Mexicans would play macho. American tricks will come as quickly as they can. Mexicans will hold back and make me work for my money. I swear to God they were doing multiplication tables in their heads to keep from having an orgasm. I would use every trick I knew to get them to finish. It was crazy!

"I was teaching school at the same time. I used *Alice in Wonderland* as the text in my English class. During the day I tutored English for fifth- and sixth-grade kids. In the evening, I worked in the call house.

"The junk down there was quite cheap and quite good. My habit was quite large. I loved dope more than anything else around. After a while I couldn't differentiate between working and not working. All men were tricks, all relationships were acting. I was completely turned off."

She quit shooting dope the moment she was slugged, brutally beaten by a dealer who wanted her. This was her revelatory experience. "It was the final indignity. I'd had tricks pulling broken bottles on me, I'd been in razor fights, but nobody had ever *hit me*." It was a threat to her status. "I was strong. I could handle myself. A tough broad. This was threatened, so . . ."

I can't talk for women who were involved with pimps. That was where I always drew the line. I always thought pimps were lower than pregnant cockroaches. I didn't want anything to do with them. I was involved from time to time with some men. They were either selling dope or stealing, but they were not depending on my income. Nor were they telling me to get my ass out on the street. I never supported a man.

As a call girl I got satisfaction, an unbelievable joy—perhaps perverted—in knowing what these reputable folks were really like. Being able to open a newspaper every morning, read about this pillar of society, and know what a pig he really was. The tremendous kick in knowing that I didn't feel anything, that I was acting and they weren't. It's sick, but no sicker than what every woman is taught, all right?

I was in *control* with every one of those relationships. You're vulnerable if you allow yourself to be involved sexually. I wasn't. They were. I called it. Being able to manipulate somebody sexually, I could determine when I wanted that particular transaction to end. 'Cause I could make the guy come. I could play all kinds of games. See? It was a tremendous sense of power.

What I did was no different from what ninety-nine percent of Ameri-can women are taught to do. I took the money from under the lamp in-stead of in Arpege. What would I do with 150 bottles of Arpege a week?

You become your job. I became what I did. I became a hustler. I became cold, I became hard, I became turned off, I became numb. Even when I wasn't hustling, I was a hustler. I don't think it's terribly different from somebody who works on the assembly line forty hours a week and comes home cut off, numb, dehumanized. People aren't built to switch on and off like water faucets.

What was really horrifying about jail is that it really isn't horrifying. You adjust very easily. The same thing with hustling. It became my life. It was too much of an effort to try to make contact with another human being, to force myself to care, to feel.

I didn't care about me. It didn't matter whether I got up or didn't get up. I got high as soon as I awoke. The first thing I'd reach for, with my eyes half-closed, was my dope. I didn't like my work. It was messy. That was the biggest feeling about it. Here's all these guys slobbering over you all night long. I'm lying there, doing math or conjugations or Spanish poetry in my head. (Laughs.) And they're slobbering. God! God! What enabled me to do it was being high—high and numb.

The overt hustling society is the microcosm of the rest of the society. The power relationships are the same and the games are the same. Only this one I was in control of. The greater one I wasn't. In the outside soci-ety, if I tried to be me, I wasn't in control of anything. As a bright, as-sertive woman, I had no power. As a cold, manipulative hustler, I had a lot. I knew I was playing a role. Most women are taught to become what they act. All I did was act out the reality of American womanhood.

III. Maggie Holmes, Domestic

What bugs me now, since I'm on welfare, is people saying they give you the money for nothin'. When I think back what we had to come through, up from the South, comin' here. The hard work we had to do. It really gets me, when I hear people . . . It do somethin' to me. I think violence.

I think what we had to work for. I used to work for $1.50 a week. This is five days a week, sometimes six. If you live in the servant quarter, your time is never off, because if they decide to have a party at night, you gotta come out. My grandmother, I remember when she used to work, we'd get milk and a pound of butter. I mean this was pay. I'm thinkin' about what my poor parents worked for, gettin' nothing. What do the white think about when they think? Do they ever think about what *they* would do?

> She had worked as a domestic, hotel chambermaid, and as "kitchen help in cafes" for the past twenty-five years, up North and down South. She lives with her four children.

When it come to housework, I can't do it now. I can't stand it, cause it do somethin' to my mind. They want you to clean the house, want you to wash, even the windows, want you to iron. You not supposed to wash no dishes. You ain't supposed to make no beds up. Lots of 'em try to sneak it in on you, think you don't know that. So the doorbell rings and I didn't answer to. The bell's ringin' and I'm still doin' my work. She ask me why I don't answer the bell, I say; "Do I come here to be a butler?" And I don't see myself to be no doormaid. I came to do some work, and I'm gonna do my work. When you end up, you's nursemaid, you's cook. They puts all this on you. If you want a job to cleanin', you ask for just cleanin'. She wants you to do in one day what she hasn't did all year.

Now this bug me: the first thing she gonna do is pull out this damn rubber thing—just fittin' for your knees. Knee pads—like you're workin' in the fields, like people pickin' cotton. No mop or nothin'. That's why you find so many black women here got rheumatism in their legs, knees. When you get on that cold floor, I don't care how warm the house is, you can feel the cold on the floor, the water and stuff. I never see nobody on their knees until I come North. In the South, they had mops. Most times, if they had real heavy work, they always had a man to come in. Washin' windows, that's a man's job. They don't think nothin' about askin' you to do that here. They don't have no feeling that that's what bothers you. I think to myself; My God, if I had somebody come and do my floors, clean up for me, I'd appreciate it. They don't say nothin' about it. Act like you haven't even done anything. They has no feelin's.

I worked for one old hen on Lake Shore Drive. You remember that big snow they had there? Remember when you couldn't get there? When I gets to work she says: "Call the office." She complained to the lady where I got the job, said I was late to work. So I called. So I said, in the phone (Shouts), "*What do you want with me?* I got home four black, beautiful kids. Before I go to anybody's job in the morning I see that my kids are at school. I gonna see that they have warm clothes on and they fed." I'm lookin' right at the woman I'm workin' for. (Laughs.) When I get through the phone I tell this employer: "That goes for you too. The only thing I live for is my kids. There's nothin', you and nobody else." The expression on her face: What is this? (Laughs.) She thought I was gonna be like (mimics "Aunt Jemima"): "Yes ma'am, I'll try to get here a little early." But it wasn't like that. (Laughs.)

When I come in the door that day she told me pull my shoes off. I said, "For what? I can wipe my feet at the door here, but I'm not gettin' out of my shoes, it's cold." She look at me like she said: Oh my God, what I got here? (Laughs.) I'm knowin' I ain't gonna make no eight hours here. I can't take it.

She had everything in there snow white. And that means work, believe me. In the dining room she had a blue set, she had sky-blue chairs. They had a bedroom with pink and blue. I look and say, "I know what this means." It means sho' 'nough-knees. I said, "I'm gonna try and make it today, *if* I can make it." Usually when they're so bad, you have to leave.

I ask her where the mop is. She say she don't have no mop. I said, "Don't tell me you mop the floor on your knees. I know you don't." They usually hid these mops in the clothes closet. I go out behind all these clothes and get the mop out. (Laughs.) They don't get on their knees, but they don't think nothin' about askin' a black woman. She says, "All you— you girls . . ." She stop. I say, "All you *niggers,* is that what you want to say?" She give me this stupid look. I say, "I'm glad you tellin' me that there's more like me." (Laughs.) I told her, "You better give me my money and let me go, 'cause I'm gettin' angry. So I made her give me my carfare and what I had worked that day.

Most when you find decent work is when you find one that work themselves. They know what it's like to get up in the morning and go to work. In the suburbs they ain't got nothin' to do. They has nothin' else to think about. Their mind's just about blowed.

It's just like they're talkin' about mental health. Poor people's mental health is different than the rich white. Mine could come from a job or not havin' enough money for my kids. Mine is from me being poor. That don't mean you're sick. His sickness is from money, graftin' where he want more. I don't have *any.* You live like that day to day, penny to penny.

I worked for a woman, her husband's a judge. I cleaned the whole house. When it was time for me to go home, she decided she wants some ironing. She goes in the basement, she turn on the air conditioner. She said, "I think you can go down in the basement and finish your day out. It's air conditioned." I said, "I don't care what you got down there, I'm not ironing. You look at that slip, it says cleanin'. Don't say no ironin'. She wanted me to wash the walls in the bathroom. I said, "If you look at that telephone book they got all kinds of ads there under house cleanin'." She said the same thing as the other one, "All you girls—" I said same thing I said to the other one; "You mean niggers." (Laughs.)

They ever call you by your last name?

Oh God, they wouldn't do that. (Laughs.)

Do you call her by her last name?

Most time I don't call her, period. I don't say anything to her. I don't talk nasty to nobody, but when I go to work I don't talk to people. Most time they don't like what you're gonna say. So I keeps quiet.

Most of her jobs were "way out in the suburbs. You get a bus and you ride til you get a subway. After you gets to Howard, you gets the El. If you get to the end of the line and there's no bus, they pick you up. I don't like to work in the city, 'cause they don't pay you nothin'. And these old buildings are so nasty. It takes so much time to clean 'em. They are not kept up so good, like suburbs. Most of the new homes out there, it's easier to clean."

A commonly observed phenomenon: during the early evening hour, trains, crowded, predominantly by young white men carrying attaché cases, pass trains headed in the opposite direction, crowded, predominantly by middle-aged black women carrying brown paper bags. Neither group, it appears, glances at the other.

"We spend most of the time ridin'. You get caught goin' out from the suburbs at nighttime, man, you're really sittin' there for hours. There's nothin' movin'. You got a certain hour to meet trains. You get a transfer, you have to get that train. It's a shuffle to get in and out of the job. If you miss that train at five o'clock, what time you gonna get out that end? Sometime you don't get home till eight o'clock. . . . "

You don't feel like washin' your own window when you come from out there, scrubbin'. If you work in one of them houses eight hours, you gotta come home do the same thing over . . . you don't feel like . . . (sighs softly) . . . tired. You gotta come home, take care of your kids, you gotta cook, you gotta wash. Most of the time, you gotta wash for the kids for somethin' to wear to school. You gotta clean up, 'cause you didn't have time in the morning. You gotta wash and iron and whatever you do, nights. You be so tired, until you don't feel like even doin' nothin'.

You get up at six, you fix breakfast for the kids, you get them ready to go on to school. Leave home about eight. Most of the time I make biscuits for my kids, cornbread you gotta make. I don't mean the canned kind. This I don't call cookin', when you go in that refrigerator and get some beans and drop 'em in a pot. And TV dinners, they go stick 'em in the stove and she say she cooked. This is not cookin'.

And *she's* tired. Tired from doin' what? You got a washing dryer, you got an electric sweeper, anything at fingertips. All she gotta do is unfroze 'em, dump 'em in the pot, and she's tired! I go to the store, I get my vegetables, greens, I wash 'em. I gotta pick 'em first. I don't eat none of that stuff, like in the cans. She don't do that, and she says she's tired.

When you work for them, when you get in that house in the morning, boy, they got one arm in their coat and a scarf on their head. And when you open that door, she shoots by you, she's gone. Know what I mean? They want you to come there and keep the kids and let them get out. What she think about how am I gonna do? Like I gets tired of my kids too. I'd like to go out too. It bugs you to think that they don't have no feelin's about that.

Most of the time I work for them and they be out. I don't like to work for 'em when they be in the house so much. They don't have no work to do. All they do is get on the telephone and talk about one another. Make you sick. I'll go and close the door. They're all the same, everybody's house is the same. You think they rehearse it. . . .

When I work, only thing I be worryin' about is my kids. I just don't like to leave 'em too long. When they get out of school, you wonder if they out on the street. The only thing I worry is if they had a place to play in easy.

I always call two, three times. When she don't like you to call, I'm in a hurry to get out of there. (Laughs.) My mind is gettin' home, what are you gonna find to cook before the stores close.

This Nixon was sayin' he don't see nothin' wrong with people doin' scrubbin'. For generations that's all we done. He should know we wants to be doctors and teachers and lawyers like him. I don't want my kids to come up and do domestic work. It's degrading. You can't see no tomorrow there. We done this for generation and generation cooks and butlers all your life. They want their kids to be lawyers, doctors, and things. You don't want 'em in no cafes workin'. . . .

When they say about the neighborhood we live in is dirty, why do they ask me to come and clean their house? We, the people in the slums, the same nasty women they have come to their house in the suburbs every day. If these women are so filthy, why you want them to clean for you? They don't go and clean for us. We go and clean for them.

I worked one day where this white person did some housework. I'm lookin' at the difference how she with me and her. She had a guilt feeling towards that lady. They feel they shouldn't ask them to do this type of work, but they don't mind askin' me.

They want you to get in a uniform. You take me and my mother, she work in what she wear. She tells you, "If that place so dirty where I can't wear my dress, I won't do the job." You can't go to work dressed like they do, 'cause they think you're not working—like you should get dirty, at least. They don't say what kind of uniform, just say uniform. This is in case anybody come in, the black be workin'. They don't want you walkin' around dressed up, lookin' like them. They asks you sometimes, "Don't you have somethin' else to put on?" I say, "No, 'cause I'm not gettin' on my knees."

They move with caution now, believe me. They want to know, "What should I call you?" I say, "Don't call me a Negro, I'm black." So they say, "Okay, I don't want to make you angry with me." (Laughs.) The old-timers, a lot of 'em was real religious. "Lord'll make a way." I say, "I'm makin' my own way." I'm not anti-Bible or anti-God, but I just let 'em know I don't think thataway.

The younger women, they don't pay you too much attention. Most of 'em work. The older women, they behind you, wiping. I don't like nobody checkin' behind me. When you go to work, they want to show you how to clean. That really gets me, somebody showin' me how to clean. I been doin' it all my life. They come and get the rag and show you how to do it. (Laughs.) I stand there, look at 'em. Lotta times I ask her, "You finished?" I say, "If there's anything you gotta go and do, I wish you'd go." I don't need nobody to show me how to clean.

I had them put money down and pretend they can't find it and have me look for it. I worked for one, she had dropped ten dollars on the floor, and I was sweepin' and I'm glad I seen it, because if I had put that sweeper on it, she coulda said I got it. I had to push the couch back and the ten dollars was there. Oh, I had 'em, when you go to dust, they put something . . . to test you.

I worked at a hotel. A hotel's the same thing. You makin' beds, scrub-bin' toilets, and things. You gotta put in linens and towels. You still cleanin'. When people come in the room—that's what bugs me—they give you that look: You just a maid. It do somethin' to me. It really gets into me.

Some of the guests are nice. The only thing you try to do is to hurry up and get this bed made and get outa here, 'cause they'll get you to do somethin' else. If they take that room, they want everything they paid for. (Laughs.) They get so many towels, they can't use 'em all. But you gotta put up all those towels. They want that pillow, they want that blanket. You gotta be trottin' back and forth and gettin' all those things.

In the meantime, when they have the hotel full, we put in extra beds—the little foldin' things. They say they didn't order the bed. They stand and look at you like you crazy. Now you gotta take this bed back all the way from the twelfth floor to the second. The guy at the desk, he got the wrong room. He don't say, "I made a mistake." You take the blame.

And you get some guys . . . you can't work with a fightin' 'em. He'll call down and say he wants some towels. When you knock, he says, "Come in." He's standing there without a stitch of clothes on, buck naked. You're not goin' in there. You only throw those towels and go back. Most of the time you wait till he got out of there.

When somethin's missin', it's always the maid took it. If we find one of those type people, we tell the house lady, "You have to go in there and clean it yourself." If I crack that door, and nobody's in, I wouldn't go in there. If a girl had been in there, they would call and tell you, "Did you see something?" They won't say you got it. It's the same thing. You say no. They say, "It *musta* been in there."

Last summer I worked at a place and she missed a purse. I didn't work on that floor that day. She called the office, "Did you see that lady's purse?" I said, "No, I haven't been in the room." He asked me again, Did I . . . ? I had to stay till twelve o'clock. She found it. It was under some pa-pers. I quit, 'cause they end up sayin' you stole somethin'.

You know what I wanted to do all my life? I wanted to play piano. And I'd want to write songs and things, that's what I really wanted to do. If I could just get myself enough to buy a piano. . . . And I'd like to write about my life, if I could sit long enough: How I growed up in the South and my grandparents and my father—I'd like to do that. I would like to dig up more of black history, too. I would love to for my kids.

Lotta times I'm tellin' 'em about things, they'll be sayin', "Mom, that's olden days." (Laughs.) They don't understand, because it's so far from what happening now. Mighty few young black women are doin' domestic work. And I'm glad. That's why I want my kids to go to school. This one lady told me, "All you people are gettin' like that." I said, "I'm glad." There's no more gettin' on their knees.

PLAYING WAR

■

Black Elk

The selection that follows is from Black Elk Speaks, *which was edited by poet and scholar John A. Neihardt.*

When it was summer again we were camping on the Rosebud, and I did not feel so much afraid, because the Wasichus seemed farther away and there was peace there in the valley and there was plenty of meat. But all the boys from five or six years up were playing war. The little boys would gather together from the different bands of the tribe and fight each other with mud balls that they threw with willow sticks. And the big boys played the game called Throwing-Them-Off-Their-Horses, which is a battle all but the killing; and sometimes they got hurt. The horsebacks from the different bands would line up and charge upon each other, yelling; and when the ponies came together on the run, they would rear and flounder and scream in a big dust, and the riders would seize each other, wrestling until one side had lost all its men, for those who fell upon the ground were counted dead.

When I was older, I, too, often played this game. We were always naked when we played it, just as warriors are when they go into battle if it is not too cold, because they are swifter without clothes. Once I fell off on my back right in the middle of a bed of prickly pears, and it took my mother a long while to pick all the stickers out of me. I was still too little to play war that summer, but I can remember watching the other boys, and I thought that when we all grew up and were big together, maybe we could kill all the Wasichus or drive them far away from our country. . . .

There was a war game that we little boys played after a big hunt. We went out a little way from the village and built some grass tepees, playing we were enemies and this was our village. We had an adviser, and when it got dark he would order us to go and steal some dried meat from the big people. He would hold a stick up to us and we had to bite off a piece of it. If we bit a big piece we had to get a big piece of meat, and if we bit a little piece, we did not have to get so much. Then we started for the big people's village, crawling on our bellies, and when we got back without getting caught, we would have a big feast and a dance and make kill talks, telling of our brave deeds like warriors. Once, I remember, I had no brave deed to tell. I crawled up to a leaning tree beside a tepee and there was meat hanging on the limbs. I wanted a tongue I saw up there in the moonlight, so I climbed up. But just as I was about to reach it, the man in the tepee yelled "Ye-a-a!" He was saying this to his dog, who was stealing some meat too, but I thought the man had seen me, and I was so scared I fell out of the tree and ran away crying.

Then we used to have what we called a chapped breast dance. Our adviser would look us over to see whose breast was burned most from not

having it covered with the robe we wore; and the boy chosen would lead
the dance while we all sang like this:

> I have a chapped breast.
> My breast is red.
> My breast is yellow.

And we practiced endurance too. Our adviser would put dry sunflower
seeds on our wrists. These were lit at the top, and we had to let them burn
clear down to the skin. They hurt and made sores, but if we knocked them
off or cried Owh!, we would be called women.

Steelworker by W. Eugene Smith, Pittsburgh Project.

THE IMPORTANCE OF WORK
■

Gloria Steinem

This essay was originally published in Steinem's 1983 book Outrageous Acts and
Everyday Rebellions.

Toward the end of the 1970s, *The Wall Street Journal* devoted an eight-
part, front-page series to "the working woman"—that is, the influx
of women into the paid-labor force—as the greatest change in American
life since the Industrial Revolution.

Many women readers greeted both the news and the definition with cynicism. After all, women have always worked. If all the productive work of human maintenance that women do in the home were valued at its replacement cost, the gross national product of the United States would go up by 26 percent. It's just that we are now more likely than ever before to leave our poorly rewarded, low-security, high-risk job of home-making (though we're still trying to explain that it's a perfectly good one and that the problem is male society's refusal both to do it and to give it an economic value) for more secure, independent, and better-paid jobs outside the home.

Obviously, the real work revolution won't come until all productive work is rewarded—including child rearing and other jobs done in the home—and men are integrated into so-called women's work as well as vice versa. But the radical change being touted by the *Journal* and other media is one part of that long integration process: the unprecedented flood of women into salaried jobs, that is, into the labor force as it has been male-defined and previously occupied by men. We are already more than 41 percent of it—the highest proportion in history. Given the fact that women also make up a whopping 69 percent of the "discouraged labor force" (that is, people who need jobs but don't get counted in the unemployment statistics because they've given up looking), plus an official female unemployment rate that is substantially higher than men's, it's clear that we could expand to become fully half of the national work force by 1990.

Faced with this determination of women to find a little independence and to be paid and honored for our work, experts have rushed to ask: "Why?" It's a question rarely directed at male workers. Their basic motivations of survival and personal satisfaction are taken for granted. Indeed, men are regarded as "odd" and therefore subjects for sociological study and journalistic reports only when they *don't* have work, even if they are rich and don't need jobs or are poor and can't find them. Nonetheless, pollsters and sociologists have gone to great expense to prove that women work outside the home because of dire financial need, or if we persist despite the presence of a wage-earning male, out of some desire to buy "little extras" for our families, or even out of good old-fashioned penis envy.

Job interviewers and even our own families may still ask salaried women the big "Why?" If we have small children at home or are in some job regarded as " men's work," the incidence of such questions increases. Condescending or accusatory versions of "What's a nice girl like you doing in a place like this?" have not disappeared from the workplace.

How do we answer these assumptions that we are "working" out of some pressing or peculiar need? Do we feel okay about arguing that it's as natural for us to have salaried jobs as for our husbands—whether or not we have young children at home? Can we enjoy strong career ambitions without worrying about being thought "unfeminine"? When we confront men's growing resentment of women competing in the work force (often in the form of such guilt-producing accusations as "You're taking men's jobs away" or "You're damaging your children"), do we simply state that a decent job is a basic human right for everybody?

I'm afraid the answer is often no. As individuals and as a movement, we tend to retreat into some version of a tactically questionable defense: "Womenworkbecausewehaveto." The phrase has become one word, one key on the typewriter—an economic form of the socially "feminine" stance of passivity and self-sacrifice. Under attack, we still tend to present ourselves as creatures of economic necessity and familial devotion. "Womenworkbecausewehaveto" has become the easiest thing to say.

Like most truisms, this one is easy to prove with statistics. Economic need *is* the most consistent work motive—for women as well as men. In 1976, for instance, 43 percent of all women in the paid-labor force were single, widowed, separated, or divorced, and working to support themselves and their dependents. An additional 21 percent were married to men who had earned less than ten thousand dollars in the previous year, the minimum then required to support a family of four. In fact, if you take men's pensions, stocks, real estate, and various forms of accumulated wealth into account, a good statistical case can be made that there are more women who "have" to work (that is, who have neither the accumulated wealth, nor husbands whose work or wealth can support them for the rest of their lives) than there are men with the same need. If we were going to ask one group "Do you really need this job?" we should ask men.

But the first weakness of the whole "have to work" defense is its deceptiveness. Anyone who has ever experienced dehumanized life on welfare or any other confidence-shaking dependency knows that a paid job may be preferable to the dole, even when the hand-out is coming from a family member. Yet the will and self-confidence to work on one's own can diminish as dependency and fear increase. That may explain why—contrary to the "have to" rationale—wives of men who earn less than three thousand dollars a year are actually *less* likely to be employed than wives whose husbands make ten thousand dollars a year or more.

Furthermore, the greatest proportion of employed wives is found among families with a total household income of twenty-five to fifty thousand dollars a year. This is the statistical underpinning used by some sociologists to prove that women's work is mainly important for boosting families into the middle or upper middle class. Thus, women's incomes are largely used for buying "luxuries" and "little extras": a neat double-whammy that renders us secondary within our families, and makes our jobs expendable in hard times. We may even go along with this interpretation (at least, up to the point of getting fired so a male can have our job). It preserves a husbandly ego-need to be seen as the primary breadwinner, and still allows us a safe "feminine" excuse for working.

But there are often rewards that we're not confessing. As noted in *The Two-Career Couple,* by Francine and Douglas Hall: "Women who hold jobs by choice, even blue-collar routine jobs, are more satisfied with their lives than are the full-time housewives."

In addition to personal satisfaction, there is also society's need for all its members' talents. Suppose that jobs were given out on only a "have to work" basis to both women and men—one job per household. It would be unthinkable to lose the unique abilities of, for instance, Eleanor Holmes Norton, the distinguished chair of the Equal Employment Opportunity Commission. But would we then be forced to question the important work of her husband, Edward Norton, who is also a distinguished lawyer? Since men earn more than twice as much as women on the average, the wife in most households would be more likely to give up her job. Does that mean the nation could do as well without millions of its nurses, teachers, and secretaries? Or that the rare man who earns less than his wife should give up his job?

It was this kind of waste of human talents on a society-wide scale that traumatized millions of unemployed or underemployed Americans during the Depression. Then, a one-job-per-household rule seemed somewhat justified, yet the concept was used to displace women workers only, create intolerable dependencies, and waste female talent that the country needed. That Depression experience, plus the energy and example of women who were finally allowed to work during the manpower shortage created by World War II, led Congress to reinterpret the meaning of the country's full-employment goal in its Economic Act of 1946. Full employment was officially defined as "the employment of those who want to work, without regard to whether their employment is, by some definition, necessary. This goal applies equally to men and to women." Since bad economic times are again creating a resentment of employed women—as well as creating more need for women to be employed—we need such a goal more than ever. Women are again being caught in a tragic double bind: We are required to be strong and then punished for our strength.

Clearly, anything less than government and popular commitment to this 1946 definition of full employment will leave the less powerful groups, whoever they may be, in danger. Almost as important as the financial penalty paid by the powerless is the suffering that comes from being shut out of paid and recognized work. Without it, we lose much of our self-respect and our ability to prove that we are alive by making some difference in the world. That's just as true for the suburban woman as it is for the unemployed steel worker.

But it won't be easy to give up the passive defense of "wework-becausewehaveto."

When a woman who is struggling to support her children and grandchildren on welfare sees her neighbor working as a waitress, even though that neighbor's husband has a job, she may feel resentful; and the waitress (of course, not the waitress's husband) may feel guilty. Yet unless we establish the obligation to provide a job for everyone who is willing and able to work, that welfare woman may herself be penalized by policies that give out only one public-service job per household. She and her daughter will have to make a painful and divisive decision about which of them gets that precious job, and the whole household will have to survive on only one salary.

A job as a human right is a principle that applies to men as well as women. But women have more cause to fight for it. The phenomenon of the "working woman" has been held responsible for everything from an increase in male impotence (which turned out, incidentally, to be attributable to medication for high blood pressure) to the rising cost of steak (which was due to high energy costs and beef import restrictions, not women's refusal to prepare the cheaper, slower-cooking cuts). Unless we see a job as part of every citizen's right to autonomy and personal fulfillment, we will continue to be vulnerable to someone else's idea of what "need" is, and whose "need" counts the most.

In many ways, women who do not have to work for simple survival, but who choose to do so nonetheless, are on the frontier of asserting this right for all women. Those with well-to-do husbands are dangerously easy for us to resent and put down. It's easier still to resent women from families of inherited wealth, even though men generally control and benefit from that wealth. (There is no Rockefeller Sisters Fund, no J. P. Morgan & Daughters, and sons-in-law may be the ones who really sleep their way to power.) But to prevent a woman whose husband or father is wealthy from earning her own living, and from gaining the self-confidence that comes with that ability, is to keep her needful of that unearned power and less willing to disperse it. Moreover, it is to lose forever her unique talents.

Perhaps modern feminists have been guilty of a kind of reverse snobbism that keeps us from reaching out to the wives and daughters of wealthy men; yet it was exactly such women who refused the restrictions of class and financed the first wave of feminist revolution.

For most of us, however, "womenworkbecausewehaveto" is just true enough to be seductive as a personal defense.

If we use it without also staking out the larger human right to a job, however, we will never achieve that right. And we will always be subject to the false argument that independence for women is a luxury affordable only in good economic times. Alternatives to layoffs will not be explored, acceptable unemployment will always be used to frighten those with jobs into accepting low wages, and we will never remedy the real cost, both to families and to the country, of dependent women and a massive loss of talent.

Worst of all, we may never learn to find productive, honored work as a natural part of ourselves and as one of life's basic pleasures.

ON POWER

—■—

Barbara Lazear Ascher

The following selection is from Ascher's 1989 book The Habit of Loving.

When I graduated from law school, I was hired by what is known in the business as a Prestigious New York Law Firm. I felt privileged to be associated with talent and money and respectability, to be in a place that promised me four weeks vacation, my own secretary, an office with a window, and, above all, a shot at power. I would not have preferred working for a single practitioner who struggled to pay rent on his windowless, one-room office in the Bronx.

There's a lot to be said for the accouterments of power. Those who asked where I worked immediately assumed, upon being told the name of the firm, that I must have been at the top of my class, an editor of the Law Review and a clerk for a federal judge. I was none of these, but being where the power is frees you from having to explain yourself.

The "outsider's" version of the "insider" is always distorted by the mental glass through which they observe. The outsider tends to think that once inside the power structure the voyage is over, destination reached. No more struggle or strain. But in fact, once you have "arrived," you discover that there are power structures within the power. You may share office space and a central switchboard, but that doesn't mean you are at the controls.

In my firm, the partners (male) took the young associates (also male), resplendent in their red suspenders and newly sported cigars, to lunch, to Dallas, Los Angeles, and Atlanta to meet the clients. The "girl" associates were sent to the library to do research. Actually, they were sent to the library to stay out of trouble.

Soon the clients with whom the associates dined were calling them for advice. These associates were learning how to practice law. Those of us hidden away in the stacks were learning how to be invisible.

A friend at a similar Prestigious New York Law Firm told me that she had tried and failed to enlist the cooperation of the one woman partner. "I suggested that we, the women associates and she, have monthly luncheons to discuss some of the problems we faced. After all, she'd been one of us." But she was no longer "one of us" and feared that if her partners perceived her as an ally of women associates, they might forget that she was, first and foremost, one of "them." She knew that hanging out with weak sisters was no way to safeguard her tentative grasp of success.

Eight years later, when my friend became a partner, she learned that the woman she had approached for help was powerless within the partnership. She was, in the eyes of the men, their token "girl" partner, and power, like beauty, is in the eye of the beholder. She was a lady and that's how she was perceived. How could her mother have known as she trained her daughter for power in the drawing room that what she would want was power in the boardroom?

However, even if hers was a token acceptance, she had entered that heady realm, she was feted around town as "the first woman partner" and she proceeded to follow a pattern not unusual for women who achieve some semblance of power. She refused to reach behind to pull other women along. It was too risky. She might fall backwards. I blush to recall that when, in fourth grade I was the only girl on the boys' baseball team, I joined in their systematic "girl trashing." I enthusiastically participated in disparaging conversations about people who were "just girls." Who threw like girls. Who giggled like girls. Who couldn't whistle through their fingers, burp on command or slide into home plate. Then, all I knew was that my power depended on keeping other girls out. Now, I know about identification with the aggressor.

Not that it makes much difference. There are uncanny similarities between being the only girl on a fourth grade baseball team and the only woman in bigger boys' games. Take, for instance, the response of Harvard Business School's tenured, female professors when their former colleague, Barbara Bund Jackson, filed suit against the school for its refusal to grant her tenure. Nonsense, these women replied to Jackson's charge of a sexist "institutional bias." Not so, they said of her contention that the school sets "impossible standards for female faculty members." Why shouldn't they? Why should Harvard deviate from the accepted wisdom that a man can occasionally goof off and still be perceived as powerful? It's kind of cute, we say. Oh, look, he's got nice human touches, an ability to have fun. How boyish. How charming. Not so for a woman. She who goofs off is a goof-off.

Tenured Harvard professor Regina E. Herzlinger's response to Jackson's claim of discrimination was, "I don't feel there is . . . friction caused by the fact that there are few women on the faculty . . . I don't think there is discrimination on the basis of sex." Of course there isn't friction for those "few women." And Regina'd better keep quiet if she thinks otherwise. Boys don't like girls who turn around and say, "But what about the other girls?" I certainly never invited my friend Linda to play baseball with us, even though she ran like the wind and threw overhand.

But power, who has it and who doesn't, is not limited to the realm of male/female strife. My husband, a physician in practice for many years, volunteers his time, one day a week at a hospital often described with the same breathless reverence as my law firm. This is the place to which ailing shahs and wealthy dowagers come to be healed. The full time attendings (those with the power) don't like the voluntary attendings (those without the power), and occasionally rise up to divest them of responsibility. How, you might ask, when wise and seasoned physicians are willing to give their time, free of charge, to teach students and treat patients, could there be a complaint? The volunteers are not part of the power structure. And power's particular drive is to grab more for itself, an act which invariably involves stripping others of any.

Recently, some of the voluntary attendings went to the head of their department and informed him, "You make us feel like second-class citizens." He listened, nodded, and assured: "You are second-class citizens."

Irrational, you say? Of course. But whoever thought that the power drive made sense?

In fifth grade, secret clubs were the order of the day. The purpose was, first of all, the secret. A secret name. Secret rules. Secret members. Secret meeting places. The purpose was to exclude, which is the first step in establishing a power base. The second is to create fear in those excluded. Those of us who assembled the group of meanest and most popular children had the run of the playground. We were a force to contend with.

Recently, when I went to choose a puppy from a litter, I was told, "Don't get the Alpha dog, whatever you do!" It seems that, like their ancestors the wolves, each litter has a leader. He or she is the power in the pack, and once the Alpha dog comes to live with your family, you become the pack.

What does the Alpha dog get for his trouble? A certain haughtiness. A certain swagger. What did the Alpha attorneys in my firm get for their power? A certain haughtiness. A certain swagger. And an occasional invitation to the Piping Rock Country Club.

So who cares? We all did. We who sat in the library working on Blue Sky Memos, something my twelve-year-old daughter could have done, given the careful and patronizing instructions we received. We were enraged at being excluded from Making It Big. What we didn't know at the time is that the ones who Make It Big are always watching their backs, but then girls rarely have the opportunity to learn these finer points.

Power sanctions self-centeredness. (It could be argued that that's why girls don't have it—"They're so giving.") It returns you, full circle, to the delicious years of being an infant and toddler when, it seemed, you were the center of the universe. But what is missing at thirty-five, forty, or fifty years of age is the innocence of the infant, the two- or three-year-old. It is a dangerous absence. Self-interest plus muscle power and experience combine to create a being more pervasively harmful than the sandbox bully.

Take, for instance, Manhattan real estate developers. They are currently a favorite target of the less powerful, and are, in some instances, a legitimate target. There are those who use their amassed fortunes to gain political sway by contributing to the campaign funds of elected officials. The elected officials then turn deaf ears to the complaints of less powerful constituents dispossessed from low rent buildings razed to make room for luxury high rises complete with Jacuzzis in every bath.

Donald Trump's song of himself is on the best-seller lists. *Vanity Fair* featured a breathlessly infatuated profile of his wife. Why? Because if you can't be powerful, the next best thing is to fancy yourself on intimate terms with those who are. There is a hunger to know how they make their deals, shop for their children's Christmas presents, stay fresh and alert from five A.M. until Peter Duchin's orchestra plays its last charity ball waltz at midnight. All this, and not a wrinkle in the brow to show for it.

People read about power for the same reason that little girls read *Cinderella*, they want to believe that someday a prince will come to deliver a subject into sovereignty.

One might ask whether adulation of those who are flagrantly self-involved makes any sense when there are thousands of dispossessed sleeping in Grand Central and Pennsylvania Station. It certainly doesn't make mature sense.

But then power is not necessarily in mature hands. It is most often achieved, and clung to by those whose passion for it is fueled by childlike greed and self-interest. What they find, once they have it, is that being the proud possessor of power bears an uncanny similarity to being the two-year-old with the biggest plastic pail and shovel on the beach. It's a life of nervous guardianship.

I left the law because I wasn't motivated to engage in the struggle required to move myself from library to the light of day and lunches with clients. The struggle would have required molding myself in the partners' images, a hard concept for them to visualize since I was female and they were male. It would have been necessary to remember when to speak and when to keep my mouth shut. I would have had to create an asexual aura. I would have had to work very, very hard.

I left the law because that wasn't the power that interested me. Which is not to say that power itself doesn't interest me. I remember the full glory of being the only girl on the boy's baseball team. I remember the total sense of worthlessness that resulted when I grew breasts and the guys banished me from the pitcher's mound to the powerless world of hopscotch. Power is as tantalizing as a hypnotist's swinging pendulum. Power promises that you will never again be stuck with "the girls." Ask Regina Herzlinger. She knows.

GREEN CARDS

———————◆———————

Alberto Alvaro Rios

The following selection first appeared in Indiana Review *in 1995.*

All colors exist to satisfy the longing for blue.

There's a folk saying in Spanish, *el que quira azul que le cueste.* One must pay for what one wants; it's a variation of the older Spanish proverb, "Take what you want and pay for it, says God." But the phrase means, more literally, *he who wants blue, let it cost him.*

A green card is what you get if you are a citizen of another country but you find yourself in, or cross over to, the United States. The card is a first step toward applying for citizenship. My wife, who was born in Mexico, had one. My mother, who was born in England, had one. My father, who was born in Mexico, didn't have one. But that's another story, involving some curious papers and shady explanations. My mother-in-law, after more than forty years here, still has one. She's never been quite sure what to do next. But she's learned well that you don't raise your hand to ask the Immigration Service anything. They notice you then. Everybody knows that.

They notice you, and then they do something. And they're everywhere, maybe. So you don't speak loudly, you don't ask questions, you don't make trouble. Run away when you have to. Don't sign anything. Get a job only where everybody else is getting one, where it's safe.

There were all kinds of stories. The one my mother-in-law lived with the longest was how, her sister in Guaymas told her, they had heard that when you become a citizen of the United States, you have to spit on the flag of Mexico. And they would all shake their heads in a *no.*

My mother, when she became a citizen, recalls a curious moment. After the ceremony, the high-school band came in to the courtroom and, because she was special—which is to say, in this border town with Mexico, she was not Mexican—they played the British national anthem. Someone thought it was a good idea. At that moment, though, she says she felt a little funny. She never forgot.

None of this is easy, and nobody knows what will happen when you come, and everybody is not treated the same. And things do happen. I think, finally, they were right.

Crossing over from Mexico, for example, was more than just being there and then being here. It was a change in how one walked, and a change in color. Over there, the ground moved one way, coiled and trailed and offered itself. Here was not there, and the coiling and trailing and offering were to the left and to the right, but never the same. To this, the legs and the body had to adjust. It was not the same ground.

And in Mexico, the color was green. Here, it is blue. And that Latin-American green is not the green of here, in the way that this blue is not the same blue in Mexico. The eyes, like the legs, have to learn over.

It is more than the music and the food and the clothing. It is the walk, and the color. And smell—not of food, but of things. And if one walked this other walk, and smells were new so the nose had to accommodate itself, one then began to look different. The body and the mirror made their changes.

I remember something from the middle of all this, from the middle of color and the middle of the century. During the '50s, I remember driving through town and seeing pickup trucks full of men dressed in white. They were *braceros,* the workers imported specifically from Mexico for a brief time, sometimes only a day, just to work. After work, either at the end of the day or the end of the growing season, they had to go back to Mexico. What that meant was taking the pickup truck to the border and dropping them all off.

Arizona was the last state to hold out against minimum wage, championing the *laissez-faire* system of government oversight: in this case, let the growers pay what the workers will accept and don't get in the way. And these workers worked for almost nothing. It seemed, for a while, like a good idea to the growers and to the government, whose program this was.

As a kid, I remember only all these men dressed in white. It was a color that meant they didn't belong anywhere.

Crossing over from Mexico to the United States is not a small thing, but not large either. This is an incorrect vocabulary. To cross over was big, but that part was easy. The big is like that. It was the small that was difficult.

To cross the border was made up of these smaller things, then. It was lived as these more difficult-to-explain changes in color, more like that, more something of the body than one might suspect. It was the different way of walking because the ground was new, in all things. A different way of walking or a different way of hiding. More surprise, or more dullness, dullness or quiet. Something.

It is a movement from green, but who would know it? How to explain it? This is what I've heard all my life. It is a movement like the planet's, a movement that is there absolute, but who can feel it? A movement from green, from green to what is next.

For my family, crossing over was crossing over from green, not from Mexico. Green from before, but sorted out, from all the moments of green in a life, sorted and lifted out and then assembled together, into a big green, into green only. Fresh from the inhuman jungles of Chiapas and farther still, somewhere middle on the Western-hemisphere map, into the green day, into the green night, into the in-between—the light and the dark greens, the green that is brown and the green that is white—but green, and inside green, green incarnate, from the back and from the front, from the shoulders and the feet, green from yesterday and green from before yesterday, all of it ocean-like, all of it water, all of it moving as claws and tendrils and tongues, as eyes, as webs, and as base and rough flight, so that to navigate upon it one needed to ride above it to move through it, and even then to be careful and to look around. One needed to paddle and to chart, the paddle as a half-weapon and a half-tool, remembering never to dangle foolishly—for the one moment green takes—an arm into it.

From green utterly and in whispers, green eyes and green tongue, green taste and green sound; green from tea, but then from coffee; from bitter, but then from sweet; green from garden, and a little then from bean and root and tuber, but then from sky and from air, and from light.

But at light, and in dream, sound and strong, four-square and, yet, in that moment of pellucid strength, in that moment also inexplicably tinged with rue, there it is that green wavers and is for a moment inconstant, is for a moment green that is hollowed, or absent; is, for a moment, blue. There is the pivotal point, the narrows in this repeating hourglass of colors, in this life. There for a second, but there absolutely: green shifts to blue, and it is done.

It is Blue. Only and just blue. It is the log sawed and in its moment of breaking. It is the yawn pushed fully and then fully engaged. It is a blue. Blue and not green. Only blue. Only blue and the memory of green. Not a desire yet—green is too close—but a memory.

So much was the green.

On the far other side of green was a yellow, somewhere out there, somewhere only in imagination perhaps, yellow and red and some other colors on the other side of memory. Yellow, then the green, but now blue. It was the end at last, or the beginning. It was not the middle. But it was the discovery of the middle.

In this way, the green stayed, the way the Virgin Mary was painted, and in the shades of the hillside houses. It stayed in the Chinese teas, in the *yerba buena*, how that green was a cure for things, and in the afternoons, in talk. Green stayed, and had a place in my family, but always as a memory. It stayed as a sadness for something.

It stayed as what used to be.

WORK, LABOR, AND PLAY

W. H. Auden

The following selection is from W. H. Auden's A Certain World: A Commonplace Book.

So far as I know, Miss Hannah Arendt was the first person to define the essential difference between work and labor. To be happy, a man must feel, firstly, free and, secondly, important. He cannot be really happy if he is compelled by society to do what he does not enjoy doing, or if what he enjoys doing is ignored by society as of no value or importance. In a society where slavery in the strict sense has been abolished, the sign that what a man does is of social value is that he is paid money to do it, but a laborer today can rightly be called a wage slave. A man is a laborer if the job society offers him is of no interest to himself but he is compelled to take it by the necessity of earning a living and supporting his family.

The antithesis to labor is play. When we play a game, we enjoy what we are doing, otherwise we should not play it, but it is a purely private activity; society could not care less whether we play it or not.

Between labor and play stands work. A man is a worker if he is personally interested in the job which society pays him to do; what from the point of view of society is necessary labor is from his own point of view voluntary play. Whether a job is to be classified as labor or work depends, not on the job itself, but on the tastes of the individual who undertakes it. The difference does not, for example, coincide with the difference between a manual and a mental job; a gardener or a cobbler may be a worker, a bank clerk a laborer. Which a man is can be seen from his attitude toward leisure. To a worker, leisure means simply the hours he needs to relax and rest in order to work efficiently. He is therefore more likely to take too little leisure than too much; workers die of coronaries and forget their wives' birthdays. To the laborer, on the other hand, leisure means freedom from compulsion, so that it is natural for him to imagine that the fewer hours he has to spend laboring, and the more hours he is free to play, the better.

What percentage of the population in a modern technological society are, like myself, in the fortunate position of being workers? At a guess I would say sixteen per cent, and I do not think that figure is likely to get bigger in the future.

Technology and the division of labor have done two things: by eliminating in many fields the need for special strength or skill, they have made a very large number of paid occupations which formerly were enjoyable work into boring labor, and by increasing productivity they have reduced the number of necessary laboring hours. It is already possible to imagine a society in which the majority of the population, that is to say, its laborers, will have almost as much leisure as in earlier times was enjoyed by the aristocracy. When one recalls how aristocracies in the past actually behaved, the prospect is not cheerful. Indeed, the problem of dealing with boredom may be even more difficult for such a future mass society than it was for aristocracies. The latter, for example, ritualized their time; there was a season to shoot grouse, a season to spend in town, etc. The masses are more likely to replace an unchanging ritual by fashion which it will be in the economic interest of certain people to change as often as possible. Again, the masses cannot go in for hunting, for very soon there would be no animals left to hunt. For other aristocratic amusements like gambling, dueling, and warfare, it may be only too easy to find equivalents in dangerous driving, drug-taking, and senseless acts of violence. Workers seldom commit acts of violence, because they can put their aggression into their work, be it physical like the work of a smith, or mental like the work of a scientist or an artist. The role of aggression in mental work is aptly expressed by the phrase "getting one's teeth into a problem."

DELUSIONS OF GRANDEUR
—■—
Henry Louis Gates, Jr.

The following essay first appeared in Sports Illustrated.

Standing at the bar of an all-black VFW post in my hometown of Piedmont, W.Va., I offered five dollars to anyone who could tell me how many African-American professional athletes were at work today. There are 35 million African-Americans, I said.

"Ten million!" yelled one intrepid soul, too far into his cups.

"No way . . . more like 500,000," said another.

"You mean *all* professional sports," someone interjected, "including golf and tennis, but not counting the brothers from Puerto Rico?" Everyone laughed.

"Fifty thousand, minimum," was another guess.

Here are the facts:

There are 1,200 black professional athletes in the U.S.

There are 12 times more black lawyers than black athletes.

There are 2½ times more black dentists than black athletes.

There are 15 times more black doctors than black athletes.

Nobody in my local VFW believed these statistics; in fact, few people would believe them if they weren't reading them in the pages of *Sports Illustrated.* In spite of these statistics, too many African-American youngsters still believe that they have a much better chance of becoming another Magic Johnson or Michael Jordan than they do of matching the achievements of Baltimore Mayor Kurt Schmoke or neurosurgeon Dr. Benjamin Carson, both of whom, like Johnson and Jordan, are black.

In reality, an African-American youngster has about as much chance of becoming a professional athlete as he or she does of winning the lottery. The tragedy for our people, however, is that few of us accept that truth.

Let me confess that I love sports. Like most black people of my generation—I'm 40—I was raised to revere the great black athletic heroes, and I never tired of listening to the stories of triumph and defeat that, for blacks, amount to a collective epic much like those of the ancient Greeks: Joe Louis's demolition of Max Schmeling; Satchel Paige's dazzling repertoire of pitches; Jesse Owens's in-your-face performance in Hitler's 1936 Olympics; Willie Mays's over-the-shoulder basket catch; Jackie Robinson's quiet strength when assaulted by racist taunts; and a thousand other grand tales.

Nevertheless, the blind pursuit of attainment in sports is having a devastating effect on our people. Imbued with a belief that our principal avenue to fame and profit is through sport, and seduced by a win-at-any-cost system that corrupts even elementary school students, far too many black kids treat basketball courts and football fields as if they were classrooms in an alternative school system. "O.K., I flunked English," a young athlete will say. "But I got an A plus in slam-dunking."

The failure of our public schools to educate athletes is part and parcel of the schools' failure to educate almost everyone. A recent survey of the Philadelphia school system, for example, stated that "more than half of all students in the third, fifth and eighth grades cannot perform minimum math and language tasks." One in four middle school students in that city fails to pass to the next grade each year. It is a sad truth that such statistics are repeated in cities throughout the nation. Young athletes—particularly young black athletes—are especially ill-served. Many of them are functionally illiterate, yet they are passed along from year to year for the greater glory of good old Hometown High. We should not be surprised to learn, then, that only 26.6% of black athletes at the collegiate level earn their degrees. For every successful educated black professional athlete, there are thousands of dead and wounded. Yet young blacks continue to aspire to careers as athletes, and it's no wonder why; when the University of North Carolina recently commissioned a sculptor to create archetypes of its student body, guess which ethnic group was selected to represent athletes?

Those relatively few black athletes who do make it in the professional ranks must be prevailed upon to play a significant role in the education of all of our young people, athlete and nonathlete alike. While some have done so, many others have shirked their social obligations: to earmark small percentages of their incomes for the United Negro College Fund; to appear on television for educational purposes rather than merely to sell sneakers; to let children know the message that becoming a lawyer, a teacher or a doctor does more good for our people than winning the Super Bowl; and to form productive liaisons with educators to help forge solutions to the many ills that beset the black community. These are merely a few modest proposals.

A similar burden falls upon successful blacks in all walks of life. Each of us must strive to make our young people understand the realities. Tell them to cheer Bo Jackson but to emulate novelist Toni Morrison or businessman Reginald Lewis or historian John Hope Franklin or Spelman College president Johnetta Cole—the list is long.

Of course, society as a whole bears responsibility as well. Until colleges stop using young blacks as cannon fodder in the big-business wars of so-called nonprofessional sports, until training a young black's mind becomes as important as training his or her body, we will continue to perpetuate a system akin to that of the Roman gladiators, sacrificing a class of people for the entertainment of the mob.

GREETINGS FROM THE
ELECTRONIC PLANTATION

■

Roger Swardson

The original version of the following selection was published in the alternative newspaper City Pages.

Out in the economic sector where you work all week but can't make a living, lots of us are fastened like barnacles to the bottom of the computer revolution. Soldering tiny leads on circuit boards. Plugging data into terminals. All sorts of things that tend to share one characteristic: repetition. Some of the jobs, like mine, consist of sitting in a chair while, all day long, people call you from all over the country to buy things like T-shirts that read "Compost Happens."

Just after 9 A.M., a tireless recorded voice in my headset tips me off. A catalog shopper is coming my way from across the continent. I press the appropriate key and say, "Good morning, welcome to Wireless. My name is Roger. How can I help you?"

Wireless is one of five direct-mail catalogs operated by Rivertown Trading Company, a shirttail relation of Minnesota Public Radio, the spawning ground of Garrison Keillor.

This morning I walk through a new industrial park to the clusters of smokers hanging around the lone door in the block-long wall of a warehouse. Once inside I show my picture ID to the guard behind the glass window and stick another plastic card in the time clock.

I initial the sheet that tells me when to take my morning and afternoon 15-minute breaks and half-hour lunch period. I nod good morning to two women at the group leader station that overlooks the room. They smile and nod back. Both are concentrating on computer terminals that identify scores of telephone service representatives (TSRs) like me who have logged onto the system this morning. The screens tell the group leaders exactly what all the TSRs are doing in the system and for how many seconds they have been doing it. In a seven-day period prior to Christmas 1991, despite the lousy economy, about 300 of us in two shifts wrote 87,642 mail or credit card orders, up 47 percent from the year before.

One supervisor in a headset has a distant look on her face. She's monitoring a TSR, tapping into a customer call to check on two dozen points that must be covered. The TSR will be told the results later in the day.

I fill up my coffee mug and check the printout taped to the wall next to the time card rack. The printout summarizes the results of our weekly monitorings. Ideally we should get 24 pieces of information from the customer (like home phone, work address, whether or not they want to be on our mailing list) during the course of the conversation. During the monitorings, we are graded according to how much of the data we have gotten, which is a difficult task when you've got a customer on the other end of the line who just wants to make a purchase and hang up without being asked a bunch of questions. We are expected to maintain an average above 90 percent. The names of all TSRs in the 90s have been highlighted with a blue marker. I'm at 89.6 percent. It has been suggested that I could use additional training.

I head down a double row of 20 stalls where the backsides of seated people stick out like the rumps of Guernsey cows. The room is done in tones of gray, and merchandise is pinned to white walls. The 80 stalls I can see are mostly occupied. There is a continuous yammer like audience noise before a concert. On two walls electronic scoreboards flash the number of calls completed for each of five catalogs. The total is around 2,200. A busy morning. Must have been a big catalog mailing.

I find an open stall, adjust the chair height, get my headset on, and log onto the phone and computer systems, using my password. An orange light on my console indicates that there are callers on hold.

I bring up the initial screen of the order process and tap the button on my phone to signal that I'm ready to take a customer call. A recorded voice instantly says "Wireless."

I swing right into it. "Good morning. Welcome to Wireless. My name is Roger. How can I help you?"

A woman from New Jersey is distressed.

"You have to help me."

"Sure, what's the problem?"

"I ordered a ring for my husband for our anniversary. Last night we went out and I gave it to him before dinner. Well, he's put on a little weight and it didn't fit. The poor man was so upset he couldn't eat his dinner. Today he's out there running around the neighborhood and getting red in the face."

"That's terrible. What can I do?"

"Well, I looked at the ring this morning and I ordered a size too small."

"Send it back. We'll send you another one right away."

"How long will it take?"

"If you want to pay extra I can send it overnight air. Regular delivery is 10 working days."

"Make it the 10-day. It won't kill him."

"Interface" is a word that tells millions of American workers where we fit. We are devices between you and a computer system. Various terms further identify the device: data entry, customer service, word processing, telemarketing, and others. We take reservations. We do market research. We sell people aluminum siding the minute they sit down to dinner. Every night we update computer records so that multinational corporations can begin the day on top of things. We type most of today's business communications. We do all those mundane tasks that provide computer systems with the raw data that makes them useful.

Even so, most of us are among the more than 14 million Americans who work every week but are still classified by the government as poor. The people Ross Perot talks about when he says, "I suppose when they are up to six bucks an hour in Mexico and down to six bucks here, American corporations will again begin creating jobs in this country."

Here's another way we are classified. The first sentence of my employee handbook tells me that the company "believes in the practice of employment at will, which means that employment is terminable by either the employee or the company at any time, for any reason." We are devices that accommodate the economic needs of our era. Flexible. Disposable.

Even recyclable.

Say a company is "downsizing" or "delayering" or whatever other term describes job cuts. Through a combination of early retirement, attrition, and layoffs they manage to take 200 current semi-skilled employees off the payroll over the course of a year. Say those employees were paid an average of $12 an hour with full benefits. The company then hires a temporary agency to fill openings as they occur. The agency may even have an office in the company's building. Job qualifications are determined, and the agency finds the people and trains them if necessary. The jobs will pay from $5 to $7 an hour. Even with the agency's commission, the company has just saved around $2 million annually in wages and benefits.

Improbable? A want ad placed by a temporary employment agency in my St. Paul newspaper lists four major corporations that need temporary workers. The agency is offering a $25 bonus to people with prior experience with any of the listed companies. Today, through the wonders of current economic policy, it is possible to replace yourself at a bargain rate.

Here's another way the system works. You have a data entry barn where the job routine is easy and repetitious. The problem is that your volume is changeable, with big bulges around some of the holidays. A permanent work force would be awkward, so you have a standing order with three temporary agencies.

When your temporaries show up, they are told their hours will vary as necessary with one week's advance notice. The temps will rarely get a full week's work. They can be sent home any time during the day or let go permanently for any reason. They will receive no benefits. They are subject to a probationary period and can be dropped with a call to the agency. In a relatively short time you have a high-performance, completely flexible work force. You can even offer the best of them permanent part-time jobs, again with no benefits but with a raise in pay. (This actually amounts to a savings, since you no longer have to pay the agency commission.)

Look at the costs and problems you have eliminated. Look how easy the system is to manage. All you have to do is keep weeding.

This is the employment system of the 1990s, made possible by a bankrupt economy and an increasingly desperate work force.

We are the vocational descendants of the dapper clerks in the better stores who knew your sizes and decided when your son ought to be ready for his first suit. Our voices, regardless of how we happen to look or feel that day, are fresh and animated and friendly. We just happen to be sitting here in jeans and a sweatshirt talking into a little foam ball.

After a while you get into a rhythm. You learn to judge how the calls will go. Women in California invariably say they have shopped with us before when they have not, men everywhere say they have no idea whether they've shopped with us before though many of them are repeaters.

Southern women sign off with "Ba-Ba" except for Texans, who just say "Ba," and people from Alaska sound like friends you can rely on, which seems fortunate in that kind of country. I never heard a shrill voice from Alaska.

You can easily tell people who are ordering with a purpose and people who love to shop or do it to feel better. One day a woman browsed through the catalog for 18 minutes and ordered more than 3,000 bucks' worth of stuff. I had a pretty good idea the order wouldn't go through, but she had a wonderful time.

This two-week pay period I'm able to get in 74 hours at $6 an hour. My take-home, after federal and state taxes and Social Security, is $355.48. With another good pay period plus the 5 percent commission I make by selling merchandise on the specials list, I could net $800 this month.

On this particular day I take 57 calls from 23 states. I write $4,096.59 in orders. The biggest is from a guy in California for a selection of videotapes that includes complete sets of the British television shows *Reilly, Ace of Spies* and *Rumpole of the Bailey*.

In just over eight months, working at a pace where I am either available for or taking orders more than 90 percent of the time I am logged on, I have taken 4,462 orders and booked nearly $300,000.

Even so, many jobs like mine, especially in urban America, are at risk. Workers in American cities cost more than elsewhere simply because it costs more to live here. As a result, there is a kind of ongoing economic cleansing. Software "upgrades" constantly eliminate some jobs, data barns move to cheaper rural locations, and the Caribbean and Mexico are claiming jobs.

In the meantime, take that $6-an-hour job that provides about $800 a month if you can get 40 hours a week in, and then add up rent, utilities, phone, food, and transportation. Then try adding a family.

It doesn't add up.

"Recovery" is a wishful term. It is also a word that means something understandable. Most of us can tell whether we are recovering. Thirty-eight million people below the poverty line is not a persuasive definition of an economic "recovery."

Leading economic indicators are used by economists to describe conditions as they may be six to nine months in the future. How, if the present constantly worsens, can the future remain perpetually bright? Even schoolchildren can see that that's denial.

How else could "downsizing" be heralded for improving corporate profits and aiding the "recovery"? Fewer livelihoods mean "recovery"? For whom?

The same with "diminished expectations" or lesser livelihoods. That must mean those economic refugees from companies that let $12-an-hour people go and replaced them with $6 temporaries. These resettled workers are a non-statistical phenomenon. They are employed. But because millions of dollars have been hacked out of their paychecks, they no longer qualify for mortgages, car loans, or credit cards no matter what the interest rate. Who will spend us into the "recovery"?

Workers are getting pushed farther down the economic ladder as laid-off skilled workers and recent college graduates secure even the menial jobs. And, on the bottom, public assistance is breaking its seams.

Surely, the term "recovery" has become a mockery of the way millions of Americans now live.

The rest of us come and go. The young. Men without jobs. People picking up some extra money. But women between 40 and 60 are always there, plugging away at countless uninspiring jobs that need doing day in and day out, year in and year out.

On break they sit together eating homemade food out of Tupperware while the rest of us use the vending machines. They show each other craft handiwork. They bring packets of photos. They take work seriously and talk about the merchandise and what kind of a day they're having. They do well at jobs many make fun of or would not do. And they succeed at life as it is.

I left a temp job at an insurance company at dusk. A woman was sitting at a terminal in word processing wearing a smock. I said something sprightly like "Working late, huh?" And that started a conversation. It happens easily with night-shift people.

Her husband put in 27 years on the production line of a company that went broke and then cheated him out of his pension. She worked for a small office-equipment firm and the same thing happened. He is now a part-time security guard. She holds down two temporary jobs. Their jobs don't provide health insurance, and they can't afford it. They put in a lifetime working, raising their kids, and they must continue working indefinitely. I was enraged but she passed it off. Gave me a brownie. Then in the lighted corner of the darkened office floor she went to work, producing letters from dictation. As I left I could hear the tape of some dayside junior exec talking through his nose about yet another intolerable situation that had come to his attention.

The caller's voice does not hold together well. I can tell he is quite old and not well. He is calling from Maryland.

"I want four boxes of the Nut Goodies," he rasps at me after giving me his credit card information in a faltering hurry.

"There are 24 bars in each box" I say in case he doesn't know the magnitude of his order. Nut Goodies are made here in St. Paul and consist of a patty of maple cream covered with milk chocolate and peanuts. Sort of a Norwegian praline.

"OK, then make it five boxes but hurry this up before my nurse gets back."

He wants the order billed to a home address but sent to a nursing home.

"I've got Parkinson's," he says. "I'm 84."

"OK, Sir. I think I've got it all. They're on the way." I put a rush on it.

"Right. Bye," he says, and in the pause when he is concentrating God knows how much energy on getting the receiver back in its cradle, I hear a long, dry chuckle.

One hundred and twenty Nut Goodies.

Way to go, buddy.

During our time together I am not sucking cough drops and scratching for rent money and she, with her mellow alto, is not calling from a condo at Sea Island. We are two grandparents talking over the selection of videos for her grandson's seventh birthday. We settle on classics, among them *The Red Balloon, Old Yeller,* and *Fantasia.*

I say "we" because when I'm on the phone I identify with the people I speak with; I'm no longer an electronic menial. And it's not just me. We all do it. I can hear my neighbors. You'd think we were at a Newport garden party.

We identify with wealth because none of us, moneyless, think of ourselves as poor. We'll be on this plantation another month. Maybe two. That $10 job will come through. That ominous feeling around the tooth will go away. The car won't break again. We'll be on our way presently.

Except there's a feeling these days that's hard to pin down. A detachment that comes out now and then as rage or despair. Many of the people I work with are bone-tired from just trying to make it week by week. A lot of people have just plain stopped believing any politician.

For years the working poor in this country have felt they had a pact with the powerful. Work hard and you'll be OK. Do your job well and you'll have the basics and a chance to move up. The rich and powerful, because they run the system, have been stewards of that promise. It means when the chips are down, the preservation of opportunity is supposed to come before the cultivation of privilege.

On the bus and in the break room today there is a great deal of frustration. The promise has been broken and people don't really know what they can do about it. Another system has taken the place of the old pact.

Those who have found a secure place in the suburbs, in government, in the corporations, in wealth, have redefined the country under a different set of rules. It is a smug new club. And those riding the bus and sitting in the break room need not apply.

At the end of my shift I log off the computer and phone system, nod goodbye to the two women at the supervisory station, punch out, open my backpack for the guard so he knows I'm not stealing anything, and head for the bus.

Not a bad day. Remarkably like yesterday.

ONE LAST TIME
—————•—————

Gary Soto

This essay is from Soto's book Living up the Street.

Yesterday I saw the movie *Gandhi* and recognized a few of the people—not in the theater but in the film. I saw my relatives, dusty and thin as sparrows, returning from the fields with hoes balanced on their shoulders. The workers were squinting, eyes small and veined, and were using their hands to say what there was to say to those in the audience with popcorn and Cokes. I didn't have anything, though. I sat thinking of my family and their years in the fields, beginning with Grandmother who came to the United States after the Mexican revolution to settle in Fresno where she met her husband and bore children, many of them. She worked in the fields around Fresno, picking grapes, oranges, plums, peaches, and cotton, dragging a large white sack like a sled. She worked in the packing houses, Bonner and Sun-Maid Raisin, where she stood at a conveyor belt passing her hand over streams of raisins to pluck out leaves and pebbles. For over twenty years she worked at a machine that boxed raisins until she retired at sixty-five.

Grandfather worked in the fields, as did his children. Mother also found herself out there when she separated from Father for three weeks. I remember her coming home, dusty and so tired that she had to rest on the porch before she trudged inside to wash and start dinner. I didn't understand the complaints about her ankles or the small of her back, even though I had been in the grape fields watching her work. With my brother and sister I ran in and out of the rows; we enjoyed ourselves and pretended not to hear Mother scolding us to sit down and behave ourselves. A few years later, however, I caught on when I went to pick grapes rather than play in the rows.

Mother and I got up before dawn and ate quick bowls of cereal. She drove in silence while I rambled on how everything was now solved, how I was going to make enough money to end our misery and even buy her a beautiful copper tea pot, the one I had shown her in Long's Drugs. When we arrived I was frisky and ready to go, self-consciously aware of my grape knife dangling at my wrist. I almost ran to the row the foreman had pointed out, but I returned to help Mother with the grape pans and jug of water. She told me to settle down and reminded me not to lose my knife. I walked at her side and listened to her explain how to cut grapes; bent down, hands on knees, I watched her demonstrate by cutting a few bunches into my pan. She stood over me as I tried it myself, tugging at a bunch of grapes that pulled loose like beads from a necklace. "Cut the stem all the way," she told me as last advice before she walked away, her shoes sinking in the loose dirt, to begin work on her own row.

I cut another bunch, then another, fighting the snap and whip of vines. After ten minutes of groping for grapes, my first pan brimmed with bunches. I poured them on the paper tray, which was bordered by a wooden frame that kept the grapes from rolling off, and they spilled like jewels from a pirate's chest. The tray was only half filled, so I hurried to jump under the vines and begin groping, cutting, and tugging at the grapes again. I emptied the pan, raked the grapes with my hands to make them look like they filled the tray, and jumped back under the vine on my knees. I tried to cut faster because Mother, in the next row, was slowly moving ahead. I peeked into her row and saw five trays gleaming in the early morning. I cut, pulled hard, and stopped to gather the grapes that missed the pan; already bored, I spat on a few to wash them before tossing them like popcorn into my mouth.

So it went. Two pans equaled one tray—or six cents. By lunchtime I had a trail of thirty-seven trays behind me while mother had sixty or more. We met about halfway from our last trays, and I sat down with a grunt, knees wet from kneeling on dropped grapes. I washed my hands with the water from the jug, drying them on the inside of my shirt sleeve before I opened the paper bag for the first sandwich, which I gave to Mother. I dipped my hand in again to unwrap a sandwich without looking at it. I took a first bite and chewed it slowly for the tang of mustard. Eating in silence I looked straight ahead at the vines, and only when we were finished with cookies did we talk.

"Are you tired?" she asked.

"No, but I got a sliver from the frame," I told her. I showed her the web of skin between my thumb and index finger. She wrinkled her forehead but said it was nothing.

"How many trays did you do?"

I looked straight ahead, not answering at first. I recounted in my mind the whole morning of bend, cut, pour again and again, before answering a feeble "thirty-seven." No elaboration, no detail. Without looking at me she told me how she had done field work in Texas and Michigan as a child. But I had a difficult time listening to her stories. I played with my grape knife, stabbing it into the ground, but stopped when Mother reminded me that I had better not lose it. I left the knife sticking up like a small, leafless plant. She then talked about school, the junior high I would be going to that fall, and then about Rick and Debra, how sorry they would be that they hadn't come out to pick grapes because they'd have no new clothes for the school year. She stopped talking when she peeked at her watch, a bandless one she kept in her pocket. She got up with an *"Ay, Dios,"* and told me that we'd work until three, leaving me cutting figures in the sand with my knife and dreading the return to work.

Finally I rose and walked slowly back to where I had left off, again kneeling under the vine and fixing the pan under bunches of grapes. By that time, 11:30, the sun was over my shoulder and made me squint and think of the pool at the Y.M.C.A. where I was a summer member. I saw myself diving face first into the water and loving it. I saw myself gleaming like something new, at the edge of the pool. I had to daydream and keep my mind busy because boredom was a terror almost as awful as the work itself. My mind went dumb with stupid things, and I had to keep it moving with dreams of baseball and would-be girlfriends. I even sang, however softly, to keep my mind moving, my hands moving.

I worked less hurriedly and with less vision. I no longer saw that copper pot sitting squat on our stove or Mother waiting for it to whistle. The wardrobe that I imagined, crisp and bright in the closet numbered only one pair of jeans and two shirts because, in half a day, six cents times thirty-seven trays was two dollars and twenty-two cents. It became clear to me. If I worked eight hours, I might make four dollars. I'd take this, even gladly, and walk downtown to look into store windows on the mall and long for the bright madras shirts from Walter Smith or Coffee's, but settling for two imitation ones from Penney's.

That first day I laid down seventy-three trays while Mother had a hundred and twenty behind her. On the back of an old envelope, she wrote out our numbers and hours. We washed at the pump behind the farm house and walked slowly to our car for the drive back to town in the afternoon heat. That evening after dinner I sat in a lawn chair listening to music from a transistor radio while Rick and David King played catch. I joined them in a game of pickle, but there was little joy in trying to avoid their tags because I couldn't get the fields out of my mind: I saw myself dropping on my knees under a vine to tug at a branch that wouldn't come off. In bed, when I closed my eyes, I saw the fields, yellow with kicked up dust, and a crooked trail of trays rotting behind me.

The next day I woke tired and started picking tired. The grapes rained into the pan, slowly filling like a belly, until I had my first tray and started my second. So it went all day, and the next, and all through the following week, so that by the end of thirteen days the foreman counted out, in tens mostly, my pay of fifty-three dollars. Mother earned one hundred and forty-eight dollars. She wrote this on her envelope, with a message I didn't bother to ask her about.

The next day I walked with my friend Scott to the downtown mall where we drooled over the clothes behind fancy windows, bought popcorn, and sat at a tier of outdoor fountains to talk about girls. Finally we went into Penney's for more popcorn, which we ate walking around, before we returned home without buying anything. It wasn't until a few days before school that I let my fifty-three dollars slip quietly from my hands, buying a pair of pants, two shirts, and a maroon T-shirt, the kind that was in style. At home I tried them on while Rick looked on enviously; later, the day before school started, I tried them on again wondering not so much if they were worth it as who would see me first in those clothes.

Along with my brother and sister I picked grapes until I was fifteen, before giving up and saying that I'd rather wear old clothes than stoop like a Mexican. Mother thought I was being stuck-up, even stupid, because there would be no clothes for me in the fall. I told her I didn't care, but when Rick and Debra rose at five in the morning, I lay awake in bed feeling that perhaps I had made a mistake but unwilling to change my mind. That fall Mother bought me two pairs of socks, a packet of colored T-shirts, and underwear. The T-shirts would help, I thought, but who would see that I had new underwear and socks? I wore a new T-shirt on the first day of school, then an old shirt on Tuesday, than another T-shirt on Wednesday, and on Thursday an old Nehru shirt that was embarrassingly out of style. On Friday I changed into the corduroy pants my brother had handed down to me and slipped into my last new T-shirt. I worked like a magician, blinding my classmates, who were all clothes conscious and small-time social climbers, by arranging my wardrobe to make it seem larger than it really was. But by spring I had to do something—my blue jeans were almost silver and my shoes had lost their form, puddling like black ice around my feet. That spring of my sixteenth year, Rick and I decided to take a labor bus to chop cotton. In his old Volkswagen, which was more noise than power, we drove on a Saturday morning to West Fresno—or Chinatown as some call it—parked, walked slowly toward a bus, and stood gawking at the winos, toothy blacks, Okies, *Tejanos* with gold teeth, whores, Mexican families, and labor contractors shouting "Cotton" or "Beets," the work of spring.

We boarded the "Cotton" bus without looking at the contractor who stood almost blocking the entrance because he didn't want winos. We boarded scared and then were more scared because two blacks in the rear were drunk and arguing loudly about what was better, a two-barrel or four-barrel Ford carburetor. We sat far from them, looking straight ahead, and only glanced briefly at the others who boarded, almost all of them broken and poorly dressed in loudly mismatched clothes. Finally when the contractor banged his palm against the side of the bus, the young man at the wheel, smiling and talking in Spanish, started the engine, idled it for a moment while he adjusted the mirrors, and started off in slow chugs. Except for the windshield there was no glass in the windows, so as soon as we were on the rural roads outside Fresno, the dust and sand began to be sucked into the bus, whipping about like irate wasps as the gravel ticked about us. We closed our eyes, clotted up our mouths that wanted to open with embarrassed laughter because we couldn't believe we were on that bus with those people and the dust attacking us for no reason.

When we arrived at a field we followed the others to a pickup where we each took a hoe and marched to stand before a row. Rick and I, self-conscious and unsure, looked around at the others who leaned on their hoes or squatted in front of the rows, almost all talking in Spanish, joking, lighting cigarettes—all waiting for the foreman's whistle to begin work. Mother had explained how to chop cotton by showing us with a broom in the backyard.

"Like this," she said, her broom swishing down weeds. "Leave one plant and cut four—and cut them! Don't leave them standing or the foreman will get mad."

The foreman whistled and we started up the row stealing glances at other workers to see if we were doing it right. But after awhile we worked like we knew what we were doing, neither of us hurrying or falling behind. But slowly the clot of men, women, and kids began to spread and loosen. Even Rick pulled away. I didn't hurry, though. I cut smoothly and cleanly as I walked at a slow pace, in a sort of funeral march. My eyes measured each space of cotton plants before I cut. If I missed the plants, I swished again. I worked intently, seldom looking up, so when I did I was amazed to see the sun, like a broken orange coin, in the east. It looked blurry, unbelievable, like something not of this world. I looked around in amazement, scanning the eastern horizon that was a taut line jutted with an occasional mountain. The horizon was beautiful, like a snapshot of the moon, in the early light of morning, in the quiet of no cars and few people.

The foreman trudged in boots in my direction, stepping awkwardly over the plants, to inspect the work. No one around me looked up. We all worked steadily while we waited for him to leave. When he did leave, with a feeble complaint addressed to no one in particular, we looked up smiling under straw hats and bandanas.

By 11:00, our lunch time, my ankles were hurting from walking on clods the size of hardballs. My arms ached and my face was dusted by a wind that was perpetual, always busy whipping about. But the work was not bad, I thought. It was better, so much better, than picking grapes, especially with the hourly wage of a dollar twenty-five instead of piece work. Rick and I walked sorely toward the bus where we washed and drank water. Instead of eating in the bus or in the shade of the bus, we kept to ourselves by walking down to the irrigation canal that ran the length of the field, to open our lunch of sandwiches and crackers. We laughed at the crackers, which seemed like a cruel joke from our Mother, because we were working under the sun and the last thing we wanted was a salty dessert. We ate them anyway and drank more water before we returned to the field, both of us limping in exaggeration. Working side by side, we talked and laughed at our predicament because our Mother had warned us year after year that if we didn't get on track in school we'd have to work in the fields and then we would see. We mimicked Mother's whining voice and smirked at her smoky view of the future in which we'd be trapped by marriage and screaming kids. We'd eat beans and then we'd see.

Rick pulled slowly away to the rhythm of his hoe falling faster and smoother. It was better that way, to work alone. I could hum made-up songs or songs from the radio and think to myself about school and friends. At the time I was doing badly in my classes, mainly because of a difficult stepfather, but also because I didn't care anymore. All through junior high and into my first year of high school there were those who said I would never do anything, be anyone. They said I'd work like a donkey and marry the first Mexican girl that came along. I was reminded so often, verbally and in the way I was treated at home, that I began to believe that chopping cotton might be a lifetime job for me. If not chopping cotton, then I might get lucky and find myself in a car wash or restaurant or junkyard. But it was clear; I'd work, and work hard.

I cleared my mind by humming and looking about. The sun was directly above with a few soft blades of clouds against a sky that seemed bluer and more beautiful than our sky in the city. Occasionally the breeze flurried and picked up dust so that I had to cover my eyes and screw up my face. The workers were hunched, brown as the clods under our feet, and spread across the field that ran without end—fields that were owned by corporations, not families.

I hoed trying to keep my mind busy with scenes from school and pretend girlfriends until finally my brain turned off and my thinking went fuzzy with boredom. I looked about, no longer mesmerized by the beauty of the landscape, no longer wondering if the winos in the fields could hold out for eight hours, no longer dreaming of the clothes I'd buy with my pay. My eyes followed my chopping as the plants, thin as their shadows, fell with each strike. I worked slowly with ankles and arms hurting, neck stiff, and eyes stinging from the dust and the sun that glanced off the field like a mirror.

By quitting time, 3:00, there was such an excruciating pain in my ankles that I walked as if I were wearing snowshoes. Rick laughed at me and I laughed too, embarrassed that most of the men were walking normally and I was among the first timers who had to get used to this work. "And what about you, wino," I came back at Rick. His eyes were meshed red and his long hippie hair was flecked with dust and gnats and bits of leaves. We placed our hoes in the back of a pickup and stood in line for our pay, which was twelve fifty. I was amazed at the pay, which was the most I had ever earned in one day, and thought that I'd come back the next day, Sunday. This was too good.

Instead of joining the others in the labor bus, we jumped in the back of a pickup when the driver said we'd get to town sooner and were welcome to join him. We scrambled into the truck bed to be joined by a heavy-set and laughing *Tejano* whose head was shaped like an egg, particularly so because the bandana he wore ended in a point on the top of his head. He laughed almost demonically as the pickup roared up the dirt path, a gray cape of dust rising behind us. On the highway, with the wind in our faces, we squinted at the fields as if we were looking for someone. The *Tejano* had quit laughing but was smiling broadly, occasionally chortling tunes he never finished. I was scared of him, though Rick, two years older and five inches taller, wasn't. If the *Tejano* looked at him, Rick stared back for a second or two before he looked away to the fields.

I felt like a soldier coming home from war when we rattled into China-town. People leaning against car hoods stared, their necks following us, owl-like; prostitutes chewed gum more ferociously and showed us their teeth; Chinese grocers stopped brooming their storefronts to raise their cadaverous faces at us. We stopped in front of the Chi Chi Club where Mexican music blared from the juke box and cue balls cracked like dull ice. The *Tejano,* who was dirty as we were, stepped awkwardly over the side rail, dusted himself off with his bandana, and sauntered into the club.

Rick and I jumped from the back, thanked the driver who said *de nada* and popped his clutch, so that the pickup jerked and coughed blue smoke. We returned smiling to our car, happy with the money we had made and pleased that we had, in a small way, proved ourselves to be tough; that we worked as well as other men and earned the same pay.

We returned the next day and the next week until the season was over and there was nothing to do. I told myself that I wouldn't pick grapes that summer, saying all through June and July that it was for Mexicans, not me. When August came around and I still had not found a summer job, I ate my words, sharpened my knife, and joined Mother, Rick, and Debra for one last time.

QUIT YOUR JOB

■

Douglas Coupland

The following selection is excerpted from Douglas Coupland's novel Generation X, *published in 1991.*

I deflected her question. I like Margaret. She tries hard. She's older, and attractive in a hair-spray-and-shoulder-pads-twice-divorced sur-vivor kind of way. A real bulldozer. She's like one of those little rooms you find only in Chicago or New York in superexpensive downtown apartments—small rooms painted intense, flaring colors like emerald or raw beef to hide the fact that they're so small. She told me my season once, too: I'm a summer.

"God, Margaret. You really have to wonder why we even bother to get *up* in the morning. I mean, really: *Why work?* Simply to buy more *stuff?*

That's just not enough. Look at us all. What's the common assumption that got us all from there to here? What makes us *deserve* the ice cream and running shoes and wool Italian suits we have? I mean, I see all of us trying so hard to acquire so much *stuff*, but I can't help but feeling that we didn't merit it, that . . ."

"But Margaret cooled me right there. Putting down her mug, she said that before I got into one of my Exercised Young Man states, I should realize that the only reason we all go to work in the morning is because we're terrified of what would happen if we *stopped*. 'We're not built for free time as a species. We think we are, but we aren't.' Then she began almost talking to herself. I'd gotten her going. She was saying that most of us have only two or three genuinely interesting moments in our lives, the rest is filler, and that at the end of our lives, most of us will be lucky if any of those moments connect together to form a story that anyone would find remotely interesting.

SICK BUILDING MIGRATION:
The tendency of younger workers to leave or avoid jobs in unhealthy office environments or workplaces affected by the Sick Building Syndrome.

"Well. You can see that morbid and self-destructive impulses were overtaking me that morning and that Margaret was more than willing to sweep her floor into my fireplace. So we sat there watching tea steep (never a fun thing to do, I might add) and in a shared moment listened to the office proles discuss whether a certain game show host had or had not had cosmetic surgery recently.

RECURVING: Leaving one job to take another that pays less but places one back on the learning curve.

" 'Hey, Margaret,' I said, 'I bet you can't think of one person in the entire history of the world who became famous without a whole lot of cash changing hands along the way.'

"She wanted to know what this meant, so I elaborated. I told her that people simply don't . . . *can't* become famous in this world unless a lot of people make a lot of money. The cynicism of this took her aback, but she answered my challenge at face value. 'That's a bit harsh, Dag. What about Abraham Lincoln?'

" 'No go. That was all about slavery and land. Tons-o'-cash happening there.'

"So she says, 'Leonardo da Vinci,' to which I could only state that he was a businessman like Shakespeare or any of those old boys and that all of his work was purely on a commission basis and even *worse*, his research was used to support the military.

" 'Well, Dag, this is just the *stupidest* argument I've ever heard," she starts saying, getting desperate. 'Of course people become famous without people making money out of it.'

" 'So name one, then.'

"I could see Margaret's thinking flail, her features dissolving and re-forming, and I was feeling just a little too full of myself, knowing that other people in the cafeteria had started to listen in on the conversation. I was the boy in the baseball cap driving the convertible again, high on his own cleverness and ascribing darkness and greed to all human endeavors. That was me.

" 'Oh, all right, you win,' she says, conceding me a pyrrhic victory, and I was about to walk out of the room with my coffee (now the Perfect-But-Somewhat-Smug Young Man), when I heard a little voice at the back of the coffee room say 'Anne Frank.'

"Well.

OZMOSIS: The inability of one's job to live up to one's self-image.

POWER MIST: The tendency of hierarchies in office environments to be diffuse and preclude crisp articulation.

I pivoted around on the ball of my foot, and who did I see, looking quietly defiant but dreadfully dull and tubby, but Charlene sitting next to the megatub of office acetaminophen tablets. Charlene with her trailer-park bleached perm, meat-extension recipes culled from *Family Circle* magazine, and neglect from her boyfriend; the sort of person who when you draw their name out of the hat for the office Christmas party gift, you say, 'Who?'

" 'Anne Frank?' I bellowed, 'Why of *course* there was money there, why . . .' but, of course, there was no money there. I had unwittingly declared a moral battle that she had deftly won. I felt awfully silly and awfully mean.

"The staff, of course, sided with Charlene—no one sides with scuzzballs. They were wearing their 'you-got-your-comeuppance' smiles, and there was a lull while the cafeteria audience waited for me to dig my hole deeper, with Charlene in particular looking righteous. But I just stood there unspeaking; all they got to watch instead was my fluffy white karma instantly converting into iron-black cannon balls accelerating to the bottom of a cold and deep Swiss lake. I felt like turning into a plant— a comatose, nonbreathing, nonthinking entity, right there and then. But, of course, plants in offices get scalding hot coffee poured into their soil by copier machine repair people, don't they? So what was I to do? I wrote off the psychic wreckage of that job, before it got any worse. I walked out of that kitchen, out the office doors, and never bothered to come back. Nor did I ever bother to gather my belongings from my veal-fattening pen.

"I figure in retrospect, though, that if they had *any* wisdom at all at the company (which I doubt), they would have made Charlene clean out my desk for me. Only because in my mind's eye I like to see her standing there, wastepaper basket in her plump sausage-fingered hands, sifting through my rubble of documents. There she would come across my framed photo of the whaling ship crushed and stuck, possibly forever, in the glassy Antarctic ice. I see her staring at this photo in mild confusion, wondering in that moment what sort of young man I am and possibly finding me not unlovable.

"But inevitably she would wonder *why* I would want to frame such a strange image and then, I imagine, she would wonder whether it has any financial value. I then see her counting her lucky stars that she doesn't understand such unorthodox impulses, and then I see her throwing the picture, already forgotten, into the trash. But in that brief moment of confusion . . . *that brief moment* before she'd decided to throw the photo out, well . . . I think I could almost love Charlene then.

"And it was this thought of loving that sustained me for a long while when, after quitting, I turned into a Basement Person and never went in to work in an office again."

OVERBOARDING: Overcompensating for fears about the future by plunging headlong into a job or life-style seemingly unrelated to one's previous life interests; i.e., Amway sales, aerobics, the Republican party, a career in law, cults, McJobs. . . .

"Now: when you become a Basement Person, you drop out of the system. You have to give up, as I did, your above-ground apartment and all of the silly black matte objects inside *as well as* the meaningless rectangles of minimalist art above the oatmeal-colored sofa and the semidisposable furniture from Sweden. Basement People rent basement suites; the air above is too middle class.

EARTH TONES: A youthful subgroup interested in vegetarianism, tie-dyed outfits, mild recreational drugs, and good stereo equipment. Earnest, frequently lacking in humor.

"I stopped cutting my hair. I began drinking too many little baby coffees as strong as heroin in small cafés where sixteen-year-old boys and girls with nose rings daily invented new salad dressings by selecting spices with the most exotic names (*'Oooh! Car*damom! Let's try a teaspoon of *that!'*). I developed new friends who yapped endlessly about South American novelists never getting enough attention. I ate lentils. I wore llama motif serapes, smoked brave little cigarettes (*Nazionali's*, from Italy, I remember). In short, I was earnest.

ETHNOMAGNETISM: The tendency of young people to live in emotionally demonstrative, more unrestrained ethnic neighborhoods: *"You wouldn't understand it there, mother— they hug where I live now."*

"Basement subculture was strictly codified: wardrobes consisted primarily of tie-dyed and faded T-shirts bearing images of Schopenhauer or Ethel and Julius Rosenberg, all accessorized with Rasta doohickeys and badges. The girls all seemed to be ferocious dykey redheads, and the boys were untanned and sullen. No one ever seemed to have sex, saving their intensity instead for discussions of social work and generating the best idea for the most obscure and politically correct travel destination (the Nama Valley in Namibia—but *only* to see the daisies). Movies were black and white and frequently Brazilian.

"And after a while of living the Basement life-style, I began to adopt more of its attitudes. I began occupational slumming: taking jobs so beneath my abilities that people would have to look at me and say, 'Well of course he could do *better*.' I also got into cult employment, the best form of which was tree planting in the interior of British Columbia one summer in a not unpleasant blitz of pot and crab lice and drag races in beat up spray painted old Chevelles and Biscaynes.

"All of this was to try and shake the taint that marketing had given me, that had indulged my need for control too bloodlessly, that had, in some way, taught me to not really *like* myself. Marketing is essentially about feeding the poop back to diners fast enough to make them think they're still getting real food. It's not creation, really, but theft, and *no one* ever feels good about stealing.

> **MID-TWENTIES BREAK-DOWN:** A period of mental collapse occurring in one's twenties, often caused by an inability to function outside of school or structured environments coupled with a realization of one's essential aloneness in the world. Often marks induction into the ritual of pharmaceutical usage.

"But basically, my life-style escape wasn't working. I was only using the *real* Basement People to my own ends—no different than the way design people exploit artists for new design riffs. I was an imposter, and in the end my situation got so bad that I finally had my Mid-twenties Breakdown. That's when things got pharmaceutical, when they hit *bottom,* and when all voices of comfort began to fail."

DOGS
—■—
Kevin Canty

This story was originally published in Canty's 1994 collection A Stranger in This World.

Let's say things stop working out for you. Let's say you run out of money in a city that doesn't know you, and the only job they find for you is killing dogs on the night shift. Your car dies. Your apartment is not quite far enough from the shelter. That distant sound of barking dogs is amplified by your memory, by dreams, so that it fills your grainy, sleepless mornings, the way that barking fills the shelter like water, a thick, swirling weight of sound that makes it hard to move, that spills out of the shelter, that ebbs and subsides and then, one dog at a time, starts again. Every kind of sound, yipping shih tzus, baying coonhounds, Pomeranians and Dobermans and vocalizing mutts. Some of the dogs bark so long and loud that they lose their voices before you can kill them, they go out with puny squeaks, shaking their heads, wondering what's wrong. You give them a shot, pile them in the chamber, pump the air out. Then the incinerator.

The trees that you remember every morning in your dreams, midwestern oaks and elms and leafy poplars, are shrunk to bitter twigs here. The only green in this city carpets the cemeteries. The remaining life is draining down into the roots: half-empty old women wander the supermarkets, the libraries, pardon me, pardon me. The knuckles of old men. While the bodies of the dogs you kill are beautiful, especially the greyhounds:

piled in the cart on their way to the incinerator, they look like sleeping ballerinas, waiting for Cinderella. They belong onstage. The racing dogs arrive on your shift, dozens of them, on the night that racing season is over for the year. You picture them under the lights, straining toward the artificial rabbit while the tourists scream their names.

You report at eleven, you kill the night's dogs at twelve, from two till four you hose down the cages, after four the shelter doesn't care what you do. Once a month the phone rings but it's a wrong number. Each dog has a little card posted on the outside of the cage, a card filled out by the owners: Name, Breed, Sex, Weight, Spayed/Neutered, Shots, Reason. You read the Reasons and wonder who could ever pass this test: Not good w/kids; Needs company; Moving to new apt. does not allow pets; Barks. You fill out cards on the owners and slip them into the card file at night, knowing that no one will ever look, tens of thousands of Names, of Reasons: Not good w/ animals.

The shelter uses these multiplying library cabinets as proof of its efficiency, but the names don't matter, just the number, the bulk of them. These empty hours before dawn, the shelter bursting with the voices of the reprieved, you review the accidents that brought you here, and the intentions. Let's say that your mother died young. You lost a picture of yourself. Some nights you bring a half-pint of Jim Beam to doctor the coffee.

There's a procedure for leaving a dog to be killed, you try to tell the girl, but she is just gone, tires smoking gravel out of the parking lot. The dog looks through you, frantic—a pretty little bitch, some sort of Border collie cross or Australian shepherd. Who will do the paperwork? You take out a card and begin to make things up: her name is Ginger, the girl that Gilligan never got. The bitch is two, more or less—you guess it from her teeth—and her owner was a college girl, so she's had her first shots but not the recent ones. Ginger's claws skitter on the linoleum floor, tying to follow the long-gone car. It's just light, quarter to five. When you get to the line for Reason you see the apparition of the college girl: bottle-blond, a little heavy, she drove some little American shitbox like a Chevette. Not one of the beautiful ones, the ones who couldn't lose. Her makeup was smeared in black profusion across her cheeks, as if she had been crying.

Think of a dog's loyalty, the weight of that uncomplicated love. You remember minutes after you first made love, staring out the window of a girl's suburban bedroom at the dirty snow in her yard, the dark bones of the trees, and wondering how you would stand up under the weight of love that had been entrusted to you, the promises you meant to keep— promises that meant everything to you, though not as much to her. Later this gets mixed up with the barking, but the idea of snow, of virginity, starts tears in your chest. You reach down, unclip the leash from Ginger's collar and hold the door for her to go, running, racing toward the college girl with all the grace of her beautiful dog's body.

Even if she finds her owner, she'll be back. And there are other futures: delivery trucks and dogcatchers, kids with .22s down in the wash, shooting rusty appliances, anything that moves. But still. The dogs in the cages behind you bark furiously, angry and begging, wanting only the chance that Ginger got: to be released into the wide and loveless world to find their owners. Let's say you retreat into the chain-link pens, where tomorrow's dead dogs race and whimper, frantic for love, barking and barking. And you have the keys to every lock, the means to open the cages, open the doors and send them racing. You'll be a hero, king of the dogs. Strangers will know your name in the world of dogs.

But in the world of men, the dogs will continue to be killed. You can be replaced, easily. You can be replaced. The morning traffic has started, the morning cars on their way to work, the big machine awakening, moving forward, spitting out junk, broken parts, dead dogs, junk. The nonstop barking drives the last thought from your mind. Quite suddenly you hate the dogs, all of them. You put the keys back in your pocket. Their barking is injuring you. You stand in the sunlight, feeling the yellow warmth of morning on your useless body.

Labor in the United States During the Early
Twentieth Century: A Rise in Power

Lyle John Jorgenson

Lyle John Jorgenson is a senior at The University of
Montana.

The organized labor movement in the United States
really began around the beginning of this century with
the maturing of industrial capitalism and the rise of big
business. At the beginning of the twentieth century, the
average worker faced wages that were low, workdays that
were long, and no benefits (medical, unemployment
insurance, compensation for sick leave, etc.). On the
whole, employees at the beginning of this century were at
the mercy of their employers. Around the turn of the
century, a movement for workers' rights began in an
effort to change the unfair employer practices of the
past.

In the later part of the nineteenth century and the
early twentieth century, antitrust laws were passed in
the United States in an attempt to regulate big business.
These antitrust laws attempted to break up previously
formed trusts and prevent the formation of new trusts
which allowed business to monopolize and control
financial, commodities, and resource markets in the
United States. While these new laws defined what business
was and was not able to do, workers were still in the
dark as to their rights under the new antitrust laws.

In response to the pressure to clarify labor's
position under the new antitrust laws, Congress passed
the first of the pro-labor acts. In 1914, Congress
enacted the <u>Clayton Act</u>, which contained several
provisions for the protection of organized labor. Among
these the Clayton Act stated:

"The Labor of a human being is not a commodity or
article of commerce" . . . and provided further that
nothing contained in the Federal antitrust laws: shall
be construed to forbid the existence and operation of
labor, labor organizations . . . nor shall such

organizations, or the members thereof, be held or
construed to be illegal combinations or conspiracies
in restraint of trade under the anti-trust laws.
(Congressional Digest, June–July 1993)

The Clayton Act was one of the earliest acts to
recognize the worker as being more than a unit of
commerce, as well as being among the first Acts passed to
recognize the right of workers to organize. In the years
following the passage of the Clayton Act, much
legislation was passed that supported and strengthened
the position of labor in the United States.

Among the most important pieces of legislation were
the Railway Labor Act, which required employers to
bargain collectively and prohibited discrimination
against unions. Originally, this act applied to
interstate railroad commerce but, in 1936, it was
expanded to include airlines that engaged in interstate
commerce. The Davis–Bacon Act, in 1931, required
contracts for construction entered into by the Federal
Government to specify a minimum wage and pay that minimum
wage to workers being employed under these contracts.

The Norris–LaGuardia Act, passed in 1932, was the
first in a series of laws passed in the 1930s which gave
Federal sanction to labor unions for the right to
organize and strike. These laws also gave sanction to
labor to use various forms of economic leverage in
dealing with employers and management. The
Norris–LaGuardia Act addressed several other issues that
were important footholds for the growth of organized
labor. Specifically, the Act prohibited Federal courts
from enforcing "yellow dog" contracts, which were
contracts or agreements made between employers and
workers under which workers promised to discontinue
association with organized labor or promised not to join
with the aforementioned. The reasoning behind this was
that oftentimes employees entered into these agreements
under the threat of job loss or other forms of coercion
on the part of the employer.

The Norris–LaGuardia Act also barred Federal courts
from issuing restraining orders or injunctions against
labor unions and workers for joining a union or

organizing for union purposes; for striking or refusing to work, or advising others to strike or organize; for publicizing acts of a labor dispute; and for providing legal aid to persons participating in a labor dispute.

These acts strengthened the position of United States labor considerably during the years preceding Franklin Roosevelt's election as president and the beginning of the New Deal era. However, the New Deal era is when organized labor in the United States truly came into the height of its power. During this period, membership in unions increased from 3,584,000 members in 1935 to 10,201,000 or nearly 24 percent membership by 1941, just before World War II (Congressional Digest, June–July 1993).

During the late nineteen-twenties and throughout the nineteen-thirties, the nation was in the midst of the Great Depression, and things were, as they say, "tough all over." During this period, the gross national product dropped from an all-time high of $103.1 billion in 1929 to a low of $55.6 billion in 1933. The GNP started to climb after this point but remained unstable for the next several years. Other economic indicators remained unstable as well. The unemployment rate, which had stabilized at about four percent during the nineteen-twenties, skyrocketed to the point that twenty-five percent of the American workforce was unemployed during the middle nineteen-thirties.

Organized labor, however, experienced tremendous growth, partially because of the economic hardships being faced by all workers, the desire of already employed persons to retain stable employment, and the need for the creation of new, stable, quality jobs for those who were unemployed. The United States Government, faced with the economic depression, was looking for solutions to fix the nation's economic problems. Some of the legislation passed during this period was extremely important to the growth of organized labor.

Among this legislation was the National Industrial Recovery Act, passed in 1933. The Act sought to provide codes of "fair competition" and to fix wages and hours in industry. However, title I of the Act, which guaranteed

the right of employees to collectively bargain without
interference or coercion of employers, was held
unconstitutional by the United States Supreme Court in
1935. So what could have been a tremendous boon to labor
was delayed until later that year with the passage of the
National Labor Relations Act or, as it is more commonly
known, The Wagner Act.

> The Wagner Act was by far the most important labor
> legislation of the nineteen-thirties. The Wagner Act
> was applicable to all firms and employees in
> activities affecting interstate commerce with the
> exception of agricultural laborers, government
> employees, and those persons subject to the Railway
> Labor Act. It guaranteed covered workers the right to
> organize and join labor movements, to choose
> representatives and to bargain collectively, and to
> strike. (Labor Relations Resources, Federal Labor
> Laws, p. 2)

The Wagner Act also established the National Labor
Relations Board (NLRB), which was an independent Federal
agency with members officially appointed by the
president. The NLRB had the power to determine whether a
particular union should be certified to represent a
particular group of workers. The NLRB was allowed to use
such methods as it deemed suitable to make these
determinations, including the holding of a representation
election among the workers concerned. The NLRB is also
the group with which all complaints of employer
violations of worker rights are registered, and is in
charge of resolving these complaints.

As well as the previously mentioned powers, the Wagner
Act also set limits on business in the following ways.
Employers were forbidden to dominate or otherwise
interfere with the formation of a labor union. Employers
were forbidden to interfere or restrain employees
exercising their rights to collectively bargain.
Employers were no longer allowed to impose any special
conditions that either encouraged or discouraged union
membership. Employers were forbidden to discharge or
discriminate against an employee because he/she had filed
charges or given testimony under the Wagner Act, and

finally, employers were forbidden to refuse to bargain collectively with unions representing a company's employees.

The Wagner Act is considered to be the most important piece of labor legislation in the history of U.S. labor. It has been cited as being one of the primary reasons for the rapid growth of unions during the nineteen-thirties and early 'forties. Lastly, and most important, the Wagner Act was the first piece of labor legislation to apply to the vast majority of workers, rather than just to a select few groups, as had previous legislation.

During the early part of this century, organized labor was supportive of the development of social welfare programs like Social Security, national health insurance, and disability pensions, but was inactive in its development. Organized labor supported the development of these policies but held strongly to the position that workers' own organizations could meet the needs of workers. The American Federation of Labor, for example, hesitated to support the development of government welfare programs. It endorsed only need-based pensions in 1909 and, until the late nineteen-twenties, refused to back government unemployment and health insurance.

It was not until the nineteen-thirties that some labor unions started to wholeheartedly back government programs. Labor unions at this point fully supported the passage of the Social Security Act of 1935. For the most part, however, labor unions were reluctant to back the expansion of the public welfare state. Rather than supporting the development of the welfare state, most unions by this time had begun to negotiate with employers for private-sector benefits which were similar to those that public welfare policy was attempting to secure for all people.

Post-World War II: The Decline of Labor's Power in the United States

The post-World War II era spelled the beginning of a decline in power for organized labor in the United States. With companies flush with war profits, employers were able to withstand labor's attempts to strengthen its positions on collective bargaining and on workers' rights. New legislative acts, pushed through by Southern conservatives backed by big business, drastically limited the power unions had gained and set back the progress made by labor in the nineteen-thirties and early 'forties. To make matters worse, public opinion of labor unions was also starting to decline and would continue to do so in the coming years. All in all, this period would be a hallmark of hard times to come for organized labor.

Early in the nineteen-forties, a dramatic push was made by corporate America and conservative politicians to limit the political power of unions. In 1943, Congress passed the War Labor Disputes Act. Southern conservatives designed the Act to reduce the power of unions by playing on the annoyance of the public at the disruption of the war effort by unions. The new Act included provisions that made it difficult for unions to exert influence in the political arena. Labor was no longer able to make direct contributions to any political candidates. Labor was now limited to contributing only to political activities that registered voters and educated the public about general political issues. Unions were now forced to collect funds for political contributions from each individual member of the union rather than being able to donate from general funds, lessening the ability of unions to place pro-labor candidates in office.

The War Labor Disputes Act was only the beginning of anti-labor sentiment in the political arena. In 1947, the Taft-Hartley Act was the first major modification to the National Labor Relations Act. The Taft-Hartley Act reinforced the restrictions put in place by the War Labor Disputes Act but also limited, in several ways, the power of labor unions to bargain with employers. First, it established procedures of delaying or averting so-called "national emergency" strikes that had previously allowed unions to come to the aid of other unions with collective strikes. It excluded supervisory employees from coverage under the Wagner Act, drawing a clearer separation between management and workers. The Act prohibited the "closed shop" altogether (closed shop is a term for the strictly union workplace) and also banned closed-shop union hiring halls that discriminated against non-union members.

The Act also added a list of other provisions that limited the power of unions. Unions could no longer strike against the government; authorization of damage suits for economic losses by secondary boycotts and certain strikes was now allowed. The Act permitted the establishment of a sixty-day no-strike-and no-lockout notice period for any party seeking to cancel an existing collective bargaining agreement. Most importantly, the Act ordered a reorganization of the National Labor Relations Board and put a limitation on its power.

Not only were unions losing much of their political power and bargaining ability due to the new government regulations that came about in the middle of this century, but public opinions of organized labor on certain important issues were slipping. At the same time, however, the public's opinion of management was becoming more favorable.

General approval of labor unions was high, but public opinion on specific labor issues was increasingly negative. Near the top of the public's list of issues that needed government attention was expansion of regulation of labor unions. In 1945, 58 percent of those in a Gallup Poll favored either the elimination of unions or increased restrictions on their behavior. And in 1946, over half of the public attributed motives of social responsibility to management, but only 7 percent gave labor leaders credit for similar sentiments. (Beth Stevens, Journal of Policy History 1990)

Another reason for the reduction of the labor movement's power is that, during this time of decreasing union membership, labor did not open itself up to new worker markets. During the decades since the end of World War II, large numbers of blacks and women have entered the labor force because of the recent developments in nationwide civil liberties. Labor failed to open itself up to new membership from women and blacks, effectively shutting itself off from fifty or more percent of the labor market. Labor also failed to make attempts to organize in the fields that were considered unskilled labor, the primary area that these new members of the workforce were moving into during this time. Not until recently has labor made attempts to draw membership from these areas of the working population.

Unlike its early conventions from 1955 through 1960 where A. Philip Randolph was practically a lone voice for the recognition of black labor, or the many subsequent ones where the issue was ignored, this year saw a lot of talk about and at least a little movement toward, diversity in the leadership. (Kim Moody, US Labor Wars: Bottom to Top) This quote is referring to the 20th biennial convention of the AFL-CIO.

Labor's relationship with public welfare policy during the period from the post-World War II era to recent times has remained similar to what it had been in the beginning of the century. With labor's continuing losses in political power and support in the public sector, labor chose to focus on gaining private-sector benefits to maintain the support of its current members. The drive of labor for employee benefits was also a reaction to the decreasing ability of the labor movement to influence public sector decisions about public social programs.

Labor and Welfare in the 1990s: A Ray of Hope?

Coming into the nineties, the power of organized labor was at a low that had not been seen since before 1920. Membership had declined from almost forty percent in the mid-fifties to barely over ten percent in the private sector in 1993 (Labor Studies Journal, Fall 1994). Labor had continually failed to gain new support and draw new membership from the workforce. Many reasons were cited for the decline in labor's power, including: a shift in the demographic and market forces away from industrial blue-collar work from which labor had drawn much of its previous strength. Some would suggest that labor's decline was a manifestation of the individualism historically found in America, and yet others say that the decline of labor has happened because of increases in employer use of sophisticated union avoidance practices.

In my opinion, it is a combination of these three factors, plus the fact that labor has made limited attempts to organize women and blacks.

Whatever the case may be, labor has, in recent years, with the passage of new Federal welfare laws, begun making attempts to adapt to the new labor markets and organize in sectors it had previously given little attention to. The reasoning behind labor's recent moves to work with welfare recipients is that the new Federal work requirements, under the new TANF (Temporary Aid to Needy Families) program, will require that states put twenty-five percent of their former AFDC (Aid to Families with Dependent Children) recipients to work by the end of 1997. By 2002, fifty percent must be working. This will create a tremendous influx of workers into the labor market; as many as 1 million workers will need to be placed in work or work programs. Unfortunately, the TANF makes these new work requirements but does not make any provisions for the creation of the new jobs that will be needed to meet the requirements in the public sector. Private-sector employers will be targeted to absorb these new workers. President Clinton was quoted as saying the following about the new job requirements

> We cannot create enough public-service jobs to hire these folks; so they have to be hired in the private sector, and I ask you to help. This is basically a private-sector show. (President Clinton, The Wall Street Journal, Oct. 31, 1996)

Not only do the new welfare laws put much pressure on private-sector employers but they also include few protections for workers that currently hold private-sector jobs. The new law only prohibits employers from laying off employees with the intent to replace them with welfare placements. Unfilled vacancies in the public and private sector can be converted into workfare slots. Lower-skilled workers are particularly threatened by the loss of protections that were contained in the old welfare law. (AFL–CIO Executive Council, February 17, 1997 statement)

Workfare participants will also suffer under the new law. TANF does not include minimum wage guarantees, health and safety coverage, or the right to join a union, or offer any protections against discrimination that previous welfare law included. This has possible ramifications that could reflect upon current workers. The new law could make it possible to lower wages and benefits for all workers because employers will have a readily available source of inexpensive laborers to whom they are not required to give benefits.

Due to these new provisions in welfare law, organized labor has recently begun to make attempts at working with workfare and welfare participants. Among the programs that labor is currently backing is Jobs with Justice. Jobs with Justice is a Washington, DC-based organization that attempts to organize communities and labor to improve the rights of working families by forming workers' rights boards in communities. These workers' rights boards are comprised of community, religious, and labor leaders. Also included in the boards are public officials and academics. These boards attempt to apply moral and public pressure to encourage fair behavior by employers. The Jobs with Justice movement has been in the past very successful in applying pressure to employers and in protecting the rights of working families. Currently, Jobs with Justice is working with organized labor to unionize workfare participants in hopes of creating a better, safer workplace for all workers. Hopefully, this effort by organized labor, Jobs with Justice, and workfare participants is indicative of a future partnership between organized labor and social welfare organizations that will be fruitful for all.

In this paper, I have attempted to follow the progress of organized labor in the United States and how it has related to the development of the U.S. welfare state through labor's early years of progress, its years of decline, and current times.

Works Cited

AFL-CIO Executive Council February 17, 1997 Statement.

   Taken from http://www.ancio.org/estatements

   /welfarea.htm

AFL-CIO. Labor Confronts Welfare Reform: An AFL-CIO Guide

   to State Activity. Copyright 1996 AFL-CIO.

Cagan, Steve. Jobs with Justice: A Campaign for Workers'

   Rights. Taken from Jobs with Justice information pack-

   age, 1997.

Early, Steve and Cohen, Larry. Jobs with Justice: Mobi-

   lizing Labor-Community Coalitions. Working USA, Novem-

   ber/December 1997.

Federal Labor Laws. Congressional Digest, June-July 1993.

   Taken from labor relations resources

   http://www.crisny.org

Foner, Philip S. Women and the American Labor Movement:

   From the First Trade Unions to the Present (New York:

   The Free Press; London: Collier Macmillan Publishers),

   1979, 1980, 1982.

Levin-Waldman, Oren M. The Political Consequences of De-

   clining Unionism. Cleveland Plain Dealer, September 1,

   1997.

Martin, George T. Jr. Union Social Services and Women's

   Work. Social Service Review, March 1985, vol. 59.

Moody, Kim. United States Labor Wars: Bottom to Top. New

    Politics (Winter, 1996).

Morand, David A. The Changing Situation of U.S. Labor

    Law: Alternative Legislative Initiatives for Workers

    and Workplaces. Labor Studies Journal, Fall 1994, vol.

    19, n. 3.

Partridge, Mark. The Effect of International Trade on

    Worker Union Choice, Journal of Economics (January,

    1994).

Rose, Joseph B. and Chaison, Gary N. The State of the

    Unions—United States and Canada. Journal of Labor Re-

    search (June, 1983), 1.

Stevens, Beth. Labor Unions, Employee Benefits, and the

    Privatization of the American Welfare State. Journal

    of Policy History, vol. 2, no. 3, 1990.

Zinn, Howard. A People's History of the United States

    1492-Present (New York: Harper Perennial Publishers),

    1980, 1995.

6

A SENSE
OF PLACE

ON SEEING ENGLAND
FOR THE FIRST TIME

Jamaica Kincaid

This essay first appeared in the journal Transition *in 1991.*

When I saw England for the first time, I was a child in school sitting at a desk. The England I was looking at was laid out on a map gently, beautifully, delicately, a very special jewel; it lay on a bed of sky blue— the background of the map—its yellow form mysterious, because though it looked like a leg of mutton, it could not really look like anything so familiar as a leg of mutton because it was England—with shadings of pink and green, unlike any shadings of pink and green I had seen before, squiggly veins of red running in every direction. England was a special jewel all right, and only special people got to wear it. The people who got to wear England were English people. They wore it well and they wore it everywhere: in jungles, in deserts, on plains, on top of the highest mountains, on all the oceans, on all the seas, in places where they were not welcome, in places they should not have been. When my teacher had pinned this map up on the blackboard, she said, "This is England"—and she said it with authority, seriousness, and adoration, and we all sat up. It was as if she had said, "This is Jerusalem, the place you will go to when you die but only if you have been good." We understood then—we were meant to understand then—that England was to be our source of myth and the source from which we got our sense of reality, our sense of what was meaningful, our sense of what was meaningless—and much about our own lives and much about the very idea of us headed that last list.

At the time I was a child sitting at my desk seeing England for the first time, I was already very familiar with the greatness of it. Each morning before I left for school, I ate a breakfast of half a grapefruit, an egg, bread and butter and a slice of cheese, and a cup of cocoa; or half a grapefruit, a bowl of oat porridge, bread and butter and a slice of cheese, and a cup of cocoa. The can of cocoa was often left on the table in front of me. It had written on it the name of the company, the year the company was established, and the words "Made in England." Those words, "Made in England," were written on the box the oats came in too. They would also have been written on the box the shoes I was wearing came in; a bolt of gray linen cloth lying on the shelf of a store from which my mother had bought three yards to make the uniform that I was wearing had written along its edge those three words. The shoes I wore were made in England; so were my socks and cotton undergarments and the satin ribbons I wore tied at the end of two plaits of my hair. My father, who might have sat next to me at breakfast, was a carpenter and cabinet maker. The shoes he wore to work would have been made in England, as were his khaki shirt and trousers, his underpants and undershirt, his socks and brown felt hat. Felt was not the proper material from which a hat that was expected to provide shade from the hot sun should be made, but my father must have seen and admired a picture of an Englishman wearing such a hat in England, and this picture that he saw must have been so compelling that it caused him to wear the wrong hat for a hot climate most of his long life. And this hat—a brown felt hat—became so central to his character that it was the first thing he put on in the morning as he stepped out of bed and the last thing he took off before he stepped back into bed at night. As we sat at breakfast a car might go by. The car, a Hillman or a Zephyr, was made in England. The very idea of the meal itself, breakfast, and its substantial quality and quantity was an idea from England; we somehow knew that in England they began the day with this meal called breakfast and a proper breakfast was a big breakfast. No one I knew liked eating so much food so early in the day; it made us feel sleepy, tired. But this breakfast business was Made in England like almost everything else that surrounded us, the exceptions being the sea, the sky, and the air we breathed.

At the time I saw this map—seeing England for the first time—I did not say to myself, "Ah, so that's what it looks like," because there was no longing in me to put a shape to those three words that ran through every part of my life, no matter how small; for me to have had such a longing would have meant that I lived in a certain atmosphere, an atmosphere in which those three words were felt as a burden. But I did not live in such an atmosphere. My father's brown felt hat would develop a hole in its crown, the lining would separate from the hat itself, and six weeks before he thought that he could not be seen wearing it—he was a very vain man—he would order another hat from England. And my mother taught me to eat my food the English way: the knife in the right hand, the fork in the left, my elbows held still close to my side, the food carefully balanced on my fork and then brought up to my mouth. When I had finally mastered it, I overheard her saying to a friend, "Did you see how nicely she can eat?" But I knew then that I enjoyed my food more when I ate it with my bare hands, and I continued to do so when she wasn't looking. And when my teacher showed us the map, she asked us to study it carefully, because no test we would ever take would be complete without this statement: "Draw a map of England."

I did not know then that the statement "Draw a map of England" was something far worse than a declaration of war, for in fact a flat-out declaration of war would have put me on alert, and again in fact, there was no need for war—I had long ago been conquered. I did not know then that this statement was part of a process that would result in my erasure, not my physical erasure, but my erasure all the same. I did not know then that this statement was meant to make me feel in awe and small whenever I heard the word "England": awe at its existence, small because I was not from it. I did not know very much of anything then—certainly not what a blessing it was that I was unable to draw a map of England correctly.

After that there were many times of seeing England for the first time. I saw England in history. I knew the names of all the kings of England. I knew the names of their children, their wives, their disappointments, their triumphs, the names of people who betrayed them, I knew the dates on which they were born and the dates they died. I knew their conquests and was made to feel glad if I figured in them; I knew their defeats. I knew the details of the year 1066 (the Battle of Hastings, the end of the reign of the Anglo-Saxon kings) before I knew the details of the year 1832 (the year slavery was abolished). It wasn't as bad as I make it sound now; it was worse. I did like so much hearing again and again how Alfred the Great, traveling in disguise, had been left to watch cakes, and because he wasn't used to this the cakes got burned, and Alfred burned his hands pulling them our of the fire, and the woman who had left him to watch the cakes screamed at him. I loved King Alfred. My grandfather was named after him; his son, my uncle, was named after King Alfred; my brother is named after King Alfred. And so there are three people in my family named after a man they have never met, a man who died over ten centuries ago. The first view I got of England then was not unlike the first view received by the person who named my grandfather.

This view, though—the naming of the kings, their deeds, their disappointments—was the vivid view, the forceful view. There were other views, subtler ones, softer, almost not there—but these were the ones that made the most lasting impression on me, these were the ones that made me really feel like nothing. "When morning touched the sky" was one phrase, for no morning touched the sky where I lived. The mornings where I lived came on abruptly, with a shock of heat and loud noises. "Evening approaches" was another, but the evenings where I lived did not approach; in fact, I had no evening—I had night and I had day and they came and went in a mechanical way: on, off; on, off. And then there were gentle mountains and low blue skies and moors over which people took walks for nothing but pleasure, when where I lived a walk was an act of labor, a burden, something only death or the automobile could relieve. And there were things that a small turn of a head could convey—entire worlds, whole lives would depend on this thing, a certain turn of a head. Everyday life could be quite tiring, more tiring than anything I was told not to do. I was told not to gossip, but they did that all the time. And they ate so much food, violating another of those rules they taught me: Do not indulge in gluttony. And the foods they ate actually: If only sometime I could eat cold cuts after theater, cold cuts of lamb and mint sauce, and Yorkshire pudding and scones, and clotted cream, and sausages that came from up-country (imagine, "up-country"). And having troubling thoughts at twilight, a good time to have troubling thoughts, apparently; and servants who stole and left in the middle of a crisis, who were born with a limp or some other kind of deformity, not nourished properly in their mother's womb (that last part I figured out for myself; the point was, oh to have an untrustworthy servant); and wonderful cobbled streets onto which solid front doors opened; and people whose eyes were blue and who had fair skins and who smelled only of lavender, or sometimes sweet pea or primrose. And those flowers with those names: delphiniums, foxgloves, tulips, daffodils, floribunda, peonies: in bloom, a striking display, being cut and placed in large glass bowls, crystal, decorating rooms so large twenty families the size of mine could fit in comfortably but used only for passing through. And the weather was so remarkable because the rain fell gently always, only occasionally in deep gusts, and it colored the air various shades of gray, each an appealing shade for a dress to be worn when a portrait was being painted; and when it rained at twilight, wonderful things happened: People bumped into each other unexpectedly and that would lead to all sorts of turns of events—a plot, the mere weather caused plots. I saw that people rushed: They rushed to catch trains, they rushed toward each other and away from each other; they rushed and rushed and rushed. That word: rushed! I did not know what it was to do that. It was too hot to do that, and so I came to envy people who would rush, even though it had no meaning to me to do such a thing. But there they are again. They loved their children; their children were sent to their own rooms as a punishment, rooms larger than my entire house. They were special, everything about them said so, even their clothes; their clothes rustled, swished, soothed. The world was theirs, not mine; everything told me so.

If now as I speak of all this I give the impression of someone on the outside looking in, nose pressed up against a glass window, that is wrong. My nose was pressed up against a glass window all right, but there was an iron vise at the back of my neck forcing my head to stay in place. To avert my gaze was to fall back into something from which I had been rescued, a hole filled with nothing, and that was the word for everything about me, nothing. The reality of my life was conquests, subjugation, humiliation, enforced amnesia. I was forced to forget. Just for instance, this: I lived in a part of St. John's, Antigua, called Ovals. Ovals was made up of five streets, each of them named after a famous English seaman—to be quite frank, an officially sanctioned criminal: Rodney Street (after George Rodney), Nelson Street (after Horatio Nelson), Drake Street (after Francis Drake), Hood Street, and Hawkins Street (after John Hawkins). But John Hawkins was knighted after a trip he made to Africa, opening up a new trade, the slave trade. He was then entitled to wear as his crest a Negro bound with a cord. Every single person living on Hawkins Street was descended from a slave. John Hawkins's ship, the one in which he transported the people he had bought and kidnapped, was called *The Jesus*. He later became the treasurer of the Royal Navy and rear admiral.

Again, the reality of my life, the life I led at the time I was being shown these views of England for the first time, for the second time, for the one-hundred-millionth time, was this: The sun shone with what sometimes seemed to be a deliberate cruelty; we must have done something to deserve that. My dresses did not rustle in the evening air as I strolled to the theater (I had no evening, I had no theater; my dresses were made of a cheap cotton, the weave of which would give way after not too many washings). I got up in the morning, I did my chores (fetched water from the public pipe for my mother, swept the yard), I washed myself, I went to a woman to have my hair combed freshly every day (because before we were allowed into our classroom our teachers would inspect us, and children who had not bathed that day, or had dirt under their fingernails, or whose hair had not been combed anew that day, might not be allowed to attend class). I ate that breakfast. I walked to school. At school we gathered in an auditorium and sang a hymn, "All Things Bright and Beautiful," and looking down on us as we sang were portraits of the Queen of England and her husband; they wore jewels and medals and they smiled. I was a Brownie. At each meeting we would form a little group around a flagpole, and after raising the Union Jack, we would say, "I promise to do my best, to do my duty to God and the Queen, to help other people every day and obey the scouts' law."

Who were these people and why had I never seen them, I mean really seen them, in the place where they lived? I had never been to England. No one I knew had ever been to England, or I should say, no one I knew had ever been and returned to tell me about it. All the people I knew who had gone to England had stayed there. Sometimes they left behind them their small children, never to see them again. England! I had seen England's representatives. I had seen the governor general at the public grounds at a ceremony celebrating the Queen's birthday. I had seen an old princess and I had seen a young princess. They had both been extremely not beautiful, but who of us would have told them that? I had never seen England, really seen it, I had only met a representative, seen a picture, read books, memorized its history. I had never set foot, my own foot, in it.

Doo word imitation

The space between the idea of something and its reality is always wide and deep and dark. The longer they are kept apart—idea of thing, reality of thing—the wider the width, the deeper the depth, the thicker and darker the darkness. This space starts out empty, there is nothing in it, but it rapidly becomes filled up with obsession or desire or hatred or love— sometimes all of these things, sometimes some of these things, sometimes only one of these things. The existence of the world as I came to know it was a result of this: idea of thing over here, reality of thing way, way over there. There was Christopher Columbus, an unlikable man, an unpleasant man, a liar (and so, of course, a thief) surrounded by maps and schemes and plans, and there was the reality on the other side of that width, that depth, that darkness. He became obsessed, he became filled with desire, the hatred came later, love was never a part of it. Eventually, his idea met the longed-for reality. That the idea of something and its reality are often two completely different things is something no one ever remembers; and so when they meet and find that they are not compatible, the weaker of the two, idea or reality, dies. That idea Christopher Columbus had was more powerful than the reality he met, and so the reality he met died.

And so finally, when I was a grown-up woman, the mother of two children, the wife of someone, a person who resides in a powerful country that takes up more than its fair share of a continent, the owner of a house with many rooms in it and of two automobiles, with the desire and will (which I very much act upon) to take from the world more than I give back to it, more than I deserve, more than I need, finally then, I saw England, the real England, not a picture, not a painting, not through a story in a book, but England, for the first rime. In me, the space between the idea of it and its reality had become filled with hatred, and so when at last I saw it I wanted to take it into my hands and tear it into little pieces and then crumble it up as if it were clay, child's clay. That was impossible, and so I could only indulge in not-favorable opinions.

There were monuments everywhere; they commemorated victories, battles fought between them and the people who lived across the sea from them, all vile people, fought over which of them would have dominion over the people who looked like me. The monuments were useless to them now, people sat on them and ate their lunch. They were like markers on an old useless trail, like a piece of old string tied to a finger to jog the memory, like old decoration in an old house, dirty, useless, in the way. Their skins were so pale, it made them look so fragile, so weak, so ugly. What if I had the power to simply banish them from their land, send boat after boatload of them on a voyage that in fact had no destination, force them to live in a place where the sun's presence was a constant? This would rid them of their pale complexion and make them look more like me, make them look more like the people I love and treasure and hold dear, and more like the people who occupy the near and far reaches of my imagination, my history, my geography, and reduce them and everything they have ever known to figurines as evidence that I was in divine favor, what if all this was in my power? Could I resist it? No one ever has.

And they were rude, they were rude to each other. They didn't like each other very much. They didn't like each other in the way they didn't like me, and it occurred to me that their dislike for me was one of the few things they agreed on.

I was on a train in England with a friend, an English woman. Before we were in England she liked me very much. In England she didn't like me at all. She didn't like the claim I said I had on England, she didn't like the views I had of England. I didn't like England, she didn't like England, but she didn't like me not liking it too. She said, "I want to show you my England, I want to show you the England that I know and love." I had told her many times before that I knew England and I didn't want to love it anyway. She no longer lived in England; it was her own country, but it had not been kind to her, so she left. On the train, the conductor was rude to her; she asked something, and he responded in a rude way. She became ashamed. She was ashamed at the way he treated her; she was ashamed at the way he behaved. "This is the new England," she said. But I liked the conductor being rude; his behavior seemed quite appropriate. Earlier this had happened: We had gone to a store to buy a shirt for my husband; it was meant to be a special present, a special shirt to wear on special occasions. This was a store where the Prince of Wales has his shirts made, but the shirts sold in this store are beautiful all the same. I found a shirt I thought my husband would like and I wanted to buy him a tie to go with it. When I couldn't decide which one to choose, the salesman showed me a new set. He was very pleased with these, he said, because they bore the crest of the Prince of Wales, and the Prince of Wales had never allowed his crest to decorate an article of clothing before. There was something in the way he said it; his tone was slavish, reverential, awed. It made me feel angry; I wanted to hit him. I didn't do that. I said, my husband and I hate princes, my husband would never wear anything that had a prince's anything on it. My friend stiffened. The salesman stiffened. They both drew themselves in, away from me. My friend told me that the prince was a symbol of her Englishness, and I could see that I had caused offense. I looked at her. She was an English person, the sort of English person I used to know at home, the sort who was nobody in England but somebody when they came to live among the people like me. There were many people I could have seen England with; that I was seeing it with this particular person, a person who reminded me of the people who showed me England long ago as I sat in church or at my desk, made me feel silent and afraid, for I wondered if, all these years of our friendship, I had had a friend or had been in the thrall of a racial memory.

I went to Bath—we, my friend and I, did this, but though we were together, I was no longer with her. The landscape was almost as familiar as my own hand, but I had never been in this place before, so how could that be again? And the streets of Bath were familiar, too, but I had never walked on them before. It was all those years of reading, starting with Roman Britain. Why did I have to know about Roman Britain? It was of no real use to me, a person living on a hot, drought-ridden island, and it is of no use to me now, and yet my head is filled with this nonsense, Roman Britain. In Bath, I drank tea in a room I had read about in a novel written in the eighteenth century. In this very same room, young women wearing those dresses that rustled and so on danced and flirted and sometimes disgraced themselves with young men, soldiers, sailors, who were on their way to Bristol or someplace like that, so many places like that where so many adventures, the outcome of which was not good for me, began. Bristol, England. A sentence that began "That night the ship sailed from Bristol, England" would end not so good for me. And then I was driving through the countryside in an English motorcar, on narrow winding roads, and they were so familiar, though I had never been on them before; and through little villages the names of which I somehow knew so well though I had never been there before. And the countryside did have all those hedges and hedges, fields hedged in. I was marveling at all the toil of it, the planting of the hedges to begin with and then the care of it, all that clipping, year after year of clipping, and I wondered at the lives of the people who would have to do this, because wherever I see and feel the hands that hold up the world, I see and feel myself and all the people who look like me. And I said, "Those hedges" and my friend said that some-one, a woman named Mrs. Rothchild, worried that the hedges weren't being taken care of properly; the farmers couldn't afford or find the help to keep up the hedges, and often they replaced them with wire fencing. I might have said to that, well if Mrs. Rothchild doesn't like the wire fenc-ing, why doesn't she take care of the hedges herself, but I didn't. And then in those fields that were now hemmed in by wire fencing that a privileged woman didn't like was planted a vile yellow flowering bush that pro-duced an oil, and my friend said that Mrs. Rothchild didn't like this either; it ruined the English countryside, it ruined the traditional look of the English countryside.

It was not at that moment that I wished every sentence, everything I knew, that began with England would end with "and then it all died; we don't know how, it just all died." At that moment, I was thinking, who are these people who forced me to think of them all the time, who forced me to think that the world I knew was incomplete, or without substance, or did not measure up because it was not England; that I was incomplete, or without substance, and did not measure up because I was not English. Who were these people? The person sitting next to me couldn't give me a clue; no one person could. In any case, if I had said to her, I find England ugly, I hate England; the weather is like a jail sentence, the English are a very ugly people, the food in England is like a jail sentence, the hair of English people is so straight, so dead looking, the English have an unbear-able smell so different from the smell of people I know, real people of course, she would have said that I was a person full of prejudice. Apart from the fact that it is I—that is, the people who look like me—who made her aware of the unpleasantness of such a thing, the idea of such a thing, prejudice, she would have been only partly right, sort of right: I may be capable of prejudice, but my prejudices have no weight to them, my preju-dices have no force behind them, my prejudices remain opinions, my prej-udices remain my personal opinion. And a great feeling of rage and disappointment came over me as I looked at England, my head full of per-sonal opinions that could not have public, my public, approval. The people I come from are powerless to do evil on grand scale.

The moment I wished every sentence, everything I knew, that began with England would end with "and then it all died, we don't know how, it just all died" was when I saw the white cliffs of Dover. I had sung hymns and recited poems that were about a longing to see the white cliffs of Dover again. At the time I sang the hymns and recited the poems, I could really long to see them again because I had never seen them at all, nor had anyone around me at the time. But there we were, groups of people long-ing for something we had never seen. And so there they were, the white cliffs, but they were not that pearly majestic thing I used to sing about, that thing that created such a feeling in these people that when they died in the place where I lived they had themselves buried facing a direction that would allow them to see the white cliffs of Dover when they were resurrected, as surely they would be. The white cliffs of Dover, when finally I saw them, were cliffs, but they were not white; you would only call them that if the word "white" meant something special to you; they were dirty and they were steep; they were so steep, the correct height from which all my views of England, starting with the map before me in my classroom and ending with the trip I had just taken, should jump and die and disappear forever.

CITIES AND THE DEAD

Italo Calvino

This piece is an excerpt from Invisible Cities, *Calvino's 1972 book.*

Never in all my travels had I ventured as far as Adelma. It was dusk when I landed there. On the dock the sailor who caught the rope and tied it to the bollard resembled a man who had soldiered with me and was dead. It was the hour of the wholesale fish market. An old man was loading a basket of sea urchins on a cart; I thought I recognized him; when I turned, he had disappeared down an alley, but I realized that he looked like a fisherman who, already old when I was a child, could no longer be among the living. I was upset by the sight of a fever victim huddled on the ground, a blanket over his head: my father a few days before his death had yellow eyes and a growth of beard like this man. I turned my gaze aside; I no longer dared look anyone in the face.

I thought: "If Adelma is a city I am seeing in a dream, where you encounter only the dead, the dream frightens me. If Adelma is a real city, inhabited by living people, I need only continue looking at them and the resemblances will dissolve, alien faces will appear, bearing anguish. In either case it is best for me not to insist on staring at them."

A vegetable vendor was weighing a cabbage on a scales and put it in a basket dangling on a string a girl lowered from a balcony. The girl was identical with one in my village who had gone mad for love and killed herself. The vegetable vendor raised her face: she was my grandmother.

I thought: "You reach a moment in life when, among the people you have known, the dead outnumber the living. And the mind refuses to accept more faces, more expressions: on every new face you encounter, it prints the old forms, for each one it finds the most suitable mask."

The stevedores climbed the steps in a line, bent beneath demijohns and barrels; their faces were hidden by sackcloth hoods; "Now they will straighten up and I will recognize them," I thought, with impatience and fear. But I could not take my eyes off them; if I turned my gaze just a little toward the crowd that crammed those narrow streets, I was assailed by un-expected faces, reappearing from far away, staring at me as if demanding recognition, as if to recognize me, as if they had already recognized me. Per-haps, for each of them, I also resembled someone who was dead. I had barely arrived at Adelma and I was already one of them, I had gone over to their side, absorbed in that kaleidoscope of eyes, wrinkles, grimaces.

I thought: "Perhaps Adelma is the city where you arrive dying and where each finds again the people he has known. This means I, too, am dead." And I also thought: "This means the beyond is not happy."

Translated by William Weaver

MY NEIGHBORHOOD

Ishmael Reed

"My Neighborhood" was published originally in California *magazine.*

My stepfather is an evolutionist. He worked for many years at the Chevrolet division of General Motors in Buffalo, a working-class auto and steel town in upstate New York, and was able to rise from rela-tive poverty to the middle class. He believes that each succeeding genera-tion of Afro-Americans will have it better than its predecessor. In 1979 I moved into the kind of neighborhood that he and my mother spent about a third of their lives trying to escape. According to the evolutionist inte-grationist ethic, this was surely a step backward, since "success" was seen as being able to live in a neighborhood in which you were the only black and joined your neighbors in trying to keep out "them."

My neighborhood, bordered by Genoa, Market Street, and 48th and 55th streets in North Oakland, is what the media refer to as a "predomi-nantly black neighborhood." It's the kind of neighborhood I grew up in before leaving for New York City in 1962. My last New York residence was an apartment in a brownstone, next door to the building in which poet W. H. Auden lived. There were trees in the backyard, and I thought it was a swell neighborhood until I read in Robert Craft's biography of [the com-poser] Stravinsky that "when Stravinsky sent his chauffeur to pick up his friend Auden, the chauffeur would ask, 'Are you sure Mr. Auden lives in this neighborhood?'" By 1968 my wife and I were able to live six months of the year in New York and the other six in California. This came to an end when one of the people I sublet the apartment to abandoned it. He had fled to England to pursue a romance. He didn't pay the rent, and so we were evicted long distance.

My first residence in California was an apartment on Santa Ynez Street, near Echo Park Lake in Los Angeles, where I lived for about six months in

1967. I was working on my second novel, and Carla Blank, my wife, a dancer, was teaching physical education at one of Eddie Rickenbacker's camps, located on an old movie set in the San Bernardino Mountains. Carla's employers were always offering me a cabin where they promised I could write without interruption. I never took them up on the offer, but for years I've wondered about what kind of reception I would have received had they discovered that I am black.

During my breaks from writing I would walk through the shopping areas near Santa Ynez, strolling by vending machines holding newspapers whose headlines screamed about riots in Detroit. On some weekends we'd visit novelist Robert Gover (*The One Hundred Dollar Misunderstanding*) and his friends in Malibu. I remember one of Gover's friends, a scriptwriter for the *Donna Reed Show,* looking me in the eye and telling me that if he were black he'd be "on a Detroit rooftop, sniping at cops," as he reclined, glass of scotch in hand, in a comfortable chair whose position gave him a good view of the rolling Pacific.

My Santa Ynez neighbors were whites from Alabama and Mississippi, and we got along fine. Most of them were elderly, left behind by white flight to the suburbs, and on weekends the street would be lined with cars belonging to relatives who were visiting. While living here I observed a uniquely Californian phenomenon. Retired men would leave their houses in the morning, enter their cars, and remain there for a good part of the day, snoozing, reading newspapers, or listening to the radio.

I didn't experience a single racial incident during my stay in this Los Angeles neighborhood of ex-southerners. Once, however, I had a strange encounter with the police. I was walking through a black working-class neighborhood on my way to the downtown Los Angeles library. Some cops drove up and rushed me. A crowd gathered. The cops snatched my briefcase and removed its contents books and notebooks having to do with my research of voodoo. The crowd laughed when the cops said they thought I was carrying a purse.

In 1968 my wife and I moved to Berkeley, where we lived in one Bauhaus box after another until about 1971, when I received a three-book contract from Doubleday. Then we moved into the Berkeley Hills, where we lived in the downstairs apartment of a very grand-looking house on Bret Harte Way. There was a Zen garden with streams, waterfalls, and bridges outside, along with many varieties of flowers and plants. I didn't drive, and Carla was away at Mills College each day, earning a master's degree in dance. I stayed holed up in that apartment for two years, during which time I completed my third novel, *Mumbo Jumbo.*

During this period I became exposed to some of the racism I hadn't detected on Santa Ynez or in the Berkeley flats. As a black male working at home, I was regarded with suspicion. Neighbors would come over and warn me about a heroin salesman they said was burglarizing the neighborhood, all the while looking over my shoulder in an attempt to pry into what I was up to. Once, while I was eating breakfast, a policeman entered through the garden door, gun drawn. "What on earth is the problem, officer?" I asked. He said they got word that a homicide had been committed in my apartment, which I recognized as an old police tactic used to gain entry into somebody's house. Walking through the Berkeley Hills on Sundays, I was greeted by unfriendly stares and growling, snarling dogs. I remember one pest who always poked her head out of her window whenever I'd walk down Bret Harte Way. She was always hassling me about parking my car in front of her house. She resembled Miss Piggy. I came to think of this section of Berkeley as "Whitetown."

Around 1974 the landlord raised the rent on the house in the hills, and we found ourselves again in the Berkeley flats. We spent a couple of peaceful years on Edith Street, and then moved to Jayne Street, where we encountered another next-door family of nosy, middle-class progressives. I understand that much time at North Berkeley white neighborhood association meetings is taken up with discussion of and fascination with blacks who move through the neighborhoods, with special concern given those who tarry, or who wear dreadlocks. Since before the Civil War, vagrancy laws have been used as political weapons against blacks. Appropriately, there has been talk of making Havana—where I understand a woman can get turned in by her neighbors for having too many boyfriends over—Berkeley's sister city.

In 1976 our landlady announced that she was going to reoccupy the Jayne Street house. I facetiously told a friend that I wanted to move to the most right-wing neighborhood he could think of. He mentioned El Cerrito. There, he said, your next-door neighbor might even be a cop. We moved to El Cerrito. Instead of the patronizing nosiness blacks complain about in Berkeley, I found the opposite on Terrace Drive in El Cerrito. The people were cold, impersonal, remote. But the neighborhood was quiet, serene even—the view was Olympian, and our rented house was secluded by eucalyptus trees. The annoyances were minor. Occasionally a car would careen down Terrace Drive full of white teenagers, and one or two would shout, "Hey, nigger!" Sometimes as I walked down The Arlington toward Kensington Market, the curious would stare at me from their cars, and women I encountered would give me nervous, frightened looks. Once, as I was walking to the market to buy magazines, a white child was sitting directly in my path. We were the only two people on the street. Two or three cars actually stopped, and their drivers observed the scene through their rearview mirrors until they were assured I wasn't going to abduct the child.

At night the Kensington Market area was lit with a yellow light, especially eerie during a fog. I always thought that this section of Kensington would be a swell place to make a horror movie—the residents would make great extras—but whatever discomfort I felt about traveling through this area at 2 A.M. was mixed with the relief that I had just navigated safely through Albany, where the police seemed always to be lurking in the shadows, prepared to ensnare blacks, hippies, and others they didn't deem suitable for such a neighborhood.

In 1979 our landlord, a decent enough fellow in comparison to some of the others we had had (who made you understand why the communists shoot the landlords first when they take over a country), announced he was going to sell the house on Terrace Drive. This was the third rented house to be sold out from under us. The asking price was way beyond our means, and so we started to search for another home, only to find that the ones within our price range were located in North Oakland, in a "predominantly black neighborhood." We finally found a huge Queen Anne Victorian, which seemed to be about a month away from the wrecker's ball if the termites and the precarious foundation didn't do it in first, but I decided that I had to have it. The oldest house on the block, it was built in 1906, the year the big earthquake hit Northern California, but left Oakland unscathed because, according to Bret Harte, "there are some things even the earth can't swallow." If I was apprehensive about moving into this neighborhood—on television all black neighborhoods resemble the commotion of the station house on *Hill Street Blues*—I was later to learn that our neighbors were just as apprehensive about us. Were we hippies? Did I have a job? Were we going to pay as much attention to maintaining our property as they did to theirs? Neglected, the dilapidated monstrosity I'd got myself into would blight the entire block.

While I was going to college I worked as an orderly in a psychiatric hospital, and I remember a case in which a man was signed into the institution, after complaints from his neighbors that he mowed the lawn at four in the morning. My neighbors aren't that finicky, but they keep very busy pruning, gardening, and mowing their lawns. Novelist Toni Cade Bambara wrote of the spirit women in Atlanta who plant by moonlight and use conjure to reap gorgeous vegetables and flowers. A woman on this block grows roses the size of cantaloupes.

On New Year's Eve, famed landscape architect John Roberts accompanied me on my nightly walk, which takes me from 53rd Street to Aileen, Shattuck, and back to 53rd Street. He was able to identify plants and trees that had been imported from Asia, Africa, the Middle East, and Australia. On Aileen Street he discovered a banana tree! And Arthur Monroe, a painter and art historian, traces the "Tabby" garden design—in which seashells and plates are mixed with lime, sand, and water to form decorative borders, found in this Oakland neighborhood, and others—to the influence of Islamic slaves brought to the Gulf Coast.

I won over my neighbors, I think, after I triumphed over a dozen generations of pigeons that had been roosting in the crevices of this house for many years. It was a long and angry war, and my five year old constantly complained to her mother about Daddy's bad words about the birds. I used everything I could get my hands on, including chicken wire and mothballs, and I would have tried the clay owls if the only manufacturer hadn't gone out of business. I also learned never to underestimate the intelligence of pigeons; just when you think you've got them whipped, you'll notice that they've regrouped on some strategic rooftop to prepare for another invasion. When the house was free of pigeons and their droppings, which had spread to the adjoining properties, the lady next door said, "Thank you."

Every New Year's Day since then our neighbors have invited us to join them and their fellow Louisianans for the traditional Afro-American good luck meal called Hoppin' John. This year the menu included black-eyed peas, ham, corn bread, potato salad, chitterlings, greens, fried chicken, yams, head cheese, macaroni, rolls, sweet potato pie, and fruitcake. I got up that morning weighing 214 pounds and came home from the party weighing 220.

We've lived on 53rd Street for three years now. Carla's dance and theater school, which she operates with her partner, Jody Roberts—Roberts and Blank Dance/Drama—is already five years old. I am working on my seventh novel and a television production of my play *Mother Hubbard*. The house has yet to be restored to its 1906 glory, but we're working on it.

I've grown accustomed to the common sights here—teenagers moving through the neighborhood carrying radios blasting music by Grandmaster Flash and Prince, men hovering over cars with tools and rags in hand, decked-out female church delegations visiting the sick. Unemployment up, one sees more men drinking from sacks as they walk through Market Street or gather in Helen McGregor Plaza, on Shattuck and 52nd Street, near a bench where mothers sit with their children, waiting for buses. It may be because the bus stop is across the street from Children's Hospital (exhibiting a brand-new antihuman, postmodern wing), but there seem to be a lot of sick black children these days. The criminal courts and emergency rooms of Oakland hospitals, both medical and psychiatric, are also filled with blacks.

White men go from door to door trying to unload spoiled meat. Incredibly sleazy white contractors and hustlers try to entangle people into shady deals that sometimes lead to the loss of a home. Everybody knows of someone, usually a widow, who has been gypped into paying thousands of dollars more than the standard cost for, say, adding a room to a house. It sure ain't El Cerrito. In El Cerrito the representatives from the utilities were very courteous. If they realize they're speaking to someone in a black neighborhood, however, they become curt and sarcastic. I was trying to arrange for the gas company to come out to fix a stove when the woman from Pacific Gas and Electric gave me some snide lip. I told her, "Lady, if you think what you're going through is an inconvenience, you can imagine my inconvenience paying the bills every month." Even she had to laugh.

The clerks in the stores are also curt, regarding blacks the way the media regard them, as criminal suspects. Over in El Cerrito the cops were professional, respectful—in Oakland they swagger about like candidates for a rodeo. In El Cerrito and the Berkeley Hills you could take your time paying some bills, but in this black neighborhood if you miss paying a bill by one day, "reminders" printed in glaring and violent typefaces are sent to you, or you're threatened with discontinuance of this or that service. Los Angeles police victim Eulia Love, who was shot in the aftermath of an argument over an overdue gas bill, would still be alive if she had lived in El Cerrito or the Berkeley Hills.

I went to a bank a few weeks ago that advertised easy loans on television, only to be told that I would have to wait six months after opening an account to be eligible for a loan. I went home and called the same bank, this time putting on my Clark Kent voice, and was informed that I could come in and get the loan the same day. Other credit unions and banks, too, have different lending practices for black and white neighborhoods, but when I try to tell white intellectuals that blacks are prevented from developing industries because the banks find it easier to lend money to communist countries than to American citizens, they call me paranoid. Sometimes when I know I am going to be inconvenienced by merchants or creditors because of my 53rd Street address, I give the address of my Berkeley studio instead. Others are not so fortunate.

Despite the inconveniences and antagonism from the outside world one has to endure for having a 53rd Street address, life in this neighborhood is more pleasant than grim. Casually dressed, well-groomed elderly men gather at the intersections to look after the small children as they walk to and from school, or just to keep an eye on the neighborhood. My next-door neighbor keeps me in stitches with his informed commentary on any number of political comedies emanating from Washington and Sacramento. Once we were discussing pesticides and the man who was repairing his porch told us that he had a great garden and didn't have to pay all that much attention to it. As for pesticides, he said, the bugs have to eat, too.

There are people on this block who still know the subsistence skills many Americans have forgotten. They can hunt and fish (and if you don't fish, there is a man who covers the neighborhood selling fresh fish and yelling, "Fishman," recalling a period of ancient American commerce when you didn't have to pay the middleman). They are also loyal Americans—they vote, they pay taxes—but you don't find the extreme patriots here that you find in white neighborhoods. Although Christmas, Thanksgiving, New Year's, and Easter are celebrated with all get-out, I've never seen a flag flying on Memorial Day, or on any holiday that calls for the showing of the flag. Blacks express their loyalty in concrete ways. For example, you rarely see a foreign car in this neighborhood. And this 53rd Street neighborhood, as well as black neighborhoods like it from coast to coast, will supply the male children who will bear the brunt of future jungle wars, just as they did in Vietnam.

We do our shopping on a strip called Temescal, which stretches from 46th to 51st streets. Temescal, according to Oakland librarian William

Sturm, is an Aztec word for "hothouse," or "bathhouse." The word was borrowed from the Mexicans by the Spanish to describe similar hothouses, early saunas, built by the California Indians in what is now North Oakland. Some say the hothouses were used to sweat out demons; others claim the Indians used them for medicinal purposes. Most agree that after a period of time in the steam, the Indians would rush en masse into the streams that flowed through the area. One still runs underneath my backyard—I have to mow the grass there almost every other day.

Within these five blocks are the famous Italian restaurant Bertola's, "Since 1932"; Siam restaurant; La Belle Creole, a French-Caribbean restaurant; Asmara, an Ethiopian restaurant; and Ben's Hof Brau, where white and black senior citizens, dressed in the elegance of a former time, congregate to talk or to have an inexpensive though quality breakfast provided by Ben's hardworking and courteous staff.

The Hof Brau shares its space with Vern's market, where you can shop to the music of DeBarge. To the front of Vern's is the Temescal Delicatessen, where a young Korean man makes the best po'boy sandwiches north of Louisiana, and near the side entrance is Ed Fraga's Automotive. The owner is always advising his customers to avoid stress, and he says goodbye with a "God bless you." The rest of the strip is taken up by the Temescal Pharmacy, which has a resident health advisor and a small library of health literature; the Aikido Institute; an African bookstore; and the internationally known Genova deli, to which people from the surrounding cities travel to shop. The strip also includes the Clausen House thrift shop, which sells used clothes and furniture. Here you can buy novels by J. D. Salinger and John O'Hara for ten cents each.

Space that was recently occupied by the Buon Gusto Bakery is now for rent. Before the bakery left, an Italian lady who worked there introduced me to a crunchy, cookie-like treat called "bones," which she said went well with Italian wine. The Buon Gusto had been a landmark since the 1940s, when, according to a guest at the New Year's Day Hoppin' John supper, North Oakland was populated by Italians and Portuguese. In those days a five-room house could be rented for $45 a month, she said.

The neighborhood is still in transition. The East Bay Negro Historical Society, which was located around the corner on Grove Street, included in its collection letters written by nineteenth-century macho man Jack London to his black nurse. They were signed, "Your little white pickaninny." It's been replaced by the New Israelite Delight restaurant, part of the Israelite Church, which also operates a day care center. The restaurant offers homemade Louisiana gumbo and a breakfast that includes grits.

Unlike the other California neighborhoods I've lived in, I know most of the people on this block by name. They are friendly and cooperative, always offering to watch your house while you're away. The day after one of the few whites who lives on the block—a brilliant muckraking journalist and former student of mine—was robbed, neighbors gathered in front of his house to offer assistance.

In El Cerrito my neighbor was indeed a cop. He used pomade on his curly hair, sported a mustache, and there was a grayish tint in his brown eyes. He was a handsome man, with a smile like a movie star's. His was the only house on the block I entered during my three-year stay in that neighborhood, and that was one afternoon when we shared some brandy. I wanted to get to know him better. I didn't know he was dead until I saw people in black gathered on his doorstep.

I can't imagine that happening on 53rd Street. In a time when dour thinkers view alienation and insensitivity toward the plight of others as characteristics of the modern condition, I think I'm lucky to live in a neighborhood where people look out for one another.

A human neighborhood.

THE SOW IN THE RIVER
■
Mary Clearman Blew

This piece is the opening essay from Blew's 1991 book All But the Waltz.

In the sagebrush to the north of the mountains in central Montana, where the Judith River deepens its channel and threads a slow, treacherous current between the cutbanks, a cottonwood log house still stands. It is in sight of the highway, about a mile downriver on a gravel road. From where I have turned off and stopped my car on the sunlit shoulder of the highway, I can see the house, a distant and solitary dark interruption of the sagebrush. I can even see the lone box elder tree, a dusty green shade over what used to be the yard.

I know from experience that if I were to keep driving over the cattle guard and follow the gravel road through the sage and alkali to the log house, I would find the windows gone and the door sagging and the floor rotting away. But from here the house looks hardly changed from the summer of my earliest memories, the summer before I was three, when I lived in that log house on the lower Judith with my mother and father and grandmother and my grandmother's boyfriend, Bill.

My memories seem to me as treacherous as the river. Is it possible, sitting here on this dry shoulder of a secondary highway in the middle of Montana where the brittle weeds of August scratch at the sides of the car, watching the narrow blue Judith take its time to thread and wind through the bluffs on its way to a distant northern blur, to believe in anything but today? The past eases away with the current. I cannot watch a single drop of water out of sight. How can I trust memory, which slips and wobbles and grinds its erratic furrows like a bald-tired truck fighting for traction on a wet gumbo road?

Light flickers. A kerosene lamp in the middle of the table has driven the shadows back into the corners of the kitchen. Faces and hands emerge in a circle. Bill has brought apples from the box in the dark closet. The coil of peel follows his pocketknife. I bite into the piece of quartered apple he hands me. I hear its snap, taste the juice. The shadows hold threats: mice and the shape of nameless things. But in the circle around the lamp, in the certainty of apples, I am safe.

The last of the kerosene tilts and glitters around the wick. I cower behind Grammy on the stairs, but she boldly walks into the shadows, which reel and retreat from her and her lamp. In her bedroom the window reflects large pale her and timorous me. She undresses herself, undresses me; she piles my pants and stockings on the chair with her dress and corset. After she uses it, her pot is warm for me. Her bed is cold, then warm. I burrow against her back and smell the smoke from the wick she has pinched out. Bill blows his nose from his bedroom on the other side of the landing. Beyond the eaves the shapeless creatures of sound, owls and coyotes, have taken the night. But I am here, safe in the center.

I am in the center again on the day we look for Bill's pigs. I am sitting between him and Grammy in the cab of the old Ford truck while the rain sheets on the windshield. Bill found the pigpen gate open when he went to feed the pigs this morning, their pen empty, and now they are nowhere to be found. He has driven and driven through the sagebrush and around the gulches, peering out through the endless gray rain as the truck spins and growls on the gumbo in low gear. But no pigs. He and Grammy do not speak. The cab is cold, but I am bundled well between them with my feet on the clammy assortment of tools and nails and chains on the floor-boards and my nose just dashboard level, and I am at home with the smell of wet wool and metal and the feel of a broken spring in the seat.

But now Bill tramps on the brakes, and he and Grammy and I gaze through the streaming windshield at the river. The Judith has risen up its cutbanks, and its angry gray current races the rain. I have never seen such a Judith, such a tumult of water. But what transfixes me and Grammy and Bill behind our teeming glass is not the ruthless condition of the river—no, for on a bare ait at midcurrent, completely surrounded and only inches above that muddy roiling water, huddle the pigs.

The flat top of the ait is so small that the old sow takes up most of it by herself. The river divides and rushes around her, rising, practically at her hooves. Surrounding her, trying to crawl under her, snorting in apprehension at the water, are her little pigs. Watching spellbound from the cab of the truck, I can feel their small terrified rumps burrowing against her sides, drawing warmth from her center even as more dirt crumbles under their hooves. My surge of understanding arcs across the current, and my flesh shrivels in the icy sheets of rain. Like the pigs I cringe at the roar of the river, although behind the insulated walls of the cab I can hear and feel nothing. I am in my center and they are in theirs. The current separates us irrevocably, and suddenly I understand that my center is as precarious as theirs, that the chill metal cab of the old truck is almost as fragile as their ring of crumbling sod.

And then the scene darkens and I see no more.

For years I would watch for the ait. When I was five my family moved, but I learned to snatch a glimpse whenever we drove past our old turnoff on the road from Lewistown to Denton. The ait was in plain view, just a hundred yards downriver from the highway, as it is today. *Ait* was a fancy word I learned afterward. It was a fifteen-foot-high steep-sided, flat-topped pinnacle of dirt left standing in the bed of the river after years of wind and water erosion. And I never caught sight of it without the same small thrill of memory: that's where the pigs were.

One day I said it out loud. I was grown by then. "That's where the pigs were."

My father was driving. We would have crossed the Judith River bridge, and I would have turned my head to keep sight of the ait and the lazy blue threads of water around the sandbars.

My father said, "What pigs?"

"The old sow and her pigs," I said, surprised. "The time the river flooded. I remember how the water rose right up to their feet."

My father said, "The Judith never got that high, and there never was any pigs up there."

"Yes there were! I remember!" I could see the little pigs as clearly as I could see my father, and I could remember exactly how my own skin had shriveled as they cringed back from the water and butted the sow for cold comfort.

My father shook his head. "How did you think pigs would get up there?" he asked.

Of course they couldn't.

His logic settled on me like an awakening in ordinary daylight. Of course a sow could not lead nine or ten suckling pigs up those sheer fifteen-foot crumbling dirt sides, even for fear of their lives. And why, after all, would pigs even try to scramble to the top of such a precarious perch when they could escape a cloudburst by following any one of the cattle trails or deer trails that webbed the cutbanks on both sides of the river?

Had there been a cloudburst at all? Had there been pigs?

No, my father repeated. The Judith had never flooded anywhere near that high in our time. Bill Hafer had always raised a few pigs when we lived down there on the river, but he kept them penned up. No.

Today I lean on the open window of my car and yawn and listen to the sounds of late summer. The snapping of grasshoppers. Another car approaching on the highway, roaring past my shoulder of the road, then fading away until I can hear the faint scratches of some small hidden creature in the weeds. I am bone-deep in landscape. In this dome of sky and river and undeflected sunlight, in this illusion of timelessness, I can almost feel my body, blood, and breath in the broken line of the bluffs and the pervasive scent of ripening sweet clover and dust, almost feel the sagging fence line of ancient cedar posts stapled across my vitals.

The only shade in sight is across the river where box elders lean over a low white frame house with a big modern house trailer parked behind it. Downstream, far away, a man works along a ditch. I think he might be the husband of a second cousin of mine who still lives on her old family place. My cousins wouldn't know me if they stopped and asked me what I was doing here.

Across the highway, a trace of a road leads through a barbed-wire gate and sharply up the bluff. It is the old cutoff to Danvers, a town that has dried up and blown away. I have heard that the cutoff has washed out, further up the river, but down here it still holds a little bleached gravel. Almost as though my father might turn off in his battered truck at fifteen miles an hour, careful of his bald wartime tires, while I lie on the seat with my head on his thigh and take my nap. Almost as though at the end of that road will be the two grain elevators pointing sharply out of the hazy olives and ochers of the grass into the rolling cumulus, and two or three graveled streets with traffic moving past the pool hall and post office and dug-out store where, when I wake from my nap and scramble down from the high seat of the truck, Old Man Longin will be waiting behind his single glass display case with my precious wartime candy bar.

Yes, that little girl was me, I guess. A three-year-old standing on the unswept board floor, looking up at rows of canned goods on shelves that were nailed against the logs in the 1880s, when Montana was still a territory. The dust smelled the same to her as it does to me now.

Across the river, that low white frame house where my cousin still lives is the old Sample place. Ninety years ago a man named Sample fell in love with a woman named Carrie. Further up the bottom—you can't see it from here because of the cottonwoods—stands Carrie's deserted house in what used to be a fenced yard. Forty years ago Carrie's house was full of three generations of her family, and the yard was full of cousins at play. Sixty years ago the young man who would be my father rode on horseback down that long hill to Carrie's house, and Sample said to Carrie, *Did your brother Albert ever have a son? From the way the kid sits his horse, he must be your brother's son.*

Or so the story goes. Sample was murdered. Carrie died in her sleep. My father died of exposure.

The Judith winds toward its mouth. Its current seems hardly to move. Seeing it in August, so blue and unhurried, it is difficult to believe how many drownings or near drownings the Judith has counted over the years. To a stranger it surely must look insignificant, hardly worth calling a river.

In 1805 the explorers Lewis and Clark, pausing in their quest for the Pacific, saw the mountains and the prairies of central Montana and the wild game beyond reckoning. They also noted this river, which they named after a girl. Lewis and Clark were the first white recorders of this place. In recording it, they altered it. However indifferent to the historical record, those who see this river and hear its name, *Judith*, see it in a slightly different way because Lewis and Clark saw it and wrote about it.

In naming the river, Lewis and Clark claimed it for a system of governance that required a wrenching of the fundamental connections between landscape and its inhabitants. This particular drab sagebrush pocket of the West was never, perhaps, holy ground. None of the landmarks here is invested with the significance of the sacred buttes to the north. For the Indian tribes that hunted here, central Montana must have been commonplace, a familiar stretch of their lives, a place to ride and breathe and be alive.

But even this drab pocket is now a part of the history of the West, which, through a hundred and fifty years of white settlement and economic development, of rapid depletion of water and coal and timber and topsoil, of dependence upon military escalation and federal subsidies, has been a history of the transformation of landscape from a place to be alive in into a place to own. This is a transformation that breaks connections, that holds little in common. My deepest associations with this sunlit river are private. Without a connection between outer and inner landscape, I cannot tell my father what I saw. "There never was a sow in the river," he said, embarrassed at my notion. And yet I know there was a sow in the river.

All who come and go bring along their own context, leave their mark, however faint. If the driver glanced out the window of that car that just roared past, what did he see? Tidy irrigated alfalfa fields, a small green respite from the dryland miles? That foreshortened man who works along the ditch, does he straighten his back from his labors and see his debts spread out in irrigation pipes and electric pumps?

It occurs to me that I dreamed the sow in the river at a time when I was too young to sort out dreams from daylight reality or to question why they should be sorted out and dismissed. As I think about it, the episode does contain some of the characteristics of a dream. That futile, endless, convoluted search in the rain, for example. The absence of sound in the cab of the truck, and the paralysis of the onlookers on the brink of that churning current. For now that I know she never existed outside my imagination, I think I do recognize that sow on her slippery pinnacle.

Memory lights upon a dream as readily as an external event, upon a set of rusty irrigation pipes and a historian's carefully detailed context through which she recalls the collective memory of the past. As memory saves, discards, retrieves, fails to retrieve, its logic may well be analogous to the river's inexorable search for the lowest ground. The trivial and the profound roll like leaves to the surface. Every ripple is suspect.

Today the Judith River spreads out in the full sunlight of August, oblivious of me and my precious associations, indifferent to the emotional context I have framed it with. My memory seems less a record of landscape and event than a superimposition upon what otherwise would continue to flow, leaf out, or crumble according to its lot. What I remember is far less trustworthy than the story I tell about it. The possibility for connection lies in story.

Whether or not I dreamed her, the sow in the river is my story. She is what I have saved, up there on her pinnacle where the river roils.

SACRED AND ANCESTRAL GROUND

N. Scott Momaday

This essay is a selection from The Names, *Momaday's 1987 book.*

There is great good in returning to a landscape that has had extraordinary meaning in one's life. It happens that we return to such places in our minds irresistibly. There are certain villages and towns, mountains and plains that, having seen them, walked in them, lived in them, even for a day, we keep forever in the mind's eye. They become indispensable to our well-being; they define us, and we say: I am who I am because I have been there, or there. There is good, too, in actual, physical return.

Some years ago I made a pilgrimage into the heart of North America. I began the journey proper in western Montana. From there I traveled across the high plains of Wyoming into the Black Hills, then southward to the southern plains, to a cemetery at Rainy Mountain, in Oklahoma. It was a journey made by my Kiowa ancestors long before. In the course of their migration they became a people of the Great Plains, and theirs was the last culture to evolve in North America. They had been for untold generations a mountain tribe of hunters. Their ancient nomadism, which had determined their way of life even before they set foot on this continent, perhaps 30,000 years ago, was raised to its highest level of expression when they entered upon the Great Plains and acquired horses. Their migration brought them to a Golden Age. At the beginning of their journey they were a people of hard circumstances, often hungry and cold, fighting always for sheer survival. At its end, and for a hundred years, they were the lords of the land, a daring race of centaurs and buffalo hunters whose love of freedom and space was profound.

Recently I returned to the old migration route of the Kiowas. I had in me a need to behold again some of the principal landmarks of that long, prehistoric quest, to descend again from the mountain to the plain.

With my close friend Charles, a professor of American literature at a South Dakota university, I headed north to the Montana-Wyoming border. I wanted to intersect the Kiowa migration route at the Bighorn Medicine Wheel, high in the Bighorn Mountains. We ascended to 8,000 feet gradually, on a well-maintained but winding highway. Then we climbed sharply, bearing upon the timberline. Although the plain below had been comfortable, even warm at midday, the mountain air was cold, and much of the ground was covered with snow. We turned off the pavement, on a dirt road that led three miles to the Medicine Wheel. The road was forbidding, it was narrow and winding, and the grades were steep and slippery; here and there the shoulders fell away into deep ravines. But at the same time something wonderful happened: we crossed the line between civilization and wilderness. Suddenly the earth persisted in its original being. Directly in front of us a huge white-tailed buck crossed our path, ambling without haste into a thicket of pines. As we drove over his tracks we saw four does above on the opposite bank, looking down at us, their great black eyes bright and benign, curious. There seemed no wariness, nothing of fear or alienation. Their presence was a good omen, we thought; somehow in their attitude they bade us welcome to their sphere of wilderness.

There was a fork in the road, and we took the wrong branch. At a steep, hairpin curve we got out of the car and climbed to the top of a peak. An icy wind whipped at us; we were among the bald summits of the Bighorns. Great flumes of sunlit snow erupted on the ridges and dissolved in spangles on the sky. Across a deep saddle we caught sight of the Medicine Wheel. It was perhaps two miles away.

When we returned to the car we saw another vehicle approaching. It was a very old Volkswagen bus, in much need of repair, cosmetic repair, at least. Out stepped a thin, bearded young man in thick glasses. He wore a wool cap, a down parka, jeans and well-worn hiking boots. "I am looking for Medicine Wheel," he said, having nodded to us. He spoke softly, with a pronounced accent. His name was Jürg, and he was from Switzerland; he had been traveling for some months in Canada and the United States. Chuck and I shook his hand and told him to follow us, and we drove down into the saddle. From there we climbed on foot to the Medicine Wheel.

The Medicine Wheel is a ring of stones, some 80 feet in diameter. Stone spokes radiate from the center to the circumference. Cairns are placed at certain points on the circumference, one in the center and one just outside the ring to the southwest. We do not know as a matter of fact who made this wheel or to what purpose. It has been proposed that it was an astronomical observatory, a solar calendar and the ground design of a Kiowa sun dance lodge. What we know without doubt is that it is a sacred expression, an equation of man's relation to the cosmos.

There was a great calm upon that place. The hard, snowbearing wind that had burned our eyes and skin only minutes before had died away altogether. The sun was warm and bright, and there was a profound silence. On the wire fence that had been erected to enclose and protect the wheel were fixed offerings, small prayer bundles. Chuck and Jürg and I walked about slowly, standing for long moments here and there, looking into the wheel or out across the great distances. We did not say much; there was little to be said. But we were deeply moved by the spirit of that place. The silence was such that it must be observed. To the north we could see down to the timberline, to the snowfields and draws that marked the black planes of forest among the peaks of the Bighorns. To the south and west the mountains fell abruptly to the plains. We could see thousands of feet down and a hundred miles across the dim expanse.

When we were about to leave, I took from my pocket an eagle-bone whistle that my father had given me, and I blew it in the four directions. The sound was very high and shrill, and it did not break the essential silence. As we were walking down we saw far below, crossing our path, a coyote sauntering across the snow into a wall of trees. It was just there, a wild being to catch sight of, and then it was gone. The wilderness which had admitted us with benediction, with benediction let us go.

When we came within a stone's throw of the highway, Chuck and I said goodbye to Jürg, but not before Jürg had got out his camp stove and boiled water for tea. There in the dusk we enjoyed a small ceremonial feast of tea and crackers. The three of us had become friends. Only later did I begin to understand the extraordinary character of that friendship. It was the friendship of those who come together in recognition of the sacred. If we never meet again, I thought, we shall not forget this day.

On the plains the fences and roads and windmills and houses seemed almost negligible, all but overwhelmed by the earth and sky. It is a landscape of great clarity; its vastness is that of the ocean. It is the near revelation of infinity. Antelope were everywhere in the grassy folds, grazing side by side with horses and cattle. Hawks sailed above, and crows scattered before us. The place names were American—Tensleep, Buffalo, Dull Knife, Crazy Woman, Spotted Horse.

The Black Hills are an isolated and ancient group of mountains in South Dakota and Wyoming. They lie very close to both the geographic center of the United States (including Alaska and Hawaii) and the geographic center of the North American continent. They form an island, an elliptical area of nearly 6,000 square miles, in the vast sea of grasses that is the northern Great Plains. The Black Hills form a calendar of geologic time that is truly remarkable. The foundation rocks of these mountains are older than much of the sedimentary layer of which the Americas are primarily composed. An analysis of this foundation, made in 1975, indicates an age of between two billion and three billion years.

A documented record of exploration in this region is found in the Lewis and Clark journals, 1804–6. The first white party known definitely to have entered the Black Hills proper was led by Jedediah Smith in 1823. The diary of this expedition, kept by one James Clyman, is notable. Clyman reports a confrontation between Jedediah Smith and a grizzly bear, in which Smith lost one of is ears. There is also reported the discovery of a petrified ("putrified," as Clyman has it) forest, where petrified birds sing petrified songs.

Toward the end of the century, after rumors of gold had made the Black Hills a name known throughout the country, Gen. (then Lieut. Col.) George Armstrong Custer led an expedition from Fort Abraham Lincoln into the Black Hills in July and August, 1874. The Custer expedition traveled 600 miles in 60 days. Custer reported proof of gold, but he had an eye to other things as well:

> Every step of our march that day was amid flowers of the most exquisite colors and perfume. So luxuriant in growth were they that men plucked them without dismounting from the saddle. . . . It was a strange sight to glance back at the advancing columns of cavalry and behold the men with beautiful bouquets in their hands, while the headgear of the horses was decorated with wreaths of flowers fit to crown a queen of May. Deeming it a most fitting appellation, I named this Floral Valley.

In the evening of that same day, sitting at mess in a meadow, the officers competed to see how many different flowers could be picked by each man, without leaving his seat. Seven varieties were gathered so. Some 50 different flowers were blooming then in Floral Valley.

The Lakota, or Teton Sioux, called these mountains Paha Sapa, "Hills That Are Black." Other tribes, besides the Kiowa and the Sioux, thought of the Black Hills as sacred ground, a place crucial in their past. The Arapaho lived here. So did the Cheyenne. Bear Butte, near Sturgis, S.D., on the northeast edge of the Black Hills, is the Cheyenne's sacred mountain. It remains, like the Medicine Wheel, a place of the greatest spiritual intensity. So great was thought to be the power inherent in the Black Hills that the Indians did not camp there. It was a place of rendezvous, a hunting ground, but above all inviolate, a place of thunder and lightning, a dwelling place of the gods.

On the edge of the Black Hills nearest the Bighorn Mountains is Devils Tower, the first of our National Monuments. The Lakotas called it Mateo Tepee, "Grizzly Bear Lodge." The Kiowas called it Tsoai, "Rock Tree." Devils Tower is a great monolith that rises high above the timber of the Black Hills. In conformation it closely resembles the stump of a tree. It is a cluster of rock columns (phonolite porphyry) 1,000 feet across at the base and 275 feet across the top. It rises 865 feet above the high ground on which it stands and 1,280 feet above the Belle Fourche River, in the valley below.

It has to be seen to be believed. "There are things in nature that engender an awful quiet in the heart of man; Devils Tower is one of them." I wrote these words almost 20 years ago. They remain true to my experience. Each time I behold this Tsoai, I am more than ever in awe of it.

Two hundred years ago, more or less, the Kiowas came upon this place. They were moved to tell a story about it:

Eight children were there at play, seven sisters and their brother. Suddenly the boy was struck dumb; he trembled and began to run upon his hands and feet. His fingers became claws and his body was covered with fur. Directly there was a bear where the boy had been. The sisters were terrified; they ran, and the bear ran after them. They came to the stump of a great tree, and the tree spoke to them. It bade them climb upon it, and as they did so it began to rise into the air. The bear came to kill them, but they were just beyond its reach. It reared against the tree and scored the bark all around with its claws. The seven sisters were borne into the sky, and they became the stars of the Big Dipper.

El Greco, *View of Toledo,* oil on canvas, 47¾ × 42¾".

This story, which I have known from the time I could first understand language, exemplifies the sacred for me. The storyteller, that anonymous, illiterate man who told the story for the first time, succeeded in raising the human condition to the level of universal significance. Not only did he account for the existence of the rock tree, but in the process he related his human race to the stars.

When Chuck and I had journeyed over this ground together, when we were about to go our separate ways, I reminded him of our friend Jürg, knowing well enough that I needn't have: Jürg was on our minds. He had touched us deeply with his trust, not unlike that of the wild animals we had seen. I can't account for it. Jürg had touched us deeply with his generosity of spirit, his concern to see beneath the surface of things, his attitude of free, direct, disinterested kindness.

"Did he tell us what he does?" I asked. "Does he have a profession?"

"I don't think he said," Chuck replied. "I think he's a pilgrim."

"Yes."

"Yes."

O ROTTEN GOTHAM: SLIDING DOWN INTO THE BEHAVIORAL SINK

Tom Wolfe

This piece is from Wolfe's book The Pump House, *published in 1968.*

I just spent two days with Edward T. Hall, an anthropologist, watching thousands of my fellow New Yorkers short-circuiting themselves into hot little twitching death balls with jolts of their own adrenalin. Dr. Hall says it is overcrowding that does it. Overcrowding gets the adrenalin going, and the adrenalin gets them hyped up. And here they are, hyped up, turning bilious, nephritic, queer, autistic, sadistic, barren, batty, sloppy, hot-in-the-pants, chancred-on-the-flankers, leering, puling, numb—the usual in New York, in other words, and God knows what else. Dr. Hall has the theory that overcrowding has already thrown New York into a state of behavioral sink. Behavioral sink is a term from ethology, which is the study of how animals relate to their environment. Among animals, the sink winds up with a "population collapse" or "massive die-off." O rotten Gotham.

It got to be easy to look at New Yorkers as animals, especially looking down from some place like a balcony at Grand Central at the rush hour Friday afternoon. The floor was filled with the poor white humans, running around, dodging, blinking their eyes, making a sound like a pen full of starlings or rats or something.

"Listen to them skid," says Dr. Hall.

He was right. The poor old etiolate animals were out there skidding on their rubber soles. You could hear it once he pointed it out. They stop short to keep from hitting somebody or because they are disoriented and they suddenly stop and look around, and they skid on their rubber-sole shoes, and a screech goes up. They pour out onto the floor down the escalators from the Pan-Am Building, from 42nd Street, from Lexington Avenue, up out of subways, down into subways, railroad trains, up into helicopters—

"You can also hear the helicopters all the way down here," says Dr. Hall. The sound of the helicopters using the roof of the Pan-Am Building nearly fifty stories up beats right through. "If it weren't for this ceiling"—he is referring to the very high ceiling in Grand Central—"this place would be unbearable with this kind of crowding. And yet they'll probably never 'waste' space like this again."

They screech! And the adrenal glands in all those poor white animals enlarge, micrometer by micrometer, to the size of cantaloupes. Dr. Hall pulls a Minox camera out of a holster he has on his belt and starts shooting away at the human scurry. The Sink!

Dr. Hall has the Minox up to his eye—he is a slender man, calm, 52 years old, young-looking, an anthropologist who has worked with Navajos, Hopis, Spanish-Americans, Negroes, Trukese. He was the most important anthropologist in the government during the crucial years of the foreign aid program, the 1950's. He directed both the Point Four training program and the Human Relations Area Files. He wrote *The Silent Language* and *The Hidden Dimension,* two books that are picking up the kind of "underground" following his friend Marshall McLuhan started picking up about five years ago. He teaches at the Illinois Institute of Technology, lives with his wife, Mildred, in a high-ceilinged town house on one of the last great residential streets in downtown Chicago, Astor Street; has a grown son and daughter, loves good food, good wine, the relaxed, civilized life—but comes to New York with a Minox at his eye to record—perfect. The Sink.

We really got down in there by walking down into the Lexington Avenue line subway stop under Grand Central. We inhaled those nice big fluffy fumes of human sweat, urine, effluvia, and sebaceous secretions. One old female human was already stroked out on the upper level, on a stretcher, with two policemen standing by. The other humans barely looked at her. They rushed into line. They bellied each other, haunch to paunch, down the stairs. Human heads shone through the gratings. The species North European tried to create bubbles of space around themselves, about a foot and a half in diameter.

"See, he's reacting against the line," says Dr. Hall.

—but the species Mediterranean presses on in. The hell with bubbles of space. The species North European resents that, this male human behind him presses forward toward the booth . . . *breathing* on him, he's disgusted, he pulls out of the line entirely, the species Mediterranean resents him for resenting it, and neither of them realizes what the hell they are getting irritable about exactly. And in all of them the old adrenals grow another micrometer.

Dr. Hall whips out the Minox. Too perfect! The bottom of The Sink.

It is the sheer overcrowding, such as occurs in the business sections of Manhattan five days a week and in Harlem, Bedford-Stuyvesant, southeast Bronx every day—sheer overcrowding is converting New Yorkers into animals in a sink pen. Dr. Hall's argument runs as follows: all animals, including birds, seem to have a built-in, inherited requirement to have a certain amount of territory, space, to lead their lives in. Even if they have all the food they need, and there are no predatory animals threatening them, they cannot tolerate crowding beyond a certain point. No more than two hundred wild Norway rats can survive on a quarter acre of ground, for example, even when they are given all the food they can eat. They just die off.

But why? To find out, ethologists have run experiments on all sorts of animals, from stickleback crabs to Sika deer. In one major experiment, an ethologist named John Calhoun put some domesticated white Norway rats in a pen with four sections to it, connected by ramps. Calhoun knew from previous experiments that the rats tend to split up into groups of ten to twelve and that the pen, therefore, would hold forty to forty-eight rats comfortably, assuming they formed four equal groups. He allowed them to reproduce until there were eighty rats, balanced between male and female, but did not let it get any more crowded. He kept them supplied with plenty of food, water, and nesting materials. In other words, all their more obvious needs were taken care of. A less obvious need—space—was not. To the human eye, the pen did not even look especially crowded. But to the rats, it was crowded beyond endurance.

The entire colony was soon plunged into a profound behavioral sink. "The sink," said Calhoun, "is the outcome of any behavioral process that collects animals together in unusually great numbers. The unhealthy connotations of the term are not accidental: a behavioral sink does act to aggravate all forms of pathology that can be found within a group."

For a start, long before the rat population reached eighty, a status hierarchy had developed in the pen. Two dominant male rats took over the two end sections, acquired harems of eight to ten females each, and forced the rest of the rats into the two middle pens. All the overcrowding took place in the middle pens. That was where the "sink" hit. The aristocrat rats at the ends grew bigger, sleeker, healthier, and more secure the whole time.

In The Sink, meanwhile, nest building, courting, sex behavior, reproduction, social organization, health—all of it went to pieces. Normally, Norway rats have a mating ritual in which the male chases the female, the female ducks down into a burrow and sticks her head up to watch the male. He performs a little dance outside the burrow, then she comes out, and he mounts her, usually for a few seconds. When The Sink set in, however, no more than three males—the dominant males in the middle sections—kept up the old customs. The rest tried everything from satyrism to homosexuality or else gave up on sex altogether. Some of the subordinate males spent all their time chasing females. Three or four might chase one female at the same time, and instead of stopping at the burrow entrance for the ritual, they would charge right in. Once mounted, they would hold on for minutes instead of the usual seconds.

Homosexuality rose sharply. So did bisexuality. Some males would mount anything—males, females, babies, senescent rats, anything. Still other males dropped sexual activity altogether, wouldn't fight and, in fact, would hardly move except when the other rats slept. Occasionally a female from the aristocrat rats' harems would come over the ramps and into the middle sections to sample life in The Sink. When she had had enough, she would run back up the ramp. Sink males would give chase up to the top of the ramp, which is to say, to the very edge of the aristocratic preserve. But one glance from one of the king rats would stop them cold and they would return to The Sink.

The slumming females from the harems had their adventures and then returned to a placid, healthy life. Females in The Sink, however were ravaged, physically and psychologically. Pregnant rats had trouble continuing pregnancy. The rate of miscarriages increased significantly, and females started dying from tumors and other disorders of the mammary glands, sex organs, uterus, ovaries, and Fallopian tubes. Typically, their kidneys, livers, and adrenals were also enlarged or diseased or showed other signs associated with stress.

Child-rearing became totally disorganized. The females lost the interest or the stamina to build nests and did not keep them up if they did build them. In the general filth and confusion, they would not put themselves out to save offspring they were momentarily separated from. Frantic, even sadistic competition among the males was going on all around them and rendering their lives chaotic. The males began unprovoked and senseless assaults upon one another, often in the form of tail-biting. Ordinarily, rats will suppress this kind of behavior when it crops up. In The Sink, male rats gave up all policing and just looked out for themselves. The "pecking order" among males in The Sink was never stable. Normally, male rats set up a three-class structure. Under the pressure of overcrowding, however, they broke up into all sorts of unstable subclasses, cliques, packs—and constantly pushed, probed, explored, tested one another's power. Anyone was fair game, except for the aristocrats in the end pens.

Calhoun kept the population down to eighty, so that the next stage, "population collapse" or "massive die-off," did not occur. But the autopsies showed that the pattern—as in the diseases among the female rats—was already there.

The classic study of die-off was John J. Christian's study of Sika deer on James Island in the Chesapeake Bay, west of Cambridge, Maryland. Four or five of the deer had been released on the island, which was 280 acres and uninhabited, in 1916. By 1955 they had bred freely into a herd of 280 to 300. The population density was only about one deer per acre at this point, but Christian knew that this was already too high for the Sikas' inborn space requirements, and something would give before long. For two years the number of deer remained 280 to 300. But suddenly, in 1958, over half the deer died; 161 carcasses were recovered. In 1959 more deer died and the population steadied at about 80.

In two years, two-thirds of the herd had died. Why? It was not starvation. In fact, all the deer collected were in excellent condition, with well-developed muscles, shining coats, and fat deposits between the muscles. In practically all the deer, however, the adrenal glands had enlarged by 50 percent. Christian concluded that the die-off was due to "shock following severe metabolic disturbance, probably as a result of prolonged adrenocortical hyperactivity. . . . There was no evidence of infection, starvation, or other obvious cause to explain the mass mortality." In other words, the constant stress of overpopulation, plus the normal stress of the cold of the winter, had kept the adrenalin flowing so constantly in the deer that their systems were depleted of blood sugar and they died of shock.

Well, the white humans are still skidding and darting across the floor of Grand Central. Dr. Hall listens a moment longer to the skidding and the darting noises, and then says, "You know, I've been on commuter trains here after everyone has been through one of these rushes and I'll tell you, there is enough acid flowing in the stomachs in every car to dissolve the rails underneath."

Just a little invisible acid bath for the linings to round off the day. The ulcers the acids cause, of course, are the one disease people have already been taught to associate with the stress of city life. But overcrowding, as Dr. Hall sees it, raises a lot more hell with the body than just ulcers. In everyday life in New York—just the usual, getting to work, working in massively congested areas like 42nd Street between Fifth Avenue and Lexington, especially now that the Pan-Am Building is set in there, working in cubicles such as those in the editorial offices at Time-Life, Inc., which Dr. Hall cites as typical of New York's poor handling of space, working in cubicles with low ceilings and, often, no access to a window, while construction crews all over Manhattan drive everybody up the Masonite wall with air-pressure generators with noises up to the boil-a-brain decibel levels, then rushing to get home, piling into subways and trains, fighting for time and for space, the usual day in New York—the whole now-normal thing keeps shooting jolts of adrenalin into the body, breaking down the body's defenses and winding up with the work-a-daddy human animal stroked out at the breakfast table with his head apoplexed like a cauliflower out of his $6.95 semispread Pima-cotton shirt, and nosed over into a plate of No-Kloresto egg substitute, signing off with the black thrombosis, cancer, kidney, liver, or stomach failure, and the adrenals ooze to a halt, the size of eggplants in July.

One of the people whose work Dr. Hall is interested in on this score is Rene Dubos at the Rockefeller Institute. Dubos's work indicates that specific organisms, such as the tuberculosis bacillus or a pneumonia virus, can seldom be considered "the cause" of a disease. The germ or virus, apparently, has to work in combination with other things that have already broken the body down in some way—such as the old adrenal hyperactivity. Dr. Hall would like to see some autopsy studies made to record the size of adrenal glands in New York, especially of people crowded into slums and people who go through the full rush-hour-work-rush-hour cycle every day. He is afraid that until there is some clinical, statistical data on how overcrowding actually ravages the human body, no one will be willing to do anything about it. Even in so obvious a thing as air pollution, the pattern is familiar. Until people can actually see the smoke or smell the sulphur or feel the sting in their eyes, politicians will not get excited about it, even though it is well known that many of the lethal substances polluting the air are invisible and odorless. For one thing, most politicians are like the aristocrat rats. They are insulated from The Sink by practically sultanic buffers—limousines, chauffeurs, secretaries, aides-de-camp, doormen, shuttered houses, high-floor apartments. They almost never ride subways, fight rush hours, much less live in the slums or work in the Pan-Am Building.

We took a cab from Grand Central to go up to Harlem, and by 48th Street we were already socked into one of those great, total traffic jams on First Avenue on Friday afternoon. Dr. Hall motions for me to survey the scene, and there they all are, humans, male and female, behind the glass of their automobile windows, soundlessly going through the torture of their own adrenalin jolts. This male over here contracts his jaw muscles so hard that they bunch up into a great cheese Danish pattern. He twists his lips, he bleeds from the eyeballs, he shouts . . . soundlessly behind glass . . . the fat corrugates on the back of his neck, his whole body shakes as he pounds the heel of his hand into the steering wheel. The female human in the car ahead of him whips her head around, she bares her teeth, she screams . . . soundlessly behind glass . . . she throws her hands up in the air, Whaddya expect me—Yah, yuh stupid—and they all sit there, trapped in their own congestion, bleeding hate all over each other, shorting out the ganglia and—goddam it—

Dr. Hall sits back and watches it all. This is it! The Sink! And where is everybody's wandering boy?

Dr. Hall says, "We need a study in which drivers who go through these rush hours every day would wear GSR bands."

GSR?

"Galvanic skin response. It measures the electric potential of the skin, which is a function of sweating. If a person gets highly nervous, his palms begin to sweat. It is an index of tension. There are some other fairly simple devices that would record respiration and pulse. I think everybody who goes through this kind of experience all the time should take his own pulse—not literally—but just be aware of what's happening to him. You can usually tell when stress is beginning to get you physically."

In testing people crowded into New York's slums, Dr. Hall would like to take it one step further—gather information on the plasma hydrocortisone level in the blood or the corticosteroids in the urine. Both have been demonstrated to be reliable indicators of stress, and testing procedures are simple.

The slums—we finally made it up to East Harlem. We drove into 101st Street, and there was a new, avant-garde little church building, the Church of the Epiphany, which Dr. Hall liked—and, next to it, a pile of rubble where a row of buildings had been torn down, and from the back windows of the tenements beyond several people were busy "airmailing," throwing garbage out the window, into the rubble, beer cans, red shreds, the No-Money-Down Eames roller stand for a TV set, all flying through the air onto the scaggy sump. We drove around some more in Harlem, and a sequence was repeated, trash, buildings falling down, buildings torn down, rubble, scaggy sumps or, suddenly, a cluster of high-rise apartment projects, with fences around the grass.

"You know what this city looks like?" Dr. Hall said. "It looks bombed out. I used to live at Broadway and 124th Street back in 1946 when I was studying at Columbia. I can't tell you how much Harlem has changed in twenty years. It looks bombed out. It's broken down. People who live in New York get used to it and don't realize how filthy the city has become. The whole thing is typical of a behavioral sink. So is something like the Kitty Genovese case—a girl raped and murdered in the courtyard of an apartment complex and forty or fifty people look on from their apartments and nobody even calls the police. That kind of apathy and anomie is typical of the general psychological deterioration of The Sink."

He looked at the high-rise housing projects and found them mainly testimony to how little planners know about humans' basic animal requirements for space.

"Even on the simplest terms," he said, "it is pointless to build one of these blocks much over five stories high. Suppose a family lives on the fifteenth floor. The mother will be completely cut off from her children if they are playing down below, because the elevators are constantly broken in these projects, and it often takes half an hour, literally half an hour, to get the elevator if it is running. That's very common. A mother in that situation is just as much a victim of overcrowding as if she were back in the tenement block. Some Negro leaders have a bitter joke about how the white man is solving the slum problem by stacking Negroes up vertically, and there is a lot to that."

For one thing, says Dr. Hall, planners have no idea of the different space requirements of people from different cultures, such as Negroes and Puerto Ricans. They are all treated as if they were minute, compact middle-class whites. As with the Sika deer, who are overcrowded at one per acre, overcrowding is a relative thing for the human animal, as well.

Each species has its own feeling for space. The feeling may be "subjective," but it is quite real.

Dr. Hall's theories on space and territory are based on the same information, gathered by biologists, ethologists, and anthropologists, chiefly, as Robert Ardrey's. Ardrey has written two well-publicized books, *African Genesis* and *The Territorial Imperative*. *Life* magazine ran big excerpts from *The Territorial Imperative,* all about how the drive to acquire territory and property and add to it and achieve status is built into all animals, including man, over thousands of centuries of genetic history, etc., and is a more powerful drive than sex. *Life*'s big display prompted Marshall McLuhan to crack, "They see this as a great historic justification for free enterprise and Republicanism. If the birds do it and the stickle-back crabs do it, then it's right for man." To people like Hall and McLuhan, and Ardrey, for that matter, the right or wrong of it is irrelevant. The only thing they find inexcusable is the kind of thinking, by influential people, that isn't even aware of all this. Such as the thinking of most city planners.

"The planners always show you a bird's-eye view of what they are doing," he said. "You've seen those scale models. Everyone stands around the table and looks down and says that's great. It never occurs to anyone that they are taking a bird's-eye view. In the end, these projects do turn out fine, when viewed from an airplane."

As an anthropologist, Dr. Hall has to shake his head every time he hears planners talking about fully integrated housing projects for the year 1980 or 1990, as if by then all cultural groups will have the same feeling for space and will live placidly side by side, happy as the happy burghers who plan all the good clean bird's-eye views. According to his findings, the very fact that every cultural group does have its own peculiar, unspoken feeling for space is what is responsible for much of the uneasiness one group feels around the other.

It is like the North European and the Mediterranean in the subway line. The North European, without ever realizing it, tries to keep a bubble of space around himself, and the moment a stranger invades that sphere, he feels threatened. Mediterranean peoples tend to come from cultures where everyone is much more involved physically, publicly, with one another on a day-to-day basis and feels no uneasiness about mixing it up in public, but may have very different ideas about space inside the home. Even Negroes brought up in America have a different vocabulary of space and gesture from the North European Americans who, historically, have been their models, according to Dr. Hall. The failure of Negroes and whites to communicate well often boils down to things like this: some white will be interviewing a Negro for a job; the Negro's culture has taught him to show somebody you are interested by looking right at him and listening intently to what he has to say. But the species North European requires something more. He expects his listener to nod from time to time, as if to say, "Yes, keep going." If he doesn't get this nodding, he feels anxious, for fear the listener doesn't agree with him or has switched off. The Negro may learn that the white expects this sort of thing, but he isn't used to the precise kind of nodding that is customary, and so he may start overresponding, nodding like mad, and at this point the North European is liable to think he has some kind of stupid Uncle Tom on his hands, and the guy still doesn't get the job.

The whole handling of space in New York is so chaotic, says Dr. Hall, that even middle-class housing now seems to be based on the bird's-eye models for slum projects. He took a look at the big Park West Village development, set up originally to provide housing in Manhattan for families in the middle-income range, and found its handling of space very much like a slum project with slightly larger balconies. He felt the time has come to start subsidizing the middle class in New York on its own terms—namely, the kind of truly "human" spaces that still remain in brownstones.

"I think New York City should seriously consider a program of encouraging the middle-class development of an area like Chelsea, which is already starting to come up. People are beginning to renovate houses there on their own, and I think if the city would subsidize that sort of thing with tax reliefs and so forth, you would be amazed at what would result. What New York needs is a string of minor successes in the housing field, just to show everyone that it can be done, and I think the middle class can still do that for you. The alternative is to keep on doing what you're doing now, trying to lift a very large lower class up by main force almost and finding it a very slow and discouraging process.

"But before deciding how to redesign space in New York," he said, "people must first simply realize how severe the problem already is. And the handwriting is already on the wall."

"A study published in 1962," he said, "surveyed a representative sample of people living in New York slums and found only 18 percent of them free from emotional symptoms. Thirty-eight percent were in need of psychiatric help, and 23 percent were seriously disturbed or incapacitated. Now, this study was published in 1962, which means the work probably went on from 1955 to 1960. There is no telling how bad it is now. In a behavioral sink, crises can develop rapidly."

Dr. Hall would like to see a large-scale study similar to that undertaken by two sociopsychologists, Chombart de Lauwe and his wife, in a French working-class town. They found a direct relationship between crowding and general breakdown. In families where people were crowded into the apartment so that there was less than 86 to 108 square feet per person, social and physical disorders doubled. That would mean that for four people the smallest floor space they could tolerate would be an apartment, say, 12 by 30 feet.

What would one find in Harlem? "It is fairly obvious," Dr. Hall wrote in *The Hidden Dimension*, "that the American Negroes and people of Spanish culture who are flocking to our cities are being very seriously stressed. Not only are they in a setting that does not fit them, but they have passed the limits of their own tolerance of stress. The United States is faced with the fact that two of its creative and sensitive peoples are in the process of being destroyed and like Samson could bring down the structure that houses us all."

Dr. Hall goes out to the airport, to go back to Chicago, and I am coming back in a cab, along the East River Drive. It is four in the afternoon, but already the damned drive is clogging up. There is a 1959 Oldsmobile just to the right of me. There are about eight people in there, a lot of popeyed silhouettes against a leopard-skin dashboard, leopard-skin seats—and the driver is classic. He has a mustache, sideburns down to his jaw socket, and a tattoo on his forearm with a Rossetti painting of Jane Burden Morris with her hair long. All right; it is even touching, like a postcard photo of the main drag in San Pedro, California. But suddenly Sideburns guns it and cuts in front of my cab so that my driver has to hit the brakes, and then hardly 100 feet ahead Sideburns hits a wall of traffic himself and has to hit his brakes, and then it happens. A stuffed white Angora animal, a dog, no, it's a Pekingese cat, is mounted in his rear window—as soon as he hits the brakes its *eyes* light up, Nighttown pink. To keep from ramming him, my driver has to hit the brakes again, too, and so here I am, out in an insane, jammed-up expressway at four in the afternoon, shuddering to a stop while a stuffed Pekingese grows bigger and bigger and brighter in the eyeballs directly in front of me. Jolt! Nighttown pink! Hey—that's me the adrenalin is hitting, *I* am this white human sitting in a projectile heading amid a mass of clotted humans toward white Angora stuffed goddam leopard-dash Pekingese freaking cat—kill that damned Angora—Jolt!—got me—another micrometer on the old adrenals—

GETTING TO KNOW MISTER LINCOLN

———————————————•———————————————

Beverly Lowry

This essay originally appeared in The New York Times Magazine *on May 14, 1995.*

In September, I moved to Washington to take up a teaching job at George Washington University. I was provided housing in a brownstone the college owns in a once-swampy area of town called Foggy Bottom. From my house, the White House was about five blocks east, the Kennedy Center about the same distance in the other direction. I found my way around Foggy Bottom quickly enough. Like that of many cities, the history of Washington is about water. There's always too much or too little. Less bossy than it used to be, the Potomac River now cradles Foggy Bottom. Parkland along the riverbank provides ample walking paths, north and south and across the river into Virginia. I walked and walked, to Cleveland Park, to Georgetown.

But the direction I headed most often was straight south down the street I lived on, past the small park where 10 to 20 homeless men lived and on warn nights danced to a whammed-out beat on metal containers, past the huge, faceless State Department building, past one of the many kiosks selling three-for-$10 T-shirts and another one selling egg rolls, hot smokies and pretzels, across Constitution Avenue, to the Mall.

Everything is there: museums, a small lake, the Capitol, the Washington Monument, the Jefferson and Lincoln Memorials, not to mention people from all over the world. I went there all the time, to watch the people or go to a museum, often to see only one exhibit, or even one painting or statue. There was one funerary statue in the National Museum of African Art I grew particularly attached to. And afterward I would come back home feeling lively and nurtured and accompanied—by the art I had seen, the observations from the walk, the people, the water, the wide long stretches of green. Because no building can be taller than the Capitol, there is a lot of sky in Washington, which I found comforting.

One night early in the fall semester I decided to go for a short run after class. But on my way home, I ran into a colleague and so by the time I had laced up my shoes and hit 21st Street, it was past 7:30 and dark.

I took the most lighted route, turning on Virginia Avenue toward the Washington Monument. The monument's up on a rise, and well lighted. When I got to 19th Street, I could see a number of people still wandering around its base.

I had my Walkman on, rock music pounding into my ears. When I got to Constitution, there was still a rosy glow in the sky but the light was failing fast. I would, I told myself, start straight back home as soon as I got to the monument, but once I did, and looked west down the reflecting pool toward the river, I stopped dead in my tracks.

After the assassination of Abraham Lincoln, it took nearly 50 years of hot dispute before a decision was made about what kind of memorial should be built in his honor, and where it should go. In the late 1800's, Tiber Creek met the Potomac on what would become Constitution Avenue. The water flowed all the way to the White House, often flooding Pennsylvania Avenue. The unfinished Washington Monument was an unsightly stump; the west end of the Mall, river bottom; the area around it, malarial marshes.

All kinds of suggestions were made: a triumphal arch, a grand memorial to the soldiers and statesmen of the Civil War. The emerging automobile industry favored a memorial highway from Washington to Gettysburg, Pa. Railwaymen wanted a statue at Union Station. Finally, in 1912, the classic design of the architect Henry Bacon was chosen. By then, Tiber Creek had been covered over, the swamps dredged and filled, the land reclaimed. The west end of the Mall was still mosquito-ridden and jungly, but Bacon's supporters won the day and Congress voted to situate the memorial on a spot some 3,000 yards down the Mall from the Washington Monument, on an axis that went from the Capitol across the river to Arlington Cemetery, and then to the house that until the Civil War had been the home of Robert E. Lee.

The sun sets behind the Lincoln Memorial, at an angle from its southernmost corner. That night it had already gone down, but that time of year sunset blessedly lasts from what seems like hours, and the sky was wildly ablaze, framing the memorial in a pulsating glow of deep reds, wild pinks and hot golds as lush and beautiful and vulgar as a cheap chiffon scarf.

I switched off my Walkman and stood there gawking, saying, "Look. Look at that," out loud and to nobody at all. The lights inside the memorial had gone on. There's a moment when, after that happens, the sky suddenly gets dark enough that the statue of Lincoln inside the memorial slowly makes a ghostly appearance from between the columns. From where I stood, I saw it happen. Like a picture coming into focus, gradually he was there, seated and in deep contemplation. With the sky on fire behind him, it was as if the whole thing had been staged, a drama of night and time, history and splendor. Beyond the memorial, the Memorial Bridge with its spotty sparkling lights pointed the way across the Potomac. In the reflecting pool, some geese honked a raucous chant, flapped their wings and took off. An airplane from National Airport flew in a diagonal line across the memorial, heading northeast.

I started for home. Beyond the statue of José de San Martín, there was a stretch of dark sidewalk to get through and—having read all the crime reports before arriving—I vowed if I made it home safely that night, never to go out that late again. But I wasn't sorry I had taken the risk. And afterward I began going to the Mall more often and for a more specific reason than for the people, the art or the sky. I went, as I said to myself in the way people alone speak aloud to themselves all the time, "to visit Abe."

Sometimes on a cool clear morning I would simply get up and go down there. The Wall, as the memorial to the veterans of the Vietnam War is called, is located just north of the Lincoln Memorial, and so I had to pass it on my way, and then the kiosks manned by Warriors Inc., and Friends of the Vietnam Veterans Memorial. No matter how early I got there, the kiosks were open, selling T-shirts and P.O.W. and M.I.A. bracelets. I would move on past them, and up the 58 steps to the memorial, where I paid Mr. Lincoln my respects, then came back home and made coffee, ready for the day.

I quickly began to develop a relationship with Abraham Lincoln. I read a couple of biographies, I went to Ford's Theater, where he was shot, and the house across the street, where he died. I stared at pictures of him for long minutes at a time. There was nothing about his life I did not find moving, and significant. And I began to depend on his presence. In my life as a visitor, Abraham Lincoln became a constant.

One day, standing on the top step leading to the reflecting pool, I heard this conversation from a group of boys in private-school jackets and ties:

"Which one is that?" He pointed.

"Lincoln I think. You taking a picture?"

"No, man. I only took Jefferson because Forrest Gump went there." And they moved on.

I have taken 10 or 12 photos of strangers who wanted a picture to take home, of themselves next to Lincoln. I would look in the lens and they would be standing there, those overhanging marble-booted toes high above them. They wouldn't do anything, not even smile, just stand there.

Not wanting to become jaded, I didn't always go up into the memorial itself. Sometimes I only walked past, looked to see who was around, nodded at the statue, and went on. About once a month, however, I allowed myself the pleasure. I devised a ceremony. I was strict. I did it the same way every time.

First I read the plaque at the foot of the steps, explaining that of the 38 columns in the memorial, 36 symbolize the 36 states that were a part of the Union during Lincoln's Presidency, all of which are named on the frieze above the columns. And then I would go up the steps, reading the names of the states, noting that states from both the North and South are on the front facade: Massachusetts, Virginia, New York, Georgia.

Henry Bacon's design was an American version of a Greek Doric temple turned sideways, so that the long side became the front facade. The inner room, therefore, is comparatively shallow, and so when you walk inside the statue looks even bigger than it actually is, it's that close and in your face. Once I got past the columns, I stopped.

For the most part, visits to graves or memorial sites are a disappointment. You expect something to be there, to give you a sign, that all the marble and greenskeeping and landscaping mean something; that some version of the dead person is still around. And mostly nothing is there except trees, grass, the stone. In the Lincoln Memorial, however, I could swear some kind of magic has been accomplished. Henry Bacon's method of working was said to have been one of "ceaseless meditation." In the memorial, the presence of Lincoln seems to be all over the place.

I took my time looking up. He's up there, 11 feet of pedestal, 19 of statue. I concentrated first on his hands, the long fingers of the right one articulately, even delicately tensed as if about to make a gesture; the left one clenched in a loose, determined fist. After the hands I took in the huge booted feet and long legs, the broad shoulders and then finally—holding off, to extend the moment—I made my way to his magnificent face, those eyes. He is looking slightly down but mostly out, as if absorbed in his own thoughts yet knowing he must not sink too far or grow too introspective; there is a country to think of, and all those dead young men.

Beyond the top of his head, the inscription carved in the marble panel always fairly took my breath away: "In this temple/ as in the hearts of the people/ for whom he saved the Union/ the memory of Abraham Lincoln/ is enshrined forever." A newspaperman wrote those words, one Royal Cortissoz, then arts editor of the New York Herald Tribune. I would move from one side of the statue to another, taking it in from all angles. Aided by carefully orchestrated artificial lighting, sunlight falls softly through skylights in the ceiling, and bounces off the reflecting pool and on a clear day fills the memorial.

On either side of the statue are the limestone tablets on which are carved, on one side, the amazing Gettysburg Address and on the other, the even more moving and eloquent Second Inaugural Address. I made a point to read them, word by word, every time I went.

Hired to teach classes in the personal essay, I suggested to my students that when feeling confused about the form, they take a walk to the memorial and read those speeches. There they would find out the difference between certainty and smugness, between modesty and ambivalence.

I read those speeches many times. And every time I did, I felt moved and grounded again, as an American and as a writer. And afterward I would go down the steps feeling nourished and clean.

THE BEAUTIFUL PLACES

Kathleen Norris

The following is an excerpt from Norris's 1993 book Dakota.

> The Scarecrow sighed. "Of course I cannot understand it," he said. "If your heads were stuffed with straw like mine, you would probably all live in the beautiful places, and then Kansas would have no people at all. It is fortunate for Kansas that you have brains."
>
> —L. *Frank Baum,* The Wizard of Oz

The high plains, the beginning of the desert West, often act as a crucible for those who inhabit them. Like Jacob's angel, the region requires that you wrestle with it before it bestows a blessing. This can mean driving through a snowstorm on icy roads, wondering whether you'll have to pull over and spend the night in your car, only to emerge under tag ends of clouds into a clear sky blazing with stars. Suddenly you know what you're seeing: the earth has turned to face the center of the galaxy, and many more stars are visible than the ones we usually see on our wing of the spiral.

Or a vivid double rainbow marches to the east, following the wild summer storm that nearly blew you off the road. The storm sky is gun-metal gray, but to the west the sky is peach streaked with crimson. The land and sky of the West often fill what Thoreau termed our "need to witness our limits transgressed." Nature, in Dakota, can indeed be an experience of the holy.

More Americans than ever, well over 70 percent, now live in urban areas and tend to see Plains land as empty. What they really mean is devoid of human presence. Most visitors to Dakota travel on interstate highways that will take them as quickly as possible through the region, past our larger cities to such attractions as the Badlands and the Black Hills. Looking at the expanse of land in between, they may wonder why a person would choose to live in such a barren place, let alone love it. But mostly they are bored: they turn up the car stereo, count the miles to civilization, and look away.

Dakota is a painful reminder of human limits, just as cities and shopping malls are attempts to deny them. This book is an invitation to a land of little rain and few trees, dry summer winds and harsh winters, a land rich in grass and sky and surprises. On a crowded planet, this is a place inhabited by few, and by the circumstance of inheritance, I am one of them. Nearly twenty years ago I returned to the holy ground of my childhood summers; I moved from New York City to the house my mother had grown up in, in an isolated town on the border between North and South Dakota.

More than any other place I lived as a child or young adult—Virginia, Illinois, Hawaii, Vermont, New York—this is my spiritual geography, the place where I've wrestled my story out of the circumstances of landscape and inheritance. The word "geography" derives from the Greek words for earth and writing, and writing about Dakota has been my means of understanding that inheritance and reclaiming what is holy in it. Of course Dakota has always been such a matrix for its Native American inhabitants. But their tradition is not mine, and in returning to the Great Plains, where two generations of my family lived before me, I had to build on my own traditions, those of the Christian West.

When a friend referred to the western Dakotas as the Cappadocia of North America, I was handed an essential connection between the spirituality of the landscape I inhabit and that of the fourth-century monastics who set up shop in Cappadocia and the deserts of Egypt. Like those monks, I made a countercultural choice to live in what the rest of the world considers a barren waste. Like them, I had to stay in this place, like a scarecrow in a field, and hope for the brains to see its beauty. My idea of what makes a place beautiful had to change, and it has. The city no longer appeals to me for the cultural experiences and possessions I might acquire there, but because its population is less homogenous than Plains society. Its holiness is to be found in being open to humanity in all its diversity. And the western Plains now seem bountiful in their emptiness, offering solitude and room to grow.

I want to make it clear that my move did not take me "back to the land" in the conventional sense. I did not strike out on my own to make a go of it with "an acre and a cow," as a Hungarian friend naively imagined. As the homesteaders of the early twentieth century soon found out, it is not possible to survive on even 160 acres in western Dakota. My move was one that took me deep into the meaning of inheritance, as I had to try to fit myself into a complex network of long-established relationships.

My husband and I live in the small house in Lemmon, South Dakota, that my grandparents built in 1923. We moved there after they died because my mother, brother, and sisters, who live in Honolulu, did not want to hold an estate auction, the usual procedure when the beneficiaries of an inheritance on the Plains live far away. I offered to move there and manage the farm interests (land and a cattle herd) that my grandparents left us. David Dwyer, my husband, also a poet, is a New York City native who spent his childhood summers in the Adirondacks, and he had enough sense of adventure to agree to this. We expected to be in Dakota for just a few years.

It's hard to say why we stayed. A growing love of the prairie landscape and the quiet of a small town, inertia, and because as freelance writers, we found we had the survival skills suitable for a frontier. We put together a crazy quilt of jobs: I worked in the public library and as an artist-in-residence in schools in both Dakotas; I also did freelance writing and bookkeeping. David tended bar, wrote computer programs for a number of businesses in the region, and did freelance translation of French literature for several publishers. In 1979 we plunged into the cable television business with some friends, one of whom is an electronics expert. David learned how to climb poles and put up the hardware, and I kept the books. It was a good investment; after selling the company we found that we had bought ourselves a good three years to write. In addition, I still do bookkeeping for my family's farm business: the land is leased to people I've known all my life, people who have rented our land for two generations and also farm their own land and maintain their own cattle herds, an arrangement that is common in western Dakota.

In coming to terms with my inheritance, and pursuing my vocation as a writer, I have learned, as both farmers and writers have discovered before me, that it is not easy to remain on the Plains. Only one of North Dakota's best-known writers—Richard Critchfield, Louise Erdrich, Lois Hudson, and Larry Woiwode—currently lives in the state. And writing the truth about the Dakota experience can be a thankless task. I recently discovered that Lois Hudson's magnificent novel of the Dakota Dust Bowl, *The Bones of Plenty,* a book arguably better than *The Grapes of Wrath,* was unknown to teachers and librarians in a town not thirty miles from where the novel is set. The shame of it is that Hudson's book could have helped these people better understand their current situation, the economic crisis forcing many families off the land. Excerpts from *The Grapes of Wrath* were in a textbook used in the school, but students could keep them at a safe distance, part of that remote entity called "American literature" that has little relation to their lives.

The Plains are full of what a friend here calls "good telling stories," and while our sense of being forgotten by the rest of the world makes it all the more important that we preserve them and pass them on, instead we often neglect them. Perversely, we do not even claim those stories which have attracted national attention. Both John Neihardt and Frederick Manfred have written about Hugh Glass, a hunter and trapper mauled by a grizzly bear in 1823 at the confluence of the Little Moreau and Grand rivers just south of Lemmon. Left for dead by his companions, he crawled and limped some two hundred miles southeast, to the trading post at Fort Kiowa on the Missouri River. Yet when Manfred wanted to give a reading in Lemmon a few years ago, the publicist was dismissed by a high school principal who said, "Who's he? Why would our students be interested?" Manfred's audience of eighty—large for Lemmon—consisted mainly of the people who remembered him from visits he'd made in the early 1950s while researching his novel *Lord Grizzly*.

Thus are the young disenfranchised while their elders drown in details, "story" reduced to the social column of the weekly newspaper that reports on family reunions, card parties, even shopping excursions to a neighboring town. But real story is as hardy as grass, and it survives in Dakota in oral form. Good storytelling is one thing rural whites and Indians have in common. But Native Americans have learned through harsh necessity that people who survive encroachment by another culture need story to survive. And a storytelling tradition is something Plains people share with both ancient and contemporary monks: we learn our ways of being and reinforce our values by telling tales about each other.

One of my favorite monastic stories concerns two fourth-century monks who "spent fifty years mocking their temptations by saying 'After this winter, we will leave here.' When the summer came, they said, 'After this summer, we will go away from here.' They passed all their lives in this way." These ancient monks sound remarkably like the farmers I know in Dakota who live in what they laconically refer to as "next-year country."

We hold on to hopes for next year every year in western Dakota: hoping that droughts will end; hoping that our crops won't be hailed out in the few rainstorms that come; hoping that it won't be too windy on the day we harvest, blowing away five bushels an acre; hoping (usually against hope) that if we get a fair crop, we'll be able to get a fair price for it. Sometimes survival is the only blessing that the terrifying angel of the Plains bestows. Still, there are those born and raised here who can't imagine living anywhere else. There are also those who are drawn here—teachers willing to take the lowest salaries in the nation; clergy with theological degrees from Princeton, Cambridge, and Zurich who want to serve small rural churches—who find that they cannot remain for long. Their professional mobility sets them apart and becomes a liability in an isolated Plains community where outsiders are treated with an uneasy mix of hospitality and rejection.

"Extremes," John R. Milton suggests in his history of South Dakota, is "perhaps the key word for Dakota . . . What happens to extremes is that they come together, and the result is a kind of tension." I make no attempt in this book to resolve the tensions and contradictions I find in the Dakotas between hospitality and insularity, change and inertia, stability and instability, possibility and limitation, between hope and despair, between open hearts and closed minds.

I suspect that these are the ordinary contradictions of human life, and that they are so visible in Dakota because we are so few people living in a stark landscape. We are at the point of transition between East and West in America, geographically and psychically isolated from either coast, and unlike either the Midwest or the desert West. South Dakota has been dubbed both the Sunshine State and the Blizzard State, and both designations have a basis in fact. Without a strong identity we become a mythic void; "the Great Desolation," as novelist Ole Rolvaag wrote early in this century, or "The American Outback," as *Newsweek* designated us a few years ago.

Geographical and cultural identity is confused even within the Dakotas. The eastern regions of both states have more in common with each other than with the area west of the Missouri, colloquially called the "West River." Although I commonly use the term "Dakota" to refer to both Dakotas, most of my experience is centered in this western region, and it seems to me that especially in western Dakota we live in tension between myth and truth. Are we cowboys or farmers? Are we fiercely independent frontier types or community builders? One myth that haunts us is that the small town is a stable place. The land around us was divided neatly in 160-acre rectangular sections, following the Homestead Act of 1863 (creating many section-line roads with 90-degree turns). But our human geography has never been as orderly. The western Dakota communities settled by whites are, and always have been, remarkably unstable. The Dakotas have always been a place to be *from:* some 80 percent of homesteaders left within the first twenty years of settlement, and our boom-and-bust agricultural and oil industry economy has kept people moving in and out (mostly out) ever since. Many small-town schools and pulpits operate with revolving doors, adding to the instability.

When I look at the losses we've sustained in western Dakota since 1980 (about one fifth of the population in Perkins County, where I live, and a full third in neighboring Corson County) and at the human cost in terms of anger, distrust, and grief, it is the prairie descendants of the ancient desert monastics, the monks and nuns of Benedictine communities in the Dakotas, who inspire me to hope. One of the vows a Benedictine makes is *stability:* commitment to a particular community, a particular place. If this vow is countercultural by contemporary American standards, it is countercultural in the way that life on the Plains often calls us to be. Benedictines represent continuity in the boom-and-bust cycles of the Plains; they incarnate, and can articulate, the reasons people want to stay.

Terrence Kardong, a monk at an abbey in Dakota founded roughly a thousand years after their European motherhouse, has termed the Great Plains "a school for humility," humility being one goal of Benedictine life. He writes, "in this eccentric environment . . . certainly one is made aware that things are not entirely in control." In fact, he says, the Plains offer constant reminders that "we are quite powerless over circumstance." His abbey, like many Great Plains communities with an agricultural base, had a direct experience of powerlessness, going bankrupt in the 1920s. Then, and at several other times in the community's history, the monks were urged to move to a more urban environment.

Kardong writes, "We may be crazy, but we are not necessarily stupid . . . We built these buildings ourselves. We've cultivated these fields since the turn of the century. We watched from our dining room window the mirage of the Killdeer Mountains rise and fall on the horizon. We collected a library full of local history books and they belong here, not in Princeton. Fifty of our brothers lie down the hill in our cemetery. We have become as indigenous as the cottonwood trees . . . If you take us somewhere else, we lose our character, our history—maybe our soul."

A monk does not speak lightly of the soul, and Kardong finds in the Plains the stimulus to develop an inner geography. "A monk isn't supposed to need all kinds of flashy surroundings. We're supposed to have a beautiful inner landscape. Watching a storm pass from horizon to horizon fills your soul with reverence. It makes your soul expand to fill the sky."

Monks are accustomed to taking the long view, another countercultural stance in our fast-paced, anything-for-a-buck society which has corrupted even the culture of farming into "agribusiness." Kardong and many other writers of the desert West, including myself, are really speaking of values when they find beauty in this land no one wants. He writes: "We who are permanently camped here see things you don't see at 55 m.p.h. . . . We see white-faced calves basking in the spring grass like the lilies of the field. We see a chinook wind in January make rivulets run. We see dust-devils and lots of little things. We are grateful."

The so-called emptiness of the Plains is full of such miraculous "little things." The way native grasses spring back from a drought, greening before your eyes; the way a snowy owl sits on a fencepost, or a golden eagle hunts, wings outstretched over grassland that seems to go on forever. Pelicans rise noisily from a lake; an antelope stands stock-still, its tattooed neck like a message in unbreakable code; columbines, their long steins beaten down by hail, bloom in the mud, their whimsical and delicate flowers intact. One might see a herd of white-tailed deer jumping a fence; fox cubs wrestling at the door of their lair; cock pheasants stepping out of a medieval tapestry into windrowed hay; cattle bunched in the southeast corner of a pasture, anticipating a storm in the approaching thunderheads. And above all, one notices the quiet, the near-absence of human noise.

My spiritual geography is a study in contrasts. The three places with which I have the deepest affinity are Hawaii, where I spent my adolescent years; New York City, where I worked after college; and western South Dakota. Like many Americans of their generation, my parents left their small-town roots in the 1930s and moved often. Except for the family home in Honolulu—its yard rich with fruits and flowers (pomegranate, tangerine, lime, mango, plumeria, hibiscus, lehua, ginger, and bird-of-paradise)—and my maternal grandparents' house in a remote village in western Dakota—its modest and hard-won garden offering columbine, daisies and mint—all my childhood places are gone.

When my husband and I moved nearly twenty years ago from New York to that house in South Dakota, only one wise friend in Manhattan understood the inner logic of the journey. Others, appalled, looked up Lemmon, South Dakota (named for George Lemmon, a cattleman and wheeler-dealer of the early 1900s, and home of the Petrified Wood Park—the world's largest—a gloriously eccentric example of American folk art) in their atlases and shook their heads. How could I leave the artists' and writers' community in which I worked, the diverse and stimulating environment of a great city, for such barrenness? Had I lost my mind? But I was young, still in my twenties, an apprentice poet certain of the rightness of returning to the place where I suspected I would find my stories. As it turns out, the Plains have been essential not only for my growth as a writer, they have formed me spiritually. I would even say they have made me a human being.

St. Hilary, a fourth-century bishop (and patron saint against snake bites) once wrote, "Everything that seems empty is full of the angels of God." The magnificent sky above the Plains sometimes seems to sing this truth; angels seem possible in the wind-filled expanse. A few years ago a small boy named Andy who had recently moved to the Plains from Pennsylvania told me he knew an angel named Andy Le Beau. He spelled out the name for me and I asked him if the angel had visited him here. "Don't you know?" he said in the incredulous tone children adopt when adults seem stupefyingly ignorant. "Don't you know?" he said, his voice rising, "*This* is where angels drown."

Andy no more knew that he was on a prehistoric sea bed than he knew what *le beau* means in French, but some ancient wisdom in him had sensed great danger here; a terrifying but beautiful landscape in which we are at the mercy of the unexpected, and even angels proceed at their own risk.

TAKE THE F

■

Ian Frazier

This essay originally appeared in The New Yorker *in 1995 and was reprinted in* Best American Essays.

Brooklyn, New York, has the undefined, hard-to-remember shape of a stain. I never know what to tell people when they ask me where in it I live. It sits at the western tip of Long Island at a diagonal that does not conform neatly to the points of the compass. People in Brooklyn do not describe where they live in terms of north or west or south. They refer instead to their neighborhoods, and to the nearest subway lines. I live on the edge of Park Slope, a neighborhood by the crest of a low ridge that runs through the borough. Prospect Park is across the street. Airplanes in the landing pattern for La Guardia Airport sometimes fly right over my building; every few minutes, on certain sunny days, perfectly detailed airplane shadows slide down my building and up the building opposite in a blink. You can see my building from the plane—it's on the left-hand side of Prospect Park, the longer patch of green you cross after the expanse of Green-Wood Cemetery.

We moved to a co-op apartment in a four-story building a week before our daughter was born. She is now six. I grew up in the country and would not have expected ever to live in Brooklyn. My daughter is a city kid, with less sympathy for certain other parts of the country. When we visited Montana, she was disappointed by the scarcity of pizza places. I overheard her explaining—she was three or four then—to a Montana kid about Brooklyn. She said, "In Brooklyn, there is a lot of broken glass, so you have to wear shoes. And, there is good pizza." She is stern in her judgment of pizza. At the very low end of the pizza-ranking scale is some pizza she once had in New Hampshire, a category now called New Hampshire pizza. In the middle is some OK pizza she once had at the Bronx Zoo, which she calls zoo pizza. At the very top is the pizza at the pizza place where the big kids go, about two blocks from our house.

Our subway is the F train. It runs under our building and shakes the floor. The F is generally a reliable train, but one spring as I walked in the park I saw emergency vehicles gathered by a concrete-sheathed hole in the lawn. Firemen lifted a metal lid from the hole and descended into it. After a while, they reappeared, followed by a few people, then dozens of people, then a whole lot of people—passengers from a disabled F train, climbing one at a time out an exit shaft. On the F, I sometimes see large women in straw hats reading a newspaper called the *Caribbean Sunrise*, and Orthodox Jews bent over Talmudic texts in which the footnotes have footnotes, and groups of teenagers wearing identical red bandannas with identical red plastic baby pacifiers in the corners of their mouths, and female couples in porkpie hats, and young men with the silhouettes of the Manhattan skyline razored into their short side hair from one temple around to the other, and Russian-speaking men with thick wrists and big wristwatches, and a hefty, tall woman with long, straight blond hair who hums and closes her eyes and absently practices cello fingerings on the metal subway pole. As I watched the F-train passengers emerge among the grass and trees of Prospect Park, the faces were as varied as usual, but the expressions of indignant surprise were all about the same.

Just past my stop, Seventh Avenue, Manhattan-bound F trains rise from underground to cross the Gowanus Canal. The train sounds different—lighter, quieter—in the open air. From the elevated tracks, you can see the roofs of many houses stretching back up the hill to Park Slope, and a bumper crop of rooftop graffiti, and neon signs for Eagle Clothes and Kentile Floors, and flat expanses of factory roofs where seagulls stand on one leg around puddles in the sagging spots. There are fuel-storage tanks surrounded by earthen barriers, and slag piles, and conveyor belts leading down to the oil-slicked waters of the canal. On certain days, the sludge at the bottom of the canal causes it to bubble. Two men fleeing the police jumped in the canal a while ago; one made it across, the other quickly died. When the subway doors open at the Smith–Ninth Street stop, you can see the bay, and sometimes smell the ocean breeze. This stretch of elevated is the highest point of the New York subway system. To the south you can see the Verrazano-Narrows Bridge, to the north the World Trade towers. For just a few moments, the Statue of Liberty appears between passing buildings. Pieces of a neighborhood—laundry on clotheslines, a standup swimming pool, a plaster saint, a satellite dish, a rectangle of lawn—slide by like quickly dealt cards. Then the train descends again; growing over the wall just before the tunnel is a wisteria bush, which blooms pale blue every May.

I have spent days, weeks on the F train. The trip from Seventh Avenue to midtown Manhattan is long enough so that every ride can produce its own minisociety of riders, its own forty-minute Ship of Fools. Once a woman an arm's length from me on a crowded train pulled a knife on a man who threatened her. I remember the argument and the principals, but mostly I remember the knife—its flat, curved wood-grain handle inlaid with brass fittings at each end, its long, tapered blade. Once a man sang the words of the Lord's Prayer to a mournful, syncopated tune, and he fitted the mood of the morning so exactly that when he asked for money at the end the riders reached for their wallets and purses as if he'd pulled a gun. Once a big white kid with some friends was teasing a small old Hispanic lady, and when he got off the train I looked at him through the window and he slugged it hard next to my face. Once a thin woman and a fat woman sitting side by side had a long and loud conversation about someone they intended to slap silly: "Her butt be in the *hospital!*" "Bring out the ar-*tillery!*" The terminus of the F in Brooklyn is at Coney Island, not far from the beach. At an off hour, I boarded the train and found two or three passengers and, walking around on the floor, a crab. The passengers were looking at the crab. Its legs clicked on the floor like varnished fingernails. It moved in this direction, then that, trying to get comfortable. It backed itself under a seat, against the wall. Then it scooted out just after some new passengers had sat down there, and they really screamed. Passengers at the next stop saw it and laughed. When a boy lifted his foot as if to stomp it, everybody cried, "Noooh!" By the time we reached Jay Street–Borough Hall, there were maybe a dozen of us in the car, all absorbed in watching the crab. The car doors opened and a heavy-set woman with good posture entered. She looked at the crab; then, sternly, at all of us. She let a moment pass. Then she demanded, "*Whose is that?*" A few stops later, a short man with a mustache took a manila envelope, bent down, scooped the crab into it, closed it, and put it in his coat pocket.

The smells in Brooklyn: coffee, fingernail polish, eucalyptus, the breath from laundry rooms, pot roast, Tater Tots. A woman I know who grew up here says she moved away because she could not stand the smell of cooking food in the hallway of her parents' building. I feel just the opposite. I used to live in a converted factory above an army-navy store, and I like being in a place that smells like people live there. In the mornings, I sometimes wake to the smell of toast, and I still don't know exactly whose toast it is. And I prefer living in a borough of two and a half million inhabitants, the most of any borough in the city. I think of all the rural places, the pine-timbered canyons and within-commuting-distance farmland, that we are preserving by not living there. I like the immensities of the borough, the unrolling miles of Eastern Parkway and Ocean Parkway and Linden Boulevard, and the disheveled outlying parks strewn with tree limbs and with shards of glass held together by liquor-bottle labels, and the tough bridges—the Williamsburg and the Manhattan—and the gentle Brooklyn Bridge. And I like the way the people talk; some really do have Brooklyn accents, really do say "dese" and "dose." A week or two ago, a group of neighbors stood on a street corner watching a peregrine falcon on a building cornice contentedly eating a pigeon it had caught, and the sunlight came through its tail feathers, and a woman said to a man, "Look at the tail, it's so ah-range," and the man replied, "Yeah, I soar it." Like many Americans, I fear living in a nowhere, in a place that is noplace; in Brooklyn, that doesn't trouble me at all.

Everybody, it seems, is here. At Grand Army Plaza, I have seen traffic tie-ups caused by Haitians and others rallying in support of President Aristide, and by St. Patrick's Day parades, and by Jews of the Lubavitcher sect celebrating the birthday of their Grand Rebbe with a slow procession of ninety-three motor homes—one for each year of his life. Local taxis have bumper stickers that say "Allah Is Great"; one of the men who made the bomb that blew up the World Trade Center used an apartment just a few blocks from me. When an election is held in Russia, crowds line up to cast ballots at a Russian polling place in Brighton Beach. A while ago, I volunteer-taught reading at a public elementary school across the park. One of my students, a girl, was part Puerto Rican, part Greek, and part Welsh. Her looks were a lively combination, set off by sea-green eyes. I went to a map store in Manhattan and bought maps of Puerto Rico, Greece, and Wales to read with her, but they didn't interest her. A teacher at the school was directing a group of students to set up chairs for a program in the auditorium, and she said to me, "We have a problem here— each of these kids speaks a different language." She asked the kids to tell me where they were from. One was from Korea, one from Brazil, one from Poland, one from Guyana, one from Taiwan. In the program that followed, a chorus of fourth and fifth graders sang "God Bless America," "You're a Grand Old Flag," and "I'm a Yankee-Doodle Dandy."

People in my neighborhood are mostly white, and middle class or above. People in neighborhoods nearby are mostly not white, and mostly middle class or below. Everybody uses Prospect Park. On summer days, the park teems with sound—the high note is kids screaming in the water sprinklers at the playground, the midrange is radios and tape players, and the bass is idling or speeding cars. People bring lawn furniture and badminton nets and coolers, and then they barbecue. Charcoal smoke drifts into the neighborhood. Last year, local residents upset about the noise and litter and smoke began a campaign to outlaw barbecuing in the park. There was much unfavorable comment about "the barbecuers." Since most of the barbecuers, as it happens, are black or Hispanic, the phrase "Barbecuers Go Home," which someone spray-painted on the asphalt at the Ninth Street entrance to the park, took on a pointed, unkind meaning. But then park officials set up special areas for barbecuing, and the barbecuers complied, and the controversy died down.

Right nearby is a shelter for homeless people. Sometimes people sleep on the benches along the park, sometimes they sleep in the foyer of our building. Once I went downstairs, my heart pounding, to evict a homeless person who I had been told was there. The immediate, unquestioning way she left made me feel bad; later I always said "Hi" to her and gave her a dollar when I ran into her. One night, late, I saw her on the street, and I asked her her last name (by then I already knew her first name) and for a moment she couldn't recall it. At this, she shook her head in mild disbelief.

There's a guy I see on a bench along Prospect Park West all the time. Once I walked by carrying my year-old son, and the man said, "Someday he be carrying you." At the local copy shop one afternoon, a crowd was waiting for copies and faxes when a man in a houndstooth fedora came in seeking signatures for a petition to have the homeless shelter shut down. To my surprise, and his, the people in the copy shop instantly turned on him. "I suppose because they're poor they shouldn't even have a place to sleep at night," a woman said as he backed out the door. On the park wall across the street from my building, someone has written in black marker:

COPS PROTECT CITIZENS
WHO PROTECT US FROM COPS.

Sometimes I walk from my building downhill and north, along the Brooklyn waterfront, where cargo ships with scuffed sides and prognathous bows lean overhead. Sometimes I walk by the Brooklyn Navy Yard, its docks now too dormant to attract saboteurs, its long expanses of chainlink fence tangled here and there with the branches of ailanthus trees growing through. Sometimes I head southwest, keeping more or less to the high ground—Bay Ridge—along Fifth Avenue, through Hispanic neighborhoods that stretch in either direction as far as you can see, and then through block after block of Irish. I follow the ridge to its steep descent to the water at the Verrazano-Narrows; Fort Hamilton, an army post dating from 1814, is there, and a small Episcopal church called the Church of the Generals. Robert E. Lee once served as a vestryman of this church, and Stonewall Jackson was baptized here. Today the church is in the shade of a forest of high concrete columns supporting an access ramp to the Verrazano-Narrows Bridge.

Sometimes I walk due south, all the way out Coney Island Avenue. In that direction, as you approach the ocean, the sky gets bigger and brighter, and the buildings seem to flatten beneath it. Dry cleaners advertise "Tallis Cleaned Free with Every Purchase Over Fifteen Dollars." Then you start to see occasional lines of graffiti written in Cyrillic. Just past a Cropsey Avenue billboard welcoming visitors to Coney Island is a bridge over a creek filled nearly to the surface with metal shopping carts that people have tossed there over the years. A little farther on, the streets open onto the beach. On a winter afternoon, bundled-up women sit on the boardwalk on folding chairs around a portable record player outside a restaurant called Gastronom Moscow. The acres of trash-dotted sand are almost empty. A bottle of Peter the Great vodka lies on its side, drops of water from its mouth making a small depression in the sand. A man with trousers rolled up to his shins moves along the beach, chopping at driftwood with an ax. Another passerby says, "He's vorking hard, that guy!" The sunset unrolls light along the storefronts like tape. From the far distance, little holes in the sand at the water's edge mark the approach of a short man wearing hip boots and earphones and carrying a long-handled metal detector. Treasure hunters dream of the jewelry that people must have lost here over the years. Some say that this is the richest treasure beach in the Northeast. The man stops, runs the metal detector again over a spot, digs with a clamming shovel, lifts some sand, brushes through it with a gloved thumb, discards it. He goes on, leaving a trail of holes behind him.

I like to find things myself, and I always try to keep one eye on the ground as I walk. So far I have found seven dollars (a five and two ones), an earring in the shape of a strawberry, several personal notes, a matchbook with a 900 number to call to hear "prison sex fantasies," and two spent .25-caliber shells. Once on Carroll Street, I saw a page of text on the sidewalk, and I bent over to read it. It was page 191 from a copy of *Anna Karenina*. I read the whole page. It described Vronsky leaving a gathering and riding off in a carriage. In a great book, the least fragment is great. I looked up and saw a woman regarding me closely from a few feet away. "You're reading," she said wonderingly. "From a distance, I t'ought you were watchin' ants."

My favorite place to walk is the Brooklyn Botanic Garden, not more than fifteen minutes away. It's the first place I take out-of-towners, who may not associate Brooklyn with flowers. In the winter, the garden is drab as pocket lint, and you can practically see all the way through from Flatbush Avenue to Washington Avenue. But then in February or March a few flowerings begin, the snowdrops and the crocuses, and then the yellow of the daffodils climbs Daffodil Hill, and then the magnolias—star magnolias, umbrella magnolias, saucer magnolias—go off all at once, and walking among them is like flying through cumulus clouds. Then the cherry trees blossom, some a soft and glossy red like makeup, others pink as a dessert, and crowds fill the paths on weekends and stand in front of the blossoms in their best clothes and have their pictures taken. Security guards tell people, "No eating, no sitting on the grass—this is a garden, not a park." There are traffic jams of strollers, and kids running loose. One security guard jokes into his radio, "There's a pterodactyl on the overlook!" In the pond in the Japanese Garden, ducks lobby for pieces of bread. A duck quacks, in Brooklynese, "Yeah, yeah, yeah," having heard it all before.

Then the cherry blossoms fall, they turn some paths completely pink next to the grass's green, and the petals dry, and people tread them into a fine pink powder. Kids visit on end-of-school-year field trips, and teachers yell "Shawon, get back on line!" and boys with long T-shirts printed from neck to knee with an image of Martin Luther King's face run by laughing and swatting at one another. The yellow boxes that photographic film comes in fall on the ground, and here and there an empty bag of Crazy Calypso potato chips. The lilacs bloom, each bush with a scent slightly different from the next, and yellow tulips fill big round planters with color so bright it ascends in a column, like a searchlight beam. The roses open on the trellises in the Rose Garden and attract a lively air traffic of bees, and June wedding parties, brides and grooms and their subsidiaries, adjust themselves minutely for photographers there. A rose called the Royal Gold smells like a new bathing suit, and is as yellow.

In our building of nine apartments, two people have died and six have been born since we moved in. I like our neighbors—a guy who works for Off-Track Betting, a guy who works for the Department of Correction, a woman who works for Dean Witter, an in-flight steward, a salesperson of subsidiary rights at a publishing house, a restaurant manager, two lawyers, a retired machinist, a Lebanese-born woman of ninety-five—as well as any I've ever had. We keep track of the bigger events in the building with the help of Chris, our downstairs neighbor. Chris lives on the ground floor and often has conversations in the hall while her foot props her door open. When our kids are sick, she brings them her kids' videos to watch, and when it rains she gives us rides to school. One year, Chris became pregnant and had to take a blood-thinning medicine and was in and out of the hospital. Finally, she had a healthy baby and came home, but then began to bleed and didn't stop. Her husband brought the baby to us about midnight and took Chris to the nearest emergency room. Early the next morning, the grandmother came and took the baby. Then for two days nobody heard anything. When we knocked on Chris's door we got no answer, and when we called we got an answering machine. The whole building was expectant, spooky, quiet. The next morning I left the house and there in the foyer was Chris. She held her husband's arm, and she looked pale, but she was returning from the hospital under her own steam. I hugged her at the door, and it was the whole building hugging her. I walked to the garden seeing glory everywhere. I went to the Rose Garden and took a big Betsy McCall rose to my face and breathed into it as if it were an oxygen mask.

PASSING THROUGH TANGIERS

Jack Kerouac

This piece is a passage from Desolation Angels, *published in 1965.*

What a crazy picture, maybe the picture of the typical American, sitting on a boat mulling over fingernails wondering where to really go, what to do next—I suddenly realized I had nowhere to turn at all.

But it was on this trip that the great change took place in my life which I called a "complete turningabout" on that earlier page, turning from a youthful brave sense of adventure to a complete nausea concerning experience in the world at large, a *revulsion* in all the six senses. And as I say the first sign of that revulsion had appeared during the dreamy solitary comfort of the two months on Desolation mountain, before Mexico, since which time I'd been melanged again with all my friends and old adventures, as you saw, and not so 'sweetly,' but now I was alone again. And the same feeling came to me: Avoid the World, it's just a lot of dust and drag and means nothing in the end. But what to do instead? And here I was relentlessly being carried to further "adventures" across the sea. But it was really in Tangiers after an overdose of opium the turningabout really clicked down and locked. In a minute—but meanwhile another experience, at sea, put the fear of the world in me, like an omen warning. This was a huge tempest that whacked at our C-4 from the North, from the Januaries and Pleniaries of Iceland and Baffin Bay. During wartime I'd actually sailed in those Northern seas of the Arctic but it was only in summertime: now, a thousand miles south of these in the void of January Seas, gloom, the cappers came glurring in gray spray as high as a house and plowed rivers all over our bow and down the washes. Furyiating howling Blakean glooms, thunders of thumping, washing waving sick manship diddling like a long cork for nothing in the mad waste. Some old Breton knowledge of the sea still in my blood now shuddered. When I saw those walls of water advancing one by one for miles in gray carnage I cried in my soul WHY DIDNT I STAY HOME!? But it was too late. When the third night came the ship was heaving from side to side so badly even the Yugoslavs went to bed and jammed themselves down between pillows and blankets. The kitchen was insane all night with crashing and toppling pots even tho they'd been secured. It scares a seaman to hear the Kitchen scream in fear. For eating at first the steward had placed dishes on a wet tablecloth, and of course no soup in soupbowls but in deep cups, but now it was too late for even that. The men chewed at biscuits as they staggered to their knees in their wet sou'westers. Out on deck where I went a minute the heel of the ship was enough to kick you over the gunwale straight *at* walls of water, sperash. Deck lashed trucks groaned and broke their cables and smashed around. It was a Biblical Tempest like an old dream. In the night I prayed with fear to God Who was now taking all of us, the souls on board, at this dread particular time, for reasons of His own, at last. In my semi delirium I thought I saw a snow white ladder being held down to us from the sky. I saw Stella Maris over the Sea like a statue of Liberty in all shining white. I thought of all the sailors that ever drowned and O the choking thought of it, from Phoenicians of 3000 years ago to poor little teenage sailors of America only last war (some of whom I'd sailed in safety with)—The carpets of sinking water all deep blue *green* in the middle of the ocean, with their damnable patterns of foam, the sickening choking *too-much* of it even tho you're only looking at the surface—beneath all that the upwell of cold miles of fathoms—swaying, rolling, smashing, the tonnages of Peligroso Roar beating, heaving, swirling—not a face in sight! Here comes more! Duck! The whole ship (only as long as a Village) ducks into it shuddering, the crazy screws furiously turn in nothingness, shaking the ship, slap, the bow's now up, thrown up, the screws are dreaming deep below, the ship hasn't gained ten feet—it's like that—It's like frost in your face, like the cold mouths of ancient fathers, like wood cracking in the sea. Not even a fish in sight. It's the thunderous jubilation of Neptune and his bloody wind god canceling men. "All I had to do was stay home, give it all up, get a little home for me and Ma, meditate, live quiet, read in the sun, drink wine in the moon in old clothes, pet my kitties, sleep good dreams—now look at this *petrain* I got me in, Oh dammit!" ("Petrain" is a 16th Century French word meaning "mess.") But God chose to let us live as at dawn the captain turned the ship the other way and gradually left the storm behind, then headed back east towards Africa and the stars.

51

I feel I didn't explain that right, but it's too late, the moving finger crossed the storm and that's the storm.

I thereafter spent ten quiet days as that old freighter chugged and chugged across the calmest seas without seeming to get anywhere and I read a book on world history, wrote notes, and paced the deck at night. (How insouciantly they write about the sinking of the Spanish fleet in the storm off Ireland, ugh!) (Or even one little Galilean fisherman, drowned forever.) But even in so peaceful and simple an act as reading world history in a comfortable cabin on comfortable seas I felt that awful revulsion for everything—the insane things done in human history even before us, enough to make Apollo cry or Atlas drop his load, my God the massacres, purges, tithes stolen, thieves hanged, crooks imperatored, dubs praetorian'd, benches busted on people's heads, wolves attacked nomad campfires, Genghiz Khans ruining—testes smashed in battle, women raped in smoke, children belted, animals slaughtered, knives raised, bones thrown—Clacking big slurry meatjuiced lips the dub Kings crapping on everybody thru silk—The beggars crapping thru burlap—The mistakes everywhere the mistakes! The smell of old settlements and their cookpots and dungheaps—The Cardinals like "Silk stockings full of mud," the American congressmen who "shine and stink like rotten mackerel in the moonlight"—The scalpings from Dakota to Tamurlane—And the human eyes at Guillotine and burning stake at dawn, the glooms, bridges, mists, nets, raw hands and old dead vests of poor mankind in all these thousands of years of "history" (they call it) and all of it an awful mistake. Why did God do it? or is there really a Devil who led the Fall? Souls in Heaven said "We want to try mortal existence, O God, Lucifer said it's great!"—Bang, down we fall, to this, to concentration camps, gas ovens, barbed wire, atom bombs, television murders, Bolivian starvation, thieves in silk, thieves in neckties, thieves in office, paper shufflers, bureaucrats, insult, rage, dismay, horror, terrified nightmares, secret death of hangovers, cancer, ulcers, strangulation, pus, old age, old age homes, canes, puffed flesh, dropped teeth, stink, tears, and goodbye. Somebody else write it, I don't know how.

How to live with glee and peace therefore? By roaming around with your baggage from state to state each one worse deeper into the darkness of the fearful heart? And the heart only a thumping tube all delicately murderable with snips of artery and vein, with chambers that shut, finally someone eats it with the knife and fork of malice, laughing. (Laughing for awhile anyway.)

Ah but as Julien would say "There's nothing you can do about it, revel in it boy—Bottoms up in every way, Fernando." I think of Fernando his puffed alcoholic eyes like mine looking out on bleak palmettos at dawn, shivering in his scarf: beyond the last Frisian Hill a big scythe is cutting down the daisies of his hope tho he's urged to celebrate this each New Years Eve in Rio or in Bombay. In Hollywood they swiftly slide the old director in his crypt. Aldous Huxley half blind watches his house burn down, seventy years old and far from the happy walnut chair of Oxford. Nothing, nothing, nothing O but *nothing* could interest me any more for one god damned minute in anything in the *world*. But where else to go?

On the overdose of opium this was intensified to the point where I actually got up and packed to go back to America and find a *home*.

SHOOTING A FARMHOUSE

Ted Kooser

This poem is from Kooser's 1980 poetry collection Sure Signs.

The first few wounds are nearly invisible;
a truck rumbles past in the dust
and a .22 hole appears in the mailbox
like a fly landing there.
In a month you can see sky
through the tail of the windmill.
The attic windows grow black and uneasy.
When the last hen is found shot in the yard,
the old man and his wife move away.

In November, a Land Rover
flattens the gate like a tank
and pulls up in the yard. Hunters spill out
and throw down their pheasants like hats.
They blow out the rest of the windows,
set beer cans up on the porch rails
and shoot from the hip.
One of them walks up and yells in,
"Is anyone home?" getting a laugh.

By sunset, they've kicked down the door.
In the soft blush of light,
they blast holes in the plaster
and piss on the floors.

When the beer and the shells are all gone,
they drive sadly away,
the blare of their radio fading.
A breeze sighs in the shelterbelt.
Back in the house,
the newspapers left over from packing
the old woman's dishes
begin to blow back and forth through the rooms.

SHILOH

—■—

Bobbie Ann Mason

The following is the title story from Mason's 1982 collection Shiloh and Other Stories.

Leroy Moffitt's wife, Norma Jean, is working on her pectorals. She lifts three-pound dumbbells to warm up, then progresses to a twenty-pound barbell. Standing with her legs apart, she reminds Leroy of Wonder Woman.

"I'd give anything if I could just get these muscles to where they're real hard," says Norma Jean. "Feel this arm. It's not as hard as the other one."

"That's cause you're right-handed," says Leroy, dodging as she swings the barbell in an arc.

"Do you think so?"

"Sure."

Leroy is a truckdriver. He injured his leg in a highway accident four months ago, and his physical therapy, which involves weights and a pulley, prompted Norma Jean to try building herself up. Now she is attending a body-building class. Leroy has been collecting temporary disability since his tractor-trailer jackknifed in Missouri, badly twisting his left leg in its socket. He has a steel pin in his hip. He will probably not be able to drive his rig again. It sits in the backyard, like a gigantic bird that has flown home to roost. Leroy has been home in Kentucky for three months, and his leg is almost healed, but the accident frightened him and he does not want to drive any more long hauls. He is not sure what to do next. In the meantime, he makes things from craft kits. He started by building a miniature log cabin from notched Popsicle sticks. He varnished it and placed it on the TV set, where it remains. It reminds him of a rustic Nativity scene. Then he tried string art (sailing ships on black velvet), a macramé owl kit, a snap-together B-17 Flying Fortress, and a lamp made out of a model truck, with a light fixture screwed in the top of the cab. At first the kits were diversions, something to kill time, but now he is thinking about building a full-scale log house from a kit. It would be considerably cheaper than building a regular house, and besides, Leroy has grown to appreciate how things are put together. He has begun to realize that in all the years he was on the road he never took time to examine anything. He was always flying past scenery.

"They won't let you build a log cabin in any of the new subdivisions," Norma Jean tells him.

"They will if I tell them it's for you," he says, teasing her. Ever since they were married, he has promised Norma Jean he would build her a new home one day. They have always rented, and the house they live in is small and nondescript. It does not even feel like a home, Leroy realizes now.

Norma Jean works at the Rexall drugstore, and she has acquired an amazing amount of information about cosmetics. When she explains to Leroy the three stages of complexion care, involving creams, toners, and moisturizers, he thinks happily of other petroleum products—axle grease, diesel fuel. This is a connection between him and Norma Jean. Since he has been home, he has felt unusually tender about his wife and guilty over his long absences. But he can't tell what she feels about him. Norma Jean has never complained about his traveling; she has never made hurt remarks, like calling his truck a "widow-maker." He is reasonably certain she has been faithful to him, but he wishes she would celebrate his permanent homecoming more happily. Norma Jean is often startled to find Leroy at home, and he thinks she seems a little disappointed about it. Perhaps he reminds her too much of the early days of their marriage, before he went on the road. They had a child who died as an infant, years ago. They never speak about their memories of Randy, which have almost faded, but now that Leroy is home all the time, they sometimes feel awkward around each other, and Leroy wonders if one of them should mention the child. He has the feeling that they are waking up out of a dream together—that they must create a new marriage, start afresh. They are lucky they are still married. Leroy has read that for most people losing a child destroys the marriage—or else he heard this on *Donahue*. He can't always remember where he learns things anymore.

At Christmas, Leroy bought an electric organ for Norma Jean. She used to play the piano when she was in high school. "It don't leave you," she told him once. "It's like riding a bicycle."

The new instrument had so many keys and buttons that she was bewildered by it at first. She touched the keys tentatively, pushed some buttons, then pecked out "Chopsticks." It came out in an amplified fox-trot rhythm, with marimba sounds.

"It's an orchestra!" she cried.

The organ had a pecan-look finish and eighteen preset chords, with optional flute, violin, trumpet, clarinet, and banjo accompaniments. Norma Jean mastered the organ almost immediately. At first she played Christmas songs. Then she bought *The Sixties Songbook* and learned every tune in it, adding variations to each with the rows of brightly colored buttons.

"I didn't like these old songs back then," she said. "But I have this crazy feeling I missed something."

"You didn't miss a thing," said Leroy.

Leroy likes to lie on the couch and smoke a joint and listen to Norma Jean play "Can't Take My Eyes Off You" and "I'll Be Back." He is back again. After fifteen years on the road, he is finally settling down with the woman he loves. She is still pretty. Her skin is flawless. Her frosted curls resemble pencil trimmings.

Now that Leroy has come home to stay, he notices how much the town has changed. Subdivisions are spreading across western Kentucky like an oil slick. The sign at the edge of town says "Pop: 11,500"—only seven hundred more than it said twenty years before. Leroy can't figure out who is living in all the new houses. The farmers who used to gather around the courthouse square on Saturday afternoons to play checkers and spit tobacco juice have gone. It has been years since Leroy has thought about the farmers, and they have disappeared without his noticing.

Leroy meets a kid named Stevie Hamilton in the parking lot at the new shopping center. While they pretend to be strangers meeting over a stalled car, Stevie tosses an ounce of marijuana under the front seat of Leroy's car. Stevie is wearing orange jogging shoes and a T-shirt that says CHATTAHOOCHEE SUPER-RAT. His father is a prominent doctor who lives in one of the expensive subdivisions in a new white-columned brick house that looks like a funeral parlor. In the phone book under his name there is a separate number, with the listing "Teenagers."

"Where do you get this stuff?" asks Leroy. "From your pappy!"

"That's for me to know and you to find out," Stevie says. He is slit-eyed and skinny.

"What else you got?"

"What you interested in?"

"Nothing special. Just wondered."

Leroy used to take speed on the road. Now he has to go slowly. He needs to be mellow. He leans back against the car and says, "I'm aiming to build me a log house, soon as I get time. My wife, though, I don't think she likes the idea."

"Well, let me know when you want me again," Stevie says. He has a cigarette in his cupped palm, as thought sheltering it from the wind. He takes a long drag, then stomps it on the asphalt and slouches away.

Stevie's father was two years ahead of Leroy in high school. Leroy is thirty-four. He married Norma Jean when they were both eighteen, and their child Randy was born a few months later, but he died at the age of four months and three days. He would be about Stevie's age now. Norma Jean and Leroy were at the drive-in, watching a double feature (*Dr. Strangelove* and *Lover Come Back*), and the baby was sleeping in the back seat. When the first movie ended, the baby was dead. It was the sudden infant death syndrome. Leroy remembers handing Randy to a nurse at the emergency room, as though he were offering her a large doll as a present. A dead baby feels like a sack of flour. "It just happens sometimes," said the doctor, in what Leroy always recalls as a nonchalant tone. Leroy can hardly remember the child anymore, but he still sees vividly a scene from *Dr. Strangelove* in which the President of the United States was talking in a folksy voice on the hot line to the Soviet premier about the bomber accidentally headed toward Russia. He was in the War Room, and the world map was lit up. Leroy remembers Norma Jean catatonically beside him in the hospital and himself thinking: Who is this strange girl? He had forgotten who she was. Now scientists are saying that crib death is caused by a virus. Nobody knows anything, Leroy thinks. The answers are always changing.

When Leroy gets home from the shopping center, Norma Jean's mother, Mabel Beasley, is there. Until this year, Leroy has not realized how much time she spends with Norma Jean. When she visits, she inspects the closets and then the plants, informing Norma Jean when a plant is droopy or yellow. Mabel calls the plants "flowers," although there are never any blooms. She always notices if Norma Jean's laundry is piling up. Mabel is a short, overweight woman whose tight, brown-dyed curls look more like a wig than the actual wig she sometimes wears. Today she has brought Norma Jean an off-white dust ruffle she made for the bed; Mabel works in a custom-upholstery shop.

"This is the tenth one I made this year," Mabel says. "I got started and couldn't stop."

"It's real pretty," says Norma Jean.

"Now we can hide things under the bed," says Leroy, who gets along with his mother-in-law primarily by joking with her. Mabel has never really forgiven him for disgracing her by getting Norma Jean pregnant. When the baby died, she said that fate was mocking her.

"What's that thing?" Mabel says to Leroy in a loud voice, pointing to a tangle of yarn on a piece of canvas.

Leroy holds it up for Mabel to see. "It's my needlepoint," he explains. "This is a *Star Trek* pillow cover."

"That's what a woman would do," says Mabel. "Great day in the morning!"

"All the big football players on TV do it," he says.

"Why, Leroy, you're always trying to fool me. I don't believe you for one minute. You don't know what to do with yourself—that's the whole trouble. Sewing!"

"I'm aiming to build us a log house," says Leroy. "Soon as my plans come."

"Like *heck* you are," says Norma Jean. She takes Leroy's needlepoint and shoves it into a drawer. "You have to find a job first. Nobody can afford to build now anyway."

Mabel straightens her girdle and says, "I still think before you get tied down y'all ought to take a little run to Shiloh."

"One of these days, Mama," Norma Jean says impatiently.

Mabel is talking about Shiloh, Tennessee. For the past few years, she has been urging Leroy and Norma Jean to visit the Civil War battleground there. Mabel went there on her honeymoon—the only real trip she ever took. Her husband died of a perforated ulcer when Norma Jean was ten, but Mabel, who was accepted into the United Daughters of the Confederacy in 1975, is still preoccupied with going back to Shiloh.

"I've been to kingdom come and back in that truck out yonder," Leroy says to Mabel, "but we never yet set foot in that battleground. Ain't that something? How did I miss it?"

"It's not even that far," Mabel says.

After Mabel leaves, Norma Jean reads to Leroy from a list she has made. "Thing you could do," she announces. "You could get a job as a guard at Union Carbide, where they'd let you set on a stool. You could get on at the lumberyard. You could do a little carpenter work, if you want to build so bad. You could—"

"I can't do something where I'd have to stand up all day."

"You ought to try standing up all day behind a cosmetics counter. It's amazing that I have strong feet, coming from two parents that never had strong feet at all." At the moment Norma Jean is holding on to the kitchen counter, raising her knees one at a time as she talks. She is wearing two-pound ankle weights.

"Don't worry," says Leroy. "I'll do something."

"You could truck calves to slaughter for somebody. You wouldn't have to drive any big old truck for that."

"I'm going to build you this house," says Leroy. "I want to make you a real home."

"I don't want to live in any log cabin."

"It's not a cabin. It's a house."

"I don't care. It looks like a cabin."

"You and me together could lift those logs. It's just like lifting weights."

Norma Jean doesn't answer. Under her breath, she is counting. Now she is marching through the kitchen. She is doing goose steps.

Before his accident, when Leroy came home he used to stay in the house with Norma Jean, watching TV in bed and playing cards. She would cook fried chicken, picnic ham, chocolate pie—all his favorites. Now he is home alone much of the time. In the mornings, Norma Jean disappears, leaving a cooling place in the bed. She eats a cereal called Body Buddies, and she leaves the bowl on the table, with soggy tan balls floating in a milk puddle. He sees things about Norma Jean that he never realized before. When she chops onions, she stares off into a corner, as if she can't bear to look. She puts on her house slippers almost precisely at nine o'clock every evening and nudges her jogging shoes under the couch. She saves bread heels for the birds. Leroy watches the birds at the feeder. He notices the peculiar way goldfinches fly past the window. They close their wings, then fall, then spread their wings to catch and lift themselves. He wonders if they close their eyes when they fall. Norma Jean closes her eyes when they are in bed. She wants the lights turned out. Even then, he is sure she closes her eyes.

He goes for long drives around town. He tends to drive a car rather carelessly. Power steering and an automatic shift make a car feel so small and inconsequential that his body is hardly involved in the driving process. His injured leg stretches out comfortably. Once or twice he has almost hit something, but even the prospect of an accident seems minor in a car. He cruises the new subdivisions, feeling like a criminal rehearsing for a robbery. Norma Jean is probably right about a log house being inappropriate here in the new subdivisions. All the houses look grand and complicated. They depress him.

One day when Leroy comes home from a drive he finds Norma Jean in tears. She is in the kitchen making a potato and mushroom-soup casserole, with grated-cheese topping. She is crying because her mother caught her smoking.

"I didn't hear her coming. I was standing here puffing away pretty as you please," Norma Jean says, wiping her eyes.

"I knew it would happen sooner or later," says Leroy, putting his arm around her.

"She don't know the meaning of the word 'knock,'" says Norma Jean. "It's a wonder she hadn't caught me years ago."

"Think of it this way," Leroy says. "What if she caught me with a joint?"

"You better not let her!" Norma Jean shrieks. "I'm warning you, Leroy Moffitt!"

"I'm just kidding. Here, play me a tune. That'll help you relax."

Norma Jean puts the casserole in the oven and sets the timer. Then she plays a ragtime tune, with horns and banjo, as Leroy lights up a joint and lies on the couch, laughing to himself about Mabel's catching him at it. He thinks of Stevie Hamilton—a doctor's son pushing grass. Everything is funny. The whole town seems crazy and small. He is reminded of Virgil Mathis, a boastful policeman Leroy used to shoot pool with. Virgil recently led a drug bust in a back room at a bowling alley, where he seized ten thousand dollars' worth of marijuana. The newspaper had a picture of him holding up the bags of grass and grinning widely. Right now, Leroy can imagine Virgil breaking down the door and arresting him with a lungful of smoke. Virgil would probably have been alerted to the scene because of all the racket Norma Jean is making. Now she sounds like a hard-rock band. Norma Jean is terrific. When she switches to a Latin-rhythm version of "Sunshine Superman," Leroy hums along. Norma Jean's foot goes up and down, up and down.

"Well, what do you think?" Leroy says, when Norma Jean pauses to search through her music.

"What do I think about what?"

His mind has gone blank. Then he says, "I'll sell my rig and build us a house." That wasn't what he wanted to say. He wanted to know what she thought—what she *really* thought—about them.

"Don't start in on that again," says Norma Jean. She begins playing "Who'll Be the Next in Line?"

Leroy used to tell hitchhikers his whole life story—about his travels, his hometown, the baby. He would end with a question: "Well, what do you think?" It was just a rhetorical question. In time, he had the feeling that he'd been telling the same story over and over to the same hitchhikers. He quit talking to hitchhikers when he realized how his voice sounded— whining and self-pitying, like some teenage-tragedy song. Now Leroy has the sudden impulse to tell Norma Jean about himself, as if he had just met her. They have known each other so long they have forgotten a lot about each other. They could become reacquainted. But when the oven timer goes off and she runs to the kitchen, he forgets why he wants to do this.

The next day, Mabel drops by. It is Saturday and Norma Jean is cleaning. Leroy is studying the plans of his log house, which have finally come in the mail. He has them spread out on the table—big sheets of stiff blue paper, with diagrams and numbers printed in white. While Norma Jean runs the vacuum, Mabel drinks coffee. She sets her coffee cup on a blueprint.

"I'm just waiting for time to pass," she says to Leroy drumming her fingers on the table.

As soon as Norma Jean switches off the vacuum, Mabel says in a loud voice, "Did you hear about the datsun dog that killed the baby?"

Norma Jeans says, "The word is 'dachshund.'"

"They put the dog on trial. It chewed the baby's legs off. The mother was in the next room all the time." She raises her voice. "They thought it was neglect."

Norma Jean is holding her ears. Leroy manages to open the refrigerator and get some Diet Pepsi to offer Mabel. Mabel still has some coffee and she waves away the Pepsi.

"Datsuns are like that," Mabel says. "They're jealous dogs. They'll tear a place to pieces if you don't keep an eye on them."

"You better watch out what you're saying, Mabel," says Leroy.

"Well, facts is facts."

Leroy looks out the window at his rig. It is like a huge piece of furniture gathering dust in the backyard. Pretty soon it will be an antique. He hears the vacuum cleaner. Norma Jean seems to be cleaning the living room rug again.

Later, she says to Leroy, "She just said that about the baby because she caught me smoking. She's trying to pay me back."

"What are you talking about?" Leroy says, nervously shuffling blueprints.

"You know good and well," Norma Jean says. She is sitting in a kitchen chair with her feet up and her arms wrapped around her knees. She looks small and helpless. She says, "The very idea, her bringing up a subject like that! Saying it was neglect."

"She didn't mean that," Leroy says.

"She might not have *thought* she meant it. She always says things like that. You don't know how she goes on."

"But she didn't really mean it. She was just talking."

Leroy opens a king-sized bottle of beer and pours it into two glasses, dividing it carefully. He hands a glass to Norma Jean and she takes it from him mechanically. For a long time, they sit by the kitchen window watching the birds at the feeder.

Something is happening. Norma Jean is going to night school. She has graduated from her six-week body-building course and now she is taking an adult-education course in composition at Paducah Community College. She spends her evenings outlining paragraphs.

"First you have a topic sentence," she explains to Leroy. "Then you divide it up. Your secondary topic has to be connected to your primary topic."

To Leroy, this sounds intimidating. "I never was any good in English," he says.

"It makes a lot of sense."

"What are you doing this for, anyhow?"

She shrugs. "It's something to do." She stands up and lifts her dumbbells a few times.

"Driving a rig, nobody cared about my English."

"I'm not criticizing your English."

Norma Jean used to say, "If I lose ten minutes' sleep, I just drag all day." Now she stays up late, writing compositions. She got a B on her first paper—a how-to theme on soup-based casseroles. Recently Norma Jean has been cooking unusual foods—tacos, lasagna, Bombay chicken. She doesn't play the organ anymore, though her second paper was called "Why Music Is Important to Me." She sits at the kitchen table, concentrating on her outlines, while Leroy plays with his log house plans, practicing with a set of Lincoln Logs. The thought of getting a truckload of notched, numbered logs scares him, and he wants to be prepared. As he and Norma Jean work together at the kitchen table, Leroy has the hopeful thought that they are sharing something, but he knows he is a fool to think this. Norma Jean is miles away. He knows he is going to lose her. Like Mabel, he is just waiting for time to pass.

One day, Mabel is there before Norma Jean gets home from work, and Leroy finds himself confiding in her. Mabel, he realizes, must know Norma Jean better than he does.

"I don't know what's got into that girl," Mabel says. "She used to go to bed with the chickens. Now you say she's up all hours. Plus her a-smoking. I like to died."

"I want to make her this beautiful home," Leroy says, indicating the Lincoln Logs. "I don't think she even wants it. Maybe she was happier with me gone."

"She don't know what to make of you, coming home like this."

"Is that it?"

Mabel takes the roof off his Lincoln Log cabin. "You couldn't get *me* in a log cabin," she says. "I was raised in one. It's no picnic, let me tell you."

"They're different now," says Leroy.

"I tell you what," Mabel says, smiling oddly at Leroy.

"What?"

"Take her on down to Shiloh. Y'all need to get out together, stir a little. Her brain's all balled up over them books."

Leroy can see traces of Norma Jean's features in her mother's face. Mabel's face has the texture of crinkled cotton, but suddenly she looks pretty. It occurs to Leroy that Mabel has been hinting all along that she wants them to take her with them to Shiloh.

"Let's all go to Shiloh," he says. "You and me and her. Come Sunday."

Mabel throws up her hands in protest. "Oh, no, not me. Young folks want to be by theirselves."

When Norma Jean comes in with groceries, Leroy says excitedly, "Your mama here's been dying to go to Shiloh for thirty-five years. It's about time we went, don't you think?"

"I'm not going to butt in on anybody's second honeymoon," Mabel says.

"Who's going on a honeymoon, for Christ's sake?" Norma Jean says loudly.

"I never raised no daughter of mine to talk that-a-way," Mabel says.

"You ain't seen nothing yet," says Norma Jean. She starts putting away boxes and cans, slamming cabinet doors.

"There's a log cabin at Shiloh." Mabel says, "It was there during the battle. There's bullet holes in it."

"When are you going to *shut up* about Shiloh, Mama?" asks Norma Jean.

"I always thought Shiloh was the prettiest place, so full of history," Mabel goes on. "I just hoped y'all could see it once before I die, so you could tell me about it." Later, she whispers to Leroy, "You do what I said. A little change is what she needs."

"Your name means 'the king,'" Norma Jean says to Leroy that evening. He is trying to get her to go to Shiloh, and she is reading a book about another century.

"Well, I reckon I ought to be right proud."

"I guess so."

"Am I still king around here?"

Norma Jean flexes her biceps and feels them for hardness. "I'm not fooling around with anybody, if that's what you mean," she says.

"Would you tell me if you were?"

"I don't know."

"What does *your* name mean?"

"It was Marilyn Monroe's real name."

"No kidding!"

"Norma comes from the Normans. They were invaders," she says. She closes her book and looks hard at Leroy. "I'll go to Shiloh with you if you'll stop staring at me."

On Sunday, Norma Jean packs a picnic and they go to Shiloh. To Leroy's relief, Mabel says she does not want to come with them. Norma Jean drives, and Leroy, sitting beside her, feels like some boring hitchhiker she has picked up. He tries some conversation, but she answers him in monosyllables. At Shiloh, she drives aimlessly through the park, past bluffs and trails and steep ravines. Shiloh is an immense place, and Leroy cannot see it as a battleground. It is not what he expected. He thought it would look like a golf course. Monuments are everywhere, showing through the thick clusters of trees. Norma Jean passes the log cabin Mabel mentioned. It is surrounded by tourists looking for bullet holes.

"That's not the kind of log house I've got in mind," says Leroy apologetically.

"I know *that*."

"This is a pretty place. Your mama was right."

"It's O.K.," says Norma Jean. "Well, we've seen it. I hope she's satisfied."

They burst out laughing together.

At the park museum, a movie on Shiloh is shown every half hour, but they decide that they don't want to see it. They buy a souvenir Confederate flag for Mabel, and then they find a picnic spot near the cemetery. Norma Jean has brought a picnic cooler, with pimiento sandwiches, soft drinks, and Yodels. Leroy eats a sandwich and then smokes a joint, hiding it behind the picnic cooler. Norma Jean has quit smoking altogether. She is picking cake crumbs from the cellophane wrapper, like a fussy bird.

Leroy says, "So the boys in gray ended up in Corinth. The Union soldiers zapped 'em finally. April 7, 1862."

They both know that he doesn't know any history. He is just talking about some of the historical plaques they have read. He feels awkward, like a boy on a date with an older girl. They are still just making conversation.

"Corinth is where Mama eloped to," says Norma Jean.

They sit in silence and stare at the cemetery for the Union dead and, beyond, at a tall cluster of trees. Campers are parked nearby, bumper to bumper, and small children in bright clothing are cavorting and squealing. Norma Jean wads up the cake wrapper and squeezes it tightly in her hand. Without looking at Leroy, she says, "I want to leave you."

Leroy takes a bottle of Coke out of the cooler and flips off the cap. He holds the bottle poised near his mouth but cannot remember to take a drink. Finally he says, "No, you don't."

"Yes, I do."

"I won't let you."

"You can't stop me."

"Don't do me that way."

Leroy knows Norma Jean will have her own way. "Didn't I promise to be home from now on?" he says.

"In some ways, a woman prefers a man who wanders," says Norma Jean. "That sounds crazy, I know."

"You're not crazy."

Leroy remembers to drink from his Coke. Then he says, "Yes, you *are* crazy. You and me could start all over again. Right back at the beginning."

"We *have* started all over again," says Norma Jean. "And this is how it turned out."

"What did I do wrong?"

"Nothing."

"Is this one of those women's lib things?" Leroy asks.

"Don't be funny."

The cemetery, a green slope dotted with white markers, looks like a subdivision site. Leroy is trying to comprehend that his marriage is breaking up, but for some reason he is wondering about white slabs in a graveyard.

"Everything was fine till Mama caught me smoking," says Norma Jean, standing up. "That set something off."

"What are you talking about?"

"She won't leave me alone—*you* won't leave me alone." Norma Jean seems to be crying, but she is looking away from him. "I feel eighteen again. I can't face that all over again." She starts walking away. "No, it *wasn't* fine. I don't know what I'm saying. Forget it."

Leroy takes a lungful of smoke and closes his eyes as Norma Jean's words sink in. He tries to focus on the fact that thirty-five hundred soldiers died on the grounds around him. He can only think of that war as a board game with plastic soldiers. Leroy almost smiles, as he compares the Confederates' daring attack on the Union camps and Virgil Mathis's raid on the bowling alley. General Grant, drunk and furious, shoved the Southerners back to Corinth, where Mabel and Jet Beasley were married years later, when Mabel was still thin and good-looking. The next day, Mabel and Jet visited the battleground, and then Norma Jean was born, and then she married Leroy and they had a baby, which they lost, and now Leroy and Norma Jean are here at the same battleground. Leroy knows he is leaving out a lot. He is leaving out the insides of history. History was always just names and dates to him. It occurs to him that building a house out of logs is similarly empty—too simple. And the real inner workings of a marriage, like most of history, have escaped him. Now he sees that building a log house is the dumbest idea he could have had. It was clumsy of him to think Norma Jean would want a log house. It was a crazy idea. He'll have to think of something else, quickly. He will wad the blueprints into tight balls and fling them into the lake. Then he'll get moving again. He opens his eyes. Norma Jean has moved away and is walking through the cemetery, following a serpentine brick path.

Leroy gets up to follow his wife, but his good leg is asleep and his bad leg still hurts him. Norma Jean is far away, walking rapidly toward the bluff by the river, and he tries to hobble toward her, Some children run past him, screaming noisily. Norma Jean has reached the bluff, and she is looking out over the Tennessee River. Now she turns toward Leroy and waves her arms. Is she beckoning to him? She seems to be doing an exercise for her chest muscles. The sky is unusually pale—the color of the dust ruffle Mabel made for their bed.

ROMAN FEVER

—■—

Edith Wharton

The following story is reprinted from Wharton's 1936 book The World Over.

From the table at which they had been lunching two American ladies of ripe but well-cared-for middle age moved across the lofty terrace of the Roman restaurant and, leaning on its parapet, looked first at each other, and then down on the out-spread glories of the Palatine and the Forum, with the same expression of vague but benevolent approval.

As they leaned there a girlish voice echoed up gaily from the stairs leading to the court below. "Well, come along, then," it cried, not to them but to an invisible companion, "and let's leave the young things to their knitting"; and a voice as fresh laughed back: "Oh, look here, Babs, not actually *knitting*—" "Well, I mean figuratively," rejoined the first. "After all, we haven't left our poor parents much else to do. . . . " and at that point the turn of the stairs engulfed the dialogue.

The two ladies looked at each other again, this time with a tingle of smiling embarrassment, and the smaller and paler one shook her head and colored slightly.

"Barbara!" she murmured, sending an unheard rebuke after the mocking voice in the stairway.

The other lady, who was fuller, and higher in color, with a small determined nose supported by vigorous black eyebrows, gave a good-humored laugh. "That's what our daughters think of us!"

Her companion replied by a deprecating gesture. "Not of us individually. We must remember that. It's just the collective modern idea of Mothers. And you see—" Half-guiltily she drew from her handsomely mounted black handbag a twist of crimson silk run through by two fine knitting needles. "One never knows," she murmured. "The new system has certainly given us a good deal of time to kill; and sometimes I get tired just looking—even at this." Her gesture was now addressed to the stupendous scene at their feet.

The dark lady laughed again, and they both relapsed upon the view, contemplating it in silence, with a sort of diffused serenity which might have been borrowed from the spring effulgence of the Roman skies. The luncheon hour was long past, and the two had their end of the vast terrace to themselves. At its opposite extremity a few groups, detained by a lingering look at the outspread city, were gathering up guidebooks and fumbling for tips. The last of them scattered, and the two ladies were alone on the air-washed height.

"Well, I don't see why we shouldn't just stay here," said Mrs. Slade, the lady of the high color and energetic brows. Two derelict basket chairs stood near, and she pushed them into the angle of the parapet, and settled herself in one, her gaze upon the Palatine. "After all, it's still the most beautiful view in the world."

"It always will be, to me," assented her friend Mrs. Ansley, with so slight a stress on the "me" that Mrs. Slade, though she noticed it, wondered if it were not merely accidental, like the random underlinings of old-fashioned letter writers.

"Grace Ansley was always old-fashioned," she thought; and added aloud, with a retrospective smile: "It's a view we've both been familiar with for a good many years. When we first met here we were younger than our girls are now. You remember?"

"Oh, yes, I remember," murmured Mrs. Ansley, with the same undefinable stress. "There's that headwaiter wondering," she interpolated. She was evidently far less sure than her companion of herself and of her rights in the world.

"I'll cure him of wondering:" said Mrs. Slade, stretching her hand toward a bag as discreetly opulent-looking as Mrs. Ansley's. Signing to the headwaiter, she explained that she and her friend were old lovers of Rome, and would like to spend the end of the afternoon looking down on the view—that is, if it did not disturb the service? The headwaiter, bowing over her gratuity, assured her that the ladies were most welcome, and would be still more so if they would condescend to remain for dinner. A full-moon night, they would remember. . . .

Mrs. Slade's black brows drew together, as though references to the moon were out of place and even unwelcome. But she smiled away her frown as the headwaiter retreated. "Well, why not? We might do worse. There's no knowing, I suppose, when the girls will be back. Do you even know back from *where?* I don't!"

Mrs. Ansley again colored slightly. "I think those young Italian aviators we met at the Embassy invited them to fly to Tarquinia for tea. I suppose they'll want to wait and fly back by moonlight."

"Moonlight—moonlight! What a part it still plays. Do you suppose they're as sentimental as we were?"

"I've come to the conclusion that I don't in the least know what they are," said Mrs. Ansley. "And perhaps we didn't know much more about each other."

"No; perhaps we didn't."

Her friend gave her a shy glance. "I never should have supposed you were sentimental, Alida."

"Well, perhaps I wasn't." Mrs. Slade drew her lids together in retrospect; and for a few moments the two ladies, who had been intimate since childhood, reflected how little they knew each other. Each one, of course, had a label ready to attach to the other's name; Mrs. Delphin Slade, for instance, would have told herself, or anyone who asked her, that Mrs. Horace Ansley, twenty-five years ago, had been exquisitely lovely—no, you wouldn't believe it, would you? . . . though, of course, still charming, distinguished. . . . Well, as a girl she had been exquisite;

far more beautiful than her daughter Barbara, though certainly Babs, according to the new standards at any rate, was more effective—had more *edge,* as they say. Funny where she got it, with those two nullities as parents. Yes; Horace Ansley was—well, just the duplicate of his wife. Museum specimens of old New York. Good-looking, irreproachable, exemplary. Mrs. Slade and Mrs. Ansley had lived opposite each other—actually as well as figuratively—for years. When the drawing-room curtains in No. 20 East 73rd Street were renewed, No. 23, across the way, was always aware of it. And of all the movings, buyings, travels, anniversaries, illnesses—the tame chronicle of an estimable pair. Little of it escaped Mrs. Slade. But she had grown bored with it by the time her husband made his big *coup* in Wall Street, and when they bought in upper Park Avenue had already begun to think: "I'd rather live opposite a speakeasy for a change; at least one might see it raided." The idea of seeing Grace raided was so amusing that (before the move) she launched it at a woman's lunch. It made a hit, and went the rounds—she sometimes wondered if it had crossed the street, and reached Mrs. Ansley. She hoped not, but didn't much mind. Those were the days when respectability was at a discount, and it did the irreproachable no harm to laugh at them a little.

A few years later, and not many months apart, both ladies lost their husbands. There was an appropriate exchange of wreaths and condolences, and a brief renewal of intimacy in the half-shadow of their mourning; and now, after another interval, they had run across each other in Rome, at the same hotel, each of them the modest appendage of a salient daughter. The similarity of their lot had again drawn them together, lending itself to mild jokes, and the mutual confession that, if in old days it must have been tiring to "keep up" with daughters, it was now, at times, a little dull not to.

No doubt, Mrs. Slade reflected, she felt her unemployment more than poor Grace ever would. It was a big drop from being the wife of Delphin Slade to being his widow. She had always regarded herself (with a certain conjugal pride) as his equal in social gifts, as contributing her full share to the making of the exceptional couple they were: but the difference after his death was irremediable. As the wife of the famous corporation lawyer, always with an international case or two on hand, every day brought its exciting and unexpected obligation: the impromptu entertaining of eminent colleagues from abroad, the hurried dashes on legal business to London, Paris or Rome, where the entertaining was so handsomely reciprocated; the amusement of hearing in her wake: "What, that handsome woman with the good clothes and the eyes is Mrs. Slade—*the* Slade's wife? Really? Generally the wives of celebrities are such frumps."

Yes; being *the* Slade's widow was a dullish business after that. In living up to such a husband all her faculties had been engaged; now she had only her daughter to live up to, for the son who seemed to have inherited his father's gifts had died suddenly in boyhood. She had fought through that agony because her husband was there, to be helped and to help; now, after the father's death, the thought of the boy had become unbearable. There was nothing left but to mother her daughter; and dear Jenny was such a perfect daughter that she needed no excessive mothering. "Now with Babs Ansley I don't know that I *should* be so quiet," Mrs. Slade sometimes half-enviously reflected; but Jenny, who was younger than her brilliant friend, was that rare accident, an extremely pretty girl who somehow made youth and prettiness seem as safe as their absence. It was all perplexing—and to Mrs. Slade a little boring. She wished that Jenny would fall in love—with the wrong man, even; that she might have to be watched, out-maneuvered, rescued. And instead, it was Jenny who watched her mother, kept her out of drafts, made sure that she had taken her tonic. . . .

Mrs. Ansley was much less articulate than her friend, and her mental portrait of Mrs. Slade was slighter, and drawn with fainter touches. "Alida Slade's awfully brilliant; but not as brilliant as she thinks," would have summed it up; though she would have added, for the enlightenment of strangers, that Mrs. Slade had been an extremely dashing girl; much more so than her daughter, who was pretty, of course, and clever in a way, but had none of her mother's—well, "vividness," someone had once called it. Mrs. Ansley would take up current words like this, and cite them in quotation marks, as unheard-of audacities. No; Jenny was not like her mother. Sometimes Mrs. Ansley thought Alida Slade was disappointed; on the whole she had had a sad life. Full of failures and mistakes; Mrs. Ansley had always been rather sorry for her. . . .

So these two ladies visualized each other, each through the wrong end of her little telescope.

2

For a long time they continued to sit side by side without speaking. It seemed as though, to both, there was a relief in laying down their somewhat futile activities in the presence of the vast Memento Mori which faced them. Mrs. Slade sat quite still, her eyes fixed on the golden slope of the Palace of the Caesars, and after a while Mrs. Ansley ceased to fidget with her bag, and she too sank into meditation. Like many intimate friends, the two ladies had never before had occasion to be silent together, and Mrs. Ansley was slightly embarrassed by what seemed, after so many years, a new stage in their intimacy, and one with which she did not yet know how to deal.

Suddenly the air was full of that deep clangor of bells which periodically covers Rome with a roof of silver. Mrs. Slade glanced at her wristwatch. "Five o'clock already," she said, as though surprised.

Mrs. Ansley suggested interrogatively: "There's bridge at the Embassy at five." For a long time Mrs. Slade did not answer. She appeared to be lost in contemplation, and Mrs. Ansley thought the remark had escaped her. But after a while she said, as if speaking out of a dream: "Bridge, did you say? Not unless you want to. . . . But I don't think I will, you know."

"Oh, no," Mrs. Ansley hastened to assure her. "I don't care to at all. It's so lovely here; and so full of old memories, as you say." She settled herself in her chair, and almost furtively drew forth her knitting. Mrs. Slade took sideway note of this activity, but her own beautifully cared-for hands remained motionless on her knee.

"I was just thinking," she said slowly, "what different things Rome stands for to each generation of travelers. To our grandmothers, Roman fever; to our mothers, sentimental dangers—how we used to be guarded!—to our daughters, no more dangers than the middle of Main Street. They don't know it—but how much they're missing!"

The long golden light was beginning to pale, and Mrs. Ansley lifted her knitting a little closer to her eyes. "Yes; how we were guarded!"

"I always used to think," Mrs. Slade continued, "that our mothers had a much more difficult job than our grandmothers. When Roman fever stalked the streets it must have been comparatively easy to gather in the girls at the danger hour; but when you and I were young, with such beauty calling us, and the spice of disobedience thrown in, and no worse risk than catching cold during the cool hour after sunset, the mothers used to be put to it to keep us in—didn't they?"

She turned again toward Mrs. Ansley, but the latter had reached a delicate point in her knitting. "One, two, three—slip two; yes, they must have been," she assented, without looking up.

Mrs. Slade's eyes rested on her with a deepened attention. "She can knit—in the face of *this!* How like her. . . . "

Mrs. Slade leaned back, brooding, her eyes ranging from the ruins which faced her to the long green hollow of the Forum, the fading glow of the church fronts beyond it, and the outlying immensity of the Colosseum. Suddenly she thought: "It's all very well to say that our girls have done away with sentiment and moonlight. But if Babs Ansley isn't out to catch that young aviator—the one who's a Marchese—then I don't know anything. And Jenny has no chance beside her. I know that too. I wonder if that's why Grace Ansley likes the two girls to go everywhere together? My poor Jenny as a foil—!" Mrs. Slade gave a hardly audible laugh, and at the sound Mrs. Ansley dropped her knitting.

"Yes—?"

"I—oh, nothing. I was only thinking how your Babs carries everything before her. That Campolieri boy is one of the best matches in Rome. Don't look so innocent, my dear—you know he is. And I was wondering, ever so respectfully, you understand . . . wondering how two such exemplary characters as you and Horace had managed to produce anything quite so dynamic." Mrs. Slade laughed again, with a touch of asperity.

Mrs. Ansley's hands lay inert across her needles. She looked straight out at the great accumulated wreckage of passion and splendor at her feet. But her small profile was almost expressionless. At length she said: "I think you overrate Babs, my dear."

Mrs. Slade's tone grew easier. "No; I don't. I appreciate her. And perhaps envy you. Oh, my girl's perfect; if I were a chronic invalid I'd—well, I think I'd rather be in Jenny's hands. There must be times . . . but there! I always wanted a brilliant daughter . . . and never quite understood why I got an angel instead."

Mrs. Ansley echoed her laugh in a faint murmur. "Babs is an angel too."

"Of course—of course! But she's got rainbow wings. Well, they're wandering by the sea with their young men; and here we sit . . . and it all brings back the past a little too acutely."

Mrs. Ansley had resumed her knitting. One might almost have imagined (if one had known her less well, Mrs. Slade reflected) that, for her also, too many memories rose from the lengthening shadows of those august rains. But no; she was simply absorbed in her work. What was there for her to worry about? She knew that Babs would almost certainly come back engaged to the extremely eligible Campolieri. "And she'll sell the New York house, and settle down near them in Rome, and never be in their way . . . she's much too tactful. But she'll have an excellent cook, and just the right people in for bridge and cocktails . . . and a perfectly peaceful old age among her grandchildren."

Mrs. Slade broke off this prophetic flight with a recoil of self-disgust. There was no one of whom she had less right to think unkindly than of Grace Ansley. Would she never cure herself of envying her? Perhaps she had begun too long ago.

She stood up and leaned against the parapet, filling her troubled eyes with the tranquilizing magic of the hour. But instead of tranquilizing her the sight seemed to increase her exasperation. Her gaze turned toward the Colosseum. Already its golden flank was drowned in purple shadow, and above it the sky curved crystal clear, without light or color. It was the moment when afternoon and evening hang balanced in mid-heaven.

Mrs. Slade turned back and laid her hand on her friend's arm. The gesture was so abrupt that Mrs. Ansley looked up, startled.

"The sun's set. You're not afraid, my dear?"

"Afraid—?"

"Of Roman fever or pneumonia? I remember how ill you were that winter. As a girl you had a very delicate throat, hadn't you?"

"Oh, we're all right up here. Down below, in the Forum, it does get deathly cold, all of a sudden . . . but not here."

"Ah, of course you know because you had to be so careful." Mrs. Slade turned back to the parapet. She thought: "I must make one more effort not to hate her." Aloud she said: "Whenever I look at the Forum from up here, I remember that story about a great-aunt of yours, wasn't she? A dreadfully wicked great-aunt?"

"Oh, yes; great-aunt Harriet. The one who was supposed to have sent her young sister out to the Forum after sunset to gather a night-blooming flower for her album. All our great-aunts and grandmothers used to have albums of dried flowers."

Mrs. Slade nodded. "But she really sent her because they were in love with the same man—"

"Well, that was the family tradition. They said Aunt Harriet confessed it years afterwards. At any rate, the poor little sister caught the fever and died. Mother used to frighten us with the story when we were children."

"And you frightened *me* with it, that winter when you and I were here as girls. The winter I was engaged to Delphin."

Mrs. Ansley gave a faint laugh. "Oh, did I? Really frighten you? I don't believe you're easily frightened."

"Not often; but I was then. I was easily frightened because I was too happy. I wonder if you know what that means?"

"I—yes . . ." Mrs. Ansley faltered.

"Well, I suppose that was why the story of your wicked aunt made such an impression on me. And I thought: 'There's no more Roman fever, but the Forum is deathly cold after sunset—especially after a hot day. And the Colosseum's even colder and damper.'"

"The Colosseum—?"

"Yes. It wasn't easy to get in, after the gates were locked for the night. Far from easy. Still, in those days it could be managed; it *was* managed, often. Lovers met there who couldn't meet elsewhere. You knew that?"

"I—I dare say. I don't remember."

"You don't remember? You don't remember going to visit some ruins or other one evening, just after dark, and catching a bad chill? You were supposed to have gone to see the moon rise. People always said that expedition was what caused your illness."

"There was a moment's silence; then Mrs. Ansley rejoined: "Did they? It was all so long ago."

"Yes. And you got well again—so it didn't matter. But I suppose it struck your friends—the reason given for your illness, I mean—because everybody knew you were so prudent on account of your throat, and your mother took such care of you. . . . You *had* been out late sight-seeing, hadn't you, that night?"

"Perhaps I had. The most prudent girls aren't always prudent. What made you think of it now?"

Mrs. Slade seemed to have no answer ready. But after a moment she broke out: "Because I simply can't bear it any longer—!"

Mrs. Ansley lifted her head quickly. Her eyes were wide and very pale. "Can't bear what?"

"Why—your not knowing that I've always known why you went."

"Why I went—?"

"Yes. You think I'm bluffing, don't you? Well, you went to meet the man I was engaged to—and I can repeat every word of the letter that took you there."

While Mrs. Slade spoke Mrs. Ansley had risen unsteadily to her feet. Her bag, her knitting and gloves, slid in a panic-stricken heap to the ground. She looked at Mrs. Slade as though she were looking at a ghost.

"No, no—don't," she faltered out.

"Why not? Listen, if you don't believe me. 'My one darling, things can't go on like this. I must see you alone. Come to the Colosseum immediately after dark tomorrow. There will be somebody to let you in. No one whom you need fear will suspect'—but perhaps you've forgotten what the letter said?"

Mrs. Ansley met the challenge with an unexpected composure. Steadying herself against the chair she looked at her friend, and replied: "No; I know it by heart too."

"And the signature? 'Only *your* D.S.' Was that it? I'm right, am I? That was the letter that took you out that evening after dark?"

Mrs. Ansley was still looking at her. It seemed to Mrs. Slade that a slow struggle was going on behind the voluntarily controlled mask of her small quiet face. "I shouldn't have thought she had herself so well in hand," Mrs. Slade reflected, almost resentfully. But at this moment Mrs. Ansley spoke. "I don't know how you knew. I burnt that letter at once."

"Yes; you would, naturally—you're so prudent!" The sneer was open now. "And if you burnt the letter you're wondering how on earth I know what was in it. That's it, isn't it?"

Mrs. Slade waited, but Mrs. Ansley did not speak.

"Well, my dear, I know what was in that letter because I wrote it!"

"You wrote it?"

"Yes."

The two women stood for a minute staring at each other in the last golden light. Then Mrs. Ansley dropped back into her chair. "Oh," she murmured, and covered her face with her hands.

Mrs. Slade waited nervously for another word or movement. None came, and at length she broke out: "I horrify you."

Mrs. Ansley's hands dropped to her knee. The face they uncovered was streaked with tears. "I wasn't thinking of you. I was thinking———it was the only letter I ever had from him!"

"And I wrote it. Yes; I wrote it! But I was the girl he was engaged to. Did you happen to remember that?"

Mrs. Ansley's head drooped again. "I'm not trying to excuse myself . . . I remembered. . . . "

"And still you went?"

"Still I went."

Mrs. Slade stood looking down on the small bowed figure at her side. The flame of her wrath had already sunk, and she wondered why she had ever thought there would be any satisfaction in inflicting so purposeless a wound on her friend. But she had to justify herself.

"You do understand? I'd found out—and I hated you, hated you. I knew you were in love with Delphin—and I was afraid; afraid of you, of your quiet ways, your sweetness . . . your . . . well, I wanted you out of the way, that's all. Just for a few weeks; just till I was sure of him. So in a blind fury I wrote that letter . . . I don't know why I'm telling you now."

"I suppose," said Mrs. Ansley slowly, "it's because you've gone on hating me."

"Perhaps. Or because I wanted to get the whole thing off my mind." She paused. "I'm glad you destroyed the letter. Of course I never thought you'd die."

Mrs. Ansley relapsed into silence, and Mrs. Slade, leaning over her, was conscious of a strange sense of isolation, of being cut off from the warm current of human communion. "You think me a monster!"

"I don't know. . . . It was the only letter I had, and you say he didn't write it?"

"Ah, how you care for him still!"

"I cared for that memory," said Mrs. Ansley.

Mrs. Slade continued to look down at her. She seemed physically reduced by the blow—as if, when she got up, the wind might scatter her like a puff of dust. Mrs. Slade's jealousy suddenly leapt up again at the sight. All these years the woman had been living on that letter. How she must have loved him, to treasure the mere memory of its ashes! The letter of the man her friend was engaged to. Wasn't it she who was the monster?

"You tried your best to get him away from me, didn't you? But you failed; and I kept him. That's all."

"Yes. That's all."

"I wish now I hadn't told you. I'd no idea you'd feel about it as you do; I thought you'd be amused. It all happened so long ago, as you say; and you must do me the justice to remember that I had no reason to think you'd ever taken it seriously. How could I, when you were married to Horace Ansley two months afterward? As soon as you could get out of bed your mother rushed you off to Florence and married you. People were rather surprised—they wondered at its being done so quickly; but I thought I knew. I had an idea you did it out of *pique*—to be able to say you'd got ahead of Delphin and me. Girls have such silly reasons for doing the most serious things. And your marrying so soon convinced me that you'd never really cared."

"Yes. I suppose it would," Mrs. Ansley assented.

The clear heaven overhead was emptied of all its gold. Dusk spread over it, abruptly darkening the Seven Hills. Here and there lights began to twinkle through the foliage at their feet. Steps were coming and going on the deserted terrace—waiters looking out of the doorway at the head of the stairs, then reappearing with trays and napkins and flasks of wine. Tables were moved, chairs straightened. A feeble string of electric lights flickered out. Some vases of faded flowers were carried away, and brought back replenished. A stout lady in a dust coat suddenly appeared, asking in broken Italian if anyone had seen the elastic band which held together her tattered Baedeker. She poked with her stick under the table at which she had lunched, the waiters assisting.

The corner where Mrs. Slade and Mrs. Ansley sat was still shadowy and deserted. For a long time neither of them spoke. At length Mrs. Slade began again: "I suppose I did it as a sort of joke—"

"A joke?"

"Well, girls are ferocious sometimes, you know. Girls in love especially. And I remember laughing to myself all that evening at the idea that you were waiting around there in the dark, dodging out of sight, listening for every sound, trying to get in—Of course I was upset when I heard you were so ill afterward."

Mrs. Ansley had not moved for a long time. But now she turned slowly toward her companion. "But I didn't wait. He'd arranged everything. He was there. We were let in at once," she said.

Mrs. Slade sprang up from her leaning position. "Delphin there? They let you in?—Ah, now you're lying!" she burst out with violence.

Mrs. Ansley's voice grew clearer, and full of surprise. "But of course he was there. Naturally he came—"

"Came? How did he know he'd find you there? You must be raving!"

Mrs. Ansley hesitated, as though reflecting. "But I answered the letter. I told him I'd be there. So he came."

Mrs. Slade flung her hands up to her face. "Oh, God—you answered! I never thought of your answering. . . ."

"It's odd you never thought of it, if you wrote the letter."

"Yes. I was blind with rage."

Mrs. Ansley rose, and drew her fur scarf about her. "It is cold here. We'd better go. . . . I'm sorry for you," she said, as she clasped the fur about her throat.

The unexpected words sent a pang through Mrs. Slade. "Yes; we'd better go." She gathered up her bag and cloak. "I don't know why you should be sorry for me," she muttered.

Mrs. Ansley stood looking away from her toward the dusky secret mass of the Colosseum. "Well—because I didn't have to wait that night."

Mrs. Slade gave an unquiet laugh. "Yes; I was beaten there. But I oughtn't to begrudge it to you, I suppose. At the end of all these years. After all, I had everything; I had him for twenty-five years. And you had nothing but that one letter that he didn't write."

Mrs. Ansley was again silent. At length she turned toward the door of the terrace. She took a step, and turned back, facing her companion.

"I had Barbara," she said, and began to move ahead of Mrs. Slade toward the stairway.

Bees and Bricks

Heather Sundheim

Heather Sundheim is a freshman at The University of
Montana.

I spent the first half of my childhood living on a
honey farm and the second half living in a junkyard.
Although they were within a few miles of each other in a
small town in Montana, they were very different.

The bees on the honey farm greatly outnumbered my
family, but they were a benign presence. In the mail, we
would get small wooden boxes full of queen bees, which we
often kept under the old desk in our living room. I loved
to lie on the floor next to them, watching them move
around and listening to them buzz. I only remember being
stung twice. As I recall, both incidents were a result of
my not seeing the bees and accidentally grabbing hold of
them.

In the center of the farm sat the honey house itself.
It was a giant, two-story building with all kinds of
interesting machines and gadgets inside. When we were
exploring, our little tennis shoes stuck to the grimy,
honey-spattered linoleum, and they pulled up with not a
little effort and loud ripping noises. My brother and I
would often go inside to find my father working, and we
would beg a piece of honeycomb from him. He was always
somewhere close by and eager to answer all of our
questions about what he was doing.

We lived in the same house my mother grew up in. It
perched on the top of a hill, and a steep embankment
dropped off behind it. My room overlooked this steep
descent, and I was certain that one day I would find
myself sliding down it, still in my bed. The house
fascinated me, and I often dreamt about it. To this day
I'm not sure how much of what I remember actually
happened, and how much I imagined.

Beneath the house was a root cellar. My brother and I
hadn't seen any horror movies yet, so we didn't know this
was a place where little children could be locked up.

Just behind the door, there was a large earthen hole. We often crawled inside and explored the cold dirt and rock beneath the foundation of our house. The house also had an attic. The only way to get up there was for an adult to pull down the trap door and stairs. This was my favorite room, because it had been my mother's room in high school. I couldn't wait to grow old enough to move up there, and to be alone. I had to share a bedroom with my baby sister. This was not an arrangement I relished, but our room did have a unique feature. There was an adjoining door to my brother's room, and he and I would often sneak back and forth, whispering to one another at night.

Several small cottages surrounded the honey house. These had been lived in by hired hands when the farm was first built. There were exactly three of them. I thought, at the time, that my brother, sister, and I would each live in one of these houses when we grew up. I loved the honey farm so much that I wanted to live there forever.

A large sloping pasture with a river winding at its base bordered the dirt road behind the honey house. We weren't allowed to walk down to the river alone. We could only go as far as our tire swing, which hung from a giant pine tree at the top of the hill. The view from there was incredible, and we always returned to the house with fists full of wildflowers for my mother. Our surroundings were as clean and pure as the honey our bees produced.

When I was nine, my father decided he had had enough bee farming, and he wanted to start his own business. He loved cars and decided to start a wrecker service and a junkyard. He towed the twelve antique cars he had stored in a shed by the river to what would be our new home. So began what would become a fenced-in yard with thousands of vehicles.

The house was a long, one-story, unremarkable house, with no points of particular interest. Having my own bedroom provided some consolation. Ugly purple carpet and lavender walls decorated my new room, but I didn't care. Purple quickly became my favorite color. It stood for independence.

The animals that outnumbered us on this property came
in the form of hundreds of filthy garter snakes. The
house's rock foundation provided these scaly pests with
ample crevices and cracks to slither through and nest in.
They often found their way up through the heating vents
in the floor and into the house. They were disgusting and
very unwelcome guests.

The property stretched out flat, treeless, and covered
with knapweed as far as the eye could see. A dry
irrigation ditch, where we sometimes played with matchbox
cars, offered the landscape's only variation. It lay
hidden way out in the weeds, and we pretended that it was
well out of earshot. We spent most of our time, though,
walking on top of the old, weathered fence that
surrounded our house, as if we were circus performers.
The only way to stay clean was to stay inside this fence.
Outside of our small dry yard, the piles of oily parts
and junk began to increase and form endless, chaotic
rows.

As the number of cars multiplied, we ventured out
among them to explore. We played games where we would
jump from bumper to bumper as if our lives depended on
it. After several injuries and infected scrapes, our
mother didn't allow us to play this game anymore. Later
on, we started mining for the endless supply of beer and
pop cans that awaited recycling under seats and inside
trunks. This became a miserable and endless undertaking,
but we were desperate for spending money so that we could
escape and go into town.

Customers started coming at all hours of the day,
and the phone rang constantly. Because my father was on
call twenty-four hours, we rarely got to see him at all.
When he was home, he was too exhausted to pay any
attention to us. Once he sat down in his recliner, we
had to compete with the newspaper for his attention.
He wouldn't even take his eyes away from the paper
when we made attempts to speak with him. Often I would
perch on the edge of the couch next to his chair and
say his name three or four times before he'd look up,
confused and unaware that I'd been trying to talk
to him.

I began to resent the business. The physical demands of time and energy, which the yard exerted on him, had, for all intents and purposes, stolen our father from us. Like so many men in his generation, he had confused financial provision for nurturing and love. Once, he kissed me on the cheek in the receiving line at my eighth-grade graduation. I remember that I nearly fell over from shock, and my mother's eyes filled with tears as she watched. Nevertheless, I harbored such feelings of hurt and resentment that I moved away from the junkyard as soon as I graduated.

The honey farm was an enchanting home, filled with hidden places to explore and endless fuel for my imagination. The quiet solitude, characterized by the low droning of the bees at their work, had all the elements of mystery required to be forever romanticized in my memory. It was a uniquely pure experience that allowed me not only to enjoy nature, but also to experience part of its process. In stark contrast, albeit barren at first, the junkyard quickly filled with rusty, smashed automobile carcasses and greasy junk. All of it baked in the sun, and its ugliness increased with each new addition to the ranks. It was unremarkable, dirty, and all too common. People were always wandering through it, and privacy was impossible.

I recently drove out to the honey farm. It seemed much smaller and a bit run down. The surroundings, however, were still charming. The quaint little cottages still encircled the honey house, sagging a little now, and I could hear the bees buzzing. The road circled all the way around the honey house, and once behind it, I could smell the wildflowers in the pasture and hear the river rushing down below me. The most nostalgic moment, though, came when I saw our old tire swing still swaying in the light breeze beneath that old pine tree. Even at twenty-six, I was tempted to pull over, climb the fence, and squeeze myself into that little tire to lean back with the wind in my hair and the scent of wildflowers filling my nostrils.

I travel to the junkyard every few weeks to visit my parents. I don't let its ugliness bother me anymore though. Looking back on the junkyard with more maturity, I can recall some happy memories there. The old weathered fence rotted away a long time ago, but I can still remember how it felt when I made it all the way around the house without failing. I can see my brother and sister climbing the elm tree in the front yard, in their torn and dirty jeans, their grubby faces grinning at one another as they climbed the battle tower. The junkyard is still ugly, but my dad is changing. He's trying to take more interest in our lives now, and kind words and hugs come a little more easily for him.

I feel nostalgic about both places now. They each shaped my experiences and contributed to my overall growth as a person. Having lived in both places has helped me to realize that the beauty and ugliness in life are both worth experiencing. If I'd never known the distastefulness of the junkyard, the honey farm might not have seemed so sweet.

7

HISTORY

THE ORIGINALITY OF
THE OLD TESTAMENT

■

Herbert Butterfield

This piece is from the essay collection Writings on Christianity and History, *published in 1979.*

The Old Testament sometimes seems very ancient, but the earliest considerable body of historical literature that we possess was being produced through a period of a thousand years and more before that. It consisted of what we call "annals," written in the first person singular by the heads of great empires which had their centre in Egypt or Mesopotamia or Asia Minor. These monarchs, often year by year, would produce accounts—quite detailed accounts sometimes—of their military campaigns. It is clear from what they say that one of their objects in life was to put their own personal achievements on record—their building feats, their prowess in the hunt, but also their victories in war. They show no sign of having had any interest in the past, but, among other things, they betray a great anxiety about the reputation they would have after they were dead. They did not look behind them to previous generations, but instead they produced what we should call the history of their own times, in a way rather like Winston Churchill producing his account of his wars against Germany in the twentieth century.

After this, however, a great surprise occurs. There emerges from nowhere a people passionately interested in the past, dominated by an historical memory. It is clear that this is due to the fact that there is a bygone event that they really cannot get over; it takes command over their whole mentality. This people were the ancient Hebrews. They had been semi-nomads, moving a great deal in the desert, but having also certain periods in rather better areas where they could grow a bit of something. Like semi-nomads in general, they had longed to have land of their own, a settled land which they could properly cultivate. This is what they expected their God to provide for them, and what he promised to provide. Indeed the semi-nomads would tend to judge his effectiveness as a god by his ability to carry out his promise. The ancient Hebrews, the Children of Israel, had to wait a long time for their due reward, and perhaps this was the reason why they were so tremendously impressed when ultimately the Promise was actually fulfilled.

The earliest thing that we know from sheer historical evidence about these people is that as soon as they appear in the light of day they are already dominated by this historical memory. In some of the earliest books of the Bible there are embedded patches of text far earlier still, far earlier than the Old Testament itself, and repeatedly they are passages about this very thing. Fresh references go on perpetually being made to the same matter throughout the many centuries during which the Old Testament was being produced, indeed also in the Jewish literature that was written for a few centuries after that. We are more sure that the memory of this historical event was the predominating thing among them than we are of the reality, the actual historicity, of the event itself.

What they commemorated in this tremendous way, of course, was the fact that God had brought them up out of the land of Egypt and into the Promised Land. In reality it seems pretty clear that some of the tribes of Israel did not come into the land of Palestine from Egypt at all. Nevertheless I think it would be a central view among scholars that some of the ancient Hebrews came to the Promised Land from Egypt, and the impression of this was so powerful that it became the common memory of the whole group of tribes which settled in the land of Canaan; it became the accepted tradition even among the tribes that had never been in Egypt. Moreover the common tradition was the very thing that became the effective bond between the tribes of Israel, helping to weld them together as a people. This sense of a common history is always a powerful factor in fusing a group of tribes into a nation, just as Homer made the various bodies of Greeks feel that they had had a common experience in the past, a consciousness that they were all Hellenes. All this was so powerful with the Children of Israel because they felt such a fabulous gratitude for what had happened. I know of no other case in history where gratitude was carried so far, no other case where gratitude proved to be such a generative thing. Their God had stepped into history and kept his ancient Promise, bringing them to freedom and the Promised Land, and they simply could not get over it.

This was not the first time in history that gratitude had been a factor in religion, for at a date earlier still there are signs amongst the Hittites that the very sincerity of their feeling of indebtedness added an attractive kind of devotion to their worship of their pagan deities. But this gratitude was such a signal thing amongst the Israelitish people that it altered the whole development of religion in that quarter of the globe; it altered the character of religion in the area from which our Western civilization sprang. It gave the Children of Israel a historical event that they could not get over, could not help remembering, and in the first place it made them historians—historians in a way that nobody had ever been before. The ancient Hebrews worshiped the God who brought them up out of the land of Egypt more than they worshipped God as the Creator of the World. By all the rules of the game, when once they had settled down in the land of Canaan and become an agricultural people, they ought to have turned to the gods of nature, the gods of fertility, and this is what some of their number wanted to do. But their historical memory was too strong. Even when they borrowed rites and ceremonies from neighboring peoples—pieces of ritual based on the cycle of nature, the succession of the seasons—they turned these into celebrations of historical events, just as I suppose Christianity may have turned the rites of Spring into a celebration of the Resurrection. The Hebrews took over circumcision, which existed among their neighbors, but they turned even this into the celebration of a historical event. A Harvest Festival is an occasion on which even among Christians today we call attention to the cycle of the seasons and the bounty of nature. But among the Children of Israel at this ceremony you handed your thankoffering to the priest and then, if you please, you did not speak of the corn or the vine—you recited your national history, you narrated the story of the Exodus. It was set down in writing that if the younger generation started asking why they were expected to obey God's commandments they should be told that it was because God had brought their forefathers out of the house of bondage. Everything was based on their gratitude for what God had done for the nation. And it is remarkable to see to what a degree the other religious ideas of the Old Testament always remained historical in character— the Promise, the Covenant, the Judgment, the Messiah, the remnant of Israel, etc.

Yet this Promised Land to which God had brought them and on which they based a religion of extravagant gratitude was itself no great catch, and if they called it a land flowing with milk and honey, this was only because it looked rich when compared to the life that they had hitherto led. In the twentieth century Palestine has demanded a tremendous wrestling with nature, and if one looks back to the state of that region in Old Testament times one cannot help feeling that Providence endowed this people with one of the riskiest bits of territory that existed in that part of the globe. They were placed in an area which had already been encircled by vast empires, based on Egypt and on Mesopotamia and on a Hittite realm in Asia Minor. And, for all their gratitude, they were one of the most unlucky peoples of history. Other great empires soon arose again in the same regions, and they were so placed that they could not be expected to keep their freedom—their independence as a state only lasted for a few centuries, something like the period between Tudor England and the present day. The one stroke of luck that they did have was that for just a space at the crucial period those surrounding empires had come into decline, and this gave the Hebrews the chance of forming an independent state for a while. They virtually stood in the cockpit in that part of the world, just as Belgium stood in the cockpit in Western Europe and Poland in Eastern Europe. The fact that the Hebrews became, along with the Greeks, one of the main contributors to the formation of Western civilization is a triumph of mind over matter, of the human spirit over misfortune and disaster. They almost built their religion on gratitude for their good fortune in having a country at all, a country that they could call their own.

Because of the great act of God which had brought them to Palestine they devoted themselves to the God of History rather than to the gods of nature. Here is their great originality, the thing that in a way enabled them to change the very nature of religion. Because they turned their intellect to the actions of God in history, they were drawn into an ethical view of God. They were continually wrestling with him about ethical questions, continually debating with him as to whether he was playing fair with them. Religion became intimately connected with morality because this was a God who was always in personal relations with human beings in the ordinary historical realm, and in any case you find that it was the worshipers of the gods of nature who ran to orgies and cruelties and immoralities. In fact, the ancient Hebrews developed their thought about God, about personality, and about ethics all together, all rolled into one. Because these things all involved what we call problems of personal relations they developed their thought about history step by step along with the rest. For a student of history, one of the interesting features of the Old Testament is that it gives us evidence of religious development from very early stages, from most primitive ideas about God, some of these ideas being quite shocking to the modern mind. Indeed, in some of the early books of the Bible there are still embedded certain ancient things that make it look as though, here as in no other parts of Western Asia, the God of History may at one stage have been really the God of War.

So far as I have been able to discover—approaching the matter as a modern historian, and rather an outsider, and using only what is available in Western languages—the Children of Israel, while still a comparatively primitive society, are the first people who showed a really significant interest in the past, the first to produce anything like a history of their nation, the first to lay out what we call a universal history, doing it with the help of some Babylonian legends but attempting to see the whole story of the human race. Because what we possess in the Old Testament is history as envisaged by the priests, or at least by the religious people, it is also a history very critical of the rulers—not like the mass of previous historical writing, a case of monarchs blowing their own trumpets. The history they wrote is a history of the people and not just of the kings, and it is very critical even of the people. So far as I know here is the only case of a nation producing a national history and making it an exposure of its national sins. In a technical sense this ancient Hebrew people became very remarkable as writers of history, some of their narratives (for example, the death of King David and the question of the succession to his throne) being quite wonderful according to modern standards of judgment. It was to be of momentous importance for the development of Western civilization, that, growing up in Europe (with Christianity presiding over its creative stages), it was influenced by the Old Testament, by this ancient Jewish passion for history. For century after century over periods of nearly 2000 years, the European could not even learn about his religion without studying the Bible, including the Old Testament—essentially a history-book, a book of very ancient history. Our civilization, unlike many others, became historically-minded, therefore, one that was interested in the past, and we owe that in a great part to the Old Testament.

A SIXTIES PARTY

———————————●———————————

Garrison Keillor

This was originally a "Talk of the Town" in The New Yorker *magazine.*

A friend writes:
About five o'clock last Sunday evening, my son burst into the kitchen and said, "I didn't know it was so late!" He was due at a party immediately—a sixties party, he said—and he needed something from the sixties to wear. My son is almost fifteen years old, the size of a grown man, and when he bursts into a room glassware rattles and the cat on your lap grabs on to your knees and leaps from the starting block. I used to think the phrase "burst into the room" was only for detective fiction, until my son got his growth. He can burst in a way that, done by an older fellow, would mean that angels had descended into the front yard and were eating apples off the tree, and he does it whenever he's late—as being my son, he often is. I have so little sense of time that when he said he needed something from the sixties it took me a moment to place that decade. It's the one he was born toward the end of.

I asked, "What sort of stuff you want to wear?"

He said, "I don't know. Whatever they wore then."

We went up to the attic, into a long, low room under the eaves where I've squirreled away some boxes of old stuff; I dug into one box, and the first thing I hauled out was the very thing he wanted. A thigh-length leather vest covered with fringe and studded with silver, it dates from around 1967, a fanciful time in college-boy fashions. Like many boys, I grew up in nice clothes my mother bought, but was meanwhile admiring Roy Rogers, Sergeant Rock, the Cisco Kid, and other sharp dressers, so when I left home I was ready to step out and be somebody. Military Surplus was the basic style then—olive drab, and navy-blue pea jackets—with a touch of Common Man in the work boots and blue work shirts, but if you showed up in Riverboat Gambler or Spanish Peasant or Rodeo King nobody blinked, nobody laughed. I haven't worn the vest in ten years, but a few weeks ago, seeing a picture of Michael Jackson wearing a fancy band jacket like the ones the Beatles wore on the cover of "Sgt. Pepper," I missed the fun I used to have getting dressed in the morning. Pull on the jeans, a shirt with brilliant-red roses, a pair of Red Wing boots. A denim jacket. Rose-tinted glasses. A cowboy hat. Or an engineer's cap. Or, instead of jeans, bib overalls. Or white trousers with blue stripes. Take off the denim jacket, take off the rose shirt, try the neon-green bowling shirt with "Moose" stitched on the pocket, the black dinner jacket. Now the dark-green Chinese Army cap. And an orange tie with hula dancers and palm trees.

Then—presto!—I pulled the rose shirt out. He put it on, and the vest, which weighs about fifteen pounds, and by then I had found him a hat— a broad-brimmed panama that ought to make you think of a cotton planter enjoying a Sazerac on a veranda in New Orleans. I followed him down to his bedroom, where he admired himself in a full-length mirror.

"Who wore this?" he asked.

I said that I did.

"Did you really? This? You?"

Yes, I really did. After he was born, in 1969, I wore it less and less, finally settling down with what I think of as the Dad look, and now I would no sooner wear my old fringed vest in public than walk around in a taffeta tutu. I loved the fact that it fitted him so well, though, and his pleasure at the heft and extravagance of the thing, the poses he struck in front of the mirror. Later, when he got home and reported that his costume was a big hit and that all his friends had tried on the vest, it made me happy again. You squirrel away old stuff on the principle of its being useful and interesting someday; it's wonderful when the day finally arrives. That vest was waiting for a boy to come along—a boy who has a flair for the dramatic, who bursts into rooms—and to jump right into the part. I'm happy to be the audience.

THE PATTERNS OF EATING

Peter Farb and George Armelagos

This piece is an excerpt from Farb and Armelagos' 1980 book, Consuming Passions.

Among the important societal rules that represent one component of cuisine are table manners. As a socially instilled form of conduct, they reveal the attitudes typical of a society. Changes in table manners through time, as they have been documented for western Europe, likewise reflect fundamental changes in human relationships. Medieval courtiers saw their table manners as distinguishing them from crude peasants; but by modern standards, the manners were not exactly refined. Feudal lords used their unwashed hands to scoop food from a common bowl and they passed around a single goblet from which all drank. A finger or two would be extended while eating, so as to be kept free of grease and thus available for the next course, or for dipping into spices and condiments—possibly accounting for today's "polite" custom of extending the finger while holding a spoon or small fork. Soups and sauces were commonly drunk by lifting the bowl to the mouth; several diners frequently ate from the same bread trencher. Even lords and nobles would toss gnawed bones back into the common dish, wolf down their food, spit onto the table (preferred conduct called for spitting under it), and blew their noses into the tablecloth.

By about the beginning of the sixteenth century, table manners began to move in the direction of today's standards. The importance attached to them is indicated by the phenomenal success of a treatise, *On Civility in Children*, by the philosopher Erasmus, which appeared in 1530; reprinted more than thirty times in the next six years, it also appeared in numerous translations. Erasmus' idea of good table manners was far from modern, but it did represent an advance. He believed, for example, that an upper class diner was distinguished by putting only three fingers of one hand into the bowl, instead of the entire hand in the manner of the lower class. Wait a few moments after being seated before you dip into it, he advises. Do not poke around in your dish, but take the first piece you touch. Do not put chewed food from the mouth back on your plate; instead, throw it under the table or behind your chair.

By the time of Erasmus, the changing table manners reveal a fundamental shift in society. People no longer ate from the same dish or drank from the same goblet, but were divided from one another by a new wall of constraint. Once the spontaneous, direct, and informal manners of the Middle Ages had been repressed, people began to feel shame. Defecation and urination were now regarded as private activities; handkerchiefs came into use for blowing the nose; nightclothes were now worn, and bedrooms were set apart as private areas. Before the sixteenth century, even nobles ate in their vast kitchens; only then did a special room designated for eating come into use away from the bloody sides of meat, the animals about to be slaughtered, and the bustling servants. These new inhibitions became the essence of "civilized" behavior, distinguishing adults from children, the upper classes from the lower, and Europeans from the "savages" then being discovered around the world. Restraint in eating habits became more marked in the centuries that followed. By about 1800, napkins were in common use, and before long they were placed on the thighs rather than wrapped around the neck; coffee and tea were no longer slurped out of the saucer; bread was genteelly broken into small pieces with the fingers rather than cut into large chunks with a knife.

Numerous paintings that depict meals—with subjects such as the Last Supper, the wedding at Cana, or Herod's feast—show what dining tables looked like before the seventeenth century. Forks were not depicted until about 1600 (when Jacopo Bassano painted one in a Last Supper), and very few spoons were shown. At least one knife is always depicted—an especially large one when it is the only one available for all the guests—but small individual knives were often at each place. Tin disks or oval pieces of wood had already replaced the bread trenchers. This change in eating utensils typified the new table manners in Europe. (In many other parts of the world, no utensils at all were used. In the Near East, for example, it was traditional to bring food to the mouth with the fingers of the right hand, the left being unacceptable because it was reserved for wiping the buttocks.) Utensils were employed in part because of a change in the attitude toward meat. During the Middle Ages, whole sides of meat, or even an entire dead animal, had been brought to the table and then carved in view of the diners. Beginning in the seventeenth century, at first in France but later elsewhere, the practice began to go out of fashion. One reason was that the family was ceasing to be a production unit that did its own slaughtering; as that function was transferred to specialists outside the home, the family became essentially a consumption unit. In addition, the size of the family was decreasing, and consequently whole animals, or even large parts of them, were uneconomical. The cuisines of Europe reflected these social and economic changes. The animal origin of meat dishes was concealed by the arts of preparation. Meat itself became distasteful to look upon, and carving was moved out of sight to the kitchen. Comparable changes had already taken place in Chinese cuisine, with meat being cut up beforehand, unobserved by the diners. England was an exception to the change in Europe, and in its former colonies—the United States, Canada, Australia, and South Africa—the custom has persisted of bringing a joint of meat to the table to be carved.

Once carving was no longer considered a necessary skill among the well-bred, changes inevitably took place in the use of the knife, unquestionably the earliest utensil used for manipulating food. (In fact, the earliest English cookbooks were not so much guides to recipes as guides to carving meat.) The attitude of diners toward the knife, going back to the Middle Ages and the Renaissance, had always been ambivalent. The knife served as a utensil, but it offered a potential threat because it was also a weapon. Thus taboos were increasingly placed upon its use: It was to be held by the point with the blunt handle presented; it was not to be placed anywhere near the face; and most important, the uses to which it was put were sharply restricted. It was not to be used for cutting soft foods such as boiled eggs or fish, or round ones such as potatoes, or to be lifted from the table for courses that did not need it. In short, good table manners in Europe gradually removed the threatening aspect of the knife from social occasions. A similar change had taken place much earlier in China when the warrior was supplanted by the scholar as a cultural model. The knife was banished completely from the table in favor of chopsticks, which is why the Chinese came to regard Europeans as barbarians at their table who "eat with swords."

The fork in particular enabled Europeans to separate themselves from the eating process, even avoiding manual contact with their food. When the fork first appeared in Europe, toward the end of the Middle Ages, it was used solely as an instrument for lifting chunks from the common bowl. Beginning in the sixteenth century, the fork was increasingly used by members of the upper classes—first in Italy, then in France, and finally in Germany and England. By then, social relations in western Europe had so changed that a utensil was needed to spare diners from the "uncivilized" and distasteful necessity of picking up food and putting it into the mouth with the fingers. The addition of the fork to the table was once said to be for reasons of hygiene, but this cannot be true. By the sixteenth century people were no longer eating from a common bowl but from their own plates, and since they also washed their hands before meals, their fingers were now every bit as hygienic as a fork would have been. Nor can the reason for the adoption of the fork be connected with the wish not to soil the long ruff that was worn on the sleeve at the time, since the fork was also adopted in various countries where ruffs were not then in fashion.

Along with the appearance of the fork, all table utensils began to change and proliferate from the sixteenth century onward. Soup was no longer eaten directly from the dish, but each diner used an individual spoon for that purpose. When a diner wanted a second helping from the serving dish, a ladle or a fresh spoon was used. More and more special utensils were developed for each kind of food: soup spoons, oyster forks, salad forks, two-tined fondue forks, blunt butter knives, special utensils for various desserts and kinds of fruit, each one differently shaped, of a different size, with differently numbered prongs and with blunt or serrated edges. The present European pattern eventually emerged, in which each person is provided with a table setting of as many as a dozen utensils at a full-course meal. With that, the separation of the human body from the taking of food became virtually complete. Good table manners dictated that even the cobs of maize were to be held by prongs inserted in each end, and the bones of lamb chops covered by ruffled paper pantalettes. Only under special conditions—as when Western people consciously imitate an earlier stage in culture at a picnic, fish fry, cookout, or campfire—do they still tear food apart with their fingers and their teeth, in a nostalgic reenactment of eating behaviors long vanished.

Today's neighborhood barbecue recreates a world of sharing and hospitality that becomes rarer each year. We regard as a curiosity the behavior of hunters in exotic regions. But every year millions of North Americans take to the woods and lakes to kill a wide variety of animals— with a difference, of course: What hunters do for survival we do for sport (and also for proof of masculinity, for male bonding, and for various psychological rewards). Like hunters, too, we stuff ourselves almost whenever food is available. Nibbling on a roasted ear of maize gives us, in addition to nutrients, the satisfaction of participating in culturally simpler ways. A festive meal, however, is still thought of in Victorian terms, with the dominant male officiating over the roast, the dominant female apportioning vegetables, the extended family gathered around the table, with everything in its proper place—a revered picture, as indeed it was so painted by Norman Rockwell, yet one that becomes less accurate with each year that passes.

THE TYRANNY OF THE CLOCK

George Woodcock

This piece is from Woodcock's 1972 book The Rejection of Politics.

In no characteristic is existing society in the West so sharply distinguished from the earlier societies, whether of Europe or the East, than in its conception of time. To the ancient Chinese or Greek, to the Arab herdsman or Mexican peon of today, time is represented by the cyclic processes of nature, the alternation of day and night, the passage from season to season. The nomads and farmers measured and still measure their day from sunrise to sunset, and their year in terms of seedtime and harvest, of the falling leaf and the ice thawing on the lakes and rivers. The farmer worked according to the elements, the craftsman for as long as he felt it necessary to perfect his product. Time was seen as a process of natural change, and men were not concerned in its exact measurement. For this reason civilizations highly developed in other respects had the most primitive means of measuring time: the hour glass with its trickling sand or dripping water, the sun dial, useless on a dull day, and the candle or lamp whose unburnt remnant of oil or wax indicated the hours. All these devices were approximate and inexact, and were often rendered unreliable by the weather or the personal laziness of the tender. Nowhere in the ancient or mediæval world were more than a tiny minority of men concerned with time in the terms of mathematical exactitude.

Modern, western man, however, lives in a world which runs according to the mechanical and mathematical symbols of clock time. The clock dictates his movements and inhibits his actions. The clock turns time from a process of nature into a commodity that can be measured and bought and sold like soap or sultanas. And because, without some means of exact time keeping, industrial capitalism could never have developed and could not continue to exploit the workers, the clock represents an element of mechanical tyranny in the lives of modern men more potent than any individual exploiter or than any other machine. It is therefore valuable to trace the historical process by which the clock influenced the social development of modern European civilization.

It is a frequent circumstance of history that a culture or civilization develops the device that will later be used for its destruction. The ancient Chinese, for example, invented gunpowder, which was developed by the military experts of the West and eventually led to the Chinese civilization itself being destroyed by the high explosives of modern warfare. Similarly, the supreme achievement of the craftsmen of the medieval cities of Europe was the invention of the clock which, with its revolutionary alteration of the concept of time, materially assisted the growth of the middle ages.

There is a tradition that the clock appeared in the eleventh century, as a device for ringing bells at regular intervals in the monasteries which, with the regimented life they imposed on their inmates, were the closest social approximation in the middle ages to the factory of today. The first authenticated clock, however, appeared in the thirteenth century, and it was not until the fourteenth century that clocks became common as ornaments of the public buildings in German cities.

These early clocks, operated by weights, were not particularly accurate, and it was not until the sixteenth century that any great reliability was attained. In England, for instance, the clock at Hampton Court, made in 1540, is said to have been the first accurate clock in the country. And even the accuracy of the sixteenth-century clocks is relative, for they were equipped only with hour hands. The idea of measuring time in minutes and seconds had been thought out by the early mathematicians as far back as the fourteenth century, but it was not until the invention of the pendulum in 1657 that sufficient accuracy was attained to permit the addition of a minute hand, and the second hand did not appear until the eighteenth century. These two centuries, it should be observed, were those in which capitalism grew to such an extent that it was able to take advantage of the techniques of the industrial revolution to establish its economic domination over society.

The clock, as Lewis Mumford has pointed out, is the key machine of the machine age, both for its influence on technics and for its influence on the habits of men. Technically, the clock was the first really automatic machine that attained any importance in the life of man. Previous to its invention, the common machines were of such a nature that their operation depended on some external and unreliable force, such as human or animal muscles, water or wind. It is true that the Greeks had invented a number of primitive automatic machines, but these were used, like Hero's steam engine, either for obtaining "supernatural" effects in the temples or for amusing the tyrants of Levantine cities. But the clock was the first automatic machine that attained public importance and a social function. Clock-making became the industry from which men learnt the elements of machine-making and gained the technical skill that was to produce the complicated machinery of the Industrial Revolution.

Socially the clock had a more radical influence than any other machine, in that it was the means by which the regularization and regimentation of life necessary for an exploiting system of industry could best be assured. The clock provided a means by which time—a category so elusive that no philosophy has yet determined its nature—could be measured concretely in the more tangible terms of space provided by the circumference of a clock dial. Time as duration became disregarded, and men began to talk and think always of "lengths" of time, just as if they were talking of lengths of calico. And time, being now measurable in mathematical symbols, was regarded as a commodity that could be bought and sold in the same way as any other commodity.

The new capitalists, in particular, became rabidly time-conscious. Time, here symbolizing the labour of the workers, was regarded by them almost as if it were the chief raw material of industry. "Time is money" was one of the key slogans of capitalist ideology, and the time-keeper was the most significant of the new types of official introduced by the capitalist dispensation.

In the early factories the employers went so far as to manipulate their clocks or sound their factory whistles at the wrong times in order to defraud the workers of a little of this valuable new commodity. Later such practices became less frequent, but the influence of the clock imposed a regularity on the lives of the majority of men that had previously been known only in the monasteries. Men actually became like clocks, acting with a repetitive regularity which had no resemblance to the rhythmic life of a natural being. They became, as the Victorian phrase put it, "as regular as clockwork." Only in the country districts where the natural lives of animals and plants and the elements still dominated existence, did any large proportion of the population fail to succumb to the deadly tick of monotony.

At first this new attitude to time, this new regularity of life, was imposed by the clock-owning masters on the unwilling poor. The factory slave reacted in his spare time by living with a chaotic irregularity which characterized the gin-sodden slums of early nineteenth-century industrialism. Men fled to the timeless worlds of drink or Methodist inspiration. But gradually the idea of regularity spread downwards and among the workers. Nineteenth-century religion and morality played their part by proclaiming the sin of "wasting time." The introduction of mass-produced watches and clocks in the 1850's spread time-consciousness among those who had previously merely reacted to the stimulus of the knocker-up or the factory whistle. In the church and the school, in the office and the workshop, punctuality was held up as the greatest of the virtues.

Out of this slavish dependence on mechanical time which spread insidiously into every class in the nineteenth century, there grew up the demoralizing regimentation which today still characterizes factory life. The man who fails to conform faces social disapproval and economic ruin—unless he drops out into a nonconformist way of life in which time ceases to be of prime importance. Hurried meals, the regular morning and evening scramble for trains or buses, the strain of having to work to time schedules, all contribute, by digestive and nervous disturbance, to ruin health and shorten life.

Nor does the financial imposition of regularity tend, in the long run, to greater efficiency. Indeed, the quality of the product is usually much poorer, because the employer, regarding time as a commodity which he has to pay for, forces the operative to maintain such a speed that his work must necessarily be skimped. Quantity rather than quality becoming the criterion, the enjoyment is taken out of the work itself, and the worker in his turn becomes a "clock-watcher," concerned only with when he will be able to escape to the scanty and monotonous leisure of industrial society, in which he "kills time" by cramming in as much time-scheduled and mechanical enjoyment of cinema, radio and newspaper as his wage packet and his tiredness will allow. Only if he is willing to accept the hazards of living by his faith or his wits can the man without money avoid living as a slave to the clock.

The problem of the clock is, in general, similar to that of the machine. Mechanized time is valuable as a means of coordinating activities in a highly developed society, just as the machine is valuable as a means of reducing unnecessary labour to a minimum. Both are valuable for the contribution they make to the smooth running of society, and should be used in so far as they assist men to co-operate efficiently and to eliminate monotonous toil and social confusion. But neither should be allowed to dominate men's lives as they do today.

Now the movement of the clock sets the tempo of men's lives—they become the servants of the concept of time which they themselves have made, and are held in fear, like Frankenstein by his own monster. In a sane and free society such an arbitrary domination of man's functions by either clock or machine would obviously be out of the question. The domination of man by man-made machines is even more ridiculous than the domination of man by man. Mechanical time would be relegated to its true function of a means of reference and co-ordination, and men would return again to a balanced view of life no longer dominated by time-regulation and the worship of the clock. Complete liberty implies freedom from the tyranny of abstractions as well as from the rule of men.

THE HISTORIAN AND HIS FACTS

Edward Hallett Carr

This essay is from Carr's book What Is History? *published in 1961.*

What is history? Lest anyone think the question meaningless or superfluous, I will take as my text two passages relating respectively to the first and second incarnations of *The Cambridge Modern History.* Here is Acton in his report of October 1896 to the Syndics of the Cambridge University Press on the work which he had undertaken to edit:

> It is a unique opportunity of recording, in the way most useful to the greatest number, the fullness of the knowledge which the nineteenth century is about to bequeath. . . . By the judicious division of labor we should be able to do it, and to bring home to every man the last document, and the ripest conclusions of international research.

Ultimate history we cannot have in this generation; but we can dispose of conventional history, and show the point we have reached on the road from one to the other, now that all information is within reach, and every problem has become capable of solution.

And almost exactly sixty years later Professor Sir George Clark, in his general introduction to the second *Cambridge Modern History*, commented on this belief of Acton and his collaborators that it would one day be possible to produce "ultimate history," and went on:

> Historians of a later generation do not look forward to any such prospect. They expect their work to be superseded again and again. They consider that knowledge of the past has come down through one or more human minds, has been "processed" by them, and therefore cannot consist of elemental and impersonal atoms which nothing can alter. . . . The exploration seems to be endless, and some impatient scholars take refuge in scepticism, or at least in the doctrine that, since all historical judgments involve persons and points of view, one is as good as another and there is no "objective" historical truth.

Where the pundits contradict each other so flagrantly the field is open to enquiry. I hope that I am sufficiently up-to-date to recognize that anything written in the 1890's must be nonsense. But I am not yet advanced enough to be committed to the view that anything written in the 1950's necessarily makes sense. Indeed, it may already have occurred to you that this enquiry is liable to stray into something even broader than the nature of history. The clash between Acton and Sir George Clark is a reflection of the change in our total outlook on society over the interval between these two pronouncements. Acton speaks out of the positive belief, the clear-eyed self-confidence of the later Victorian age; Sir George Clark echoes the bewilderment and distracted scepticism of the beat generation. When we attempt to answer the question, What is history?, our answer, consciously or unconsciously, reflects our own position in time, and forms part of our answer to the broader question, what view we take of the society in which we live. I have no fear that my subject may, on closer inspection, seem trivial. I am afraid only that I may seem presumptuous to have broached a question so vast and so important.

The nineteenth century was a great age for facts. "What I want," said Mr. Gradgrind in *Hard Times*, "is Facts. . . . Facts alone are wanted in life." Nineteenth-century historians on the whole agreed with him. When Ranke in the 1830's, in legitimate protest against moralizing history, remarked that the task of the historian was "simply to show how it really was [*wie es eigentlich gewesen*]" this not very profound aphorism had an astonishing success. Three generations of German, British, and even French historians marched into battle intoning the magic words, *"Wie es eigentlich gewesen"* like an incantation—designed, like most incantations, to save them from the tiresome obligation to think for themselves. The Positivists, anxious to stake out their claim for history as a science, contributed the weight of their influence to this cult of facts. First ascertain the facts, said the positivists, then draw your conclusions from them. In Great Britain, this view of history fitted in perfectly with the empiricist tradition which was the dominant strain in British philosophy from Locke to Bertrand Russell. The empirical theory of knowledge presupposes a complete separation between subject and object. Facts, like sense-impressions, impinge on the observer from outside, and are independent of his consciousness. The process of reception is passive: having received the data, he then acts on them. *The Shorter Oxford English Dictionary*, a useful but tendentious work of the empirical school, clearly marks the separateness of the two processes by defining a fact as "a datum of experience as distinct from conclusions." This is what may be called the common-sense view of history. History consists of a corpus of ascertained facts. The facts are available to the historian in documents, inscriptions, and so on, like fish on the fishmonger's slab. The historian collects them, takes them home, and cooks and serves them in whatever style appeals to him. Acton, whose culinary tastes were austere, wanted them served plain. In his letter of instructions to contributors to the first *Cambridge Modern History* he announced the requirement "that our Waterloo must be one that satisfies French and English, German and Dutch alike; that nobody can tell, without examining the list of authors where the Bishop of Oxford laid down the pen, and whether Fairbairn or Gasquet, Liebermann or Harrison took it up." Even Sir George Clark, critical as he was of Acton's attitude, himself contrasted the "hard core of facts" in history with the "surrounding pulp of disputable interpretation"—forgetting perhaps that the pulpy part of the fruit is more rewarding than the hard core. First get your facts straight, then plunge at your peril into the shifting sands of interpretation—that is the ultimate wisdom of the empirical, common-sense school of history. It recalls the favorite dictum of the great liberal journalist C. P. Scott: "Facts are sacred, opinion is free."

Now this clearly will not do. I shall not embark on a philosophical discussion of the nature of our knowledge of the past. Let us assume for present purposes that the fact that Caesar crossed the Rubicon and the fact that there is a table in the middle of the room are facts of the same or of a comparable order, that both these facts enter our consciousness in the same or in a comparable manner, and that both have the same objective character in relation to the person who knows them. But, even on this bold and not very plausible assumption, our argument at once runs into the difficulty that not all facts about the past are historical facts, or are treated as such by the historian. What is the criterion which distinguishes the facts of history from other facts about the past?

What is a historical fact? This is a crucial question into which we must look a little more closely. According to the common-sense view, there are certain basic facts which are the same for all historians and which form, so to speak, the backbone of history—the fact, for example, that the Battle of Hastings was fought in 1066. But this view calls for two observations.

In the first place, it is not with facts like these that the historian is primarily concerned. It is no doubt important to know that the great battle was fought in 1066 and not in 1065 or 1067, and that it was fought at Hastings and not at Eastbourne or Brighton. The historian must not get these things wrong. But when points of this kind are raised, I am reminded of Housman's remark that "accuracy is a duty, not a virtue." To praise a historian for his accuracy is like praising an architect for using well-seasoned timber or properly mixed concrete in his building. It is a necessary condition of his work, but not his essential function. It is precisely for matters of this kind that the historian is entitled to rely on what have been called the "auxiliary sciences" of history—archaeology, epigraphy, numismatics, chronology, and so forth. The historian is not required to have the special skills which enable the expert to determine the origin and period of a fragment of pottery or marble, or decipher an obscure inscription, or to make the elaborate astronomical calculations necessary to establish a precise date. These so-called basic facts which are the same for all historians commonly belong to the category of the raw materials of the historian rather than of history itself. The second observation is that the necessity to establish these basic facts rests not on any quality in the facts themselves, but on an *a priori* decision of the historian. In spite of C. P. Scott's motto, every journalist knows today that the most effective way to influence opinion is by the selection and arrangement of the appropriate facts. It used to be said that facts speak for themselves. This is, of course, untrue. The facts speak only when the historian calls on them: It is he who decides to which facts to give the floor, and in what order or context. It was, I think, one of Pirandello's characters who said that a fact is like a sack—it won't stand up till you've put something in it. The only reason why we are interested to know that the battle was fought at Hastings in 1066 is that historians regard it as a major historical event. It is the historian who has decided for his own reasons that Caesar's crossing of that petty stream, the Rubicon, is a fact of history, whereas the crossing of the Rubicon by millions of other people before or since interests nobody at all. The fact that you arrived in this building half an hour ago on foot, or on a bicycle, or in a car, is just as much a fact about the past as the fact that Caesar crossed the Rubicon. But it will probably be ignored by historians. Professor Talcott Parsons once called science "a selective system of cognitive orientations to reality." It might perhaps have been put more simply. But history is, among other things, that. The historian is necessarily selective. The belief in a hard core of historical facts existing objectively and independently of the interpretation of the historian is a preposterous fallacy, but one which it is very hard to eradicate.

Let us take a look at the process by which a mere fact about the past is transformed into a fact of history. At Stalybridge Wakes in 1850, a vendor of gingerbread, as the result of some petty dispute, was deliberately kicked to death by an angry mob. Is this a fact of history? A year ago I should unhesitatingly have said "no." It was recorded by an eyewitness in some little-known memoirs; but I had never seen it judged worthy of mention by any historian. A year ago Dr. Kitson Clark cited it in his Ford lectures in Oxford. Does this make it into a historical fact? Not, I think, yet. Its present status, I suggest, is that it has been proposed for membership of the select club of historical facts. It now awaits a seconder and sponsors. It may be that in the course of the next few years we shall see this fact appearing first in footnotes, then in the text, of articles and books about nineteenth-century England, and that in twenty or thirty years' time it may be a well established historical fact. Alternatively nobody may take it up, in which case it will relapse into the limbo of unhistorical facts about the past from which Dr. Kitson Clark has gallantly attempted to rescue it. What will decide which of these two things will happen? It will depend, I think, on whether the thesis or interpretation in support of which Dr. Kitson Clark cited this incident is accepted by other historians as valid and significant. Its status as a historical fact will turn on a question of interpretation. This element of interpretation enters into every fact of history.

May I be allowed a personal reminiscence? When I studied ancient history in this university many years ago, I had as a special subject "Greece in the period of the Persian Wars." I collected fifteen or twenty volumes on my shelves and took it for granted that there, recorded in these volumes, I had all the facts relating to my subject. Let us assume—it was very nearly true—that those volumes contained all the facts about it that were then known, or could be known. It never occurred to me to enquire by what accident or process of attrition that minute selection of facts, out of all the myriad facts that must have once been known to somebody, had survived to become *the* facts of history. I suspect that even today one of the fascinations of ancient and mediaeval history is that it gives us the illusion of having all the facts at our disposal within a manageable compass: the nagging distinction between the facts of history and other facts about the past vanishes because the few known facts are all facts of history. As Bury, who had worked in both periods, said, "the records of ancient and mediaeval history are starred with lacunae." History has been called an enormous jig-saw with a lot of missing parts. But the main trouble does not consist of the lacunae. Our picture of Greece in the fifth century *b.c.* is defective not primarily because so many of the bits have been accidentally lost, but because it is, by and large, the picture formed by a tiny group of people in the city of Athens. We know a lot about what fifth-century Greece looked like to an Athenian citizen; but hardly anything about what it looked like to a Spartan, a Corinthian, or a Theban—not to mention a Persian, or a slave or other non-citizen resident in Athens. Our picture has been preselected and predetermined for us, not so much by accident as by people who were consciously or unconsciously imbued with a particular view and thought the facts which supported that view worth preserving. In the same way, when I read in a modern history of the Middle Ages that the people of the Middle Ages were deeply concerned with religion, I wonder how we know this, and whether it is true. What we know as the facts of mediaeval history have almost all been selected for us by generations of chroniclers who were professionally occupied in the theory and practice of religion, and who therefore thought it supremely important, and recorded everything relating to it, and not much else. The picture of the Russian peasant as devoutly religious was destroyed by the revolution of 1917. The picture of mediaeval man as devoutly religious, whether true or not, is indestructible, because nearly all the known facts about him were preselected for us by people who believed it, and wanted others to believe it, and a mass of other facts, in which we might possibly have found evidence to the contrary, has been lost beyond recall. The dead band of vanished generations of historians, scribes, and chroniclers has determined beyond the possibility of appeal the pattern of the past. "The history we read," writes Professor Barraclough, himself trained as a mediaevalist, "though based on facts, is, strictly speaking, not factual at all, but a series of accepted judgments."

But let us turn to the different, but equally grave, plight of the modern historian. The ancient or mediaeval historian may be grateful for the vast winnowing process which, over the years, has put at his disposal a manageable corpus of historical facts. As Lytton Strachey said in his mischievous way, "ignorance is the first requisite of the historian, ignorance which simplifies and clarifies, which selects and omits." When I am tempted, as I sometimes am, to envy the extreme competence of colleagues engaged in writing ancient or mediaeval history, I find consolation in the reflection that they are so competent mainly because they are so ignorant of their subject. The modern historian enjoys none of the advantages of this built-in ignorance. He must cultivate this necessary ignorance for himself—the more so the nearer he comes to his own times. He has the dual task of discovering the few significant facts and turning them into facts of history, and of discarding the many insignificant facts as unhistorical. But this is the very converse of the nineteenth-century heresy that history consists of the compilation of a maximum number of irrefutable and objective facts. Anyone who succumbs to this heresy will either have to give up history as a bad job, and take to stamp-collecting or some other form of antiquarianism, or end in a madhouse. It is this heresy, which during the past hundred years has had such devastating effects on the modern historian, producing in Germany, in Great Britain, and in the United States a vast and growing mass of dry-as-dust factual histories, of minutely specialized monographs, of would-be historians knowing more and more about less and less, sunk without trace in an ocean of facts. It was, I suspect, this heresy—rather than the alleged conflict between liberal and Catholic loyalties—which frustrated Acton as a historian. In an early essay he said of his teacher Döllinger: "He would not write with imperfect materials, and to him the materials were always imperfect." Acton was surely here pronouncing an anticipatory verdict on himself, on that strange phenomenon of a historian whom many would regard as the most distinguished occupant the Regius

Chair of Modern History in this university has ever had—but who wrote no history. And Acton wrote his own epitaph in the introductory note to the first volume of the *Cambridge Modern History,* published just after his death, when he lamented that the requirements pressing on the historian "threaten to turn him from a man of letters into the compiler of an encyclopedia." Something had gone wrong. What had gone wrong was the belief in this untiring and unending accumulation of hard facts as the foundation of history, the belief that facts speak for themselves and that we cannot have too many facts, a belief at that time so unquestioning that few historians then thought it necessary—and some still think it unnecessary today—to ask themselves the question: What is history?

The nineteenth-century fetishism of facts was completed and justified by a fetishism of documents. The documents were the Ark of the Covenant in the temple of facts. The reverent historian approached them with bowed head and spoke of them in awed tones. If you find it in the documents, it is so. But what, when we get down to it, do these documents—the decrees, the treaties, the rent-rolls, the blue books, the official correspondence, the private letters and diaries—tell us? No document can tell us more than what the author of the document thought—what he thought had happened, what he thought ought to happen or would happen, or perhaps only what he wanted others to think he thought, or even only what he himself thought he thought. None of this means anything until the historian has got to work on it and deciphered it. The facts, whether found in documents or not, have still to be processed by the historian before he can make any use of them: the use he makes of them is, if I may put it that way, the processing process.

Let me illustrate what I am trying to say by an example which I happen to know well. When Gustav Stresemann, the Foreign Minister of the Weimar Republic, died in 1929, he left behind him an enormous mass—300 boxes full—of papers, official, semiofficial, and private, nearly all relating to the six years of his tenure of office as Foreign Minister. His friends and relatives naturally thought that a monument should be raised to the memory of so great a man. His faithful secretary Bernhardt got to work; and within three years there appeared three massive volumes, of some 600 pages each, of selected documents from the 300 boxes, with the impressive title *Stresemanns Vermächtnis.* In the ordinary way the documents themselves would have moldered away in some cellar or attic and disappeared for ever; or perhaps in a hundred years or so some curious scholar would have come upon them and set out to compare them with Bernhardt's text. What happened was far more dramatic. In 1945 the documents fell into the hands of the British and the American governments, who photographed the lot and put the photostats at the disposal of scholars in the Public Record Office in London and in the National Archives in Washington, so that, if we have sufficient patience and curiosity, we can discover exactly what Bernhardt did. What he did was neither very unusual nor very shocking. When Stresemann died, his Western policy

seemed to have been crowned with a series of brilliant successes—
Locarno, the admission of Germany to the League of Nations, the Dawes
and Young plans and the American loans, the withdrawal of allied occupation armies from the Rhineland. This seemed the important and rewarding part of Stresemann's foreign policy; and it was not unnatural
that it should have been over-represented in Bernhardt's selection of
documents. Stresemann's Eastern policy, on the other hand, his relations
with the Soviet Union, seemed to have led nowhere in particular; and,
since masses of documents about negotiations which yielded only trivial
results were not very interesting and added nothing to Stresemann's
reputation, the process of selection could be more rigorous. Stresemann
in fact devoted a far more constant and anxious attention to relations
with the Soviet Union, and they played a far larger part in his foreign policy as a whole, than the reader of the Bernhardt selection would surmise.
But the Bernhardt volumes compare favorably, I suspect, with many published collections of documents on which the ordinary historian implicitly relies.

This is not the end of my story. Shortly after the publication of
Bernhardt's volumes, Hitler came into power. Stresemann's name was
consigned to oblivion in Germany, and the volumes disappeared from circulation: many, perhaps most, of the copies must have been destroyed.
Today *Stresemanns Vermächtnis* is a rather rare book. But in the West
Stresemann's reputation stood high. In 1935 an English publisher brought
out an abbreviated translation of Bernhardt's work—a selection from
Bernhardt's selection; perhaps one third of the original was omitted.
Sutton, a well-known translator from the German, did his job compe-
tently and well. The English version, he explained in the preface, was
"slightly condensed, but only by the omission of a certain amount of
what, it was felt, was more ephemeral matter . . . of little interest to
English readers or students." This again is natural enough. But the result
is that Stresemann's Eastern policy, already under-represented in
Bernhardt, recedes still further from view, and the Soviet Union appears
in Sutton's volumes merely as an occasional and rather unwelcome
intruder in Stresemann's predominantly Western foreign policy. Yet it
is safe to say that, for all except a few specialists, Sutton and not
Bernhardt—and still less the documents themselves—represents for the
Western world the authentic voice of Stresemann. Had the documents
perished in 1945 in the bombing, and had the remaining Bernhardt volumes disappeared, the authenticity and authority of Sutton would never
have been questioned. Many printed collections of documents gratefully
accepted by historians in default of the originals rest on no securer basis
than this.

But I want to carry the story one step further. Let us forget about
Bernhardt and Sutton, and be thankful that we can, if we choose, consult
the authentic papers of a leading participant in some important events in
recent European history. What do the papers tell us? Among other things

they contain records of some hundreds of Stresemann's conversations with the Soviet ambassador in Berlin and of a score or so with Chicherin. These records have one feature in common. They depict Stresemann as having the lion's share of the conversations and reveal his arguments as invariably well put and cogent, while those of his partner are for the most part scanty, confused, and unconvincing. This is a familiar characteristic of all records of diplomatic conversations. The documents do not tell us what happened, but only what Stresemann thought had happened. It was not Sutton or Bernhardt, but Stresemann himself, who started the process of selection. And, if we had, say Chicherin's records of these same conversations, we should still learn from them only what Chicherin thought, and what really happened would still have to be reconstructed in the mind of the historian. Of course, facts and documents are essential to the historian. But do not make a fetish of them. They do not by themselves constitute history; they provide in themselves no ready-made answer to this tiresome question: What is history?

At this point I should like to say a few words on the question of why nineteenth-century historians were generally indifferent to the philosophy of history. The term was invented by Voltaire, and has since been used in different senses; but I shall take it to mean, if I use it at all, our answer to the question: What is history? The nineteenth century was, for the intellectuals of Western Europe, a comfortable period exuding confidence and optimism. The facts were on the whole satisfactory; and the inclination to ask and answer awkward questions about them was correspondingly weak. Ranke piously believed that divine providence would take care of the meaning of history if he took care of the facts; and Burckhardt with a more modern touch of cynicism observed that "we are not initiated into the purposes of the eternal wisdom." Professor Butterfield as late as 1931 noted with apparent satisfaction that "historians have reflected little upon the nature of things and even the nature of their own subject." But my predecessor in these lectures, Dr. A. L. Rowse, more justly critical, wrote of Sir Winston Churchill's *The World Crisis*—his book about the First World War—that, while it matched Trotsky's *History of the Russian Revolution* in personality, vividness, and vitality, it was inferior in one respect: it had "no philosophy of history behind it." British historians refused to be drawn, not because they believed that history had no meaning, but because they believed that its meaning was implicit and self-evident. The liberal nineteenth-century view of history had a close affinity with the economic doctrine of *laissez-faire*—also the product of a serene and self-confident outlook on the world. Let everyone get on with his particular job, and the hidden hand would take care of the universal harmony. The facts of history were themselves a demonstration of the supreme fact of a beneficent and apparently infinite progress towards higher things. This was the age of innocence, and historians walked in the Garden of Eden, without a scrap of philosophy to cover them, naked and unashamed before the god of history. Since then, we have known Sin and experienced a Fall; and those historians who today pretend to dispense with a philosophy of history are merely trying, vainly and self-consciously, like members of a nudist colony, to recreate the Garden of Eden in their garden suburb. Today the awkward question can no longer be evaded.

During the past fifty years a good deal of serious work has been done on the question: What is history? It was from Germany, the country which was to do so much to upset the comfortable reign of nineteenth-century liberalism, that the first challenge came in the 1880's and 1890's to the doctrine of the primacy and autonomy of facts in history. The philosophers who made the challenge are now little more than names: Dilthey is the only one of them who has recently received some belated recognition in Great Britain. Before the turn of the century, prosperity and confidence were still too great in this country for any attention to be paid to heretics who attacked the cult of facts. But early in the new century, the torch passed to Italy, where Croce began to propound a philosophy of history which obviously owed much to German masters. All history is "contemporary history," declared Croce meaning that history consists essentially in seeing the past through the eyes of the present and in the light of its problems, and that the main work of the historian is not to record, but to evaluate; for, if he does not evaluate, how can he know what is worth recording? In 1910 the American philosopher, Carl Becker, argued in deliberately provocative language that "the facts of history do not exist for any historian till he creates them." These challenges were for the moment little noticed. It was only after 1920 that Croce began to have a considerable vogue in France and Great Britain. This was not perhaps because Croce was a subtler thinker or a better stylist than his German predecessors, but because, after the First World War, the facts seemed to smile on us less propitiously than in the years before 1914, and we were therefore more accessible to a philosophy which sought to diminish their prestige. Croce was an important influence on the Oxford philosopher and historian Collingwood, the only British thinker in the present century who has made a serious contribution to the philosophy of history. He did not live to write the systematic treatise he had planned; but his published and unpublished papers on the subject were collected after his death in a volume entitled *The Idea of History*, which appeared in 1945.

The views of Collingwood can be summarized as follows. The philosophy of history is concerned neither with "the past by itself" nor with "the historian's thought about it by itself," but with "the two things in their mutual relations." (This dictum reflects the two current meanings of the word "history"—the enquiry conducted by the historian and the series of past events into which he enquires.) "The past which a historian studies is not a dead past, but a past which in some sense is still living in the present." But a past act is dead, *i.e.* meaningless to the historian, unless he can understand the thought that lay behind it. Hence "all history is the history of thought," and "history is the re-enactment in the historian's mind of the thought whose history he is studying." The reconstitution of the past in the historian's mind is dependent on empirical evidence. But it is not in itself an empirical process, and cannot consist in a mere recital of facts. On the contrary, the process of reconstitution governs the selection and interpretation of the facts: this, indeed, is what makes them historical facts. "History," says Professor Oakeshott, who on this point stands near to Collingwood, "is the historian's experience. It is 'made' by nobody save the historian: to write history is the only way of making it."

This searching critique, though it may call for some serious reservations, brings to light certain neglected truths.

In the first place, the facts of history never come to us "pure," since they do not and cannot exist in a pure form: they are always refracted through the mind of the recorder. It follows that when we take up a work of history, our first concern should be not with the facts which it contains but with the historian who wrote it. Let me take as an example the great historian in whose honor and in whose name these lectures were founded. Trevelyan, as he tells us in his autobiography, was "brought up at home on a somewhat exuberantly Whig tradition"; and he would not, I hope, disclaim the title if I described him as the last and not the least of the great English liberal historians of the Whig tradition. It is not for nothing that he traces back his family tree, through the great Whig historian George Otto Trevelyan, to Macaulay, incomparably the greatest of the Whig historians. Dr. Trevelyan's finest and maturest work *England under Queen Anne* was written against that background, and will yield its full meaning and significance to the reader only when read against that background. The author, indeed, leaves the reader with no excuse for failing to do so. For if, following the technique of connoisseurs of detective novels, you read the end first, you will find on the last few pages of the third volume the best summary known to me of what is nowadays called the Whig interpretation of history; and you will see that what Trevelyan is trying to do is to investigate the origin and development of the Whig tradition, and to root it fairly and squarely in the years after the death of its founder, William III. Though this is not, perhaps, the only conceivable interpretation of the events of Queen Anne's reign, it is a valid and, in Trevelyan's hands, a fruitful interpretation. But, in order to appreciate it at its full value, you have to understand what the historian is doing. For if, as Collingwood says, the historian must re-enact in thought what has gone on in the mind of his *dramatis personae,* so the reader in his turn must re-enact what goes on in the mind of the historian. Study the historian before you begin to study the facts. This is, after all, not very abstruse. It is what is already done by the intelligent undergraduate who, when recommended to read a work by that great scholar Jones of St. Jude's, goes round to a friend at St. Jude's to ask what sort of chap Jones is, and what bees he has in his bonnet. When you read a work of history, always listen out for the buzzing. If you can detect none, either you are tone deaf or your historian is a dull dog. The facts are really not at all like fish on the fishmonger's slab. They are like fish swimming about in a vast and some-times inaccessible ocean; and what the historian catches will depend partly on chance, but mainly on what part of the ocean he chooses to fish in and what tackle he chooses to use—these two factors being, of course, determined by the kind of fish he wants to catch. By and large, the histo-rian will get the kind of facts he wants. History means interpretation. In-deed, if, standing Sir George Clark on his head, I were to call history "a hard core of interpretation surrounded by a pulp of disputable facts," my statement would, no doubt, be one-sided and misleading, but no more so, I venture to think, than the original dictum.

The second point is the more familiar one of the historian's need of imaginative understanding for the minds of the people with whom he is dealing, for the thought behind their acts: I say "imaginative understand-ing," not "sympathy," lest sympathy should be supposed to imply agree-ment. The nineteenth century was weak in mediaeval history, because it was too much repelled by the superstitious beliefs of the Middle Ages and by the barbarities which they inspired, to have any imaginative un-derstanding of mediaeval people. Or take Burckhardt's censorious re-mark about the Thirty Years' War: "It is scandalous for a creed, no matter whether it is Catholic or Protestant, to place its salvation above the in-tegrity of the nation." It was extremely difficult for a nineteenth-century liberal historian, brought up to believe that it is right and praiseworthy to kill in defense of one's country, but wicked and wrongheaded to kill in defense of one's religion, to enter into the state of mind of those who fought the Thirty Years' War. This difficulty is particularly acute in the field in which I am now working. Much of what has been written in English-speaking countries in the last ten years about the Soviet Union, and in the Soviet Union about the English-speaking countries, has been vitiated by this inability to achieve even the most elementary measure of imaginative understanding of what goes on in the mind of the other party, so that the words and actions of the other are always made to ap-pear malign, senseless, or hypocritical. History cannot be written unless the historian can achieve some kind of contact with the mind of those about whom he is writing.

The third point is that we can view the past, and achieve our under-standing of the past, only through the eyes of the present. The historian is of his own age, and is bound to it by the conditions of human existence. The very words which he uses—words like democracy, empire, war, revo-lution—have current connotations from which he cannot divorce them. Ancient historians have taken to using words like *polis* and *plebs* in the original, just in order to show that they have not fallen into this trap. This does not help them. They, too, live in the present, and cannot cheat them-selves into the past by using unfamiliar or obsolete words, any more than they would become better Greek or Roman historians if they delivered their lectures in a *chlamys* or a *toga*. The names by which successive French historians have described the Parisian crowds which played so prominent a role in the French revolution—*les sansculottes, le peuple, la canaille, les bras-nus*—are all, for those who know the rules of the game, manifestos of a political affiliation and of a particular interpretation. Yet the historian is obliged to choose: the use of language forbids him to be neutral. Nor is it a matter of words alone. Over the past hundred years the changed balance of power in Europe has reversed the attitude of British historians to Frederick the Great. The changed balance of power within the Christian churches between Catholicism and Protestantism has profoundly altered their attitude to such figures as Loyola, Luther, and Cromwell. It requires only a superficial knowledge of the work of French historians of the last forty years on the French revolution to recognize how deeply it has been affected by the Russian revolution of 1917. The historian belongs not to the past but to the present. Professor Trevor-Roper tells us that the historian "ought to love the past." This is a dubious injunction. To love the past may easily be an expression of the nostalgic romanticism of old men and old societies, a symptom of loss of faith and interest in the present or future. *Cliché* for *cliché*, I should prefer the one about freeing oneself from "the dead hand of the past." The function of the historian is neither to love the past nor to emancipate himself from the past, but to master and understand it as the key to the understanding of the present.

If, however, these are some of the sights of what I may call the Collingwood view of history, it is time to consider some of the dangers. The emphasis on the role of the historian in the making of history tends, if pressed to its logical conclusion, to rule out any objective history at all: history is what the historian makes. Collingwood seems indeed, at one moment, in an unpublished note quoted by his editor, to have reached this conclusion:

> St. Augustine looked at history from the point of view of the early Christian; Tillemont, from that of a seventeenth-century Frenchman; Gibbon, from that of an eighteenth-century Englishman; Mommsen, from that of a nineteenth-century German. There is no point in asking which was the right point of view. Each was the only one possible for the man who adopted it.

This amounts to total scepticism, like Froude's remark that history is "a child's box of letters with which we can spell any word we please." Collingwood, in his reaction against "scissors-and-paste history," against the view of history as a mere compilation of facts, comes perilously near to treating history as something spun out of the human brain, and leads back to the conclusion referred to by Sir George Clark in the passage which I quoted earlier, that "there is no 'objective' historical truth." In place of the theory that history has no meaning, we are offered here the theory of an infinity of meanings, none any more right than any other—which comes to much the same thing. The second theory is surely as untenable as the first. It does not follow that, because a mountain appears to take on different shapes from different angles of vision, it has objectively either no shape at all or an infinity of shapes. It does not follow that, because interpretation plays a necessary part in establishing the facts of history, and because no existing interpretation is wholly objective, one interpretation is as good as another, and the facts of history are in principle not amenable to objective interpretation. I shall have to consider at a later stage what exactly is meant by objectivity in history.

But a still greater danger lurks in the Collingwood hypothesis. If the historian necessarily looks at his period of history through the eyes of his own time, and studies the problems of the past as a key to those of the present, will he not fall into a purely pragmatic view of the facts, and maintain that the criterion of a right interpretation is its suitability to some present purpose? On this hypothesis, the facts of history are nothing, interpretation is everything. Nietzsche had already enunciated the principle: "The falseness of an opinion is not for us any objection to it. . . . The question is how far it is life-furthering, life-preserving, species-preserving, perhaps species-creating." The American pragmatists moved, less explicitly and less wholeheartedly, along the same line. Knowledge is knowledge for some purpose. The validity of the knowledge depends on the validity of the purpose. But, even where no such theory has been professed, the practice has often been no less disquieting. In my own field of study, I have seen too many examples of extravagant interpretation riding roughshod over facts, not to be impressed with the reality of this danger. It is not surprising that perusal of some of the more extreme products of Soviet and anti-Soviet schools of historiography should sometimes breed a certain nostalgia for that illusory nineteenth-century heaven of purely factual history.

How then, in the middle of the twentieth century, are we to define the obligation of the historian to his facts? I trust that I have spent a sufficient number of hours in recent years chasing and perusing documents, and stuffing my historical narrative with properly footnoted facts, to escape the imputation of treating facts and documents too cavalierly. The duty of the historian to respect his facts is not exhausted by the obligation to see that his facts are accurate. He must seek to bring into the picture all known or knowable facts relevant, in one sense or another, to the theme on which he is engaged and to the interpretation proposed. If he seeks to depict the Victorian Englishman as a moral and rational being, he must not forget what happened at Stalybridge Wakes in 1850. But this, in turn, does not mean that he can eliminate interpretation, which is the life-blood of history. Laymen—that is to say, non-academic friends or friends from other academic disciplines—sometimes ask me how the historian goes to work when he writes history. The commonest assumption appears to be that the historian divides his work into two sharply distinguishable phases or periods. First, he spends a long preliminary period reading his source and filling his notebooks with facts: then, when this is over, he puts away his sources, takes out his notebooks, and writes his book from beginning to end. This is to me an unconvincing and unplausible picture. For myself, as soon as I have got going on a few of what I take to be the capital sources, the itch becomes too strong and I begin to write—not necessarily at the beginning, but somewhere, anywhere. Thereafter, reading and writing go on simultaneously. The writing is added to, subtracted from, re-shaped, cancelled, as I go on reading. The reading is guided and directed and made fruitful by the writing: the more I write, the more I know what I am looking for, the better I understand the significance and relevance of what I find. Some historians probably do all this preliminary writing in their head without using pen, paper, or typewriter, just as some people play chess in their heads without recourse to board and chess-men: this is a talent which I envy, but cannot emulate. But I am convinced that, for any historian worth the name, the two processes of what economists call "input" and "output" go on simultaneously and are, in practice, parts of a single process. If you try to separate them, or to give one priority over the other, you fall into one of two heresies. Either you write scissors-and-paste history without meaning or significance; or you write propaganda or historical fiction, and merely use facts of the past to embroider a kind of writing which has nothing to do with history.

Our examination of the relation of the historian to the facts of history finds us, therefore, in an apparently precarious situation, navigating delicately between the Scylla of an untenable theory of history as an objective compilation of facts, of the unqualified primacy of fact over interpretation, and the Charybdis of an equally untenable theory of history as the subjective product of the mind of the historian who establishes the facts of history and masters them through the process of interpretation, between a view of history having the center of gravity in the past and the view having the center of gravity in the present. But our situation is less precarious than it seems. We shall encounter the same dichotomy of fact and interpretation again in these lectures in other guises—the particular and the general, the empirical and the theoretical, the objective and the subjective. The predicament of the historian is a reflection of the nature of man. Man, except perhaps in earliest infancy and in extreme old age, is not totally involved in his environment and unconditionally subject to it. On the other hand, he is never totally independent of it and its unconditional master. The relation of man to his environment is the relation of the historian to his theme. The historian is neither the humble slave, nor the tyrannical master, of his facts. The relation between the historian and his facts is one of equality, of give-and-take. As any working historian knows, if he stops to reflect on what he is doing as he thinks and writes, the historian is engaged in a continuous process of molding his facts to his interpretation and his interpretation to his facts. It is impossible to assign primacy to one over the other.

The historian starts with the provisional selection of facts and a provisional interpretation in the light of which that selection has been made—

by others as well as by himself. As he works, both the interpretation and the selection and ordering of facts undergo subtle and perhaps partly unconscious changes through the reciprocal action of one or the other. And this reciprocal action also involves reciprocity between present and past, since the historian is part of the present and the facts belong to the past. The historian and the facts of history are necessary to one another. The historian without his facts is rootless and futile; the facts without their historian are dead and meaningless. My first answer therefore to the question, What is history?, is that it is a continuous process of interaction between the historian and his facts, an unending dialogue between the present and the past.

Street Fair, ca. 1955, Photograph by W. Eugene Smith.

"THIS IS THE END OF THE WORLD":
THE BLACK DEATH

——————■——————

Barbara Tuchman

This is an excerpt from Tuchman's 1978 book A Distant Mirror: The Calamitous Fourteenth Century.

In October 1347, two months after the fall of Calais, Genoese trading ships put into the harbor of Messina in Sicily with dead and dying men at the oars. The ships had come from the Black Sea port of Caffa (now Feodosiya) in the Crimea, where the Genoese maintained a trading post. The diseased sailors showed strange black swellings about the size of an egg or an apple in the armpits and groin. The swellings oozed blood and pus and were followed by spreading boils and black blotches on the skin from internal bleeding. The sick suffered severe pain and died quickly within five days of the first symptoms. As the disease spread, other symptoms of continuous fever and spitting of blood appeared instead of the swellings or buboes. These victims coughed and sweated heavily and died even more quickly, within three days or less, sometimes in 24 hours. In both types everything that issued from the body—breath, sweat, blood from the buboes and lungs, bloody urine, and blood-blackened excrement—smelled foul. Depression and despair accompanied the physical symptoms, and before the end "death is seen seated on the face."

The disease was bubonic plague, present in two forms: one that infected the bloodstream, causing the buboes and internal bleeding, and was spread by contact; and a second, more virulent pneumonic type that infected the lungs and was spread by respiratory infection. The presence of both at once cause the high mortality and speed of contagion. So lethal was the disease that cases were known of persons going to bed well and dying before they woke, of doctors catching the illness at a bedside and dying before the patient. So rapidly did it spread from one to another that to a French physician, Simon de Covino, it seemed as if one sick person "could infect the whole world." The malignity of the pestilence appeared more terrible because its victims knew no prevention and no remedy.

The physical suffering of the disease and its aspect of evil mystery were expressed in a strange Welsh lament which saw "death coming into our midst like black smoke, a plague which cuts off the young, a rootless phantom which has no mercy for fair countenance. Woe is me of the shilling in the armpit! It is seething, terrible . . . a head that gives pain and causes a loud cry . . . a painful angry knob . . . Great is its seething like a burning cinder . . . a grievous thing of ashy color." Its eruption is ugly like the "seeds of black peas, broken fragments of brittle sea-coal . . . the early ornaments of black death, cinders of the peelings of the cockle weed, a mixed multitude, a black plague like half-pence, like berries. . . . "

Rumors of a terrible plague supposedly arising in China and spreading through Tartary (Central Asia) to India and Persia, Mesopotamia, Syria, Egypt, and all of Asia Minor had reached Europe in 1346. They told of a death toll so devastating that all of India was said to be depopulated, whole territories covered by dead bodies, other areas with no one left alive. As added up by Pope Clement VI at Avignon, the total of reported dead reached 23,840,000. In the absence of a concept of contagion, no serious alarm was felt in Europe until the trading ships brought their black burden of pestilence into Messina while other infected ships from the Levant carried it to Genoa and Venice.

By January 1348 it penetrated France via Marseille, and North Africa via Tunis. Shipborne along coasts and navigable rivers, it spread westward from Marseille through the ports of Languedoc to Spain and northward up the Rhône to Avignon, where it arrived in March. It reached Narbonne, Montpellier, Carcassonne, and Toulouse between February and May, and at the same time in Italy spread to Rome and Florence and their hinterlands. Between June and August it reached Bordeaux, Lyon, and Paris, spread to Burgundy and Normandy, and crossed the Channel from Normandy into southern England. From Italy during the same summer it crossed the Alps into Switzerland and reached eastward to Hungary.

In a given area the plague accomplished its kill within four to six months and then faded, except in the larger cities, where, rooting into the close-quartered population, it abated during the winter, only to reappear in spring and rage for another six months.

In 1349 it resumed in Paris, spread to Picardy, Flanders, and the Low Countries, and from England to Scotland and Ireland as well as to Norway, where a ghost ship with a cargo of wool and a dead crew drifted offshore until it ran aground near Bergen. From there the plague passed into Sweden, Denmark, Prussia, Iceland, and as far as Greenland. Leaving a strange pocket of immunity in Bohemia, and Russia unattacked until 1351, it had passed from most of Europe by mid-1350. Although the mortality rate was erratic, ranging from one fifth in some places to nine tenths or almost total elimination in others, the overall estimate of modern demographers has settled—for the area extending from India to Iceland—around the same figure expressed in Froissart's casual words: "a third of the world died." His estimate, the common one at the time, was not an inspired guess but a borrowing of St. John's figure for mortality from plague in Revelation, the favorite guide to human affairs of the Middle Ages.

A third of Europe would have meant about 20 million deaths. No one knows in truth how many died. Contemporary reports were an awed impression, not an accurate count. In crowded Avignon, it was said, 400 died daily; 7,000 houses emptied by death were shut up; a single graveyard received 11,000 corpses in six weeks; half the city's inhabitants reportedly died, including 9 cardinals or one third of the total, and 70 lesser prelates.

Watching the endlessly passing death carts, chroniclers let normal exaggeration take wings and put the Avignon death toll at 62,000 and even at 120,000, although the city's total population was probably less than 50,000.

When graveyards filled up, bodies at Avignon were thrown into the Rhône until mass burial pits were dug for dumping the corpses. In London in such pits corpses piled up in layers until they overflowed. Everywhere reports speak of the sick dying too fast for the living to bury. Corpses were dragged out of homes and left in front of doorways. Morning light revealed new piles of bodies. In Florence the dead were gathered up by the Compagnia della Misericordia—founded in 1244 to care for the sick—whose members wore red robes and hoods masking the face except for the eyes. When their efforts failed, the dead lay putrid in the streets for days at a time. When no coffins were to be had, the bodies were laid on boards, two or three at once, to be carried to graveyards or common pits. Families dumped their own relatives into the pits, or buried them so hastily and thinly "that dogs dragged them forth and devoured their bodies."

Amid accumulating death and fear of contagion, people died without last rites and were buried without prayers, a prospect that terrified the last hours of the stricken. A bishop in England gave permission to laymen to make confession to each other as was done by the Apostles, "or if no man is present then even to a woman," and if no priest could be found to administer extreme unction, "then faith must suffice." Clement VI found it necessary to grant remissions of sin to all who died of the plague because so many were unattended by priests. "And no bells tolled," wrote a chronicler of Siena, "and nobody wept no matter what his loss because almost everyone expected death. . . . And people said and believed, 'This is the end of the world.'"

In Paris, where the plague lasted through 1349, the reported death rate was 800 a day, in Pisa 500, in Vienna 500 to 600. The total dead in Paris numbered 50,000 or half the population. Florence, weakened by the famine of 1347, lost three to four fifths of its citizens, Venice two thirds, Hamburg and Bremen, though smaller in size, about the same proportion. Cities, as centers of transportation, were more likely to be affected than villages, although once a village was infected, its death rate was equally high. At Givry, a prosperous village in Burgundy of 1,200 to 1,500 people, the parish register records 615 deaths in the space of fourteen weeks, compared to an average of thirty deaths a year in the previous decade. In three villages of Cambridgeshire, manorial records show a death rate of 47 percent, 57 percent, and in one case 70 percent. When the last survivors, too few to carry on, moved away, a deserted village sank back into the wilderness and disappeared from the map altogether, leaving only a grass-covered ghostly outline to show where mortals once had lived.

In enclosed places such as monasteries and prisons, the infection of one person usually meant that of all, as happened in the Franciscan convents of Carcassonne and Marseille, where every inmate without exception died. Of the 140 Dominicans at Montpellier only seven survived. Petrarch's brother Gherardo, member of a Carthusian monastery, buried the prior and 34 fellow monks one by one, sometimes three a day, until he was left alone with his dog and fled to look for a place that would take him in. Watching every comrade die, men in such places could not but wonder whether the strange peril that filled the air had not been sent to exterminate the human race. In Kilkenny, Ireland, Brother John Clyn of the Friars Minor, another monk left alone among dead men, kept a record of what had happened lest "things which should be remembered perish with time and vanish from the memory of those who come after us." Sensing "the whole world, as it were, placed within the grasp of the Evil One," and waiting for death to visit him too, he wrote, "I leave parchment to continue this work, if perchance any man survive and any of the race of Adam escape this pestilence and carry on the work which I have begun." Brother John, as noted by another hand, died of the pestilence, but he foiled oblivion.

The largest cities of Europe, with populations of about 100,000, were Paris and Florence, Venice and Genoa. At the next level, with more than 50,000, were Ghent and Bruges in Flanders, Milan, Bologna, Rome, Naples, and Palermo, and Cologne. London hovered below 50,000, the only city in England except York with more than 10,000. At the level of 20,000 to 50,000 were Bordeaux, Toulouse, Montpellier, Marseille, and Lyon in France, Barcelona, Seville, and Toledo in Spain, Siena, Pisa, and other secondary cities in Italy, and the Hanseatic trading cities of the Empire. The plague raged through them all, killing anywhere from one third to two thirds of their inhabitants. Italy, with a total population of 10 to 11 million, probably suffered the heaviest toll. Following the Florentine bankruptcies, the crop failures and workers' riots of 1346–47, the revolt of Cola di Rienzi that plunged Rome into anarchy, the plague came as the peak of successive calamities. As if the world were indeed in the grasp of the Evil One, its first appearance on the European mainland January 1348 coincided with a fearsome earthquake that carved a path of wreckage from Naples up to Venice. Houses collapsed, church towers toppled, villages were crushed, and the destruction reached as far as Germany and Greece. Emotional response, dulled by horrors, underwent a kind of atrophy epitomized by the chronicler who wrote, "And in these days was burying without sorrowe and wedding without friendschippe."

In Siena, where more than half the inhabitants died of the plague, work was abandoned on the great cathedral, planned to be the largest in the world, and never resumed, owing to loss of workers and master masons and "the melancholy and grief" of the survivors. The cathedral's truncated transept still stands in permanent witness to the sweep of death's scythe. Agnolo di Tura, a chronicler of Siena, recorded the fear of contagion that froze every other instinct. "Father abandoned child, wife husband, one brother another," he wrote, "for this plague seemed to strike through the breath and sight. And so they died. And no one could be found to bury the dead for money or friendship. . . . And I, Agnolo di Tura, called the Fat, buried my five children with my own hands, and so did many others likewise."

There were many to echo his account of inhumanity and few to balance it, for the plague was not the kind of calamity that inspired mutual help. Its loathsomeness and deadliness did not herd people together in mutual distress, but only prompted their desire to escape each other. "Magistrates and notaries refused to come and make the wills of the dying," reported a Franciscan friar of Piazza in Sicily; what was worse, "even the priests did not come to hear their confessions." A clerk of the Archbishop of Canterbury reported the same of English priests who "turned away from the care of their benefices from fear of death." Cases of parents deserting children and children their parents were reported across Europe from Scotland to Russia. The calamity chilled the hearts of men, wrote Boccaccio in his famous account of the plague in Florence that serves as introduction to the *Decameron*. "One man shunned another . . . kinsfold held aloof, brother was forsaken by brother, oftentimes husband by wife; nay, what is more, and scarcely to be believed, fathers and mothers were found to abandon their own children to their fate, untended, unvisited as if they had been strangers." Exaggeration and literary pessimism were common in the 14th century, but the Pope's physician, Guy de Chauliac, was a sober, careful observer who reported the same phenomenon: "A father did not visit his son, nor the son his father. Charity was dead."

Yet not entirely. In Paris, according to the chronicler Jean de Venette, the nuns of the Hôtel Dieu or municipal hospital, "having no fear of death, tended the sick with all sweetness and humility." New nuns repeatedly took the places of those who died, until the majority "many times renewed by death now rest in peace with Christ as we may piously believe."

When the plague entered northern France in July 1348, it settled first in Normandy and, checked by winter, gave Picardy a deceptive interim until the next summer. Either in mourning or warning, black flags were flown from church towers of the worst-stricken villages of Normandy. "And in that time," wrote a monk of the abbey of Fourcarment, "the mortality was so great among the people of Normandy that those of Picardy mocked them." The same unneighborly reaction was reported of the Scots, separated by a winter's immunity from the English. Delighted to hear of the disease that was scourging the "southrons," they gathered forces for an invasion, "laughing at their enemies." Before they could move, the savage mortality fell upon them too, scattering some in death and the rest in panic to spread the infection as they fled.

In Picardy in the summer of 1349 the pestilence penetrated the castle of Coucy to kill Enguerrand's mother, Catherine, and her new husband. Whether her nine-year-old son escaped by chance or was perhaps living elsewhere with one of his guardians is unrecorded. In nearby Amiens, tannery workers, responding quickly to losses in the labor force, combined to bargain for higher wages. In another place villagers were seen dancing to drums and trumpets, and on being asked the reason, answered that, seeing their neighbors die day by day while their village remained immune, they believed they could keep the plague from entering "by the jollity that is in us. That is why we dance." Further north in Tournai on the border of Flanders, Gilles li Muisis, Abbot of St. Martin's, kept one of the epidemic's most vivid accounts. The passing bells rang all day and all night, he recorded, because sextons were anxious to obtain their fees while they could. Filled with the sound of mourning, the city became oppressed by fear, so that the authorities forbade the tolling of bells and the wearing of black and restricted funeral services to two mourners. The silencing of funeral bells and of criers' announcements of deaths was ordained by most cities. Siena imposed a fine on the wearing of mourning clothes by all except widows.

Flight was the chief recourse of those who could afford it or arrange it. The rich fled to their country places like Boccaccio's young patricians of Florence, who settled in a pastoral palace "removed on every side from the roads" with "wells of cool water and vaults of rare wines." The urban poor died in their burrows, "and only the stench of their bodies informed neighbors of their death." That the poor were more heavily afflicted than the rich was clearly remarked at the time, in the north as in the south. A Scottish chronicler, John of Fordun, stated flatly that the pest "attacked especially the meaner sort and common people—seldom the magnates." Simon de Covino of Montpellier made the same observation. He ascribed it to the misery and want and hard lives that made the poor more susceptible, which was half the truth. Close contact and lack of sanitation was the unrecognized other half. It was noticed too that the young died in greater proportion than the old; Simon de Covino compared the disappearance of youth to the withering of flowers in the fields.

In the countryside peasants dropped dead on the roads, in the fields, in their houses. Survivors in growing helplessness fell into apathy, leaving ripe wheat uncut and livestock untended. Oxen and asses, sheep and goats, pigs and chickens ran wild and they too, according to local reports, succumbed to the pest. English sheep, bearers of the precious wool, died throughout the country. The chronicler Henry Knighton, canon of Leicester Abbey, reported 5,000 dead in one field alone, "their bodies so corrupted by the plague that neither beast nor bird would touch them," and spreading an appalling stench. In the Austrian Alps wolves came down to prey upon sheep and then, "as if alarmed by some invisible warning, turned and fled back into the wilderness." In remote Dalmatia bolder wolves descended upon a plague-stricken city and attacked human survivors. For want of herdsmen, cattle strayed from place to place and died in hedgerows and ditches. Dogs and cats fell like the rest.

The dearth of labor held a fearful prospect because the 14th century lived close to the annual harvest both for food and for next year's seed. "So few servants and laborers were left," wrote Knighton, "that no one knew where to turn for help." The sense of a vanishing future created a kind of dementia of despair. A Bavarian chronicler of Neuberg on the Danube recorded that "Men and women . . . wandered around as if mad" and let their cattle stray "because no one had any inclination to concern themselves about the future." Fields went uncultivated, spring seed unsown. Second growth with nature's awful energy crept back over cleared land, dikes crumbled, salt water reinvaded and soured the lowlands. With so few hands remaining to restore the work of centuries, people felt, in Walsingham's words, that "the world could never again regain its former prosperity."

Though the death rate was higher among the anonymous poor, the known and the great died too. King Alfonso XI of Castile was the only reigning monarch killed by the pest, but his neighbor King Pedro of Aragon lost his wife, Queen Leonora, his daughter Marie, and a niece in the space of six months. John Cantacuzene, Emperor of Byzantium, lost his son. In France the lame Queen Jeanne and her daughter-in-law Bonne de Luxemburg, wife of the Dauphin, both died in 1349 in the same phase that took the life of Enguerrand's mother. Jeanne, Queen of Navarre, daughter of Louis X, was another victim. Edward III's second daughter, Joanna, who was on her way to marry Pedro, the heir of Castile, died in Bordeaux. Women appear to have been more vulnerable than men, perhaps because, being more housebound, they were more exposed to fleas. Boccaccio's mistress Fiammetta, illegitimate daughter of the King of Naples, died, as did Laura, the beloved—whether real or fictional—of Petrarch. Reaching out to us in the future, Petrarch cried, "Oh happy posterity who will not experience such abysmal woe and will look upon our testimony as a fable."

In Florence Giovanni Villani, the great historian of his time, died at 68 in the midst of an unfinished sentence: ". . . *e dure questo pistolenza fino a . . .* (in the midst of this pestilence there came to an end . . .)." Siena's master painters, the brothers Ambrogio and Pietro Lorenzetti, whose names never appear after 1348, presumably perished in the plague, as did Andrea Pisano, architect and sculptor of Florence. William of Ockham and the English mystic Richard Rolle of Hampole both disappear from mention after 1349. Francisco Datini, merchant of Prato, lost both his parents and two siblings. Curious sweeps of mortality afflicted certain bodies of merchants in London. All eight wardens of the Company of Cutters, all six wardens of the Hatters, and four wardens of the Goldsmiths died before July 1350. Sir John Pulteney, master draper and four times Mayor of London, was a victim, likewise Sir John Montgomery, Governor of Calais.

Among the clergy and doctors the mortality was naturally high because of the nature of their professions. Out of 24 physicians in Venice, 20 were said to have lost their lives in the plague, although, according to another account, some were believed to have fled or to have shut themselves up in their houses. At Montpellier, site of the leading medieval medical school, the physician Simon de Covino reported that, despite the great number of doctors, "hardly one of them escaped." In Avignon, Guy de Chauliac confessed that he performed his medical visits only because he dared not stay away for fear of infamy, but "I was in continual fear." He claimed to have contracted the disease but to have cured himself by his own treatment; if so, he was one of the few who recovered.

Clerical mortality varied with rank. Although the one-third toll of cardinals reflects the same proportion as the whole, this was probably due to their concentration in Avignon. In England, in strange and almost sinister procession, the Archbishop of Canterbury, John Stratford, died in August 1348, his appointed successor died in May 1349, and the next appointee three months later, all three within a year. Despite such weird vagaries, prelates in general managed to sustain a higher survival rate than the lesser clergy. Among bishops the deaths have been estimated at about one in twenty. The loss of priests, even if many avoided their fearful duty of attending the dying, was about the same as among the population as a whole.

Government officials, whose loss contributed to the general chaos, found, on the whole, no special shelter. In Siena four of the nine members of the governing oligarchy died, in France one third of the royal notaries, in Bristol 15 out of the 52 members of the Town Council or almost one third. Tax-collecting obviously suffered, with the result that Philip VI was unable to collect more than a fraction of the subsidy granted him by the Estates in the winter of 1347–48.

Lawlessness and debauchery accompanied the plague as they had during the great plague of Athens of 430 B.C., when according to Thucydides, men grew bold in the indulgence of pleasure: "For seeing how the rich died in a moment and those who had nothing immediately inherited their property, they reflected that life and riches were alike transitory and they resolved to enjoy themselves while they could." Human behavior is timeless. When St. John had his vision of plague in Revelation, he knew from some experience or race memory that those who survived "repented not of the work of their hands. . . . Neither repented they of their murders, nor of their sorceries, nor of their fornication, nor of their thefts."

Ignorance of the cause augmented the sense of horror. Of the real carriers, rats and fleas, the 14th century had no suspicion, perhaps because they were so familiar. Fleas, though a common household nuisance, are not once mentioned in contemporary plague writings, and rats only incidentally, although folklore commonly associated them with pestilence. The legend of the Pied Piper arose from an outbreak of 1284. The actual plague bacillus, *Pasturella pestis*, remained undiscovered for another 500 years. Living alternately in the stomach of the flea and the bloodstream of the rat who was the flea's host, the bacillus in its bubonic form was transferred to humans and animals by the bite of either rat or flea. It traveled by virtue of *Rattus rattus,* the small medieval black rat that lived on ships, as well as by the heavier brown or sewer rat. What precipitated the turn of the bacillus from innocuous to virulent form is unknown, but the occurrence is now believed to have taken place not in China but somewhere in central Asia and to have spread along the caravan routes. Chinese origin was a mistaken notion of the 14th century based on real but belated reports of huge death tolls in China from drought, famine, and pestilence which have since been traced to the 1330s, too soon to be responsible for the plague that appeared in India in 1346.

The phantom enemy had no name. Called the Black Death only in later recurrences, it was known during the first epidemic simply as the Pestilence or Great Mortality. Reports from the East, swollen by fearful imaginings, told of strange tempests and "sheets of fire" mingled with huge hailstones that "slew almost all," or a "vast rain of fire" that burned up men, beasts, stones, trees, villages, and cities. In another version, "foul blasts of wind" from the fires carried the infection to Europe "and now as some suspect it cometh round the seacoast." Accurate observation in this case could not make the mental jump to ships and rats because no idea of animal- or insect-borne contagion existed.

The earthquake was blamed for releasing sulfurous and foul fumes from the earth's interior, or as evidence of a titanic struggle of planets and oceans causing waters to rise and vaporize until fish died in masses and corrupted the air. All these explanations had in common a factor of poisoned air, of miasmas and thick, stinking mists traced to every kind of natural or imagined agency from stagnant lakes to malign conjunction of the planets, from the hand of the Evil One to the wrath of God. Medical thinking, trapped in the theory of astral influences, stressed air as the communicator of disease, ignoring sanitation or visible carriers. The existence of two carriers confused the trail, the more so because the flea could live and travel independently of the rat for as long as a month and, if infected by the particularly virulent septicemic form of the bacillus, could infect humans without reinfecting itself from the rat. The simultaneous presence of the pneumonic form of the disease, which was indeed communicated through the air, blurred the problem further.

The mystery of the contagion was "the most terrible of all the terrors," as an anonymous Flemish cleric in Avignon wrote to a correspondent in Bruges. Plagues had been known before, from the plague of Athens (believed to have been typhus) to the prolonged epidemic of the 6th century A.D., to the recurrence of sporadic outbreaks in the 12th and 13th centuries, but they had left no accumulated store of understanding. That the infection came from contact with the sick or with their houses, clothes, or corpses was quickly observed but not comprehended. Gentile da Foligno, renowned physician of Perugia and doctor of medicine at the universities of Bologna and Padua, came close to respiratory infection when he surmised that poisonous material was "communicated by means of air breathed out and in." Having no idea of microscopic carriers, he had to assume that the air was corrupted by planetary influences. Planets, however, could not explain the ongoing contagion. The agonized search for an answer gave rise to such theories as transference by sight. People fell ill, wrote Guy de Chauliac, not only by remaining with the sick but "even by looking at them." Three hundred years later Joshua Barnes, the 17th century biographer of Edward III, could write that the power of infection had entered into beams of light and "darted death from the eyes."

Doctors struggling with the evidence could not break away from the terms of astrology, to which they believed all human physiology was subject. Medicine was the one aspect of medieval life, perhaps because of its links with the Arabs, not shaped by Christian doctrine. Clerics detested astrology, but could not dislodge its influence. Guy de Chauliac, physician to three popes in succession, practiced in obedience to the zodiac. While his *Cirurgia* was the major treatise on surgery of its time, while he understood the use of anesthesia made from the juice of opium, mandrake, or hemlock, he nevertheless prescribed bleeding and purgatives by the planets and divided chronic from acute diseases on the basis of one being under the rule of the sun and the other of the moon.

In October 1348 Philip VI asked the medical faculty of the University of Paris for a report on the affliction that seemed to threaten human survival. With careful thesis, antithesis, and proofs, the doctors ascribed it to a triple conjunction of Saturn, Jupiter, and Mars in the 40th degree of Aquarius said to have occurred on March 20, 1345. They acknowledged, however, effects "whose cause is hidden from even the most highly trained intellects." The verdict of the masters of Paris became the official version. Borrowed, copied by scribes, carried abroad, translated from Latin into various vernaculars, it was everywhere accepted, even by the Arab physicians of Cordova and Granada, as the scientific if not the popular answer. Because of the terrible interest of the subject, the translations of the plague tracts stimulated use of national languages. In that one respect, life came from death.

To the people at large there could be but one explanation—the wrath of God. Planets might satisfy the learned doctors, but God was closer to the average man. A scourge so sweeping and unsparing without any visible cause could only be seen as Divine punishment upon mankind for its sins. It might even be God's terminal disappointment in his creature. Matteo Villani compared the plague to the Flood in ultimate purpose and believed he was recording "the extermination of mankind." Efforts to appease Divine wrath took many forms, as when the city of Rouen ordered that everything that could anger God, such as gambling, cursing, and drinking, must be stopped. More general were the penitent processions authorized at first by the Pope, some lasting as long as three days, some attended by as many as 2,000, which everywhere accompanied the plague and helped to spread it.

Barefoot in sackcloth, sprinkled with ashes, weeping, praying, tearing their hair, carrying candles and relics, sometimes with ropes around their necks or beating themselves with whips, the penitents wound through the streets, imploring the mercy of the Virgin and saints at their shrines. In a vivid illustration for the *Très Riches Heures* of the Duc de Berry, the Pope is shown in a penitent procession attended by four cardinals in scarlet from hat to hem. He raises both arms in supplication to the angel on top of the Castel Sant'Angelo, while white-robed priests bearing banners and relics in golden cases turn to look as one of their number, stricken by the plague, falls to the ground, his face contorted with anxiety. In the rear, a gray-clad monk falls beside another victim already on the ground as the towns-people gaze in horror. (Nominally the illustration represents a 6th century plague in the time of Pope Gregory the Great, but as medieval artists made no distinction between past and present, the scene is shown as the artist would have seen it in the 14th century.) When it became evident that these processions were sources of infection, Clement VI had to prohibit them.

In Messina, where the plague first appeared, the people begged the Archbishop of neighboring Catania to lend them the relics of St. Agatha. When the Catanians refused to let the relics go, the Archbishop dipped them in holy water and took the water himself to Messina, where he carried it in a procession with prayers and litanies through the streets. The demonic, which shared the medieval cosmos with God, appeared as "demons in the shape of dogs" to terrify the people. "A black dog with a drawn sword in his paws appeared among them, gnashing his teeth and rushing upon them and breaking all the silver vessels and lamps and candlesticks on the altars and casting them hither and thither. . . . So the people of Messina, terrified by this prodigious vision, were all strangely overcome by fear."

The apparent absence of earthly cause gave the plague a supernatural and sinister quality. Scandinavians believed that a Pest Maiden emerged from the mouth of the dead in the form of a blue flame and flew through the air to infect the next house. In Lithuania the Maiden was said to wave a red scarf through the door or window to let in the pest. One brave man, according to legend, deliberately waited at his open window with drawn sword and, at the fluttering of the scarf, chopped off the hand. He died of his deed, but his village was spared and the scarf long preserved as a relic in the local church.

Beyond demons and superstition the final hand was God's. The Pope acknowledged it in a Bull of September 1348, speaking of the "pestilence with which God is afflicting the Christian people." To the Emperor John Cantacuzene it was manifest that a malady of such horrors, stenches, and agonies, and especially one bringing the dismal despair that settled upon its victims before they died, was not a plague "natural" to mankind but "a chastisement from Heaven." To Piers Plowman "these pestilences were for pure sin."

The general acceptance of this view created an expanded sense of guilt, for if the plague were punishment there had to be terrible sin to have occasioned it. What sins were on the 14th century conscience? Primarily greed, the sin of avarice, followed by usury, worldliness, adultery, blasphemy, falsehood, luxury, irreligion. Giovanni Villani, attempting to account for the cascade of calamity that had fallen upon Florence, concluded that it was retribution for the sins of avarice and usury that oppressed the poor. Pity and anger about the condition of the poor, especially victimization of the peasantry in war, was often expressed by writers of the time and was certainly on the conscience of the century. Beneath it all was the daily condition of medieval life, in which hardly an act or thought, sexual, mercantile, or military, did not contravene the dictates of the Church. Mere failure to fast or attend mass was sin. The result was an underground lake of guilt in the soul that the plague now tapped.

That the mortality was accepted as God's punishment may explain in part the vacuum of comment that followed the Black Death. An investigator has noticed that in the archives of Périgord references to the war are innumerable, to the plague few. Froissart mentions the great death but once, Chaucer gives it barely a glance. Divine anger so great that it contemplated the extermination of man did not bear close examination.

INFLUENZA 1918

■

Jane Brox

This essay appeared in The Georgia Review *in 1995 and was reprinted in* Best American Essays.

In ordinary times, the bankers, lawyers, and mill owners who lived on Tower Hill opened their doors to a quiet broken only by the jostle of a laden milk wagon, the first stirrings of a wind in the elms, or the quavering notes of a sparrow. It was the height of country; the air, sweet and clear. Looking east from their porches they could survey miles of redbrick textile mills that banked the canals and the sluggish Merrimack, as well as the broad central plain mazed with tenements. To their west was a patchwork of small dairy holdings giving over to the blue distance. But for the thirty-one mornings of October 1918 those men adjusted gauze masks over their mouths and noses as they set out for work in the cold-tinged dawn, and they kept their eyes to the ground so as not to see what they couldn't help but hear: the clatter of motorcars and horse-drawn wagons over the paving stones, as day and night without ceasing the ambulances ran up the hill bringing sufferers from the heart of the city and the hearses carried them away.

It had started as a seemingly common thing—what the line-storm season always brings, born on its wind and on our breath, something that would run its course in the comfort of camphor and bed rest. At first there had been no more than six or eight or ten cases a day reported in the city, and such news hardly took up a side column in the papers, which were full of soldiers' obituaries and reports of a weakening Germany. As September wore on, however, the death notices of victims of the flu began to outnumber the casualties of war. Finally it laid low so many the Lawrence Board of Health set aside its usual work of granting permits to keep roosters, charting the milk supply, and inspecting tenements. The flu took up all its talk—how it was to be treated, how contained, how to stay ahead of the dead. The sufferers needed fresh air and isolation, and their care had to be consolidated to make the most of the scarce nurses and orderlies. So the board took a page from other stricken cities and voted to construct a makeshift tent hospital on their highest, most open land that offered the best air, which was the leeward side of Tower Hill where a farm still spread across the slope.

Lawrence, Massachusetts, in 1918 was largely a city of immigrants who had come for work in the textile mills. Most had been in the city for only a short time and still spoke Polish, Arabic, French, Italian, German—forty-five different languages and dialects within the few square miles of the central district. They made worsteds and woolens; they were dyers, cutters, and weavers. They fixed the looms, rigged the warps, and felt along the yardage for slubs, working more than fifty hours a week, breathing in air white with cloth dust. At home they breathed in the smells of rubbish and night soil that drifted up from the alleyways between tenements. Where they lived was low-lying, so such smells, together with smoke and ash, hung in the air. Their heat was sparse. They were crowded into their rooms. The flu cut right through, spreading ahead of its own rumors, passing on a handshake and on the wind and with the lightest kiss. No spitting. No sharing food. Keep your hands clean. Avoid crowds. Walk everywhere. Sleep with your windows open.

They slept to the sound of rain—rain pouring from their gutterless roofs turning the alleyways into thick mud, rain on the wandering hens pecking at stones in the streets, rain on the silenced pigeons puffed and caged in their coops. At times it was hard, driven from the north like mare's hooves on their roofs, drowning the parsley and oregano set in enamel basins on the window ledges. Other times it fell soft and fine out of a pale gray sky, making circles fragile as wrists on the surfaces of the canals before being lost to the brown, frothy water there. And sometimes it was no more than a mist that settled in the low places, obscuring the bottoms of the stairwells and the barrels and the piles of sawdust, only to shift and reveal the same world as always. Then the rain would gather its strength again, seeming to rake their lives all that much harder. Scrap coal couldn't keep away its chill.

A doctor may as well have gone house to house down Common, Haverhill, and Jackson streets, so numerous were the cases. Often his knock would go unanswered, since it wasn't the family who had sought him out. More likely the sickness had been reported by their landlord or neighbor—afraid that the influenza would spread—so the doctor heard a sudden silence within and a face at the window disappearing into shadow. What kept the families from responding wasn't a lack of a common language so much as the fear that the doctor would tack a card to the door warning of the infection within, and the greater fear that their sick children would be ordered to the tent hospital. Once there, they wouldn't be seen again until they were dead or cured.

When the doctor finally gained entrance—at times with the help of the police—he could find whole families had been laid low, with the sick tending those who were sicker. They had sacks of camphor around their necks, or mustard spread on their chests, a cup of chamomile by the cot. Whiskey. Garlic and onions weighed in the air. Some sufferers lay in windowless rooms where the damp had kept in the smoke from a low coal fire, and what light there was wavered from a kerosene lamp. Almost always the disease had gone beyond a cough and aches and a runny nose. There was blood mixed in with their phlegm, and they couldn't move from their beds. In the worst cases their skin was tinted blue.

One doctor could see hundreds of cases a day, and in his haste to complete his records, he sometimes left out the ages of the victims and often the names. They come down now in the *Influenza Journal* distinguished only by their address or their nationality: *four Cases, 384 Common Street (downstairs).* Or: *Mother and Child. Baby Rossano. Father and Son. A Syrian fellow. Polish man.* When the rain finally let up and days of mist lifted to bring on clear dry air, the number of influenza cases still didn't slow. Every woman who gave birth, it seems, died. The elderly, schoolchildren, and infants, yes—but strangest of all was how it took the young and healthy who had never been sick in their lives. Just yesterday they had worked a full day.

The entrance to the tent hospital on Tower Hill was clotted with ambulances arriving with patients and standing ambulances awaiting their dispatch orders. Many were still horse drawn, and the mares stood uneasy in the confusion. The motorized cars idled and choked the air with gasoline, the tang of which overlay the warm, familiar smells of hay and animal sweat. Everyone wore gauze masks, and there was no talk but orders. *Don't back up. Bring that one over here.* Nurses checked the pulse and color of patients and listened to their lungs. *We need more masks. Find me a doctor. Help me with this one.* The gate was patrolled by a military guard to assure that only the sufferers and those who tended them went beyond. Waiting black hacks stood three deep.

Every day at 5 A.M. a soldier blew reveille. The quick, bright notes parted the confusion at the entrance and gleamed above the hospital grounds—a far call from a country those patients no longer came from. The general din at the gate may as well have been the sound of a market day in a port city, and they, drowsing on a ship that had pulled away. They didn't stir. It was no concern of theirs, each in his or her own tent, the tent flap open to the back of a neighboring tent. Tents were arranged in rows, in wards, and in precincts, making a grid of the old hayfield. Its crickets were silent. Its summer birds had flown. Electrical wires hung on make-shift poles, and you could hear them swaying in the storms. The soaked canvas flanks of the tents ballooned in a wind and settled back on their frames. Boardwalks had been laid down between the tents, and foot-falls, softened by the drenched wood, came near and receded. The nuns' habits swished. What country was this? A cough. A groan. The stricken tossed in their fevers. Their muscles ached. One moment they had the sweats; the next, chills. In forty-five different languages and dialects they called for water and warmth.

Many were cared for in words they couldn't understand. The student nurses and sisters of Saint Jeanne d'Arc spoke both English and French, but to the Germans and Italians and Syrians their voices may just as well have been more soft rain. A face half covered with gauze leaned near their own. They were given water to drink. Cool cloths were placed on their brows. They were wrapped in blankets and wheeled outside for more air. Someone listened to their hearts and then to their bogged-down lungs. A spoonful of thick serum was lifted to their lips. Their toes and fingertips turned blue from a lack of oxygen. In many pneumonia set in.

It was the same suffering in each tent, in each ward, in each precinct of the hospital. And the same in the surrounding country, in all cities, in all the known nations of the world. It struck those already stricken with war in the military camps, the troop ships, the trenches, in the besieged villages along the Meuse, in the devastated plain called the Somme, in the Argonne woods. It struck those who knew nothing of the war—all the Eskimos in a remote outpost, villagers in China. Some died without hav-ing given it a name. Others called it "the grippe," the flu—influenza—meaning "under the influence of the stars," under Orion and the Southern Cross, under the Bear, the Pole Star, and the Pleiades.

When care failed in the Tower Hill hospital, the sisters of Saint Jeanne d'Arc closed the eyes of the dead, blessed the body in the language that they knew, blessed themselves, and closed the tent flap. The sisters on the next shift said a last prayer in front of each closed tent and turned to the living.

In the central city those who were spared became captive to a strange, altered music. All the sounds of their streets—voices and songs, teams hauling loads over paving stones, elm whips cracking the air and animals, bottles nudging one another in the back of a truck, the deliberate tread of the iceman on their stairs—all these were no longer heard. Or they weren't heard as usual. Survivors strained at the absence, as if they were listening for flowing water after a cold snap, water now trapped and nearly silenced by clear ice. Schools and movie houses had been ordered closed and bolted shut; public gatherings were curtailed. Workers, their numbers halved, walked down Essex Street to the mills in a slackened ribbon. Their tamped-down gossip touched only on who had been stricken, who had died in the night. They traded preventions and cures, some wearing masks, others with garlic hung around their necks. More pronounced than the usual smells of the fouled canals or lanolin or grease were the head-clearing scents of camphor and carbolic soap.

The flow of supply wagons slowed as well. There was no commerce in bolts of velvet, silk puffs, worsted suits, or pianos. Bakers who used to shape one hundred granary loaves a day—split and seeded and washed with a glaze of milk—took to preparing fifty or sixty unadorned loaves. In the corner groceries, scab spread on the early apple crop, grapes softened then soured, and pears turned overripe in their crates.

The absence filled with uncommon sounds. Children with nowhere to go played in the streets and in the parks as if it were another kind of summer. They sang their jump-rope songs and called out sides in the letups between rains. The pharmacies swarmed with customers looking for Vaporub, germicide, and ice. And all the carpenters—whether they had formerly spent their days roughing out tenements or carving details into table legs—had turned to making pine boxes. Their sawing and the sound of bright nails driving into soft wood could be heard long into the night. Even so, coffins remained scarce and expensive.

The streets running up to Tower Hill rushed with ambulances, police cars, and fire engines. The alleyways and side streets were clogged with passing funerals. Meager corteges where everywhere—there, out of the corner of an eye, or coming straight on. In hopes of slowing the spread of the epidemic, the board of health had limited the size of the funerals to one carriage. They prohibited church services for the dead, and forbade anyone other than the immediate family to accompany the coffin. So, a black hack or a utility wagon with a loose knot of mourners following on foot behind was all. Some of the grieving were sick themselves, some barely recovered, and they had trouble keeping up if the hack driver was proceeding faster than he should—there were so many, had been so many, and someone else was waiting for his services. The processions appeared to be blown by a directionless wind down home streets past the mill-works and across the bridge to the burial grounds on the outskirts of the city.

The mourners entered a place starred with freshly closed graves and open graves with piles of earth next to them—clay, sea-worn gravel, sodden sandy loam. The gravediggers kept on shoveling—they had long stopped looking up from their work. Even so, they couldn't stay ahead, and most of the coffins had to be escorted to the yard and left near the entrance along with others to await a later burial. Few of the processions were accompanied by ministers or priests. The parents or children or sisters of the deceased bowed their heads and said their own prayers. Perhaps they threw a handful of earth on the set-aside box. Maybe they lay a clutch of asters on the top. So plain and unsacred, it may just as well have been a death in the wilderness. Small. A winter spider crawling across an old white wall.

"We knew it was serious, but we didn't know how serious," my father says. The farm is less than five miles to the west of Lawrence, but by the time news reached here, it was muted and slowed—no more than a rumor on the sea winds biting in from Cape Ann. Their eastward view was open then, and they could see the leeward slope of Tower Hill, though it was far enough away to appear plainly blue. On the first of October 1918 they woke to see the flanks of those white canvas tents set in columns and rows across the hill. And that night the horizon was so crowded with lights that it must have seemed as if the heart of the city had grown closer.

As in the city, whole families on some farms were stricken, others spared. His family was spared—all he knew of the flu then was white chips of camphor in an old sock around his neck, and his mother whispering to his father in the evenings: "You'll bring it here. . . . " His aunt and uncle, who had a nearby farm, and his cousins all came down with it in turn. It had begun when his uncle, for all his old strength, just couldn't get up. His aunt cared for him, until the whole household was confined to their beds. No doctor came. My grandfather, after he had tended his own herd, saw to theirs—to their water and grain, as well as the milking. He drew water for the house and brought them bread. He'd light the fires and bring in a day's supply of wood. Even so, with the windows open the rooms felt as cold as quarried granite.

The last to contract it, the youngest boy, died. The parents, still weak, were slow to perform the offices of the strong. They washed the body and had to rest. It seemed to take most of a day to make a respectable, small pine coffin. They cleaned the front room, set the coffin in the bay window, and took their turns sitting beside it. Not even small things were the same. Not the rust-colored chrysanthemums blooming against the kitchen door. Not the lingering fragrance of thyme and mint in the yard.

And the large things to be done—the work that had waited all through their sickness—waited still and weighed heavier. It was late enough in the year so that the weeding didn't matter anymore. But carrots, potatoes, and cabbages had to be harvested and stored. Wood to be gotten in. The late apple tree was laden with fruit—Ben Davis apples would cling to the branches all winter if you let them. Enough work to fill their days for as long as they could foresee.

There are two small, walled-in graveyards in the middle of our farm. They seem odd and adrift now among our fields and woods, though in the early part of this century there had been a Protestant church adjoining them. It was pulled down for salvage sometime in the forties, and its granite steps are now my parents' doorstone. My father sits on one of the pews when he pulls off his work boots. He will be buried among those graves, just up the hill behind a white birch. But in those years only the names of the settlers—Richardson, Coburn, Clough—had been chiseled into the stones. It wasn't a place for recent immigrants to be buried, so his uncle's family walked behind the coffin to Lawrence and set their child beside all the recent victims in the city. The mounds of earth beside the open graves were composed of heavier and stonier soils than any they had cultivated in the arid land they had been born to. Impossible to return to that country now, though they said their words in Arabic before turning west out of the gate.

For another week after the funeral they could still see the tents, white in the new days, just like yesterday. Then at the end of October the epidemic broke, the fires were banked. The tent hospital was taken down in a driving rain, and the stricken were moved to winter quarters at the General Hospital. At night Tower Hill once again appeared darker than the night sky. Predictable quiet returned to the neighborhood of mill owners, bankers, lawyers. The schools opened again, then the theaters. The policemen and firemen took off their gauze masks. On the twelfth of November, even the Red Cross workers marched in the Victory Day parade. When the city looked up, they counted more dead of the flu than of the war.

    The winter of 1918 was so cold that the water over the Lawrence dam froze and had to be dynamited. The following spring, the field where the tent hospital had stood was seeded in hay. It was mown three times that summer and winds swept the timothy and redtop. Here, after the child had become bone, a liturgy was said for him. A child whose life is no longer given a name or a length, so short it is remembered by the one fact of his death.

    It is a summer evening, and my father sits on his porch, looking at our own horizon. The long simple line of the hill is gone. Pine and maple have grown up and buildings square off against the sky. Out of nowhere he mentions the lights of the tent hospital, as if he could still see them, strange and clear.

DEATH OF ABRAHAM LINCOLN

Walt Whitman

This piece is an excerpt from poet Whitman's memoir Specimen Days, *published in 1882.*

I shall not easily forget the first time I ever saw Abraham Lincoln. It must have been about the 18th or 19th of February, 1861. It was rather a pleasant afternoon, in New York City, as he arrived there from the West, to remain a few hours, and then pass on to Washington, to prepare for his inauguration. I saw him in Broadway, near the site of the present Post-office. He came down, I think from Canal street, to stop at the Astor House. The broad spaces, sidewalks, and streets in the neighborhood, and for some distance, were crowded with solid masses of people, many thousands. The omnibuses and other vehicles had all been turn'd off, leaving an unusual hush in that busy part of the city. Presently two or three shabby hack barouches made their way with some difficulty through the crowd, and drew up at the Astor House entrance. A tall figure stepp'd out of the centre of these barouches, paus'd leisurely on the sidewalk, look'd up at the granite walls and looming architecture of the grand old hotel—then, after a relieving stretch of arms and legs, turn'd round for over a minute to slowly and good-humoredly scan the appearance of the vast and silent crowds. There were no speeches—no compliments—no welcome—as far as I could hear, not a word said. Still much anxiety was conceal'd in the quiet. Cautious persons had fear'd some mark'd insult or indignity to the President-elect—for he possess'd no personal popularity at all in New York City, and very little political. But it was evidently tacitly agreed that if the few political supporters of Mr. Lincoln present would entirely abstain from any demonstration on their side, the immense majority, who were anything but supporters, would abstain on their sides also. The result was a sulky, unbroken silence, such as certainly never before characterized so great a New York crowd.

Almost in the same neighborhood I distinctly remember'd seeing Lafayette on his visit to America in 1825. I had also personally seen and heard, various years afterward, how Andrew Jackson, Clay, Webster, Hungarian Kossuth, Filibuster Walker, the Prince of Wales on his visit, and other *célèbres*, native and foreign, had been welcom'd there—all that indescribable human roar and magnetism, unlike any other sound in the universe—the glad exulting thunder-shouts of countless unloos'd throats of men! But on this occasion, not a voice—not a sound. From the top of an omnibus, (driven up one side, close by, and block'd by the curbstone and the crowds), I had, I say, a capital view of it all, and especially of Mr. Lincoln, his look and gait—his perfect composure and coolness—his unusual and uncouth height, his dress of complete black, stovepipe hat push'd back on the head, dark-brown complexion, seam'd and wrinkled yet canny-looking face, black, bushy head of hair, disproportionately long neck, and his hands held behind as he stood observing the people. He look'd with curiosity upon that immense sea of faces, and the sea of faces return'd the look with similar curiosity. In both there was a dash of comedy, almost farce, such as Shakspere puts in his blackest tragedies. The crowd that hemm'd around consisted I should think of thirty to forty thousand men, not a single one his personal friend—while I have no doubt, (so frenzied were the ferments of the time,) many an assassin's knife and pistol lurk'd in hip or breast-pocket there, ready, soon as break and riot came.

But no break or riot came. The tall figure gave another relieving stretch or two of arms and legs; then with moderate pace, and accompanied by a few unknown-looking persons, ascended the portico-steps of the Astor House, disappear'd through its broad entrance—and the dumb-show ended.

I saw Abraham Lincoln often the four years following that date. He changed rapidly and much during his Presidency—but this scene, and him in it, are indelibly stamp'd upon my recollection. As I sat on the top of my omnibus, and had a good view of him, the thought, dim and inchoate then, has since come out clear enough, that four sorts of genius, four mighty and primal hands, will be needed to the complete limning of this man's future portrait—the eyes and brains and finger-touch of Plutarch and Eschylus and Michel Angelo, assisted now by Rabelais.

And now—(Mr. Lincoln passing on from this scene to Washington, where he was inaugurated, amid armed cavalry, and sharpshooters at every point—the first instance of the kind in our history—and I hope it will be the last)—now the rapid succession of well-known events, (too well-known—l believe, these days, we almost hate to hear them mention'd)—the national flag fired on at Sumter—the uprising of the North, in paroxysms of astonishment and rage—the chaos of divided councils— the call for troops—the first Bull Run—the stunning cast-down, shock, and dismay of the North—and so in full flood the Secession war. Four years of lurid, bleeding, murky, murderous war. Who paint those years, with all their scenes?—the hard-fought engagements—the defeats, plans, failures—the gloomy hours, days, when our Nationality seem'd hung in pall of doubt, perhaps death—the Mephistophelean sneers of foreign lands and attachés—the dreaded Scylla of European interference, and the Charybdis of the tremendously dangerous latent strata of seccession sympathizers throughout the free States, (far more numerous than is supposed)—the long marches in summer—the hot sweat, and many a sunstroke, as on the rush to Gettysburg in '63—the night battles in the woods, as under Hooker at Chancellorsville—the camps in winter—the military prisons—the hospitals—(alas! alas! the hospitals.)

The Secession war? Nay, let me call it the Union war. Though whatever call'd, it is even yet too near us—too vast and too closely over-shadowing— its branches unform'd yet, (but certain,) shooting too far into the future— and the most indicative and mightiest of them yet ungrown. A great literature will yet arise out of the era of those four years, those scenes—era compressing centuries of native passion, first-class pictures, tempests of life and death—an inexhaustible mine for the histories, drama, romance, and even philosophy, of peoples to come—indeed the verteber of poetry and art, (of personal character too,) for all future America—far more grand, in my opinion, to the hands capable of it, than Homer's siege of Troy, or the French wars to Shakspere.

But I must leave these speculations, and come to the theme I have assign'd and limited myself to. Of the actual murder of President Lincoln, though so much has been written, probably the facts are yet very indefinite in most persons' minds. I read from my memoranda, written at the time, and revised frequently and finally since.

The day, April 14, 1865, seems to have been a pleasant one throughout the whole land—the moral atmosphere pleasant too—the long storm, so dark, so fratricidal, full of blood and doubt and gloom, over and ended at last by the sunrise of such an absolute National victory, and utter breakdown of Secessionism—we almost doubted our own senses! Lee had capitulated beneath the apple-tree of Appomattox. The other armies, the flanges of the revolt, swiftly follow'd. And could it really be, then? Out of all the affairs of this world of woe and failure and disorder, was there really come the confirm'd, unerring sign of plan, like a shaft of pure light—of rightful rule—of God? So the day, as I say, was propitious. Early herbage, early flowers, were out. (I remember where I was stopping at the time, the season being advanced, there were many lilacs in full bloom. By one of those caprices that enter and give tinge to events without being at all a part of them, I find myself always reminded of the great tragedy of that day by the sight and odor of these blossoms. It never fails.)

But I must not dwell on accessories. The deed hastens. The popular afternoon paper of Washington, the little *Evening Star*, has spatter'd all over its third page, divided among the advertisements in a sensational manner, in a hundred different places, *"The President and his Lady will be at the Theatre this evening. . . ."* (Lincoln was fond of the theatre. I have myself seen him there several times. I remember thinking how funny it was that he, in some respects the leading actor in the stormiest drama known to real history's stage through centuries, should sit there and be so completely interested and absorb'd in those human jackstraws, moving about with their silly little gestures, foreign spirit, and flatulent text.)

On this occasion the theatre was crowded, many ladies in rich and gay costumes, officers in their uniforms, many well-known citizens, young folks, the usual clusters of gas-lights, the usual magnetism of so many people, cheerful, with perfumes, music of violins and flutes—(and over all, and saturating all, that vast, vague wonder, *Victory*, the nation's victory, the triumph of the Union, filling the air, the thought, the sense, with exhilaration more than all music and perfumes.)

The President came betimes, and, with his wife, witness'd the play from the large stage-boxes of the second tier, two thrown into one, and profusely drap'd with the national flag. The acts and scenes of the piece—one of those singularly written compositions which have at least the merit of giving entire relief to an audience engaged in mental action or business excitements and cares during the day, as it makes not the slightest call on either the moral, emotional, esthetic, or spiritual nature—a piece, *(Our American Cousin,)* in which, among other characters so call'd, a Yankee, certainly such a one as was never seen, or the least like it ever seen, in North America, is introduced in England, with a varied fol-de-rol of talk, plot, scenery, and such phantasmagoria as goes to make up a modern popular drama—had progress'd through perhaps a couple of its acts, when in the midst of this comedy, or non-such, or whatever it is to be call'd, and to offset it, or finish it out, as if in Nature's and the great Muse's mockery of those poor mimes, came interpolated that scene, not really or exactly to be described at all, (for on the many hundreds who were there it seems to this hour to have left a passing blur, a dream, a blotch)—and yet partially to be described as I now proceed to give it. There is a scene in the play representing a modern parlor, in which two unprecedented English ladies are inform'd by the impossible Yankee that he is not a man of fortune, and therefore undesirable for marriage-catching purposes; after which, the comments being finish'd, the dramatic trio make exit, leaving the stage clear for a moment. At this period came the murder of Abraham Lincoln. Great as all its manifold train, circling round it, and stretching into the future for many a century, in the politics, history, art &c., of the New World, in point of fact the main thing, the actual murder, transpired with the quiet and simplicity of any commonest occurrence—the bursting of a bud or pod in the growth of vegetation, for instance. Through the general hum following the stage pause, with the change of positions, came the muffled sound of a pistol-shot, which not one-hundredth part of the audience heard at the time—and yet a moment's hush—somehow, surely, a vague startled thrill—and then, through the ornamented, draperied, starr'd and striped space-way of the President's box, a sudden figure, a man, raises himself with hands and feet, stands a moment on the railing, leaps below to the stage, (a distance of perhaps fourteen or fifteen feet), falls out of position, catching his boot-heel in the copious drapery, (the American flag,) falls on one knee, quickly recovers himself, rises as if nothing had happen'd, (he really sprains his ankle, but unfelt then)—and so the figure, Booth, the murderer, dress'd in plain black broadcloth, bare-headed, with full, glossy, raven hair, and his eyes like some mad animal's flashing with light and resolution, yet with a certain strange calmness, holds aloft in one hand a large knife—walks along not much back from the footlights—turns fully toward the audience his face of statuesque beauty, lit by those basilisk eyes, flashing with desperation, perhaps insanity—launches out in a firm and steady voice the words *Sic semper tyrannis*—and then walks with neither slow nor very rapid pace diagonally across to the back of the stage, and disappears. (Had not all this terrible scene—making the mimic ones preposterous— had it not all been rehears'd, in blank, by Booth, beforehand?)

A moment's hush—a scream—the cry of *"murder"*—Mrs. Lincoln leaning out of the box, with ashy cheeks and lips, with involuntary cry, pointing to the retreating figure, *"He has kill'd the President."* And still a moment's strange, incredulous suspense—and then the deluge! then that mixture of horror, noises, uncertainty—(the sound, somewhere back, of a horse's hoofs clattering with speed)—the people burst through chairs and railings, and break them up—there is inextricable confusion and terror— women faint—quite feeble persons fall, and are trampl'd on—many cries of agony are heard—the broad stage suddenly fills to suffocation with a dense and motley crowd, like some horrible carnival—the audience rush generally upon it, at least the strong men do—the actors and actresses are all there in their play-costumes and painted faces, with mortal fright showing through the rouge—the screams and calls, confused talk—redoubled, trebled—two or three manage to pass up water from the stage to the President's box—others try to clamber up—&c., &c.

In the midst of all this, the soldiers of the President's guard, with others, suddenly drawn to the scene, burst in—(some two hundred altogether)—they storm the house, through all the tiers, especially the upper ones, inflam'd with fury, literally charging the audience with fix'd bayonets, muskets, and pistols, shouting *"Clear out! clear out! you sons of——"* . . . . Such a wild scene, or a suggestion of it rather, inside the play-house that night.

Outside, too, the atmosphere of shock and craze, crowds of people, fill'd with frenzy, ready to seize any outlet for it, come near committing murder several times on innocent individuals. One such case was especially exciting. The infuriated crowd, through some chance, got started against one man, either for words he utter'd, or perhaps without any cause at all, and were proceeding at once to actually hang him on a neighboring lamp-post, when he was rescued by a few heroic policemen, who placed him in their midst, and fought their way slowly and amid great peril toward the station-house. It was a fitting episode of the whole affair. The crowd rushing and eddying to and fro—the night, the yells, the pale faces, many frighten'd people trying in vain to extricate themselves—the attack'd man, not yet freed from the jaws of death, looking like a corpse— the silent, resolute, half-dozen policemen, with no weapons but their little clubs, yet stern and steady through all those eddying swarms—made a fitting side-scene to the grand tragedy of the murder. They gain'd the station house with the protected man, whom they placed in security for the night, and discharged him in the morning.

And in the midst of that pandemonium, infuriated soldiers, the audience and the crowd, the stage, and all its actors and actresses, its paint-pots, spangles, and gas-lights—the life blood from those veins, the best and sweetest of the land, drips slowly down, and death's ooze already begins its little bubbles on the lips.

Thus the visible incidents and surroundings of Abraham Lincoln's murder, as they really occur'd. Thus ended the attempted secession of these States: thus the four years' war. But the main things come subtly and invisibly afterward, perhaps long afterward—neither military, political, nor (great as those are,) historical. I say, certain secondary and indirect results, out of the tragedy of this death, are, in my opinion, greatest. Not the event of the murder itself. Not that Mr. Lincoln strings the principal points and personages of the period, like beads, upon the single string of his career. Not that his idiosyncrasy, in its sudden appearance and disappearance, stamps this Republic with a stamp more mark'd and enduring than any yet given by any one man—(more even than Washington's;)—but, join'd with these, the immeasurable value and meaning of that whole tragedy lies, to me, in senses finally dearest to a nation, (and here all our own)—the imaginative and artistic senses—the literary and dramatic ones. Not in any common or low meaning of those terms, but a meaning precious to the race, and to every age. A long and varied series of contradictory events arrives at last at its highest poetic, single, central, pictorial *dénouement*. The whole involved, baffling, multiform whirl of the secession period comes to a head, and is gather'd in one brief flash of lightning-illumination—one simple, fierce deed. Its sharp culmination, and as it were solution, of so many bloody and angry problems, illustrates those climax-moments on the stage of universal Time, where the historic Muse at one entrance, and the tragic Muse at the other, suddenly ringing down the curtain, close an immense act in the long drama of creative thought, and give it radiation, tableau, stranger than fiction. Fit radiation—fit close! How the imagination—how the student loves these things! America, too, is to have them. For not in all great deaths, not far or near—not Caesar in the Roman senate-house, or Napoleon passing away in the wild night-storm at St. Helena—not Paleologus, falling, desperately fighting, piled over dozens deep with Grecian corpses—not calm old Socrates, drinking the hemlock—outvies that terminus of the secession war, in one man's life, here in our midst, in our time—that seal of the emancipation of three million slaves—that parturition and delivery of our at last really free Republic, born again, henceforth to commence its career of genuine homogeneous Union, compact, consistent with itself.

Nor will ever future American Patriots and Unionists, indifferently over the whole land, or North or South, find a better moral to their lesson. The final use of the greatest men of a Nation is, after all, not with reference to their deeds in themselves, or their direct bearing on their times or lands. The final use of a heroic-eminent life—especially of a heroic-eminent death—is its indirect filtering into the nation and the race, and to give, often at many removes, but unerringly, age after age, color and fibre to the personalism of the youth and maturity of that age, and of mankind. Then, there is a cement to the whole people, subtler, more underlying, than any thing in written constitution, or courts or armies—namely, the cement of a death identified thoroughly with that people, at its head, and for its sake. Strange, (is it not?) that battles, martyrs, agonies, blood, even assassination, should so condense—perhaps only really, lastingly condense—a Nationality.

I repeat it—the grand deaths of the race—the dramatic deaths of every nationality—are its most important inheritance-value—in some respects beyond its literature and art—(as the hero is beyond his finest portrait, and the battle itself beyond its choicest song or epic). Is not here indeed the point underlying all tragedy? the famous pieces of the Grecian masters—and all masters? Why, if the old Greeks had had this man, what trilogies of plays—what epics—would have been made out of him! How the rhapsodes would have recited him! How quickly that quaint tall form would have enter'd into the region where men vitalize gods, and gods divinify men! But Lincoln, his times, his death—great as any, any age—belong altogether to our own, and are autochthonic. (Sometimes indeed I think our American days, our own stage—the actors we know and have shaken hands, or talk'd with—more fateful than any thing in Eschylus—more heroic than the fighters around Troy—afford kings of men for our Democracy prouder than Agamemnon—models of character cute and hardy as Ulysses—deaths more pitiful than Priam's.)

When centuries hence, (as it must, in my opinion, be centuries hence before the life of these States, or of Democracy, can be really written and illustrated,) the leading historians and dramatists seek for some personage, some special event, incisive enough to mark with deepest cut, and mnemonize, this turbulent nineteenth century of ours, (not only these States, but all over the political and social world)—something, perhaps, to close that gorgeous procession of European feudalism, with all its pomp and caste-prejudices, (of whose long train we in America are yet so inextricably the heirs)—something to identify with terrible identification, by far the greatest revolutionary step in the history of the United States, (perhaps the greatest of the world, our century)—the absolute extirpation and erasure of slavery from the States—those historians will seek in vain for any point to serve more thoroughly their purpose, than Abraham Lincoln's death.

Dear to the Muse—thrice dear to Nationality—to the whole human race—precious to this Union—precious to Democracy—unspeakably and forever precious—their first great Martyr Chief.

GALLIPOLI
·

Kildare Dobbs

The following piece is excerpted from Dobbs' 1989 book Anatolian Suite.

Most visitors to the First World War battlefields and cemeteries of Gallipoli are Australians or New Zealanders who want to see the place where their countrymen died in such numbers. And perhaps the Australian movie *Gallipoli* has given them the idea that this catastrophic campaign in 1915 was entirely an ANZAC (Australia New Zealand Army Corps) affair. But the spearhead of the operation was the British 29th Division, made up of regular army units, among them a number of famous Irish regiments. It was because of one young officer in the 1st Battalion, the Royal Dublin Fusiliers, that I came to Gallipoli that gray morning in early spring.

My middle names, Robert and Eric, commemorate two uncles killed in the First World War before I was born. Lieutenant Robert Bernard of the Dublins was one of them. He fell on the second day of the assault on the Gallipoli peninsula in one of its most desperate battles.

I could recall little of the facts when I arrived.

Next morning I visited the office of the Commonwealth War Graves Commission, where a pleasant Turkish assistant had just arrived. Soft-spoken, plump, of fiery complexion, he gave me a glass of tea and a stack of tattered printed lists of the fallen—about a hundred thousand names. I did not succeed in finding that of Robert Bernard. Nor could the Englishman in charge help me when he arrived.

I found an agency called Troyanzac and asked the proprietor to arrange a taxi to the Helles monument at the entrance to the Dardanelles on the Gallipoli peninsula. I would not need a guide. Two young couples, Australian and New Zealander, were also taking a Gallipoli tour, but they were going to Anzac cove, a different area from the one I sought. I would have to go alone and it would cost about thirty American dollars. Mr. Husseyin, the proprietor, made a little speech before we set out. The British, he said, had undertaken the Gallipoli campaign in 1915 in an attempt to force a passage through the Dardanelles, capture Constantinople and open a new front against the Central Powers. British and Commonwealth troops had fought gallantly for many months, but the fierce resistance of the Turks under Mustafa Kemal had in the end defeated them. At least 36,000 men on each side had been killed.

Mr. Husseyin, a small, tweedy gentleman with a fine mustache, looked suitably melancholy as he said this. I noticed his gleaming shoes, perhaps a tribute to men who had died with their boots clean. "Their name," he added sombrely, "liveth for evermore." And I thought that was one of the lies of history, that the dead would be remembered, a lie to comfort the next-of-kin. I would be the first of Robbie Bernard's kin to come to this remote place.

After a pause Husseyin Bey told us that we would cross the Dardanelles in a private launch. We were to follow his assistant now to the wharf.

The launch turned out to be an ancient, private-enterprise ferry. The official one went to Eceabat. Ours crossed directly to Kilitbahir, a medieval Ottoman fortress built by Mehmet II, the conqueror of Constantinople. From the upper deck I could see a Turkish war memorial scarring a hillside opposite. Akin to those prehistoric images cut into the turf of the British downs, this was a white figure on a gray ground, a soldier with one arm thrown out toward a poem in Turkish. The words were translated in my guidebook, no doubt losing something in the process: "Stop O Passer By . . ." and then something to the effect that this soil was where the heart of a nation throbbed. The poet's unlucky name was Onan, though verse so publicly exposed on a hillside could hardly be called a solitary vice.

On the wharf my yellow taxi was waiting. The driver spoke a few words of English. He had carefully carpeted the floor of his car with pieces of clean cardboard, to protect it from muddy feet.

As we headed toward open sea along the Gallipoli shore I saw many ships passing through the Dardanelles, to and from Istanbul and the Black Sea. The sky was gray and overcast. My spirits were raised by the sight of a large school of dolphins leaping through the waves near the shore. I remembered Yeats's line in the poem "Byzantium":

> That dolphin-torn, that gong-tormented sea.

Symbols of rebirth, I recalled, dolphins were among the earliest images in Christian art, ferrying spirits over death's river. Yeats had never been in these waters except in imagination. He got his gongs and dolphins from books. Yet, such is the power of genius, here they were in this haunted channel. On the far side, the land was flat along the Asian shore, easier country for an attacker to capture, reason enough why the strategic city of Troy, buried for centuries a few miles from the Hellespont, had fallen at least seven times. The Turks' German advisors had expected the British to make their assault over there; and in fact a French contingent did attack Kumkale, as diversion from the main thrust, suffering heavy casualties before they withdrew.

Soon we turned inland where the ground was high. Orchards and broom were in blossom. There were olive groves and stands of pine and myrtle, and a few patches of green wheat or barley. This was April, the same month in which the campaign had begun. The grass was green, spring was reawakening the land with daisies, poppies and anemones. We passed shepherds with flocks of shivering sheep and goats, a village, two or three small cemeteries. At last we came to the Helles Memorial, at the south western point of the Gallipoli peninsula.

This rough stone obelisk, designed by Sir John Burnet, commemorates the Gallipoli campaign itself, together with the names of some twenty thousand dead whose bodies were never found and a roll call of the ships and regiments that took part. Among the latter I found the 6th Royal Irish Rifles, the 5th Connaught Rangers, the 6th Leinster Regiment, the 6th and 7th Royal Munster Fusiliers, the 6th and 7th Royal Dublin Fusiliers, the 5th and 6th Inniskiling Fusiliers, the 5th and 6th Royal Irish Fusiliers. Ireland itself had forgotten the military virtue of these soldiers and regiments, whose battle honors were part of the imperial myth. The official Irish myth had eclipsed them. Gallipoli, 1915, was overshadowed by the Easter Rising of 1916.

A little to my right there was a lighthouse, slightly to the left the ruins of a redoubt where a couple of big guns had been blown off their mountings, and farther off along the beach the wreck of a fortress and a village, clustered around its minaret.

"What is the name of that village?" I asked the driver.

After some shouting and gesticulating I made myself understood. He told me the place was called Sedd-el-Bahr.

Vaguely I recalled having been told that that was the place where Uncle Robbie had been killed. Was there another cemetery down there? I asked. The driver led me to the edge of a bluff and pointed. There it was, below us, just inshore from the beach. This was V Beach Cemetery.

Telling the driver to wait for me, I walked down a rough, dirt road, passing a shepherd and some very dirty sheep on the way. *"Merhaba!"* I said. The man gave a grunt.

The cemetery was beautifully kept, with trim lawn and flowering judas trees. Some instinct led me straight to the marker. "Believed to be buried in this cemetery," I read. "Lieutenant Robert Bernard, Royal Dublin Fusiliers. 26 April 1915. Age 23. Dearly loved son of Most Rev. J. H. Bernard D. D. and Maud his wife."

At his son's death, Dr. Bernard was bishop of Ossory, residing in Kilkenny, thus Right Rev. Later that year he became archbishop of Dublin, distinguished as Most Rev.

I stared for a while at the beach, at the cliffs on the left, the hill behind it and the fortress on the right, fixing them in my memory. I took photographs despite the uninteresting light.

So that now, weeks later, I am able to see in my mind the desperate fighting and the horror that took place here in April 1915. I can do so because Dr. Bernard in his grief brought all the weight of his meticulous scholarship to bear on the problem of finding out how his son died. And he used his access to the inner councils of empire to collect the evidence. It is all here, in a thick album in my possession, along with every letter Robbie Bernard wrote to his parents in the entire course of his short life. Only three letters are withheld, Dr. Bernard notes, and those contain nothing dishonorable.

Men in the front line, at the cutting edge of battle, are not aware of the big picture. They know only what confronts them. They know their own unit's objectives, and as much of the general plan as their commanders think they need to understand. Robbie Bernard did not live to see the failure of the whole campaign, but the staff had not deceived the fighting units about what faced them. Historians see that the whole thing was a muddle, a project backed by young Winston Churchill (then first lord of the admiralty) that was never adequately thought through by the admiralty or the war office. The Royal Navy failed to blast a passage through the Dardanelles on March 18. All they had achieved, apart from the loss of three capital ships, was to put the enemy on notice that they would be attacked again, so that the Turks, guided by their German advisers, were able to fortify the beaches and dig in.

The Royal Dublin Fusiliers were to be shock troops of the Covering Force, that is, among the units detailed to capture the beaches at Cape Helles and their defences, and hold them while the main body of the army came ashore. The Dublins were an elite regiment of Irishmen. The 1st Battalion, until its disbandment in 1922, was one of the oldest units in the British army, raised in 1646 and assigned to the East India Company as the Madras Fusiliers; the 2nd Battalion, raised in 1662, became the Bombay Fusillers when the port was ceded to the Company.

"Clive led you to Arcot and Plassey," King George V told them as he received their colors at disbandment; "Eyre Coote to Wandewash; Forde to Condore. Your history is the history of the early British dominance in India. . . ."

As the spearhead of the 29th Division the 1st Dublins and 1st Munsters were to attack V Beach at dawn, April 25, after heavy bombardment of the defences by the big guns of the Royal Navy. They were to seize the beach, capture and hold the hill behind it and the village of Sedd-el-Bahr with its fortress. An Englishman who met them before the attack described them as "typical paddies," long-service professionals for whom war was a big joke. Certainly they were a cheerful lot, officers no less than the men.

On April 12, Robbie Bernard wrote a note in pencil to his parents. He was annoyed with the Senior Service (the navy): "They seem to have done absolutely nothing and if they were not so infernally jealous of our Service they would have called us in long ago and finished things off. Now, when our adversaries have had time to get things together we come in." Yet on April 22 he wrote in his diary—the last entry: "Hurrah! Off today. At least we have left the harbour."

Robbie had joined the regiment in March 1912, after passing out of Sandhurst Royal Military College. A photograph shows him in full dress uniform, scarlet tunic with gold bullion epaulets, blue facings and trews, a magenta sash, sword and heavy bearskin hat. Six feet in height, athletic in build, he had blue eyes, reddish mustache and hair parted in the middle. His letters reveal an affectionate character, without intellectual leanings, perhaps somewhat oppressed by the desire to please his scholarly father. His father's brief sketch supports this view.

"He was a very small baby," Dr. Bernard wrote, "but grew into a powerfully built man of six feet high. He was a jolly, cheerful child—much fonder of games than of books, as he continued to be throughout his life. But he would work hard, as he proved when he read for the army. He was always a good trier (as his teachers said) and 'did his best.'" One of the boy's earliest letters begins, "Dear father How are you I doing my best to please you."

After schooling at Arnold House in Wales (where Evelyn Waugh was to teach) and at Marlborough, Robbie took three tries at the army examination before he succeeded. He had served in Ludlow, Shropshire, where he fell in love with a girl called Eva Macaulay; and then in India and Egypt. His father hoped to get him transferred to the Indian army, which offered better pay than the imperial service, and where his uncle Colonel Herbert Bernard had kept a place for him in the 45th (Rattray's) Sikhs, the illustrious regiment he commanded. These plans were derailed by the world war, in which not only poor Robbie fell, but Uncle Herbie as well, leading his men, Irish this time, at the Somme.

Back in England, in January 1915, he found that Eva was tired of waiting for him. "She won't climb down and I won't so there's an end of the matter," he told his parents, "—sickening I call it." He left her his diaries, watches and a small camera. There is no picture of her in the album.

Two friends of Robbie's survived to tell the story of the landing on Sunday, April 25, at V Beach, described by Lieutenant Desmond O'Hara as "a small sandy bay about 200 yards long, very like the Silver Sand at Wicklow; it was commanded by high ground all round, and into this the ships poured such shellfire, that you would never believe a living thing could survive it for a minute."

O'Hara's company was in a tramp steamer, the *River Clyde*, which had had doors cut in her sides through which the troops could disembark when she ran aground on the beach. The rest of the lst Dublins, in pith helmets and khaki, and loaded down with heavy packs, ammunition and iron rations, were in cutters towed by pinnaces. Dawn was breaking as the thunder of the naval guns suddenly stopped. There was an ominous silence as the tows neared the beach. Some of the men must have hoped that the bombardment had knocked out all resistance.

They were within a few yards of the shore when a hurricane of fire from rifles, maxim-guns and pom-poms tore into the crowded boats. Within seconds about half of the first wave of Dublins was killed or wounded. In a letter to his mother O'Hara wrote, "The whole of the high ground round was honeycombed with the enemy's trenches, and they waited till the boats which were crammed full got about five yards from the shore when they let drive at them. . . . Numbers of men were killed in the boats, others as they waded ashore, and more on the sand before they could take cover behind a sandbank some twelve or fifteen yards from the shore."

Today the sandbank is simply a low scarp marking the highest point of spring tides.

Lieutenant-Colonel R. A. Rooth, commanding the battalion, was killed as he stepped ashore with his men. His second-in-command, Major E. Fetherstonhaugh, was mortally wounded before he could leave his boat. Captain G. M. Dunlop "just managed to crawl into the sand and died there. Poor young [Lieutenant R. V. C.] Corbet was horribly wounded in the boat, and died an hour later, in awful pain, I am afraid. [Captain and Adjutant W. F.] Higginson was able to get under cover, but put his head up and was killed. . . . [Captain D. V. F.] Anderson was shot through the body and killed almost instantly." Second Lieutenants Maffet and Walters were wounded, as was Lieutenant Lanigan O'Keeffe, a particular friend of Robbie's who had only just rejoined his unit after recovering from serious wounds suffered in France.

O'Keeffe described his ordeal to his sister in a letter written from a hospital ship May 3, 1915: "Well, here I am on my back again, having been whacked in both legs almost as soon as the show started. . . . We had to land from open boats on the shore of a small bay under fierce fire from either side and in front.

"Tremendous numbers of our fellows were killed or wounded even before the boats grounded, and then it was another 50 yards or so to the shore.

"They got me twice between the boat and the shore, but I was able to struggle ashore and into a more or less safe spot where I remained all that day and night and half the next day before being taken off by the ambulance people. No fault of theirs at all as we didn't drive the enemy from the cliffs just over my head until the next morning, and they couldn't do much by day, as our friends have a happy knack of firing at stretcher parties. I don't feel strong enough to describe that 30 hours minutely just yet. Suffice it to say it was extremely unpleasant.

"Poor old Robbie Bernard was killed on the morning of the 2nd day (Monday), I believe and hope instantaneously. Poor old lad—there were few better in every way on this earth."

Somehow Robbie Bernard had survived the carnage of the first, terrible day. The men in the tramp steamer were so cut up as they tried to sally from the doors into boats that the attempt to land them was postponed till dark. O'Hara wrote: "I got our company ashore about 12 o'clock that night. Next morning we attacked a small village [Sedd-el-Bahr] to clear the snipers out of it. Bernard was killed by a hand grenade." But O'Hara had not witnessed this, and it was to be corrected by Sergeant-Major George Baker of Robbie's company, who saw what actually happened. In the horror of battle men were none too sure of what was going on.

Among the soldiers Dr. Bernard wrote to in his quest for information was a private in the Dublins who had been wounded. His letter gives some idea of the confusion: "1st-6-1915. Dear Sir in answer to your letter as regards the death of your son I could not tell you what he was doeing when he got shot for the last time I seen him was on the night of the 25 that is the day before he got shot but I think he was in charge of his company or the 26 as his capation got wounded the first day but on the 26 we made a bayonet charge on the front and great number of officers fell in the charge as they where all in front of there companies. Dear Sir I am very sorry I can not give you very much information about the brave officer. Pte. R. McGillin 1st Royal Dublin Fusiliers Clarendon House Keneton."

The bayonet charge referred to was carried out by the shattered remnant of the Dublins and the Munsters. They captured the hill inland from the beach, a desperate exploit that more than one commentator called glorious. "One of the most magnificent deeds of the whole war," said the French General Gouraud, who witnessed it. War correspondents took pride in it as a feat of "British" arms.

The Dublins lost twenty-one officers in the two days of fighting, and more than two-thirds of the rank and file. Sergeant-Major Baker reported the death of Robbie Bernard: "Lieutenant Bernard fell too bravely leading a charge through the village." That was how Baker recalled it from a military hospital on May 30. On June 3 he wrote in more detail: "Y company was ordered to go through the village of Seddul Bahr which was rather strongly held, but it had to be cleared and we were getting weaker and the men dubious of doing it, when Lieut. Bernard led the rush to their positions which cleared them out, but both he and Lieut. Andrews were shot dead at point-blank range by rifle fire, for he led the rush right up to the house without trying to take cover."

Dr. Bernard's inquiries would continue. On May 1 a blizzard of telegrams had descended on Dublin and the southern Irish counties, each with its shocking bulletin. One of them was delivered around nine A.M. to the Palace, Kilkenny, the gray mansion that stands next to St. Canice's Cathedral and its ancient round tower. Robbie's mother dashed off a note to her sister Alice: "I know how you will grieve with us when I tell you our darling Robbie was killed on the 25th—The cruel wire has just come, it seems quite unbearable, your loving Nan." Addressed to the Bishop of Ossory, the wire, scribbled in pencil, said, "Deeply regret to inform you that Lieutenant R. Bernard R Dublin Fusiliers is reported from Alexandria to have been killed in action 25th April Lord Kitchener expresses his sympathy. Secy War Office." It is noticeable that the date of death is wrong in this official notification, an error that was repeated in newspaper notices, and even in a regimental history.

Early in December 1915 Dr. Bernard was able to interview Baker in person about his son: "He saw him killed. It was quite instantaneous. Baker says that Robert was not in any way foolhardy. What gave rise to this suggestion probably was this: Robert, being in command, should (in theory) have kept behind and not exposed himself. But the thing was very dangerous, and the men were doubtful. If Robert had said 'Go on' and not 'Come on,' the men might have hesitated. He had crept up to the corner of the village street with his men, and was peering about with his revolver out. He saw a Turk and fired at him. But the Turk had already fired, and that was the end. No pain, for the Sergeant saw him hours afterwards and there were no signs of struggle or movement at all. He was hit twice—in the shoulder and behind the ear . . . I am thankful. It could not have been more merciful, or more gallant."

Lieutenant O'Hara, who was killed in August of that year, was awarded the Distinguished Service Order for his courage and competence. After Robbie's death the Turks were driven out of Sedd-el-Bahr, and in the afternoon the "Dubsters" carried their other objective, the hill behind the village. "When the Turks had been driven off," O'Hara wrote, "we entrenched for the night, and had a few hours rest next day. Then, on the following day, we had a tremendous battle, and gained four miles of land, and next morning attacked again with disastrous results. The French gave way on the right, and the whole division retired in disorder—a very little more, and it would have been a rout. It was an awful time, and at the end I was the only officer left in the regiment. The Turks made no attempt to follow up their advantage, and we were able to dig in. We remained there for two nights, and on the third the Turks advanced, 20,000 strong, and tried to break through the line. The fight went on from 10.30 at night till 5 o'c next morning—a desperate fight the whole time. My regiment alone got through 150,000 rounds, and they were only 360 strong. The Turks were simply driven on to the barbed wire in front of the trenches by the German officers, and shot down by the score. They must have lost thousands. The fighting is of the most desperate kind—very little quarter on either side. One wounded German officer was found just in front of our trenches when day broke, and was instantly riddled by bullets. The men are absolutely mad to get at them, as they mutilate our wounded when they catch them. For the first three nights I did not have a wink of sleep, and actually fell asleep once during the big night attack. We had no food for about 36 hours after landing, as we were fighting incessantly. There were only 1600 left in the brigade out of 4000. I have only had my boots off once since landing." It was now May 1.

Thanks to the tenacity of the Dublins and the Munsters, and of the Royal Lancashire Fusiliers on an adjacent beach, the invading army was ashore by the next day. The failure to break out of the beachhead was in the end fatal to the enterprise. Ignorance of topography, even of geography, seems to have been a failing of Churchill's. In the Second World War, he would speak of "the soft underbelly of Europe," referring to an area that presents an almost unbroken barrier of mountains.

According to a letter from Captain A. W. Molony, Bernard's company commander, who was wounded the first day, "The Turks fought extremely well, and hung on with the greatest tenacity. They made very clever use of their machine guns, which were very well concealed and did a lot of damage. Our losses were terribly heavy."

Eventual victory at Gallipoli gave the Turks, under Mustafa Kemal, a new confidence. For them it was the first of many ordeals on the blood-soaked road to a new nation. The virus of nationalism which had eaten away the Ottoman Empire was to create the Republic of Turkey, and to make Kemal the first of the twentieth-century dictators and the founding hero of his country.

And now, some seventy-three springs later, I see in my mind, not the quiet and remote beach where the Aegean enters the Dardanelles and the judas blossom trembles in the breeze, but the inferno of 1915 where Irishmen died gallantly in a vain cause with friends and countrymen.

Under Robbie Bernard's photo, his father has written: *"Qui ante diem periit sed miles, sed pro patria."*

Gallipoli is today a national park, but Turkish country people live there. In spring and winter when visitors come there is a little money to be made selling souvenirs or driving taxis. One enterprising villager has even built a tiny motel on V Beach.

The day I went to Cape Helles I was the only visitor, not only at the British memorial but also at the colossal Turkish one, whose principal merit is sheer magnitude and visibility from far off. And the small group from down under at Anzac cove was there largely because it was the scene of a famous movie. The world of shadows is more real than that of memory or history.

And in the afternoon I would take a minibus to the site of ancient Troy, surely because it was the scene of a famous poem called the *Iliad*.

DENMARK AND THE JEWS

Hannah Arendt

This excerpt is from Arendt's book Eichmann in Jerusalem: A Report on the Banality of Evil, *published in 1963.*

At the Wannsee Conference, Martin Luther, of the Foreign Office, warned of great difficulties in the Scandinavian countries, notably in Norway and Denmark. (Sweden was never occupied, and Finland, though in the war on the side of the Axis, was one country the Nazis never even approached on the Jewish question. This surprising exception of Finland, with some two thousand Jews, may have been due to Hitler's great esteem for the Finns, whom perhaps he did not want to subject to threats and humiliating blackmail.) Luther proposed postponing evacuations from Scandinavia for the time being, and as far as Denmark was concerned, this really went without saying, since the country retained its independent government, and was respected as a neutral state, until the fall of 1943, although it, along with Norway, had been invaded by the German Army in April, 1940. There existed no Fascist or Nazi movement in Denmark worth mentioning, and therefore no collaborators. In Norway, however, the Germans had been able to find enthusiastic supporters; indeed, Vidkun Quisling, leader of the pro-Nazi and anti-Semitic Norwegian party, gave his name to what later became known as a "quisling government." The bulk of Norway's seventeen hundred Jews were stateless, refugees from Germany; they were seized and interned in a few lightning operations in October and November, 1942. When Eichmann's office ordered their deportation to Auschwitz, some of Quisling's own men resigned their government posts. This may not have come as a surprise to Mr. Luther and the Foreign Office, but what was much more serious, and certainly totally unexpected, was that Sweden immediately offered asylum, and even Swedish nationality, to all who were persecuted. Dr. Ernst von Weizsäcker, Undersecretary of State of the Foreign Office, who received the proposal, refused to discuss it, but the offer helped nevertheless. It is always relatively easy to get out of a country illegally, whereas it is nearly impossible to enter the place of refuge without permission and to dodge the immigration authorities. Hence, about nine hundred people, slightly more than half of the small Norwegian community, could be smuggled into Sweden.

It was in Denmark, however, that the Germans found out how fully justified the Foreign Office's apprehensions had been. The story of the Danish Jews is *sui generis,* and the behavior of the Danish people and their government was unique among all the countries in Europe—whether occupied, or a partner of the Axis, or neutral and truly independent. One is tempted to recommend the story as required reading in political science for all students who wish to learn something about the enormous power potential inherent in non-violent action and in resistance to an opponent possessing vastly superior means of violence. To be sure, a few other countries in Europe lacked proper "understanding of the Jewish question," and actually a majority of them were opposed to "radical" and "final" solutions. Like Denmark, Sweden, Italy, and Bulgaria proved to be nearly immune to anti-Semitism, but of the three that were in the German sphere of influence, only the Danes dared speak out on the subject to their German masters. Italy and Bulgaria sabotaged German orders and indulged in a complicated game of double-dealing and double-crossing, saving their Jews by a tour de force of sheer ingenuity, but they never contested the policy as such. That was totally different from what the Danes did. When the Germans approached them rather cautiously about introducing the yellow badge, they were simply told that the King would be the first to wear it, and the Danish government officials were careful to point out that anti-Jewish measures of any sort would cause their own immediate resignation. It was decisive in this whole matter that the Germans did not even succeed in introducing the vitally important distinction between native Danes of Jewish origin, of whom there were about sixty-four hundred, and the fourteen hundred German Jewish refugees who had found asylum in the country prior to the war and who now had been declared stateless by the German government. This refusal must have surprised the Germans no end, since it appeared so "illogical" for a government to protect people to whom it had categorically denied naturalization and even permission to work. (Legally, the prewar situation of refugees in Denmark was not unlike that in France, except that the general corruption in the Third Republic's civil services enabled a few of them to obtain naturalization papers, through bribes or "connections," and most refugees in France could work illegally, without a permit. But Denmark, like Switzerland, was no country *pour se débrouiller.*) The Danes, however, explained to the German officials that because the stateless refugees were no longer German citizens, the Nazis could not claim them without Danish assent. This was one of the few cases in which statelessness turned out to be an asset, although it was of course not statelessness per se that saved the Jews but, on the contrary, the fact that the Danish government had decided to protect them. Thus, none of the preparatory moves, so important for the bureaucracy of murder, could be carried out, and operations were postponed until the fall of 1943.

What happened then was truly amazing; compared with what took place in other European countries, everything went topsy-turvey. In August, 1943—after the German offensive in Russia had failed, the Afrika Korps had surrendered in Tunisia, and the Allies had invaded Italy—the Swedish government canceled its 1940 agreement with Germany which had permitted German troops the right to pass through the country. Thereupon, the Danish workers decided that they could help a bit in hurrying things up; riots broke out in Danish shipyards, where the dock workers refused to repair German ships and then went on strike. The German military commander proclaimed a state of emergency and imposed martial law, and Himmler thought this was the right moment to tackle the Jewish question, whose "solution" was long overdue. What he did not reckon with was that—quite apart from Danish resistance—the German officials who had been living in the country for years were no longer the same. Not only did General von Hannecken, the military commander, refuse to put troops at the disposal of the Reich plenipotentiary, Dr. Werner Best; the special S.S. units (*Einsatz-kommandos*) employed in Denmark very frequently objected to "the measures they were ordered to carry out by the central agencies"—according to Best's testimony of Nuremberg. And Best himself, an old Gestapo man and former legal adviser to Heydrich, author of a then famous book on the police, who had worked for the military government in Paris to the entire satisfaction of his superiors, could not longer be trusted, although it is doubtful that Berlin ever learned the extent of his unreliability. Still, it was clear from the beginning that things were not going well, and Eichmann's office sent one of its best men to Denmark—Rolf Günther, whom no one had ever accused of not possessing the required "ruthless toughness." Günther made no impression on his colleagues in Copenhagen, and now von Hannecken refused even to issue a decree requiring all Jews to report for work.

Best went to Berlin and obtained a promise that all Jews from Denmark would be sent to Theresienstadt regardless of their category—a very important concession, from the Nazis' point of view. The night of October 1 was set for their seizure and immediate departure—ships were ready in the harbor—and since neither the Danes nor the Jews nor the German troops stationed in Denmark could be relied on to help, police units arrived from Germany for a door-to-door search. At the last moment, Best told them that they were not permitted to break into apartments, because the Danish police might then interfere, and they were not supposed to fight it out with the Danes. Hence they could seize only those Jews who voluntarily opened their doors. They found exactly 477 people, out of a total of more then 7,800, at home and willing to let them in. A few days before the date of doom, a German shipping agent, Georg F. Duckwitz, having probably been tipped off by Best himself, had revealed the whole plan to Danish government officials, who, in turn, had hurriedly informed the heads of the Jewish community. They, in marked contrast to Jewish leaders in other countries, had then communicated the news openly in the synagogues on the occasion of the New Year services. The Jews had just time enough to leave their apartments and go into hiding, which was very easy in Denmark, because, in the words of the judgment, "all sections of the Danish people, from the King down to simple citizens," stood ready to receive them.

They might have remained in hiding until the end of the war if the Danes had not been blessed with Sweden as a neighbor. It seemed reasonable to ship the Jews to Sweden, and this was done with the help of the Danish fishing fleet. The cost of transportation for people without means—about a hundred dollars per person—was paid largely by wealthy Danish citizens, and that was perhaps the most astounding feat of all, since this was a time when Jews were paying for their own deportation, when the rich among them were paying fortunes for exit permits (in Holland, Slovakia, and, later, in Hungary) either by bribing the local authorities or by negotiating "legally" with the S.S., who accepted only hard currency and sold exit permits, in Holland, to the tune of five or ten thousand dollars per person. Even in places where Jews met with genuine sympathy and a sincere willingness to help, they had to pay for it, and the chances poor people had of escaping were nil.

It took the better part of October to ferry all the Jews across the five to fifteen miles of water that separates Denmark from Sweden. The Swedes received 5,919 refugees, of whom at least 1,000 were of German origin, 1,310 were half-Jews, and 686 were non-Jews married to Jews. (Almost half the Danish Jews seem to have remained in the country and survived the war in hiding.) The non-Danish Jews were better off than ever before, they all received permission to work. The few hundred Jews whom the German police had been able to arrest were shipped to Theresienstadt. They were old or poor people, who either had not received the news in time or had not been able to comprehend its meaning. In the ghetto, they enjoyed greater privileges than any other group because of the never-ending "fuss" made about them by Danish institutions and private persons. Forty-eight persons died, a figure that was not particularly high, in view of the average age of the group. When everything was over, it was the considered opinion of Eichmann that "for various reasons the action against the Jews in Denmark has been a failure," whereas the curious Dr. Best declared that "the objective of the operation was not to seize a great number of Jews but to clean Denmark of Jews, and this objective has now been achieved."

Politically and psychologically, the most interesting aspect of this incident is perhaps the role played by the German authorities in Denmark, their obvious sabotage of orders from Berlin. It is the only case we know of in which the Nazis met with *open* native resistance, and the result seems to have been that those exposed to it changed their minds. They themselves apparently no longer looked upon the extermination of a whole people as a matter of course. They had met resistance based on principle, and their "toughness" had melted like butter in the sun, they had even been able to show a few timid beginnings of genuine courage. That the ideal of "toughness," except, perhaps, for a few half-demented brutes, was nothing but a myth of self-deception, concealing a ruthless desire for conformity at any price, was clearly revealed at the Nuremberg Trials, where the defendants accused and betrayed each other and assured the world that they "had always been against it" or claimed, as Eichmann was to do, that their best qualities had been "abused" by their superiors. (In Jerusalem, he accused "those in power" of having abused his "obedience." "The subject of a good government is lucky, the subject of a bad government is unlucky. I had no luck.") The atmosphere had changed, and although most of them must have known that they were doomed, not a single one of them had the guts to defend the Nazi ideology. Werner Best claimed at Nuremberg that he had played a complicated double role and that it was thanks to him that the Danish officials had been warned of the impending catastrophe; documentary evidence showed, on the contrary, that he himself had proposed the Danish operation in Berlin, but he explained that this was all part of the game. He was extradited to Denmark and there condemned to death, but he appealed the sentence, with surprising results; because of "new evidence," his sentence was commuted to five years in prison, from which he was released soon afterward. He must have been able to prove to the satisfaction of the Danish court that he really had done his best.

THE BATTLE OF THE ANTS

Henry David Thoreau

This is an excerpt from Thoreau's 1854 book Walden.

One day when I went out to my wood-pile, or rather my pile of stumps, I observed two large ants, the one red, the other much larger, nearly half an inch long, and black, fiercely contending with one another. Having once got hold they never let go, but struggled and wrestled and rolled on the chips incessantly. Looking farther, I was surprised to find that the chips were covered with such combatants, that it was not a *duellum*, but a *bellum*, a war between two races of ants, the red always pitted against the black, and frequently two red ones to one black. The legions of these Myrmidons covered all the hills and vales in my wood-yard, and the ground was already strewn with the dead and dying, both red and black. It was the only battle which I have ever witnessed, the only battle-field I ever trod while the battle was raging; internecine war; the red republicans on the one hand, and the black imperialists on the other. On every side they were engaged in deadly combat, yet without any noise that I could hear, and human soldiers never fought so resolutely. I watched a couple that were fast locked in each other's embraces, in a little sunny valley amid the chips, now at noonday prepared to fight till the sun went down, or life went out. The smaller red champion had fastened himself like a vice to his adversary's front, and through all the tumblings on that field never for an instant ceased to gnaw at one of his feelers near the root, having already caused the other to go by the board; while the stronger black one dashed him from side to side, and, as I saw on looking nearer, had already divested him of several of his members. They fought with more pertinacity than bulldogs. Neither manifested the least disposition to retreat. It was evident that their battle-cry was "Conquer or die." In the meanwhile there came along a single red ant on the hillside of this valley, evidently full of excitement, who either had despatched his foe, or had not yet taken part in the battle; probably the latter, for he had lost none of his limbs; whose mother had charged him to return with his shield or upon it. Or perchance he was some Achilles, who had nourished his wrath apart, and had now come to avenge or rescue his Patroclus. He saw this unequal combat from afar—for the blacks were nearly twice the size of the red—he drew near with rapid pace till he stood on his guard within half an inch of the combatants; then, watching his opportunity, he sprang upon the black warrior, and commenced his operations near the root of his right fore leg, leaving the foe to select among his own members; and so there were three united for life, as if a new kind of attraction had been invented which put all other locks and cements to shame. I should not have wondered by this time to find that they had their respective musical bands stationed on some eminent chip, and playing their national airs the while, to excite the slow and cheer the dying combatants. I was myself excited somewhat even as if they had been men. The more you think of it, the less the difference. And certainly there is not the fight recorded in Concord history, at least, if in the history of America, that will bear a moment's comparison with this, whether for the numbers engaged in it, or for the patriotism and heroism displayed. For numbers and for carnage it was an Austerlitz or Dresden. Concord Fight! Two killed on the patriots' side, and Luther Blanchard wounded! Why here every ant was a Buttrick—"Fire! for God's sake fire!"—and thousands shared the fate of Davis and Hosmer. There was not one hireling there. I have no doubt that it was a principle they fought for, as much as our ancestors, and not to avoid a three-penny tax on their tea; and the results of this battle will be as important and memorable to those whom it concerns as those of the battle of Bunker Hill, at least.

I took up the chip on which the three I have particularly described were struggling, carried into my house, and placed it under a tumbler on my window-sill, in order to see the issue. Holding a microscope to the first-mentioned red ant, I saw that, though he was assiduously gnawing at the near fore leg of his enemy, having severed his remaining feeler, his own breast was all torn away, exposing what vitals he had there to the jaws of the black warrior, whose breastplate was apparently too thick for him to pierce; and the dark carbuncles of the sufferer's eyes shone with ferocity such as war only could excite. They struggled half an hour longer under the tumbler, and when I looked again the black soldier had severed the heads of his foes from their bodies, and the still living heads were hanging on either side of him like ghastly trophies at his saddle-bow, still apparently as firmly fastened as ever, and he was endeavoring with feeble struggles, being without feelers, and with only the remnant of a leg, and I know not how many other wounds, to divest himself of them; which at length, after half an hour more, he accomplished. I raised the glass, and he went off over the window-sill in that crippled state. Whether he finally survived that combat, and spent the remainder of his days in some Hôtel des Invalides, I do not know; but I thought that his industry would not be worth much thereafter. I never learned which party was victorious, nor the cause of the war, but I felt for the rest of that day as if I had my feelings excited and harrowed by witnessing the struggle, the ferocity and carnage, of a human battle before my door.

Kirby and Spence tell us that the battles of ants have long been celebrated and the date of them recorded, though they say that Huber is the only modern author who appears to have witnessed them. "Aeneas Sylvius," say they, "after giving a very circumstantial account of one contested with great obstinacy by a great and small species on the trunk of a pear tree," adds that "'this action was fought in the pontificate of Eugenius the Fourth, in the presence of Nicholas Pistoriensis, an eminent lawyer, who related the whole history of the battle with the greatest fidelity.' A similar engagement between great and small ants is recorded by Olaus Magnus, in which the small ones, being victorious, are said to have buried the bodies of their own soldiers, but left those of their giant enemies a prey to the birds. This event happened previous to the expulsion of the tyrant Christiern the Second from Sweden." The battle which I witnessed took place in the Presidency of Polk, five years before the passage of Webster's Fugitive-Slave Bill.

CATTLEKILLING WINTER, 1889-90

Jana Harris

This poem originally appeared in Harris's 1993 book Oh How Can I Keep on Singing? Voices of Pioneer Women.

> We walked, of course.
> Omaha to Walla Walla: 5 months, 3 days.
> My husband, Nathan Sloan (known as Kentucky),
> a fireman on the Missouri-Louisville line,
> worked years tallowing valves
> before the railroads fell on slack times.
> He lost his job and the farm.

In Walla Walla, rested our oxen before
the baby—christened Caleb—was born,
walked another week north to where
Loop Loop Creek crosses the Okanogan.

Long days, high clouds, temperatures in the 90's.

Made a land claim, went to Buzzard Lake
to wash and water our stock,
met a miner, Dutch Jake, and his dog,
who infected my husband with gold fever.
Came back, found our claim jumped,
went up creek, made another. The only law
against selling black powder to an Indian.

Milled lumber too costly—not even a board
for a coffin. So cut and hewed logs for a cabin,
our lead ox hauling through mire.
Local talk had it winters too mild
to necessitate a barn.

Humidity high. Nighttime temperatures falling.

Mosquitoes so thick, Nathan had to stand
above me as I cooked, battling them off
with a towel. Morning coffee required
constant skimming, while bugs
in our mash appeared as caraway.
Deer were so plentiful they staggered
for lack of forage and could be had by clubbing.
November 1, ten venison hams hung from our eaves.

Nights getting longer, though unseasonably warm.

Just before New Year's, I awoke to ice
in the washbasin. Snowed nineteen inches.
Temperatures dropped. Snow crusted hard enough
to cut the lead ox's tendon.
John Other Day, Cut Nose, and their squaws
came daily to our door demanding flour.
Oats: six cents a pound; potatoes, five;
hay, a hundred a ton if you could find it.

Forty below by mid-month. The sun never shone.

Our oxen froze in the fields,
the twin calves dead at the milch cow's side,
the last of our hay in front of her.
Five feet of snow and blizzarding winds
for thirteen consecutive days.

The only drinking water, melted snow;
the only wood, our furniture.
Nathan sawed frozen meat from the dead,
feeding it to what stock remained.
I soaked rags in the blood of offal, giving
the baby suck. God Be Praised, he thrived.

Up on Buzzard Mountain, prospectors
were trapped in their mines—the artillery
of avalanche thundered through our valley.
When he tried to leave, Dutch, his mule and hound,
were buried—the dog dug its way out.
Ours was the first cabin he came to.

Brought the two living cows and one horse
into our lean-to kitchen, supped with us
on flour mash and seed potato.
If we went anywhere, it was hand-over-hand
over ice. No mail for weeks,
river frozen, the railroad snowbound.
A stranger who went through on snowshoes,
said a neighbor's wife died of laudanum
taken with suicidal intent.
Flour and sugar gone, rumor our daily bread.

When the ice melted, the creeks swelled
bringing typhoid which weakened my husband.
After pneumonia, he looked worse
than any at Andersonville and was unable
to help with chores.

First day of March. Days longer. Heavy fog.

The stock were enfeebled by hunger.
Balding from rain scald, hair fell in sheets
from their hides. When the spring grass
came on, they were too weak to graze,
collapsing like long-legged insects.
Ill myself, I crawled out to help, Caleb on my back:
right hoof forward, left knee bent, sometimes
it took a rail under the rump to raise them.

Most ranchers went under.
Some took twenty years to repay loans
on herds that perished, and then
only when they sold off their farms.
But the two cows left to us begat others
who begat the thousand head
Caleb and his sons graze in this valley.

I was born Effie Rebecca, named for my mother,
but forever after that cattle-killing winter,
my husband called me by another.
Years ago he went to the stone orchard,
my place beside him ready: "SLOAN, Nathan
known as Kentucky, and Wife, Born Again '89
as God's handmaiden, Faith."

Long Days. High clouds. Temperatures in the 90's.

FROM FOOLS CROW
—■—

James Welch

This is an excerpt from Welch's novel Fools Crow, *published in 1986 by Viking Penguin.*

On the morning of the thirteenth sleep of sickness in the Lone Eater camp, Fools Crow and his father, Rides-at-the-door, walked through the village. They went from lodge to lodge and called to the people within. There were still many sick and dying, but the number of new victims had gone down. The rage of the white-scabs was subsiding. It seemed impossible that it would last such a short time and leave so many dead or scarred for life by the draining sores. Others were out walking listlessly in the warm sun or just sitting outside their lodges. There was none of the bustle that usually occurred on a morning of winter camp. The people did not greet each other. If they met on the path to the river, they would move off the path and circle warily until they were well beyond. If a child was caught playing with the children from a family hard hit by the bad spirit, he would be called inside and scolded. But it was one old woman, the only survivor of her lodge, who sat and wailed and dug at the frozen ground until her fingers were raw and bloody—it was this old woman who made the people realize the extent of their loss. Gradually they emerged from the deep void of sickness and death and saw that they had become a different people.

As Fools Crow and Rides-at-the-door continued their count, they passed the painted ermine lodge of Three Bears. Prairie Runner Woman knelt outside the entrance, her eyes closed, her face raised to the sun. Neither man spoke out in greeting, for she was still numb with the death of the old chief. Rides-at-the-door had been present when Three Bears died. During one of his last lucid moments, the old man had given Rides-at-the-door his red-stone pipe. In that way he chose the younger man as his successor. Young Bird Chief had died, so there would be no opposition.

"There are thirty-seven dead ones," said Fools Crow.

"There will be more." They were walking in the shadows of a grove of big-leaf trees. They stopped to watch a man leading two packhorses from camp. There were two robe-draped bundles across the horses' backs. Rides-at-the-door pulled his capote tight around his neck. "The time before, the disease hit three different times. Just when it would appear to be over, a new wave of sickness would visit the people. I pray to the Above Ones that such a thing not occur again, but we must not allow ourselves to think we are out of it."

"There are only five newly stricken."

Rides-at-the-door grunted. After a time he said, "We must organize a hunt while some are still healthy. I'm afraid Cold Maker will visit any day and then it will go hard on us."

"The blackhorns will be south of the Big River, maybe along the Yellow River, maybe farther south." Fools Crow, even as he spoke, remembered the vision on the yellow skin, the vast plains empty of blackhorns. He had told his father and Three Bears—just before the old man got sick—of this vision, and of the others as well. After much deliberation, the two men had decided that the people should be kept ignorant of these designs until they grew stronger and were capable of deciding what should be done. But a feeling had been growing inside Fools Crow that there would be little deciding, that any decisions would be puny in the face of such powerful designs. He did not mention this feeling to his father.

"Go see the camp crier," Rides-at-the-door was saying. "Tell him to announce a meeting of all the men's societies for tonight. Our hunting parties will have a long way to go, and the sooner they start the better."

As Fools Crow hurried off, he realized that he was passing the lodge of Heavy Shield Woman. The only sign of activity was two dogs playing tug-of-war with a strip of deerskin. They were flattened almost to the ground and their low growling made a buffalo-runner, tethered in front of the next lodge, dance warily, his ears forward and eyes trained on the dogs.

Good Young Man had died the day after Fools Crow had performed his healing ritual. The convulsions had lasted a long time, and both Fools Crow and Heavy Shield Woman had breathed exhausted sighs when the end finally came. Fools Crow got directions from his mother-in-law and took the young body out to the quaking-leaf grove where Yellow Kidney rested. Heavy Shield Woman stayed behind to care for One Spot. And the boy survived. He came up out of his delirium and asked for soup. Because of his youth, he recovered rapidly. For the second time in three moons, he pulled back from the shadow of the Sand Hills. But he was changed, like all the Lone Eaters.

For two days Wind Maker howled from the north and kept the hunters in camp. The snow drifted into Two Medicine valley, until in some places it was as high as a man's waist. It covered the debris of the camp and filled in the prints of man, dog and horse as soon as they were made. Soon, nothing moved and only the smoke from the tops of the lodges gave away the existence of life in the village.

Each day at midmorning Fools Crow made his round of the camp, taking count of the sickness. Two of the five newly afflicted had died, and there were three new cases, including one of Boss Ribs' wives. She had been very active during the height of the plague, going from lodge to lodge, bathing the sick ones, feeding the others, caring for the children. Now she lay in her own robes, the disease sucking the life from her breast in spite of Boss Ribs' desolate songs.

Fools Crow reported his findings to Rides-at-the-door, then returned to his lodge. He drank a cup of broth and watched Red Paint, who had been quiet for the last couple of sleeps. He thought it was because of the death of her brother, and he thought she would get over her sadness in time, maybe when the weather broke, when she could safely visit her mother's lodge. But something about her made him think of Feather Woman and the way she looked that morning in the clearing, shoulders slumped, chin on her breast, oblivious to everything but her failed plea to Morning Star. Fools Crow picked up his many-shots gun and ran a greasy rag over the action. He had not shot it in a long time.

The third day dawned clear and cold. The sun was pale and high and the air was gray. The snow had ended and the hunters stood ready at the edge of camp. There were to be three groups of seven each. One group would go south, another southeast, and the third, of which Fools Crow was a member, would go directly east, following the course of the Two Medicine and Bear rivers until they reached the country between the Sweet Grass Hills and the Bear Paws. Although there would be hunters from other camps, maybe even from the Entrails People and the Cutthroats, the herd that often wintered there was large. The thought of encountering an enemy was almost welcome to the hunters after the ordeal within their own camp. They were mostly young and restless and, in spite of the intense cold, ready to risk anything out on the ground-of-many-gifts.

Fools Crow and the others made good time down the valley of the Two Medicine River. They kept to the open ground where the wind had scoured the snow away, and the packhorses drove easily before them. Sits-in-the-middle, who had a reputation as a good meat provider, led the party, and the others had great faith in his power to lead them to the blackhorns. By the time Sun was behind them, they had reached the confluence of the Two Medicine and Bear. They saw a winter camp and recognized it as that of the Hard Topknots. They drove the horses around the southern edge of the camp and Sits-in-the-middle and Fools Crow galloped over to the lodge of Crow Foot. Fools Crow rode apprehensively, several paces behind Sits-in-the-middle, for he remembered the design on the yellow skin. Again, he saw Little Bird Woman, Crow Foot's daughter, lugging the bucket of guts from the agency compound. He shuddered as he thought that at one time she had been chosen to become his wife.

Crow Foot welcomed them but he did not offer them a smoke. Although he had not been affected by the white-scabs, the hunters were almost frightened to see how thin he had become. Then he began to talk of the empty lodges in his camp—over half of the Hard Topknots had been carried away. He spoke the names of the dead as though he had memorized them. He told of the suffering and the desertions and the falling apart of the band. He spoke rapidly and he signed as he talked, as he would to strangers. And then he stopped talking and stared out at the camp, as if in a trance. Fools Crow looked around and he didn't see any of the Hard Topknots. This was unusual, for visitors brought the curious from their lodges to look, to laugh and point, to come join in the conversation. Now there was none of that. Not even dogs. The two hunters wished Crow Foot well and promised him meat on their return, but he didn't seem to hear them. They left him there, still staring in disbelief at the quiet camp.

That night they made camp in a thicket of willows on the north side of the Bear River. They had seen no game all day and so they ate handfuls of pemmican before sleeping. Fools Crow awoke twice during the night to the howling of the little-wolves, and each time he felt the cold sense of dread that had accompanied him since the party left their camp. When he finally slept, he dreamed of enemies.

The hunting party was up and on the move long before daylight. If they pushed hard this day, they would be in the blackhorn country within two more sleeps. Fools Crow rode beside Sits-in-the-middle at the head of the small group. Behind them, the others drove the pack animals. After a long period of silence in which the only sound was the rubbing of cold leather and the steady clopping of the horses' hooves, Fools Crow told the hunt leader of his dream of enemies. He had not seen them clearly in his dream, and in the darkness before dawn, the vision seemed less significant.

But Sits-in-the-middle listened and then he said, "This dream of yours does not make me happy. I am responsible for these young men and I must return them to their families. But the Lone Eaters need meat, that is our first concern, and so we must chance an encounter with our enemies."

Fools Crow glanced at Sits-in-the-middle. The light had increased enough so that he could see the dark frown on the hunt leader's face. It was a round, almost puffy face. Many in the camp secretly ridiculed Sits-in-the-middle, for his mother was a Snake woman who had been captured by the Loan Eaters many winters ago. She had been a slave until the Pikuni Hears-in-the-wind took her as a wife. Sits-in-the-middle was her only offspring. Fools Crow felt pity for him, for he was barely listened to in councils and was deemed capable only of leading a small party of young hunters.

"Perhaps our enemies are also down with the white-scabs," said Fools Crow. "My dream was less than clear. I do not attach much importance to it."

By midmorning the sun was high to the southeast and the hunters stopped to stretch their bodies and to slap the circulation back into their calves and thighs and arms. Again they had seen no sign of game, but they hadn't expected to. Because of the winter camps in the valley, the animals were scarce and moved only at night. After eating a handful of pemmican, Fools Crow mounted his black buffalo-runner. He felt the animal's warmth beneath his thighs and was grateful for it. Although there was no wind, the air was as cold as it had been that winter. He pulled his robe up over his capote and sat, waiting for the others to finish their cold meal. He gazed absently down the valley.

At first he didn't believe what he was seeing. He jumped up and stood on his horse's back and he could see more clearly the patches of color beneath a cutbank far in the distance. It took a while to see their movement, but soon he saw that the patches were people, on foot, and they were coming toward the hunters.

"What is it you look at?" said Sits-in-the-middle. He began to hurry to a piece of higher ground. The others followed, suddenly alert and expectant.

"Human beings. On foot. They are coming our way." He jumped down to the ground. He could only think of enemies. Only horse stealers traveled on foot in the winter.

After a quick look, Sits-in-the-middle ran down the small rise. The others followed, breathing hard, their excitement causing the horses to move restlessly. One of the pack animals began to whinny until a hunter reached him and clamped his hand over the muzzle.

"We must be ready," said Sits-in-the-middle. 'They are coming straight down the river beneath the cutbank." There was no cover near, but the swale they were in hid them from view. The hunt leader instructed one of the young men to drive the pack animals back upstream and into a gully that opened out onto the river bottom.

Then the hunters waited, Fools Crow and Sits-in-the-middle lying below the lip of the rise. Both had repeating rifles, but the others had only bows. None of them had encountered an enemy before. Fools Crow looked back at them and they looked like prairie birds, crouched together, facing up at him. They are too young, he thought. If the raiders are experienced warriors it will go hard on us. He almost expressed his fear to Sits-in-the-middle, but as he looked down the valley at the approaching party, he felt his apprehension leave him.

"There are children among them," he whispered. "Little ones. And some of them move out slowly, like old people." He lifted himself from the ground and knelt. 'They carry nothing with them—no weapons."

Soon the people were close enough for Fools Crow to count. There were three old people, two young women, a youth of twelve or thirteen winters and two children. One of the young women was limping badly. The other was helping her. They were Pikunis. Fools Crow recognized the wounded one—White Crane Woman, a member of Heavy Runner's band. He looked downstream, in the direction the group had come from, but there were no others.

"Something has happened, something bad!" Fools Crow ran down the rise and threw himself on his horse. The others still crouched motionless, their mouths open like birds.

As he galloped the black buffalo-runner down the valley, he knew this scene had something to do with the yellow skin and the designs. It was the same weather, the same kind of day that the seizers rode north. He felt the fear and guilt rise and spread throughout his limbs and he was almost too weak to stay up. He had seen the design. "Why didn't I warn them?" he cried. "Why didn't I tell them?" The wind was in his eyes and the hoofbeats filled his ears and he pushed the horse even faster.

As he reined in, the horse skidded almost to his rump, and the people began to scramble back against the cutbank. Only the children, a boy and a girl, stood and watched him.

"It is Fools Crow—of the Lone Eaters! I have come to help you!"

White Crane Woman had fallen when her companion deserted her, but now she stood, her eyes dark and hard.

"White Crane Woman! You know me. Our families visit during the Sun Dance encampment." Fools Crow slid from his horse and ran to her. He caught her just as her energy faded and gently lowered her to the frozen ground. The old ones and the other woman slowly approached. The youth still clung to the side of the cutbank.

"What has happened to you?"

No one spoke. They stood and Fools Crow saw the fear return to their eyes. Then he heard the harsh thumping of the horses as the other hunters rode up. "They are also Lone Eaters. They too come to help." Fools Crow knelt beside White Crane Woman. The hem of her dress was bloody. He raised it and saw the bullet wound through the fleshy part of her calf. The skin was red and shredded where it had exited. Fools Crow had no medicine but he did have a piece of soft-tanned skin in his war bag. As he wrapped the wound, one of the old ones, a woman, knelt beside him and spoke. "It was the seizers. They sneaked up on us while we were still asleep. There was only a little light, just enough to see by, and they shot us in our lodges. Pretty soon, our people were running in all directions and still they shot us. Many of us are killed. We managed to slip away, down to the river, and run away below the cutbank. But one of the greased shooters found this one's leg. We ran away and now you have found us."

"The others—are they all dead?"

"I do not know this. We had to run and keep on going. But the shooters were still buzzing until finally we were beyond hearing."

The young woman who had been helping White Crane Woman came forward and squatted beside the old woman. Her eyes were flat with shock.

"They killed Heavy Runner," she said. She pointed with her lips to the youth who was now leaning back against the cutbank.

"That boy there saw him fall."

Fools Crow tied off the bandage, then looked up at the two women. He was surprised at the calmness with which they related their news. They could have been telling him about a relative's visit or a berrying party.

But as he looked into their eyes, he saw that the immensity of what had happened had left them numb.

"Where is your camp?" he said.

"In the big bend below the Medicine Rock. It is not long by horseback."

Fools Crow stood and turned to Sits-in-the-middle. "I will go there and see for myself."

A look of hesitancy came into Sits-in-the-middle's eyes, as though he too might be expected to go to the massacred camp.

"These people can find shelter in Crow Foot's camp," said Fools Crow. "They will need you to lead them."

"Yes, that is true. We will take them on the packhorses and wait for you there."

First there was the smoke, only slightly darker than the gray air. It rose from behind a bluff where the river curved to the south. The sun was behind it, and it looked orange and sharp-edged.

Then the black horse smelled it and stiffened beneath his rider. It was a smell not of smoke but of burnt things, and the smell was heavy in the air. Even though the bluff stood between the horse and the smell, he stopped, his shoulders and forelegs trembling. Fools Crow kicked the horse in the ribs, but still he did not move.

"You know what we are about to see. You have known for a long time, Heavy-charging-in-the-brush." Fools Crow let the horse settle down. "We will see it now. We will take heart from Wolverine, who always faces into the wind."

The horse moved forward and soon they were around the bluff and they saw the remains of the camp. There were no fires visible but the smoke was darker and thicker. It rose from many places until it became a cloud above the south bank of the river. As they moved up to higher ground, Fools Crow began to pick out the blackened lumps that emitted the smoke. Between the lumps, the snow was still white. Then a small wind blew the smoke toward him and the snow became yellow and dirty and the smell hit his nostrils, the smell of burnt skin. Fools Crow could almost taste it, and it was smoky and pleasant in his mouth. He began to weep and still the horse moved forward.

Then they were at the edge of the camp and the black lumps were lodges that had burned. A dog lay in the snow a few paces away. Most of his hair had been burned off and his tongue was black against the white teeth. Then Fools Crow saw something else lying in a patch of blackened, melted snow. He kicked the horse in the ribs and moved toward it. The sight made his stomach come up against his ribs. It was an infant and its head was black and hairless. Specks of black ash lay in its wide eyes. Fools Crow fell from his horse and vomited up the handful of pemmican he had eaten earlier that morning. He was on his hands and knees and the convulsions wracked his body until only a thin yellow strand of saliva hung from his lips. He stayed in that position and gulped hard until the wracking stopped. He wiped his mouth and eyes, then stood. And he began to pick out the other bodies. Most of them had been thrown onto the burning lodges but they were not all black like the infant. There were scraps of clothes that hadn't burned. There was skin and hair and eyes. There were teeth and bone and arms and legs. One old woman lay on top on one of the smoking lumps, only the underside of her skin dress burned. Her feet were bare. Fools Crow, through his tears, saw the purple welts on her legs where she had slashed herself a long time ago in mourning a lost one.

As he wandered from smoking ruin to ruin, he didn't really know that his eyes had quit seeing, that his nose no longer burned with the smell of death. He didn't even notice that his feet had gotten wet from walking through the trampled melted snow. On the far side of camp, he kept moving until he came to a downed big-leaf. He sat slowly, carefully down on the smooth trunk and buried his face in his hands. He rubbed his eyes and there were no more tears, not from the smoke, not from his heart. He sat for a long time, tired and numb, until his mind came back and he remembered where he was, what he had seen. Still he was in no hurry to open his eyes.

Then he felt something on his knee. He opened his eyes and saw a red puppy standing before him, one paw on his knee, the other swiping the air as though he wanted to play. He reached out and touched the head and ran his hand all the way down to the tail. The puppy yipped and bit the air. Fools Crow smiled and the puppy sat back and scratched himself behind the ear.

Through the smoke, on the other side of the camp, Fools Crow saw a figure standing motionless, looking at him. It was a man and Fools Crow's heart quickened. He had only his knife in his belt. But the man was dressed in the way of the Pikunis. The knees of his leggings were black. Fools Crow stood quickly and the puppy tumbled away, yipping in fear. Then another figure emerged from the brush behind the man. It was an old woman, bent with age. Two more figures came forward, and they too were old.

When he reached them, Fools Crow saw that the first man was hardly more than a youth. He was tall but his shoulders slumped. Fools Crow looked at the others and he recognized Black Prairie Runner, once a man who had led many war parties against the enemies. His eyes were cloudy now and his long fingers, clutching a blanket over his shoulders, were bent and stiff.

"They drove off our horses," he said. His words were mild and flimsy in the cold air.

"Are there others? Others who survived?"

"Our horses are all gone. You see"—he waved his free arm around them—"there are no horses."

Fools Crow looked questioningly at the others.

The young man stepped forward. "I am called Bear Head. My father was also called Bear Head, and he was killed by Owl Child some winters ago."

"Yes," said Fools Crow. "They argued over who had killed a Cutthroat in battle. It is said that Owl Child made a false claim."

"All there knew that the Cutthroat was my father's kill. But Owl Child was crazy and he killed my father rather than admit his falsehood." Bear Head stood straighter. "I will have my revenge."

Fools Crow was moved by this small introduction, for he knew Bear Head would have no satisfactory revenge. Even revenge had been slaughtered.

"I met some of your band, escaping up the river. The other hunters I was with have taken them to Crow Foot's camp. They told of the seizers."

"It was the seizers. I left camp before first light to get my horses. I had planned to do some hunting this day and I needed pack animals. The herds were down near the foot of Three Persons. I picked out four animals and was leading them back when I saw some movement on that low ridge over there. It was still dark down here but there was a faint light in the sky behind the ridge. At first I thought it was a pack of little-wolves up there, thinking to look for scraps around the camp. But then one of the shapes stood and I knew it for a man. I became frightened and began to run toward camp, leaving my horses where they stood. But just before entering that stand of spear-leafs, I saw the dark shapes before me. There was a man behind each tree. Then all at once came the thunder and fire of the big guns. I froze against a tree. All I could do was listen and pray that the thunder would end, but it went on and on until it was light enough to see the cloud of blue smoke from the guns. It hung in the trees and drifted toward me. I could taste it in my mouth. When I looked up at the ridge I could see hundreds of fire flashes through the smoke. But I still could not see my village so I began to run around the seizers in the trees. They were so intent on their work that they did not look around. Finally I was on the lower side, near the river and I saw my people—" Bear Head stopped, and Fools Crow could see his eyes wander beyond him to the remains of the camp. He seemed to focus on one of the smoking lumps. Fools Crow turned and saw that it had burned nearly to the ground.

"Besides my mother, I had three near-mothers and four sisters and a brother. Now they are gone from me. I do not know where they have gone—they did not have time to prepare themselves."

As Fools Crow stared out at the smoking ruins, he began to notice what was missing. The mention of Bear Head's mothers and sisters made him realize that he had seen only the bodies of old men and young boys among the women.

"Where are the men?" he said. He turned back to Bear Head. "Where are the warriors?"

One of the old women lifted her head. She had been watching the red puppy, who had followed Fools Crow and now lay with his head between his paws.

"Off hunting," she said. "There was no meat in camp, and a Pikuni does not live without meat." She said this fiercely.

"Those who weren't dead or sick with the white-scabs," said Bear Head. He looked uncomfortable. "I myself was leaving for the hunt this morning."

"A Pikuni does not live without meat," muttered the old woman.

Bear Head looked down at her. "Curlew Woman's two sons were to go with me. Now they are burned up."

Fools Crow could envision the hunters' return. Whether laden with meat or empty-handed, they would see something they would mourn for the rest of their lives.

"Where are the seizers now?" Fools Crow's voice was sharp. Anger welled up within him, an anger that was directed at the futility of attempting to make the seizers pay. He had always thought that the Pikunis could fight these hairy-faces. He had prepared himself for this fight, he was ready to die a good death to defend this country. Now he knew that his father had been right all along—the Pikunis were no match for the seizers and their weapons. That the camps were laid low with the white-scabs disease did not even matter. The disease, this massacre—Sun Chief favored the Napikwans. The Pikunis would never possess the power to make them cry.

He listened to Bear Head's weary voice recount the details of the massacre. "Curlew Woman says Heavy Runner was among the first to fall. He had a piece of paper that was signed by a seizer chief. It said that he and his people were friends to the Napikwans. But they shot him many times. By the time I could see the camp, there were only a few running, trying to escape. They were all cut down by the greased shooters. There were several lodges already on fire. Some of the seizers were aiming at the lodge bindings. Many of the lodge covers fell into the fires within and started burning. Then there was no more movement and I heard a seizer chief shout and the shooting stopped. By that time there was too much smoke in the air, dark smoke from the burning lodges, blue smoke from the shooting. The seizers waited awhile, then they came down from the ridge and out of the trees. I felt naked and exposed beside the river, so I crawled into some brush here behind us. The seizers walked among the lodges, at first quietly; then they became bolder and began to talk and laugh. Whenever they saw a movement from under one of the lodge covers they shot at it until it moved no more. They rounded up the bodies and threw them onto the fires. Those lodges that stood untouched by fire were ragged with bullet holes. The seizers cut the bindings and set these lodges on fire. They took what they valued and threw all the rest onto the fires. They drove off all our horses."

"Did any others get away?"

"I saw three women and their children. The seizers did not shoot them even though they stood beside these trees and watched the burning. I search for them after the seizers left but I did not find them. Perhaps they left for Mountain Chief 's camp. The Many Chiefs are camped just downriver."

Fools Crow suddenly remembered the rumor he had heard in his own camp. Owl Child had supposedly returned to Mountain Chief's village and was down with the white-scabs. He wondered if Fast Horse was there too, if he was sick—or dead. He knew that the Many Chiefs would be gone as soon as they learned of this disaster.

"Which way did the seizers go?"

Curlew Woman looked up again. She pointed to the hills behind the ridge from which the seizers slaughtered the camp. "Up there. Black Prairie Runner and Good Kill here"—she indicated the other old woman—"we ran up a draw over there. The seizers rode right by us—they saw us but they didn't shoot. Oh, how I wish they had! I cursed them, I stole their honor, but they only laughed."

"They will probably make camp at Dry Fork. Perhaps we could recover the horses if the hunters return." Fools Crow felt his spirit rise slightly. He turned to Curlew Woman. "It is good that you are alive. You will have much to teach the young ones about the Napikwans. Many of them will come into the world and grow up thinking that the Napikwans are their friends because they will be given a blanket or a tin of the white man's water. But here, you see, this is the Napikwan's real gift."

Black Prairie Runner, as though he had just come out of a trance, started, then spoke. "What you say is true, young man. But these women and I are old. We have seen much, we have seen the winter counts add up—some years were good, some were bad, but each design on the skin was something we could understand. Now they are all bad and we do not understand why. This world has changed and we do not belong to it. We would be better off to join our before-people in the Sand Hills. It is as Curlew woman says. We would rather be killed by the Napikwans than live in their world."

"I listen to you with a good heart and I hear the truth in your voice. Many of our people feel this way. As we stand here, I see this tragedy that Sun Chief permits. I am tempted to wish that all the Pikuni people could go to that other world where there are no Napikwans. There the hunting is good and the people live according to the old ways. But this is the land of the Pikunis. This is where the long-ago people were born and lived and died. They would be angry with us if we just gave it up. They would say the Pikunis had become puny, that we would not fight for this land that they left us."

"But how can we fight?" Bear Head's voice was tense, as though a fire had begun to burn within him. "You see what they do to us. There are too many of them and their weapons are more powerful than ours. More Pikunis died this one day than in all the days since I have been alive. They kill our women and children. They kill our old ones!" Then, just as suddenly as it began, the fire went out. "They kill my mother, my sisters, my near-mothers. They kill us all. I, who have no family left, welcome it."

"This is bad talk," said Fools Crow, but he felt young and powerless, as though he talked into a strong wind. Listening to Curlew Woman and

Black Prairie Runner, and now Bear Head, he felt his small hope fading and he wished for the presence of his father. Rides-at-the-door would say some words that would make them all see a reason to go on. He could talk with the wind's strength. Even Black Prairie Runner and Curlew Woman, who had lived so long and now wished to die, would feel that strength and they would know it was important to think of the children.

Fools Crow thought of the final design on the yellow skin in Feather Woman's lodge. He saw the Napikwan children playing and laughing in a world that they possessed. And he saw the Pikuni children, quiet and huddled together, alone and foreign in their own country.

"We must think of our children," he said. He lowered his eyes to the red puppy and it was quiet all around. The few survivors stared at the red puppy, who had rolled onto his back, his front legs tucked against his chest. They had no children.

WICKEDNESS

———————■———————

Ron Hansen

This short story is from Hansen's 1989 story collection Nebraska.

At the end of the nineteenth century a girl from Delaware got on a milk train in Omaha and took a green wool seat in the second-class car. August was outside the window, and sunlight was a yellow glare on the trees. Up front, a railway conductor in a navy-blue uniform was gingerly backing down the aisle with a heavy package in a gunnysack that a boy was helping him with. They were talking about an agreeable seat away from the hot Nebraska day that was persistent outside, and then they were setting their cargo across the runnered aisle from the girl and tilting it against the shellacked wooden wall of the railway car before walking back up the aisle and elsewhere into August.

She was sixteen years old and an Easterner just recently hired as a county schoolteacher, but she knew enough about prairie farming to think the heavy package was a crank-and-piston washing machine or a boxed plowshare and coulter, something no higher than the bloody stump where the poultry were chopped with a hatchet and then wildly high-stepped around the yard. Soon, however, there was a juggling movement and the gunnysack slipped aside, and she saw an old man sitting there, his limbs hacked away, and dark holes where his ears ought to have been, the skin pursed at his jaw hinge like pink lips in a kiss. The milk train jerked into a roll through the railway yard, and the old man was jounced so that his gray cheek pressed against the hot window glass. Although he didn't complain, it seemed an uneasy position, and the girl wished she had the courage to get up from her seat and tug the jolting body upright. She instead got to her page in *Quo Vadis* and pretended to be so rapt by the book that she didn't look up again until Columbus, where a doctor with liquorice on his breath sat heavily beside her and openly stared over his newspaper before whispering that the poor man was a carpenter in Genoa who'd been caught out in the great blizzard of 1888. Had she heard of that one?

The girl shook her head.

She ought to look out for their winters, the doctor said. Weather in Nebraska could be the wickedest thing she ever saw.

She didn't know what to say, so she said nothing. And at Genoa a young teamster got on in order to carry out the old man, whose half body was heavy enough that the boy had to yank the gunnysack up the aisle like 60 pounds of mail.

In the year 1888, on the twelfth day of January, a pink sun was up just after seven and southeastern zephyrs of such soft temperature were sailing over the Great Plains that squatters walked their properties in high rubber boots and April jackets and some farmhands took off their Civil War greatcoats to rake silage into the cattle troughs. However, sheep that ate whatever they could the night before raised their heads away from food and sniffed the salt tang in the air. And all that morning streetcar mules were reported to be acting up, nipping each other, jingling the hitch rings, foolishly waggling their dark manes and necks as though beset by gnats and horseflies.

A Danish cattleman named Axel Hansen later said he was near the Snake River and tipping a teaspoon of slaeratus into a yearling's mouth when he heard a faint groaning in the north that was like the noise of a high waterfall at a fair distance. Axel looked toward Dakota, and there half the sky was suddenly gray and black and indigo blue with great storm clouds that were seething up as high as the sun and wrangling toward him at horse speed. Weeds were being uprooted, sapling trees were bullwhipping and the top inches of snow and prairie soil were being sucked up and stirred like the dirty flour that was called red dog. And then the onslaught hit him hard as furniture, flying him onto his back so that when Axel looked up, he seemed to be deep undersea and in icehouse cold. Eddying snow made it hard to breathe any way but sideways, and getting up to just his knees and hands seemed a great attainment. Although his sod house was but a quarter-mile away, it took Axel four hours to get there. Half his face was frozen gray and hard as weather-boarding so the cattleman was speechless until nightfall, and then Axel Hansen simply told his wife, That was not pleasant.

Cow tails stuck out sideways when the wind caught them. Sparrows and crows whumped hard against the windowpanes, their eyes seeking out an escape, their wings fanned out and flattened as though pinned up in an ornithologist's display. Cats died, dogs died, pigeons died. Entire farms of cattle and pigs and geese and chickens were wiped out in a single night. Horizontal snow that was hard and dry as salt dashed and seethed over everything, sloped up like rooftops, tricked its way across creek beds and ditches, milkily purled down city streets, stole shanties and coops and pens from a bleak landscape that was even then called the Great American Desert. Everything about the blizzard seemed to have personality and hateful intention. Especially the cold. At 6 A.M., the temperature at Valentine, Nebraska, was 30 degrees above zero. Half a day later the temperature was 14 below, a drop of 44 degrees and the difference between having toes and not, between staying alive overnight and not, between ordinary concerns and one overriding idea.

Ainslie Classen was hopelessly lost in the whiteness and tilting low under the jamming gale when his right elbow jarred against a joist of his pigsty. He walked around the sty by skating his sore red hands along the upright shiplap and then squeezed inside through the slops trough. The pigs scampered over to him, seeking his protection, and Ainslie put himself among them, getting down in their stink and their body heat, socking them away only when they ganged up or when two or three presumed he was food. Hurt was nailing into his finger joints until he thought to work his hands into the pigs' hot wastes, and smeared some onto his skin. The pigs grunted around him and intelligently snuffled at his body with their pink and tender noses, and Ainslie thought, *You are not me but I am you,* and Ainslie Classen got through the night without shame or injury.

Whereas a Harrington woman took two steps out her door and disappeared until the snow sank away in April and raised her body up from her garden patch.

An Omaha cigar maker got off the Leavenworth Street trolley that night, 50 yards from his own home and 5 yards from another's. The completeness of the blizzard so puzzled him that the cigar maker tramped up and down the block more than 20 times and then slept against a lamppost and died.

A cattle inspector froze to death getting up on his quarter horse. The next morning he was still tilting the saddle with his upright weight, one cowboy boot just inside the iced stirrup, one bear-paw mitten over the horn and reins. His quarter horse apparently kept waiting for him to complete his mount, and then the quarter horse died too.

A Chicago boy visiting his brother for the holidays was going to a neighbor's farm to borrow a scoop shovel when the night train of blizzard raged in and overwhelmed him. His tracks showed the boy mistakenly slanted past the sod house he'd just come from, and then tilted forward with perhaps the vain hope of running into some shop or shed or railway depot. His body was found four days later and 27 miles from home.

A forty-year-old wife sought out her husband in the open range land near O'Neill and days later was found standing up in her muskrat coat and black bandanna, her scarf-wrapped hands tightly clenching the top strand of rabbit wire that was keeping her upright, her blue eyes still open but cloudily bottled by a half inch of ice, her jaw unhinged as though she'd died yelling out a name.

The 1 A.M. report from the Chief Signal Officer in Washington, D.C., had said Kansas and Nebraska could expect "fair weather, followed by snow, brisk to high southerly winds gradually diminishing in force, becoming westerly and warmer, followed by colder."

Sin Thomas undertook the job of taking Emily Flint home from their Holt County schoolhouse just before noon. Sin's age was sixteen, and Emily was not only six years younger but also practically kin to him, since her stepfather was Sin's older brother. Sin took the girl's hand and they haltingly tilted against the uprighting gale on their walk to a dark horse, gray-maned and gray-tailed with ice. Sin cracked the reins loose of the crowbar tie-up and helped Emily up onto his horse, jumping up onto the croup from a soapbox and clinging the girl to him as though she were groceries he couldn't let spill.

Everything she knew was no longer there. She was in a book without descriptions. She could put her hand out and her hand would disappear. Although Sin knew the general direction to Emily's house, the geography was so duned and drunk with snow that Sin gave up trying to nudge his horse one way or another and permitted its slight adjustments away from the wind. Hours passed and the horse strayed southeast into Wheeler County, and then in misery and pneumonia it stopped, planting its overworked legs like four parts of an argument and slinging its head away from Sin's yanks and then hanging its nose in anguish. Emily hopped down into the snow and held on to the boy's coat as Sin uncinched the saddle and jerked off a green horse blanket and slapped it against his iron leggings in order to crack the ice from it. And then Sin scooped out a deep nook in a snow slope that was as high and steep as the roof of a New Hampshire house. Emily tightly wrapped herself in the green horse blanket and slumped inside the nook in the snow, and the boy crept on top of her and stayed like that, trying not to press into her.

Emily would never say what was said or was cautiously not said that night. She may have been hysterical. In spite of the fact that Emily was out of the wind, she later said that the January night's temperature was like wire-cutting pliers that snipped at her ears and toes and fingertips until the horrible pain became only a nettling and then a kind of sleep and her feet seemed as dead as her shoes. Emily wept, but her tears froze cold as penny nails and her upper lip seemed candlewaxed by her nose and she couldn't stop herself from feeling the difference in the body on top of her. She thought Sin Thomas was responsible, that the night suited his secret purpose, and she so complained of the bitter cold that Sin finally took off his Newmarket overcoat and tailored it around the girl; but sixty years later, when Emily wrote her own account of the ordeal, she forgot to say anything about him giving her his overcoat and only said in an ordinary way that they spent the night inside a snowdrift and that "by morning the storm had subsided."

With daybreak Sin told Emily to stay there and, with or without his Newmarket overcoat, the boy walked away with the forlorn hope of chancing upon his horse. Winds were still high, the temperature was 35 degrees below zero, and the snow was deep enough that Sin pulled lop-sidedly with every step and then toppled over just a few yards away. And then it was impossible for him to get to his knees, and Sin only sank deeper when he attempted to swim up into the high wave of snow hanging over him. Sin told himself that he would try again to get out, but first he'd build up his strength by napping for just a little while. He arranged his body in the snow gully so that the sunlight angled onto it, and then Sin Thomas gave in to sleep and within twenty minutes died.

His body was discovered at noon by a Wheeler County search party, and shortly after that they came upon Emily. She was carried to a nearby house where she slumped in a kitchen chair while girls her own age dipped Emily's hands and feet into pans of ice water. She could look up over a windowsill and see Sin Thomas's body standing upright on the porch, his hands woodenly crossed at his chest, so Emily kept her brown eyes on the pinewood floor and slept that night with jars of hot water against her skin. She could not walk for two months. Even scissoring tired her hands. She took a cashier's job with the Nebraska Farm Implements Company and kept it for forty-five years, staying all her life in Holt County. She died in a wheelchair on a hospital porch in the month of April. She was wearing a glamorous sable coat. She never married.

The T. E. D. Schusters' only child was a seven-year-old boy named Cleo who rode his Shetland pony to the Westpoint school that day and had not shown up on the doorstep by 2 P.M., when Mr. Schuster went down into the root cellar, dumped purple sugar beets onto the earthen floor, and up-ended the bushel basket over his head as he slung himself against the on-slaught in his second try for Westpoint. Hours later Mrs. Schuster was tapping powdered salt onto the night candles in order to preserve the wax when the door abruptly blew open and Mr. Schuster stood there without Cleo and utterly white and petrified with cold. She warmed him up with okra soup and tenderly wrapped his frozen feet and hands in strips of gauze that she'd dipped in kerosene, and they were sitting on milking stools by a red-hot stove, their ankles just touching, only the usual senti-ments being expressed, when they heard a clopping on the wooden stoop and looked out to see the dark Shetland pony turned gray and shaggy-bearded with ice, his legs as wobbly as if he'd just been born. Jammed under the saddle skirt was a damp, rolled-up note from the Scottish schoolteacher that said, Cleo is safe. The Schusters invited the pony into the house and bewildered him with praises as Cleo's mother scraped ice from the pony's shag with her own ivory comb, and Cleo's father gave him sugar from the Dresden bowl as steam rose up from the pony's back.

Even at 6 o'clock that evening, there was no heat in Mathias Aachen's house, and the seven Aachen children were in whatever stockings and clothing they owned as they put their hands on a Hay-burner stove that was no warmer than soap. When a jar of apricots burst open that night and the iced orange syrup did not ooze out, Aachen's wife told the children, You ought now to get under your covers. While the seven were crying and crowding onto their dirty floor mattresses, she ran the green tent cloth along the iron wire dividing the house and slid underneath horse blankets in Mathias Aachen's gray wool trousers and her own gray dress and a ghastly muskrat coat that in hot weather gave birth to insects.

Aachen said, Every one of us will be dying of cold before morning. Freezing here. In Nebraska.

His wife just lay there, saying nothing.

Aachen later said he sat up bodingly until shortly after 1 P.M., when the house temperature was so exceedingly cold that a gray suede of ice was on the teapot and his pretty girls were whimpering in their sleep. You are not meant to stay here, Aachen thought, and tilted hot candle wax into his right ear and then his left, until he could only hear his body drumming blood. And then Aachen got his Navy Colt and kissed his wife and killed her. And then walked under the green tent cloth and killed his seven children, stopping twice to capture a scuttling boy and stopping once more to reload.

Hattie Benedict was in her Antelope County schoolyard overseeing the noon recess in a black cardigan sweater and gray wool dress when the January blizzard caught her unaware. She had been impatiently watching four girls in flying coats playing Ante I Over by tossing a spindle of chartreuse yarn over the one-room schoolhouse, and then a sharp cold petted her neck and Hattie turned toward the open fields of hoarfrosted scraggle and yellow grass. Just a half mile away was a gray blur of snow underneath a dark sky that was all hurry and calamity, like a nighttime city of sin-black buildings and havoc in the streets. Wind tortured a creekside cottonwood until it cracked apart. A tin water pail rang in a skipping toll to the horse path. One quarter of the tar-paper roof was torn from the schoolhouse and sailed southeast 40 feet. And only then did Hattie yell for the older boys with their cigarettes and clay pipes to hurry in from the prairie 20 rods away, and she was hustling a dallying girl inside just as the snowstorm socked into her Antelope County schoolhouse, shipping the building awry off its timber skids so that the southwest side heavily dropped 6 inches and the oakplank floor became a slope that Hattie ascended unsteadily while ordering the children to open their *Webster Franklin Fourth Reader* to the Lord's Prayer in verse and to say it aloud. And then Hattie stood by her desk with her pink hands held theatrically to her cheeks as she looked up at the walking noise of bricks being jarred from the chimney and down the roof. Every window view was as white as if butchers' paper had been tacked up. Winds pounded into the windowpanes and dry window putty trickled onto the unpainted sills. Even the slough grass fire in the Hay-burner stove was sucked high into the tin stack pipe so that the soot on it reddened and snapped. Hattie could only stare. Four of the boys were just about Hattie's age, so she didn't say anything when they ignored the reading assignment and earnestly got up from the wooden benches in order to argue *oughts* and *ought nots* in the cloakroom. She heard the girls saying Amen and then she saw Janusz Vasko, who was fifteen years old and had grown up in Nebraska weather, gravely exiting the cloakroom with a cigarette behind one ear and his right hand raised high overhead. Hattie called on him, and Janusz said the older boys agreed that they could get the little ones home, but only if they went out right away. And before she could even give it thought, Janusz tied his red handkerchief over his nose and mouth and jabbed his orange corduroy trousers inside his antelope boots with a pencil.

Yes, Hattie said, please go, and Janusz got the boys and girls to link themselves together with jump ropes and twine and piano wire, and twelve of Hattie Benedict's pupils walked out into a nothingness that the boys knew from their shoes up and dully worked their way across as though each crooked stump and tilted fence post was a word they could spell in a plain-spoken sentence in a book of practical knowledge. Hours later the children showed up at their homes, aching and crying in raw pain. Each was given cocoa or the green tea of the elder flower and hot bricks were put next to their feet while they napped and newspapers printed their names incorrectly. And then, one by one, the children disappeared from history.

Except for Johan and Alma Lindquist, aged nine and six, who stayed behind in the schoolhouse, owing to the greater distance to their ranch. Hattie opened a week-old Omaha newspaper on her desktop and with caution peeled a spotted yellow apple on it, eating tan slices from her scissor blade as she peered out at children who seemed irritatingly sad and pathetic. She said, You wish you were home.

The Lindquists stared.

Me too, she said. She dropped the apple core onto the newspaper page and watched it ripple with the juice stain. Have you any idea where Pennsylvania is?

East, the boy said. Johan was eating pepper cheese and day-old rye bread from a tin lunch box that sparked with electricity whenever he touched it. And his sister nudged him to show how her yellow hair was beguiled toward her green rubber comb whenever she brought it near.

Hattie was talking in such quick English that she could tell the Lindquists couldn't quite understand it. She kept hearing the snow pinging and pattering against the windowpanes, and the storm howling like clarinets down the stack pipe, but she perceived the increasing cold in the room only when she looked to the Lindquists and saw their Danish sentences grayly blossoming as they spoke. Hattie went into the cloakroom and skidded out the poorhouse box, rummaging from it a Scotch plaid scarf that she wrapped twice around her skull and ears just as a squaw would, and snipping off the fingertips of some red knitted gloves that were only slightly too small. She put them on and then she got into her secondhand coat and Alma whispered to her brother but Hattie said she'd have no whispering, she hated that, she couldn't wait for their kin to show up for them, she had too many responsibilities, and nothing interesting ever happened in the country. Everything was stupid. Everything was work. She didn't even have a girlfriend. She said she'd once been sick for four days, and two by two practically every woman in Neligh mistrustfully visited her rooming house to squint at Hattie and palm her forehead and talk about her symptoms. And then they'd snail out into the hallway and prattle and whisper in the hawk and spit of the German language.

Alma looked at Johan with misunderstanding and terror, and Hattie told them to get out paper and pencils; she was going to say some necessary things and the children were going to write them down. She slowly paced as she constructed a paragraph, one knuckle darkly striping the blackboard, but she couldn't properly express herself. She had forgotten herself so absolutely that she thought forgetting was a yeast in the air; or that the onslaught's only point was to say over and over again that she was next to nothing. Easily bewildered. Easily dismayed. The Lindquists were shying from the crazy woman and concentrating their shame on a nickel pad of Wisconsin paper. And Hattie thought, *You'll give me an ugly name and there will be cartoons and snickering and the older girls will idly slay me with jokes and imitations.*

She explained she was taking them to her rooming house, and she strode purposefully out into the great blizzard as if she were going out to a garden to fetch some strawberries, and Johan dutifully followed, but Alma stayed inside the schoolhouse with her purple scarf up over her mouth and nose and her own dark sandwich of pepper cheese and rye bread clutched to her breast like a prayer book. And then Johan stepped out of the utter whiteness to say Alma had to hurry up, that Miss Benedict was angrily asking him if his sister had forgotten how to use her legs. So Alma stepped out of the one-room schoolhouse, sinking deep in the snow and sloshing ahead in it as she would in a pond until she caught up with Hattie Benedict, who took the Lindquists' hands in her own and walked them into the utter whiteness and night of the afternoon. Seeking to blindly go north to her rooming house, Hattie put her high button shoes in the deep tracks that Janusz and the schoolchildren had made, but she misstepped twice, and that was enough to get her on a screw-tape path over snow humps and hillocks that took her south and west and very nearly into a great wilderness that was like a sea in high gale.

Hattie imagined herself reaching the Elkhorn River and discovering her rooming house standing high and honorable under the sky's insanity. And then she and the Lindquist children would duck over their teaspoons of tomato soup and soda crackers as the town's brooms and scarecrows teetered over them, hooking their green hands on the boy and girl and saying, Tell us about it. She therefore created a heroine's part for herself and tried to keep to it as she floundered through drifts as high as a four-poster bed in a white room of piety and weeping. Hattie pretended gaiety by saying once, See how it swirls! but she saw that the Lindquists were tucking deep inside themselves as they trudged forward and fell and got up again, the wind drawing tears from their squinting eyes, the hard, dry snow hitting their skin like wildly flying pencils. Hours passed as Hattie tipped away from the press of the wind into country that was a puzzle to her, but she kept saying, Just a little farther, until she saw Alma playing Gretel by secretly trailing her right hand along a high wave of snow in order to secretly let go yet another crumb of her rye bread. And then, just ahead of her, she saw some pepper cheese that the girl dropped some time ago. Hissing spindrifts tore away from the snow swells and spiked her face like sharp pins, but then a door seemed to inch ajar and Hattie saw the slight, dark change of a haystack and she cut toward it, announcing that they'd stay there for the night.

She slashed away an access into the haystack and ordered Alma to crawl inside, but the girl hesitated as if she were still thinking of the gingerbread house and the witch's oven, and Hattie acidly whispered, You'll be a dainty mouthful. She meant it as a joke but her green eyes must have seemed crazy, because the little girl was crying when Hattie got inside the haystack next to her, and then Johan was crying, too, and Hattie hugged the Lindquists to her body and tried to shush them with a hymn by Dr. Watts, gently singing, Hush, my dears, lie still and slumber. She couldn't get her feet inside the haystack, but she couldn't feel them anyway just then, and the haystack was making everything else seem right and possible. She talked to the children about hot pastries and taffy and Christmas presents, and that night she made up a story about the horrible storm being a wicked old man whose only thought was to eat them up, but he couldn't find them in the haystack even though he looked and looked. The old man was howling, she said, because he was so hungry.

At daybreak a party of farmers from Neligh rode out on their high plowhorses to the Antelope County schoolhouse in order to get Hattie and the Lindquist children, but the room was empty and the bluetick hound that was with them kept scratching up rye bread until the party walked along behind it on footpaths that wreathed around the schoolyard and into a haystack 20 rods away where the older boys smoked and spit tobacco juice at recess. The Lindquist girl and the boy were killed by the cold, but Hattie Benedict had stayed alive inside the hay, and she wouldn't come out again until the party of men yanked her by the ankles. Even then she kept the girl's body hugged against one side and the boy's body hugged to the other, and when she was put up on one horse, she stared down at them with green eyes that were empty of thought or understanding and inquired if they'd be okay. Yes, one man said. You took good care of them.

Bent Lindquist ripped down his kitchen cupboards and carpentered his own triangular caskets, blacking them with shoe polish, and then swaddled Alma and Johan in black alpaca that was kindly provided by an elder in the Church of Jesus Christ of Latter-Day Saints. And all that night Danish women sat up with the bodies, sopping the Lindquists' skin with vinegar so as to impede putrefaction.

Hattie Benedict woke up in a Lincoln hospital with sweet oil of spermaceti on her hands and lips, and weeks later a Kansas City surgeon amputated her feet with a polished silver hacksaw in the presence of his anatomy class. She was walking again by June, but she was attached to cork-and-iron shoes and she sighed and grunted with every step. Within a year she grew so overweight that she gave up her crutches for a wicker-backed wheelchair and stayed in Antelope County on a pension of 40 dollars per month, letting her dark hair grow dirty and leafy, reading one popular romance per day. And yet she complained so much about her helplessness, especially in winter, that the Protestant churches took up a collection and Hattie Benedict was shipped by train to Oakland, California, whence she sent postcards saying she'd married a trolley repairman and she hated Nebraska, hated their horrible weather, hated their petty lives.

On Friday the thirteenth some pioneers went to the upper stories of their houses to jack up the windows and crawl out onto snow that was like a jeweled ceiling over their properties. Everything was sloped and planed and caped and whitely furbelowed. One man couldn't get over his boyish delight in tramping about on deerhide snowshoes at the height of his roof gutters, or that his dogwood tree was forgotten but for twigs sticking out of the snow like a skeleton's fingers. His name was Eldad Alderman, and he jabbed a bamboo fishing pole in four likely spots a couple of feet below his snowshoes before the bamboo finally thumped against the plank roof of his chicken coop. He spent two hours spading down to the coop and then squeezed in through the one window in order to walk among the fowl and count up. Half his sixty hens were alive; the other half were still nesting, their orange beaks lying against their white hackles, sitting there like a dress shop's hats, their pure white eggs not yet cold underneath them. In gratitude to those thirty chickens that withstood the ordeal, Eldad gave them Dutch whey and curds and eventually wrote a letter praising their constitutions in the *American Poultry Yard*.

Anna Shevschenko managed to get oxen inside a shelter sturdily constructed of oak scantling and a high stack of barley straw, but the snow powder was so fine and fiercely penetrating that it sifted through and slowly accumulated on the floor. The oxen tamped it down and inchingly rose toward the oak scantling rafters, where they were stopped as the snow flooded up, and by daybreak were overcome and finally asphyxiated. Widow Schevschenko decided then that an old woman could not keep a Nebraska farm alone, and she left for the East in February.

One man lost 300 Rhode Island Red chickens; another lost 26 Hereford cattle and sold their hides for 2 dollars apiece. Hours after the Hubenka boy permitted 21 hogs to get out of the snowstorm and join their 40 Holsteins in the upper barn, the planked floor in the cattle linter collapsed under the extra weight and the livestock perished. Since even coal picks could no more than chip the earth, the iron-hard bodies were hauled aside until they could be put underground in April, and just about then some Pawnee Indians showed up outside David City. Knowing their manner of living, Mr. Hubenka told them where the carcasses were rotting in the sea wrack of weed tangles and thaw-water jetsam, and the Pawnee rode their ponies onto the property one night and hauled the carrion away.

And there were stories about a Union Pacific train being arrested by snow on a railway siding near Lincoln, and the merchandizers in the smoking car playing euchre, high five, and flinch until sunup; about cowboys staying inside a Hazard bunkhouse for three days and getting bellyaches from eating so many tins of anchovies and saltine crackers; about the Omaha YMCA where shop clerks paged through inspirational pamphlets or played checkers and cribbage or napped in green leather Chesterfield chairs until the great blizzard petered out.

Half a century later, in Atkinson, there was a cranky talker named Bates, who maintained he was the fellow who first thought of attaching the word *blizzard* to the onslaught of high winds and slashing dry snow and ought to be given credit for it. And later, too, a Lincoln woman remembered herself as a little girl peering out through yellowed window paper at a yard and countryside that were as white as the first day of God's creation. And then a great white Brahma bull with street-wide horns trotted up to the house, the night's snow puffing up from his heavy footsteps like soap flakes, gray funnels of air flaring from his nostrils and wisping away in the horrible cold. With a tilt of his head the great bull sought out the hiding girl under a Chesterfield table and, having seen her, sighed and trotted back toward Oklahoma.

Wild turkey were sighted over the next few weeks, their wattled heads and necks just above the snow like dark sticks, some of them petrified that way but others simply waiting for happier times to come. The onslaught also killed prairie dogs, jackrabbits, and crows, and the coyotes that relied upon them for food got so hungry that skulks of them would loiter like juveniles in the yards at night and yearn for scraps and castaways in old songs of agony that were always misunderstood.

Addie Dillingham was seventeen and irresistible that January day of the great blizzard, a beautiful English girl in an hourglass dress and an ankle-length otter-skin coat that was sculpted brazenly to display a womanly bosom and bustle. She had gently agreed to join an upperclassman at the Nebraska School of Medicine on a journey across the green ice of the Missouri River to Iowa, where there was a party at the Masonic Temple in order to celebrate the final linking of Omaha and Council Bluffs. The medical student was Repler Hitchcock of Council Bluffs—a good companion, a Republican, and an Episcopalian—who yearned to practice electrotherapeutics in Cuernavaca, Mexico. He paid for their three-course luncheon at the Paxton Hotel and then the couple strolled down Douglas Street with 400 other partygoers, who got into cutters and one-horse open sleighs just underneath the iron legs and girders of what would eventually be called the Ak-Sar-Ben Bridge. At a cap-pistol shot the party jerked away from Nebraska and there were champagne toasts and cheers and yahooing, but gradually the party scattered and Addie could only hear the iron shoes of the plowhorse and the racing sleigh hushing across the shaded window glass of river, like those tropical flowers shaped like saucers and cups that slide across the green silk of a pond of their own accord.

At the Masonic Temple there were coconut macaroons and hot syllabub made with cider and brandy, and quadrille dancing on a puncheon floor to songs like the "Butterfly Whirl" and "Cheater Swing" and "The Girl I Left Behind Me." Although the day was getting dark and there was talk about a great snowstorm roistering outside, Addie insisted on staying out on the dance floor until only twenty people remained and the quadrille caller had put away his violin and his sister's cello. Addie smiled and said, Oh what fun! as Repler tidily helped her into her mother's otter-skin coat and then escorted her out into a grand empire of snow that Addie thought was thrilling. And then, although the world by then was wrathfully meaning everything it said, she walked alone to the railroad depot at Ninth and Broadway so she could take the one-stop train called The Dummy across to Omaha.

Addie sipped hot cocoa as she passed sixty minutes up close to the railroad depot's coal stoker oven and some other partygoers sang of Good King Wenceslaus over a parlor organ. And then an old yardman who was sheeped in snow trudged through the high drifts by the door and announced that no more trains would be going out until morning.

Half the couples stranded there had family in Council Bluffs and decided to stay overnight, but the idea of traipsing back to Repler's house and sleeping in his sister's trundle bed seemed squalid to Addie, and she decided to walk the iron railway trestle across to Omaha.

Addie was a half hour away from the Iowa railway yard and up on the tracks over the great Missouri before she had second thoughts. White hatchings and tracings of snow flew at her horizontally. Wind had rippled snow up against the southern girders so that the high white skin was pleated and patterned like oyster shell. Every creosote tie was tented with snow that angled down into dark troughs that Addie could fit a leg through. Everything else was night sky and mystery, and the world she knew had disappeared. And yet she walked out onto the trestle, teetering over to a catwalk and sidestepping along it in high-button shoes, 40 feet above the ice, her left hand taking the yield from one guy wire as her right hand sought out another. Yelling winds were yanking at her, and the iron trestle was swaying enough to tilt her over into nothingness, as though Addie Dillingham were a playground game it was just inventing. Halfway across, her gray tam-o'shanter was snagged out just far enough into space that she could follow its spider-drop into the night, but she only stared at the great river that was lying there moon-white with snow and intractable. Wishing for her to jump.

Years later Addie thought that she got to Nebraska and did not give up and was not overfrightened because she was seventeen and could do no wrong, and accidents and dying seemed a government you could vote against, a mother you could ignore. She said she panicked at one jolt of wind and sank down to her knees up there and briefly touched her forehead to iron that hurt her skin like teeth, but when she got up again, she could see the ink-black stitching of the woods just east of Omaha and the shanties on timber piers just above the Missouri River's jagged stacks of ice. And she grinned as she thought how she would look to a vagrant down there plying his way along a rope in order to assay his trotlines for gar and catfish and then, perhaps, appraising the night as if he'd heard a crazy woman screaming in a faraway hospital room. And she'd be jauntily up there on the iron trestle like a new star you could wish on, and as joyous as the last high notes of "The Girl I Left Behind Me."

Human Rights Violations in Tibet

Heidi Fehlhaber

Heidi Fehlhaber is working on a degree in resource
conservation with a minor in wilderness studies. She
devotes a good portion of her free time to
organizing meetings and training sessions for the
Western Montana Mountain Rescue Team.

Tibet, known as the "roof of the world" due to an
average elevation exceeding 4,000 meters, lies adjacent to
China's southwestern border (Almanac of China's economy,
1982). Tibetans are overwhelmingly devout followers of
their own sect of Buddhism. For them, Buddhism defines the
very essence of their way of life, rather than just a
religious aspect. That is why their religious leader, the
Dalai Lama (see appendix 1 for further information) is
also their true political leader. In fact, Tibet was a
self-determined country until May 23, 1951, when China
used military force to seize control of its government. In
the decades following that takeover, China has completely
restructured the political, social, and religious aspects
of Tibetan culture. To accomplish such drastic
alterations, the Chinese have resorted to imprisonment,
torture, and even execution of Tibetans who attempt to
pursue their traditional lifestyle. Although the Chinese
government claims to be the liberator of Tibet, it is in
fact the perpetrator of extreme human rights violations
against Tibetans.

Tibetan-Chinese Relations

Due to Tibet's proximity to China, these two cultures
have intermingled for centuries. Chinese artisans have
visibly influenced the artwork and statues found in
Tibetan monasteries of all ages. And in the year 641, the
Chinese Princess Wencheng married the Tibetan king,
Songsten Gampo (Chan 1994). Throughout the centuries,
China's military has alternately attacked and defended
Tibet, according to shifts in power in the leadership of
both countries. During the last two hundred years of the

Manchu dynasty, however, an emissary of the Chinese
emperor was stationed in Lhasa, the capital city, as well
as his support troops. Tibet asserted its independence in
1913, expelling all members of the Chinese entourage.
Next, the British expeditions began to arrive, but,
unlike China, Britain allowed Tibet freedom of religion
and political self-determination. Tibet was a de facto
independent land until Chinese Communist troops invaded
the army-less country once again in 1951 (Michael 1988).
This final transfer of power was far from peaceful.

China claims, nonetheless, that this action actually
liberated Tibetans from English imperialists and, more
importantly, the peasant populace from serfdom under
feudal lords. Dawa Norbu writes, "Tibetans . . . were
deeply rooted in Tibet and in anything that was Tibetan.
The majority were quite unreceptive to new ideas,
especially to communism, which directly opposed the
spirit of their ways of life (1979)." Despite Tibet's
appeal to the United Nations stating that it did indeed
wish to remain independent and that the Chinese attack
was unprovoked, the situation was ignored by the more
powerful countries of the world. In 1951, a Tibetan
delegation sent to Beijing agreed to a seventeen-point
treaty in which the People's (China's) government
promised regional autonomy, recognition of the status and
power of the Dalai Lama, and protection of the
monasteries. This paper will demonstrate that China has
undoubtedly rescinded on all these points.

Tensions between the two sides escalated in 1959,
prompting China to violently crack down on demonstrators
in Lhasa. The fourteenth (current) Dalai Lama, fearing
for his life, fled into exile at this time with 100,000
supporters. The Tibetan government-in-exile and many
refugees reside in Dharamsala, India (Chan 1994). To this
day, they are unable to return to their homeland for fear
of horrific torture, imprisonment, and death.

China's Imprisonment and Torture of Tibetans

Thousands of Tibetans have become political prisoners
and victims in their homeland simply for attempting to
live as they have for centuries. Essentially, the heart of

Tibetan culture revolves around the Gelugpa sect of
Buddhism, of which the Dalai Lama is the central figure.
He not only guides Tibetans along the spiritual path, but
the political one as well. Monasteries and/or temples
rise among the homes of nearly every village,
demonstrating the desire and need for Tibetans to worship
frequently. Unfortunately, the Han ethnic majority of
China does not share their belief in Buddhism. In this
"autonomous" region of China, religion is seen by the
authorities as a potential threat to national security
because of its close association with the cultural and
national identity of ethnic groups (Amnesty International
1996).

China has specifically targeted Tibetan monks and nuns
for continuing to display their faith in Tibetan Buddhism
and its leader, the Dalai Lama. In an attempt to control
the scope of Buddhism's influence on Tibetans, Chinese
officials have begun to strictly enforce numerous anti-
Buddhist codes and regulations. To illustrate,
authorities are regulating the acceptable number of monks
and nuns permitted to live at a given monastery. On
March 13, 1996, the Tibet Daily reported that "the size
and influence of monasteries and monks has grown out of
control" and that "efforts should be made to . . . weaken
the influence of religion" (Amnesty International 1996).
Authorities have made corresponding evictions of nuns and
monks from their nunneries and monasteries, and even
ordered the demolition of their living quarters. Chinese
troops had already destroyed over 6,000 monasteries
during the invasions of the 1950s. Fearing a lack of
influence and control over Tibetan Buddhists, the Chinese
government forced monks to sign pledges denouncing the
Dalai Lama as their spiritual and thus temporal leader.
Many monks refusing to do so were given "reeducation
through labour" sentences without trial by local public
security (police) officers, who have the power to
circumvent the judicial system. The conditions in these
prison camps are reminiscent of the inhumanity practiced
by Nazi Germany. The labor camp's goal is to effectively
break down prisoners' physical, emotional, and spiritual
strength until they will submit to the demands of the

government. At the same time, these prisoners provide a wage-free workforce for government projects such as mines, irrigation ditches, and road building (Michael 1988). Beatings and torture are commonplace (Lawson 1996). Other monks refusing to accept a five-point declaration of opposition to the pro-independence movement face expulsion from their monasteries (Human Rights Watch 1995).

In yet another bold move by the Chinese to discredit and undermine the people's faith in the Dalai Lama, they banned possession and display of all Dalai Lama photographs. To enforce the ban, police raided private homes, hotels, restaurants, and shops in Lhasa. After a resulting confrontation between citizens and police, over ninety monks were arrested and held for their participation. Often, the methods of torture used during a suspect's detainment leave little physical evidence of abuse, as prisoners are subjected to extremes of temperature, deprivation of food and water, application of electricity, and forcibly injected drugs (Human Rights Watch 1995). Tibetan citizens now live in fear of more police invasions of their private premises where the discovery of so much as a cardsize photo of the Dalai Lama could lead to arrest and detainment—or worse.

The Chinese forces of suppression make no exception for women, either. In the case of Ngawang Sangdrol, arrested at age fifteen for taking part in a pro-independence demonstration in 1992, imprisonment has become a way of life. While serving her three-year sentence, she received, first, a six-year extension for singing nationalist songs, followed by an additional nine-year sentence for failing to stand up in the presence of a prison official, for not making her bed, and for shouting a political slogan. A former fellow inmate, Gyaltsen Pelsang, who has escaped from Tibet, affirms that Sangdrol had been singled out for especially harsh treatment, including being held in an isolation cell without windows or light, and being fed a very restricted diet. At age nineteen, she is now facing longer jail time than any other female political prisoner in Tibet (Tibet News, 1997). Another woman, Damchoe

Pema, who participated in the same protest, was quickly arrested. The twenty-weeks-pregnant Tibetan businesswoman miscarried her child as a result of being forced to remain standing for twelve hours, while being beaten with an electric baton by prison guards.

According to Amnesty International, "Torture using electro-shock weapons is common, with batons applied to the feet, armpits, genitals, and inside the mouth or vagina" (13 March 1996). To obtain firsthand accounts of such excruciating and humiliating torture, an American doctor interviewed Tibetan refugees in India. One young nun named Dechen spoke of a twenty-year-old friend being held in Drapchi Prison for her participation in Lhasa's October 1, 1987, demonstration, along with thousands of fellow Tibetans. The young woman "'received daily beatings and torture. The police forced Tamdy and eleven other women to run for hours while they beat them with cattle prods. The dogs attacked Tamdy many times. The dogs must have had very sharp teeth because there is one place in her right thigh with a large hunk of flesh missing.'" Furthermore, Dechen herself experienced abuse and denial of legal rights at the hands of Chinese police. Following the October 1 demonstration, they took her from her workplace to the police station, where they exhibited a thick book which they claimed contained all her crimes. Though she maintained innocence, the officers never opened the book, yet proceeded to apply electricity to her mouth many times with an electric stick. "This felt as though her mouth had exploded," and she lost consciousness. Later, the Chinese police—both male and female—stripped off her clothes to continue beating her body, breasts, mouth, and head with the electric rod. She lost consciousness many times over the course of those three days. Ever since, Dechen has had difficulty remembering things and learning new words. Before being released from Drapchi, Dechen was warned not to speak of her ordeals in prison, nor to participate in another demonstration, or she would receive even more severe treatment the next time (Kerr 1993). These few alarming incidents represent hundreds more—if not thousands—of similar nature, all of which violate international human rights standards.

Indeed, political repression in Tibet has increased sharply since 1994, and there are more political prisoners in custody there than at any time in the past six years (Human Rights Watch/Asia 1996). One of these detainees, the Panchen Lama, is also the youngest political prisoner in the world. The exiled Dalai Lama's selection of this young boy, who is the eleventh reincarnate of the Panchen Lama, Tibetan Buddhism's second most influential leader, is viewed as a threat to Chinese control over Tibetans and their religious worship. Therefore, China abducted the then six-year-old boy, Choekyi Nyima, and his family in 1995. Chinese officials do not deny that they are holding the boy and his family under house arrest at an undisclosed location. Meanwhile, they have made their own selection of a different boy from a communist family, and declared him the true Panchen Lama (Forney 1995). Moreover, the Chinese-appointed head of the search committee and abbot of the Tashilhunpo monastery, Chadrel Rimpoche, and two fellow lamas were also secretly detained for two years before receiving official charges and sentences. In a closed trial on April 21, 1997, Rimpoche was sentenced to six years' imprisonment, and deprivation of political rights for an additional three years, on charges of "conspiring to split the country" and "leaking state secrets," based on his suspected conferral with the Dalai Lama during the course of the search (Amnesty International 1997). In the eyes of Tibetans, these men have, to the best of their abilities, attempted to carry out an important religious tradition, and should not be the subjects of a public denunciation campaign nor questionable justice proceedings. Regardless of who is playing the role of perpetrator or victim, these abuses of young and old, male and female, exceed all acceptable limits of due process and punishment.

Genocide in Tibet

The population density in Tibet gives little justification for the governmentally regulated birthrate restrictions; it is only one one-hundredth of China's (Zechner 1994). Even so, China actively enforces a

population control policy in Tibet limiting every woman
to two births, one being considered ideal. If they have a
sterilization procedure performed after their first
child, they will be praised for being a good citizen. A
thirdborn child, however, is considered illegal, and it
will have no rights to food rations, education, organized
work, travel, or property ownership. Furthermore, women
are fined excessively for having a third or fourth child.
Often, "unauthorized" pregnancies are terminated by
abortion or lethal injection (Kerr 1993).

In 1982, China initiated the use of "mobile birth-
control teams" which travel from village to village
performing abortions and sterilizations. Despite the
influx of Chinese settlers throughout Tibet, only Tibetan
women are ordered to report to the operation tents, or
face fines and no post-procedure medical care (Kerr
1993). These mobile units, as well as the segregated
Tibetan hospital wards, have visibly unhygienic
conditions. Dr. Dolma, a Tibetan obstetrician in a
Chinese hospital, related how long it takes her to
perform a sterilization: fifteen minutes. Her quickness
is due to the fact that everything is done under local
anesthetic, which is painful, but allows the woman to
walk home immediately afterward. According to a monk
named Tashi, many women, especially in rural areas, are
misled about the procedures being performed on them, and
told "that sterilization was part of a world
constitution; women all over the world have this done."
Others have witnessed nurses killing their healthy
newborns with an injection in the soft spot on the
forehead. Perhaps this explains why the Tibetan infant
mortality rate is one in six babies, one of the highest
in the world (Kerr 1993).

The emotional stress caused by the social, economic,
and political sanctions used to enforce this birth policy
is reflected in the increased number of Tibetan divorces
and families separating—an uncommon occurrence before
Chinese interference. Undeniably, the Chinese have no
justification other than genocide to endorse such cruel
procedures and limitations of women's rights over their
own bodies.

Conclusion

Given the available information on conditions in Tibet, it is obvious that the Chinese have done little to improve the Tibetan quality of life. Franz Michael, professor emeritus at George Washington University and former director of the Institute for Sino-Soviet Studies, writes:

> One of the major propaganda myths about rural transformation was the claim that Tibetan society had been feudal, that the Tibetan people were serfs of the estates, and that Tibetans had suffered under the cruel exploitation, economic and otherwise, of their monastic and aristocratic masters. This assessment was reported widely even outside China, and affected international public opinion. The facts were otherwise. (Michael 1998)

This is merely one of the reasons China uses to justify its forceful 1959 seizure of defenseless Tibet. Likewise, China claims to have implemented beneficial agricultural reforms and land redistribution measures, yet "many Tibetans regard the years of subsequent Chinese rule as years of repression and ecological destruction" (Leckie 1995). These issues, however, barely begin to rival the enormous affronts to human rights perpetuated by the Chinese government. It has blatantly ignored the universal beliefs that "all people have an equal right to live in peace and happiness; people can only be happy when able to realize their inherent human affinities for freedom, equality and dignity; and protection of human rights is a precondition for the expression of these natural affinities" (Dalai Lama 1994/1995). In fact, countless Tibetans have been arrested, detained, imprisoned, tortured, and killed at Chinese hands in recent decades, simply for expressing their desire to be free, to live as human beings.

Appendix 1

Definition and Description of the Dalai Lama

Introduction

Knowledge of the Dalai Lama and his role in Tibetan leadership are crucial to understanding Tibetan culture and its human rights struggles. This appendix will provide the reader with both a definition of the Dalai Lama and a detailed description of his role in Tibetan culture.

Expanded Definition and Description

Word Origin

According to the Oxford English Dictionary's primary definition of the term, "Lama" is "the title given to the Buddhist priests of Mongolia and Tibet. The chief Lamas of Tibet and Mongolia are called respectively Dalai (dalae or delli)-lama, or simply Dalai, and Tesho- or Teshu-lama." "Lama" stems from the Tibetan word "blama," of which the "b" is silent. "Dalai," on the other hand, actually hails from the sixteenth-century Mongol ruler, Altan Khan, who gave the high Lama of that time "the honorific title 'ta-le' (Anglicized as 'dalai'), meaning 'ocean' and presumably suggesting breadth and depth of wisdom." This name was subsequently applied posthumously to this Dalai's two predecessors. In addition, the Tibetans themselves call the Dalai Lama "Rgyal-ba Rinpo-che," or "Great Precious Conqueror" (Encyclopedia Britannica, 1993. Vol. 3).

History of the Dalai Lama

Early in the fifteenth century, amidst much political rivalry and dissension in Tibet, a scholarly monk called Blo-bzang grags-pa formed his own monastery at Dga-Idan. This sect of Buddhism, now known as Dge-lugs-pa, or Yellow Hat sect, emphasized strict monastic discipline and was soon also drawn into the political arena by ambitious disciples. The second reincarnate—the physical manifestation of the compassionate bodhisattva

("Buddha-to-be"), Avalokitesvara—became the head abbot of the 'Bras-spungs monastery on the outskirts of Lhasa. Lhasa has ever since been considered Tibet's capital city, housing the Dalai Lama's magnificent 999-room Potala Palace, as well as other Lamas and political advisers within its walls. It was the third Dge-lug-pa hierarch whom Altan Khan invited to his court and on whom he bestowed the title of "Dalai" Lama, officially signifying his belief in the Yellow Hat sect as the dominant religious and political group in Tibet. The fourth Dalai Lama was then conveniently discovered in the Mongolian royal family.

Following many more decades of political and military confrontations between Tibetan sects and their various Mongol supporters, the next Dalai Lama—"The Great Fifth"— rose to power and succeeded in unifying the country and government. His enthronement (1642) coincides almost exactly with the birth of the Manchu dynasty in neighboring China (1644), which at that time became a Tibetan ally (Encyclopedia Britannica, 1993, Vol. 16). Since that time, the number of Dalai Lamas has increased to fourteen, and interactions with China have escalated to oppressive and violent levels.

Searching for the Dalai Lama

Upon the death of the Dalai Lama, the search for his successor begins. A head abbot, usually the Panchen Lama (of Drepung monastery), heads the search team, which consists of other lamas. This delegation travels extensively through populated and rural areas of Tibet, seeking news of a recently born child—historically, a male. These holy men also ask villagers if there have been any recent miracles, signifying the birth of a great reincarnate spirit in the proximity. This process may continue for years until the seekers believe they have found the correct child, who must then pass certain tests to prove himself. The exact nature of these tests is unknown to Westerners. When the lamas are certain of their choice, the boy, and often his whole family, make the trek back to Lhasa where the new Dalai Lama will begin his monastic life and formal education. The typical

age of the Dalai Lama upon discovery is five or six
years old.

Traditional Lifestyle of the Dalai Lama

The child who is identified as the successor to the
previous Dalai Lama is brought to the Potala Palace with
great ceremony and reverence. At such a young age, the
boy is unfit to make political decisions, which
subsequently fall into the hands of political advisers
(regents), lamas, or lay noblemen, depending on the
regime of that era. Meanwhile, distinguished lamas see to
the youth's spiritual and academic tutelage.

Furthermore, "the Dalai Lama lives in the strictest
seclusion, and is worshiped with almost divine honours"
(Oxford English Dictionary, 1989). To illustrate, no one
may be seated higher than him nor speak without being
spoken to, and it is considered disrespectful not to
prostrate oneself multiple times when greeting him.

Modern Lifestyle of the Dalai Lama

Ironically, neither the leader of Tibet nor the rest
of its councils have set foot in their country for nearly
four decades. In 1959, the Chinese communists sought to
forcibly silence all opposition to their hostile seizure
of Tibet from its peace-loving populace, thus forcing the
fourteenth Dalai Lama to flee his home for refuge in
India. Accompanied by other lamas, officials, and
approximately 100,000 followers, he reestablished the
exiled Tibetan government in Dharamsala, India
(Encyclopedia Britannica, 1993, Vol. 3).

His usual routine there consists of rising at two
o'clock in the morning in order to meditate for several
hours before eating the first of two modest daily meals.
The remainder of the day also allows time for gardening,
study, and more meditation. He has a compassionate, wise,
laughing countenance, decorated by a pair of eyeglasses,
and topped by a shaved head. Moreover, the Dalai Lama has
been globally recognized for his books, including several
works on Buddhist theology, and his autobiography.

In addition to writing, the Dalai Lama has actively
pursued compromises with China in hopes of being allowed

to safely reenter his homeland and guide his people. This effort was rewarded only with a Nobel Peace Prize in 1988, the money from which he donated entirely to the Tibetan struggle (Oberman, 1990). Undaunted by China's treaty refusals, he continues to travel the world in an effort to raise awareness and backing for this humanitarian cause. More recently, he has even befriended the likes of supporter Richard Gere (a Hollywood actor)—a far cry from the seclusion of Potala, which prohibited the presence of foreigners—all the while clad in the humble orange robes and shaved head of a Tibetan monk.

Conclusion

Political strife between Tibet and its neighbors is certainly nothing new, yet its people have always persisted, held together by their unquestioning faith in the Dalai Lama. His very image is enough to sustain their spirituality and hope during this period of extreme religious and political oppression. More than anyone or anything else, the ancient soul of the Dalai Lama embodies the essence of Tibetan culture.

Bibliography

Almanac of China's economy. 1982. The Economic Research
Centre, the State Council of the People's Republic of
China, and the State Statistical Bureau. Xue Muqiao,
editor. Modem Cultural Co. Ltd., New York and Hong
Kong.

Amnesty International. 20 May 1996. China: Amnesty International condemns violent crackdown. Amnesty International News Release (On-Line). 1 p. Internet. 24 Nov.
1997.

Amnesty International. 13 March 1996. China: World can no
longer ignore human rights of 1.2 billion people.
Amnesty International News Release (On-Line). 2 pp.
Internet. 23 Nov. 1997.

Amnesty International. 26 February 1996. Media Advisory.
Amnesty International News Release (On-Line). 1 p. Internet. 23 Nov. 1997.

Amnesty International. July 1996. People's Republic of
China: Repression against Buddhists. Amnesty International Library (On-Line). 30 pp. Internet. 23 Nov.
1997.

Amnesty International. 27 May 1997. People's Republic of
China: Three Tibetans sentenced on political charges
in Panchen Lama dispute. Amnesty International Country
Report (On-Line). 6 pp. Internet. 23 Nov. 1997.

Bowers, Stephen. 1994. Tibet since Mao Zedong. Journal of
Social, Political and Economic Studies. 19:409-432.

Chan, Victor. 1994. Tibet Handbook. Moon Publications.
Chico.

Critchfield, Richard. 1973. The golden bowl be broken:
Peasant life in four cultures. Indiana University
Press, Bloomington and London.

The Dalai Lama. 1994/1995. Human rights and the future of
Tibet. Harvard International Review. 17(1):46-50.

Forney, Matt. 30 Nov. 1995. Divide and rule—Beijing seeks
to split Tibetan Buddhism. Far Eastern Economic Review. 158:26.

Human Rights Watch. 1993. Human Rights Watch world report
1994. Human Rights Watch. New York, Washington, DC,
Los Angeles, London.

Human Rights Watch. 1994. Human Rights Watch world report
1995. Human Rights Watch. New York, Washington, DC,

Human Rights Watch. 1994. Human Rights Watch world report 1995. Human Rights Watch. New York, Washington, DC, Los Angeles, London.

Human Rights Watch. 1995. Human Rights Watch world report 1996. Human Rights Watch. New York, Washington, DC, London, Brussels.

Human Rights Watch/Asia. 29 March 1996. Dramatic increase in political imprisonment in Tibet. One World News Service (On-Line). 2 pp. Internet. 24 Nov. 1997.

Jiaqi, Yan. 1996. China's national minorities and feder- alism. Dissent. 43(3):139-144.

Kaye, Lincoln and Kranti, Vijay. 1995. Eleventh coming: Designation of Panchen Lama stirs a storm. Far Eastern Economic Review. 158:17.

Kerr, Blake. 1993. Sky burial: An eyewitness account of China's brutal crackdown in Tibet. The Noble Press, Inc., Chicago.

Kolodner, Eric. 1994. Religious rights in China: A com- parison of international human rights law and Chinese domestic legislation. Human Rights Quarterly. 16(3):455-490.

Lawson, Edward. 1996. Encyclopedia of human rights, sec- ond edition. Taylor and Francis, Washington, DC.

Leckie, Scott. 1995. Housing as social control in Tibet. Ecologist. 25:8-10+.

Michael, Franz. 1988. Non-Chinese nationalities and reli- gious communities: Human rights in the People's Repub- lic of China. Westview Press, Boulder and London.

The New Encyclopedia Britannica. 1993. Vol. 3:854. Ency- clopedia Britannica, Ltd., Chicago.

The New Encyclopedia Britannica. 1993. Vol. 16:210-211. Encyclopedia Britannica, Ltd., Chicago.

Norbu, Dawa. Mar. 1979. The 1959 Tibetan rebellion: An interpretation. The China Quarterly. pp. 74-93.

Oberman, Bonnie. 1990. Dalai Lama. Britannica Book of the Year. Encyclopedia Britannica, Ltd., Chicago.

Simpson, J.A. and Weiner, E.S.C. 1989. The Oxford English dictionary, second ed. Vol. 8. Clarendon Press, Oxford.

Tibet News. 1994. Dissident nun given harsh new sentence. 1 p. Internet. 23 Nov. 1997.

Women's Issues Desk of the Department of Information and International Relations, Tibetan Government-in-Exile. Aug. 1995. National Report on Tibet Women. 17 pp. Internet. 23 Nov. 1997.

Wu, Harry. 1996. The need to restrain China. The Journal of International Affairs 49(2):355–360.

Zechner, Rosa. 1994. Population politics. Connexions. 46:17–18.

8

FILM, TELEVISION, AND MUSIC

GOING TO THE MOVIES

———————■———————

Susan Allen Toth

This piece is an excerpt from Toth's 1988 book How to Prepare for Your High-School Reunion.

Aaron takes me only to art films. That's what I call them, anyway: strange movies with vague poetic images I don't always understand, long dreamy movies about a distant Technicolor past, even longer black-and-white movies about the general meaninglessness of life. We do not go unless at least one reputable critic has found the cinematography superb. We went to *The Devil's Eye,* and Aaron turned to me in the middle and said, "My God, this is *funny.*" I do not think he was pleased.

When Aaron and I go to the movies, we drive our cars separately and meet by the box office. Inside the theater he sits tentatively in his seat, ready to move if he can't see well, poised to leave if the film is disappointing. He leans away from me, careful not to touch the bare flesh of his arm against the bare flesh of mine. Sometimes he leans so far I am afraid he may be touching the woman on his other side instead. If the movie is very good, he leans forward too, peering between the heads of the couple in front of us. The light from the screen bounces off his glasses; he gleams with intensity, sitting there on the edge of his seat, watching the screen. Once I tapped him on the arm so I could whisper a comment in his ear. He jumped.

After *Belle de Jour* Aaron said he wanted to ask me if he could stay overnight. "But I can't," he shook his head mournfully before I had a chance to answer, "because I know I never sleep well in strange beds." Then he apologized for asking. "It's just that after a film like that," he said, "I feel the need to assert myself."

II

Bob takes me only to movies that he thinks have a redeeming social conscience. He doesn't call them films. They tend to be about poverty, war, injustice, political corruption, struggling unions in the 1930s, and the military-industrial complex. Bob doesn't like propaganda movies, though, and he doesn't like to be too depressed, either. We stayed away from *The Sorrow and the Pity;* it would be, he said, just too much. Besides, he assured me, things are never that hopeless. So most of the movies we see are made in Hollywood. Because they are always very topical, these movies offer what Bob calls "food for thought." When we saw *Coming Home,* Bob's jaw set so firmly with the first half hour that I knew we would end up at Poppin' Fresh Pies afterward.

When Bob and I go to the movies, we take turns driving so no one owes anyone else anything. We park far away from the theater so we don't have to pay for a space. If it's raining or snowing, Bob offers to let me off at the door, but I can tell he'll feel better if I go with him while he parks, so we share the walk too. Inside the theater Bob will hold my hand when I get scared if I ask him. He puts my hand firmly on his knee and covers it completely with his own hand. His knee never twitches. After a while, when the scary part is past, he loosens his hand slightly and I know that is a signal to take mine away. He sits companionably close, letting his jacket just touch my sweater, but he does not infringe. He thinks I ought to know he is there if I need him.

One night after *The China Syndrome* I asked Bob if he wouldn't like to stay for a second drink, even though it was past midnight. He thought awhile about that, considering my offer from all possible angles, but finally he said no. Relationships today, he said, have a tendency to move too quickly.

III

Sam likes movies that are entertaining. By that he means movies that Will Jones in the *Minneapolis Tribune* loved and either *Time* or *Newsweek* rather liked; also movies that do not have sappy love stories, are not musicals, do not have subtitles, and will not force him to think. He does not go to movies to think. He liked *California Suite* and *The Seduction of Joe Tynan*, though the plots, he said, could have been zippier. He saw it all coming too far in advance, and that took the fun out. He doesn't like to know what is going to happen. "I just want my brain to be tickled," he says. It is very hard for me to pick out movies for Sam.

When Sam takes me to the movies, he pays for everything. He thinks that's what a man ought to do. But I buy my own popcorn, because he doesn't approve of it; the grease might smear his flannel slacks. Inside the theater, Sam makes himself comfortable. He takes off his jacket, puts one arm around me, and all during the movie he plays with my hand, stroking my palm, beating a small tattoo on my wrist. Although he watches the movie intently, his body operates on instinct. Once I inclined my head and kissed him lightly just behind his ear. He beat a faster tattoo on my wrist, quick and musical, but he didn't look away from the screen.

When Sam takes me home from the movies, he stands outside my door and kisses me long and hard. He would like to come in, he says regretfully, but his steady girlfriend in Duluth wouldn't like it. When the *Tribune* gives a movie four stars, he has to save it to see with her. Otherwise her feelings might be hurt.

IV

I go to some movies by myself. On rainy Sunday afternoons I often sneak into a revival house or a college auditorium for old Technicolor musicals, *Kiss Me Kate, Seven Brides for Seven Brothers, Calamity Jane,* even, once, *The*

Sound of Music. Wearing saggy jeans so I can prop my feet on the seat in front, I sit toward the rear where no one will see me. I eat large handfuls of popcorn with double butter. Once the movie starts, I feel completely at home. Howard Keel and I are old friends; I grin back at him on the screen, admiring all his teeth. I know the sound tracks by heart. Sometimes when I get really carried away I hum along with Kathryn Grayson, remembering how I once thought I would fill out a formal like that. Skirts whirl, feet tap, acrobatic young men perform impossible feats, and then the camera dissolves into a dream sequence I know I can comfortably follow. It is not, thank God, Bergman.

If I can't find an old musical, I settle for Hepburn and Tracy, vintage Grant or Gable, on adventurous days Claudette Colbert or James Stewart. Before I buy my ticket I make sure it will all end happily. If necessary, I ask the girl at the box office. I have never seen *Stella Dallas* or *Intermezzo.* Over the years I have developed other peccadilloes: I will, for example, see anything that is redeemed by Thelma Ritter. At the end of *Daddy Long Legs* I wait happily for the scene when Fred Clark, no longer angry, at last pours Thelma a convivial drink. They smile at each other, I smile at them, I feel they are smiling at me. In the movies I go to by myself, the men and women always like each other.

CHALLENGING THE ASIAN ILLUSION

Gish Jen

This piece first appeared in The New York Times *in 1991.*

For a very long time, when people talked about race, they talked about black America and white America. Where did that put Asian-Americans?

Spike Lee touches on the Asian-American dilemma in *Do the Right Thing* when the Korean grocer, afraid of having his business attacked by rioting blacks, yells: "I not white! I black! Like you! Same!"

Unlike the grocer, though, my family and I identified mostly with white America, which, looking back, was partly wishful thinking, partly racism and partly an acknowledgment that, whatever else we did face, at least we did not have to contend with the legacy of slavery.

Yet we were not white. We were somehow borderline; we did not quite belong. Now, not only has the number of Asian-Americans in this country doubled in the last decade, we are growing faster than any other ethnic group. How meaningful it will ultimately prove to lump the Hmong with the Filipinos with the Japanese remains to be seen. Still, to be perceived as a significant minority is a development for which I, at least, am grateful.

There is a sense that to be perceived at all, a minority group must be plagued with problems—a problem in itself, to be sure. But what about our problems—were they significant enough to warrant attention? Who cared, for instance, that we did not see ourselves reflected on movie screens? Until recently, it did not occur to most of us that the absence of Asian and Asian-American images was symptomatic of a more profound invisibility.

Today, though, it is shocking to behold how little represented we have been, and in how blatantly distorted a manner. There has been some progress now that more Asian-Americans like David Henry Hwang and Philip Kan Gotanda have begun to write for stage and screen: also, some recent Caucasian-directed television shows, including *Shannon's Deal* and *Davis Rules*, are breaking new ground.

For the most part, however, film, television and theater, from *Miss Saigon* to *Teen-Age Mutant Ninja Turtles*, have persisted in perpetuating stereotypes. Mostly this has been through the portrayal of Asian characters; Asian-Americans have rarely been represented at all.

This invisibility is essentially linked to the process by which fanciful ideas are superimposed onto real human beings. How are everyday Asians transformed into mysterious "Orientals," after all, if not by distance? Americans can be led to believe anything about people living in a far-off land, or even a distinctly unfamiliar place like Chinatown. It is less easy with a kid next door who plays hockey and air guitar.

Over the years, Asians have been the form onto which white writers have freely projected their fears and desires. That this is a form of colonialism goes almost without saying; it can happen only when the people whose images are appropriated are in no position to object.

For certainly anyone would object to being identified with a figure as heartlessly evil and preternaturally cunning as Fu Manchu, a brilliant but diabolical force set on taking over the world. The character's prototype was invented in 1916, in a climate of hysteria over the "threat" that Asian workers posed to native labor. We behold its likeness in figures like Odd Job in *Goldfinger* (1964); his influence can be seen in depictions of Chinatown as a den of iniquity in movies like *The Year of the Dragon* (1985) and *True Believer* (1988). *Chinatown* (1974) used it as a symbol of all that is rotten in the city of Los Angeles, despite the fact that no Chinese person had much to do with the evil turnings of the plot.

What fuels these images is xenophobia. In periods of heightened political tension, they tend to recur; in more secure times, they are replaced by more benign images. Charlie Chan for example, arose in 1926, shortly after the last of a series of laws restricting Chinese immigration had been passed and the "Yellow Peril" seemed to be over.

The benign images, however, are typically no more tied to reality than their malign counterparts; vilification is merely replaced by glorification. The aphorism-spouting Charlie Chan (played by Warner Oland, a white actor in yellowface) is godlike in his intelligence, the original Asian whiz kid; you would not be surprised to hear he had won a Westinghouse prize in his youth. More message than human being, he recalls the ever-smiling black mammy that proliferated during Reconstruction: Don't worry, he seems to say, no one's going to go making any trouble.

ONE GOOD GUY, BUT HE'S A RAT

In today's social climate of multi-culturalism, movies like *Rambo,* which made the Vietnamese out to be so much cannon fodder, seem to be behind us, at least temporarily. Instead, reflecting the American preoccupation with Japan, there is *Teen-Age Mutant Ninja Turtles.* Here the Japanese enemy gang leader is once again purely demonic and bestial, a hairless, barbaric figure who wears a metal claw for ornament. What gives the movie a more contemporary stamp is the fact that Master Splinter, the good-guy rodent leader of the Mutant Turtles, is also Japanese. It is as if Fu Manchu and Charlie Chan were cast into a single movie—seemingly presenting a balanced view of the Japanese as good and bad.

But the fact that the "good" Japanese is a rat means that slanty eyes belong to the bad guy. And as individuals the Japanese are still portrayed as sub- or superhuman, possessing fabulous abilities and arcane knowledge that center on (another contemporary twist) martial arts.

Is it a sign of a fitness-crazed age that this single aspect of Asian culture is so enthralling? So perennially popular are movies like *The Karate Kid* (1984) and this year's *Iron and Silk* that one begins to wonder whether Asian males pop out of the womb doing mid-air gyrations. The audience marvels: How fantastic, these people! Meanwhile, the non-Asian roles are the more recognizably human ones.

Real humanity similarly eludes the Asian characters in the Broadway play *Miss Saigon.* As in *Teen-Age Mutant Ninja Turtles,* they are either simply evil or simply good, with the possible exception of the Engineer (Jonathan Pryce) who, loathsome as he is, seems more self-interested than evil. Half-white, he seems to be, correspondingly, halfway human. In contrast, Thuy, the major Vietnamese character, is portrayed as so inhuman that he would kill a child in cold blood. Is this what Communists do? Asians? When Kim (Lea Salonga), the heroine, shoots her erstwhile loyal fiancé, the audience applauds, feeling no more for him than for Rambo's victims. The subhuman brute has got what he deserved.

At the same time, the audience does feel, horribly, for Kim, who has been forced to pull the trigger and now must live with blood on her hands. What a fate for a paragon of virtue! She is Madame Butterfly unpinned from her specimen board and let loose to flutter around the room again: abandoned, virtuous, she waits faithfully for her white lover, only to discover that he has married. He returns for his son (it's always a son); she kills herself.

Isn't this a beautiful story? Annette Kolodny, a feminist critic, has observed that when the Western mind feels free to remake a place and people according to its liking, it conceives of that place and people as a woman. This has been nowhere so true as in the case of the "Orient," and correspondingly, no woman, it seems, has been portrayed as more exquisitely feminine than an Oriental.

Take any play in which both Oriental and Caucasian women appear—say, *South Pacific*—and it is immediately obvious which is more delicate, more willing to sacrifice for her man, more docile. Never mind that there are in the world real women who might object to having their image appropriated for such use.

But of course, women do object. I object, especially since the only possible end for this invented Butterfly is suicide. For how would the white characters go on with their lives?

It is an irony of stage history that a musical as conventional in its use of the Butterfly story should follow so closely on the heels of another play that turns the same narrative on its head. The 1988 Broadway play *M. Butterfly* offers not just the "beautiful story" itself, but also a white man who has been taken in by it. So enthralled is René Gallimard by the idea of his Butterfly, the projection of his own desire, that he forgets there is a real person—Song Liling, a man and a spy—upon which his notions are imposed.

Ultimately, *M. Butterfly* makes clear that for the "game" of Orientalism, there is a price to pay, not only by those whose images are appropriated, but by the appropriators.

Do stereotypes lurk even here? It might seem so, but would a stereotype wonder, as does Song Liling, whether he and Gallimard might not continue on together, even after the truth has been revealed. When Song asks, "What do I do now?" he conveys how helpless he is too, how powerless. This is a human being. That he should be is maybe not so surprising, given that he was invented by David Henry Hwang, an Asian-American.

ONE STEP FORWARD: SPOOF THE STEREOTYPE

Are Asian-American writers the only hope for new forms of characterization? Perhaps, when even directors as intelligent as Woody Allen portray Chinatown as having opium dens. In his most recent movie, *Alice*, Mr. Allen's recycling of an Asian sage is likewise problematic. Could he not have created a spoof of a sage—a character who winked at the stereotype even as he played it—without any damage to the plot?

Spoofing the stereotype was the strategy taken last spring in an episode of the now-cancelled television series *Shannon's Deal* that featured a pony-tailed Korean immigrant. Here were clear signs for hope: the immigrant at first appeared to be an all-knowing Charlie Chan, but turned out to be at once less and more. At moments way ahead of the investigator Shannon, he proved to be way behind at others; he knew all the aphorisms but had trouble passing the bar exam, and discussed his own tendency to drop pronouns.

Other signs of change include a jeans-wearing, face-making, poker-playing Japanese character in *Davis Rules.* Unexotic Mrs. Yamagami (Tamayo Otsuki) even shows a sense of humor, characterizing a coworker as "a rebel without a car." Similarly, in *Twin Peaks,* the figure of Jocelyn (Joan Chen), evil as she is, does not stand in contrast to the good, white characters the way a female Fu Manchu—a dragon lady—might. Neither, certainly, is she any Butterfly. She is, within the show's offbeat context, just one of the gang.

All these characters are heartening, since they are not simply unexamined projections onto the Asian race. Still, as might be expected, directors like Wayne Wang and playwrights like Philip Kan Gotanda are not only more likely to present Asian-Americans in their work, but to present Asian-Americans who are not of the immigrant generation. In Mr. Wang's movie *Dim Sum* (1987) and Mr. Gotanda's film *The Wash* (1988), Asian-Americans are presented in far greater complexity than is typical of the mainstream media; the characters seem more captured than constructed, more like flesh-and-blood than cartoons. This is partly a matter of their status as protagonists rather than peripheral figures.

And more images are needed if the few that exist now are not to become new stereotypes. Since the much publicized success of Connie Chung, for example, Asian-American anchorwomen have become a staple in films like *Year of the Dragon* and *Moscow on the Hudson.* With real-life repercussions: the San Francisco newscaster Emerald Yeh tells of an interview with CNN, during which she was more or less asked why she couldn't do her hair like Connie Chung's.

Ridiculous, right? And yet such is the power of image. We would not have to insist that images reflect life, except that all too often we ask life to reflect images.

DANCES WITH INDIANS

Michael Dorris

This essay first appeared in The New York Times *in February of 1991.*

In *Dances with Wolves,* the Sioux and Lt. John Dunbar meet cute: he's naked, and that fact so throws a group of mounted warriors off their normal stride that the ingenuous young soldier lives to tell the tale, a sort of Boy Scout "Order of the Arrow" ritual carried to the *n*th power. The plot begins when Dunbar (Kevin Costner), a Civil War-era recruit, arrives at his western frontier post after it has been completely deserted. Alone, he is befriended first by the eponymous wolf. Then, taken in by local Indians and aptly renamed Dances with Wolves, he quickly earns merit badges in Pawnee bashing and animal telepathy. In short order, he marries Stands with a Fist (Mary McDonnell), a passionate young widow who just happens to herself be a white captive/campfire girl of impressive cross-cultural accomplishments. Eventually the "With" family strikes out on their own—the nucleus of a handsome new Anglo tribe—sadder, wiser, and certainly more sensitive as a result of their Native American immersion.

Kevin Costner's Dunbar follows in a long tradition of literary and cinematic heroes who have discovered Indians. Robinson Crusoe did it off the coast of Brazil, Natty Bumppo did it in New York State, and everyone from Dustin Hoffman (*Little Big Man*, 1970) to Richard Harris (*A Man Called Horse*, 1970, and *Return of a Man Called Horse*, 1976) to Debra Paget (*Broken Arrow*, 1950), Natalie Wood (*The Searchers*, 1956), and Robert Redford (*Tell Them Willie Boy Is Here*, 1969) has done it in Hollywood.

The first time I saw a white guy get spiritually redeemed by life among the Indians was at a matinee in 1958, when I was in the sixth grade. Of course, when push came to shove at the end of *The Light in the Forest*, little James MacArthur sold out his adopted people and went back to his own kind.

Usually these visits by outsiders do not bode well for the Indians involved—just ask the Mohicans! Appreciative white folks always seem to show up shortly before the cavalry (who are often searching for them) or Manifest Destiny, and record the final days of peace before the tribe is annihilated. Readers and viewers of such sagas are left with a predominant emotion of regret for a golden age now but a faint memory. In the imaginary mass media world of neat beginnings, middles, and ends, American Indian society, whatever its virtues and fascinations as an arena for Euro-American consciousness raising, is definitely past tense.

Thematically, virtually all such films share a subtle (or not so subtle) message: Indians may be poor, they may at first seem strange or forbidding or primitive, but, by golly, once you get to know them they have a thing or two to teach us about The Meaning of Life.

The tradition goes back a long way. Europeans like French philosopher Jean-Jacques Rousseau and turn-of-this-century novelist Karl May (whose many books, a mixture of Louis L'Amour and the Hardy Boys, have been a rite of passage for generations of German youth) laid out a single range for Indians to inhabit: savage-savage to noble-savage. Indians embody the concept of "the other"—a foreign, exotic panorama against which "modem" (i.e., white) men can measure and test themselves, and eventually, having proved their mettle in battle, be anointed as natural leaders by their hosts.

Placed within the genre, *Dances with Wolves* shows some signs of evolution. Director/star Kevin Costner obviously worked hard and spared no expense in order to achieve a sense of authenticity in his production. He filmed on the Pine Ridge reservation in South Dakota and defied conventional Hollywood wisdom to assemble a large and talented

Native American supporting cast. Great attention was clearly paid to dressing the actors in ethnographically correct costumes, and if the streets in the native camp seem a tad too spotless to be believed, at least the tipis are museum-quality.

Impressively, large segments of the film are spoken in Lakota, the language of the western Sioux, and though the subtitles are stilted (Indians in the movies seem incapable of using verbal contractions and are overly fond of explaining the minute details of their motivation), they at least convey the impression that Native Americans carried on an intellectual life among themselves.

When I saw *Dances with Wolves* at an advance screening, I predicted to a friend that it would be less than a box-office smash. Though spectacular to look at, it struck me as too long, too predictable, too didactic to attract a large audience. One hundred million dollars in revenues and twelve Academy Award nominations later, was I ever wrong. In fact, it's possible that the movie sells tickets precisely because it delivers the old-fashioned Indians whom the ticket-buying audience expects to find. Kevin Costner is our national myth's everyman—blandly handsome, Robert Bly-sensitive, flexible, politically correct. He passes the test of the frontier, out-Indians the Indians, achieves a pure soul by encountering and surmounting the wilderness.

A ☆ Yet, if *Dances with Wolves* had been about people who happen to be Indians, rather than about INDIANS (uniformly stoic, brave, nasty to their enemies, nice to their friends), it might have stood a better chance of forming a bridge between societies that for too long have woodenly characterized each other. The film's tremendous popularity is sure to generate a bubble of sympathy for the Sioux, but hard questions remain: will this sentiment be practical, translating into public support for Native American legal cases before the U.S. Supreme Court, for restoration of Lakota sacred lands (the Black Hills) or water rights, for tribal sovereignty, for providing the funding desperately needed by reservation health-care clinics? Pine Ridge is today, according to the U.S. Census Bureau, the most economically impoverished corner of America, but will its modern Indian advocates in business suits, men and women equipped with laptop computers and articulate English, be the recipients of a tidal wave of popcorn-fed good will?

Or will it turn out, once again, that the only good Indians, the only Indians whose causes and needs this country can embrace, are lodged safely in the past, wrapped neatly in the blankets of history, comfortable magnets for our sympathy because they require nothing of us but tears in a dark theater?

A CENTURY OF CINEMA

Susan Sontag

The New York Times Magazine *first published this essay in 1996. It was reprinted in* Best American Essays.

C inema's hundred years seem to have the shape of a life cycle: an inevitable birth, the steady accumulation of glories, and the onset in the last decade of an ignominious, irreversible decline. This doesn't mean that there won't be any more new films that one can admire. But such films won't simply be exceptions; that's true of great achievement in any art. They have to be heroic violations of the norms and practices which now govern movie-making everywhere in the capitalist and would-be capitalist world—which is to say, everywhere. And ordinary films, films made purely for entertainment (that is, commercial) purposes, will continue to be astonishingly witless; already the vast majority fail resoundingly to appeal to their cynically targeted audiences. While the point of a great film is now, more than ever, to be a one-of-a-kind achievement, the commercial cinema has settled for a policy of bloated, derivative film-making, a brazen combinatory or re-combinatory art, in the hope of re-producing past successes. Every film that hopes to reach the largest possible audience is designed as some kind of remake. Cinema, once heralded as *the* art of the twentieth century, seems now, as the century closes numerically, to be a decadent art.

Perhaps it is not cinema which has ended . . . but only cinephilia—the name of the very specific kind of love that cinema inspired. Each art breeds its fanatics. The love that cinema inspired, however, was special. It was born of the conviction that cinema was an art unlike any other: quintessentially modern; distinctively accessible; poetic and mysterious and erotic and moral—all at the same time. Cinema had apostles (it was like religion). Cinema was a crusade. Cinema was a world view. Lovers of poetry or opera or dance don't think there is *only* poetry or opera or dance. But lovers of cinema could think there was only cinema. That the movies encapsulated everything—and they did. It was both the book of art and the book of life.

As many people have noted, the start of movie-making a hundred years ago was, conveniently, a double start. In that first year, 1895, two kinds of films were made, proposing two modes of what cinema could be: cinema as the transcription of real unstaged life (the Lumière brothers) and cinema as invention, artifice, illusion, fantasy (Meliés). But this was never a true opposition. For those first audiences watching the Lumière brothers. "The Arrival of a Train at La Ciotat Station," the camera's transmission of a banal sight was a fantastic experience. Cinema began in wonder, the wonder that reality can be transcribed with such magical immediacy. All of cinema is an attempt to perpetuate and to re-invent that sense of wonder.

Everything begins with that moment, one hundred years ago, when the train pulled into the station. People took movies into themselves, just as the public cried out with excitement, actually ducked, as the train seemed to move toward *them*. Until the advent of television emptied the movie theatres, it was from a weekly visit to the cinema that you learned (or tried to learn) how to walk, to smoke, to kiss, to fight, to grieve. Movies gave you tips about how to be attractive, such as . . . it looks good to wear a raincoat even when it isn't raining. But whatever you took home from the movies was only a part of the larger experience of losing yourself in faces, in lives that were *not* yours—which is the more inclusive form of desire embodied in the movie experience. The strongest experience was simply to surrender to, to be transported by, what was on the screen. You wanted to be kidnapped by the movie.

The first condition of being kidnapped was to be overwhelmed by the physical presence of the image. And the conditions of "going to the movies" was essential to that. To see a great film only on TV isn't to have really seen that film. (This is equally true of those made for TV, like Fassbinder's *Berlin Alexanderplatz* and the two Helmat films of Edgar Reitz.) It's not only the difference of dimensions: the superiority of the larger-than-you image in the theatre to the little image on the box at home. The conditions of paying attention in a domestic space are radically disrespectful of film. Since film no longer has a standard size, home screens *can* be as big as living room or bedroom walls. But you are still in a living room or a bedroom, alone or with familiars. To be kidnapped, you have to be in a movie theatre, seated in the dark among anonymous strangers.

No amount of mourning will revive the vanished rituals—erotic, ruminative—of the darkened theatre. The reduction of cinema to assaultive images, and the unprincipled manipulation of images (faster and faster cutting) to be more attention-grabbing, has produced a disincarnated, lightweight cinema that doesn't demand anyone's full attention. Images now appear in any size and on a variety of surfaces: on a screen in a theatre, on home screens as small as the palm of your hand or as big as a wall, on disco walls and mega-screens hanging above sports arenas and the outsides of tall public buildings. The sheer ubiquity of moving images has steadily undermined the standards people once had both for cinema as art at its most serious and for cinema as popular entertainment.

In the first years there was, essentially, no difference between cinema as art and cinema as entertainment. And *all* films of the silent era—from the masterpieces of Feuillade, D. W. Griffith, Djiga Vertov, Pabst, Murnau, King Vidor to the most formula-ridden melodramas and comedies—are on a very high artistic level, compared with most of what was to follow. With the coming of sound, the image-making lost much of its brilliance and poetry, and commercial standards tightened. This way of making movies—the Hollywood system—dominated film-making for about twenty-five years (roughly from 1930 to 1955). The most original directors, like Erich von Stroheim and Orson Welles, were defeated by the system and eventually went into artistic exile in Europe—where more or less the same quality-defeating system was now in place, with lower budgets; only in France were a large number of superb films produced throughout this period. Then, in the mid-1950s, vanguard ideas took hold again, rooted in the idea of cinema as a craft pioneered by the Italian films of the immediate post-war period. A dazzling number of original, passionate films of the highest seriousness got made with new actors and tiny crews, went to film festivals (of which there were more and more), and from there, garlanded with festival prizes, into movie theatres around the world. This golden age actually lasted as long as twenty years.

It was at this specific moment in the hundred-year history of cinema that going to movies, thinking about movies, talking about movies became a passion among university students and other young people. You fell in love not just with actors but with cinema itself. Cinephilia had first become visible in the 1950s in France: Its forum was the legendary film magazine, *Cahiers du Cinéma* (followed by similarly fervent magazines in Germany, Italy, Great Britain, Sweden, the United States, Canada). Its temples, as it spread throughout Europe and the Americas, were the many cinemathèques and film clubs specializing in films from the past and directors' retrospectives which sprang up. The 1960s and early 1970s was the feverish age of movie-going, with the full-time cinephile always hoping to find a seat as close as possible to the big screen, ideally the third row center. "One can't live without Rossellini," declares a character in Bertolucci's *Before the Revolution* (1964)—and means it.

Cinephilia—a source of exultation in the films of Godard and Truffaut and the early Bertolucci and Syberberg; a morose lament in some recent films of Nanni Moretti—was mostly a Western European affair. The great directors of "the other Europe" (Zanussi in Poland, Angelopolous in Greece, Tarkovsky and Sokurov in Russia, Jancso and Tarr in Hungary) and the great Japanese directors (Ozu, Mizoguchi, Kurosawa, Oshima, Imamura) have tended not to be cinephiles, perhaps because in Budapest or Moscow or Tokyo or Warsaw or Athens there wasn't a chance to get a cinemathèque education. The distinctive thing about cinephile taste was that it embraced both "art" films and popular films. Thus, European cinephilia had a romantic relation to the films of certain directors in Hollywood at the apogee of the studio system: Godard for Howard Hawks, Fassbinder for Douglas Sirk. Of course, this moment—when cinephilia emerged—was also the moment when the Hollywood studio system was breaking up. It seemed that movie-making had re-won the right to experiment; cinephiles could *afford* to be passionate (or sentimental) about the old Hollywood genre films. A host of new people came into cinema, including a generation of young film critics from *Cahiers du Cinéma;* the towering figure of that generation, indeed of several decades of film-making anywhere, was Jean-Luc Godard. A few writers turned out to be wildly talented film-makers: Alexander Kluge in Germany, Pier Paolo Pasolini in Italy. (The model for the writer who turns to film-making actually emerged earlier, in France, with Pagnol in the 1930s and Cocteau in the 1940s; but it was not until the 1960s that this seemed, at least in Europe, normal.) Cinema seemed reborn.

For some fifteen years there were new masterpieces every month, and one allowed oneself to imagine that this would go on forever. How far away that era seems now. To be sure, there was always a conflict between cinema as an industry and cinema as an art, cinema as routine and cinema as experiment. But the conflict was not such as to make impossible the making of wonderful films, sometimes within and sometimes outside of mainstream cinema. Now the balance has tipped decisively in favor of cinema as an industry. The great cinema of the 1960s and 1970s has been thoroughly repudiated. Already in the 1970s Hollywood was plagiarizing and banalizing the innovations in narrative method and editing of successful new European and ever-marginal independent American films. Then came the catastrophic rise in production costs in the 1980s, which secured the world-wide reimposition of industry standards of making and distributing films on a far more coercive, this time truly global scale. The result can be seen in the melancholy fate of some of the greatest directors of the last decades. What place is there today for a maverick like Hans Jurgen Syberberg, who has stopped making films altogether, or for the great Godard, who now makes films about the history of film, on video? Consider some other cases. The internationalizing of financing and therefore of casts was a disaster for Andrei Tarkovsky in the last two films of his stupendous (tragically abbreviated) career. And these conditions for making films have proved to be as much an artistic disaster for two of the most valuable directors still working: Krzysztof Zanussi (*The Structure of Crystals, Illumination, Spiral, Contract*) and Theo Angelopolous (*Reconstruction, Days of '36, The Travelling Players*). And what will happen now to Bela Tarr (*Damnation, Satantango*)? And how will Aleksandr Sokurov (*Save and Protect, Days of Eclipse, The Second Circle, Stone, Whispering Pages*) find the money to go on making films, his sublime films, under the rude conditions of Russian capitalism?

Predictably, the love of cinema has waned. People still like going to the movies, and some people still care about and expect something special, necessary from a film. And wonderful films are still being made: Mike Leigh's *Naked*, Gianni Amelio's *Lamerica*, Fred Kelemen's *Fate*. But one hardly finds any more, at least among the young, the distinctive cinephilic love of movies, which is not simply love of but a certain *taste* in films (grounded in a vast appetite for seeing and re-seeing as much as possible of cinema's glorious past). Cinephilia itself has come under attack, as something quaint, outmoded, snobbish. For cinephilia implies that films are unique, unrepeatable, magic experiences. Cinephilia tells us that the Hollywood remake of Godard's *Breathless* cannot be as good as the original. Cinephilia has no role in the era of hyper-industrial films.

For cinephilia cannot help, by the very range and eclecticism of its passions, from sponsoring the idea of the film as, first of all, a poetic object; and cannot help from inciting those outside the movie industry, like painters and writers, to want to make films, too. It is precisely this that must be defeated. That has been defeated.

If cinephilia is dead, then movies are dead too . . . no matter how many movies, even very good ones, go on being made, If cinema can be resurrected, it will only be through the birth of a new kind of cine-love.

WHERE THE BOYS ARE
———————◆———————

Steven Stark

This essay appeared in the September 1994 issue of The Atlantic Monthly.

Over the past several years American pop culture has spawned a wide range of wildly popular offerings that appear remarkably similar in sensibility. Although at first glance little appears to link the infamous syndicated-radio talk-meisters Howard Stern and Don Imus with the movies *Jurassic Park* and *Field of Dreams,* the comedy of David Letterman and Jerry Seinfeld, the cartoon series *Beavis and Butt-head* and *The Simpsons,* and journalism's *The McLaughlin Group,* they in fact share a motif: though for the most part aimed at adults, these are all offerings that strongly echo the world of boys in early adolescence, ages eleven to fifteen. The unspoken premise of much of American pop culture today is that a large group of men would like nothing better than to go back to their junior high school locker rooms and stay there.

There is nothing new, of course, about men acting like boys, as anyone who has read the The *Odyssey* or *Don Quixote* knows. But something different is going on today: never before have so many seemed to produce so much that is so popular to evoke what is, after all, a brief and awkward stage of life. What's more, the trend spans the range of popular culture. Take talk radio: One of its most popular approaches today is to offer the listener a world of close-knit boyish pals. The style of Stern and Imus is that of the narcissistic class cutup in seventh grade: both sit in a playhouse-like radio studio with a bunch of guys and horse around for hours talking about sex or sports, along with political and show-biz gossip, all the while laughing at the gang's consciously loutish, subversive jokes. To the extent that women participate, they are often treated to a barrage of sexual and scatological humor. It's no wonder the audience for both shows is predominantly male.

Late Show With David Letterman and *Seinfeld* similarly echo the ethos of young teenage boys. Late-night television has always been a chiefly male world, but until recently it wasn't a boy's world. One of Letterman's contributions to late-night entertainment has been to take its humor out of the nightclub-act tradition—replete with all of Johnny Carson's jokes about drinking or adult sex—and place it firmly in that prankish, subversive, back-of-the-classroom seventh-grade realm that has become so culturally prominent. Although Letterman rarely greets women guests with filthy jokes (you can't do that on network television), he often treats them with the exaggerated deference and shyness typical of fourteen-year-old boys.

Like a group of fourteen-year-olds, the men on *Seinfeld* seem not to hold regular jobs, the better to devote time to "the gang." One woman, Elaine, is allowed to tag along with the boys, much like those younger sisters who are permitted to hang out with their brothers. It's not simply that everyone in Seinfeld's gang is unmarried and pushing fortysomething. It's that given their personas, it's difficult to imagine any of them having a real relationship with any woman but his mother. (Note how much more often parents of adult children appear here than on other shows.) Compare this situation comedy with the one that was roughly its cultural predecessor, *Cheers*, which appeared in the same time slot. On that show, too, the men didn't spend much time at work, but they did hang out in a traditional domain of adults (the tavern), and the hero, Sam Malone, spent many of his waking hours chasing women. Seinfeld is better known for sitting in a diner eating french fries with his pals. One of the show's most celebrated "risqué" episodes was about—what else?—masturbation.

And so it goes in various ways, as the early-teen male sensibility is celebrated in everything from *Wayne's World* (the adventures of two adolescent goofballs) to *The Simpsons* (starring the proud underachiever Bart) to *Beavis and Butt-head* (MTV's notorious early-adolescent icons). The heavy-metal sound of bands with names like Danzig, Gwar, and Genitorturers is in vogue now, and with its constant evocation of sexism, violence, and hostility for hostility's sake, that rock genre has always reeked of the adolescent experience more than others have.

Like many recent cinema hits, ranging from the Indiana Jones series to most Arnold Schwarzenegger offerings, last year's blockbuster film *Jurassic Park* was largely a traditional teenage "boys' movie"—heavy on adventure and violence, light on romance and relationships. Psychologists have observed that the culture-wide trend toward "pumped-up" male heroes—Schwarzenegger, Sylvester Stallone, and half the guys at your local health club—is a pre-teen male fantasy brought to life. Even popular "adult" movies, such as *City Slickers* and *Big*, often revolve around the premise that once a man has passed through puberty, it's pretty much all downhill.

The cult of baseball can be seen as an intensely nostalgic return to early adolescence for many Americans. The rite of Rotisserie League baseball—an activity in which men spend hours every week poring over sheets of statistics, as they did when they were young—is part of this phenomenon, as are the wearing of baseball hats and the collecting of autographs and baseball cards by men of all ages. So, too, are baseball-movie parables like the quasi-religious *Field of Dreams,* in which male adolescence, the pastoral life, and baseball are linked in a way that would make both Jean Jacques Rousseau and Casey Stengel proud. In these visions of utopia, of course, women are again peripheral—except, perhaps, when baking cookies or waving in maternal fashion from the front porch as Dad and Son play catch. In the 1955 America that is usually the baseball lover's Paradise Lost, there are no Astroturf, no new stadiums, and no western teams to challenge the prominence of New York and the eastern urban society it represents. That America is not only a man's world but also, by and large, a white man's world.

Today's early-adolescent attitude is certainly on display throughout the news media. It's not simply that in a tabloid age many publications have adopted a kind of sneering, sophomoric attitude toward public affairs, or that shows such as *Crossfire* and *The McLaughlin Group*—with their mostly male screaming casts—resemble nothing so much as a junior high social-studies debate (in which the girls were always shouted down by the boys regardless of what they had to say). It's that today's journalism is obsessed with the kinds of things that tend to preoccupy thirteen-year-old boys: sports, sex, crime, and narcissism—that is, itself. Also in journalism as currently practiced, reporters often set themselves up as passive observers of events and then spend much of their time identifying with those who exercise real power—a point of view that is reminiscent of the way a young teenager views his parents. Moreover, if today's journalism has a driving principle, that principle centers on an obsession with hypocrisy. Journalism is about many things, but these days it is often about revealing that public figures are phonies. Covering Bill Clinton, or Prince Charles, or Michael Jackson, reporters frame their stories by saying implicitly, "These people aren't what they say they are. Look, they lied to you." Although there is a cultural role for balloon deflators, journalism has brought this characteristic attitude of the early adolescent to the adult world and elevated it to the status of cultural religion. That's why much of journalism today is really a form of institutionalized early adolescence.

Because the press tends to set the agenda for our culture, these sentiments have enormous ramifications. Whether in the form of the media's obsession with violence or its preoccupation with polls and popularity, the fantasy life of the adolescent male ends up defining much of our political reality. Political coverage tends to focus on gaffes, girlfriends, and youthful indiscretions while far more important, "adult" issues go underreported.

The press has also seen to it that the cardinal sin in American politics today is not to run up a deficit or lose an important court case but to change one's mind: like a fourteen-year-old, the press always takes a switch as evidence of hypocrisy. Thus George Bush was skewered by the media in 1990 for flip-flopping on the issue of taxes, and Bill Clinton was attacked unmercifully last year for going back on his promise of a tax cut for the middle class. Maybe both men had misled the voters during their campaigns, but a less iconoclastic press corps might have concluded that both men changed their minds for unselfish policy reasons. While an adolescent often looks at a change in direction and sees deceit, an adult realizes that life is usually more complex than that. Mature leaders recognize their mistakes and often adjust accordingly—though not without peril in today's climate.

Admittedly, too much can be made of all this. Entertainment has always evoked certain stages of life in ways that appeal to the masses: think of *The Wizard of Oz* and *Rebel Without a Cause*. The fourteen-year-old sensibility is certainly not the only one celebrated in a culture that includes *The Golden Girls, Murphy Brown,* and Barney the dinosaur. And it's true that other eras in America have celebrated youth in various forms, from Shirley Temple to the Brady Bunch. But it's hard to make the case that the male early-adolescent mind-set was as pervasive or influential in those eras as it is in this one.

There are, of course, antecedents in our cultural life for this veneration of male early adolescence. The western often celebrated the young cowboy or outlaw like Billy the Kid, who, surrounded by his loyal gang in a world without commitment to women, broke the rules. In his recent book, *American Manhood*, E. Anthony Rotundo shows how American culture came to celebrate the misbehavior of boys as a way of idolizing the traits of childishness without idolizing children. In *Love and Death in the American Novel* (1960) Leslie Fiedler traces the evolution of the "bad boy" in American fiction from its roots in late-nineteenth-century bestsellers like *Peck's Bad Boy* and *The Story of a Bad Boy.* He also describes American fiction's traditional preoccupation with "The Good Bad Boy"—from Huckleberry Finn to Holden Caulfield to the characters in Jack Kerouac's *On the Road.* Fiedler wrote, "The Good Bad Boy is, of course, America's vision of itself, crude and unruly in his beginnings, but endowed by his creator with an instinctive sense of what is right."

Thirty-four years ago Fiedler wrote that from the Puritan-influenced Hawthorne and Melville on, Americans had been drawn to tales of boys and neutered women as a way of avoiding the subject of sex. In a tabloid era of penis-mutilation trials, prime-time network nudity, condom ads, and endless talk-show discussions of sexual fetishes, however, it's hard to continue to make his case. Still, if early-adolescent boys are notable for their inclinations to look at dirty pictures and talk about sex, they aren't quite ready to do something about it responsibly with a woman. That propensity to be in the world of sex but not really of it is certainly a sign of the times.

What's more, even if men aren't trying to avoid sex today, a retreat into teenhood may be a convenient way to avoid the opposite sex. As Susan Faludi and other writers have noted, the women's movement—perhaps the greatest social change of our time—has triggered something of a well-documented backlash. One result may be the creation of this boyish countermovement that looks with nostalgic longing on perhaps the last period in life when it's socially acceptable for males to exclude women, if not deride them.

The reasons for the cultural ubiquity of male early adolescence have little to do with puritanism. Many psychologists consider that stage of life, when one is acutely aware of being powerless, to be the time when individuals are most subversive of the society at large. That idea also fits a wider cultural mood, always somewhat prevalent in America, that exalts the outsider. Such an anti-establishment mood, rooted in powerlessness, is particularly strong today, and the proof is not simply in the Ross Perot phenomenon. Whether the subject is how the tabloid press now eagerly tears down public figures or the pervasiveness of gossip masquerading as news (to demonstrate how the famous are no better than anyone else) or the rise of anti-establishment talk radio and comedy clubs where the humor grows more derisive by the day, America is full of the defiant, oppositional anger that often characterizes the early adolescent.

That anger is also an asset for TV programmers in the cable era. Television, of course, tends to encourage a kind of passivity that isn't ultimately much different from the angry powerlessness early teens tend to feel: Beavis and Butt-head have become cultural symbols precisely because a nation of couch potatoes feels like a nation of fifteen-year-olds. Moreover, in an age of multiple offerings and channel surfing, what tends to draw these passive audiences is the irately outrageous and exhibitionistic—the Howard Sterns, not the Arthur Godfreys. It also doesn't hurt that adolescents tend to be what advertisers call "good consumers"—narcissistic, with a fair amount of disposable income, and with no one but themselves to spend it on. A culture that is obsessed with this stage of life is arguably in a better frame of mind to buy—to run up the limit on Dad's (or Uncle Sam's) credit card—than one that worships, say, thrifty middle age.

In a country whose citizens have always had tendencies that remind observers of those of a fourteen-year-old boy, it would be wrong to lay all the blame for society's vulgarity and violence, its exhibitionist inclinations, its fear of powerful women, its failure to grow up and take care of its real children, and its ambivalence about paternal authority at the feet of Howard Stern, John McLaughlin, and Jerry Seinfeld. But they have helped, and many of us have willingly obliged. After all, as Fiedler reminded us, boys will be boys.

TV ADDICTION

—■—

Marie Winn

This excerpt is from Winn's 1977 book The Plug-in Drug: Television, Children, and Family, *which was revised in 1985.*

The word "addiction" is often used loosely and wryly in conversation. People will refer to themselves as "mystery book addicts" or "cookie addicts." E. B. White wrote of his annual surge of interest in gardening: "We are hooked and are making an attempt to kick the habit." Yet nobody really believes that reading mysteries or ordering seeds by catalogue is serious enough to be compared with addictions to heroin or alcohol. The word "addiction" is here used jokingly to denote a tendency to overindulge in some pleasurable activity.

People often refer to being "hooked on TV." Does this, too, fall into the lighthearted category of cookie eating and other pleasures that people pursue with unusual intensity, or is there a kind of television viewing that falls into the more serious category of destructive addiction?

When we think about addiction to drugs or alcohol we frequently focus on negative aspects, ignoring the pleasures that accompany drinking or drug-taking. And yet the essence of any serious addiction is a pursuit of pleasure, a search for a "high" that normal life does not supply. It is only the inability to function without the addictive substance that is dismaying, the dependence of the organism upon a certain experience and an increasing inability to function normally without it. Thus people will take two or three drinks at the end of the day not merely for the pleasure drinking provides, but also because they "don't feel normal" without them.

Real addicts do not merely pursue a pleasurable experience one time in order to function normally. They need to *repeat* it again and again. Something about that particular experience makes life without it less than complete. Other potentially pleasurable experiences are no longer possible, for under the spell of the addictive experience, their lives are peculiarly distorted. The addict craves an experience and yet is never really satisfied. The organism may be temporarily sated, but soon it begins to crave again.

Finally, a serious addiction is distinguished from a harmless pursuit of pleasure by its distinctly destructive elements. Heroin addicts, for instance, lead a damaged life: their increasing need for heroin in increasing doses prevents them from working, from maintaining relationships, from developing in human ways. Similarly alcoholics' lives are narrowed and dehumanized by their dependence on alcohol.

Let us consider television viewing in the light of the conditions that define serious addictions.

Not unlike drugs or alcohol, the television experience allows the participant to blot out the real world and enter into a pleasurable and passive mental state. The worries and anxieties of reality are as effectively deferred by becoming absorbed in a television program as by going on a "trip" induced by drugs or alcohol. And just as alcoholics are only vaguely aware of their addiction, feeling that they control their drinking more than they really do ("I can cut it out any time I want—I just like to have three or four drinks before dinner"), people similarly overestimate their control over television watching. Even as they put off other activities to spend hour after hour watching television, they feel they could easily resume living in a different, less passive style. But somehow or other, while the television set is present in their homes, the click doesn't sound. With television pleasures available, those other experiences seem less attractive, more difficult somehow.

A heavy viewer (a college English instructor) observes:

"I find television almost irresistible. When the set is on, I cannot ignore it. I can't turn it off. I feel sapped, will-less, enervated. As I reach out to turn off the set, the strength goes out of my arms. So I sit there for hours and hours."

Self-confessed television addicts often feel they "ought" to do other things—but the fact that they don't read and don't plant their garden or sew or crochet or play games or have conversations means that those activities are no longer as desirable as television viewing. In a way the lives of heavy viewers are as imbalanced by their television "habit" as a drug addict's or an alcoholic's. They are living in a holding pattern, as it were, passing up the activities that lead to growth or development or a sense of accomplishment. This is one reason people talk about their television viewing so ruefully, so apologetically. They are aware that it is an unproductive experience, that almost any other endeavor is more worthwhile by any human measure.

Finally it is the adverse effect of television viewing on the lives of so many people that defines it as a serious addiction. The television habit distorts the sense of time. It renders other experiences vague and curiously unreal while taking on a greater reality for itself. It weakens relationships by reducing and sometimes eliminating normal opportunities for talking, for communicating.

And yet television does not satisfy, else why would the viewer continue to watch hour after hour, day after day? "The measure of health," writes Lawrence Kubie, "is flexibility . . . and especially the freedom to cease when sated." But heavy television viewers can never be sated with their television experiences—they do not provide the true nourishment that satiation requires—and thus they find that they cannot stop watching.

A former heavy watcher (filmmaker) describes such a syndrome:

"I remember when we first got the set I'd watch for hours and hours, whenever I could, and I remember that feeling of tiredness and anxiety that always followed those orgies, a sense of time terribly wasted. It was like eating cotton candy; television promised so much richness, I couldn't wait for it, and then it just evaporated into air. I remember feeling terribly drained after watching for a long time."

Similarly a nursery school teacher remembers her own childhood television experience:

"I remember bingeing on television when I was a child and having that vapid feeling after watching hours of TV. I'd look forward to watching whenever I could, but it just didn't give back a real feeling of pleasure. It was like no orgasm, no catharsis, very frustrating. Television just wasn't giving me the promised satisfaction, and yet I kept on watching. It filled some sort of need, or had to do with an inability to get something started."

The testimonies of ex-television addicts often have the evangelistic overtones of stories heard at Alcoholics Anonymous meetings.

A handbag repair shop owner says:

"I'd get on the subway home from work with the newspaper and immediately turn to the TV page to plan out my evening's watching. I'd come home, wash, change my clothes, and tell my wife to start the machine so it would be warmed up. (We had an old-fashioned set that took a few seconds before an image appeared.) And then we'd watch TV for the rest of the evening. We'd eat our dinner in the living room while watching, and we'd only talk every once in a while, during the ads, if at all. I'd watch anything, good, bad, or indifferent.

"All the while we were watching I'd feel terribly angry at myself for wasting all that time watching junk. I could never go to sleep until at least the eleven o'clock news, and then sometimes I'd still stay up for the late-night talk show. I had a feeling that I *had* to watch the news programs, that I *had* to know what was happening, even though most of the time nothing much was happening and I could easily find out what was by reading the paper the next morning. Usually my wife would fall asleep on the couch while I was watching. I'd get angry at her for doing that. Actually, I was angry at myself. I had a collection of three years of back issues of different magazines that I planned to read sometime, but I never got around to reading them. I never got around to sorting or labeling my collection of slides I had made when traveling. I only had time for television. We'd take the telephone off the hook while watching so we wouldn't be interrupted! We like classical music, but we never listened to any, never!

"Then one day the set broke. I said to my wife, 'Let's not fix it. Let's just see what happens.' Well, that was the smartest thing we ever did. We haven't had a TV in the house since then.

"Now I look back and I can hardly believe we could have lived like that. I feel that my mind was completely mummified for all those years. I was glued to that machine and couldn't get loose, somehow. It really frightens me to think of it. Yes, I'm frightened of TV now. I don't think I could control it if we had a set in the house again. I think it would take over no matter what I did."

A further sign of addiction is that "an exclusive craving for something is accompanied by a loss of discrimination towards the object which satisfies the craving ... the alcoholic is not interested in the taste of liquor that is available; likewise the compulsive eater is not particular about what he eats when there is food around," write the authors of a book about the nature of addiction. And just so, for many viewers the process of *watching* television is far more important than the actual contents of the programs being watched. The knowledge that the act of watching is more important than *what* is being watched lies behind the practice of "road-blocking," invented by television advertisers and adopted by political candidates who purchase the same half-hour on all three channels in order to force-feed their message to the public. As one prominent candidate put it, "People will watch television no matter what is on, and if you allow them no other choice they will watch your show."

FUTURE SCHLOCK

Neil Postman

This piece comes from Postman's book Conscientious Objections, *published in 1988.*

Human intelligence is among the most fragile things in nature. It doesn't take much to distract it, suppress it, or even annihilate it. In this century, we have had some lethal examples of how easily and quickly intelligence can be defeated by any one of its several nemeses: ignorance, superstition, moral fervor, cruelty, cowardice, neglect. In the late 1920s, for example, Germany was, by any measure, the most literate, cultured nation in the world. Its legendary seats of learning attracted scholars from every corner. Its philosophers, social critics, and scientists were of the first rank; its humane traditions an inspiration to less favored nations. But by the mid-1930s—that is, in less than ten years—this cathedral of human reason had been transformed into a cesspool of barbaric irrationality. Many of the most intelligent products of German culture were forced to flee—for example, Einstein, Freud, Karl Jaspers, Thomas Mann, and Stefan Zweig. Even worse, those who remained were either forced to submit their minds to the sovereignty of primitive superstition, or—worse still—willingly did so: Konrad Lorenz, Werner Heisenberg, Martin Heidegger, Gerhardt Hauptmann. On May 10, 1933, a huge bonfire was kindled in Berlin and the books of Marcel Proust, André Gide, Emile Zola, Jack London, Upton Sinclair, and a hundred others were committed to the flames, amid shouts of idiot delight. By 1936, Joseph Paul Goebbels, Germany's Minister of Propaganda, was issuing a proclamation which began with the following words: "Because this year has not brought an improvement in art criticism, I forbid once and for all the continuance of art criticism in its past form, effective as of today." By 1936, there was no one left in Germany who had the brains or courage to object.

Exactly why the Germans banished intelligence is a vast and largely unanswered question. I have never been persuaded that the desperate economic depression that afflicted Germany in the 1920s adequately explains what happened. To quote Aristotle: Men do not become tyrants in order to keep warm. Neither do they become stupid—at least not *that* stupid. But the matter need not trouble us here. I offer the German case only as the most striking example of the fragility of human intelligence. My focus here is the United States in our own time, and I wish to worry you about the rapid erosion of our own intelligence. If you are confident that such a thing cannot happen, your confidence is misplaced, I believe, but it is understandable.

After all, the United States is one of the few countries in the world founded by intellectuals—men of wide learning, of extraordinary rhetorical powers, of deep faith in reason. And although we have had our moods of anti-intellectualism, few people have been more generous in support of intelligence and learning than Americans. It was the United States that initiated the experiment in mass education that is, even today, the envy of the world. It was America's churches that laid the foundation of our admirable system of higher education; it was the Land-Grant Act of 1862 that made possible our great state universities; and it is to America that scholars and writers have fled when freedom of the intellect became impossible in their own nations. This is why the great historian of American civilization Henry Steele Commager called America "the Empire of Reason." But Commager was referring to the United States of the eighteenth and nineteenth centuries. What term he would use for America today, I cannot say. Yet he has observed, as others have, a change, a precipitous decline in our valuation of intelligence, in our uses of language, in the disciplines of logic and reason, in our capacity to attend to complexity. Perhaps he would agree with me that the Empire of Reason is, in fact, gone, and that the most apt term for America today is the Empire of Shlock.

In any case, this is what I wish to call to your notice: the frightening displacement of serious, intelligent public discourse in American culture by the imagery and triviality of what may be called show business. I do not see the decline of intelligent discourse in America leading to the barbarisms that flourished in Germany, of course. No scholars, I believe, will ever need to flee America. There will be no bonfires to burn books. And I cannot imagine any proclamations forbidding once and for all art criticism, or any other kind of criticism. But this is not a cause for complacency, let alone celebration. A culture does not have to force scholars to flee to render them impotent. A culture does not have to burn books to assure that they will not be read. And a culture does not need a Minister of Propaganda issuing proclamations to silence criticism. There are other ways to achieve stupidity, and it appears that, as in so many other things, there is a distinctly American way.

To explain what I am getting at, I find it helpful to refer to two films, which taken together embody the main lines of my argument. The first film is of recent vintage and is called *The Gods Must Be Crazy*. It is about a tribal people who live in the Kalahari Desert plains of southern Africa, and what happens to their culture when it is invaded by an empty Coca-Cola bottle tossed from the window of a small plane passing overhead. The bottle lands in the middle of the village and is construed by these gentle people to be a gift from the gods, for they not only have never seen a bottle before but have never seen glass either. The people are almost immediately charmed by the gift, and not only because of its novelty. The bottle, it turns out, has multiple uses, chief among them the intriguing music it makes when one blows into it.

But gradually a change takes place in the tribe. The bottle becomes an irresistible preoccupation. Looking at it, holding it, thinking of things to do with it displace other activities once thought essential. But more than this, the Coke bottle is the only thing these people have ever seen of which there is only one of its kind. And so those who do not have it try to get it from the one who does. And the one who does refuses to give it up. Jealousy, greed, and even violence enter the scene, and come very close to destroying the harmony that has characterized their culture for a thousand years. The people begin to love their bottle more than they love themselves, and are saved only when the leader of the tribe, convinced that the gods must be crazy, returns the bottle to the gods by throwing it off the top of a mountain.

The film is great fun and it is also wise, mainly because it is about a subject as relevant to people in Chicago or Los Angeles or New York as it is to those of the Kalahari Desert. It raises two questions of extreme importance to our situation: How does a culture change when new technologies are introduced to it? And is it always desirable for a culture to accommodate itself to the demands of new technologies? The leader of the Kalahari tribe is forced to confront these questions in a way that Americans have refused to do. And because his vision is not obstructed by a belief in what Americans call "technological progress," he is able with minimal discomfort to decide that the songs of the Coke bottle are not so alluring that they are worth admitting envy, egotism, and greed to a serene culture.

The second film relevant to my argument was made in 1967. It is Mel Brooks's first film, *The Producers*. *The Producers* is a rather raucous comedy that has at its center a painful joke: An unscrupulous theatrical producer has figured out that it is relatively easy to turn a buck by producing a play that fails. All one has to do is induce dozens of backers to invest in the play by promising them exorbitant percentages of its profits. When the play fails, there being no profits to disperse, the producer walks away with thousands of dollars that can never be claimed. Of course, the central problem he must solve is to make sure that his play is a disastrous failure. And so he hits upon an excellent idea: he will take the most tragic and grotesque story of our century—the rise of Adolf Hitler—and make it into a musical.

Because the producer is only a crook and not a fool, he assumes that the stupidity of making a musical on this theme will be immediately grasped by audiences and that they will leave the theater in dumbfounded rage. So he calls his play *Springtime for Hitler*, which is also the name of its most important song. The song begins with the words:

Springtime for Hitler and Germany;
Winter for Poland and France.

The melody is catchy, and when the song is sung it is accompanied by a happy chorus line. (One must understand, of course, that *Springtime for Hitler* is no spoof of Hitler, as was, for example, Charlie Chaplin's *The Great Dictator*. The play is instead a kind of denial of Hitler in song and dance; as if to say, it was all in fun.)

The ending of the movie is predictable. The audience loves the play and leaves the theater humming *Springtime for Hitler.* The musical becomes a great hit. The producer ends up in jail, his joke having turned back on him. But Brooks's point is that the joke is on us. Although the film was made years before a movie actor became President of the United States, Brooks was making a kind of prophecy about that—namely, that the producers of American culture will increasingly turn our history, politics, religion, commerce, and education into forms of entertainment, and that we will become as a result a trivial people, incapable of coping with complexity, ambiguity, uncertainty, perhaps even reality. We will become, in a phrase, a people amused into stupidity.

For those readers who are not inclined to take Mel Brooks as seriously as I do, let me remind you that the prophecy I attribute here to Brooks was, in fact, made many years before by a more formidable social critic than he. I refer to Aldous Huxley, who wrote *Brave New World* at the time that the modern monuments to intellectual stupidity were taking shape: Nazism in Germany, fascism in Italy, communism in Russia. But Huxley was not concerned in his book with such naked and crude forms of intellectual suicide. He saw beyond them, and mostly, I must add, he saw America. To be more specific, he foresaw that the greatest threat to the intelligence and humane creativity of our culture would not come from Big Brother and Ministries of Propaganda, or gulags and concentration camps. He prophesied, if I may put it this way, that there is tyranny lurking in a Coca-Cola bottle; that we could be ruined not by what we fear and hate but by what we welcome and love, by what we construe to be a gift from the gods.

And in case anyone missed his point in 1932, Huxley wrote *Brave New World Revisited* twenty years later. By then, George Orwell's *1984* had been published, and it was inevitable that Huxley would compare Orwell's book with his own. The difference, he said, is that in Orwell's book people are controlled by inflicting pain. In *Brave New World,* they are controlled by inflicting pleasure.

The Coke bottle that has fallen in our midst is a corporation of dazzling technologies whose forms turn all serious public business into a kind of *Springtime for Hitler* musical. Television is the principal instrument of this disaster, in part because it is the medium Americans most dearly love, and in part because it has become the command center of our culture. Americans turn to television not only for their light entertainment but for their news, their weather, their politics, their religion, their history—all of which may be said to be their serious entertainment. The light entertainment is not the problem. The least dangerous things on television are its junk. What I am talking about is television's preemption of our culture's most serious business. It would be merely banal to say that television presents us with entertaining subject matter. It is quite another thing to say that on television all subject matter is presented as entertaining. And that is how television brings ruin to any intelligent understanding of public affairs.

Political campaigns, for example, are now conducted largely in the form of television commercials. Candidates forgo precision, complexity, substance—in some cases, language itself—for the arts of show business: music, imagery, celebrities, theatrics. Indeed, political figures have become so good at this, and so accustomed to it, that they do television commercials even when they are not campaigning, as, for example, Geraldine Ferraro for Diet Pepsi and former vice-presidential candidate William Miller and the late Senator Sam Ervin for American Express. Even worse, political figures appear on variety shows, soap operas, and sitcoms. George McGovern, Ralph Nader, Ed Koch, and Jesse Jackson have all hosted "Saturday Night Live." Henry Kissinger and former President Gerald Ford have done cameo roles on "Dynasty." Tip O'Neill and Governor Michael Dukakis have appeared on "Cheers." Richard Nixon did a short stint on "Laugh-In." The late Senator from Illinois, Everett Dirksen, was on "What's My Line?" a prophetic question if ever there was one. What *is* the line of these people? Or, more precisely, *where* is the line that one ought to be able to draw between politics and entertainment? I would suggest that television has annihilated it.

It is significant, I think, that although our current President, a former Hollywood movie actor, rarely speaks accurately and never precisely, he is known as the Great Communicator; his telegenic charm appears to be his major asset, and that seems to be quite good enough in an entertainment-oriented politics. But lest you think his election to two terms is a mere aberration, I must remind you that, as I write [1988], Charlton Heston is being mentioned as a possible candidate for the Republican nomination in 1988. Should this happen, what alternative would the Democrats have but to nominate Gregory Peck? Two idols of the silver screen going one on one. Could even the fertile imagination of Mel Brooks have foreseen this? Heston giving us intimations of Moses as he accepts the nomination; Peck re-creating the courage of his biblical David as he accepts the challenge of running against a modern Goliath. Heston going on the stump as Michelangelo; Peck countering with Douglas MacArthur. Heston accusing Peck of insanity because of *The Boys From Brazil.* Peck replying with the charge that Heston blew the world up in *Return to Planet of the Apes. Springtime for Hitler* could be closer than you think.

But politics is only one arena in which serious language has been displaced by the arts of show business. We have all seen how religion is packaged on television, as a kind of Las Vegas stage show, devoid of ritual, sacrality, and tradition. Today's electronic preachers are in no way like America's evangelicals of the past. Men like Jonathan Edwards, Charles Finney, and George Whitefield were preachers of theological depth, authentic learning, and great expository power. Electronic preachers such as Jimmy Swaggart, Jim Bakker, and Jerry Falwell are merely performers who exploit television's visual power and their own charisma for the greater glory of themselves.

We have also seen "Sesame Street" and other educational shows in which the demands of entertainment take precedence over the rigors of learning. And we well know how American businessmen, working under the assumption that potential customers require amusement rather than facts, use music, dance, comedy, cartoons, and celebrities to sell their products.

vague pronoun reference

Even our daily news, which for most Americans means television news, is packaged as a kind of show, featuring handsome news readers, exciting music, and dynamic film footage. Most especially, film footage. When there is no film footage, there is no story. Stranger still, commercials may appear anywhere in a news story—before, after, or in the middle. This reduces all events to trivialities, sources of public entertainment and little more. After all, how serious can a bombing in Lebanon be if it is shown to us prefaced by a happy United Airlines commercial and summarized by a Calvin Klein jeans commercial? Indeed, television newscasters have added to our grammar a new part of speech—what may be called the "Now . . . this" conjunction, a conjunction that does not connect two things, but disconnects them. When newscasters say, "Now . . . this," they mean to indicate that what you have just heard or seen has no relevance to what you are about to hear or see. There is no murder so brutal, no political blunder so costly, no bombing so devastating that it cannot be erased from our minds by a newscaster saying, "Now . . . this." He means that you have thought long enough on the matter (let us say, for forty seconds) and you must now give your attention to a commercial. Such a situation is not "the news." It is merely a daily version of *Springtime for Hitler,* and in my opinion accounts for the fact that Americans are among the most ill-informed people in the world. To be sure, we know *of* many things; but we know *about* very little.

To provide some verification of this, I conducted a survey a few years back on the subject of the Iranian hostage crisis. I chose this subject because it was alluded to on television *every day for more than a year.* I did not ask my subjects for their opinions about the hostage situation. I am not interested in opinion polls; I am interested in knowledge polls. The questions I asked were simple and did not require deep knowledge. For example, Where is Iran? What language do the Iranians speak? Where did the Shah come from? What religion do the Iranians practice, and what are its basic tenets? What does "Ayatollah" mean? I found that almost everybody knew practically nothing about Iran. And those who did know something said they had learned it from *Newsweek* or *Time* or the *New York Times.* Television, in other words, is not the great information machine. It is the great disinformation machine. A most nerve-wracking confirmation of this came some time ago during an interview with the producer and the writer of the TV mini-series *Peter the Great.* Defending the historical inaccuracies in the drama—which included a fabricated meeting between Peter and Sir Isaac Newton—the producer said that no one would watch a dry, historically faithful biography. The writer added that it is better for audiences to learn something that is untrue, if it is entertaining, than not to learn anything at all. And just to put some icing on the cake, the actor who played Peter, Maximilian Schell, remarked that he does not believe in historical truth and therefore sees no reason to pursue it.

I do not mean to say that the trivialization of American public discourse is all accomplished on television. Rather, television is the paradigm for all our attempts at public communication. It conditions our minds to apprehend the world through fragmented pictures and forces other media to orient themselves in that direction. You know the standard question we put to people who have difficulty understanding even simple language: we ask them impatiently, "Do I have to draw a picture for you?" Well, it appears that, like it or not, our culture will draw pictures for us, will explain the world to us in pictures. As a medium for conducting public business, language has receded in importance; it has been moved to the periphery of culture and has been replaced at the center by the entertaining visual image.

Please understand that I am making no criticism of the visual arts in general. That criticism is made by God, not by me. You will remember that in His Second Commandment, God explicitly states that "Thou shalt not make unto thee any graven image, nor any likeness of anything that is in Heaven above, or that is in the earth beneath, or the waters beneath the earth." I have always felt that God was taking a rather extreme position on this, as is His way. As for myself, I am arguing from the standpoint of a symbolic relativist. Forms of communication are neither good nor bad in themselves. They become good or bad depending on their relationship to other symbols and on the functions they are made to serve within a social order. When a culture becomes overloaded with pictures; when logic and rhetoric lose their binding authority; when historical truth becomes irrelevant; when the spoken or written word is distrusted or makes demands on our attention that we are incapable of giving; when our politics, history, education, religion, public information, and commerce are expressed largely in visual imagery rather than words, then a culture is in serious jeopardy.

Neither do I make a complaint against entertainment. As an old song has it, life is not a highway strewn with flowers. The sight of a few blossoms here and there may make our journey a trifle more endurable. But in America, the least amusing people are our professional entertainers. In our present situation, our preachers, entrepreneurs, politicians, teachers, and journalists are committed to entertaining us through media that do not lend themselves to serious, complex discourse. But these producers of our culture are not to be blamed. They, like the rest of us, believe in the supremacy of technological progress. It has never occurred to us that the gods might be crazy. And even if it did, there is no mountaintop from which we can return what is dangerous to us.

We would do well to keep in mind that there are two ways in which the spirit of a culture may be degraded. In the first—the Orwellian—culture becomes a prison. This was the way of the Nazis, and it appears to be the way of the Russians. In the second—the Huxleyan—culture becomes a burlesque. This appears to be the way of the Americans. What Huxley reaches is that in the Age of Advanced Technology, spiritual devastation is more likely to come from an enemy with a smiling countenance than from one whose face exudes suspicion and hate. In the Huxleyan prophecy, Big Brother does not watch us, by his choice; we watch him, by ours. When a culture becomes distracted by trivia; when political and so-cial life arc redefined as a perpetual round of entertainments; when pub-lic conversation becomes a form of baby talk; when a people become, in short, an audience and their public business a vaudeville act, then— Huxley argued—a nation finds itself at risk and culture-death is a clear possibility. I agree.

WHY BLAME TV?

———————●———————

John Leonard

This piece was first printed in The Nation *magazine in 1993.*

Like a warrior-king of Sumer, daubed with sesame oil, gorged on goat, hefting up his sword and drum, Senator Ernest Hollings looked down November 23 from a ziggurat to intone, all over the op-ed page of the *New York Times:* "If the TV and cable industries have no sense of shame, we must take it upon ourselves to stop licensing their violence-saturated programming."

Hollings, of course, is co-sponsor in the Senate, with Daniel Inouye, of a ban on any act of violence on television before, say, midnight. Never mind whether this is constitutional, or what it would do to the local news. Never mind, either, that in Los Angeles last August, in the International Ballroom of the Beverly Hilton, in front of 600 industry executives, the talking heads—a professor here, a producer there, a child psychologist and a network veep for program standards—couldn't even agree on a definition of violence. (Is it only violent if it hurts or kills?) And they dis-agreed on which was worse, a "happy" violence that sugarcoats aggres-sive behavior or a "graphic" violence that at least suggests consequences. (How, anyway, does television manage somehow simultaneously to *desen-sitize* and to *incite?*) Nor were they really sure what goes on in the dreamy heads of our children as they crouch in the dark to commune with the tube while their parents, if they have any, aren't around. (*Road Runner?* Beep-beep.) Nor does the infamous scarlet V "parent advisory" warning even apply to cartoons, afternoon soaps, or Somalias.

Never mind, because everybody agrees that watching television causes anti-social behavior, especially among the children of the poor; that there seems to be more violent programming on the air now than there ever was before; that *Beavis and Butt-head* inspired an Ohio 5-year-old to burn down the family trailer; that in the blue druidic light of television we will have spawned generations of toadstools and triffids.

In fact, there is less violence on network television than there used to be; because of ratings, it's mostly sitcoms. The worst stuff is the Hollywood splatterflicks; they're found on premium cable, which means the poor are less likely to be watching. Everywhere else on cable, not counting the court channel or home shopping and not even to think about blood sports and Pat Buchanan, the fare is innocent to the point of stupefaction (Disney, Discovery, Family, Nickelodeon). That Ohio trailer wasn't even wired for cable, so the littlest firebird must have got his MTV elsewhere in the dangerous neighborhood. (And kids have been playing with matches since, at least, Prometheus. I recall burning down my very own bedroom when I was 5 years old. The fire department had to tell my mother that the evidence pointed to me.) Since the '60s, according to statistics cited by Douglas Davis in *The Five Myths of Television Power,* more Americans than ever before are going out to eat in restaurants, see films, plays, and baseball games, visit museums, travel abroad, jog, even *read.* Watching television, everybody does *something else* at the same time. While our children are playing with their Adobe Illustrators and Domark Virtual Reality Toolkits, the rest of us eat, knit, smoke, dream, read magazines, sign checks, feel sorry for ourselves, think about Hillary, and plot shrewd career moves or revenge.

Actually watching television, unless it's C-Span, is usually more interesting than the proceedings of Congress. Or what we read in hysterical books like Jerry Mander's *Four Arguments for the Elimination of Television,* or George Gilder's *Life After Television,* or Marie Winn's *The Plug-In Drug,* or Neal Postman's *Amusing Ourselves to Death,* or Bill McKibben's *The Age of Missing Information.* Or what we'll hear at panel discussions on censorship, where right-wingers worry about sex and left-wingers worry about violence. Or just lolling around an academic deep think-tank, trading mantras like "violence profiles" (George Gerbner), "processed culture" (Richard Hoggart), "narcoleptic joys" (Michael Sorkin), and "glass teat" (Harlan Ellison).

Of *course* something happens to us when we watch television; networks couldn't sell their millions of pairs of eyes to advertising agencies, nor would ad agencies buy more than $21 billion worth of commercial time each year, if speech (and sound, and motion) didn't somehow modify action. But what happens is far from clear and won't be much clarified by lab studies, however longitudinal, of habits and behaviors isolated from the larger feedback loop of a culture full of gaudy contradictions. The only country in the world that watches more television than we do is Japan, and you should see its snuff movies and pornographic comic books; but the Japanese are pikers compared with us when we compute per capita rates of rape and murder. Some critics in India tried to blame the recent rise in communal violence there on a state-run television series dramatizing the *Mahabharata,* but not long ago they were blaming Salman Rushdie, as in

Bangladesh they have decided to blame the writer Taslima Nasrin. No Turk I know of attributes skinhead violence to German TV. It's foolish to pretend that all behavior is mimetic, and that our only model is Spock or Brokaw. Or Mork and Mindy. Why, after so many years of *M*A*S*H*, weekly in prime time and nightly in reruns, aren't all of us out there hugging trees and morphing dolphins? Why, with so many sitcoms, aren't all of us comedians?

But nobody normal watches television the way congressmen, academics, symposiasts, and Bill McKibbens do. We are less thrilling. For instance:

On March 3, 1993, a Wednesday, midway through the nine-week run of *Homicide* on NBC, in an episode written by Tom Fontana and directed by Martin Campbell, Baltimore detectives Bayliss (Kyle Secor) and Pembleton (Andre Braugher) had 12 hours to wring a confession out of "Arab" Tucker (Moses Gunn) for the strangulation and disemboweling of an 11-year-old girl. In the dirty light and appalling intimacy of a single claustrophobic room, with a whoosh of wind sound like some dread blowing in from empty Gobi spaces, among maps, library books, diaries, junk food, pornographic crime-scene photographs, and a single black overflowing ashtray, these three men seemed as nervous as the hand-held cameras—as if their black coffee were full of jumping beans, amphetamines, and spiders; as if God himself were jerking them around.

Well, you may think the culture doesn't really need another cop show. And, personally, I'd prefer a weekly series in which social problems are solved through creative nonviolence, after a Quaker meeting, by a collective of vegetarian carpenters. But in a single hour, for which Tom Fontana eventually won an Emmy, I learned more about the behavior of fearful men in small rooms than from any number of better-known movies, plays, and novels on the topic by the likes of Don DeLillo, Mary McCarthy, Alberto Moravia, Heinrich Böll, and Doris Lessing.

This, of course, was an accident, as it usually is when those of us who watch television like normal people are startled in our expectations. We leave home expecting, for a lot of money, to be exalted, and almost never are. But staying put, slumped in an agnosticism about sentience itself, suspecting that our cable box is just another bad-faith credit card enabling us to multiply our opportunities for disappointment, we are ambushed in our lethargy. And not so much by "event" television, like Ingmar Bergman's *Scenes from a Marriage*, originally a six-hour miniseries for Swedish television; or Marcel Ophuls' *The Sorrow and the Pity*, originally conceived for French television; or Rainer Werner Fassbinder's *Berlin Alexanderplatz*, commissioned by German television; or *The Singing Detective*; or *The Jewel in the Crown*. On the contrary, we've stayed home on certain nights to watch television, the way on other nights we'll go out to a neighborhood restaurant, as if on Mondays we ordered in for laughs, as on Fridays we'd rather eat Italian. We go to television—message center, mission control, Big Neighbor, electronic Elmer's glue-all—to look at Oscars, Super Bowls, moon shots, Watergates, Pearlygates, ayatollahs, dead Kings, dead Kennedys; and also, perhaps, to experience some "virtual" community as a nation. But we also go because we are hungry, angry, lonely, or tired, and television is always there for us, a 24-hour user-friendly magic box grinding out narrative, novelty, and distraction, news and laughs, snippets of high culture, remedial seriousness and vulgar celebrity, an incitement and a sedative, a place to celebrate and a place to mourn, a circus and a wishing well.

And suddenly Napoleon shows up, like a popsicle, on *Northern Exposure*, while Chris on the radio is reading Proust. Or Roseanne is about lesbianism instead of bowling. Or *Picket Fences* has moved on, from serial bathers and elephant abuse to euthanasia and gay-bashing.

Kurt Vonnegut on Showtime! David ("Masturbation") Mamet on TNT! Norman Mailer wrote the TV screenplay for *The Executioner's Song*, and Gore Vidal gave us *Lincoln* with Mary Tyler Moore as Mary Todd. In just the past five years, if I hadn't been watching television, I'd have missed *Tanner '88*, when Robert Altman and Garry Trudeau ran Michael Murphy for president of the United States; *My Name Is Bill W.*, with James Woods as the founding father of Alcoholics Anonymous; *The Final Days*, with Theodore Bikel as Henry Kissinger; *No Place Like Home*, where there wasn't one for Christine Lahti and Jeff Daniels, as there hadn't been for Jane Fonda in *The Dollmaker* and Mare Winningham in *God Bless the Child*; *Eyes on the Prize*, a home movie in two parts about America's second civil war; *The Last Best Year*, with Mary Tyler Moore and Bernadette Peters learning to live with their gay sons and HIV; *Separate but Equal*, with Sidney Poitier as Thurgood Marshall; and *High Crimes and Misdemeanors*, the Bill Moyers special on Irangate and the scandal of our intelligence agencies; Graham Greene, John Updike, Philip Roth, Gloria Naylor, Arthur Miller, and George Eliot, plus Paul Simon and Stephen Sondheim. Not to mention—guiltiest of all our secrets—those hoots without which any popular culture would be as tedious as a John Cage or an Anaïs Nin, like Elizabeth Taylor in *Sweet Bird of Youth* and the Redgrave sisters in a remake of *Whatever Happened to Baby Jane?*

What all this television has in common is narrative. Even network news—which used to be better than most newspapers before the bean counters started closing down overseas bureaus and the red camera lights went out all over Europe and Asia and Africa—is in the story-telling business. And so far no one in Congress has suggested banning narrative.

Because I watch all those despised network TV movies, I know more about racism, ecology, homelessness, gun control, child abuse, gender confusion, date rape, and AIDS than is dreamt of by, say, Katie Roiphe, the Joyce Maynard of Generation X, or than Hollywood has ever bothered to tell me, especially about AIDS. Imagine, Jonathan Demme's *Philadelphia* opened in theaters around the country well after at least a dozen TV movies on AIDS that I can remember without troubling my hard disk. And I've learned something else, too:

We were a violent culture before television, from Wounded Knee to the lynching bee, and we'll be one after all our children have disappeared by video game into the pixels of cyberspace. Before television, we blamed public schools for what went wrong with the Little People back when classrooms weren't overcrowded in buildings that weren't falling down in neighborhoods that didn't resemble Beirut, and whose fault is that? *The A-Team?* We can't control guns, or drugs, and each year two million American women are assaulted by their male partners, who are usually in an alcoholic rage, and whose fault is that? *Miami Vice?* The gangs that menace our streets aren't home watching Cinemax, and neither are the sociopaths who make bonfires, in our parks, from our homeless, of whom there are at least a million, a supply-side migratory tide of the deindustrialized and dispossessed, of angry beggars, refugee children, and catatonic nomads, none of them traumatized by *Twin Peaks.* So cut Medicare, kick around the Brady Bill, and animadvert Amy Fisher movies. But children who are loved and protected long enough to grow up to have homes and respect and lucky enough to have jobs don't riot in the streets. Ours is a tantrum culture that measures everyone by his or her ability to produce wealth, and morally condemns anybody who fails to prosper, and now blames Burbank for its angry incoherence. Why not recessive genes, angry gods, lousy weather? The mafia, the zodiac, the *Protocols of the Elders of Zion?* Probability theory, demonic possession, Original Sin? George Steinbrenner? Sunspots?

FIDDLING WHILE AFRICA STARVES

P. J. O'Rourke

This excerpt is taken from O'Rourke's 1992 book Give War a Chance.

When the "We Are the World" video first slithered into public view, I was sitting around with a friend who himself happens to be in show business. The thing gave him the willies. Me too. But neither of us could figure exactly why. "Whenever you see people that pleased with themselves on a stage," said my friend, "you know you're in for a bad show." And the USA for Africa performers did have that self-satisfied look of toddlers on a pot. But in this world of behemoth evils, such a minor lapse of taste shouldn't have upset us. We changed the channel.

Half a year later, in the middle of the Live Aid broadcast, my friend called me. "Turn on your television," he said. "This is horrible. They're in a frenzy."

"Well," I said, "at least it's a frenzy of charity."

"Oh, no," he said, "it could be *anything.* Next time it might be 'Kill the Jews.'"

A mob, even an eleemosynary mob, is an ugly thing to see. No good ever came of mass emotion. The audience that's easily moved to tears is as easily moved to sadistic dementia. People are not thinking under such circumstances. And poor, dreadful Africa is something which surely needs thought.

The Band Aid, Live Aid, USA for Africa concerts and records (and videos, posters, T-shirts, lunch buckets, thermos bottles, bath toys, etc.) are supposed to illuminate the plight of the Africans. Note the insights provided by these lyrics:

> We are the world [solipsism], we are the children [average age near forty]
> We are the ones to make a brighter day [unproven]
> So let's start giving [logical inference supplied without argument]
> There's a choice we're making [true as far as it goes]
> We're saving our own lives [absurd]
> It's true we'll make a better day [see line 2 above]
> Just you and me [statistically unlikely]

That's three palpable untruths, two dubious assertions, nine uses of a first-person pronoun, not a single reference to trouble or anybody in it and no facts. The verse contains, literally, neither rhyme nor reason.

And these musical riots of philanthropy address themselves to the wrong problems. There is, of course, a shortage of food among Africans, but that doesn't mean there's a shortage of food *in* Africa. "A huge backlog of emergency grain has built up at the Red Sea port of Assab," says the *Christian Science Monitor*. "Food sits rotting in Ethiopia," reads a headline in the *St. Louis Post-Dispatch*. And according to hunger maven William Shawcross, 200,000 tons of food aid delivered to Ethiopia is being held in storage by the country's government.

There's also, of course, a lack of transport for that food. But that's not the real problem either. The authorities in Addis Ababa have plenty of trucks for their military operations against the Eritrean rebels, and much of the rest of Ethiopia's haulage is being used for forcibly resettling people instead of feeding them. Western governments are reluctant to send more trucks, for fear they'll be used the same way. And similar behavior can be seen in the rest of miserable Africa.

The African relief fad serves to distract attention from the real issues. There is famine in Ethiopia, Chad, Sudan and areas of Mozambique. All these countries are involved in pointless civil wars. There are pockets of famine in Mauritania, Niger and Mali—the result of desertification caused mostly by idiot agricultural policies. African famine is not a visitation of fate. It is largely man-made, and the men who made it are largely Africans.

Enormous irrigation projects have been put onto lands that cannot support them and into cultures that cannot use them. Feeble-witted nationalism puts borders in the way of nomadic peoples who used to pick up and move when things got dry, Rural poverty drives populations to African cities where governments keep food prices artificially low, thus increasing rural poverty. Bumbling and corrupt central planning stymies farm production. And the hideous regimes use hunger as a weapon to suppress rebellion. People are not just starving. They are *being* starved.

"Socialist" ideals infest Africa like malaria or dengue fever. African leaders, lost in the frippery of centrist thinking, fail to deal with market forces or any other natural phenomena. Leave it to a Marxist to see the world as the world is not. It's not unusual for African intellectuals to receive their education at such august bodies of learning as Patrice Lumumba U. in Moscow. That is, they are trained by a nation which intentionally starved millions of its citizens in order to collectivize farming.

Death is the result of bad politics. And the Aid concerts are examples of the bad logic that leads to bad politics. It's probably not going too far to say that Africa's problems have been produced by the same kind of dim, ignorant thinking found among American pop artists. "If we take, say, six months and not spend any money on nuclear weapons, and just spend it on food, I think we could make a big dent," says Waylon Jennings in the USA for Africa publicity packet. In fact, a small nuclear weapon placed directly under Haile Mariam Mengistu and his pals would probably make a more beneficial dent than a whole U.S. defense budget worth of canned goods.

Anyway, money is not going to solve the problem. Yet the concert nonsense is all put strictly in terms of cash. Perhaps it is the only thing the idiot famous understand.

Getting people to give vast amounts of money when there's no firm idea what that money will do is like throwing maidens down a well. It's an appeal to magic. And the results are likely to be as stupid and disappointing as the results of magic usually are.

But, say some, Live Aid sets a good example for today's selfish youth, reminding them to be socially concerned. Nonsense. The circus atmosphere of the Live Aid concerts makes the world's problems seem easy and fun to solve and implies that the solutions are naturally uncontroversial. As an example of charity, Live Aid couldn't be worse. Charity entails sacrifice. Yet the Live Aid performers are sacrificing nothing. Indeed, they're gaining public adulation and a thoroughly unmerited good opinion of themselves. Plus it's free advertising. These LPs, performances and multiform by-products have nothing in common with charity. Instead they levy a sort of regressive alms tax on the befuddled millions. The performers donate their time, which is wholly worthless. Big corporations donate their services, which are worth little enough. Then the poor audience pledges all the contributions and buys all the trash with money it can ill afford. The worst nineteenth-century robber barons wouldn't have had the cheek to put forward such a bunco scheme. They may have given away tainted money, but at least they didn't ask you to give away yours.

One more thing, the music's lousy. If we must save the world with a song, what's the matter with the Metropolitan Opera Company?

Rock and roll's dopey crusade against African hunger has, I posit, added to the stock of human misery. And not just audibly. Any religious person—whether he worships at a pile of gazelle bones or in the Cathedral of St. Paul—will tell you egotism is the source of sin. The lust for power that destroys the benighted Ethiope has the same fountainhead as the lust for fame that propels the lousy pop band. "Not every one that saith unto me, Lord, Lord, shall enter into the kingdom of heaven." Let alone everyone that saith sha la la la la and doobie doobie do.

HOW WE LISTEN TO MUSIC
■

Aaron Copland

This piece, originally entitled "Listening To Music," is from Copland's 1957 book What To Listen For In Music.

We all listen to music according to our separate capacities. But, for the sake of analysis, the whole listening process may become clearer if we break it up into its component parts, so to speak. In a certain sense we all listen to music on three separate planes. For lack of a better terminology, one might name these: (1) the sensuous plane, (2) the expressive plane, (3) the sheerly musical plane. The only advantage to be gained from mechanically splitting up the listening process into these hypothetical planes is the clearer view to be had of the way in which we listen.

The simplest way of listening to music is to listen for the sheer pleasure of the musical sound itself. That is the sensuous plane. It is the plane on which we hear music without thinking, without considering it in any way. One turns on the radio while doing something else and absent-mindedly bathes in the sound. A kind of brainless but attractive state of mind is engendered by the mere sound appeal of the music.

You may be sitting in a room reading this book. Imagine one note struck on the piano. Immediately that one note is enough to change the atmosphere of the room—providing that the sound element in music is a powerful and mysterious agent, which it would be foolish to deride or belittle.

The surprising thing is that many people who consider themselves qualified music lovers abuse that plane in listening. They go to concerts in order to lose themselves. They use music as a consolation or an escape. They enter an ideal world where one doesn't have to think of the realities of everyday life. Of course they aren't thinking about the music either. Music allows them to leave it, and they go off to a place to dream, dreaming because of and apropos of the music yet never quite listening to it.

Yes, the sound appeal of music is a potent and primitive force, but you must not allow it to usurp a disproportionate share of your interest. The sensuous plane is an important one in music, a very important one, but it does not constitute the whole story.

There is no need to digress further on the sensuous plane. Its appeal to every normal human being is self-evident. There is, however, such a thing as becoming more sensitive to the different kinds of sound stuff as used by various composers. For all composers do not use that sound stuff in the same way. Don't get the idea that the value of music is commensurate with its sensuous appeal or that the loveliest sounding music is made by the greatest composer. If that were so, Ravel would be a greater creator than Beethoven. The point is that the sound element varies with each composer, that his usage of sound forms an integral part of his style and must be taken into account when listening. The reader can see, therefore, that a more conscious approach is valuable even on this primary plane of music listening.

The second plane on which music exists is what I have called the expressive one. Here, immediately, we tread on controversial ground. Composers have a way of shying away from any discussion of music's expressive side. Did not Stravinsky himself proclaim that his music was an "object," a "thing," with a life of its own, and with no other meaning than its own purely musical existence? This intransigent attitude of Stravinsky's may be due to the fact that so many people have tried to read different meanings into so many pieces. Heaven knows it is difficult enough to say precisely what it is that a piece of music means, to say it definitely, to say it finally so that everyone is satisfied with your explanation. But that should not lead one to the other extreme of denying to music the right to be "expressive."

My own belief is that all music has an expressive power, some more and some less, but that all music has a certain meaning behind the notes and that the meaning behind the notes constitutes, after all, what the piece is saying, what the piece is about. The whole problem can be stated quite simply by asking, "Is there a meaning to music?" My answer to that would be, "Yes." And "Can you state in so many words what the meaning is?" My answer to that would be, "No." Therein lies the difficulty.

Simple-minded souls will never be satisfied with the answer to the second of these questions. They always want music to have a meaning, and the more concrete it is the better they like it. The more the music reminds them of a train, a storm, a funeral, or any other familiar conception the more expressive it appears to be to them. This popular idea of music's meaning—stimulated and abetted by the usual run of musical commentator—should be discouraged wherever and whenever it is met. One timid lady once confessed to me that she suspected something seriously lacking in her appreciation of music because of her inability to connect it with anything definite. That is getting the whole thing backward, of course.

Still, the question remains, How close should the intelligent music lover wish to come to pinning a definite meaning to any particular work? No closer than a general concept, I should say. Music expresses, at different moments, serenity or exuberance, regrets or triumph, fury or delight. It expresses each of these moods, and many others, in a numberless variety of subtle shadings and differences. It may even express a state of meaning for which there exists no adequate word in any language. In that case, musicians often like to say that it has only a purely musical meaning. They sometimes go further and say that *all* music has only a purely musical meaning. What they really mean is that no appropriate word can be found to express the music's meaning and that, even if it could, they do not feel the need of finding it.

But whatever the professional musician may hold, most musical novices still search for specific words with which to pin down their musical reactions. That is why they always find Tschaikovsky easier to "understand" than Beethoven. In the first place, it is easier to pin a meaning-word on a Tschaikovsky piece than on a Beethoven one. Much easier. Moreover, with the Russian composer, every time you come back to a piece of his it almost always says the same thing to you, whereas with Beethoven it is often quite difficult to put your finger right on what he is saying. And any musician will tell you that that is why Beethoven is the greater composer. Because music which always says the same thing to you will necessarily soon become dull music, but music whose meaning is slightly different with each hearing has a greater chance of remaining alive.

Listen, if you can, to the forty-eight fugue themes of Bach's *Well Tempered Clavichord*. Listen to each theme, one after another. You will soon realize that each theme mirrors a different world of feeling. You will also soon realize that the more beautiful a theme seems to you the harder it is to find any word that will describe it to your complete satisfaction. Yes, you will certainly know whether it is a gay theme or a sad one. You will be able, in other words, in your own mind, to draw a frame of emotional feeling around your theme. Now study the sad one a little closer. Try to pin down the exact quality of its sadness. Is it pessimistically sad or resignedly sad; is it fatefully sad or smilingly sad?

Let us suppose that you are fortunate and can describe to your own satisfaction in so many words the exact meaning of your chosen theme. There is still no guarantee that anyone else will be satisfied. Nor need they be. The important thing is that each one feel for himself the specific expressive quality of a theme or, similarly, an entire piece of music. And if it is a great work of art, don't expect it to mean exactly the same thing to you each time you return to it.

Themes or pieces need not express only one emotion, of course. Take such a theme as the first main one of the *Ninth Symphony*, for example. It is clearly made up of different elements. It does not say only one thing. Yet anyone hearing it immediately gets a feeling of strength, a feeling of power. It isn't a power that comes simply because the theme is played loudly. It is a power inherent in the theme itself. The extraordinary strength and vigor of the theme results in the listener's receiving an impression that a forceful statement has been made. But one should never try to boil it down to "the fateful hammer of life," etc. That is where the trouble begins. The musician, in his exasperation, says it means nothing but the notes themselves, whereas the nonprofessional is only too anxious to hang on to any explanation that gives him the illusion of getting closer to the music's meaning.

Now, perhaps, the reader will know better what I mean when I say that music does have an expressive meaning but that we cannot say in so many words what that meaning is.

The third plane on which music exists is the sheerly musical plane. Besides the pleasurable sound of music and the expressive feeling that it gives off, music does exist in terms of the notes themselves and of their manipulation. Most listeners are not sufficiently conscious of this third plane. . . .

Professional musicians, on the other hand, are, if anything, too conscious of the mere notes themselves. They often fall into the error of becoming so engrossed with their arpeggios and staccatos that they forget the deeper aspects of the music they are performing. But from the layman's standpoint, it is not so much a matter of getting over bad habits on the sheerly musical plane as of increasing one's awareness of what is going on, in so far as the notes are concerned.

When the man in the street listens to the "notes themselves" with any degree of concentration, he is most likely to make some mention of the melody. Either he hears a pretty melody or he does not, and he generally lets it go at that. Rhythm is likely to gain his attention next, particularly if it seems exciting. But harmony and tone color are generally taken for granted, if they are thought of consciously at all. As for music's having a definite form of some kind, that idea seems never to have occurred to him.

It is very important for all of us to become more alive to music on its sheerly musical plane. After all, an actual musical material is being used. The intelligent listener must be prepared to increase his awareness of the musical material and what happens to it. He must hear the melodies, the rhythms, the harmonies, the tone colors in a more conscious fashion. But above all he must, in order to follow the line of the composer's thought, know something of the principles of musical form. Listening to all of these elements is listening on the sheerly musical plane.

Let me repeat that I have split up mechanically the three separate planes on which we listen merely for the sake of greater clarity. Actually, we never listen on one or the other of these planes. What we do is to correlate them—listening in all three ways at the same time. It takes no mental effort, for we do it instinctively.

Perhaps an analogy with what happens to us when we visit the theater will make this instinctive correlation clearer. In the theater, you are aware of the actors and actresses, costumes and sets, sounds and movements. All these give one the sense that the theater is a pleasant place to be in. They constitute the sensuous plane in our theatrical reactions.

The expressive plane in the theater would be derived from the feeling that you get from what is happening on the stage. You are moved to pity, excitement, or gayety. It is this general feeling, generated aside from the particular words being spoken, a certain emotional something which exists on the stage, that is analogous to the expressive quality in music.

The plot and plot development is equivalent to our sheerly musical plane. The playwright creates and develops a character in just the same way that a composer creates and develops a theme. According to the degree of your awareness of the way in which the artist in either field handles his material you will become a more intelligent listener.

It is easy enough to see that the theatergoer never is conscious of any of these elements separately. He is aware of them all at the same time. The same is true of music listening. We simultaneously and without thinking listen on all three planes.

In a sense, the ideal listener is both inside and outside the music at the same moment, judging it and enjoying it, wishing it would go one way and watching it go another—almost like the composer at the moment he composes it; because in order to write his music, the composer must also be inside and outside his music, carried away by it and yet coldly critical of it. A subjective and objective attitude is implied in both creating and listening to music.

What the reader should strive for, then, is a more *active* kind of listening. Whether you listen to Mozart or Duke Ellington, you can deepen your understanding of music only by being a more conscious and aware listener—not someone who is just listening, but someone who is listening *for* something.

ROCK AND ROLL AS MUSIC; ROCK AND ROLL AS CULTURE

Jack Santino

This article first appeared in the July 1990 issue of The World and I *(a publication of the Washington Times Corporation).*

Here we are, in the 1990s, and rock and roll music, in some form or other, is still the dominant popular musical form in the USA, and maybe the world. Who would have thought, almost forty years ago, when Big Joe Turner, Fats Domino, and Bo Diddley began having hit records that crossed over to the white charts, that rock and roll music would become the business and cultural force that it is today? Who would have thought, when Bill Haley's "Rock Around the Clock," or Hank Ballard and the Midnighters' "Work With Me Annie" were attacked for their supposed ill effects on youth, that a similar debate would be raging almost forty years later about songs and music that evolved and developed out of their efforts?

Rock and roll was seen as a menace to society by many in the fifties. Much of the reaction to the early crossover and cover hits was overtly racist. When a song intended for one market, such as blacks, becomes popular with another market, such as whites, it is called a crossover hit. When a song that has been recorded by one artist, for example, Little Richard, is recorded by another—for instance, Pat Boone—the re-recording is called a cover record. There were crossovers and covers of country and western material, but most of the early rock and roll crossovers did in fact go from the "race" or rhythm and blues charts to the pop charts. This meant an influx of black music on popular radio. Likewise, the cover records tended to be by whites of black artists' work. During the wave of rock and roll bashing and record smashing that began almost simultaneously with the music's sudden popularity, the very fact that much of the music was derived from black tradition was frequently raised as an issue. That the music had a beat, and that this syncopation was African American in origin, was pointed to as self-evident proof that the music was both inferior and corrupting.

On the other hand, rock and roll was also considered by many to be simply a fad, the latest in a long line of trivialities embraced by whimsical youth. This attitude continued well into the 1960s. The Beatles, for instance, were dismissed for years before it dawned on people that they were (1) not a fad, (2) important, and (3) good. It took a long time before adults figured out what the kids knew all along—rock and roll is here to stay.

The Origins of Rock and Roll

I remember seeing Elvis Presley on the *Ed Sullivan Show* in 1956. Although I was young, I knew who he was because my two older sisters had told me all about him. They were very interested in seeing him, and so was I. Watching him on television, I was fascinated by the performance and my sisters loved him, but my parents decided he was "on dope." "Look at his eyes!" my mother said, as if offering proof. Recently I was discussing Elvis with a colleague who also remembered seeing him on television for the first time. His story was identical to mine, right down to his mother's exclamation: "He must be on dope. Look at his eyes!" Actually, despite Presley's later addiction to drugs, at that time he was not "on" anything. But he managed to divide parents from children with his looks, his singing, and his stage movements. At that moment in 1956, a generation gap was created.

A similar thing happened in 1964, when the Beatles performed on the *Ed Sullivan Show.* Kids loved them and parents hated them—both their music and their appearance. In 1982, however, when Michael Jackson achieved a similar kind of superfame, also after national exposure on television, many parents took their children to see him on the Jacksons' Victory Tour. They viewed Jackson as the functional equivalent of the Elvis or the Beatles they remembered and cherished in their own youth and wanted to give their children the opportunity to see this generation's rock hero live. In fact, this is one of the reasons Michael Jackson declined in popularity rather quickly—too many parents liked him. Along with overexposure and his well-publicized idiosyncracies, Jackson was immediately cast into a "good boy" role, as Elvis and the Beatles had been before him, thus clearing the way for such "bad boy" artists as Jerry Lee Lewis, the Rolling Stories, and Prince.

ROCK AND ROLL'S EVOLVING AUDIENCE

We live in a rock and roll culture. Since the 1950s, generations have grown up with the music—and to some extent it has grown up with them— while new artists and new styles continue to emerge. A generation gap still exists, however, although somewhat narrowed. Young people today may enjoy musicians who were popular before they were born, such as Chuck Berry, but how many parents today who grew up with fifties and sixties rock music enjoy Prince, or Bon Jovi, or the Dead Milkmen? "Rock and roll" means different things to people, depending on, among other things, how old they are, and although a great many adults consider themselves rock fans, they have difficulty in understanding, much less appreciating, the music that their kids enjoy.

I teach popular music, from a sociocultural as well as an aesthetic perspective, in the nation's only academic Department of Popular Culture, at Bowling Green State University in Bowling Green, Ohio. I believe that the best teaching involves learning on the part of both the students and the instructor, and this is certainly true in my case. Through my teaching I am continually exposed to the various tastes and perceptions of the current generation of college students. From them, I find out not merely who is currently popular, who they like and dislike and why, but also how they view the artists of the past in the light of their own experiences. For instance, during the sixties, the Monkees were viewed as a "plastic" band, consisting of nonmusician actors hired by a corporate entrepreneur (Don Kirshner) to play the roles of imitation Beatles, singing songs written for them by professional songwriters. Although they sold a lot of records, the counterculture hated them. Today, the issues of authenticity and sincerity I alluded to above simply are not relevant to the audience that hears, buys, and enjoys listening to the Monkees' records. Most of my students see no difference whatsoever between the Beatles and the Monkees, while many consumers in the sixties viewed the two bands as polar opposites. Moreover, this example points to another fact: The audience for popular music is diversified. The so-called counterculture may have despised the Monkees, but somebody liked them. They had the best selling album of 1966, along with several No. 1 singles.

If we accept the fact that there is such diversity in the tastes of the consumers of rock and roll music, we must then realize that the term is frequently used in a general way to encompass a great number of musical styles, both black and white. This is how I am using it. With this in mind, I would say that despite the fact that their view of the rock/pop music is different from mine, my students and I share a rock and roll culture.

Rock music (I am using the terms rock and roll and rock interchange-ably, although not everyone does) is one of the distinctive features of post-war life, along with television, the Cold War, space travel, and the atomic bomb. For instance, I can expect that everyone in my classroom will be fa-miliar with most of the more popular songs of Elvis Presley, Chuck Berry, or Buddy Holly. They hear them on the radio and on television, they are used in commercials, they are covered by later artists—in short, it is diffi-cult to be alive in America and not know these songs. The same thing is true for popular sixties music, especially the Beatles, the Beach Boys, and Detroit's Motown artists such as the Supremes, the Four Tops, and the Temptations.

However, if I play songs that were popular a year or two preceding the first nationally popular rock hits, or if I drop back to the forties and play something from the Big Band era, these college-age young people are to-tally unfamiliar with the material, no matter how popular it was in its day. Neither do they know much about other genres, such as blues or country. This is not to say, however, that within the apparently limited category of "rock" that there is not a wide variety of musical styles avail-able to them. Often, these styles give rise to specific subcultures which have their own dress code and concomitant values, such as the punks.

INTERWEAVING AND EVOLVING STYLES

This has always been the case. In his important and influential work *The Sound of the City*, Charlie Gillett says that when the music we call rock and roll achieved national popularity in the mid-fifties, it actually included five distinct regional styles: Memphis rockabilly (Elvis, Carl Perkins, Jerry Lee Lewis), Chicago rhythm and blues (Bo Diddley, Chuck Berry), New Orleans piano boogie (Fats Domino, Little Richard), the group har-mony singing known as doo-wop, centered in New York but found in other urban areas as well (the Platters, the Moonglows, the Penguins), and Northern band rock and roll (Bill Haley and the Comets, from Chester, Pennsylvania). While one may question the specific number of styles Gillett identifies or argue for the inclusion of other styles as well, the principle is a sound one. Different styles of music, derived from blues, country, and gospel—often tied to a geographical region and sometimes to ethnicity as well—all became identified as rock and roll largely be-cause they shared an emphasis on a beat that was appealing to a genera-tion of young people.

Since then, we have seen styles come and go, some to return again, oth-ers to wield an influence on later music. If rock is, generally speaking, a synthesis of rhythm and blues (i.e., black) music and country and western (i.e., white) music, and I believe it is, the music that resulted was the be-ginning, not the end, of a dynamic process. For instance, an interest in American blues inspired young, white British musicians to form bands such as the Rolling Stones and Cream. Their music led in turn to the de-velopment of heavy metal music in the 1970s through such blues-based

British bands as Led Zeppelin. And heavy metal itself has changed greatly and spun new subgenres in the past twenty years: speed metal, glam metal, bubblegum metal, and so forth. England's Beatles, who were heavily influenced by Americans such as Buddy Holly and the Everly Brothers, went on to influence virtually every rock act in the world, including the early art-rockers, who also contributed to the rise of heavy metal. New styles are created out of the syntheses of the old, but these new styles became the raw materials for further developments.

There are and have been so many styles of rock or rock-derived music in the past thirty years that I could not exhaustively list them all in the space of this article, let alone describe, define, or discuss each of them. A partial list would include surf music, girl-group, Merseybeat, California country rock, psychedelic, punk, new wave, doo-wop, Motown, soul, funk, rap, disco, industrial, and synth-pop. Each has its audience, though neither the audiences nor the musical styles are mutually exclusive. For many adolescents, music becomes a basis of personal and group identity. The music is something they can relate to and feel is their own; they signal their taste by their dress, their hair styles, perhaps even the words they use. They associate with others who share their tastes and, implicitly, their values. Many such subcultures have formed around musical styles over the years. Rockabilly musicians in Memphis were "cats." In the sixties rock had unprecedented influence, giving rise to the hippie life-style. Rock in Britain became associated with Teddy Boys, mods, rockers, and, later, punks. Often, these rock subcultures are shocking and threatening to the rest of us, because the symbols that are used to identify one as a member are loaded with antisocial or rebellions meaning: motorcycle jackets, shoulder-length hair on men, spiked bracelets, and razor blades.

However, we should be aware that the members of these subgroups— the people wearing such things—have redefined these symbols in their own terms and are usually not the threats they appear to be. Wearing forbidden items, breaking the rules for acceptable public appearance, helps define the group in many ways. Of course, it helps individuals identify each other as having reasonably similar tastes, but it also defines an in-group/out-group dichotomy, an " us against them" outlook. The choice of sacrilegious and taboo paraphernalia, such as crucifixes or swastikas, brings forth the wrath of outsiders and helps the kids perpetuate in their own mind their sense that they are both prejudged and misunderstood by adults.

ROCK AND ROLL AS BIG BUSINESS

Rock and roll is a way of life; certainly it is music, but it is also big business. Selling records, compact discs, tapes, and concert appearances is at the center of a multi-billion-dollar international industry. The success of a popular musician depends as much on monetary backing, good publicity, and sharp business agents as it does on talent. Creating an image is an all-important part of the process. The leather-jacketed Beatles, for instance, were cleaned up and put into suits by their manager, Brian Epstein, to help them achieve commercial success. Ironically, their being marketed as cheeky but cute and cuddly British boys led to the self-conscious image-mongering of the Rolling Stones as unkempt ruffians.

Today, the music video has become a major marketing tool which has intensified the importance of visual image, often at the expense of the musicianship. Legend has it that Fabian was discovered sitting on the front step of his Philadelphia row house. His dark good looks appealed to the "talent scouts," but when the sixteen-year-old Fabian Forte explained that he could not sing, he was assured that this was not a problem. More recently, certain bands such as Duran Duran are said to be the contemporary versions of essentially the same process. They are routinely described as having been created by and for videos.

Such assessment may not be fair. Most popular musicians are groomed for a mass audience; not all make it. Artists who create music aimed at the widest possible market are not necessarily poor musicians. I have noticed that my students feel that artists have "sold out" when they achieve great popularity, for example, artists such as Bruce Springsteen and such former college favorites as Genesis and U2. The question really has to do with the extent to which an artist is willing to change in order to achieve this popularity, and whether the artist considers this change morally or aesthetically compromising. Forgotten in such judgments is the fact that rock music is indeed an industry whose first concern is making money, and that most if not all popular recording artists hope to appeal to a broad audience and, yes, make a lot of money. Sociologist Simon Frith sees this as a central contradiction in rock and roll music: It is and always has been an outlaw form, rebellious, renegade, at odds with authority. On the other hand, it is very much a part of the Establishment it apparently rejects: It is a commercial endeavor that generates fortunes for large corporations. Thus, Frith feels that the image of rock as an outlaw form is illusory, designed to add to its mystique and help sell more units. Nevertheless, rock's most enduring artists are unquestionably talented musicians.

THE CULTURAL IMPACT OF ROCK AND ROLL

Beyond all of this, however, is the question of rock as a social force. As a genre that breaks social rules, rock remains true to itself and appealing to its mostly younger audience specifically by stirring up controversy and angering adults. The kids' aesthetics are the reverse of the adults': the more tasteless and shocking the better. As a product of big business, however, rock is scrutinized for songs and lyrics that might tarnish the corporations' image or offend consumers, or rather, consumers' parents. Despite such well-publicized philanthropic and humanitarian efforts such as the Live-Aid concert or the song "We Are the World," both of which raised money for famine-plagued Ethiopia, rock music is seen as a threat to the young, and to society in general. Satanic imagery, references to violence, rape, drugs, and sex, along with provocatively explicit music videos, frighten the very parents who grew up with rock in the fifties and sixties. The current situation is different, they say, more extreme, more vile, and I have no doubt that it is. However, my students have taught me that the situation is more complex than it seems.

Often songs are judged out of the context of the entire album in which the kids will usually hear them. The Rolling Stones' "Under Cover of the Night" has been cited for its violence; my students answer that if you listen to the entire 1983 album *Undercover*, although the song showcases violence, the entire album is actually antiviolent. Likewise, some songs that are about suicide are not necessarily promoting it but rather attempting to demonstrate the futility of it. Nevertheless, many people feel that these songs (and others with less redeeming social qualities) contribute to the proliferation of society's evils. Companies have responded by initiating a labeling system that cautions consumers about potentially offensive material contained in the recordings. Opponents maintain this is censorship and a curtailment of free speech. From practical experience I can say that the labels in actuality do little to prevent the sale of these recordings to minors, but proponents of the system feel it is a necessary step, and that the free speech issue is outweighed by social urgency.

What is the effect of music—or any other popular medium, such as television or movies—on its audience? No one really knows. It has not been systematically measured and it may be immeasurable. One thing we do know: It depends on the person listening. There are a great many other factors involved as well, such as which specific music are we talking about, under what conditions is it being listened to, and in what situation? A youngster may be more vulnerable to suggestion at certain times, such as after the death of a parent, for instance, than at others. Lawsuits have been brought against singers such as Ozzy Osbourne by parents who feel that his work influenced—in fact, caused—their child to commit suicide. Under such circumstances, parents are distraught and feel understandably passionate about the issue. I am not a fan of Ozzy Osbourne's, and I believe that artists do have a responsibility to consider the effects of their work on their young audience, but it is hard to believe that a child could be driven to such an extreme act by a single piece of music unless there were many other problems already involved. I am not a psychologist, but it occurs to me that a teenager who spends a great deal of time listening to death-oriented music may in fact be asking for help. A fascination with this kind of material may be symptomatic of a deeper problem, one that parents should address before things get to the point of irrevocable tragedy.

It is too easy to blame rock stars for the existence of troubled teenagers. Millions of young people listen to the same records without killing themselves or committing crimes against others. I think we have to consider the personality of the listener as the primary rather than the secondary factor. People seek out music that reinforces their own attitudes and moods; they bring themselves to the music. Charles Manson heard the Beatles' "Helter Skelter" as a call for mass murder, but the rest of us did not.

Furthermore, we need to look closely at the great variety of material that is routinely lumped together in discussions of rock lyrics. There are many different genres, styles, and songs involved, and they may not all be of the same order. Is a song about masturbation to be treated the same as a song that urges its audience to kill? How much of the negative reaction to some of this material has to do with personal morality or individual political points of view? People have defended the use of Satanic imagery to me as simply an artistic use of mythological symbolism, and they frequently point to Milton's *Paradise Lost* as the epitome of an artistic use of the story of Satan. Indeed, Milton portrays Satan sympathetically. Are we to deny Milton the use of the Bible for poetic purposes? Should we take Milton off the library shelves? Many of the people who want to curtail such symbolism believe in the literal, biblical truth of Satan, and see any reference to him as evil. However, not everyone in the United States shares this belief. Are we then dealing with constitutional issues of religious freedom?

It seems obvious that people have a right to write and sing what they want. But parents also have a right and a duty to monitor their children's entertainments. To the extent that rock remains a music of the young, we find a clash of two principles: the artists' right to free expression versus the parents' right to raise their children as they see fit. However, it is important to remind ourselves that rock stars are no longer exclusively in their teens and twenties. A forty-year-old Bruce Springsteen might well write about sex, as poets have always done. It would be unrealistic to expect him not to. In the past, rock performers were themselves young, and this is still true to a large extent, but as the decades have passed, both the audience and the musicians have aged. Last year (1989) saw tours by the Who, the Jefferson Airplane, the Kinks, the Rolling Stones, Bob Dylan, Ringo Starr, and Paul McCartney, all veterans of the sixties. Certainly there are younger musicians playing today, but the point is that these adult musicians cannot be expected to write or sing about teenage concerns.

Furthermore, such things as suicide, drugs, sex, and violence *are* teenage concerns. While artists have a responsibility not to glamorize them, that does not mean these themes should not be explored. Rock songs often work as fantasy explorations of situations that a young person has confronted or at least can imagine confronting. A teenager imagines him or herself into the song, explores it, but does not necessarily live it. Adolescence is a time of identity formation, when peer-group pressure is very powerful, and when one explores any number of alternative identities:

Today, I am a vegetarian, deeply concerned about world ecology; tomorrow I wear leather and chains. Rock music is a part of this testing out of identities, of ideas. It is a fictive form, and it may in fact *help* young people gain a sense of their identity.

Moreover, rock does not exist in a vacuum. It is not the only popular entertainment that has grown more violent and more sexually explicit in recent years. Compare the slasher films of today with the horror films of the sixties or fifties. Even a superheroic movie such as *Robocop*, whose audience would obviously contain a great many children, came very close to receiving an X-rating for violence. Language restrictions have loosened in film and television, and popular television shows are certainly much more explicit than ever before. Comic books are undergoing a similar controversy, due again to their traditional appeal to youngsters. Today's comics are often labeled "Intended For Mature Audiences," and feature the same range of subjects and themes as described above for rock. Creators say that comics are a medium like any other, and that they are free to produce what they want, for readers of all age groups, while others feel that comics are and will always be for kids, and therefore should not contain certain materials under any circumstances. My point is that, in the midst of all this opening up across all the popular media, why should anyone expect that rock music would not reflect the same changes? Is it any more exploitative when rock deals with these themes than television shows such as, say, *Dynasty*, or *Geraldo?* Songs may in fact be written about gang rape, and I find these reprehensible, but I find the slasher films reprehensible also. Rock music is a part of society. It should not be singled out as the single effective agent of change within society.

REDEEMING QUALITIES

Rock also has its positive side, seldom addressed in this debate. Beyond such altruistic efforts as the above-mentioned Live-Aid concert, or Quake-Aid, held to raise money for earthquake victims in Northern California, or benefits to save the whales, or George Harrison's Concert for Bangladesh (way back in 1971), rock can be inspirational on a personal level. Most rock songs do *not* contain off-color lyrics or deal with extremely antisocial behavior. What of all the songs that celebrate fidelity, or that reject drug-taking as a way of life? The truth is, it is far more convincing for kids to bear Rolling Stone Keith Richards talk of the dangers of heroin than to hear Nancy Reagan pronounce "Just say no."

Ultimately, rock and roll is as much a creation of its audience as it is of the artists or the businessmen. Songs that deal with taboo subjects, such as Prince's "Darling Nikki" (masturbation), do not necessarily corrupt their listeners. Prince's fans are quite aware of his tendency to write explicitly about sex. He also writes frequently about God, leading some to see him as a kind of contemporary mystic, using sexual imagery to describe spiritual yearning. As I said, these issues are much more complex than the simpleminded arguments being raised on both sides suggest, and until we deal with them in all their complexity, we will continue to get nowhere. We need to hear out the young people who listen to Prince, or Madonna, or heavy metal, or rap. How do *they* perceive the music? What does it mean to them? They can tell us more about it than we can tell them. Which kids are attracted to which styles, and which musicians? While some rock and roll is nihilistic, much of it is romantic and often melodramatic. This is what has always appealed to me about it, and I think today's youth feel the same. How often do they hear something positive, something altruistic, in rock and roll? Two decades ago, Crosby, Stills, and Nash exhorted parents to "teach your children well," and also, for children, to "teach your parents well." The advice is still good. Let us learn from each other.

A BLACK FAN OF COUNTRY MUSIC FINALLY TELLS ALL

Lena Williams

This essay appeared in The New York Times *in 1994.*

I heard that Reba McEntire's new album, "Read My Mind," shot to No. 5 on the Billboard chart the first weekend of its release.

Well, she got my $11.95.

I'm a 40-something black woman who spent her youth in Washington, lip-syncing to the Supremes and slow dancing to the Temptations. Now I often come home to my Manhattan apartment and put on Vince Gill, Randy Travis or Reba. Consider me a fan of country music. So there. Deal with it.

For most of my adult life, I was a closet country music fan. I'd hide my Waylon Jennings and Willie Nelson albums between the dusty, psychedelic rock. I'd listen to Dolly Parton on my earphones, singing along softly, afraid my neighbors might mistake my imitation twang for a cry for help. I'd enter a music store, looking over my shoulder in search of familiar faces and flip through the rhythm-and-blues section for about five minutes before sneaking off to the country aisle where I'd surreptitiously grab a Travis Tritt tape off the rack and make a beeline for the shortest cashier's line.

Just when I'd reached for my American Express card, I'd spot a tall, dark, handsome type in an Armani suit standing behind me with a puzzled look. What's he going to think? "The sister seems down, but what's she doing with that Dwight Yoakum CD?"

So now I'm publicly coming out of the closet and proclaiming my affection for country perennials like Ms. McEntire.

When I told a friend I was preparing this confessional, he offered a word of caution: "No self-respecting black person would ever admit to that in public."

I thought about his comment. As a child growing up in the 1950's, in a predominantly black community, I wasn't allowed to play country-and-western music in my house. Blacks weren't supposed to like country—or classical for that matter—but that's another story. Blacks' contribution to American music was in jazz, blues and funk. Country music was dismissed as poor white folks' blues and associated with regions of the nation that symbolized prejudice and racial bigotry. Even mainstream white America viewed country as lower class and less desirable, often poking fun at its twangy chords and bellyaching sentiments.

But I was always a cowgirl at heart. I liked country's wild side; its down-home, aw-shucks musicians with the yodel in their voices and the angst in their lyrics. I saw an honesty in country and its universal tales of love lost and found. Besides, the South didn't have a monopoly on racial hatred, and country artists, like everybody else, were stealing black music, so why should I hold it against country?

And while snickering at country, white America also demonstrated a similar cultural backwardness toward black music, be it gospel, ragtime or the blues. So I allowed country to enter my heart and my mind, in spite of its faults. Indeed, when prodded, some blacks who rejected country conceded that there was a spirituality that resounded in the music and that in its heartfelt sentiment, country was a lot like blues. Yet they could never bring themselves to spend hard-earned dollars on Hank Williams Jr.

The 1980's saw country (western was dropped, much to my chagrin) become mainstream. Suddenly there was country at the Copa and at Town Hall. WYNY-FM radio in New York now claims the largest audience of any country station, with more than one million listeners. Dolly Parton and Kenny Rogers became movie stars. Garth Brooks became an American phenomenon.

Wall Street investment bankers bought cowboy boots and hats and learned to do the two-step. And black and white artists like Patti La Belle and Lyle Lovett and Natalie Cole and Ms. McEntire now sing duets and clearly admire one another's music.

Perhaps the nation's acceptance of country has something to do with an evolutionary change in the music. Country has got edge. It has acquired an attitude. Womens' voices have been given strength. Oh, the hardship and misery is still there. But the stuff about "standing by your man" has changed to a more assertive posture.

In "I Won't Stand in Line," a song on Ms. McEntire's new album, she makes it clear to a skirt-chasing lover that "I'd do almost anything just to make you mine, but I won't stand in line." That line alone makes me think of Aretha Franklin's "Respect."

One other thing: I don't like sad songs. I've cried enough for a lifetime. Country makes me laugh, always has. Maybe because it never took itself so seriously. Think about it. "Drop-Kick Me, Jesus, Through the Goal Posts of Life." "A Boy Named Sue."

Ms. McEntire serves up a humorous touch in "Why Haven't I Heard From You." "That thing they call the telephone/Now there's one on every corner, in the back of every bar/You can get one in your briefcase, on a plane or in your car/So tell me why haven't I heard from you, darlin', honey, what is your excuse?" Call it Everywoman's lament.

Well, it's off my chest, and it feels good.

I will no longer make excuses for my musical tastes. Not when millions are being made by performers exhorting listeners to "put your hands in the air and wave 'em like you just don't care."

Compare that with the haunting refrain of Ms. McEntire's "I Think His Name Was John," a song about a woman, a one-night stand and AIDS: "She lays all alone and cries herself to sleep/'Cause she let a stranger kill her hopes and her dreams/And in the end when she was barely hanging on/All she could say is she thinks his name was John."

THE DEATH OF MARILYN MONROE

■

Sharon Olds

This poem is from Olds's 1993 book Dead and the Living.

> The ambulance men touched her cold
> body, lifted it, heavy as iron,
> onto the stretcher, tried to close the
> mouth, closed the eyes, tied the
> arms to the sides, moved a caught
> strand of hair, as if it mattered,
> saw the shape of her breasts, flattened by
> gravity, under the sheet,
> carried her, as if it were she,
> down the steps.
>
> These men were never the same. They went out
> afterwards, as they always did,
> for a drink or two, but they could not meet
> each other's eyes.
>
> Their lives took
> a turn—one had nightmares, strange
> pains, impotence, depression. One did not
> like his work, his wife looked
> different, his kids. Even death

seemed different to him—a place where she
would be waiting,

And one found himself standing at night
in the doorway to a room of sleep, listening to
a woman breathing, just an ordinary
woman
breathing.

BECAUSE MY MOTHER WAS DEAF
SHE PLAYED THE PIANO

Patricia Goedicke

This poem is from Goedicke's 1996 book Invisible Horses.

Because my mother was deaf she played the piano
And golfed. Skied. Harangued the mild editors
of several newspapers. Like so many others, Hispanic
Chinese Haitian Indian Japanese
Italian mothers, in every language
obsessed, muttering angrily to themselves in parking lots
at rush hour, this particular one studied Russian

imagine, just to feel it
in her own throat, then make fun of it
embarrassed, because she was deaf
or because she was Irish, was that
bad? Ripped up the
celery. For the lamb chops, the boiled
potatoes for supper, who rang
                    the front doorbell? She'd run
Quick, into the closet,
turn the hearing aid down, tune out the loud, pithy
green kiwi fruit of the present with its too many
anxious blips, tiny beards in the salad, sure, why not

switch stations? From Marian Anderson to the great
Eleanor Roosevelt to Amy to Gertrude to Sylvia on the radio
my mother knew them all, but she liked piano best:
Bach, Mozart, Chopin and Scott Joplin too, also the Debussy
Petite Suite we'd play together
with me taking *Parte Secondo,* often after school
I'd come home and not find her, only Beethoven blasting
all over the house, then almost stumble over her
crouched, hidden behind the sofa

on all fours in front of the phonograph listening
with her whole body, she'd get right down there on the floor
on top of them, each undulating vibration, as even Beethoven
might have listened before her; first having plucked the notes
out of the upper and lower registers and then fiddled with them
so brilliantly, the remembered growl of the
bass clef or more delicate gymnastics, higher variations
he'd swing from so why not Mother?
                       She'd leap up all by herself,
flinging her tanned arms out
to Horowitz, Rubenstein, Dame Myra and Wanda,
even Art Tatum, sometimes she'd keep going
all afternoon until later, after supper
quieter. Washing the dishes, she'd wrap her cigarette tenor
gently around Billie. Judy. Or Edith Piaf or a Mexican
cradle song, slowly, with fires banked

when just that morning, in flames, she'd have been hatcheting at me
with pickaxes in the kitchen! No genteel
ladylike pecking order for her but outrage: after the scorched tendernesses
of the dutiful wife, in the fury of burned toast,
she couldn't help it, weeping and frantically shrieking
at everyone in her path, in between kisses
all her life patronized, scorned, ignored,
what else could she do?
                   In the middle of America, alone
all day in the house with nothing but yesterday's
dirty laundry. With squadrons of button-down shirts
out there soiling themselves. Dragging socks from the
churning dryer, with only the washing machine's
dull thumps for company.
                 Most body language is dumb
they kept telling her, they tried to keep her quiet
but couldn't: what they forgot
was the ground under her feet, swaying in its chains
but still rolling, even as earth turns
from multitude to multitude, so many stilled voices,
trees fallen, mountains stripped and leveled
cannot be silenced forever:
                     for all she could not hear,
daily my mother laid down her body
for me and my sister, sputtering
Your father he . . . Who cares if they . . . Go, Move, Speak Up . . .
Make your own music or get out; no pre-ordained
hand-me-down hierarchies for her
or me either, her kid
from bassinet to grave, she lives in me like a crowd
of love songs and loud static,
                   because what's missing in our lives

is not cordless. Nor any kind of bodiless
information network; what she knew was touch,
velvet keys she pressed
tenderly, with pedals lumbering, just think of it,
                     my mother and maybe yours
pounding the ivories or not, with the same pulsing
up from the guts *obbligato* that's always changing
and never, Tallulah Bankhead, your huskiness
is ours. And Mae West, and Lauren Bacall.
Hoarse, throaty. Curling inside us like smoke
but so arrogant, passionate, peppery
everyone stops to listen to you,
                  nobody can shut you up
ever, my mother and I hear you with our toenails
the minute you open your mouths: *Hi, you*
I greet you and all the rest of you,
some say it makes no difference
in the long run, who says what
or how, but the body's dark
sheet music never stops tingling,
                the ways we move are earthquakes
that won't go away: as every vibration shakes itself
into smaller and smaller fractions, as the vocal chords tremble
in sympathy with whatever lullaby
or struck tongue rouses us to wake up, step out to the beat

of the rhythm that's always there, waiting for the slightest
tap of a listening foot, ruffle of melody
in the ears, the quietest tune ribbons
all through us, which is why my mother is still waltzing
and playing the piano, from sleek suburb to farm,
from ghetto to desert city,
so what if she's gone, if the milk's long since dried up,
I'm still taking my shoes off
this spring, with the first pieces of pale grass
poking through hairless sidewalks because listen, friends,
whatever happens we're together,
              however altered
a few frogs still keep creaking,
the seas still shake with fish, the moon shrugs,
oil gushes from the mines, bread rises
against all odds: I only wish
my real mother were alive and could come too
but you'll do, you'll do.

THE ENORMOUS RADIO

John Cheever

This short story is from Cheever's 1953 collection The Enormous Radio and Other Stories.

Jim and Irene Westcott were the kind of people who seem to strike that satisfactory average of income, endeavor, and respectability that is reached by the statistical reports in college alumni bulletins. They were the parents of two young children, they had been married nine years, they lived on the twelfth floor of an apartment house near Sutton Place, they went to the theatre on an average of 10.3 times a year, and they hoped someday to live in Westchester. Irene Westcott was a pleasant, rather plain girl with soft brown hair and a wide, fine forehead upon which nothing at all had been written, and in the cold weather she wore a coat of fitch skins dyed to resemble mink. You could not say that Jim Westcott looked younger than he was, but you could at least say of him that he seemed to feel younger. He wore his graying hair cut very short, he dressed in the kind of clothes his class had worn at Andover, and his manner was earnest, vehement, and intentionally naïve. The Westcotts differed from their friends, their classmates, and their neighbors only in an interest they shared in serious music. They went to a great many concerts—although they seldom mentioned this to anyone—and they spent a good deal of time listening to music on the radio.

Their radio was an old instrument, sensitive, unpredictable, and beyond repair. Neither of them understood the mechanics of radio—or of any of the other appliances that surrounded them—and when the instrument faltered, Jim would strike the side of the cabinet with his hand. This sometimes helped. One Sunday afternoon, in the middle of a Schubert quartet, the music faded away altogether. Jim struck the cabinet repeatedly, but there was no response; the Schubert was lost to them forever. He promised to buy Irene a new radio, and on Monday when he came home from work he told her that he had got one. He refused to describe it, and said it would be a surprise for her when it came.

The radio was delivered at the kitchen door the following afternoon, and with the assistance of her maid and the handyman Irene uncrated it and brought it into the living room. She was struck at once with the physical ugliness of the large gumwood cabinet. Irene was proud of her living room, she had chosen its furnishings and colors as carefully as she chose her clothes, and now it seemed to her that the new radio stood among her intimate possessions like an aggressive intruder. She was confounded by the number of dials and switches on the instrument panel, and she studied them thoroughly before she put the plug into a wall socket and turned the radio on. The dials flooded with a malevolent green light, and in the distance she heard the music of a piano quintet. The quintet was in the distance for only an instant; it bore down upon her with a speed greater than light and filled the apartment with the noise of music amplified so mightily that it knocked a china ornament from a table to the floor. She rushed to the instrument and reduced the volume. The violent forces that were snared in the ugly gumwood cabinet made her uneasy. Her children came home from school then, and she took them to the Park. It was not until later in the afternoon that she was able to return to the radio.

The maid had given the children their suppers and was supervising their baths when Irene turned on the radio, reduced the volume, and sat down to listen to a Mozart quintet that she knew and enjoyed. The music came through clearly. The new instrument had a much purer tone, she thought, than the old one. She decided that tone was most important and that she could conceal the cabinet behind a sofa. But as soon as she had made her peace with the radio, the interference began. A crackling sound like the noise of a burning powder fuse began to accompany the singing of the strings. Beyond the music, there was a rustling that reminded Irene unpleasantly of the sea, and as the quintet progressed, these noises were joined by many others. She tried all the dials and switches but nothing dimmed the interference, and she sat down, disappointed and bewildered, and tried to trace the flight of the melody. The elevator shaft in her building ran beside the living-room wall, and it was the noise of the elevator that gave her a clue to the character of the static. The rattling of the elevator cables and the opening and closing of the elevator doors were reproduced in her loudspeaker, and, realizing that the radio was sensitive to electrical currents of all sorts, she began to discern through the Mozart the ringing of telephone bells, the dialing of phones, and the lamentation of a vacuum cleaner. By listening more carefully, she was able to distinguish doorbells, elevator bells, electric razors, and Waring mixers, whose sounds had been picked up from the apartments that surrounded hers and transmitted through her loudspeaker. The powerful and ugly instrument, with its mistaken sensitivity to discord, was more than she could hope to master, so she turned the thing off and went into the nursery to see her children.

When Jim Westcott came home that night, he went to the radio confidently and worked the controls. He had the same sort of experience Irene had had. A man was speaking on the station Jim had chosen, and his voice swung instantly from the distance into a force so powerful that it shook the apartment. Jim turned the volume control and reduced the voice. Then, a minute or two later, the interference began. The ringing of telephones and doorbells set in, joined by the rasp of the elevator doors and the whir of cooking appliances. The character of the noise had changed since Irene had tried the radio earlier; the last of the electric razors was being unplugged, the vacuum cleaners had all been returned to their closets, and the static reflected that change in pace that overtakes the city after the sun goes down. He fiddled with the knobs but couldn't get rid of the noises, so he turned the radio off and told Irene that in the morning he'd call the people who had sold it to him and give them hell.

The following afternoon, when Irene returned to the apartment from a luncheon date, the maid told her that a man had come and fixed the radio. Irene went into the living room before she took off her hat or her furs and tried the instrument. From the loudspeaker came a recording of the "Missouri Waltz." It reminded her of the thin, scratchy music from an old-fashioned phonograph that she sometimes heard across the lake where she spent her summers. She waited until the waltz had finished, expecting an explanation of the recording, but there was none. The music was followed by silence, and then the plaintive and scratchy record was repeated. She turned the dial and got a satisfactory burst of Caucasian music—the thump of bare feet in the dust and the rattle of coin jewelry—but in the background she could hear the ringing of bells and a confusion of voices. Her children came home from school then, and she turned off the radio and went to the nursery.

When Jim came home that night, he was tired, and he took a bath and changed his clothes. Then he joined Irene in the living room. He had just turned on the radio when the maid announced dinner, so he left it on, and he and Irene went to the table.

Jim was too tired to make even a pretense of sociability, and there was nothing about the dinner to hold Irene's interest, so her attention wandered from the food to the deposits of silver polish on the candlesticks and from there to the music in the other room. She listened for a few moments to a Chopin prelude and then was surprised to hear a man's voice break in. "For Christ's sake, Kathy," he said, "do you always have to play the piano when I get home?" The music stopped abruptly. "It's the only chance I have," a woman said. "I'm at the office all day." "So am I," the man said. He added something obscene about an upright piano, and slammed a door. The passionate and melancholy music began again.

"Did you hear that?" Irene asked.

"What?" Jim was eating his dessert.

"The radio. A man said something while the music was still going on—something dirty."

"It's probably a play."

"I don't think it *is* a play," Irene said.

They left the table and took their coffee into the living room. Irene asked Jim to try another station. He turned the knob. "Have you seen my garters?" a man asked. "Button me up," a woman said. "Have you seen my garters?" the man said again. "Just button me up and I'll find your garters," the woman said. Jim shifted to another station. "I wish you wouldn't leave apple cores in the ashtrays," a man said. "I hate the smell."

"This is strange," Jim said.

"Isn't it?" Irene said.

Jim turned the knob again. "'On the coast of Coromandel where the early pumpkins blow,'" a woman with a pronounced English accent said, "'in the middle of the woods lived the Yonghy-Bonghy-Bò. Two old chairs, and a candle, one old jug without a handle . . .'"

"My God!" Irene cried. "That's the Sweeneys' nurse."

"'These were all his worldly goods,'" the British voice continued.

"Turn that thing off," Irene said. "Maybe they can hear *us*." Jim switched the radio off. "That was Miss Armstrong, the Sweeneys' nurse," Irene said. "She must be reading to the little girl. They live in 17-B. I've talked with Miss Armstrong in the Park. I know her voice very well. We must be getting other people's apartments."

"That's impossible," Jim said.

"Well, that was the Sweeneys' nurse," Irene said hotly. "I know her voice. I know it very well. I'm wondering if they can hear us."

Jim turned the switch. First from a distance and then nearer, nearer, as if borne on the wind, came the pure accents of the Sweeneys' nurse again: "'Lady Jingly! Lady Jingly!'" she said, "'*Sitting where the pumpkins blow, will you come and be my wife,* said the Yonghy-Bonghy-Bò . . .'"

Jim went over to the radio and said "Hello" loudly into the speaker.

"'*I am tired of living singly,*'" the nurse went on, "'*on this coast so wild and shingly, I'm a-weary of my life; if you'll come and be my wife, quite serene would be my life . . .*'"

"I guess she can't hear us," Irene said. "Try something else."

Jim turned to another station, and the living room was filled with the uproar of a cocktail party that had overshot its mark. Someone was playing the piano and singing the Whiffenpoof Song, and the voices that surrounded the piano were vehement and happy. "Eat some more sandwiches," a woman shrieked. There were screams of laughter and a dish of some sort crashed to the floor.

"Those must be the Fullers, in 11-E," Irene said. "I knew they were giving a party this afternoon. I saw her in the liquor store. Isn't this too divine? Try something else. See if you can get those people in 18-C."

The Westcotts overheard that evening a monologue on salmon fishing in Canada, a bridge game, running comments on home movies of what had apparently been a fortnight at Sea Island, and a bitter family quarrel about an overdraft at the bank. They turned off their radio at midnight and went to bed, weak with laughter. Sometime in the night, their son began to call for a glass of water and Irene got one and took it to his room. It was very early. All the lights in the neighborhood were extinguished, and from the boy's window she could see the empty street. She went into the living room and tried the radio. There was some faint coughing, a moan, and then a man spoke. "Are you all right, darling?" he asked. "Yes," a woman said wearily. "Yes, I'm all right, I guess," and then she added with great feeling, "but, you know, Charlie, I don't feel like myself any more. Sometimes there are about fifteen or twenty minutes in the week when I feel like myself. I don't like to go to another doctor, because the doctor's bills are so awful already, but I just don't feel like myself, Charlie. I just never feel like myself." They were not young, Irene thought. She guessed from the timbre of their voices that they were middle-aged. The restrained melancholy of the dialogue and the draft from the bedroom window made her shiver, and she went back to bed.

The following morning, Irene cooked breakfast for the family—the maid didn't come up from her room in the basement until ten—braided her daughters' hair, and waited at the door until her children and her husband had been carried away in the elevator. Then she went into the living room and tried the radio. "I don't want to go to school," a child screamed. "I hate school. I won't go to school. I hate school." "You will go to school," an enraged woman said. "We paid eight hundred dollars to get you into that school and you'll go if it kills you." The next number on the dial produced the worn record of the "Missouri Waltz." Irene shifted the control and invaded the privacy of several breakfast tables. She overheard demonstrations of indigestion, carnal love, abysmal vanity, faith, and despair. Irene's life was nearly as simple and sheltered as it appeared to be, and the forthright and sometimes brutal language that came from the loudspeaker that morning astonished and troubled her. She continued to listen until her maid came in. Then she turned off the radio quickly, since this insight, she realized, was a furtive one.

Irene had a luncheon date with a friend that day, and she left her apartment at a little after twelve. There were a number of women in the elevator when it stopped at her floor. She stared at their handsome and impassive faces, their furs, and the cloth flowers in their hats. Which one of them had been to Sea Island, she wondered. Which one had overdrawn her bank account? The elevator stopped at the tenth floor and a woman with a pair of Skye terriers joined them. Her hair was rigged high on her head and she wore a mink cape. She was humming the "Missouri Waltz."

Irene had two Martinis at lunch, and she looked searchingly at her friend and wondered what her secrets were. They had intended to go shopping after lunch, but Irene excused herself and went home. She told the maid that she was not to be disturbed; then she went into the living room, closed the doors, and switched on the radio. She heard, in the course of the afternoon, the halting conversation of a woman entertaining her aunt, the hysterical conclusion of a luncheon party, and a hostess briefing her maid about some cocktail guests. "Don't give the best Scotch to anyone who hasn't white hair," the hostess said. "See if you can get rid of that liver paste before you pass those hot things, and could you lend me five dollars? I want to tip the elevator man."

As the afternoon waned, the conversations increased in intensity. From where Irene sat, she could see the open sky above the East River. There were hundreds of clouds in the sky, as though the south wind had broken the winter into pieces and were blowing it north, and on her radio she could hear the arrival of cocktail guests and the return of children and businessmen from their schools and offices. "I found a good-sized diamond on the bathroom floor this morning," a woman said. "It must have fallen out of that bracelet Mrs. Dunston was wearing last night." "We'll sell it," a man said. "Take it down to the jeweller on Madison Avenue and sell it. Mrs. Dunston won't know the difference, and we could use a couple of hundred bucks . . ." "'Oranges and lemons, say the bells of St. Clement's,'" the Sweeneys' nurse sang. "'Half-pence and farthings, say the bells of St. Martin's. When will you pay me? say the bells at old Bailey . . .'" "It's not a hat," a woman cried, and at her back roared a cocktail party. "It's not a hat, it's a love affair. That's what Walter Florell said. He said it's not a hat, it's a love affair," and then, in a lower voice, the same woman added, "Talk to somebody, for Christ's sake, honey, talk to somebody. If she catches you standing here not talking to anybody, she'll take us off her invitation list, and I love these parties."

The Westcotts were going out for dinner that night, and when Jim came home, Irene was dressing. She seemed sad and vague, and he brought her a drink. They were dining with friends in the neighborhood, and they walked to where they were going. The sky was broad and filled with light. It was one of those splendid spring evenings that excite memory and desire, and the air that touched their hands and faces felt very soft. A Salvation Army band was on the corner playing "Jesus Is Sweeter." Irene drew on her husband's arm and held him there for a minute, to hear the music. "They're really such nice people, aren't they?" she said. "They have such nice faces. Actually, they're so much nicer than a lot of the people we know." She took a bill from her purse and walked over and dropped it into the tambourine. There was in her face, when she returned to her husband, a look of radiant melancholy that he was not familiar with. And her conduct at the dinner party that night seemed strange to him, too. She interrupted her hostess rudely and stared at the people across the table from her with an intensity for which she would have punished her children.

It was still mild when they walked home from the party, and Irene looked up at the spring stars. "'How far that little candle throws its beams,'" she exclaimed. "'So shines a good deed in a naughty world.'" She waited that night until Jim had fallen asleep, and then went into the living room and turned on the radio.

Jim came home at about six the next night. Emma, the maid, let him in, and he had taken off his hat and was taking off his coat when Irene ran into the hall. Her face was shining with tears and her hair was disordered. "Go up to 16-C, Jim!" she screamed. "Don't take off your coat. Go up to 16-C. Mr. Osborn's beating his wife. They've been quarrelling since four o'clock, and now be's hitting her. Go up there and stop him."

From the radio in the living room, Jim heard screams, obscenities, and thuds. "You know you don't have to listen to this sort of thing," he said. He strode into the living room and turned the switch. "It's indecent," he said. "It's like looking in windows. You know you don't have to listen to this sort of thing. You can turn it off."

"Oh, it's so horrible, it's so dreadful," Irene was sobbing. "I've been listening all day, and it's so depressing."

"Well, if it's so depressing, why do you listen to it? I bought this damned radio to give you some pleasure," he said. "I paid a great deal of money for it. I thought it might make you happy. I wanted to make you happy."

"Don't, don't, don't, don't quarrel with me," she moaned, and laid her head on his shoulder. "All the others have been quarrelling all day. Everybody's been quarrelling. They're all worried about money. Mrs. Hutchinson's mother is dying of cancer in Florida and they don't have enough money to send her to the Mayo Clinic. At least, Mr. Hutchinson says they don't have enough money. And some woman in this building is having an affair with the handyman—with that hideous handyman. It's too disgusting. And Mrs. Melville has heart trouble and Mr. Hendricks is going to lose his job in April and Mrs. Hendricks is horrid about the whole thing and that girl who plays the 'Missouri Waltz' is a whore, a common whore, and the elevator man has tuberculosis and Mr. Osborn has been beating Mrs. Osborn." She wailed, she trembled with grief and checked the stream of tears down her face with the heel of her palm.

"Well, why do you have to listen?" Jim asked again. "Why do you have to listen to this stuff if it makes you so miserable?"

"Oh, don't, don't, don't," she cried. "Life is too terrible, too sordid and awful. But we've never been like that, have we, darling? Have we? I mean we've always been good and decent and loving to one another, haven't we? And we have two children, two beautiful children. Our lives aren't sordid, are they, darling? Are they?" She flung her arms around his neck and drew his face down to hers. "We're happy, aren't we, darling? We are happy, aren't we?"

"Of course we're happy," he said tiredly. He began to surrender his resentment. "Of course we're happy. I'll have that damned radio fixed or taken away tomorrow." He stroked her soft hair. "My poor girl," he said.

"You love me, don't you?" she asked. "And we're not hypercritical or worried about money or dishonest, are we?"

"No, darling," he said.

A man came in the morning and fixed the radio. Irene turned it on cautiously and was happy to hear a California-wine commercial and a recording of Beethoven's Ninth Symphony, including Schiller's "Ode to Joy." She kept the radio on all day and nothing untoward came from the speaker.

A Spanish suite was being played when Jim came home. "Is everything all right?" he asked. His face was pale, she thought. They had some cocktails and went in to dinner to the "Anvil Chorus" from "Il Trovatore." This was followed by Debussy's "La Mer."

"I paid the bill for the radio today," Jim said. "It cost four hundred dollars. I hope you'll get some enjoyment out of it."

"Oh, I'm sure I will," Irene said.

"Four hundred dollars is a good deal more than I can afford," he went on. "I wanted to get something that you'd enjoy. It's the last extravagance we'll be able to indulge in this year. I see that you haven't paid your clothing bills yet. I saw them on your dressing table." He looked directly at her. "Why did you tell me you'd paid them? Why did you lie to me?"

"I just didn't want you to worry, Jim," she said. She drank some water. "I'll be able to pay my bills out of this month's allowance. There were the slipcovers last month, and that party."

"You've got to learn to handle the money I give you a little more intelligently, Irene," he said. "You've got to understand that we won't have as much money this year as we had last. I had a very sobering talk with Mitchell today. No one is buying anything. We're spending all our time promoting new issues, and you know how long that takes. I'm not getting any younger, you know. I'm thirty-seven. My hair will be gray next year. I haven't done as well as I'd hoped to do. And I don't suppose things will get any better."

"Yes, dear," she said.

"We've got to start cutting down," Jim said. "We've got to think of the children. To be perfectly frank with you, I worry about money a great deal. I'm not at all sure of the future. No one is. If anything should happen to me, there's the insurance, but that wouldn't go very far today. I've worked awfully hard to give you and the children a comfortable life," he said bitterly. I don't like to see all of my energies, all of my youth, wasted in fur coats and radios and slipcovers and—"

"Please, Jim," she said. "Please. They'll hear us."

"*Who'll hear us?* Emma can't hear us."

"The radio."

"Oh, I'm sick!" he shouted. "I'm sick to death of your apprehensiveness. The radio can't hear us. Nobody can hear us. And what if they can hear us? Who cares?"

Irene got up from the table and went into the living room. Jim went to the door and shouted at her from there. "Why are you so Christly all of a sudden? What's turned you overnight into a convent girl? You stole your mother's jewelry before they probated her will. You never gave your sister a cent of that money that was intended for her—not even when she needed it. You made Grace Howland's life miserable, and where was all your piety and your virtue when you went to that abortionist? I'll never forget how cool you were. You packed your bag and went off to have that child murdered as if you were going to Nassau. If you'd had any reasons, if you'd had any good reasons—"

Irene stood for a minute before the hideous cabinet, disgraced and sickened, but she held her hand on the switch before she extinguished the music and the voices, hoping that the instrument might speak to her kindly, that she might hear the Sweeneys' nurse. Jim continued to shout at her from the door. The voice on the radio was suave and noncommital. "An early-morning railroad disaster in Tokyo," the loudspeaker said, "killed twenty-nine people. A fire in a Catholic hospital near Buffalo for the care of blind children was extinguished early this morning by nuns. The temperature is forty-seven. The humidity is eighty-nine."

SONNY'S BLUES

James Baldwin

The Partisan Review *first published this short story in 1957.*

I read about it in the paper, in the subway, on my way to work. I read it, and I couldn't believe it, and I read it again. Then perhaps I just stared at it, at the newsprint spelling out his name, spelling out the story. I stared at it in the swinging lights of the subway car, and in the faces and bodies of the people, and in my own face, trapped in the darkness which roared outside.

It was not to be believed and I kept telling myself that, as I walked from the subway station to the high school. And at the same time I couldn't doubt it. I was scared, scared for Sonny. He became real to me again. A great block of ice got settled in my belly and kept melting there slowly all day long, while I taught my classes algebra. It was a special kind of ice. It kept melting, sending trickles of ice water all up and down my veins, but it never got less. Sometimes it hardened and seemed to expand until I felt my guts were going to come spilling out or that I was going to choke or scream. This would always be at a moment when I was remembering some specific thing Sonny had once said or done.

When he was about as old as the boys in my classes his face had been bright and open, there was a lot of copper in it; and he'd had wonderfully direct brown eyes, and great gentleness and privacy. I wondered what he looked like now. He had been picked up, the evening before, in a raid on an apartment downtown, for peddling and using heroin.

I couldn't believe it: but what I mean by that is that I couldn't find any room for it anywhere inside me. I had kept it outside me for a long time. I hadn't wanted to know. I had had suspicions, but I didn't name them, I kept putting them away. I told myself that Sonny was wild, but he wasn't crazy. And he'd always been a good boy, he hadn't ever turned hard or evil or disrespectful, the way kids can, so quick, so quick, especially in Harlem. I didn't want to believe that I'd ever see my brother going down, coming to nothing, all that light in his face gone out, in the condition I'd already seen so many others. Yet it had happened and here I was, talking about algebra to a lot of boys who might, every one of them for all I knew, be popping off needles every time they went to the head. Maybe it did more for them than algebra could.

I was sure that the first time Sonny had ever had horse, he couldn't have been much older than these boys were now. These boys, now, were living as we'd been living then, they were growing up with a rush and their heads bumped abruptly against the low ceiling of their actual possibilities. They were filled with rage. All they really knew were two darknesses, the darkness of their lives, which was now closing in on them, and the darkness of the movies, which had blinded them to that other darkness, and in which they now, vindictively, dreamed, at once more together than they were at any other time, and more alone.

When the last bell rang, the last class ended, I let out my breath. It seemed I'd been holding it for all that time. My clothes were wet—I may have looked as though I'd been sitting in a steam bath, all dressed up, all afternoon. I sat alone in the classroom a long time. I listened to the boys outside, downstairs, shouting and cursing and laughing. Their laughter struck me for perhaps the first time. It was not the joyous laughter which—God knows why—one associates with children. It was mocking and insular, its intent was to denigrate. It was disenchanted, and in this, also, lay the authority of their curses. Perhaps I was listening to them because I was thinking about my brother and in them I heard my brother. And myself.

One boy was whistling a tune, at once very complicated and very simple, it seemed to be pouring out of him as though he were a bird, and it sounded very cool and moving through all that harsh, bright air, only just holding its own through all those other sounds.

I stood up and walked over to the window and looked down into the courtyard. It was the beginning of the spring and the sap was rising in the boys. A teacher passed through them every now and again, quickly, as though he or she couldn't wait to get out of that courtyard, to get those boys out of their sight and off their minds. I started collecting my stuff. I thought I'd better get home and talk to Isabel.

The courtyard was almost deserted by the time I got downstairs. I saw this boy standing in the shadow of a doorway, looking just like Sonny. I almost called his name. Then I saw that it wasn't Sonny, but somebody we used to know, a boy from around our block. He'd been Sonny's friend. He'd never been mine, having been too young for me, and, anyway, I'd never liked him. And now, even though he was a grown-up man, he still hung around that block, still spent hours on the street corners, was always high and raggy. I used to run into him from time to time and he'd often work around to asking me for a quarter or fifty cents. He always had some real good excuse, too, and I always gave it to him. I don't know why.

But now, abruptly, I hated him. I couldn't stand the way he looked at me, partly like a dog, partly like a cunning child. I wanted to ask him what the hell he was doing in the school courtyard.

He sort of shuffled over to me, and he said, "I see you got the papers. So you already know about it."

"You mean about Sonny? Yes, I already know about it. How come they didn't get you?"

He grinned. It made him repulsive and it also brought to mind what he'd looked like as a kid. "I wasn't there. I stay away from them people."

"Good for you." I offered him a cigarette and I watched him through the smoke. "You come all the way down here just to tell me about Sonny?"

"That's right." He was sort of shaking his head and his eyes looked strange, as though they were about to cross. The bright sun deadened his damp dark brown skin and it made his eyes look yellow and showed up the dirt in his kinked hair. He smelled funky. I moved a little away from him and I said, "Well, thanks. But I already know about it and I got to get home."

"I'll walk you a little ways," he said. We started walking. There were a couple of kids still loitering in the courtyard and one of them said good-night to me and looked strangely at the boy beside me.

"What're you going to do?" he asked me. "I mean, about Sonny?"

"Look. I haven't seen Sonny for over a year, I'm not sure I'm going to do anything. Anyway, what the hell *can* I do?"

"That's right," he said quickly, "ain't nothing you can do. Can't much help old Sonny no more, I guess."

It was what I was thinking and so it seemed to me he had no right to say it.

"I'm surprised at Sonny, though," he went on—he had a funny way of talking, he looked straight ahead as though he were talking to himself—"I thought Sonny was a smart boy, I thought he was too smart to get hung."

"I guess he thought so too," I said sharply, "and that's how he got hung. And how about you? You're pretty goddamn smart, I bet."

Then he looked directly at me, just for a minute. "I ain't smart," he said. "If I was smart, I'd have reached for a pistol a long time ago."

"Look. Don't tell *me* your sad story, if it was up to me, I'd give you one." Then I felt guilty—guilty, probably, for never having supposed that the poor bastard *had* a story of his own, much less a sad one, and I asked, quickly, "What's going to happen to him now?"

He didn't answer this. He was off by himself some place.

"Funny thing," he said, and from his tone we might have been dis-cussing the quickest way to get to Brooklyn, "when I saw the papers this morning, the first thing I asked myself was if I had anything to do with it. I felt sort of responsible."

I began to listen more carefully. The subway station was on the corner, just before us, and I stopped. He stopped, too. We were in front of a bar and he ducked slightly, peering in, but whoever he was looking for didn't seem to be there. The juke box was blasting away with something black and bouncy and I half watched the barmaid as she danced her way from the juke box to her place behind the bar. And I watched her face as she laughingly responded to something someone said to her, still keeping time to the music. When she smiled one saw the little girl, one sensed the doomed, still-struggling woman beneath the battered face of the semi-whore.

"I never *give* Sonny nothing," the boy said finally, "but a long time ago I come to school high and Sonny asked me how it felt." He paused, I couldn't bear to watch him, I watched the barmaid, and I listened to the music which seemed to be causing the pavement to shake. "I told him it felt great." The music stopped, the barmaid paused and watched the juke box until the music began again. "It did."

All this was carrying me some place I didn't want to go. I certainly didn't want to know how it felt. It filled everything, the people, the houses, the music, the dark, quicksilver barmaid, with menace; and this menace was their reality.

"What's going to happen to him now?" I asked again.

"They'll send him away some place and they'll try to cure him." He shook his head. "Maybe he'll even think he's kicked the habit. Then they'll let him loose"—he gestured, throwing his cigarette into the gutter. "That's all."

"What do you mean, that's *all?*"

But I knew what he meant.

"I *mean*, that's *all*." He turned his head and looked at me, pulling down the corners of his mouth. "Don't you know what I mean?" he asked, softly.

"How the hell *would* I know what you mean?" I almost whispered it. I don't know why.

"That's right," he said to the air, "how would *he* know what I mean?" He turned toward me again, patient and calm, and yet I somehow felt him shaking, shaking as though he were going to fall apart. I felt that ice in my guts again, the dread I'd felt all afternoon; and again I watched the barmaid, moving about the bar, washing glasses, and singing. "Listen. They'll let him out and then it'll just start all over again. That's what I mean."

"You mean—they'll let him out. And then he'll just start working his way back in again. You mean he'll never kick the habit. Is that what you mean?"

"That's right," he said, cheerfully. "*You* see what I mean."

"Tell me," I said at last, "why does he want to die? He must want to die, he's killing himself, why does he want to die?"

He looked at me in surprise. He licked his lips. "He don't want to die. He wants to live. Don't nobody want to die, ever."

Then I wanted to ask him—too many things. He could not have answered, or if he had, I could not have borne the answers. I started walking. "Well, I guess it's none of my business."

"It's going to be rough on old Sonny," he said. We reached the subway station. "This is your station?" he asked. I nodded. I took one step down.

"Damn!" he said, suddenly. I looked up at him. He grinned again. "Damn it if I didn't leave all my money home. You ain't got a dollar on you, have you? Just for a couple of days, is all."

All at once something inside gave and threatened to come pouring out of me. I didn't hate him any more. I felt that in another moment I'd start crying like a child.

"Sure," I said. "Don't sweat." I looked in my wallet and didn't have a dollar, I only had a five. "Here," I said. "That hold you?"

He didn't look at it—he didn't want to look at it. A terrible, closed look came over his face, as though he were keeping the number on the bill a secret from him and me. "Thanks," he said, and now he was dying to see me go. "Don't worry about Sonny. Maybe I'll write him or something."

"Sure," I said. "You do that. So long."

"Be seeing you," he said. I went on down the steps.

And I didn't write Sonny or send him anything for a long time. When I finally did, it was just after my little girl died, and he wrote me back a letter which made me feel like a bastard.

Here's what he said:

Dear brother,

You don't know how much I needed to hear from you. I wanted to write you many a time but I dug how much I must have hurt you and so I didn't write. But now I feel like a man who's been trying to climb up out of some deep, real deep and funky hole and just saw the sun up there, outside. I got to get outside.

I can't tell you much about how I got here. I mean I don't know how to tell you. I guess I was afraid of something or I was trying to escape from something and you know I have never been very strong in the head (smile). I'm glad Mama and Daddy are dead and can't see what's happened to their son and I swear if I'd known what I was doing I would never have hurt you so, you and a lot of other fine people who were nice to me and who believed in me.

I don't want you to think it had anything to do with me being a musician. It's more than that. Or maybe less than that. I can't get anything straight in my head down here and I try not to think about what's going to happen to me when I get outside again. Sometime I think I'm going to flip and *never* get outside and sometime I think I'll come straight back. I tell you one thing, though, I'd rather blow my brains out than go through this again. But that's what they all say, so they tell me. If I tell you when I'm coming to New York and if you could meet me, I sure would appreciate it. Give my love to Isabel and the kids and I was sure sorry to hear about little Gracie. I wish I could be like Mama and say the Lord's will be done, but I don't know it seems to me that trouble is the one thing that never does get stopped and I don't know what good it does to blame it on the Lord. But maybe it does some good if you believe it.

Your brother,

Sonny

Then I kept in constant touch with him and I sent him whatever I could and I went to meet him when he came back to New York. When I saw him many things I thought I had forgotten came flooding back to me. This was because I had begun, finally, to wonder about Sonny, about the life that Sonny lived inside. This life, whatever it was, had made him older and thinner and it had deepened the distant stillness in which he had always moved. He looked very unlike my baby brother. Yet, when he smiled, when we shook hands, the baby brother I'd never known looked out from the depths of his private life, like an animal waiting to be coaxed into the light.

"How you been keeping?" he asked me.

"All right. And you?"

"Just fine." He was smiling all over his face. "It's good to see you again."

"It's good to see you."

The seven years' difference in our ages lay between us like a chasm: I wondered if these years would ever operate between us as a bridge. I was remembering, and it made it hard to catch my breath, that I had been there when he was born; and I had heard the first words he had ever spoken. When he started to walk, he walked from our mother straight to me. I caught him just before he fell when he took the first steps he ever took in this world.

"How's Isabel?"

"Just fine. She's dying to see you."

"And the boys?"

"They're fine, too. They're anxious to see their uncle."

"Oh, come on. You know they don't remember me."

"Are you kidding? Of course they remember you."

He grinned again. We got into a taxi. We had a lot to say to each other, far too much to know how to begin.

As the taxi began to move, I asked, "You still want to go to India?"

He laughed. "You still remember that. Hell, no. This place is Indian enough for me."

"It used to belong to them," I said.

And he laughed again. "They damn sure knew what they were doing when they got rid of it."

Years ago, when he was around fourteen, he'd been all hipped on the idea of going to India. He read books about people sitting on rocks, naked, in all kinds of weather, but mostly bad, naturally, and walking barefoot through hot coals and arriving at wisdom. I used to say that it sounded to me as though they were getting away from wisdom as fast as they could. I think he sort of looked down on me for that.

"Do you mind," he asked, "if we have the driver drive alongside the park? On the west side—I haven't seen the city in so long."

"Of course not," I said. I was afraid that I might sound as though I were humoring him, but I hoped he wouldn't take it that way.

So we drove along, between the green of the park and the stony, lifeless elegance of hotels and apartment buildings, toward the vivid, killing streets of our childhood. These streets hadn't changed, though housing projects jutted up out of them now like rocks in the middle of a boiling sea. Most of the houses in which we had grown up had vanished, as had the stores from which we had stolen, the basements in which we had first tried sex, the rooftops from which we had hurled tin cans and bricks. But houses exactly like the houses of our past yet dominated the landscape, boys exactly like the boys we once had been found themselves smothering in these houses, came down into the streets for light and air and found themselves encircled by disaster. Some escaped the trap, most didn't. Those who got out always left something of themselves behind, as some animals amputate a leg and leave it in the trap. It might be said, perhaps, that I had escaped, after all, I was a school teacher; or that Sonny had, he hadn't lived in Harlem for years. Yet, as the cab moved uptown through streets which seemed, with a rush, to darken with dark people, and as I covertly studied Sonny's face, it came to me that what we both were seeking through our separate cab windows was that part of ourselves which had been left behind. It's always at the hour of trouble and confrontation that the missing member aches.

We hit 110th Street and started rolling up Lenox Avenue. And I'd known this avenue all my life, but it seemed to me again, as it had seemed on the day I'd first heard about Sonny's trouble, filled with a hidden menace which was its very breath of life.

"We almost there," said Sonny.

"Almost." We were both too nervous to say anything more.

We live in a housing project. It hasn't been up long. A few days after it was up it seemed uninhabitably new, now, of course, it's already run-down. It looks like a parody of the good, clean, faceless life—God knows the people who live in it do their best to make it a parody. The beat-looking grass lying around isn't enough to make their lives green, the hedges will never hold out the streets, and they know it. The big windows fool no one, they aren't big enough to make space out of no space. They don't bother with the windows, they watch the TV screen instead. The play-ground is most popular with the children who don't play at jacks, or skip rope, or roller skate, or swing, and they can be found in it after dark. We moved in partly because it's not too far from where I teach, and partly for the kids; but it's really just like the houses in which Sonny and I grew up. The same things happen, they'll have the same things to remember. The moment Sonny and I started into the house I had the feeling that I was simply bringing him back into the danger he had almost died trying to escape.

Sonny has never been talkative. So I don't know why I was sure he'd be dying to talk to me when supper was over the first night. Everything went fine, the oldest boy remembered him, and the youngest boy liked him, and Sonny had remembered to bring something for each of them; and

544

Isabel, who is really much nicer than I am, more open and giving, had gone to a lot of trouble about dinner and was genuinely glad to see him. And she's always been able to tease Sonny in a way that I haven't. It was nice to see her face so vivid again and to hear her laugh and watch her make Sonny laugh. She wasn't, or, anyway, she didn't seem to be, at all uneasy or embarrassed. She chatted as though there were no subject which had to be avoided and she got Sonny past his first, faint stiffness. And thank God she was there, for I was filled with that icy dread again. Everything I did seemed awkward to me, and everything I said sounded freighted with hidden meaning. I was trying to remember everything I'd heard about dope addiction and I couldn't help watching Sonny for signs. I wasn't doing it out of malice. I was trying to find out something about my brother. I was dying to hear him tell me he was safe.

"Safe!" my father grunted, whenever Mama suggested trying to move to a neighborhood which might be safer for children. "Safe, hell! Ain't no place safe for kids, nor nobody."

He always went on like this, but he wasn't, ever, really as bad as he sounded, not even on weekends, when he got drunk. As a matter of fact, he was always on the lookout for "something a little better," but he died before he found it. He died suddenly, during a drunken weekend in the middle of the war, when Sonny was fifteen. He and Sonny hadn't ever got on too well. And this was partly because Sonny was the apple of his father's eye. It was because he loved Sonny so much and was frightened for him, that he was always fighting with him. It doesn't do any good to fight with Sonny. Sonny just moves back, inside himself, where he can't be reached. But the principal reason that they never hit it off is that they were so much alike. Daddy was big and rough and loud-talking, just the opposite of Sonny, but they both had—that same privacy.

Mama tried to tell me something about this, just after Daddy died. I was home on leave from the army.

This was the last time I ever saw my mother alive. Just the same, this picture gets all mixed up in my mind with pictures I had of her when she was younger. The way I always see her is the way she used to be on a Sunday afternoon, say, when the old folks were talking after the big Sunday dinner. I always see her wearing pale blue. She'd be sitting on the sofa. And my father would be sitting in the easy chair, not far from her. And the living room would be full of church folks and relatives. There they sit, in chairs all around the living room, and the night is creeping up outside, but nobody knows it yet. You can see the darkness growing against the windowpanes and you hear the street noises every now and again, or maybe the jangling beat of a tambourine from one of the churches close by, but it's real quiet in the room. For a moment nobody's talking, but every face looks darkening, like the sky outside. And my mother rocks a little from the waist, and my father's eyes are closed. Everyone is looking at something a child can't see. For a minute they've forgotten the children. Maybe a kid is lying on the rug, half asleep. Maybe somebody's got a kid in his lap and is absent-mindedly stroking the kid's head. Maybe there's a kid, quiet and big-eyed, curled up in a big chair in the corner. The silence, the darkness coming, and the darkness in the faces frighten the child obscurely. He hopes that the hand which strokes his forehead will never stop—will never die. He hopes that there will never come a time when the old folks won't be sitting around the living room, talking about where they've come from, and what they've seen, and what's happened to them and their kinfolk.

But something deep and watchful in the child knows that this is bound to end, is already ending. In a moment someone will get up and turn on the light. Then the old folks will remember the children and they won't talk any more that day. And when light fills the room, the child is filled with darkness. He knows that every time this happens he's moved just a little closer to that darkness outside. The darkness outside is what the old folks have been talking about. It's what they've come from. It's what they endure. The child knows that they won't talk any more because if he knows too much about what's happened to *them,* he'll know too much too soon, about what's going to happen to *him.*

The last time I talked to my mother, I remember I was restless. I wanted to get out and see Isabel. We weren't married then and we had a lot to straighten out between us.

There Mama sat, in black, by the window. She was humming an old church song, *Lord, you brought me from a long ways off.* Sonny was out somewhere. Mama kept watching the streets.

"I don't know," she said, "if I'll ever see you again, after you go off from here. But I hope you'll remember the things I tried to teach you."

"Don't talk like that," I said, and smiled. "You'll be here a long time yet."

She smiled, too, but she said nothing. She was quiet for a long time. And I said, "Mama, don't you worry about nothing. I'll be writing all the time, and you be getting the checks. . . . "

"I want to talk to you about your brother," she said, suddenly. "If anything happens to me he ain't going to have nobody to look out for him."

"Mama," I said, "ain't nothing going to happen to you *or* Sonny. Sonny's all right. He's a good boy and he's got good sense."

"It ain't a question of his being a good boy," Mama said, "nor of his having good sense. It ain't only the bad ones, nor yet the dumb ones that gets sucked under." She stopped, looking at me. "Your Daddy once had a brother," she said, and she smiled in a way that made me feel she was in pain. "You didn't never know that, did you?"

"No," I said, "I never knew that," and I watched her face.

"Oh, yes," she said, "your Daddy had a brother." She looked out of the window again. "I know you never saw your Daddy cry. But I did—many a time, through all these years."

I asked her, "What happened to his brother? How come nobody's ever talked about him?"

This was the first time I ever saw my mother look old.

"His brother got killed," she said, "when he was just a little younger than you are now. I knew him. He was a fine boy. He was maybe a little full of the devil, but he didn't mean nobody no harm."

Then she stopped and the room was silent, exactly as it had sometimes been on those Sunday afternoons. Mama kept looking out into the streets.

"He used to have a job in the mill," she said, "and, like all young folks, he just liked to perform on Saturday nights. Saturday nights, him and your father would drift around to different places, go to dances and things like that, or just sit around with people they knew, and your father's brother would sing, he had a fine voice, and play along with himself on his guitar. Well, this particular Saturday night, him and your father was coming home from some place, and they were both a little drunk and there was a moon that night, it was bright like day. Your father's brother was feeling kind of good, and he was whistling to himself, and he had his guitar slung over his shoulder. They was coming down a hill and beneath them was a road that turned off from the highway. Well, your father's brother, being always kind of frisky, decided to run down this hill, and he did, with that guitar banging and clanging behind him, and he ran across the road, and he was making water behind a tree. And your father was sort of amused at him and he was still coming down the hill, kind of slow. Then he heard a car motor and that same minute his brother stepped from behind the tree, into the road, in the moonlight. And he started to cross the road. And your father started to run down the hill, he says he don't know why. This car was full of white men. They was all drunk, and when they seen your father's brother they let out a great whoop and holler and they aimed the car straight at him. They was having fun, they just wanted to scare him, the way they do sometimes, you know. But they was drunk. And I guess the boy, being drunk, too, and scared, kind of lost his head. By the time he jumped it was too late. Your father says he heard his brother scream when the car rolled over him, and he heard the wood of that guitar when it give, and he heard them strings go flying, and he heard them white men shouting, and the car kept on a-going and it ain't stopped till this day. And, time your father got down the hill, his brother weren't nothing but blood and pulp."

Tears were gleaming on my mother's face. There wasn't anything I could say.

"He never mentioned it," she said, "because I never let him mention it before you children. Your Daddy was like a crazy man that night and for many a night thereafter. He says he never in his life seen anything as dark as that road after the lights of that car had gone away. Weren't nothing, weren't nobody on that road, just your Daddy and his brother and that busted guitar. Oh, yes. Your Daddy never did really get right again. Till the day he died he weren't sure but that every white man he saw was the man that killed his brother."

She stopped and took out her handkerchief and dried her eyes and looked at me.

"I ain't telling you all this," she said, "to make you scared or bitter or to make you hate nobody. I'm telling you this because you got a brother. And the world ain't changed."

I guess I didn't want to believe this. I guess she saw this in my face. She turned away from me, toward the window again, searching those streets.

"But I praise my Redeemer," she said at last, "that He called your Daddy home before me. I ain't saying it to throw no flowers at myself, but, I declare, it keeps me from feeling too cast down to know I helped your father get safely through this world. Your father always acted like he was the roughest, strongest man on earth. And everybody took him to be like that. But if he hadn't had me there—to see his tears!"

She was crying again. Still, I couldn't move. I said, "Lord, Lord, Mama, I didn't know it was like that."

"Oh, honey," she said, "there's a lot that you don't know. But you are going to find out." She stood up from the window and came over to me. "You got to hold on to your brother," she said, "and don't let him fall, no matter what it looks like is happening to him and no matter how evil you gets with him. You going to be evil with him many a time. But don't you forget what I told you, you hear?"

"I won't forget," I said. "Don't you worry, I won't forget. I won't let nothing happen to Sonny."

My mother smiled as though she was amused at something she saw in my face. Then, "You may not be able to stop nothing from happening. But you got to let him know you's *there*."

Two days later I was married, and then I was gone. And I had a lot of things on my mind and I pretty well forgot my promise to Mama until I got shipped home on a special furlough for her funeral.

And, after the funeral, with just Sonny and me alone in the empty kitchen, I tried to find out something about him.

"What do you want to do?" I asked him.

"I'm going to be a musician," he said.

For he had graduated, in the time I had been away, from dancing to the juke box to finding out who was playing what, and what they were doing with it, and he had bought himself a set of drums.

"You mean, you want to be a drummer?" I somehow had the feeling that being a drummer might be all right for other people but not for my brother Sonny.

"I don't think," he said, looking at me very gravely, "that I'll ever be a good drummer. But I think I can play a piano."

I frowned. I'd never played the role of the oldest brother quite so seriously before, had scarcely ever, in fact, *asked* Sonny a damn thing. I sensed myself in the presence of something I didn't really know how to handle, didn't understand. So I made my frown a little deeper as I asked: "What kind of musician do you want to be?"

He grinned. "How many kinds do you think there are?"

"Be *serious*," I said.

He laughed, throwing his head back, and then looked at me. "I *am* serious."

"Well, then, for Christ's sake, stop kidding around and answer a serious question. I mean, do you want to be a concert pianist, you want to play classical music and all that, or—or what?" Long before I finished he was laughing again. "For Christ's *sake*, Sonny!"

He sobered, but with difficulty. "I'm sorry. But you sound so—*scared!*" and he was off again.

"Well, you may think it's funny now, baby, but it's not going to be so funny when you have to make your living at it, let me tell you *that*." I was furious because I knew he was laughing at me and I didn't know why.

"No," he said, very sober now, and afraid, perhaps, that he'd hurt me, "I don't want to be a classical pianist. That isn't what interests me. I mean"—he paused, looking hard at me, as though his eyes would help me to understand, and then gestured helplessly, as though perhaps his hand would help—"I mean, I'll have a lot of studying to do, and I'll have to study *everything*, but, I mean, I want to play *with*—jazz musicians." He stopped. "I want to play jazz," he said.

Well, the word had never before sounded as heavy, as real, as it sounded that afternoon in Sonny's mouth. I just looked at him and I was probably frowning a real frown by this time. I simply couldn't see why on earth he'd want to spend his time hanging around nightclubs, clowning around on bandstands, while people pushed each other around a dance floor. It seemed—beneath him, somehow. I had never thought about it before, had never been forced to, but I suppose I had always put jazz musicians in a class with what Daddy called "good-time people."

"Are you *serious*?"

"Hell, *yes*, I'm serious."

He looked more helpless than ever, and annoyed, and deeply hurt.

I suggested, helpfully: "You mean—like Louis Armstrong?"

His face closed as though I'd struck him. "No. I'm not talking about none of that old-time, down home crap."

"Well, look, Sonny, I'm sorry, don't get mad. I just don't altogether get it, that's all. Name somebody—you know, a jazz musician you admire."

"Bird."

"Who?"

"Bird! Charlie Parker! Don't they teach you nothing in the goddamn army?"

I lit a cigarette. I was surprised and then a little amused to discover that I was trembling. "I've been out of touch," I said. "You'll have to be patient with me. Now. Who's this Parker character?"

"He's just one of the greatest jazz musicians alive," said Sonny, sullenly, his hands in his pockets, his back to me. "Maybe *the* greatest," he added, bitterly, "that's probably why *you* never heard of him."

"All right," I said, "I'm ignorant. I'm sorry. I'll go out and buy all the cat's records right away, all right?"

"It don't," said Sonny, with dignity, "make any difference to me. I don't care what you listen to. Don't do me no favors."

I was beginning to realize that I'd never seen him so upset before. With another part of my mind I was thinking that this would probably turn out to be one of those things kids go through and that I shouldn't make it seem important by pushing it too hard. Still, I didn't think it would do any harm to ask: "Doesn't all this take a lot of time? Can you make a living at it?"

He turned back to me and half leaned, half sat, on the kitchen table. "Everything takes time," he said, "and—well, yes, sure, I can make a living at it. But what I don't seem to be able to make you understand is that it's the only thing I want to do."

"Well, Sonny," I said gently, "you know people can't always do exactly what they *want* to do—"

"*No,* I don't know that," said Sonny, surprising me. "I think people *ought* to do what they want to do, what else are they alive for?"

"You getting to be a big boy," I said desperately, "it's time you started thinking about your future."

"I'm thinking about my future," said Sonny, grimly. "I think about it all the time."

I gave up. I decided, if he didn't change his mind, that we could always talk about it later. "In the meantime," I said, "you got to finish school." We had already decided that he'd have to move in with Isabel and her folks. I knew this wasn't the ideal arrangement because Isabel's folks are inclined to be dicty and they hadn't especially wanted Isabel to marry me. But I didn't know what else to do. "And we have to get you fixed up at Isabel's."

There was a long silence. He moved from the kitchen table to the window. "That's a terrible idea. You know it yourself."

"Do you have a *better* idea?"

He just walked up and down the kitchen for a minute. He was as tall as I was. He had started to shave. I suddenly had the feeling that I didn't know him at all.

He stopped at the kitchen table and picked up my cigarettes. Looking at me with a kind of mocking, amused defiance, he put one between his lips. "You mind?"

"You smoking already?"

He lit the cigarette and nodded, watching me through the smoke. "I just wanted to see if I'd have the courage to smoke in front of you." He grinned and blew a great cloud of smoke to the ceiling. "It was easy." He looked at my face. "Come on, now. I bet you was smoking at my age, tell the truth."

I didn't say anything but the truth was on my face, and he laughed. But now there was something very strained in his laugh. "Sure. And I bet that ain't all you was doing."

He was frightening me a little. "Cut the crap," I said. "We already decided that you was going to go and live at Isabel's. Now what's got into you all of a sudden?"

"*You* decided it," he pointed out. "*I* didn't decide nothing." He stopped in front of me, leaning against the stove, arms loosely folded. "Look, brother. I don't want to stay in Harlem no more, I really don't." He was very earnest. He looked at me, then over toward the kitchen window. There was something in his eyes I'd never seen before, some thoughtfulness, some worry all his own. He rubbed the muscle of one arm. "It's time I was getting out of here."

"Where do you want to *go*, Sonny?"

"I want to join the army. Or the navy, I don't care. If I say I'm old enough, they'll believe me."

Then I got mad. It was because I was so scared. "You must be crazy. You goddamn fool, what the hell do you want to go and join the *army* for?"

"I just told you. To get out of Harlem."

"Sonny, you haven't even finished *school*. And if you really want to be a musician, how do you expect to study if you're in the *army*?"

He looked at me, trapped, and in anguish. "There's ways. I might be able to work out some kind of deal. Anyway, I'll have the G.I. Bill when I come out."

"*If* you come out." We stared at each other. "Sonny, please. Be reasonable. I know the setup is far from perfect. But we got to do the best we can."

"I ain't learning nothing in school," he said. "Even when I go." He turned away from me and opened the window and threw his cigarette out into the narrow alley. I watched his back. "At least, I ain't learning nothing you'd want me to learn." He slammed the window so hard I thought the glass would fly out, and turned back to me. "And I'm sick of the stink of these garbage cans!"

"Sonny," I said, "I know how you feel. But if you don't finish school now, you're going to be sorry later that you didn't." I grabbed him by the shoulders. "And you only got another year. It ain't so bad. And I'll come back and I swear I'll help you do *whatever* you want to do. Just try to put up with it till I come back. Will you please do that? For me?"

He didn't answer and he wouldn't look at me.

"Sonny. You hear me?"

He pulled away. "I hear you. But you never hear anything *I* say."

I didn't know what to say to that. He looked out of the window and then back at me. "OK," he said, and sighed. "I'll try."

Then I said, trying to cheer him up a little, "They got a piano at Isabel's. You can practice on it."

And as a matter of fact, it did cheer him up for a minute. "That's right," he said to himself. "I forgot that." His face relaxed a little. But the worry, the thoughtfulness, played on it still, the way shadows play on a face which is staring into the fire.

But I thought I'd never hear the end of that piano. At first, Isabel would write me, saying how nice it was that Sonny was so serious about his music and how, as soon as he came in from school, or wherever he had been when he was supposed to be at school, he went straight to that piano and stayed there until suppertime. And, after supper, he went back to that piano and stayed there until everybody went to bed. He was at the piano all day Saturday and all day Sunday. Then be bought a record player and started playing records. He'd play one record over and over again, all day long sometimes, and he'd improvise along with it on the piano. Or he'd play one section of the record, one chord, one change, one progression, then he'd do it on the piano. Then back to the record. Then back to the piano.

Well, I really don't know how they stood it. Isabel finally confessed that it wasn't like living with a person at all, it was like living with sound. And the sound didn't make any sense to her, didn't make any sense to any of them—naturally. They began, in a way, to be afflicted by this presence that was living in their home. It was as though Sonny were some sort of god, or monster. He moved in an atmosphere which wasn't like theirs at all. They fed him and he ate, he washed himself, he walked in and out of their door; he certainly wasn't nasty or unpleasant or rude, Sonny isn't any of those things; but it was as though he were all wrapped up in some cloud, some fire, some vision all his own; and there wasn't any way to reach him.

At the same time, he wasn't really a man yet, he was still a child, and they had to watch out for him in all kinds of ways. They certainly couldn't throw him out. Neither did they dare to make a great scene about that piano because even they dimly sensed, as I sensed, from so many thousands of miles away, that Sonny was at that piano playing for his life.

But he hadn't been going to school. One day a letter came from the school board and Isabel's mother got it—there had, apparently, been other letters but Sonny had torn them up. This day, when Sonny came in, Isabel's mother showed him the letter and asked where he'd been spending his time. And she finally got it out of him that he'd been down in Greenwich Village, with musicians and other characters, in a white girl's apartment. And this seared her and she started to scream at him and what came up, once she began—though she denies it to this day—was what sacrifices they were making to give Sonny a decent home and how little he appreciated it.

Sonny didn't play the piano that day. By evening, Isabel's mother had calmed down but then there was the old man to deal with, and Isabel herself. Isabel says she did her best to be calm but she broke down and started crying. She says she just watched Sonny's face. She could tell, by watching him, what was happening with him. And what was happening was that they penetrated his cloud, they had reached him. Even if their fingers had been a thousand times more gentle than human fingers ever are, he could hardly help feeling that they had stripped him naked and were spitting on that nakedness. For he also had to see that his presence, that music, which was life or death to him, had been torture for them and that they had endured it, not at all for his sake, but only for mine. And Sonny couldn't take that. He can take it a little better today than he could then but he's still not very good at it and, frankly, I don't know anybody who is.

The silence of the next few days must have been louder than the sound of all the music ever played since time began. One morning, before she went to work, Isabel was in his room for something and she suddenly realized that all of his records were gone. And she knew for certain that he was gone. And he was. He went as far as the navy would carry him. He finally sent me a postcard from some place in Greece and that was the first I knew that Sonny was still alive. I didn't see him any more until we were both back in New York and the war had long been over.

He was a man by then, of course, but I wasn't willing to see it. He came by the house from time to time, but we fought almost every time we met. I didn't like the way he carried himself, loose and dreamlike all the time, and I didn't like his friends, and his music seemed to be merely an excuse for the life he led. It sounded just that weird and disordered.

Then we had a fight, a pretty awful fight, and I didn't see him for months. By and by I looked him up, where he was living, in a furnished room in the Village, and I tried to make it up. But there were lots of other people in the room and Sonny just lay on his bed, and he wouldn't come downstairs with me, and he treated these other people as though they were his family and I weren't. So I got mad and then he got mad, and then I told him that he might just as well be dead as live the way he was living. Then he stood up and he told me not to worry about him any more in life, that he *was* dead as far as I was concerned. Then he pushed me to the door and the other people looked on as though nothing were happening, and he slammed the door behind me. I stood in the hallway, staring at the door. I heard somebody laugh in the room and then the tears came to my eyes. I started down the steps, whistling to keep from crying. I kept whistling to myself, *You going to need me, baby, one of these cold, rainy days.*

I read about Sonny's trouble in the spring. Little Grace died in the fall. She was a beautiful little girl. But she only lived a little over two years. She died of polio and she suffered. She had a slight fever for a couple of days, but it didn't seem like anything and we just kept her in bed. And we would certainly have called the doctor, but the fever dropped, she seemed to be all right. So we thought it had just been a cold. Then, one day, she was up, playing, Isabel was in the kitchen fixing lunch for the two boys when they'd come in from school, and she heard Grace fall down in the living room. When you have a lot of children you don't always start running when one of them falls, unless they start screaming or something. And, this time, Gracie was quiet. Yet, Isabel says that when she heard that *thump* and then that silence, something happened to her to make her afraid. And she ran to the living room and there was little Grace on the floor, all twisted up, and the reason she hadn't screamed was that she couldn't get her breath. And when she did scream, it was the worst sound, Isabel says, that she'd ever heard in all her life, and she still hears it sometimes in her dreams. Isabel will sometimes wake me up with a low, moaning, strangling sound and I have to be quick to awaken her and hold her to me and where Isabel is weeping against me seems a mortal wound.

I think I may have written Sonny the very day that little Grace was buried. I was sitting in the living room in the dark, by myself, and I suddenly thought of Sonny. My trouble made his real.

One Saturday afternoon, when Sonny had been living with us, or anyway, been in our house, for nearly two weeks, I found myself wandering aimlessly about the living room, drinking from a can of beer, and trying to work up courage to search Sonny's room. He was out, he was usually out whenever I was home, and Isabel had taken the children to see their grandparents. Suddenly I was standing still in front of the living room window, watching Seventh Avenue. The idea of searching Sonny's room made me still. I scarcely dared to admit to myself what I'd be searching for. I didn't know what I'd do if I found it. Or if I didn't.

On the sidewalk across from me, near the entrance to a barbecue joint, some people were holding an old-fashioned revival meeting. The barbecue cook, wearing a dirty white apron, his conked hair reddish and metallic in the pale sun, and a cigarette between his lips, stood in the doorway, watching them. Kids and older people paused in their errands and stood there, along with some older men and a couple of very tough-looking women who watched everything that happened on the avenue, as though they owned it, or were maybe owned by it. Well, they were watching this, too. The revival was being carried on by three sisters in black, and a brother. All they had were their voices and their Bibles and a tambourine. The brother was testifying and while he testified two of the sisters stood together, seeming to say, amen, and the third sister walked around with the tambourine outstretched and a couple of people dropped coins into it. Then the brother's testimony ended and the sister who had been taking up the collection dumped the coins into her palm and transferred them to the pocket of her long black robe. Then she raised both hands, striking the tambourine against the air, and then against one hand, and she started to sing. And the two other sisters and the brother joined in.

It was strange, suddenly, to watch, though I had been seeing these meetings all my life. So, of course, had everybody else down there. Yet, they paused and watched and listened and I stood still at the window. "'Tis the old ship of Zion," they sang, and the sister with the tambourine kept a steady, jangling beat, "it has rescued many a thousand!" Not a soul under the sound of their voices was hearing this song for the first time, not one of them had been rescued. Nor had they seen much in the way of rescue work being done around them. Neither did they especially believe in the holiness of the three sisters and the brother, they knew too much about them, knew where they lived, and how. The woman with the tambourine, whose voice dominated the air, whose face was bright with joy, was divided by very little from the woman who stood watching her, a cigarette between her heavy, chapped lips, her hair a cuckoo's nest, her face scarred and swollen from many beatings, and her black eyes glittering like coal. Perhaps they both knew this, which was why, when, as rarely, they addressed each other, they addressed each other as Sister. As the singing filled the air the watching, listening faces underwent a change, the eyes focusing on something within; the music seemed to soothe a poison out of them; and time seemed, nearly, to fall away from the sullen, belligerent, battered faces, as though they were fleeing back to their first condition, while dreaming of their last. The barbecue cook half shook his head and smiled, and dropped his cigarette and disappeared into his joint. A man fumbled in his pockets for change and stood holding it in his hand impatiently, as though he had just remembered a pressing appointment further up the avenue. He looked furious. Then I saw Sonny, standing on the edge of the crowd. He was carrying a wide, flat notebook with a green cover, and it made him look, from where I was standing, almost like a schoolboy. The coppery sun brought out the copper in his skin, he was very faintly smiling, standing very still. Then the singing stopped, the tambourine turned into a collection plate again. The furious man dropped in his coins and vanished, so did a couple of the women, and Sonny dropped some change in the plate, looking directly at the woman with a little smile. He started across the avenue, toward the house. He has a slow, loping walk, something like the way Harlem hipsters walk, only he's imposed on this his own half-beat. I had never really noticed it before.

I stayed at the window, both relieved and apprehensive. As Sonny disappeared from my sight, they began singing again. And they were still singing when his key turned in the lock.

"Hey," he said.

"Hey, yourself. You want some beer?"

"No. Well, maybe." But he came up to the window and stood beside me, looking out. "What a warm voice," he said.

They were singing *If I could only hear my mother pray again!*

"Yes," I said, "and she can sure beat that tambourine."

"But what a terrible song," he said, and laughed. He dropped his notebook on the sofa and disappeared into the kitchen. "Where's Isabel and the kids?"

"I think they want to see their grandparents. You hungry?"

"No." He came back into the living room with his can of beer. "You want to come some place with me tonight?"

I sensed, I don't know how, that I couldn't possibly say no. "Sure. Where?"

He sat down on the sofa and picked up his notebook and started leafing through it. "I'm going to sit in with some fellows in a joint in the Village."

"You mean, you're going to play, tonight?"

"That's right." He took a swallow of his beer and moved back to the window. He gave me a sidelong look. "If you can stand it."

"I'll try," I said.

He smiled to himself and we both watched as the meeting across the way broke up. The three sisters and the brother, heads bowed, were singing *God be with you till we meet again.* The faces around them were very quiet. Then the song ended. The small crowd dispersed. We watched the three women and the lone man walk slowly up the avenue.

"When she was singing before," said Sonny, abruptly, "her voice reminded me for a minute of what heroin feels like sometimes—when it's in your veins. It makes you feel sort of warm and cool at the same time. And distant. And—and sure." He sipped his beer, very deliberately not looking at me. I watched his face. "It makes you feel—in control. Sometimes you've got to have that feeling."

"Do you?" I sat down slowly in the easy chair.

"Sometimes." He went to the sofa and picked up his notebook again. "Some people do."

"In order," I asked, "to play?" And my voice was very ugly, full of contempt and anger.

"Well"—he looked at me with great, troubled eyes, as though, in fact, he hoped his eyes would tell me things he could never otherwise say— "they *think* so. And *if* they think so—!"

"And what do *you* think?" I asked.

He sat on the sofa and put his can of beer on the floor. "I don't know," he said, and I couldn't be sure if he were answering my question or pursuing his thoughts. His face didn't tell me. "It's not so much to *play.* It's to *stand* it, to be able to make it at all. On any level." He frowned and smiled: "In order to keep from shaking to pieces."

"But these friends of yours," I said, "they seem to shake themselves to pieces pretty goddamn fast."

"Maybe." He played with the notebook. And something told me that I should curb my tongue, that Sonny was doing his best to talk, that I should listen. "But of course you only know the ones that've gone to pieces. Some don't—or at least they haven't *yet* and that's just about all *any* of us can say." He paused. "And then there are some who just live, really, in hell, and they know it and they see what's happening and they go right on. I don't know." He sighed, dropped the notebook, folded his arms. "Some guys, you can tell from the way they play, they on something *all* the time. And you can see that, well, it makes something real for them. But of course," he picked up his beer from the floor and sipped it and put the can down again, "they *want* to, too, you've got to see that. Even some of them that say they don't—*some,* not all."

"And what about you?" I asked—I couldn't help it. "What about you? Do *you* want to?"

He stood up and walked to the window and I remained silent for a long time. Then he sighed. "Me," he said. Then: "While I was downstairs before, on my way here, listening to that woman sing, it struck me all of a sudden how much suffering she must have had to go through—to sing like that. It's *repulsive* to think you have to suffer that much."

I said: "But there's no way not to suffer—is there, Sonny?"

"I believe not," he said and smiled, "but that's never stopped anyone from trying." He looked at me. "Has it?" I realized, with this mocking look, that there stood between us, forever, beyond the power of time or forgiveness, the fact that I had held silence—so long!—when he had needed human speech to help him. He turned back to the window. "No, there's no way not to suffer. But you try all kinds of ways to keep from drowning in it, to keep on top of it, and to make it seem—well, like *you*. Like you did something, all right, and now you're suffering for it. You know?" I said nothing. "Well you know," he said, impatiently, "why *do* people suffer? Maybe it's better to do something to give it a reason, *any* reason."

"But we just agreed," I said, "that there's no way not to suffer. Isn't it better, then, just to—take it?"

"But nobody just takes it," Sonny cried, "that's what I'm telling you! *Everybody* tries not to. You're just hung up on the *way* some people try—it's not *your* way!"

The hair on my face began to itch, my face felt wet. "That's not true." I said, "that's not true. I don't give a damn what other people do, I don't even care how they suffer. I just care how *you* suffer." And he looked at me. "Please believe me," I said, "I don't want to see you—die—trying not to suffer."

"I won't," he said flatly, "die trying not to suffer. At least, not any faster than anybody else."

"But there's no need," I said, trying to laugh, "is there? in killing yourself."

I wanted to say more, but I couldn't. I wanted to talk about will power and how life could be—well, beautiful. I wanted to say that it was all within; but was it? or, rather, wasn't that exactly the trouble? And I wanted to promise that I would never fail him again. But it would all have sounded—empty words and lies.

So I made the promise to myself and prayed that I would keep it.

"It's terrible sometimes, inside," he said, "that's what's the trouble. You walk these streets, black and funky and cold, and there's not really a living ass to talk to, and there's nothing shaking, and there's no way of getting it out—that storm inside. You can't talk it and you can't make love with it, and when you finally try to get with it and play it, you realize *nobody's* listening. So *you've* got to listen. You got to find a way to listen."

And then he walked away from the window and sat on the sofa again, as though all the wind had suddenly been knocked out of him. "Sometimes you'll do *anything* to play, even cut your mother's throat." He laughed and looked at me. "Or your brother's." Then he sobered. "Or your own." Then: "Don't worry. I'm all right now and I think I'll *be* all right. But I can't forget—where I've been. I don't mean just the physical place I've been, I mean where I've *been*. And *what* I've been."

"What have you been, Sonny?" I asked.

He smiled—but sat sideways on the sofa, his elbow resting on the back, his fingers playing with his mouth and chin, not looking at me. "I've been something I didn't recognize, didn't know I could be. Didn't know anybody could be." He stopped, looking inward, looking helplessly young, looking old. "I'm not talking about it now because I feel *guilty* or anything like that—maybe it would be better if I did, I don't know. Anyway, I can't really talk about it. Not to you, not to anybody," and now he turned and faced me. "Sometimes, you know, and it was actually when I was most *out* of the world, I felt that I was in it, that I was *with* it, really, and I could play or I didn't really have to *play*, it just came out of me, it was there. And I don't know how I played, thinking about it now, but I know I did awful things, those times, sometimes, to people. Or it wasn't that I *did* anything to them—it was that they weren't real." He picked up the beer can; it was empty; he rolled it between his palms: "And other times—well, I needed a fix, I needed to find a place to lean, I needed to clear a space to *listen*—and I couldn't find it, and I—went crazy, I did terrible things to *me*, I was terrible *for* me." He began pressing the beer can between his hands, I watched the metal begin to give. It glittered, as he played with it like a knife, and I was afraid he would cut himself, but I said nothing. "Oh well. I can never tell you. I was all by myself at the bottom of something, stinking and sweating and crying and shaking, and I smelled it, you know? *my* stink, and I thought I'd die if I couldn't get away from it and yet, all the same, I knew that everything I was doing was just locking me in with it. And I didn't know," he paused, still flattening the beer can, "I didn't know, I still *don't* know, something kept telling me that maybe it was good to smell your own stink, but I didn't think that *that* was what I'd been trying to do—and—who can stand it?" and he abruptly dropped the ruined beer can, looking at me with a small, still smile, and then rose, walking to the window as though it were the lodestone rock. I watched his face, he watched the avenue. "I couldn't tell you when Mama died—but the reason I wanted to leave Harlem so bad was to get away from drugs. And then, when I ran away, that's what I was running from— really. When I came back, nothing had changed, *I* hadn't changed, I was just—older." And he stopped, drumming with his fingers on the windowpane. The sun had vanished, soon darkness would fall. I watched his face. "It can come again," he said, almost as though speaking to himself. Then he turned to me. "It can come again," he repeated. "I just want you to know that."

"All right," I said, at last. "So it can come again. All right."

He smiled, but the smile was sorrowful. "I had to try to tell you," he said.

"Yes," I said. "I understand that."

"You're my brother," he said, looking straight at me, and not smiling at all.

"Yes," I repeated, "yes. I understand that."

He turned back to the window, looking out. "All that hatred down there," he said, "all that hatred and misery and love. It's a wonder it doesn't blow the avenue apart."

We went to the only nightclub on a short, dark street, downtown. We squeezed through the narrow, chattering, jampacked bar to the entrance of the big room, where the bandstand was. And we stood there for a moment, for the lights were very dim in this room and we couldn't see. Then, "Hello, boy," said the voice and an enormous black man, much older than Sonny or myself, erupted out of all that atmospheric lighting and put an arm around Sonny's shoulder. "I been sitting right here," he said, "waiting for you."

He had a big voice, too, and heads in the darkness turned toward us.

Sonny grinned and pulled a little away, and said, "Creole, this is my brother. I told you about him."

Creole shook my hand. "I'm glad to meet you, son," he said, and it was clear that he was glad to meet me *there*, for Sonny's sake. And he smiled, "You got a real musician in *your* family," and he took his arm from Sonny's shoulder and slapped him, lightly, affectionately, with the back of his hand.

"Well. Now I've heard it all," said a voice behind us. This was another musician, and a friend of Sonny's, a coal-black, cheerful-looking man, built close to the ground. He immediately began confiding to me, at the top of his lungs, the most terrible things about Sonny, his teeth gleaming like a lighthouse and his laugh coming up out of him like the beginning of an earthquake. And it turned out that everyone at the bar knew Sonny, or almost everyone; some were musicians, working there, or nearby, or not working, some were simply hangers-on, and some were there to hear Sonny play. I was introduced to all of them and they were all very polite to me. Yet, it was clear that, for them, I was only Sonny's brother. Here, I was in Sonny's world. Or, rather: his kingdom. Here, it was not even a question that his veins bore royal blood.

They were going to play soon and Creole installed me, by myself, at a table in a dark corner. Then I watched them, Creole, and the little black man, and Sonny, and the others, while they horsed around, standing just below the bandstand. The light from the bandstand spilled just a little short of them and, watching them laughing and gesturing and moving about, I had the feeling that they, nevertheless, were being most careful not to step into that circle of light too suddenly; that if they moved into the light too suddenly, without thinking, they would perish in flame.

Then, while I watched, one of them, the small black man, moved into the light and crossed the bandstand and started fooling around with his drums. Then—being funny and being, also, extremely ceremonious—Creole took Sonny by the arm and led him to the piano. A woman's voice called Sonny's name and a few hands started clapping. And Sonny, also being funny and being ceremonious, and so touched, I think, that he could have cried, but neither hiding it nor showing it, riding it like a man, grinned, and put both hands to his heart and bowed from the waist.

Creole then went to the bass fiddle and a lean, very bright-skinned brown man jumped up on the bandstand and picked up his horn. So there they were, and the atmosphere on the bandstand and in the room began to change and tighten. Someone stepped up to the microphone and announced them. Then there were all kinds of murmurs. Some people at the bar shushed others. The waitress ran around, frantically getting in the last orders, guys and chicks got closer to each other, and the lights on the bandstand, on the quartet, turned to a kind of indigo. Then they all looked different there. Creole looked about him for the last time, as though he were making certain that all his chickens were in the coop, and then he—jumped and struck the fiddle. And there they were.

All I know about music is that not many people ever really hear it. And even then, on the rare occasions when something opens within, and the music enters, what we mainly hear, or hear corroborated, are personal, private, vanishing evocations. But the man who creates the music is hearing something else, is dealing with the roar rising from the void and imposing order on it as it hits the air. What is evoked in him, then, is of another order, more terrible because it has no words, and triumphant, too, for that same reason. And his triumph, when he triumphs, is ours. I just watched Sonny's face. His face was troubled, he was working hard, but he wasn't with it. And I had the feeling that, in a way, everyone on the bandstand was waiting for him, both waiting for him and pushing him along. But as I began to watch Creole, I realized that it was Creole who held them all back. He had them on a short rein. Up there, keeping the beat with his whole body, wailing on the fiddle, with his eyes half closed, he was listening to everything, but he was listening to Sonny. He was having a dialogue with Sonny. He wanted Sonny to leave the shoreline and strike out for the deep water. He was Sonny's witness that deep water and drowning were not the same thing—he had been there, and he knew. And he wanted Sonny to know. He was waiting for Sonny to do the things on the keys which would let Creole know that Sonny was in the water.

And, while Creole listened, Sonny moved, deep within, exactly like someone in torment. I had never before thought of how awful the relationship must be between the musician and his instrument. He has to fill it, this instrument, with the breath of life, his own. He has to make it do what he wants it to do. And a piano is just a piano. It's made out of so much wood and wires and little hammers and big ones, and ivory. While there's only so much you can do with it, the only way to find this out is to try; to try and make it do everything.

And Sonny hadn't been near a piano for over a year. And he wasn't on much better terms with his life, not the life that stretched before him now. He and the piano stammered, started one way, got scared, stopped; started another way, panicked, marked time, started again; then seemed to have found a direction, panicked again, got stuck. And the face I saw on Sonny I'd never seen before. Everything had been burned out of it, and, at the same time, things usually hidden were being burned in, by the fire and fury of the battle which was occurring in him up there.

Yet, watching Creole's face as they neared the end of the first set, I had the feeling that something had happened, something I hadn't heard. Then they finished, there was scattered applause, and then, without an instant's warning, Creole started into something else, it was almost sardonic, it was *Am I Blue.* And, as though he commanded, Sonny began to play. Something began to happen. And Creole let out the reins. The dry, low, black man said something awful on the drums, Creole answered, and the drums talked back. Then the horn insisted, sweet and high, slightly detached perhaps, and Creole listened, commenting now and then, dry, and driving, beautiful and calm and old. Then they all came together again, and Sonny was part of the family again. I could tell this from his face. He seemed to have found, right there beneath his fingers, a damn brand-new piano. It seemed that he couldn't get over it. Then, for a while, just being happy with Sonny, they seemed to be agreeing with him that brand-new pianos certainly were a gas.

Then Creole stepped forward to remind them that what they were playing was the blues. He hit something in all of them, he hit something in me, myself, and the music tightened and deepened, apprehension began to beat the air. Creole began to tell us what the blues were all about. They were not about anything very new. He and his boys up there were keeping it new, at the risk of ruin, destruction, madness, and death, in order to find new ways to make us listen. For, while the tale of how we suffer, and how we are delighted, and how we may triumph is never new, it always must be beard. There isn't any other tale to tell, it's the only light we've got in all this darkness.

And this tale, according to that face, that body, those strong hands on those strings, has another aspect in every country, and a new depth in every generation. Listen, Creole seemed to be saying, listen. Now these are Sonny's blues. He made the little black man on the drums know it, and the bright, brown man on the horn. Creole wasn't trying any longer to get Sonny in the water. He was wishing him Godspeed. Then he stepped back, very slowly, filling the air with the immense suggestion that Sonny speak for himself.

Then they all gathered around Sonny and Sonny played. Every now and again one of them seemed to say, amen. Sonny's fingers filled the air with life, his life. But that life contained so many others. And Sonny went all the way back, he really began with the spare, flat statement of the opening phrase of the song. Then he began to make it his. It was very beautiful because it wasn't hurried and it was no longer a lament. I seemed to hear with what burning he had made it his, and what burning we had yet to make it ours, how we could cease lamenting. Freedom lurked around us and I understood, at last, that he could help us to be free if we would listen, that he would never be free until we did. Yet, there was no battle in his face now, I heard what he had gone through, and would continue to go through until he came to rest in earth. He had made it his: that long line, of which we knew only Mama and Daddy. And he was giving it back, as everything must be given back, so that, passing through death, it can live forever. I saw my mother's face again, and felt, for the first time, how the stones of the road she had walked on must have bruised her feet. I saw the moonlit road where my father's brother died. And it brought something else back to me, and carried me past it, I saw my little girl again and felt Isabel's tears again, and I felt my own tears begin to rise. And I was yet aware that this was only a moment, that the world waited outside, as hungry as a tiger, and that trouble stretched above us, longer than the sky.

Then it was over. Creole and Sonny let out their breath, both soaking wet, and grinning. There was a lot of applause and some of it was real. In the dark, the girl came by and I asked her to take drinks to the bandstand. There was a long pause, while they talked up there in the indigo light and after awhile I saw the girl put a Scotch and milk on top of the piano for Sonny. He didn't seem to notice it, but just before they started playing again, he sipped from it and looked toward me, and nodded. Then he put it back on top of the piano. For me, then, as they began to play again, it glowed and shook above my brother's head like the very cup of trembling.

Wished on the Moon

Ben Hausmann

In addition to being a college freshman, Ben
Hausmann is also a DJ. Ben was recently promoted
from dishwasher to busboy at a Missoula, Montana,
restaurant.

The moon was spectacular the other night—a single,
golden crescent—like a moon from a painting or a
children's storybook. It was so beautiful. It brought me
nearly to tears. Blinking them away, I turned from it in
the dark and back to my mother who was standing behind me
in the driveway.

"Do you remember?" I asked, " . . . I think it's from a
movie. There is a scene where a man and a woman are
talking, and the woman mentions something, a song, a poem;
I'm not sure what, and the man says to her about it, '. . .
a little sad, don't you think?' And the woman pauses for a
sec and replies, 'Melancholy maybe, but never sad.'"

She shrugged, "I don't think I've heard that."

"It's from an old movie, I think," I tried to jog her
memory, but she had already started for the house. I gave
up, followed her in, and closed the door on the moon.

A few hours later, after my mother and everyone else
in the house had gone off to bed, I crept back up the
stairs and out of the door.

The moon had just begun to set, and I could barely see
it over the very tops of the trees. I tried to climb a
tree in the yard to get a better look, but the sprinklers
had come on and my bare feet couldn't get a hold on the
wet bark. I stood back, away from the mist of the
sprinklers, and watched as the moon sank slowly behind
the spreading branches. I whispered under my breath to
the moon as I stood there half-naked in the dewy grass,
until all that was left of the bright, watery orb was a
soft glow through the trees. I set off back down stairs,
closing and locking the door softly behind me, and dug
out a Bille Holiday CD. I put it in, hit *Play* and, having
made my wish, I got ready to go to bed.

9

NATURE AND
THE ENVIRONMENT

THE LAND ETHIC

Aldo Leopold

This selection is from the Sand County Almanac, *published in 1949.*

When God-like Odysseus returned from the wars in Troy, he hanged all on one rope a dozen slave-girls of his household whom he suspected of misbehavior during his absence.

This hanging involved no question of propriety. The girls were property. The disposal of property was then, as now, a matter of expediency, not of right and wrong.

Concepts of right and wrong were not lacking from Odysseus' Greece: witness the fidelity of his wife through the long years before at last his black-prowed galleys clove the wine-dark seas for home. The ethical structure of that day covered wives, but had not yet been extended to human chattels. During the three thousand years which have since elapsed, ethical criteria have been extended to many fields of conduct, with corresponding shrinkages in those judged by expediency only.

THE ETHICAL SEQUENCE

This extension of ethics, so far studied only by philosophers, is actually a process in ecological evolution. Its sequences may be described in ecological as well as in philosophical terms. An ethic, ecologically, is a limitation on freedom of action in the struggle for existence. An ethic, philosophically, is a differentiation of social from anti-social conduct. These are two definitions of one thing. The thing has its origin in the tendency of interdependent individuals or groups to evolve modes of co-operation. The ecologist calls these symbioses. Politics and economics are advanced symbioses in which the original free-for-all competition has been replaced, in part, by co-operative mechanisms with an ethical content.

The complexity of co-operative mechanisms has increased with population density, and with the efficiency of tools. It was simpler, for example, to define the anti-social uses of sticks and stones in the days of the mastodons than of bullets and billboards in the age of motors.

The first ethics dealt with the relation between individuals; the Mosaic Decalogue is an example. Later accretions dealt with the relation between the individual and society. The Golden Rule tries to integrate the individual to society; democracy to integrate social organization to the individual.

There is as yet no ethic dealing with man's relation to land and to the animals and plants which grow upon it. Land, like Odysseus' slave-girls, is still property. The land-relation is still strictly economic, entailing privileges but not obligations.

The extension of ethics to this third element in human environment is, if I read the evidence correctly, an evolutionary possibility and an ecological necessity. It is the third step in a sequence. The first two have already been taken. Individual thinkers since the days of Ezekiel and Isaiah have asserted that the despoliation of land is not only inexpedient but wrong. Society, however, has not yet affirmed their belief. I regard the present conservation movement as the embryo of such an affirmation.

An ethic may be regarded as a mode of guidance for meeting ecological situations so new or intricate, or involving such deferred reactions, that the path of social expediency is not discernible to the average individual. Animal instincts are modes of guidance for the individual in meeting such situations. Ethics are possibly a kind of community instinct in-the-making.

THE COMMUNITY CONCEPT

All ethics so far evolved rest upon a single premise: that the individual is a member of a community of interdependent parts. His instincts prompt him to compete for his place in the community, but his ethics prompt him also to co-operate (perhaps in order that there may be a place to compete for).

The land ethic simply enlarges the boundaries of the community to include soils, waters, plants, and animals, or collectively: the land.

This sounds simple: do we not already sing our love for and obligation to the land of the free and the home of the brave? Yes, but just what and whom do we love? Certainly not the soil, which we are sending helter-skelter downriver. Certainly not the waters, which we assume have no function except to turn turbines, float barges, and carry off sewage. Certainly not the plants, of which we exterminate whole communities without batting an eye. Certainly not the animals, of which we have already extirpated many of the largest and most beautiful species. A land ethic of course cannot prevent the alteration, management, and use of these "resources," but it does affirm their right to continued existence, and, at least in spots, their continued existence in a natural state.

In short, a land ethic changes the role of *Homo sapiens* from conqueror of the land-community to plain member and citizen of it. It implies respect for his fellow-members, and also respect for the community as such.

In human history, we have learned (I hope) that the conqueror role is eventually self-defeating. Why? Because it is implicit in such a role that the conqueror knows, *ex cathedra*, just what makes the community clock tick, and just what and who is valuable, and what and who is worthless, in community life. It always turns out that he knows neither, and this is why his conquests eventually defeat themselves.

In the biotic community, a parallel situation exists. Abraham knew exactly what the land was for: it was to drip milk and honey into Abraham's mouth. At the present moment, the assurance with which we regard this assumption is inverse to the degree of our education.

The ordinary citizen today assumes that science knows what makes the community clock tick; the scientist is equally sure that he does not. He knows that the biotic mechanism is so complex that its workings may never be fully understood.

That man is, in fact, only a member of a biotic team is shown by an ecological interpretation of history. Many historical events, hitherto explained solely in terms of human enterprise, were actually biotic interactions between people and land. The characteristics of the land determined the facts quite as potently as the characteristics of the men who lived on it.

Consider, for example, the settlement of the Mississippi valley. In the years following the Revolution, three groups were contending for its control: the native Indian, the French and English traders, and the American settlers. Historians wonder what would have happened if the English at Detroit had thrown a little more weight into the Indian side of those tipsy scales which decided the outcome of the colonial migration into the cane-lands of Kentucky. It is time now to ponder the fact that the cane-lands, when subjected to the particular mixture of forces represented by the cow, plow, fire, and axe of the pioneer, became bluegrass. What if the plant succession inherent in this dark and bloody ground had, under the impact of these forces, given us some worthless sedge, shrub, or weed? Would Boone and Kenton have held out? Would there have been any overflow into Ohio, Indiana, Illinois, and Missouri? Any Louisiana Purchase? Any transcontinental union of new states? Any Civil War?

Kentucky was one sentence in the drama of history. We are commonly told what the human actors in this drama tried to do, but we are seldom told that their success, or the lack of it, hung in large degree on the reaction of particular soils to the impact of the particular forces exerted by their occupancy. In the case of Kentucky, we do not even know where the bluegrass came from—whether it is a native species, or a stowaway from Europe.

Contrast the cane-lands with what hindsight tells us about the Southwest, where the pioneers were equally brave, resourceful, and persevering. The impact of occupancy here brought no bluegrass, or other plant fitted to withstand the bumps and buffetings of hard use. This region, when grazed by livestock, reverted through a series of more and more worthless grasses, shrubs, and weeds to a condition of unstable equilibrium. Each recession of plant types bred erosion; each increment to erosion bred a further recession of plants. The result today is a progressive and mutual deterioration, not only of plants and soils, but of the animal community subsisting thereon. The early settlers did not expect this: on the ciénegas of New Mexico some even cut ditches to hasten it. So subtle has been its progress that few residents of the region are aware of it. It is quite invisible to the tourist who finds this wrecked landscape colorful and charming (as indeed it is, but it bears scant resemblance to what it was in 1848).

This same landscape was "developed" once before, but with quite different results. The Pueblo Indians settled the Southwest in pre-Columbian times, but they happened *not* to be equipped with range livestock. Their civilization expired, but not because their land expired.

In India, regions devoid of any sod-forming grass have been settled, apparently without wrecking the land, by the simple expedient of carrying the grass to the cow, rather than vice versa. (Was this the result of some deep wisdom, or was it just good luck? I do not know.)

In short, the plant succession steered the course of history; the pioneer simply demonstrated, for good or ill, what successions inhered in the land. Is history taught in this spirit? It will be, once the concept of land as a community really penetrates our intellectual life.

THE ECOLOGICAL CONSCIENCE

Conservation is a state of harmony between men and land. Despite nearly a century of propaganda, conservation still proceeds at a snail's pace; progress still consists largely of letterhead pieties and convention oratory. On the back forty we still slip two steps backward for each forward stride.

The usual answer to this dilemma is "more conservation education." No one will debate this, but is it certain that only the *volume* of education needs stepping up? Is something lacking in the *content* as well?

It is difficult to give a fair summary of its content in brief form, but, as I understand it, the content is substantially this: obey the law, vote right, join some organizations, and practice what conservation is profitable on your own land; the government will do the rest.

Is not this formula too easy to accomplish anything worth-while? It defines no right or wrong, assigns no obligation, calls for no sacrifice, implies no change in the current philosophy of values. In respect of land-use, it urges only enlightened self-interest. Just how far will such education take us? An example will perhaps yield a partial answer.

By 1930 it had become clear to all except the ecologically blind that southwestern Wisconsin's topsoil was slipping seaward. In 1933 the farmers were told that if they would adopt certain remedial practices for five years, the public would donate CCC labor to install them, plus the necessary machinery and materials. The offer was widely accepted, but the practices were widely forgotten when the five-year contract period was up. The farmers continued only those practices that yielded an immediate and visible economic gain for themselves.

This led to the idea that maybe farmers would learn more quickly if they themselves wrote the rules. Accordingly the Wisconsin Legislature in 1937 passed the Soil Conservation District Law. This said to farmers, in effect: *We, the public, will furnish you free technical service and loan you specialized machinery, if you will write your own rules for land-use. Each county may write its own rules, and these will have the force of law.* Nearly all the counties promptly organized to accept the proffered help, but after a decade of operation, *no county has yet written a single rule.* There has been visible progress in such practices as strip-cropping, pasture renovation, and soil liming, but none in fencing woodlots against grazing, and none in excluding plow and cow from steep slopes. The farmers, in short, have selected those remedial practices which were profitable anyhow, and ignored those which were profitable to the community, but not clearly profitable to themselves.

When one asks why no rules have been written, one is told that the community is not yet ready to support them; education must precede rules. But the education actually in progress makes no mention of obligations to land over and above those dictated by self-interest. The net result is that we have more education but less soil, fewer healthy woods, and as many floods as in 1937.

The puzzling aspect of such situations is that the existence of obligations over and above self-interest is taken for granted in such rural community enterprises as the betterment of roads, schools, churches, and baseball teams. Their existence is not taken for granted, nor as yet seriously discussed, in bettering the behavior of the water that falls on the land, or in the preserving of the beauty or diversity of the farm landscape. Land-use ethics are still governed wholly by economic self-interest, just as social ethics were a century ago.

To sum up: we asked the farmer to do what he conveniently could to save his soil, and he has done just that, and only that. The farmer who clears the woods off a 75 per cent slope, turns his cows into the clearing, and dumps its rainfall, rocks, and soil into the community creek, is still (if otherwise decent) a respected member of society. If he puts lime on his fields and plants his crops on contour, he is still entitled to all the privileges and emoluments of his Soil Conservation District. The District is a beautiful piece of social machinery, but it is coughing along on two cylinders because we have been too timid, and too anxious for quick success, to tell the farmer the true magnitude of his obligations. Obligations have no meaning without conscience, and the problem we face is the extension of the social conscience from people to land.

No important change in ethics was ever accomplished without an internal change in our intellectual emphasis, loyalties, affections, and convictions. The proof that conservation has not yet touched these foundations of conduct lies in the fact that philosophy and religion have not yet heard of it. In our attempt to make conservation easy, we have made it trivial.

SUBSTITUTES FOR A LAND ETHIC

When the logic of history hungers for bread and we hand out a stone, we are at pains to explain how much the stone resembles bread. I now describe some of the stones which serve in lieu of a land ethic.

One basic weakness in a conservation system based wholly on economic motives is that most members of the land community have no economic value. Wildflowers and songbirds are examples. Of the 22,000 higher plants and animals native to Wisconsin, it is doubtful whether more than 5 per cent can be sold, fed, eaten, or otherwise put to economic use. Yet these creatures are members of the biotic community, and if (as I believe) its stability depends on its integrity, they are entitled to continuance.

When one of these non-economic categories is threatened, and if we happen to love it, we invent subterfuges to give it economic importance. At the beginning of the century songbirds were supposed to be disappearing. Ornithologists jumped to the rescue with some distinctly shaky evidence to the effect that insects would eat us up if birds failed to control them. The evidence had to be economic in order to be valid.

It is painful to read these circumlocutions today. We have no land ethic yet, but we have at least drawn nearer the point of admitting that birds should continue as a matter of biotic right, regardless of the presence or absence of economic advantage to us.

A parallel situation exists in respect of predatory mammals, raptorial birds, and fish-eating birds. Time was when biologists somewhat overworked the evidence that these creatures preserve the health of game by killing weaklings, or that they control rodents for the farmer, or that they prey only on "worthless" species. Here again, the evidence had to be economic in order to be valid. It is only in recent years that we hear the more honest argument that predators are members of the community, and that no special interest has the right to exterminate them for the sake of a benefit, real or fancied, to itself. Unfortunately this enlightened view is still in the talk stage. In the field the extermination of predators goes merrily on: witness the impending erasure of the timber wolf by fiat of Congress, the Conservation Bureaus, and many state legislatures.

Some species of trees have been "read out of the party" by economics-minded foresters because they grow too slowly, or have too low a sale value to pay as timber crops: white cedar, tamarack, cypress, beech, and hemlock are examples. In Europe, where forestry is ecologically more advanced, the non-commercial tree species are recognized as members of the native forest community, to be preserved as such, within reason. Moreover some (like beech) have been found to have a valuable function in building up soil fertility. The interdependence of the forest and its constituent tree species, ground flora, and fauna is taken for granted.

Lack of economic value is sometimes a character not only of species or groups, but of entire biotic communities: marshes, bogs, dunes, and "deserts" are examples. Our formula in such cases is to relegate their conservation to government as refuges, monuments, or parks. The difficulty is that these communities are usually interspersed with more valuable private lands; the government cannot possibly own or control such scattered parcels. The net effect is that we have relegated some of them to ultimate extinction over large areas. If the private owner were ecologically minded, he would be proud to be the custodian of a reasonable proportion of such areas, which add diversity and beauty to his farm and to his community.

In some instances, the assumed lack of profit in these "waste" areas has proved to be wrong, but only after most of them had been done away with. The present scramble to reflood muskrat marshes is a case in point.

There is a clear tendency in American conservation to relegate to government all necessary jobs that private landowners fail to perform. Government ownership, operation, subsidy, or regulation is now widely prevalent in forestry, range management, soil and watershed management, park and wilderness conservation, fisheries management, and migratory bird management, with more to come. Most of this growth in governmental conservation is proper and logical, some of it is inevitable. That I imply no disapproval of it is implicit in the fact that I have spent most of my life working for it. Nevertheless the question arises: What is the ultimate magnitude of the enterprise? Will the tax base carry its eventual ramifications? At what point will governmental conservation, like the mastodon, become handicapped by its own dimensions? The answer, if there is any, seems to be in a land ethic, or some other force which assigns more obligation to the private landowner.

Industrial landowners and users, especially lumbermen and stockmen, are inclined to wail long and loudly about the extension of government ownership and regulation to land, but (with notable exceptions) they show little disposition to develop the only visible alternative: the voluntary practice of conservation on their own lands.

When the private landowner is asked to perform some unprofitable act for the good of the community, he today assents only with outstretched palm. If the act costs him cash this is fair and proper, but when it costs only fore-thought, open-mindedness, or time, the issue is at least debatable. The overwhelming growth of land-use subsidies in recent years must be ascribed, in large part, to the government's own agencies for conservation education: the land bureaus, the agricultural colleges, and the extension services. As far as I can detect, no ethical obligation toward land is taught in these institutions.

To sum up: a system of conservation based solely on economic self-interest is hopelessly lopsided. It tends to ignore, and thus eventually to eliminate, many elements in the land community that lack commercial value, but that are (as far as we know) essential to its healthy functioning. It assumes, falsely, I think, that the economic parts of the biotic clock will function without the uneconomic parts. It tends to relegate to government many functions eventually too large, too complex, or too widely dispersed to be performed by government.

An ethical obligation on the part of the private owner is the only visible remedy for these situations.

THE LAND PYRAMID

An ethic to supplement and guide the economic relation to land presupposes the existence of some mental image of land as a biotic mechanism.

We can be ethical only in relation to something we can see, feel, understand, love, or otherwise have faith in.

The image commonly employed in conservation education is "the balance of nature." For reasons too lengthy to detail here, this figure of speech fails to describe accurately what little we know about the land mechanism. A much truer image is the one employed in ecology: the biotic pyramid. I shall first sketch the pyramid as a symbol of land, and later develop some of its implications in terms of land-use.

Plants absorb energy from the sun. This energy flows through a circuit called the biota, which may be represented by a pyramid consisting of layers. The bottom layer is the soil. A plant layer rests on the soil, an insect layer on the plants, a bird and rodent layer on the insects, and so on up through various animal groups to the apex layer, which consists of the larger carnivores.

The species of a layer are alike not in where they came from, or in what they look like, but rather in what they eat. Each successive layer depends on those below it for food and often for other services, and each in turn furnishes food and services to those above. Proceeding upward, each successive layer decreases in numerical abundance. Thus, for every carnivore there are hundreds of his prey, thousands of their prey, millions of insects, uncountable plants. The pyramidal form of the system reflects this numerical progression from apex to base. Man shares an intermediate layer with the bears, raccoons, and squirrels which eat both meat and vegetables.

The lines of dependency for food and other services are called food chains. Thus soil-oak-deer-Indian is a chain that has now been largely converted to soil-corn-cow-farmer. Each species, including ourselves, is a link in many chains. The deer eats a hundred plants other than oak, and the cow a hundred plants other than corn. Both, then, are links in a hundred chains. The pyramid is a tangle of chains so complex as to seem disorderly, yet the stability of the system proves it to be a highly organized structure. Its functioning depends on the co-operation and competition of its diverse parts.

In the beginning, the pyramid of life was low and squat; the food chains short and simple. Evolution has added layer after layer, link after link. Man is one of thousands of accretions to the height and complexity of the pyramid. Science has given us many doubts, but it has given us at least one certainty: the trend of evolution is to elaborate and diversify the biota.

Land, then, is not merely soil; it is a fountain of energy flowing through a circuit of soils, plants, and animals. Food chains are the living channels which conduct energy upward; death and decay return it to the soil. The circuit is not closed; some energy is dissipated in decay, some is added by absorption from the air, some is stored in soils, peats, and long-lived forests; but it is a sustained circuit, like a slowly augmented revolving fund of life. There is always a net loss by downhill wash, but this is normally small and offset by the decay of rocks. It is deposited in the ocean and, in the course of geological time, raised to form new lands and new pyramids.

The velocity and character of the upward flow of energy depend on the complex structure of the plant and animal community, much as the upward flow of sap in a tree depends on its complex cellular organization. Without this complexity, normal circulation would presumably not occur. Structure means the characteristic numbers, as well as the characteristic kinds and functions, of the component species. This interdependence between the complex structure of the land and its smooth functioning as an energy unit is one of its basic attributes.

When a change occurs in one part of the circuit, many other parts must adjust themselves to it. Change does not necessarily obstruct or divert the flow of energy; evolution is a long series of self-induced changes, the net result of which has been to elaborate the flow mechanism and to lengthen the circuit. Evolutionary changes, however, are usually slow and local. Man's invention of tools has enabled him to make changes of unprecedented violence, rapidity, and scope.

One change is in the composition of floras and faunas. The larger predators are lopped off the apex of the pyramid; food chains, for the first time in history, become shorter rather than longer. Domesticated species from other lands are substituted for wild ones, and wild ones are moved to new habitats. In this world-wide pooling of faunas and floras, some species get out of bounds as pests and diseases, others are extinguished. Such effects are seldom intended or foreseen; they represent unpredicted and often untraceable readjustments in the structure. Agricultural science is largely a race between the emergence of new pests and the emergence of new techniques for their control.

Another change touches the flow of energy through plants and animals and its return to the soil. Fertility is the ability of soil to receive, store, and release energy. Agriculture, by overdrafts on the soil, or by too radical a substitution of domestic for native species in the superstructure, may derange the channels of flow or deplete storage. Soils depleted of their storage, or of the organic matter which anchors it, wash away faster than they form. This is erosion.

Waters, like soil, are part of the energy circuit. Industry, by polluting waters or obstructing them with dams, may exclude the plants and animals necessary to keep energy in circulation.

Transportation brings about another basic change: the plants or animals grown in one region are now consumed and returned to the soil in another. Transportation taps the energy stored in rocks, and in the air, and uses it elsewhere; thus we fertilize the garden with nitrogen gleaned by the guano birds from the fishes of seas on the other side of the Equator. Thus the formerly localized and self-contained circuits are pooled on a world-wide scale.

The process of altering the pyramid for human occupation releases stored energy, and this often gives rise, during the pioneering period, to a deceptive exuberance of plant and animal life, both wild and tame. These releases of biotic capital tend to becloud or postpone the penalties of violence.

■ ■ ■

This thumbnail sketch of land as an energy circuit conveys three basic ideas:

1. That land is not merely soil.
2. That the native plants and animals kept the energy circuit open; others may or may not.
3. That man-made changes are of a different order than evolutionary changes, and have effects more comprehensive than is intended or foreseen.

These ideas, collectively, raise two basic issues: Can the land adjust itself to the new order? Can the desired alterations be accomplished with less violence?

Biotas seem to differ in their capacity to sustain violent conversion. Western Europe, for example, carries a far different pyramid than Caesar found there. Some large animals are lost; swampy forests have become meadows or plowland; many new plants and animals are introduced, some of which escape as pests; the remaining natives are greatly changed in distribution and abundance. Yet the soil is still there and, with the help of imported nutrients, still fertile; the waters flow normally; the new structure seems to function and to persist. There is no visible stoppage or derangement of the circuit.

Western Europe, then, has a resistant biota. Its inner processes are tough, elastic, resistant to strain. No matter how violent the alterations, the pyramid, so far, has developed some new *modus vivendi* which preserves its habitability for man, and for most of the other natives.

Japan seems to present another instance of radical conversion without disorganization.

Most other civilized regions, and some as yet barely touched by civilization, display various stages of disorganization, varying from initial symptoms to advanced wastage. In Asia Minor and North Africa diagnosis is confused by climatic changes, which may have been either the cause or the effect of advanced wastage. In the United States the degree of disorganization varies locally; it is worst in the Southwest, the Ozarks, and parts of the South, and least in New England and the Northwest. Better land-uses may still arrest it in the less advanced regions. In parts of Mexico, South America, South Africa, and Australia a violent and accelerating wastage is in progress, but I cannot assess the prospects.

This almost world-wide display of disorganization in the land seems to be similar to disease in an animal, except that it never culminates in complete disorganization or death. The land recovers, but at some reduced level of complexity, and with a reduced carrying capacity for people, plants, and animals. Many biotas currently regarded as "lands of opportunity" are in fact already subsisting on exploitative agriculture, i.e. they have already exceeded their sustained carrying capacity. Most of South America is overpopulated in this sense.

In arid regions we attempt to offset the process of wastage by reclamation, but it is only too evident that the prospective longevity of reclamation projects is often short. In our own West, the best of them may not last a century.

The combined evidence of history and ecology seems to support one general deduction: the less violent the man-made changes, the greater the probability of successful readjustment in the pyramid. Violence, in turn, varies with human population density; a dense population requires a more violent conversion. In this respect, North America has a better chance for permanence than Europe, if she can contrive to limit her density.

This deduction runs counter to our current philosophy, which assumes that because a small increase in density enriched human life, that an indefinite increase will enrich it indefinitely. Ecology knows of no density relationship that holds for indefinitely wide limits. All gains from density are subject to a law of diminishing returns.

Whatever may be the equation for men and land, it is improbable that we as yet know all its terms. Recent discoveries in mineral and vitamin nutrition reveal unsuspected dependencies in the up-circuit: incredibly minute quantities of certain substances determine the value of soils to plants, of plants to animals. What of the down-circuit? What of the vanishing species, the preservation of which we now regard as an esthetic luxury? They helped build the soil; in what unsuspected ways may they be essential to its maintenance? Professor Weaver proposes that we use prairie flowers to reflocculate the wasting soils of the dust bowl; who knows for what purpose cranes and condors, otters and grizzlies may some day be used?

LAND HEALTH AND THE A-B CLEAVAGE

A land, ethic, then, reflects the existence of an ecological conscience, and this in turn reflects a conviction of individual responsibility for the health of the land. Health is the capacity of the land for self-renewal. Conservation is our effort to understand and preserve this capacity.

Conservationists are notorious for their dissensions. Superficially these seem to add up to mere confusion, but a more careful scrutiny reveals a single plane of cleavage common to many specialized fields. In each field one group (A) regards the land as soil, and its function as commodity-production; another group (B) regards the land as a biota, and its function as something broader. How much broader is admittedly in a state of doubt and confusion.

In my own field, forestry, group A is quite content to grow trees like cabbages, with cellulose as the basic forest commodity. It feels no inhibition against violence; its ideology is agronomic. Group B, on the other hand, sees forestry as fundamentally different from agronomy because it employs natural species, and manages a natural environment rather than creating an artificial one. Group B prefers natural reproduction on principle. It worries on biotic as well as economic grounds about the loss of species like chestnut, and the threatened loss of the white pines. It worries about a whole series of secondary forest functions: wildlife, recreation, watersheds, wilderness areas. To my mind, Group B feels the stirrings of an ecological conscience.

In the wildlife field, a parallel cleavage exists. For Group A the basic commodities are sport and meat; the yardsticks of production are ciphers of take in pheasants and trout. Artificial propagation is acceptable as a permanent as well as a temporary recourse—if its unit costs permit. Group B, on the other hand, worries about a whole series of biotic side-issues. What is the cost in predators of producing a game crop? Should we have further recourse to exotics? How can management restore the shrinking species, like prairie grouse, already hopeless as shootable game? How can management restore the threatened rarities, like trumpeter swan and whooping crane? Can management principles be extended to wild-flowers? Here again it is clear to me that we have the same A-B cleavage as in forestry.

In the larger field of agriculture I am less competent to speak, but there seem to be somewhat parallel cleavages. Scientific agriculture was actively developing before ecology was born, hence a slower penetration of ecological concepts might be expected. Moreover the farmer, by the very nature of his techniques, must modify the biota more radically than the forester or the wildlife manager. Nevertheless, there are many discontents in agriculture which seem to add up to a new vision of "biotic farming."

Perhaps the most important of these is the new evidence that poundage or tonnage is no measure of the food-value of farm crops; the products of fertile soil may be qualitatively as well as quantitatively superior. We can bolster poundage from depleted soils by pouring on imported fertility, but we are not necessarily bolstering food-value. The possible ultimate ramifications of this idea are so immense that I must leave their exposition to abler pens.

The discontent that labels itself "organic farming," while bearing some of the earmarks of a cult, is nevertheless biotic in its direction, particularly in its insistence on the importance of soil flora and fauna.

The ecological fundamentals of agriculture are just as poorly known to the public as in other fields of land-use. For example, few educated people realize that the marvelous advances in technique made during recent decades are improvements in the pump, rather than the well. Acre for acre, they have barely sufficed to offset the sinking level of fertility.

In all of these cleavages, we see repeated the same basic paradoxes: man the conqueror *versus* man the biotic citizen; science the sharpener of his sword *versus* science the searchlight on his universe; land the slave and servant *versus* land the collective organism. Robinson's injunction to

Tristram may well be applied, at this juncture, to *Homo sapiens* as a species in geological time:

> Whether you will or not
> You are a King, Tristram, for you are one
> Of the time-tested few that leave the world,
> When they are gone, not the same place it was.
> Mark what you leave.

THE OUTLOOK

It is inconceivable to me that an ethical relation to land can exist without love, respect, and admiration for land, and a high regard for its value. By value, I of course mean something far broader than mere economic value; I mean value in the philosophical sense.

Perhaps the most serious obstacle impeding the evolution of a land ethic is the fact that our educational and economic system is headed away from, rather than toward, an intense consciousness of land. Your true modern is separated from the land by many middlemen, and by innumerable physical gadgets. He has no vital relation to it; to him it is the space between cities on which crops grow. Turn him loose for a day on the land, and if the spot does not happen to be a gold links or a "scenic" area, he is bored stiff. If crops could be raised by hydroponics instead of farming, it would suit him very well. Synthetic substitutes for wood, leather, wool, and other natural land products suit him better than the originals. In short, land is something he has "outgrown."

Almost equally serious as an obstacle to a land ethic is the attitude of the farmer for whom the land is still an adversary, or a taskmaster that keeps him in slavery. Theoretically, the mechanization of farming ought to cut the farmer's chains, but whether it really does is debatable.

One of the requisites for an ecological comprehension of land is an understanding of ecology, and this is by no means co-extensive with "education"; in fact, much higher education seems deliberately to avoid ecological concepts. An understanding of ecology does not necessarily originate in courses bearing ecological labels; it is quite as likely to be labeled geography, botany, agronomy, history, or economics. This is as it should be, but whatever the label, ecological training is scarce.

The case for a land ethic would appear hopeless but for the minority which is in obvious revolt against these "modern" trends.

The "key-log" which must be moved to release the evolutionary process for an ethic is simply this: quit thinking about decent land-use as solely an economic problem. Examine each question in terms of what is ethically and esthetically right, as well as what is economically expedient. A thing is right when it tends to preserve the integrity, stability, and beauty of the biotic community. It is wrong when it tends otherwise.

It of course goes without saying that economic feasibility limits the tether of what can or cannot be done for land. It always has and it always will. The fallacy the economic determinists have tied around our collective neck, and which we now need to cast off, is the belief that economics determines *all* land-use. This is simply not true. An innumerable host of actions and attitudes, comprising perhaps the bulk of all land relations, is determined by the land-users' tastes and predilections, rather than by his purse. The bulk of all land relations hinges on investments of time, forethought, skill, and faith rather than on investments of cash. As a land-user thinketh, so is he.

I have purposely presented the land ethic as a product of social evolution because nothing so important as an ethic is ever "written." Only the most superficial student of history supposes that Moses "wrote" the Decalogue; it evolved in the minds of a thinking community, and Moses wrote a tentative summary of it for a "seminar." I say tentative because evolution never stops.

The evolution of a land ethic is an intellectual as well as emotional process. Conservation is paved with good intentions which prove to be futile, or even dangerous, because they are devoid of critical understanding either of the land, or of economic land-use. I think it is a truism that as the ethical frontier advances from the individual to the community, its intellectual content increases.

The mechanism of operation is the same for any ethic: social approbation for right actions: social disapproval for wrong actions.

By and large, our present problem is one of attitudes and implements. We are remodeling the Alhambra with a steam-shovel, and we are proud of our yardage. We shall hardly relinquish the shovel, which after all has many good points, but we are in need of gentler and more objective criteria for its successful use.

SONNET 33
◼

William Shakespeare

Shakespeare's sonnets were composed in the late 1590s. They first appeared in printed form in 1609.

> Full many a glorious morning have I seen
> Flatter the mountaintops with sovereign eye,
> Kissing with golden face the meadows green,
> Gilding pale streams with heavenly alchemy,
> Anon permit the basest clouds to ride
> With ugly rack on his celestial face
> And from the forlorn world his visage hide,
> Stealing unseen to west with this disgrace.
> Even so my sun one early morn did shine
> With all-triumphant splendor on my brow.

But out, alack! he was but one hour mine,
The region cloud hath masked him from me now.
Yet him for this my love no whit disdaineth.
Suns of the world may stain when heaven's sun
staineth.

GONE BACK INTO THE EARTH

Barry Lopez

This essay is from the 1988 Lopez collection Crossing Open Ground.

I am up to my waist in a basin of cool, acid-clear water, at the head of a box canyon some 600 feet above the Colorado River. I place my out-stretched hands flat against a terminal wall of dark limestone which rises more than a hundred feet above me, and down which a sheet of water falls—the thin creek in whose pooled waters I now stand. The water splits at my fingertips into wild threads; higher up, a warm canyon wind lifts water off the limestone in a fine spray; these droplets intercept and shat-ter sunlight. Down, down another four waterfalls and fern-shrouded pools below, the water spills into an eddy of the Colorado River, in the shadow of a huge boulder. Our boat is tied there.

This lush crease in the surface of the earth is a cleft in the precipitous desert walls of Arizona's Grand Canyon. Its smooth outcrops of purple-tinged travertine stone, its heavy air rolled in the languid perfume of columbine, struck by the sharp notes of a water ouzel, the trill of a dis-turbed black phoebe—all this has a name: Elves Chasm.

A few feet to my right, a preacher from Maryland is staring straight up at a blue sky, straining to see what flowers those are that nod at the top of the falls. To my left a freelance automobile mechanic from Colorado sits with an impish smile by helleborine orchids. Behind, another man, a builder and sometime record producer from New York, who comes as often as he can to camp and hike in the Southwest, stands immobile at the pool's edge.

Sprawled shirtless on a rock is our boatman. He has led twelve or fif-teen of us on the climb up from the river. The Colorado entrances him. He has a well-honed sense of the ridiculous, brought on, one believes, by so much time in the extreme remove of this canyon.

In our descent we meet others in our group who stopped climbing at one of the lower pools. At the second to the last waterfall, a young woman with short hair and dazzling blue eyes walks with me back into the canyon's narrowing V. We wade into a still pool, swim a few strokes to its head, climb over a boulder, swim across a second pool and then stand to-gether, giddy, in the press of limestone, beneath the deafening cascade—filled with euphoria.

One at a time we bolt and glide, fishlike, back across the pool, grounding in fine white gravel. We wade the second pool and continue our descent, stopping to marvel at the strategy of a barrel cactus and at the pale shading of color in the ledges to which we cling. We share few words. We know hardly anything of each other. We share the country.

The group of us who have made this morning climb are in the middle of a ten-day trip down the Colorado River. Each day we are upended, if not by some element of the landscape itself then by what the landscape does, visibly, to each of us. It has snapped us like fresh-laundered sheets.

After lunch, we reboard three large rubber rafts and enter the Colorado's quick, high flow. The river has not been this high or fast since Glen Canyon Dam—135 miles above Elves Chasm, 17 miles above our starting point at Lee's Ferry—was closed in 1963. Jumping out ahead of us, with its single oarsman and three passengers, is our fourth craft, a twelve-foot rubber boat, like a water strider with a steel frame. In Sockdolager Rapid the day before, one of its welds burst and the steel pieces were bent apart. (Sockdolager: a nineteenth-century colloquialism for knockout punch.)

Such groups as ours, the members all but unknown to each other on the first day, almost always grow close, solicitous of each other, during their time together. They develop a humor that informs similar journeys everywhere, a humor founded in tomfoolery, in punning, in a continuous parody of the life-in-civilization all have so recently (and gleefully) left. Such humor depends on context, on an accretion of small, shared events; it seems silly to those who are not there. It is not, of course. Any more than that moment of fumbling awe one feels on seeing the Brahma schist at the dead bottom of the canyon's Inner Gorge. Your fingertips graze the 1.9-billion-year-old stone as the boat drifts slowly past.

With the loss of self-consciousness, the landscape opens.

There are forty-one of us, counting a crew of six. An actor from Florida, now living in Los Angeles. A medical student and his wife. A supervisor from Virginia's Department of Motor Vehicles. A health-store owner from Chicago. An editor from New York and his young son.

That kind of diversity seems normal in groups that seek such vacations—to trek in the Himalaya, to dive in the Sea of Cortez, to go birding in the Arctic. We are together for two reasons: to run the Colorado River, and to participate with jazz musician Paul Winter, who initiated the trip, in a music workshop.

Winter is an innovator and a listener. He had thought for years about coming to the Grand Canyon, about creating music here in response to this particular landscape—collared lizards and prickly pear cactus, Anasazi Indian ruins and stifling heat. But most especially he wanted music evoked by the river and the walls that flew up from its banks—Coconino sandstone on top of Hermit shale on top of the Supai formations, stone exposed to sunlight, a bloom of photons that lifted colors—saffron and ochre, apricot, madder orange, pearl and gray green, copper reds, umber and terra-cotta browns—and left them floating in the air.

Winter was searching for a reintegration of music, landscape and people. For resonance. Three or four times during the trip he would find it for sustained periods: drifting on a quiet stretch of water below Bass Rapids with oboist Nancy Rumbel and cellist David Darling; in a natural amphitheater high in the Muav limestone of Matkatameba Canyon; on the night of a full June moon with euphonium player Larry Roark in Blacktail Canyon.

Winter's energy and passion, and the strains of solo and ensemble music, were sewn into the trip like prevailing winds, like the canyon wren's clear, whistled, descending notes, his glissando—seemingly present, close by or at a distance, whenever someone stopped to listen.

But we came and went, too, like the swallows and swifts that flicked over the water ahead of the boats, intent on private thoughts.

On the second day of the trip we stopped at Redwall Cavern, an undercut recess that spans a beach of fine sand, perhaps 500 feet wide by 150 feet deep. Winter intends to record here, but the sand absorbs too much sound. Unfazed, the others toss a Frisbee, practice Tai-chi, jog, meditate, play recorders, and read novels.

No other animal but the human would bring to bear so many activities, from so many different cultures and levels of society, with so much energy, so suddenly in a new place. And no other animal, the individuals so entirely unknown to each other, would chance together something so unknown as this river journey. In this frenetic activity and difference seems a suggestion of human evolution and genuine adventure. We are not the first down this river, but in the slooshing of human hands at the water's edge, the swanlike notes of an oboe, the occasional hugs among those most afraid of the rapids, there *is* exploration.

Each day we see or hear something that astounds us. The thousand-year-old remains of an Anasazi footbridge, hanging in twilight shadow high in the canyon wall above Harding Rapid. Deer Creek Falls, where we stand knee-deep in turquoise water encircled by a rainbow. Havasu Canyon, wild with grapevines, cottonwoods and velvet ash, speckled dace and mule deer, wild grasses and crimson monkey flowers. Each evening we enjoy a vespers: cicadas and crickets, mourning doves, vermilion flycatchers. And the wind, for which chimes are hung in a salt cedar. These notes leap above the splash and rattle, the grinding of water and the roar of rapids.

The narrow, damp, hidden worlds of the side canyons, with their scattered shards of Indian pottery and ghost imprints of 400-million-year-old nautiloids, open onto the larger world of the Colorado River itself; but nothing conveys to us how far into the earth's surface we have come. Occasionally we glimpse the South Rim, four or five thousand feet above. From the rims the canyon seems oceanic; at the surface of the river the feeling is intimate. To someone up there with binoculars we seem utterly remote down here. It is this known dimension of distance and time and the perplexing question posed by the canyon itself—What is consequential? (in one's life, in the life of human beings, in the life of a planet)—that reverberate constantly, and make the human inclination to judge (another person, another kind of thought) seem so eerie.

Two kinds of time pass here: sitting at the edge of a sun-warmed pool watching blue dragonflies and black tadpoles. And the rapids: down the glassy-smooth tongue into a yawing trench, climb a ten-foot wall of standing water and fall into boiling, ferocious hydraulics, sucking whirlpools, drowned voices, stopped hearts. Rapids can fold and shatter boats and take lives if the boatman enters at the wrong point or at the wrong angle.

Some rapids, like one called Hermit, seem more dangerous than they are and give us great roller-coaster rides. Others—Hance, Crystal, Upset—seem less spectacular, but are technically difficult. At Crystal, our boat screeches and twists against its frame. Its nose crumples like cardboard in the trough; our boatman makes the critical move to the right with split-second timing and we are over a standing wave and into the haystacks of white water, safely into the tail waves. The boatman's eyes cease to blaze.

The first few rapids—Badger Creek and Soap Creek—do not overwhelm us. When we hit the Inner Gorge—Granite Falls, Unkar Rapid, Horn Creek Rapid—some grip the boat, rigid and silent. (On the ninth day, when we are about to run perhaps the most formidable rapid, Lava Falls, the one among us who has had the greatest fear is calm, almost serene. In the last days, it is hard to overestimate what the river and the music and the unvoiced concern for each other have washed out.)

There are threats to this separate world of the Inner Gorge. Down inside it one struggles to maintain a sense of what they are, how they impinge.

In 1963, Glen Canyon Dam cut off the canyon's natural flow of water. Spring runoffs of more than two hundred thousand cubic feet per second ceased to roar through the gorge, clearing the main channel of rock and stones washed down from the side canyons. Fed now from the bottom of Lake Powell backed up behind the dam, the river is no longer a warm, silt-laden habitat for Colorado squawfish, razorback sucker and several kinds of chub, but a cold, clear habitat for trout. With no annual scouring and a subsequent deposition of fresh sand, the beaches show the evidence of continuous human use: they are eroding. The postflood eddies where squawfish bred have disappeared. Tamarisk (salt cedar) and camel thorn, both exotic plants formerly washed out with the spring floods, have gained an apparently permanent foothold. At the old high-water mark, catclaw acacia, mesquite and Apache plume are no longer watered and are dying out.

On the rim, far removed above, such evidence of human tampering seems, and perhaps is, pernicious. From the river, another change is more wrenching. It floods the system with a kind of panic that in other animals induces nausea and the sudden evacuation of the bowels: it is the descent of helicopters. Their sudden arrival in the canyon evokes not jeers but staring. The violence is brutal, an intrusion as criminal and as random as rape. When the helicopter departs, its rotor-wind walloping against the stone walls, I want to wash the sound off my skin.

The canyon finally absorbs the intrusion. I focus quietly each day on the stone, the breathing of time locked up here, back to the Proterozoic, before there were seashells. Look up to wisps of high cirrus overhead, the hint of a mare's tail sky. Close my eyes: tappet of water against the boat, sound of an Anasazi's six-hole flute. And I watch the bank for beaver tracks, for any movement.

The canyon seems like a grandfather.

One evening, Winter and perhaps half the group carry instruments and recording gear back into Blacktail Canyon to a spot sound engineer Mickey Houlihan says is good for recording.

Winter likes to quote from Thoreau: "The woods would be very silent if no birds sang except those that sing best." The remark seems not only to underscore the ephemeral nature of human evolution but the necessity in evaluating any phenomenon—a canyon, a life, a song—of providing for change.

After several improvisations dominated by a cappella voice and percussion, Winter asks Larry Roark to try something on the euphonium; he and Rumbel and Darling will then come up around him. Roark is silent. Moonlight glows on the canyon's lips. There is the sound of gurgling water. After a word of encouragement, feeling shrouded in anonymous darkness like the rest of us, Larry puts his mouth to the horn.

For a while he is alone. God knows what visions of waterfalls or wrens, of boats in the rapids, of Bach or Mozart, are in his head, in his fingers, to send forth notes. The whine of the soprano sax finds him. And the flutter of the oboe. And the rumbling of the choral cello. The exchange lasts perhaps twenty minutes. Furious and sweet, anxious, rolling, delicate and raw. The last six or eight hanging notes are Larry's. Then there is a long silence. Winter finally says, "My God."

I feel, sitting in the wet dark in bathing suit and sneakers and T-shirt, that my fingers have brushed one of life's deep, coursing threads. Like so much else in the canyon, it is left alone. Speak, even notice it, and it would disappear.

I had come to the canyon with expectations. I had wanted to see snowy egrets flying against the black schist at dusk; I saw blue-winged teal against the deep green waters at dawn. I had wanted to hear thunder rolling in the thousand-foot depths; I heard Winter's soprano sax resonating in Matkatameba Canyon, with the guttural caws of four ravens which circled above him. I had wanted to watch rattlesnakes; I saw in an abandoned copper mine, in the beam of my flashlight, a wall of copper sulphate that looked like a wall of turquoise. I rose each morning at dawn and washed in the cold river. I went to sleep each night listening to the cicadas, the pencil-ticking sound of some other insect, the soughing of river waves in tamarisk roots, and watching bats plunge and turn, looking like leaves blown around against the sky. What any of us had come to see or do fell away. We found ourselves at each turn with what we had not imagined.

The last evening it rained. We had left the canyon and been carried far out onto Lake Mead by the river's current. But we stood staring backward, at the point where the canyon had so obviously and abruptly ended.

A thought that stayed with me was that I had entered a private place in the earth. I had seen exposed nearly its oldest part. I had lost my sense of urgency, rekindled a sense of what people were, clambering to gain access to high waterfalls where we washed our hair together; and a sense of our endless struggle as a species to understand time and to estimate the consequences of our acts.

It rained the last evening. But before it did, Nancy Rumbel moved to the highest point on Scorpion Island in Lake Mead and played her oboe before a storm we could see hanging over Nevada. Sterling Smyth, who would return to programming computers in twenty-four hours, created a twelve-string imitation of the canyon wren, a long guitar solo. David Darling, revealed suddenly stark, again and then again, against a white-lightning sky, bowed furious homage to the now overhanging cumulonimbus.

In the morning we touched the far shore of Lake Mead, boarded a bus and headed for the Las Vegas airport, We were still wrapped in the journey, as though it were a Navajo blanket. We departed on various planes and arrived home in various cities and towns and at some point the world entered again and the hardest thing, the translation of what we had touched, began.

I sat in the airport in San Francisco, waiting for a connecting flight to Oregon, dwelling on one image. At the mouth of Nankoweap Canyon, the river makes a broad turn, and it is possible to see high in the orange rock what seem to be four small windows. They are entrances to granaries, built by the Anasazi who dwelled in the canyon a thousand years ago. This was provision against famine, to ensure the people would survive.

I do not know, really, how we will survive without places like the Inner Gorge of the Grand Canyon to visit. Once in a lifetime, even, is enough. To feel the stripping down, an ebb of the press of conventional time, a radical change of proportion, an unspoken respect for others that elicits keen emotional pleasure, a quick, intimate pounding of the heart.

Some parts of the trip will emerge one day on an album. Others will be found in a gesture of friendship to some stranger in an airport, in a letter of outrage to a planner of dams, in a note of gratitude to nameless faces in the Park Service, in wondering at the relatives of the ubiquitous wren, in the belief, passed on in whatever fashion—a photograph, a chord, a sketch—that nature can heal.

The living of life, any life, involves great and private pain, much of which we share with no one. In such places as the Inner Gorge the pain trails away from us. It is not so quiet there or so removed that you can hear yourself think, that you would even wish to; that comes later. You can hear your heart beat. That comes first.

EARTH FIRST

Dave Foreman

This declaration of principles was first published in the October 1981 issue of The Progressive.

... Maybe—some of us began to feel, even before Reagan's election—it was time for a new joker in the deck: a militant, uncompromising group unafraid to say what needed to be said or to back it up with stronger actions than the established organizations were willing to take. This idea had been kicking around for a couple of years; finally last year several of us (including, among others, Susan Morgan, formerly educational director for the Wilderness Society: Howie Wolke, former Wyoming representative for Friends of the Earth: Bart Koehler, former Wyoming representative for the Wilderness Society, and myself) decided that the time for talk was past. We formed a new national group. EARTH FIRST! We set out to be radical in style, positions, philosophy, and organization in order to be effective and to avoid the pitfalls of co-option and moderation which we had already experienced.

What, we asked ourselves as we sat around a campfire in the Wyoming mountains, were the advantages, the reasons for environmental radicalism?

- To state honestly the views held by many conservationists.
- To demonstrate that the Sierra Club and its allies were raging moderates, believers in the system, and to refute the Reagan/Watt contention that they were "extremist environmentalists."
- To balance such anti-environmental radicals as the Grand County commission and provide a broader spectrum of viewpoints.
- To return some vigor, joy, and enthusiasm to the allegedly tired environmental movement.
- To keep the established groups honest. By stating a pure, noncompromise pro-Earth position, we felt EARTH FIRST! could help keep the other groups from straying too far from their philosophical base.
- To give an outlet to many hard-line conservationists who were no longer active because of disenchantment with compromise politics and the co-option of environmental organizations.

- To provide a productive fringe since it seems that ideas, creativity, and energy spring up on the fringe and later spread into the middle.

- To inspire others to carry out activities straight from the pages of *The Monkey Wrench Gang* even though EARTH FIRST!, we agreed, would itself be ostensibly law-abiding.

- To question the system; to help develop a new world view, a biocentric paradigm, an Earth philosophy. To fight, with uncompromising passion, for Mother Earth.

The name—EARTH FIRST!—was chosen deliberately because it succinctly summed up the one thing on which we could all agree: That in *any* decision, consideration for the health of the Earth must come first, or, as Aldo Leopold said, "A thing is right when it tends to preserve the integrity, stability, and beauty of the biotic community It is wrong when it tends otherwise."

In a true Earth-radical group, concern for wilderness preservation must be the keystone. The idea of wilderness, after all, is the most radical in human thought—more radical than Paine, than Marx, than Mao. Wilderness says: Human beings are not dominant, Earth is not for *Homo sapiens* alone, human life is but one life form on the planet and has no right to take exclusive possession. Yes, wilderness for its own sake, without any need to justify it for human benefit. Wilderness for wilderness. For grizzlies and whales and titmice and rattlesnakes and stink bugs. And . . . wilderness for human beings. Because it is the laboratory of three million years of human evolution—and because it is home.

It is not enough to protect our few remaining bits of wilderness. The only hope for Earth (and humanity for that matter) is to withdraw huge areas as inviolate natural sanctuaries from the depredations of modern industry and technology. Keep Cleveland, Los Angeles. Contain them. Try to make them habitable. But identify areas—big areas—that can be restored to a semblance of natural conditions, reintroduce the griz and wolf and prairie grasses, and declare them off limits to modern civilization.

In the United States pick an area for each of our major ecosystems and recreate the American wilderness—not in little pieces of a thousand acres but in chunks of a million or ten million. Move out the people and cars. Reclaim the roads and plowed land. It is not enough any longer to say no more dams on our wild rivers. We must begin tearing down some dams already built—beginning with Glen Canyon, Hetch Hetchy, Tellico, and New Melones—and freeing shackled rivers.

This emphasis on wilderness is not to ignore other environmental issues or to abandon the people who suffer because of them. In the United States blacks and Chicanos of the inner cities are the ones most affected by air and water pollution, the ones most trapped by the unnatural confines of urbanity. So we decided that not only should ecomilitants be concerned with these human environmental problems; we should also make common ground with other progressive elements of society whenever possible.

Obviously, for a group more committed to Gila monsters and mountain lions than to people, there will not be a total alliance with the other social movements. But there are issues where Earth radicals can cooperate with feminist, Indian rights, anti-nuke, peace, civil rights, and civil liberties groups. The inherent conservatism of the conservation community has made it wary of snuggling too close to these questionable (in their minds) leftist organizations. We hoped that the way might be paved for better cooperation from the entire conservation movement.

We believed that new tactics were needed—something more than commenting on dreary environmental impact statements and writing letters to members of Congress. Politics in the streets. Civil disobedience. Media stunts. Holding the villains up to ridicule. Using music to charge the cause.

Action is the key. Action is more important than philosophical hairsplitting or endless refining of dogma (for which radicals are so well known). Let our actions set the finer points of our philosophy. And let us recognize that diversity is not only the spice of life, it is also the strength. All that would be required to join us, we decided, was a belief in Earth first. Apart from that, EARTH FIRST! would be big enough to contain street poets and cowboy bar bouncers, agnostics and pagans, vegetarians and raw steak eaters, pacifists and those who think that turning the other cheek is a good way to get a sore face.

Radicals frequently verge toward a righteous seriousness. But we felt that if we couldn't laugh at ourselves we would be merely another bunch of dangerous fanatics who should be locked up (like the oil companies). Not only does humor preserve individual and group sanity, it retards hubris, a major cause of environmental rape, and it is also an effective weapon. Additionally, fire, passion, courage, and emotionalism are called for. We have been too reasonable, too calm, too understanding. It's time to get angry, to cry, to let rage flow at what the human cancer is doing to Mother Earth, to be uncompromising. For EARTH FIRST! it is all or nothing. Win or lose. No truce or cease fire. No surrender. No partitioning of the territory.

Ever since the Earth goddesses of ancient Greece were supplanted by the macho Olympians, repression of women and Earth has gone hand in hand with imperial organization. EARTH FIRST! decided to be nonorganizational: no officers, no bylaws or constitution, no incorporation, no tax status; just a collection of women and men committed to the Earth. At the turn of the century William Graham Sumner wrote a famous essay entitled "The Conquest of the United States by Spain." His thesis was that Spain had ultimately won the Spanish-American War because the United States took on the imperialism and totalitarianism of Spain as a result. We felt that if we took on the organization of the industrial state, we would soon accept their anthropocentric paradigm (much as Audubon and the Sierra Club already had).

In keeping with that view, EARTH FIRST! took the shape of a circle, a group of thirteen women and men around the country who more or less direct the movement, and a collection of regional contacts. We also have local affiliates (so far in Alaska, Montana, Wyoming, Colorado, Arizona, New Mexico, Utah, Arkansas, Maine, and Virginia). We publish a newsletter eight times a year and are developing position papers on a range of issues from automobiles to overgrazing. We also send out press releases. Membership is free, although we do encourage members to kick in ten bucks or more, if they can afford it, to help with expenses. We have not sought any grants or funding with strings attached, nor do we plan to have paid staff (although we hope to have field organizers receiving expenses in the tradition of the Wobblies).

And, when we are inspired, we *act*.

Massive, powerful, like some creation of Darth Vader's. Glen Canyon Dam squats in the canyon of the Colorado River on the Arizona-Utah border and backs the cold dead waters of Lake Powell some 180 miles upstream, drowning the most awesome and magical canyon on Earth. More than any other single entity, Glen Canyon Dam is the symbol of the destruction of wilderness, of the technological rape of the West. The finest fantasy of *eco*-warriors in the West is the destruction of the dam and the liberation of the Colorado. So it was only proper that on March 21, 1981—on the Spring Equinox, the traditional time of rebirth—EARTH FIRST! held its first national gathering at Glen Canyon Dam.

On that morning, seventy-five members of EARTH FIRST! lined the walkway of the Colorado River Bridge 700 feet above the once free river and watched five compatriots busy at work with an awkward black bundle on the massive dam just upstream. Those on the bridge carried placards reading "Damn Watt, Not Rivers," "Free the Colorado," and "Let It Flow." The four men and one woman on the dam attached ropes to a grill on the dam, shouted out "Earth first!" and let 300 feet of black plastic unfurl down the side of the dam, creating the impression of a growing crack. Those on the bridge returned the cheer.

A few minutes later, Edward Abbey, author of *The Monkey Wrench Gang*, a novel of environmental sabotage in the Southwest, told the protesters of the "green and living wilderness" that was Glen Canyon only nineteen years ago:

"And they took it away from us. The politicians of Arizona, Utah, New Mexico, and Colorado, in cahoots with the land developers, city developers, industrial developers of the Southwest, stole this treasure from us in order to pursue and promote their crackpot ideology of growth, profit, and power—growth for the sake of power, power for the sake of growth."

Speaking toward the future, Abbey offered this advice: "Oppose. Oppose the destruction of our homeland by these alien forces from Houston, Tokyo, Manhattan, Washington, D.C., and the Pentagon. And if opposition is not enough, we must resist. And if resistance is not enough, then subvert."

Abbey then launched a nationwide petition campaign demanding the dismantling of Glen Canyon Dam. Hardly had he finished speaking when Park Service police and Coconino County sheriffs deputies arrived on the scene. While they questioned the organizers of the illegal assembly and tried to disperse it, outlaw country singer Johnny Sagebrush led the demonstrators in song for another twenty minutes.

The Glen Canyon Dam caper brought EARTH FIRST! an unexpected degree of media attention. Membership in our group has spiraled to more than a thousand with members from Maine to Hawaii. Even the Government is interested—according to reliable reports, the FBI dusted the entire Glen Canyon Dam crack for fingerprints!

Last Fourth of July more than 200 EARTH FIRSTers gathered in Moab, Utah, for the first Sagebrush Patriot Rally to express support for Federal public lands and to send a message to anti-Earth fanatics that there are Americans who are patriotic about *their* wilderness.

When a few of us kicked off EARTH FIRST! we sensed a growing environmental radicalism in the country but we did not expect the response we have received. Maybe EARTH FIRST! is in the right place at the right time. Tom Turner, editor of Friends of the Earth's *Not Man Apart,* recently wrote to us to say:

"Russ Train once said, 'Thank God for Dave Brower—he makes it so easy for the rest of us to appear reasonable.' Youze guys are about to make Dave Brower look reasonable, and more power to you!"

The cynical may smirk. "But what can you really accomplish? How can you fight Exxon, Coors, David Rockefeller, Japan, and the other great corporate giants of the Earth? How, indeed, can you fight the dominant dogmas of Western Civilization?"

Perhaps it *is* a hopeless quest. But is that relevant? Is that important? No, what is important is that one who loves Earth can do no less. Maybe a species will be saved or a forest will go uncut or a dam will be torn down. Maybe not. A monkey wrench thrown into the gears of the machine may not stop it. But it might delay it. Make it cost more. And it feels good to put it there.

SHIPS IN THE DESERT

Al Gore

This is the first chapter of Gore's 1992 book Earth in the Balance.

I was standing in the sun on the hot steel deck of a fishing ship capable of processing a fifty-ton catch on a good day. But it wasn't a good day. We were anchored in what used to be the most productive fishing site in all of central Asia, but as I looked out over the bow, the prospects of a good catch looked bleak. Where there should have been gentle blue-green waves lapping against the side of the ship, there was nothing but hot dry sand—as far as I could see in all directions. The other ships of the fleet were also at rest in the sand, scattered in the dunes that stretched all the way to the horizon.

Oddly enough, it made me think of a fried egg I had seen back in the United States on television the week before. It was sizzling and popping the way a fried egg should in a pan, but it was in the middle of a sidewalk in downtown Phoenix. I guess it sprang to mind because, like the ship on which I was standing, there was nothing wrong with the egg itself. Instead, the world beneath it had changed in an unexpected way that made the egg seem—through no fault of its own—out of place. It was illustrating the newsworthy point that at the time Arizona wasn't having an especially good day, either, because for the second day in a row temperatures had reached a record 122 degrees.

As a camel walked by on the dead bottom of the Aral Sea, my thoughts returned to the unlikely ship of the desert on which I stood, which also seemed to be illustrating the point that its world had changed out from underneath it with sudden cruelty. Ten years ago the Aral was the fourth-largest inland sea in the world, comparable to the largest of North America's Great Lakes. Now it is disappearing because the water that used to feed it has been diverted in an ill-considered irrigation scheme to grow cotton in the desert. The new shoreline was almost forty kilometers across the sand from where the fishing fleet was now permanently docked. Meanwhile, in the nearby town of Muynak the people were still canning fish—brought not from the Aral Sea but shipped by rail through Siberia from the Pacific Ocean, more than a thousand miles away.

I had come to the Aral Sea in August 1990 to witness at first hand the destruction taking place there on an almost biblical scale. But during the trip I encountered other images that also alarmed me. For example, the day I returned to Moscow from Muynak, my friend Alexei Yablokov, possibly the leading environmentalist in the Soviet Union, was returning from an emergency expedition to the White Sea, where he had investigated the mysterious and unprecedented death of several *million* starfish, washed up into a knee-deep mass covering many miles of beach. That night, in his apartment, he talked of what it was like for the residents to wade through the starfish in hip boots, trying to explain their death.

Later investigations identified radioactive military waste as the likely culprit in the White Sea deaths. But what about all of the other mysterious mass deaths washing up on beaches around the world? French scientists recently concluded that the explanation for the growing number of dead dolphins washing up along the Riviera was accumulated environmental stress, which, over time, rendered the animals too weak to fight off a virus. This same phenomenon may also explain the sudden increase in dolphin deaths along the Gulf Coast in Texas as well as the mysterious deaths of 12,000 seals whose corpses washed up on the shores of the

North Sea in the summer of 1988. Of course, the oil-covered otters and seabirds of Prince William Sound a year later presented less of a mystery to science, if no less an indictment of our civilization.

As soon as one of these troubling images fades, another takes its place, provoking new questions. What does it mean, for example, that children playing in the morning surf must now dodge not only the occasional jellyfish but the occasional hypodermic needle washing in with the waves? Needles, dead dolphins, and oil-soaked birds—are all these signs that the shores of our familiar world are fast eroding, that we are now standing on some new beach, facing dangers beyond the edge of what we are capable of imagining?

With our backs turned to the place in nature from which we came, we sense an unfamiliar tide rising and swirling around our ankles, pulling at the sand beneath our feet. Each time this strange new tide goes out, it leaves behind the flotsam and jetsam of some giant shipwreck far out at sea, startling images washed up on the sands of our time, each a fresh warning of hidden dangers that lie ahead if we continue on our present course.

My search for the underlying causes of the environmental crisis has led me to travel around the world to examine and study many of these images of destruction. At the very bottom of the earth, high in the Trans-Antarctic Mountains, with the sun glaring at midnight through a hole in the sky, I stood in the unbelievable coldness and talked with a scientist in the late fall of 1988 about the tunnel he was digging through time. Slipping his parka back to reveal a badly burned face that was cracked and peeling, he pointed to the annual layers of ice in a core sample dug from the glacier on which we were standing. He moved his finger back in time to the ice of two decades ago. "Here's where the U.S. Congress passed the Clean Air Act," he said. At the bottom of the world, two continents away from Washington, D.C., even a small reduction in one country's emissions had changed the amount of pollution found in the remotest and least accessible place on earth.

But the most significant change thus far in the earth's atmosphere is the one that began with the industrial revolution early in the last century and has picked up speed ever since. Industry meant coal, and later oil, and we began to burn lots of it—bringing rising levels of carbon dioxide (CO_2), with its ability to trap more heat in the atmosphere and slowly warm the earth. Fewer than a hundred yards from the South Pole, upwind from the ice runway where the ski plane lands and keeps its engines running to prevent the metal parts from freeze-locking together, scientists monitor the air several times every day to chart the course of that inexorable change. During my visit, I watched one scientist draw the results of that day's measurements, pushing the end of a steep line still higher on the graph. He told me how easy it is—there at the end of the earth—to see that this enormous change in the global atmosphere is still picking up speed.

Two and a half years later I slept under the midnight sun at the other end of our planet, in a small tent pitched on a twelve-foot-thick slab of ice floating in the frigid Arctic Ocean. After a hearty breakfast, my companions and I traveled by snowmobiles a few miles farther north to a rendezvous point where the ice was thinner—only three and a half feet thick—and a nuclear submarine hovered in the water below. After it crashed through the ice, took on its new passengers, and resubmerged, I talked with scientists who were trying to measure more accurately the thickness of the polar ice cap, which many believe is thinning as a result of global warming. I had just negotiated an agreement between ice scientists and the U.S. Navy to secure the release of previously top secret data from submarine sonar tracks, data that could help them learn what is happening to the north polar cap. Now, I wanted to see the pole itself, and some eight hours after we met the submarine, we were crashing through that ice, surfacing, and then I was standing in an eerily beautiful snowscape, windswept and sparkling white, with the horizon defined by little hummocks, or "pressure ridges" of ice that are pushed up like tiny mountain ranges when separate sheets collide. But here too, CO_2 levels are rising just as rapidly, and ultimately temperatures will rise with them—indeed global warming is expected to push temperatures up much more rapidly in the polar regions than in the rest of the world. As the polar air warms, the ice here will thin; and since the polar cap plays such a crucial role in the world's weather system, the consequences of a thinning cap could be disastrous.

Considering such scenarios is not a purely speculative exercise. Six months after I returned from the North Pole, a team of scientists reported dramatic changes in the pattern of ice distribution in the Arctic, and a second team reported a still controversial claim (which a variety of data now suggest) that, overall, the north polar cap has thinned by 2 percent in just the last decade. Moreover, scientists established several years ago that in many land areas north of the Arctic Circle, the spring snowmelt now comes earlier every year, and deep in the tundra below, the temperature of the earth is steadily rising.

As it happens, some of the most disturbing images of environmental destruction can be found exactly halfway between the North and South poles—precisely at the equator in Brazil—where billowing clouds of smoke regularly blacken the sky above the immense but now threatened Amazon rain forest. Acre by acre, the rain forest is being burned to create fast pasture for fast-food beef, as I learned when I went there in early 1989, the fires are set earlier and earlier in the dry season now, with more than one Tennessee's worth of rain forest being slashed and burned each year. According to our guide, the biologist Tom Lovejoy, there are more different species of birds in each square mile of the Amazon than exist in all of North America—which means we are silencing thousands of songs we have never even heard.

But for most of us the Amazon is a distant place, and we scarcely notice the disappearance of these and other vulnerable species. We ignore these losses at our peril, however. They're like the proverbial miners' canaries, silent alarms whose message in this case is that living species of animals and plants are now vanishing around the world *one thousand times faster* than at any time in the past 65 million years (see illustration).

To be sure, the deaths of some of the larger and more spectacular animal species now under siege do occasionally capture our attention. I have also visited another place along the equator, East Africa, where I encountered the grotesquely horrible image of a dead elephant, its head mutilated by poachers who had dug out its valuable tusks with chain saws. Clearly, we need to change our purely aesthetic consideration of ivory, since its source is now so threatened. To me, its translucent whiteness seems different now, like evidence of the ghostly presence of a troubled spirit, a beautiful but chill apparition, inspiring both wonder and dread.

A similar apparition lies just beneath the ocean. While scuba diving in the Caribbean, I have seen and touched the white bones of a dead coral reef. All over the earth, coral reefs have suddenly started to "bleach" as warmer ocean temperatures put unaccustomed stress on the tiny organisms that normally live in the skin of the coral and give the reef its natural coloration. As these organisms—nicknamed "zooks"—leave the membrane of the coral, the coral itself becomes transparent, allowing its

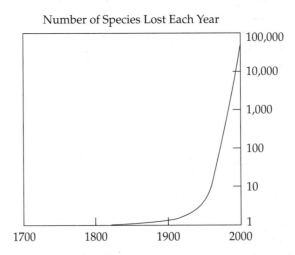

Number of Species Lost Each Year

This graph portrays the estimated loss of living species from 1700 to 1992. The normal or "background" rate of extinction remained essentially unchanged for the last 65 million years—from the disappearance of the dinosaurs along with countless other species at the end of the Cretaceous era until the present century.

white limestone skeleton to shine through—hence its bleached appearance. In the past, bleaching was almost always an occasional and temporary phenomenon, but repeated episodes can exhaust the coral. In the last few years, scientists have been shocked at the sudden occurrence of extensive worldwide bleaching episodes from which increasing numbers of coral reefs have failed to recover. Though dead, they shine more brightly than before, haunted perhaps by the same ghost that gives spectral light to an elephant's tusk.

But one doesn't have to travel around the world to witness humankind's assault on the earth. Images that signal the distress of our global environment are now commonly seen almost anywhere. A few miles from the Capitol, for example, I encountered another startling image of nature out of place. Driving in the Arlington, Virginia, neighborhood where my family and I live when the Senate is in session, I stepped on the brake to avoid hitting a large pheasant walking across the street. It darted between the parked cars, across the sidewalk, and into a neighbor's backyard. Then it was gone. But this apparition of wildness persisted in my memory as a puzzle: Why would a pheasant, let alone such a large and beautiful mature specimen, be out for a walk in my neighborhood? Was it a much wilder place than I had noticed? Were pheasants, like the trendy Vietnamese potbellied pigs, becoming the latest fashion in unusual pets? I didn't solve the mystery until weeks later, when I remembered that about three miles away, along the edge of the river, developers were bulldozing the last hundred acres of untouched forest in the entire area. As the woods fell to make way for more concrete, more buildings, parking lots, and streets, the wild things that lived there were forced to flee. Most of the deer were hit by cars; other creatures—like the pheasant that darted into my neighbor's backyard—made it a little farther.

Ironically, before I understood the mystery, I felt vaguely comforted to imagine that perhaps this urban environment, so similar to the one in which many Americans live, was not so hostile to wild things after all. I briefly supposed that, like the resourceful raccoons and possums and squirrels and pigeons, all of whom have adapted to life in the suburbs, creatures as wild as pheasants might have a fighting chance. Now I remember that pheasant when I take my children to the zoo and see an elephant or a rhinoceros. They too inspire wonder and sadness. They too remind me that we are creating a world that is hostile to wildness, that seems to prefer concrete to natural landscapes. We are encountering these creatures on a path we have paved—one that ultimately leads to their extinction.

On some nights, in high northern latitudes, the sky itself offers another ghostly image that signals the loss of ecological balance now in progress. If the sky is clear after sunset—and if you are watching from a place where pollution hasn't blotted out the night sky altogether—you can sometimes see a strange kind of cloud high in the sky. This "noctilucent cloud" occasionally appears when the earth is first cloaked in the evening darkness; shimmering above us with a translucent whiteness, these clouds seem quite unnatural. And they should: noctilucent clouds have begun to appear more often because of a huge buildup of methane gas in the atmosphere. (Also called natural gas, methane is released from landfills, from coal mines and rice paddies, from billions of termites that swarm through the freshly cut forestland, from the burning of biomass and from a variety of other human activities.) Even though noctilucent clouds were sometimes seen in the past, all this extra methane carries more water vapor into the upper atmosphere, where it condenses at much higher altitudes to form more clouds that the sun's rays still strike long after sunset has brought the beginning of night to the surface far beneath them.

What should we feel toward these ghosts in the sky? Simple wonder or the mix of emotions we feel at the zoo? Perhaps we should feel awe for our own power: just as men tear tusks from elephants' heads in such quantity as to threaten the beast with extinction, we are ripping matter from its place in the earth in such volume as to upset the balance between daylight and darkness. In the process, we are once again adding to the threat of global warming, because methane has been one of the fastest-growing greenhouse gases, and is third only to carbon dioxide and water vapor in total volume, changing the chemistry of the upper atmosphere. But, without even considering that threat, shouldn't it startle us that we have now put these clouds in the evening sky which glisten with a spectral light? Or have our eyes adjusted so completely to the bright lights of civilization that we can't see these clouds for what they are—a physical manifestation of the violent collision between human civilization and the earth?

Even though it is sometimes hard to see their meaning, we have by now all witnessed surprising experiences that signal the damage from our assault on the environment—whether it's the new frequency of days when the temperature exceeds 100 degrees, the new speed with which the sun burns our skin, or the new constancy of public debate over what to do with growing mountains of waste. But our response to these signals is puzzling. Why haven't we launched a massive effort to save our environment? To come at the question another way: Why do some images startle us into immediate action and focus our attention on ways to respond effectively? And why do other images, though sometimes equally dramatic, produce instead a kind of paralysis, focusing our attention not on ways to respond but rather on some convenient, less painful distraction?

In a roundabout way, my visit to the North Pole caused me to think about these questions from a different perspective and gave them a new urgency. On the submarine, I had several opportunities to look through the periscope at the translucent bottom of the ice pack at the North Pole. The sight was not a little claustrophobic, and at one point I suddenly thought of the three whales that had become trapped under the ice of the

Beaufort Sea a couple of years earlier. Television networks from four continents came to capture their poignant struggle for air and in the process so magnified the emotions felt around the world that soon scientists and rescue workers flocked to the scene. After several elaborate schemes failed, a huge icebreaker from the Soviet Union cut a path through the ice for the two surviving whales. Along with millions of others, I had been delighted to see them go free, but there on the submarine it occurred to me that if we are causing 100 extinctions each day—and many scientists believe we are—approximately 2,000 living species had disappeared from the earth during the whales' ordeal. They disappeared forever—unnoticed.

Similarly, when a little girl named Jessica McClure fell into a well in Texas, her ordeal and subsequent rescue by a legion of heroic men and women attracted hundreds of television cameras and journalists who sent the story into the homes and minds of hundreds of millions of people. Here, too, our response seems skewed: during the three days of Jessica's ordeal, more than 100,000 boys and girls her age or younger died of preventable causes—mostly starvation and diarrhea—due to failures of both crops and politics. As they struggled for life, none of these children looked into a collection of television cameras, anxious to send word of their plight to a waiting world. They died virtually unnoticed. Why?

Perhaps one part of the answer lies in the perceived difficulty of an effective response. If the problem portrayed in the image is one whose solution appears to involve more effort or sacrifice than we can readily imagine, or if even maximum effort by any one individual would fail to prevent the tragedy, we are tempted to sever the link between stimulus and moral response. Then, once a response is deemed impossible, the image that briefly caused us to consider responding becomes not just startling but painful. At that point, we begin to react not to the image but to the pain it now produces, thus severing a more basic link in our relationship to the world: the link between our senses and our emotions. Our eyes glaze over as our hearts close. We look but we don't see. We hear but we refuse to listen.

Still, there are so many distressing images of environmental destruction that sometimes it seems impossible to know how to absorb or comprehend them. Before considering the threats themselves, it may be helpful to classify them and thus begin to organize our thoughts and feelings so that we may be able to respond appropriately.

A useful system comes from the military, which frequently places a conflict in one of three different categories, according to the theater in which it takes place. There are "local" skirmishes, "regional" battles, and "strategic" conflicts. This third category is reserved for struggles that can threaten a nation's survival and must be understood in a global context.

Environmental threats can be considered in the same way. For example, most instances of water pollution, air pollution, and illegal waste dumping are essentially local in nature. Problems like acid rain, the contamination of underground aquifers, and large oil spills are fundamentally regional. In both of these categories, there may be so many similar instances of particular local and regional problems occurring simultaneously all over the world that the pattern appears to be global, but the problems themselves are still not truly strategic because the operation of the global environment is not affected and the survival of civilization is not at stake.

However, a new class of environmental problems does affect the global ecological system, and these threats are fundamentally strategic. The 600 percent increase in the amount of chlorine in the atmosphere during the last forty years has taken place not just in those countries producing the chlorofluorocarbons responsible but in the air above every country, above Antarctica, above the North Pole and the Pacific Ocean—all the way from the surface of the earth to the top of the sky. The increased levels of chlorine disrupt the global process by which the earth regulates the amount of ultraviolet radiation from the sun that is allowed through the atmosphere to the surface; and if we let chlorine levels continue to increase, the radiation levels will also increase—to the point that all animal and plant life will face a new threat to their survival.

Global warming is also a strategic threat. The concentration of carbon dioxide and other heat-absorbing molecules has increased by almost 25 percent since World War II, posing a worldwide threat to the earth's ability to regulate the amount of heat from the sun retained in the atmosphere. This increase in heat seriously threatens the global climate equilibrium that determines the pattern of winds, rainfall, surface temperatures, ocean currents, and sea level. These in turn determine the distribution of vegetative and animal life on land and sea and have a great effect on the location and pattern of human societies.

In other words, the entire relationship between humankind and the earth has been transformed because our civilization is suddenly capable of affecting the entire global environment, not just a particular area. All of us know that human civilization has usually had a large impact on the environment; to mention just one example, there is evidence that even in prehistoric times, vast areas were sometimes intentionally burned by people in their search for food. And in our own time we have reshaped a large part of the earth's surface with concrete in our cities and carefully tended rice paddies, pastures, wheatfields, and other croplands in the countryside. But these changes, while sometimes appearing to be pervasive, have, until recently, been relatively trivial factors in the global ecological system. Indeed, until our lifetime, it was always safe to assume that nothing we did or could do would have any lasting effect on the global environment. But it is precisely that assumption which must now be discarded so that we can think strategically about our new relationship to the environment.

Human civilization is now the dominant cause of change in the global environment. Yet we resist this truth and find it hard to imagine that our effect on the earth must now be measured by the same yardstick used to calculate the strength of the moon's pull on the oceans or the force of the wind against the mountains. And if we are now capable of changing something so basic as the relationship between the earth and the sun, surely we must acknowledge a new responsibility to use that power wisely and with appropriate restraint. So far, however, we seem oblivious of the fragility of the earth's natural systems.

This century has witnessed dramatic changes in two key factors that define the physical reality of our relationship to the earth: a sudden and startling surge in human population, with the addition of one China's worth of people every ten years, and a sudden acceleration of the scientific and technological revolution, which has allowed an almost unimaginable magnification of our power to affect the world around us by burning, cutting, digging, moving, and transforming the physical matter that makes up the earth.

The surge in population is both a cause of the changed relationship and one of the clearest illustrations of how startling the change has been, especially when viewed in a historical context. From the emergence of modern humans 200,000 years ago until Julius Caesar's time, fewer than 250 million people walked on the face of the earth. When Christopher Columbus set sail for the New World 1,500 years later, there were approximately 500 million people on earth. By the time Thomas Jefferson wrote the Declaration of Independence in 1776, the number had doubled again, to 1 billion. By midway through this century, at the end of World War II, the number had risen to just above 2 billion people.

In other words, from the beginning of humanity's appearance on earth to 1945, it took more than ten thousand generations to reach a world population of 2 billion people. Now, in the course of one human lifetime—mine—the world population will increase from 2 to more than 9 billion, and it is already more than halfway there (see the graph on the following page).

Like the population explosion, the scientific and technological revolution began to pick up speed slowly during the eighteenth century. And this ongoing revolution has also suddenly accelerated exponentially. For example, it is now an axiom in many fields of science that more new and important discoveries have taken place in the last ten years than in the entire previous history of science. While no single discovery has had the kind of effect on our relationship to the earth that nuclear weapons have had on our relationship to warfare, it is nevertheless true that taken together, they have completely transformed our cumulative ability to exploit the earth for sustenance—making the consequences of unrestrained exploitation every bit as unthinkable as the consequences of unrestrained nuclear war.

Now that our relationship to the earth has changed so utterly, we have to see that change and understand its implications. Our challenge is to

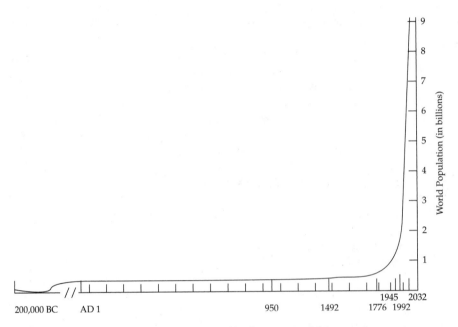

World population, after remaining stable for most of history, began to grow gradually after the agricultural revolution a few thousand years ago. This slow rate of increase continued until the onset of the industrial revolution, when the curve began sloping upward. In this century, the rate of increase has accelerated so rapidly that an extra billion people are being added to the population each decade. By the beginning of 1992, the population had climbed to almost 5.5 billion. By the year 2032, it is expected to reach 9 billion.

recognize that the startling images of environmental destruction now occurring all over the world have much more in common than their ability to shock and awaken us. They are symptoms of an underlying problem broader in scope and more serious than any we have ever faced. Global warming, ozone depletion, the loss of living species, deforestation—they all have a common cause: the new relationship between human civilization and the earth's natural balance.

There are actually two aspects to this challenge. The first is to realize that our power to harm the earth can indeed have global and even permanent effects. The second is to realize that the only way to understand our new role as a co-architect of nature is to see ourselves as part of a complex system that does not operate according to the same simple rules of cause and effect we are used to. The problem is not our effect *on* the environment so much as our relationship *with* the environment. As a result, any solution to the problem will require a careful assessment of that relationship as well as the complex interrelationship among factors within civilization and between them and the major natural components of the earth's ecological system.

There is only one precedent for this kind of challenge to our thinking, and again it is military. The invention of nuclear weapons and the subsequent development by the United States and the Soviet Union of many thousands of strategic nuclear weapons forced a slow and painful recognition that the new power thus acquired forever changed not only the relationship between the two superpowers but also the relationship of humankind to the institution of warfare itself. The consequences of all-out war between nations armed with nuclear weapons suddenly included the possibility of the destruction of both nations—completely and simultaneously. That sobering realization led to a careful reassessment of every aspect of our mutual relationship to the prospect of such a war. As early as 1946 one strategist concluded that strategic bombing with missiles "may well tear away the veil of illusion that has so long obscured the reality of the change in warfare—from a fight to a process of destruction."

Nevertheless, during the earlier stages of the nuclear arms race, each of the superpowers assumed that its actions would have a simple and direct effect on the thinking of the other. For decades, each new advance in weaponry was deployed by one side for the purpose of inspiring fear in the other. But each such deployment led to an effort by the other to leapfrog the first one with a more advanced deployment of its own. Slowly, it has become apparent that the problem of the nuclear arms race is not primarily caused by technology. It is complicated by technology, true; but it arises out of the relationship between the superpowers and is based on an obsolete understanding of what war is all about.

The eventual solution to the arms race will be found, not in a new deployment by one side or the other of some ultimate weapon or in a decision by either side to disarm unilaterally, but rather in new understandings and in a mutual transformation of the relationship itself. This transformation will involve changes in the technology of weaponry and the denial of nuclear technology to rogue states. But the key changes will be in the way we think about the institution of warfare and about the relationship between states.

The strategic nature of the threat now posed *by* human civilization to the global environment and the strategic nature of the threat *to* human civilization now posed by changes in the global environment present us with a similar set of challenges and false hopes. Some argue that a new ultimate technology, whether nuclear power or genetic engineering, will solve the problem. Others hold that only a drastic reduction of our reliance on technology can improve the conditions of life—a simplistic notion at best. But the real solution will be found in reinventing and finally healing the relationship between civilization and the earth. This can only be accomplished by undertaking a careful reassessment of all the factors that led to the relatively recent dramatic change in the relationship. The transformation of the way we relate to the earth will of course involve new technologies, but the key changes will involve new ways of thinking about the relationship itself.

SAVE THE WHALES, SCREW THE SHRIMP

Joy Williams

This essay originally appeared in Esquire *magazine in 1989.*

I don't want to talk about *me,* of course, but it seems as though far too much attention has been lavished on *you* lately—that your greed and vanities and quest for self-fulfillment have been catered to far too much. You just want and want and want. You haven't had a mandala dream since the eighties began. To have a mandala dream you'd have to instinctively know that it was an attempt at self-healing on the part of Nature, and you don't believe in Nature anymore. It's too isolated from you. You've abstracted it. It's so messy and damaged and sad. Your eyes glaze as you travel life's highway past all the crushed animals and the Big Gulp cups. You don't even take pleasure in looking at nature photographs these days. Oh, they can be just as pretty, as always, but don't they make you feel increasingly . . . anxious? Filled with more trepidation than peace? So what's the point? You see the picture of the baby condor or the panda munching on a bamboo shoot, and your heart just sinks, doesn't it? A picture of a poor old sea turtle with barnacles on her back, all ancient and exhausted, depositing her five gallons of doomed eggs in the sand hardly fills you with joy, because you realize, quite rightly, that just outside the frame falls the shadow of the condo. What's cropped from the shot of ocean waves crashing on a pristine shore is the plastics plant, and just beyond the dunes lies a parking lot. Hidden from immediate view in the butterfly-bright meadow, in the dusky thicket, in the oak and holly wood, are the surveyors' stakes, for someone wants to build a mall exactly there—some gas stations and supermarkets, some pizza and video shops, a health club, maybe a bulimia treatment center. Those lovely pictures of leopards and herons and wild rivers, well, you just know they're going to be accompanied by a text that will serve only to bring you down. You don't want to think about it! It's all so uncool. And you don't want to feel guilty either. Guilt is uncool. Regret maybe you'll consider. *Maybe.* Regret is a possibility, but don't push me, you say. Nature photographs have become something of a problem, along with almost everything else. Even though they leave the bad stuff out—maybe because you *know* they're leaving all the bad stuff out—such pictures are making you increasingly aware that you're a little too late for Nature. Do you feel that? Twenty years too late, maybe only ten? Not *way* too late, just a little too late? Well, it appears that you are. And since you are, you've decided you're just not going to attend this particular party.

Pascal said that it is easier to endure death without thinking about it than to endure the thought of death without dying. This is how you manage to dance the strange dance with that grim partner, nuclear annihilation. When the U.S. Army notified Winston Churchill that the first atom bomb had been detonated in New Mexico, it chose the code phrase BABIES SATIS-FACTORILY BORN. So you entered the age of irony, and the strange double life you've been leading with the world ever since. Joyce Carol Oates suggests that the reason writers—*real* writers, one assumes—don't write about Nature is that it lacks a sense of humor and registers no irony. It just doesn't seem to be of the times—these slick, sleek, knowing, objective, indulgent times. And the word *Environment*. Such a bloodless word. A flat-footed word with a shrunken heart. A word increasingly disengaged from its association with the natural world. Urban planners, industrialists, economists, and developers use it. It's a lost word, really. A cold word, mechanistic, suited strangely to the coldness generally felt toward Nature. It's their word now. You don't mind giving it up. As for *Environmentalist*, that's one that can really bring on the yawns, for you've tamed and tidied it, neutered it quite nicely. An environmentalist must be calm, rational, reasonable, and willing to compromise, otherwise you won't listen to him. Still, his beliefs are *opinions* only, for this is the age of radical subjectivism. Not long ago, Barry Commoner spoke to the Environmental Protection Agency. He scolded them. They loved it. The way they protect the environment these days is apparently to find an "acceptable level of harm from a pollutant and then issue rules allowing industry to pollute to that level." Commoner suggested that this was inappropriate. An EPA employee suggested that any other approach would place limits on economic growth and implied that Commoner was advocating this. Limits on economic growth! Commoner vigorously denied this. Oh, it was a healthy exchange of ideas, healthier certainly than our air and water. We needed that little spanking, the EPA felt. It was refreshing. The agency has recently lumbered into action in its campaign to ban dinoseb. You seem to have liked your dinoseb. It's been a popular weed killer, even though it has been directly linked with birth defects. You must hate weeds a lot. Although the EPA appears successful in banning the poison, it will still have to pay the disposal costs and compensate the manufacturers for the market value of the chemicals they still have in stock.

That's ironic, you say, but farmers will suffer losses, too, oh dreadful financial losses, if herbicide and pesticide use is restricted.

Farmers grow way too much stuff anyway. They grow surplus crops with subsidized water created by turning rivers great and small into a plumbing system of dams and canals. Rivers have become *systems*. Wetlands are increasingly being referred to as *filtering systems*—things deigned *useful* because of their ability to absorb urban run-off, oil from roads, et cetera.

We know that. We've known that for years about farmers. We know a lot these days. We're very well informed. If farmers aren't allowed to make a profit by growing surplus crops, they'll have to sell their land to developers, who'll turn all that *arable land* into office parks. Arable land isn't Nature anyway, and besides, we like those office parks and shopping plazas, with their monster supermarkets open twenty-four hours a day with aisle after aisle after aisle of *products*. It's fun. Products are fun.

Farmers like their poisons, but ranchers like them even more. There are well-funded predominantly federal and cooperative programs like the Agriculture Department's Animal Damage Control Unit that poison, shoot, and trap several thousand animals each year. This unit loves to kill things. It was created to kill things—bobcats, foxes, black bears, mountain lions, rabbits, badgers, countless birds—all to make this great land safe for the string bean and the corn, the sheep and the cow, even though you're not consuming as much cow these days. A burger now and then, but burgers are hardly cows at all, you feel. They're not all *our* cows in any case, for some burger matter is imported. There's a bit of Central American burger matter in your bun. Which is contributing to the conversion of tropical rain forest into cow pasture. Even so, you're getting away from meat these days. You're eschewing cow. It's seafood you love, shrimp most of all. And when you love something, it had better watch out, because you have a tendency to love it to death. Shrimp, shrimp, shrimp. It's more common on menus than chicken. In the wilds of Ohio, far, far from watery shores, four out of the six entrées on a menu will be shrimp, for some modest sum. Everywhere, it's all the shrimp you can eat or all you *care* to eat, for sometimes you just don't feel like eating all you *can*. You are intensively *harvesting* shrimp. Soon there won't be any left and then you can stop. It takes that, often, to make you stop. Shrimpers shrimp, of course. That's their *business*. They put out these big nets and in these nets, for each pound of shrimp, they catch more than ten times that amount of fish, turtles, and dolphins. These, quite the worse for wear, they dump back in. There is an object called TED (Turtle Excluder Device), which would save thousands of turtles and some dolphins from dying in the nets, but the shrimpers are loath to use TEDs, as they say it would cut the size of their shrimp catch.

We've heard about TED, you say.

They want you, all of you, to have all the shrimp you can eat and more. At Kiawah Island, off the coast of South Carolina, visitors go out on Jeep "safaris" through the part of the island that hasn't been developed yet. ("Wherever you see trees," the guide says, "really, that's a lot.") The safari comprises six Jeeps, and these days they go out at least four times a day, with more trips promised soon. The tourists drive their own Jeeps and the guide talks to them by radio. Kiawah has nice beaches, and the guide talks about turtles. When he mentions the shrimpers' role in the decline of the turtle, the shrimpers, who share the same frequency, scream at him. Shrimpers and most commercial fishermen (many of them working with drift and gill nets anywhere from six to thirty miles long) think of themselves as an *endangered species*. A recent newspaper headline said, "Shrimpers Spared Anti-Turtle Devices." Even so, with the continuing wanton depletion of shrimp beds, they will undoubtedly have to find some other means of employment soon. They might, for instance, become part of that vast throng laboring in the *tourist industry.*

Tourism has become an industry as destructive as any other. You are no longer benign in your traveling somewhere to look at the scenery. You never thought there was much gain in just looking anyway, you've always preferred to *use* the scenery in some manner. In your desire to get away from what you've got, you've caused there to be no place to get away *to.* You're just all bumpered up out there. Sewage and dumps have become prime indicators of America's lifestyle. In resort towns in New England and the Adirondacks, measuring the flow into the sewage plant serves as a business barometer. Tourism is a growth industry. You believe in growth. *Controlled* growth, of course. Controlled exponential growth is what you'd really like to see. You certainly don't want to put a moratorium or a cap on anything. That's illegal, isn't it? Retro you're not. You don't want to go back or anything. Forward. Maybe ask directions later. Growth is *desirable* as well as being *inevitable.* Growth is the one thing you seem to be powerless before, so you try to be realistic about it. Growth is—it's weird—it's like cancer or something.

Recently you, as tourist, have discovered your national parks and are quickly *overburdening* them. Spare land and it belongs to you! It's exotic land too, not looking like all the stuff around it that looks like everything else. You want to take advantage of this land, of course, and use it in every way you can. Thus the managers—or *stewards,* as they like to be called—have developed *wise* and *multiple-use* plans, keeping in mind exploiters' interests (for they have their needs, too) as well as the desires of the backpackers. Thus mining, timbering, and ranching activities take place in the national forests, where the Forest Service maintains a system of logging roads eight times larger than the interstate highway system. The national parks are more of a public playground and are becoming increasingly Europeanized in their look and management. Lots of concessions and motels. You deserve a clean bed and a hot meal when you go into the wilderness. At least your stewards think that you do. You keep your stewards busy. Not only must they cater to your multiple and conflicting desires, they have to manage your wildlife *resources.* They have managed wildfowl to such an extent that the reasoning has become, if it weren't for hunters, ducks would disappear. Duck stamps and licensing fees support the whole rickety duck-management system. Yes! If it weren't for the people who killed them, wild ducks wouldn't exist! Managers are managing all wild creatures, not just those that fly. They track and tape and tag and band. They relocate, restock, and reintroduce. They cull and control. It's hard to keep it all straight. Protect or poison? Extirpate or just mostly eliminate? Sometimes even the stewards get mixed up.

This is the time of machines and models, hands-on management and master plans. Don't you ever wonder as you pass that billboard advertising another MASTER-PLANNED COMMUNITY just what master they are actually talking about? Not the Big Master, certainly. Something brought to you by one of the tiny masters, of which there are many. But you like these tiny masters and have even come to expect and require them. In Florida they've just started a ten-thousand-acre city in the Everglades. It's a *megaproject*, one of the largest ever in the state. Yes, they must have thought you wanted it. No, what you thought of as the Everglades, the Park, is only a little bitty part of the Everglades. Developers have been gnawing at this irreplaceable, strange land for years. It's like they just *hate* this ancient sea of grass. Maybe you could ask them about this sometime. Roy Rogers is the senior vice president of strategic planning, and the old cowboy says that every tree and bush and inch of sidewalk in the project has been planned. Nevertheless, because the whole thing will take twenty-five years to complete, the plan is going to be constantly changed. You can understand this. The important thing is that there be a blueprint. You trust a blueprint. The tiny masters know what you like. You like *a secure landscape* and *access to services*. You like grass—that is, lawns. The ultimate lawn is the golf course, which you've been told has "some ecological value." You believe this! Not that it really matters, you just like to play golf. These golf courses require a lot of watering. So much that the more inspired of the masters have taken to watering them with effluent, *treated* effluent, but yours, from all the condos and villas built around the stocked artificial lakes you fancy.

I really don't want to think about sewage, you say, but it sounds like progress.

It is true that the masters are struggling with the problems of your incessant flushing. Cuisine is also one of their concerns. Advances in sorbets—sorbet intermezzos—in their clubs and fine restaurants. They know what you want. You want A HAVEN FROM THE ORDINARY WORLD. If you're A NATURE LOVER in the West you want to live in a $200,000 home in A WILD ANIMAL HABITAT. If you're eastern and consider yourself more hip, you want to live in new towns—brand-new reconstructed-from-scratch towns—in a house of NINETEENTH-CENTURY DESIGN. But in these new towns the masters are building, getting around can be confusing. There is an abundance of curves and an infrequency of through streets. It's the new wilderness without any trees. You can get lost, even with all the "mental bread crumbs" the masters scatter about as visual landmarks—the windmill, the water views, the various groupings of landscape "material." You *are* lost, you know. But you trust a Realtor will show you the way. There are many more Realtors than tiny masters, and many of them have to make do with less than a loaf—that is, trying to sell stuff that's already been built in an environment already "enhanced" rather than something being planned—but they're everywhere, willing to show you the path. If Dante returned to Hell today, he'd probably be escorted down by a Realtor, talking all the while about how it was just another level of Paradise.

When have you last watched a sunset? Do you remember where you were? With whom? At Loews Ventana Canyon Resort, the Grand Foyer will provide you with that opportunity through lighting which is computerized to diminish with the approaching sunset!

The tiny masters are willing to arrange Nature for you. They will compose it into a picture that you can look at at your leisure, when you're not doing work or something like that. Nature becomes scenery, a prop. At some golf courses in the Southwest, the saguaro cacti are reported to be repaired with green paste when balls blast into their skin. The saguaro can attempt to heal themselves by growing over the balls, but this takes time, and the effect can be somewhat . . . baroque. It's better to get out the pastepot. Nature has become simply a visual form of entertainment, and it had better look snappy.

Listen, you say, we've been at Ventana Canyon. It's in the desert, right? It's very, very nice, a world-class resort. A totally self-contained environment with everything that a person could possibly want, on more than a thousand acres in the middle of zip. It sprawls but nestles, like. And they've maintained the integrity of as much of the desert ecosystem as possible. Give them credit for that. *Great* restaurant, too. We had baby bay scallops there. Coming into the lobby there are these two big hand-carved coyotes, mutely howling. And that's the way we like them, *mute.* God, why do those things howl like that?

Wildlife is a personal matter, you think. The attitude is up to you. You can prefer to see it dead or not dead. You might want to let it mosey about its business or blow it away. Wild things exist only if you have the graciousness to allow them to. Just outside Tucson, Arizona, there is a brand-new structure modeled after a French foreign legion outpost. It's the *International Wildlife Museum,* and it's full of dead animals. Three hundred species are there, at least a third of them—the rarest ones—killed and collected by one C. J. McElroy, who enjoyed doing it and now shares what's left with you. The museum claims to be educational because you can watch a taxidermist at work or touch a lion's tooth. You can get real close to these dead animals, closer than you can in a zoo. Some of you prefer zoos, however, which are becoming bigger, better, and bioclimatic. New-age zoo designers want the animals to *flow right out into your space.* In Dallas there will soon be a Wilds of Africa exhibit; in San Diego there's a simulated rain forest, where you can thread your way "down the side of a lush canyon, the air filled with a fine mist from 300 high-pressure nozzles"; in New Orleans you've constructed a swamp, the real swamp not far away on the verge of disappearing. Animals in these places are abstractions—wandering relics of their true selves, but that doesn't matter.

Animal behavior in a zoo is nothing like natural behavior, but that doesn't really matter, either. Zoos are pretty, contained, and accessible. These new habitats can contain one hundred different species—not more than one or two of each thing, of course—on seven acres, three, one. You don't want to see *too much* of anything, certainly. An *example* will suffice. Sort of like a biological Crabtree & Evelyn basket selected with *you* in mind. You like things reduced, simplified. It's easier to take it all in, park it in your mind. You like things inside better than outside anyway. You are increasingly looking at and living in proxy environments created by substitution and simulation. *Resource economists* are a wee branch in the tree of tiny masters, and one, Martin Krieger, wrote, "Artificial prairies and wildernesses have been created, and there is no reason to believe that these artificial environments need be unsatisfactory for those who experience them. . . . We will have to realize that the way in which we experience nature is conditioned by our society—which more and more is seen to be receptive to responsible intervention."

Nature has become a world of appearances, a mere source of materials. You've been editing it for quite some time; now you're in the process of deleting it. Earth is beginning to look like not much more than a launching pad. Back near Tucson, on the opposite side of the mountain from the dead-animal habitat, you're building Biosphere II (as compared with or opposed to Biosphere I, more commonly known as Earth)—a 2½-acre terrarium, an artificial ecosystem that will include a rain forest, a desert, a thirty-five-foot ocean, and several thousand species of life (lots of microbes), including eight human beings, who will cultivate a bit of farmland. You think it would be nice to colonize other worlds after you've made it necessary to leave this one.

Hey, that's pretty good, you say, all that stuff packed into just 2½ acres. That's only about three times bigger than my entire *house.*

It's small all right, but still not small enough to be, apparently, useful. For the purposes of NASA, say, it would have to be smaller, oh much smaller, and energy-efficient too. Fiddle, fiddle, fiddle. You support fiddling, as well as meddling. This is how you learn. Though it's quite apparent the environment has been grossly polluted and the natural world abused and defiled, you seem to prefer to continue pondering effects rather than preventing causes. You want proof, you insist on proof. A Dr. Lave from Carnegie-Mellon—and he's an expert, an economist, and an environmental *expert*—says that scientists will have to prove to you that you will suffer if you don't become less of a "throwaway society." *If you really want me to give up my car or my air conditioner, you'd better prove to me first that the earth would otherwise be uninhabitable,* Dr. Lave says. *Me* is *you,* I presume, whereas *you* refers to them. You as in me—that is, *me, me, me*—certainly strike a hard bargain. Uninhabitable the world has to get before you rein in your requirements. You're a consumer after all, *the* consumer upon whom so much attention is lavished, the ultimate user of a commodity that has become, these days, everything. To try to appease your appetite for proof, for example, scientists have been leasing for experimentation forty-six pristine lakes in Canada.

They don't want to *keep* them, they just want to *borrow* them.

They've been intentionally contaminating many of the lakes with a variety of pollutants dribbled into the propeller wash of research boats. *It's one of the boldest experiments in lake ecology ever conducted.* They've turned these remote lakes into huge *real-world test tubes.* They've been doing this since 1976! And what they've found so far in these *preliminary* studies is that pollutants are really destructive. The lakes get gross. Life in them ceases. It took about eight years to make this happen in one of them, everything carefully measured and controlled all the while. Now the scientists are slowly reversing the process. But it will take hundreds of years for the lakes to recover. They think.

Remember when you used to like rain, the sound of it, the feel of it, the way it made the plants and trees all glisten. We needed that rain, you would say. It looked pretty too, you thought, particularly in the movies. Now it rains and you go, Oh-oh. A nice walloping rain these days means *overtaxing our sewage treatment plants.* It means *untreated waste discharged directly into our waterways.* It means . . .

Okay. Okay.

Acid rain! And we all know what this is. Or most of us do. People of power in government and industry still don't seem to know what it is. Whatever it is, they say, they don't want to curb it, but they're willing to study it some more. Economists call air and water pollution "externalities" anyway. Oh, acid rain. You do get so sick of hearing about it. The words have already become a white-noise kind of thing. But you think in terms of *mitigating* it maybe. As for *the greenhouse effect,* you think in terms of *countering* that. One way that's been discussed recently is the planting of new forests, not for the sake of the forests alone, oh my heavens, no. Not for the sake of majesty and mystery or of Thumper and Bambi, are you kidding me, but because, as every schoolchild knows, trees absorb carbon dioxide. They just soak it up and store it. They just love it. So this is the plan: you plant millions of acres of trees, and you can go on doing pretty much whatever you're doing—driving around, using staggering amounts of energy, keeping those power plants fired to the max. Isn't Nature remarkable? So willing to serve? You wouldn't think it had anything more to offer, but it seems it does. Of course these "forests" wouldn't exactly be forests. They would be more like trees. *Managed* trees. The Forest Service, which now manages our forests by cutting them down, might be called upon to evolve in their thinking and allow these trees to grow. They would probably be patented trees after a time. Fast-growing, uniform, genetically-created-to-be-toxin-eating *machines.* They would be *new-age* trees, because the problem with planting the old-fashioned variety to *combat* the greenhouse effect, which is caused by pollution, is that they're already dying from it. All along the crest of the Appalachians from Maine to Georgia, forests struggle to survive in a toxic soup of poisons. They can't *help* us if we've killed them, now can they?

All right, you say, wow, lighten up will you? Relax. Tell about yourself.

Well, I say, I live in Florida . . .

Oh my God, you say. Florida! Florida is a joke! How do you expect us to take you seriously if you still live there! Florida is crazy, it's pink concrete. It's paved, it's over. And a little girl just got eaten by an alligator down there. It came out of some swamp next to a subdivision and just carried her off. That set your Endangered Species Act back fifty years, you can bet.

I . . .

Listen, we don't want to hear any more about Florida. We don't want to hear about Phoenix or Hilton Head or California's Central Valley. If our wetlands—our *vanishing* wetlands—are mentioned one more time, we'll scream. And the talk about condors and grizzlies and wolves is becoming too de trop. We had just managed to get whales out of our minds when those three showed up under the ice in Alaska. They even had *names.* Bone is the dead one, right? It's almost the twenty-first century! Those last condors are *pathetic.* Can't we just get this over with?

Aristotle said that all living things are ensouled and striving to participate in eternity.

Oh, I just bet he said that, you say. That doesn't sound like Aristotle. He was a humanist. We're all humanists here. This is the age of humanism. And it has been for a long time.

You are driving with a stranger in the car, and it is the stranger behind the wheel. In the back seat are your pals for many years now—DO WHAT YOU LIKE and his swilling sidekick, WHY NOT. A deer, or some emblematic animal, something from that myriad natural world you've come from that you now treat with such indifference and scorn—steps from the dimming woods and tentatively upon the highway. The stranger does not decelerate or brake, not yet, maybe not at all. The feeling is that whatever it is *will get out of the way.* Oh, it's a fine car you've got, a fine machine, and oddly you don't mind the stranger driving it, because in a way, everything has gotten too complicated, way, way out of your control. You've given the wheel to the masters, the managers, the comptrollers. Something is wrong, *maybe,* you feel a little sick, *actually,* but the car is luxurious and fast and you're *moving,* which is the most important thing by far.

Why make a fuss when you're so comfortable? Don't make a fuss, make a baby. Go out and get something to eat, build something. Make *another* baby. Babies are cute. Babies show you have faith in the future. Although faith is perhaps too strong a word. They're everywhere these days, in all the crowds and traffic jams, there are the babies too. You don't seem to associate them with the problems of population increase. They're just babies! And you've come to believe in them again. They're a lot more tangible than the afterlife, which, of course, you haven't believed in in ages. At least not for yourself. The afterlife now belongs to plastics and poisons. Yes, plastics and poisons will have a far more extensive afterlife than you, that's known. A disposable diaper, for example, which is all plastic and wood pulp—you like them for all those babies, so easy to use and toss—will take around four centuries to degrade. Almost all plastics do, centuries and centuries. In the sea, many marine animals die from ingesting or being entangled in discarded plastic. In the dumps, plastic squats on more than 25 percent of dump space. But your heart is disposed toward plastic. Someone, no doubt the plastics industry, told you it was convenient. This same industry is now looking into recycling in an attempt to get the critics of their nefarious, multifarious products off their backs. That should make you feel better, because *recycling* has become an honorable word, no longer merely the hobby of Volvo owners. The fact is that people in plastics are born obscurants. Recycling (practically, impossible) won't solve the plastic glut, only reduction of production will, and the plastics industry isn't looking into that, you can be sure. Waste is not just the stuff you throw away, of course, it's the stuff you use to excess. With the exception of *hazardous waste*, which you do worry about from time to time, it's even thought you have a declining sense of emergency about the problem. Builders are building bigger houses because you want bigger. You're trading up. Utility companies are beginning to worry about your constantly rising consumption. Utility companies! You haven't entered a new age at all but one of upscale nihilism, deluxe nihilism.

In the summer, particularly in the *industrial Northeast*, you did get a little excited. The filth cut into your fun time. Dead stuff floating around. Sludge and bloody vials. Hygienic devices—appearing not quite so hygienic out of context—all coming in on the tide. The air smelled funny, too. You tolerate a great deal, but the summer of '88 was truly creepy. It was even thought for a moment that the environment would become a political issue. But it didn't. You didn't want it to be, preferring instead to continue in your politics of subsidizing and advancing avarice. The issues were the same as always—jobs, defense, the economy, maintaining and improving the standard of living in this greedy, selfish, expansionistic, industrialized society.

You're getting a little shrill here, you say.

You're pretty well off. You expect to be better off soon. You do. What does this mean? More software, more scampi, more square footage? You have created an ecological crisis. The earth is infinitely variable and alive, and you are killing it. It seems safer this way. But you are not safe. You want to find wholeness and happiness in a land increasingly damaged and betrayed, and you never will. More than material matters. You must change your ways.

What is this? *Sinners in the Hands of an Angry God?*

The ecological crisis cannot be resolved by politics. It cannot be solved by science or technology. It is a crisis caused by culture and character, and a deep change in personal consciousness is needed. Your fundamental attitudes toward the earth have become twisted. You have made only brutal contact with Nature, you cannot comprehend its grace. You must change. Have few desires and simple pleasures. Honor nonhuman life. Control yourself, become more authentic. Live lightly upon the earth and treat it with respect. Redefine the word *progress* and dismiss the managers and masters. Grow inwardly and with knowledge become truly wiser. Make connections. Think differently, behave differently. For this is essentially a moral issue we face and moral decisions must be made.

A *moral issue!* Okay, this discussion is now toast. A *moral* issue . . . And who's this *we* now? Who are *you* is what I'd like to know. You're not me, anyway. I admit, someone's to blame and something should be done. But I've got to go. It's getting late. That's dusk out there. That is dusk, isn't it? It certainly doesn't look like any dawn I've ever seen. Well, take care.

FROM THE END OF NATURE

Bill McKibbin

This piece is the last section of "A Path of More Resistance," the final chapter of McKibbin's 1989 book The End of Nature. *Several sections of the book were first published in* The New Yorker.

The inertia of affluence, the push of poverty, the soaring population—these and the other reasons listed earlier make me pessimistic about the chances that we will dramatically alter our ways of thinking and living, that we will turn humble in the face of our troubles.

A purely personal effort is, of course, just a gesture—a good gesture, but a gesture. The greenhouse effect is the first environmental problem we can't escape by moving to the woods. There are no personal solutions. There is no time to just decide we'll raise enlightened children and they'll slowly change the world. (When the problem was that someone might drop the Bomb, it perhaps made sense to bear and raise sane, well-adjusted children in the hope that they'd help prevent the Bomb from being dropped. But the problem now is precisely too many children, well adjusted or otherwise.) We have to be the ones to do it, and simply driving less won't matter, except as a statement, a way to get other people—many other people—to drive less. *Most* people have to be persuaded, and persuaded quickly, to change.

But saying that something is difficult is not the same as saying it is impossible. After all, George Bush decided in the wake of the 1988 heat that he was an environmentalist. Margaret Thatcher, who in 1985 had linked environmental groups with other "subversives" as "the enemy within," found the religion at about the same time, after the death of the North Sea seals and the odyssey of the *Karin B*, the wandering toxic-waste barge. "Protecting the balance of nature," she said, is "one of the great challenges of the twentieth century."

I've been using the analogy of slavery throughout this discussion: we feel it our privilege (and we feel it a necessity) to dominate nature to our advantage, as whites once dominated blacks. When one method of domination seems to be ending—the reliance on fossil fuels, say—we cast about for another, like genetic tinkering, much as Americans replaced slavery with Jim Crow segregation. However, in my lifetime that official segregation ended. Through their courage, men and women like Martin Luther King and Fannie Lou Hamer managed to harness the majority's better qualities—idealism, love for one's neighbor—to transform the face of American society. Racism, it is true, remains virulent, but the majority of Americans have voted for legislators who passed laws—radical laws—mandating affirmative action programs. Out of some higher motive, (and, of course, some base motives, such as the fear of black revolt) whites have sacrificed at least a little potential wealth and power. It would be wrong to say categorically that such a shift couldn't happen with regard to the environment—that a mixture of fear and the love for nature buried in most of us couldn't rise to the surface. Some small but significant steps have been taken. Los Angeles, for instance, recently enacted a series of laws to improve air quality that will change at least the edges of the lives of every resident. Los Angelenos will drive different cars, turn in their gas-powered lawn mowers, start their barbecues without lighter fluid.

Most of my hope, however, fades in the face of the uniqueness of the situation. As we have seen, nature is already ending, its passing quiet and accidental. And not only does its ending prevent us from returning to the world we previously knew, but it also, for two powerful reasons, makes any of the fundamental changes we've discussed even more unlikely than they might be in easier times. If the end of nature were still in the future, a preventable possibility, the equation might be different. But it isn't in the future—it's in the recent past, and the present.

The end of nature is a plunge into the unknown, fearful as much because it is unknown as because it might be hot or dry or whipped by hurricanes. This lack of security is the first reason that fundamental change will be much harder, for the changes we've been discussing—the deep ecology alternative, for instance—would make life even more unpredictable. One would have to begin to forgo the traditional methods of securing one's future—many children, many possessions, and so on. Jeremy Rifkin, in his book on genetic engineering, said there was still a chance we would choose to sacrifice "a measure of our own future security in order to represent the interests of the rest of the cosmos. . . . If we have been saving that spirit up for a propitious moment, then certainly now is the time for it to pour forth."

But now isn't the time—now, as the familiar world around us starts to change, is the moment when every threatened instinct will push us to scramble to preserve at least our familiar style of life. We can—and we may well—make the adjustments necessary for our survival. For instance, much of the early work in agricultural biotechnology has focused on inventing plants able to survive heat and drought. It seems the sensible thing to do—the way to keep life as "normal" as possible in the face of change. It leads, though, as I have said, to the second death of nature: the imposition of our artificial world in place of the broken natural one.

The rivers of the American Southwest, in particular the Colorado, provide a perfect example of this phenomenon. Though Ed Abbey wrote about the entire Southwest, the one spot he kept returning to, the navel of his universe, was Glen Canyon dam. The dam, built a couple of decades ago near the Utah-Arizona line, is just upstream of the Grand Canyon. It backs up the waters of the Colorado into Lake Powell, a reservoir that rises and falls with the demand for hydroelectric power. The water covers Glen Canyon, a place so sweet Abbey called it "paradise"—and the description of his raft trip through the gorge shortly before the dam was finished makes the term sound weak, understated.

Since the degradation of this canyon stood in his mind for all human arrogance, its salvation would be the sign that man had turned the corner, begun the long trek back toward his proper station. (Blowing up the dam is the great aim of the Monkey Wrench Gang.) If we decide to take out the dam, it would signal many things, among them that perhaps the desert should not house huge numbers of people—that some should move, and others take steps to ensure smaller future generations. True, if we decide to take out the dam and the lake flowed away toward Mexico, it would "no doubt expose a drear and hideous scene: immense mul flats and whole plateaus of sodden garbage strewn with dead trees, sunken boats, the skeletons of long-forgotten, decomposing waterskiers," Abbey writes. "But to those who find the prospect too appalling, I say give nature a little time. In five years, at most in ten, the sun and wind and storms will cleanse and sterilize the repellent mess. The inevitable floods will soon remove all that does not belong within the canyons. Fresh green willow, box elder, and redbud will reappear; and the ancient drowned cottonwoods (noble monuments to themselves) will be replaced by young of their own kind. . . . Within a generation—thirty years—I predict the river and canyons will bear a decent resemblance to their former selves. Within the lifetime of our children Glen Canyon and the living river, heart of the canyonlands, will be restored to us. The wilderness will again belong to God, the people, and the wild things that call it home."

Such a vision is, of course, romantically unlikely under any circumstances. But the new insecurity that accompanies the end of nature makes it even more farfetched. As we have seen, the projected increases in evaporation and decreases in rainfall in the Colorado watershed could cut flows along the river nearly in half. As a result, noted an EPA report, the reluctance in recent years to build big dams, for fear of environmental opposition, "may be re-evaluated in light of possible new demands for developed water under warm-dry climate change scenarios." Specifically, "climate change may create pressure to build the Animas-LaPlata and Narrows projects proposed for Colorado." In other words, where Abbey hoped for box elder and redbud more dams will bloom. The authors of *Gaia: An Atlas for Planet Management* are quite explicit about dam building. In a section on water conservation they put forth a lot of good ideas for fixing leaky mains and such, but they also sing the praises of damming rivers, a process that "can help satisfy a number of needs at once: it helps control flooding, provides the potential for generating hydropower, and stores water for a variety of purposes, including irrigation. The resulting reservoirs represent a multi-purpose resource, with potential for aqua-culture and leisure activities." A flood-washed paradise of cottonwood or a "multipurpose resource"—that is the choice, and it is not hard to guess, if the heat is on, what the voters of Arizona will demand.

I got a glimpse of this particular future a few years ago when I spent some time along the La Grande River, in sub-Arctic Quebec. It is barren land but beautiful—a tundra of tiny ponds and hummocks stretching to the horizon, carpeted in light-green caribou moss. There are trees—al-most all black spruce, and all spindly, sparse. A number of Indians and Eskimos lived there—about the number the area could support. Then, a decade or so ago, Hydro-Quebec, the provincial utility, decided to exploit the power of the La Grande by building three huge dams along the river's 350-mile length. The largest, said the Hydro-Quebec spokesman, is the size of 54,000 two-story houses or sixty-seven billion peas. Its spillway could carry the combined flow of all the rivers of Europe. And erecting it was a Bunyanesque task: eighteen thousand men carved the roads north through the tundra and poured the concrete. (Photos show the cooks stir-ring spaghetti sauce with canoe paddles.) On the one hand, this is a per-fect example of "environmentally sound" energy generation; it produces an enormous amount of power without giving off so much as a whiff of any greenhouse gas. This is the sort of structure we'll be clamoring to build as the warming progresses.

But environmentally sound is not the same as natural. The dams have al-tered an area larger than Switzerland—the flow of the Caniapiscau River, for instance, has been partly reversed to provide more water for the tur-bines. In September of 1984, at least ten thousand caribou drowned trying to cross the river during their annual migration. They were crossing at their usual spot, but the river was not its usual size; it was so swollen that many of the animals were swept forty-five miles downstream. Every good argument—the argument that fossil fuels cause the greenhouse effect; the argument that in a drier, hotter world we'll need more water; the argument that as our margin of security dwindles we must act to restore it—will lead us to more La Grande projects, more dams on the Colorado, more "management." Every argument—that the warmer weather and increased ultraviolet is killing plants and causing cancer; that the new weather is causing food shortages—will have us looking to genetic engineering for salvation. And with each such step we will move farther from nature.

At the same time—and this is the second kicker—the only real counterargument, the argument for an independent, eternal, ever-sweet nature, will grow ever fainter and harder to make. Why? Because nature, independent nature, is already ending. Fighting for it is like fighting for an independent Latvia except that it's harder, since the end of nature may be permanent. Take out Glen Canyon dam and let the Colorado run free, let the "inevitable floods" wash away the debris? But floods may be a thing of the past on the Colorado; the river may, in effect, be dammed at the source—in the clouds that no longer dump their freight on its upper reaches, and in the heat that evaporates the water that does fall.

If nature were about to end, we might muster endless energy to stave it off; but if nature has already ended, what are we fighting for? Before any redwoods had been cloned or genetically improved, one could understand clearly what the fight against such tinkering was about. It was about the idea that a redwood was somehow sacred, that its fundamental identity should remain beyond our control. But once that barrier has been broken, what is the fight about, then? It's not like opposing nuclear reactors or toxic waste dumps, each one of which poses new risks to new areas. This damage is to an idea, the idea of nature, and all the ideas that descend from it. It is not cumulative. Wendell Berry once argued that without a "fascination" with the wonder of the natural world "the energy needed for its preservation will never be developed"—that "there must be a mystique of the rain if we are ever to restore the purity of the rainfall." This makes sense when the problem is transitory—sulfur from a smokestack drifting over the Adirondacks. But how can there be a mystique of the rain now that every drop—even the drops that fall as snow on the Arctic, even the drops that fall deep in the remaining forest primeval—bears the permanent stamp of man? Having lost its separateness, it loses its special power. Instead of being a category like God—something beyond our control—it is now a category like the defense budget or the minimum wage, a problem we must work out. This in itself changes its meaning completely, and changes our reaction to it.

A few weeks ago, on the hill behind my house, I almost kicked the biggest rabbit I had ever seen. She had nearly finished turning white for the winter, and we stood there watching each other for a pleasant while, two creatures linked by curiosity. What will it mean to come across a rabbit in the woods once genetically engineered "rabbits" are widespread?

Why would we have any more reverence or affection for such a rabbit than we would for a Coke bottle?

The end of nature probably also makes us reluctant to attach ourselves to its remnants, for the same reason that we usually don't choose friends from among the terminally ill. I love the mountain outside my back door—the stream that runs along its flank, and the smaller stream that slides down a quarter-mile mossy chute, and the place where the slope flattens into an open plain of birch and oak. But I know that some part of me resists getting to know it better—for fear, weak-kneed as it sounds, of getting hurt. If I knew as well as a forester what sick trees looked like, I fear I would see them everywhere. I find now that I like the woods best in winter, when it is harder to tell what might be dying. The winter woods might be perfectly healthy come spring, just as the sick friend, when she's sleeping peacefully, might wake up without the wheeze in her lungs.

Writing on a different subject, the bonds between men and women, Allan Bloom describes the difficulty of maintaining a committed relationship in an age when divorce—the end of that relationship—is so widely accepted: "The possibility of separation is already the fact of separation, inasmuch as people today must plan to be whole and self-sufficient and cannot risk interdependence." Instead of working to strengthen our attachments, our energies "are exhausted in preparation for independence." How much more so if that possible separation is definite, if that hurt and confusion is certain. I love winter best now, but I try not to love it too much, for fear of the January perhaps not so distant when the snow will fall as warm rain. There is no future in loving nature.

And there may not even be much past. Though Thoreau's writings grew in value and importance the closer we drew to the end of nature, the time fast approaches when he will be inexplicable, his notions less sensible to future men than the cave paintings are to us. Thoreau writes, on his climb up Katahdin, that the mountain "was vast, Titanic, and such as man never inhabits. Some part of the beholder, even some vital part, seems to escape through the loose grating of his ribs. . . . Nature has got him at a disadvantage, caught him alone, and pilfers him of some of his divine faculty. She does not smile on him as in the plains. She seems to say sternly, why came ye here before your time. This ground is not prepared for you." This sentiment describes perfectly the last stage of the relationship of man to nature—though we had subdued her in the low places, the peaks, the poles, the jungles still rang with her pure message. But what sense will this passage make in the years to come, when Katahdin, the "cloud factory," is ringed by clouds of man's own making? When the massive pines that ring its base have been genetically improved for straightness of trunk and "proper branch drop," or, more likely, have sprung from the cones of genetically improved trees that began a few miles and a few generations distant on some timber plantation? When the moose that ambles by is part of a herd whose rancher is committed to the enlightened, Gaian notion that "conservation and profit go hand in hand"?

Thoreau describes an afternoon of fishing at the mouth of Murch Brook, a dozen miles from the summit of Katahdin. Speckled trout "swallowed the bait as fast as we could throw in; and the finest specimens . . . that I have ever seen, the largest one weighing three pounds, were heaved upon the shore." He stood there to catch them as "they fell in a perfect shower" around him. "While yet alive, before their tints had faded, they glistened like the fairest flowers, the product of primitive rivers; and he could hardly trust his senses, as he stood over them, that these jewels should have swam away in that Aboljacknagesic water for so long, some many dark ages—these bright fluviatile flowers, seen of Indians only, made beautiful, the Lord only knows why, to swim there!" But through biotechnology we have already synthesized growth hormone for trout. Soon pulling them from the water will mean no more than pulling cars from an assembly line. We won't have to wonder why the Lord made them beautiful and put them there; we will have created them to increase protein supplies or fish-farm profits. If we want to make them pretty, we may. Soon Thoreau will make no sense. And when that happens, the end of nature—which began with our alteration of the atmosphere, and continued with the responses to our precarious situation of the "planetary managers" and the "genetic engineers"—will be final. The loss of memory will be the eternal loss of meaning.

In the end, I understand perfectly well that defiance may mean prosperity and a sort of security—that more dams will help the people of Phoenix, and that genetic engineering will help the sick, and that there is so much progress that can still be made against human misery. And I have no great desire to limit my way of life. If I thought we could put off the decision, foist it on our grandchildren, I'd be willing. As it is, I have no plans to live in a cave, or even an unheated cabin. If it took ten thousand years to get where we are, it will take a few generations to climb back down. But this could be the epoch when people decide at least to go no farther down the path we've been following—when we make not only the necessary technological adjustments to preserve the world from overheating but also the necessary mental adjustments to ensure that we'll never again put our good ahead of everything else's. This is the path I choose, for it offers at least a shred of hope for a living, eternal, meaningful world.

The reasons for my choice are as numerous as the trees on the hill outside my window, but they crystallized in my mind when I read a passage from one of the brave optimists of our managed future. "The existential philosophers—particularly Sartre—used to lament that man lacked an essential purpose," writes Walter Truett Anderson. "We find now that the human predicament is not quite so devoid of inherent purpose after all.

To be caretakers of a planet, custodians of all its life forms and shapers of its (and our own) future is certainly purpose enough." This intended rallying cry depresses me more deeply than I can say. That is our destiny? To be "caretakers" of a managed world, "custodians" of all life? For that job security we will trade the mystery of the natural world, the pungent mystery of our own lives and of a world bursting with exuberant creation? Much better, Sartre's neutral purposelessness. But much better than that, another vision, of man actually living up to his potential.

As birds have flight, our special gift is reason. Part of that reason drives the intelligence that allows us, say, to figure out and master DNA, or to build big power plants. But our reason could also keep us from following blindly the biological imperatives toward endless growth in numbers and territory. Our reason allows us to conceive of our species as a species, and to recognize the danger that our growth poses to it, and to feel something for the other species we threaten. Should we so choose, we could exercise our reason to do what no other animal can do: we could limit ourselves voluntarily, *choose* to remain God's creatures instead of making ourselves gods. What a towering achievement that would be, so much more impressive than the largest dam (beavers can build dams) because so much harder. Such restraint—not genetic engineering or planetary management—is the real challenge, the hard thing. Of course we can splice genes. But can we *not* splice genes?

The momentum behind our impulse to control nature may be too strong to stop. But the likelihood of defeat is not an excuse to avoid trying. In one sense it's an aesthetic choice we face, much like Thoreau's, though what is at stake is less the shape of our own lives than the very practical question of the lives of all the other species and the creation they together constitute. But it is, of course, for our benefit, too. Jeffers wrote, "Integrity is wholeness, the greatest beauty is / organic wholeness of life and things, the divine beauty of the universe. Love that, not man / Apart from that, or else you will share man's pitiful confusions, or drown in despair when his days darken." The day has come when we choose between that wholeness and man in it or man apart, between that old clarity or new darkness.

The strongest reason for choosing man apart is, as I have said, the idea that nature has ended. And I think it has. But I cannot stand the clanging finality of the argument I've made, any more than people have ever been able to stand the clanging finality of their own deaths. So I hope against hope. Though not in our time, and not in the time of our children, or their children, if we now, *today*, limited our numbers and our desires and our ambitions, perhaps nature could someday resume its independent working. Perhaps the temperature could someday adjust itself to its own setting, and the rain fall of its own accord.

Time, as I said at the start of this essay, is elusive, odd. Perhaps the ten thousand years of our encroaching, defiant civilization, an eternity to us and a yawn to the rocks around us, could give way to ten thousand years of humble civilization when we choose to pay more for the benefits of nature, when we rebuild the sense of wonder and sanctity that could protect the natural world. At the end of that span we would still be so young, and perhaps ready to revel in the timelessness that surrounds us. I said, much earlier, that one of the possible meanings of the end of nature is that God is dead. But another, if there was or is any such thing as God, is that he has granted us free will and now looks on, with great concern and love, to see how we exercise it: to see if we take the chance offered by this crisis to bow down and humble ourselves, or if we compound original sin with terminal sin.

And if what I fear indeed happens? If the next twenty years sees us pump ever more gas into the sky, and if it sees us take irrevocable steps into the genetically engineered future, what solace then? The only ones in need of consolation will be those of us who were born in the transitional decades, too early to adapt completely to a brave new ethos.

I've never paid more than the usual attention to the night sky, perhaps because I grew up around cities, on suburban blocks lined with streetlights. But last August, on a warm Thursday afternoon, my wife and I hauled sleeping bags high into the mountains and laid them out on a rocky summit and waited for night to fall and the annual Perseid meteor shower to begin. After midnight, it finally started in earnest—every minute, every thirty seconds, another spear of light shot across some corner of the sky, so fast that unless you were looking right at it you had only the sense of a flash. Our bed was literally rock-hard, and when, toward dawn, an unforecast rain soaked our tentless clearing, it was cold—but the night was glorious, and I've since gotten a telescope. When, in *Paradise Lost,* Adam asks about the movements of the heavens, Raphael refuses to answer. "Let it speak," he says, "the Maker's high magnificence, who built / so spacious, and his line stretcht out so far; / That man may know he dwells not in his own; / An edifice too large for him to fill, / Lodg'd in a small partition, and the rest / Ordain'd for uses to his Lord best known." We may be creating microscopic nature; we may have altered the middle nature all around us; but this vast nature above our atmosphere still holds mystery and wonder. The occasional satellite does blip across, but it is almost a self-parody. Someday, man may figure out a method of conquering the stars, but at least for now when we look into the night sky, it is as Burroughs said: "We do not see ourselves reflected there—we are swept away from ourselves, and impressed with our own insignificance."

As I lay on the mountaintop that August night I tried to pick out the few constellations I could identify—Orion's Belt, the Dippers. The ancients, surrounded by wild and even hostile nature, took comfort in seeing the familiar above them—spoons and swords and nets. But we will need to train ourselves not to see those patterns. The comfort we need is inhuman.

THE CLAN OF ONE-BREASTED WOMEN

Terry Tempest Williams

This selection is from Williams's 1991 book Refuge.

I belong to a Clan of One-breasted Women. My mother, my grand-mothers, and six aunts have all had mastectomies. Seven are dead. The two who survive have just completed rounds of chemotherapy and radiation.

I've had my own problems: two biopsies for breast cancer and a small tumor between my ribs diagnosed as "a borderline malignancy."

This is my family history.

Most statistics tell us breast cancer is genetic, hereditary, with rising percentages attached to fatty diets, childlessness, or becoming pregnant after thirty. What they don't say is living in Utah may be the greatest haz-ard of all.

We are a Mormon family with roots in Utah since 1847. The word-of-wisdom, a religious doctrine of health, kept the women in my family aligned with good foods: no coffee, no tea, tobacco, or alcohol. For the most part, these women were finished having their babies by the time they were thirty. And only one faced breast cancer prior to 1960. Tradi-tionally, as a group of people, Mormons have a low rate of cancer.

Is our family a cultural anomaly? The truth is we didn't think about it. Those who did, usually the men, simply said, "bad genes." The women's attitude was stoic. Cancer was part of life. On February 16, 1971, the eve before my mother's surgery, I accidently picked up the telephone and overheard her ask my grandmother what she could expect.

"Diane, it is one of the most spiritual experiences you will ever encounter."

I quietly put down the receiver.

Two days later, my father took my three brothers and me to the hospi-tal to visit her. She met us in the lobby in a wheelchair. No bandages were visible. I'll never forget her radiance, the way she held herself in a purple velour robe and how she gathered us around her.

"Children, I am fine. I want you to know I felt the arms of God around me."

We believed her. My father cried. Our mother, his wife, was thirty-eight years old.

Two years ago, after my mother's death from cancer, my father and I were having dinner together. He had just returned from St. George where his construction company was putting in natural gas lines for towns in southern Utah. He spoke of his love for the country: the sandstoned land-scape, bare-boned and beautiful. He had just finished hiking the Kolob trail in Zion National Park. We got caught up in reminiscing, recalling with fondness our walk up Angle's Landing on his fiftieth birthday and the years our family had vacationed there. This was a remembered landscape where we had been raised.

Over dessert, I shared a recurring dream of mine. I told my father that for years, as long as I could remember, I saw this flash of light in the night in the desert. That this image had so permeated my being, I could not venture south without seeing it again, on the horizon, illuminating buttes and mesas.

"You did see it," he said.

"Saw what?" I asked, a bit tentative.

"The bomb. The cloud. We were driving home from Riverside, California. You were sitting on your mother's lap. She was pregnant. In fact, I remember the date, September 7, 1957. We had just gotten out of the Service. We were driving north, past Las Vegas. It was an hour or so before dawn, when this explosion went off. We not only heard it, but felt it. I thought the oil tanker in front of us had blown up. We pulled over and suddenly, rising from the desert floor, we saw it, clearly, this golden-stemmed cloud, the mushroom. The sky seemed to vibrate with an eerie pink glow. Within a few minutes, a light ash was raining on the car."

I stared at my father. This was new information to me.

"I thought you knew that," my father said. "It was a common occurrence in the fifties."

It was at this moment I realized the deceit I had been living under. Children growing up in the American Southwest, drinking contaminated milk from contaminated cows, even from the contaminated breasts of their mother, my mother—members, years later, of the Clan of One-breasted Women.

It is a well-known story in the Desert West, "The Day We Bombed Utah," or perhaps, "The Years We Bombed Utah."[1] Above ground atomic testing in Nevada took place from January 27, 1951, through July 11, 1962. Not only were the winds blowing north, covering "low use segments of the population" with fallout and leaving sheep dead in their tracks, but the climate was right.[2] The United States of the 1950s was red, white, and blue, The Korean War was raging. McCarthyism was rampant. Ike was it and the Cold War was hot. If you were against nuclear testing, you were for a Communist regime.

Much has been written about this "American nuclear tragedy." Public health was secondary to national security. The Atomic Energy Commissioner, Thomas Murray, said, "Gentlemen, we must not let anything interfere with this series of tests, nothing."[3]

---

[1] Fuller, John G., *The Day We Bombed Utah* (New York: New American Library, 1984).

[2] Discussion on March 14, 1998, with Carole Gallagher, photographer and author, *Nuclear Towns: The Secret War in the American Southwest,* to be published by Doubleday, Spring, 1990.

[3] Szasz, Ferenc M., "Downwind From the Bomb," *Nevada Historical Society Quarterly,* Fall, 1987 Vol. XXX, No. 3, p. 185.

Again and again, the American public was told by its government, in spite of burns, blisters, and nausea, "It has been found that the tests may be conducted with adequate assurance of safety under conditions prevailing at the bombing reservations."[4] Assuaging public fears was simply a matter of public relations. "Your best action," an Atomic Energy Commission booklet read, "is not to be worried about fallout." A news release typical of the times stated, "We find no basis for concluding that harm to any individual has resulted from radioactive fallout."[5]

On August 30, 1979, during Jimmy Carter's presidency, a suit was filed entitled "Irene Allen vs. the United States of America." Mrs. Allen was the first to be alphabetically listed with twenty-four test cases, representative of nearly 1200 plaintiffs seeking compensation from the United States government for cancers caused from nuclear testing in Nevada.

Irene Allen lived in Hurricane, Utah. She was the mother of five children and had been widowed twice. Her first husband with their two oldest boys had watched the tests from the roof of the local high school. He died of leukemia in 1956. Her second husband died of pancreatic cancer in 1978.

In a town meeting conducted by Utah Senator Orrin Hatch, shortly before the suit was filed, Mrs. Allen said, "I am not blaming the government, I want you to know that, Senator Hatch. But I thought if my testimony could help in any way so this wouldn't happen again to any of the generations coming up after us . . . I am really happy to be here this day to bear testimony of this."[6]

God-fearing people. This is just one story in an anthology of thousands.

On May 10, 1984, Judge Bruce S. Jenkins handed down his opinion. Ten of the plaintiffs were awarded damages. It was the first time a federal court had determined that nuclear tests had been the cause of cancers. For the remaining fourteen test cases, the proof of causation was not sufficient. In spite of the split decision, it was considered a landmark ruling.[7] It was not to remain so for long.

In April, 1987, the 110th Circuit Court of Appeals overturned Judge Jenkins' ruling on the basis that the United States was protected from suit by the legal doctrine of sovereign immunity, the centuries-old idea from England in the days of absolute monarchs.[8]

In January, 1988, the Supreme Court refused to review the Appeals Court decision. To our court system, it does not matter whether the

---

[4] Fradkin, Philip L., *Fallout* (Tuscon: University of Arizona Press, 1989), 98.

[5] Ibid., 109.

[6] Town meeting held by Senator Orrin Hatch in St. George, Utah, April 17, 1979, transcript, 26–28.

[7] Fradkin, Op. cit., 228.

[8] U.S. vs. Allen, 816 Federal Reporter, 2d/1417 (10th Circuit Court 1987), cert. denied, 108 S. CT. 694 (1988).

United States Government was irresponsible, whether it lied to its citizens or even that citizens died from the fallout of nuclear testing. What matters is that our government is immune. "The King can do no wrong."

In Mormon culture, authority is respected, obedience is revered, and independent thinking is not. I was taught as a young girl not to "make waves" or "rock the boat."

"Just let it go—" my mother would say. "You know how you feel, that's what counts."

For many years, I did just that—listened, observed, and quietly formed my own opinions within a culture that rarely asked questions because they had all the answers. But one by one, I watched the women in my family die common, heroic deaths. We sat in waiting rooms hoping for good news, always receiving the bad. I cared for them, bathed their scarred bodies and kept their secrets. I watched beautiful women become bald as cytoxan, cisplatin and adriamycin were injected into their veins. I held their foreheads as they vomited green-black bile and I shot them with morphine when the pain became inhuman. In the end, I witnessed their last peaceful breaths, becoming a midwife to the rebirth of their souls. But the price of obedience became too high.

The fear and inability to question authority that ultimately killed rural communities in Utah during atmospheric testing of atomic weapons was the same fear I saw being held in my mother's body. Sheep. Dead sheep. The evidence is buried.

I cannot prove that my mother, Diane Dixon Tempest, or my grandmothers, Lettie Romney Dixon and Kathryn Blackett Tempest, along with my aunts contracted cancer from nuclear fallout in Utah. But I can't prove they didn't.

My father's memory was correct, the September blast we drove through in 1957 was part of Operation Plumbbob, one of the most intensive series of bomb tests to be initiated. The flash of light in the night in the desert I had always thought was a dream developed into a family nightmare. It took fourteen years, from 1957 to 1971, for cancer to show up in my mother—the same time, Howard L. Andrews, an authority on radioactive fallout at the National Institutes of Health, says radiation cancer requires to become evident.[9] The more I learn about what it means to be a "downwinder," the more questions I drown in.

What I do know, however, is that as a Mormon woman of the fifth generation of "Latter-Day-Saints," I must question everything, even if it means losing my faith, even if it means becoming a member of a border tribe among my own people. Tolerating blind obedience in the name of patriotism or religion ultimately takes our lives.

---

[9] Fradkin, Op. cit., 116.

When the Atomic Energy Commission described the country north of the Nevada Test Site as "virtually uninhabited desert terrain," my family members were some of the "virtual uninhabitants."

One night, I dreamed women from all over the world circling a blazing fire in the desert. They spoke of change, of how they hold the moon in their bellies and wax and wane with its phases. They mocked at the presumption of even-tempered beings and made promises that they would never fear the witch inside themselves. The women danced wildly as sparks broke away from the flames and entered the night sky as stars.

And they sang a song given to them by Shoshoni grandmothers:

> Ah ne nah, nah
> nin nah nah—
> Ah ne nah, nah
> nin nah nah—
> Nyaga mutzi
> oh ne nay—
> Nyaga mutzi
> oh ne nay—[10]

The women danced and drummed and sang for weeks, preparing themselves for what was to come. They would reclaim the desert for the sake of their children, for the sake of the land.

A few miles downwind from the fire circle, bombs were being tested. Rabbits felt the tremors. Their soft leather pads on paws and feet recognized the shaking sands while the roots of mesquite and sage were smoldering. Rocks were hot from the inside out and dust devils hummed unnaturally. And each time there was another nuclear test, ravens watched the desert heave. Stretch marks appeared. The land was losing its muscle.

The women couldn't bear it any longer. They were mothers. They had suffered labor pains but always under the promise of birth. The red hot pains beneath the desert promised death only as each bomb became a stillborn. A contract had been broken between human beings and the land. A new contract was being drawn by the women who understood the fate of the earth as their own.

Under the cover of darkness, ten women slipped under the barbed wire fence and entered the contaminated country. They were trespassing. They walked toward the town of Mercury in moonlight, taking their cues from coyote, kit fox, antelope squirrel, and quail. They moved quietly and deliberately through the maze of Joshua trees. When a hint of daylight appeared they rested, drinking tea and sharing their rations of food. The

---

[10] This song was sung by the Western Shoshone women as they crossed the line at the Nevada Test Site on March 18, 1988, as part of their "Reclaim the Land" action. The translation they gave was: "Consider the rabbits how gently they walk on the earth. Consider the rabbits how gently they walk on the earth. We remember them. We can walk gently also. We remember them. We can walk gently also."

women closed their eyes. The time had come to protest with the heart, that to deny one's genealogy with the earth was to commit treason against one's soul.

At dawn, the women draped themselves in mylar, wrapping long streamers of silver plastic around their arms to blow in the breeze. They wore clear masks that became the faces of humanity. And when they arrived on the edge of Mercury, they carried all the butterflies of a summer day in their wombs. They paused to allow their courage to settle.

The town which forbids pregnant women and children to enter because of radiation risks to their health was asleep. The women moved through the streets as winged messengers, twirling around each other in slow motion, peeking inside homes and watching the easy sleep of men and women. They were astonished by such stillness and periodically would utter a shrill note or low cry just to verify life.

The residents finally awoke to what appeared as strange apparitions. Some simply stared. Others called authorities, and in time, the women were apprehended by wary soldiers dressed in desert fatigues. They were taken to a white, square building on the other edge of Mercury. When asked who they were and why they were there, the women replied, "We are mothers and we have come to reclaim the desert for our children."

The soldiers arrested them. As the ten women were blindfolded and handcuffed, they began singing:

> You can't forbid us everything
> You can't forbid us to think—
> You can't forbid our tears to flow
> And you can't stop the songs that we sing.

The women continued to sing louder and louder, until they heard the voices of their sisters moving across the mesa.

> Ah ne nah, nah
> nin nah nah—
> Ah ne nah, nah
> nin nah nah—
> Nyaga mutzi
> oh ne nay—
> Nyaga mutzi
> oh ne nay—

"Call for re-enforcement," one soldier said.

"We have," interrupted one woman. "We have—and you have no idea of our numbers."

On March 18, 1988, I crossed the line at the Nevada Test Site and was arrested with nine other Utahns for trespassing on military lands. They are still conducting nuclear tests in the desert. Ours was an act of civil disobedience. But as I walked toward the town of Mercury, it was more than a gesture of peace. It was a gesture on behalf of the Clan of One-breasted Women.

As one officer cinched the handcuffs around my wrists, another frisked my body. She found a pen and a pad of paper tucked inside my left boot.

"And these?" she asked sternly.

"Weapons," I replied.

Our eyes met. I smiled. She pulled the leg of my trousers back over my boot.

"Step forward, please," she said as she took my arm.

We were booked under an afternoon sun and bussed to Tonapah, Nevada. It was a two-hour ride. This was familiar country to me. The Joshua trees standing their ground had been named by my ancestors who believed they looked like prophets pointing west to the promised land. These were the same trees that bloomed each spring, flowers appearing like white flames in the Mojave. And I recalled a full moon in May when my mother and I had walked among them, flushing out mourning doves and owls.

The bus stopped short of town. We were released. The officials thought it was a cruel joke to leave us stranded in the desert with no way to get home. What they didn't realize is that we were home, soul-centered and strong, women who recognized the sweet smell of sage as fuel for our spirits.

ELIXIRS OF DEATH

Rachel Carson

This is the third chapter of Carson's 1962 book Silent Spring.

For the first time in the history of the world, every human being is now subjected to contact with dangerous chemicals, from the moment of conception until death. In the less than two decades of their use, the synthetic pesticides have been so thoroughly distributed throughout the animate and inanimate world that they occur virtually everywhere. They have been recovered from most of the major river systems and even from streams of groundwater flowing unseen through the earth. Residues of these chemicals linger in soil to which they may have been applied a dozen years before. They have entered and lodged in the bodies of fish, birds, reptiles, and domestic and wild animals so universally that scientists carrying on animal experiments find it almost impossible to locate subjects free from such contamination. They have been found in fish in remote mountain lakes, in earthworms burrowing in soil, in the eggs of birds—and in man himself. For these chemicals are now stored in the bodies of the vast majority of human beings, regardless of age. They occur in the mother's milk, and probably in the tissues of the unborn child.

All this has come about because of the sudden rise and prodigious growth of an industry for the production of man-made or synthetic chemicals with insecticidal properties. This industry is a child of the Second World War. In the course of developing agents of chemical warfare, some of the chemicals created in the laboratory were found to be lethal to insects. The discovery did not come by chance: insects were widely used to test chemicals as agents of death for man.

The result has been a seemingly endless stream of synthetic insecticides. In being man-made—by ingenious laboratory manipulation of the molecules, substituting atoms, altering their arrangement—they differ sharply from the simpler insecticides of prewar days. These were derived from naturally occurring minerals and plant products—compounds of arsenic, copper, lead, manganese, zinc, and other minerals, pyrethrum from the dried flowers of chrysanthemums, nicotine sulphate from some of the relatives of tobacco, and rotenone from leguminous plants of the East Indies.

What sets the new synthetic insecticides apart is their enormous biological potency. They have immense power not merely to poison but to enter into the most vital processes of the body and change them in sinister and often deadly ways. Thus, as we shall see, they destroy the very enzymes whose function is to protect the body from harm, they block the oxidation processes from which the body receives its energy, they prevent the normal functioning of various organs, and they may initiate in certain cells the slow and irreversible change that leads to malignancy.

Yet new and more deadly chemicals are added to the list each year and new uses are devised so that contact with these materials has become practically worldwide. The production of synthetic pesticides in the United States soared from 124,259,000 pounds in 1947 to 637,666,000 pounds in 1960—more than a fivefold increase. The wholesale value of these products was well over a quarter of a billion dollars. But in the plans and hopes of the industry this enormous production is only a beginning.

A Who's Who of pesticides is therefore of concern to us all. If we are going to live so intimately with these chemicals—eating and drinking them, taking them into the very marrow of our bones—we had better know something about their nature and their power.

Although the Second World War marked a turning away from inorganic chemicals as pesticides into the wonder world of the carbon molecule, a few of the old materials persist. Chief among these is arsenic, which is still the basic ingredient in a variety of weed and insect killers. Arsenic is a highly toxic mineral occurring widely in association with the ores of various metals, and in very small amounts in volcanoes, in the sea, and in spring water. Its relations to man are varied and historic. Since many of its compounds are tasteless, it has been a favorite agent of homicide from long before the time of the Borgias to the present. [Arsenic was the first recognized elementary carcinogen (or cancer-causing substance), identified in chimney soot and linked to cancer nearly two centuries ago by an English physician.] Epidemics of chronic arsenical poisoning involving whole populations over long periods are on record. Arsenic-contaminated environments have also caused sickness and death among horses, cows, goats, pigs, deer, fishes, and bees; despite this record arsenical sprays and dusts are widely used. In the arsenic-sprayed cotton country of southern United States beekeeping as an industry has nearly died out. Farmers using arsenic dusts over long periods have been afflicted with chronic arsenic poisoning; livestock have been poisoned by crop sprays or weed killers containing arsenic. Drifting arsenic dusts from blueberry lands have spread over neighboring farms, contaminating streams, fatally poisoning bees and cows, and causing human illness. "It is scarcely possible . . . to handle arsenicals with more utter disregard of the general health than that which has been practiced in our country in recent years," said Dr. W. C. Hueper, of the National Cancer Institute, an authority on environmental cancer. "Anyone who has watched the dusters and sprayers of arsenical insecticides at work must have been impressed by the almost supreme carelessness with which the poisonous substances are dispensed."

Modern insecticides are still more deadly. The vast majority fall into one of two large groups of chemicals. One, represented by DDT, is known as the "chlorinated hydrocarbons." The other group consists of the organic phosphorus insecticides, and is represented by the reasonably familiar malathion and parathion. All have one thing in common. As mentioned above, they are built on a basis of carbon atoms, which are also the indispensable building blocks of the living world, and thus classed as "organic." To understand them, we must see of what they are made, and how, although linked with the basic chemistry of all life, they lend themselves to the modifications which make them agents of death.

The basic element, carbon, is one whose atoms have an almost infinite capacity for uniting with each other in chains and rings and various other configurations, and for becoming linked with atoms of other substances. Indeed, the incredible diversity of living creatures from bacteria to the great blue whale is largely due to this capacity of carbon. The complex protein molecule has the carbon atom as its basis, as have molecules of fat, carbohydrates, enzymes, and vitamins. So, too, have enormous numbers of nonliving things, for carbon is not necessarily a symbol of life.

Some organic compounds are simply combinations of carbon and hydrogen. The simplest of these is methane, or marsh gas, formed in nature by the bacterial decomposition of organic matter under water. Mixed with air in proper proportions, methane becomes the dreaded "fire damp" of coal mines. Its structure is beautifully simple, consisting of one carbon atom to which four hydrogen atoms have become attached:

$$\begin{array}{ccc} H & & H \\ \diagdown & & \diagup \\ & C & \\ \diagup & & \diagdown \\ H & & H \end{array}$$

Chemists have discovered that it is possible to detach one or all of the hydrogen atoms and substitute other elements. For example, by substituting one atom of chlorine for one of hydrogen we produce methyl chloride:

$$\begin{array}{ccc} H & & Cl \\ \diagdown & & \diagup \\ & C & \\ \diagup & & \diagdown \\ H & & H \end{array}$$

Take away three hydrogen atoms and substitute chlorine and we have the anesthetic chloroform:

$$\begin{array}{ccc} H & & Cl \\ \diagdown & & \diagup \\ & C & \\ \diagup & & \diagdown \\ Cl & & Cl \end{array}$$

Substitute chlorine atoms for all of the hydrogen atoms and the result is carbon tetrachloride, the familiar cleaning fluid:

$$\begin{array}{ccc} Cl & & Cl \\ \diagdown & & \diagup \\ & C & \\ \diagup & & \diagdown \\ Cl & & Cl \end{array}$$

In the simplest possible terms, these changes rung upon the basic molecule of methane illustrate what a chlorinated hydrocarbon is. But this illustration gives little hint of the true complexity of the chemical world of the hydrocarbons, or of the manipulations by which the organic chemist creates his infinitely varied materials. For instead of the simple methane molecule with its single carbon atom, he may work with hydrocarbon molecules consisting of many carbon atoms, arranged in rings or chains, with side chains or branches, holding to themselves with chemical bonds not merely simple atoms of hydrogen or chlorine but also a wide variety of chemical groups. By seemingly slight changes the whole character of the substance is changed; for example, not only what is attached but the place of attachment to the carbon atom is highly important. Such ingenious manipulations have produced a battery of poisons of truly extraordinary power.

DDT (short for dichloro-diphenyl-trichloro-ethane) was first synthe-sized by a German chemist in 1874, but its properties as an insecticide were not discovered until 1939. Almost immediately DDT was hailed as a means of stamping out insect-borne disease and winning the farmers' war against crop destroyers overnight. The discoverer, Paul Müller of Switzerland, won the Nobel Prize.

DDT is now so universally used that in most minds the product takes on the harmless aspect of the familiar. Perhaps the myth of the harmless-ness of DDT rests on the fact that one of its first uses was the wartime dusting of many thousands of soldiers, refugees, and prisoners, to combat lice. It is widely believed that since so many people came into extremely intimate contact with DDT and suffered no immediate ill effects the chemical must certainly be innocent of harm. This understandable mis-conception arises from the fact that—unlike other chlorinated hydrocar-bons—DDT *in powder form* is not readily absorbed through the skin. Dissolved in oil, as it usually is, DDT is definitely toxic. If swallowed, it is absorbed slowly through the digestive tract; it may also be absorbed through the lungs. Once it has entered the body it is stored largely in organs rich in fatty substances (because DDT itself is fat-soluble) such as the adrenals, testes, or thyroid. Relatively large amounts are deposited in the liver, kidneys, and the fat of the large, protective mesenteries that enfold the intestines.

This storage of DDT begins with the smallest conceivable intake of the chemical (which is present as residues on most foodstuffs) and continues until quite high levels are reached. The fatty storage depots act as biologi-cal magnifiers, so that an intake of as little as $\frac{1}{10}$ of 1 part per million in the diet results in storage of about 10 to 15 parts per million, an increase of one hundredfold or more. These terms of reference, so commonplace to the chemist or the pharmacologist, are unfamiliar to most of us. One part in a million sounds like a very small amount—and so it is. But such substances are so potent that a minute quantity can bring about vast changes in the body. In animal experiments, 3 parts per million has been found to inhibit an essential enzyme in heart muscle; only 5 parts per million has brought about necrosis or disintegration of liver cells; only 2.5 parts per million of the closely related chemicals dieldrin and chlordane did the same.

This is really not surprising. In the normal chemistry of the human body there is just such a disparity between cause and effect. For example, a quantity of iodine as small as two ten-thousandths of a gram spells the difference between health and disease. Because these small amounts of pesticides are cumulatively stored and only slowly excreted, the threat of chronic poisoning and degenerative changes of the liver and other organs is very real.

Scientists do not agree upon how much DDT can be stored in the human body. Dr. Arnold Lehman, who is the chief pharmacologist of the Food and Drug Administration, says there is neither a floor below which DDT is not absorbed nor a ceiling beyond which absorption and storage ceases. On the other hand, Dr. Wayland Hayes of the United States Public Health Service contends that in every individual a point of equilibrium is reached, and that DDT in excess of this amount is excreted. For practical purposes it is not particularly important which of these men is right. Storage in human beings has been well investigated, and we know that the average person is storing potentially harmful amounts. According to various studies, individuals with no known exposure (except the inevitable dietary one) store an average of 5.3 parts per million to 7.4 parts per million; agricultural workers 17.1 parts per million; and workers in insecticide plants as high as 648 parts per million! So the range of proven storage is quite wide and, what is even more to the point, the minimum figures are above the level at which damage to the liver and other organs or tissues may begin.

One of the most sinister features of DDT and related chemicals is the way they are passed on from one organism to another through all the links of the food chains. For example, fields of alfalfa are dusted with DDT; meal is later prepared from the alfalfa and fed to hens; the hens lay eggs which contain DDT. Or the hay, containing residues of 7 to 8 parts per million, may be fed to cows. The DDT will turn up in the milk in the amount of about 3 parts per million, but in butter made from this milk the concentration may run to 65 parts per million. Through such a process of transfer, what started out as a very small amount of DDT may end as a heavy concentration. Farmers nowadays find it difficult to obtain uncontaminated fodder for their milk cows, though the Food and Drug Administration forbids the presence of insecticide residues in milk shipped in interstate commerce.

The poison may also be passed on from mother to offspring. Insecticide residues have been recovered from human milk in samples tested by Food and Drug Administration scientists. This means that the breast-fed human infant is receiving small but regular additions to the load of toxic chemicals building up in his body. It is by no means his first exposure, however: there is good reason to believe this begins while he is still in the womb. In experimental animals the chlorinated hydrocarbon insecticides freely cross the barrier of the placenta, the traditional protective shield between the embryo and harmful substances in the mother's body. While the quantities so received by human infants would normally be small, they are not unimportant because children are more susceptible to poisoning than adults. This situation also means that today the average individual almost certainly starts life with the first deposit of the growing load of chemicals his body will be required to carry thenceforth.

All these facts—storage at even low levels, subsequent accumulation, and occurrence of liver damage at levels that may easily occur in normal diets—caused Food and Drug Administration scientists to declare as early as 1950 that it is "extremely likely the potential hazard of DDT has been underestimated." There has been no such parallel situation in medical history. No one yet knows what the ultimate consequences may be.

Chlordane, another chlorinated hydrocarbon, has all these unpleasant attributes of DDT plus a few that are peculiarly its own. Its residues are long persistent in soil, on foodstuffs, or on surfaces to which it may be applied. [Yet it is also quite volatile and poisoning by inhalation is a definite risk to anyone handling or exposed to it.] Chlordane makes use of all available portals to enter the body [It penetrates the skin easily, is breathed in as vapor,] and of course is absorbed from the digestive tract if residues are swallowed. Like all other chlorinated hydrocarbons, its deposits build up in the body in cumulative fashion. A diet containing such a small amount of chlordane as 2.5 parts per million may eventually lead to storage of 75 parts per million in the fat of experimental animals.

So experienced a pharmacologist as Dr. Lehman has described chlordane as "one of the most toxic of industrial insecticides—anyone handling it could be poisoned." Judging by the carefree liberality with which dusts for lawn treatments by suburbanites are laced with chlordane, . . . this warning has not been taken to heart. The fact that the suburbanite is not instantly stricken has little meaning, for the toxins may sleep long in the body, to become manifest months or years later in an obscure disorder almost impossible to trace to its origins. On the other hand, death may strike quickly. One victim who accidentally spilled a 25 per cent solution on his skin developed symptoms of poisoning within 40 minutes and died before medical help could be obtained. No reliance can be placed on receiving advance warning which might allow treatment to be had in time.

Heptachlor, one of the constituents of chlordane, is marketed as a separate formulation. It has a particularly high capacity for storage in fat. If the diet contains as little as 1/10 of 1 part per million there will be measurable amounts of heptachlor in the body. It also has the curious ability to undergo change into a chemically distinct substance known as heptachlor epoxide. It does this in soil and in the tissues of both plants and animals. Tests on birds indicate that the epoxide that results from this change is [about four times as toxic as] the original chemical, which in turn is four times as toxic as chlordane.

As long ago as the mid-1930's a special group of hydrocarbons, the chlorinated naphthalenes, was found to cause hepatitis, and also a rare and almost invariably fatal liver disease in persons subjected to occupational exposure. They have led to illness and death of workers in electrical industries; and more recently, in agriculture, they have been considered a cause of a mysterious and usually fatal disease of cattle. In view of these antecedents, it is not surprising that three of the insecticides that [belong] to this group are among the most violently poisonous of all the hydrocarbons. These are dieldrin, aldrin, and endrin.

Dieldrin, named for a German chemist, Diels, is about 5 times as toxic as DDT when swallowed but 40 times as toxic when absorbed through the skin in solution. It is notorious for striking quickly and with terrible effect at the nervous system, sending the victims into convulsions. Persons thus poisoned recover so slowly as to indicate chronic effects. As with other chlorinated hydrocarbons, these long-term effects include severe damage to the liver. The long duration of its residues and the effective insecticidal action make dieldrin one of the most used insecticides today, despite the appalling destruction of wildlife that has followed its use. As tested on quail and pheasants, it has proved to be about 40 to 50 times as toxic as DDT.

There are vast gaps in our knowledge of how dieldrin is stored or distributed in the body, or excreted, for the chemists' ingenuity in devising insecticides has long ago outrun biological knowledge of the way these poisons affect the living organism. However, there is every indication of long storage in the human body, where deposits may lie dormant like a slumbering volcano, only to flare up in periods of physiological stress when the body draws upon its fat reserves. Much of what we do know has been learned through hard experience in the antimalarial campaigns carried out by the World Health Organization. As soon as deildrin was substituted for DDT in malaria-control work (because the malaria mosquitoes had become resistant to DDT), cases of poisoning among the spraymen began to occur. The seizures were severe—from half to all (varying in the different programs) of the men affected went into convulsions and several died. Some had convulsions as long as *four months* after the last exposure.

Aldrin is a somewhat mysterious substance, for although it exists as a separate entity it bears the relation of alter ego to dieldrin. When carrots are taken from a bed created with aldrin they are found to contain residues of dieldrin. This change occurs in living tissues and also in soil. Such alchemistic transformations have led to many erroneous reports, for if a chemist, knowing aldrin has been applied, tests for it he will be deceived into thinking all residues have been dissipated. The residues are there, but they are dieldrin and this requires a different test.

Like dieldrin, aldrin is extremely toxic. It produces degenerative changes in the liver and kidneys. A quantity the size of an aspirin tablet is enough to kill more than 400 quail. Many cases of human poisonings are on record, most of them in connection with industrial handling.

Aldrin, like most of this group of insecticides, projects a menacing shadow into the future, the shadow of sterility. Pheasants fed quantities too small to kill them nevertheless laid few eggs, and the chicks that hatched soon died. The effect is not confined to birds. Rats exposed to aldrin had fewer pregnancies and their young were sickly and short-lived. Puppies born of treated mothers died within three days. By one means or another, the new generations suffer for the poisoning of their parents. No one knows whether the same effect will be seen in human beings, yet this chemical has been sprayed from airplanes over suburban areas and farmlands.

Endrin is the most toxic of all the chlorinated hydrocarbons. Although chemically rather closely related to dieldrin, a little twist in its molecular structure makes it 5 times as poisonous. It makes the progenitor of all this group of insecticides, DDT, seem by comparison almost harmless. It is 15 times as poisonous as DDT to mammals, 30 times as poisonous to fish, and about 300 times as poisonous to some birds.

In the decade of its use, endrin has killed enormous numbers of fish, has fatally poisoned cattle that have wandered into sprayed orchards, has poisoned wells, and has drawn a sharp warning from at least one state health department that its careless use is endangering human lives.

In one of the most tragic cases of endrin poisoning there was no apparent carelessness; efforts had been made to take precautions apparently considered adequate. A year-old child had been taken by his American parents to live in Venezuela. There were cockroaches in the house to which they moved, and after a few days a spray containing endrin was used. The baby and the small family dog were taken out of the house before the spraying was done about nine o'clock one morning. After the spraying the floors were washed. The baby and dog were returned to the house in midafternoon. An hour or so later the dog vomited, went into convulsions, and died. At 10 P.M. on the evening of the same day the baby also vomited, went into convulsions, and lost consciousness. After that fateful contact with endrin, this normal, healthy child became little more than a vegetable—unable to see or hear, subject to frequent muscular spasms, apparently completely cut off from contact with his surroundings. Several months of treatment in a New York hospital failed to change his condition or bring hope of change. "It is extremely doubtful," reported the attending physicians, "that any useful degree of recovery will occur."

The second major group of insecticides, the alkyl or organic phosphates, are among the most poisonous chemicals in the world. The chief and most obvious hazard attending their use is that of acute poisoning of people applying the sprays or accidentally coming in contact with drifting spray, with vegetation coated by it, or with a discarded container. In Florida, two children found an empty bag and used it to repair a swing. Shortly thereafter both of them died and three of their playmates became ill. The bag had once contained an insecticide called parathion, one of the organic phosphates; tests established death by parathion poisoning. On another occasion two small boys in Wisconsin, cousins, died on the same night. One had been playing in his yard when spray drifted in from an adjoining field where his father was spraying potatoes with parathion; the other had run playfully into the barn after his father and had put his hand on the nozzle of the spray equipment.

The origin of these insecticides has a certain ironic significance. Although some of the chemicals themselves—organic esters of phosphoric acid—had been known for many years, their insecticidal properties remained to be discovered by a German chemist, Gerhard Schrader, in the late 1930's. Almost immediately the German government recognized the value of these same chemicals as new and devastating weapons in man's war against his own kind, and the work on them was declared secret.

Some became the deadly nerve gases. Others, of closely allied structure, became insecticides.

The organic phosphorus insecticides act on the living organism in a peculiar way. They have the ability to destroy enzymes—enzymes that perform necessary functions in the body. Their target is the nervous system, whether the victim is an insect or a warm-blooded animal. Under normal conditions, an impulse passes from nerve to nerve with the aid of a "chemical transmitter" called acetylcholine, a substance that performs an essential function and then disappears. Indeed, its existence is so ephemeral that medical researchers are unable, without special procedures, to sample it before the body has destroyed it. This transient nature of the transmitting chemical is necessary to the normal functioning of the body. If the acetylcholine is not destroyed as soon as a nerve impulse has passed, impulses continue to flash across the bridge from nerve to nerve, as the chemical exerts its effects in an ever more intensified manner. The movements of the whole body become uncoordinated: tremors, muscular spasms, convulsions, and death quickly result.

This contingency has been provided for by the body. A protective enzyme called cholinestrase is at hand to destroy the transmitting chemical once it is no longer needed. By this means a precise balance is struck and the body never builds up a dangerous amount of acetylcholine. But on contact with the organic phosphorus insecticides, the protective enzyme is destroyed, and as the quantity of the enzyme is reduced that of the transmitting chemical builds up. In this effect, the organic phosphorus compounds resemble the alkaloid poison muscarine, found in a poisonous mushroom, the fly amanita.

Repeated exposures may lower the cholinesterase level until an individual reaches the brink of acute poisoning, a brink over which he may be pushed by a very small additional exposure. For this reason it is considered important to make periodic examinations of the blood of spray operators and others regularly exposed.

Parathion is one of the most widely used of the organic phosphates. It is also one of the most powerful and dangerous. Honeybees become "wildly agitated and bellicose" on contact with it, perform frantic cleaning movements, and are near death within half an hour. A chemist, thinking to learn by the most direct possible means the dose acutely toxic to human beings, swallowed a minute amount, equivalent to about .00424 ounce. Paralysis followed so instantaneously that he could not reach the antidotes he had prepared at hand, and so he died. Parathion is now said to be a favorite instrument of suicide in Finland. In recent years the State of California has reported an average of more than 200 cases of accidental parathion poisoning annually. In many parts of the world the fatality rate from parathion is startling: 100 fatal cases in India and 67 in Syria in 1958, and an average of 336 deaths per year in Japan.

Yet some 7,000,000 pounds of parathion are now applied to fields and orchards of the United States—by hand sprayers, motorized blowers and dusters, and by airplane. The amount used on California farms alone could, according to one medical authority, "provide a lethal dose for 5 to 10 times the whole world's population."

One of the few circumstances that save us from extinction by this means is the fact that parathion and other chemicals of this group are decomposed rather rapidly. Their residues on the crops to which they are applied are therefore relatively short-lived compared with the chlorinated hydrocarbons. However, they last long enough to create hazards and produce consequences that range from the merely serious to the fatal. In Riverside, California, eleven out of thirty men picking oranges became violently ill and all but one had to be hospitalized. Their symptoms were typical of parathion poisoning. The grove had been sprayed with parathion some two and a half weeks earlier; the residues that reduced them to retching, half-blind, semiconscious misery were sixteen to nineteen days old. And this is not by any means a record for persistence. Similar mishaps have occurred in groves sprayed a month earlier, and residues have been found in the peel of oranges six months after treatment with standard dosages.

The danger to all workers applying the organic phosphorus insecticides in fields, orchards, and vineyards, is so extreme that some states using these chemicals have established laboratories where physicians may obtain aid in diagnosis and treatment. Even the physicians themselves may be in some danger, unless they wear rubber gloves in handling the victims of poisoning. So may a laundress washing the clothing of such victims, which may have absorbed enough parathion to affect her.

Malathion, another of the organic phosphates, is almost as familiar to the public as DDT, being widely used by gardeners, in household insecticides, in mosquito spraying, and in such blanket attacks on insects as the spraying of nearly a million acres of Florida communities for the Mediterranean fruit fly. It is considered the least toxic of this group of chemicals and many people assume they may use it freely and without fear of harm. Commercial advertising encourages this comfortable attitude.

The alleged "safety" of malathion rests on rather precarious ground, although—as often happens—this was not discovered until the chemical had been in use for several years. Malathion is "safe" only because the mammalian liver, an organ with extraordinary protective powers, renders it relatively harmless. The detoxification is accomplished by one of the enzymes of the liver. If, however, something destroys this enzyme or interferes with its action, the person exposed to malathion receives the full force of the poison.

Unfortunately for all of us, opportunities for this sort of thing to happen are legion. A few years ago a team of Food and Drug Administration scientists discovered that when malathion and certain other organic phosphates are administered simultaneously a massive poisoning results—up to 50 times as severe as would be predicted on the basis of adding together the toxicities of the two. In other words, $\frac{1}{100}$ of the lethal dose of each compound may be fatal when the two are combined.

This discovery led to the testing of other combinations. It is now known that many pairs of organic phosphate insecticides are highly dangerous, the toxicity being stepped up or "potentiated" through the combined action. Potentiation seems to take place when one compound destroys the liver enzyme responsible for detoxifying the other. The two need not be given simultaneously. The hazard exists not only for the man who may spray this week with one insecticide and next week with another; it exists also for the consumer of sprayed products. The common salad bowl may easily present a combination of organic phosphate insecticides. Residues well within the legally permissible limits may interact.

The full scope of the dangerous interaction of chemicals is as yet little known, but disturbing findings now come regularly from scientific laboratories. Among these is the discovery that the toxicity of an organic phosphate can be increased by a second agent that is not necessarily an insecticide. For example, one of the plasticizing agents may act even more strongly than another insecticide to make malathion more dangerous. Again, this is because it inhibits the liver enzyme that normally would "draw the teeth" of the poisonous insecticide.

What of other chemicals in the normal human environment? What, in particular, of drugs? A bare beginning has been made on this subject, but already it is known that some organic phosphates (parathion and malathion) increase the toxicity of some drugs used as muscle relaxants, and that several others (again including malathion) markedly increase the sleeping time of barbiturates.

In Greek mythology the sorceress Medea, enraged at being supplanted by a rival for the affections of her husband Jason, presented the new bride with a robe possessing magic properties. The wearer of the robe immediately suffered a violent death. This death-by-indirection now finds its counterpart in what are known as "systemic insecticides." These are chemicals with extraordinary properties which are used to convert plants or animals into a sort of Medea's robe by making them actually poisonous. This is done with the purpose of killing insects that may come in contact with them, especially by sucking their juices or blood.

The world of systemic insecticides is a weird world, surpassing the imaginings of the brothers Grimm—perhaps most closely akin to the cartoon world of Charles Addams. It is a world where the enchanted forest of the fairy tales has become the poisonous forest in which an insect that chews a leaf or sucks the sap of a plant is doomed. It is a world where a flea bites a dog, and dies because the dog's blood has been made poisonous, where an insect may die from vapors emanating from a plant it has never touched, where a bee may carry poisonous nectar back to its hive and presently produce poisonous honey.

The entomologists' dream of the built-in insecticide was born when workers in the field of applied entomology realized they could take a hint from nature: they found that wheat growing in soil containing sodium selenate was immune to attack by aphids or spider mites. Selenium, a naturally occurring element found sparingly in rocks and soils of many parts of the world, thus became the first systemic insecticide.

What makes an insecticide a systemic is the ability to permeate all the tissues of a plant or animal and make them toxic. This quality is possessed by some chemicals of the chlorinated hydrocarbon group and by others of the organophosphorus group, all synthetically produced, as well as by certain naturally occurring substances. In practice, however, most systemics are drawn from the organophosphorus group because the problem of residues is somewhat less acute.

Systemics act in other devious ways. Applied to seeds, either by soaking or in a coating combined with carbon, they extend their effects into the following plant generation and produce seedlings poisonous to aphids and other sucking insects. Vegetables such as peas, beans, and sugar beets are sometimes thus protected. Cotton seeds coated with a systemic insecticide have been in use for some time in California, where 25 farm laborers planting cotton in the San Joaquin Valley in 1959 were seized with sudden illness, caused by handling the bags of treated seeds.

In England someone wondered what happened when bees made use of nectar from plants treated with systemics. This was investigated in areas treated with a chemical called schradan. Although the plants had been sprayed before the flowers were formed, the nectar later produced contained the poison. The result, as might have been predicted, was that the honey made by the bees also was contaminated with schradan.

Use of animal systemics has concentrated chiefly on control of the cattle grub, a damaging parasite of livestock. Extreme care must be used in order to create an insecticidal effect in the blood and tissues of the host without setting up a fatal poisoning. The balance is delicate and government veterinarians have found that repeated small doses can gradually deplete an animal's supply of the protective enzyme cholinesterase, so that without warning a minute additional dose will cause poisoning.

There are strong indications that fields closer to our daily lives are being opened up. You may now give your dog a pill which, it is claimed, will rid him of fleas by making his blood poisonous to them. The hazards discovered in treating cattle would presumably apply to the dog. As yet no one seems to have proposed a human systemic that would make us lethal to a mosquito. Perhaps this is the next step.

So far . . . we have been discussing the deadly chemicals that are being used in our war against the insects. What of our simultaneous war against the weeds?

The desire for a quick and easy method of killing unwanted plants has given rise to a large and growing array of chemicals that are known as herbicides, or, less formally, as weed killers. . . . The question that here concerns us is whether the weed killers are poisons and whether their use is contributing to the poisoning of the environment.

The legend that the herbicides are toxic only to plants and so pose no threat to animal life has been widely disseminated, but unfortunately it is not true. The plant killers include a large variety of chemicals that act on animal tissue as well as on vegetation. They vary greatly in their action on the organism. Some are general poisons, some are powerful stimulants of metabolism, causing a fatal rise in body temperature, some induce malignant tumors either alone or in partnership with other chemicals, some strike at the genetic material of the race by causing gene mutations. The herbicides, then, like the insecticides, include some very dangerous chemicals, and their careless use in the belief that they are "safe" can have disastrous results.

Despite the competition of a constant stream of new chemicals issuing from the laboratories, arsenic compounds are still liberally used, both as insecticides (as mentioned above) and as weed killers, where they usually take the chemical form of sodium arsenite. The history of their use is not reassuring. As roadside sprays, they have cost many a farmer his cow and killed uncounted numbers of wild creatures. As aquatic weed killers in lakes and reservoirs they have made public waters unsuitable for drinking or even for swimming. As a spray applied to potato fields to destroy the vines they have taken a toll of human and nonhuman life.

In England this latter practice developed about 1951 as a result of a shortage of sulfuric acid, formerly used to burn off the potato vines. The Ministry of Agriculture considered it necessary to give warning of the hazard of going into the arsenic-sprayed fields, but the warning was not understood by the cattle (nor, we must assume, by the wild animals and birds) and reports of cattle poisoned by the arsenic sprays came with monotonous regularity. When death came also to a farmer's wife through arsenic-contaminated water, one of the major English chemical companies (in 1959) stopped production of arsenical sprays and called in supplies already in the hands of dealers, and shortly thereafter the Ministry of Agriculture announced that because of high risks to people and cattle restrictions on the use of arsenites would be imposed. In 1961, the Australian government announced a similar ban. No such restrictions impede the use of these poisons in the United States, however.

Some of the "dinitro" compounds are also used as herbicides. They are rated as among the most dangerous materials of this type in use in the United States. Dinitrophenol is a strong metabolic stimulant. For this reason it was at one time used as a reducing drug, but the margin between the slimming dose and that required to poison or kill was slight—so slight that several patients died and many suffered permanent injury before use of the drug was finally halted.

A related chemical, pentachlorophenol, sometimes known as "penta," is used as a weed killer as well as an insecticide, often being sprayed along railroad tracks and in waste areas. Penta is extremely toxic to a wide variety of organisms from bacteria to man. Like the dinitros, it interferes, often fatally, with the body's source of energy, so that the affected organism almost literally burns itself up. Its fearful power is illustrated in a fatal accident recently reported by the California Department of Health. A tank truck driver was preparing a cotton defoliant by mixing diesel oil with pentachlorophenol. As he was drawing the concentrated chemical out of a drum, the spigot accidentally toppled back. He reached in with his bare hand to regain the spigot. Although he washed immediately, he became acutely ill and died the next day.

While the results of weed killers such as sodium arsenite or the phenols are grossly obvious, some other herbicides are more insidious in their effects. For example, the now famous cranberry-weed-killer aminotriazole, or amitrol, is rated as having relatively low toxicity. But in the long run its tendency to cause malignant tumors of the thyroid may be far more significant for wildlife and perhaps also for man.

Among the herbicides are some that are classified as "mutagens," or agents capable of modifying the genes, the materials of heredity. We are rightly appalled by the genetic effects of radiation; how then, can we be indifferent to the same effect in chemicals that we disseminate widely in our environment?

FOREVER VIRGIN:
THE AMERICAN VIEW OF AMERICA

Noel Perrin

This essay was first published in the journal Anteus *in 1986.*

If there is one novel that nearly all educated Americans have read, it's F. Scott Fitzgerald's *The Great Gatsby*. If there's a single most famous passage in that novel, it's the one on the last page where Fitzgerald talks about Gatsby's belief in the green light ahead. He has in mind two or three kinds of green light at once. There's the literal green dock-identification light that Gatsby can see from his Long Island mansion, glimmering across the bay where Daisy lives. There's the metaphorical green traffic light: the future is open, the future is GO. And finally there's the green light that nature produces: the reflection from trees, and especially from a whole forest, a forest crowding right up to the shore of Long Island Sound.

In that famous last passage, the narrator of the book is standing in front of Gatsby's mansion at night—a summer night. He is looking across the bay, just as Gatsby used to do. There is a bright moon. As he looks, "the inessential houses began to melt away until gradually I came aware of the old island here that flowered once for Dutch sailors' eyes—a fresh, green breast of the new world. Its vanished trees, the trees that had made way for Gatsby's house, had once pandered in whispers to the last and greatest of all human dreams; for a transitory enchanted moment man must have held his breath in the presence of this continent . . . face to face for the last time in history with something commensurate to his capacity for wonder."

Fitzgerald says in this passage that it was just for a moment that men and women beheld the new world as a fresh, untouched place, a virgin world, a place where the future is open and green. But, of course, it wasn't. We still see it that way—or most of us do most of the time. Certainly that was how Jay Gatsby saw it sixty years ago. In the narrator's vision, there on the last page, that is how he, too, sees it: Long Island with the houses invisible in the moonlight, the island like a green breast, the breast of Mother Nature, inexhaustibly nourishing. As I am going to try to show in a little while, that is how most Americans still perceive the country now: morning in America, a green light ahead, nature glad and strong and free. Or at least we do in our dominant mood, and that's why the majority of us don't really worry much about acid rain, or recycling, or any of that. We have a consciousness below knowledge that the big country can handle all that.

But there are two things I want to do before I come to the relationship between human beings and nature in America in the 1980s: a short thing and a long thing. The short one is simply to make clear what I mean by nature. And the long one is to give some of the history of the encounter between us and nature since we got here. Because of course I am not claiming we feel exactly the same as Henryk Hudson's sailors did in 1609. We have changed, and the country has changed since then. A lot. All I'm claiming is that we still see the green light.

First, what nature is. Among other things, it's a word that if you look it up turns out to have twelve meanings, plus eight more submeanings. They vary so widely that Robert Frost could and did once write a poem on the subject. In the poem, he and an anonymous college official are arguing about what the word means in the epitaph that the Victorian poet Walter Savage Landor wrote for himself. Landor summed up his life thus:

> I strove with none, for none was worth my strife.
> Nature I loved, and next to Nature, Art.
> I warm'd both hands before the fire of life;
> It sinks, and I am ready to depart.

Frost and the administrator can't agree on what it was that Landor loved, and the result is a mocking little poem that begins

> Dean, adult education may seem silly.
> What of it, though? I got some willy-nilly
> The other evening at your college deanery.
> And grateful for it (let's not be facetious!)
> For I thought Epicurus and Lucretius
> By Nature meant the Whole Goddamn Machinery
> But you say that in college nomenclature
> The only meaning possible for Nature
> In Landor's quatrain would be Pretty Scenery.

Well, what I mean by nature is more than pretty scenery, but slightly less than the whole goddam machinery. I mean everything that exists on this planet (or elsewhere) that was not made by man. It's what most people mean. Only the minute you look closely, it turns out to be very hard to decide what was made by man and what wasn't. A plastic bag or a beer can is easy: Both were made by man—though of course out of natural materials, since that's all there are. But what about a garden? Nature made the carrot, but man modified it, planted it, grew it. There are two wills in collaboration here—the will of the carrot to be orange and to taste carroty and so forth—and the will of human beings to have it be a large carrot that travels well, keeps in cold storage, and so forth. What about a lake that exists because someone has built a dam, a so-called man-made or artificial lake? What about a tree? Only God—or nature—can make them, as Joyce Kilmer pointed out. But then, there are hybrid poplars: designed, planted, shaped by human beings. Again, a collaboration. Almost the entire surface of England is such a collaboration, and most of the United States, too. Only a wilderness area is not at least partly a collaboration. Lots of the prettiest scenery *is*.

So what I'm going to call nature is everything on this planet that is at least partially under the control of some other will than ours. Pure nature is of course what exists entirely without our will. In terms of landscape, there isn't much of it.

That still leaves one big question unanswered. Is man himself part of nature? Our remote ancestors certainly were: They evolved without planning to. But we ourselves? Well, I think we're partly in and partly out of nature—and the balance varies from age to age. But for the moment I'm going to say we're outside of nature. Certainly we thought of ourselves that way when we came to America. The Dutch sailors did, the pioneer settlers did. The authors of the Bible did.

Now let me drop back a little, and talk history. Not as far back as 1609—the Dutch sailors didn't leave much record of what they thought when they saw Long Island—but back to the eighteenth century and to a book called *Letters From an American Farmer,* which was written in the 1770s (though not published until 1782), and which was one of the very early American best-sellers. Basically, it's a report to Europeans on conditions in America just before the Revolution. Most of it is about what it's like to come to be a farmer in one of the thirteen colonies, though there is one long section on what it's like to live on Nantucket and be a sailor.

At that time "America" was a strip of land about 300 miles wide, going south from Maine to Georgia. In the absence of airplanes, satellites, and so forth, no one knew exactly how much more land there was west of the frontier.

But the general feeling was that for all practical purposes this continent was infinite. As Hector St. John de Crèvecoeur says in *Letters From an American Farmer,* "Many ages will not see the shores of our great lakes replenished with inland nations, nor the unknown bounds of North America entirely peopled. Who can tell how far it extends?"

St. John was wrong, of course. It did not take many ages to start inland nations on the shores of our Great Lakes. It took about two generations.

Fifty years after he wrote the book, the inland nation of Illinois came into being. Another fifty years and Chicago was a large city, another forty and it had two million people. But he couldn't know that. He and everyone else in 1770 thought we would still have a frontier in, say, the twenty-fifth century, and that the still-growing country could absorb all the immigrants who might ever wish to come, that it, in fact, would always *need* more. "There is room for everybody in America," he wrote. And, remember, America had already existed for a century and a half when he wrote that: The image was firmly fixed that this was an infinite country.

The other thing that St. John took for granted was that pure nature is an appalling thing. He saw no beauty in wilderness whatsoever. Trackless forests did not appeal to him, and he considered frontiersmen corrupt and degenerate barbarians. What he liked, what he thought beautiful was the collaboration between man and nature that a farm is, and he considered that the best possible use of a person's time lay in taming wild nature.

> To examine how the world is gradually settled, how the howling swamp is converted into a pleasing meadow, the rough ridge into a fine field; and to hear the cheerful whistling, the rural song, where there was no sound heard before save . . . the screech of the owl or the hissing of the snake—

that, says St. John, gives him enormous pleasure. He explains to his European audience how the first thing an American does when he comes into a new piece of wilderness is to build a bridge over whatever creek or little river runs through it, and the second is to take his axe and chop down as many acres of trees as he has energy to do that year, and the third is to start draining swamps and other wetlands. And perfectly reasonable, too, since the woods, the swamps, and the rivers are infinite. But St. John's assumptions are that nature is not in any way sacred, or precious, or to be treasured just because it exists; on the contrary it is badly in need of collaboration with man, and only under our governance can it become the beautiful thing it should be. And he also assumes, as the Bible told him to, that nature has no other important function than to serve us. He even thinks that God intended the wolves, the bears, the snakes, and the Indians themselves to give way before us. He doesn't worry about their becoming extinct, because the continent is infinite—but I think if you pressed him, he'd say that had to be their eventual fate.

One other observation of St. John's demands mention, even though it has little to do with nature, only nurture. I mentioned that one long section of the book is about Nantucket, a place St. John greatly admired. It was a Quaker community, and already deep into whaling—the people St. John met there were the great-grandfathers of the people Melville wrote about in *Moby-Dick*. St. John also admired the women of Nantucket, who ran the farms while their husbands were off whaling—and whom he regarded as the most spirited, independent, and, incidentally, good-looking women in America—which for him means they were the most spirited, independent, and good-looking women in the world. But, he says, "a singular custom prevails here among the women, at which I was greatly surprised.... They have adopted these many years the Asiatic custom of taking a dose of opium every morning, and so deeply rooted is it that they would be at a loss how to live without this indulgence; they would rather be deprived of any necessary than forego their favorite luxury." Nantucket men, St. John says, didn't touch opium.

Now I want to move ahead to 1804, which was the year that President Jefferson sent Captains Meriwether Lewis and William Clark of the U.S. Army across the continent on foot, the first human beings, so far as I know, to make that entire trip across what is now the United States. It took them and their party of twenty-five enlisted men and a couple of guides two years to get to the Pacific ocean and back again. Plus, as usual, rather more money than the government had anticipated. President Jefferson budgeted the two-year trip for thirty people, including boats, a newly invented airgun to impress the Indians, all supplies, at $2,500. The actual cost of the expedition was nearly $5,000. But it did reach the Pacific.

After Lewis and Clark, no one could think that North America was infinite. They returned with maps and mileage estimates. The shrinking process had begun. But it was still huge—a place that takes you a year to cross in each direction—and it was still largely pure nature.

Lewis and Clark did not see the wilderness quite the way St. John did— partly because the region he knew was all woods, and a great deal of their time was spent crossing the Great Plains, the grassy open plains with herds of antelope and buffalo. What struck them was that nature had already made the center of America into a garden, just waiting for the settlers to come cultivate it. In fact, some of it God or nature had already cultivated for us. On July 10, 1804, going up the Missouri River, they passed a piece of bottom-land: 2,000 acres covered with wild potatoes. At any time, there were hordes of deer, wild turkeys, elk, just waiting to be killed. Lewis gave it as his professional army captain's opinion that two hunters could keep a regiment supplied with meat. On August 5, 1804, Captain Clark noticed how abundant the fresh fruit was. "Great quantities of grapes on the banks. I observe three kinds, at this time ripe." On August 16, 1804, Captain Lewis and twelve men spent the morning fishing. Here's the report: "Caught upwards of 800 fine fish: 79 pike, 8 salmon resembling trout, 1 rock, 1 flat back, 127 buffalo and red horse, 4 bass, 490 cats, with many small silver fish and shrimp."

Sometimes, when the captains climbed a hill for the view, a whole section of what is now Iowa or Nebraska would remind them of a giant stock farm back in Virginia. Lewis described one view in which there was a forest of wild plum trees on one side—"loaded with fruit and now ripe"— and on the other twenty miles of open grassland, smooth as a bowling green. "This scenery," he says, "already rich, pleasing, and beautiful, was still further heightened by immense herds of buffalo, deer, elk, and antelopes, which we saw in every direction.... I do not think I exaggerate when I estimate the number of buffalo which could be comprehended at one view to be 3,000." The wolves prowling around the edge of each herd even reminded him of the sheepdogs back in Virginia.

Again, the sense is that nature is so bounteous that we could never possibly run short of anything. Nor was this some special white prejudice. The Indians felt the same. Lewis and Clark watched several times while a small tribe of Plains Indians drove a whole herd of buffalo over a cliff, took the tongues and humps of a couple of dozen to eat, and left all the rest to rot. Why not? There was no more need to be frugal with buffalo than we feel the need to be frugal with, say, ice cubes. Don't think I'm blaming either Lewis and Clark or the Indians. Their behavior made perfect sense at the time.

Nature wasn't all bounty, though. For example, the whole region was swarming with grizzly bears: eating plums, waiting at the bottoms of cliffs for someone to drive a herd of buffalo over, and just generally enjoying life. They were not a bit afraid of American soldiers. And in fact a soldier with a single-shot rifle was in no way a match for a grizzly. By experience, Lewis and Clark found that about six soldiers equaled one grizzly. If all six shot, they were pretty likely to kill the bear with no one being hurt or chased up a tree. If fewer shot, there was apt to be trouble.

There was other trouble, too. When the expedition reached the Rocky Mountains, they found the peaks terrifying. Not beautiful (except snow-capped from a distance), not fun to be in. Instead, a place where you were very apt to starve to death, freeze to death, fall off a cliff. A typical campsite was by the mountain stream they called Hungry Creek—"at that place we had nothing to eat"—where they spent the night of September 18, 1805. A typical adventure occurred the next morning when Private Robert Frazer's packhorse bought from the Indians, lost its footing and rolled a hundred yards down a precipice.

Most of the year, the only food you were going to find in the Rockies was what you carried in on your back, and when you ran out of that, there was no store to buy more at, nor could you decide to quit and hitch a ride back to Virginia, much less catch a plane to Denver. In short, not only was nature huge, but man was weak. Clever—clever enough to have invented axes and to drive stupid buffalo off cliffs— but weak. Nature, Mother Nature, was a worthy opponent as well as a worthy partner. In fact, let me make a sort of metaphor out of the grizzly and the buffalo, the two of them standing for wild nature. Both are physically stronger than men, and can run faster. One, the grizzly, is untameable, and more or less useless to us. So the thing to do is kill them, and that's a heroic and dangerous task: one part of subduing the wilderness. The other, the buffalo, is partially tameable, and very useful to us. Kill them, too, but not all of them, because we want them around to eat. Or else replace them with cattle, which are completely tameable. That's another part of subduing the wilderness—less heroic, maybe, but still a big job, and still nature offers plenty of resistance to the changes we make. The collaboration is not entirely on our terms, but partly on hers.

In sum, for the first two centuries that Europeans lived in North America, they saw the continent as a giant wilderness or desert—they used the two words interchangeably—the motto of Dartmouth College, *Vox clamantis in deserto,* translates to "A voice crying in the wilderness." They saw a vast, powerful, and immensely rich wilderness, which it would be the bounden duty of their descendants to turn into farms and gardens and alabaster cities, but which we would never entirely do, because the country was so damned big and the power of the axe and plow so limited.

All that began to change in the nineteenth century with the growth of technology. Railroads and steamboats were, of course, the first major manifestations. They made the wilderness accessible and the continent (relatively) small. In so doing, they produced the first few converts to a new point of view. Henry David Thoreau was one. Thoreau lived right next to the Fitchburg Railroad. He saw quite clearly the threat steam posed to untamed nature. Steam engines are bigger and faster than grizzlies. Steam saws can cut trees up far more quickly than forests can grow them. Steam shovels can drain an everglade.

Wilderness threatened became wilderness desirable—for the handful of converts. Thoreau was, as far as I know, the first American who publicly concluded that wilderness as wilderness—that is, pure nature—was a good thing to have around. In the 1850s he made a proposal that each town in Massachusetts save a 500-acre piece of woods which would be forever wild: no lumbering, no changes at all. Needless to say, he got nowhere, not even in Concord itself. It was still too much like going down to McDonald's and suggesting to the manager that he put 500 ice cubes in permanent deep freeze, against the time when ice may be scarce.

John Muir was a slightly later convert. It's a coincidence, but a nice coincidence, that the year in which he began to describe the western mountains as wonderful places, sacred ground, God's outdoor temples, was the same year in which the transcontinental railroad was completed. That was 1869. Henceforth the Lewis and Clark journey of a year could be done in a few days. Muir, like Thoreau before him, sensed the growth of man's power against nature, though in 1869 nature was still stronger. And, of course, Muir could be romantic about mountains in part because by now the country had been so much tamed that within one day's walk of most of his camping places in the Sierras he could borrow or buy flour to make bread with, sometimes even go to a regular store. He could even be worried about the ecological harm that overgrazing by sheep was doing in the Sierras, and eventually have some success in banning sheep from portions.

Ever since then, human power has grown at an almost geometric rate, while the forces of nature have remained static. The ascending line was bound eventually to cross the level one. It's not possible to pinpoint the year in which this happened, but it is possible to suggest a decade. I think the 1950s represent the swing point in man's relationship to nature, certainly in the United States, and probably in the whole world. During that decade we became stronger than our surroundings. Certainly not in all ways—such physical phenomena as earthquakes and hurricanes and volcanoes remain quite beyond our power to control. But in most ways. The biggest river isn't even difficult for us to bridge, or to dam. No other living creature can seriously dispute us, certainly not on a one-to-one basis. In Melville's day, six men in a whaleboat were generally a match for one whale—but not always; sometimes the whale won. By the 1950s, one man with a harpoon gun could do in any number of whales. There's not even any thrill to it.

More important than any of this, by the 1950s our science and our engineering enabled us to produce new substances and to distribute old substances on a scale equal to nature's own. For example, we can put sulfur dioxide in the air at a rate faster than the volcanoes do. One single refinery in Sudbury, Ontario, became the source of 5 percent of all the sulfur dioxide that entered the air of the entire planet, there to become sulfuric acid and to come down again as acid rain and snow. One fleet of jet airplanes could seriously affect the ozone layer.

We have earth-moving machinery that can rearrange a whole landscape. We have new chemical compounds that can affect the whole chain of life. Nature cannot easily absorb the effect of DDT or of Sevin; nature is no longer resilient. We can nearly eliminate whales, sort of half-meaning to, and we can all but extinguish peregrine falcons as an unintended by-product of raising crops. We really are what our ancestors only claimed to be: the masters of nature—or at least we're the dominant partner in the collaboration. To use one more metaphor, we are like goldfish who have been living in an aquarium for as long as we can remember; and being clever goldfish, we have discovered how to manipulate the controls of the aquarium: put more oxygen in the water, get rid of the pesky turtle we never liked anyway, triple the supply of goldfish food. Only once we realize we're partly running the aquarium, it scares some of us. What if we make a mistake, and wreck the aquarium entirely? We couldn't live outside it.

That has been the actual position since the 1950s, and it is what our rational minds clearly report. The green light has turned yellow, and there is a real possibility it will go to red. But it is not what our emotions tell us. Emotionally, almost all of us still believe what the Dutch sailors thought: that here is an inexhaustible new world, with plenty of everything for everybody.

And because of that emotion, which I, too, share, we have had a double response since the 1950s. One is to do our damndest to keep part of our continent still virgin—pure nature, wilderness. That's the nature-lover's response, the Sierra Club response, and sometimes the environmentalist's response. It's almost uniquely American. I have a friend, for example, who is a Spanish environmentalist, and I know from him that there is exactly one national park in Spain, the former hunting forest of the dukes of Medina, and even that is by no means a wilderness area. Spain is not virgin country. At the moment, about 2 percent of the United States is official wilderness, just about the same amount that is paved. And in a country this big, 2 percent is quite a lot: something like 60,000 square miles, twelve times as big as the state of Connecticut.

In terms of our whole population, to be sure, it's less impressive: If you put all of us in the wilderness at once, we'd each have a fifth of an acre. But it's enough to give a comforting illusion that pure nature is still going, independent of us. And most people who seek that illusion also want to downplay their separateness from nature, and to say that we have no right to meddle, our collaboration is deadly. We goldfish should stand back and let the aquarium run itself as it always has.

The other response involves a much greater illusion—or I think it does, anyway. And that is simply to deny that anything has changed significantly since the days of Hector St. John de Crèvecoeur and Lewis and Clark. This is the response, for example, of the present United States government. We're still just collaborators with nature, people who hold this view say, more effective collaborators than we used to be, certainly; and if we do our part, nature will do its. Nature is still resilient; it can still absorb anything we do. Besides, we were meant to rule the planet—this aquarium was designed specially for us—and what we do was pretty much all allowed for in the original design.

One group wants to re-create the world the Dutch sailors saw, and the other denies that it has ever ceased to exist. If I have to choose, of course I choose to be one of the re-creators—to try to protect as much wilderness as possible. I'd like to get the proportion of untouched land up to 3 percent. I've even dreamt of 4 percent.

But neither group, I think, is right. Neither has really dealt with the fact that a generation ago the green light turned yellow. If there is anything that is really, really worth doing in the rest of this century, I think, it's to find a third and better way of dealing with the relationship between man and nature.

ROLLING NAKED IN THE MORNING DEW

Pattiann Rogers

This poem comes from Rogers's fourth book of poetry, Splitting and Binding, *published in 1989.*

> Out among the wet grasses and wild barley-covered
> Meadows, backside, frontside, through the white clover
> And feather peabush, over spongy tussocks
> And shaggy-mane mushrooms, the abandoned nests

Of larks and bobolinks, face to face
With vole trails, snail niches, jelly
Slug eggs; or in a stone-walled garden, level
With the stemmed bulbs of orange and scarlet tulips,
Cricket carcasses, the bent blossoms of sweet william,
Shoulder over shoulder, leg over leg, clear
To the ferny edge of the goldfish pond—some people
Believe in the rejuvenating powers of this act—naked
As a toad in the forest, belly and hips, thighs
And ankles drenched in the dew-filled gulches
Of oak leaves, in the soft fall beneath yellow birches,
All of the skin exposed directly to the *killy* cry
Of the kingbird, the buzzing of grasshopper sparrows,
Those calls merging with the dawn-red mists
Of crimson steeplebush, entering the bare body then
Not merely through the ears but through the skin
Of every naked person willing every event and potentiality
Of a damp transforming dawn to enter.

Lillie Langtry practiced it, when weather permitted,
Lying down naked every morning in the dew,
With all of her beauty believing the single petal
Of her white skin could absorb and assume
That radiating purity of liquid and light.
And I admit to believing myself, without question,
In the magical powers of dew on the cheeks
And breasts of Lillie Langtry believing devotedly
In the magical powers of early morning dew on the skin
Of her body lolling in purple beds of bird's-foot violets,
Pink prairie mimosa. And I believe, without doubt,
In the mystery of the healing energy coming
From that wholehearted belief in the beneficent results
Of the good delights of the naked body rolling
And rolling through all the silked and sun-filled,
Dusky-winged, sheathed and sparkled, looped
and dizzied effluences of each dawn
Of the rolling earth.

Just consider how the mere idea of it alone
Has already caused me to sing and sing
This whole morning long.

READING PLATO

—■—

Jorie Graham

This poem is from Graham's 1983 poetry collection Erosion.

This is the story
    of a beautiful
lie, what slips
    through my fingers,
your fingers. It's winter,
    it's far

in the lifespan
    of man.
Bareheaded, in a soiled
    shirt,
speechless, my friend
    is making

lures, his hobby. Flies
    so small
he works with tweezers and
    a magnifying glass.
They must be
    so believable

they're true—feelers,
    antennae,
quick and frantic
    as something
drowning. His heart
    beats wildly

in his hands. It is
    blinding
and who will forgive him
    in his tiny
garden? He makes them
    out of hair,

deer hair, because it's hollow
    and floats.
Past death, past sight,
    this is
his good idea, what drives
    the silly days

together. Better than memory. Better
    than love.

Then they are done, a hook
        under each pair
of wings, and it's Spring,
        and the men

wade out into the riverbed
        at dawn. Above,
the stars still connect-up
        their hungry animals.
Soon they'll be satisfied
        and go. Meanwhile

upriver, downriver, imagine, quick
        in the air,
in flesh, in a blue
        swarm of
flies, our knowledge of
        the graceful

deer skips easily across
        the surface.
Dismembered, remembered,
        it's finally
alive. Imagine
        the body

they were all once
        a part of,
these men along the lush
        green banks
trying to slip in
        and pass

for the natural world.

FROM THE RIVER WHY

David James Duncan

"The Warble of the Water Owl" is Chapter 3 of Duncan's 1983 novel The River Why.

3
THE WARBLE OF THE WATER OWL

In our aquarium we may witness all the cruelties of an embittered struggle
for existence. . . . Before the glorious male, the modestly garbed female lowers the flag . . . and, if she is unwilling to mate, flees immediately. . . . The

male must never obtain so much as a glimpse of her flanks; otherwise he will immediately become . . . unchivalrous.

—*Konrad Lorenz*

I awoke before dawn. The morning star was twinkling through the same opening in the cedars and the world was too wide and lovely to leave unexplored. I jumped up, got dressed, dashed to the truck and—empty-stomached, shivering, and the stars still out—started down Highway 101 with no particular destination.

After an amount of time I can't disclose (lest it hint at the location of the Tamanawis) I pulled into Otis for a depth-charge breakfast of pancakes and coffee which I choked down in huge quantities for the inane reason that some loggers were sitting by me and I wanted to impress them. I think one *was* impressed; at least he gave me a crooked little smile as he stirred his piping-hot coffee—with his thumb! I was glad to find a early-opening grocery in Lincoln City: I bought ten pounds of oranges, figuring it would take at least that to flush the batter from my bowels. Then I headed up into the Coast Range to explore the Siletz River country.

By early afternoon I'd wandered well into the mountains. The sun was hot, the pickup dusty, and I was finally getting hungry, so I thought I'd eat oranges somewhere along the river, bake in the sun, then go for a skinny-dip. It is a strange fact that I had never deliberately been swimming in all my twenty years; I'd fallen in fishing, but I'd never gone swimming for swimming's sake. Since I am, like most hermits, modest, I picked a place where the river wound away from the road into a canyon. There were deserted places all along that hundred-mile river; there was nothing outstanding about this place: but this was, inexplicably, the place I picked.

A DIGRESSION: INEXPLICABILITIES

There appear to be, generally speaking, two explanations for the inexplicable. One is logical, crediting the random operation of a principle known variously as Fate, Destiny or Chance. Fate, Destiny or Chance, in its extreme manifestations, is said to be capable of descending upon a room full of monkeys playing with typewriters and causing one monkey to type *an entire Shakespeare play*—provided the number of monkeys and the amount of time are sufficient to allow for those frustrating cases wherein a monkey types its way clear to the end of *Hamlet*, only to conclude, ". . . Take up the bodies: such a sight as this becomes the field but here shows much amiss. Go, bid the soldiers sh&$bznx¢ ¼grntnokyirt."

The other explanation of inexplicabilities is *mytho*-logical, crediting (or Warning) various mischievous, machinating gods with names like Pan, Cupid, Kama, Khizr, Coyote, Raven and even Narayana Himself for the stranger experiences we endure. I ask the reader to remember these two explanations, and to ask which of the two most plausibly accounts for my selecting that nondescript parking place on the Siletz.

end of digression

Lugging five of the ten pounds of oranges, I hiked down a hellish incline through firs, alders, salal, devil's club and cooties, and came out by a rapids. I've never liked lingering beside rapids: they're noisy, you can't catch fish in them, and if you fall in you die, so I wandered upstream till I came to a long, slow glide. Above the glide was a big quiet pool with a massive broken-topped alder hanging out over it and a number of moss-covered sunlit boulders just past, any of which would make an admirable picnic table for my oranges and me . . .

but before proceeding I happened to glance once more at the broken-topped alder——————and there was a person in that alder. Way up in the top. Way out over the river. I scrambled closer, hoping the person in the alder wouldn't see me. Finding the five pounds of oranges inconducive to furtivity, I set them down, thinking to return for them soon after . . . but I returned for them neither soon nor ever after—and the reason I didn't was up in the alder.

I stopped a spin-cast or so below that alder and looked again. The person in the tree hadn't seen me. In fact, the person in the tree hadn't moved a muscle. I didn't know why the person was so motionless, but I did know this: it was no ordinary person up in that tree, way up in the top, way out over the pool, all alone in that desolate canyon. No. It was a *girl* up in that tree. A barefoot girl. A full-grown one. One who wore the top tenth or so of what had long ago been a pair of blue jeans. One who wore a short, skin-tight, sleeveless sky-colored t-shirt through which I could see the, which showed the, which revealed the shape of the . . . well, I really couldn't see her very well through all those branches. Not as well as I wanted to. I crept closer, stopping a fly-cast or so below the broken alder. I looked again. What was that girl doing up there? Why didn't she ever move? Why did she hold her golden right arm before her like Moses had done waging war against the Amalekites? My angle-ridden memory supplied me with a Biblical verse:

> Thy rod, wherewith thou smotest the river,
> take in thine hand, and go.

And I saw it—the dangling line, the rod in the extended hand . . . of course! The girl was fishing. I slunk closer, stopping a mere roll-cast below the broken alder: I could see her very clearly now. From where I stood it was impossible not to observe that there were no problems pertaining to her appearance. None at all. Because, well, she was fishing. It would, um, it would be, uh, *interesting*, yes, it would be interesting. I told myself to unobtrusively observe the way the girl in the tree fished. A kind of research project. A study in fishing methods. Nothing voyeuristic about it. It would simply be best not to disturb her concentration and sense of privacy. Clearly, there was much to learn. Take, for instance, the innovative and utter lack of waders and vest and every sort of cumbersome clothing. This interested me very much. More freedom of movement and so on. Something to consider. Very practical and so forth. I could hardly have been more interested. . . . Her fishing equipment was innovative also: she appeared to have no creel or equipage or container of any kind apart form her pole and line and whatever was on the end of it. There was the possibility of a few spare hooks or leaders in the pockets of the fraction of blue jeans, certainly, but given their fit, given the fact that from my excellent vantage point there were only anatomical contours discernible within their sparse confines, the spare-hooks-or-weights-or-baits theory grew tenuous. As to the possibility of fishing tackle concealed within the sky-colored t-shirt, this was even less likely. Nevertheless I considered the problem long and carefully, scanning every least curve of the thin material, reluctant to give up the search. All in all her angling costume was so thought-provoking, so fundamental yet satisfactory, that it was difficult to proceed to an examination of pole and line. There was something so pleasing to the eye about it. I wasn't used to looking at such things, let alone in trees, let alone fishing, let alone slender and golden-skinned and young and blond and solitary and, um—the pole. It must be mentioned that the pole and the line and the whatever-was-tied-to-the-line were the only other tackle to be considered: there was *no reel* on the pole. I'd never seen anyone before without a reel like her in trees dressed like she was fishing up there ever ever before that way, for which reason I couldn't help but feel she must be an extraordinary person, well worth watching, well worth meeting, well worth thinking about, an exceptional fisherman, and I was, what was I, I was learning, yes, *learning:* I was learning like crazy. I'd never learned so much so fast before, all sorts of new things about my sport, for instance how important it is to learn by watching others, how valuable it can be to meet other fishermen and share ideas, get to know them and so forth, after watching them for awhile up in the tree, fishing like that, in those clothes, with, um . . . the pole. I should describe it: it was a *huge sucker.* That's not slang: that's a literal fact. It was a huge hazelnut sucker, fourteen feet long, with the bark and even a few leaves still hanging on it. It had two wire guide-loops and a third loop attached at the tip, but there were no real guides. And there was no reel: what line wasn't in the air or the water was coiled in her left hand, which also clasped a branch for balance while her right hand held the rod high. Which brings us to her posture. It was a superb fishing posture. Extremely alert. Among other things. Lots of other things. I could only see the edge of her face. Fishermen's faces can tell an experienced observer a lot about the fishing and all, so I craned my neck to see it as clearly as possible. It was an excellent edge of a face—lips the color of silver salmon roe; long lashes curved like the hind legs of mayflies; a nose that gave you the same sort of feeling a baby cottontail rabbit's nose gives you. Not that her nose looked like a baby cottontail rabbit's nose. That would have looked ridiculous. Just like *her* nose would have looked ridiculous on a baby cottontail rabbit. I just meant the *feeling*. You know. How baby cottontail rabbit noses, the little fuzzy ones, make you feel? You know, how when they scrunch them up to smell something, how cute it looks and everything . . . Oh forget it.

Anyhow her nose was nice. It was a part complete unto itself. Which was the sort of parts all the parts of her were: you saw one part—just a nose, or a foot, or a t-shirt—and you'd no desire to look elsewhere. But you did look elsewhere anyhow, because you didn't want to miss anything going on up there. Those sorts of parts. To me, anyway.

But when I kept looking all over her not to miss anything, watching how she was getting along up there—the *entire her*, that is, apart from the parts—I realized something: there was something more going on, something on the wind, some impending thing impending. My native intelligence, enfeebled though it was by fractions and parts, still sensed it: something spectacular was afoot—

because she never once moved. She hadn't budged since I first laid eyes on her. It was remembering Moses that clued me in. I don't know why I remembered Moses, but I did. I remembered how when the Israelites battled away against the Amalekites ol' Moses held his arms extended so the Israelites would win, and his arms got "heavy as stones," and Aaron and some other guy had to come hold his arms up for him. I always felt sorry for the Amalekites, whoever they were. Seemed like Moses should have had to hold his own dang arms up. Like the girl in the tree was doing with her arm. And with five or six pounds of hazelnut sucker at the end of it! Her poor arm must have been killing her, but you'd never guess it by the edge of her face. I could think of only one thing that would inspire such strength in a fisherman and put such a feeling in the wind: Big Fish. There *had* to be a big fish in the pool down there, and judging by the signs it must be watching her bait about as closely as I was watching her and she was watching it. . . .

Suddenly she flexed, and O! the entire up and down of her rippled like a zephyr across a lake. Her line began wandering slowly upstream: something big had taken the bait! Like a ballerina she leaned and twisted, extending the rod out over the water as far as she could reach. Then, savagely, she struck! and sang out like a meadowlark as a bright summer steelhead of eight or nine pounds took a tail-walk across the top of the river. It tore upstream on a powerful run and would have her handful of line in seconds so I figured the game was up, but still her face was undismayed. She let the coils fly from her fingers as though she expected it. What came next took maybe ten seconds; but as those ten seconds contained the three most spectacular and profound fish-fighting maneuvers I have ever witnessed, I will take some time to describe them:

First she pulled some sort of release string and the three guide-loops fell into the water. Her line was now attached only at the butt, so the long rod would be useless for battling the steelhead; yet her expression was still undismayed. . . .

Next, she leapt to the very tip of the snag, turned the rod around backwards and *threw* it, like a javelin, upstream after the speeding fish! The hazel disappeared in the Siletz, then surfaced, speeding along butt-first like a whale boat on a Nantucket sleigh ride! Seeing in a flash that the attachment of line to butt made the hazel a truer-flying spear, a straighter-gliding sled, and a more resistant barge for the fish to tow, I felt for the first time in my life that I was in the presence of a fishing genius exceeding my own. It seemed no tactic could possibly surpass the two I'd just seen. *But they were nothing. . . .*

When I looked back up in the alder my eyes met with a sight beyond hope: the small fraction of blue jeans, the t-shirt, and a pair of blue panties fluttered from a twig. . . .

And the lithe and blinding figure of the naked girl was airborne, soaring out in an arc and flashing down through the leaves in a swan dive next to which the gliding flight of swans was a sorry, lumbering sight. She shot through the tree—sun and shadow streaking across her body—flying more than falling through the blue-green air, past glowing leaf and dark deadly limbs, vanishing with a fish-soft splash in the pool. Surfacing far upstream, she struck out after the speeding rod in an otter-swift crawl stroke. I scrambled through brush and boulders, gashing slits and gouging holes in my person, not about to take my eyes from the girl for a purpose so mundane as watching where I was going.

The hazel stopped at the head of the pool. I ducked behind the long-forgotten picnic boulders. She waded up and grabbed her pole then started for the far shore, but the steelhead turned and ran downriver so she launched the pole again, but gently, like a toy boat, and breaststroked after. The fish jumped twice more, but sluggishly; then the line slackened and the steelhead wove, weary and confused. She waded o my god into the thigh-deep water. She detached the line from the rod butt while the fish rested, tied it to the tip, then backed toward shore. When the line came taut the steelhead reacted with a last, slow-motion leap and a few short runs, but she'd calculated its strength perfectly and now used the length and suppleness of the rod to keep it from gaining line. She led it into the shallows, and by the time she'd beached and killed it my bloodstream was pulsating with so many outrageous romantic goads that I had to turn away to stave off the head-staggers. When I caught my breath I turned back—and she was swimming, rod and fish in tow, right toward me!

I ducked behind a boulder and looked madly for a way into the trees. There was none. Any way I took would expose me, and the conglomeration of heat, scratches and emotion must have had me looking like the Mad Rapist of the River. I heard her wading toward me through the shallows. I heard water dripping from her body onto the rocks. I heard her quick, soft breathing as she climbed onto a moss-topped boulder *very* near mine . . . then I heard nothing. She must have seen me! I could picture her face—gaping in horror, too terrified to begin the screaming sure to follow. I didn't move a muscle: huddled in a ball, head in arms, arms round knees, I vowed to stay that way for a day, a week, as long as it took. I wouldn't move for anything. Sooner or later she'd take me for dead or crazy and go away.

But after an eternity of silence I heard a low humming. It was not the low humming of a horror-stricken nude. With a furtiveness that far surpassed any fish-stalking furtiveness I have ever accomplished, I peeked over my boulder. . . . She was sunbathing on a stone not a flyrod's length away, in an utterly unsuspecting, utterly alone pose of poses.

O ye frogs and fevers, ye coots and constellations, the fisher-girl was the loveliest of lovely sights! On the sunbaked boulder, on green moss she lay, the quicksilver trout, rose-hued and stippled, glimmering by her side, glistening by her side, a pale, paltry thing by her gleaming side. As she ran a slender finger through the moss, over the stone, along the wretched fish, only Heaven and myself knew the pain that I was in. And when at last I remembered to breathe, that breath came, that breath went, with a fall and rise of rose-tipped breasts. Birds flew, crickets sang, stone and river spoke together in the shallows, and her music low and lovely and the beauty of her body and the wind's soft singing and the beauty of her body O the beauty of her body beat upon me like a storm. Ah, what became of my mother's boy as he watched beside the river? What became of her fisher-son gazing on the gleaming girl?

> The warble of the water owl poor Gus became.
> A salmon in a gill-net little Gus became.
> The ouzel's cry on a frozen deck,
> the field mouse in the kestrel's clasp,
> the otter whelp weeping in the nettle patch
> poor Gus became.
> The grass blade growing in the asphalt slab,
> the baying of a lone hound in bare winter,
> a gnat in a cobweb,
> a trout in a creel,
> a child in a night wood without a trail
> poor Gus's heart became. . . .

At last she stirred and I hid again. I heard her slide off the boulder. I watched her return to the alder and climb it with the grace and agility that marked everything she'd done. She dressed in her fishing perch. As she climbed down I broke at last out of hiding, striving hopelessly to feign innocence, ignorance and a fresh arrival. To give her fair warning I crashed through the underbrush like a great landed nabob, whistling, mumbling, resolved on an attempt at bluff gruff fishermanly good humor. Just as I prepared my jolly hello I saw her face full on for the first time . . . Piteous Christ it was beautiful! I croaked, "Wet luke!"

She froze, and said nothing. I tried to laugh: what emerged from my gullet was the death rattle of a wen-headed Hoosier. Attempting to explain my initial utterance, I gave vent to these sounds: "Oh! Me, I say Wet luke but A meant to snay 'What muck,' I mean 'Lut,' orm, um . . ."

That did it. Still silent, the lovely girl leaned over and picked up a big rock. Grinning my face off, I blurted, "AWrr! Yore rock hown!"

O ye hodags and ye ditzels! I imagined what she must be going through. . . . Just got her clothes on—what few she had—when a blubbering Sasquatch comes heaving out of the underplants making incomprehensible mating gurgles in its hairy throat! I imagined my beard full of lint, my teeth yellow, my fly open and undershorts showing there the color of my teeth, and thick green boogers clogging both my nostrils. I stared at the ground: there was a wee little snail crawling peacefully along down there. O ye Newark New Jersey how I wished I was that snail! How softly I'd sneak under the nearest rock and die! She stood before me, terribly beautiful, terribly frightened, while I gawked on, helpless to hide, feeling my face was the size of a billboard. I had to do something. "Don't get scored," I burbled. "Me gog peech inspediment. M-m-my-I juss a marmless fissamren!"

"Oh," she said, clutching the rock tighter, lips quivering, eyes the size of ripe blue apples.

It was too awful. I gurbled, "Ope! Got go now . . . Goodo, mmm, Good lerk! Bye." I stumbled to the river, waded in, and kept on wading till it swallowed me alive. I swam and swam along the very bottom where the slime and mudsuckers and fish-shit lived, hoping I'd black out, take a deep lungful of river, get it over with then and there. But I came unexpectedly to the far shore and surfaced against my will, gasping for air. Then I waded up the bank and barged into the brush on a beeline, refusing to veer to either side for anything; I tore through devil's club, briars, wildrose thickets and choked, evil copses; I left a legacy of flesh and clothing on stickers and snags; then I came to a cedar—a great stinking monster of a tree—and since I wouldn't move for it and it wouldn't move for me I jumped up, caught the lowest branch, shinnied it to the trunk and started climbing, intending to keep on climbing till I ran out of tree.

As I labored up I encountered a red ant laboring down and was moved by my misery to interrogate it: I asked it why I was ever born, why my parents lacked the sense to expose me at infancy on some icy mountain, why I failed to drown, why some compassionate disease didn't ravage and kill me, why some rabid squirrel didn't come open my throat, and other questions of similar description. But the ant, like the girl, took one look at me and began to brandish its tiny pincers. I climbed on alone.

HEART OF A CHAMPION

●

T. Coraghessan Boyle

The following short story is from Boyle's 1979 collection The Descent of Man.

We scan the cornfields and the wheatfields winking gold and gold-brown and yellowbrown in the midday sun, on up the grassy slope to the barn redder than red against the sky bluer than blue, across the smooth stretch of the barnyard with its pecking chickens, and then right on up to the screen door at the back of the house. The door swings open, a black hole in the sun, and Timmy emerges with his corn-silk hair, corn-fed face. He is dressed in crisp overalls, striped T-shirt, stubby blue Keds. There'd have to be a breeze—and we're not disappointed—his clean fine cup-cut hair waves and settles as he scuffs across the barnyard and out to the edge of the field. The boy stops there to gaze out over the nodding wheat, eyes unsquinted despite the sun, and blue as tinted lenses. Then he brings three fingers to his lips in a neat triangle and whistles long and low, sloping up sharp to cut off at the peak. A moment passes: he whistles again. And then we see it—way out there at the far corner of the field—the ripple, the dashing furrow, the blur of the streaking dog, white chest, flashing feet.

They're in the woods now. The boy whistling, hands in pockets, kicking along with his short baby-fat strides; the dog beside him wagging the white tip of her tail like an all-clear flag. They pass beneath an arching old black-barked oak. It creaks. And suddenly begins to fling itself down on them: immense, brutal: a panzer strike. The boy's eyes startle and then there's a blur, a smart snout clutching his pantleg, the thunderblast of the trunk, the dust and spinning leaves. "Golly, Lassie . . . I didn't even see it," says the boy sitting safe in a mound of moss. The collie looks up at him (the svelte snout, the deep gold logician's eyes), and laps at his face.

And now, they're down by the river. The water is brown with angry suppurations, spiked with branches, fence posts, tires and logs. It rushes like the sides of boxcars—and chews deep and insidious at the bank under Timmy's feet. The roar is like a jetport: little wonder he can't hear the dog's warning bark. We watch the crack appear, widen to a ditch; then the halves separating (snatch of red earth, writhe of worm), the poise and pitch, and Timmy crushing down with it. Just a flash—but already he's way downstream, his head like a plastic jug, dashed and bobbed, spinning toward the nasty mouth of the falls. But there's the dog—fast as a struck match—bursting along the bank all white and gold melded in motion, hair sleeked with the wind of it, legs beating time to the panting score. . . . Yet what can she hope to do?—the current surges on, lengths ahead, sure bet to win the race to the falls. Timmy sweeps closer, sweeps closer, the falls loud now as a hundred tympani, the war drums of the Sioux, Africa gone bloodlust mad! The dog strains, lashing over the wet earth like a whipcrack; strains every last ganglion and dendrite until finally she draws abreast of him. Then she's in the air, the foaming yellow water. Her paws churning like pistons, whiskers chuffing with the exertion—oh the roar!—and there, she's got him, her sure jaws clamping down on the shirt collar, her eyes fixed on the slip of rock at the falls' edge. Our blood races, organs palpitate. The black brink of the falls, the white paws digging at the rock—and then they're safe. The collie sniffs at Timmy's inert little form, nudges his side until she manages to roll him over. Then clears his tongue and begins mouth-to-mouth.

Night: the barnyard still, a bulb burning over the screen door. Inside, the family sit at dinner, the table heaped with pork chops, mashed potatoes, applesauce and peas, a pitcher of clean white milk. Home-baked bread. Mom and Dad, their faces sexless, bland, perpetually good-humored and sympathetic, poise stiff-backed, forks in midswoop, while Timmy tells his story: "So then Lassie grabbed me by the collar and golly I musta blanked out cause I don't remember anything more till I woke up on the rock—"

"Well I'll be," says Mom.

"You're lucky you've got such a good dog, son," says Dad, gazing down at the collie where she lies patiently, snout over paw, tail wapping the floor. She is combed and washed and fluffed, her lashes mascaraed and curled, her chest and paws white as dishsoap. She looks up humbly. But then her ears leap, her neck jerks round—and she's up at the door, head cocked, alert. A high yipping yowl like a stuttering fire whistle shudders through the room. And then another. The dog whines.

"Darn," says Dad. "I thought we were rid of those coyotes—next thing they'll be after the chickens again."

The moon blanches the yard, leans black shadows on the trees, the barn. Upstairs in the house, Timmy lies sleeping in the pale light, his hair fastidiously mussed, his breathing gentle. The collie lies on the throw rug beside the bed. We see that her eyes are open. Suddenly she rises and slips to the window, silent as a shadow. And looks down the long elegant snout to the barnyard below, where the coyote slinks from shade to shade, a limp pullet dangling from his jaws. He is stunted, scabious, syphilitic, his forepaw trap-twisted, his eyes running. The collie whimpers softly from behind the window. And the coyote stops in mid-trot, frozen in a cold shard of light, ears high on his head. Then drops the chicken at his feet, leers up at the window and begins a soft, crooning, sad-faced song.

The screen door slaps behind Timmy as he bolts from the house, Lassie at his heels. Mom's head emerges on the rebound. "Timmy!" (He stops as if jerked by a rope, turns to face her.) "You be home before lunch, hear?"

"Sure, Mom," he says, already spinning off, the dog by his side. We get a close-up of Mom's face: she is smiling a benevolent boys-will-be-boys smile. Her teeth are perfect.

In the woods Timmy steps on a rattler and the dog bites its head off. "Gosh," he says. "Good girl, Lassie." Then he stumbles and slips over an embankment, rolls down the brushy incline and over a sudden precipice, whirling out into the breath-taking blue space like a sky diver. He thumps down on a narrow ledge twenty feet below. And immediately scrambles to his feet, peering timorously down the sheer wall to the heap of bleached bone at its base. Small stones break loose, shoot out like asteroids. Dirt-slides begin. But Lassie yarps reassuringly from above, sprints back to the barn for a winch and cable, hoists the boy to safety.

On their way back for lunch Timmy leads them through a still and leaf-darkened copse. We remark how odd it is that the birds and crickets have left off their cheeping, how puzzling that the background music has begun to rumble so. Suddenly, round a bend in the path before them, the coyote appears. Nose to the ground, intent, unaware of them. But all at once he jerks to a halt, shudders like an epileptic, the hackles rising, tail dipping between his legs. The collie too stops short, just yards away, her chest proud and shaggy and white. The coyote cowers, bunches like a cat, glares at them. Timmy's face sags with alarm. The coyote lifts his lip. But then, instead of leaping at her adversary's throat, the collie prances up and stretches her nose out to him, her eyes soft as a leading lady's, round as a doe's. She's balsamed and perfumed; her full chest tapers a lovely S to her sleek haunches and sculpted legs. He is puny, runted, half her size, his coat like a discarded doormat. She circles him now, sniffing. She whimpers, he growls: throaty and tough, the bad guy. And stands stiff while she licks at his whiskers, noses at his rear, the bald black scrotum. Timmy is horror-struck. Then, the music sweeping off in birdtrills of flute and harpstring, the coyote slips round behind, throat thrown back, black lips tight with anticipation.

"What was she doing, Dad?" Timmy asks over his milk and sandwich.

"The sky was blue today, son," he says.

"But she had him trapped, Dad—they were stuck together end to end and I thought we had that wicked old coyote but then she went and let him go—what's got into her, Dad?"

"The barn was red today, son," he says.

Late afternoon: the sun mellow, more orange than white. Purpling clots of shadow hang from the branches, ravel out from the tree trunks. Bees and wasps and flies saw away at the wet full-bellied air. Timmy and the dog are far out beyond the north pasture, out by the old Indian burial mound, where the boy stoops now to search for arrowheads. Oddly, the collie is not watching him: instead she's pacing the crest above, whimpering softly, pausing from time to time to stare out across the forest, her eyes distant and moonstruck. Behind her, storm clouds squat on the horizon like dark kidneys or brains.

We observe the wind kicking up: leaves flapping like wash, saplings quivering, weeds whipping. It darkens quickly now, the clouds scudding low and smoky over the treetops, blotting the sun from view. Lassie's white is whiter than ever, highlighted against the dark horizon, the wind-whipped hair foaming around her. Still she doesn't look down at the boy: he digs, dirty-kneed, stoop-backed, oblivious. Then the first fat random drops, a flash, the volcanic blast of thunder. Timmy glances over his shoulder at the noise: he's just in time to watch the scorched pine plummeting toward the constellated freckles in the center of his forehead. Now the collie turns—too late!—the *swoosh-whack!* of the tree, the trembling needles. She's there in an instant, tearing at the green welter, struggling through to his side. He lies unconscious in the muddying earth, hair artistically arranged, a thin scratch painted on his cheek. The trunk lies across the small of his back like the tail of a brontosaurus. The rain falls.

Lassie tugs doggedly at a knob in the trunk, her pretty paws slipping in the wet—but it's no use—it would take a block and tackle, a crane, an army of Bunyans to shift that stubborn bulk. She falters, licks at his ear, whimpers. We observe the troubled look in her eyes as she hesitates, uncertain, priorities warring: should she stand guard, or dash for help? The decision is sure and swift—her eyes firm with purpose and she's off like a shard of shrapnel, already up the hill, shooting past the dripping trees, over the river, already cleaving through the high wet banks of wheat.

A moment later she's dashing through the puddled and rain-screened barnyard, barking right on up to the back door, where she pauses to scratch daintily, her voice high-pitched and insistent. Mom swings open the door and the collie pads in, claws clacking on the shiny linoleum. "What is it girl? What's the matter? Where's Timmy?"

"Yarf! Yarfata-yarf-yarf!"

"Oh my! Dad! Dad, come quickly!"

Dad rushes in, his face stolid and reassuring as the Lincoln Memorial. "What is it, dear? . . . Why, Lassie?"

"Oh Dad, Timmy's trapped under a pine tree out by the old Indian burial ground—"

"Arpit-arp."

"—a mile and a half past the north pasture."

Dad is quick, firm, decisive. "Lassie—you get back up there and stand watch over Timmy . . . Mom and I'll go for Doc Walker. Hurry now!"

The collie hesitates at the door: "Rarf-arrar-ra!"

"Right," says Dad. "Mom, fetch the chain saw."

We're back in the woods now. A shot of the mud-running burial mound locates us—yes, there's the fallen pine, and there: Timmy. He lies in a puddle, eyes closed, breathing slow. The hiss of the rain is loud as static. We see it at work: scattering leaves, digging trenches, inciting streams to swallow their banks. It lies deep now in the low areas, and in the mid areas, and in the high areas. Then a shot of the dam, some indeterminate (but short we presume) distance off, the yellow water churning over its lip like urine, the ugly earthen belly distended, blistered with the pressure. Raindrops pock the surface like a plague.

Suddenly the music plunges to those thunderous crouching chords—we're back at the pine now—what is it? There: the coyote. Sniffing, furtive, the malicious eyes, the crouch and slink. He stiffens when he spots the boy—but then slouches closer, a rubbery dangle drooling from between his mismeshed teeth. Closer. Right over the prone figure now, those ominous chords setting up ominous vibrations in our bowels. He stoops, head dipping between his shoulders, irises caught in the corners of his eyes: wary, sly, predatory: the vulture slavering over the fallen fawn.

But wait!—here comes the collie, sprinting out of the wheatfield, bounding rock to rock across the crazed river, her limbs contourless with sheer speed and purpose, the music racing in a mad heroic prestissimo!

The jolting front seat of a Ford. Dad, Mom and the Doctor, all dressed in rain slickers and flap-brimmed rain hats, sitting shoulder to shoulder behind the clapping wipers. Their jaws set with determination, eyes aflicker with pioneer gumption.

The coyote's jaws, serrated grinders, work at the tough bone and cartilage of Timmy's left hand. The boy's eyelids flutter with the pain, and he lifts his head feebly—but almost immediately it slaps down again, flat and volitionless, in the mud. At that instant Lassie blazes over the hill like a cavalry charge, show-dog indignation aflame in her eyes. The scrag of a coyote looks up at her, drooling blood, choking down frantic bits of flesh. Looks up at her from eyes that go back thirty million years, savage and bloodlustful and free. Looks up unmoved, uncringing, the bloody snout and steady yellow eyes less a physical challenge than philosophical. We watch the collie's expression alter in midbound—the look of offended AKC morality giving way, dissolving. She skids to a halt, drops her tail and approaches him, a buttery gaze in her golden eyes. She licks the blood from his lips.

The dam. Impossibly swollen, rain festering the yellow surface, a hundred new streams a minute rampaging in, the pressure of those millions of gallons hard-punching those millions more. There! the first gap, the water spewing out, a burst bubo. And now the dam shudders, splinters, falls to pieces like so much cheap pottery. The roar is devastating.

The two animals start at that terrible rumbling, and still working their gummy jaws, they dash up the far side of the hill. We watch the white-tipped tail retreating side by side with the hacked and tick-blistered gray one—wagging like raggled banners as they disappear into the trees at the top of the rise. We're left with a tableau: the rain, the fallen pine in the crotch of the valley's V, the spot of the boy's head. And that chilling roar in our ears. Suddenly the wall of water appears at the far end of the V, smashing through the little declivity like a god-sized fist, prickling with shattered trunks and boulders, grinding along like a quick-melted glacier, like planets in collision. We cut to Timmy: eyes closed, hair plastered, his left arm looking as though it should be wrapped in butcher's paper. How? we wonder. How will they ever get him out of this? But then we see them—Mom, Dad and the Doctor—struggling up that same rise, rushing with the frenetic music now, the torrent seething closer, booming and howling. Dad launches himself in full charge down the hillside—but the water is already sweeping over the fallen pine, lifting it like paper— there's a blur, a quick clip of a typhoon at sea (is that a flash of blond hair?), and it's over. The valley is filled to the top of the rise, the water ribbed and rushing like the Colorado in adolescence. Dad's pants are wet to the crotch.

Mom's face, the Doctor's. Rain. And then the opening strains of the theme song, one violin at first, swelling in mournful mid-American triumph as the full orchestra comes in, tearful, beautiful, heroic, sweeping us up and out of the dismal rain, back to the golden wheatfields in the midday sun. The boy cups his hands to his mouth and pipes: "Laahh-sie! Laahh-sie!" And then we see it—way out there at the end of the field—the ripple, the dashing furrow, the blur of the streaking dog, white chest, flashing feet.

The Pursuit of Life

Jesse Scott

Jesse Scott is a former meat cutter. He is currently
a pre-pharmacy major at The University of Montana.

   I enjoy participating in nature in almost all of its
aspects. One method I enjoy involves hunting. I don't
mean being the "great white hunter," exploiting nature
with my hand cannon. I enjoy a more personal approach. I
suppose that is why I was drawn to archery and bow
hunting. I believe that humans and the wild can live in
harmony, and I do what I can to live with nature instead
of against it. Even though I also hunt with the same
attitude when I hunt with a gun, the fact that I can
extinguish a life from several hundred meters away seems
very impersonal. Due to modern technology, almost any
inexperienced, nonappreciative moron can snuff out life
by simply squeezing a trigger. I feel more attached to my
surroundings by limiting my disturbance of nature and
wildlife. I prefer that I am never noticed as having been
present in the forest. When I release an arrow from my
bow, the sound is rarely heard; fear of man doesn't have
the opportunity or time to enter the head of my quarry.
Many times an animal's companions never know what has
transpired between me and my mark.
   Being a conscientious archery hunter takes many hours
of devoted preparation. I practice shooting in varied
positions and ranges. Many times, in my mind, I envision
the precise spot I will place my lethal projectiles for a
humane and quick kill. With the onset of spring and
summer, I enjoy watching the deer. They shed their dark
brown coats and don bright orange-brown sleek ones. I
watch the new spotted fawns develop over the summer, and
I enjoy watching the fuzzy antlers grow on the bucks'
heads. I observe their travel patterns and attempt to
place my tree stands in the positions that will give me
an ideal shot. These hours of enjoyable observation and
preparation lead up to one time in the fall of each
year . . . hunting season.

One late afternoon when the season had been opened for a while, I had the opportunity to go hunting at my local spot. I gathered my gear and headed to the woods. I enjoyed the sunny afternoon as I crept stealthily to my stand—"stealthily" is relative in my case, because I am blessed with clumsy, human feet. I climbed onto my stand, buckled my safety harness and positioned my equipment for readiness. As I relaxed, I enjoyed the many sounds of the forest around me. The squirrels chattered, and the many birds added to the music. Even a curious chickadee came and perched on a close branch and said its greetings. Ants were busy traveling on their tree highway in search of food and building materials. I soon got caught up in my enjoyment in the world around me.

I started daydreaming of the day's events and of future aspirations. A leaf crackled, and my dream world was gone. I focused my attention on the sound as my eyes groped for movement or color. I laughed inside when I found out what the source of the noise was. It was a house cat, and he seemed to be in pursuit of his own game. He left, and soon I caught some movement a short way off. I could feel the excitement as a mature doe stepped into my range. She picked her way toward me on a familiar trail. I enjoyed studying her attentive and graceful movements. She moved closer and presented a perfect shot angle, and the thought crossed my mind to take her. The twin fawns that burst from the brush and joined their mom quickly vanquished this thought. I was caught up by their white-spotted fur and playful attitude. They paused for a brief moment and grabbed a quick snack from mom's milk factory before they continued their journey. As I enjoyed their beauty, many more does, fawns and young bucks passed by me. I was not concerned about passing these deer by because I had many more weeks of the season left. I was enjoying being out in the woods and being mere feet from such beautiful creatures. As my mind traveled peacefully through this blissful, natural world, I caught more movement a long way off. My eyes concentrated on the movement and deciphered what it was.

A mature buck stepped out of the brush about 200 yards from me and sniffed the air. He traveled the ground between us in what seemed to be seconds, and then paused, just out of range. He looked cautiously around and proceeded toward me. He turned and walked beside my tree. He walked too quickly for a clean shot, so I waited. My patience paid off, and he walked out and presented a perfect angle for a shot. He paused, and at that moment—the moment I had prepared for months to encounter—I released my deadly projectile. As the startled buck trotted off a few feet, I could see my shot was true. He walked a few more feet and lay down. The excitement of what I had just done came rushing in on me. My hands and legs were shaking, and it took me a few minutes to regain my composure. I waited and watched the buck for what seemed like an hour, but it actually was only minutes. Slowly, he lay his head down and passed away. The buck never realized my presence and died in a dignified manner without fear of humans. Twenty minutes later, I descended my tree and retrieved my animal.

I knelt beside where he lay and ran my hands down his beautiful coat. I admired his wide and tall antlers. I thought, "What a beautiful creature." I was somewhat saddened by taking this life, and I felt a sense of gratitude to this animal. This was partially because through this animal I would have some sustenance. I thanked our creator for this beautiful animal's life, and I commenced the unpleasant, but necessary, job of dressing my deer. As I walked home, I couldn't help but feel a sense of pride, accomplishment, and appreciation for being able to partake in one of the age-old traditions of the wild. My pursuit of life was over for that day.

10

HEALTH, SCIENCE, AND TECHNOLOGY

CYBERSCARED
———————— ■ ————————
Emelye

The piece is from Cupsize, *a zine.*

It is the end of the twentieth century. Those in their early twenties should feel blessed (by whatever deity or lack thereof they wish) to experience the approaching millennium in the prime of youth. In an abstract, romantic sense, it truly is a wonderful event. But there are down sides. Right now, AT&T bombards America with advertisements for products we are not even sure exist yet. They blatantly admit that we do not need these products now, and only promise, as their slogan says, *"you will."* Will I? With the failure of any one religion or system of thought to prevail universally, humankind is instinctively constructing a secular medium that all can ascribe to; cyberspace [the on-line world, a word used by William Gibson in his novel, *Neuromancer*]. In the global world of multi-culturalism, relativism, and deconstruction, there can be no right and wrong, no great and bad or boring, just an accumulative mass of information being misidentified as *knowledge,* submitted piece by piece to databases through computers. Through the development of cyberspace, we are building the collective mind. Humankind's inclination to progress is not at its most fundamental about greed, accumulation, or human accomplishment, but a race for the tangible institution of collective being, an accessibility of information so complete that it provides instant omniscience to the participant in it.

In the haze of history that accompanies a liberal arts education, students are told a story of progress, change, and evolution. At our times of greatest nihilism, perhaps after having read Pynchon's *The Crying of Lot 49* and related to the self-conscious paranoia of its protagonist, we, exasperated, ask, "haven't I heard this story before?"; the story of the sense of a generation encroaching on doom. Has Generation X a right to fear the technological age that awaits it? Is their seeming laziness a rightful conservative reaction to the whirlwind of their first twenty years? In the span of their mean twenty years, the 8-track tape player has stayed around just long enough to be mocked, the cassette has been overrun by the compact disc, CD challenged by DAT systems, and all along vinyl has been loved the most. The generation approaching the millennium should distinguish their precise, distinct, and unique fears. In effect, learn to build an argument against progress—that not everything can be entered into cyberspace as data and retain its "essence."

In a recent AT&T commercial, a child sits in front of a computer terminal. She is smiling. On the screen are graphics of a book. An encyclopedia. In this case, not only is the information of the book entered as data, but the form itself. With a click of the mouse, the pages turn before her.

Graphically-produced images of pages turning. Setting aside obvious environmental advantages of on-line encyclopedias (less paper, less trees slaughtered, more forests) we must examine the urge to make this transition. Or how it is being sold to America. There is a seemingly instinctive drive to immediately turn all of life into an image of itself. Weddings are staged so that they look more real in the videotape than when they are actually taking place. This is more than a universal increase in vanity; we are building things to produce images, to represent the real objects and happenings of our lives. In cyberspace, rather than being the mere spectators of images, like in the local movie house, we are participants—creating the images, changing them, shaping them, interacting with them. Are we moving swiftly to a time when real actions and events and objects will be kept around merely for their anachronistic appeal? If this is the instinctive drive of humankind, is it ultimately a doomed process—can we distinguish when cyberspace has enveloped too many aspects of our physical and sensible world? If a series of generations only viewed books on cyberspace, would the graphics eventually just represent random blocks of color, no longer attached to the original object?

The vastness of the super highway scares me and does not intrigue me. I e-mail and that's it. I don't even use the PHONE function of most e-mail lines. It just all seems so ephemeral to me. When people try to teach me the rules to use MUDS and other databases, my brain shuts off, because I know the rules will probably be revised tomorrow or the whole "world" may be deleted in an hour. If a piece of information has a life-span of a day, I may just as well bypass it. Why do I want to go cruising through an arena of graphically produced sensations, "getting to know" cyberspace, when I haven't even been to Europe yet for real.

I am scared that the job market will insist that I exist in cyberspace. My humanity screams out against it. Am I a conservative, a reactionary? If I were around when the printing press was developed, would I have protested against that too, saying handwriting dictates nature's natural text reproduction rate and we shouldn't tamper with it? It's all changing so fast that I just can't get the energy to learn today what may be obsolete tomorrow. I don't want to spend my free-time existing bodiless in cyberspace. I could spend my whole life walking the streets of New York and not know everything. I'd rather start there than at a computer prompt.

I admit that I like limits. I like books with a beginning and an end. Is being able to remix Todd Rudgren's new album on CD-ROM really progress? Our forthcoming technological age overcomes boundaries like time, place, location. By global communication linkage, we can all be present all places at once. All information is accessible at all times. Time is not lost in tracking down books in libraries. Projected into a perfect future, all history and human discourse would be downloadable. The role of chance and limitation in shaping human life becomes less, or becomes limited to the function of technology. I had a hard enough time carving an existence for myself in my high school, learning the quirks of my peers, where I fit in. The prospect of existing with meaning in the infinite world of cyberspace makes me yearn for the simple days when my Commodore 64 was hot news on the block, but my neighbor's new BMX ruled over all.

ALIENATED
AND PROUD

DREAMING OF DISCONNECTING
A RESPIRATOR

■

Elissa Ely

The Boston Globe *first published this piece on July 1, 1989.*

L ate one night in the Intensive Care Unit, one eye on the cardiac monitor and one on the Sunday paper, I read this story:

An infant lies in a hospital, hooked to life by a respirator. He exists in a "persistent vegetative state" after swallowing a balloon that blocked the oxygen to his brain. This "vegetative state," I've always thought, is a metaphor inaccurately borrowed from nature, since it implies that with only the proper watering and fertilizer, a comatose patient will bloom again.

One day his father comes to visit. He disconnects the respirator and, with a gun in hand, cradles his son until the infant dies. The father is arrested and charged with murder.

In the ICU where I read this, many patients are bound to respirators. I look to my left and see them lined up, like potted plants. Some will eventually be "weaned" back to their own lung power. Others will never draw an independent breath again.

In Bed No. 2, there is a woman who has been on the respirator for almost two months. When she was admitted with a simple pneumonia, there were no clues she would come apart so terribly. On her third day, she had a sudden and enigmatic seizure. She rolled rapidly downhill. Her pneumonia is now gone, but her lungs refuse independence: she can't come off the machine.

I know little about this patient except that she is elderly and European. (It is the peculiar loss of hospital life that patients often exist here with a medical history, but not a personal one.) I sometimes try to picture her as she might have been: busy in a chintz kitchen smelling of pastries. She might have hummed, rolling dough. Now there is a portable radio by the bed, playing Top Ten, while the respirator hisses and clicks 12 times a minute.

The family no longer visits. They have already signed the autopsy request, which is clipped to the front of her thick chart. Yet in their pain, they cannot take the final step and allow us to discontinue her respirator. Instead, they have retired her here, where they hope she is well cared for, and where she exists in a state of perpetual mechanical life.

I have dreamed of disconnecting my patient's respirator. Every day I make her death impossible and her life unbearable. Each decision—the blood draws, the rectal temperatures, the oxygen concentration—is one for or against life. No action in the ICU is neutral. Yet many of these decisions are made with an eye toward legal neutrality—and this has little to do with medical truth. The medical truth is that this patient exists without being alive. The legal neutrality is that existence is all that is required.

Late at night, reading in the ICU, the story of that father—so dangerous and impassioned—puts me to shame. I would never disconnect my patient from her respirator; it is unthinkable. But this is not because I am a doctor. It is because I feel differently toward her than the father toward his son.

I do not love her enough.

SOCIETY WRITES BIOLOGY

—■—

Anne Fausto-Sterling

This piece is an excerpt from "Society Writes Biology/Biology Constructs Gender," first published in Daedalus, *Journal of the American Academy of Arts and Sciences, Fall 1987.*

Truth, bias, objectivity, prejudice. In recent years both defenders and critics of the activities of the modern Western scientific community have used these words with a certain abandon as they engage in debate about the role of science and the scientist in our culture. Perhaps the best-known voice in this discussion is that of Thomas Kuhn, whose historical analyses of the "progress" of science threw into sharp relief the uneven nature of the development of scientific ideas. In the past decade feminist analysts of science have joined the discussion. Historians, philosophers, anthropologists, and scientists who write from a feminist perspective have raised varied and complex questions about modern science.

In this essay I propose to examine the process by which cultural understandings of gender become building blocks in supposedly objective understandings of nature. The two case studies (one historical, one contemporary) will illustrate how cultural understandings or beliefs, whether conscious or unconscious, influence the construction of scientific theory. The writings of a famous and highly imaginative Italian scientist, Abbé Lazzaro Spallanzani (1729–1799), illustrate that the inner workings of the mind of a dedicated experimental scientist are complex and often under subconscious wraps. Although Spallanzami is probably best known for his experimental disproof of the idea of spontaneous generation, he also made an important contribution to eighteenth-century thinking about fertilization and embryonic development. The presence of spermatozoa in the semen had been discovered in Spallanzani's time, but the role of these "vermicelli" (or "spermatozoan worms," as they were often called) remained a subject of considerable debate within the context of a long-lived controversy about the origin of the embryo. Ovists believed that it arose solely from the egg, while spermists maintained that the womb was a passive vessel that offered fertile ground for the growth and development of the semen.

The most famous of early biologists belonged to different camps. The frontispiece of William Harvey's *Concerning the Generation of Living Animals* depicts Zeus sitting on a throne and opening what looks like a bird's egg, out of which hop, fly, and crawl all manner of beasts, mythical and otherwise. On the egg is written *Ex ovo omnia*. On the other side we find Antony van Leeuwenhoek arguing that the animalcules in semen find their way to the womb, where they act as seed; he dismisses eggs as "emunctorys . . . adhering to the bowels of animals."

Spallanzani, an ovist, performed a series of experiments with mating frogs to disprove Carolus Linnaeus's claim that insemination must always be internal. In a classic demonstration of the scientific method, he observed that the male frog, grasping the female frog as she lays eggs, deposits semen on the eggs as they emerge from her uterus. To test the semen's function, he constructed little taffeta breeches for the male frogs (unwittingly presaging Kenneth Grahame's *The Wind in the Willows*, in which toads wear clothes and drive cars) and made the following observations:

> The males, notwithstanding this incumbrance, seek the females with equal eagerness and perform, as well as they can, the act of generation, but the event is such as may be expected: the eggs are never prolific for want of having been bedewed with semen, which sometimes may be seen in the breeches in the form of drops. That these drops are real seed, appeared clearly from the artificial fecondation that was obtained by means of them.

In other words, Spallanzani showed not only that preventing semen deposition prevented egg development, but also that when he spread semen on the eggs, fertilization resulted. A model of good experimentation indeed.

But Spallanzani did not conclude from these or other experiments that the vermicelli were necessary for the embryo to develop. Instead he conducted a series of experiments in an attempt to find out how much semen was needed to achieve fertilization. Observing that even very tiny amounts were sufficient, he concluded that the important factor was something he called the "seminal aura," which he thought to be "nothing but the vapor of the seed exceedingly rarified." Believing that his results proved the ovists's theory, he proceeded to perform a series of experiments on the seminal aura, all of which he designed to disprove the role of the spermatozoan in fertilization. He diluted semen samples until he could see no more sperm and found the diluted fluid still capable of fertilization. He also filtered semen so thoroughly that it could no longer induce development. The former results he took as proof of the existence of a seminal aura; the latter he ignored.

In Spallanzani we have an example of a highly talented eighteenth-century scientist doing careful experiments that prove, to our modern-day eyes, the opposite of what he concluded. Because he interpreted his investigations within a particular theoretical framework—that of ovism—his mind was closed to alternative conclusions that seem obvious to those not so committed. Because Spallanzani was a scientist of considerable authority and influence, his conclusions, rather than his experimental results, dominated biological thought on fertilization. A correct account of the role of the sperm in fertilization and development was not generally accepted for another 100 years. The point here is not that an incompetent scientist made a series of experimental errors, but that an extremely good scientist performed a series of beautifully controlled experiments but did not draw from them the correct conclusions. The process by which cultural categories shape perception and influence reasoning is little studied. The case of Spallanzani and his experiments on spermatozoa and their role in fertilization would be an excellent starting point for a cultural anthropologist who wished to analyze this process. That this phenomenon holds true for modern scientific activity can be seen in the next, more contemporary example.

During mammalian development all embryos (regardless of their potential sex) pass through a stage that embryologists have dubbed the "indifferent period." Examination of XX and XY embryos during this period shows no evidence of sex differences in either the embryonic gonad or sexually-related somatic structures such as the oviducts or the vas deferens. Present are a single gonad that will later take either a male or female path of development, and two sets of accessory structures known as the mesonephric and paramesonephric ducts. In female development the mesonephric ducts disintegrate while the paramesonephric ducts form the oviducts, uterus, and part of the vagina. In male development the paramesonephric ducts degenerate while the mesonephric ducts develop into the epididymal duct and the vas deferens. In general, then, mammals first develop a single pair of gonads, which subsequently takes either a male or a female direction, and both male and female accessory structures, only one set of which survives while the other degenerates. Baldly stated, up to a certain point all embryos are completely bisexual.

The choice of whether to follow a male or a female path of development is made through the intervention of the sex chromosomes and hormones present in utero. It is at this point in the story that a curious use of language that has set limits on the experimental questions asked about sexual development enters in. I will first recount the tale as it is told in text books, popular literature, and the vast majority of scientific papers, and then underline some of the story's peculiarities, showing how they have resulted in a supposedly general account of the development of the sexes that is in actuality only an account of male development. This example illustrates a case in which the meaning of *man* as a supposedly inclusive universal has slipped unnoticed into its meaning as an exclusive biological category. What biologists turn out to have provided as our account of the development of gender from a mechanistic point of view is really only an account of male differentiation.

The following excerpts come from an up-to-date and heavily used undergraduate embryology text written by Dr. Bruce M. Carlson. My intent is not to attack Carlson, who recounts an almost universally held set of beliefs, but merely to analyze the text to uncover some of the underlying structures of those beliefs. Carlson writes:

> The sex-determining function of the Y chromosome is intimately bound with the activity of the H-Y antigen . . . its major function is to cause the organization of the primitive gonad into the testis. In the *absence* of the H-Y antigen the gonad later becomes transformed into the ovary. (Italics added.)

The account continues with a discussion of the formation of non-gonadal (somatic) sex organs such as the uterus and vas deferens.

> The early embryo develops a dual set of potential genital ducts [the mesonephric and paramesonephric ducts]. . . . Under the *influence of testosterone* secreted by the testes, the mesonephric ducts develop into the duct system through which spermatozoa are conveyed from the testes to the urethra. . . . The potentially female paramesonephric ducts regress *under the influence* of another secretion of the embryonic testes, the Mullerian Inhibitory Factor. (Italics added.)
>
> In genetically female embryos neither testosterone nor Mullerian Inhibitory Factor is secreted by the gonads. In the *absence of testosterone* the mesonephric ducts regress and the *lack of Mullerian Inhibitory Factor* permits the paramesonephric ducts to develop into the oviducts, uterus and part of the vagina. The external genitalia also first take form in a morphologically indifferent condition and then develop either in the male direction *under the influence of testosterone* or in the female direction *if the influence of testosterone is lacking.* (Italics added.)

Carlson also writes of "the natural tendency of the body to develop along female lines in the absence of other modifying influences." The presence-or-absence-of-maleness concept is an old one. Simone de Beauvoir quoted Aristotle as saying that "the female is a female by virtue of a certain *lack* of qualities." Psychologist Dr. John Money calls accounts of sexual development similar to Carlson's an example of "the Adam Principle" that something is *added* to an embryo to make it a male. A well-known reproductive biologist, Dr. R. V. Short, concludes an introductory account of sex determination differentiation by spelling out what he sees as the implications of that viewpoint:

> In all systems that we have considered, maleness means mastery; the Y-chromosome over the X, the medulla [of the indifferent gonad] over the cortex, androgen over oestrogen. So physiologically speaking, there is no justification for believing in the equality of the sexes; *vive la différence!*

The idea that the female represents some natural, fundamental "ground state" is also familiar. Strangely, although biologists emulate physicists by reducing organisms to smaller and smaller parts in order to investigate causes that precede causes ad infinitum, they are generally satisfied to accept the idea that a female direction of development occurs passively in the absence of instructions from so-called male sex hormones. How does it happen? What are the mechanisms? Investigators ask these questions about male development (generically referred to as sexual differentiation), but only a few express interest in applying the same scrutiny to development of the female. This imbalance in levels of intellectual curiosity is reflected in the etymologies of the words that name sex hormones: *androgen* comes from the Greek *andros* and the Latin *generare* (to make a male), *estrogen* from the Latin *oestrus* (gadfly or frenzy). In fact, the word *gynogen,* which would be the etymologically and biologically correct counterpart to *androgen,* cannot be found in biological accounts of sexual development (or, for that matter, in any dictionary).

If we look carefully at the existing biological literature, we can see how we might construct a narrative that treats female sexual differentiation as requiring as much investigation and explanation as male sexual differentiation. We could begin by examining the many studies on hormonal control of sexual development in cold-blooded vertebrates. Some examples: the addition of estrogen to the water of certain XY (potentially male) fish causes them to develop as females rather than males; similarly, the addition of estrogen to the water of amphibian tadpoles before and during their metamorphosis to adults results in all exposed larvae becoming females. Clearly, such research provides evidence that so-called female hormones actively induce female development; that is, they behave as gynogens. But the findings of studies on cold-blooded vertebrates are usually considered inapplicable to mammals. Only rarely does a publication on mammalian development include a consideration of the active role of female hormones.

Estrogen and progesterone (another female hormone) are not absent during female mammalian development. In addition to estrogen synthesis in the fetal ovary, all sexual development, both male and female, takes place in the presence of high concentrations of placentally-produced female hormones, especially the estrogens and progesterones. That sexual development occurs in a sea of female placental hormones is recognized and viewed as a "problem" for male development. A variety of hypotheses have been proposed and experiments carried out to explain why the developing male embryo is not feminized by maternal hormones. Yet the scientist who is concerned about the potential feminizing effect of female hormones in male development is often the same one who writes that female development is not directed by hormones at all, but is an event that results from a lack of male hormones. This lopsided logic requires both attention and explanation.

What I've just written is, of course, an oversimplification. In some parts of the scientific literature the idea of a positive role for estrogen has begun to creep in. This is partly due to the discovery that testosterone may be converted into estrogen by certain cells in the body, and that what was long believed to be an effect of testosterone on male behavior in rodents is actually caused by the conversion of testosterone to estrogen by cells in the brain. Nevertheless, the associations of male/presence/active and female/absence/passive still govern our concepts of human development and influence the language used to explain them in the current literature.

There is one other etymological/scientific issue to be teased out of the account of male and female development in vertebrates. It is the designation of the male gamete-transporting ducts as mesonephric (middle kidney) and the female's as paramesonephric (sitting next to the middle kidney). Three different types of kidneys have evolved during the evolution of vertebrates: the pronephros, the mesonephros, and the metanephros. In mammals the pronephros is vestigial in the embryo and completely absent in the adult. The mesonephros functions as a kidney in the embryos of some mammals, and its ducts become part of the adult postembryonic male gonadal duct system (this ancient connection between gamete transport and waste excretion is also seen in vertebrates such as those fish and amphibia whose kidney tubules are the means of transporting both sperm and urine to the outside). The metanephros becomes the functional kidney at birth.

In female mammals there evolved a separate set of ducts (dubbed the paramesonephric ducts) having nothing to do with the kidneys, apparently designed only for the transport of ova. The prefix *para* has several meanings, including near, beside, adjacent to, closely resembling, almost, beyond, remotely or indirectly relating to, faulty or abnormal condition, and associated in an accessory capacity. The use of the prefix is common in the language of anatomy and certainly not restricted to structures related to sexual organs. The adrenal glands, for example, are sometimes referred to as the paranephros because of their location atop the kidneys, so the naming of the paramesonephric ducts for their positional relationship to ducts in the male (note that they have no separate name of their own as do the adrenals) could be nothing more than happenstance. It would be easier to sustain that argument, however, if the literature revealed further interest in both the embryonic and evolution-ary origins of these ducts. Yet knowledge about them is lacking.

The changing function of an organ such as the embryonic kidney is a well-known evolutionary phenomenon. Front limbs, for example, have evolved into wings, arms, legs, and flippers. Bones that form parts of the jaw in reptiles have become the functional sound-receiving and -transferring bones of the inner ear in mammals. On the other hand, the appearance of a brand new structure is less common and presents a pro-foundly difficult explanatory problem for evolutionary biologists. Yet the evolutionary and embryological origins of the paramesonephric duct, which might be such a de novo structure, have been little studied; as one author writes, "The phylogenetic origin of paramesonephric ducts is again obscure." As in the case of estrogen's role in governing fe-male development, our lack of understanding of the origin and develop-ment of the paramesonephric duct represents a research path not taken. The reasons for this are probably multiple, but at least one of them must be that the road to understanding these ducts has been considered a side path, one lying next to or away from the main road that one must follow in order to understand male development.

Another example of how scientific language betrays a one-sided curios-ity can be found in the literature on the study of male and female sexual differentiation of the rat brain, which until very recently has been framed around the idea that testosterone provides an "organizing effect" on the "intrinsic tendency to develop according to a female pattern of body structure and behavior." (Does this phraseology imply that the female brain is disorganized?) Or consider the fact that mutations affecting an-drogen metabolism in humans and other mammals have been extensively studied and well-cataloged, but that none affecting estrogen metabolism have been isolated. Some authors have suggested that because implanta-tion in the uterus is impossible without estrogen, an ovum affected by a mutation that interferes with estrogen metabolism would not survive. In other words, estrogen metabolism may be more poorly understood than androgen metabolism because it is essential for mammalian life. From this perspective, the focus on the role of androgens in sexual develop-ment, while not misplaced, certainly seems one-sided. Correcting the im-balance is not technically impossible; estrogen metabolism studies could be conducted with laboratory animals in ways that avoid the problem of lethality. It seems, though, that our considerable scientific and experi-mental ingenuity has not yet been directed toward solving this particular puzzle.

These cases from the biological literature strongly suggest that broad cultural paradigms about the nature of male and female have had a con-siderable effect on biological theory. The language used to describe "the facts" has channeled experimental thought along certain lanes, leaving others not only unexplored but unnoticed.

FROM WORKING SCIENTIST
TO FEMINIST CRITIC

■

Evelyn Fox Keller

This essay is from Keller's 1992 book Secrets of Life/Secrets of Death: Essays on Language, Gender and Sciences.

I begin with three vignettes, all drawn from memory.

1965. In my first few years out of graduate school, I held quite conventional beliefs about science. I believed not only in the possibility of clear and certain knowledge of the world, but also in the uniquely privileged access to this knowledge provided by science in general, and by physics in particular. I believed in the accessibility of an underlying (and unifying) "truth" about the world we live in, and I believed that the laws of physics gave us the closest possible approximation of this truth. In short, I was well trained in both the traditional realist worldviews assumed by virtually all scientists and in the conventional epistemological ordering of the sciences. I had, after all, been trained, first, by theoretical physicists, and later, by molecular biologists. This is not to say that I lived my life according to the teachings of physics (or molecular biology), only that when it came to questions about what "really is," I knew where, and how, to look. Although I had serious conflicts about my own ability to be part of this venture, I fully accepted science, and scientists, as arbiters of truth. Physics (and physicists) were, of course, the highest arbiters.

Somewhere around this time, I came across the proceedings of the first major conference held in the United States on "Women and the Scientific Professions" (Mattfield and Van Aiken 1965)—a subject of inevitable interest to me. I recall reading in those proceedings an argument for more women in science, made by both Erik Erikson and Bruno Bettelheim, based on the invaluable contributions a "specifically female genius" could make to science. Although earlier in their contributions both Erikson and Bettelheim had each made a number of eminently reasonable observations and recommendations, I flew to these concluding remarks as if waiting for them, indeed forgetting everything else they had said. From the vantage point I then occupied, my reaction was predictable: To put it quite bluntly, I laughed. Laws of nature are universal—how could they possibly depend on the sex of their discoverers? Obviously, I snickered, these psychoanalysts know little enough about science (and by implication, about truth).

1969. I was living in a suburban California house and found myself with time to think seriously about my own mounting conflicts (as well as those of virtually all my female cohorts) about being a scientist. I had taken a leave to accompany my husband on his sabbatical, remaining at home to care for our two small children. Weekly, I would talk to the colleague I had left back in New York and hear his growing enthusiasm as he reported the spectacular successes he was having in presenting our joint work. In between, I would try to understand why my own enthusiasm was not only not growing, but actually diminishing. How I went about seeking such an understanding is worth noting: What I did was to go to the library to gather data about the fate of women scientists in general—more truthfully, to document my own growing disenchantment (even in the face of manifest success) as part of a more general phenomenon reflecting an underlying misfit between women and science. And I wrote to Erik Erikson for further comment on the alarming (yet somehow satisfying) attrition data I was collecting. In short, only a few years after ridiculing his thoughts on the subject, I was ready to at least entertain if not embrace an argument about women in, or out of, science based on "women's nature." Not once during that entire year did it occur to me that at least part of my disenchantment might be related to the fact that I was in fact not sharing in the *kudos* my colleague was reaping for our joint work.

1974. I had not dropped out of science, but I had moved into interdisciplinary, undergraduate teaching. And I had just finished teaching my first women's studies course when I received an invitation to give a series of "Distinguished Lectures" on my work in mathematical biology at the University of Maryland. It was a great honor and I wanted to do it, but I had a problem. In my women's studies course, I had yielded to the pressure of my students and colleagues to talk openly about what it had been like, as a woman, to become a scientist. In other words, I had been persuaded to publicly air the exceedingly painful story of the struggle that had actually been—a story I had previously only talked about in private, if at all. The effect of doing this was that I actually came to *see* that story as public, that is, of political significance, rather than as simply private, of merely personal significance. As a result, the prospect of continuing to present myself as a disembodied scientist, of talking about my work as if it had been done in a vacuum, as if the fact of my being a woman was entirely irrelevant, had come to feel actually dishonest.

I resolved the conflict by deciding to present in my last lecture a demographic model of women in science—an excuse to devote the bulk of that lecture to a review of the many barriers that worked against the survival of women as scientists, and to a discussion of possible solutions. I concluded my review with the observation that perhaps the most important barrier to success for women in science derived from the pervasive belief in the intrinsic masculinity of scientific thought. Where, I asked, does such a belief come from? What is it doing in science, reputedly the most objective, neutral, and abstract endeavor we know? And what consequences does that belief have for the actual doing of science?

In 1974 "women in science" was not a proper subject for academic or scientific discussion; I was aware of violating professional protocol. Having given the lecture—having "carried it off"—I felt profoundly liberated. I had passed an essential milestone.

Although I did not know it then, and wouldn't recognize it for another two years, this lecture marked the beginning of my work as a feminist critic of science. In it I raised three of the central questions that were to mark my research and writing over the next decade. I can now see that, with the concluding remarks of that lecture, I had also completed the basic shift in mind-set that made it possible to begin such a venture. Even though my views about gender, science, knowledge, and truth were to evolve considerably over the years to come, I had already made the two most essential steps: I had shifted attention from the question of male and female nature to that of *beliefs about* male and female nature, that is, to gender ideology. And I had admitted the possibility that such beliefs could affect science itself.

In hindsight, these two moves may seem simple enough, but when I reflect on my own history, as well as that of other women scientists, I can see that they were not. Indeed, from my earlier vantage point, they were unthinkable. In that mind-set, there was room neither for a distinction between sexual identity and beliefs about sexual identity (not even for the prior distinction between sex and gender upon which it depends), nor for the possibility that beliefs could affect science—a possibility that requires a distinction analogous to that between sex and gender, only now between nature and science. I was, of course, able to accommodate a distinction between belief and reality, but only in the sense of "false" beliefs—that is, mere illusion, or mere prejudice; "true" beliefs I took to be synonymous with the "real."

It seems to me that in that mind-set, beliefs per se were not seen as having any real force—neither the force to shape the development of men and women, nor the force to shape the development of science. Some people may "misperceive" nature, human or otherwise, but properly seen, men and women simply *are*, faithful reflections of male and female biology—just as science simply *is*, a faithful reflection of nature. Gravity has (or is) a force, DNA has force, but beliefs do not. In other words, as scientists, we are trained to see the locus of real force in the world as physical, not mental.

There is of course a sense in which they are right: Beliefs per se cannot exert force on the world. But the people who carry such beliefs can. Furthermore, the language in which their beliefs are encoded has the force to shape what others—as men, as women, and as scientists—think, believe, and, in turn, actually do. It may have taken the lens of feminist theory to reveal the popular association of science, objectivity, and masculinity as a statement about the social rather than natural (or biological) world, referring not to the bodily and mental capacities of individual men and women, but to a collective consciousness; that is, as a set of beliefs given existence by language rather than by bodies, and by that language, granted the force to shape what individual men and women might (or might not) do. But to see how such culturally laden language could contribute to the shaping of science takes a different kind of lens. That requires, first and foremost, a recognition of the social character (and force) of the enterprise we call "science," a recognition quite separable from—and in fact, historically independent of—the insights of contemporary feminism.

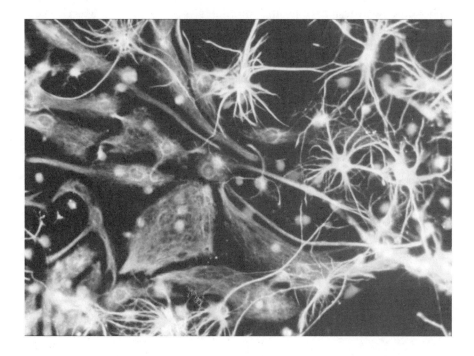

THE MONKEY WARS

■

Deborah Blum

The following piece was published in The Sacramento Bee *in 1992.*

On the days when he's scheduled to kill, Allen Merritt summons up his ghosts.

They come to him from the shadows of a 20-year-old memory. Eleven human babies from his first year out of medical school. All born prematurely. All lost within one week when their lungs failed.

"We were virtually helpless," said Merritt, now head of the neonatal intensive care unit at the University of California–Davis Medical Center.

"There's nothing worse than being a new physician and standing there watching babies die. It's a strong motivator to make things different."

On this cool morning, he needs that memory. The experiment he's doing is deceptively simple: a test of a new chemical to help premature babies breathe. But it's no clinical arrangement of glass tubes. He's trying the drug on two tiny rhesus monkeys, each weighing barely one-third of a pound. At the end of the experiment, he plans to cut their lungs apart, to see how it worked.

Even his ghosts don't make that easy. Nestled in a towel on a surgical table, eyes shut, hands curled, the monkeys look unnervingly human. "The link between people and monkeys is very close," Merritt said. "Much closer than some people would like to think. There's a real sense of sadness, that we can only get the information we need if we kill them."

Once, there was no such need to justify. Once, American researchers could go through 200,000 monkeys a year, without question. Now, the numbers are less—perhaps 20,000 monkeys will die every year, out of an estimated 40,000 used in experiments. But the pressures are greater.

These days, it seems that if researchers plan one little study—slicing the toes off squirrel monkeys, siphoning blood from rhesus macaques, hiding baby monkeys from their mothers—they face not just questions, but picket signs, lawsuits and death threats phoned in at night.

The middle ground in the war over research with monkeys and apes has become so narrow as to be nearly invisible. And even that is eroding.

Intelligent, agile, fast, but not fast enough, these non-human primates are rapidly being driven from the planet, lost to heavy trapping and vanishing rain forests. Of 63 primate species in Asia—where most research monkeys come from—only one is not listed as vulnerable.

Primate researchers believe they are making the hard choice, using non-human primates for medical research because they must, because no other animal so closely mirrors the human body and brain. During the 1950s, American scientists did kill hundreds of thousands of monkeys for polio research, using the animals' organs to grow virus, dissecting their brains to track the spread of the infection. But out of those experiments came a polio vaccine. Using monkeys, scientists have created vaccines for measles, learned to fight leprosy, developed anti-rejection drugs that make organ transplants possible.

Outside the well-guarded laboratory wall, that choice can seem less obvious. Animal rights advocates draw a dark description of research. They point out that AIDS researchers have used endangered chimpanzees, without, so far, managing to help people dying of the disease. Further, conservationists fear that the research is introducing dangerous infection into the country's chimpanzee breeding program, badly needed to help counter the loss of wild animals.

"They're guzzling up money and animals, and for what?" asked Shirley McGreal, head of the non-profit International Primate Protection League. "Why not use those resources in helping sick people, why infect healthy animals?"

Her argument is that of animal advocates across the country—that scientists are sacrificing our genetic next-of-kin for their own curiosity, dubious medical gains and countless tax dollars.

No one is sure exactly how much money scientists spend experimenting on monkeys, although the National Institutes of Health alone allocates almost $40 million annually to its primate research programs, including one in Davis. Overall, more than half of NIH's research grants—approaching $5 billion—involve at least some animal research.

Rats and mice are the most abundant, some 15 million are used in experiments every year. But primates are the most expensive; monkeys cost a basic $1,000, chimpanzees start at $50,000.

For people such as McGreal, these are animals in a very wrong place. McGreal's long-term goal for monkeys is simple: out of the laboratory, back into what remains of the rain forests.

"I used to think that we could persuade those people to understand what we do," said Frederick King, director of the Yerkes Regional Primate Research Center in Atlanta. "But it's impossible. And that's why I no longer describe this as a battle. I describe it as a war."

The rift is so sharp that it is beginning to reshape science itself.

"Science has organized," marveled Alex Pacheco, founder of the country's most powerful animal rights group, People for Ethical Treatment of Animals. "Researchers are out-lobbying us and outspending us. They've become so aggressive that it puts new pressure on us. We're going to have to fight tougher too."

In the past year, researchers have made it clear just how much they dislike the role of victim. If Pacheco wants to call scientists "sadistic bastards"—which he does frequently—then Fred King is more than ready to counter with his description of PETA: "Fanatic, fringe, one of the most despicable organizations in the country."

But beyond name-calling, the research community is realizing its political power. Its lobbyists are pushing for laws that would heavily penalize protesters who interfere with research projects. And this year, to the fury of animal rights groups, primate researchers were able to win a special exemption from the public records laws, shielding their plans for captive monkey care.

For researchers, the attention focused on them is an almost dizzying turnabout. Not so long ago, they could have hung their monkey care plans as banners across streets and no one would have read them.

"When I first started, 20 years ago, monkeys were $25 each," said Roy Henrickson, chief of lab animal care at the University of California, Berkeley. "You'd use one once and you'd throw it away. I'd talk to lab vets who were under pressure about dogs and I'd say, I'm sure glad I'm in non-human primates. Nobody cares about them."

He can date the change precisely, back to 1981, the year Pacheco went undercover in the laboratory of Edward Taub. Taub was a specialist in nerve damage, working in Silver Springs, Md. To explore the effects of ruined nerves, he took 17 rhesus monkeys and sliced apart nerves close to the spinal column, crippling their limbs. Then he studied the way they coped with the damage.

Pacheco left the laboratory with an enduring mistrust of scientists and an armload of inflammatory photographs: monkeys wrenched into vices, packed into filthy cages. Monkeys who, with no feeling in their hands, had gnawed their fingers to the bone. Some of the wounds were oozing with infection, darkening with gangrene.

Many believe those battered monkeys were the fuse, lighting the current, combative cycle of animal rights. In the fury over the Silver Springs monkeys, Pacheco was able to build People for Ethical Treatment of Animals into a national force, and across the country, the movement gained power. Today, membership in animal advocacy groups tops 12 million; the 30 largest organizations report a combined annual income approaching $70 million.

And primate researchers have suddenly found themselves under scrutiny of the most hostile kind.

There are experiments, such as Allen Merritt's work to salvage premature infants, that the critics will sometimes reluctantly accept. The compound that Merritt is testing on young monkeys is a kind of lubricant for the lungs, a slippery ooze that coats the tissues within, allowing them to flex as air comes in and out.

Without the ooze—called surfactant—the tissues don't stretch. They rip. The problem for premature babies is that the body doesn't develop surfactant until late in fetal development, some 35 weeks into a pregnancy.

Although artificial surfactants are now available, Merritt doesn't believe they're good enough. Two-thirds of the tiniest premature babies, weighing less than a pound at birth, still die as their lungs shred. He's trying to improve the medicine.

"There could be a scientific defense for doing that, even though it's extremely cruel," said Elliot Katz, head of In Defense of Animals, a national animal rights group, headquartered in San Rafael.

But Katz finds most of the work indefensible. He can rapidly cite examples of a different sort: a U.S. Air Force experiment, which involved draining 40 percent of the blood from rhesus macaques and then spinning them on a centrifuge, to simulate injured astronauts; a New York University study of addiction in which monkeys were strapped into metal boxes and forced to inhale concentrated cocaine fumes.

Last year, animal advocates rallied against a proposed study at the Seattle center, a plan to take 13 baby rhesus macaques from their mothers and try to drive them crazy through isolation, keeping them caged away from their mothers and without company. The scientists acknowledged that they might drive the monkeys to self-mutilation; rhesus macaques do badly in isolation, rocking, pulling out their hair, sometimes tearing their skin open.

This year, protesters have been holding candlelight vigils outside the home of a researcher at a Maryland military facility, the Uniformed Services University of the Health Sciences. That project involves cutting the toes from kittens and young squirrel monkeys and then, after they've wobbled into adjustment, killing them to look at their brains.

In both cases, there are scientific explanations. The Washington scientists wanted to analyze the chemistry of a troubled brain, saying that it could benefit people with mental illness. The Maryland researchers are brain-mapping, drafting a careful picture of how the mind reorganizes itself to cope with crippling injury.

But these are not—and may never be—explanations acceptable to those crusading for animal rights. "This is just an example of someone doing something horrible to animals because he can get paid for it," said Laurie Raymond, of Seattle's Progressive Animal Welfare Society, which campaigned against the baby monkey experiment and takes credit for the fact that it failed to get federal funding.

Researchers are tired of telling the public about their work, documenting it in public records—and having that very openness used against them. The Washington protesters learned about the baby monkey experiment through a meeting of the university's animal care committee—which is public. The Maryland work came to light through a listing of military funded research—which is public.

When the U.S. Department of Agriculture, which inspects research facilities annually, complained about the housekeeping at the Tulane Regional Primate Research Center in Louisiana, the director wrote the agency a furious letter. Didn't administrators realize that the report was public—and made scientists look bad?

"The point I am making is that USDA, without intending to do so, is playing into the hands of the animal rights/anti-vivisectionists whose stated goal is to abolish animal research," wrote center head Peter Gerone, arguing that the complaints could have been handled privately. "If you are trying to placate the animal rights activists by nitpicking inspections . . . you will only serve to do us irreparable harm."

When Arnold Arluke, a sociologist at Boston's Northeastern University, spent six years studying lab workers and drafted a report saying that some actually felt guilty about killing animals, he found himself suddenly under pressure. "I was told putting that information out would be like giving ammunition to the enemy," he said.

He titled his first talk "Guilt Among Animal Researchers." The manager of the laboratory where he spoke changed "guilt" to stress. When he published that in a journal, the editors thought that stress was too controversial. They changed the tide to "Uneasiness Among Lab Workers." When he gave another talk at a pharmaceutical company, he was told uneasiness was too strong. They changed the tide to "How to Deal with Your Feelings." Arluke figures his next talk will be untitled.

"People in animal research don't even want to tell others what they do," he said. "One woman I talked to was standing in line at a grocery store, and when she told the person next to her what she did, the woman started yelling at her: 'You should be ashamed of yourself.'"

And when new lab animal care rules were published this year, it was clear that researchers were no longer willing to freely hand over every record of operation.

The new regulations resulted from congressional changes in 1985 to the Animal Welfare Act. They included a special provision for the care of laboratory primates; legislators wanted scientists to recognize that these were sociable, intelligent animals.

The provision—perhaps the most controversial in the entire act—was called "psychological well-being of primates." When the USDA began drafting rules, in response to the new law, it received a record 35,000 letters of comment. And 14,000 consisted of a written shouting match over how to make primates happy. It took six years before the agency could come up with rules that the research community could accept.

Originally, the USDA proposed firm standards: Laboratories would have to give monkeys bigger cages, let them share space, provide them with puzzles and toys from a list.

Researchers argued that was unreasonable: Every monkey species was different, the rigid standards might satisfy one animal and make another miserable. Now, each institution is asked to do what it thinks best for its monkeys; USDA inspectors will be free to study, criticize and ask for changes in those plans.

But animal rights groups will not. Research lobbyists persuaded the USDA to bypass the federal Freedom of Information Act; the president of the American Society of Primatologists told the agency that making the plans public would be like giving a road map to terrorists. Under the new rules, the plans will be kept at the individual institutions rather than filed with the federal government, as has been standard practice. That makes them institutional property—exempted from any requests for federal records.

Tom Wolfle, director of the Institute for Laboratory Animal Resources in Washington, D.C., the federal government's chief advisory division on animal issues, said the research community simply needed some clear space. "The idea was to prevent unreasonable criticism by uninformed people," he said.

Advocacy groups have sued the government over the new rules, saying they unlawfully shut the public out of research that it pays for. "In the end, they just handed everything back to the researchers and said, here, it's all yours," said Christine Stevens, an executive with the non-profit Animal Welfare Institute.

Stevens, daughter of a Michigan physiology researcher, finds this the ultimate contradiction, as well as "foolish and short-sighted." She thinks that science, of all professions, should be one of open ideas.

On this point, she has some unlikely allies. Frederick King, of Yerkes, no friend to the animal rights movement, is also unhappy with the research community's tendency to withdraw. "I don't know about the law," he said. "But our plans for taking care of our primates will be open.

"We are using taxpayers' money. In my judgment, we have an obligation to tell the public what we're about. And the fact that we haven't done that, I think, is one of the greatest mistakes over the last half-century, hell, the last century, that scientists have made."

Against that conflict, Allen Merritt's decision to make public an experiment in which he kills monkeys was not an easy one. His wife worried that anti-research fanatics would stalk their home. His supervisors worried that animal lovers would be alienated; one administrator even called the Davis primate center, suggesting that Merritt's work should not be publicly linked to the medical school's pediatrics department.

But Merritt, like King, believes that his profession will only lose if it remains hidden from the public. "People need to understand what we're doing. If I were to take a new drug first to a nursery, and unforeseen complications occurred, and a baby died—who would accept that?"

So, on a breezy morning, he opens the way to the final test of lung-lubricating surfactants that he will do this year, a 24-hour-countdown for two baby monkeys. Those hours are critical to whether these drugs work. If human premature babies last from their first morning to the next one, their survival odds soar.

The tiny monkeys—one male, one female—taken by C-section, are hurried into an intensive care unit, dried and warmed with a blow drier, put onto folded towels, hooked up to ventilators, heart monitors, intravenous drip lines. During the experiment, they will never be conscious, never open their eyes.

"OK, let's treat," Merritt says. His technician gently lifts the tube from the ventilator, which carries oxygen into the monkey's lungs. A white mist of surfactant fills the tube, spraying into the lungs. And then, through the night, the medical team watches and waits.

The next morning, they decide to kill the female early. An intravenous line going into her leg is starting to cause bleeding problems. The monkey is twitching a little in her unconsciousness, as if in pain. Merritt sees no point in dragging her through the experiment's official end.

But the male keeps breathing. As the sun brightens to midday, the scientists inject a lethal dose of anesthesia. Still, the monkey's chest keeps moving, up and down, up and down with the push of the ventilator. But, behind him, the heart monitor shows only a straight green line.

For a few seconds, before they shut the machines down and begin the lung dissection, Allen Merritt stands quietly by the small dead monkey, marshaling the ghosts of the babies he couldn't save, a long time ago.

EWEGENICS

Jean Bethke Elshtain

This essay appeared in the March 31, 1997 issue of The New Republic.

For a change, there was no waffling. The president acted decisively and boldly, and, what's more, rightly, when he called for a moratorium on all cloning experiments involving humans. The alarm and moral clarity behind the president's action, however, has been absent in much of the media. The newspapers' ubiquitous search for "balance" is unbalanced when the matter at hand is as extraordinarily unsettling as cloning. I read a half-dozen pieces pairing a techno-enthusiast against a hand-wringing theologian. A professional ethicist is usually brought onstage as an arbiter between two obviously one-sided points of view. A comforting sense of moderation is achieved. The article ends.

But listen to the radio call-in shows and you get a rather different picture. For every wild-eyed optimist there are, by my count, a good half-dozen alarmists. Talk to the man and woman on the street and you hear murmurs and rumblings and dark portents of the "end-of-times" and "now we've gone too far." The airwaves and the street win this one hands down. They represent a humane and sobering contrast to the celebratory glitz of, say, *USA Today*, which trumpeted "hello dolly!"—the name of the fetching ewe staring at us in a front-page color photo. The sub-head read: "sheep cloning prompts ethical debate." The sheep looks perfectly normal, of course, and not terribly exercised about her historic significance. That she is the child of no one will probably not haunt her nights and days. But we—we humans, that is—should be haunted, by Dolly and all the Dollies to come and by the prospect others will appear on this earth as the progeny of our omnipotent striving, our yearning to create without pausing to reflect on what we are simultaneously destroying.

A few nights ago, I watched the Chicago Bulls clobber the San Antonio Spurs. Michael Jordan performed one of his typically superhuman feats, an assist that suggested he had eyes in the back of his head and two sets of arms. To one citizen who called a local program, the prospect of "more Michael Jordans" made the whole "cloning thing" not only palatable but desirable. "Can you imagine a whole basketball team of Michael Jordans?" he asked giddily.

Unfortunately, I can. It's a nightmare. If there were basketball teams fielding Jordans against Jordans, we wouldn't be able to recognize the one, the only, Michael Jordan. It's like suggesting that forty Mozarts are better than one. There would be no Mozart if there were forty Mozarts. We know the singularity of the one, the extraordinary genius—a Jordan, a Mozart—because they stand apart from and above the rest. Absent that irreducible singularity, their gifts and glorious accomplishments would mean nothing. They would be the norm, commonplace: another dunk, another concerto. In fact, lots of callers made this point, or one similar to it, in reacting to the Michael Jordan Clonetopia scenario.

A research librarian at a small college in Indiana, who had given me a drive to her campus for the purpose of delivering a lecture, offered a spontaneous, sustained and troubling critique of cloning that rivals the best dystopian fictions. Her cloning nightmare was a veritable army of Hitlers, ruthless and remorseless bigots who kept reproducing themselves until they had finished what the historic Hitler had failed to do: annihilate us. It occurred to me that an equal number of Mother Teresas would probably not be a viable deterrent, not if the Hitler clones were behaving like, well, Hitler.

But I had my own nightmare scenario: a society that clones human beings to serve as spare parts for the feeble. Because the cloned entities are not fully human, our moral queasiness is somewhat disarmed. We could then "harvest" organs to our heart's content—organs from human beings of every age, race and phenotype. Anencephalic newborns, whose organs are now "harvested," would, in that world, be the equivalent of the Model T—an early and, it turns out, very rudimentary prototype of glorious, gleaming things to come.

Far-fetched? No longer. Besides, the far-fetched often gets us nearer to the truth than the cautious, persnickety pieces that fail to come anywhere close to the pity and terror this topic evokes.

Consider Stanislaw Lem's science fiction classic *The Star Diaries*, in which his protagonist, Ijon Tichy, described as a "hapless Candide of the Cosmos," ventures into space and encounters one weird situation after another. Lem's "Thirteenth Voyage" takes Tichy to a planet called Panta, where he runs afoul of local custom and is accused of the worst of crimes, "the crime of personal differentiation." The evidence against him is incriminating. Nonetheless, Tichy is given an opportunity to conform. A planet spokesman instructs Tichy on the benefits of his planet, on which there are no separate entities—"only the collective."

The denizens of Panta have come to understand that the source of all "the cares, sufferings and misfortunes to which beings, gathered together in societies, are prone" lies in the individual, "in his private identity." The individual, by contrast to the collective, is "characterized by uncertainty, indecision, inconsistency of action, and above all—by impermanence." Having "completely eliminated individuality," the people of planet Panta have achieved "the highest degree of social interchangeability." It works rather the way the Marxist utopia was to function: everyone at any moment can be anything else. Functions or roles are commutable. On Panta you occupy a role for twenty-four hours only: one day a gardener, the next an engineer, then a mason, now a judge.

The same principle holds with families. "Each is composed of relatives—there's a father, mother, children. Only the functions remain constant; the ones who perform them are changed every day." All feelings and emotions are entirely abstract. One never needs to grieve or to mourn as everyone is infinitely replaceable. "Affection, respect, love were at one time gnawed by constant anxiety, by the fear of losing the person held dear," Lem writes. "This dread we have conquered. For in point of fact whatever upheavals, diseases or calamities may be visited upon us, we shall always have a father, a mother, a spouse and children." Indeed, there is no "I." And there can be no death, "where there are no individuals." In this commutable void, we do not die. Tichy, like most of us, can't quite get with the program. Brought before a court, he is "found guilty and condemned to life identification." He blasts off and sets his course for Earth.

Only this time, if Lem were writing an addendum to his brilliant tale, Tichy would probably land on terra firma—in both the literal and metaphorical sense—only to discover the greeting party at the rocket-port a bit strange: there are forty very tall basketball players all wearing identical #23 jerseys, dribbling on one side and, on the other side, forty men in powdered wigs, suited up in breeches and satin frock coats, all playing *The Marriage of Figaro*.

HUMAN CLONING? DON'T JUST SAY NO

Ruth Macklin

This essay first appeared in U.S. News and World Report *on March 10, 1997.*

Last week's news that scientists had cloned a sheep sent academics and the public into a panic at the prospect that humans might be next. That's an understandable reaction. Cloning is a radical challenge to the most fundamental laws of biology, so it's not unreasonable to be concerned that it might threaten human society and dignity. Yet much of the ethical opposition seems also to grow out of an unthinking dust—a sort of "yuk factor." And that makes it hard for even trained scientists and ethicists to see the matter clearly. While human cloning might not offer great benefits to humanity, no one has yet made a persuasive case that it would do any real harm, either.

Theologians contend that to clone a human would violate human dignity. That would surely be true if a cloned individual were treated as a lesser being, with fewer rights or lower stature. But why suppose that cloned persons wouldn't share the same rights and dignity as the rest of us? A leading lawyer-ethicist has suggested that cloning would violate the "right to genetic identity." Where did he come up with such a right? It makes perfect sense to say that adult persons have a right not to be cloned without their voluntary, informed consent. But if such consent is given, whose "right" to genetic identity would be violated?

Many of the science-fiction scenarios prompted by the prospect of human cloning turn out, upon reflection, to be absurdly improbable. There's the fear, for instance, that parents might clone a child to have "spare parts" in case the original child needs an organ transplant. But parents of identical twins don't view one child as an organ farm for the other. Why should cloned children's parents be any different?

Vast difference. Another disturbing thought is that cloning will lead to efforts to breed individuals with genetic qualities perceived as exceptional (math geniuses, basketball players). Such ideas are repulsive, not only because of the "yuk factor" but also because of the horrors perpetrated by the Nazis in the name of eugenics. But there's a vast difference between "selective breeding" as practiced by totalitarian regimes (where the urge to propagate certain types of people leads to efforts to eradicate other types) and the immeasurably more benign forms already practiced in democratic societies (where, say, lawyers freely choose to marry other lawyers). Banks stocked with the frozen sperm of geniuses already exist. They haven't created a master race because only a tiny number of women have wanted to impregnate themselves this way. Why think it will be different if human cloning becomes available?

So who will likely take advantage of cloning? Perhaps a grieving couple whose child is dying. This might seem psychologically twisted. But a cloned child born to such dubious parents stands no greater or lesser chance of being loved, or rejected, or warped than a child normally conceived. Infertile couples are also likely to seek out cloning. That such couples have other options (in vitro fertilization or adoption) is not an argument for denying them the right to clone. Or consider an example raised by Judge Richard Posner: a couple in which the husband has some tragic genetic defect. Currently, if this couple wants a genetically related child, they have four not altogether pleasant options. They can reproduce naturally and risk passing on the disease to the child. They can go to a sperm bank and take a chance on unknown genes. They can try in vitro fertilization and dispose of any afflicted embryo—though that might be objectionable, too. Or they can get a male relative of the father to donate sperm, if such a relative exists. This is one case where even people unnerved by cloning might see it as not the worst option.

Even if human cloning offers no obvious benefits to humanity, why ban it? In a democratic society we don't usually pass laws outlawing something before there is actual or probable evidence of harm. A moratorium on further research into human cloning might make sense, in order to consider calmly the grave questions it raises. If the moratorium is then lifted, human cloning should remain a research activity for an extended period, And if it is ever attempted, it should—and no doubt will—take place only with careful scrutiny and layers of legal oversight. Most important, human cloning should be governed by the same laws that now protect human rights. A world not safe for cloned humans would be a world not safe for the rest of us.

GET A CYBERLIFE

Peggy Orenstein

This piece first appeared in Mother Jones Magazine *in 1991.*

I've never been wed to reality. I've never even been engaged to it. I'll fling myself wholeheartedly into anything that can help me forget, at least momentarily, the thrum of war, toxic waste, ecological disaster, nuclear annihilation, poverty, destitution, or the fact that the tremendous amount of effort I just put into redecorating my apartment may be for naught if the entire city that I live in shakes, rattles, and rolls into the sea. There are times when I've looked at the world's problems and wished that I could just go find another world, one I would populate only with people I like. Sometimes I'm not so sure about them. There are people out there in California's Silicon Valley, at the University of Washington in

Seattle, and at the University of North Carolina who are responding to such escapist fantasies. They're using computers to generate three-dimensional alternative environments—of, say, Tahiti to the inside of the human brain or Mars—that, at least some day, will be as photographically "real" as the room you're sitting in right now. This winter I got a preview of that future at Cyberthon, a twenty-four-hour marathon conference and demonstration of Virtual Reality, the newest, fringiest, most talked about technological boom since artificial intelligence went bust.

Standard VR gear consists of heavy, computerized, blacked-out goggles and a Lycra glove. When you move your goggled head, the computer responds by changing your perspective on the scene around you, just like in "real" reality. If you grab an image with your gloved hand, the computer notes that too and moves the image accordingly.

Some architects are using VR (also called "cyberspace," a term coined by writer William Gibson, who dreamed up VR in his novel *Neuromancer*) to show clients what a structure will look like before it's built. Doctors are using it to practice surgery without making a single cut. A cyberpunk counterculture, spearheaded by people like Brian Eno and director George Coates, is creating a whole new technology-driven spectrum of post-postmodern, nihilistic art. And, of course, NASA and the Defense Department (which hopes to replace jet pilots with VR screens) have been following—and funding—VR since its inception.

Cyberthon took place at a soundstage at the edge of San Francisco, in a specially built maze designed with a calculated irreverence toward day, night, right, left, and the entire history of empiricist philosophy. The exhibits within these virtual walls were mostly technological pupae: visual, tactile, and aural bits and bytes, which, their inventors believe, will someday achieve the sum of their parts and blossom into something revolutionary.

In the nethermost reaches of the maze I found Sense8. Among the big three VR companies (the others being VR granddaddy Virtual Programming Languages Research [VPL] and Autodesk, Inc., which caters primarily to architects), Sense8 is the cheap seats, either the lowest tech or the most practical, depending on your perspective. Whereas VPL uses two computers to generate its virtual world, Sense8 and Autodesk use only a single computer. The difference in quality is significant, and so is the difference in price: about $15,000 a pop as opposed to VPL's $250,000. (In fact, VPL declined to haul its more complex, high-wattage gear down to San Francisco for a demo.)

I waited in line impatiently for my turn at the Cyberhood, a long, View-Master-like contraption, which focuses your eyes on a computer-generated 3-D image; you manipulate yourself, or "fly," by gripping a ball to the left of the machine. The ball, Sense8 president Eric Gullichsen kept repeating to the users, is like your head, think of it as your head. The trouble with that notion is that most people don't yank, twist, twirl, and push their heads, so most people were having trouble with the image: flipping it upside down, pulling their "head" back so far that the image became tiny and distant, hitting the floor with their wide-open eyeballs.

The man in front of me, a shortish, plump guy in a blue shirt and jeans, was muttering to himself as he yanked at his "head." Finally he gave in and straightened up. He turned out to be Robin Williams, but no one paid much attention in this crowd—the machines were the celebrities.

I asked him what it was like.

"Try it," he said, then dropped his voice to a Bela Lugosi whisper. "Don't be scared."

Was it fun?

"Yeah," he said, unconvincingly. "In a vertigo kind of way."

In the Cyberhood I saw a room with a purple-and-chartreuse linoleum floor. There was a red chair, a brown desk, preternaturally blue walls, a book, a lamp, a painting on the wall. None of it looked particularly "real." It looked flat and cartoonish—I've heard it compared to Toontown, a sort of two-dimensional three-dimensionality, if you can grok that.

I yanked my "head" and moved in on the chair. Suddenly the purple-and-green floor cracked me in the "face." I pulled back and the whole thing flipped over. I took a deep breath and steadied myself. I'm not very good at Nintendo either. To my right (my real right, not my virtual right) there was a joystick. I hit the button and a red-and-white-checked missile flew down from the ceiling and bounced on the floor. A woman's rude laugh followed. Gullichsen explained that you're supposed to move the joystick to make the missiles hit the target. I tried again; this time a yellow airplane came out and I manipulated it toward the chair. It hit and exploded with a crash of broken glass.

I'd had enough.

Back in the real room, Gullichsen introduced me to Alison Kennedy, a.k.a. Queen Mu, the "domineditrix" of the sporadically published cyberpunk rag *Mondo2000* as well as the anthropologist who first explained that licking a certain genus of toad can induce a hallucinogenic experience. Genuinely pleased to initiate a sister-in-publishing into the VR scene, she broke into a wide, ethereal grin and invited me to visit her house in the Berkeley hills once she returned from a Druid festival in Graz. Queen Mu and her stunning smile seem to have many of the VR boys wrapped like the gold bracelet around her upper arm. The new cyberians all publish in *M2*, which is as hot hot hot as Mickey Rourke and Jerry Lewis in France and Japan.

She was chatting with Stephen Beck about his Virtual Light exhibit, which wasn't working (and never did). Virtual Light? I asked. Don't we already have that? Isn't it called the light bulb?

"I guess you could think of it that way," Beck answered thoughtfully. "But no, the light bulb is artificial light. This is Virtual Light. You can see it with your eyes closed."

"I can see electric light with my eyes closed."

At this, Beck launched into a long explanation of Virtual Light, the only word of which I recognized was "photon." And I'm not quite sure what that means.

By now I was hungry, so I strolled over to the virtual eating exhibit that a group of local art students had set up. I didn't know what to expect—perhaps it could make me feel virtually full. Perhaps no calories would be involved. There was a reservation book graced with a real red rose outside the closed-off room. I wrote my name down. There was a ten- to fifteen-minute wait for a table. Just like real life, I thought. I wondered where I could get a virtual Stoli while I waited.

I told the man in front of me in line, a guy with a stringy ponytail down to the center of his back, that I had done Virtual Reality. He asked how it was. I told him the most exciting thing about it was that Robin Williams was next to me.

"You mean you were virtually with Robin Williams? That's great!"

No, I tried to explain, he was really next to me.

"You mean virtually really, or really really?"

I began to get a headache.

"Robin Williams was actually next to me, in line, waiting for a turn on the machine."

Mr. Ponytail looked crestfallen. "Well, did he say anything funny?" he asked, perking up some.

Virtual eating turned out to be a bunch of 3-D video images of food, projected onto a plate-shaped screen. A well-rounded meal, yes, but inedible.

Since I was already experiencing a taste of the third dimension, I hustled over to something called a Flying Mouse. If you've ever used an Apple computer, you know that you move the cursor with something that does not resemble but is nevertheless called a mouse. You move the mouse up and down to make the cursor move up and down, left and right to move the cursor back and forth. If you're feeling really crazy, you can spin the mouse in a circle, but that's about the most exciting effect you could achieve. Up until now.

The Flying Mouse is shaped like a manta ray and operates in 3-D. Simgraphics president Steve Tice called up a double image of Gumby's twin sister on screen and handed me a pair of LCD glasses. The lenses blink so rapidly—sixty times a second—that the eye can't perceive it. Suddenly, the two images on the screen merged into one three-dimensional figure. I could move her back and forth and up and down the conventional way, but, by lifting the mouse up off the table, I could also pull her out toward my face, push her back deep into the screen, or make her legs and arms kick and twist in agony. And when I "selected" a body part, I felt a tingly pressure on my index finger—tactile feedback! It didn't reflect notions of hard or soft or round or sharp, but I definitely felt like I'd touched something.

Habitat, an interactive, two-dimensional, animated program originally designed for Commodore computers, touched something in me, too. Like a raw nerve. To its users, Habitat is clearly much more than a computer game: it's truly an alternative universe, a mythical place where cartoon figures representing users throughout the country travel about, talk via typed overhead balloons, earn "money" through entrepreneurial ventures to purchase various luxury items, and observe strict codes of etiquette (if someone talks to you, it's rude not to talk back). Habitat users, programmer Randy Farmer explained to me, can go to a head shop and trade in their heads and bodies for new ones. Farmer himself had a large, blue dragon head. On screen, that is. In real life, he conformed to the stereotype of a hacker: shaggy hair, scruffy clothes, glasses, bad skin, paunchy.

And self-aware: "A lot of these people," he told me, "buy Marilyn Monroe heads, or Robert Redford heads, or some other gorgeous head-body combination. But the truth is, the kind of people who stare into a computer screen for hours and hours a day probably aren't the most beautiful people. On the outside, anyway. They're beautiful on the inside. So sometimes you meet one of these people who've represented themselves with these beautiful faces, and you're disappointed. You think, 'Oh, she doesn't look like Marilyn Monroe at all.' I figure, if I have a monster head and someone meets me someday, I come out ahead. The way I really look won't seem so bad."

As he talked, two figures appeared on the screen, a "man" with a nondescript head and body (all the men's bodies are nondescript, all the women's bodies have huge breasts and wasp waists. Guess which gender designed Habitat?) who said he was from Nebraska, and a headless female with major mamambas from North Carolina.

The man reached out and grabbed the woman's breasts. "Nice boobs," he said.

Randy told me the gesture was bad form, but then again, so was walking around without a head. In the meantime, the woman had begun to talk.

"I'm a man, you idiot," she said.

"What's with the boobs, then?" typed man number one, in consternation.

"They're muscles. Now get off 'em."

Let's talk about the birds and the cyberbees. Everyone I told about Cyberthon (including the editors of *Mother Jones*) asked if virtual sex was possible. At first I thought maybe that was just the kind of lowlife I hang around with, but during a question-and-answer session later that night, Jaron Lanier—the thirty-one-year-old founder of VPL, who is renowned for his spherical belly and the light-brown, lichen-like dreadlocks that sprout from his visionary skull—rolled his eyes when he was asked what he calls "the sex question."

But "the sex question" is really a misnomer. These guys, the bedrock of this new technology, didn't, and don't, really ask "the sex question"; they ask "the porn question": they don't want to know how to enhance intimacy with a partner; they want to know if they can make that Habitat babe 3-D and then spend all day feeling her virtual breasts.

There's even a word for VR sex: "dildonics." Note the emphasis here. It's not ovanics, or clitonics, or even cybersex. Dildonics. And Lanier, who has struggled to keep his Virtual Reality squeaky-clean, denied that people will want to use his machine for dildonic ends. "VR won't be used successfully as a porn media," he insisted. "Porn is cinema and photography that leaves something to the imagination. Completely knowing makes you deal with what's really on your plate. The reality here, the virtual reality, is that you'd have a girl made of polygons. And no one wants to have sex with a bunch of polygons."

Lanier went on to tout VR as a great equalizer. "Virtual Reality is the ultimate lack of class or race distinctions or any other form of pretense, since all form is variable," he said. In VR, said Lanier, gender, race, age— all become invention. You can be who or even what you want. If you can choose your form, you don't have to make it a human one: you can appear as a cat, a table, a piano. He told the crowd that, because VR is interactive, it can be community-enhancing, like the telephone or the light bulb, rather than reinforcing the numbing alienation of the television. "We live in this very weird time in history where we're passive recipients of a very immature, noninteractive broadcast media," he said. "Mission number one is to kill TV."

Someone commented that Nintendo is interactive, but it doesn't seem like a stride toward establishing an authentic electronic community.

"Nintendo is a little interactive," Lanier corrected. "You're being guided down a narrow set of predetermined possibilities, like a rat in a maze. VR is an endless range. If we're going to call Nintendo interactive, then I want a different word for VR."

Throughout Cyberthon, William Gibson played Darth Vader to Lanier's Luke Skywalker. His vision of Virtual Reality, as articulated in *Neuromancer,* was a bleak one, in which those unfortunate enough to be mired in the physical world were called "meat" by those who roamed the cyberrange. When someone subsequently asked *him* whether he believed VR could be an electronic utopia, he shot back, "I think it could be lethal, like freebasing American TV." Disheveled, hunched over, looking like he'd rather be out back smoking, Gibson leaned into the microphone. "I don't think that anyone who read my book seems to have understood it," he said in his adenoidal twang. "It was supposed to be ironic. The book was really a metaphor about how I felt about the media. I didn't expect anyone to actually go out and build one of these things."

You want VR? Try staying among black-walled mazes for eighteen hours straight. Try making a Jif peanut butter and generic white bread sandwich in "Mom's Kitchen," assuming Mom was just thawed after being cryonically frozen in 1932 (and, given this crowd, that's a pretty fair assumption). Walk into a big room at 3 A.M. and have Timothy Leary tell you all reality is virtual. Believe him.

At six in the morning, Kit Galloway, the ponytailed artist whose "Electronic Cafe" provides communal video-telephone hookups in public places, free of charge, got up to speak. He suggested that cyber-elitism could be avoided by using the technology we already have. "To get into computer-shared electronic space, you need to be rich," he said to a bleary-eyed but attentive audience. "The telephone has all kinds of potential. There are gridlocks in the cities, and people can't run around the country in jet planes, punching holes in the ozone, for an ecology conference in Chicago—it doesn't make sense. Why not telecommute or teleconference by videophone? Telephones are the only thing that will get cheaper—they're our magic, our epitaph."

Galloway said that the new technology we need to achieve VR's grand claims could be found in the least likely places, and, just before breakfast, I discovered he was right. Chris Hardman, whose Antenna Theater produces taped tours that re-create the pivotal events of historical sites like Dallas's School Book Depository, was exhibiting his virtual jump off the Golden Gate Bridge.

I strapped on a Walkman and stood by a waist-high cadmium-red-painted wooden fence overlooking a blue plastic ocean. Voices came from all sides—a soft, seductive man's voice telling me: "Tense your shoulders, clench your fists. Relax your shoulders. Don't look down. Don't look down . . . look down. Put one foot on the rail. Feel the rail. . . . " A nasal, Brooklyn-accented woman's voice relating the story of her averted suicide: "So he said: 'You're gonna jump? So jump. I haven't got all day.' And I said: 'You shit! I'm going to kill myself, and you're not going to stay here and talk to me?'" A young, angry woman, out for a walk on the bridge to get some air. . . . "Don't look down. Look down." The voices rising like so many waves, swirling together, repeating themselves, urging me up and over the rail. . . .

". . . Everyone jumps off the east side. Why? They face the city. You jump off the west side, you face nothing as you go down. . . ."

". . . What keeps you from doing it is, what if you changed your mind halfway down? That would be horrible."

". . . Don't look down. Look down."

". . . If you don't do it, it's okay. Because after that, everything is a gift. Everything in life that comes after is a gift. . . ."

As I listened, the fog rolled out of machines; the plastic ocean covering a soft mattress beckoned.

Some of the people around me climbed the wooden railing.

Some people jumped.

I did not, although I'm not sure why. Shyness, perhaps. Or maybe the spell was broken by the sound of bodies crunching on plastic instead of being swallowed silently by waves. Or maybe the whole thing was, finally, just too real.

I came to Cyberthon curious, but terribly smug (indeed superior) in my neoluddism. By daybreak, though, I was convinced that people who care about media, art, and education shouldn't just pass this off as the latest trend among techno-weenies with weird hair. This time, we have the chance to enter the debate about the direction of a revolutionary technology, before that debate has been decided for us.

How to do that is, of course, hard to say, if you're the kind of person who still hasn't mastered all ten function keys on your PC. During a panel on the social implications of VR, a woman who identified herself as an artist and educator stepped up to the microphone and announced, "Who gets to use this should be part of the design."

It was a nice idea, and everyone agreed, but the discussion went no further. How could it? You can't prevent technology from being abused. There will be those who use VR rudely, stupidly, dangerously—just as they do the telephone or the computer. Like the telephone and the modem, its popular rise will also eliminate the need for certain fundamental kinds of human contact, even as it enhances our ability to communicate. That's not comforting, but it is inevitable, and worth noting. At the very least, Cyberthon, where nontechnicians—teachers, artists, and writers—were included in the discourse, gave me hope that if we all are plugged into VR someday, there's a possibility that more than just one hand will control the switch.

Before I left Cyberthon, I watched the crowd around Atari's Hard Drivin' computer game. Drivers were surrounded on three sides by screens, which projected various racecourse scenes. They drove as fast as they could around curves (watch those cows!), through loops (accelerate . . . now!), along straightaways (gun it, man, gun it!). When they crashed, the computer showed an instant replay from the third-person perspective. As it turns out, it's a lot more fun (not to mention boffo yucks) to watch devastation from the outside. I watched the game for half an hour, then walked into the bright light of what I still perceive as the real world and hopped into my car.

As I rode down the freeway, I found myself going a little faster than usual, edging my curves a little sharper, coming a little closer than was really comfortable to the truck merging in the lane ahead of me. Maybe I was just tired. It had been a long night. But maybe it just doesn't take the mind that long to grab onto the new and make it real. Even when you don't want it to.

FLAMERS

—■—

Gary Chapman

The New Republic *published this essay on April 10, 1995.*

A joke floating around the Internet:
Q: How many Internet contributors does it take to change a lightbulb?
A: What are you trying to say, you worthless, scumbag jerk?

Computer networks are increasingly hyped as a new medium of virtuous democratic and social discourse, the cyber-version of the Acropolis. A *Time* magazine reviewer recently called the Internet "the ultimate salon" of conversation, and *The Utne Reader* is promising "electronic salons" to soothe the anomie and coarseness of contemporary life. Author Howard Rheingold has celebrated the "virtual community" as a source of solace and fraternity, and columnist David Broder has written paeans to the new spirit of civic participation allegedly found on computer networks.

Electronic conversations—if that's what they are to be called—on the Internet and various other computer networks such as America Online, Prodigy and CompuServe, are certainly a new and interesting feature of American social life and manners. The terabytes of gab on these systems, engaging millions of people, are perhaps the first display of the direct voice of the American people in an ongoing, semi-organized, public forum. People are talking about everything under the sun—politics, pet care, even deliberate gibberish. Consequently, politicians, pollsters, reporters, marketers and social analysts are keenly interested in what our fellow citizens are thinking and saying on-line. Electronic conversations, to our benefit, allow people to circumvent the managed public dialogue that politicians and P.R.-types try to shape to serve their own ends.

But the evidence of public virtue in cyberspace is so far more discouraging and alarming than noble and salutary. Electronic salons already contain broken furniture and have mud on their walls. The notorious phenomenon of "flaming"—issuing a nasty and often profane diatribe—is now a familiar sociological curiosity. UseNet news groups—open, topical conversations accessible over the Internet and other systems—have become vast libraries of pyrotechnic insults. Mark Dery, editor of a new book, *Flame Wars,* offers a few choice examples: "You syphilitic bovine harpy." "You heaving purulent mammoth." "You twitching gelatinous yolk of rancid smegma." You get the idea. Many retorts are merely terse, obscene snarls, but Internet users have also developed a competition in rococo, smart-alecky taunts, such as this one: "Your reply was most impressive. You seem to have the ability to respond to mail with either profanity, inanity or pointless threats of physical violence. Why don't you try those pills the doctor gave you, and take a nice long rest. It may do you no good, but I am sure the remainder of the viewers would be pleased by the absence of your moronic and asinine diatribes." It's hard to imagine such exchanges at a PTA meeting or a cocktail party. Electronic communication is providing a disturbing glimpse of what may be smoldering, heretofore unsaid, in the minds of many Americans.

More generally, electronic conversations appear to be prone to misinterpretation, sudden and rapidly escalating hostility between the participants, and a weird kind of implosion when the conversants express their anger with sulking silence. This may be because, unlike in face-to-face conversation, there are no visual cues, what linguist Peter Farb calls "paralanguage." It may also be because people who are completely removed from one another physically can assault each other verbally without fear of bodily harm, a suggestion that our evolutionary heritage is still at work in restraining our behavior in everyday encounters.

Electronic anonymity also encourages fantasy life, often tilting toward the dark side. Dedicated network denizens frequently inhabit alter egos attached to their computer names. Some computer users have identities in cyberspace that correspond to exotic names, such as Phreak or Acid, two well-known hacker monikers, rather than to their prosaically named real-world personae. While a middle-class, suburban white man may tend not to adopt a *nom d'ordinateur,* millions of electronic Walter Mittys nationwide do take on a more aggressive personality behind a computer and a modem—ferociously pouring out their otherwise sublimated middle-class angst.

A cyberspace alter ego often goes beyond a new name and a release of inhibition. Network users lie, sometimes spectacularly. Pavel Curtis, a Xerox researcher who runs a fascinating Multi-User Dimension (or MUD)—a kind of a "virtual world" within the Internet with its own simulated geography, characters and interactions—reports that a significant portion of people logging into his system switch genders for the identities they assume. Most common are young men who portray themselves as women; indeed, it's become a rule of thumb that any sexually aggressive female on this MUD is really a man. Peter Lewis, *The New York Times*'s cyberspace reporter, tells a story about a man who conducted a protracted and intimate electronic romance over the Internet with a pen pal, who said she was a 26-year-old graduate student. When he met her in person, he learned that she was in fact a 13-year-old girl.

As the French discovered in their national Minitel system, sex often dominates electronic encounters. The majority of messages on Minitel have been advertisements for sex or sex talk, and, national character notwithstanding, Americans are no slackers in this regard. Computer communication seems to bring out the id screaming for attention. In

February, a University of Michigan student, Jake Baker, was arrested for posting to the university's computer network a graphic fantasy of the rape, torture and murder of a fellow student; though such stories are common on a few news groups, Baker actually named his victim, which police interpreted as a threat. A reporter for *Computer Life* magazine posed on the Internet as a 15-year-old cheerleader and got more than thirty e-mail messages of a sexual nature, including requests for her panties and her telephone number. Harassment of women is so common that women often pretend to be men to avoid sexually suggestive e-mail.

Bigotry and misogyny are prevalent as well. As Amy Harmon noted recently in *The Los Angeles Times,* bigots are showing up on computer networks with increasing frequency because they can't get a hearing anywhere else. Networks are a cheap means for white supremacists and neo-Nazis to get their hate messages to thousands of people at once. The Simon Wiesenthal Center has protested to Prodigy about frequent anti-Semitic rants on that system. Prodigy officials are caught, to their embarrassment, in a tug-of-war between freedom of speech and the basic civilities that many users expect.

Finally, the general quality of the rhetoric on the Internet is discouraging in itself. Even without all the cranks, poseurs, charlatans, fetishists, single-issue monomaniacs, sex-starved lonely hearts, mischievous teenagers, sexists, racists and right-wing haranguers, many participants in unstructured Internet conversations have little of interest to say but a lot of room in which to say it. Goofy opinions and comical disregard for facts are rampant. Spelling is haphazard and even simple typos sometimes produce absurd flaming firefights. Nearly every reasonable discussion is sooner or later discovered by someone with a hobby horse or an abrasive personality or both, and there are few reliable ways to shunt such people elsewhere. It's pretty clear, too, that quite a few messages come from people who must be drunk; there are as yet no sobriety checkpoints on the "information superhighway." The new electronic Acropolis seems to foster rhetoric stylistically closer to Beavis and Butthead than to Pericles.

Fifteen years ago, the forerunner of the Internet, the Arpanet, was used almost exclusively by top computer scientists and other elite engineers and scientists, who tend to be a refined bunch, partial to classical music and good books. Many are now appalled by what networking has become. Some have dropped off the net altogether.

This suggests that the Internet may be on a path similar to that followed by television and other communications media: the introduction of the masses so alienates well-educated, cosmopolitan people that they abandon the medium or resort to a specialized class of cultural material that advertises its disdain for mass tastes. There are already signs that this is happening on the Internet: while veterans of the net have tended to narrow their presence to a select group of exclusive and low-profile mailing lists, more recent users are complaining loudly about the influx of hundreds of thousands of newcomers via America Online, "newbies" who are stumbling around the net asking greenhorn questions and committing faux pas of "netiquette." Many people with pressing schedules are starting to regard the cacophonous noise as a waste of time. Their exits raise the proportion of nuts, creeps and boors. Thus an inevitable backlash against the lofty hype surrounding the Internet is building, such as in Cliff Stoll's new book, *Silicon Snake Oil: Second Thoughts on the Information Highway.*

This all sounds like an anti-democratic trend, in contrast to the democratization that computer networks are supposed to both exemplify and support. Is cyberspace already sorting itself into two camps, a jaded, invisible elite and a teeming mass of wrassling rubes? This image wouldn't be unusual in the history of American popular culture. It seems clear that cultural polarization and low behavior in cyberspace reflect trends in American society as a whole, but the peculiar features of computer communication are amplifying the decline of our national mores and manners, and, at the same time, giving us an unprecedented bird's-eye view of what we've become.

Of course, we can always hope that computer networks are undergoing a metamorphosis from childhood to adolescence these days, with an anticipated maturation into adulthood sometime in the future. We'll have to develop manners in cyberspace just as we have in our everyday, real-world encounters, and that could entail a long process of evolution and refinement. If we don't develop virtual manners, cyberspace will continue to resemble a mud wrestling event. But if we can treat each other with respect over e-mail, we may go a long way toward solving some of the basic dilemmas of democracy.

WHEN I HEARD THE LEARN'D ASTRONOMER

Walt Whitman

This poem is from the longer work Leaves of Grass, *first published in 1855.*

When I heard the learn'd astronomer,
When the proofs, the figures, were ranged in columns before me,
When I was shown the charts and diagrams, to add, divide, and measure them,
When I sitting heard the astronomer where he lectured with much applause in
    the lecture-room,
How soon unaccountable I became tired and sick,
Till rising and gliding out I wander'd off by myself,
In the mystical moist night-air, and from time to time,
Look'd up in perfect silence at the stars.

THE TABLES TURNED

William Wordsworth

This poem was first published in 1850.

Up! up! my friend, and clear your looks,
Why all this toil and trouble?
Up! up! my friend, and quit your books,
Or surely you'll grow double.

The sun above the mountain's head,
A freshening lustre mellow,
Through all the long green fields has spread,
His first sweet evening yellow.

Books! 'tis a dull and endless strife,
Come, hear the woodland linnet,
How sweet his music; on my life
There's more of wisdom in it.

And hark! how blithe the throstle sings!
And he is no mean preacher;
Come forth into the light of things,
Let Nature be your teacher.

She has a world of ready wealth,
Our minds and hearts to bless—
Spontaneous wisdom breathed by health,
Truth breathed by chearfulness.

One impulse from a vernal wood
May teach you more of man;
Of moral evil and of good,
Than all the sages can.

Sweet is the lore which nature brings;
Our meddling intellect
Mis-shapes the beauteous forms of things;
—We murder to dissect.

Enough of science and of art;
Close up these barren leaves;
Come forth, and bring with you a heart
That watches and receives.

THE GERNSBACK CONTINUUM

Willam Gibson

"The Gernsback Continuum," first published in Universe II *in 1981, was reprinted in the collection* Burning Chrome *(1986).*

Mercifully, the whole thing is starting to fade, to become an episode. When I do still catch the odd glimpse, it's peripheral; mere fragments of mad-doctor chrome, confining themselves to the corner of the eye. There was that flying-wing liner over San Francisco last week, but it was almost translucent. And the shark-fin roadsters have gotten scarcer, and freeways discreetly avoid unfolding themselves into the gleaming eighty-lane monsters I was forced to drive last month in my rented Toyota. And I know that none of it will follow me to New York; my vision is narrowing to a single wavelength of probability. I've worked hard for that. Television helped a lot.

I suppose it started in London, in that bogus Greek taverna in Battersea Park Road, with lunch on Cohen's corporate tab. Dead steam-table food and it took them thirty minutes to find an ice bucket for the retsina. Cohen works for Barris-Watford, who publish big, trendy "trade" paperbacks: illustrated histories of the neon sign, the pinball machine, the windup toys of Occupied Japan. I'd gone over to shoot a series of shoe ads; California girls with tanned legs and frisky Day-Glo jogging shoes had capered for me down the escalators of St. John's Wood and across the platforms of Tooting Bec. A lean and hungry young agency had decided that the mystery of London Transport would sell waffle-tread nylon runners. They decide; I shoot. And Cohen, whom I knew vaguely from the old days in New York, had invited me to lunch the day before I was due out of Heathrow. He brought along a very fashionably dressed young woman named Dialta Downes, who was virtually chinless and evidently a noted pop-art historian. In retrospect, I see her walking in beside Cohen under a floating neon sign that flashes THIS WAY LIES MADNESS in huge sans-serif capitals.

Cohen introduced us and explained that Dialta was the prime mover behind the latest Barris-Watford project, an illustrated history of what she called "American Streamlined Modern." Cohen called it "raygun Gothic." Their working title was *The Airstream Futuropolis: The Tomorrow That Never Was.*

There's a British obsession with the more baroque elements of American pop culture, something like the weird cowboys-and-Indians fetish of the West Germans or the aberrant French hunger for old Jerry Lewis films. In Dialta Downes this manifested itself in a mania for a uniquely American form of architecture that most Americans are scarcely aware of. At first I wasn't sure what she was talking about, but gradually it began to dawn on me. I found myself remembering Sunday morning television in the Fifties.

Sometimes they'd run old eroded newsreels as filler on the local station. You'd sit there with a peanut butter sandwich and a glass of milk, and a static-ridden Hollywood baritone would tell you that there was A Flying Car in Your Future. And three Detroit engineers would putter around with this big old Nash with wings, and you'd see it rumbling furiously down some deserted Michigan runway. You never actually saw it take off, but it flew away to Dialta Downes's never-never land, true home of a generation of completely uninhibited technophiles. She was talking about those odds and ends of "futuristic" Thirties and Forties architecture you pass daily in American cities without noticing; the movie marquees ribbed to radiate some mysterious energy, the dime stores faced with fluted aluminum, the chrome-tube chairs gathering dust in the lobbies of transient hotels. She saw these things as segments of a dreamworld, abandoned in the uncaring present; she wanted me to photograph them for her.

The Thirties had seen the first generation of American industrial designers; until the Thirties, all pencil sharpeners had looked like pencil sharpeners—your basic Victorian mechanism, perhaps with a curlicue of decorative trim. After the advent of the designers, some pencil sharpeners looked as though they'd been put together in wind tunnels. For the most part, the change was only skin-deep; under the streamlined chrome shell, you'd find the same Victorian mechanism. Which made a certain kind of sense, because the most successful American designers had been recruited from the ranks of Broadway theater designers. It was all a stage set, a series of elaborate props for playing at living in the future.

Over coffee, Cohen produced a fat manila envelope full of glossies. I saw the winged statues that guard the Hoover Dam, forty-foot concrete hood ornaments leaning steadfastly into an imaginary hurricane. I saw a dozen shots of Frank Lloyd Wright's Johnson's Wax Building, juxtaposed with the covers of old *Amazing Stories* pulps, by an artist named Frank R. Paul; the employees of Johnson's Wax must have felt as though they were walking into one of Paul's spray-paint pulp utopias. Wright's building looked as though it had been designed for people who wore white togas and Lucite sandals. I hesitated over one sketch of a particularly grandiose prop-driven airliner, all wing, like a fat symmetrical boomerang with windows in unlikely places. Labeled arrows indicated the locations of the grand ballroom and two squash courts. It was dated 1936.

"This thing couldn't have flown . . . ?" I looked at Dialta Downes,

"Oh, no, quite impossible, even with those twelve giant props; but they loved the look, don't you see? New York to London in less than two days, first-class dining rooms, private cabins, sun decks, dancing to jazz in the evening . . . The designers were populists, you see; they were trying to give the public what it wanted. What the public wanted was the future."

I'd been in Burbank for three days, trying to suffuse a really dull-looking rocker with charisma, when I got the package from Cohen. It is possible to photograph what isn't there; it's damned hard to do, and consequently a very marketable talent. While I'm not bad at it, I'm not exactly the best, either, and this poor guy strained my Nikon's credibility. I got out, depressed because I do like to do a good job, but not totally depressed, because I did make sure I'd gotten the check for the job, and I decided to restore myself with the sublime artiness of the Barris-Watford assignment. Cohen had sent me some books on Thirties design, more photos of streamlined buildings, and a list of Dialta Downes's fifty favorite examples of the style in California.

Architectural photography can involve a lot of waiting; the building becomes a kind of sundial, while you wait for a shadow to crawl away from a detail you want, or for the mass and balance of the structure to reveal itself in a certain way. While I was waiting, I thought myself in Dialta Downes's America. When I isolated a few of the factory buildings on the ground glass of the Hasselblad, they came across with a kind of sinister totalitarian dignity, like the stadiums Albert Speer built for Hitler. But the rest of it was relentlessly tacky: ephemeral stuff extruded by the collective American subconscious of the Thirties, tending mostly to survive along depressing strips lined with dusty motels, mattress wholesalers, and small used-car lots. I went for the gas stations in a big way.

During the high point of the Downes Age, they put Ming the Merciless in charge of designing California gas stations. Favoring the architecture of his native Mongo, he cruised up and down the coast erecting raygun emplacements in white stucco. Lots of them featured superfluous central towers ringed with those strange radiator flanges that were a signature motif of the style, and made them look as though they might generate potent bursts of raw technological enthusiasm, if you could only find the switch that turned them on. I shot one in San Jose an hour before the bulldozers arrived and drove right through the structural truth of plaster and lathing and cheap concrete.

"Think of it," Dialta Downes had said, "as a kind of alternate America: a 1980 that never happened. An architecture of broken dreams."

And that was my frame of mind as I made the stations of her convoluted socioarchitectural cross in my red Toyota—as I gradually tuned in to her image of a shadowy America-that-wasn't, of Coca-Cola plants like beached submarines, and fifth-run movie houses like the temples of some lost sect that had worshiped blue mirrors and geometry. And as I moved among these secret ruins, I found myself wondering what the inhabitants of that lost future would think of the world I lived in. The Thirties dreamed white marble and slipstream chrome, immortal crystal and burnished bronze, but the rockets on the covers of the Gernsback pulps had fallen on London in the dead of night, screaming. After the war, everyone had a car—no wings for it—and the promised superhighway to drive it down, so that the sky itself darkened, and the fumes ate the marble and pitted the miracle crystal. . . .

And one day, on the outskirts of Bolinas, when I was setting up to shoot a particularly lavish example of Ming's martial architecture, I penetrated a fine membrane, a membrane of probability. . . .

Ever so gently, I went over the Edge—

And looked up to see a twelve-engined thing like a bloated boomerang, all wing, thrumming its way east with an elephantine grace, so low that I could count the rivets in its dull silver skin, and hear—maybe—the echo of jazz.

I took it to Kihn.

Merv Kihn, free-lance journalist with an extensive line in Texas pterodactyls, redneck UFO contactees, bush-league Loch Ness monsters, and the Top Ten conspiracy theories in the loonier reaches of the American mass mind.

"It's good," said Kihn, polishing his yellow Polaroid shooting glasses on the hem of his Hawaiian shirt, "but it's not *mental;* lacks the true quill."

"But I saw it, Mervyn." We were seated poolside in brilliant Arizona sunlight. He was in Tucson waiting for a group of retired Las Vegas civil servants whose leader received messages from Them on her microwave oven. I'd driven all night and was feeling it.

"Of course you did. Of course you saw it. You've read my stuff, haven't you grasped my blanket solution to the UFO problem? It's simple, plain and country simple: people"—he settled the glasses carefully on his long hawk nose and fixed me with his best basilisk glare—"*see* . . . things. People see things. Nothing's there, but people *see* them anyway. Because they need to, probably. You've read Jung, you should know the score. . . . In your case, it's so obvious: You admit you were thinking about this crackpot architecture, having fantasies. . . . Look, I'm sure you've taken your share of drugs, right? How many people survived the Sixties in California without having the odd hallucination? All those nights when you discovered that whole armies of Disney technicians had been employed to weave animated holograms of Egyptian hieroglyphs into the fabric of your jeans, say, or the times when—"

"But it wasn't like that."

"Of course not. It wasn't like that at all; it was 'in a setting of clear reality,' right? Everything normal, and then there's the monster, the mandala, the neon cigar. In your case, a giant Tom Swift airplane. It happens *all the time.* You aren't even crazy. You know that, don't you?" He fished a beer out of the battered foam cooler beside his deck chair.

"Last week I was in Virginia. Grayson County. I interviewed a sixteen-year-old girl who'd been assaulted by a *bar hade.*"

"A what?"

"A bear head. The severed head of a bear. This *bar hade,* see, was floating around on its own little flying saucer, looked kind of like the hubcaps on cousin Wayne's vintage Caddy. Had red, glowing eyes like two cigar stubs and telescoping chrome antennas poking up behind its ears." He burped.

"It assaulted her? How?"

"You don't want to know; you're obviously impressionable. 'It was cold'"—he lapsed into his bad southern accent—"'and metallic.' It made electronic noises. Now that is the real thing, the straight goods from the mass unconscious, friend; that little girl is a witch. There's just no place for her to function in this society. She'd have seen the devil, if she hadn't been brought up on 'The Bionic Man' and all those 'Star Trek' reruns. She is clued into the main vein. And she knows that it happened to her. I got out ten minutes before the heavy UFO boys showed up with the polygraph."

I must have looked pained, because he set his beer down carefully beside the cooler and sat up.

"If you want a classier explanation, I'd say you saw a semiotic ghost. All these contactee stories, for instance, are framed in a kind of sci-fi imagery that permeates our culture. I could buy aliens, but not aliens that look like Fifties' comic art. They're semiotic phantoms, bits of deep cultural imagery that have split off and taken on a life of their own, like the Jules Verne airships that those old Kansas farmers were always seeing. But you saw a different kind of ghost, that's all. That plane was part of the mass unconscious, once. You picked up on that, somehow. The important thing is not to worry about it."

I did worry about it, though.

Kihn combed his thinning blond hair and went off to hear what they had had to say over the radar range lately, and I drew the curtains in my room and lay down in air-conditioned darkness to worry about it. I was still worrying about it when I woke up. Kihn had left a note on my door; he was flying up north in a chartered plane to check out a cattle-mutilation rumor ("muties," he called them; another of his journalistic specialties).

I had a meal, showered, took a crumbling diet pill that had been kicking around in the bottom of my shaving kit for three years, and headed back to Los Angeles.

The speed limited my vision to the tunnel of the Toyota's headlights. The body could drive, I told myself, while the mind maintained. Maintained and stayed away from the weird peripheral window dressing of amphetamine and exhaustion, the spectral, luminous vegetation that grows out of the corners of the mind's eye along late-night highways. But the mind had its own ideas, and Kihn's opinion of what I was already thinking of as my "sighting" rattled endlessly through my head in a tight, lopsided orbit. Semiotic ghosts. Fragments of the Mass Dream, whirling past in the wind of my passage. Somehow this feedback-loop aggravated the diet pill, and the speed-vegetation along the road began to assume the colors of infrared satellite images, glowing shreds blown apart in the Toyota's slipstream.

I pulled over, then, and a half-dozen aluminum beer cans winked goodnight as I killed the headlights. I wondered what time it was in London, and tried to imagine Dialta Downes having breakfast in her Hampstead flat, surrounded by streamlined chrome figurines and books on American culture.

Desert nights in that country are enormous; the moon is closer. I watched the moon for a long time and decided that Kihn was right. The main thing was not to worry. All across the continent, daily, people who were more normal than I'd ever aspired to be saw giant birds, Bigfeet, flying oil refineries; they kept Kihn busy and solvent. Why should I be upset by a glimpse of the 1930s pop imagination loose over Bolinas? I decided to go to sleep, with nothing worse to worry about than rattlesnakes and cannibal hippies, safe amid the friendly roadside garbage of my own familiar continuum. In the morning I'd drive down to Nogales and photograph the old brothels, something I'd intended to do for years. The diet pill had given up.

The light woke me, and then the voices.

The light came from somewhere behind me and threw shifting shadows inside the car. The voices were calm, indistinct, male and female, engaged in conversation.

My neck was stiff and my eyeballs felt gritty in their sockets. My leg had gone to sleep, pressed against the steering wheel. I fumbled for my glasses in the pocket of my work shirt and finally got them on.

Then I looked behind me and saw the city.

The books on Thirties design were in the trunk; one of them contained sketches of an idealized city that drew on *Metropolis* and *Things to Come,* but squared everything, soaring up through an architect's perfect clouds to zeppelin docks and mad neon spires. That city was a scale model of the one that rose behind me. Spire stood on spire in gleaming ziggurat steps that climbed to a central golden temple tower ringed with the crazy radiator flanges of the Mongo gas stations. You could hide the Empire State Building in the smallest of those towers. Roads of crystal soared between the spires, crossed and recrossed by smooth silver shapes like beads of running mercury. The air was thick with ships: giant wing-liners, little darting silver things (sometimes one of the quicksilver shapes from the sky bridges rose gracefully into the air and flew up to join the dance), mile-long blimps, hovering dragonfly things that were gyrocopters . . .

I closed my eyes tight and swung around in the seat. When I opened them, I willed myself to see the mileage meter, the pale road dust on the black plastic dashboard, the overflowing ashtray.

"Amphetamine psychosis," I said. I opened my eyes. The dash was still there, the dust, the crushed filtertips. Very carefully, without moving my head, I turned the headlights on.

And saw them.

They were blond. They were standing beside their car, an aluminum avocado with a central shark-fin rudder jutting up from its spine and smooth black tires like a child's toy. He had his arm around her waist and was gesturing toward the city. They were both in white: loose clothing, bare legs, spotless white sun shoes. Neither of them seemed aware of the beams of my headlights. He was saying something wise and strong, and she was nodding, and suddenly I was frightened, frightened in an entirely different way. Sanity had ceased to be an issue; I knew, somehow, that the city behind me was Tucson—a dream Tucson thrown up out of the collective yearning of an era. That it was real, entirely real. But the couple in front of me lived in it, and they frightened me.

They were the children of Dialta Downes's '80-that-wasn't; they were Heirs to the Dream. They were white, blond, and they probably had blue eyes. They were American. Dialta had said that the Future had come to America first, but had finally passed it by. But not here, in the heart of the Dream. Here, we'd gone on and on, in a dream logic that knew nothing of pollution, the finite bounds of fossil fuel, or foreign wars it was possible to lose. They were smug, happy, and utterly content with themselves and their world. And in the Dream, it was *their* world.

Behind me, the illuminated city: Searchlights swept the sky for the sheer joy of it. I imagined them thronging the plazas of white marble, orderly and alert, their bright eyes shining with enthusiasm for their flood-lit avenues and silver cars.

It had all the sinister fruitiness of Hitler Youth propaganda.

I put the car in gear and drove forward slowly, until the bumper was within three feet of them. They still hadn't seen me. I rolled the window down and listened to what the man was saying. His words were bright and hollow as the pitch in some Chamber of Commerce brochure, and I knew that he believed in them absolutely.

"John," I heard the woman say, "we've forgotten to take our food pills." She clicked two bright wafers from a thing on her belt and passed one to him. I backed onto the highway and headed for Los Angeles, wincing and shaking my head.

I phoned Kihn from a gas station. A new one, in bad Spanish Modern. He was back from his expedition and didn't seem to mind the call.

"Yeah, that is a weird one. Did you try to get any pictures? Not that they ever come out, but it adds an interesting *frisson* to your story, not having the pictures turn out. . . ."

But what should I do?

"Watch lots of television, particularly game shows and soaps. Go to porn movies. Ever see *Nazi Love Motel?* They've got it on cable, here. Really awful. Just what you need."

What was he talking about?

"Quit yelling and listen to me. I'm letting you in on a trade secret: Really bad media can exorcise your semiotic ghosts. If it keeps the saucer

pe...   ...ods off yours. Try it.
WI

                                                         date with the Elect.

"These oldsters from Vegas; the one...   microwaves."

I considered putting a collect call through to London, getting Cohen at Barris-Watford and telling him his photographer was checked out for a protracted season in the Twilight Zone. In the end, I let a machine mix me a really impossible cup of black coffee and climbed back into the Toyota for the haul to Los Angeles.

Los Angeles was a bad idea, and I spent two weeks there. It was prime Downes country; too much of the Dream there, and too many fragments of the Dream waiting to snare me, I nearly wrecked the car on a stretch of overpass near Disneyland, when the road fanned out like an origami trick and left me swerving through a dozen minilanes of whizzing chrome teardrops with shark fins. Even worse, Hollywood was full of people who looked too much like the couple I'd seen in Arizona. I hired an Italian director who was making ends meet doing darkroom work and installing patio decks around swimming pools until his ship came in; he made prints of all the negatives I'd accumulated on the Downes job. I didn't want to look at the stuff myself. It didn't seem to bother Leonardo, though, and when he was finished I checked the prints, riffling through them like a deck of cards, sealed them up, and sent them air freight to London. Then I took a taxi to a theater that was showing *Nazi Love Motel*, and kept my eyes shut all the way.

Cohen's congratulatory wire was forwarded to me in San Francisco a week later. Dialta had loved the pictures. He admired the way I'd "really gotten into it," and looked forward to working with me again. That afternoon I spotted a flying wing over Castro Street, but there was something tenuous about it, as though it were only half there. I rushed into the nearest newsstand and gathered up as much as I could find on the petroleum crisis and the nuclear energy hazard. I'd just decided to buy a plane ticket for New York.

"Hell of a world we live in, huh?" The proprietor was a thin black man with bad teeth and an obvious wig. I nodded, fishing in my jeans for change, anxious to find a park bench where I could submerge myself in hard evidence of the human near-dystopia we live in. "But it could be worse, huh?"

"That's right," I said, "or even worse, it could be perfect."

He watched me as I headed down the street with my little bundle of condensed catastrophe.

1986

A 36-Hour Day

Renee Tietz

Renee Tietz is a freshman at the University of
Montana.

> ". . . the major diseases of human beings have
>   become approachable biological puzzles
>   ultimately solvable. Stroke and senile
>   dementia . . . are not natural aspects of the
> human condition, and we ought to rid ourselves of
>   such impediments as quickly as we can."
>   —Lewis Thomas, The Medusa and the Snail

Dementia is a condition characterized by a progressive
decline in an individual's mental abilities, most often
accompanied by changes in personality and behavior. More
specifically, senile dementia is a loss of memory and
judgment, as seen in the elderly, caused by the
deterioration of brain tissues due to arteriosclerotic
disorders. Under such conditions, the arteries begin to
harden and become less flexible, thus restricting blood
flow to the brain. Dementia is not a single disease, but
rather is seen as a form of brain damage from various
diseases, injury, or senile deterioration. It consists of
a common loss of memory and the skills needed to carry
out everyday functions. Dementia is considered a
syndrome, or cluster of symptoms, but not a consequence
of the normal process of aging.

Dementia, in a literal sense, means "deprived of mind."
It affects less than one person in a thousand under the
age of 65, but from 4 to 5 persons in one hundred over
the age of 65. Nearly two percent are affected from the
age of 65 to 75, and more than 20 percent over the age of
80 are likely to experience symptoms of dementia
(Kingshill Research Centre, n. pag.). Dementia is the
most common nursing home diagnosis, given to
approximately two-thirds of the residents.

More than 50 causes of dementia have been identified.
It can be associated with infection, tumor, toxicity, or

improper nutrition. "True" dementia is typically caused by diseases that have no known cure. Among these are Alzheimer's disease, Huntington's disease, multiple sclerosis, Parkinson's disease, and multiple infarct dementia, which is caused by repeated strokes. Alzheimer's disease is the primary cause for dementia. Postmortem studies show that 50 to 60 percent of those who experienced symptoms of dementia did in fact have Alzheimer's. (Norrgard and Kraft, n. pag.) In general, dementia is caused by an increase in damaged nerve cells in the brain. The information that was once stored and processed in these cells is unavailable for the person's use.

Theories that continue to develop help explain why an individual experiences symptoms of dementia. The first is backed by genetic reasoning. Of those diagnosed that are younger than the age of 65 or 70, frequent cases occur within families. A second theory follows the belief that the onset of dementia is caused by a "slow virus" that gradually takes over the brain. These viruses can live in the brains of people who appear healthy for 20 or more years before any signs of dementia are shown. Associated with the virus theory is that of an immunological factor. As people grow older, their immune defenses weaken. The individual becomes less able to resist viral and other infections. Still yet another theory is related to substances in the environment, for example, aluminum. Over time, these materials can form a plaque around nerve cells in the brain, possibly contributing to the development of the disease.

If a person is suspected to be suffering from dementia, many symptoms can become apparent over a period of time. The individual may become more forgetful of recent events, but will have the capability to recall the distant past. He or she will also more likely be repetitious in conversation and become less concerned with other people and activities, especially those previously enjoyed. The person may have difficulty understanding the results of one's actions, sometimes causing one to overreact and strike out unpredictably. Dementia sufferers become less able to grasp or

comprehend new ideas, are less adaptable to change, and
can be more anxious about decision making. The individual
may also become more easily irritated or upset if a task
cannot be managed, whether it be very simple or difficult.

Those affected by dementia will eventually have a
decline in their intellectual ability. For instance, they
may not remember the correct sequence of dressing and
will put their undergarments over the rest of their
clothing. These persons may also show a lack of emotion
and become less interested in occurrences around them.
Perhaps the symptom that may weigh heaviest on the family
is the forgetfulness of names and individuals, either
temporarily or altogether. In the case of a 72-year-old
man named Jim, he noticed that he was forgetting the
names of his good friends, and found himself having to
memorize names to associate with people (Bayles and
Kaszniak, pg. 205). If dementia progresses, more and more
brain cells will cease to function. The person affected
by the disease may lose voluntary control over the body,
which can lead to a difficulty in walking, sitting up
straight, or even swallowing or smiling. But the person
suffering is not responsible for these actions because
there is no brain power to decipher between right and
wrong.

In the diagnosing of dementia, the physician will
first determine what the patient does not have, rather
than what the patient has. Studies indicate that 10 to 33
percent of adults with characteristics of dementia suffer
from a condition that has a reversible cause (Bayles and
Kaszniak, 1987). It is best to seek help early on and
begin by eliminating the treatable causes. One factor
that distinguishes reversible dementias from irreversible
dementias is that in irreversible cases, there are
structural changes in the brain. The physician will look
for symptoms such as increased forgetfulness and
confusion, difficulty in concentrating, and a lack of
concern for the patient's appearance. They will also look
for an increase in restlessness, irritability, agitation,
depression, wandering, and hallucinating.

To determine it a treatable disease is present, the
physician will perform various tests. These tests

include: a mental status test, a blood test, an EEG
(electroencephalogram, or brain wave tracing), an EKG
(electrocardiogram, or heart tracing), or a head CT scan
(computerized tomography, or brain scan). The mental
status test most often used is known as the Mental Status
Questionnaire (MSQ). Physicians use this method to
determine the patient's degree of confusion. The test
consists of ten simple questions that have proven to be
good indicators of the patient's alertness, recognition
of time and place, and recent and remote memory.

The MSQ questions are:

* Where are we now?
* Where is this place located?
* What is today's date?
* What month is it?
* What year is it?
* How old are you?
* When is your birthday?
* What year were you born?
* Who is the president of the United States?
* Who was the president before him?

A score of 9 to 10 correct means the patient is not
confused; 6 to 8, slightly confused; 3 to 5, moderately
confused; and 0 to 2, severely confused (Bair, pg. 14).
The physician will carefully observe the patient's
performance and behavior, concentrating less on the
person's overall knowledge.

Upon completion of the Mental Status Questionnaire,
the physician may ask the patient to repeat a list of
three items and remember them. After a lapse of five
minutes, the patient will be asked to repeat those items
again. The physician may also ask the patient to make
monetary change, count backward from 100 by 7s, interpret
proverbs, or explain cartoons. Once again, the physician
is focusing mainly on the patient's performance and
behavior.

Another test that is often used is referred to as the
Face-Hand Test. During this procedure, the physician sits
facing the patient. The patient is asked to close his or
her eyes and place the hands on the knees. The physician
strokes the patient's cheek, while at the same time

stroking the back of one hand. The face-hand combinations are alternated: right cheek and left hand, left cheek and right hand, right cheek and right hand, and left cheek and left hand. The patient is asked to tell which hand and which cheek are being touched. The physician may repeat the process with the patient's eyes open, but 80 percent of those who perform poorly when their eyes are closed do no better (Bair, pg. 16).

As more research is completed, innovations are being made in the mechanisms used to test an individual's mental state. One such method is the improved CT scanning technique used to trace blood flow in the brain. It is useful in studying multiple infarct dementia and other neurological disorders. One of the newest research tools is a method of recording brain images known as positron emission tomography (PET). By using this technique, physicians are able to observe what parts of the brain are active during certain mental activities. Researchers are then able to use the results and compare a normal brain with the brain of a patient with a dementing illness.

Though many tests exist that can determine an individual's mental capabilities, no known physical or psychological tests exist to definitely diagnose a person with dementia. A true diagnosis is only possible if an autopsy is done on the brain after the person's death.

When an individual is known to be suffering from dementia, certain behaviors may become increasingly noticeable as the disease progresses. These behaviors, known as <u>agitated behaviors</u>, range from moderate to severe (Sachdev, pg. 25). They include hostility, aggression, and destructiveness. The person may be disruptive of others' activities, show an increase in uncooperativeness, or be noncompliant with someone's requests. Dementia sufferers can display episodes of attention-seeking behaviors, much like those of a young child. Their actions may be sexually inappropriate, or they may inflict injury on themselves. These agitated behaviors can be aggressive or nonaggressive, and are usually more frequent when the individual is experiencing pain.

Those who suffer from dementia will usually experience many emotions associated with their illness. Most often, these persons will feel very confused. They realize that something is happening to their ability to work, but they are not sure what it is or why it is happening. These persons may also feel frustration when it becomes evident that they cannot do things they previously could. They can become angry at their impairment of abilities and develop fear from their loss of memory. Because progression of dementia varies, these persons will usually feel uncertain and unsure of what to expect. They may experience grief or depression due to their deteriorating state.

There are no known cures for dementias or brain deterioration, but there are medications that can help in slowing the process and improving the lives of those who are diagnosed with the syndrome. So far, two drugs have been approved to treat Alzheimer's disease: Cognex and Aricept. Both work by increasing the availability of a brain chemical called acetylcholine, which is a nerve-impulse transmitter involved in memory. They do not cure the disease, but do produce improvement for a time in some patients. Also available are prescription tranquilizers and antidepressants which help reduce anxiety, control outbursts, and improve the patient's mood. Vitamin E, aspirin, and other anti-inflammatory drugs may also slow the progression of dementing illnesses.

Some years ago, Dutch investigators began working with the hormone vasopressin, which is produced by the pituitary gland. The hormone was used in learning experiments with rats. The rats received mild electric shock if they made a wrong turn in a simple T-shaped maze. If the rats were given vasopressin shortly after exploring the maze, their memories improved when placed back in the course. Through these animal studies, vasopressin was shown to improve the process by which memories are stored in the brain and to increase the recall of events.

Another method of treatment involves nutrition, or diet therapy. The enzyme needed to produce acetylcholine is in short supply in dementia sufferers. Patients are given foods rich in the raw materials that make up acetylcholine. Results of diet therapy have been inconclusive, showing no proof that the treatment is beneficial.

Most important throughout the progression of dementia is the care that the patient receives, though it can be a very time-consuming and emotional process for the caregiver. "It's like a 36-hour day," as one man described it (Bair, pg. 154). Individuals suffering from dementia need much family support and flexibility in care. Many voluntary health organizations provide counseling and therapy for the patient and the family. Patients are encouraged to learn to help themselves. They are aided in relearning everyday activities, which stimulates them and encourages independence. Patients are also urged to exercise to reduce anxiety and restlessness. New facilities offer services for the diagnosis and research of dementia. Among them are the memory disorder clinic at the New England Medical Center in Boston, and the Center for the Study of Dementia at the Johns Hopkins University School of Medicine in Baltimore. Early treatment and positive caring techniques can slow the decline of a person's mental abilities.

Dementia is not a consequence of the normal process of aging. Aging does not necessarily mean mental decline. Too many people today believe that aging is a disease, but the myths of former years are beginning to fade, due to facts drawn from continuing research. Dementia patients need to be reassured that life can still be enjoyed and that people will go on caring regardless of the problem. The belief that getting old means getting senile is simply not true.

Works Cited

1. Bayles, Kathryn and Kaszniak, Alfred. <u>Communication and Cognition in Normal Aging and Dementia</u>. Boston: Little, Brown and Company, 1987

2. Channing L. Bete Co., Inc. (1997), <u>About Alzheimer's Disease</u>, pamphlet

3. Encyclopedia America (Vol. 8) Connecticut: Grolier Inc. (1995) pgs. 681–682

4. Health Reference Series Vol. 2, <u>Alzheimer's, Stroke, and 29 Other Neurological Disorders Sourcebook</u>, Bair, Frank E., Omnigraphics, Inc. (1993), pgs. 13–18, 137–155, 534–538

5. Kahn, Carol. "New Drugs and Hope for Alzheimer's Patients." <u>Parade</u> magazine (Nov. 8, 1998), pgs. 16–18

6. Kingshill Research Centre. "Dementia: What it is and what to look for" (accessed 31 Oct 1998): 3pp. Online. Internet. Available: http://www.kingshillresearch.org/pages/whatis.htm

7. Norrgard, Carolyn and Matheis-Kraft, Carol. "General Information About Dementia," Clinical Reference Systems (Dec 1997): p. 2066. Online. 3 Nov 1998. Available: http://web4.searchbank.com/infotrac/session/643/923/27713639w3/sig!n1.0

8. Sachdev, Perminder. <u>Akathisia and Restless Legs</u>. Massachusetts: Cambridge University Press, 1995. pgs. 25-6, 30-2, 40-1, 43-4

11

ART AND ARCHITECTURE

Interior of the Mosque. Islamic architecture, 9th c. Mosque, Cordoba, Spain.

HARD ARCHITECTURE

●

Robert Sommer

This selection comes from Tight Spaces, *a study of contemporary public architecture.*

Prison fixtures are being installed in the restrooms of city parks. According to the manufacturers' statements, they are supposed to be vandal-proof. One advertisement shows a man attacking a toilet with a sledgehammer. According to Sacramento, California, Recreation Director Solon Wishmam, Jr., "There is no exposed plumbing in the new buildings. The external fixtures are made of cast aluminum covered with hard epoxy. The buildings themselves are made of concrete blocks rather than wood or brick." This same trend toward hard buildings is evident in public facilities across the country. Picnic tables are being cast of concrete rather than built of wood and are embedded several feet into the ground. It isn't possible to move these tables to a shady place or combine two tables to accommodate a large group, but that is an inconvenience for the users rather than the park officials. The older wood and metal tables remaining from a happier era are chained to blocks of concrete or steel posts.

The original inspiration for the park restroom, the prison cell, illustrates the hard facts of hard architecture. Human beings are enclosed in steel cages with the bare minimum of furnishings or amenities. In some cells there may be no furniture whatever except for the furthest advance in the field of vandal-proof plumbing, the hole in the concrete floor, otherwise known as a Chinese toilet. Because nothing is provided that the inmate might destroy, he may have to sleep on a bare concrete floor without mattress or blanket. I am not talking about the Middle Ages or some backward part of the nation. I have a clear image of an isolation cell circa 1973 with a man in a steel cage for 23 hours a day with nothing to do but pace the floor and curse the guard watching him through the slit in a steel door. The architecture of the isolation cell is based on a variant of Murphy's Law—if something can be destroyed, it will be destroyed. In mental hospitals of the early 1950s, the line was, "If you give the patients anything nice, they won't take care of it." For public housing tenants it went "If you provide good architecture they won't appreciate it." There is the same denigrating we/they dichotomy in all these assessments of people's response to their surroundings. We know what's best for them and they don't. Even if we provide what they say they'd like, they won't take care of it and will probably destroy it. Ergo, it is best for everyone, especially the taxpayers who foot the bill, to design things that cannot be destroyed.

The result is that architecture is designed to be strong and resistant to human imprint. To the inhabitants it seems impervious, impersonal, and inorganic. Lady Allen, who pioneered the adventure playground in Great

Britain, was appalled at American play yards which she described as "an administrator's heaven and a child's hell . . . asphalt barracks yards behind wire mesh screen barriers" built primarily for ease and economy of maintenance. There is a whole industry built around supplying steel cages for prisons, wire mesh fences for city parks, and graffiti-resistant paint for public buildings. On a larger scale, the hardening of the landscape is evident in the ever-growing freeway system, the residential and second-home subdivisions pushing aside orchards and forests, the straightening and cementing of river beds, the walled and guarded cities of suburbia, and the TV cameras in banks and apartment buildings.

Another characteristic of hard architecture is a lack of permeability between inside and out. Often this means an absence of windows, a style referred to in Berkeley as post-revolutionary architecture. At first glance the Bank of America on Berkeley's Telegraph Avenue seems to have windows but these are really reflecting metal surfaces. The new postal center in Oakland, with its tiny slit windows, looks as if it were intended for urban guerilla warfare. Older buildings that still have plate glass use steel shutters and gates that can be drawn across the exterior in a matter of minutes. Some corporations are moving their data-processing machinery underground where they are less vulnerable to attack. The fact that employees must work underground forty hours a week is a minor cost borne by the employees rather than the architect.

Hard architecture means wall surfaces that resist human imprint. Dark colors and rough cement were satisfactory prior to the advent of the aerosol can. The counter response of the hard-line designers has taken two forms. The first is the legal effort to remove aerosol cans from the hands of potential graffitists. Ordinances have been proposed to make it illegal to carry open aerosol cans on city streets. A New York State Senator has proposed a bill to make it illegal for people under eighteen to purchase cans of spray paint. The other approach is to develop vandal-resistant surfaces and stronger kinds of paint remover. In a six-month period New York City purchased 7,000 gallons of a yellow jelly called DWR (dirty word remover) from a Moorestown, N.J., manufacturer of industrial chemicals. The remover comes in two strengths and the heavier duty version is optimistically called Enzitall. Planners of President Nixon's inauguration sprayed the trees alongside the motorcade route with a material that prevented birds from roosting there. They didn't want the president being embarrassed by an occasional bird-dropping. The two-year interval during which the birds would be unable to roost on these trees is a minor inconvenience again borne by the users.

Most of these efforts to harden the environment have had the avowed purpose of increasing security. Frequently this reason is a coverup for a desire to maintain order, discipline, or control. Although these motives are related to security, there are important differences between security and control that must be recognized and heeded if a democratic society is to continue. . . .

IDEOLOGICAL SUPPORTS FOR HARD BUILDINGS

Any effort to soften hard buildings and improve the lot of the public housing tenant, the prisoner, or the park user will encounter the popular prejudice against "frills" in public facilities. As they say about army buildings, "It doesn't have to be cheap, it just has to look cheap." The tax-payer doesn't want to believe that people living in public housing are better off than he is. Almost every prison official advocates individual cells for prisoners. The logic behind single cells is compelling; it includes the physical protection of weaker inmates, reduces homosexual relationships, enables better control of inmates in single cells, as well as increased privacy and personal dignity. However, whenever prison officials argue for single cells, they are accused of coddling convicts. The apocryphal question from the state legislature is how single rooms can be justified for people who have broken the law when army recruits are compelled to live in open barracks. Is it reasonable to provide more amenities for lawbreakers than for draftees?

There are several good answers to this question. First we can turn to Florence Nightingale's dictum that the first requisite of a hospital is that it do the patients no harm. The minimum criterion of a prison should be that an inmate emerges no worse than when he entered. At present this is not the case and prisons are accurately described as breeding grounds for criminal behavior. When someone is hurt and angry, there is no reason to believe that putting him in a degrading and dehumanizing environment will improve his outlook or behavior. Indeed there is every reason to suppose that this will worsen whatever antisocial attitudes presently exist.

The logic of subjecting the poor, the criminal, and the deviant to degrading conditions is also based on a puritanical attitude toward comfort. A belief in the redemptive value of hard work and frugality pervades much of our thinking about people who are public charges. The first American prison was developed in Pennsylvania in response to demands for the humane treatment of criminals by the Quaker sect, a group characterized both by its humane impulses and a disdain for anything beyond the minimum in personal comfort. Following Quaker precepts, lawbreakers were confined in solitary cells with ample time to consider their transgressions and become penitent. The cells were quite large and the inmate remained in his cell most of the day apart from a one-hour exercise period. Later, when large-scale workshops proved more efficient than individual craft work performed in a single cell, the solitary system of the Pennsylvania prison was replaced by the silent system of the Auburn Prison, in which inmates also lived in single cells but came together to work and eat but had to remain silent. The idea that an ascetic life would help to rehabilitate prisoners was used against any effort to humanize the institutions.

Even today, efforts to improve the drab conditions of army life, to permit recruits to personalize their sleeping quarters or choose their own hair styles, are regarded by many senior officers as responsible for breakdowns in order and discipline. Not too long ago architects who planned college classrooms and dormitories were advised against making the furnishings too pleasant or comfortable lest the students become distracted or fall asleep. Guidebooks for undergraduate students still warn against too many amenities in the student's room. Here is a sampling of advice on dormitory furnishing: "Choose a straight backed chair rather than a very comfortable one. . . ." "All of the votes are in favor of a simple, rugged, straightbacked chair with no cushion. You study best when you are not too comfortable or relaxed. . . ." "For obvious reasons, avoid studying on a couch, easy chair, or in bed. . . ." "A bed is no place to study. Neither is a sofa, nor a foam rubber lounge chair. When you are too relaxed and comfortable physically, your concentration also relaxes. A straight-backed wooden chair is best for most students; it allows them to work at maximum concentration for longer periods." Before analyzing the attitudes behind these recommendations, let me state emphatically that there is no evidence that people work better when they are uncomfortable. Let the reader examine his or her own circumstances while reading this book. Are you sitting bolt upright in a straight-backed chair or lying on a couch with your head against a cushion? My own observations of the way students read suggest that when a couch or easy chair is available, it will be chosen almost every time over the rugged, virtuous, and uncomfortable straight-backed chair.

Another ideological prop behind hard architecture is neo-behaviorism. Providing decent housing for public charges would be "rewarding" poverty or criminal behavior. The argument goes beyond the accusation of simply coddling convicts to the idea that improved conditions will actually "reinforce" criminal tendencies. Neo-behaviorism maintains that people won't be deterred from crime if the consequences are not sufficiently dire. This requires some form of punishment—if not actual torture then at least confinement without amenity. The critical question is whether confinement and removal from society constitute sufficient punishment or whether the transgressor must be punished still further during confinement. There is no evidence to indicate that such punishment exerts any positive influences on an inmate's character. Instead it increases his alienation from and his bitterness toward society. There is not much basis for believing that dehumanizing public housing will help to reduce welfare rolls, juvenile delinquency, or anything else society considers bad. Poor housing lowers the self-image of the tenant and helps to convince him how little society cares about his plight. This is not a terribly important consideration to a philosophy that is unabashedly beyond freedom and dignity. Hard, hard, hard, ain't it hard? Yes it is. But does it work? No, it doesn't. City officials across the country will testify that there is no such thing as a vandal-proof restroom or picnic bench. If restrooms are built out of concrete they will be dynamited and have concrete poured down the toilet holes. Vandals, thousands of helmeted Huns riding out of the East, have managed to dig out concrete blocks and haul away picnic tables weighing hundreds of pounds. Bolt cutters and wire snippers can sever any chain-link fence manufactured today. In the People's Park disturbance of 1972, the metal poles for the fence were used to break up the macadam of the parking lot. Local police were very cooperative in carting away the broken macadam pieces lest they in turn be used to break the windows of local stores. The harder the architecture, the greater its potential as a weapon if it is used against the authorities. Prison inmates have learned how to make deadly knives from steel bedsprings. Hard architecture also costs more to adapt or remove. Pennsylvania's Eastern Penitentiary, built in 1829, was closed down in 1966, but has yet to be removed from the site because of the high razing expense. The extra costs of hard architecture are manifold; first in the initial purchase price because it costs twice as much as ordinary items, second in its potential for abuse once it is destroyed as well as the greater cost in repairing or removing a heavy and rigid item designed to be installed permanently, and finally the human costs resulting from being in cold, ugly, and impersonal buildings.

Challenge people to destroy something and they will find a way to do it. Many people prefer to ignore the great amount of technological ingenuity released in wartime. Although only sketchy accounts of the automated battlefield have been made public, it is evident that the Vietnam War has produced the most sophisticated gadgetry in the history of warfare. If city agencies use remote sensors and infrared photography to detect the presence of people in parks after closing time, it is likely that such methods will have the same success in New York parks that they had in Vietnam. Authorities who go the route of vandal-proof facilities are deluding themselves. They are short-range thinkers who cost everyone money in the long run. Adversity puts human ingenuity to the test and the prison inmate naked in his strip cell is tested more severely. By law the California authorities are required to provide even strip-cell inmates with their own Bibles. The result is that the Bible has become a weapon in a manner unintended by the most ardent missionary. Inmates stuff the pages into the ventilator shaft and use the covers to stop up the Chinese toilet. Think of what the inmate could do if he had a table and chair to work with! An advisory committee on dental hygiene ran into problems when it suggested to the California Department of Corrections that inmates should be allowed to use dental floss. Prison officials pointed out that dental floss "when coated with an abrasive substance, could be as effective as metal blades in cutting through iron bars."

The major defects of hard architecture are that it is costly, dehumanizing, and it isn't effective. Besides that, it doesn't look very nice. The prototype of hard architecture is the strip cell in the maximum security prison containing nothing but reinforced concrete poured over a steel cage without any amenities. If we can develop ways of humanizing the prison cell, perhaps we can also do so for schools, parks, and other public facilities.

The rationale of the hard prison is that the inmate will destroy anything that is provided for him. It is easy to prove the correctness of this view by giving a wooden chair to an inmate in a strip cell. It is likely that he will bang the chair against the wall until the legs have come loose and he has several clubs in his possession. Give him a mattress and sooner or later the authorities will have a fire or smoke problem on their hands. Just what does this prove? One can also supply numerous examples of maximum security cells that are equally secure and full of amenities including rugs, tables, desks, television sets, and stereo systems. In prison disturbances, where inmates are rampaging against virtually every part of the prison building, television sets purchased with inmate welfare funds remain undisturbed. Nor do inmates destroy the paintings made by their fellow prisoners.

The arguments against providing amenities for inmates do not discuss the costs of denying a human existence to the lawbreakers. I have never heard anyone maintain that the inmate's mental or physical health is improved by a bare, unheated cell with no exercise yard or outside stimulation. This experience does not teach him a greater respect for the law or the society that maintains him under such dehumanizing conditions. However, guards legitimately object to providing chairs for inmates who are going to break them apart and fashion clubs from the pieces. The typical solution has been to harden prison furnishings with indestructible materials and attach them to the walls. But human ingenuity can always find a way to destroy things that are physically or spiritually oppressive.

Another assumption behind hard architecture is that security through steel, concrete, and electronic surveillance is cheaper and more effective than security through public access. Stated another way, security can be gained through technological control of the environment. This is perhaps valid when one is working *with* people rather than against them. To design a highway to minimize ambiguity, error, and accidents increases everyone's sense of security. I feel more comfortable riding my bike on a well-planned bicycle path than on a street or highway that was designed with automobiles in mind. However, we have not been discussing situations in which everyone gains from good design, but rather those in which hard architecture is used by one group to exclude or oppress another.

The emulation of the prison as a security environment is the more ironic because the prison is a failing institution from everyone's standpoint. It provides no security for inmates, guards, wardens, and visitors. It does provide a short-run protection to outside society by segregating offenders for brief periods, but this must be weighed against the corrosive effects of incarceration in an oppressive and unnatural environment.

SOFT ARCHITECTURE

If experience has shown that hard architecture isn't working from the standpoint of economics, aesthetics, or human dignity, what then is the answer? The solution, I believe, is to reverse course and make buildings more rather than less responsive to their users. Instead of hardening things to resist human imprint, let us design buildings, parks, and cities to welcome and reflect the presence of human beings—let us abandon the fruitless and costly search for ever more secure cell furnishings. There is another alternative to the completely empty cell. This would involve materials such as foam and inflatables as well as other types of plastics. Provided one selects materials that are fire proof, the security implications of an inexpensive air mattress or styrofoam chair are virtually zero, or at least they are considerably less than with ordinary prison furnishings. There is no justification for inmates in maximum security cells sleeping on hard concrete floors when the wholesale cost of an air mattress is twenty cents. At least an inmate should be offered a choice between the bare concrete floor and an air mattress which he can destroy if he chooses. If he elects to destroy the air mattress, the security implications to the guard as well as the cost to the taxpayers are minimal. However, if he does not destroy it, an equally inexpensive foam chair might be tried next. In this way a valid transaction between the inmate and the authorities regarding cell furnishings could be established.

Soft architecture can change the relationship between keeper and inmate. New Jersey State Penitentiary in Leesburg was deliberately built by the architects to include breakable materials; a necessary adjunct to a humane environment. Glass abounds and each cell has natural light with an exterior window in addition to the glazed walls separating cells from courtyards. Locally some people refer to this medium security facility as "the glass house." All windows face the interior courtyards and exterior security is provided by the back wall of the residential units, a deep overhang of the roof to prevent climbing, and a cyclone fence surrounding the entire site. However the interior of the prison contains a great amount of breakable material requiring inmates and guards to reach a mutually satisfactory accommodation, because any burst of anger would result in shattered glass. It would indeed be difficult to run a repressive prison in "the glass house." On the other hand, it requires tremendous tact, patience, and sensitivity to run such a prison. Let the reader answer whether he or she would prefer to work (or be confined) in Leesburg or in a traditional institution.

Several years ago, the dormitories on my campus had strict rules against students hanging pictures or posters on the walls. There were constant inspections by university officials who removed illegal posters and fined the offenders. The basis for these regulations was that the tacks or tape used to mount these posters would scratch the walls. The prohibition against decorating dormitory rooms continued for years even though it was a constant irritant as well as being costly and ineffective. Besides the inspections there was the annual repainting bill, which mounted steadily over the years. Eventually the administration decided that it would be cheaper and happier for everyone to let students hang anything they wanted on their walls. The housing office now provides paint at the beginning of the year so that students can erase anything done by the previous occupants and have the colors they want. Students living on the same floor can decide jointly how the corridors and stairwells are to be painted. New dormitories now contain soft wall materials such as cork or burlap on wood so that students can hang pictures, mobiles, or macramé without marring the surface. They are built to be largely maintained by the users. This has proven cheaper and more satisfying than the previous arrangement of bare walls accompanied by constant inspections, fines, and reprimands, as well as periodic repainting by the maintenance staff. It costs $15 per room to allow students to do the painting themselves, compared to $75 charged by the physical plant office. In 1970, the repaint rate was 10 percent—that is, only one out of ten rooms was repainted by the subsequent occupant.

On any college campus there is always a shortage of study space, particularly around exam time. There is also a great deal of unused space in the evenings, in the form of academic offices, laboratories, and even cafeterias, but it is difficult to get these opened for student use. I don't know of a single campus where faculty offices are available in the evenings as study space—the territorial feelings of the faculty toward their offices are too strong. However on a number of campuses there have been successful campaigns to open up the cafeterias in the evenings. These campaigns have been successful only sporadically and probably less than one-third of university cafeterias are routinely opened for evening studiers, another third are opened during examination periods, and the remainder are locked and available only during specified meal hours. The arguments against opening up cafeterias are custodial and security-oriented—the students will disturb the table arrangements and will steal the utensils and perhaps even the chairs and tables themselves. At a large university in Los Angeles where the silverware is automatically returned to the locked kitchen after meals, the explanation for closing the cafeteria in the evenings is that the students would steal the salt and pepper shakers. Like the belief that mental patients will flush magazines down the toilets, prisoners will destroy decent furnishings if they have them, or park users will chop up wooden benches, a few instances can always be cited, but the trade-offs in social utility and aesthetics are rarely considered. The best counterargument for opening up college cafeterias for evening studiers is that the system works on scores of campuses across the nation. The loss of twenty salt and pepper shakers and perhaps an extra $10 per evening in janitorial services to open up two cafeterias for around-the-clock use might provide the campus with an additional 15,000 feet of prime study space already equipped with tables and chairs. If need be, the student government or some dormitory organization can provide proctors or monitors in the late evening hours.

In all such illustrations—magazines for mental patients, amenities for prisoners, and study space for college students—the security and custodial opposition is largely specious, but this is obvious only to someone knowledgeable about the situation elsewhere. The argument that mental patients will immediately tear up magazines and flush them down the toilet has at least minimal logic *unless* one has worked on a psychiatric ward where magazines and newspapers are freely available. The arguments against amenity for prisoners seem equally ridiculous if one has seen maximum security cells equipped with carpets, stereos, green plants, and tropical fish. To the criticism that inmates will hide knives and drugs in flower pots and stereos, one can cite the fact that inmates presently secrete weapons and contraband even in the barest cells and sometimes as suppositories. It is also true that the majority of stabbings and other serious injuries have occurred at the most security-conscious institutions. The explanation always returns to the "type of inmate" and never to the type of place. The mental patients who had free access to newspapers and magazines and didn't flush them down the toilets were presumably a "better class of patients." Similarly, students at University *A* who have access to cafeterias for evening study and leave the salt and pepper shakers undisturbed are a "better class of students." This "class logic" treats people apart from their surroundings, as if there is some intrinsic self independent of the environment. This is a false model of any natural process, including person/environment transactions. There is no behavior apart from environment even *in utero*. People adapt themselves to their surroundings in diverse and complex ways. When those surroundings are cold and oppressive, people who can will avoid them. Unfortunately many people, for economic, social, or statutory reasons, cannot avoid places that oppress them. The result may be somatic disorders, anxiety, and irritation, but the probable outcome will be numbness to one's surroundings, with psychological withdrawal substituting for physical avoidance. . . .

The dream of a society in which people who share common goals will trust and respect one another is being suffocated in a torrent of concrete, steel, and sophisticated security equipment. I would feel less strongly if windowless buildings, barbed-wire fences, and electronic surveillance equipment were infrequent aberrations of paranoid homeowners and public officials, but they are not. Housing projects, schools, playgrounds, courtrooms, and commercial buildings reveal the hardening process at an advanced stage. If there is truth to Churchill's dictum that the buildings we shape will eventually shape us, then the inevitable result of hard buildings will be withdrawn, callous, and indifferent people. A security emphasis is being poured into concrete that will harden our children's children fifty years from now. . . .

PERSONALIZATION

There is no single best arrangement of office furniture and no way for a designer, building manager, or psychologist to intuit someone's space needs without meeting the person, seeing the sort of job he or she has to do, and how he or she does it. Every faculty office on my campus comes equipped with a standard complement of furniture—a desk, filing cabinet, table, two or three bookcases, coat rack, and so on. Because all these people have the same job title (professor) and the size and shape of all office pieces are identical, one could conceive of standardized office arrangements. However a walk down the hallways reveals a great diversity of arrangements. One man has placed his bookcase between his desk and the door for maximum privacy. Another has joined together his desk and table to yield a large work area and writing surface as well as considerable distance from any visitor, and a third has placed all furniture against the walls to remove any barriers between himself and the students. Numerous attempts at personalization are evident. Out of their own pocket, faculty purchased rugs, drapes, wall-hangings, and pictures of every description, as well as artifacts and symbols of their respective professions. The same diversity of arrangements is evident in the student dormitories, which also come equipped with a standardized complement of similar furniture. Sometimes I think I have seen every conceivable arrangement of two desks, two beds, two chairs, and two dressers, but invariably I am surprised to find a novel pattern.

Instead of guessing "user needs" one should aim at providing access to a pool or selection of furnishings and allow people to arrange their office areas as they see fit. During the occupation of the administration building during Berkeley's Free Speech Movement crisis in 1964, it was reported that the students had broken into and ransacked the office of President Emeritus Robert Gordon Sproul. When the police had removed the demonstrators, they found Sproul's office in disarray with papers strewn about the floor. The situation was resolved when Sproul's secretary reported that her employer often worked on the floor and left papers strewn about.

The idea that people should be able to control and personalize their work spaces is well within the technical capability of the building industry. It does call for a reversal of the tendency to centralize services and decision-making regarding the physical environment. In the short run it may be cheaper to omit the light switches in an office building, but this makes it difficult to show slides and it is also terribly wasteful of electric power. The same point applies to heating, air conditioning, and humidity controls. There is something tragic about an employee who is officially reprimanded for placing cardboard over her air conditioning vent or a poster on the wall to brighten an otherwise drab office. There is no contradiction between central design and local control provided one develops an overall design scheme that makes allowance for local inputs. One can design a soft building in which each occupant controls his own temperature—hotels and motels do this routinely—or one can design a hard building in which the custodian controls everyone's temperature. In the work on classroom seating . . . it was found that janitors arranged chairs in accordance with their educational philosophies. They also followed their own standards of temperature, humidity, and illumination. The custodian in my building has a clear conception of where my desk and chair belong. Every morning I move my chair over to the side of the room and every evening he returns it to my desk. He arranges the room according to his scheme and I to mine. Fortunately the rules allow me to move my chair. I visited a conference room in one government agency and found taped to the wall under the President's picture a diagram specifying how every item of furniture in the room was to be arranged.

Pleas for personalizing offices and work spaces are academic and even precious until one sees the drab and impersonal conditions under which many people work. At the offices of a large insurance company I found hundreds of clerk's desks in straight rows in a large open room with phones ringing, people scurrying about, and no one having any control over the thermal, acoustical, or visual environment. A federal agency building is liable to be a maze of offices of identical size, shape, and decor. All the furniture, including desks and bookcases, is government-issue grey and on every wall there is a framed photograph of the President and the agency director. A few executives are able to place maps on the walls for visual relief, but that is all. The quest for stimulating and attractive work places, the right to personalize one's own spaces and control temperature and illumination and noise are not academic issues to people who must spend eight hours a day in these settings. I don't feel it is necessary to "prove" that people in colorful offices will type more accurately, stay healthier, or buy more government bonds than people in drab offices. People should have the right to attractive and humane working conditions. Somehow the onus of the argument for a decent environment always falls upon the person who wants to improve things; the custodians and the rest of the grey wall crowd never have to defend drab and unresponsive buildings. This is a curious double standard. If an employee hangs up a poster by his desk, he is imposing his values and artistic tastes on the other employees, but if the management paints all the walls in the building grey or institutional green, that is part of the natural order. We eventually tune them out and thereby become alienated from the very buildings in which we spend our daylight hours.

Ugly and drab furnishings cannot be justified economically. For a corporation or government agency, colored items would cost only slightly more than grey ones and on a large order the difference would disappear entirely. There is some poetic justice that many of the drab furnishings of state office buildings are manufactured by the state prison system. In private corporations, which buy their furniture in the free market where a wide variety of styles and colors is available, standardization is less a result of economics or efficiency than of insensitivity and deliberate unconcern. There is also more than a hint of authoritarianism in the idea that each employee must accept the specific furniture arrangement provided by the company. In a large corporation or agency it would be feasible to give each employee a choice of desk, chair, file cabinet, table, and waste basket from a central furniture pool, not only at the time of employment, but every six months if the person felt like changing things around. This may sound utopian but it isn't. It doesn't take all that long to move furniture. The main objective is not so much to keep the furniture moving as it is to sensitize people to the connection between themselves and their surroundings and counteract the pervasive numbness and apathy. The idea of so many millions of people singlemindedly going to dingy little work stations in large skyscrapers, completely turned off to other people and places, is profoundly disturbing. This kind of numbness to one's surroundings can become a life style.

QUICK! BEFORE IT CRUMBLES!

Paul Goldberger

This piece originally appeared in Esquire *in 1975.*

AN ARCHITECTURE CRITIC LOOKS AT COOKIE ARCHITECTURE

SUGAR WAFER (NABISCO)

There is no attempt to imitate the ancient forms of traditional, individually baked cookies here—this is a modern cookie through and through. Its simple rectangular form, clean and pure, just reeks of mass production and modern technological methods. The two wafers, held together by the sugar-cream filling, appear to float, and the Nabisco trademark, stamped re-

peatedly across the top, confirms that this is a machine-age object. Clearly the Sugar Wafer is the Mies van der Rohe of cookies.

FIG NEWTON (NABISCO)

This, too, is a sandwich but different in every way from the Sugar Wafer. Here the imagery is more traditional, more sensual even; a rounded form of cookie dough arcs over the fig concoction inside, and the whole is soft and pliable. Like all good pieces of design, it has an appropriate form for its use, since the insides of Fig Newtons can ooze and would not be held in place by a more rigid form. The thing could have had a somewhat different shape, but the rounded top is a comfortable, familiar image, and it's easy to hold. Not a revolutionary object but an intelligent one.

MILANO (PEPPERIDGE FARMS)

This long, chocolate-filled cookie summons up contradictory associations. Its rounded ends suggest both the traditional image of stodgy ladyfingers and the curves of Art Deco, while the subtle yet forceful "V" embossed onto the surface creates an abstract image of force and movement. The "V" is the kind of ornament that wishes to appear modern without really being modern, which would have meant banning ornament altogether. That romantic symbolism of the modern was an Art Deco characteristic, of course; come to think of it the Milano is rather Art Deco in spirit.

MALLOMAR (NABISCO)

This marshmallow, chocolate and cracker combination is the ultimate sensual cookie—indeed, its resemblance to the female breast has been cited so often as to sound rather trite. But the cookie's imagery need not be read so literally—the voluptuousness of the form, which with its nipped waist rather resembles the New Orleans Superdome, is enough. Like all good pieces of design, the

form of the cookie is primarily derived from functional needs, but with just enough distinction to make it instantly identifiable. The result is a cultural icon—the cookie equivalent, surely, of the Coke bottle.

LORNA DOONE (NABISCO)

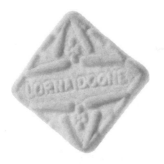

Like the Las Vegas casino that is overwhelmed by its sign, image is all in the Lorna Doone. It is a plain, simple cookie (of shortbread, in fact), but a cookie like all other cookies—except for its sign. The Lorna Doone logo, a four-pointed star with the cookie's name and a pair of fleur-de-lis-like decorations, covers the entire surface of the cookie in low relief. Cleverly, the designers of this cookie have placed the logo so that the points of the star align with the corners of the square, forcing one to pivot the cookie forty-five degrees, so that its shape appears instead to be a diamond. It is a superb example of the ordinary made extraordinary.

DWELLINGS

◆

Linda Hogan

This selection is from Hogan's 1995 book Dwellings: Reflections on the Natural World.

Not far from where I live is a hill that was cut into by the moving water of a creek. Eroded this way, all that's left of it is a broken wall of earth that contains old roots and pebbles woven together and exposed. Seen from a distance, it is only a rise of raw earth. But up close it is something wonderful, a small cliff dwelling that looks almost as intricate and well made as those the Anasazi left behind when they vanished mysteriously centuries ago. This hill is a place that could be the starry skies at night turned inward into the thousand round holes where solitary bees have lived and died. It is a hill of tunneling rooms. At the mouths of some of the excavations, half-circles of clay beetle out like awnings shading a doorway. It is earth that was turned to clay in the mouths of the bees and spit out as they mined deeper into their dwelling places.

This place is where the bees reside at an angle safe from rain. It faces the southern sun. It is a warm and intelligent architecture of memory, learned by whatever memory lives in the blood. Many of the holes still contain gold husks of dead bees, their faces dry and gone, their flat eyes gazing out from death's land toward the other uninhabited half of the hill that is across the creek from the catacombs.

The first time I found the residence of the bees, it was dusty summer. The sun was hot, and land was the dry color of rust. Now and then a car rumbled along the dirt road and dust rose up behind it before settling back down on older dust. In the silence, the bees made a soft droning hum. They were alive then, and working the hill, going out and returning with pollen, in and out through the holes, back and forth between daylight and the cooler, darker regions of the inner earth. They were flying an invisible map through air, a map charted by landmarks, the slant of light, and a circling story they told one another about the direction of food held inside the center of yellow flowers.

Sitting in the hot sun, watching the small bees fly in and out around the hill, hearing the summer birds, the light breeze, I felt right in the world. I belonged there. I thought of my own dwelling places, those real and those imagined. Once I lived in a town called Manitou, which means "Great Spirit," and where hot mineral springwater gurgled beneath the streets and rose into open wells. I felt safe there. With the underground movement of water and heat a constant reminder of other life, of what lives beneath us, it seemed to be the center of the world.

A few years after that, I wanted silence. My daydreams were full of places I longed to be, shelters and solitudes. I wanted a room apart from others, a hidden cabin to rest in. I wanted to be in a redwood forest with trees so tall the owls called out in the daytime. I daydreamed of living in a vapor cave a few hours away from here. Underground, warm, and moist, I thought it would be the perfect world for staying out of cold winter, for escaping the noise of living.

And how often I've wanted to escape to a wilderness where a human hand has not been in everything. But those were only dreams of peace, of comfort, of a nest inside stone or woods, a sanctuary where a dream or life wouldn't be invaded.

Years ago, in the next canyon west of here, there was a man who followed one of those dreams and moved into a cave that could only be reached by climbing down a rope. For years he lived there in comfort, like a troglodite. The inner weather was stable, never too hot, too cold, too wet, or too dry. But then he felt lonely. His utopia needed a woman. He went to town until he found a wife. For a while after the marriage, his wife climbed down the rope along with him, but before long she didn't want the mice scurrying about in the cave, or the untidy bats that wanted to hang from the stones of the ceiling. So they built a door. Because of the closed entryway, the temperature changed. They had to put in heat. Then the inner moisture of earth warped the door, so they had to have air-conditioning, and after that the earth wanted to go about life in its own way and it didn't give in to the people.

In other days and places, people paid more attention to the strong-headed will of earth. Once homes were built of wood that had been felled from a single region in a forest. That way, it was thought, the house would hold together more harmoniously, and the family of walls would not fall or lend themselves to the unhappiness or arguments of the inhabitants.

An Italian immigrant to Chicago, Aldo Piacenzi, built birdhouses that were dwellings of harmony and peace. They were the incredible spired shapes of cathedrals in Italy. They housed not only the birds, but also his memories, his own past. He painted them the watery blue of his Mediterranean, the wild rose of flowers in a summer field. Inside them was straw and the droppings of lives that layed eggs, fledglings who grew there. What places to inhabit, the bright and sunny birdhouses in dreary alleyways of the city.

One beautiful afternoon, cool and moist, with the kind of yellow light that falls on earth in these arid regions, I waited for barn swallows to return from their daily work of food gathering. Inside the tunnel where they live, hundreds of swallows had mixed their saliva with mud and clay, much like the solitary bees, and formed nests that were perfect as a potter's bowl. At five in the evening, they returned all at once, a dark, flying shadow. Despite their enormous numbers and the crowding together of nests, they didn't pause for even a moment before entering the nests, nor did they crowd one another. Instantly they vanished into the nests. The tunnel went silent. It held no outward signs of life.

But I knew they were there, filled with the fire of living. And what a marriage of elements was in those nests. Not only mud's earth and water, the fire of sun and dry air, but even the elements contained one another. The bodies of prophets and crazy men were broken down in that soil.

I've noticed often how when a house is abandoned, it begins to sag. Without a tenant, it has no need to go on. If it were a person, we'd say it is depressed or lonely. The roof settles in, the paint cracks, the walls and floorboards warp and slope downward in their own natural ways, telling us that life must stay in everything as the world whirls and tilts and moves through boundless space.

One summer day, cleaning up after long-eared owls where I work at a rehabilitation facility for birds of prey, I was raking the gravel floor of a flight cage. Down on the ground, something looked like it was moving. I bent over to look into the pile of bones and pellets I'd just raked together. There, close to the ground, were two fetal mice. They were new to the planet, pink and hairless. They were so tenderly young. Their faces had swollen blue-veined eyes. They were nestled in a mound of feathers, soft as velvet, each one curled up smaller than an infant's ear, listening to the first sounds of earth. But the ants were biting them. They turned in agony, unable to pull away, not yet having the arms or legs to move, but feeling, twisting away from, the pain of the bites. I was horrified to see them bitten out of life that way. I dipped them in water, as if to take away the sting, and let the ants fall in the bucket. Then I held the tiny mice in the palm of my hand. Some of the ants were drowning in the water. I was trading one life for another, exchanging the lives of the ants for those of mice, but I hated their suffering, and hated even more that they had not yet grown to a life, and already they inhabited the miserable world of pain. Death and life feed each other. I know that.

Inside these rooms where birds are healed, there are other lives besides those of mice. There are fine gray globes the wasps have woven together, the white cocoons of spiders in a corner, the downward tunneling anthills. All these dwellings are inside one small walled space, but I think most about the mice. Sometimes the downy nests fall out of the walls where their mothers have placed them out of the way of their enemies. When one of the nests falls, they are so well made and soft, woven mostly from the chest feathers of birds. Sometimes the leg of a small quail holds the nest together like a slender cornerstone with dry, bent claws. The mice have adapted to life in the presence of their enemies, adapted to living in the thin wall between beak and beak, claw and claw. They move their nests often, as if a new rafter or wall will protect them from the inevitable fate of all our returns home to the deeper, wider nests of earth that houses us all.

One August at Zia Pueblo during the corn dance I noticed tourists picking up shards of all the old pottery that had been made and broken there. The residents of Zia know not to take the bowls and pots left behind by the older ones. They know that the fragments of those earlier lives need to be smoothed back to earth, but younger nations, travelers from continents across the world who have come to inhabit this land, have little of their own to grow on. The pieces of earth that were formed into bowls, even on their way home to dust, provide the new people a lifeline to an unknown land, help them remember that they live in the old nest of earth.

It was in early February, during the mating season of the great horned owl. It was dusk, and I hiked up the back of a mountain to where I'd heard the owls a year before. I wanted to hear them again, the voices so tender, so deep, like a memory of comfort. I was halfway up the trail when I found a soft, round nest. It had fallen from one of the bare-branched trees. It was a delicate nest, woven together of feathers, sage, and strands of wild grass. Holding it in my hand in the rosy twilight, I noticed that a blue thread was entwined with the other gatherings there. I pulled at the thread a little, and then I recognized it. It was a thread from one of my skirts. It was blue cotton. It was the unmistakable color and shape of a pattern I knew. I liked it, that a thread of my life was in an abandoned nest, one that had held eggs and new life. I took the nest home. At home, I held it to the light and looked more closely. There, to my surprise, nestled into the gray-green sage, was a gnarl of black hair. It was also unmistakable. It was my daughter's hair, cleaned from a brush and picked up out in the sun beneath the maple tree, or the pit cherry where the birds eat from the overladen, fertile branches until only the seeds remain on the trees.

I didn't know what kind of nest it was, or who had lived there. It didn't matter. I thought of the remnants of our lives carried up the hill that way and turned into shelter. That night, resting inside the walls of our home, the world outside weighed so heavily against the thin wood of the house. The sloped roof was the only thing between us and the universe. Everything outside of our wooden boundaries seemed so large. Filled with the night's citizens, it all came alive. The world opened in the thickets of the dark. The wild grapes would soon ripen on the vines. The burrowing ones were emerging. Horned owls sat in treetops. Mice scurried here and there. Skunks, fox, the slow and holy porcupine, all were passing by this way. The young of the solitary bees were feeding on the pollen in the dark. The whole world was a nest on its humble tilt, in the maze of the universe, holding us.

MARY CASSATT

Mary Gordon

The following selection is from Mary Gordon's 1991 collection of essays Good Boys and Dead Girls.

When Mary Cassatt's father was told of her decision to become a painter, he said: "I would rather see you dead." When Edgar Degas saw a show of Cassatt's etchings, his response was: "I am not willing to admit that a woman can draw that well." When she returned to Philadelphia after twenty-eight years abroad, having achieved renown as an Impressionist painter and the esteem of Degas, Huysmans, Pissarro, and Berthe Morisot, the *Philadelphia Ledger* reported: "Mary Cassatt, sister of Mr. Cassatt, president of the Pennsylvania Railroad, returned from Europe yesterday. She has been studying painting in France and owns the smallest Pekingese dog in the world."

Mary Cassatt exemplified the paradoxes of the woman artist. Cut off from the experiences that are considered the entitlement of her male counterpart, she has access to a private world a man can only guess at. She has, therefore, a kind of information he is necessarily deprived of. If she has almost impossible good fortune—means, self-confidence, heroic energy and dedication, the instinct to avoid the seductions of ordinary domestic life, which so easily become a substitute for creative work—she may pull off a miracle: she will combine the skill and surety that she has stolen from the world of men with the vision she brings from the world of women.

Mary Cassatt pulled off such a miracle. But if her story is particularly female, it is also American. She typifies one kind of independent American spinster who keeps reappearing in our history in forms as various as Margaret Fuller and Katharine Hepburn. There is an astringency in such women, a fierce discipline, a fearlessness, a love of work. But they are not inhuman. At home in the world, they embrace it with a kind of aristocratic greed that knows nothing of excess. Balance, proportion, an instinct for the distant and the formal, an exuberance, a vividness, a clarity of line: the genius of Mary Cassatt includes all these elements. The details of the combination are best put down to grace; the outlines may have been her birthright.

She was one of those wealthy Americans whose parents took the children abroad for their education and medical care. The James family comes to mind and, given her father's attitude toward her career, it is remarkable that Cassatt didn't share the fate of Alice James. But she had a remarkable mother, intelligent, encouraging of her children. When her daughter wanted to study in Paris, and her husband disapproved, Mrs. Cassatt arranged to accompany Mary as her chaperone.

From her beginnings as an art student, Cassatt was determined to follow the highest standards of craftsmanship. She went first to Paris, then to Italy, where she studied in Parma with Raimondi and spent many hours climbing up scaffolding (to the surprise of the natives) to study the work of Correggio and Parmigianino. Next, she was curious to visit Spain to look at the Spanish masters and to make use of the picturesque landscape and models. Finally, she returned to Paris, where she was to make her home, and worked with Degas, her sometime friend and difficult mentor. There has always been speculation as to whether or not they were lovers; her burning their correspondence gave the rumor credence. But I believe that they were not; she was, I think, too protective of her talent to make herself so vulnerable to Degas as a lover would have to be. But I suppose I don't believe it because I cherish, instead, the notion that a man and a woman can be colleagues and friends without causing an excuse for raised eyebrows. Most important, I want to believe they were not lovers because if they were, the trustworthiness of his extreme praise grows dilute.

She lived her life until late middle age among her family. Her beloved sister, Lydia, one of her most cherished models, had always lived as a semi-invalid and died early, in Mary's flat, of Bright's disease. Mary was closely involved with her brothers and their children. Her bond with her mother was profound: when Mrs. Cassatt died, in 1895, Mary's work began to decline. At the severing of her last close familial tie, when her surviving brother died as a result of an illness he contracted when traveling with her to Egypt, she broke down entirely. "How we try for happiness, poor things, and how we don't find it. The best cure is hard work—if only one has the health for it," she said, and lived that way.

Not surprisingly, perhaps, Cassatt's reputation has suffered because of the prejudice against her subject matter. Mothers and children: what could be of lower prestige, more vulnerable to the charge of sentimentality. Yet if one looks at the work of Mary Cassatt, one sees how triumphantly she avoids the pitfalls of sentimentality because of the astringent rigor of her eye and craft. The Cassatt iconography dashes in an instant the notion of the comfortable, easily natural fit of the maternal embrace. Again and again in her work, the child's posture embodies the ambivalence of his or her dependence. In *The Family,* the mother and child exist in positions of unease; the strong diagonals created by their postures of opposition give the pictures their tense strength, a strength that renders sentimental sweetness impossible. In *Ellen Mary Cassatt in a White Coat* and *Girl in the Blue Arm Chair,* the children seem imprisoned and dwarfed by the trappings of respectable life. The lines of Ellen's coat, which create such a powerful framing device, entrap the round and living child. The sulky little girl in the armchair seems about to be swallowed up by the massive cylinders of drawing room furniture and the strong curves of emptiness that are the floor. In *The Bath,* the little girl has all the unformed charming awkwardness of a young child: the straight limbs, the loose stomach. But these are not the stuff of Gerber babies—even of the children of Millais. In this picture, the center of interest is not the relationship between the mother and the child but the strong vertical and diagonal stripes of the mother's dress, whose opposition shape the picture with an insistence that is almost abstract.

Cassatt changed the iconography of the depiction of mothers and children. Hers do not look out into and meet the viewer's eye; neither supplicating nor seductive, they are absorbed in their own inner thoughts. Minds are at work here, a concentration unbroken by an awareness of themselves as objects to be gazed at by the world.

The brilliance of Cassatt's colors, the clarity and solidity of her forms, are the result of her love and knowledge of the masters of European painting. She had a second career as adviser to great collectors: she believed passionately that America must, for the sake of its artists, possess master-pieces, and she paid no attention to the outrage of her European friends, who felt their treasures were being sacked by barbarians. A young man visiting her in her old age noted her closed mind regarding the movement of the moderns. She thought American painters should stay home and not become "café loafers in Paris. Why should they come to Europe?" she demanded. "When I was young it was different. . . . Our Museums had not great paintings for the students to study. Now that has been corrected and something must be done to save our young over here."

One can hear the voice of the old, irascible, still splendid aunt in that comment and see the gesture of her stick toward the Left Bank. Cassatt

Diego Velazquez, *Las Meninas* 1656. Approx. 10′ 5″ × 9′.

was blinded by cataracts; the last years of her life were spent in a fog. She became ardent on the subjects of suffragism, socialism, and spiritualism; the horror of the First World War made her passionate in her conviction that mankind itself must change. She died at her country estate near Grasse, honored by the French, recipient of the Légion d'honneur, but unappreciated in America, rescued only recently from misunderstanding, really, by feminist art critics. They allowed us to begin to see her for what she is: a master of line and color whose great achievement was to take the "feminine" themes of mothers, children, women with their thoughts alone, to endow them with grandeur without withholding from them the tenderness that fits so easily alongside the rigor of her art.

LOSING THE WAR FOR AMERICA'S CULTURE?

Patrick Buchanan

The following essay appeared in the Washington Times, *May 22, 1989.*

As altarpiece of his exhibit, Andres Serrano has a photograph of a crucifix, a replica of Christ dying on the cross. The unusual feature of Mr. Serrano's exhibit, however, is that his crucifix is submerged in a vat of urine, his own. Lest one miss the point, it is titled *Piss Christ;* others are *Piss God* and *Piss Pope.*

Mr. Serrano's pièce de résistance apparently captivated judges of The Awards in the Visual Arts program of the Southeastern Center for Contemporary Art of Winston-Salem, N.C., who chose it for display and tour.

According to James Cooper, art critic of *The New York City Tribune,* AVA is funded by the National Endowment for the Arts, which, in 1985, gave Mr. Serrano its own grant of $15,000 for "creating art works composed from human body parts and decapitated heads of animals exhibited in glass vats." Your tax dollars at work.

The downhill slide of American culture gathers momentum. In a year, we have seen Martin Scorsese's *The Last Temptation of Christ*—portraying Jesus as an adulterous wimp—nominated for an Academy Award, and a modern art exhibit in Chicago where patrons were invited to walk on an American flag.

Rising above New York's West Side Highway, for a late summer unveiling, is a 75-foot-high mural celebrating Marx, Lenin, Trotsky, Mao, Castro and Che, a six-story shrine to communism, a Marxist Mount Rushmore in Greenwich Village. Funding for the *Pathfinder Mural* comes in part from Managua's Ministry of Culture.

"[F]or those who create the popular culture . . . patriotism is no longer in style," President Ronald Reagan warned in his farewell address. It was a dramatic understatement; America's art and culture are, more and more, openly anti-Christian, anti-American, nihilistic.

About last year's "Committed to Print" exhibit at the New York Museum of Modern Art, Mr. Cooper writes:

> The visitor is bombarded with picture after picture, gallery after gallery, of supposed crimes that the United States has inflicted. . . . President Reagan is portrayed . . . as a bloodthirsty vampire urging a rabid fanged dog to kill innocent Latin American peasants. Another picture portrays an ocean of skulls filling the mall in front of the United States Capital. . . . Pictures of Lt. William Calley, blackened skulls, dead babies, all serve to inculcate in the mind of the viewer one continuous unending image of America's past and present "sins." Nowhere is there any evidence of the achievements of American capitalism or democracy. Instead, posters of heroic Red Chinese soldiers . . . and Malcolm X are offered to remind us of the glorious political alternatives available by embracing socialism, communism, or worse.

While the right has been busy winning primaries and elections, cutting taxes and funding anti-communist guerrillas abroad, the left has been quietly seizing all the commanding heights of American art and culture. Mr. Cooper, who edits the excellent little magazine *American Arts Quarterly*, is direct in his blame, scathing in his commentary:

> Conservatives have not even made the attempt of creating their own culture program during the last 100 years. Nor has the religious community, despite a tradition of glorious art that has produced Gothic cathedrals, the Sistine Chapel, the music of Johann Sebastian Bach and the art of Raphael, Durer and Rembrandt.
>
> American churches, business corporations, and government and educational institutions have . . . meekly embraced without protest a nihilist, existential, relativist, secular humanist culture they profess to abhor. Later, they wonder why films are made that are as sacrilegious as *The Last Temptation of Christ* . . . or why art shows that are blatantly pro-communist can . . . be seen at such locations as the Museum of Modern Art.
>
> The reason for all of this is simple. Those who believe in absolute values such as God and beauty do nothing, and those who believe in existential humanism have captured the culture. Businessmen, political leaders and bankers have failed to recognize the importance of culture as a force for good and a force for evil. . . .
>
> Political leaders in Washington believe that the battle against communism is being fought in the jungles of Asia and Central America, while failing to realize the war is also raging on the battlefield of the arts within our own borders.
>
> The United States spends $5 billion a year on the arts, but no one questions the nihilist values this art disseminates to the American public. The conservatives simply bury their heads in the sand and do nothing.

Is he wrong? So, what is to be done?

Conservatives and the religious community that comprise the vast middle-American population should actively support those artists that advocate the same values and ideas as they do. They should also choose to withdraw support and funding from the modernist culture they profess to despise. In short, they should do what the liberals did long ago—"capture the culture."

Surely the place to begin is with the National Endowment of the Arts, whose new chairman is to be selected, soon, by president George Bush.

A nation absorbs its values through its art. A corrupt culture will produce a corrupt people, and vice versa; between rotten art, films, plays and books—and rotten behavior—the correlation is absolute. The hour is late; America needs a cultural revolution in the '90s as sweeping as its political revolution in the '80s.

End of sermon. Amen.

SUITABLE ART—STATEMENT TO THE SENATE
■

John Danforth

The following selection is a reprint of a statement made on the floor of the United States Senate on September 29, 1989.

Mr. President, I have unfortunately had the opportunity to look very briefly at the exhibits that the Senator from North Carolina has brought to the floor and everything that has been said about them is true. These are gross. These are terrible. These are totally indefensible. I do not think they are art.

Mr. President, however I do not believe that the issue before us tonight is whether we like or do not like these pictures. I do not like them and my guess is that not a single resident of my State would like them. They would not like the idea of the Government paying for them. I am sorry Government did pay for them.

That is not the issue before us. The issue is very simple: The Senator from Texas used the expression, and I think it was very well chosen, the question is: What is suitable art? And the issue before the Senate is very simple, and it is whether we in the U.S. Senate should attempt to make definitions of what we consider to be suitable art.

Maybe there should not be any National Endowment for the Arts. Maybe the Government should never be in the business of making judgments of taste, because that is what the NEA does. I think that is an arguable position. But the question is not whether the NEA should do it or not do it. We have already decided that the NEA is in that business.

The question is whether we in the Congress of the United States should try to establish some criteria by which we define what is or is not suitable art. That is what the Senator from North Carolina does by his amendment. His amendment does not say that the Mapplethorpe exhibition is pornography and it should not be funded. He does not say that. He goes much more broadly than that. He does not say that Mr. Serrano should or should not be funded by the NEA.

He goes much more broadly than that in the terms of his amendment, and I want to read a couple paragraphs because we have been focusing on obscenity and I think everybody knows that obscenity has been a problem for the Supreme Court of the United States. But he also says in paragraph 2 that the amendment covers material which denigrates the object or beliefs of the adherents of a particular religion or nonreligion.

Mr. President, consider what that means: Material which denigrates the object or beliefs of the adherents of a particular religion or nonreligion.

Does it denigrate the object of a religion to portray Christ as a clown? Well, the musical *Godspell* did just that. It portrayed Christ as a clown. Could it be found by some administrator that the portrayal of Christ as a clown denigrates the object of somebody's religion? Of course it could.

Godspell probably would be covered by the breadth of this amendment. How about a portrayal of Christ as a wild animal? Would that portrayal denigrate a person's religion? Well, C.S. Lewis did that in *The Lion, the Witch and the Wardrobe.* It was a book about Christianity and the Christ figure was a lion and some administrator, some bureaucrat could have said that denigrates a person's religion. C.S. Lewis spent his academic and literary life describing his religious beliefs which were very, very profound beliefs.

How about in the world of music? Could it be said that the beliefs of the Quaker faith are denigrated by "Onward Christian Soldiers Marching as to War"?

And then how about the question of race. I remember from my own part the country, *Tom Sawyer* and *Huckleberry Finn.* There have been those throughout the last number of decades who have tried for one reason or another to get *Tom Sawyer* and *Huckleberry Finn* off of the shelves of our schools.

This amendment would say that *Tom Sawyer* would not have qualified for an NEA grant and *Huckleberry Finn* because it could be argued that they denigrated an individual, namely Nigger Jim, as he was called according to his race.

Or how about creed? Can we think of anything in the annals of literature that denigrates an individual because of his religion? How about the *Merchant of Venice?* How about William Shakespeare himself? Would that be covered by this amendment? I think it would be. This amendment is not just about Mapplethorpe. It is also about Shakespeare.

And in our own time in American literature Alice Walker's great little book, *The Color Purple* made into a movie, clearly denigrates men. And this amendment says that material that denigrates or reviles a person on the basis of sex falls within the parameters. I take it that *The Color Purple* would not have qualified for an NEA grant.

How about age? I do not remember the name of the book, but I do remember that Bill Cosby, the famous comedian, wrote a book about kids. It is a spoof of children, and his television programs are always doing that. And I take it that those programs and that book denigrate people on the basis of age.

Then there is national origin which is also covered material that denigrates or reviles on the basis of national origin. Perhaps *The Godfather.* The head of Paramount Theaters was visiting with me recently. I said. "What is the greatest movie you ever made?" He said, "The two Godfather movies taken together, absolutely the essence of American art" and it would be covered by this amendment.

I am not for Mapplethorpe. I am sick that a dollar of taxpayer money went to pay for this kind of junk. I am sick about it. I could just see the faces of the people of Sedalia, or Cabool, or Mountain Grove, MO, if they were told that they had to pay for this. It truly is outlandish. That is not the issue.

The issue is: How good are we at defining whether something is suitable art or not-suitable art and how do we draw those definitions? And should we really write definitions on the floor of the Senate which cover *Godspell,* and *Tom Sawyer,* and *The Merchant of Venice,* and *The Color Purple,* and *The Godfather?* Mr. President, I think the answer is no.

PORTRAIT OF THE ARTIST
AS A FOCUS GROUP

Michiko Kakutani

This essay was originally published in the March 1, 1998 New York Times Magazine.

If you took a poll, what would America's best-loved painting look like? In their playful new book, "Painting by Numbers," two Russian émigré conceptual artists decided to find out. With a little help from some polling experts, Vitaly Komar and Alexander Melamid queried 1,001 Americans about their tastes in color, form and style, and concluded that the most wanted painting in the country is a bluish landscape painting, populated by George Washington, a family of tourists and a pair of frolicking deer. The canvas is the size of a dishwasher and looks like something that might adorn the walls of a third-rate motel. It is the apotheosis of art created by consensus.

Komar and Melamid's exercise, of course, is a sly comment on the democratization of creativity and America's mania for polls. What is more disturbing is that their satiric project unwittingly underscores another trend at work in American culture: our eagerness to substitute public opinion for personal belief, market demands for authentic artistic and political vision.

From the world of advertising, consumer research has already spread to Washington, where President Clinton has rarely made a move without checking with his pollsters, and to Hollywood, where test audiences can affect the content, pacing and tone of big-budget pictures and determine which TV pilots get scheduled. From Hollywood, it is now spreading into music, theater, novels and journalism. The result is a new brand of carefully positioned art and a culture-wide embrace of that old advertising slogan *"The customer is always right"—even if that customer has no expertise, no knowledge and no taste.*

MTV's new show "12 Angry Viewers" gives audience members a chance to add a video to the station's playlist, and focus groups similarly determine what songs many radio stations will or will not play. In his insightful new book, "Dreaming Out Loud," Bruce Feiler points out that a growing number of country-music stations now employ market-research companies to tell them exactly what their audiences want. The process, he suggests, systematically excludes tracks that provoke the strongest reaction, positive as well as negative—and the resulting picks tend to be predictable, homogenized and cheerfully upbeat.

The sales imperative—be popular, be accessible, be liked—is also threatening to turn writing into another capitalist tool. In an effort to raise circulation, newspapers like The Miami Herald and The Boca Raton News have used reader-preference surveys to determine their "coverage priorities," and some novelists are adopting the literary equivalent of the applause-o-meter as well. The best-selling author Andrew Greeley has used focus groups to shape his marketing campaigns, and the novelist James Patterson has conscripted groups of test readers to analyze his books before publication. Patterson recently changed the ending of his new thriller, "Cat & Mouse," in response to reader feedback; the novel reached No. 2 on the Times best-seller list.

This shameless second-guessing is not simply a money-grubbing attempt to give audiences what they think they want. It also represents the abdication by creative types of their artistic freedom and judgment. Just as today's poll-driven politicians have elected to become mirrors of the national Zeitgeist rather than leaders, so have poll-driven "artists" elected to become assembly-line manufacturers, in thrall to the opinions of mall rats deemed demographically correct.

No one has tried harder to turn the messy process of artistic creation into a systematic, risk-free proposition than Garth Drabinsky, the producer of the Broadway musical "Ragtime." A 20-year veteran of the movie business, Drabinsky is methodically transferring Hollywood practices to the stage. He insists that a show's prospective book writer submit an initial treatment to insure that the writer is not "going off on a tangent and doing something that is incongruous to the philosophy or ideas of the producer." For "Ragtime," he hired a polling firm to help calibrate audience reactions. The show's book eventually went through some 20 drafts.

"We want to hear what audiences have to say about what they're seeing," Drabinsky says, "and most importantly, we want to find out if the work is coherent—if it's making sense emotionally and dramatically." The "Ragtime" focus groups, he argues, helped his creative team "learn about the response of audiences to what characters we've chosen to put in the show," as well as "whether they feel the show is too long."

So what if critics complained that "Ragtime" lacked a distinctive voice? So what if they thought it had the feel of a corporate committee? "Ragtime" has already racked up a $17.5 million advance, and other producers and theater owners are being encouraged to use surveys and exit polls as a means of boosting business. In an article in the theatrical magazine Back Stage, George A. Wachtel, president of a firm called Audience Research & Analysis, writes: "Response cards distributed during previews can produce objective feedback from which the creative team can learn what is working and what isn't." In five years, Wachtel says, "when you open the Playbill for a show and it says, advertising by . . . , publicity by . . . , it will also say market research by . . . , because it's going to become part of what happens on Broadway. In five years, I predict that most shows will be doing audience surveys and will be better understanding their audience from the get-go, and that the majority of new shows will have some kind of preview research."

Such predictions eerily limn a future in which Pop Art gives way to Poll Art—a future in which reproductions of Komar and Melamid's cloying painting will hang on every museum's walls.

LETTER TO HIS BROTHER, THEO

Vincent Van Gogh

Vincent Van Gogh wrote the following letter to his brother, Theo, in 1885.

My dear Theo,

It's more than time I thanked you for the 50 fr. you sent, which enabled me to get through the month, although from today onwards things will be more or less back to normal.

But—a few more studies have been done and the more I paint the more progress I think I make. The moment I received the money I took on a beautiful model and did a life-size painting of her head. It's all quite light, except for the black hair. Yet the head itself stands out in tone against a background into which I have tried to put a golden glimmer of light.

Anyway, here is the colour range: a flesh colour full of tonal values, with more bronze in the neck, jet-black hair—black which I had to do with carmine and Prussian blue—off-white for the little jacket, light yellow, much lighter than the white, for the background. A touch of flame red in the jet-black hair and again a flame-coloured bow in the off-white.

She's a girl from a café-chantant and yet the expression I was looking for was somewhat 'ecce homo-like.' But that was because I was aiming for the truth, especially in the expression, though I also wanted to put my own thoughts into it. When the model arrived, it was obvious she had had quite a few busy nights—and she said something that was fairly characteristic: 'Pour moi le champagne ne m'égaye pas, il me rend tout triste.' Then I knew how matters stood and tried to produce something voluptuous and at the same time heart-rending.

I've started a second study of the same subject in profile.

Apart from that I've done the portrait about which, as I told you, I'd been negotiating, and a study of the same head for myself. And now, during these last few days of the month, I'm hoping to paint another head of a man. I feel very cheerful, especially as far as work is concerned, and being here is doing me good.

I imagine that no matter what the girls may be, one can make money painting them, sooner than anything else. There's no denying that they can be damned beautiful, and that it is in keeping with the times that just that kind of painting should be gaining ground. Nor can there be any objections to that from even the highest artistic standpoint—painting *human beings*, that was the old Italian art, that was Millet and that is Breton.

The only question is whether one should start from the soul or from the clothes, and whether one allows the form to serve as a peg for hanging ribbons and bows from, or if one looks upon the form as a means of conveying an impression, a sentiment—or again, if one does modelling for the sake of modelling because it is such an infinitely beautiful thing to do. Only the first is ephemeral, the other two are high art.

What rather pleased me was that the girl who posed for me wanted to have one of the portraits for herself, preferably just like the one I'd done. And that she's promised to let me paint a study of her in a dancer's costume at her room, as soon as possible. It can't be done right away because the man who runs the café where she stays objects to her posing, but she's about to take lodgings with another girl, and both she and the other girl would like to have their portraits done. And I really very much hope that I'll get her back, for she has a remarkable head, and she's witty.

However, I must first get into practice because it certainly takes a special knack—they don't have much time or patience. Actually, the work needn't be the worse for being done fairly quickly, and one must be able to paint even if the model doesn't sit stock-still.

Well, you can see that I am working with a will. If I could sell something so that I could earn a bit more, I should work even harder.

As for Portier—I haven't lost heart yet—but poverty is dogging my steps and at present all dealers are suffering a little from the same defect, that of being more or less 'une nation retirée du monde'—they are so much sunk in gloom that how is one really to feel inspired to go grubbing about in all that indifference and apathy—the more so as the disease is catching.

For it's just a lot of nonsense that business is slack, one has to work quand bien même with self-confidence and enthusiasm, in short with some zeal.

And as for Portier—you wrote to me yourself that he was the first to show the impressionists & that he was overwhelmed by Durand-Ruel— well, one is bound to conclude from this that he has the initiative not just to say things but also to <u>do</u> them. It could be put down to his 60 years, however—and anyway, perhaps it was just one of those many cases when, at the time when paintings were all the rage, and trade was doing well, a great many intelligent people were being wantonly brushed aside, as if they were incompetent and of no importance, simply because they couldn't bring themselves to believe that the sudden rage for paintings and the enormous rise in prices would last. <u>Now</u> that business is hanging fire, one sees those same dealers who were so very entreprenant a few years ago—let's say about 10 years ago—turning more or less into 'une nation retirée du monde'. And we haven't yet seen the end of it.

Personal initiative with little or no capital is perhaps the seed corn for the future. We shall see.

Yesterday I saw a large phot. of a Rembrandt I didn't know—I was tremendously impressed by it—it was the head of a woman, the light falling on breast, throat, chin, the tip of the nose and the lower jaw. Forehead and eyes in the shadow of a large hat, with feathers that are probably red. Probably more red or yellow in the low-necked jacket. Dark background. The expression a mysterious smile like that of Rembrandt himself in his self-portrait with Saskia on his knee and a glass of wine in his hand.

My thoughts are full of Rembrandt and Hals these days, not because I see many of their paintings but because I see so many types amongst the people here that remind me of that period. I still keep going to those bals populaires to look at the heads of the women and of the sailors and soldiers. One pays an entrance fee of 20 or 30 centimes and drinks a glass of beer—for there isn't much hard drinking and one can have a first-rate time all evening, or at least I can, just watching the people's en-train.

I must do a lot of work from the model, it's the only way to ensure real progress.

I've discovered that my appetite has been held in check a bit too long and when I received your money I couldn't stomach any food. But I shall certainly do my best to remedy that. It doesn't take away from the fact that I have all my wits and energy about me when I'm painting. But when I'm out of doors, work in the open air is too much for me and I come over all weak.

Well, painting is something that wears one out. However, Van der Loo said, when I consulted him shortly before I came here, that I am reasonably strong après tout. That I needn't despair of reaching the requisite age to produce a complete body of work. I told him that I knew several painters who, for all their nervousness, etc., had reached the age of 60, or even 70, fortunately for themselves, and that I should like to do the same.

I also believe that if one aims for serenity, and retains one's zest for living, one's state of mind helps a great deal. And in that respect I have gained by coming here, for I've new ideas and new means of expressing what I want; the better brushes are going to prove a great help, and I'm very excited by those two colours carmine & cobalt.

Cobalt—is a divine colour and there is nothing as fine for putting an atmosphere round things. Carmine is the red of wine and is warm and lively like wine. The same goes for emerald green too. It's false economy to dispense with them, with those colours. Cadmium as well.

Something about my constitution that has pleased me a great deal is that a doctor in Amsterdam, with whom I once discussed a few things that sometimes made me think that I wasn't long for this world, and whose opinion I didn't ask for directly, wanting simply to gauge the first impression of someone who didn't know me at all and availing myself of a small upset I had at the time to bring the conversation round to my general constitution—I was absolutely delighted that this doctor took me for an ordinary worker, saying, 'I daresay you're an ironworker by trade.' That's exactly what I'd been trying to achieve—when I was younger you could tell that my mind was overwrought, and now I look like a bargee or an ironworker.

And changing one's constitution so that one gets 'le cuir dur' is no easy matter. However, I must go on being careful, try to hold on to what I have and to improve on it still.

Above all, I should like you to tell me if you think it absurd of me to suggest that now might be a good time for us to sow the seeds of a future business. As far as my present work is concerned, I feel I can do better— however, I do need more air and space, in other words I must be able to spread my wings a little. Above all, above all, I still haven't enough models. I could soon produce work of higher quality, but my expenses would be heavier. Still, one should aim at something lofty, genuine, something distinguished, shouldn't one?

The female figures I see among the people here impress me enormously—far more for the purpose of painting them than of having them, though if the truth be told I should like both.

I am again rereading de Goncourt's book, it is first-rate. In the preface to Chérie, which you should read, there is an account of what the de Goncourts went through—and of how, at the end of their lives, they were pessimistic, yes—but also sure of themselves, knowing that they had done something, that their work would last. What fellows they were! If only we got on together better than we do now, if only we too could be in complete accord—we could be the same, couldn't we?

By the way, since, après tout, I've been virtually fasting for 4 or 5 days at this year's end—send your letter no later than 1 January.

You may well find it difficult to imagine, but it is a fact—when I receive the money my greatest craving will not be for food, though I shall have been fasting, but even more so for painting—and I shall immediately go on a hunt for models and continue until all the money is gone. Meanwhile what will be keeping me going is my breakfast with the people where I live, and a cup of coffee and some bread in the crêmerie in the evening. Supplemented, when I can, by a second cup of coffee and bread in the crêmerie for my supper or else some rye bread I keep in my trunk. As long as I am painting that is more than enough, but when my models have left, a feeling of weakness does come over me.

The models here appeal to me because they're so completely unlike the models in the country. And more especially because their character is completely different. And the contrast has given me some new ideas for the flesh colours in particular. And though I'm still not satisfied with what I've achieved with my last head, it does differ from the earlier ones.

I think you value the truth enough for me to speak freely to you. For much the same reasons that if I paint peasant women I want them to be peasant women—so I want to get a whore's expression when I paint whores.

That is precisely why a whore's head by Rembrandt struck me so forcefully. Because he had caught that mysterious smile in such an infinitely beautiful way, with a sérieux of his very own—the magician of magicians.

This is something new for me, and I want to achieve it at all costs. Manet has done it and Courbet—well, sacrebleu, I've the same ambition too, the more so as I've felt the infinite beauty of the study of women by the giants of literature—Zola, Daudet, de Goncourt, Balzac—in the very marrow of my bones.

Even Stevens fails to satisfy me, because his women are not like any I know personally. And those he chooses are not the most interesting there are, I find.

Well, be that as it may—I want to get on à tout prix, and—I want to be myself. I am feeling obstinate, too, and no longer care what people say about me or about my work.

It seems more difficult to get a nude model here—the girl I used wouldn't do it, at any rate. Of course, that 'wouldn't' is probably relative, but you certainly can't take it for granted. Still, the fact is she would be splendid.

From a business point of view I can only say that we are in what people have already begun to call 'la fin d'un siècle'—that the women have the same charm as at a time of revolution—and just as much to say—and that one would be 'retiré du monde' if one worked without them. It is the same everywhere, in the country as much as in the city—one has to take women into account if one wants to be up to date.

Goodbye, have a happy New Year, with a handshake,

Ever yours,
Vincent

THE WHITE BIRD

John Berger

The following essay is from Berger's 1985 book The Sense of Sight.

From time to time I have been invited by institutions—mostly American—to speak about aesthetics. On one occasion I considered accepting and I thought of taking with me a bird made of white wood. But I didn't go. The problem is that you can't talk about aesthetics without talking about the principle of hope and the existence of evil. During the long winters the peasants in certain parts of the Haute Savoie used to make wooden birds to hang in their kitchens and perhaps also in their chapels. Friends who are travellers have told me that they have seen similar birds, made according to the same principle, in certain regions of Czechoslovakia, Russia and the Baltic countries. The tradition may be more widespread.

The principle of the construction of these birds is simple enough, although to make a fine bird demands considerable skill. You take two bars of pine wood, about six inches in length, a little less than one inch in height and the same in width. You soak them in water so that the wood has the maximum pliability, then you carve them. One piece will be the head and body with a fan tail, the second piece will represent the wings. The art principally concerns the making of the wing and tail feathers. The whole block of each wing is carved according to the silhouette of a single feather. Then the block is sliced into thirteen thin layers and these are gently opened out, one by one, to make a fan shape. Likewise for the second wing and for the tail feathers. The two pieces of wood are joined together to form a cross and the bird is complete. No glue is used and there is only one nail where the two pieces of wood cross. Very light, weighing only two or three ounces, the birds are usually hung on a thread from an overhanging mantelpiece or beam so that they move with the air currents.

It would be absurd to compare one of these birds to a van Gogh self-portrait or a Rembrandt crucifixion. They are simple, home-made objects, worked according to a traditional pattern. Yet, by their very simplicity, they allow one to categorize the qualities which make them pleasing and mysterious to everyone who sees them.

First there is a figurative representation—one is looking at a bird, more precisely a dove, apparently hanging in mid-air. Thus, there is a reference to the surrounding world of nature. Secondly, the choice of subject (a flying bird) and the context in which it is placed (indoors where live birds are unlikely) render the object symbolic. This primary symbolism then joins a more general, cultural one. Birds, and doves in particular, have been credited with symbolic meanings in a very wide variety of cultures.

Thirdly, there is a respect for the material used. The wood has been fashioned according to its own qualities of lightness, pliability and texture. Looking at it, one is surprised by how well wood becomes bird. Fourthly, there is a formal unity and economy. Despite the object's apparent complexity, the grammar of its making is simple, even austere. Its richness is the result of repetitions which are also variations. Fifthly, this man-made object provokes a kind of astonishment: how on earth was it made? I have given rough indications above, but anyone unfamiliar with the technique wants to take the dove in his hands and examine it closely to discover the secret which lies behind its making.

These five qualities, when undifferentiated and perceived as a whole, provoke at least a momentary sense of being before a mystery. One is looking at a piece of wood that has become a bird. One is looking at a bird that is somehow more than a bird. One is looking at something that has been worked with a mysterious skill and a kind of love.

Thus far I have tried to isolate the qualities of the white bird which provoke an aesthetic emotion. (The word "emotion," although designating a motion of the heart and of the imagination, is somewhat confusing for we are considering an emotion that has little to do with the others we experience, notably because the self here is in a far greater degree of abeyance.) Yet my definitions beg the essential question. They reduce aesthetics to art. They say nothing about the relation between art and nature, art and the world.

Before a mountain, a desert just after the sun has gone down, or a fruit tree, one can also experience aesthetic emotion. Consequently we are forced to begin again—not this time with a man-made object but with the nature into which we are born.

Urban living has always tended to produce a sentimental view of nature. Nature is thought of as a garden, or a view framed by a window, or as an arena of freedom. Peasants, sailors, nomads have known better. Nature is energy and struggle. It is what exists without any promise. If it can be thought of by man as an arena, a setting, it has to be thought of as one which lends itself as much to evil as to good. Its energy is fearsomely indifferent. The first necessity of life is shelter. Shelter against nature. The first prayer is for protection. The first sign of life is pain. If the Creation was purposeful, its purpose is a hidden one which can only be discovered intangibly within signs, never by the evidence of what happens.

It is within this bleak natural context that beauty is encountered, and the encounter is by its nature sudden and unpredictable. The gale blows itself out, the sea changes from the colour of grey shit to aquamarine. Under the fallen boulder of an avalanche a flower grows. Over the shanty town the moon rises. I offer dramatic examples so as to insist upon the bleakness of the context. Reflect upon more everyday examples. However it is encountered, beauty is always an exception, always *in despite of*. This is why it moves us.

It can be argued that the origin of the way we are moved by natural beauty was functional. Flowers are a promise of fertility, a sunset is a reminder of fire and warmth, moonlight makes the night less dark, the bright colours of a bird's plumage are (atavistically even for us) a sexual stimulus. Yet such an argument is too reductionist, I believe. Snow is useless. A butterfly offers us very little.

Of course the range of what a given community finds beautiful in nature will depend upon its means of survival, its economy, its geography. What Eskimos find beautiful is unlikely to be the same as what the Ashanti found beautiful. Within modern class societies there are complex ideological determinations: we know, for instance, that the British ruling class in the eighteenth century disliked the sight of the sea. Equally, the social use to which an aesthetic emotion may be put changes according to the historical moment: the silhouette of a mountain can represent the home of the dead or a challenge to the initiative of the living. Anthropology, comparative studies of religion, political economy and Marxism have made all this clear.

Yet there seem to be certain constants which all cultures have found 'beautiful': among them—certain flowers, trees, forms of rock, birds, animals, the moon, running water . . .

One is obliged to acknowledge a coincidence or perhaps a congruence. The evolution of natural forms and the evolution of human perception have coincided to produce the phenomenon of a potential recognition: what *is* and what we can see (and by seeing also feel) sometimes meet at a point of affirmation. This point, this coincidence, is two-faced: what has been seen is recognized and affirmed and, at the same time, the seer is affirmed by what he sees. For a brief moment one finds oneself—without the pretensions of a creator—in the position of God in the first chapter of Genesis . . . And he saw that *it was* good. The aesthetic emotion before nature derives, I believe, from this double affirmation.

Yet we do not live in the first chapter of Genesis. We live—if one follows the biblical sequence of events—after the Fall. In any case, we live in a world of suffering in which evil is rampant, a world whose events do not confirm our Being, a world that has to be resisted. It is in this situation that the aesthetic moment offers hope. That we find a crystal or a poppy beautiful means that we are less alone, that we are more deeply inserted into existence than the course of a single life would lead us to believe. I try to describe as accurately as possible the experience in question; my starting point is phenomenological, not deductive; its form, perceived as such, becomes a message that one receives but cannot translate because, in it, all is instantaneous. For an instant, the energy of one's perception becomes inseparable from the energy of the creation.

The aesthetic emotion we feel before a man-made object—such as the white bird with which I started—is a derivative of the emotion we feel before nature. The white bird is an attempt to translate a message received from a real bird. All the languages of art have been developed as an attempt to transform the instantaneous into the permanent. Art supposes that beauty is not an exception—is not *in despite of*—but is the basis for an order.

Several years ago, when considering the historical face of art, I wrote that I judged a work according to whether or not it helped men in the modern world claim their social rights. I hold to that. Art's other, transcendental face raises the question of man's ontological right.

The notion that art is the mirror of nature is one that only appeals in periods of scepticism. Art does not imitate nature, it imitates a creation, sometimes to propose an alternative world, sometimes simply to amplify, to confirm, to make social the brief hope offered by nature. Art is an organized response to what nature allows us to glimpse occasionally. Art sets out to transform the potential recognition into an unceasing one. It proclaims man in the hope of receiving a surer reply . . . the transcendental face of art is always a form of prayer.

The white wooden bird is wafted by the warm air rising from the stove in the kitchen where the neighbours are drinking. Outside, in minus 25°C, the real birds are freezing to death!

LANDMARK KITSCH

Paul Goldberger

This piece originally appeared in the August 18, 1997, New Yorker.

John Krawchuk's view of New York City was formed by the television shows that he watched growing up in California in the early nineteen-seventies: "The Courtship of Eddie's Father," "Family Affair," and the PBS documentary "An American Family," in which Lance Loud, the gay son, resettles in Manhattan. Krawchuk's idea of architecture was shaped by "The Jetsons" and "The Brady Bunch." So it is not altogether surprising that his favorite building is the old Huntington Hartford Gallery of Modern Art, on Columbus Circle—the confection of white marble designed by Edward Durell Stone, which less generous souls have likened to a Hollywood version of a Persian whorehouse. Krawchuk, a thirty-one-year-old landscape architect with a degree in historic preservation from Columbia, is one of the leaders of a movement to save the building. He also likes Stone's General Motors Building, on Fifth Avenue—a white marble skyscraper with forty-eight stories of bay windows—which is despised by most architects who were around when it was built, in 1968. Krawchuk was three years old then. He doesn't know a New York without the GM Building—or without the glass boxes of Sixth Avenue, or the Pan Am Building, or Lincoln Center, or the white brick apartment blocks on Second Avenue. To him, those buildings define the city, just as the Art Deco skyscrapers epitomized New York for a previous generation, and the Beaux-Arts monuments and brownstones for earlier generations still.

But is the former Gallery of Modern Art, now known as 2 Columbus Circle, the equivalent of the Frick Collection in the greater scheme of architectural history? If so, Kennedy Airport belongs on the list that begins with Grand Central Terminal. That is precisely what Krawchuk and plenty of other young architects and historic preservationists are saying. And they have been increasingly successful in persuading their elders, the people who grew up hating the buildings of the postwar era, to go along with them.

That tastes change, and have always changed, is the premise on which landmarks laws are based: they are intended to protect worthy architecture from the whims of fashion. In the fifties and sixties, there were few things lower on the scale of aesthetic values than Victorian and Edwardian architecture, and all kinds of buildings that would be cherished today were summarily demolished, often to make room for the very buildings that are now the subject of anguished debate. That paradox has not gone unnoticed. "A lot of the buildings that have to be preserved are the ones the preservationists came of age attacking, the ones they thought were the horrible buildings of the fifties and sixties," says Nina Rappaport, an architectural historian affiliated with DOCO-MOMO, an organization formed in the Netherlands in 1988 to preserve modernist architecture.

Still, even among those who believe that there is postwar architecture worth saving, 2 Columbus Circle has become the subject of controversy. "It's a flashy, vulgar building built by an architect who wanted to be elegant and original and failed miserably," Donald Oresman, the chairman of the Landmarks Conservancy, said the other day. "The thing looks like a stork whose legs were cut off at the knees."

"People talk about that building the way they once talked about the Jefferson Market Courthouse, in Greenwich Village," Krawchuk says, speaking of the once reviled 1887 brick-and-stone castle, by Vaux & Withers, whose rescue was one of the preservation movement's first triumphs, in the nineteen-sixties. "They say it's gawky and awkward. Well, so is the Jefferson Market Courthouse, and that's now an icon."

"If it weren't where it is, nobody would think twice about it," Oresman claims. So far, he has succeeded in preventing his colleagues on the Landmarks Conservancy board from adding the building to the list of structures they are recommending for official designation as landmarks.

The debate over the fate of 2 Columbus Circle began last year, when the city put the place up for sale. Given to the city by Gulf & Western seventeen years ago, it had been used as offices for the Department of Cultural Affairs and the Convention and Visitors Bureau. A private art collection, called the Dahesh Museum, expressed interest in buying it recently, but the Giuliani administration, considering the fourth-coming redevelopment of the Coliseum, next door, decided that more money could be made by selling the building to a developer. It would be a preservation scandal—"CITY SELLS OFF MUSEUM TO DEVELOPER!"—if the preservation community weren't so deeply ambivalent about Stone's handiwork.

Unfortunately for advocates of 2 Columbus Circle, no one has yet made a persuasive case that the building is much more than kitsch. And it's harder still to make a case for it as a historic artifact: it was put up in 1965 by a supermarket heir in a bizarre bid to overthrow the Museum of Modern Art's cultural power. The paintings in Hartford's collection, long gone, were undistinguished, and the building's vertically organized galleries, bereft of windows, would have doomed it even with better pictures. About the only thing that this eerily dumb building has ever done successfully is stand as a kind of amiable monumental presence at the foot of Central Park West. Its curved façade, dainty pillars, and porthole windows create a strangely innocent, fanciful quality, and perhaps the only argument for giving it landmark status is that it has become familiar, and hence a source of comfort. It's less like a building than like a Claes Oldenburg sculpture.

"I grew up thinking that everything modern was ticky-tacky and all the same," Peg Breen, who is the president of the Landmarks Conservancy, said recently. "Well, to me these buildings are a lot less huggable than older ones, but I'm learning that there is architecture there, too, and we need to include them in our definition of landmarks." To that end, the conservancy sponsored a lecture by the architect Robert A. M. Stern last October, in which Stern, best known as a designer of traditional houses for the rich, listed thirty-five modern buildings in New York that he deemed worthy of designation as landmarks, and proclaimed that the time had come to treat modern architecture as reverentially as the architecture of the distant past, for, after all, modernism now *is* the past. The Gallery of Modern Art is No. 26 on Stern's list. "People of a certain age think I'm out of my mind," he said. "But it's the only building on Columbus Circle that actually honors the idea of a circle: it was built to be a monument."

There is a real difference between modern buildings that are lovably eccentric, like 2 Columbus Circle, or Morris Lapidus's curving blue brick Summit Hotel, now Loews New York, on Lexington Avenue (the one that everyone said was nice but a little far from the beach); those that are dreary and banal, like the office towers of Park Avenue; and those that achieve a more profound degree of architectural experience, like the sumptuously elegant Seagram Building, on Park Avenue, or the Ford Foundation headquarters, built around a glassed-in garden on East Forty-second Street. The Landmarks Preservation Commission is as conscious of these distinctions as anyone. And it has remained, so far, solidly on the side of the modernist icons, declining even to hold a hearing on 2 Columbus Circle but enthusiastically designating Lever House, the green glass slab on Park Avenue that was among the city's first glass buildings, the Seagram Building, and the old Pepsi-Cola headquarters, at 500 Park Avenue. This fall, it will consider three more: the Ford Foundation, the black granite CBS Building, and the Chase Manhattan Bank on Fifth Avenue at Forty-third Street, the glass box built in 1954 for the Manufacturers Bank.

These buildings were all acclaimed when they were new and have never gone entirely out of fashion. To have a problem with them, you would have to believe that architecture stopped with Stanford White. As for the eccentric modern buildings and the banal ones—the architecture that the critics never liked but that a younger generation clings to as part of the texture of the city it has inherited—Jennifer Raab, the chairman of the commission, says only, "I'm very open to learning, but I do not think we have to rush."

Every generation enjoys embracing what the previous one disdained, of course, but in architecture the tension may be more acute. If modernism failed at anything, it was at creating a workable, comfortable vernacular—a design vocabulary out of which appealing everyday buildings could be made. Ordinary modern architecture was about making things quick and cheap, not about making civilized cities. Robert Stern recalls hearing an executive of one of New York's biggest builders of office towers in the fifties and sixties say that the glass-and-metal boxes his company erected were intended to last for the life of their mortgages, and no longer.

So why preserve buildings that even their creators thought so little of? You sometimes hear high-flown talk about the importance of postwar modernism to the "narrative" of New York, but the real reason a lot of these buildings are going to be saved is that people have got used to them. Like John Krawchuk, architects under forty view them as having always been there. No thirty-year-old remembers McKim, Mead & White's Savoy-Plaza, which once stood on the site of the GM Building, or the vista that existed on Park Avenue before the Pan Am Building blocked it, or the lower Manhattan skyline before the World Trade Center tipped it toward New Jersey. You don't regret the loss of what you never had.

As for the rest of us—people like me, who remember staring down into the hole that was to become the Time-Life Building in 1959, when I was nine—well, you get used to anything. Architecture, because its presence is constant, has a strangely benign effect over time: even the ugliest buildings become tolerable—and actually comforting. We expect to see them, and thus in some small way we come to value them. It is an odd irony that modernism, an architectural style that was anything but sentimental, has come to be the object of considerable sentiment.

Modern architecture was invented to obliterate history, not to make it. When the modern style evolved—in Europe, in the early decades of this century—its goal was to sweep away the clutter of the past, including classical columns and Gothic arches. Modernists were going to invent the world anew and, through the clean simplicity of their buildings, create a better life for all. It worked for a few years—the modernist buildings of the twenties and thirties almost always seem to wear a halo of utopian idealism—but by the end of the Second World War the dream had disintegrated into a kind of corporate dullness. Modern architecture meant the new American corporation, not a new way of living. Treating quick, cheap modern buildings as permanent presences requires a lot of rethinking on the part of preservationists. "We know what to recommend for a limestone building with a deteriorating façade," Jennifer Raab says, "but what do you do with a glass-curtain wall? We're not yet experts in how to preserve modern buildings."

The commission faced its first such situation earlier this year, when the owners of Lever House decided to replace the green glass façade that gives the building its character. The glass had deteriorated badly after more than forty winters, and had always been problematic in terms of energy conservation. Engineers first proposed putting a new glass skin over the existing one, for added insulation. The Landmarks Commission was less than enthusiastic about the proposal, arguing that it would change the building's appearance, and urged the company to consult with Skidmore, Owings & Merrill, the original architects. Gordon Bunshaft, who designed the building, died in 1990, but David Childs, one of the firm's chief design partners, and a man who had made his reputation designing postmodern skyscrapers with classical details, came up with a new glass skin that will look, he says, exactly like the original. The glass is scheduled to be replaced later this year.

Lever House's face-lift brings up another paradox of modern landmarks: in the case of older buildings, authenticity is usually a matter of retaining genuine and original pieces that bear the patina of age, but modern buildings can often be made *more* authentic by having their parts replaced. Like the Bionic Man, they are truest to form when they are forever new.

Modern buildings need to be protected by a different set of standards. Most landmark designations cover only the exterior of a building. But what if a building is made of glass, and the exterior is transparent? Change the inside, and you have changed the outside, too. The former Manufacturers Bank at the corner of Fifth Avenue and Forty-third Street once had a pristine, simple interior that was entirely visible from the street. Now Chase has put colored signs with its logo everywhere on the second floor, and has rented out part of the ground floor as a showroom for office machines. From the outside, the bank is a different building altogether, even though not an inch of its original structure has been changed.

When there isn't much ornament, windows and surface mean everything. In the Look Building, the "wedding cake-like" pile of alternating horizontal ribbons of brick and glass at 488 Madison Avenue, the rhythm of stripes wrapping around curved corners makes a definite architectural statement—enough, at least, so that the building is on most modern preservationists' priority lists. All those setbacks and curves do confer a certain presence—a somewhat endearing combination of the flamboyant and the boring, sort of like a 1955 DeSoto.

I know that I once thought nothing of this building, and now I like it, and could even begin to make a case for it as a serious work of architecture.

But do I like it because I am used to seeing it at the corner of Fifty-first Street—because it has become the architectural equivalent of comfort food? Isn't that the kind of criterion John Krawchuk would use?

Not a chance. He is actually quite tough. "I don't like everything," he said. "Sure, I like old things like the Pan Am Building and Lincoln Center. But some of this new architecture—I don't know about it. Take the Millennium, that apartment building on the West Side that just went up. I look at it, and I wonder how it could ever be a landmark. I just see a lot of glass and brick."

ON PAINTING

Leon Battista Alberti

The following selection was published in Latin in 1435 and in Italian a year later.

Because this [process of] learning may perhaps appear a fatiguing thing to young people, I ought to prove here that painting is not unworthy of consuming all our time and study.

Painting contains a divine force which not only makes absent men present, as friendship is said to do, but moreover makes the dead seem almost alive. Even after many centuries they are recognized with great pleasure and with great admiration for the painter. Plutarch says that Cassander, one of the captains of Alexander, trembled through all his body because he saw a portrait of his King. Agesilaos, the Lacedaemonian, never permitted anyone to paint him or to represent him in sculpture; his own form so displeased him that he avoided being known by those who would come after him. Thus the face of a man who is already dead certainly lives a long life through painting. Some think that painting shaped the gods who were adored by the nations. It certainly was their greatest gift to mortals, for painting is most useful to that piety which joins us to the gods and keeps our souls full of religion. They say that Phidias made in Aulis a god Jove so beautiful that it considerably strengthened the religion then current.

The extent to which painting contributes to the most honourable delights of the soul and to the dignified beauty of things can be clearly seen not only from other things but especially from this: you can conceive of almost nothing so precious which is not made far richer and much more beautiful by association with painting. Ivory, gems and similar expensive things become more precious when worked by the hand of the painter. Gold worked by the art of painting outweighs an equal amount of unworked gold. If figures were made by the hand of Phidias or Praxiteles from lead itself—the lowest of metals—they would be valued more highly than silver. The painter, Zeuxis, began to give away his things because, as he said, they could not be bought. He did not think it possible to come to a just price which would be satisfactory to the painter, for in painting animals he set himself up almost as a god.

Therefore, painting contains within itself this virtue that any master painter who sees his works adored will feel himself considered another god. Who can doubt that painting is the master art or at least not a small ornament of things? The architect, if I am not mistaken, takes from the painter architraves, bases, capitals, columns, façades and other similar things. All the smiths, sculptors, shops and guilds are governed by the rules and art of the painter. It is scarcely possible to find any superior art which is not concerned with painting, so that whatever beauty is found can be said to be born of painting. *But also this, a dignified painting is held in high honour by many so that among all artists some smiths are named, only this is not the rule among smiths.* For this reason, I say among my friends that Narcissus who was changed into a flower, according to the poets, was the inventor of painting. Since painting is already the flower of every art, the story of Narcissus is most to the point. What else can you call painting but a similar embracing with art of what is presented on the surface of the water in the fountain?

Quintilian said that the ancient painters used to circumscribe shadows cast by the sun, and from this our art has grown. There are those who say that a certain Philocles, an Egyptian, and a Cleantes were among the first inventors of this art. The Egyptians affirm that painting was in use among them a good 6000 years before it was carried into Greece. They say that painting was brought to us from Greece after the victory of Marcellus over Sicily. But we are not interested in knowing who was the inventor of the art or the first painter, since we are not telling stories like Pliny. We are, however, building anew an art of painting about which nothing, as I see it, has been written in this age. They say that Euphranor of Isthmus wrote something about measure and about colours, that Antigonos and Xenocrates exchanged something in their letters about painting, and that Apelles wrote to Pelleus about painting. Diogenes Laertius recounts that Demetrius made commentaries on painting. Since all the other arts were recommended in letters by our great men, and since painting was not neglected by our Latin writers, I believe that our ancient Tuscan [ancestors] were already most expert masters in painting.

Trismegistus, an ancient writer, judged that painting and sculpture were born at the same time as religion, *for thus he answered Aesclepius: mankind portrays the gods in his own image from his memories of nature and his own origins.* Who can here deny that in all things public and private, profane and religious, painting has taken all the most honourable parts to itself so that nothing has ever been so esteemed by mortals?

The incredible prices of painted pictures have been recorded. Aristides the Theban sold a single picture for one hundred talents. They say that Rhodes was not burned by King Demetrius for fear that a painting of Protogenes' should perish. It could be said that the city of Rhodes was ransomed from the enemy by a single painting. Pliny collected many other such things in which you can see that good painters have always been greatly honoured by all. The most noble citizens, philosophers and quite a few kings not only enjoyed painted things but also painted with their own hands. Lucius Manilius, Roman citizen, and Fabius, a most noble man, were painters. Turpilius, a Roman knight, painted at Verona. Sitedius, praetor and proconsul, acquired renown as a painter. Pacuvius, tragic poet and nephew of the poet Ennuis, painted Hercules in the Roman forum. Socrates, Plato, Metrodorus, Pyrrho were connoisseurs of painting. The emperors Nero, Valentinian, and Alexander Severus were most devoted to painting. It would be too long, however, to recount here how many princes and kings were pleased by painting. Nor does it seem necessary to me to recount all the throng of ancient painters. Their number is seen in the fact that 360 statues, part on horseback and part in chariots, were completed in four hundred days for Demetrius Phalerius, son of Phanostratus. In a land in which there was such a great number of sculptors, can you believe that painters were lacking? I am certain that both these arts are related and nurtured by the same genius, painting with sculpture. But I always give higher rank to the genius of the painter because he works with more difficult things.

However, let us return to our work. Certainly the number of sculptors and painters was great in those times when princes and plebeians, learned and unlearned enjoyed painting, and when painted panels and portraits, considered the choicest booty from the provinces, were set up in the theatres. Finally L. Paulus Aemilius and not a few other Roman citizens taught their sons painting along with the fine arts and the art of living piously and well. This excellent custom was frequently observed among the Greeks who, because they wished their sons to be well educated, taught them painting along with geometry and music. It was also an honour among women to know how to paint. Martia, daughter of Varro, is praised by the writers because she knew how to paint. Painting had such reputation and honour among the Greeks that laws and edicts were passed forbidding slaves to learn painting. It was certainly well that they did this, for the art of painting has always been most worthy of liberal minds and noble souls.

As for me, I certainly consider a great appreciation of painting to be the best indication of a most perfect mind, even though it happens that this art is pleasing to the uneducated as well as to the educated. It occurs rarely in any other art that what delights the experienced also moves the inexperienced. In the same way you will find that many greatly desire to be well versed in painting. Nature herself seems to delight in painting, for in the cut faces of marble she often paints centaurs and faces of bearded and curly headed kings. It is said, moreover, that in a gem from Pyrrhus all nine Muses, each with her symbol, are to be found clearly painted by nature. Add to this that in no other art does it happen that both the experienced and the inexperienced of every age apply themselves so voluntarily to the learning and exercising of it. Allow me to speak of myself here. Whenever I turn to painting for my recreation, which I frequently do when I am tired of more pressing affairs, I apply myself to it with so much pleasure that I am surprised that three or four hours have passed. Thus this art gives pleasure and praise to whoever is skilled in it; riches and perpetual fame to one who is master of it. Since these things are so, since painting is the best and most ancient ornament of things, worthy of free men, pleasing to learned and unlearned, I greatly encourage our studious youth to exert themselves as much as possible in painting.

Therefore, I recommend that he who is devoted to painting should learn this art. The first great care of one who seeks to obtain eminence in painting is to acquire the fame and renown of the ancients. It is useful to remember that avarice is always the enemy of virtue. Rarely can anyone given to acquisition of wealth acquire renown. I have seen many in the first flower of learning suddenly sink to money-making. As a result they acquire neither riches nor praise. However, if they had increased their talent with study, they would have easily soared into great renown. Then they would have acquired much riches and pleasure. . . .

MUSÉE DES BEAUX ARTS

■

W. H. Auden

The following poem was written by Auden in 1940.

About suffering they were never wrong,
The Old Masters: how well they understood
Its human position; how it takes place
While someone else is eating or opening a window or just walking dully along;
How, when the aged are reverently, passionately waiting
For the miraculous birth, there always must be
Children who did not specially want it to happen, skating
On a pond at the edge of the wood:
They never forgot
That even the dreadful martyrdom must run its course
Anyhow in a corner, some untidy spot
Where the dogs go on with their doggy life and the torturer's horse
Scratches its innocent behind on a tree.

In Brueghel's *Icarus*, for instance: how everything turns away
Quite leisurely from the disaster; the ploughman may
Have heard the splash, the forsaken cry,
But for him it was not an important failure; the sun shone

As it had to on the white legs disappearing into the green
Water; and the expensive delicate ship that must have seen
Something amazing, a boy falling out of the sky,
Had somewhere to get to and sailed calmly on.

CATHEDRAL

Raymond Carver

This short story was first published in 1983.

This blind man, an old friend of my wife's, he was on his way to
spend the night. His wife had died. So he was visiting the dead
wife's relatives in Connecticut. He called my wife from his in-laws'.
Arrangements were made. He would come by train, a five-hour trip, and
my wife would meet him at the station. She hadn't seen him since she
worked for him one summer in Seattle ten years ago. But she and the
blind man had kept in touch. They made tapes and mailed them back
and forth. I wasn't enthusiastic about his visit. He was no one I knew.
And his being blind bothered me. My idea of blindness came from the
movies. In the movies, the blind moved slowly and never laughed. Sometimes they were led by seeing-eye dogs. A blind man in my house was
not something I looked forward to.

That summer in Seattle she bad needed a job. She didn't have any
money. The man she was going to marry at the end of the summer was in
officers' training school. He didn't have any money, either. But she was in
love with the guy, and he was in love with her, etc. She'd seen something
in the paper: HELP WANTED—*Reading to Blind Man,* and a telephone
number. She phoned and went over, was hired on the spot. She'd worked
with this blind man all summer. She read stuff to him, case studies, reports, that sort of thing. She helped him organize his little office in the
county social-service department. They'd become good friends, my wife
and the blind man. How do I know these things? She told me. And she
told me something else. On her last day in the office, the blind man asked
if he could touch her face. She agreed to this. She told me he touched his
fingers to every part of her face, her nose—even her neck! She never forgot
it. She even tried to write a poem about it. She was always trying to write
a poem. She wrote a poem or two every year, usually after something
really important had happened to her.

When we first started going out together, she showed me the poem. In
the poem, she recalled his fingers and the way they had moved around
over her face. In the poem, she talked about what she had felt at the time,
about what went through her mind when the blind man touched her nose
and lips. I can remember I didn't think much of the poem. Of course, I

didn't tell her that. Maybe I just don't understand poetry. I admit it's not the first thing I reach for when I pick up something to read.

Anyway, this man who'd first enjoyed her favors, the officer-to-be, he'd been her childhood sweetheart. So okay. I'm saying that at the end of the summer she let the blind man run his hands over her face, said goodbye to him, married her childhood etc., who was now a commissioned officer, and she moved away from Seattle. But they'd kept in touch, she and the blind man. She made the first contact after a year or so. She called him up one night from an Air Force base in Alabama. She wanted to talk. They talked. He asked her to send him a tape and tell him about her life. She did this. She sent the tape. On the tape, she told the blind man about her husband and about their life together in the military. She told the blind man she loved her husband but she didn't like it where they lived and she didn't like it that he was a part of the military-industrial thing. She told the blind man she'd written a poem about what it was like to be an Air Force officer's wife. The poem wasn't finished yet. She was still writing it. The blind man made a tape. He sent her the tape. She made a tape. This went on for years. My wife's officer was posted to one base and then another. She sent tapes from Moody AFB, McGuire, McConnell, and finally Travis, near Sacramento, where one night she got to feeling lonely and cut off from people she kept losing in that moving-around life. She got to feeling she couldn't go it another step. She went in and swallowed all the pills and capsules in the medicine chest and washed them down with a bottle of gin. Then she got into a hot bath and passed out.

But instead of dying, she got sick. She threw up. Her officer—why should he have a name? he was the childhood sweetheart, and what more does he want?—came home from somewhere, found her, and called the ambulance. In time, she put it all on a tape and sent the tape to the blind man. Over the years, she put all kinds of stuff on tapes and sent the tapes off lickety-split. Next to writing a poem every year, I think it was her chief means of recreation. On one tape, she told the blind man she'd decided to live away from her officer for a time. On another tape, she told him about her divorce. She and I began going out, and of course she told her blind man about it. She told him everything, or so it seemed to me. Once she asked me if I'd like to hear the latest tape from the blind man. This was a year ago. I was on the tape, she said. So I said okay, I'd listen to it. I got us drinks and we settled down in the living room. We made ready to listen. First she inserted the tape into the player and adjusted a couple of dials. Then she pushed a lever. The tape squeaked and someone began to talk in this loud voice. She lowered the volume. After a few minutes of harmless chitchat, I heard my own name in the mouth of this stranger, this blind man I didn't even know! And then this: "From all you've said about him, I can only conclude—" But we were interrupted, a knock at the door, something, and we didn't ever get back to the tape. Maybe it was just as well. I'd heard all I wanted to.

Now this same blind man was coming to sleep in my house.

"Maybe I could take him bowling," I said to my wife. She was at the draining board doing scalloped potatoes. She put down the knife she was using and turned around.

"If you love me," she said, "you can do this for me. If you don't love me, okay. But if you had a friend, any friend, and the friend came to visit, I'd make him feel comfortable." She wiped her hands with the dish towel.

"I don't have any blind friends," I said.

"You don't have *any* friends," she said. "Period. Besides," she said, "goddamn it, his wife's just died! Don't you understand that? The man's lost his wife!"

I didn't answer. She'd told me a little about the blind man's wife. Her name was Beulah. Beulah! That's a name for a colored woman.

"Was his wife a Negro?" I asked.

"Are you crazy?" my wife said. "Have you just flipped or something?" She picked up a potato. I saw it hit the floor, then roll under the stove. "What's wrong with you?" she said. "Are you drunk?"

"I'm just asking," I said.

Right then my wife filled me in with more detail than I cared to know. I made a drink and sat at the kitchen table to listen. Pieces of the story began to fall into place.

Beulah had gone to work for the blind man the summer after my wife had stopped working for him. Pretty soon Beulah and the blind man had themselves a church wedding. It was a little wedding—who'd want to go to such a wedding in the first place?—just the two of them, plus the minister and the minister's wife. But it was a church wedding just the same. It was what Beulah had wanted, he'd said. But even then Beulah must have been carrying the cancer in her glands. After they had been inseparable for eight years—my wife's word, *inseparable*—Beulah's health went into a rapid decline. She died in a Seattle hospital room, the blind man sitting beside the bed and holding on to her hand. They'd married, lived and worked together, slept together—had sex, sure—and then the blind man had to bury her. All this without his having ever seen what the goddamned woman looked like. It was beyond my understanding. Hearing this, I felt sorry for the blind man for a little bit. And then I found myself thinking what a pitiful life this woman must have led. Imagine a woman who could never see herself as she was seen in the eyes of her loved one. A woman who could go on day after day and never receive the smallest compliment from her beloved. A woman whose husband could never read the expression on her face, be it misery or something better. Someone who could wear makeup or not—what difference to him? She could, if she wanted, wear green eye-shadow around one eye, a straight pin in her nostril, yellow slacks and purple shoes, no matter. And then to slip off into death, the blind man's hand on her hand, his blind eyes streaming tears—I'm imagining now—her last thought maybe this: that he never even knew what she looked like, and she on an express to the grave. Robert was left with a small insurance policy and half of a twenty-peso Mexican coin. The other half of the coin went into the box with her. Pathetic.

So when the time rolled around, my wife went to the depot to pick him up. With nothing to do but wait—sure, I blamed him for that—I was having a drink and watching the TV when I heard the car pull into the drive. I got up from the sofa with my drink and went to the window to have a look.

I saw my wife laughing as she parked the car. I saw her get out of the car and shut the door. She was still wearing a smile. Just amazing. She went around to the other side of the car to where the blind man was already starting to get out. This blind man, feature this, he was wearing a full beard! A beard on a blind man! Too much, I say. The blind man reached into the back seat and dragged out a suitcase. My wife took his arm, shut the car door, and, talking all the way, moved him down the drive and then up the steps to the front porch. I turned off the TV. I finished my drink, rinsed the glass, dried my hands. Then I went to the door.

My wife said, "I want you to meet Robert. Robert, this is my husband. I've told you all about him." She was beaming. She had this blind man by his coat sleeve.

The blind man let go of his suitcase and up came his hand.

I took it. He squeezed hard, held my hand, and then he let it go.

"I feel like we've already met," he boomed.

"Likewise," I said. I didn't know what else to say. Then I said, "Welcome. I've heard a lot about you." We began to move then, a little group, from the porch into the living room, my wife guiding him by the arm. The blind man was carrying his suitcase in his other hand. My wife said things like, "To your left here, Robert. That's right. Now watch it, there's a chair. That's it. Sit down right here. This is the sofa. We just bought this sofa two weeks ago."

I started to say something about the old sofa. I'd liked that old sofa. But I didn't say anything. Then I wanted to say something else, small-talk, about the scenic ride along the Hudson. How going *to* New York, you should sit on the right-hand side of the train, and coming *from* New York, the left-hand side.

"Did you have a good train ride?" I said. "Which side of the train did you sit on, by the way?"

"What a question, which side!" my wife said. "What's it matter which side?" she said.

"I just asked," I said.

"Right side," the blind man said. "I hadn't been on a train in nearly forty years. Not since I was a kid. With my folks. That's been a long time. I'd nearly forgotten the sensation. I have winter in my beard now," he said. "So I've been told, anyway. Do I look distinguished, my dear?" the blind man said to my wife.

"You look distinguished, Robert," she said. "Robert," she said. "Robert, it's just so good to see you."

My wife finally took her eyes off the blind man and looked at me. I had the feeling she didn't like what she saw. I shrugged.

I've never met, or personally known, anyone who was blind. This blind man was late forties, a heavy-set, balding man with stooped shoulders, as if he carried a great weight there. He wore brown slacks, brown shoes, a light-brown shirt, a tie, a sports coat. Spiffy. He also had this full beard. But he didn't use a cane and he didn't wear dark glasses. I'd always thought dark glasses were a must for the blind. Fact was, I wished he had a pair. At first glance, his eyes looked like anyone else's eyes. But if you looked close, there was something different about them. Too much white in the iris, for one thing, and the pupils seemed to move around in the sockets without his knowing it or being able to stop it. Creepy. As I stared at his face, I saw the left pupil turn in toward his nose while the other made an effort to keep in one place. But it was only an effort, for that eye was on the roam without his knowing it or wanting it to be.

I said, "Let me get you a drink. What's your pleasure? We have a little of everything. It's one of our pastimes."

"Bub, I'm a Scotch man myself," he said fast enough in this big voice.

"Right," I said. Bub! "Sure you are. I knew it."

He let his fingers touch his suitcase, which was sitting alongside the sofa. He was taking his bearings. I didn't blame him for that.

"I'll move that up to your room," my wife said.

"No, that's fine," the blind man said loudly. "It can go up when I go up."

"A little water with the Scotch?" I said.

"Very little," he said.

"I knew it," I said.

He said, "Just a tad. The Irish actor, Barry Fitzgerald? I'm like that fellow. When I drink water, Fitzgerald said, I drink water. When I drink whiskey, I drink whiskey." My wife laughed. The blind man brought his hand up under his beard. He lifted his beard slowly and let it drop.

I did the drinks, three big glasses of Scotch with a splash of water in each. Then we made ourselves comfortable and talked about Robert's travels. First the long flight from the West Coast to Connecticut, we covered that. Then from Connecticut up here by train. We had another drink concerning that leg of the trip.

I remembered having read somewhere that the blind didn't smoke because, as speculation had it, they couldn't see the smoke they exhaled. I thought I knew that much and that much only about blind people. But this blind man smoked his cigarette down to the nubbin and then lit another one. This blind man filled his ashtray and my wife emptied it.

When we sat down at the table for dinner, we had another drink. My wife heaped Robert's plate with cube steak, scalloped potatoes, green beans. I buttered him up two slices of bread. I said, "Here's bread and butter for you." I swallowed some of my drink. "Now let us pray," I said, and the blind man lowered his head. My wife looked at me, her mouth agape. "Pray the phone won't ring and the food doesn't get cold," I said.

We dug in. We ate everything there was to eat on the table. We ate like there was no tomorrow. We didn't talk. We ate. We scarfed. We grazed that table. We were into serious eating. The blind man had right away located his foods, he knew just where everything was on his plate. I watched with admiration as he used his knife and fork on the meat. He'd cut two pieces of meat, fork the meat into his mouth, and then go all out for the scalloped potatoes, the beans next, and then he'd tear off a hunk of buttered bread and eat that. He'd follow this up with a big drink of milk. It didn't seem to bother him to use his fingers once in a while, either.

We finished everything, including half a strawberry pie. For a few moments, we sat as if stunned. Sweat beaded on our faces. Finally, we got up from the table and left the dirty plates. We didn't look back. We took ourselves into the living room and sank into our places again. Robert and my wife sat on the sofa. I took the big chair. We had us two or three more drinks while they talked about the major things that had come to pass for them in the past ten years. For the most part, I just listened. Now and then I joined in. I didn't want him to think I'd left the room, and I didn't want her to think I was feeling left out. They talked of things that had happened to them—to them!—these past ten years. I waited in vain to hear my name on my wife's sweet lips: "And then my dear husband came into my life"— something like that. But I heard nothing of the sort. More talk of Robert. Robert had done a little of everything, it seemed, a regular blind jack-of-all-trades. But most recently he and his wife had had an Amway distributorship, from which, I gathered, they'd earned their living, such as it was. The blind man was also a ham radio operator. He talked in his loud voice about conversations he'd had with fellow operators in Guam, in the Philippines, in Alaska, and even in Tahiti. He said he'd have a lot of friends there if he ever wanted to go visit those places. From time to time, he'd turn his blind face toward me, put his hand under his beard, ask me something. How long had I been in my present position? (Three years.) Did I like my work? (I didn't.) Was I going to stay with it? (What were the options?) Finally, when I thought he was beginning to run down, I got up and turned on the TV.

My wife looked at me with irritation. She was heading toward a boil. Then she looked at the blind man and said, "Robert, do you have a TV?"

The blind man said, "My dear, I have two TVs. I have a color set and a black-and-white thing, an old relic. It's funny, but if I turn the TV on, and I'm always turning it on, I turn on the color set. It's funny, don't you think?"

I didn't know what to say to that. I had absolutely nothing to say to that. No opinion. So I watched the news program and tried to listen to what the announcer was saying.

"This is a color TV," the blind man said. "Don't ask me how, but I can tell."

"We traded up a while ago," I said.

The blind man had another taste of his drink. He lifted his beard, sniffed it, and let it fall. He leaned forward on the sofa. He positioned his ashtray on the coffee table, then put the lighter to his cigarette. He leaned back on the sofa and crossed his legs at the ankles.

My wife covered her mouth, and then she yawned. She stretched. She said, "I think I'll go upstairs and put on my robe. I think I'll change into something else. Robert, you make yourself comfortable," she said,

"I'm comfortable," the blind man said.

"I want you to feel comfortable in this house," she said.

"I am comfortable," the blind man said.

After she'd left the room, he and I listened to the weather report and then to the sports roundup. By that time, she'd been gone so long I didn't know if she was going to come back. I thought she might have gone to bed. I wished she'd come back downstairs. I didn't want to be left alone with a blind man. I asked him if he wanted to smoke some dope with me. I said I'd just rolled a number. I hadn't, but I planned to do so in about two shakes.

"I'll try some with you," he said.

"Damn right," I said. "That's the stuff."

I got our drinks and sat down on the sofa with him. Then I rolled us two fat numbers. I lit one and passed it. I brought it to his fingers. He took it and inhaled.

"Hold it as long as you can," I said. I could tell he didn't know the first thing.

My wife came back downstairs wearing her pink robe and her pink slippers.

"What do I smell?" she said.

"We thought we'd have us some cannabis," I said.

My wife gave me a savage look. Then she looked at the blind man and said, "Robert, I didn't know you smoked."

He said, "I do now, my dear. There's a first time for everything. But I don't feel anything yet."

"This stuff is pretty mellow," I said. "This stuff is mild. It's dope you can reason with," I said. "It doesn't mess you up."

"Not much it doesn't, bub," he said, and laughed.

My wife sat on the sofa between the blind man and me. I passed her the number. She took it and toked and then passed it back to me. "Which way is this going?" she said. Then she said, "I shouldn't be smoking this. I can hardly keep my eyes open as it is. That dinner did me in. I shouldn't have eaten so much."

"It was the strawberry pie," the blind man said. "That's what did it," he said, and he laughed his big laugh. Then he shook his head.

"There's more strawberry pie," I said.

"Do you want some more, Robert?" my wife said.

"Maybe in a little while," he said.

We gave our attention to the TV. My wife yawned again. She said, "Your bed is made up when you feel like going to bed, Robert. I know you must have had a long day. When you're ready to go to bed, say so." She pulled his arm. "Robert?"

He came to and said, "I've had a real nice time. This beats tapes, doesn't it?"

I said, "Coming at you," and I put the number between his fingers. He inhaled, held the smoke, and then let it go. It was like he'd been doing it since he was nine years old.

"Thanks, bub," he said. "But I think this is all for me. I think I'm beginning to feel it," he said. He held the burning roach out for my wife.

"Same here," she said. "Ditto. Me, too." She took the roach and passed it to me. "I may just sit here for a while between you two guys with my eyes closed. But don't let me bother you, okay? Either one of you. If it bothers you, say so. Otherwise, I may just sit here with my eyes closed until you're ready to go to bed," she said. "Your bed's made up, Robert, when you're ready. It's right next to our room at the top of the stairs. We'll show you up when you're ready. You wake me up now, you guys, if I fall asleep." She said that and then she closed her eyes and went to sleep.

The news program ended. I got up and changed the channel. I sat back down on the sofa. I wished my wife hadn't pooped out. Her head lay across the back of the sofa, her mouth open. She'd turned so that her robe had slipped away from her legs, exposing a juicy thigh. I reached to draw her robe back over her, and it was then that I glanced at the blind man. What the hell! I flipped the robe open again.

"You say when you want some strawberry pie," I said.

"I will," he said.

I said, "Are you tired? Do you want me to take you up to your bed? Are you ready to hit the hay?"

"Not yet," he said. "No, I'll stay up with you, bub. If that's all right. I'll stay up until you're ready to turn in. We haven't had a chance to talk. Know what I mean? I feel like me and her monopolized the evening." He lifted his beard and he let it fall. He picked up his cigarettes and lighter.

"That's all right," I said. Then I said, "I'm glad for the company."

And I guess I was. Every night I smoked dope and stayed up as long as I could before I fell asleep. My wife and I hardly ever went to bed at the same time. When I did go to sleep, I had these dreams. Sometimes I'd wake up from one of them, my heart going crazy.

Something about the church and the Middle Ages was on the TV. Not your run-of-the-mill TV fare. I wanted to watch something else. I turned to the other channels. But there was nothing on them, either. So I turned back to the first channel and apologized.

"Bub, it's all right," the blind man said. "It's fine with me. Whatever you want to watch is okay. I'm always learning something. Learning never ends. It won't hurt me to learn something tonight. I got ears," he said.

We didn't say anything for a time. He was leaning forward with his head turned at me, his right ear aimed in the direction of the set. Very disconcerting. Now and then his eyelids dropped and then they snapped open again. Now and then he put his fingers into his beard and tugged, like he was thinking about something he was hearing on the television.

On the screen, a group of men wearing cowls was being set upon and tormented by men dressed in skeleton costumes and men dressed as devils. The men dressed as devils wore devil masks, horns, and long tails. This pageant was part of a procession. The Englishman who was narrating the thing said it took place in Spain once a year. I tried to explain to the blind man what was happening.

"Skeletons," he said. "I know about skeletons," he said, and he nodded.

The TV showed this one cathedral. Then there was a long, slow look at another one. Finally, the picture switched to the famous one in Paris, with its flying buttresses and its spires reaching up to the clouds. The camera pulled away to show the whole of the cathedral rising above the skyline.

There were times when the Englishman who was telling the thing would shut up, would simply let the camera move around over the cathedrals. Or else the camera would tour the countryside, men in fields walking behind oxen. I waited as long as I could. Then I felt I had to say something. I said, "They're showing the outside of this cathedral now. Gargoyles. Little statues carved to look like monsters. Now I guess they're in Italy. Yeah, they're in Italy. There's paintings on the walls of this one church."

"Are those fresco paintings, bub?" he asked, and he sipped from his drink.

I reached for my glass. But it was empty. I tried to remember what I could remember. "You're asking me are those frescoes?" I said. "That's a good question, I don't know."

The camera moved to a cathedral outside Lisbon. The differences in the Portuguese cathedral compared with the French and Italian were not that great. But they were there. Mostly the interior stuff. Then something occurred to me, and I said, "Something has occurred to me. Do you have any idea what a cathedral is? What they look like, that is? Do you follow me? If somebody says cathedral to you, do you have any notion what they're talking about? Do you know the difference between that and a Baptist church, say?"

He let the smoke dribble from his mouth. "I know they took hundreds of workers fifty or a hundred years to build," he said. "I just heard the man say that, of course. I know generations of the same families worked on a cathedral. I heard him say that, too. The men who began their life's work on them, they never lived to see the completion of their work. In that wise, bub, they're no different from the rest of us, right?" He laughed. Then his eyelids drooped again. His head nodded. He seemed to be snoozing. Maybe he was imagining himself in Portugal. The TV was showing another cathedral now. This one was in Germany. The Englishman's voice droned on. "Cathedrals," the blind man said. He sat up and rolled his head back and forth. "If you want the truth, bub, that's about all I know. What I just said. What I heard him say. But maybe you could describe one to me? I wish you'd do it. I'd like that. If you want to know, I really don't have a good idea."

I stared hard at the shot of the cathedral on the TV. How could I even begin to describe it? But say my life depended on it. Say my life was being threatened by an insane guy who said I had to do it or else.

I stared some more at the cathedral before the picture flipped off into the countryside. There was no use. I turned to the blind man and said, "To begin with, they're very tall." I was looking around the room for clues. "They reach way up. Up and up. Toward the sky. They're so big, some of them, they have to have these supports. To help hold them up, so to speak. These supports are called buttresses. They remind me of viaducts, for some reason. But maybe you don't know viaducts, either? Sometimes the cathedrals have devils and such carved into the front. Sometimes lords and ladies. Don't ask me why this is," I said.

He was nodding. The whole upper part of his body seemed to be moving back and forth.

"I'm not doing so good, am I?" I said.

He stopped nodding and leaned forward on the edge of the sofa. As he listened to me, he was running his fingers through his beard. I wasn't getting through to him, I could see that. But he waited for me to go on just the same. He nodded, like he was trying to encourage me. I tried to think what else to say. "They're really big," I said. "They're massive. They're built of stone. Marble, too, sometimes. In those olden days, when they built cathedrals, men wanted to be close to God. In those olden days, God was an important part of everyone's life. You could tell this from their cathedral-building. I'm sorry," I said, "but it looks like that's the best I can do for you. I'm just no good at it."

"That's all right, bub," the blind man said. "Hey, listen. I hope you don't mind my asking you. Can I ask you something? Let me ask you a simple question, yes or no. I'm just curious and there's no offense. You're my host. But let me ask if you are in any way religious? You don't mind my asking?"

I shook my head. He couldn't see that, though. A wink is the same as a nod to a blind man. "I guess I don't believe in it. In anything. Sometimes it's hard. You know what I'm saying?"

"Sure, I do," he said.

"Right," I said.

The Englishman was still holding forth. My wife sighed in her sleep. She drew a long breath and went on with her sleeping.

"You'll have to forgive me," I said. "But I can't tell you what a cathedral looks like. It just isn't in me to do it. I can't do any more than I've done."

The blind man sat very still, his head down, as he listened to me.

I said, "The truth is, cathedrals don't mean anything special to me. Nothing. Cathedrals. They're something to look at on late-night TV. That's all they are."

It was then that the blind man cleared his throat. He brought something up. He took a handkerchief from his back pocket. Then be said, "I get it, bub. It's okay. It happens. Don't worry about it," he said. "Hey, listen to me. Will you do me a favor? I got an idea. Why don't you find us some heavy paper? And a pen. We'll do something. We'll draw one together. Get us a pen and some heavy paper. Go on, bub, get the stuff," he said.

So I went upstairs. My legs felt like they didn't have any strength in them. They felt like they did after I'd done some running. In my wife's room, I looked around. I found some ballpoints in a little basket on her table. And then I tried to think where to look for the kind of paper he was talking about.

Downstairs, in the kitchen, I found a shopping bag with onion skins at the bottom of the bag. I emptied the bag and shook it. I brought it into the living room and sat down with it near his legs. I moved some things, smoothed the wrinkles from the bag, spread it out on the coffee table.

The blind man got down from the sofa and sat next to me on the carpet.

He ran his fingers over the paper. He went up and down the sides of the paper. The edges, even the edges. He fingered the corners.

"All right," he said. "All right, let's do her."

He found my hand, the hand with the pen. He closed his hand over my hand. "Go ahead, bub, draw," he said. "Draw. You'll see. I'll follow along with you. It'll be okay. Just begin now like I'm telling you. You'll see. Draw," the blind man said.

So I began. First I drew a box that looked like a house. It could have been the house I lived in. Then I put a roof on it. At either end of the roof, I drew spires. Crazy.

"Swell," he said. "Terrific. You're doing fine," he said. "Never thought anything like this could happen in your lifetime, did you, bub? Well, it's a strange life, we all know that. Go on now. Keep it up."

I put in windows with arches. I drew flying buttresses. I hung great doors. I couldn't stop. The TV station went off the air. I put down the pen and closed and opened my fingers. The blind man felt around over the paper. He moved the tips of his fingers over the paper, all over what I had drawn, and he nodded.

"Doing fine," the blind man said.

I took up the pen again, and he found my hand. I kept at it. I'm no artist. But I kept drawing just the same.

My wife opened up her eyes and gazed at us. She sat up on the sofa, her robe hanging open. She said, "What are you doing? Tell me, I want to know."

I didn't answer her.

The blind man said, "We're drawing a cathedral. Me and him are working on it. Press hard," he said to me. "That's right. That's good," he said. "Sure. You got it, bub. I can tell. You didn't think you could. But you can, can't you? You're cooking with gas now. You know what I'm saying? We're going to really have us something here in a minute. How's the old arm?" he said. "Put some people in there now. What's a cathedral without people?"

My wife said, "What's going on? Robert, what are you doing? What's going on?"

"It's all right," he said to her. "Close your eyes now," the blind man said to me.

I did it. I closed them just like he said.

"Are they closed?" he said. "Don't fudge."

"They're closed," I said.

"Keep them that way," he said. He said, "Don't stop now. Draw."

So we kept on with it. His fingers rode my fingers as my hand went over the paper. It was like nothing else in my life up to now.

Then he said, "I think that's it. I think you got it," he said. "Take a look. What do you think?"

But I had my eyes closed. I thought I'd keep them that way for a little longer. I thought it was something I ought to do.

"Well?" he said. "Are you looking?"

My eyes were still closed. I was in my house. I knew that. But I didn't feel like I was inside anything.

"It's really something," I said.

Entartete Kunst

Hadley Skinner

Hadley Skinner is a college senior majoring in art
and music.

When Hitler came into power, he influenced the artists
of Germany in many ways. He had a very strong opinion
about what was good art and bad art or "Entartete Kunst,"
which translates into "degenerate art." He argued that
degenerate art should be thought of as irregular because
it went against the aesthetic rules of the Nazi party.
This art was often avant-garde in style, and displayed
images that criticized the Nazis and challenged Nazi
goals for the nation. This art often contained images of
destruction, despair, cruelty, and madness.

Hitler believed that good art should be Neoclassical
in style, and was meant to glorify and celebrate what was
good in German culture. It was realistic art that
idealized the supremacy of the German race by simply
leaving other races out of the work, and it also
idealized the leader, Hitler. Bad art was modern art that
belittled the country, its people, and its dictator, and
was created in an abstract, unrealistic style. The Nazis
discouraged such art.

Many of the traditional subjects, such as landscapes,
portraits, images of peasants, still-lifes, animals, and
nudes, were soon replaced with images of war, the
military, sportsmen, industrial work, and merchants. It
was important to convey a sense of production. Many
artists painted works that idealized warriors, heroes,
and the family. Warriors were painted or sculpted with
bulging muscles and with fixed hard gazes directed
against their opponents.

The peasants and farmers were painted in scenes where
they appeared to be engaged in doing noble work for the
advancement of the German nation. Images that displayed
the difficulties of unemployment and the hardships of the
labor of the peasant workers were not allowed. They were
considered to be the work of the degenerate artists.

It was also unacceptable to include any races other than the German Aryan race in works because the presence of these people was thought to encourage a mixture of races within a culture. All other races were considered inferior to the German race, and the Nazis believed that it would do themselves harm to be associated with weaker races. Thus, paintings depicting other races were labeled as degenerate.

Propaganda art was another form of artistic communication of Hitler's ideas, like the famous propaganda poster for the Hitler Youth Movement, painted by Ludwig Holwein. The poster shows a young boy who is holding up the Nazi flag in a very militaristic manner. He is dressed in his uniform, which has the swastika symbol on his left arm. The poster was created to encourage the youth of Germany to join the military. Many propaganda posters were created to emphasize Hitler's aspirations for the future. These were displayed in public sites and became constant reminders of what people should think and do in their loyalty to Germany.

The Nazis also attacked architecture that did not, in their view, glorify Nazi power and German traditions. It was required that certain modern materials, such as steel and concrete, be concealed behind facings of wood and stone. Steel and concrete were considered to be modern materials, and thus, were not natural and did not reinforce the desired effect of monumentality. It was important to preserve the German culture and these materials enforced this concept. This culture was celebrated by the erection of memorials to soldiers who died in the Franco-Prussian War and in World War I, as well as many military and cultural buildings.

One example is the Haus der Deutschen Kunst in Munich (1933-7), designed by Paul Ludwig Troost, who was one of the major architects for the Nazis until his death in 1934. This building was built as a showpiece for Nazi paintings and sculptures. It is a great example of Nazi architecture because it was designed using large, classical-style colonnades in the front, combined with flat unornamented surfaces that give the structure a feeling of power and presence.

After the death of Paul Ludwig Troost, Albert Speer
rose to the position of being one of the most famous
Nazi architects. He trained and worked with some of the
more well known architects of his time, including a man
by the name of Heinrich Tessenow. This was considered
quite an honor for a man as young as he. Speer joined
the Nazi party after the Great Depression—which was a
time when architectural work was scarce—in an attempt to
understand the economic and political crisis in Germany
better. He was very taken with Hitler's personality and
quickly accepted the offer to become his principal
architect.

Hitler and Speer had many discussions about what the
criteria of each design should be. One thing that was
important to Hitler was that these buildings stand the
test of time. He wanted them to keep all their beauty
even when they started to decay. One of the ways Speer
attempted to accomplish this was by creating a well-
structured steel and concrete interior that would support
a beautiful stone exterior. His designs included
characteristically thick walls that rose high above the
ground. Most of his buildings were very centrally located
within a city and easily visible.

Albert Speer was remembered for much more than this
one design, though. Between 1934 and 1942, Speer
completed the designs and building of the Zeppelinfeld
stadium in Nuremburg, the German pavilion at the
Exposition Internationale des Arts et Techniques dans la
Vie Moderne in Paris, and the new Reichskanzlei in
Berlin. He was also involved in the designing and
planning of transport networks, and concentration camp
construction (1). One of Speer's great projects was the
designing of the new remodel plans for Berlin. The plan
was to reconstruct the city so that it could accommodate
more people than it already did. Only one of the designs
was ever completed, and that was of the House of German
Tourism. Speer was one of the lucky architects during the
time of the Nazis; he worked so closely with Hitler. With
Hitler's many restrictions and rules for the architects
of Germany, it was much easier to be part of his party
than against it.

As the Nazi party grew and Hitler rose to power, strict rules were imposed upon the artists of Germany as well. First, "degenerate art" was confiscated from public and private collections throughout Germany, and later from such countries as France and The Netherlands. The records available show that 15,997 works of art were confiscated from 101 German museums under the Law on the Confiscation of Products of Degenerate Art, which was passed on May 31, 1938 (2). The museum directors who supported "degenerate" art were told to resign and close down their museums, under the Law for the Restoration of Civil Service with Tenure, passed on April 7, 1933 (3).

The next step the Nazis took was to destroy the art of these controversial artists nationwide. (Some works survived, however, as it was discovered much later that about 1,000 works of art had been hidden away in underground repositories in Germany and Austria. One of the most serious acts of destruction occurred in the courtyard of the Berlin Fire Brigade where 4,829 works of art were burned. The artists themselves were termed inferior and, thus, it was thought that they should be removed from society. They were forbidden to paint or exhibit such art, and if they disobeyed, they were sent to concentration camps.

The final step Hitler and the Nazi party took in promoting their beliefs was the exhibition of <u>Entartete Kunst</u>, which was opened on July 19, 1937, in the Archeologisches Institute in Munich. This was a special art exhibit which displayed the works of degenerate artists in such a manner as to convince the public of their inferiority. Nazis went to every measure to ensure the proper message by displaying the art in an anti-aesthetic hanging and installation of the works. They crowded so many pieces together in one room that each piece fought with another for attention. They took little care in the arrangement and the hanging. Each work had a written interpretation by the Nazis, who ridiculed the artist and the work. The producers of this exhibition wanted nothing other than for the people to walk through each room and think, "What horrible work and craftsmanship these artists produced."

One of the more prominent artists of his time was Max Beckman (1884-1950), who was branded by the Nazis as a "degenerate" artist in the 1930s. He was known for his paintings, drawings, prints, and teachings. From 1900-1903 he trained at the Kunstschule in Weimar, and later was a student of Julius Meier-Graefe in Paris. He moved back to Germany and lived near Berlin until the start of World War I. During this time, he painted many nude figures that drew from traditional ideas as well as modern concepts as symbolism. His paintings conveyed strong feelings of fear, suffering, and death. He was also a portraitist and a painter of seascapes and landscapes. He would often place man-made objects within these environments.

At the outbreak of World War I, Beckman joined the medical corps. Due to health problems, he was discharged from service in 1915, and returned to his art work. The experience of the war changed his subject matter drastically, and he became more concerned with his drawings and prints than his paintings. He no longer was creating traditional art, but devoted himself to the creation of imaginary pictorial spaces in which he collaged massive groups of people. He also began to incorporate the cubist style into the picture plane.

It wasn't until the 1920s that Beckman returned to painting as his main focus. His painting style was similar to that of his early years, but his colors were much brighter and the paint much thicker. He continued with imagery of nudes, portraits, landscapes, and still-lifes, which all varied greatly in mood. The Dream (1921) was one of his great works at this time in his life. It was originally entitled The Madhouse because the people in the painting are shown as a crowded mass of misery. He also includes several seemingly symbolic images, such as fish and trumpets. It was with this painting that he was invited to join an exhibition in Mannheim in 1925 through an organization called the Neue Sachlichkeit.

Years later, The Dream was strongly criticized and eventually banned because of its dark nature. Several people look as if their eyes are black, and they crease their eyebrows in a look of sorrow. They are all composed in a cramped space showing no room for individual space. The painting suggests that not all aspects of life are ones of happiness and joy, and that there is a side of misery. The Nazis didn't allow painters to express such emotions because the goal of the artist was to glorify Germany. Beckman's work was also criticized for its unrealistic execution. The Nazis dismissed the modern avant-garde style as being too chaotic and full of conflicting emotions.

In 1925, Beckman became an art professor at the Stadelsches Kunstinstitut in Frankfurt. Through his teaching, he encouraged his students to express all the emotional states through their art. In this same year, he also renewed a contract which allowed him to exhibit his works in the Newman's Art Circle in New York. By the 1930s, Beckman was exhibiting his work nationally and internationally, was published widely, and emerged as one of Germany's most prominent artists.

When the Nazis came into power in 1933, things changed drastically for Beckman. His works were removed from existing exhibitions, and future display of his art was prohibited. He was forced to resign his position at the Stadelsches Kunstinstitut, and to discontinue his artistic practices. In hopes that he would be able to continue in a different location, he left Frankfurt and moved back to Berlin. It was here that he produced a two-year-long work titled The Departure.

In this triptych, he collaged his knowledge of East Asian philosophy, the German philosopher Schopenhauer, and the Cabbala. It explored the ordeals of an earthly existence. The piece depicts bound and tortured figures on the outer panels, which contrast with the brightly colored center panel. In this center panel, a man, woman, and child are being taken across a sea by a hooded boatman. This is an ominous picture in which the middle panel suggests someone trying to escape from the world depicted in the other two panels.

In contrast, many Nazi paintings idealized the German family. These paintings include both the mother and father with their son and daughter, in a healthy and happy environment. The people are always painted as the blond-haired and blue-eyed physical ideal of the German race. These paintings idealize the German family as healthy, serious, contemplative, orderly, hardworking, and sincere people who were exclusively devoted to one another.

After Beckman's works were exhibited in the Entartete Kunst exhibition, he left for Amsterdam, living there in exile until 1947. Many of the "degenerate" artists left Germany in exile, such as Christian Schad and George Grosz, or they faced the possibility of imprisonment at a concentration camp. These artists wouldn't be able to return to Germany until the end of the Nazi era in 1945.

Works Cited

"Speer, Albert." The Dictionary of Art, pg. 378. Because
     of Speer's involvement with Hitler, and his inter-
     est in designing the concentration camps, he was
     sentenced to twenty years in prison in 1945 at the
     Spandau prison in Berlin.
"Entartete Kunst," pg. 413.
Id., pg. 414.

12

PHILOSOPHY
AND RELIGION

Gustav Klimt (1862–1918). *Death and Life,* ca. 1911–15. Collection Leopold, Vienna, Austria.

THE RIDDLE OF INEQUALITY

Paul Tillich

The following piece is from Tillich's 1963 book The Eternal Now.

> For to him who has will more be given; and from him
> who has not, even what he has will be taken away.
>
> —*MARK iv. 25*

One day a learned colleague called me up and said to me with angry excitement: "There is a saying in the New Testament which I consider to be one of the most immoral and unjust statements ever made!" And then he started quoting our text: "To him who has will more be given," and his anger increased when he continued: "and from him who has not, even what he has will be taken away." We all, I think, feel offended with him. And we cannot easily ignore the offense by suggesting what *he* suggested—that the words may be due to a misunderstanding of the disciples. It appears at least four times in the gospels with great emphasis. And even more, we can clearly see that the writers of the gospels felt exactly as we do. For them it was a stumbling block, which they tried to interpret in different ways. Probably none of these explanations satisfied them fully, for with this saying of Jesus, we are confronted immediately with the greatest and perhaps most painful riddle of life, that of the inequality of all beings. We certainly cannot hope to solve it when neither the Bible nor any other of the great religions and philosophies was able to do so. But we can do two things: We can show the breadth and the depth of the riddle of inequality and we can try to find a way to live with it, even if it is unsolved.

I

If we hear the words, "to him who has will more be given," we ask ourselves: What *do* we have? And then we may find that much is given to us in terms of external goods, of friends, of intellectual gifts and even of a comparatively high moral level of action. So we can expect that more will be given to us, while we must expect that those who are lacking in all that will lose the little they already have. Even further, according to Jesus' parable, the one talent they have will be given to us who have five or ten talents. We shall be richer because they will be poorer. We may cry out against such an injustice. But we cannot deny that life confirms it abundantly. We cannot deny it, but we can ask the question, do we *really* have what we believe we have so that it cannot be taken from us? It is a question full of anxiety, confirmed by a version of our text rendered by Luke. "From him who has not, even what he *thinks* that be has will be taken away." Perhaps our having of those many things is not the kind of having which is increased. Perhaps the having of few things by the poor ones is the kind of having which makes them grow. In the parable of the talents, Jesus confirms this. Those talents which are used, even with a risk of losing them, are those which we really have; those which we try to preserve without using them for growth are those which we do not really have and which are being taken away from us. They slowly disappear, and suddenly we feel that we have lost these talents, perhaps forever.

Let us apply this to our own life, whether it is long or short. In the memory of all of us many things appear which we had without having them and which were taken away from us. Some of them became lost because of the tragic limitations of life; we had to sacrifice them in order to make other things grow. We all were given childish innocence; but innocence cannot be used and increased. The growth of our lives is possible only because we have sacrificed the original gift of innocence. Nevertheless, sometimes there arises in us a melancholy longing for a purity which has been taken from us. We all were given youthful enthusiasm for many things and aims. But this also cannot be used and increased. Most of the objects of our early enthusiasm must be sacrificed for a few, and the few must be approached with soberness. No maturity is possible without this sacrifice. Yet often a melancholy longing for the lost possibilities and enthusiasm takes hold of us. Innocence and youthful enthusiasm: we had them and had them not. Life itself demanded that they were taken from us.

But there are other things which we had and which were taken from us, because we let them go through our own guilt. Some of us had a deep sensitivity for the wonder of life as it is revealed in nature. Slowly under the pressure of work and social life and the lure of cheap pleasures, we lose the wonder of our earlier years when we felt intense joy and the presence of the mystery of life through the freshness of the young day or the glory of the dying day, the majesty of the mountains or the infinity of the sea, a flower breaking through the soil or a young animal in the perfection of its movements. Perhaps we try to produce such feelings again, but we are empty and do not succeed. We had it and had it not, and it has been taken from us.

Others had the same experience with music, poetry, the great novels and plays. One wanted to devour all of them, one lived in them and created for oneself a life above the daily life. We *had* all this and did not have it; we did not let it grow; our love towards it was not strong enough and so it was taken from us.

Many, especially in this group, remember a time in which the desire to learn to solve the riddles of the universe, to find truth has been the driving force in their lives. They came to college and university, not in order to buy their entrance ticket into the upper middle classes or in order to provide for the preconditions of social and economic success, but they came, driven by the desire for knowledge. They had something and more could have been given to them. But in reality they did not have it. They did not make it grow and so it was taken from them and they finished their academic work in terms of expediency and indifference towards truth. Their love for truth has left them and in some moments they are sick in their hearts because they realize that what they have lost they may never get back.

We all know that any deeper relation to a human being needs watchfulness and growth, otherwise it is taken away from us. And we cannot get it back. This is a form of having and not having which is the root of innumerable human tragedies. We all know about them. And there is another, the most fundamental kind of having and not having—our having and losing God. Perhaps we were rich towards God in our childhood and beyond it. We may remember the moments in which we felt his ultimate presence. We may remember prayers with an overflowing heart, the encounter with the holy in word and music and holy places. We had communication with God; but it was taken from us because we had it and had it not. We did not let it grow, and so it slowly disappeared leaving an empty space. We became unconcerned, cynical, indifferent, not because we doubted about our religious traditions—such doubt belongs to being rich towards God—but because we turned away from that which once concerned us infinitely.

Such thoughts are a first step in approaching the riddle of inequality. Those who have, receive more if they really have it, if they use it and make it grow. And those who have not, lose what they have because they never had it really.

II

But the question of inequality is not yet answered. For one now asks: Why do some receive more than others in the very beginning, before there is even the possibility of using or wasting our talents? Why does the one servant receive five talents and the other two and the third one? Why is the one born in the slums and the other in a well-to-do suburban family? It does not help to answer that of those to whom much is given much is demanded and little of those to whom little is given. For it is just this inequality of original gifts, internal and external, which arouses our question. Why is it given to one human being to gain so much more out of his being human than to another one? Why is so much given to the one that much *can* be asked of him, while to the other one little is given and little *can* be asked? If this question is asked, not only about individual men but also about classes, races and nations, the everlasting question of political inequality arises, and with it the many ways appear in which men have tried to abolish inequality. In every revolution and in every war, the will to solve the riddle of inequality is a driving force. But neither war nor revolution can remove it. Even if we imagine that in an indefinite future most social inequalities are conquered, three things remain: the inequality of talents in body and mind, the inequality created by freedom and destiny, and the fact that all generations before the time of such equality would be excluded from its blessings. This would be the greatest possible inequality! No! In face of one of the deepest and most torturing problems of life, it is unpermittably shallow and foolish to escape into a social dreamland. We have to live now; we have to live this our life, and we must face today the riddle of inequality.

Let us not confuse the riddle of inequality with the fact that each of us is a unique incomparable self. Certainly our being individuals belongs to our dignity as men. It is given to us and must be used and intensified and not drowned in the gray waters of conformity which threaten us today. One should defend every individuality and the uniqueness of every human self. But one should not believe that this is a way of solving the riddle of inequality. Unfortunately, there are social and political reactionaries who use this confusion in order to justify social injustice. They are at least as foolish as the dreamers of a future removal of inequality. Whoever has seen hospitals, prisons, sweatshops, battlefields, houses for the insane, starvation, family tragedies, moral aberrations should be cured from any confusion of the gift of individuality with the riddle of inequality. He should be cured from any feelings of easy consolation.

III

And now we must make the third step in our attempt to penetrate the riddle of inequality and ask: Why do some use and increase what was given to them, while others do not, so that it is taken from them? Why does God say to the prophet in our Old Testament lesson that the ears and eyes of a nation are made insensible for the divine message?

Is it enough to answer: Because some use their freedom responsibly and do what they ought to do while others fail through their own guilt? Is this answer, which seems so obvious, sufficient? Now let me first say that it *is* sufficient if we apply it to ourselves. Each of us must consider the increase or the loss of what is given to him as a matter of his own responsibility. Our conscience tells us that we cannot put the blame for our losses on anybody or anything else than ourselves.

But if we look at others, this answer is not sufficient. On the contrary: If we applied the judgment which we *must* apply to anyone else we would be like the Pharisee in Jesus' parable. You cannot tell somebody who comes to you in distress about himself: Use what has been given to you; for he may come to you just because be is unable to do so! And you cannot tell those who are in despair about what they are: Be something else; for this is just what despair means—the inability of getting rid of oneself. You cannot tell those who did not conquer the destructive influences of their surroundings and were driven into crime and misery that they should have been stronger; for it was just of this strength they had been deprived by heritage or environment. Certainly they all are men, and to all of them freedom is given; but they all are also subject to destiny. It is not up to us to condemn them because they were free, as it is not up to us to excuse them because they were under their destiny. We cannot judge them. And when we judge ourselves, we must be conscious that even this is not the last word, but that we like them are under an ultimate judgment. In it the riddle of inequality is eternally answered. But this answer is not ours. It is our predicament that we must ask. And we ask with an uneasy conscience. Why are they in misery, why not we? Thinking of some who are near to us, we can ask: Are we partly responsible? But even if we are, it does not solve the riddle of inequality. The uneasy conscience asks about the farthest as well as about the nearest: Why they, why not we?

Why has my child, or any of millions and millions of children, died before even having a chance to grow out of infancy? Why is my child, or any child, born feeble-minded or crippled? Why has my friend or relative, or anybody's friend or relative, disintegrated in his mind and lost both his freedom and his destiny? Why has my son or daughter, gifted as I believe with many talents, wasted them and been deprived of them? And why does this happen to any parent at all? Why have this boy's or this girl's creative powers been broken by a tyrannical father or by a possessive mother?

In all these questions it is not the question of our own misery which we ask. It is not the question: Why has this happened to *me?*

It is not the question of Job which God answers by humiliating him and then by elevating him into communion with him. It is not the old and urgent question: Where is the divine justice, where is the divine love towards me? But it is almost the opposite question: Why has this *not* happened to me, why has it happened to the other one, to the innumerable other ones to whom not even the power of Job is given to accept the divine answer? Why—and Jesus has asked the same question—are many called and few elected?

He does not answer; he only states that this is the human predicament. Shall we therefore cease to ask and humbly accept the fact of a divine judgment which condemns most human beings away from the community with him into despair and self-destruction? Can we accept the eternal victory of judgment over love? We cannot; and nobody ever could, even if he preached and threatened in these terms. As long as he could not see himself with complete certainty as eternally rejected, his preaching and threatening would be self-deceiving. And who could see himself eternally rejected?

But if this is not the solution of the riddle of inequality at its deepest level, can we trespass the boundaries of the Christian tradition and listen to those who tell us that this life does not decide about our eternal destiny? There will be occasions in other lives, as our present life is determined by previous ones and what we have achieved or wasted in them. It is a serious doctrine and not completely strange to Christianity. But if we don't know and never will know what each of us has been in the previous or future lives, then it is not really *our* destiny which develops from life to life, but in each life it is the destiny of someone else. This answer also does not solve the riddle of inequality.

There is no answer at all if we ask about the temporal and eternal destiny of the single being separated from the destiny of the whole. Only in the unity of all beings in time and eternity can a humanly possible answer to the riddle of inequality be found. *Humanly* possible does not mean an answer which removes the riddle of inequality, but an answer with which we can live.

There is an ultimate unity of all beings, rooted in the divine life from which they come and to which they go. All beings, nonhuman as well as human, participate in it. And therefore they all participate in each other. We participate in each other's having and we participate in each other's not-having. If we become aware of this unity of all beings, something happens. The fact that others have-not changes in every moment the character of my having: It undercuts its security, it drives me beyond myself, to understand, to give, to share, to help. The fact that others fall into sin, crime and misery changes the character of the grace which is given to me: It makes me realize my own hidden guilt, it shows to me that those who suffer for their sin and crime, suffer also for me; for I am guilty of their guilt—at least in the desire of my heart—and ought to suffer as they do. The awareness that others who *could* have become fully developed human beings and never *have*, changes my state of full humanity. Their early death, their early or late disintegration, makes my life and my health a continuous risk, a dying which is not yet death, a disintegration which is not yet destruction. In every death which we encounter, something of us dies; in every disease which we encounter, something of us tends to disintegrate.

Can we live with this answer? We can to the degree in which we are liberated from the seclusion within ourselves. But nobody can be liberated from himself unless he is grasped by the power of that which is present in everyone and everything—the eternal from which we come and to which we go, which gives us to ourselves and which liberates us *from* ourselves. It is the greatness and the heart of the Christian message that God—as manifest in the Cross of the Christ—participates totally in the dying child, in the condemned criminal, in the disintegrating mind, in the starving one and in him who rejects him. There is no extreme human condition into which the divine presence would not reach. This is what the Cross, the most extreme of all human conditions, tells us. The riddle of inequality cannot be solved on the level of our separation from each other. It is eternally solved in the divine participation in all of us and every being. The certainty of the divine participation gives us the courage to stand the riddle of inequality, though finite minds cannot solve it. Amen.

DEATH—THE TIME OF YOUR LIFE

Neil Gaiman

The following selection is excerpted from Gaiman's trade paperback, Death—The Time of Your Life, *which was published in 1997.*

⑨

EXISTENTIALISM
Jean-Paul Sartre

The piece that follows was originally published in Sartre's 1947 book Existentialism.

Man is nothing else but what he makes of himself. Such is the first principle of existentialism. It is also what is called subjectivity, the name we are labeled with when charges are brought against us. But what do we mean by this, if not that man has a greater dignity than a stone or table? For we mean that man first exists, that is, that man first of all is the being who hurls himself toward a future and who is conscious of imagining himself as being in the future. Man is at the start a plan which is aware of itself, rather than a patch of moss, a piece of garbage, or a cauliflower; nothing exists prior to this plan; there is nothing in heaven; man will be what he will have planned to be. Not what he will want to be. Because by the word "will" we generally mean a conscious decision, which is subsequent to what we have already made of ourselves. I may want to belong to a political party, write a book, get married; but all that is only a manifestation of an earlier, more spontaneous choice that is called "will." But if existence really does precede essence, man is responsible for what he is. Thus, existentialism's first move is to make every man aware of what he is and to make the full responsibility of his existence rest on him. And when we say that a man is responsible for himself, we do not only mean that he is responsible for his own individuality, but that he is responsible for all men.

The word "subjectivism" has two meanings, and our opponents play on the two. Subjectivism means, on the one hand, that an individual chooses and makes himself; and, on the other, that it is impossible for man to transcend human subjectivity. The second of these is the essential meaning of existentialism. When we say that man chooses his own self, we mean that every one of us does likewise; but we also mean by that that in making this choice he also chooses all men. In fact, in creating the man that we want to be, there is not a single one of our acts which does not at the same time create an image of man as we think he ought to be. To choose to be this or that is to affirm at the same time the value of what we choose, because we can never choose evil. We always choose the good, and nothing can be good for us without being good for all.

If, on the other hand, existence precedes essence, and if we grant that we exist and fashion our image at one and the same time, the image is valid for everybody and for our whole age. Thus, our responsibility is much greater than we might have supposed, because it involves all mankind. If I am a workingman and choose to join a Christian trade union rather than be a Communist, and if by being a member, I want to show that the best thing for man is resignation, that the kingdom of man is not of this world, I am not only involving my own case—I want to be resigned for everyone. As a result, my action has involved all humanity. To take a more individual matter, if I want to marry, to have children, even if this marriage depends solely on my own circumstances or passion or wish, I am involving all humanity in monogamy and not merely myself. Therefore, I am responsible for myself and for everyone else. I am creating a certain image of man of my own choosing. In choosing myself, I choose man.

This helps us understand what the actual content is of such rather grandiloquent words as anguish, forlornness, despair. As you will see, it's all quite simple.

First, what is meant by anguish? The existentialists say at once that man is anguish. What that means is this: the man who involves himself and who realizes that he is not only the person he chooses to be, but also a lawmaker who is, at the same time, choosing all mankind as well as himself, cannot help escape the feeling of his total and deep responsibility. Of course, there are many people who are not anxious; but we claim that they are hiding their anxiety, that they are fleeing from it. Certainly, many people believe that when they do something, they themselves are the only ones involved, and when someone says to them, "What if everyone acted that way?" they shrug their shoulders and answer, "Everyone doesn't act that way." But really, one should always ask himself, "What would happen if everybody looked at things that way?" There is no escaping this disturbing thought except by a kind of double-dealing. A man who lies and makes excuses for himself by saying "not everybody does that," is someone with an uneasy conscience, because the act of lying implies that a universal value is conferred upon the lie.

Anguish is evident even when it conceals itself. This is the anguish that Kierkegaard called the anguish of Abraham. You know the story: an angel has ordered Abraham to sacrifice his son; if it really were an angel who has come and said, "You are Abraham, you shall sacrifice your son," everything would be all right. But everyone might first wonder, "Is it really an angel, and am I really Abraham? What proof do I have?"

There was a madwoman who had hallucinations; someone used to speak to her on the telephone and give her orders. Her doctor asked her, "Who is it who talks to you?" She answered, "He says it's God." What proof did she really have that it was God? If an angel comes to me, what proof is there that it's an angel? And if I hear voices, what proof is there that they come from heaven and not from hell, or from the subconscious, or a pathological condition? What proves that they are addressed to me? What proof is there that I have been appointed to impose my choice and my conception of man on humanity? I'll never find any proof or sign to convince me of that. If a voice addresses me, it is always for me to decide that this is the angel's voice; if I consider that such an act is a good one, it is I who will choose to say that it is good rather than bad.

Now, I'm not being singled out as an Abraham, and yet at every moment I'm obliged to perform exemplary acts. For every man, everything happens as if all mankind had its eyes fixed on him and were guiding itself by what he does. And every man ought to say to himself, "Am I really the kind of man who has the right to act in such a way that humanity might guide itself by my actions?" And if he does not say that to himself, he is masking his anguish.

There is no question here of the kind of anguish which would lead to quietism, to inaction. It is a matter of a simple sort of anguish that anybody who has had responsibilities is familiar with. For example, when a military officer takes the responsibility for an attack and sends a certain number of men to death, he chooses to do so, and in the main he alone makes the choice. Doubtless, orders come from above, but they are too broad; he interprets them, and on this interpretation depend the lives of ten or fourteen or twenty men. In making a decision he cannot help having a certain anguish. All leaders know this anguish. That doesn't keep them from acting; on the contrary, it is the very condition of their action. For it implies that they envisage a number of possibilities, and when they choose one, they realize that it has value only because it is chosen. We shall see that this kind of anguish, which is the kind that existentialism describes, is explained, in addition, by a direct responsibility to the other men whom it involves. It is not a curtain separating us from action, but is part of action itself.

When we speak of forlornness, a term Heidegger was fond of, we mean only that God does not exist and that we have to face all the consequences of this. This existentialist is strongly opposed to a certain kind of secular ethics which would like to abolish God with the least possible expense. About 1880, some French teachers tried to set up a secular ethics which went something like this: God is a useless and costly hypothesis; we are discarding it; but, meanwhile, in order for there to be an ethics, a society, a civilization, it is essential that certain values be taken seriously and that they be considered as having an *a priori* existence. It must be obligatory, *a priori*, to be honest, not to lie, not to beat your wife, to have children, etc., etc. So we're going to try a little device which will make it possible to show that values exist all the same, inscribed in a heaven of ideas, though otherwise God does not exist. In other words—and this, I believe, is the tendency of everything called reformism in France—nothing will be changed if God does not exist. We shall find ourselves with the same norms of honesty, progress, and humanism, and we shall have made of God an outdated hypothesis which will peacefully die off by itself.

The existentialist, on the contrary, thinks it very distressing that God does not exist, because all possibility of finding values in a heaven of ideas disappears along with Him; there can no longer be an *a priori* Good, since there is no infinite and perfect consciousness to think it. Nowhere is it written that the Good exists, that we must be honest, that we must not lie; because the fact is we are on a plane where there are only men. Dostoievsky said, "If God didn't exist, everything would be possible." That is the very starting point of existentialism. Indeed, everything is permissible if God does not exist, and as a result man is forlorn, because neither within him nor without does he find anything to cling to. He can't start making excuses for himself.

If existence really does precede essence, there is no explaining things away by reference to a fixed and given human nature. In other words, there is no determinism, man is free, man is freedom. On the other hand, if God does not exist, we find no values or commands to turn to which legitimize our conduct. So, in the bright realm of values, we have no excuse behind us, nor justification before us. We are alone, with no excuses.

That is the idea I shall try to convey when I say that man is condemned to be free. Condemned, because he did not create himself, yet, in other respects is free; because, once thrown into the world, he is responsible for everything he does. The existentialist does not believe in the power of passion. He will never agree that a sweeping passion is a ravaging torrent which fatally leads a man to certain acts and is therefore an excuse. He thinks that man is responsible for his passion.

The existentialist does not think that man is going to help himself by finding in the world some omen by which to orient himself. Because he thinks that man will interpret the omen to suit himself. Therefore, he thinks that man, with no support and no aid, is condemned every moment to invent man. Ponge, in a very fine article, has said, "Man is the future of man." That's exactly it. But if it is taken to mean that this future is recorded in heaven, that God sees it, then it is false, because it would really no longer be a future. If it is taken to mean that, whatever a man may be, there is a future to be forged, a virgin future before him, then this remark is sound. But then we are forlorn.

To give you an example which will enable you to understand forlornness better, I shall cite the case of one of my students who came to see me under the following circumstances: his father was on bad terms with his mother, and, moreover, was inclined to be a collaborationist, his older brother had been killed in the German offensive of 1940, and the young man, with somewhat immature but generous feelings, wanted to avenge him. His mother lived alone with him, very much upset by the half-treason of her husband and the death of her older son; the boy was her only consolation.

The boy was faced with the choice of leaving for England and joining the Free French forces—that is, leaving his mother behind—or remaining with his mother and helping her to carry on. He was fully aware that the woman lived only for him and that his going off—and perhaps his death—would plunge her into despair. He was also aware that every act that he did for his mother's sake was a sure thing, in the sense that it was helping her to carry on, whereas every effort he made toward going off and fighting was an uncertain move which might run aground and prove completely useless; for example, on his way to England he might, while passing through Spain, be detained indefinitely in a Spanish camp; he might reach England or Algiers and be stuck in an office at a desk job. As a result, he was faced with two very different kinds of action: one, concrete, immediate, but concerning only one individual; the other concerned an incomparably vaster group, a national collectivity, but for that very reason was dubious, and might be interrupted en route. And, at the same time, he was wavering between two kinds of ethics. On the one hand, an ethics of sympathy, of personal devotion; on the other, a broader ethics, but one whose efficacy was more dubious. He had to choose between the two.

Who could help him choose? Christian doctrine? No. Christian doctrine says, "Be charitable, love your neighbor, take the more rugged path, etc., etc." But which is the more rugged path? Whom should he love as a brother? The fighting man or his mother? Which does the greater good, the vague act of fighting in a group, or the concrete one of helping a particular human being to go on living? Who can decide *a priori?* Nobody. No book of ethics can tell him. The Kantian ethics says, "Never treat any person as a means, but as an end." Very well, if I stay with my mother, I'll treat her as an end and not as a means; but by virtue of this very fact, I'm running the risk of treating the people around me who are fighting, as means; and, conversely, if I go to join those who are fighting, I'll be treating them as an end, and, by doing that, I run the risk of treating my mother as a means.

If values are vague, and if they are always too broad for the concrete and specific case that we are considering, the only thing left for us is to trust our instincts. That's what this young man tried to do; and when I saw him, he said, "In the end, feeling is what counts. I ought to choose whichever pushes me in one direction. If I feel that I love my mother enough to sacrifice everything else for her—my desire for vengeance, for action, for adventure—then I'll stay with her. If, on the contrary, I feel that my love for my mother isn't enough, I'll leave."

But how is the value of a feeling determined? What gives his feeling for his mother value? Precisely the fact that he remained with her. I may say that I like so-and-so well enough to sacrifice a certain amount of money for him, but I may say so only if I've done it. I may say "I love my mother well enough to remain with her" if I have remained with her. The only way to determine the value of this affection is, precisely, to perform an act which confirms and defines it. But, since I require this affection to justify my act, I find myself caught in a vicious circle.

On the other hand, Gide has well said that a mock feeling and a true feeling are almost indistinguishable; to decide that I love my mother and will remain with her, or to remain with her by putting on an act, amount somewhat to the same thing. In other words, the feeling is formed by the acts one performs; so, I cannot refer to it in order to act upon it. Which means that I can neither seek within myself the true condition which will impel me to act, nor apply to a system of ethics for concepts which will permit me to act. You will say, "At least, he did go to a teacher for advice." But if you seek advice from a priest, for example, you have chosen this priest; you already knew, more or less, just about what advice he was going to give you. In other words, choosing your adviser is involving yourself. The proof of this is that if you are a Christian, you will say, "Consult a priest." But some priests are collaborating, some are just marking time, some are resisting. Which to choose? If the young man chooses a priest who is resisting or collaborating, he has already decided on the kind of advice he's going to get. Therefore, in coming to see me he knew the answer I was going to give him, and I had only one answer to give: "You're free, choose, that is, invent." No general ethics can show you what is to be done; there are no omens in the world. The Catholics will reply, "But there are." Granted—but, in any case, I myself choose the meaning they have.

When I was a prisoner, I knew a rather remarkable young man who was a Jesuit. He had entered the Jesuit order in the following way: he had had a number of very bad breaks; in childhood, his father died, leaving him in poverty, and he was a scholarship student at a religious institution where he was constantly made to feel that he was being kept out of charity; then, he failed to get any of the honors and distinctions that children like; later on, at about eighteen, he bungled a love affair; finally, at twenty-two, he failed in military training, a childish enough matter, but it was the last straw.

This young fellow might well have felt that he had botched everything. It was a sign of something, but of what? He might have taken refuge in bitterness or despair. But he very wisely looked upon all this as a sign that he was not made for secular triumphs, and that only the triumphs of religion, holiness, and faith were open to him. He saw the hand of God in all this, and so he entered the order. Who can help seeing that he alone decided what the sign meant?

Some other interpretation might have been drawn from this series of setbacks; for example, that he might have done better to turn carpenter or revolutionist. Therefore, he is fully responsible for the interpretation. Forlornness implies that we ourselves choose our being. Forlornness and anguish go together.

As for despair, the term has a very simple meaning. It means that we shall confine ourselves to reckoning only with what depends upon our will, or on the ensemble of probabilities which make our action possible. When we want something, we always have to reckon with probabilities. I may be counting on the arrival of a friend. The friend is coming by rail or streetcar; this supposes that the train will arrive on schedule, or that the streetcar will not jump the track. I am left in the realm of possibility; but possibilities are to be reckoned with only to the point where my action comports with the ensemble of these possibilities, and no further. The moment the possibilities I am considering are not rigorously involved by my action, I ought to disengage myself from them, because no God, no scheme, can adapt the world and its possibilities to my will. When Descartes said, "Conquer yourself rather than the world," he meant essentially the same thing.

The Marxists to whom I have spoken reply, "You can rely on the support of others in your action, which obviously has certain limits because you're not going to live forever. That means: rely on both what others are doing elsewhere to help you, in China, in Russia, and what they will do later on, after your death, to carry on the action and lead it to its fulfillment, which will be the revolution. You even *have* to rely upon that, otherwise you're immoral." I reply at once that I will always rely on fellow-fighters insofar as these comrades are involved with me in a common struggle, in the unity of a party or a group in which I can more or less make my weight felt; that is, one whose ranks I am in as a fighter and whose movements I am aware of at every moment. In such a situation, relying on the unity and will of the party is exactly like counting on the fact that the train will arrive on time or that the car won't jump the track. But, given that man is free and that there is no human nature for me to depend on, I cannot count on men whom I do not know by relying on human goodness or man's concern for the good of society. I don't know what will become of the Russian revolution; I may make an example of it to the extent that at the present time it is apparent that the proletariat plays a part in Russia that it plays in no other nation. But I can't swear that this will inevitably lead to a triumph of the proletariat. I've got to limit myself to what I see.

Given that men are free and that tomorrow they will freely decide what man will be, I cannot be sure that, after my death, fellow-fighters will carry on my work to bring it to its maximum perfection. Tomorrow, after my death, some men may decide to set up Fascism, and the others may be cowardly and muddled enough to let them do it. Fascism will then be the human reality, so much the worse for us.

Actually, things will be as man will have decided they are to be. Does that mean that I should abandon myself to quietism? No. First, I should involve myself; then, act on the old saw, "Nothing ventured, nothing gained." Nor does it mean that I shouldn't belong to a party, but rather that I shall have no illusions and shall do what I can. For example, suppose I ask myself, "Will socialization, as such, ever come about?" I know nothing about it. All I know is that I'm going to do everything in my power to bring it about. Beyond that, I can't count on anything. Quietism is the attitude of people who say, "Let others do what I can't do." The doctrine I am presenting is the very opposite of quietism, since it declares, "There is no reality except in action." Moreover, it goes further, since it adds, "Man is nothing else than his plan; he exists only to the extent that he fulfills himself; he is therefore nothing else than the ensemble of his acts, nothing else than his life."

According to this, we can understand why our doctrine horrifies certain people. Because often the only way they can bear their wretchedness is to think, "Circumstances have been against me. What I've been and done doesn't show my true worth. To be sure, I've had no great love, no great friendship, but that's because I haven't met a man or woman who was worthy. The books I've written haven't been very good because I haven't had the proper leisure. I haven't had children to devote myself to because I didn't find a man with whom I could have spent my life. So there remains within me, unused and quite viable, a host of propensities, inclinations, possibilities, that one wouldn't guess from the mere series of things I've done."

Now, for the existentialist there is really no love other than one which manifests itself in a person's being in love. There is no genius other than one which is expressed in works of art; the genius of Proust is the sum of Proust's works; the genius of Racine is his series of tragedies. Outside of that, there is nothing. Why say that Racine could have written another tragedy, when he didn't write it? A man is involved in life, leaves his impress on it, and outside of that there is nothing. To be sure, this may seem a harsh thought to someone whose life hasn't been a success. But, on the other hand, it prompts people to understand that reality alone is what counts, that dreams, expectations, and hopes warrant no more than to define a man as a disappointed dream, as miscarried hopes, as vain expectations. In other words, to define him negatively and not positively. However, when we say, "You are nothing else than your life," that does not imply that the artist will be judged solely on the basis of his works of art; a thousand other things will contribute toward summing him up. What we mean is that a man is nothing else than a series of undertakings, that he is the sum, the organization, the ensemble of the relationships which make up these undertakings.

When all is said and done, what we are accused of, at bottom, is not our pessimism, but an optimistic toughness. If people throw up to us our works of fiction in which we write about people who are soft, weak, cowardly, and sometimes even downright bad, it's not because these people are soft, weak, cowardly, or bad; because if we were to say, as Zola did, that they are that way because of heredity, the workings of environment, society, because of biological or psychological determinism, people would be reassured. They would say, "Well, that's what we're like, no one can do anything about it." But when the existentialist writes about a coward, he says that this coward is responsible for his cowardice. He's not like that because he has a cowardly heart or lung or brain; he's not like that on account of his physiological make-up; but he's like that because he has made himself a coward by his acts. There's no such thing as a cowardly constitution; there are nervous constitutions; there is poor blood, as the common people say, or strong constitutions. But the man whose blood is poor is not a coward on that account, for what makes cowardice is the act of renouncing or yielding. A constitution is not an act; the coward is defined on the basis of the acts he performs. People feel, in a vague sort of way, that this coward we're talking about is guilty of being a coward, and the thought frightens them. What people would like is that a coward or a hero be born that way. . . .

From these few reflections it is evident that nothing is more unjust than the objections that have been raised against us. Existentialism is nothing else than an attempt to draw all the consequences of a coherent atheistic position. It isn't trying to plunge man into despair at all. But if one calls every attitude of unbelief despair, like the Christians, then the word is not being used in its original sense. Existentialism isn't so atheistic that it wears itself out showing that God doesn't exist. Rather, it declares that even if God did exist, that would change nothing. There you've got our point of view. Not that we believe that God exists, but we think that the problem of His existence is not the issue. In this sense existentialism is optimistic, a doctrine of action, and it is plain dishonesty for Christians to make no distinction between their own despair and ours and then to call us despairing.

THE ALLEGORY OF THE CAVE

Plato

The following selection was first published in the fourth century B.C.

And now, I said, let me show in a figure how far our nature is enlightened or unenlightened: Behold! human beings living in an underground den, which has a mouth open towards the light and reaching all along the den; here they have been from their childhood, and have their legs and necks chained so that they cannot move, and can only see before them, being prevented by the chains from turning round their heads. Above and behind them a fire is blazing at a distance, and between the fire and the prisoners there is a raised way; and you will see, if you look, a low wall built along the way, like the screen which marionette players have in front of them, over which they show the puppets.

I see.

And do you see, I said, men passing along the wall carrying all sorts of vessels, and statues and figures of animals made of wood and stone and various materials, which appear over the wall? Some of them are talking, others silent.

You have shown me a strange image, and they are strange prisoners.

Like ourselves, I replied; and they see only their own shadows, or the shadows of one another, which the fire throws on the opposite wall of the cave?

True, he said; how could they see anything but the shadows if they were never allowed to move their heads?

And of the objects which are being carried in like manner they would only see the shadows?

Yes, he said.

And if they were able to converse with one another, would they not suppose that they were naming what was actually before them?

Very true.

And suppose further that the prison had an echo which came from the other side, would they not be sure to fancy when one of the passers-by spoke that the voice which they heard came from the passing shadow?

No question, he replied.

To them, I said, the truth would be literally nothing but the shadows of the images.

That is certain.

And now look again, and see what will naturally follow if the prisoners are released and disabused of their error. At first, when any of them is liberated and compelled suddenly to stand up and turn his neck round and walk and look towards the light, he will suffer sharp pains; the glare will distress him and he will be unable to see the realities of which in his former state he had seen the shadows; and then conceive some one saying to him, that what he saw before was an illusion, but that now, when he is approaching nearer to being and his eye is turned towards more real existence, he has a clearer vision—what will be his reply? And you may further imagine that his instructor is pointing to the objects as they pass and requiring him to name them—will he not be perplexed? Will he not fancy that the shadows which he formerly saw are truer than the objects which are now shown to him?

Far truer.

And if he is compelled to look straight at the light, will he not have a pain in his eyes which will make him turn away to take refuge in the objects of vision which he can see, and which he will conceive to be in reality clearer than the things which are now being shown to him?

True, he said.

And suppose once more, that he is reluctantly dragged up a steep and rugged ascent, and held fast until he is forced into the presence of the sun himself, is he not likely to be pained and irritated? When he approaches the light his eyes will be dazzled and he will not be able to see anything at all of what are now called realities.

Not all in a moment, he said.

He will require to grow accustomed to the sight of the upper world. And first he will see the shadows best, next the reflections of men and other objects in the water, and then the objects themselves; then he will gaze upon the light of the moon and the stars and the spangled heaven; and he will see the sky and the stars by night better than the sun or the light of the sun by day?

Certainly.

Last of all he will be able to see the sun, and not mere reflections of him in the water, but he will see him in his own proper place, and not in another; and he will contemplate him as he is.

Certainly.

He will then proceed to argue that this is he who gives the season and the years, and is the guardian of all that is in the visible world, and in a certain way the cause of all things which he and his fellows have been accustomed to behold?

Clearly, he said, he would first see the sun and then reason about him.

And when he remembered his old habitation, and the wisdom of the den and his fellow-prisoners, do you not suppose that he would felicitate himself on the change, and pity them?

Certainly, he would.

And if they were in the habit of conferring honors among themselves on those who were quickest to observe the passing shadows and to remark which of them went before, and which followed after, and which were together; and who were therefore best able to draw conclusions as to the future, do you think that he would care for such honors and glories, or envy the possessors of them? Would he not say with Homer,

> Better to be the poor servant of a poor master,

and to endure anything, rather than think as they do and live after their manner?

Yes, he said, I think that he would rather suffer anything than entertain these false notions and live in this miserable manner.

Imagine once more, I said, such an one coming suddenly out of the sun to be replaced in his old situation; would he not be certain to have his eyes full of darkness?

To be sure, he said.

And if there were a contest, and he had to compete in measuring the shadows with the prisoners who had never moved out of the den, while his sight was still weak, and before his eyes had become steady (and the time which would be needed to acquire this new habit of sight might be very considerable) would he not be ridiculous? Men would say of him that up he went and down he came without his eyes; and that it was better not even to think of ascending; and if any one tried to loose another and lead him up to the light, let them only catch the offender, and they would put him to death.

No question, he said.

This entire allegory, I said, you may now append, dear Glaucon, to the previous argument; the prison-house is the world of sight, the light of the fire is the sun, and you will not misapprehend me if you interpret the journey upwards to be the ascent of the soul into the intellectual world according to my poor belief, which, at your desire, I have expressed— whether rightly or wrongly God knows. But, whether true or false, my opinion is that in the world of knowledge the idea of good appears last of all, and is seen only with an effort; and, when seen, is also inferred to be the universal author of all things beautiful and right, parent of light and of the lord of light in this visible world, and the immediate source of reason and truth in the intellectual; and that this is the power upon which he who would act rationally either in public or private life must have his eye fixed.

I agree, he said, as far as I am able to understand you.

Moreover, I said, you must not wonder that those who attain to this beatific vision are unwilling to descend to human affairs; for their souls are ever hastening into the upper world where they desire to dwell; which desire of theirs is very natural, if our allegory may be trusted.

Yes, very natural.

And is there anything surprising in one who passes from divine contemplations to the evil state of man, misbehaving himself in a ridiculous manner; if, while his eyes are blinking and before he has become accustomed to the surrounding darkness, he is compelled to fight in courts of law, or in other places, about the images or the shadows of images of justice, and is endeavouring to meet the conceptions of those who have never yet seen absolute justice?

Anything but surprising, he replied.

Any one who has common sense will remember that the bewilderments of the eyes are of two kinds, and arise from two causes, either from coming out of the light or from going into the light, which is true of the mind's eye, quite as much as of the bodily eye; and he who remembers this when he sees any one whose vision is perplexed and weak, will not be too ready to laugh; he will first ask whether that soul of man has come out of the brighter life, and is unable to see because unaccustomed to the dark, or having turned from darkness to the day is dazzled by excess of light. And he will count the one happy in his condition and state of being, and he will pity the other; or, if he have a mind to laugh at the soul which comes from below into the light, there will be more reason in this than in the laugh which greets him who returns from above out of the light into the den.

That, he said, is a very just distinction.

THE DEATH OF THE MOTH

Virginia Woolf

This selection was originally published in 1942.

Moths that fly by day are not properly to be called moths; they do not excite that pleasant sense of dark autumn nights and ivy-blossom which the commonest yellow-underwing asleep in the shadow of the curtain never fails to rouse in us. They are hybrid creatures, neither gay like butterflies nor sombre like their own species. Nevertheless the present specimen, with his narrow hay-coloured wings, fringed with a tassel of the same colour, seemed to be content with life. It was a pleasant morning, mid-September, mild, benignant, yet with a keener breath than that of the summer months. The plough was already scoring the field opposite the window, and where the share had been, the earth was pressed flat and gleamed with moisture. Such vigour came rolling in from the fields and the down beyond that it was difficult to keep the eyes strictly turned upon the book. The rooks too were keeping one of their annual festivities; soaring round the tree tops until it looked as if a vast net with thousands of black knots in it had been cast up into the air; which, after a few moments sank slowly down upon the trees until every twig seemed to have a know at the end of it. Then, suddenly, the net would be thrown into the air again in a wider circle this time, with the utmost clamour and vociferation, as though to be thrown into the air and settle slowly down upon the tree tops were a tremendously exciting experience.

The same energy which inspired the rooks, the ploughmen, the horse, and even, it seemed, the lean bare-backed downs, sent the moth fluttering from side to side of his square of the window-pane. One could not help watching him. One was, indeed, conscious of a queer feeling of pity for him. The possibilities of pleasure seemed that morning so enormous and so various that to have only a moth's part in life, and a day moth's at that, appeared a hard fate, and his zest in enjoying his meagre opportunities to the full, pathetic. He flew vigorously to one corner of his compartment, and, after waiting there a second, flew across to the other. What remained for him but to fly to a third corner and then to a fourth? That was all he could do, in spite of the size of the downs, the width of the sky, the far-off smoke of houses, and the romantic voice, now and then, of a steamer out at sea. What he could do he did. Watching him, it seemed as if a fibre, very thin but pure, of the enormous energy of the world had been thrust into his frail and diminutive body. As often as he crossed the pane, I could fancy that a thread of vital light became visible. He was little or nothing but life.

Yet, because he was so small, and so simple a form of the energy that was rolling in at the open window and driving its way through so many narrow and intricate corridors in my own brain and in those of other human beings, there was something marvellous as well as pathetic about him. It was as if someone had taken a tiny bead of pure life and decking it as lightly as possible with down and feathers, had set it dancing and zigzagging to show us the true nature of life. Thus displayed one could not get over the strangeness of it. One is apt to forget all about life, seeing it humped and bossed and garnished and cumbered so that it has to move with the greatest circumspection and dignity. Again, the thought of all that life might have been had he been born in any other shape caused one to view his simple activities with a kind of pity.

After a time, tired by his dancing apparently, he settled on the window ledge in the sun, and, the queer spectacle being at an end, I forgot about him. Then, looking up, my eye was caught by him. He was trying to resume his dancing, but seemed either so stiff or so awkward that he could only flutter to the bottom of the window-pane; and when he tried to fly across it he failed. Being intent on other matters I watched these futile attempts for a time without thinking, unconsciously waiting for him to resume his flight, as one waits for a machine, that has stopped momentarily, to start again without considering the reason of its failure. After perhaps a seventh attempt he slipped from the wooden ledge and fell, fluttering his wings, on to his back on the window sill. The helplessness of his attitude roused me. It flashed upon me that he was in difficulties; be could no longer raise himself; his legs struggled vainly. But, as I stretched out a pencil, meaning to help him to right himself, it came over me that the failure and awkwardness were the approach of death. I laid the pencil down again.

The legs agitated themselves once more. I looked as if for the enemy against which he struggled. I looked out of doors. What had happened there? Presumably it was midday, and work in the fields had stopped. Stillness and quiet had replaced the previous animation. The birds had taken themselves off to feed in the brooks. The horses stood still. Yet the power was there all the same, massed outside indifferent, impersonal, not attending to anything in particular. Somehow it was opposed to the little hay-coloured moth. It was useless to try to do anything. One could only watch the extraordinary efforts made by those tiny legs against an oncoming doom which could, had it chosen, have submerged an entire city, not merely a city, but masse of human beings; nothing, I knew, had any chance against death. Nevertheless after a pause of exhaustion the legs fluttered again. It was superb this last protest, and so frantic that he succeeded at last in righting himself. One's sympathies, of course, were all on the side of life. Also, when there was nobody to care or to know, this gigantic effort on the part of an insignificant little moth, against a power of such magnitude, to retain what no one else valued or desired to keep, moved one strangely. Again, somehow, one saw life, a pure bead. I lifted the pencil again, useless though I knew it to be. But even as I did so, the unmistakable tokens of death showed themselves. The body relaxed, and instantly grew stiff. The struggle was over. The insignificant little creature now knew death. As I looked at the dead moth, this minute wayside triumph of so great a force over so mean an antagonist filled me with wonder. Just as life had been strange a few minutes before, so death was now as strange. The moth having righted himself now lay most decently and uncomplainingly composed. 0 yes, he seemed to say, death is stronger than I am.

Masolino da Panicale, *The Annunciation*, probably 1425/1430, tempera on panel. 58¼ × 45¼.

ANGER IN AN UNJUST WORLD

———————————————————■———————————————————

Carol Tavris

The following selection is excerpted from Tavris's 1982 book The Misunderstood Emotion.

St. Thomas Aquinas imagined that people feel angry only when they are offended by their inferiors: "Thus a nobleman is angry if he be insulted by a peasant; a wise man, if by a fool; a master, if by a servant." If the nobleman insults the peasant, on the other hand, "anger does not ensue, but only sorrow." The irritating habit of modern peasants to react to insult with anger instead of sorrow, is, of course, the story of revolution.

Yet Aquinas was making an important point about the power of authority to establish legitimacy, and legitimacy is death to anger. For, in fact, most peasants, fools, and servants have not protested the injustices done them, nor even regarded them as injustices. The sense of injustice is made, not born, and although we think of anger as the handmaiden of justice, it is not its inevitable companion. Anger depends on our perceptions of a situation, perceptions of injustice included.

Many people believe that if they feel angry now about something, they must always have felt that way, although the anger may previously have been repressed, distorted, or displaced. A woman who, in 1975, feels angry with herself for having dropped out of medical school for marriage in 1955 wonders what she did with the anger she assumes she felt at the time. A man who, as an adult, feels angry with his parents for making him eat all the food on his plate when he was young thinks he felt as angry when he *was* young. The ex-medical student and the little boy may truly have felt angry in the past, but it's more likely that they were just going along with the times, following the rules, with perhaps a squawk or two of protest. Not only do people attribute their emotions backward to what they felt years ago, but they attribute them sideways, to what they think others should be feeling. Some attribute anger to women or minorities of previous generations and even centuries. When they wonder why a battered woman stays with a vicious husband, blaming herself instead of him for her abuse; or why a slave does not rebel; or why the Untouchables accept their caste of degradation; they are assuming that these sufferers interpret the situation as they do—and see a way out of it, as well.

The forces that keep people in their places, if not entirely contented then at least not angry, are not always as irrational as they seem. The decision that a particular situation is unjust must overcome a few psychological and practical hurdles, and so must the next decision: that the injustice merits anger instead of apathy. The question, therefore, is not simply "Why do people become angry?" but why they do not.

THE RATIONALIZING SPECIES

Golfer Tom Watson seemed to be cruising to an easy victory in the $300,000 Bryon Nelson Classic a few years ago when the weather and his luck turned suddenly against him. From a comfortable score of eight under par he dropped to four over par. "It doesn't upset me," Watson told a reporter. "Golf is not a fair game."

Life is not a fair game, either, but people have a curious capacity to behave as if it were. We tend to equate what is with what ought to be, and react with outrage to attacks on our way of doing things. We accept injustices more readily when they are built into the system, because the roles we play seem so normal and inevitable. For example, we take it for granted that it is within a boss's right to set working hours; but Eskimo workers in factories in Alaska found it hilarious that the white workers responded so obediently to the whistles summoning them to stop work or start it. To the Eskimo, the only authority that determines when people shall work is the tide. Yet American workers would find it just as hilarious, to say nothing of an infringement on their liberty, if they had to sing the company song in unison every morning, as many Japanese workers do, without question or anger.

What happens when people's faith in the legitimacy of the system is put to the test? Usually, it is the test that fails. The very organization of our mental faculties seems designed to screen out information we don't want to hear, information that is at odds with our basic beliefs. Psychologist Anthony G. Greenwald calls the self "The Totalitarian Ego," arguing that the ego organizes its knowledge, perceptions, and memory in predictably biased ways that are designed (like totalitarian governments) primarily to protect its organization.

The ego, says Greenwald, is a "self justifying historian," which seeks only that information that agrees with it, rewrites history when it needs to, and does not even see the evidence that threatens it. The organization of knowledge in the mind is like a library system: our built-in biases allow us to retrieve any specific information that we need rapidly; once we make a commitment to a particular cataloging system (say, a conservative ideology or a religious framework of belief), we spend more time maintaining the system than revising it. The biases of the mind persist because they work: they preserve self-confidence, they keep our mental organization in order, and they keep us persevering toward our goals, whatever those may be. The mind's cautiousness about accepting new ideas may seem foolhardy in a world bursting with innovation and discovery, but (at least until recently) it has been an adaptive success for our species. The flash of anger that people may feel when they are threatened with conflicting information is the mind's way of protecting its organization. "My mind's made up—don't confuse me with the facts" seems to have been an oddly successful strategy in the evolution of the brain. After all, if we kept "changing our minds" with each new bit of experience and observation, we would never know how to behave, what to think, or why we were working so hard for a future reward.

Many psychologists have by now posed theories of cognitive consistency to predict how people handle information that conflicts with their beliefs: we shall shift the belief slightly, or more likely the new information, to make the two coexist harmoniously.

Consistency theories all assume that human beings have a fundamental need to find meaning and order in life's experiences. Psychologist Melvin J. Lerner adds that we need to believe in a just world, one in which people get what they deserve, good is rewarded, the sinful punished. The Belief in a Just World, he argues, is "a fundamental delusion" that is central to the way we organize experience, making sense out of confusion, justice out of cruelty and unfairness, and orderliness out of random events. And it protects the legitimacy of the established order. Researchers have by now conducted dozens of experiments that show what happens when the belief in a just world clashes with an obvious fact of injustice. If you cannot do anything about the injustice, you will tend to denigrate the victim, deny the evidence, or reinterpret the event entirely. You will go to great lengths to protect the basic faith.

DENIGRATE THE VICTIM

In a just world, innocent women are not raped. Women who are raped, therefore, must have "invited it"—by being seductive, or perhaps by merely being. In one experiment that simulated a jury trial, a defendant was depicted as having raped a married woman, a virgin, or a divorcee. The subjects in the study gave longer sentences to rapists of virgins than to rapists of divorcees, as you might expect, but, more interesting, they attributed more responsibility for the rape to the virgins and wives than to the divorcees. Apparently the knowledge that innocent, "respectable" women can be raped was too threatening to the jurors' belief in a just world, and so they found fault with the victims' behavior.

Similarly, many vehement antiabortionists cannot accept the statistics of rape, incest, poverty, contraceptive ignorance, and woman battering, preferring to believe that it is only immoral women who have abortions. Women are blamed for "getting themselves pregnant," as one Congressman put it, in that bizarre, anachronistic phrasing that exonerates the role of the male in conception. (The same Congressmen who advise that "the best contraceptive is the word no" would not take it kindly, I bet, if their women applied that word to them.)

Women are not the only objects of rationalizing denigration. The poor bring their suffering on themselves (say many of the well-to-do) because they are lazy, conniving, drunk, and violent. A man who is fired for trying to improve working conditions must have deserved it; he should have kept his mouth shut. Neoconservative Jews such as Norman Podhoretz and Irving Kristol must, to preserve their commitment to fascist but anticommunist nations such as Argentina, denigrate victims of Argentine anti-Semitism, most notably Jacobo Timerman; accepting his testimony threatens their political philosophy and their sense of religious security. Fighter pilots, on hearing that a buddy has been killed in a plane crash, will blame the buddy for having made a stupid error; if it was the plane that failed or the Air Force's error, the survivors are in danger too. All of these rationalizations help people avoid the panicky thought that poverty, job loss, anti-Semitism, or death could strike *them*.

DENIAL

Here's a familiar term for the psychoanalytic archives, this time referring not to an unconscious process but often a perfectly conscious one: screening out unpleasant information that might threaten one's convictions. Fundamentalist parents are fighting to have their children taught absolute values of right and wrong: they worry that schools are subjecting their children to information that might jeopardize their religious certainty. When writer Frances FitzGerald asked one such mother whether she would consider sending her children to a nonfundamentalist school, the mother said, "No, because our eternal destiny is all-important, so you can't take a chance. College so often throws kids into confusion." To avoid confusion, many people prefer ignorance.

Denial seems to be at the heart of political philosophies. As a particularly depressing (if extreme) case, there are people who will tell you that the Holocaust never happened. But you can see garden-variety denial in the way individuals respond to the news that innocent people have been imprisoned or murdered by the Soviet Union, the United States, China, Vietnam, Argentina, Chile, France, Japan, South Africa, Haiti, Cuba . . . (fill in your choice for infamy). Depending on your politics, you will tend to deny the crimes committed by your favorite nations (for such crimes jeopardize your desire to believe in your allies' basic integrity and justice, and possibly jeopardize your economic interests as well), and emphasize those committed by your enemies (it is perfectly consistent to believe in the sins of your opponents). If you believe in the basic corruptibility of most political systems, however, you won't find it inconsistent evidence to be denied when one of them does something criminal or stupid.

REINTERPRETATION OF THE INJUSTICE AND ITS OUTCOME

This mechanism to preserve faith in a world requires some flights of imagination: people "rewrite" the injustice they hear about so that it simply disappears, taking with it the need to be emotionally disturbed. For example, you might reinterpret the result of injustice, deciding that the victim wasn't such a victim after all; suffering is a good thing that builds moral character and makes the sufferer a better person. Or you might decide that the cause of the injustice was, let's say, not the government's decision to release Agent Orange on Vietnam, but a result of something the victim did or failed to do; perhaps those servicemen who now complain they were poisoned just forgot to take adequate precautions. Or might extend the time frame of the whole event to maintain your belief in ultimate justice: eventually, heroes and bastards will get their just deserts, but it may take a few years. Maybe a lifetime. Maybe in the afterlife . . .

So great is the need to believe in justice and order, says Lerner, that many people will even assume a large burden of anguish, blaming themselves, rather than yield the belief. Parents of terminally ill children, the most poignantly undeserving of victims, frequently berate themselves for their children's fate: "If I had only done this . . ." "If we'd never done that . . ." This self-blame, paradoxically, allays the anxiety of the intolerable conclusion that no one is responsible.

In the laboratory, psychologists have watched before their very eyes as the belief in a just world "cools out" anger. Young adults observed a videotape of what they thought was a real experiment in learning (in fact, it was staged), in which another young woman suffered a series of severe shocks whenever she made "errors." At first the observers would flinch empathetically with each televised shock, and many expressed fury and indignation at the treatment they were watching; "I was really mad." "I felt like getting up and walking out." "I thought it was disgusting." In spite of these strong affirmations of anger, *not one* of the thousand people who have by now participated in this experiment have actually complained. Instead, most of them decided that the victim was a fool or a weakling for sitting still and allowing herself to be shocked. "I would never let anyone do that to me!" they asserted. Unable as they were to do anything about the injustice they observed, they condemned the victim and evaluated her critically. The more strongly the experimenters portrayed the innocent victim as a martyr, the more vehemently the observers condemned her.

Religion, of course, offers the ultimate just world, if not in this life then in the next. Religion and political ideology organize our angers as they legitimize our social systems. Indeed all the great religions have made the management of anger a central concern, with prescriptions designed to protect the social order and to generate anger, if at all, only on its behalf.

For instance, although the Old Testament itself is a veritable catalog of family squabbles, internecine wars, and the smiting of heathens, it continually reminds its readers that "He that is slow to anger is better than the mighty"—surely a sermon that would reassure the mighty. Jehovah of the Old Testament and Allah of Islam are angry gods, who require anger to be used freely in their service against enemies, infidels, and the wicked; but anger *within* the community is to be suppressed. This was a smart and successful philosophy for small nations surrounded by competing groups, the situation then and now in the Middle East.

In contrast, the religions of Taoism, Vishnuism, and Buddhism advocate the complete eradication of anger and any other emotion that serves a this-worldly desire (such as lust and greed). Because everything that happens in this world is predestined, according to these theologies, there is no point in getting riled up about evil, war, and sin. There is certainly no point in protesting one's caste; obedient behavior in this life will be rewarded with caste advancement in the next incarnation. (War and anger may be an occasional necessity, but they are not to be sought after or celebrated.)

Christianity stands between the martial religions and the pacifist ones: anger may be used to combat evil and injustice; anger is good or bad depending on its use, not its nature. Although in the New Testament divine vengeance has subsided in favor of divine forgiveness, human beings are still supposed to wait for forgiveness in heaven and not raise their voices too loudly for justice on earth. If we consider the secular results of Christianity, however, we see that those who turned the other check usually got a slap in return; and that the meek did indeed inherit the earth—to plow, to plant, and to harvest for their masters.

Ideas about justice are not all in the mind. Realistic, practical motives hold people in roles as victims of manipulation or injustice without their perceiving either. Sociologist Barrington Moore, Jr., calls their condition one of "exploitative reciprocity," and if revolutionaries emphasize the "exploitative," the people involved tend to emphasize the "reciprocity." Every social system, from the family to a nation, is based on a social contract of the rights and duties of its participants. The contract may be written or implicit, but the rules are usually clear to all, or become clear once they are broken.

Some feminists, for example, who feel angry about genital mutilation, such as circumcision or even excision of the clitoris that women in many Third World cultures endure, cannot understand why the women tolerate these practices and continue them. Yet these horrendous, painful customs are as essential to the women's security and survival—because they guarantee that the woman will continue to be protected by men—as a job contract is to a union worker here. (Many Third World feminists themselves put food, education and work at the top of their list of reforms for this reason.) In any relationship between authority and subordinate, the subordinate gives up something to get something: the benefits of the authority's protection, expertise, talent, access to the rain god, earnings.

The anger that fuels revolt does not arise, therefore, from objective conditions of deprivation or misery; as long as people regard those conditions as natural and inevitable, as God's law or man's way, they do not feel angry about them. So sociologists speak instead of "relative deprivation," the subjective comparisons that people make when they compare their actual lives to *what might be possible*. Alexis de Tocqueville observed that "evils which are patiently endured when they seem inevitable become intolerable when once the idea of escape from them is suggested," and the freed slave Frederick Douglass put the same idea more passionately: "Beat and cuff your slave," he wrote, "keep him hungry and spiritless, and he will follow the chain of his master like a dog, but feed and clothe him well, work him moderately, surround him with physical comfort, and dreams of freedom intrude."

In this country, the civil rights, women's rights, and human rights movements have been organized and sustained primarily by those who already had more education, opportunities, and success in the system than the less-fortunate members of their race, sex, or class.

Margaret Mead once said of liberals that they are "the yeast within the body politic upon which American society relies to keep its dream worth following. Without them, we should be lost. Yet with them, we are uncomfortable. For they draw their strength from the discrepancies in the very heart of American life." Rebels and dissidents challenge the complacent belief in a just world, and, as the theory would predict, they are usually denigrated for their efforts. While they are alive, they may be called "cantankerous," "crazy," "hysterical," "uppity," or "duped." Dead, some of them become saints and heroes, the sterling characters of history. It's a matter of proportion. One angry rebel is crazy, three is a conspiracy, 50 is a movement.

SALVATION

Langston Hughes

The following piece is from Hughes's 1940 memoir The Big Sea.

I was saved from sin when I was going on thirteen. But not really saved. It happened like this. There was a big revival at my Auntie Reed's church. Every night for weeks there had been much preaching, singing, praying, and shouting, and some very hardened sinners had been brought to Christ, and the membership of the church had grown by leaps and bounds. Then just before the revival ended, they held a special meeting for children, "to bring the young lambs to the fold." My aunt spoke of it for days ahead. That night I was escorted to the front row and placed on the mourners' bench with all the other young sinners, who had not yet been brought to Jesus.

My aunt told me that when you were saved you saw a light, and something happened to you inside! And Jesus came into your life! And God was with you from then on! She said you could see and hear and feel Jesus in your soul. I believed her. I had heard a great many old people say the same thing and it seemed to me they ought to know. So I sat there calmly in the hot, crowded church, waiting for Jesus to come to me.

The preacher preached a wonderful rhythmical sermon, all moans and shouts and lonely cries and dire pictures of hell, and then he sang a song about the ninety and nine safe in the fold, but one little lamb was left out in the cold. Then he said: "Won't you come? Won't you come to Jesus? Young lambs, won't you come?" And he held out his arms to all us young sinners there on the mourners' bench. And the little girls cried. And some of them jumped up and went to Jesus right away. But most of us just sat there.

A great many old people came and knelt around us and prayed, old women with jet-black faces and braided hair, old men with work-gnarled hands. And the church sang a song about the lower lights are burning, some poor sinners to be saved. And the whole building rocked with prayer and song.

Still I kept waiting to *see* Jesus.

Finally all the young people had gone to the altar and were saved, but one boy and me. He was a rounder's son named Westley. Westley and I were surrounded by sisters and deacons praying. It was very hot in the church, and getting late now. Finally Westley said to me in a whisper: "God damn! I'm tired o' sitting here. Let's get up and be saved." So he got up and was saved.

Then I was left all alone on the mourners' bench. My aunt came and knelt at my knees and cried, while prayers and song swirled all around me in the little church. The whole congregation prayed for me alone, in a mighty wail of moans and voices. And I kept waiting serenely for Jesus, waiting, waiting—but he didn't come. I wanted to see him, but nothing happened to me. Nothing! I wanted something to happen to me, but nothing happened.

I heard the songs and the minister saying: "Why don't you come? My dear child, why don't you come to Jesus? Jesus is waiting for you. He wants you. Why don't you come? Sister Reed, what is this child's name?"

"Langston," my aunt sobbed.

"Langston, why don't you come? Why don't you come and be saved? Oh, Lamb of God! Why don't you come?"

Now it was really getting late. I began to be ashamed of myself, holding everything up so long. I began to wonder what God thought about Westley, who certainly hadn't seen Jesus either, but who was now sitting proudly on the platform, swinging his knickerbockered legs and grinning down at me, surrounded by deacons and old women on their knees praying. God had not struck Westley dead for taking his name in vain or for lying in the temple. So I decided that maybe to save further trouble, I'd better lie, too, and say that Jesus had come, and get up and be saved.

So I got up.

Suddenly the whole room broke into a sea of shouting, as they saw me rise. Waves of rejoicing swept the place. Women leaped in the air. My aunt threw her arms around me. The minister took me by the hand and led me to the platform.

When things quieted down, in a hushed silence, punctuated by a few ecstatic "Amens," all the new young lambs were blessed in the name of God. Then joyous singing filled the room.

That night, for the first time in my life but one—for I was a big boy twelve years old—I cried. I cried, in bed alone, and couldn't stop. I buried my head under the quilts, but my aunt heard me. She woke up and told my uncle I was crying because the Holy Ghost had come into my life, and because I had seen Jesus. But I was really crying because I couldn't bear to tell her that I had lied, that I had deceived everybody in the church, that I hadn't seen Jesus, and that now I didn't believe there was a Jesus anymore, since he didn't come to help me.

BORN AMONG THE BORN AGAIN

Garrison Keillor

This piece is an excerpt from Keillor's 1985 book Lake Wobegon Days.

In a town where everyone was either Lutheran or Catholic, our family was not and never had been. We were Sanctified Brethren, a sect so tiny that nobody but us and God knew about it, so when kids asked what I was, I just said Protestant. It was too much to explain, like having six toes. You would rather keep your shoes on.

Grandpa Cotten was once tempted toward Lutheranism by a preacher who gave a rousing sermon on grace that Grandpa heard as a young man while taking Aunt Esther's dog home who had chased a Model T across town. He sat down on the church steps and listened to the voice boom out the open windows until he made up his mind to go in and unite with the truth, but he took one look from the vestibule and left. "He was dressed up like the Pope of Rome," said Grandpa, "and the altar and paintings and the gold candlesticks—my gosh, it was just a big show. And he was reading the whole darn thing off a page, like an actor."

Jesus said, "Where two or three are gathered together in my name, there am I in the midst of them," and the Brethren believed that was enough. We met in Uncle Al and Aunt Flo's bare living room, with plain folding chairs arranged facing in toward the middle. No clergyman in a black smock. No organ or piano, for that would make one person too prominent. No upholstery—it would lead to complacence. No picture of Jesus—He was in our Hearts. The faithful sat down at the appointed hour and waited for the Spirit to move one of them to speak or to pray or to give out a hymn from our Little Flock hymnal. No musical notation, for music must come from the heart and not off a page. We sang the texts to a tune that fit the meter, of the many tunes we all knew. The idea of reading a prayer was sacrilege to us—"If a man can't remember what he wants to say to God, let him sit down and think a little harder," Grandpa said.

"There's the Lord's Prayer," said Aunt Esther meekly. We were sitting on the porch after Sunday dinner. Esther and Harvey were visiting from

Minneapolis and had attended Lake Wobegon Lutheran, she having turned Lutheran when she married him, a subject that was never brought up in our family.

"You call that prayer? Sitting and reciting like a bunch of school-children?"

Harvey cleared his throat and turned to me and smiled, "Speaking of school, how are you doing?" he asked.

There was a lovely silence in the Brethren assembled on Sunday morning as we waited for the Spirit. Either the Spirit was moving someone to speak who was taking his sweet time or else the Spirit was playing a wonderful joke on us and letting us sit, or perhaps silence was the point of it. We sat listening to rain on the roof, distant traffic, a radio playing from across the street, kids whizzing by on bikes, dogs barking, as we waited for the Spirit to inspire us. It was like sitting on the porch with your family, when nobody feels that they have to make talk. So quiet in church. Minutes drifted by in silence that was sweet to us. The old Regulator clock ticked, the rain stopped, and the room changed light as the sun broke through—shafts of brilliant sun through the windows and motes of dust falling through it—the smell of clean clothes and floor wax and wine and the fresh bread of Aunt Flo, which was Christ's body given for us. Jesus in our midst, who loved us. So peaceful; and we loved each other, too. I thought perhaps the Spirit was leading me to say that, but I was just a boy, and children were supposed to keep still.

And my affections were not pure. They were tainted with a sneaking admiration of Catholics—Catholic Christmas, Easter, the Living Rosary, and the Blessing of the Animals, all magnificent. Everything we did was plain, but they were regal—especially the Feast Day of Saint Francis, which they did right out in the open, a feast for the eyes. Cows, horses, some pets, right on the church lawn. The turmoil, animals bellowing and barking and clucking and a cat scheming how to escape and suddenly leaping out of the girl's arms who was holding on tight, the cat dashing through the crowd, dogs straining at the leash, and the ocarina band of third graders playing a song, and the great calm of the sisters, and the flags, and the Knights of Columbus decked out in their handsome black suits—the whole thing was gorgeous. I stared at it until my eyes almost fell out, and then I wished it would go on much longer.

"Christians," my Uncle Al used to say, "do not go in for show," referring to the Catholics. We were sanctified by the blood of the Lord; therefore we were saints, like Saint Francis, but we didn't go in for feasts or ceremonies, involving animals or not. We went in for sitting, all nineteen of us, in Uncle Al and Aunt Flo's living room on Sunday morning and having a plain meeting and singing hymns in our poor thin voices, while not far away the Catholics were whooping it up. I wasn't allowed inside Our Lady, of course, but if the Blessing of the Animals on the Feast Day of Saint Francis was any indication, Lord, I didn't know but what they had elephants in there and acrobats. I sat in our little group and envied them for the splendor and gorgeousness, as we tried to sing without even so much as a harmonica to give us the pitch. Hymns, Uncle Al said, didn't have to be sung perfect, because God looks on the heart, and if you are In The Spirit, then all praise is good.

The Brethren, also known as The Saints Gathered in the Name of Christ Jesus, who met in the living room were all related to each other and raised in the Faith from infancy except Brother Mel, who was rescued from a life of drunkenness, saved as a brand from the burning, a drowning sailor, a sheep on the hillside, whose immense red nose testified to his previous condition. I envied his amazing story of how he came to be with us. Born to godly parents, Mel left home at fifteen and joined the Navy. He sailed to distant lands in a submarine and had exciting experiences while traveling the downward path, which led him finally to the Union Gospel Mission in Minneapolis, where he heard God's voice "as clear as my voice speaking to you." He was twenty-six, he slept under bridges and in abandoned buildings, he drank two quarts of white muscatel every day, and then God told him that he must be born again, and so he was, and became the new Mel, except for his nose.

Except for his nose, Mel Burgess looked like any forty-year-old Brethren man: sober, preferring dark suits, soft-spoken, tending toward girth. His nose was what made you look twice: battered, swollen, very red with tiny purplish lines, it looked ancient and dead on his otherwise fairly handsome face, the souvenir of what he had been saved from, the "Before" of his "Before . . . and After" advertisement for being born again.

For me, there was nothing before. I was born among the born-again. This living room so hushed, the Brethren in their customary places on folding chairs (the comfortable ones were put away on Sunday morning) around the end table draped with a white cloth and the glass of wine and loaf of bread (unsliced), was as familiar to me as my mother and father, before whom there was nobody. I had always been here.

I never saw the "Before" until the Sunday we drove to St. Cloud for dinner and traipsed into a restaurant that a friend of Dad's had recommended, Phil's House of Good Food. The waitress pushed two tables together and we sat down and studied the menu. My mother blanched at the prices. A chicken dinner went for $2.50, the roast beef for $3.75. "It's a nice place," Dad said, multiplying the five of us times $2.50. "I'm not so hungry, I guess," he said. "Maybe I'll just have soup." We weren't restaurantgoers—"Why pay good money for food you could make better at home?" was Mother's philosophy—so we weren't at all sure about restaurant customs. For example, could a person who had been seated in a restaurant simply get up and walk out? Would it be proper? Would it be *legal*?

The waitress came and stood by Dad. "Can I get you something from the bar?" she said. Dad blushed a deep red. The question seemed to imply that he looked like a drinker.

"No," he whispered, as if he were turning down her offer to take off her clothes and dance on the table.

Then another waitress brought a tray of glasses to a table of four couples next to us. "Martini," she said, setting the drink down, "whiskey sour, whiskey sour, Manhattan, whiskey sour, gin and tonic, martini, whiskey sour."

"Ma'am? Something from the bar?" Mother looked at her in disbelief.

Suddenly the room changed for us. Our waitress looked hardened, rough, cheap; across the room a woman laughed obscenely, "Haw, haw, haw"; the man with her lit a cigarette and blew a cloud of smoke; a swearword drifted out from the kitchen like a whiff of urine; even the soft lighting seemed suggestive, diabolical. To be seen in such a place on the Lord's Day—*what had we done?*

"Ed," my mother said, rising.

"We can't stay, I'm sorry," Dad told the waitress. We all got up and put on our coats. Everyone in the restaurant had a good long look at us. A bald little man in a filthy white shirt emerged from the kitchen, wiping his hands. "Folks? Something wrong?" he said.

"We're in the wrong place," Mother told him. Mother always told the truth, or something close to it.

"This is *humiliating*," I said out on the sidewalk. "I feel like a *leper* or something. Why do we always have to make such a big production out of everything? Why can't we be like regular people?"

She put her hand on my shoulder. "Be not conformed to this world," she said. I knew the rest by heart ". . . but be ye transformed by the renewing of your mind, that ye may prove what is that good and acceptable and perfect will of God."

"Where we gonna eat?" Phyllis asked.

"We'll find someplace reasonable," said Mother, and we walked six blocks across the river and found a lunch counter and ate sloppy joes (called Maid-Rites) for fifteen cents apiece. They did not agree with us, and we were aware of them all afternoon through prayer meeting and Young People's.

WHOLLY WRIT: WOMEN'S SPIRITUALITY

Charlene Spretnak

The following piece was originally published in Ms. *magazine in 1993.*

In our time women's spirituality—in both perception and expression—has been constrained by two overarching social forces: the patriarchal biases in most religions and the modern worldview that devalues and marginalizes spiritual concerns in general. Consequently, the growing presence of feminist spirituality over the past 20 years has challenged not only patriarchal religion but the underpinnings of the sterile, modern view that human life is a drama apart from the larger

Earth community and the sacred whole that is the cosmos. The goal of feminist spirituality has never been the simple substitution of Yahweh-with-a-skirt. Rather, it seeks, in all its diversity, to revitalize relational, body-honoring, cosmologically grounded spiritual possibilities for women and all others.

The tensions that arose during the 1970s—between feminists who remained in mainstream religions and those who left to pursue other spiritual paths—have largely subsided. Today there is greater appreciation of common ground in many areas: recognizing the interrelatedness of all life, honoring the dignity of the female, discovering the power of creating ritual, perceiving work for ecological and social justice as a spiritual responsibility, and cultivating sensitivity to diverse multicultural experiences. Moreover, there is now greater respect for a woman's self-determination in her choice of spiritual orientation as well as in other aspects of her life.

The images and metaphors of spiritual traditions have often overshadowed the perceptions that evoked them and have fueled divisiveness among religions. At the core of each orientation is an expression of relationship to the ultimate mystery inherent in the cosmos, its self-organizing, self-regulating rhythms of creativity. The universe unfolds through an intricate play of novelty, allurement, relation, and engagement—all rising and passing away in lifetimes of a microsecond or in arcs of billions of years. Humans have only partial apprehension of this unimaginably complex web of forces, so we call on metaphor, symbol, myth or poetry to name and portray it. We call it the divine, God, Goddess, The Way, The Great Holy, Cosmic Consciousness, or other names. Many feminists feel there is good reason to use female metaphors for the divine. First, it overturns a cornerstone of gender politics in patriarchal cultures. Second, the symbolization matches physical reality; has anyone ever seen anything spring into existence because a male finger was pointed toward it? We are not amused by mythic narratives that steal the generative power of the female; womb envy should find less aggressive outlets.

The honoring of the female body in feminist spirituality has been experienced by hundreds of thousands of women as a healing corrective. It also figures, however, in a current debate in academic circles: the argument over "essentialism." Feminists subscribing to the worldview of deconstructive postmodernism assert that (1) any talk of "women's experience" is oppressive because it generalizes and thereby denies the particular experience of individuals, and (2) any talk of the (female) body is misleading because one can know only the social concepts about the body that one's particular society puts forth. Such feminists often cite "women's spirituality" as one of the worst offenders on both counts. I feel that the debate has been framed too crudely. The issue is not belief in a universal, essential female personality structure, but this: Does the fact that females, in all our cultural and individual diversity, bleed in rhythm with the moon and have the capability to grow people from our flesh (plus transform milk into food for the newborn) affect the ways women experience life? Deconstruction slams the door on that question; women's spirituality explores it. The deconstructionist "erasure of the body" is foremost a denial of the elemental power of the female body.

These and other issues are explored in a wide variety of books on women's spirituality, which address such subjects as pastoral work, contemplative expression (prayers and poems), ritual, art, literature, cultural history, psychology, and political activism. The following is a sampling of recently published works.

The poet Muriel Rukeyser wrote that if one woman told the truth about her life, the world would split open. That seems to be the goal of *Sermons Seldom Heard: Women Proclaim Their Lives* (Crossroad, $15.95), edited by Annie Lally Milhaven. A few years ago, it occurred to Milhaven, a former nun, that she had been listening to sermons for 50 years and had never heard one about the suffering that typically befalls women and children: surviving incest, battering, rape, depression, the financial struggles of single mothers, and unwanted divorce for middle-aged wives. She commissioned sermons on these and other topics from women with and without theological academic degrees who had lived through the particular hell discussed in each piece. The power of this collection results from the wrenching personal stories combined with the commonplace occurrence (according to statistics) of such violations. The silence of religious institutions on these topics has long protected the violators. This book is intended for two audiences: clergy, and women who find themselves in the situations described and who might be inspired by learning how other women freed themselves through spiritual self-empowerment that led to action. Each sermon is followed by a factual presentation on the syndrome or situation, a reading list, and a list of relevant organizations. I hope this book will be put into the hands of every clergy person in the country with a simple message: *Here! Pick any three and read them aloud for your next three sermons! Break the silence!*

Feminist theology's emphasis on articulating women's experience as the basis of our spiritual reflections is expressed in the full flowering of *Four Centuries of Jewish Women's Spirituality* (Beacon Press, $18), edited by Ellen M. Umansky and Dianne Ashton. The pieces are arranged in four chronological groupings: "1560–1800: Traditional Voices"; "1800–1890: Stronger Voices"; "1890–1960: Urgent Voices"; and "1960–1990: Contemporary Voices." Piety, the inculcating of spiritual values, and friendship are the informing themes that link the diversity of contributions. A related anthology is *A Ceremonies Sampler: New Rites, Celebrations, and Observances of Jewish Women* (Woman's Institute for Continuing Jewish Education, $9.95), edited by Elizabeth Resnick Levine. By inviting 22 women to describe rituals they have created to mark passages, events, or healing, Levine is providing models to inspire her Jewish sisterhood. The book succeeds in demonstrating that the creation of effective ceremonies is within the reach of grass-roots women, but the examples selected often fail to reach the poetic depth of ritual pieces in the previous book.

Woman-centered spiritual traditions are valued by Annette Van Dyke because they offer a bridge between lesbian and heterosexual feminists and because they honor "the female principle,' which she defines as the force that creates, nourishes, and transmutes everything in the cosmos. In *The Search for a Woman-Centered Spirituality* (New York University Press, $13.95), she interprets novels and nonfiction by women in spiritual traditions "outside of the dominant Euro-American culture's ideas of religion": Leslie Marmon Silko, Paula Gunn Allen, the late Audre Lorde, Alice Walker, Starhawk, Marion Zimmer Bradley, Sonia Johnson, and Mary Daly. Van Dyke concludes that the works she explores by these authors are healing ceremonies, and she demonstrates an understanding of the profoundly political nature of self-defining that is core to feminist spirituality.

In *The Dancing Goddess: Principles of a Matriarchal Aesthetic* (Beacon Press, $17.95), Heide Göttner-Abendroth presents an insightful feminist rebuttal of the patriarchal assumptions embedded in both formalist and neo-Marxist theories of art. She suggests a radical conceptualization of art as cosmologically grounded processes of self-healing and "complex social counterpractice." This book was originally published in Germany in 1982. Most North American feminists would call Göttner-Abendroth's vision "postpatriarchal" and "Goddess-oriented" rather than "matriarchal." While her presentation of prepatriarchal, matrifocal cultures is too generalized and her prescription sometimes too doctrinaire, Göttner-Abendroth's analysis of contemporary feminist art and ritual practice illuminates the presence of a counterforce that "oversteps the system."

The Myth of the Goddess: Evolution of an Image (Viking Arkana, $40) is a substantive work of cultural history. Anne Baring and Jules Cashford, both Jungian analysts, set out to compile stories and images of Western goddess figures, beginning with Paleolithic sculptures from 20,000 B.C.E. They soon became absorbed in tracing the decline and disappearance of "the myth of the goddess," which they define as the vision of life as a living unity. They conclude that the diminishing influence of that myth throughout the Bronze and Iron Ages was paralleled by the rise of the myth of the god, which extols humanity's *dissociation* from nature. The authors were surprised to discover the extent to which Judaism and Christianity inherited the paradigm of Babylonian mythology: the influential story of Marduk's slaying of the goddess-creator (depicted for the first time as menacing and evil, in the form of Tiamat) established the concept of opposition between Creative Spirit and Chaotic Nature, introducing a range of dualistic thinking that is still with us. The book ends with musings on the possibility of reclaiming "'a goddess myth' without a Goddess"—recovering a sense of the Earth community as a sacred unity without having to believe in a literal divine being. Toward this end, the authors are encouraged by holistic discoveries of contemporary science.

This comprehensive survey is written in an accessible style; the imposition of Jungian theory is minimal.

As Baring and Cashford note, what Heinrich Schliemann did for Troy, Marija Gimbutas has done for the Neolithic era of "Old Europe," unearthing the treasures of a culturally rich and advanced cluster of societies that flourished between 7000 and 3500 B.C.E. In *The Civilization of the Goddess* HarperSanFrancisco, $50), Gimbutas draws together her pioneering work of several decades to present essential aspects of European prehistory that have not previously been treated on a pan-European scale. The book is a companion piece to *The Language of the Goddess* (HarperSanFrancisco, $24.95), which presents Gimbutas' interpretation of the symbol system of Old Europe. Gimbutas' text is clear and specific; unfortunately, admirers and critics alike have sometimes transformed her findings into a version resembling a Neolithic paradisiacal Disneyland.

The effect of negative images of the female in the West from the Bronze Age onward is pondered by Patricia Reis in *Through the Goddess: A Woman's Way of Healing* (Continuum, $24.95). She presents a feminist analysis of ways in which "the patriarchal imagination" has structured much of psychology as a campaign against the ubiquitous "bad mother" and the supposedly looming threat of a domineering matriarchy. For a healthier alternative, Reis proposes a "feminist archetypal psychology" that focuses attention on the dynamics of our biological bodies as well as of "the cultural body," the ways in which "the female body-events" have been perceived and interpreted. Because her skillful use of archetypal theory is evocative rather than dogmatic, this wise and gentle book is a healing work.

The critical perspective of ecofeminism is the vantage point from which the theologian Rosemary Radford Ruether seeks to evaluate the heritage of Western Christian culture and to contribute to "a healed relationship" between women and men, between humans and the earth, and among nations and classes. In *Gaia & God: An Ecofeminist Theology of Earth Healing* (HarperSanFrancisco, $22), she proposes that the work of ecojustice and spirituality can best be viewed as the outer and inner aspects of transformation. Ruether begins by revealing the ideological biases in foundational belief systems of Western culture, which sacralized patriarchal relations of domination and projected evil onto nature. Drawing on her vision of a transformed, ecological version of both the sacramental and covenantal traditions within Christianity, she arrives at pragmatic, political suggestions for moving beyond patterns of destruction. The only problematic chapter in the book is on "the fall into patriarchy," in which Ruether dismisses a major theory about the origins of patriarchy in Europe that is supported by many feminist scholars without citing the main evidence for it.

Spiritual concerns combined with political activism are also the focus of *Ecofeminism and the Sacred* (Crossroad, $14.95), edited by Carol J. Adams. This multicultural anthology explores topics illuminated by the central insight of ecofeminism: the historical, political, and symbolic relationship between the domination of nature and the female. Some contributors discuss the effects of bringing ecofeminist values into institutionalized religion; all share their diverse visions, including "emergent Afrocentric ecowomanism." Interrelationship, solidarity, transformation, and embodiment are recurrent themes. Animal rights, nuclear power, abortion rights, and community resistance to degrading conditions in poor urban areas are some of the topics. This collection—the first devoted exclusively to ecofeminism and spirituality—is a thoughtful contribution to an evolving body of analysis and action.

Much of the cutting-edge political analysis of Italy today seeks to identify and redress the "ethnocide" of the peasant cultures. Regarding these cultures with new respect, political theorists discover an ethos of justice, equality, and the rights of the poor—all symbolized by the living tradition of the black madonnas, according to Lucia Chiavola Birnbaum. In a fascinating study, *Black Madonnas: Feminism, Religion, and Politics in Italy* (forthcoming from Northeastern University Press, $35), she identifies the expression of contemporary Italian liberation theology in the beliefs and observances surrounding the dark (black, brown, or gray) madonnas of Italy, whose worshipers are often fiercely anticlerical and antiestablishment. Birnbaum sees continuity between those earth-based images of the sacred female and their Neolithic predecessors found on or near the same sites. She asserts that Italy is currently undergoing a cultural revolution through the delegitimizing of patriarchal symbols and the rise of "heretical old/new vernacular beliefs."

The range of these books demonstrates feminist spirituality's challenge to the modern compartmentalization that limits spiritual concerns to the private realm. A full, rich unfolding of the person cannot proceed when society is distorted by a manipulative political economy in which survival depends on relentless competition, orchestrated greed, and a callous disregard for others. Women's spirituality seeks a renewed understanding that being is being-in-relation and that the web of life deserves attentive care.

RELIGIOUS BELIEF AND PUBLIC MORALITY

Mario Cuomo

The following was an address to the Department of Theology at the University of Notre Dame.

I speak here as a politician. And also as a Catholic, a lay person baptized and raised in the pre-Vatican II Church, educated in Catholic schools, attached to the Church first by birth, then by choice, now by love. An old-fashioned Catholic who sins, regrets, struggles, worries, gets confused, and most of the time feels better after confession. The Catholic Church is my spiritual home. My heart is there, and my hope.

There is, of course, more to being a Catholic than having a sense of spiritual and emotional resonance. Catholicism is a religion of the head as well as the heart, and to be a Catholic is to say "I believe" to the essential core of dogmas that distinguishes our faith. The acceptance of this faith requires a lifelong struggle to understand it more fully and to live it more truly, to translate truth into experience, to practice as well as to believe. That's not easy: applying religious belief to everyday life often presents difficult challenges.

It's always been that way. It certainly is today. The America of the late twentieth century is a consumer society, filled with endless distractions, where faith is more often dismissed than challenged, where the ethnic and other loyalties that once fastened us to our religion seem to be weakening.

In addition to all the weaknesses, dilemmas, and temptations that impede every pilgrim's progress, the Catholic who holds political office in a pluralistic democracy—who is elected to serve Jews and Moslems, atheists and Protestants, as well as Catholics—bears special responsibility. He or she undertakes to help create conditions under which *all* can live with a maximum of dignity and with a reasonable degree of freedom; where everyone who chooses may hold beliefs different from specifically Catholic ones—sometimes contradictory to them; where the laws protect people's right to divorce, to use birth control, and even to choose abortion.

In fact, Catholic public officials take an oath to preserve the Constitution that guarantees this freedom. And they do so gladly. Not because they love what others do with their freedom, but because they realize that in guaranteeing freedom for all, they guarantee *our* right to be Catholics; *our* right to pray, to use the sacraments, to refuse birth control devices, to reject abortion, not to divorce and remarry if we believe it to be wrong.

The Catholic public official lives the political truth most Catholics, throughout most of American history, have accepted and insisted on: the truth that to assure our freedom we must allow others the same freedom, even if occasionally it produces conduct by them that we would hold to be sinful.

I protect my right to be a Catholic by preserving your right to believe as a Jew, a Protestant, or nonbeliever, or as anything else you choose. We know that the price of seeking to force our beliefs on others is that they might someday force theirs on us. This freedom is the fundamental strength of our unique experiment in government. In the complex interplay of forces and considerations that go into the making of our laws and policies, its preservation must be a pervasive and dominant concern.

But insistence on freedom is easier to accept as a general proposition than in its applications to specific situations. There are other valid general principles firmly embedded in our Constitution, which, operating at the same time, create interesting and occasionally troubling problems. Thus the same amendment of the Constitution that forbids the establishment of a state church affirms my legal right to argue that my religious belief would serve well as an article of our universal public morality. I may use the prescribed processes of government—the legislative and executive and judicial processes—to convince my fellow citizens—Jews and Protestants and Buddhists and nonbelievers—that what I propose is as beneficial for them as I believe it is for me; that it is not just parochial or narrowly sectarian but fulfills a human desire for order, peace, justice, kindness, love, any of the values most of us agree are desirable even apart from their specific religious base or context.

I am free to argue for a governmental policy for a nuclear freeze not just to avoid sin but because I think my democracy should regard it as a desirable goal. I can, if I wish, argue that the state should not fund the use of contraceptive devices not because the pope demands it but because I think that the whole community—for the good of the whole community—should not sever sex from an openness to the creation of life.

And surely I can, if so inclined, demand some kind of law against abortion not because my bishops say it is wrong but because I think that the whole community, regardless of its religious beliefs, should agree on the importance of protecting life—including life in the womb, which is at the very least potentially human and should not be extinguished casually.

No law prevents us from advocating any of these things: I am free to do so. So are the bishops. And so is Reverend Falwell. In fact, the Constitution guarantees my right to try. And theirs. And his.

But should I? Is it helpful? Is it essential to human dignity? Does it promote harmony and understanding? Or does it divide us so fundamentally that it threatens our ability to function as a pluralistic community? When should I argue to make my religious value your morality? My rule of conduct your limitation? What are the rules and policies that should influence the exercise of this right to argue and promote?

I believe I have a salvific mission as a Catholic. Does that mean I am in conscience required to do everything I can as governor to translate *all* my religious values into the laws and regulations of the state of New York or the United States? Or be branded a hypocrite if I don't?

As a Catholic, I respect the teaching authority of the bishops. But must I agree with everything in the bishops' pastoral letter on peace and fight to include it in party platforms? And will I have to do the same for the forthcoming pastoral on economics even if I am an unrepentant supply-sider? Must I, having heard the pope renew the Church's ban on birth control devices, veto the funding of contraceptive programs for non-Catholics or dissenting Catholics in my state?

I accept the Church's teaching on abortion. Must I insist you do? By law? By denying you Medicaid funding? By a constitutional amendment? If so, which one? Would that be the best way to avoid abortions or to prevent them? These are only some of the questions for Catholics. People with other religious beliefs face similar problems.

Let me try some answers. Almost all Americans accept some religious values as a part of our public life. We are a religious people, many of us descended from ancestors who came here expressly to live their religious faith free from coercion or repression. But we are also a people of many religions, with no established church, who hold different beliefs on many matters.

Our public morality, then—the moral standards we maintain for everyone, not just the ones we insist on in our private lives—depends on a consensus view of right and wrong. The values derived from religious belief will not—and should not—be accepted as part of the public morality unless they are shared by the pluralistic community at large, by consensus.

That values happen to be religious values does not deny them acceptability as a part of this consensus. But it does not require their acceptability either. The agnostics who joined the civil rights struggle were not deterred because that crusade's values had been nurtured and sustained in black Christian churches. Those on the political left are not perturbed today by the religious basis of the clergy and lay people who join them in the protest against the arms race and hunger and exploitation.

The arguments start when religious values are used to support positions which would impose on other people restrictions they find unacceptable. Some people *do* object to Catholic demands for an end to abortion, seeing it as a violation of the separation of Church and State. And some others, while they have no compunction about invoking the authority of the Catholic bishops in regard to birth control and abortion, might reject out of hand their teaching on war and peace and social policy.

Ultimately, therefore, the question "whether or not we admit religious values into our public affairs" is too broad to yield a single answer. "Yes," we create our public morality through consensus and in this country that consensus reflects to some extent religious values of a great majority of Americans. But "no," all religiously based values don't have an a priori place in our public morality.

The community must decide if what is being proposed would be better left to private discretion than public policy; whether it restricts freedoms, and if so to what end, to whose benefit; whether it will produce a good or bad result; whether overall it will help the community or merely divide it. The right answers to these questions can be elusive. Some of the wrong answers, on the other hand, are quite clear. For example, there are those who say there is a simple answer to *all* these questions; they say that by history and practice of our people we were intended to be—and should be—a Christian country in law.

But where would that leave the nonbelievers? And whose Christianity would be law, yours or mine?

The "Christian nation" argument should concern—even frighten—two groups: non-Christians and thinking Christians. I believe it does. I think it's already apparent that a good part of this nation understands—if only instinctively—that anything which seems to suggest that God favors a political party or the establishment of a state church, is wrong and dangerous.

Way down deep the American people are afraid of an entangling relationship between formal religions—or whole bodies of religious belief—and government. Apart from constitutional law and religious doctrine, there is a sense that tells us it's wrong to presume to speak for God or to claim God's sanction of our particular legislation and His rejection of all other positions. Most of us are offended when we see religion being trivialized by its appearance in political throwaway pamphlets.

The American people need no course in philosophy or political science or church history to know that God should not be made into a celestial party chairman. To most of us, the manipulative invoking of religion to advance a politician or a party is frightening and divisive. The American people will tolerate religious leaders taking positions for or against candidates, although I think the Catholic bishops are right in avoiding that position. But the American people are leery about large religious organizations, powerful churches or synagogue groups, engaging in such activities—again, not as a matter of law or doctrine, but because our innate wisdom and democratic instinct teaches us that these things are dangerous.

Today there are a number of issues involving life and death that raise questions of public morality. They are also questions of concern to most religions. Pick up a newspaper and you are almost certain to find a bitter controversy over any one of them: Baby Jane Doe, the right to die, artificial insemination, embryos in vitro, abortion, birth control . . . not to mention nuclear war and the shadow it throws across all existence. Some of these issues touch the most intimate recesses of our lives, our roles as someone's mother or child or husband; some affect women in a unique way. But they are also public questions, for all of us.

Put aside what God expects—assume if you like that there is no God—then the greatest thing still left to us is life. Even a radically secular world must struggle with the questions of when life begins, under what circumstances it can be ended, when it must be protected, by what authority; it too must decide what protection to extend to the helpless and the dying, to the aged and the unborn, to life in all its phases.

As a Catholic, I have accepted certain answers as the right ones for myself and my family, and because I have, they have influenced me in special ways, as Matilda's husband, as a father of five children, as a son who stood next to his own father's deathbed trying to decide if the tubes and needles no longer served a purpose. As a governor, however, I am involved in defining policies that determine *other* people's rights in these same areas of life and death. Abortion is one of these issues, and while it is one issue among many, it is one of the most controversial and affects me in a special way as a Catholic public official. So let me spend some time considering it.

I should start, I believe, by noting that the Catholic Church's actions with respect to the interplay of religious values and public policy make clear that there is no inflexible moral principle that determines what our *political* conduct should be. For example, on divorce and birth control, without changing its moral teaching, the Church abides the civil law as it now stands, thereby accepting—without making much of a point of it— that in our pluralistic society we are not required to insist that *all* our religious values be the law of the land.

Abortion is treated differently. Of course there are differences both in degree and quality between abortion and some of the other religious positions the Church takes: abortion is a "matter of life and death," and degree counts. But the differences in approach reveal a truth, I think, that is not well enough perceived by Catholics and therefore still further complicates the process for us. That is, while we always owe our bishops' words respectful attention and careful consideration, the question whether to engage the political system in a struggle to have it adopt certain articles of our belief as part of public morality is not a matter of doctrine: it is a matter of prudential political judgment.

Recently, Michael Novak put it succinctly: "Religious judgment and political judgment are both needed," he wrote. "But they are not identical." My Church and my conscience require me to believe certain things about divorce, birth control, and abortion. My Church does not order me—under pain of sin or expulsion—to pursue my salvific mission according to a precisely defined political plan.

As a Catholic I accept the Church's teaching authority. While in the past some Catholic theologians may appear to have disagreed on the morality of some abortions (it wasn't, I think, until 1869 that excommunication was attached to all abortions without distinction), and while some theologians still do, I accept the bishops' position that abortion is to be avoided.

As Catholics, my wife and I were enjoined never to use abortion to destroy the life we created, and we never have. We thought Church doctrine was clear on this, and—more than that—both of us felt it in full agreement with what our hearts and our consciences told us. For me life or fetal life in the womb should be protected, even if five of nine justices of the Supreme Court and my neighbor disagree with me. A fetus is different from an appendix or a set of tonsils. At the very least, even if the argument is made by some scientists or some theologians that in the early stages of fetal development we can't discern human life, the full potential of human life is indisputably there. That—to my less subtle mind—by itself should demand respect, caution, indeed . . . reverence. But not everyone in our society agrees with Matilda and me.

And those who don't—those who endorse legalized abortions—aren't a ruthless, callous alliance of anti-Christians determined to overthrow our moral standards. In many cases, the proponents of legal abortion are the very people who have worked with Catholics to realize the goals of social justice set out in papal encyclicals: the American Lutheran Church, the Central Conference of American Rabbis, the Presbyterian Church in the United States, B'nai B'rith Women, the Women of the Episcopal Church. These are just a few of the religious organizations that don't share the Church's position on abortion.

Certainly, we should not be forced to mold Catholic morality to conform to disagreement by non-Catholics however sincere or severe their disagreement. Our bishops should be teachers, not pollsters. They should not change what we Catholics believe in order to ease our consciences or please our friends or protect the Church from criticism. But if the breadth, intensity, and sincerity of opposition to Church teaching shouldn't be allowed to shape our Catholic morality, it can't help but determine our ability—our realistic, political ability—to translate our Catholic morality into civil law, a law not for the believers who don't need it but for the disbelievers who reject it. And it is here, in our attempt to find a political answer to abortion—an answer beyond our private observance of Catholic morality—that we encounter controversy within and without the Church over how and in what degree to press the case that our morality should be everybody else's, and to what effect.

I repeat, there is no Church teaching that mandates the best political course for making our belief everyone's rule, for spreading this part of our Catholicism. There is neither an encyclical or a catechism that spells out a political strategy for achieving legislative goals. And so the Catholic trying to make moral and prudent judgments in the political realm must discern which, if any, of the actions one could take would be best.

This latitude of judgment is not something new in the Church, not a development that has arisen only with the abortion issue. Take, for example, the question of slavery. It has been argued that the failure to endorse a legal ban on abortions is equivalent to refusing to support the cause of abolition before the Civil War. This analogy has been advanced by the bishops of my own state.

But the truth of the matter is, few if any Catholic bishops spoke for abolition in the years before the Civil War. It wasn't, I believe, that the bishops endorsed the idea of some humans owning and exploiting other humans; Pope Gregory XVI, in 1840, had condemned the slave trade. Instead it was a practical political judgment that the bishops made. They weren't hypocrites; they were realists. At the time, Catholics were a small minority, mostly immigrants, despised by much of the population, often vilified and the object of sporadic violence. In the face of a public controversy that aroused tremendous passions and threatened to break the country apart, the bishops made a pragmatic decision. They believed their opinion would not change people's minds. Moreover they knew that there were southern Catholics, even some priests, who owned slaves. They concluded that under the circumstances arguing for a constitutional amendment against slavery would do more harm than good, so they were silent.

As they have been, generally, in recent years, on the question of birth control. And as the Church has been on even more controversial issues in the past, even ones that dealt with life and death.

What is relevant to this discussion is that the bishops were making judgments about translating Catholic teachings into public policy, not about the moral validity of the teachings. In so doing they grappled with the unique political complexities of their time. The decision they made to remain silent on a constitutional amendment to abolish slavery or on the repeal of the Fugitive Slave Law wasn't a mark of their moral indifference: it was a measured attempt to balance moral truths against political realities. Their decision reflected their sense of complexity, not their diffidence. As history reveals, Lincoln behaved with similar discretion.

The parallel I want to draw here is not between or among what we Catholics believe to be moral wrongs. It is in the Catholic response to those wrongs. Church teaching on slavery and abortion is clear. But in the application of those teachings—the exact way we translate them into action, the specific laws we propose, the exact legal sanctions we seek—there was and is no one, clear, absolute route that the Church says, as a matter of doctrine, we must follow.

The bishops' pastoral letter, "The Challenge of Peace," speaks directly to this point. "We recognize," the bishops wrote,

> that the Church's teaching authority does not carry the same force when it deals with technical solutions involving particular means as it does when it speaks of principles or ends. People may agree in abhorring an injustice, for instance, yet sincerely disagree as to what practical approach will achieve justice. Religious groups are entitled as others to their opinion in such cases, but they should not claim that their opinions are the only ones that people of good will may hold.

With regard to abortion, the American bishops have had to weigh Catholic moral teaching against the fact of a pluralistic country where our view is in the minority, acknowledging that what is ideally desirable isn't always feasible, that there can be different political approaches to abortion besides unyielding adherence to an absolute prohibition. This is in the American-Catholic tradition of political realism. In supporting or opposing specific legislation the Church in this country has never retreated into a moral fundamentalism that will settle for nothing less than total acceptance of its views.

Indeed, the bishops have already confronted the fact that an absolute ban on abortion doesn't have the support necessary to be placed in our Constitution. In 1981, they put aside earlier efforts to describe a law they could accept and get passed, and supported the Hatch amendment instead. Some Catholics felt the bishops had gone too far with that action, some not far enough. Such judgments were not a rejection of the bishops' teaching authority: the bishops even disagreed among themselves. Catholics are allowed to disagree on these technical political questions without having to confess.

Respectfully, and after careful consideration of the position and arguments of the bishops, I have concluded that the approach of a constitutional amendment is not the best way for us to seek to deal with abortion.

I believe that legally interdicting abortion by either the federal government or the individual states is not a plausible possibility and even if it could be obtained, it wouldn't work. Given present attitudes, it would be "Prohibition" revisited, legislating what couldn't be enforced and in the process creating a disrespect for law in general. And as much as I admire the bishops' hope that a constitutional amendment against abortion would be the basis for a full, new bill of rights for mothers and children, I disagree that this would be the result.

I believe that, more likely, a constitutional prohibition would allow people to ignore the causes of many abortions instead of addressing them, much the way the death penalty is used to escape dealing more fundamentally and more rationally with the problem of violent crime.

Other legal options that have been proposed are, in my view, equally ineffective. The Hatch amendment, by returning the question of abortion to the states, would have given us a checkerboard of permissive and restrictive jurisdictions. In some cases people might have been forced to go elsewhere to have abortions and that might have eased a few consciences but it wouldn't have done what the Church wants to do—it wouldn't have created a deep-seated respect for life. Abortions would have gone on, millions of them.

Nor would a denial of Medicaid funding for abortion achieve our objectives. Given *Roe* v. *Wade,* it would be nothing more than an attempt to do indirectly what the law says cannot be done directly; worse, it would do it in a way that would burden only the already disadvantaged. Removing funding for the Medicaid program would not prevent the rich and middle classes from having abortions. It would not even assure that the disadvantaged wouldn't have them; it would only impose financial burdens on poor women who want abortions.

Apart from that unevenness, there is a more basic question. Medicaid is designed to deal with health and medical needs. But the arguments for the cutoff of Medicaid abortion funds are not related to those needs. They are moral arguments. If we assume health and medical needs exist, our personal view of morality ought not to be considered a relevant basis for discrimination.

We must keep in mind always that we are a nation of laws—when we like those laws, and when we don't. The Supreme Court has established a woman's constitutional right to abortion. The Congress has decided the federal government should not provide federal funding in the Medicaid program for abortion. That, of course, does not bind states in the allocation of their own state funds. Under the law, individual states need not follow the federal lead, and in New York I believe we *cannot* follow that lead. The equal protection clause in New York's constitution has been interpreted by the courts as a standard of fairness that would preclude us from denying only the poor—indirectly, by a cutoff of funds—the practical use of the constitutional right given by *Roe* v. *Wade.*

In the end, even if after a long and divisive struggle we were able to remove all Medicaid funding for abortion and restore the law to what it was—if we could put most abortions out of our sight, return them to the back rooms where they were performed for so long—I don't believe our responsibility as Catholics would be any closer to being fulfilled than it is now, with abortion guaranteed by the law as a woman's right.

The hard truth is that abortion isn't a failure of government. No agency or department of government forces women to have abortions, but abortion goes on. Catholics, the statistics show, support the right to abortion in equal proportion to the rest of the population. Despite the teaching in our homes and schools and pulpits, despite the sermons and pleadings of parents and priests and prelates, despite all the effort at defining our opposition to the sin of abortion, collectively we Catholics apparently believe—and perhaps act—little differently from those who don't share our commitment.

Are we asking government to make criminal what we believe to be sinful because we ourselves can't stop committing the sin? The failure here is not Caesar's. This failure is our failure, the failure of the entire people of God.

Nobody has expressed this better than a bishop in my own state, Joseph Sullivan, a man who works with the poor in New York City, is resolutely opposed to abortion, and argues, with his fellow bishops, for a change of law, "The major problem the Church has is internal," the bishop said last month in reference to abortion. "How do we teach? As much as I think we're responsible for advocating public policy issues, our primary responsibility is to teach our own people. We haven't done that. We're asking politicians to do what we haven't done effectively ourselves."

I agree with the bishop. I think our moral and social mission as Catholics must begin with the wisdom contained in the words "Physician, heal thyself." Unless we Catholics educate ourselves better to the values that define—and can ennoble—our lives, following those teachings better than we do now, unless we set an example that is clear and compelling then we will never convince this society to change the civil laws to protect what we preach is precious human life.

Better than any law or rule or threat of punishment would be the moving strength of our own good example, demonstrating our lack of hypocrisy, proving the beauty and worth of our instruction. We must work to find ways to avoid abortions without otherwise violating our faith. We should provide funds and opportunities for young women to bring their child to term, knowing both of them will be taken care of if that is necessary; we should teach our young men better than we do now their responsibilities in creating and caring for human life.

It is this duty of the Church to teach through its practice of love what Pope John Paul II has proclaimed so magnificently to all peoples. "The Church," he wrote in *Redemptor Hominis* (1979),

> which has no weapons at her disposal apart from those of the spirits, of the word and of love, cannot renounce her proclamation of "the word . . . in season and out of season." For this reason she does not cease to implore . . . everybody in the name of God and in the name of man: Do not kill! Do not prepare destruction and extermination for each other! Think of your brothers and sisters who are suffering hunger and misery! Respect each one's dignity and freedom!

The weapons of the word and of love are already available to us: we need no statute to provide them. I am not implying that we should stand by and pretend indifference to whether a woman takes a pregnancy to its conclusion or aborts it. I believe we should in all cases try to teach a respect for life. And I believe with regard to abortion that, despite *Roe v. Wade*, we can, in practical ways. Here, in fact, it seems to me that all of us can agree.

Without lessening their insistence on a woman's right to an abortion, the people who call themselves "pro-choice" can support the development of government programs that present an impoverished mother with the full range of support she needs to bear and raise her children, to have a real choice. Without dropping their campaign to ban abortion, those who gather under the banner of "pro-life" can join in developing and enacting a legislative bill of rights for mothers and children, as the bishops have already proposed.

While we argue over abortion, the United States' infant mortality rate places us sixteenth among the nations of the world. Thousands of infants die each year because of inadequate medical care. Some are born with birth defects that, with proper treatment, could be prevented. Some are stunted in their physical and mental growth because of improper nutrition. If we want to prove our regard for life in the womb, for the helpless infant—if we care about women having real choices in their lives and not being driven to abortions by a sense of helplessness and despair about the future of their child—then there is work enough for all of us. Lifetimes of it.

In New York, we have put in place a number of programs to begin this work, assisting women in giving birth to healthy babies. This year we doubled Medicaid funding to private-care physicians for prenatal and delivery services. The state already spends $20 million a year for prenatal care in out-patient clinics and for in-patient hospital care. One program in particular we believe holds a great deal of promise. It's called "new avenues to dignity," and it seeks to provide a teen-age mother with the special service she needs to continue with her education, to train for a job, to become capable of standing on her own, to provide for herself and the child she is bringing into the world.

My dissent, then, from the contention that we can have effective and enforceable legal prohibitions on abortion is by no means an argument for religious quietism, for accepting the world's wrongs because that is our fate as "the poor banished children of Eve."

Let me make another point. Abortion has a unique significance but not a preemptive significance. Apart from the question of the efficacy of using legal weapons to make people stop having abortions, we know our Christian responsibility doesn't end with any one law or amendment. That it doesn't end with abortion. Because it involves life and death, abortion will always be a central concern of Catholics. But so will nuclear weapons. And hunger and homelessness and joblessness, all the forces diminishing human life and threatening to destroy it. The "seamless garment" that Cardinal Bernardin has spoken of is a challenge to all Catholics in public office, conservatives as well as liberals.

We cannot justify our aspiration to goodness simply on the basis of the vigor of our demand for an elusive and questionable civil law declaring what we already know, that abortion is wrong. Approval or rejection of legal restrictions on abortion should not be the exclusive litmus test of Catholic loyalty. We should understand that whether abortion is outlawed or not, our work has barely begun: the work of creating a society where the right to life doesn't end at the moment of birth; where an infant isn't helped into a world that doesn't care if it's fed properly, housed decently, educated adequately; where the blind or retarded child isn't condemned to exist rather than empowered to live.

The bishops stated this duty clearly in 1974, in their statement to the Senate subcommittee considering a proposed amendment to restrict abortions. They maintained such an amendment could not be seen as an end in itself. "We do not see a constitutional amendment as the final product of our commitment or of our legislative activity," they said.

> It is instead the constitutional base on which to provide support and assistance to pregnant women and their unborn children. This would include nutritional, prenatal, childbirth and postnatal care for the mother, and also nutritional and pediatric care for the child through the first year of life. . . . We believe that all of these should be available as a matter of right to all pregnant women and their children.

The bishops reaffirmed that view in 1976, in 1980, and again this year when the United States Catholic Committee asked Catholics to judge candidates on a wide range of issues—on abortion, yes; but also on food policy, the arms race, human rights, education, social justice, and military expenditures. The bishops have been consistently "pro-life" in the full meaning of that term, and I respect them for that.

The problems created by the matter of abortion are complex and confounding. Nothing is clearer to me than my inadequacy to find compelling solutions to all of their moral, legal, and social implications. I—and many others like me—am eager for enlightenment, eager to learn new and better ways to manifest respect for the deep reverence for life that is our religion and our instinct. I hope that this public attempt to describe the problems as I understand them will give impetus to the dialogue in the Catholic community and beyond, a dialogue that could show me a better wisdom than I've been able to find so far. It would be tragic if we let that dialogue become a prolonged, divisive argument that destroys or impairs our ability to practice any part of the morality given us in the Sermon on the Mount, to touch, heal, and affirm the human life that surrounds us.

We Catholic citizens of the richest, most powerful nation that has ever existed are like the stewards made responsible over a great household: from those to whom so much has been given, much shall be required. It is worth repeating that ours is not a faith that encourages its believers to stand apart from the world, seeking their salvation alone, separate from the salvation of those around them. We speak of ourselves as a body. We come together in worship as companions, in the ancient sense of that word, those who break bread together, and who are obliged by the commitment we share to help one another, everywhere, in all we do, and in the process, to help the whole human family. We see our mission to be "the completion of the work of creation."

This is difficult work today. It presents us with many hard choices. The Catholic Church has come of age in America. The ghetto walls are gone, our religion no longer a badge of irredeemable foreignness. This newfound status is both an opportunity and a temptation. If we choose, we can give in to the temptation to become more and more assimilated into a larger, blander culture, abandoning the practice of the specific values that made us different, worshiping whatever gods the marketplace has to sell while we seek to rationalize our own laxity by urging the political system to legislate on others a morality we no longer practice ourselves.

Or we can remember where we come from, the journey of two millennia, clinging to our personal faith, to its insistence on constancy and service and on hope. We can live and practice the morality Christ gave us, maintaining His truth in this world, struggling to embody His love, practicing it especially where that love is most needed, among the poor and the weak and the dispossessed. Not just by trying to make laws for others to live by, but by living the laws already written for us by God, in our hearts and our minds.

We can be fully Catholic; proudly, totally at ease with ourselves, a people in the world, transforming it, a light to this nation. Appealing to the best in our people not the worst. Persuading not coercing. Leading people to truth by love. And still, all the while, respecting and enjoying our unique pluralistic democracy. And we can do it even as politicians.

ADIRONDACK FUNDAMENTALISM

Randall Balmer

This selection is excerpted from Balmer's 1989 book Mine Eyes Have Seen the Glory.

I n the early morning hours, Schroon Lake is gray and placid. Wispy clouds tumble over the pine-covered hillsides that surround the lake. Steam rises from the water. A lone canoe paddles by. For a brief moment, the sun pushes past the clouds but then settles back into exile.

When the receding glaciers carved Schroon Lake into the Adirondack mountains of upstate New York, they left a ninety-acre island at the north end of the lake. There, pine trees sprouted among the glacial rocks, and thus surrounded by frigid mountain water, the island became an ideal location for a youth camp.

Jack Wyrtzen, a fundamentalist Bible teacher from New York City, took possession in 1946, at about the same time that motor travel began to diminish the attractiveness of the resorts dotting the Adirondacks. He has since added an inn, a family campground, a ranch, and a Bible institute— hundreds of acres, all told—to his empire, the Word of Life Fellowship, in and around Schroon Lake. Word of Life also includes radio broadcasts on more than one hundred stations around the world, mission enterprises in places as diverse as Peru, Hungary, Israel, and New Zealand, various traveling evangelists, musicians, and drama troupes, and over a thousand Bible clubs held in churches throughout the country. All of this consumes an annual budget of about $12 million, but the youth camp, "for young people and college-career young adults aged 13 to 30," remains the centerpiece of Word of Life.

I'm not sure there is any way I could document this, but I suspect that the greatest fear that haunts evangelical parents is that their children will not follow in their footsteps, that they will not sustain the same level of piety as their parents—stated baldly, that they are headed for hell rather than heaven. Such themes as waywardness and redemption provide the grist for countless evangelical sermons; the parable of the prodigal son, I am convinced, is one of the most popular texts in the evangelical subculture. Prayer meetings fairly reverberate with petitions for this or that son or daughter who has wandered from the faith. In recent decades, many churches, reflecting the concerns of parents in the congregation, have hired youth pastors, whose job it is to keep children safely within the evangelical fold, to shield them from the perils of worldliness.

Indeed, there is ample cause for concern. What can be harder than passing on religious verve and vitality from one generation to the next, especially within a tradition that defines itself by the conversion process, that transition from darkness to light, from sinfulness to redemption?

The Puritans of the seventeenth century faced this problem and never fully resolved it. New England's founding generation had forsaken fortune and family in England in order to carve a godly commonwealth out of the wilderness of Massachusetts. By the time the second generation approached adulthood, the spirituality of the founding generation had taken on heroic proportions, and when this next generation was asked as a requirement for church membership to stand before their elders in the meetinghouse and give an account of their conversions, most of them refused, knowing full well that their piety paled before that of their elders. Before long, the Puritans discerned in their midst a spiritual malaise that they called declension, and by the latter half of the seventeenth century the pulpits of New England resounded with calls to repentance.

In his novel *The Chosen*, Chaim Potok illustrates how this generational problem plays itself out within a different context. Reb Saunders, a pious, learned man venerated by his Hasidic followers, wants desperately to pass along the mantle of religious leadership to his eldest son, Danny, a precocious child who has studied the Talmud exhaustively all of his life and who regularly astounds his father's congregation with his grasp of even the most recondite Jewish sacred writings. Danny Saunders, the elders all agree, would be a worthy spiritual successor to his father.

But Danny Saunders's restless mind leads him in other directions, to intellectual pursuits outside the narrow confines of his father's calling and to friendships outside of his Hasidic community. When it finally becomes clear that Danny will not follow in his father's footsteps, Reb Saunders bids his son an anguished farewell, whereupon Danny Saunders, shorn of his earlocks and no longer dressed in black Hasidic hat and coat, walks down the street and toward a new life very different from the sheltered existence he has known.

It doesn't take much imagination to appreciate the quandary of parents who want to pass along to their children the faith that has shaped their lives and solved for them the riddle of eternity. You want to shelter your children from the temptations that assail them at every turn. You want to school them in the Scriptures and in the theology that you know to be correct. And you also want them to be models of godliness, a credit not only to the faith but also to you as wise, godly parents.

Yet at the same time, such sheltering diminishes the drama of their own spiritual conversions when—and if—those conversions do occur. Whereas your embracing of the gospel had delivered you from a life of, say, alcohol or drugs or promiscuity, theirs serves merely as a ratification of the beliefs and lifestyle that you, their parents, have drilled into them since infancy. (The prodigal son's older brother who stayed at home, after all, never knew the contrast between the perils of the world and the security of home, and he envied the lavish party his father threw for his brother's homecoming.) On the other hand, neglecting your children's spiritual nurture will not suffice either, for that entails the considerable risk of trusting them (through God's leading, of course) to come to Christ of their own volition.

Ever since the 1925 Scopes Trial convinced fundamentalists that the broader American culture had turned hostile to their interests, fundamentalists have busied themselves devising various institutions to insulate themselves and their children from the depredations of the world. (In fact, the terms *worldly* and *worldliness* are probably the closest most evangelicals come to epithets; these words are often spoken sneeringly, in a tone at the same time condescending and cautionary.) First, the fundamentalists separated out of mainline denominations so that they could maintain a theology untainted by liberalism or, in the argot of the day, "modernism." Evangelicals then established their own mission boards, Christian schools, Bible institutes, colleges, and, eventually, seminaries. For children, Sunday school provided socialization and instruction in the rudiments of evangelical theology. Once the children had grown, you could ship them off to a Bible institute where they might prepare for the pastorate, missionary work, or some other kind of "Christian service."

But by the 1940s many fundamentalist parents recognized a gap in this system. How do you shelter your children from the onslaughts of the world during those critical teenage years when, with hormones swirling furiously, temptations reach their zenith?

About this time Jack Wyrtzen devised a summer Bible camp for teenagers, a sanctuary for fundamentalist parents to send their children, a place where strict parietal rules would be enforced and, more important, where some sort of religious commitment would be exacted.

A small pontoon provides ferry service between the western shores of Schroon Lake and Word of Life Island. As you approach, a boathouse with the legend A VERY SPECIAL ISLAND comes into view. Once on the landing, a sign welcomes you to Word of Life Island and, beyond that, a second notice warns: ALL VISITORS MUST REPORT TO THE OFFICE AND SIGN IN! A winding pathway leads to a large frame building called the Pine Pavilion.

The Pine Pavilion is a squarish building constructed on a hillside, with terraces of long, wooden benches sloping down toward the stage. Flags and red-white-and-blue bunting festoon the interior. In the northeast corner, a large wooden sign reads:

> **CHRIST WALKS ON THIS ISLAND**
> **WILL YOU MEET HIM HERE?**

Green porcelain warehouse-style lamps hang from the rafters.

The evening service begins at seven, and several announcements over a public-address system warn campers to be on time. Soon, a torrent of energetic campers tumbles into the building. Most of them are white and dressed in standard teenage fashions—tee-shirts, denims, sneakers, large, oversized sweatshirts.

Ten minutes into the meeting, as the sun sets across Schroon Lake, the Pine Pavilion is rocking. It's military week on the island, and the campers have been divided into Army and Navy teams. A series of games, challenges, and good-natured rivalry has been devised by the camp directors to generate spirit, teamwork, and enthusiasm. Apparently they've succeeded. Some of the counselors wear camouflage fatigues, and not infrequently amidst the singing of various evangelical songs and choruses, the pavilion erupts in rival chants of "Army! Army!" and "Navy! Navy!" Each team sings its fight song—"Anchors Aweigh" and "The Caissons Keep Rolling Along"—accompanied by spirited stomping, and soon, amidst all this excitement, the building begins to smell faintly of adolescent sweat.

The crowd reverts to rhythmic clapping and stomping when a middle-aged man in a plaid, open-necked shirt plays "When the Roll Is Called Up Yonder" on his trumpet, triple-tonguing the second verse. When he finishes, more applause, shouting, hooting, and stomping. The pavilion quiets somewhat as a pretty blonde woman in her late teens, wearing a khaki skirt and a navy blazer, mounts the stage. She sings several songs to the accompaniment of taped music played over the sound system. After one of the songs, she exhorts the audience in a kind of breathless whisper: "It's so important to keep your standards high. You know, it's a nasty world out there." The next song, "Build on Higher Ground," reiterates that theme:

> Build your house above the ocean.
> Build your house on higher ground.
> Build above the world's commotion
> And its mesmerizing sound.

The music finishes with a flourish, and after an announcement encouraging campers to purchase a Ryrie Study Bible and books by Chuck Swindoll at the bookstore, the young soprano joins the trumpet player for a duet, "I've Just Seen Jesus," a fitting complement, I thought, to the sign in the northeast corner of the pavilion.

Jack Wyrtzen, a snowy-haired man in white pants and a floral-print tropical shirt, comes to the podium. He reminds the campers about some of the rules that govern life on the island. Everyone must wear a robe or sweat clothes to the beach. Shorts must be at least fingertip length. Word of Life promotional literature has already spelled out these regulations in some detail. "Please keep modesty in mind regarding all clothing," the literature counsels, adding that campers should bring a Bible and "sportswear for daytime activities, dress-up clothes (dress shirt and slacks for guys, dress for girls) for Sunday and some evening meals, modest one-piece bathing suit (I Tim. 2:9) and beach robe."

Wyrtzen is an old fashioned, unvarnished fundamentalist. An affable, bespeckled man, his photographs in Word of Life promotional materials invariably show him with a large, open-mouthed grin, wearing an expression that suggests he has just told you the funniest joke in the world and is awaiting your reaction. He opens with a prayer asking God that everyone in the building will be "born again by the Word of God." Immediately thereafter, he asks how many in the audience have Bibles. Virtually everyone thrusts a Bible high into the air. As he announces this evening's text, he tells the audience that he hopes "before the night is done you will come to the Lamb of God." For the first nineteen years of his life, he says, "nobody told me about Jesus Christ" in the liberal churches he attended. The United States Army, in fact, is "the greatest denomination in the U.S.," because that's where Wyrtzen became a Christian.

Fundamentalists are fond of belittling the pretensions of mainline, liberal churches, and Wyrtzen is no exception. He uses certain code words or phrases to indicate his derision of theological liberals. The one he employs most often is "First Church." He will tell of some member of "First Church" who came to one of Wyrtzen's rallies, heard the gospel for the first time, and went away born again. Or some worldly woman, also a member of "First Church," who "got saved" at Word of Life and now is "on fire for the Lord." The audience, many of whom have apparently heard this nomenclature before, picks up on this right away, snorting disapprovingly at the reference to theological liberals and the putative name of their churches.

But tonight Wyrtzen is not interested in preaching to the converted; be wants to bring more of the unsaved into the fold. After telling of various sinners—including a woman he refers to as the "blonde bomber"—whose lives have been transformed by Jesus, and after warning of the torments of hell, he asks, "Have you been to Calvary?" He implores the campers to come to Jesus and leads them in a slow, mournful chorus that evokes Jesus's death at Calvary:

> Dying there for me,
> Dying there for me.
> Jesus died, was crucified.
> Dying there for me.

"You need to confess you are a sinner and believe Jesus died for you," Wyrtzen says. "Invite Him into your heart right now." Wyrtzen makes it easy, providing a formula prayer for the wavering: "Dear Jesus, I confess that I am a sinner. Thank you for dying on the cross for me. Come into my heart and save me now. Amen."

All heads are bowed. All eyes closed. The meeting's raucous beginning is long forgotten. Wyrtzen asks for a show of hands from those who prayed the prayer. A few timid arms reach upward. Wyrtzen acknowledges each one. "Yes, I see that hand. Is there another?" He pleads a bit longer and then closes the meeting with this stark admonition: "If you leave this building without Jesus, you're guilty of His crucifixion."

The harvest tonight is disappointing, but it's still early in the week. Wyrtzen has a whole stable of speakers, Bible teachers, and counselors who will hammer the message home in the next few days. The entire schedule, in fact, is calculated to produce a maximum yield of converts and rededications, those who publicly reaffirm their conversions and resolve to live holier lives.

The day begins with breakfast at eight, followed by a morning of Bible study. After lunch, the campers have an afternoon of play—swimming, water skiing, basketball, volleyball—before supper and the evening meeting, either a rally in the pavilion or around a campfire. After the meeting, the counselors organize more competitive games between the Army and Navy teams. Even with lights-out at ten-thirty, fatigue sets in, what with all the fresh air, sunshine, and just plain fun. But that's part of the scheme as well, for there is a certain rhythm the organizers are trying to impose. The religious appeals begin early in the week at the rallies and in the morning sessions. By Wednesday evening's campfire, a sense of camaraderie, of shared experience, has set in. Campers are beginning to see their friends profess conversions or rededications, and nothing motivates an adolescent better than the example of his or her peers.

Figuring unpredictably into this mix is that confounding, exhilarating phenomenon: the summer romance. The people at Word of Life Island tolerate such courtships and even encourage them with a special dinner on Wednesday night to which boys are encouraged to bring dates. Parents back home, who are praying fervently for their child's spiritual renewal, also tolerate the courting that takes place at teen camp. They figure that their child's chances of meeting a nice Christian girl or boy at Bible camp are certainly greater than back home in a public high school. They trust Jack Wyrtzen and his staff, moreover, to police such romances carefully, lest passions run awry.

I kissed a girl for the first time at Bible camp—and, come to think of it, the second, third, and fourth times—all of it quite innocent, of course. Somewhere along the shores of Rainbow Lake a tree still bears the initials "R.B. + C.S.," chiseled into the bark with a jackknife. Word of Life Island bears the markings of similar romances and infatuations, flames that burn brightly, last through several exchanges of letters, but then generally flicker and die before the leaves fall:

> Erika & Howard
> I love Dave
> Dawn & John
> Kyle + Deanna
> Leon and Joan

Some have thoughtfully included the date in their memorials, as if establishing a statute of limitations:

> 85 Denise -n- John
> I ♥ Joel Hoffman '86

Adolescent love is a sweet and wonderful thing, and if your beloved is a good Christian girl— "wholesome" is the adjective my parents always favored—then your resistance to the gospel weakens further.

By the time the Friday night campfire comes around, you are tired to the bone. You've never played so hard, swum so far, or slept so little. You are sunburned and mosquito-bitten; you have several proud bruises to show your sister. A sense of melancholy sets in because you know that tomorrow you must say goodbye to all the friends you've made at camp that week: the cabinmates who put corn flakes and shaving cream in the bottom of your sleeping bag and who helped you ambush one of the girls' cabins, the counselor who listened and became a friend, and most of all the lovely girl with the cornflower-blue eyes seated next to you: You have been peppered all week with invitations to receive Christ into your life and warnings about the fate of those who refuse. You may not have another chance, you are told; Jesus may come at any time—before the week is out, before morning, even before the campfire ends. Don't let Him find you unsaved. It's easy. Come to Jesus. Just ask Him into your heart and live for Him.

The counselors at Word of Life Island refer to the Friday campfire as the "say so" meeting, taken from Psalm 107:2: "Let the redeemed of the Lord say so." Other Bible camps have different names. "Testimony service" or "afterglow" are rather common. Some camps used to refer to the final campfire, quite seriously, as a "faggot fire," a reference to the practice of grabbing the unburned end of one of the embers and tossing it into the fire as you begin your testimony about what Jesus has done in your life that past week. There is an illusion of spontaneity in these services, but for anyone who has witnessed more than a couple of them at Bible camps across the country, there is a remarkable uniformity to these gatherings. Having stared into a few fundamentalist campfires myself, I well remember the rhythms, the emotions, the ritualized adolescent behavior that takes place around the fire.

The service at Word of Life Island opens with singing; one of the counselors has supplied a guitar. The purpose of the say so meeting, another counselor informs the gathering, is to provide a chance for campers to tell what the Lord has done in their lives. He continues: "I'd just like to begin by saying that I've grown a lot this week. Pastor Jim's Bible studies have taught me a lot about what it means to be a Christian and to live for the Lord. I don't know about the rest of you, but I just praise the Lord for Pastor Jim and for the insight God has given him into the Scriptures."

A few appreciative murmurs follow and then a short silence as half a dozen people sitting there in the encroaching darkness summon the courage to stand and address the other campers. The fire is still struggling to take hold. The sun has just disappeared beyond the ridge at the west end of the lake, and all eyes are adjusting to the twilight.

There are no takers yet, the Spirit hasn't yet moved, so the guitarist begins strumming the chords for "Cum by Yah," and after the first few bars everyone joins in:

> Cum by yah, my Lord, cum by yah.
> Cum by yah, my Lord, cum by yah.

Cum by yah, my Lord, cum by yah.
O, Lord, cum by yah.

The plaintive, doleful melody functions as a kind of invocation: Come here, Jesus, and grace this gathering with Your presence.

Once the music dies, Joyce Johnson is ready. She rises confidently to her feet. All eyes move briefly from the fire to see who is talking and then, after a moment, settle back on the flames. There will be no dramatic confession here; Joyce Johnson, everyone at camp knows by now, is too good for that. Instead, this is a kind of homily disguised as self-disclosure. "I've been coming to camp ever since I was eight years old," she begins, "and once again the Lord has really worked in my life. He's shown me some new things out of His Word this week, and I know I'll be a better witness for the Lord during this next year." The tone then shifts from self-congratulatory to admonitory. "If anybody here isn't a Christian, my prayer is that you'll accept Jesus as your savior before tonight is over, before you leave this island tomorrow. You may never have another chance to receive Jesus into your heart."

After a decent interval, Candy Schroeder stands. "I'm not sure what I'm gonna say," she confesses with an uneasy chuckle, "but I wanted to tell you what the Lord has been doing in my life. For a while now I've been seeking the Lord's will for my life, and I've been praying for His guidance—especially to know what to do after I graduate from high school next year." She pauses, then wipes the corners of her eyes with the back of her hand. The length of the silence is uncomfortable for those seated around the fire, and only a few steal a glance at Candy, standing there in denims and a loose, gray sweatshirt. "I'm just so grateful to my parents," she continues between sobs, "and to everyone who has prayed for me. On Tuesday during the missionary hour, the Lord just spoke to my heart. When Reverend Hunt told about the millions of unsaved people down in Argentina, I just knew that the Lord was calling me to be a missionary to all those people who have never heard the gospel, to all those people—" she pauses again, biting her lower lip, "to all those people who are lost without Jesus." A dozen "amens" greet this happy news, and they are repeated sporadically as Candy Schroeder reveals her plans to attend a Bible institute after high school and then go to South America as a missionary.

Paul Snyder, a big, strapping kid of fourteen, is next. "I didn't grow up in a Christian home," he says. "In fact, my parents are members of the Lutheran church back in Easton, Pennsylvania, and they didn't want me to come. When my friend Mike here invited me to Word of Life, I wasn't sure, either, but then he told me how much fun it was, so I convinced my mom and dad to let me come." The fire was thriving now, shooting flames and sparks upward into the darkness like a kind of offering. The mosquitos have arrived, searching for patches of flesh. A small motorboat trolls by, its green and red lights slicing through the darkness. "I sure am glad

I came, though, because on Thursday night after the rally I gave my life to Christ. I had always thought I was a Christian because I went to church with my parents. But when I asked Don, my counselor, if I was going to heaven, he told me that unless I asked Jesus into my heart I would go to hell when I died. Well," Paul continues, halting slightly, "I gave my life to Christ. I'm a new, baby Christian. I'm going to read my Bible every day and tell all my friends at school about the Lord."

The guitarist thinks it's time for another song:

> Seek ye first the kingdom of God
> and His righteousness
> and all these things shall be added unto you.
> Hallelu-hallelujah.

The sweet, soft words echo across the lake. Paul Snyder's testimony has stirred something inside of Amy Durkin, because last year at this time she, too, gave her life to Jesus for the first time. She remembers now the feeling, the euphoria, and also her resolve to live a Christian life.

"I became a Christian here at camp last summer," Amy says, almost apologetically. "But once school started I fell in with the wrong crowd. Many of my friends are worldly, and I thought I was a strong enough Christian to stand up to them—" she begins to cry, "but I wasn't. Pretty soon I was just as worldly as the rest of them—going to movies and dances and stuff like that." Amy stops to regain her composure. The mournful cry of a loon reverberates across the lake. "But this year is going to be different. I've rededicated my life to the Lord this week, and I'm going to live for Him and bring my Bible with me to school every day and witness to my friends."

There are countless subtle variations to this rededication soliloquy, but most of them recount a previous commitment to Christ and a resolve to maintain high standards of godliness in the midst of a sinful and decadent world. But somehow, something went wrong—perhaps the lack of parental support or the absence of a good church youth program. Most often, however, even the most resolute convert from Bible camp caves in to peer pressure. "It's not easy being a Christian in my high school," is a familiar refrain.

Indeed not. If being a Christian as the people here define it means abstaining from drinking, smoking, dancing, movies, and perhaps even bowling and roller-skating (because of their "worldly" connotations), it doesn't take long for an evangelical high school student to become a pariah among his or her peers—or, more frequently, a kind of cipher on the social scene. The options then become either finding a new support network—a church youth group, perhaps—or compromising your fundamentalist scruples in order to fit in with your peers. If your parents are evangelical Christians, they want you to do the former, of course, but doing so exacts a price. It's not easy turning your back on your peers, rejecting the companionship and approval of friends at school for the comparatively unfulfilling friendships of people your own age at church.

No, it's not easy being an evangelical in high school. Carl Watkins, I think, understands that. For some time now I had been watching him shift uneasily on the stony ground; he seemed to be summoning the courage to get up and speak. Now, finally, Carl unfolds his tall, gangly frame, shuffles his feet uneasily, and clears his throat.

"My father is a preacher," Carl begins, "so I was raised in a Christian home. But I haven't always lived a good Christian witness. I'm not even sure that the kids at school know I'm a Christian." Carl stares at his shoe-tops. "I mean, sometimes I go out drinking with my friends. I know that's not right. I know that's not what the Lord wants me to do, but, I don't know, I just do it."

As he continues his halting confession, I begin to see myself in Carl Watkins. I see a Little Leaguer who had to miss all his Wednesday games, even the all-star game, because Wednesday was prayer-meeting night. I see in Carl Watkins an eighth-grader forced to sit on the sidelines during square dances in gym class and a teenager who couldn't wear bluejeans to school because his parents thought they would damage his Christian testimony. I see a high school graduate who never overcame his sense of alienation from his peers.

"I don't mean to hurt my parents," Carl continues, his voice cracking now, "but I guess, I don't know, that I always feel like I'm supposed to be perfect, to be this super-Christian at church and at school. But I'm not." Carl thrusts his hands deep into his pockets and shrugs his shoulders. "I really love my mom and dad. And I'm so grateful to the Lord for allowing me to grow up in a Christian home."

I also see in Carl Watkins a teenager contemplating the consequences of his rebellion, recounting sermon illustrations about eternity—time utterly without end, going on and on and on. If a tiny sparrow flew around the world and took a sip from the ocean at each pass, so the sermon illustration goes, by the time the ocean was dry, eternity would only have begun. Eternity was an awfully long time to be burning in hell, that lake of fire and brimstone.

"I ask you to pray for me this year," Carl concludes, "as I try to live a good Christian life." His gaze rests on the flames for a brief moment, and then he sits down. The fire crackles and spits sparks into the air. Carl Watkins reaches back and turns up the collar of his jacket against the sudden autumn chill that whips across the lake. Off to the east, a new moon hangs in the late-August darkness. Carl shifts once more and squeezes the hand of the girl with the cornflower-blue eyes seated next to him.

In another era, in another camp, I sat next to a fire and shifted uneasily on the stony ground. My repeated attempts to appropriate the faith of my parents were desultory and imperfect, as I realized even then. Summer camp was where I tried annually to get it right, to conjure the same piety that my elders showed, to claim the elusive "victory in Christ" that they professed. More often than not, what I felt instead was defeat and inadequacy, a gnawing sense that the persistent doubts I harbored about God and Christianity or my occasional transgressions of the fundamentalist behavioral codes would consign me to damnation.

Therein lay the conundrum. What I did not see then—indeed, *could* not have seen—was that the "gospel" presented to me was really an adumbration of the New Testament "good news." Much of the news I heard was bad—that I deserved damnation for my sinfulness and that if I didn't do something about it quickly I would certainly receive my just desserts. The solution to the predicament, as I understood it, was not to rely utterly on the grace of God, as Martin Luther recognized in the sixteenth century; rather, the way of salvation seemed to lay in subscribing to a set of doctrines and then hewing to strict standards of morality, usually expressed in negative terms: Don't dance, drink, smoke, swear, or attend movies.

That differed, I suspect, from the message that brought my parents into the evangelical fold. They heard about their sinfulness, yes, but the complementary element of the law is God's grace, which saves us in spite of ourselves. Therein, as Luther realized, lies true freedom and liberation—not in the observance of tiresome moralistic schemes, but in the celebration of deliverance from sin in Christ. In time, first-generation evangelical converts learn the canon of evangelical taboos, but only *after* their experience of grace. For their children, however, the sequence often is reversed. As an evangelical parent, if you are concerned (understandably) about the spiritual welfare of your children, you will establish guidelines for them so they will grow up in the faith, or, more accurately, grow up with all the trappings of godliness. Their "conversions" then become adolescent (or pre-adolescent) rites of passage, often accompanied by fabricated emotions in order to convince their peers, their parents, and, most important, themselves of their sincerity.

The difficulty, however, is that Christianity has already been defined for them in behavioral terms—do this, don't do that—rather than in terms that Luther would have approved: We all are sinners by dint of *who we are*, not *what we do*, and therefore we rely abjectly on God's mercy. For a child in a fundamentalist household, a second-generation evangelical who already adheres to most of the standards of "godly" behavior, it is difficult to grasp the significance of any such conversion, since it demands no alteration of behavior. Instead of assurance, very often they feel anger and resentment because their conversions failed to deliver the religious euphoria and freedom from doubt implied in their parents' promises.

What brings Carl Watkins and Amy Durkin back to Word of Life Island year after year, I suspect, is the same mixture of motivations that took me back to Rainbow Lake summer after summer during my teenage years. Our parents want us there, in the first place, not only because Bible camp offers a sheltered, protective environment, but also because of their abiding hope that we will someday, somehow claim their faith as our own. That's easier to do, of course, in the company of those who have professed their own conversions—certainly much easier than in the alien, godless environment of the public schools back home.

Aside from the perennial, elusive quest for summer romance, we are at camp, many of us, for the same reason that our parents want us there. We too want to claim the faith, not merely to win our parents' approval, but also because of a deep yearning for a religious experience that will meet our expectations and dispel our anxieties. We seek above all an experience that will yield the spiritual fulfillment we see (or think we see) in our parents. That experience comes to some. Others grasp it for a time and then lose it, year after year. Still others find the standards too high and abandon the quest in frustration or despair.

For people of faith, of course, and for people who want to pass their faith to the next generation, there is no easy solution to this predicament. Abandoning children to their own devices violates everything evangelicals believe about nurture, and yet mapping their children's spiritual pilgrimages may, in the end, deprive them of the kind of forceful, dramatic conversion that shaped the parents' lives.

Will evangelicalism, then, inevitably suffer from a gradual enervation of religious ardor as the faith passes from one generation to the next? Sociologists like Max Weber, who talks about the routinization of religion, insist that the answer is yes. Fervent evangelical parents pray that the answer is no.

A GOOD MAN IS HARD TO FIND

Flannery O'Connor

The following short story is from O'Connor's 1955 collection of the same name.

The grandmother didn't want to go to Florida. She wanted to visit some of her connections in east Tennessee and she was seizing every chance to change Bailey's mind. Bailey was the son she lived with, her only boy. He was sitting on the edge of his chair at the table, bent over the orange sports section of the *Journal*. "Now look here, Bailey," she said, "see here, read this," and she stood with one hand on her thin hip and the other rattling the newspaper at his bald head. "Here this fellow that calls himself The Misfit is aloose from the Federal Pen and headed toward Florida and you read here what it says he did to these people. Just you read it. I wouldn't take my children in any direction with a criminal like that aloose in it. I couldn't answer to my conscience if I did."

Bailey didn't look up from his reading so she wheeled around then and faced the children's mother; a young woman in slacks, whose face was as broad and innocent as a cabbage and was tied around with a green head-kerchief that had two points on the top like rabbit's ears. She was sitting on the sofa, feeding the baby his apricots out of a jar. "The children have been to Florida before," the old lady said. "You all ought to take them somewhere else for a change so they would see different parts of the world and be broad. They never have been to east Tennessee."

The children's mother didn't seem to hear her, but the eight-year-old boy, John Wesley, a stocky child with glasses, said, "If you don't want to go to Florida, why dontcha stay at home?" He and the little girl, June Star, were reading the funny papers on the floor.

"She wouldn't stay at home to be queen for a day," June Star said without raising her yellow head.

"Yes, and what would you do if this fellow, The Misfit, caught you?" the grandmother asked.

"I'd smack his face," John Wesley said.

"She wouldn't stay at home for a million bucks," June Star said. "Afraid she'd miss something. She has to go everywhere we go."

"All right, Miss," the grandmother said. "Just remember that the next time you want me to curl your hair."

June Star said her hair was naturally curly.

The next morning the grandmother was the first one in the car, ready to go. She had her big black valise that looked like the head of a hippopotamus in one corner, and underneath it she was hiding a basket with Pitty Sing, the cat, in it. She didn't intend for the cat to be left alone in the house for three days because he would miss her too much and she was afraid he might brush against one of the gas burners and accidentally asphyxiate himself. Her son, Bailey, didn't like to arrive at a motel with a cat.

She sat in the middle of the back seat with John Wesley and June Star on either side of her. Bailey and the children's mother and the baby sat in the front and they left Atlanta at eight forty-five with the mileage on the car at 55890. The grandmother wrote this down because she thought it would be interesting to say how many miles they had been when they got back. It took them twenty minutes to reach the outskirts of the city.

The old lady settled herself comfortably, removing her white cotton gloves and putting them up with her purse on the shelf in front of the back window. The children's mother still had on slacks and still had her head tied up in a green kerchief, but the grandmother had on a navy blue straw sailor hat with a bunch of white violets on the brim and a navy blue dress with a small white dot in the print. Her collar and cuffs were white organdy trimmed with lace and at her neckline she had pinned a purple spray of cloth violets containing a sachet. In case of an accident, anyone seeing her dead on the highway would know at once that she was a lady.

She said she thought it was going to be a good day for driving, neither too hot nor too cold, and she cautioned Bailey that the speed limit was fifty-five miles an hour and that the patrolmen hid themselves behind billboards and small clumps of trees and sped out after you before you had a chance to slow down. She pointed out interesting details of the scenery: Stone Mountain; the blue granite that in some places came up to both sides of the highway; the brilliant red clay banks slightly streaked with purple; and the various crops that made rows of green lace-work on the ground. The trees were full of silver-white sunlights and the meanest of them sparkled. The children were reading comic magazines and their mother had gone back to sleep.

"Let's go through Georgia fast so we won't have to look at it much," John Wesley said.

"If I were a little boy," said the grandmother, "I wouldn't talk about my native state that way. Tennessee has the mountains and Georgia has the hills."

"Tennessee is just a hillbilly dumping ground," John Wesley said, "and Georgia is a lousy state too."

"You said it," June Star said.

"In my time," said the grandmother, folding her thin veined fingers, "children were more respectful of their native states and their parents and everything else. People did right then. Oh look at the cute little pick-aninny!" she said and pointed to a Negro child standing in the door of a shack. "Wouldn't that make a picture, now?" she asked and they all turned and looked at the little Negro out of the back window. He waved.

"He didn't have any britches on," June Star said.

"He probably didn't have any," the grandmother explained. "Little niggers in the country don't have things like we do. If I could paint, I'd paint that picture," she said.

The children exchanged comic books.

The grandmother offered to hold the baby and the children's mother passed him over the front seat to her. She set him on her knee and bounced him and told him about the things they were passing. She rolled her eyes and screwed up her mouth and stuck her leathery thin face into his smooth bland one. Occasionally he gave her a faraway smile. They passed a large cotton field with five or six graves fenced in the middle of it, like a small island. "Look at the graveyard!" the grandmother said, pointing it out. "That was the old family burying ground. That belonged to the plantation."

'Where's the plantation?" John Wesley asked.

"Gone With the Wind," said the grandmother. "Ha. Ha."

When the children finished all the comic books they had brought, they opened the lunch and ate it. The grandmother ate a peanut butter sandwich and an olive and would not let the children throw the box and the paper napkins out the window. When there was nothing else to do they played a game by choosing a cloud and making the other two guess what shape it suggested. John Wesley took one the shape of a cow and June Star guessed a cow and John Wesley said, no, an automobile, and June Star said he didn't play fair, and they began to slap each other over the grandmother.

The grandmother said she would tell them a story if they would keep quiet. When she told a story, she rolled her eyes and waved her head and was very dramatic. She said once when she was a maiden lady she had been courted by a Mr. Edgar Atkins Teagarden from Jasper, Georgia. She said he was a very good-looking man and a gentleman and that he brought her a watermelon every Saturday afternoon with his initials cut in it, E.A.T. Well, one Saturday, she said, Mr. Teagarden brought the watermelon and there was nobody at home and he left it on the front porch and returned in his buggy to Jasper, but she never got the watermelon, she said, because a nigger boy ate it when he saw the initials, E.A.T.! This story tickled John Wesley's funny bone and he giggled and giggled but June Star didn't think it was any good. She said she wouldn't marry a man that just brought her a watermelon on Saturday. The grandmother said she would have done well to marry Mr. Teagarden because he was a gentleman and had bought Coca-Cola stock when it first came out and that he had died only a few years ago, a very wealthy man.

They stopped at The Tower for barbecued sandwiches. The Tower was a part-stucco and part-wood filling station and dance hall set in a clearing outside of Timothy. A fat man named Red Sammy Butts ran it and there were signs stuck here and there on the building and for miles up and down the highway saying, TRY RED SAMMY'S FAMOUS BARBECUE. NONE LIKE FAMOUS RED SAMMY'S! RED SAM! THE FAT BOY WITH THE HAPPY LAUGH. A VETERAN! RED SAMMY'S YOUR MAN!

Red Sammy was lying on the bare ground outside The Tower with his head under a truck while a gray monkey about a foot high, chained to a small chinaberry tree, chattered nearby. The monkey sprang back into the tree and got on the highest limb as soon as he saw the children jump out of the car and run toward him.

Inside, The Tower was a long dark room with a counter at one end and tables at the other and dancing space in the middle. They all sat down at a broad table next to the nickelodeon and Red Sam's wife, a tall burnt-brown woman with hair and eyes lighter than her skin, came and took their order. The children's mother put a dime in the machine and played "The Tennessee Waltz," and the grandmother said that tune always made her want to dance. She asked Bailey if he would like to dance but he only glared at her. He didn't have a naturally sunny disposition like she did and trips made him nervous. The grandmother's brown eyes were very bright. She swayed her head from side to side and pretended she was dancing in her chair. June Star said play something she could tap to so the children's mother put in another dime and played a fast number and June Star stepped out onto the dance floor and did her tap routine.

"Ain't she cute?" Red Sam's wife said, leaning over the counter. "Would you like to come be my little girl?"

"No, I certainly wouldn't," June Star said. "I wouldn't live in a broken-down place like this for a million bucks!" and she ran back to the table.

"Ain't she cute?" the woman repeated, stretching her mouth politely.

"Aren't you ashamed?" hissed the grandmother.

Red Sam came in and told his wife to quit lounging on the counter and hurry up with these people's order. His khaki trousers reached just to his hip bones and his stomach hung over them like a sack of meal swaying under his shirt. He came over and sat down at a table nearby and let out a combination sigh and yodel. "You can't win," he said. "You can't win," and he wiped his sweating red face off with a gray handerchief. "These days you don't know who to trust," he said. "Ain't that the truth?"

"People are certainly not nice like they used to be," said the grandmother.

"Two fellers come in here last week," Red Sammy said, "driving a Chrysler. It was an old beat-up car but it was a good one and these boys looked all right to me. Said they worked at the mill and you know I let them fellers charge the gas they bought? Now why did I do that?"

"Because you're a good man!" the grandmother said at once.

"Yes'm, I suppose so," Red Sam said as if he were struck with this answer.

His wife brought the orders, carrying the five plates all at once without a tray, two in each hand and one balanced on her arm. "It isn't a soul in this green world of God's that you can trust," she said. "And I don't count nobody out of that, not nobody," she repeated, looking at Red Sammy.

"Did you read about that criminal, The Misfit, that's escaped?" asked the grandmother.

"I wouldn't be a bit surprised if he didn't attack this place right here," said the woman. "If he hears about it being here, I wouldn't be none surprised to see him. If he hears it's two cent in the cash register, I wouldn't be a tall surprised if he . . ."

"That'll do," Red Sam said. "Go bring these people their Co'-Colas," and the woman went off to get the rest of the order.

"A good man is hard to find," Red Sammy said. "Everything is getting terrible. I remember the day you could go off and leave your screen door unlatched. Not no more."

He and the grandmother discussed better times. The old lady said that in her opinion Europe was entirely to blame for the way things were now. She said the way Europe acted you would think we were made of money and Red Sam said it was no use talking about it, she was exactly right. The children ran outside into the white sunlight and looked at the monkey in the lacy chinaberry tree. He was busy catching fleas on himself and biting each one carefully between his teeth as if it were a delicacy.

They drove off again into the hot afternoon. The grandmother took cat naps and woke up every few minutes with her own snoring. Outside of Toombsboro she woke up and recalled an old plantation that she had visited in this neighborhood once when she was a young lady. She said the house had six white columns across the front and that there was an avenue of oaks leading up to it and two little wooden trellis arbors on either side in front where you sat down with your suitor after a stroll in the garden. She recalled exactly which road to turn off to get to it. She knew that Bailey would not be willing to lose any time looking at an old house, but the more she talked about it, the more she wanted to see it once again and find out if the little twin arbors were still standing. "There was a secret panel in this house," she said craftily, not telling the truth but wishing that she were, "and the story went that all the family silver was hidden in it when Sherman came through but it was never found . . ."

"Hey!" John Wesley said. "Let's go see it! We'll find it! We'll poke all the woodwork and find it! Who lives there? Where do you turn off at? Hey Pop, can't we turn off there?"

"We never have seen a house with a secret panel!" June Star shrieked. "Let's go to the house with the secret panel! Hey, Pop, can't we go see the house with the secret panel!"

"It's not far from here, I know," the grandmother said. "It wouldn't take over twenty minutes."

Bailey was looking straight ahead. His jaw was as rigid as a horseshoe. "No," he said.

The children began to yell and scream that they wanted to see the house with the secret panel. John Wesley kicked the back of the front seat and June Star hung over her mother's shoulder and whined desperately into her ear that they never had any fun even on their vacation, that they could never do what THEY wanted to do. The baby began to scream and John Wesley kicked the back of the seat so hard that his father could feel the blows in his kidney.

"All right!" he shouted and drew the car to a stop at the side of the road. "Will you all shut up? Will you all just shut up for one second? If you don't shut up, we won't go anywhere."

"It would be very educational for them," the grandmother murmured.

"All right," Bailey said, "but get this. This is the only time we're going to stop for anything like this. This is the one and only time."

"The dirt road that you have to turn down is about a mile back," the grandmother directed. "I marked it when we passed."

"A dirt road," Bailey groaned.

After they had turned around and were headed toward the dirt road, the grandmother recalled other points about the house, the beautiful glass over the front doorway and the candle lamp in the hall. John Wesley said that the secret panel was probably in the fireplace.

"You can't go inside this house," Bailey said. "You don't know who lives there."

"While you all talk to the people in front, I'll run around behind and get in a window," John Wesley suggested.

"We'll all stay in the car," his mother said.

They turned onto the dirt road and the car raced roughly along in a swirl of pink dust. The grandmother recalled the times when there were no paved roads and thirty miles was a day's journey. The dirt road was hilly and there were sudden washes in it and sharp curves on dangerous embankments. All at once they would be on a hill, looking down over the blue tops of trees for miles around, then the next minute, they would be in a red depression with the dust-coated trees looking down on them.

"This place had better turn up in a minute," Bailey said, "or I'm going to turn around."

The road looked as if no one had traveled on it in months.

"It's not much farther," the grandmother said and just as she said it, a horrible thought came to her. The thought was so embarrassing that she turned red in the face and her eyes dilated and her feet jumped up, upsetting her valise in the corner. The instant the valise moved, the newspaper top she had over the basket under it rose with a snarl and Pitty Sing, the cat, sprang onto Bailey's shoulder.

The children were thrown to the floor and their mother, clutching the baby, was thrown out the door onto the ground; the old lady was thrown into the front seat. The car turned over once and landed right-side-up in a gulch on the side of the road. Bailey remained in the driver's seat with the cat—gray-striped with a broad white face and an orange nose—clinging to his neck like a caterpillar.

As soon as the children saw they could move their arms and legs, they scrambled out of the car, shouting, "We've had an ACCIDENT!" The grandmother was curled up under the dashboard, hoping she was injured so that Bailey's wrath would not come down on her all at once. The horrible thought she had had before the accident was that the house she had remembered so vividly was not in Georgia but in Tennessee.

Bailey removed the cat from his neck with both hands and flung it out the window against the side of a pine tree. Then he got out of the car and started looking for the children's mother. She was sitting against the side of the red gutted ditch, holding the screaming baby, but she only had a cut down her face and a broken shoulder. "We've had an ACCIDENT!" the children screamed in a frenzy of delight.

"But nobody's killed," June Star said with disappointment as the grandmother limped out of the car, her hat still pinned to her head but the broken front brim standing up at a jaunty angle and the violet spray hanging off the side. They all sat down in the ditch, except the children, to recover from the shock. They were all shaking.

"Maybe a car will come along," said the children's mother hoarsely.

"I believe I have injured an organ," said the grandmother, pressing her side, but no one answered her. Bailey's teeth were clattering. He had on a yellow sport shirt with bright blue parrots designed in it and his face was as yellow as the shirt. The grandmother decided that she would not mention that the house was in Tennessee.

The road was about ten feet above and they could see only the tops of the trees on the other side of it. Behind the ditch they were sitting in there were more woods, tall and dark and deep. In a few minutes they saw a car some distance away on top of a hill, coming slowly as if the occupants were watching them. The grandmother stood up and waved both arms dramatically to attract their attention. The car continued to come on slowly, disappeared around a bend and appeared again, moving even slower, on top of the hill they had gone over. It was a big black battered hearselike automobile. There were three men in it.

It came to a stop over them and for some minutes, the driver looked down with a steady expressionless gaze to where they were sitting, and didn't speak. Then he turned his head and muttered something to the other two and they got out. One was a fat boy in black trousers and a red sweat shirt with a silver stallion embossed on the front of it. He moved around on the right side of them and stood staring, his mouth partly open in a kind of loose grin. The other had on khaki pants and a blue striped coat and a gray hat pulled down very low, hiding most of his face. He came around slowly on the left side. Neither spoke.

The driver got out of the car and stood by the side of it, looking down at them. He was an older man than the other two. His hair was just beginning to gray and he wore silver-rimmed spectacles that gave him a scholarly look. He had a long creased face and didn't have on any shirt or undershirt. He had on blue jeans that were too tight for him and was holding a black hat and a gun. The two boys also had guns.

"We've had an ACCIDENT!" the children screamed.

The grandmother had the peculiar feeling that the bespectacled man was someone she knew. His face was as familiar to her as if she had known him all her life but she could not recall who he was. He moved away from the car and began to come down the embankment, placing his feet carefully so that he wouldn't slip. He had on tan and white shoes and no socks, and his ankles were red and thin. "Good afternoon," he said. "I see you all had you a little spill."

"We turned over twice!" said the grandmother.

"Oncet," he corrected. "We seen it happen. Try their car and see will it run, Hiram," he said quietly to the boy with the gray hat.

"What you got that gun for?" John Wesley asked. "Watcha gonna do with that gun?"

"Lady," the man said to the children's mother, "would you mind calling them children to sit down by you? Children make me nervous. I want all you all to sit down right together there were you're at."

"What are you telling us what to do for?" June Star asked.

Behind them the line of woods gaped like a dark open mouth. "Come here," said their mother.

"Look here now," Bailey began suddenly, "we're in a predicament! We're in . . ."

The grandmother shrieked. She scrambled to her feet and stood staring. "You're The Misfit!" she said. "I recognized you at once!"

"Yes'm," the man said, smiling slightly as if he were pleased in spite of himself to be known, "but it would have been better for all of you, lady, if you hadn't of reckernized me."

Bailey turned his head sharply and said something to his mother that shocked even the children. The old lady began to cry and The Misfit reddened.

"Lady," he said, "don't you get upset. Sometimes a man says things he don't mean. I don't reckon he meant to talk to you thataway."

"You wouldn't shoot a lady, would you?" the grandmother said and removed a clean handkerchief from her cuff and began to slap at her eyes with it.

The Misfit pointed the toe of his shoe into the ground and made a little hole and then covered it up again. "I would hate to have to," he said.

"Listen," the grandmother almost screamed, "I know you're a good man. You don't look a bit like you have common blood. I know you must come from nice people!"

"Yes mam," he said, "finest people in the world." When he smiled he showed a row of strong white teeth. "God never made a finer woman than my mother and my daddy's heart was pure gold," he said. The boy with the red sweat shirt had come around behind them and was standing with his gun at his hip. The Misfit squatted down on the ground. "Watch them children, Bobby Lee," he said. "You know they make me nervous." He looked at the six of them huddled together in front of him and he seemed to be embarrassed as if he couldn't think of anything to say. "Ain't a cloud in the sky," he remarked, looking up at it. "Don't see no sun but don't see no cloud neither."

"Yes, it's a beautiful day," said the grandmother. "Listen," she said, "you shouldn't call yourself The Misfit because I know you're a good man at heart. I can just look at you and tell."

"Hush!" Bailey yelled. "Hush! Everybody shut up and let me handle this!" He was squatting in the position of a runner about to spring forward but he didn't move.

"I pre-chate that, lady," The Misfit said and drew a little circle in the ground with the butt of his gun.

"It'll take a half a hour to fix this here car," Hiram called, looking over the raised hood of it.

"Well, first you and Bobby Lee get him and that little boy to step over yonder with you," The Misfit said, pointing to Bailey and John Wesley. "The boys want to ask you something," he said to Bailey. "Would you mind stepping back in them woods there with them?"

"Listen," Bailey began, "we're in a terrible predicament! Nobody realizes what this is," and his voice cracked. His eyes were as blue and intense as the parrots in his shirt and he remained perfectly still.

The grandmother reached up to adjust her hat brim as if she were going to the woods with him but it came off in her hand. She stood staring at it and after a second she let it fall on the ground. Hiram pulled Bailey up by the arm as if he were assisting an old man. John Wesley caught hold of his father's hand and Bobby Lee followed. They went off toward the woods and just as they reached the dark edge, Bailey turned and supporting himself against a gray naked pine trunk, he shouted, "I'll be back in a minute, Mamma, wait on me!"

"Come back this instant!" his mother shrilled but they all disappeared into the woods.

"Bailey Boy!" the grandmother called in a tragic voice but she found she was looking at The Misfit squatting on the ground in front of her. "I just know you're a good man," she said desperately. "You're not a bit common!"

"Nome, I ain't a good man," The Misfit said after a second as if he had considered her statement carefully, "but I ain't the worst in the world neither. My daddy said I was a different breed of dog from my brothers and sisters. 'You know,' Daddy said, 'it's some that can live their whole life out without asking about it and it's others has to know why it is, and this boy is one of the latters. He's going to be into everything!'" He put on his black hat and looked up suddenly and then away deep into the woods as if he were embarrassed again. "I'm sorry I don't have on a shirt before you ladies," he said, hunching his shoulders slightly. "We buried our clothes that we had on when we escaped and we're just making do until we can get better. We borrowed these from some folks we met," he explained.

"That's perfectly all right," the grandmother said. "Maybe Bailey has an extra shirt in his suitcase."

"I'll look and see terrectly," The Misfit said.

"Where are they taking him?" the children's mother screamed.

"Daddy was a card himself," The Misfit said. "You couldn't put anything over on him. He never got in trouble with the Authorities though. Just had the knack of handling them."

"You could be honest too if you'd only try," said the grandmother. "Think how wonderful it would be to settle down and live a comfortable life and not have to think about somebody chasing you all the time."

The Misfit kept scratching in the ground with the butt of his gun as if he were thinking about it. "Yes'm, somebody is always after you," he murmured.

The grandmother noticed how thin his shoulder blades were just behind his hat because she was standing up looking down on him. "Do you ever pray?" she asked.

He shook his head. All she saw was the black hat wiggle between his shoulder blades. "Nome," he said.

There was a pistol shot from the woods, followed closely by another. Then silence. The old lady's head jerked around. She could hear the wind move through the tree tops like a long satisfied insuck of breath. "Bailey Boy!" she called.

"I was a gospel singer for a while," The Misfit said. "I been most everything. Been in the arm service, both land and sea, at home and abroad, been twict married, been an undertaker, been with the railroads, plowed Mother Earth, been in a tornado, seen a man burnt alive oncet," and he looked up at the children's mother and the little girl who were sitting close together, their faces white and their eyes glassy; "I even seen a woman flogged," he said.

"Pray, pray," the grandmother began, "pray, pray . . ."

"I never was a bad boy that I remember of," The Misfit said in an almost dreamy voice, "but somewheres along the line I done something wrong and got sent to the penitentiary. I was buried alive," and he looked up and held her attention to him by a steady stare.

"That's when you should have started to pray," she said. "What did you do to get sent to the penitentiary that first time?"

"Turn to the right, it was a wall," The Misfit said, looking up again at the cloudless sky. "Turn to the left, it was a wall. Look up it was a ceiling, look down it was a floor. I forget what I done, lady. I set there and set there, trying to remember what it was I done and I ain't recalled it to this day. Oncet in a while, I would think it was coming to me, but it never come."

"Maybe they put you in by mistake," the old lady said vaguely.

"Nome," he said. "It wasn't no mistake. They had the papers on me."

"You must have stolen something," she said.

The Misfit sneered slightly. "Nobody had nothing I wanted," he said. "It was a head-doctor at the penitentiary said what I had done was kill my daddy but I known that for a lie. My daddy died in nineteen ought nineteen of the epidemic flu and I never had a thing to do with it. He was buried in the Mount Hopewell Baptist churchyard and you can go there and see for yourself."

"If you would pray," the old lady said, "Jesus would help you."

"That's right," The Misfit said.

"Well then, why don't you pray?" she asked trembling with delight suddenly.

"I don't want no hep," he said. "I'm doing all right by myself."

Bobby Lee and Hiram came ambling back from the woods. Bobby Lee was dragging a yellow shirt with bright blue parrots in it.

"Throw me that shirt, Bobby Lee," The Misfit said. The shirt came flying at him and landed on his shoulder and he put it on. The grandmother couldn't name what the shirt reminded her of. "No, lady," The Misfit said while he was buttoning up, "I found out the crime don't matter. You can do one thing or you can do another, kill a man or take a tire off his car, because sooner or later you're going to forget what it was you done and just be punished for it."

The children's mother had begun to make heaving noises as if she couldn't get her breath. "Lady," he asked, "would you and that little girl like to step off yonder with Bobby Lee and Hiram and join your husband?"

"Yes, thank you," the mother said faintly. Her left arm dangled helplessly and she was holding the baby, who had gone to sleep, in the other. "Hep that lady up, Hiram," The Misfit said as she struggled to climb out of the ditch, "and Bobby Lee, you hold onto that little girl's hand."

"I don't want to hold hands with him," June Star said. "He reminds me of a pig."

The fat boy blushed and laughed and caught her by the arm and pulled her off into the woods after Hiram and her mother.

Alone with The Misfit, the grandmother found that she had lost her voice. There was not a cloud in the sky nor any sun. There was nothing around her but woods. She wanted to tell him that he must pray. She opened and closed her mouth several times before anything came out. Finally she found herself saying, "Jesus, Jesus," meaning, Jesus will help you, but the way she was saying it, it sounded as if she might be cursing.

"Yes'm," The Misfit said as if he agreed. "Jesus thrown everything off balance. It was the same case with Him as with me except He hadn't committed any crime and they could prove I had committed one because they had the papers on me. Of course," he said, "they never shown me my papers. That's why I sign myself now. I said long ago, you get you a signature and sign everything you do and keep a copy of it. Then you'll know what you done and you can hold up the crime to the punishment and see do they match and in the end you'll have something to prove you ain't been treated right. I call myself The Misfit," he said, "because I can't make what all I done wrong fit what all I gone through in punishment."

There was a piercing scream from the woods, followed closely by a pistol report. "Does it seem right to you, lady, that one is punished a heap and another ain't punished at all?"

"Jesus!" the old lady cried. "You've got good blood! I know you wouldn't shoot a lady! I know you come from nice people! Pray! Jesus, you ought not to shoot a lady. I'll give you all the money I've got!"

"Lady," The Misfit said, looking beyond her far into the woods, "there never was a body that give the undertaker a tip."

There were two more pistol reports and the grandmother raised her head like a parched old turkey hen crying for water and called, "Bailey Boy, Bailey Boy!" as if her heart would break.

"Jesus was the only One that ever raised the dead," The Misfit continued, "and He shouldn't have done it. He thrown everything off balance. If He did what He said, then it's nothing for you to do but throw away everything and follow Him, and if He didn't then it's nothing for you to do but enjoy the few minutes you got left the best way you can—by killing somebody or burning down his house or doing some other meanness to him. No pleasure but meanness," he said and his voice had become almost a snarl.

"Maybe He didn't raise the dead," the old lady mumbled, not knowing what she was saying and feeling so dizzy that she sank down in the ditch with her legs twisted under her.

"I wasn't there so I can't say He didn't," The Misfit said. "I wisht I had of been there," he said, hitting the ground with his fist. "It ain't right I wasn't there because if I had of been there I would of known. Listen lady," he said in a high voice, "if I had of been there I would of known and I wouldn't be like I am now." His voice seemed about to crack and the grandmother's head cleared for an instant. She saw the man's face twisted close to her own as if he were going to cry and she murmured, "Why, you're one of my babies. You're one of my own children!" She reached out and touched him on the shoulder. The Misfit sprang back as if a snake had bitten him and shot her three times through the chest. Then he put his gun down on the ground and took off his glasses and began to clean them.

Hiram and Bobby Lee returned from the woods and stood over the ditch, looking down at the grandmother who half sat and half lay in a puddle of blood with her legs crossed under her like a child's and her face smiling up at the cloudless sky.

Without his glasses, The Misfit's eyes were red-rimmed and pale and defenseless-looking. "Take her off and throw her where you thrown the others," he said, picking up the cat that was rubbing itself against his leg.

"She was a talker, wasn't she?" Bobby Lee said, sliding down the ditch with a yodel.

"She would of been a good woman," The Misfit said, "if it had been somebody there to shoot her every minute of her life."

"Some fun!" Bobby Lee said.

"Shut up, Bobby Lee," The Misfit said. "It's no real pleasure in life."

HORIZONTAL SNOW

—■—

Rick DeMarinis

This short story is from DeMarinis's 1991 collection The Voice of America: Stories.

Because of a snag in my thinking I lost interest in both vector analysis and differential equations and had to drop out of college and hitchhike home twelve credits short of graduation. Home was half a continent away and I didn't have a car or bus money and was afraid to ask my folks for help. They had paid my way through three and a half years of engineering school at Platteville, Wisconsin, and I couldn't have said to Dad, for instance, that I wanted to come home because the laws of thermodynamics bored the life out of me. He wouldn't have understood my reasoning.

I didn't have any reasoning. Something down at the underpinnings of reason had given way, and there was no explanation for it. I couldn't even explain it to myself. All I knew was that every time I opened a textbook something numbing, like pain, would stab the back of my head. Or my eyelids would feel thick, as if stuffed with sand. Or I would read the same page over ten, fifteen times and not one word would register.

I kissed my girlfriend goodbye, packed my suitcase, and headed for the highway west. "What's *wrong* with you?" she'd asked, and I had no answer. I'd hurt her, I was aware of that, but my own feelings were in cold storage. I observed her pain in the way a surgeon observes the pain of his patient: with compassion but without involvement or remorse. I was strong and healthy, my appetite was good, I slept well, but nothing interested me. I felt like an animated corpse, moving through a world I had left behind. Greeting myself in the bathroom mirror each morning I would say: Hello, Zombie.

The first ride I hitched was with a family. They dropped me off on the far edge of Minnesota, in the middle of nowhere. It was a lonely stretch of road, and though the weather had been springlike for several weeks, the wind from Canada still had a threat of winter in it. My second ride came minutes before hypothermia set in.

A pickup truck with a homemade camper stuck on the back rolled to a gradual stop ahead of me. The camper was made of scrap wood and had a peaked roof, like a house, covered with tar paper. It looked like an out-building of a farm, modified for travel. The man driving said he was going all the way to Bonners Ferry, Idaho, four hundred miles short of my destination. I hesitated before getting in because the man was so ugly he took my breath away. He may have been the ugliest man in the world. At least I had never seen anyone up to that time as ugly as he was, and I have not seen anyone uglier since. His face was flat as a skillet, even concave. His hammered-down nose was five fingers wide, and his short forehead had prominent supraorbital ridges thick as cables. He looked like something you'd see in an anthropology textbook, as if forty thousand years of evolution had skipped over him. This was 1958, and so much has happened since then that much of what follows seems more like a dream than personal history.

His name was Lot Stoner and he claimed to be a preacher. He drove slowly, under fifty, with both hands on the wheel. He had huge, amply scarred, thick-fingered hands that had seen decades of punishing work. We rode along without speaking for several hours, though now and then he would glance over at me and at the suitcase wedged between my legs. "I specialize in the defeated," he finally said. When I didn't respond to this, he went on to explain that he was a preacher of the gospel. He didn't have a church or a degree from a recognized seminary, but was a self-taught man of God. "You just lost a big tussle, didn't you?" he said. He had yellowing, wide-spaced eyes. They were slightly wall-eyed so that when he looked at you directly it seemed as if he was seeing two of you—one slightly to the right, one slightly to the left. I guessed his age at about sixty, but his hair was bright red and youthful.

Again he waited for my response. I didn't have one. I shrugged and turned my gaze out the side window, where snow-patched fields drifted by.

"I saw defeat in your posture," he said, "while you were standing out there in the elements with your thumb out. I said to myself, 'Lot, there is a young buck who has been in the toilet. There is a boy who hit bottom but did not bounce,' Am I wrong?"

I didn't see myself as that bad off, but he was at least partly right. Articulated, the snag in my thinking went something like this: "The struggle is not worth the reward." It loomed in my mind like a huge door that had just shut, locking itself. I couldn't formulate it in words at the time, but I sensed that it had the clear-cut, irrefutable perfection of Einstein's discovery of the absolute equivalency of matter and energy. I had been an honors student headed for a job in the aerospace industry to help build rockets so that we could catch up to the Russians. Sputnik had been put into orbit the previous fall, and things did not look good for the U.S.A.

"Your hand looked like the hand of a mendicant, upraised for alms," Lot said. "I said to myself, 'Lot, there is a boy who has lost his way.' I am hardly ever off the target about such things."

Lot talked about himself for a while. He said he felt more like a traveling teacher than a pulpit-bound Bible thumper. He said he was too footloose to have his own church, and also that he was too broad-minded and generous with his Biblical interpretations to follow the narrow and self-interested theologies of the fat-cat denominations. He gave examples of his broad-mindedness. "This may astound you, son," he said, "but I can see evidence of divinity in a cow pie, and again in the maggots that devour it." He reached under his seat and pulled out a microphone that had some wires dangling loosely from it. "Ain't that right, Willie?" he shouted into the mike.

A woman's voice crackled over a loud speaker that was wedged between the seat and the back of the cab. "Ain't *what* right?" she said. She sounded sleepy and annoyed at being disturbed. I figured, correctly, that she was lying in a bunk back in the wood-slat-and-tar-paper camper.

"About me seeing the Almighty Himself in commonplace cow shit," Lot said into his microphone.

"Yeah," said the voice through an unrestrained yawn.

"I can see the Lord in all of it," he said. "In every piece of flotsam and jetsam, in every gnat and mosquito—there He is, doing business like He has every day for twenty billion years. History means nothing to Him. Yours, mine, or that of the damn fool nations."

Lot told me that he'd spent a good part of his life in prison. "I killed a man," he said. "I took his head into my hands and squeezed it until the pressure on his brain became intolerable. There were ruptures under the bone and then the bone itself gave way. He was stone dead before I released him, and the blood from his ears ran in abundance through my fingers. They said later they had to pry my fingers off of him with cold chisels and pliers. I had momentarily lost the sense of myself." He took his right hand off the wheel and showed it to me. The hard, walnut-size knuckles looked like the joints of a machine, the thick wrist timbered with straight shafts of bone.

He picked up his microphone. "Am I sorry? Tell him, Willie, if I am sorry."

"He ain't," Willie said.

"And I tell you why," Lot said. "The man deserved what he got. He was worthless. Worthless scum. I know I just told you I can see divinity in flotsam and jetsam. But this man was below that. He was filled to capacity with nothing. He was nothingness incarnate. He was a hole in God's blue air."

"He's getting up steam," Willie's crackling voice warned from the loudspeaker.

We were in the flat rich farm country of central North Dakota, the landscape of boredom itself. A few years later, after having got past my motivational problems, I would be installing Minuteman missiles into this same wheatland for the U.S. Air Force.

"The man I killed was a two-legged lamprey," Lot said. "He attached himself to the helpless underbelly of goodhearted people and sucked their lifeblood from them until they were pale effigies of their former selves. He would fill his nothingness with their somethingness. He was a con artist who had taken my daddy's last dime for an electrical arthritis cure, coupled with painful injections of a useless saline solution. Can you blame me?"

"No," I said.

"And I accept no blame. But while I was up at the state farm I had myself a long time to ponder it. My meditations led me to the light, the holy light, pure and simple. And I am going to reveal this holy light to you, son, free of charge. Spreading the truth is my goal in life. I doff my cap to no sect, denomination, figurehead, or dogma. I do not take my notions from someone else's larder of so-called religious verities."

We passed a small lake and drove through a town where, four years later, I would betray my young wife by going to bed with a farmer's widow named Zola Faye Metkovich. My young wife would leave me, I would leave Zola Faye, but I would stay on at Minot Air Force Base, helping to redesign ICBM parts and support equipment that had failed their stress and endurance tests. I would make a lot of money, drive a big car—an air-conditioned Chrysler Imperial—and have a string of five girlfriends who lived far away from each other in the small isolated towns of North Dakota where people, though born in the United States of America, still spoke with foreign accents, German and Russian. It would be the most exciting time of my life, but of course I did not know it, and could not have imagined it, as I bounced along toward Idaho with Lot Stoner and the unseen woman he called Willie.

Now and then, Lot would take a dried-out sandwich from a paper sack on the floorboards or lift a thermos to his lips. He offered these to me, but I refused. Food from his hand was automatically unappetizing, as if contaminated by his ugliness. He hummed to himself for a while, ate a little more, gazed out at the slow-moving scenery from time to time. It took me a while to realize that he'd quit talking, and that I had been waiting for him to reveal this holy-light business to me, not that I believed in such things or had ever given them much thought. I began to think that he'd just forgotten about it, or had something more pressing on his mind. And then it occurred to me that I was being conned, or that he was self-deluded, maybe even brain-damaged. I leaned my head against the window and pretended to doze off. And then I did doze off.

A crackling electrical scream woke me up. It was Willie, yelling for someone to come back to her.

Lot slowed the truck and pulled off onto the shoulder of the highway. "Go climb into the back and take a look will you, son?" he said wearily. He crossed his arms on the wheel and rested his knobbed forehead on them. "I'll catch a couple of winks while you're back there."

I got out of the truck into a northern gale. The false spring was over. A new storm from the Arctic was blowing in. In these latitudes you can smell snow in the air. It's not so much a smell as it is a pinching in of your nose, a tightening of the membranes inside. You turn your face into the wind, lift your nose to it, sniff in. "Snow," you say to yourself. "Blizzard."

When I climbed into the camper I saw a narrow-faced woman with Indian cheekbones curled up under a heavy blanket. She had thin, stringy hair, and her hunted eyes looked like those of a trapped wolverine.

"Come here, dammit," she said.

She was lying on a bunk that ran the length of the camper. There was an electric light glowing in the ceiling. The only other light came through the back door, which I left open. She was trying to push herself up on her elbows.

"What's the matter?" I said.

"Lift me up," she said through gritted teeth.

She was young. Maybe twenty, but probably closer to seventeen. I slid a hand behind her back and muscled her forward. "Quit it," she said. "I just needed to get up a little so's I can get set. It's coming."

She scooted forward a little, then lay back down. Her knees were up and her belly was very big. She pulled the blanket aside and her naked belly rose up, tight and shiny.

"You're having a baby," I said.

"You don't say," she said. She spread her knees and screamed, loud and terrible, more rage in it than pain. I stepped back and my head hit the roof. Her microphone was on the floor, next to her bunk. I picked it up.

"She's having a baby, Lot," I said.

"Joy to the world," replied his weary voice from a tiny loudspeaker that had been stuck to the ceiling with electrician's tape.

I put the mike down. Willie was growling between clenched teeth, her head rolling side to side on her pillow. "Is there anything I can do?" I asked.

She waved her arm. It flapped like a broken wing. "Get me that pint-sized green bottle out of the icebox," she said. "And don't be an asshole and faint."

We looked at each other for a few seconds. If anything, my heart was beating slower. "Don't worry," I said.

The icebox was a homemade affair with a heavy lid fitted into its top. Among cans of soda and beer and packages of food were a half-dozen pint bottles of gin. I took one of these out and uncapped it. She took a long pull from it, and then I did the same. It was cold in my mouth and warm going down.

"Glory, glory," said Lot, his grainy voice dropping like sand from the ceiling.

"Maybe you ought to be back here with your wife," I said into the microphone.

"We all can't fit back there, son," he said. "There's not that much to do, anyway. You just do what the girl tells you. She ain't new at this."

Wind from Canada mauled the truck. It howled in the wooden slats of the camper. I looked out the door and saw the blizzard, the horizontal snow.

"Give me your hand," Willie said. She squeezed hard enough to make the separate bones touch. The skin of her stomach was pulled so tight I could see my shadowy reflection in it. "Take a look, will you?" she said. "I want to know if he's coming out ass end first. I had two others that did, both stillborns."

She let go of my hand and I moved down to the foot of the bunk and peered between her upraised knees. There, at the dark joining of her thighs, was a little face. It looked like a dried apple. Crimped as it was in those bearded jaws, it looked Chinese and ancient. Its eyes were shut tight, the mouth a stubborn line. The unbreathing nose was flat and wide. The idea occurred to me that this wasn't an infant at all but a tiny old man who had serious second thoughts about the wisdom of leaving the comfortable and nourishing dark for the starved light of North Dakota. The notion made me smile. "Welcome home, chump," I whispered.

"Well?" Willie said. "Is it coming out frontwards or backwards?"

"Frontwards," I said, "Frontwards," I repeated into the mike. "And I think it's got red hair."

"I'm kissing the Good Book," said Lot.

Once the head cleared the birth canal, the rest was easy. Willie leaned forward and took the baby up in her arms, nipped the cord with her teeth, tied it off with a length of nylon fishing line, and wrapped him in the blanket. A small cry—more like the ratchety chirping of a newly hatched bird than that of a baby—came from the blanket. I wiped the sweat off Willie's face with my handkerchief, and she took another swig of gin.

"You're a nice fella," Willie said, smiling up at me.

I thought about that. "I don't think so," I said.

I went back up to the cab. "Fatherhood," Lot said, "is a great responsibility." He gave me a sidelong look of high significance, his off-center eyes splitting me into twins. Then he started the truck and we moved down the white highway.

"You probably ought to get them to a hospital," I said. "Or at least to a doctor."

"We'll stop in Minot," he said. "We'll get some warm food and a place to rest. Doctors aren't important to our thinking. Are they to yours?"

I looked at him, but he was squinting out into the painfully bright air of the storm. "Yes, I think so," I said.

"Someday you'll wake up out of your little nightmare and click your heels, son," he said, shifting down to second as snowdrifts began to collect in the road. He picked up his microphone and said, "What are we going to name him, Willie?"

"Jesus Dakota Stoner," Willie said without hesitating a beat.

"Merry Christmas," Lot hooted into the mike.

"We'll called him J.D. for short," Willie said.

Lot drove even slower as night came on and the blizzard got worse. We stopped in Rugby, an hour or so short of Minot, at an all-night café called Mud and Sinkers. Lot pulled a tobacco can out from under the seat. It was packed with dollar bills. He counted out five, smoothed them out on his thigh. "We'll get us some coffee and doughnuts and sit out this storm. When it gets light, we'll hit the road again."

We found a booth near the warm kitchen and a waitress brought us coffee and three glazed doughnuts. Willie had Jesus Dakota tucked in a blanket. The dried blood and mucus of his recent birth still mottled his skin, which otherwise would have been a bright saffron-pink, but Willie didn't seem too concerned. She opened her wool shirt and drew out a long thin breast and gave it to the baby. The baby hadn't been crying, but he pulled at his mother with urgent power.

"It'll be good to get home," I said, for conversation's sake, but I said it mostly to myself.

"J.D.'s home already," Lot chuckled. "Home is a warm teat, wherever you happen to be."

"Seattle," I said. "That's home for me."

Lot sipped his coffee, squinted at me through the steam. "Better to be in exile sustained by a dream of home than to endure the disappointments of home itself. Home itself is an idea that never measures up. I speak from experience."

"You're too deep for me, Lot," I said.

"Don't mock him," Willie said. She said it simply, without taking her eyes off her baby.

"You'll find one day that what I said is true," Lot said.

And what good will it do me? I wanted to say, but held back. I was tired and a little fed up with his homespun homilies. I wanted to be back in West Seattle, in my parent's big house overlooking the Sound. I wanted to be in my upstairs room, at my desk, watching the ferryboats at night brilliantly spangled with lights. I wanted to listen to the lonesome call of their foghorns while snuggling deeper and deeper into my old bed.

There was some names etched by knifeblade into the table before me. Rena + Yank. Pete + Vicki. Remember Me, Annette. I concentrated on those names and sipped my coffee, willing the night to pass quickly. I would come back to Mud and Sinkers four years later as a Boeing field engineer, after completing my degree at the University of Washington, the snag in my thinking long gone and forgotten. Carline Minsky from the town of Balfour would be with me, and those carved names would still be here, among half a dozen more. Carline was pregnant and wanted to get married, but I told her I already was married—even though my wife had left several months earlier. Carline broke down, but what could I do? I said I'd pay for the abortion. She took the money, but our little romantic episode ended then and there. Maybe she got the abortion and maybe she didn't. I never found out, nor wanted to.

We'd gotten carried away down in a silo, next to a recently installed Minuteman missile. We were on a service platform, adjacent to the missile's third-stage motor, near the warhead access ramp, and Carline said, "Let's do it, right here." She wasn't supposed to be in this Top Secret area, but there was no one else around within miles who might object. "This motor is fueled by a ton of nitro glycerine, stabilized by cotton filaments," I told her. "It's very dangerous." This was a partial truth, but it made her moan with fear and excitement. We did it standing up, her bending over the rail and leaning out close enough to the Minuteman to kiss the megaton hydrogen warhead. "I'm so hot," she said, and I was too. Too hot, it turned out, because we neglected the usual precautions, and she got pregnant, somewhere under North Dakota.

"I saw something else in your posture," Lot said, startling me. He was slumped over on his side in the booth, and I thought he'd been asleep. "I saw something besides defeat, or maybe it wasn't defeat I saw at all. Maybe it was this other thing all along."

I held a picture of blue water and white boats in my mind, so as not to get caught up again in his stagey pronouncements.

"Don't you care to know what I saw?" he said.

Willie stirred. Jesus Dakota turned his face left and right before finding the breast she half-consciously offered him.

"Not especially," I said.

"I'm going to tell you anyway. I saw a dangerous hunger. I saw an unfeedable hunger."

His primitive head, his bright red hair, the fatigue that lined his face—the complete aspect of an outcast and loser. I smiled and shook my head, affecting dismay.

"You were going to tell me something about a holy light. You must have forgotten," I said.

The need for sleep pulled him lower in the booth. He closed his eyes. "I already did. You weren't paying attention, son."

After a while, they were all sound asleep, that odd and aimless family with no future and a harrowing past. Even when a trucker came stomping into the café, kicking snow off his boots, flapping his arms against his chest, and cursing the storm at the top of his lungs, Lot, Willie, and Jesus

Dakota didn't wake up. It was 3:00 A.M., and the trucker ordered hot cakes and coffee. He talked constantly at the waitress, and from this I learned that he was on his way to the West Coast. I saw my chance and sat next to him at the counter. He was a tall, thin, nervous man, but he was friendly. He was a talker who was starved for conversation, and so when I asked if I could ride along with him to the Coast, he said "Just don't ask me to stop every fifty miles so you can piss. I've got to make Tacoma by tomorrow afternoon."

I went back to the booth. Willie had scooted over so that my coat was partly under her. I didn't want to wake her up, so I just left it there. It was just an unlined windbreaker anyway. I took one last look at them. I hoped they'd make it to Bonners Ferry, but given what they were it didn't seem to matter much where they wound up. They'd be back on the road again before long, the road being the only place where they would feel welcome.

In the truck, a huge Diamond T hauling double trailers, the driver said, "Who was that ugly fuck and the bony squaw you were with?"

"Just a ride," I said, tossing my suitcase behind the seat.

The trucker poured himself a cup of coffee from a thermos, shook two white pills from a small envelope. He placed the pills carefully on his tongue, then swallowed them with coffee.

"Got to jump-start my fucking *brain*," he said, winking.

Then we roared out into the blinding storm.

The Tender Bough of Youth

John Thaggard

John Thaggard is a senior at The University of
Montana majoring in broadcast journalism.

Pedigree

I was born the fourth of five sons to a devout Irish-
Catholic Mother and a whiskey-guzzling, guitar-playing
Father. My existence—as well as my little brother's—was a
miracle of sorts.

Faith

My Mom was diagnosed with a rare blood disorder after
the birth of my older brother. Her doctor told her that
she had a 25 percent chance of surviving her next
preganacy. He prescribed birth control. She took the
pills home, flushed them down the toilet, and ten months
later I was born.

Ungrateful Little . . .

My Mom's faith is the only reason I'm alive. However,
faith is something I've been without for most of my life.
I needed to see God in order to believe in God. I used to
ask God to show himself, but I never caught a glimpse.

Nice House

I was sure I would never see God at church. The
Catholic church scared me as a kid. I only encountered it
on Sundays, holidays, and funerals. To me it was hushed
tones, crying, and cemeteries. I thought that God—like my
dad—made every excuse he could to stay away from the
church.

Last Meal

As I grew older my fear increased. I looked upon my
approaching confirmation as a condemned man might look
upon his execution. Transubstatiation—the belief that
Christ is present in the wafer and wine presented at the
Holy Communion—was something I couldn't swallow.

Henry IX

Fate—or common lechery—intervened when my dad ran off with a young cocktail waitress. In the ensuing turmoil I was able to play hooky from Catholic instructions. Mom was so tired from working three jobs that she had little fight left over to make me attend confirmation class.

Here's Another Clue for You All

Around the time I hit puberty I started to search for God. I read the Bible from the Book of Genesis through one of Paul's Letters. I didn't really buy his story. I imagined him winking and grinning. Saying that he met God on the road, and that God told him to tell me not to masturbate. I gave up.

Temporal Insanity

I spent the next five years dating women. Frankly, I was a real letch. I used women. I burrowed into their hearts with lies and left after I was sated. I cared nothing for them or their feelings.

I'm Beginning to See the Light

One night I was at dinner with this lady named Teresa. It was our second date. I was about to launch into one of my surefire heart-opening monologues when I saw the strangest thing. It was God.

There's Something in Your Eye

God was in her eyes. In that moment, as I was poised to possibly sacrifice her faith in love for my pleasure, I discovered my faith in God.

Why the Chicken Really Crossed the Road

To me, God can be seen whenever I make a choice about communicating with someone. Every exchange presents me with a chance to experience God. When I see a transient on the road and I turn my gaze from him (because the dollar in my pocket is worth more than his humanity), I see nothing. But, if I choose to look beyond his surface, past my fears and stereotypes, the stranger becomes a person. Humanity is our bond. We share fear, hope, need, and a yearning to be acknowledged.

Sappy Ending

It's been a long time since my Mom and I beat the odds. She's alive and healthy and stubborn as ever. When I told her that I was no longer an agnostic, she didn't seem too surprised. Faith.

CREDITS

LEON BATTISTA ALBERTI, From *On Painting* by Leon Battista Alberti. Reprinted by permission of Yale University Press and Taylor & Francis Books Ltd.

SHERMAN ALEXIE, "White Men Can't Drum" by Sherman Alexie from *The New York Times,* October 4, 1992. Copyright © 1992 by *The New York Times.* Reprinted by permission.

DOROTHY ALLISON, "Gun Crazy" by Dorothy Allison from *Skin.* Copyright © 1994 by Dorothy Allison. Reprinted by permission of Firebrand Books.

HANNAH ARENDT, "Deportations from Western Europe," from *Eichmann in Jerusalem* by Hannah Arendt. Copyright © 1963, 1964 by Hannah Arendt. Used by permission of Viking Penguin, a division of Penguin Putnam Inc.

MICHAEL J. ARLEN, "The Tyranny of the Visual" from *The Camer Age* by Michael J. Arlen. Copyright © 1981 by Michael J. Arlen. Reprinted by permission of Farrar, Straus & Giroux, Inc.

BARBARA LAZEAR ASCHER, "On Power" from *The Habit of Loving* by Barbara Lazear Ascher. Copyright © 1986, 1987, 1989 by Barbara Lazear Ascher. Reprinted by permission of Random House, Inc.

W. H. AUDEN, "Musée des Beaux Arts" from *W. H. Auden: Collected Poems* by W. H. Auden, edited by Edward Mendelson. Copyright © 1940 and renewed © 1948 by W. H. Auden. Reprinted by permission of Random House, Inc. "Work, Labor, and Play" by W. H. Auden from *A Certain World.* Copyright © 1970 by W. H. Auden. Reprinted by permission of Curtis Brown, Ltd.

JAMES BALDWIN, "Sonny's Blues," copyright © 1965 by James Baldwin was originally published in Partisan Review. Copyright renewed. Collected in *Going to Meet the Man,* published by Vintage Books. Reprinted by arrangement with the James Baldwin Estate.

RANDALL BALMER, "Adirondack Fundamentalism" from *Mine Eyes Have Seen the Glory: A Journey into the Evangelical Subculture in America, Expanded Edition* by Randall Balmer. Copyright © 1989, 1993 by Oxford University Press, Inc. Used by permission of Oxford University Press, Inc.

JOHN BERGER, "The White Bird" from *The Sense of Sight* by John Berger. Copyright © 1985 by John Berger. Reprinted by permission of Pantheon Books, a division of Random House, Inc.

MARY CLEARMAN BLEW, "The Sow in the River," from *All but the Waltz* by Mary Clearman Blew. Copyright © 1991 Mary Clearman Blew. Used by permission of Viking Penguin, a division of Penguin Putnam Inc.

DEBORAH BLUM, "The Monkey Wars" by Deborah Blum from *The Sacramento Bee,* 1992. Copyright, The Sacramento Bee, 1992. Reprinted by permission.

JUDY J. BLUNT, "Breaking Clean" by Judy J. Blunt, as appeared in *Northern Lights,* Vol. 1, No. 4, pp. 4–5, Fall 1991. Reprinted by permission of Judy Blunt. All rights reserved. Copyright © 1991 by Judy Blunt.

T. CORAGHESSAN BOYLE, "Descent of Man" by T. Coraghessan Boyle. (Boston: Little, Brown and Company, 1979). Copyright © 1974, 1976, 1977, 1978, 1979 by T. Coraghessan Boyle. Originally appeared in *Esquire* Magazine. Reprinted by permission of Georges Brochardt, Inc. for the author.

JANE BROX, "Influenza 1918" from *Five Thousand Days Like This One* by Jane Brox. Reprinted by permission of Beacon Press.

PATRICK BUCHANAN, "Losing the War for America's Culture?" by Patrick Buchanan from *The Washington Times,* May 22, 1989. Reprinted by permission of Creators Syndicate.

HERBERT BUTTERFIELD, "The Originality of the Old Testament," from *Herbert Butterfield: Writings on Christianity and History* by Herbert Butterfield, edited by C. Thomas McIntire. Copyright © 1979 by Oxford University Press, Inc. Used by permission of Oxford University Press, Inc.

ITALO CALVINO, "Cities and the Dead" from *Invisible Cities* by Italo Calvino, copyright © 1972 by Giulio Einaudi editore s.p.a., English translation by William Weaver copyright © 1974 by Harcourt, Inc., reprinted by permission of Harcourt, Inc. Copyright © 1988 by Palomar S.r.1. No changes shall be made to the text of the above work without the express written consent of The Wylie Agency, Inc.

KEVIN CANTY, "Dogs" from *A Stranger in This World* by Kevin Canty. Copyright © 1994 by Kevin Canty. Used by permission of Doubleday, a division of Random House, Inc.

EDWARD HALLETT CARR, "The Historian and His Facts" from *What Is History?* by Edward Hallett Carr. Copyright © 1961 by Edward Hallett Carr. Reprinted by permission of Alfred A. Knopf, Inc.

RACHEL CARSON, "Elixirs of Death," from *Silent Spring* by Rachel Carson. Copyright © 1962 by Rachel L. Carson, renewed 1990 by Roger Christie. Reprinted by permission of Houghton Mifflin Company. All rights reserved.

RAYMOND CARVER, "Cathedral" from *Cathedral* by Raymond Carver. Copyright © 1981 by Raymond Carver. Reprinted by permission of Alfred A. Knopf, Inc.

GARY CHAPMAN, "Flamers" by Gary Chapman from *The New Republic,* April 10, 1995. Copyright © 1995, The New Republic, Inc. Reprinted by permission.

JOHN CHEEVER, "The Enormous Radio" from *The Stories of John Cheever* by John Cheever. Copyright © 1947 by John Cheever. Reprinted by permission of Alfred A. Knopf, Inc.

JUDITH ORTIZ COFER, "Silent Dancing" by Judith Ortiz Cofer is reprinted with permission from the publisher of *Silent Dancing: A Partial Remembrance of a Puerto Rican Childhood* (Houston: Arte Publico Press, University of Houston, 1990).

BERNARD COOPER, "A Clack of Tiny Sparks" by Bernard Cooper. Copyright © 1990 by *Harper's* Magazine. All rights reserved. Reproduced from the January 1991 issue by special permission.

AARON COPLAND, "Listening to Music" in *What to Listen for in Music* by Aaron Copland. Reprinted by permission of the Aaron Copland Fund for Music, Inc., copyright owner.

DOUGLAS COUPLAND, Copyright © 1991 by Douglas Coupland. From *Generation X* by Douglas Coupland. Reprinted by permission of St. Martin's Press, LLC.

RONALD DE LEEUW, From *The Letters of Vincent Van Gogh* selected and edited by Ronald de Leeuw, translated by Arnold Pomerans (Penguin Books, 1977). This collection copyright © Ronald de Leeuw, 1996. This translation copyright © Sdu Publishers, 1996. Reproduced by permission of Penguin Books Ltd.

RICK DEMARINIS, "Horizontal Snow," from *The Voice of America: Stories by Rick DeMarinis.* Copyright © 1991 by Rick DeMarinis. Reprinted by permission of W.W. Norton & Company, Inc.

JOAN DIDION, "On Self-Respect" from *Slouching Towards Bethlehem* by Joan Didion. Copyright © 1968 and copyright renewed © 1996 by Joan Didion. Reprinted by permission of Farrar, Straus & Giroux, Inc.

KILDARE DOBBS, "Gallipoli" from *Anatolian Suite* by Kildare Dobbs. Copyright © 1989 Kildare Dobbs. Reprinted by permission of Aurora Artistis Inc.

MARY CROW DOG with RICHARD ERDOES, From *Lakota Woman* by Mary Crow Dog with Richard Erdoes. Copyright © 1990 by Mary Crow Dog and Richard Erdoes. Used by permission of Grove/Atlantic, Inc.

MICHAEL DORRIS, "Dances with Indians" by Michael Dorris from *The New York Times,* September 4, 1988. Copyright © 1998 by *The New York Times.* Reprinted by permission.

DAVID JAMES DUNCAN, From *The River Why* by David James Duncan. Copyright © 1983 by David James Duncan. Reprinted with permission of Sierra Club Books.

JEAN BETHKE ELSHTAIN, "Ewegenics" by Jean Bethke Elsthain from *The New Republic,* March 31, 1997. Copyright © 1997, The New Republic, Inc. Reprinted by permission.

ELISSA ELY, "Dreaming of Disconnecting a Respirator" by Elissa Ely as appeared in *The Boston Globe,* July 1, 1989. Reprinted by permission of the author.

PETER FARB and GEORGE ARMELAGOS, "Patterns of Eating" from *Consuming Passions* by Peter Farb and George Armelagos. Copyright © 1980 by The Estate of Peter Farb. Reprinted by permission of Houghton Mifflin Company. All rights reserved.

DAVE FOREMAN, "Earth First" by Dave Foreman from *The Progressive,* October 1981. Reprinted by permission.

IAN FRAZIER, "Take the F" by Ian Frazier as appeared in *The New Yorker,* February 20, 1995. Copyright © Ian Frazier. Reprinted by permission of the author.

NEIL GAIMAN, *Death: The Time of Your Life,* copyright © 1997 DC Comics. All rights reserved. Used with permission.

HENRY LOUIS GATES JR., "In the Kitchen" from *Colored People* by Henry Louis Gates Jr. Copyright © 1994 by Henry Louis Gates Jr. Reprinted by permission of Alfred A. Knopf, Inc. "Delusions of Grandeur" by Henry Louis Gates Jr. as appeared in *Sports Illustrated,* August 19, 1991. Reprinted by permission of the author.

WILLIAM GIBSON, "The Gernsback Continuum" by William Gibson from *Burning Chrome,* pp. 28–40. Reprinted by permission of William Gibson, Martha Millard Literary Agency.

PATRICIA GOEDICKE, "Because My Mother Was Deaf She Played the Piano" by Patricia Goedicke was published in *Invisible Horses* (Milkweed, 1996). Copyright © 1996 by Patricia Goedicke. Reprinted with permission from Milkweed Editions.

PAUL GOLDBERGER, "Landmark Kitsch" by Paul Goldberger from *The New Yorker* Magazine, August 18, 1997. Copyright © 1997 by *The New Yorker.* Reprinted by permission of *The New Yorker* and Paul Goldberger. "Quick! Before It Crumbles" by Paul Goldberger from *Esquire* Magazine, September 1975. Reprinted by permission of the author.

MARY GORDON, "Mary Cassatt," from *Good Boys and Dead Girls* by Mary Gordon. Copyright © 1991 by Mary Gordon. Used by permission of Viking Penguin, a division of Penguin Putnam Inc.

AL GORE, "Ships in the Desert" from *Earth in the Balance* by Al Gore. Copyright © 1992 by Senator Al Gore. Reprinted by permission of Hougton Mifflin Company. All rights reserved.

JORIE GRAHAM, "Reading Plato" from *The Dream of the Unified Field* by Jorie Graham. Copyright © 1980, 1983, 1987, 1991, 1993, 1995 by Jorie Graham. Reprinted by permission of The Ecco Press.

DICK GREGORY, "Shame," copyright © 1964 by Dick Gregory Enterprises, In., from *Nigger: An Autobiography* by Dick Gregory. Used by permission of Dutton, a division of Penguin Putnam Inc.

PATRICIA HAMPL, "Memory and Imagination" by Patricia Hampl. Copyright © 1985 by Patricia Hampl. Reprinted from *The Dolphin Reader.* Permission granted by The Rhoda Weyr Agency, New York.

RON HANSEN, "Wickedness" from *Nebraska* by Ron Hansen. Copyright © 1989 by Ron Hansen. Used by permission of Grove/Atlantic, Inc.

JANA HARRIS, "Cattlekilling Winter" by Jana Harris from *O How Can I Keep on Singing? Voices of Pioneer Women.* Reprinted by permission of Ontario Review Press and the author.

MAGGIE HELWIG, "Hunger" by Maggie Helwig. Copyright © 1989. Reprinted with permission of the author.

AL HOFF, "The Best Worst Job I Ever Had" by Al Hoff from *McJob* (Julie Peasley). Reprinted by permission of the author.

LINDA HOGAN, "Dwellings," from *Dwellings: A Spiritual History of the Living World* by Linda Hogan. Copyright © 1995 by Linda Hogan. Reprinted by permission of W.W. Norton & Company, Inc.

BELL HOOKS, "Keeping Close to Home" from *Talking Back: Thinking Feminist, Thinking Black* by bell hooks, 1989. Reprinted by permission of the Institute for Social and Cultural Change (South End Press).

MARIE HOWE, "The Boy," from *What the Living Do* by Marie Howe. Copyright © 1997 by Marie Howe. Reprinted by permission of W.W. Norton & Company, Inc.

LANGSTON HUGHES, "Theme for English B" from *Collected Poems* by Langston Hughes. Copyright © 1994 by the Estate of Langston Hughes. Reprinted by permission of Alfred A. Knopf, Inc. "Salvation" from *The Big Sea* by Langston Hughes. Copyright © 1940 by Langston Hughes. Copyright renewed © 1968 by Arna Bontemps and George Houston Bass. Reprinted by permission of Hill and Wang, a division of Farrar, Straus & Giroux, Inc.

GISH JEN, "Challenging the Asian Illusion" by Gish Jen. Copyright © 1991 by Gish Jen. First published in *The New York Times*. Reprinted by permission of the author.

MICHIKO KAKUTANI, "Portrait of the Artist as a Focus Group" by Michiko Kakutani from *The New York Times*, March 1, 1998. Copyright © 1998 by *The New York Times*. Reprinted by permission.

GARRISON KEILLOR, "A Sixties Party" by Garrison Keillor. Copyright © 1984 by Garrison Keillor. Reprinted by permission of Garrison Keillor. "Protestant," from *Lake Wobegon Days* by Garrison Keillor. Copyright © 1985 by Garrison Keillor. Used by permission of Viking Penguin, a division of Penguin Putnam Inc.

EVELYN FOX KELLER, Copyright © 1992. From *Secrets Of Life, Secrets Of Death* edited by Evelyn Fox Keller. Reproduced by permission of Routledge, Inc.

JACK KEROUAC, From "Passing through Tangiers" in *Desolation Angels* by Jack Kerouac. Reprinted by permission of Sterling Lord Literistic, Inc.

JAMAICA KINCAID, "On Seeing England for the First Time" by Jamaica Kincaid. Copyright © 1991 by Jamaica Kincaid, first printed in *The New Yorker*, reprinted with permission of The Wylie Agency, Inc.

TED KOOSER, "Shooting a Farmhouse" from *Sure Signs: New and Selected Poems*, by Ted Kooser, copyright © 1980. Reprinted by permission of the University of Pittsburgh Press.

JONATHAN KOZOL, From *Rachel and Her Children* by Jonathan Kozol. Copyright © 1988 by Jonathan Kozol. Reprinted by permission of Crown Publishers, a division of Random House, Inc.

NATALIE KUSZ, "Ring Leader" by Natalie Kusz. First published in *Allure*, February 1996. All rights reserved. Copyright © 1996 by Natalie Kusz. Reprinted by permission of Brandt & Brandt Literary Agents, Inc.

STEPHEN KUUSISTO, "Navigating the Dark World" as appeared in *Harper's* Magazine, August 1996. This material appeared in a slightly different form in *Planet of the Blind* by Stephen Kuusisto, The Dial Press 1998; Delta 1999. Copyright © 1996 by Stephen Kuusisto. Reprinted by permission of Irene Skolnick Literary Agency.

JOHN LEONARD, "TV and the Decline of Civilization" by John Leonard. Reprinted with permission from the December 27, 1993 issue of *The Nation*.

ALDO LEOPOLD, "The Land Ethic" from *A Sand County Almanac: And Sketches Here and There* by Aldo Leopold. Copyright © 1949, 1977 by Oxford University Press, Inc. Used by permission of Oxford University Press, Inc.

BARRY HOLSTUN LOPEZ, "Gone Back Into the Earth" by Barry Holstun Lopez. Reprinted by permission of Sterling Lord Literistic, Inc. Copyright © 1988 by Barry Holstun Lopez.

BEVERLY LOWRY, "Getting to Know Mr. Lincoln" by Beverly Lowry from *The New York Times*, May 14, 1995. Copyright © 1995 by *The New York Times*. Reprinted by permission.

RUTH MACKLIN, "Human Cloning? Don't Just Say No" by Ruth Macklin from *U.S. News & World Report*, March 10, 1997. Copyright, March 10, 1997, *U.S. News & World Report*. Reprinted by permission.

BOBBIE ANN MASON, "Shiloh" from *Shiloh and Other Stories* by Bobbie Ann Mason. Reprinted by permission of International Creative Management, Inc. Copyright © Bobbie Ann Mason.

WILLIAM McKIBBIN, "A Path of More Resistance" from *The End of Nature* by William McKibben. Copyright © 1989 by William McKibben. Reprinted by permission of Random House, Inc.

MEGAN McNAMER, Reprinted courtesy of *Sports Illustrated* March 6, 1995. Copyright © 1995, Time Inc., "Longing and Bliss" by Megan McNamer. All rights reserved.

N. SCOTT MOMADAY, "Sacred and Ancestral Ground" by N. Scott Momaday from *The New York Times*, March 13, 1998. Copyright © 1998 by *The New York Times*. Reprinted by permission.

TARA EMELYE NEEDHAM, "Cyberscared: Alienated and Proud" by Tara Emelye Needham. Originally published in Issue #3 of the author's zine, *Cupsize*.

JOHN G. NEIHARDT, Reprinted from *Black Elk Speaks*, by John G. Neihardt, by permission of the University of Nebraska Press. Copyright © 1932, 1959, 1972, by John G. Neihardt. Copyright © 1961 by the John G. Neihardt Trust.

KATHLEEN NORRIS, "The Beautiful Places" from *Dakota*. Copyright © 1993 by Kathleen Norris. Reprinted by permission of Ticknor & Fields/Houghton Mifflin Co. All rights reserved.

TIM O'BRIEN, "The Things They Carried" from *The Things They Carried*. Copyright © 1990 by Tim O'Brien. Reprinted by permission of Houghton Mifflin Co./Seymour Lawrence. All rights reserved.

FLANNERY O'CONNOR, "A Good Man Is Hard to Find" from *A Good Man Is Hard to Find and Other Stories*, copyright © 1953 by Flannery O'Connor and renewed 1981 by Regina O'Connor, reprinted by permission of Harcourt, Inc.

SHARON OLDS, "The Death of Marilyn Monroe" from *The Dead and the Living* by Sharon Olds. Copyright © 1983 by Sharon Olds. Reprinted by permission of Alfred A. Knopf, Inc.

PEGGY ORENSTEIN, "Get a Cyberlife" by Peggy Orenstein from *Mother Jones* Magazine, 1991. Reprinted with permission from *Mother Jones* Magazine, © 1991, Foundation for National Progress.

P. J. O'ROURKE, "Fiddling While Africa Starves" from *Give War a Chance* by P. J. O'Rourke. Copyright © 1992 by P. J. O'Rourke. Used by permission of Grove/Atlantic, Inc.

CAROLINE PATTERSON, "Spikes and Slow Waves" by Caroline Patterson from *Epoch*, Cornell University, Vol. 44, No. 3, 1995. Reprinted by permission of the author.

NOEL PERRIN, "Forever Virgin: The American View of America" by Noel Perrin. First published in *Antaeus*, Autumn 1986. Copyright © 1986 by Noel Perrin. Published in *The Nature Reader* by The Ecco Press in 1997. Reprinted by permission of The Ecco Press.

NEIL POSTMAN, "Future Schlock" from *Conscientious Objections* by Neil Postman. Copyright © 1988 by Neil Postman. Reprinted by permission of Alfred A. Knopf, Inc.

ISHMAEL REED, "My Oakland, There Is a There," Part I from *Writin' Is Fightin': Thirty-Seven Years of Boxing on Paper* by Ishmael Reed. Reprinted with permission of the author.

ADRIENNE RICH, "Split at the Root: An Essay on Jewish Identity," from *Blood, Bread, and Poetry: Selected Prose 1979–1985* by Adrienne Rich. Copyright © 1986 by Adrienne Rich. Reprinted by permission of W.W. Norton & Company, Inc.

ALBERTO ALVARO RIOS, "Green Cards" by Alberto Rios. Copyright © Alberto Rios. Reprinted by permission of author.

RICHARD RODRIGUEZ, "Asians," from *Days of Obligation* by Richard Rodriguez. Copyright © 1992 by Richard Rodriguez. Used by permission of Viking Penguin, a division of Penguin Putnam Inc.

PATTIANN ROGERS, "Rolling Naked in the Morning Dew" in *Firekeeper, New and Selected Poems*. Minneapolis, Minnesota: Milkweed Editions, 1984. Copyright © by Pattiann Rogers, 1994. Reprinted by permission of the author.

BERTRAND RUSSELL, "Work," from *The Conquest of Happiness* by Bertrand Russell. Copyright © 1930 by Horace Liveright, Inc., renewed © 1958 by Bertrand Russell. Reprinted by permission of Liveright Publishing Corporation.

LUC SANTE, "Living in Tongues" by Luc Sante as appeared in *The New York Times*, June 28, 1997. Copyright © 1997 by Luc Sante. Reprinted by permission of the author.

JACK SANTINO, "Rock and Roll as Music; Rock and Roll as Culture" by Jack Santino from *The World and I*, 1990. Reprinted by permission.

JEAN-PAUL SARTRE, From *Existentialism and Human Emotions* by Jean-Paul Sartre. Copyright © 1957, 1985 by Philosophical Library, Inc. Published by arrangement with Carol Publishing Group. A Citadel Press Book.

ROBERT SOMMER, From *Personal Space: The Behavioral Basis of Design* by Robert Sommer. Reprinted by permission of the author.

SUSAN SONTAG, "A Century of Cinema" by Susan Sontag. Copyright © 1997 by Susan Sontag. Reprinted with the permission of The Wylie Agency, Inc.

GARY SOTO, "One Last Time" is copyrighted 1985 by Gary Soto and is reprinted from *Living Up the Street* (Dell, 1992). Used by permission of the author.

CHARLENE SPRETNAK, "Wholly Writ: Women's Spirituality" by Charlene Spretnal from *MS.* Magazine. Reprinted by permission of *MS.* Magazine, © 1993.

BRENT STAPLES, "Just Walk on By: A Black Man Ponders His Power to Alter Public Space" by Brent Staples from *MS.* Magazine, 1986. Reprinted by permission of the author. Brent Staples writes editorials for *The New York Times* and is author of the memoir, "Parallel Time: Growing Up in Black and White."

STEVEN STARK, "Where the Boys Are" by Steven Stark from *The Atlantic Monthly*, September 1994. Reprinted by permission of the author.

GLORIA STEINEM, "The Importance of Work" from *Outrageous Acts and Everyday Rebellions* by Gloria Steinem. Copyright © 1984 by East Toledo Productions, Inc. Copyright © 1983, 1995 by Gloria Steinem. Reprinted by permission of Henry Holt and Company, LLC.

ANNE FAUSTO-STERLING, "Society Writes Biology/Biology Constructs Gender" by Anne Fausto-Sterling reprinted by permission of DAEDALUS, *Journal of the American Academy of Arts and Sciences,* from the issue entitled, "Learning About Women: Gender, Politics, and Power," Fall 1987, Vol. 116, No. 4.

ROGER E. SWARDSON, "Greetings from the Electronic Plantation" by Roger E. Swardson from *The UTNE Reader*, March/April 1993. Reprinted by permission of the author.

AMY TAN, Copyright © 1996 by Amy Tan. Originally appeared in *The Threepenny Review*. Used by permission of Amy Tan and the Sandra Dijkstra Literary Agency.

CAROL TAVRIS, Reprinted with the permission of Simon & Schuster, Inc. from *Anger: The Misunderstood Emotion* by Carol Tavris. Copyright © 1982, 1989 by Carol Tavris.

STUDS TERKEL, From *Working: People Talk About What They Do All Day and How They Feel About It* by Studs Terkel. Reprinted by permission of Donadio & Olson, Inc. Copyright © 1974 by Studs Terkel.

PAUL THEROUX, "Being a Man" from *Sunrise with Seamonsters* by Paul Theroux. Copyright © 1985 by Cape Cod Scriveners Co. Reprinted by permission of Houghton Mifflin Co. All rights reserved.

LÊ THI DIEM THÚY, "The Gangster We Are All Looking For" by Lê Thi Diem Thúy from *The Massachusetts Review*, 1997. Reprinted by permission.

PAUL TILLICH, Reprinted with the permission of Scribner, a Division of Simon & Schuster from *The Eternal Now* by Paul Tillich. Copyright © 1963 by Paul Tillich, renewed 1991 by Mutie Tillich Farris.

SUSAN ALLEN TOTH, "Going to the Movies" from *How to Prepare for Your High School Reunion* by Susan Allen Toth. Copyright © Susan Allen Toth. Reprinted by permission of the Aaron Priest Literary Agency.

BARBARA TUCHMAN, "This is the End of the World" from *A Distant Mirror* by Barbara W. Tuchman. Copyright © 1978 by Barbara W. Tuchman. Reprinted by permission of Alfred A. Knopf, Inc.

STEPHANIE VAUGHN, "Sweet Talk" by Stephanie Vaughn (New York: Random House, 1990). Copyright © 1978, 1979, 1981, 1990 by Stephanie Vaughn. Reprinted by permission of Georges Borchardt, Inc. for the author.

James Welch, From *Fool's Crow* by James Welch. Copyright © 1986 by James Welch. Used by permission of Viking Penguin, a division of Penguin Putnam Inc.

Edith Wharton, Reprinted with the permission of Scribner, a Division of Simon & Schuster from *Roman Fever and Other Stories* by Edith Wharton. Copyright © 1934 by Liberty Magazine; copyright renewed © 1962 by William R. Tyler.

Joy Williams, "Train" from *Taking Care* by Joy Williams. Copyright © 1981 by Joy Williams. Reprinted by permission of Random House, Inc. "Save the Whales, Screw the Shrimp" by Joy Williams. Reprinted by permission of International Creative Management, Inc. Copyright © 1989 by Joy Williams.

Lena Williams, "A Black Fan of Country Music Finally Tells All" by Lena Williams from *The New York Times,* June 19, 1994. Copyright © 1994 by *The New York Times.* Reprinted by permission.

Terry Tempest Williams, "The Clan of One-Breasted Women" from *Refuge* by Terry Tempest Williams. Copyright © 1991 by Terry Tempest Williams. Reprinted by permission of Pantheon Books, a division of Random House, Inc.

Marie Winn, "Television Addiction," from *The Plug-in Drug, Revised Edition* by Marie Winn. Copyright © 1977, 1985 by Marie Winn Miller. Used by permission of Viking Penguin, a division of Penguin Putnam Inc.

Tom Wolfe, "O Rotten Gotham—Sliding Down into the Behavioral Sink" from *The Pump House Gang* by Tom Wolfe. Copyright © 1968 and copyright renewed © 1996 by Tom Wolfe. Reprinted by permission of Farrar, Straus & Giroux, Inc.

George Woodcock, "The Tyranny of the Clock" by George Woodcock from *The Rejection of Politics.* Reprinted by permission of Ingeborg Woodcock, Executor.

Virginia Woolf, "The Death of the Moth" from *The Death of the Moth and Other Essays* by Virginia Woolf, copyright © 1942 by Harcourt, Inc. and renewed 1970 by Marjorie T. Parsons, Executrix, reprinted by permission of the publisher.

Malcolm X, "The Shoeshine Boy" from *The Autobiography of Malcolm X* by Malcolm X, with the assistance of Alex Haley. Copyright © 1964 by Alex Haley and Malcolm X. Copyright © 1965 by Alex Haley and Betty Shabazz. Reprinted by permission of Random House, Inc.

PHOTO CREDITS

The authors are indebted to the following for photographs and permissions to reproduce them. Copyright for each photograph belongs to the photographer or agency credited, unless specified otherwise.

p. 1   Gift of Mrs. Mellon Bruce in memory of her father, Andrew W. Mellon. Photograph © 1999 Board of Trustees, National Gallery of Art, Washington.

p. 9   Iola Franz/Vermont Study

p. 17   "Emily Hide and Seek" Lucy Capehart

p. 45   Jesse DeMartino

p. 111   Alison Gadbow

p. 132   Hadley Skinner

p. 199   Linton Park, Flax Scutching Bee, 1885, 31½ × 50½." Gift of Edgar William and Bernice Chrysler Garbisch. Photograph © 1999

Board of Trustees, National Gallery of Art, Washington.

p. 233   Carnegie Museum of Art, Pittsburgh; Gift of the Carnegie Library of Pittsburgh. W. Eugene Smith/Black Star

p. 279   Tim Cooper

p. 305   The Metropolitan Museum of Art, H. O. Havemeyer Collection, Bequest of Mrs. H. O. Havemeyer, 1929. (29.100.6)

p. 363   J. H. Sherburne from Sherburne Collection, K. Ross Toole Archives, University of Montana

p. 391   W. Eugene Smith/Black Star

p. 473   Rex Hardy/Life Magazine ©
         Time Inc.
p. 495   Sylwia Kapuscinski
p. 563   Raymond Gehman
p. 600   Mike Smith
p. 669   © Original design by Tomato
         Cards. All Rights Reserved.
         Recycled Paper Greetings, Inc.
         Reprinted by permission.
p. 683   Nancy Kedersha, Harvard
         Medical School

p. 723   Giraudon/Art Resource, NY
p. 735 t Courtesy of Nabisco, Inc.
p. 736 b Courtesy of Nabisco, Inc.
p. 743   Museo del Prado, Madrid.
p. 787   Erich Lessing/Art Resource, NY
p. 813   Andrew W. Mellon Collection.
         Photograph © 1999 Board of
         Trustees, National Gallery of Art,
         Washington.

INDEX OF AUTHORS

Title of works are in italics. Authors names are in small caps.